A Legal Guide to Recovering for Flood Losses

DOUGLAS SCOTT MACGREGOR

AMERICAN BAR ASSOCIATION
Tort Trial and Insurance Practice Section

Cover design by Betsy Kulak/ABA Design

Printed in the United States of America.

27 26 25 24 23 5 4 3 2 1

A catalog record for this book is on file with the Library of Congress.

For Leslie Greene, M.S.W, Nancy Horton, D.M.D., and Katie Everlove-Stone, J.D., L.L.M., who through integrity, diligence, and compassion, bring honor on their chosen professions.

Contents

Preface

I experienced my first flood one summer when I was in high school. My family lived on an island just north of downtown St. Petersburg, Florida. A tropical storm brushed the coast. It brought little wind but a formidable storm surge. Water covered our dock and backed up storm drains into the street. We were trapped on the island for several days. The homes in our neighborhood were not inundated, but many nearby homes in even more low-lying areas were. Flooding has only grown more common since then.

Much of my professional work has involved the law of insurance. My interest in flood insurance originated when I was asked to write on the subject for the *New Appleman on Insurance Law Library Edition*. I was surprised to learn that there was no standalone treatise devoted solely to the topic of recovering for flood losses. While researching case law for the *Appleman* flood chapter, I came across many cases in which flood damage was covered by policies other that the Standard Flood Insurance Policy issued by the Federal Emergency Management Agency (FEMA). In some cases, the coverage came through a privately issued flood policy. However, I also found that exceptions in standard property policies—as well as Builder's Risk, Boiler and Machinery, and even Commercial General Liability policies—could be a source of recovery.

This treatise was born of the belief that there should be a single work that examines, comprehensively, the potential sources for recovery from flood losses. My hope is that when a client presents to an attorney with water damage to his or her property, the attorney will be able to compare the facts presented by the client with information in this work—and thereby develop a comprehensive recovery strategy. For example, consider a client who owns two commercial buildings—an office and a warehouse—and is having a second warehouse built alongside the existing one. The two warehouses sit alongside a creek. One night a storm with 50 mph winds dumps five inches of water on already saturated ground. The creek overflows and floods the warehouse buildings. The wind blows off part of the roof of the office building, filling it with water. The damage to the existing warehouse may be covered by a FEMA flood policy. A Builder's Risk policy may have coverage for flood damage to the building under construction. The standard commercial property policy likely covers the "flooding" to the office building. What is more, if the creek overflowed its banks due to negligent downstream work by a road construction contractor, uncovered losses to the two warehouses may be covered by the contractor's liability insurance. In the past, the attorney would have needed to consult a number of treatises to evaluate each of the potential claims, and, importantly, those treatises would not focus specifically on flood loss. This book brings all the information together and cites the cases in which flooding was the cause of the loss.

About the Author

Douglas Scott MacGregor is a graduate of Eckerd College and the Levin College of Law at the University of Florida and also earned an M.S.W. at the University of South Florida. He is the author of more than 20 books and the chapter on flood insurance in the New Appleman on Insurance Law Library Edition. He lives in the town of Gulfport on Florida's West Coast.

1

Introduction

1.1 The Flood Crisis

Virtually every corner of America is susceptible to one or more natural disasters: earthquakes, tornadic and tropical windstorms, destructive hailstorms, avalanches, and even volcanoes. But the most frequent and costly natural disasters, according to the Federal Emergency Management Agency (FEMA), are floods, which cause billions of dollars in damage each year.[1] Nine out of ten natural disasters are flood related.[2] A flood can happen almost anywhere. FEMA says 98 percent of counties in the United States have experienced a flood,[3] even though only 7 percent of land is considered to be floodplains.[4]

Floods can be caused by a number of events: tropical storm surge; rivers and streams overflowing their banks with stormwater runoff or snow melt (fluvial or riverine flooding); torrential rains overwhelming storm drains (pluvial flooding); dam or levee failures; tsunamis; and increasingly greater than usual high tides (nuisance flooding), such as spring tides, which occur twice each lunar month.[5]

1. *Why Buy Flood Insurance*, FEMA, https://www.fema.gov/sites/default/files/2020-05/Why_Buy_Flood_Factsheet_0418.pdf. *See also* Parsons, *Common Flood Insurance Myths Debunked* (June 9, 2022), PropertyCasualty360, https://www.propertycasualty360.com/2022/06/09/common-flood-insurance-myths-debunked/?kw=Common%20flood%20insurance%20myths%20debunked (between 2010 and 2021, flooding and flood-related events accounted for 26 percent of billion-dollar natural disasters).

2. Klein & Zellmer, *Mississippi River Stories: Lessons from a Century of Unnatural Disasters*, 60 SMU L. Rev. 1471, 1473 (2007).

3. *Why Buy Flood Insurance*, FEMA, https://www.fema.gov/sites/default/files/2020-05/Why_Buy_Flood_Factsheet_0418.pdf.

4. Klein & Zellmer, *Mississippi River Stories: Lessons from a Century of Unnatural Disasters*, 60 SMU L. Rev. 1471, 1473 (2007).

5. *What Are Spring and Neap Tides?*, NOAA, https://oceanservice.noaa.gov/facts/springtide.html.

Flooding can be expected to worsen. The intensity of coastal storm surges is expected to increase.[6] River flood stages have risen markedly, causing so-called 100-year floods to occur more often.[7] Flood controls designed to protect against what is known as a 500-year flood are in danger of being overtopped, and the flood hazard control system in the United States has been called broken.[8] With rising sea levels, "nuisance flooding," which is now experienced in a few particularly low-lying communities, is expected by the mid-2030s to affect a majority of the nation's coastlines.[9]

Most scientists and meteorologists ascribe the increasing flood risk to climate change. For example, a 2017 report from the National Academy of Sciences states that sea level rise (SLR) is a well-documented and urgent aspect of anthropogenic global warming.[10] The World Meteorological Organization has asserted that by the late 21st century, global warming will likely cause the average strength of tropical cyclones to increase as much as 10 percent and near-storm rainfall rates to increase by around 20 percent.[11]

In many quarters, especially in legislative corridors, climate change is a controversial subject and many deny it even exists. However, "[t]he one industry that's not debating the nature of climate change is the insurance industry."[12] Indeed, almost a decade ago industry giant Lloyd's of London issued a report

---

6. *State of the Science FACT SHEET: Atlantic Hurricanes, Climate Variability and Global Warming*, at 2 (National Oceanic and Atmospheric Administration, May 2012) (vulnerability of coastal regions to storm-surge flooding is expected to increase with future sea-level rise).

7. Davidson, *How Quickly We Forget: The National Flood Insurance Program and Floodplain Development in Missouri*, 19 Wash. U. J.L. & Pol'y 365, 390 (2005) ("100-year floods" can in the future be expected every 15–20 years or fewer).

8. Klein & Zellmer, *Mississippi River Stories: Lessons from a Century of Unnatural Disasters*, 60 SMU L. Rev. 1471, 1473 (2007).

9. Morrison, *Sunny-Day Flooding Is about to Become More than a Nuisance* (Aug. 2, 2021), WIRED, https://www.wired.com/story/sunny-day-flooding-is-about-to-become-more-than-a-nuisance/.

10. Moftakhari, Salvadori, AghaKouchak, Sanders & Matthew, *Compounding Effects of Sea Level Rise and Fluvial Flooding* at 1 (Proceedings of the National Academy of Sciences 2017), http://amir.eng.uci.edu/publications/17_PNAS_Compound_Flood_SI.pdf.

11. *State of the Science FACT SHEET: Atlantic Hurricanes, Climate Variability and Global Warming*, at 2 (National Oceanic and Atmospheric Administration, May 2012).

12. Passy, *This 'Incredibly Powerful' Home-Insurance Policy Will Make Payouts Even if Your Property Isn't Damaged* (Jan. 27, 2020), MarketWatch, https://www.marketwatch.com/story/this-powerful-home-insurance-policy-it-pays-out-even-if-your-property-isnt-damaged-2020-01-17. *See also* Parsons, *Common Flood Insurance Myths Debunked* (June 9, 2022), PropertyCasualty360, https://www.propertycasualty360.com/2022/06/09/common-flood-insurance-myths-debunked/?kw=Common%20flood%20insurance%20myths%20debunked (urbanization, undermaintained infrastructure, and weather events caused by climate change threaten more, and more costly, floods; cost of flood damage may rise another 25 percent to over $40 billion on average per year by 2050).

that stated bluntly "The Earth's global climate system is warming."[13] Allianz, a business insurer with a global presence, said in 2017 that global average sea levels have risen; the cause is attributed to glacier melt and thermal expansion, which are likely to result in an increase in severity of storm surge along American coastlines.[14] There is a very simple reason why the insurance industry is taking global warming and its potential effect on property loss seriously. The essence of insurance is assessment of risk. An insurance company must gather empirical data to evaluate which perils it will insure and at what price. It operates in a competitive market and has to provide a product consumers want at a price they will pay. If an insurance company overcharges for a low-risk peril, it will lose out to competitors; if it undercharges for high-risk perils, it risks insolvency. So, insurers eschew ideology and monitor data on the effects of global warming to make sound underwriting decisions.

1.2 What Is a Flood?

The clause in the standard property policy that is commonly referred to as a "flood exclusion" is actually much broader. It is a water loss exclusion that initially defines "water" as flood; surface water; waves, including tidal wave and tsunami; tides; tidal water; overflow of any body of water; or spray from any of these, all whether or not driven by wind including storm surge.[15] None of those components of "water" is defined in property policies. Usually, the only policies that define "flood" are those that cover it—such as the FEMA Standard Flood Insurance Policy (SFIP)—not those that exclude it.

An entire section of Chapter 2 is devoted to judicial definitions of the term "flood." However, one theme of this treatise is that laypersons may describe their property as flooded even when there has not been a flood as understood by courts. For instance, despite the long list of components of "water," from the perspective of a layperson, if property is inundated by surface water, the overflow of a body of water, or storm surge, it was flooded. If the dishwasher malfunctions or a pipe breaks, and the result is six inches of water on the floor, to the homeowner, that is a flood. It is then incumbent on counsel to examine the facts to determine if there may be coverage.

---

13. Toumi & Restell, *Catastrophe Modelling and Climate Change*, at 5 (Lloyd's of London 2014), https://assets.lloyds.com/assets/pdf-modelling-and-climate-change-cc-and-modelling-template-v6/2/pdf-modelling-and-climate-change-CC-and-modelling-template-V6.pdf.

14. *From Sandy to Maria: Increasingly Destructive "Perfect Storms"* (Allianz Global Corporate & Specialty SE, 2017), *available at* https://docslib.org/doc/2776717/how-to-prepare-for-the-new-normal-hurricane-sandy-five-year.

15. The commonly used residential policy omits tsunami and tides. ISO Form HO 00 03 10 00 (Exclusions), § A.3.a.

For example, a client calls to say that he arrived home several evenings ago to find the street outside his home knee-deep in water. The homes across the street that sit lower than his were clearly flooded. When he opened the front door, water poured forth and he could see it cascading down the stairs from the second floor. The following morning, he called the insurance broker who sold him both a homeowners and a flood policy. The broker contacted the respective insurers. The homeowners insurer said its policy did not cover flood losses. The flood insurer said there was not a flood. It had sent an adjuster to view the outside of the property, and the adjuster found no evidence that flood waters reached the home. Counsel advises the client to hire an expert to examine the property. The expert finds that a roof opening that appeared to be caused by gusty winds allowed a large amount of water to flow through the roof and "flood" the house. That is a loss covered under almost all homeowners policies regardless of whether it is called a flood. The expert discovers something else. Around the back of the house, he finds that a subsurface window in the basement wall is broken. He sees the basement floor is damp. He determines that the land at the back of the house was actually lower than the street and that the backyard flooded. That water broke the window and entered the basement. If the expert is correct, some damage in the basement will likely be covered by the flood policy. The point is that the characterization of an event is irrelevant. What *is* relevant is the specific facts and how they compare to the language of any policies.

Readers will note that cases are discussed in this volume that involve water damage that would not be considered a flood even under the loosest lay use of the word. There are two reasons for that. First, the legal principles are often the same whether or not the water damage is a flood in the legal sense. Second, in those cases, had the amount of the water been greater, there would have been a flood, at least in the layperson's sense of the word.

1.3 Topics Covered

Almost any client who presents with flood or water damage will have property insurance, either commercial or residential. For that reason, the first question to answer is whether the flood/water exclusion applies to the loss. Thus, the second chapter of this treatise explores the interpretation of the component parts of the standard flood/water exclusion. Almost every standard property policy also has some narrow exceptions to that exclusion either in the principal policy or in endorsements. The third chapter, therefore, examines the applicability of those exceptions.

Some clients will have flood insurance. The fourth chapter explains private flood coverage, both primary and excess, and the fifth chapter examines recovery under a FEMA Standard Flood Insurance Policy.

Business clients with commercial property insurance may not have flood coverage in that policy, but they generally will have coverage for business interruption and what are called extra and expediting expenses. Chapter 6 explores recovery for those losses when caused by flood or water damage.

Two specialized forms of property insurance are Builder's Risk and Equipment Breakdown. As the name suggests, the former is a type of property insurance that covers projects under construction, renovation, or repair and insures against accidental losses, damages, or destruction of property. Equipment Breakdown insurance fills a gap in coverage in standard property policies that do not cover accidental breakdown of machinery. Recovering for flood and water damage losses under these coverages is addressed in Chapters 7 and 8.

In some cases, a client may be able to recover losses caused by flood or water damage from a tortfeasor's liability insurer. Chapter 9 explains recovery under a Commercial General Liability policy, and Chapter 10 describes recovery under a Directors and Officers policy.

Comprehensive coverage under standard automobile policies encompasses losses from flooding. Chapter 11 illustrates recovery under those policies.

It is not uncommon for clients facing an uninsured flood or water damage loss to assert that they thought they had coverage or specifically asked for it and did not get it. Chapter 12 briefly reviews the circumstances under which a broker or agent can be held liable for failure to procure coverage.

This treatise is primarily concerned with recovering loss from insurance. However, there are circumstances in which recovery might be sought from a tortfeasor who may or may not be insured for the loss. One example is mentioned above: the broker or agent who fails to procure coverage and whose negligence may be covered by professional liability insurance. Of course, almost any organization or individual could negligently cause water or flood damage to another. That is a general tort law topic beyond the scope of this treatise. There are, however, some discrete categories of wrongdoers that merit attention. Chapter 13 addresses the duties owed by landlords and tenants to each other and when one is responsible to the other for flood or water damage losses. Governments engage in a variety of activities—for example, road building or dam maintenance—that can cause flooding or water damage. Despite sovereign immunity, it is possible to recover from governmental entities whose negligence causes a loss; this is discussed in Chapter 14. Finally, weather is the cause of flooding. What obligations do those who forecast the weather have to others? When a business has knowledge of dangerous weather conditions, what are its obligations to its customers? These questions are examined in Chapter 15.

2

The Standard Water Damage Exclusions and Limitations

2.1 Introduction

Standard property policies typically bar coverage for water damage in four clauses. The first is the exclusion for water.[1] It generally bars coverage for losses caused by the following:

- Flood; surface water; waves, including tidal wave and tsunami; tides; tidal water; overflow of any body of water; or spray from any of these, all whether or not driven by wind including storm surge;[2]
- Mudslide or mudflow;[3]
- Water that backs up or overflows or is otherwise discharged from a sewer, drain, sump, sump pump, or related equipment.[4]
- Water under the ground surface pressing on or flowing or seeping through foundations, walls, floors or paved surfaces, basements—whether paved or not—or doors, windows, or other openings;[5] and
- Waterborne material carried or otherwise moved by water, mudslide, or mudflow.[6]

1. ISO Form CP 10 30 09 17, § B.1.g.

2. The commonly used residential policy omits tsunami and tides. ISO Form HO 00 03 10 00 (Exclusions), § A.3.a.

3. These perils are omitted from an ISO residential policy. ISO Form HO 00 03 10 00 (Exclusions), § A.3.

4. The ISO residential form exclusion is slightly different. It applies to water and waterborne material that backs up through sewers or drains or overflows or is discharged from a sump, sump pump, or related equipment. HO 00 03 10 00 (Exclusions), § A.3.b.

5. The residential form excludes coverage for damage by water or waterborne material below the surface of the ground including water that exerts pressure on or seeps or leaks through a building, sidewalk, driveway foundation, swimming pool, or other structure. ISO Form HO 00 03 10 00 (Exclusions), § A.3.c.

6. This peril is not in the residential exclusion.

The second exclusion is for continuous or repeated seepage or leakage of water, or the presence or condensation of humidity, moisture, or vapor.[7] There is a third exclusion for water that leaks or flows from plumbing, heating, air conditioning, or other equipment caused by or resulting from freezing.[8]

Finally, there is a limitation under which the insurer will not pay for any loss that is a consequence of loss or damage to the interior of any building or structure, or to personal property in the building or structure, caused by or that results from rain, snow, sleet, or ice, whether driven by wind or not, unless the building or structure first sustains damage by a covered cause of loss to its roof or walls through which the rain, snow, sleet, or ice enters or the loss or damage is caused by or results from thawing of snow, sleet, or ice on the building or structure.[9]

Additionally, there is a standard provision that covers accidental discharge or leakage of water, with exclusions from its definition of water damage.[10] That coverage and the exceptions to it are discussed elsewhere.[11] This chapter addresses the three exclusions and the single limitation outlined above followed by a discussion of the weather conditions exclusion.

Any of the proscriptions discussed in this chapter may be modified or eliminated by endorsement.[12] Chapter 3 addresses some of these endorsements while a subsection in Chapter 4 discusses endorsements that add flood coverage.[13]

2.2 The Water Damage Exclusion: Flood, Surface Water, Waves, and Tides

[1] Generally

When a client presents with what he or she characterizes as flood damage and has a commercial or residential property policy but no flood coverage, the initial chore is to determine whether there is an applicable exclusion in the property policy. Most, but not all, commercial and residential property policies include what is often referred to as a flood exclusion. Those exclusions are

7. ISO Form CP 10 30 09 17, § B.2.f.

8. ISO Form CP 10 30 09 17, § B.2.g. *See also* ISO Form HO 00 03 10 00 (Perils Insured Against), § A.2.c.

9. ISO Form CP 10 30 09 17, § C.1.c.

10. *See, e.g.*, ISO Form CP 10 20 04 02, § A.14.a. (Commercial Property Causes of Loss); ISO Form HO 00 03 10 00 (Perils Insured Against), § 12.a.

11. *See* § 3.2[2], *infra.*

12. *See, e.g.*, Geovera Specialty Ins. Co. v. Glasser, 2022 Fla. App. LEXIS 1113 (Fla. 4th DCA Feb. 16, 2022) (endorsement replaced standard water exclusion with one that defined excluded water damage as "damage by water in any form" before listing usual source of water damage).

13. *See* § 4.2[6], *infra.*

actually broader and typically proscribe coverage for loss or damage caused directly or indirectly by *water*, which is defined as flood, surface water, waves, tides, tidal waves, or overflow of any body of water, all whether driven by wind or not.[14] The water damage exclusion is broad, but it does not encompass *all* water damage.[15] Indeed, as discussed elsewhere, most named risk property policies include certain types of water damage as a named peril.[16]

Even though a client says his or her property was "flooded," it should not be assumed that there was a "flood" or that the exclusion applies. As the Maryland Court of Appeals once noted, people "commonly speak of a cellar or basement being 'flooded' without regard to whether the water comes from the overflow of a stream, from a hard downpour, or from the bursting of pipes."[17] Counsel, therefore, needs to determine the source of the water and examine the water exclusion to determine if it applies. Three considerations need to be kept in mind. First, there may be more than one source of water. Second, an expert may be required to identify the source or sources and to determine what source caused which damage. Third, the water exclusion can vary from policy to policy, especially in policies that are not standard ISO forms. Therefore, the attorney should never assume the exclusion applies before a careful analysis of the language.

[2] Defining the Terms of the Exclusion

[a] Indirectly

Standard property policies exclude coverage for loss or damage caused directly or *indirectly* by water, but they do not define "indirectly." An Ohio federal court said simply that the term means "beyond direct, mechanical causation."[18] Other courts have employed a lay dictionary definition of "circuitous, not leading to the aim or result by the plainest course or method or obvious means, roundabout, or not resulting directly from an act or cause but more or less remotely connected with or growing out of it." [19] The Utah Supreme Court has explained that:

---

14. *See, e.g.*, ISO Form CP 10 30 09 17, § B.1.g.(1).

15. Hatley v. Truck Ins. Exchange, 261 Ore. 622, 625, 495 P.2d 1196, 1198 (1972) (insurer argued that as all water must be either on surface or below surface of ground, water exclusions should be interpreted so broadly as to exclude all damage by water, but court held that insurer obviously did not intend to exclude all water damage or it would have said so). *See also* Davidson Hotel Co. v. St. Paul Fire & Marine Ins. Co., 136 F. Supp. 2d 901 (W.D. Tenn. 2001) (standard water exclusion did not apply to damage caused by water flowing from corroded water heater; standard exclusion also did not bar coverage for leakage from water heater).

16. See § 3.2[2], *infra*.

17. Mateer v. Reliance Ins. Co., 233 A.2d 797, 799, 247 Md. 643, 648 (1967).

18. Sherwin-Williams Co. v. Insurance Co. of the State of Pa., 863 F. Supp. 542, 546 (N.D. Ohio 1994), *aff'd in part and rev'd in part*, 105 F.3d 258 (6th Cir. 1997).

19. Cahen Trust v. United States, 292 F.2d 33, 36 (7th Cir. 1961) (citing *Webster's New International Dictionary*). *See also* Maryland Casualty Co. v. Scharlack, 31 F. Supp. 931 (S.D.

> An indirect cause is a cause of a cause. It is a cause which sets in operation an active cause. A cause which contributes to a result is an independent cause, not set in operation by the other cause and operating independently of it in tending to produce the result. If the second, or secondary cause, is set in motion or in operation by the primary cause, or if its operation is controlled, directed or influenced in its action or behavior, by the primary or first cause, then the second or secondary cause is not an independent cause, not a contributing cause, operating in parallel, but operates in series and is a result of the first cause.[20]

These definitions are illustrated in an Illinois case in which a plate glass policy excluded coverage for any loss or damage resulting directly or indirectly from any "inundation." The buildings containing the insured plate glass windows were flooded when a river overflowed its banks. However, the windows were not damaged until boats being rowed through flooded streets crashed into them. The court said that under the policy, it appeared that if an injury resulted indirectly or remotely from an inundation, then no liability of the insurer could attach. People rowing boats in the streets, concluded the court, was a condition that contributed to the results: were it not for the inundation, the boats could not have been rowing on water in the streets and could not have run into the windows. Thus, the injuries sustained resulted, at least *indirectly*, from the inundation.[21] Indirect, however, does have its limits. A cause can be too remote to be reasonably thought to be indirect.[22]

[b] Flood

[i] Generally

Given the importance of the flood exclusion to property coverage, one might expect policies to define the term or courts to have developed a widely accepted definition; however, neither is true. While there are some policies that define "flood,"[23] the standard ISO commercial property and homeowners policies do

Tex. 1939), *aff'd*, 115 F.2d 719 (5th Cir. 1940) (citing *Webster's*); Amicable Life Ins. Co. v. O'Reilly, 97 S.W.2d 246, 247 (Tex. Civ. App.—Beaumont 1936) (citing Webster's New International Dictionary); Southern Traction Co. v. Gee, 198 S.W. 992, 1917 (Tex. Civ App.—Dallas 1917) (citing *Century Dictionary* for definition of "'not direct in relation or connection; not having an immediate bearing or application; not related in the natural way'").

20. Browning v. Equitable Life Assurance Soc'y, 94 Utah 570, 576, 80 P.2d 348, 352 (1938).

21. Feehrer v. Fidelity & Casualty Co., 188 Ill. App. 398 (1914).

22. *See, e.g.*, Commerical Union Assurance Co. v. Pacific Union Club, 169 F. 776 (9th Cir. 1909), where the policy insured against all direct loss or damage by fire except that the company would not be liable for a loss caused directly or indirectly by an earthquake. The insured property was totally destroyed by fire, and the insurer contended that the loss would have been prevented by the use of the city water supply had it not been prevented by the breaking of the water mains in an earthquake. Therefore, the insurer said there was no coverage. The court disagreed and found the earthquake was too remote a cause to bar coverage.

23. *See, e.g.*, Salcetti v. AIG Prop. Cas. Co., __ F. Supp. 3d __, 2021 U.S. Dist. LEXIS 71585 (S.D. Tex. Mar. 26, 2021) (policy defined "flood" as inundation of normally dry land area from

not. The argument has been put forward that the word is ambiguous.[24] However, some courts state definitively that the word "flood" is unambiguous,[25] while others say it may be ambiguous in certain circumstances.[26] After Hurricane

overflow of inland or tidal waters); K.J.D.E. Corp. v. Hartford Fire Ins. Co., 89 A.D.3d 1531, 932 N.Y.S.2d 778 (2011) (exclusion for which policy defined as in part surface water or overflow of any natural or human-made body of water from its boundaries); E.B. Metal & Rubber Industries, Inc. v. Federal Ins. Co., 84 A.D.2d 662, 444 N.Y.S.2d 321 (1981) (exclusion defined flood as waves, tidal water, or tidal wave, rising, including overflowing or breaking of boundaries, of lakes, reservoirs, rivers, streams, or other bodies of water, whether driven by wind or not). Policies that provide flood coverage generally define the term. *See, e.g.*, SEACOR Holdings, Inc. v. Commonwealth Ins. Co., 635 F.3d 675, 679 (5th Cir. 2011) (all-risk policy covered flood, which it defined to mean "waves, tide or tidal water, inundation, rainfall and/or resultant runoff, and the rising (including overflowing or breakage of boundaries) of lakes, ponds, reservoirs, rivers, harbors, streams, or similar bodies of water whether wind-driven or not"); Northrop Grumman Corp. v. Factory Mut. Ins. Co., 563 F.3d 777, 781 (9th Cir. 2008) (all-risk policy covered flood and defined it as "all physical loss or damage caused by or resulting from flood waters, rising waters, waves, tide or tidal water, surface waters, or the rising, overflowing, or breaking of boundaries of lakes, reservoirs, rivers, streams or other bodies of water, whether driven by wind or not, including spray and sewer back-up resulting from any of the foregoing, all regardless of any other cause or event contributing concurrently or in any other sequence of loss"); 4 NYP Ventures LLC v. Factory Mut. Ins. Co., 197 F. Supp. 3d 634 (S.D.N.Y. 2016) (policy covered physical loss or damage caused by or resulting from flood, which it defined as, among other things, surface waters, rising waters, storm surge, or sea surge, as well as physical loss or damage from flood associated with a storm or weather disturbance whether or not identified by name); Long Motor Lines, Inc. v. Home Fire & Marine Ins. Co., 220 S.C. 335, 67 S.E.2d 512 (S.C. 1951) (carrier of freight and merchandise had policy insuring its liability for direct loss or damage to any property transported caused by flood, meaning rising of streams or navigable waters); Sun Underwriters Ins. Co. v. Bunkley, 233 S.W.2d 153 (Tex. Civ. App. 1950) (policy covering chickens insured against direct loss or damage caused by flood, meaning rising of natural bodies of water).

24. Fossett, *What Does Flood Mean to You? The Louisiana Courts' Struggle to Define in Sher v. Lafayette Insurance Company*, 37 S.U. L. Rev. 289 (2010) (term "flood" is ambiguous as doubt exists as to parties' common intent in employing that word and opinions differ on its generally prevailing meaning).

25. Hudson Enters. v. Certain Underwriters at Lloyd's London Ins. Cos., 855 F.3d 874 (8th Cir. 2017); Whitt v. State Farm Fire & Cas. Co., 248 Ill. Dec. 620, 315 Ill. App. 3d 658, 734 N.E.2d 911, *app. den.*, 252 Ill. Dec. 86, 192 Ill. 2d 710, 742 N.E.2d 336 (2000); Ebbing v. State Farm Fire & Cas. Co., 67 Ark. App. 381, 1 S.W.3d 459 (1999). *See also* White v. West Am. Ins. Co., 2008 U.S. Dist. LEXIS 99034 (M.D. Pa. Dec. 8, 2008) ("flood" is term with specific definition and is not ambiguous).

26. Wallis v. Country Mut. Ins. Co., 309 Ill. App. 3d 566, 723 N.E.2d 376 (2000) (finding term "flood" was not ambiguous under facts of case, but acknowledging that under some circumstances it could result in ambiguity); Bartlett v. Continental Divide Ins. Co., 697 P.2d 412 (Colo. App. 1984) (although use of term "flood" may in some cases result in ambiguity, there was no ambiguity in case before the court); Mateer v. Reliance Ins. Co., 247 Md. 643, 233 A.2d 797 (1967) (by dictionary definition, the word "flood" has many meanings; while originally "flood" had riparian connotation, through centuries of change it has come to have less restricted meaning; finding latent ambiguity in term "flood"). *See also* Industrial Enclosure Corp. v. Northern Ins. Corp., 2000 U.S. Dist. LEXIS 11567 (N.D. Ill. July 25, 2000) (there may be circumstances in which "flood" may be considered ambiguous as applied to particular fact pattern); Kane v. Royal Ins. Co., 768 P.2d 678 (Colo. 1989) (term "flood" is not ambiguous as applied to the facts of case).

Katrina, the Fifth Circuit handed down one of the most important decisions on the meaning of flood. The cases of four policyholders were consolidated. The property of each was damaged when levees failed in the midst of the hurricane and canals running through the city of New Orleans overflowed their normal boundaries. The court said the flood exclusions in the policies were "unambiguous in the context of the facts of this case."[27] While the court rejected every argument on ambiguity put forward by the insureds, its holding appears to leave room for the term "flood" to be ambiguous "in the context" of other facts.

Courts agree that "flood" should be given its plain and ordinary meaning,[28] but they do not agree on exactly what that meaning is. If "flood" is to be given its plain and ordinary meaning, then the place to start to understand that meaning is a lay dictionary. The Merriam-Webster online dictionary says a flood is a "rising and overflowing of a body of water especially onto normally dry land."[29] A law dictionary begins simply by calling it an "overflow of water" but ends with the recondite statement that flood is a "relative term which may refer to mere surface water causing temporary inconvenience or which may refer to a collection of water so great as to amount to an inundation."[30] A leading treatise describes "flood waters" as "those waters above the highest line of the ordinary flow of a stream, and generally speaking they have overflowed a river, stream, or natural water course and have formed a continuous body with the water flowing in the ordinary channel."[31]

Courts have adopted a variety of definitions of "flood." They say a flood is an inundation of water over land not usually covered by it (and not necessarily an overflow of a body of water),[32] that it is a rising and overflowing of a body of water that covers land not usually under water,[33] that it is the

---

27. Vanderbrook v. Unitrin Preferred Ins. Co. (*In re* Katrina Canal Breaches Litig.), 495 F.3d 191, 221 (5th Cir. 2007).

28. Wallis v. Country Mut. Ins. Co., 309 Ill. App. 3d 566, 723 N.E.2d 376 (2000). *See also* Park Ridge Presbyterian Church v. Am. States Ins. Co., 2014 U.S. Dist. LEXIS 130492 (N.D. Ill. Sept. 17, 2014); E.K.S., Inc. v. United States Fire Ins. Co., 1999 U.S. Dist. LEXIS 7012 (N.D. Ill. May 3, 1999).

29. *Flood*, Merriam-Webster, https://www.merriam-webster.com/dictionary/flood. A second definition is "the flowing in of the tide."

30. *Ballentine's Law Dictionary*, 3rd Edition. *See also* City of Tulsa v. Grier, 114 Okla. 93, 97, 243 P. 753, 757 (1924) (word "flood" is relative term and may refer to mere surface water causing temporary inconvenience or to such quantities of water as cause damage).

31. *Appleman & Appleman, Insurance Law and Practice*, § 3145 (Matthew Bender 2011).

32. Whitt v. State Farm Fire & Cas. Co., 248 Ill. Dec. 620, 315 Ill. App. 3d 658, 734 N.E.2d 911, *app. den.*, 252 Ill. Dec. 86, 192 Ill. 2d 710, 742 N.E.2d 336 (2000). *See also* Lapa v. Sentinel Ins. Co., 2018 Ill. App. Unpub. LEXIS 569 (Mar. 30, 2018) (flood does not necessarily involve overflow from body of water, but can be inundation of water over land not usually covered by it).

33. Industrial Enclosure Corp. v. Northern Ins. Corp., 2000 U.S. Dist. LEXIS 11567 (N.D. Ill. July 25, 2000). *See also* Vanderbrook v. Unitrin Preferred Ins. Co. (*In re* Katrina Canal

coming of a great quantity of water over a place that is usually dry,[34] that it connotes an inundation,[35] that it is a deluge,[36] and that it is water above the highest line of ordinary flow of a stream.[37] "Flood water" has been defined by courts as water above the highest line of the regular or ordinary flow of a stream;[38] "water that escapes from a watercourse in large volumes and flows over adjoining property in no regular channel ending up in an area where it would not normally be expected";[39] a body of water, including moving water, overflowing or inundating land not usually covered;[40] waters flowing out of a natural watercourse, but which yet were once a part of a stream and have escaped from it;[41] and those waters that breach their containment.[42] Implicit in the definitions is that flooding is "abnormal."[43]

The principal disagreement among courts is whether the term "flood" encompasses only natural sources or whether it includes those that are human-made.

Breaches Litig.), 495 F.3d 191 (5th Cir. 2007) (event is a flood when body of water overflows its normal boundaries and inundates area of land that is normally dry).

34. E.K.S., Inc. v. United States Fire Ins. Co., 1999 U.S. Dist. LEXIS 7012 (N.D. Ill. May 3, 1999).

35. The word "inundation" is used frequently to describe "flood" and simply means "a great flow of water or of something that overwhelms." *Inundation*, Merriam-Webster, https://www.merriam-webster.com/thesaurus/inundation. *See also* Wilson v. National Auto. & Casualty Ins. Co., 22 Ill. App. 2d 34, 159 N.E.2d 504 (1959) (normal dictionary definition of "inundation" refers to overflow of waters coming out of their bed).

36. Popkin v. Security Mut. Ins. Co., 48 A.D.2d 46, 367 N.Y.S.2d 492 (1975).

37. Hudson Enters. v. Certain Underwriters at Lloyd's London Ins. Cos., 855 F.3d 874 (8th Cir. 2017); Employers' Fire Ins. Co. v. Howsley, 432 S.W.2d 578 (Tex. Civ. App.—Amarillo 1968).

38. Texas Co. v. Burkett, 117 Tex. 16, 28, 296 S.W. 273, 277 (1927) (flood waters of a stream are those above highest line of ordinary flow of stream); State Farm Lloyds v. Marchetti, 962 S.W.2d 58 (Tex. App.—Houston, 1st Dist. 1997).

39. Wallis v. Country Mut. Ins. Co., 309 Ill. App. 3d 566, 723 N.E.2d 376 (2000). *See also* Barneck v. Utah DOT, 353 P.3d 140 (Utah 2015) (*only* after water joins a watercourse, whether natural or artificial, and then spills out over its banks, whether the cause is natural or artificial, does it become "flood water"), *overruled on other grounds*, Scott v. Wingate Wilderness Therapy, LLC, 2021 Utah LEXIS 85 (July 9, 2021); Maricopa County Municipal Water Conservation Dist. No. 1 v. Warford, 69 Ariz. 1, 206 P.2d 1168 (1949); McManus v. Otis, 61 Cal. App. 2d 432, 143 P.2d 380 (1943) (that errant waters make temporary channel or follow some natural channel, gully, or depression does not affect their character as flood waters).

40. Bartlett v. Continental Divide Ins. Co., 697 P.2d 412 (Colo. App. 1984).

41. Southern Pac. Co. v. Proebstel, 61 Ariz. 412, 419, 150 P.2d 81, 84 (1944) (waters flowing out of natural watercourse, but which yet were once a part of a stream and have escaped from it, are flood waters); Le Brun v. Richards, 210 Cal. 308, 315, 291 P. 825, 828 (1930). *See also* Kennecott Copper Corp. v. McDowell, 100 Ariz. 276, 281, 413 P.2d 749, 752 (1966) (there was evidence that diverted waters were not flood waters in legal sense as they had not broken away from confines of natural channel).

42. M & M Corp. v. Auto-Owners Ins. Co., 390 S.C. 255, 701 S.E.2d 33 (S.C. 2010).

43. Milbert v. Carl Carbon, Inc., 89 Idaho 471, 478, 406 P.2d 113, 117 (1965) (flood waters are those that escape, because of their height, from confinement of a stream and overflow adjoining territory; implicit in definition is element of abnormality).

The majority of dictionaries, treatises, and courts[44] agree that the word "flood" generally means overflow of a body of water on a normally dry area, *regardless* of whether that water comes from a *natural* or *human-made* source.[45] One commentary contends that relating the term "flood" to its cause forces the distinction between natural and human-made floods, both of which may involve "bodies of water." Therefore, the author argues that courts should not ask what caused an event to determine whether it was a "flood," but should instead determine whether there was an overflow of a body of water, "an answer which is easily determinable."[46]

The court's definition of "flood" can be critical as two Illinois cases demonstrate. A federal court defined "flood" as rising and overflowing of a body of water covering land not usually under water. During a storm, water from light well walkways and stairs leading down to them caused a basement to fill with water. The court found there was no flood because the water did not escape from a body of water. There was, noted the court, no nearby stream or river that could have caused the flood, and the light well walkways were not watercourses or defined water channels.[47] In contrast, a state court defined "flood" as an inundation of water over land not usually covered by it. It considered a case in which water entered the insured home around basement window casings, through a hole in the furnace room wall, and under doors to the house and the garage after a massive rainstorm. The court said rain fell and inundated land not usually covered by water and where water would not be expected to be. There was, therefore, a flood.[48]

[ii] Natural Sources Only

Some courts hold that a flood can *only* consist of water from a natural source.[49] There are, therefore, a number of cases holding that water from broken water

---

44. *See, e.g.*, Kane v. Royal Ins. Co., 768 P.2d 678, 680–81 (Colo. 1989) (generally accepted meaning of "flood" does not include distinction between artificial and natural floods).

45. Taylor, Park & O'Brien, *Unique Coverage Issues in Flood Losses*, 48 Tort & Ins. L.J. 619 (2013).

46. Fossett, *What Does Flood Mean to You? The Louisiana Courts' Struggle to Define in* Sher v. Lafayette Insurance Company, 37 S.U. L. Rev. 289, 313 (2010).

47. Park Ridge Presbyterian Church v. Am. States Ins. Co., 2014 U.S. Dist. LEXIS 130492 (N.D. Ill. Sept. 17, 2014).

48. Whitt v. State Farm Fire & Cas. Co., 248 Ill. Dec. 620, 315 Ill. App. 3d 658, 734 N.E.2d 911, *app. den.*, 252 Ill. Dec. 86, 192 Ill. 2d 710, 742 N.E.2d 336 (2000).

49. *See, e.g.*, Broome v. Allstate Ins. Co., 144 Ga. App. 318, 241 S.E.2d 34 (1977) (finding it is more reasonable to construe water exclusion as applying only to natural flooding as opposed to flooding caused by artificial means; thus, policy covered damage from water that had leaked from faulty swing joint connecting plumbing system of house to public water supply at point just outside foundation).

lines cannot constitute flood waters.[50] In a typical case, insured property was damaged because of a broken water main, and the court found that the water exclusion concerns water damage from natural phenomena, not a ruptured water main.[51] The Kentucky Supreme Court reached the same conclusion and added that the phrase "regardless of the cause" preceding the word "flood" did not negate the distinction between naturally occurring and artificially made water disasters. That phrase, said the court, did not change the fact that the event at issue still has to constitute a flood or one of the other enumerated forms of water before the modifying phrase applies.[52]

In another case, a city water main ruptured, leaking large amounts of water into subsurface soils around the insured property that caused a large area of ground to collapse and undermine the foundation. Water also infiltrated the basement, causing significant water damage. The court said the water damage exclusion barred coverage only for damage from natural causes and not for that caused by a defective municipal water system. The amount of water that caused the damages was not a natural phenomenon and, therefore, the insurer had not established that the exclusion was applicable.[53]

[iii] Artificial or Human-Made Source

Probably the best-known decision rejecting a dichotomy between floods with natural causes and those with non-natural causes is that of the Fifth Circuit

---

50. *See, e.g.*, Auto-Owners Ins. Co. v. United Way of E. Cent. Ala., 497 F. Supp. 3d 1115, 1121 (N.D. Ala. 2020) (finding that water that escaped from ruptured water main and flowed across parking lot was not a "flood"); Veloz v. Foremost Ins. Co. Grand Rapids, 306 F. Supp. 3d 1271 (D. Ore. 2018) ("flood water" unambiguously refers to natural water sources, and no reasonable insured would interpret term to refer to water that escapes from human-made source such as water main); Change, Inc. v. Westfield Ins. Co., 208 W. Va. 654, 542 S.E.2d 475 (2000) (words of the exclusion—flood, waves, tides—referred to water arising from natural causes); Rovelli v. Allstate Ins. Co., 38 A.D.3d 241, 831 N.Y.S.2d 150 (2007) (exclusion for flood coverage did not apply where pipe had burst); Ebbing v. State Farm Fire & Cas. Co., 67 Ark. App. 381, 1 S.W.3d 459 (1999) ("flood" is unambiguous, and its common usage applies to water occasioned from natural events rather than a burst water main); Ender v. National Fire Ins. Co., 169 A.D.2d 420, 563 N.Y.S.2d 85 (1991) (insured sued insurer over water damage arising from break in city water main located approximately one block away from insured property, and court found flood exclusion was not a bar to claim as it precluded only recovery for damages arising from natural causes, not from artificial devices); Popkin v. Security Mut. Ins. Co., 48 A.D.2d 46, 367 N.Y.S.2d 492 (1975) ("flood" does not encompass water damage sustained as result of broken water main); Ferndale Dev. Co. v. Great American Ins. Co., 34 Colo. App. 258, 527 P.2d 939 (1974) ("flood" does not include water escaping from burst water mains).

51. Robert Dorsen, Inc. v. Aetna Casualty & Surety Co., 562 F. Supp. 495 (D.D.C. May 5, 1983).

52. Comley v. Auto-Owners Ins. Co., 563 S.W.3d 9, 11 (Ky. 2018) (flood exclusion barred from coverage damage caused entirely by natural forces).

53. Simmons v. Dryden Mut. Ins. Co., 22 Misc. 3d 1111(A), 880 N.Y.S.2d 227 (2009).

in the Katrina Canal Breaches Litigation.[54] As the name suggests, the case concerned claims for damage to property after levees in New Orleans failed during Hurricane Katrina. The policyholders argued that the inundation of water into the city was the result of negligent design, construction, and maintenance of the levees. The flood exclusion, they further contended, should not apply where the cause of their loss was human error. The court did not agree. The term "flood" was not, it said, limited to natural events, and it noted that dictionaries make no distinction between floods with natural causes and those with non-natural causes.[55] The court distinguished the many cases holding that water from a broken water main is not a flood because it emanates from an artificial source.[56] The Fifth Circuit noted that unlike a canal, a water main is not a body of water or watercourse, and many dictionary definitions define "flood" as the overflow of a body of water or watercourse.[57]

A Texas case brought after Hurricane Harvey is similar in reasoning. In that case the Army Corps of Engineers released water impounded in reservoirs to protect areas of a downstream bayou from additional flooding. However, water overflowing from that bayou flooded the plaintiffs' home. They argued that water released into the bayou from reservoirs was somehow a "distinct category of water," not flood water. The court responded that nothing in the policy said the water damage exclusion depended on the underlying cause of the overflow of a body of water. Damage that resulted from waters overflowing the bayou would be excluded whether the water fell directly from the sky into the bayou or was first held in a reservoir and later released into the bayou. The policy excluded water damage from the overflow of the bayou, regardless of the role the reservoir releases played in that overflow. Even when water moves through artificial structures after it overflows from a natural body, concluded the court, the character of that water does not change.[58]

---

54. Vanderbrook v. Unitrin Preferred Ins. Co. (*In re* Katrina Canal Breaches Litig.), 495 F.3d 191 (5th Cir. 2007).

55. *See also* Bartlett v. Continental Divide Ins. Co., 697 P.2d 412 (Colo. App. 1984) (refusing to distinguish between natural and artificial causes of loss, finding that only event alleged as cause of loss was flood caused by failure of dam, and loss by flood was specifically excluded from coverage). *And see* Morris v. Auto-Owners Ins. Co., 2016 U.S. Dist. LEXIS 179715 (D.S.C. Dec. 29, 2016) (release of contained water due to failed and eroded construction of body of dam itself, as well as lack of maintenance needed to protect its integrity still constituted flood).

56. *See also* Sosa v. Massachusetts Bay Ins. Co., 458 N.J. Super. 639, 648–49, 206 A.3d 1011, 1017 (2019) (flood is commonly understood to involve overflow of body of water—whether natural or not—and a water main is not a body of water).

57. *See also* Barneck v. Utah DOT, 353 P.3d 140 (Utah 2015) (only after water joins a watercourse and then spills out over its banks, whether the cause is natural or artificial, does it become "flood water"), *overruled on other grounds*, Scott v. Wingate Wilderness Therapy, LLC, 2021 Utah LEXIS 85 (July 9, 2021).

58. Salcetti v. AIG Prop. Cas. Co., 529 F. Supp. 3d 681 (S.D. Tex. 2021).

[iv] A General and Temporary Condition

One definition of "flood" is a "general and temporary condition of partial or complete inundation of normally dry land areas."[59] It is part of the definition in Federal Emergency Management Agency (FEMA) Standard Flood Insurance Policies, but it is not typically found in the water damage exclusions of commercial and residential property policies.[60] Nevertheless, a court might adopt that definition as did a New Jersey court. In the case, a municipal water main broke under a public street and water inundated the insured home. The court noted that the insurer defined "flood" as a *general* and temporary condition. In this case, said the court, the condition was *not* a "general" one. The word "general" means that the inundation must affect a wide area and precluded the "isolated water condition that specifically damaged plaintiff's property."[61]

[v] Human-Made Watercourse

Courts have held that a flood can be caused by a human-made watercourse. In one case for example, a human-made irrigation channel overflowed its banks, causing water damage to an insured house. The court said that for the purpose of defining "flood" under the water damage exclusion in the policy, it found the attempt of the policyholder to characterize the channel as an artificial source of water to be unavailing. Simply because the watercourse from which water escapes was originally human-made, asserted the court, is of no consequence if it has a defined bed, visible banks, and a recurrent water flow. The channel met those criteria and, therefore, the court held that the water that overflowed its banks and entered the insured home constituted a flood under the plain and ordinary meaning of that term.[62]

[vi] Storm Surge

Courts hold that "storm surge" is a type of flood.[63] For example, the Fifth Circuit has said repeatedly that storm surge is "little more than a synonym

59. *See* 44 C.F.R. § 59.1. See § 5.2, *infra*, for a discussion of the FEMA definition of "flood."

60. *But see* Gage Bros. Concrete Prods. v. Cincinnati Ins. Co., 535 F. Supp. 3d 865 (D.S.D. 2021), where the policy defined "flood" as the partial or complete inundation of normally dry land areas. Under that definition the court said there did not need to be a complete inundation of normally dry land. A partial inundation of normally dry land areas would meet the definition.

61. Sosa v. Massachusetts Bay Ins. Co., 458 N.J. Super. 639, 206 A.3d 1011 (2019).

62. Wallis v. Country Mut. Ins. Co., 309 Ill. App. 3d 566, 723 N.E.2d 376 (2000). *See also* Park Ridge Presbyterian Church v. Am. States Ins. Co., 2014 U.S. Dist. LEXIS 130492 (N.D. Ill. Sept. 17, 2014) (it does not matter whether water escapes from watercourse that was originally human-made or not, if watercourse has defined bed, visible banks, and recurrent water flow).

63. *See, e.g.*, New Sea Crest Healthcare Ctr., LLC v. Lexington Ins. Co., 2014 U.S. Dist. LEXIS 86585 (E.D.N.Y. June 24, 2014) (storm surge is type of flood).

for a 'tidal wave' or 'wind-driven flood.'"[64] Courts in other jurisdictions have agreed.[65] The fact that the specific term "storm surge" is omitted from the definition of water does not create an ambiguity or entitle policyholders to recover for their "flood-induced damages."[66]

[vii] Rain[67]

Courts have drawn a distinction between rain diffused over the surface of the ground and flood waters. Rain diffused over the surface of the ground constitutes surface water, not flood water.[68] The Utah Supreme Court, for example, has said that rainwater falling and accumulating outside of a watercourse—even in significant quantities—is surface water, not flood water.[69]

On the other hand, rain and flood have been said not to be distinct perils when a flood is rain induced. For example, heavy rains and snowmelt caused water to overtop dikes surrounding a lagoon. The dikes then failed, and water inundated the insured home. The court said that it believed the average purchaser of insurance would expect the term "flood" to encompass rain-induced flood and that rain is a "well-recognized and common part of a flood."[70] In another case, the insureds argued a "flood" could not be caused simply by excess rainfall. The court, with tongue in collective cheek, said that would

64. Leonard v. Nationwide Mut. Ins. Co., 499 F.3d 419, 437 (5th Cir. 2007). *See also* Bilbe v. Belsom, 530 F.3d 314, 316 (5th Cir. 2008) (damage to home was caused by inundation of tidal water from lake, and that was water damage within meaning of water damage exclusion that excluded damage for all flooding, whether driven by hurricane winds or not; term "flood" includes storm surges); Tuepker v. State Farm Fire & Cas. Co., 507 F.3d 346 (5th Cir. 2007) (storm surge is peril that is unambiguously excluded by water damage exclusion).

65. *See, e.g.*, AMTRAK v. Arch Specialty Ins. Co., 124 F. Supp. 3d 264, 269 (S.D.N.Y. 2015), *aff'd in part and vacated in part*, 661 Fed. Appx. 10 (2d Cir. 2016) (term "flood" unambiguously encompasses inundation of normally dry land that is caused by storm surge; storm surge pushes water beyond its usual borders and onto normally dry land); Lower Chesapeake Assocs. v. Valley Forge Ins. Co., 260 Va. 77, 532 S.E.2d 325 (2000) (no coverage for damage to docks caused by wind-driven water and gradual deterioration); Corban v. United Servs. Auto. Ass'n, 20 So. 3d 601 (Miss. 2009) ("storm surge" is plainly encompassed within "flood" or "overflow of a body of water" portions of "water damage" definition); Kitson v. National Retailers Mut. Ins. Co., 22 Pa. D. & C. 414 (1935) (wind-driven water was flood). *See also* Paulson v. Fire Ins. Exchange, 393 S.W.2d 316 (Tex. 1965) (coverage excluded where wind brought high water to insured property).

66. Leonard v. Nationwide Mut. Ins. Co., 499 F.3d 419, 438 (5th Cir. 2007). *See also* Corban v. United Servs. Auto. Ass'n, 20 So. 3d 601 (Miss. 2009).

67. *See* State Farm Fire & Casualty Co. v. Paulson, 756 P.2d 764 (Wyo. 1988) ("rain" is ordinarily and commonly thought of as water falling from the sky, and after it stops falling, one does not say that it is "raining," although there may still be wet sidewalks and streets, puddles of water resulting from rain, or water running through gutters and elsewhere as a result of rain).

68. Poole v. Sun Underwriters Ins. Co., 65 S.D. 422, 274 N.W. 658 (1937).

69. Barneck v. Utah DOT, 353 P.3d 140 (Utah 2015), *overruled on other grounds*, Scott v. Wingate Wilderness Therapy, LLC, 2021 Utah LEXIS 85 (July 9, 2021).

70. Kish v. Insurance Co. of N. Am., 125 Wn.2d 164, 883 P.2d 308 (1994).

be news to Noah. It held that the plain meaning of "flood" includes deluges caused by excess rainfall.[71]

[viii] Intentionally Released Water

Sometimes water is purposefully released and damages property. Property owners may then argue that intentionally released water does not constitute a flood. A Pennsylvania federal court disagreed in a case where a power company opened its floodgates and released water from a lake. The water damaged the insured home. The court found there was a flood and that the flood exclusion applied.[72] In a Massachusetts case, the insured home was flooded when authorities opened a flood valve to lower a reservoir out of concern for the integrity of the dam. The court held there was no coverage for any additional flood damage caused by the intentional release of water from the reservoir.[73]

The South Carolina Supreme Court reached a different conclusion. The state Department of Transportation was improving a road. The improvements included installation of a new underground stormwater drainage system. Before the installation was complete, heavy rains fell and the property suffered significant water damage when rainwater exited the incomplete drainage system. The court said that flood waters are those that breach their containment, as a result of either a natural phenomenon or a failure in a human-made system. In the case before the court the water was not flood water because it did not breach any containment, but it was deliberately channeled and cast on the land of the insured.[74]

[ix] Present or Past Location of Flood Water

If a loss is caused by a flood, but the waters never touch the insured property, does the exclusion apply? In one case, a power failure caused by severe tidal flooding at a substation caused the insured to lose business income and suffer food spoilage. The insurer denied coverage because the power failure was caused by the excluded peril of flood. The policyholder countered that there was no flood at the insured premises and the cause of loss was an off-premises power failure. The court said that the policy clearly excluded losses caused

---

71. Horvath v. State Farm Gen. Ins. Co., 2014 Cal. App. Unpub. LEXIS 4706 (June 30, 2014).

72. White v. West Am. Ins. Co., 2008 U.S. Dist. LEXIS 99034 (M.D. Pa. Dec. 5, 2008). *See also* Salcetti v. AIG Prop. Cas. Co., 259 F. Supp. 3d 681 (S.D. Tex. 2021) (no coverage where water intentionally released from reservoirs into bayou during hurricane, overflowed bayou, and entered plaintiff's home).

73. Cortina Realty Trust v. Pac. Ins. Co., 2010 Mass. Super. LEXIS 307 (Sept. 27, 2010).

74. M & M Corp. v. Auto-Owners Ins. Co., 390 S.C. 255, 701 S.E.2d 33 (S.C. 2010).

"indirectly" by flood and the fact that the flood occurred at a substation did not matter as the exclusion applied regardless of the location of the flood.[75]

If flood waters are retained at another location and then released, are they still flood waters? In an Illinois case, rainwater overflowed the tributary of a creek and inundated a building. The water caused a wall to collapse and release a large volume of water in a brief time that flowed back to the tributary, overwhelmed it, and entered the insured building. The policyholder argued that if the loss was caused by water from a nearby building, there was no flood, as it was not the result of a natural overflow of a watercourse. The court said the contention appeared to be that the water would not have flowed toward the insured building without the collapse of the wall of the nearby building that redirected the water toward the insured building. The water overflowed a natural watercourse, said the court, which made it flood water by definition, and the fact that its most recent location was an artificial structure—the nearby building—did not mean it was not flood water. The court added that a flood does not become something else simply because its source is water contained in an artificial structure.[76]

[x] Rising and Overflowing of a Body of Water

A common definition of flood is the "rising and overflowing of a body of water." The meaning of this phrase was significant in an Ohio case where the insured property was lower than adjacent farm land. The farm land was drained by an intermittent stream from which water would flow through a culvert under an earth embankment used as a roadway. A severe storm deposited a large amount of rainwater in a short time and washed debris into the stream channel, which sealed off the culvert. The force of the water caused the embankment to give way, creating a wall of water six feet high that crashed against the side of the insured structure, resulting in extensive damage to the building and its contents. The parties agreed with the finding of a professional engineer that the damage was not the result of the rising of a body of water. The court, citing that finding, decided that a "'flood' as defined in the exclusions did not occur."[77] The court added that "[c]learly, there was no 'body of water' here until the blocked culvert created one in the space of less than two hours after the deluge commenced." The court did, however, concede that the question of whether a flood caused the claimed damage was

75. Northern Spy Food Co., LLC v. Tower Natl. Ins., 2016 N.Y. Misc. LEXIS 1033 (Mar. 22, 2016).

76. Industrial Enclosure Corp. v. Northern Ins. Corp., 2000 U.S. Dist. LEXIS 11567 (N.D. Ill. July 25, 2000).

77. There was a policy definition of "flood" under which the term included "waves, tide or tidal water, and the rising (including the overflowing or breaking of boundaries) of lakes, ponds, reservoirs, rivers, harbors, streams and other similar bodies of water, whether driven wind or not."

"not without some doubt;" but said that doubts and ambiguities ought to be resolved against the insurer.[78] Indeed, in a footnote the court said that the stream was "body of water" only when it drained water, and not when it was a dry bed, an observation that seems to cloud the holding.

[xi] Contaminants in Flood Water

Flood waters may carry contaminants including sewage. Policyholders sometimes insist that those contaminants be treated as a separate peril. Courts have not been receptive to the argument. As one court said, property loss caused by flood damage includes damage caused by water and by toxic substances carried by those flood waters and left behind after they recede.[79]

[xii] Policies Defining "Flood"

While standard policies do not define the word "flood," a few others do, so one must always be careful to check for a definition and not assume there is not one. For example, some polices define the word "flood" as "[s]urface water, waves, tidal water, tidal waves, tsunamis, or overflow of any natural or man made body of water from its boundaries, all whether driven by wind or not."[80] Under that definition a court found no coverage for flooding caused by a creek that overflowed as the result of heavy rains and by road culverts that were blocked by a buildup of debris. The court rejected the insured's argument that the terms of the flood exclusion clause were ambiguous and concluded there was sufficient evidence to establish that the cause of the flooding was heavy rain over a two-day period and that the property was damaged by the overflow of surface water.[81] Coverage was also denied where a downspout that detached from a gutter allowed rain from the gutter to flow into a door well where a storm drain became clogged with debris carried by the rain, causing the door well to fill with water and back up onto and damage a gymnasium wood floor. The court noted the policy definition of "flood" included "surface water," which the court said was "waters on the surface of the ground, usually created by rain or snow." Given that definition, the court found that the floor damage was caused by, resulted from, or arose out of "surface water."[82]

---

78. Northland Ice Center, Inc. v. Centennial Ins. Co., 1979 Ohio App. LEXIS 10249 (Apr. 18, 1979) (unpublished). *See also* Sosa v. Massachusetts Bay Ins. Co., 458 N.J. Super. 639, 206 A.3d 1011 (2019) (broken water main was not a "body of water").

79. Riccio v. Allstate N.J. Ins. Co., 2015 N.J. Super. Unpub. LEXIS 2417 (Oct. 22, 2015). *See also* White v. West Am. Ins. Co., 2008 U.S. Dist. LEXIS 99034 (M.D. Pa. Dec. 5, 2008) (even if rainwater combined with sewage, damage caused was still barred under exclusion for flood or surface water).

80. These policies typically also define "flood" to include a mudslide or mudflow and water that backs up or overflows from any sewer or septic tank in certain circumstances.

81. K.J.D.E. Corp. v. Hartford Fire Ins. Co., 89 A.D.3d 1531, 932 N.Y.S.2d 778 (2011).

82. Dr. Mark Piechota Crefeld Sch. v. Hartford Fire Ins. Co., 2013 U.S. Dist. LEXIS 10792 (E.D. Pa. Jan. 23, 2013).

Another policy defined "flood" as the partial or complete inundation of normally dry land because of unusual or rapid accumulation or runoff of rain or surface waters from any source, waves, tidal waters, tidal waves (including tsunami), or water from rivers, ponds, lakes, streams, or any other body of water that rises above, overflows from, or is not contained within its natural or human-made boundary, and all whether driven by wind or not, including storm surge. Under that definition, a federal court found that a "flood" did not need to be a complete inundation of normally dry land areas, but it could also result from a partial inundation. Also, a flood could result from "unusual or rapid accumulation" of rain, but puddles of standing rainwater would not constitute a "flood."[83]

[c] Surface Water

[i] Common Law Definition of Surface Water

"Surface water" is a component of the water damage exclusion. Insurance policies do not define "surface water." The Restatement of Torts has a broad definition. It says that the phrase means "water from rain, melting snow, springs or seepage, or detached from subsiding floods, that lies or flows on the surface of the earth but does not form a part of a watercourse or lake."[84] The South Carolina Supreme Court has noted that courts "have not attempted to give any complete and full definition of surface waters."[85] Nevertheless, the highest courts in many states have devised a definition. The Restatement description incorporates the two features commonly found in them: (1) water from rain, melted snow, or springs that (2) flows on the Earth's surface and does not form part of a stream or lake.[86] For example, in the late 19th century

83. Gage Bros. Concrete Prods. v. Cincinnati Ins. Co., 535 F. Supp. 3d 865 (D.S.D. 2021).

84. Restatement (Second) of Torts, § 846. A comment adds that the term is used to describe water that occasionally accumulates from natural sources and has not yet evaporated, percolated into the earth, or found its way into a stream or lake. Restatement (Second) of Torts, § 846, comment b. *See* Thomson v. Public Service Commission, 241 Wis. 243, 5 N.W.2d 769 (1942) (citing comment b for meaning of surface water).

85. Lawton v. South Bound R.R. Co., 61 S.C. 548, 553, 39 S.E. 752, 753 (S.C. 1901).

86. *See, e.g.*, Oklahoma Water Resources Board v. Central Oklahoma Master Conservancy Dist., 464 P.2d 748, 751 (Okla. 1968) (surface waters are those that, in their natural state, occur on surface of earth in places other than definite streams or lakes or ponds and may originate from any source and flow vagrantly over broad lateral areas or, occasionally for brief periods, in natural depressions; essential characteristics of surface waters are their short-lived flows are diffused over the ground and are not concentrated or confined in channel flows of definite streams or concentrated or confined in bodies of water conforming to the definition of lakes or ponds); Hartle v. Neighbauer, 142 Minn. 438, 441, 172 N.W. 498, 499 (1919) (surface waters include those that come from rains and snows and do not belong to any well-defined body of water or natural stream); Lawton v. South Bound R.R. Co., 61 S.C. 548, 553, 39 S.E. 752, 753 (S.C. 1901) (surface water has no banks or channels and includes waters diffused over surface of ground and derived from rains and melting snows). *Compare* Alexander v. Muenscher, 7

the Ohio Supreme Court said that surface water is that "which is diffused over the surface of the ground, derived from falling rains and melting snows, and continues to be such until it reaches some well defined channel in which it is accustomed to, and does flow with other waters, whether derived from the surface or springs; and it then becomes the running water of a stream, and ceases to be surface water."[87] There are courts that, instead of describing surface water as "diffused over the surface of the ground,"[88] have portrayed it colorfully as "casual and vagrant."[89] When those "vagrant" waters enter a "natural water course," they are said to lose their character as surface water,[90] but not when "absorbed by or soak[ed] into the marshy or boggy land where collected."[91] Indeed, occasionally courts characterize water as being of the surface while it is "oozing through the soil"[92] or beneath the surface in swamps.[93]

The California Supreme Court famously distinguished flood from surface water, saying the former escapes from a body of water and overflows the adjacent territory,[94] while the latter is produced by rainfall, melting snow, or

---

Wn.2d 557, 559–60, 110 P.2d 625, 626 (1941) (surface waters are produced by rain, melting snow, or springs and may be said to form watercourse at point where it begins to form reasonably well-defined channel).

87. Crawford v. Rambo, 44 Ohio St. 279, 282, 7 N.E. 429, 431 (1886). *See also* Miller v. Eastern Ry. & Lumber Co., 84 Wash. 31, 146 P. 171 (1915) (surface water is water on surface of ground whose source is so temporary or limited as not to be able to maintain for any considerable time a stream or body of water having a well-defined and substantial existence). *Compare* Curtiss v. Ayrault, 47 N.Y. 73, 77 (1871) (waters that stood on marsh or were held in partial suspense in earth were, in legal effect, surface waters). *And see* Lenain, *Toward a Universal Rule for the Reasonable Disposition of Surface Waters in California*, 32 San Diego L. Rev. 637, 639 (1995) ("surface water" refers to water diffused over surface of land or contained in depressions, and which results from rain or snow, or which rises to surface from springs and does not flow in fixed channel or collect in abody of water—for example, a lake).

88. *See* Dellapenna, *The Legal Regulation of Diffused Surface Water*, 2 Vill. Envtl. L.J. 285, 288–89 (1991) (diffused surface water is water on or at surface without being in defined body of water and flows generally over land after rain falls, snow melts, or the like, or perhaps after arising from springs, but does not flow regularly).

89. *See* Thompson v. New Haven Water Co., 86 Conn. 597, 603, 86 A. 585, 588 (1913); Lawton v. South Bound R.R. Co., 61 S.C. 548, 553, 39 S.E. 752, 753 (S.C. 1901); Neal v. Ohio R.R., 47 W. Va. 316, 320, 34 S.E. 914, 915 (1899).

90. Neal v. Ohio R.R., 47 W. Va. 316, 321, 34 S.E. 914, 915 (1899).

91. Hartle v. Neighbauer, 142 Minn. 438, 441, 172 N.W. 498, 499 (1919).

92. *See, e.g.*, Thompson v. New Haven Water Co., 86 Conn. 597, 603–04, 86 A. 585, 588 (1913) (water is surface water while it is oozing through soil or diffusing and squandering itself over surface following no defined course).

93. *See, e.g.*, Hartle v. Neighbauer, 142 Minn. 438, 441, 172 N.W. 498, 499 (1919) (surface waters do not belong to any well-defined body of water or natural stream, but are confined partly to surface and partly beneath surface in swamps or sloughs where they lie stagnant and inactive).

94. *Compare* O'Connell v. East Tennessee, V. & G. R. Co., 87 Ga. 246, 247, 13 S.E. 489 (1891) (water that forms continuous body flowing in ordinary channel, or if it departs from that presently to return by recession of those waters, is to be regarded as still part of river).

rising in a spring.[95] Some courts have, like the Restatement, included water detached from a flood in their definition of surface water. For example, Georgia's highest court said over a century ago that if flood water becomes severed from the main current, or leaves a stream never to return, and spreads out over the lower ground, it becomes surface water.[96] By contrast, its sister court in Arizona said that it is "thoroughly settled" that flood water that escapes a stream is not surface water and does not lose its character as flood water while flowing wild.[97] In the insurance context, distinctions between flood and surface water are usually academic, as losses caused by either are excluded from coverage.

[ii] Meaning of "Surface Water" in Policy Exclusions[98]

"Surface water" is not defined in insurance policies, and policyholders often argue that the term as used in exclusions is ambiguous. Courts nearly unanimously reject that contention.[99] As the Wyoming Supreme Court has said, "it is difficult to understand how an item can be more plainly labeled. It is water

---

See also Lenain, *Toward a Universal Rule for the Reasonable Disposition of Surface Waters in California*, 32 San Diego L. Rev. 637, 640 (1995) (when extraordinary overflow of streams or rivers takes place, overflow is known as "flood water," not "surface water" or water flowing within "natural watercourse").

95. Le Brun v. Richards, 210 Cal. 308, 315, 291 P. 825, 828 (1930) (surface waters are not those that may be on or moving across surface of land without being collected into natural watercourse but are those falling on land by precipitation or rising from springs). *See also* Sun Underwriters Ins. Co. v. Bunkley, 233 S.W.2d 153 (Tex. Civ. App. 1950) (courts have often had occasion to draw distinction between floodwaters and surface waters; rainwater that collected on ground surface and had not backed up from a river, creek, or other natural watercourse could be regarded only as surface waters and not as a flood); Poole v. Sun Underwriters Ins. Co., 65 S.D. 422, 274 N.W. 658 (1937) (rainwater that diffused and squandered itself over land surface could in no sense be called flood waters, but had characteristics contained in various definitions of what constitutes surface water).

96. O'Connell v. East Tennessee, V. & G. R. Co., 87 Ga. 246, 247, 13 S.E. 489 (1891).

97. Southern Pac. Co. v. Proebstel, 61 Ariz. 412, 418, 150 P.2d 81, 83 (1944).

98. *See generally* Taylor, Park & O'Brien, *Unique Coverage Issues in Flood Losses*, 48 Tort & Ins. L.J. 619 (2013).

99. *See, e.g.*, White v. West Am. Ins. Co., 2008 U.S. Dist. LEXIS 99034 (M.D. Pa. Dec. 5, 2008) ("surface water" is not ambiguous term); ABK, LLC v. Mid-Century Ins. Co., 166 Idaho 92, 454 P.3d 1175 (2019); Am. Family Mut. Ins. Co. v. Schmitz, 330 Wis. 2d 263, 793 N.W.2d 111 (Wisc. App. 2010); Florida Residential Prop. & Cas. Joint Underwriting Ass'n v. Kron, 721 So. 2d 825 (Fla. 3d DCA 1998) (term "surface water" is not ambiguous as applied to water on surface of ground); Heller v. Fire Insurance Exchange, 800 P.2d 1006 (Colo. 1990). *But see* Sosa v. Massachusetts Bay Ins. Co., 458 N.J. Super. 639, 206 A.3d 1011 (2019) (finding term "surface water" to be ambiguous); Ferndale Dev. Co. v. Great American Ins. Co., 34 Colo. App. 258, 527 P.2d 939 (1974); Wilson v. National Auto. & Casualty Ins. Co., 22 Ill. App. 2d 34, 159 N.E.2d 504 (1959) (exclusion clause did not define "surface water," and term had to be strictly construed against insurer).

on the surface,[100] other than in streams, lakes and ponds."[101] Courts interpreting the term in insurance policies fall back on the long-standing common law definition: "surface water" means water diffused over the surface of the ground.[102] More specifically, it is water derived from falling rain or melting snow, or that rises to the surface in springs, that is diffused over the surface of the ground, follows no defined course or channel, and does not gather into or form a natural body of water.[103] Policies do not specify or imply that the term requires a large volume of water.[104]

The common definition suggests that rainwater that never reaches the ground is not surface water. Thus, in one case, water in a burst interior drainage pipe carrying rainwater from the roof to a storm sewer was not surface

---

100. *But see* Al Berman, Inc. v. Aetna Casualty & Surety Co., 216 F.2d 626, 628 (3d Cir. 1954) (water from rain spout that entered "soil pipe" and that escaped at break in soil pipe just below ground level to flow through hole in foundation wall into basement was "surface water").

101. State Farm Fire & Casualty Co. v. Paulson, 756 P.2d 764, 772 (Wyo. 1988). *See also* Iser v. Csaa Fire & Cas. Ins. Co., 506 F. Supp. 3d 1145 (N.D. Okla. 2020) (lake is not surface water).

102. Hatley v. Truck Ins. Exchange, 261 Ore. 622, 495 P.2d 1196 (1972). *See also* Union St. Furniture & Carpet, Inc. v. Peerless Indem. Ins. Co., 2013 Conn. Super. LEXIS 1504 (July 3, 2013) (water that flowed into insured premises through area adjacent to loading dock and through front doorway was surface water, and damages from it were excluded under plain meaning of language of policy); Thorell v. Union Ins. Co., 242 Neb. 57, 492 N.W.2d 879 (1992) (heavy rain diffused over surface of ground was surface water).

103. *See* Williams v. State Farm Fire & Cas. Ins. Co., 581 Fed. Appx. 733 (11th Cir. 2014) (stormwater that flowed in diffused state downhill from culvert located on hill and across insured property and a neighbor's yard entered insured home on surface of the ground and was surface water); Johnson v. State Farm Fire & Cas. Co., 2021 U.S. Dist. LEXIS 220996 (W.D. Tenn. Nov. 16, 2021) (surface water does not mean a permanent body of water, and rainwater lying on surface of the earth is surface water); Pomon v. Davis, 2009 R.I. Super. LEXIS 68 (June 24, 2009); State Farm Lloyds v. Marchetti, 962 S.W.2d 58, 61 (Tex. App.—Houston, 1st Dist. 1997) (surface water is defined as water or natural precipitation diffused over surface of ground until it either evaporates, is absorbed by the land, or reaches channels where water naturally flows and is terranean nature—that is, it is not water below surface, whether from natural or unnatural source); Employers' Fire Ins. Co. v. Howsley, 432 S.W.2d 578 (Tex. Civ. App.—Amarillo, 1968) (surface water is generally defined as that which is derived from rain or melting snow, and is diffused over the surface of ground while it remains in such diffused state); Dent v. Allstate Indem. Co., 82 Va. Cir. 386 (Mar. 23, 2011) (damage to home fell under surface water exclusion where heavy rainfall travelled as surface water across completely clogged drain as if no drain existed); Richman v. Home Ins. Co. of N.Y., 172 Pa. Super. 383, 94 A.2d 164 (1953). *See also* Hirschfield v. Continental Casualty Co., 199 Ga. App. 654, 405 S.E.2d 737 (1991), where a grate-covered opening to an underground storm drain was located adjacent to the insured home. Debris in the underground drain caused rainwater that had previously entered the drain to be diverted upward through the grate, across the surface area, and into the basement. The court held that the rainwater that entered the basement fit squarely within the "surface water" exclusion in the policy.

104. Harinderpal Ahluwalia v. Allied Prop. & Cas. Ins. Co., 2012 U.S. Dist. LEXIS 93820 (E.D. Cal. July 6, 2012).

water, as it had not reached the ground.[105] Many courts, however, say that water that pools or collects on the surface of a roof, deck, patio, or pavement *is* surface water, as those surfaces are in effect a substitute for the ground.[106] There is a contrary view that is apparently in the minority.[107]

---

105. Amish Connection, Co. v. State Farm Fire & Cas. Co., 861 N.W.2d 230 (Iowa 2015) (rainwater that caused damage had not reached outside ground to become surface water).

106. *See* Danville Commer. Indus. Storage, LLC v. Selective Ins. Co., 442 F. Supp. 3d 921, 926 (D. W.Va. 2020) (surface water includes ponded or standing water on a roof); Oak Hill Inv. IV LLC v. State Farm Fire & Cas. Co., 2017 U.S. Dist. LEXIS 158851 (D. Ohio Sept. 27, 2017) (surface water is not narrowly defined as only water that lands on dirt; plain meaning of word "ground" includes roof and water that pooled on roof because of clogged drain was surface water); Martinez v. Am. Family Mut. Ins. Co., 413 P.3d 201 (Colo. App. 2017) (rooftop is continuation of earth's surface, and precipitation that falls on it is surface water); Intrepid Ins. Co. v. Prestige Imps., Inc., 78 So. 3d 583 (Fla. 3d DCA 2011) (if falling rain pooled in areas adjacent to insured property and then flowed into it, damage was caused by surface water and would be excluded); Crocker v. American Nat'l Gen. Ins. Co., 211 S.W.3d 928 (Tex. App. 2007) (ordinary meaning of surface water reasonably includes rainwater that collects on surface of patio); Cameron v. USAA Prop. & Cas. Ins. Co., 733 A.2d 965 (D.C. App. 1999) (snow on patio was surface water when it melted); Casey v. General Accident Ins. Co., 178 A.D.2d 1001, 578 N.Y.S.2d 337 (1991) (where heavy rainfall caused rain from roof to collect outside basement door and enter basement because of failure of rain gutter and drainage system, cause of loss was surface water); Kossoff v. Rathgeb-Walsh, Inc., 170 N.Y.S.2d 789, 3 N.Y.2d 583, 148 N.E.2d 132 (1958) (water coming from adjacent paved lot seeped through upper wall of insured building and damaging personal property in basement was diffused surface water); McCullough v. Hartpence, 141 N.J. Eq. 499, 58 A.2d 233 (1948) (surface water includes waters derived from falling rain and melting snow, whether on ground or on roofs of buildings); Fenmode, Inc. v. Aetna Cas. & Sur. Co. of Hartford, 303 Mich. 188, 6 N.W.2d 479 (1942) (water on paved lot was surface water); Bringhurst v. O Donnell, 14 Del. Ch. 225, 124 A. 795 (1924) (in case of building erected on land, roof is artificial elevation of earth's surface and when it intercepts falling rain or snow, it gathers surface waters). *See also* Union St. Furniture & Carpet, Inc. v. Peerless Indem. Ins. Co., 2013 Conn. Super. LEXIS 1504 (July 3, 2013), where the court described the question of whether water that entered through a roof was surface water as a close one. It noted that the insurer offered some case law that stood for the proposition that water that pools or collects on the surface of a roof is by its nature surface water.

107. Cochran v. Travelers Ins. Co., 606 So. 2d 22 (La. App. 1992) (reference to "surface water" in policy is to body of water that collects and lays on surface of ground, and there is no indication that it was meant to encompass rainwater falling from sky, overflowing rooftop, and seeping into interior of building); McCorkle v. Penn Mut. Fire Ins. Co., 213 So. 2d 272 (Fla. 3d DCA 1968) (rainwater that backed up on roof because of clogged drain was not surface water); American Ins. Co. v. Guest Printing Co., 114 Ga. App. 775, 152 S.E.2d 794 (1966) (while some courts characterize water on roofs as surface water, majority of cases apply term strictly to water on surface of ground). *See also* Bethany Boardwalk Grp. LLC v. Everest Sec. Ins. Co., 2020 U.S. Dist. LEXIS 38427 (D. Md. Mar. 5, 2020) (it is far from obvious that Maryland Court of Appeals would treat rain that collected on roof as surface water); Ridgewood Grp., LLC v. Millers Capital Ins. Co., 161 A.3d 392 (Pa. Super. 2017) (unpublished) (rainwater that traveled directly from roof into channel created by window well and then entered basement was not surface water). *And see* Flamingo S. Beach Condo. Ass'n, Inc. v. Selective Ins. Co. of Se., 492 F. App'x 16 (11th Cir. 2012) (surface waters would not encompass water that pooled on surface of deck).

Water that exits a drainage pipe and flows over ground or that collects on the ground and fails to drain because of an obstruction has been considered to be surface water.[108]

While most courts consider the term "surface water" to be unambiguous, that has not stopped there from being considerable debate over its meaning. For example, are "rain" and "surface water" the same? Courts have said they are not.[109] Rain that falls is no longer rain after it reaches the ground. It becomes water and is then within the classification known as surface water.[110] On the other hand, rain that falls directly into a building through holes in a roof or broken windows without first hitting the ground would probably not be surface water.[111] What about groundwater that bubbles up to the surface?

---

108. Lucky Leather, Inc. v. Mitsui Sumitomo Ins. Grp., 650 Fed. Appx. 364 (9th Cir. 2016) (water that pooled on ground after exiting neighbor's drainage pipe was surface water); Surabian Realty Co. v. NGM Ins. Co., 462 Mass. 715, 971 N.E.2d 268 (2012) (rainwater that collects on ground is considered surface water even when, but for an obstruction, that water would have entered a drainage system); Sunshine Motors, Inc. v. New Hampshire Ins. Co., 209 Mich. App. 58, 530 N.W.2d 120 (1995) (finding no coverage where heavy rainfall created surface water that failed to drain away because of debris blocking drainage system); Montanaro v. Nationwide Ins. Co., 2003 Conn. Super. LEXIS 588 (Feb. 27, 2003) (water that may have backed up from brook pipe onto the plaintiff's parking lot was surface water).

109. *But see* Goldfarb v. Maryland Casualty Co., 311 Ill. App. 568, 37 N.E.2d 376 (1941) (determining line of demarcation between rain and surface water is difficult).

110. Poole v. Sun Underwriters Ins. Co., 65 S.D. 422, 274 N.W. 658 (1937). *See also* Florida Residential Prop. & Cas. Joint Underwriting Ass'n v. Kron, 721 So. 2d 825 (Fla. 3d DCA 1998) (term "surface water" clearly includes water derived from falling rain); State Farm Fire & Casualty Co. v. Paulson, 756 P.2d 764 (Wyo. 1988) (where some water that entered basement had diffused over surface of ground was derived from falling rains and had not reached any well-defined channel, lake, or pond, it fit plain meaning of surface water); Wilson v. National Auto. & Casualty Ins. Co., 22 Ill. App. 2d 34, 159 N.E.2d 504 (1959) (where insured building collapsed after portion of basement collapsed following unusual and excessive amount of rainfall, court concluded it was obvious that collapse resulted from surface water); Unobskey v. Continental Ins. Co., 147 Me. 249, 86 A.2d 160 (1952) (where rain and large quantities of thawed snow exerted pressure on door, causing it to break and flood building, there was no coverage for loss as damage was caused by running surface water from rainstorm and melting snow that overflowed catch basins and parking area). *And see* Anderson v. State Farm Fire & Cas. Co., 2009 U.S. Dist. LEXIS 66613 (D. Ariz. July 30, 2009) (long-established Arizona precedent holds that flows across ground of rainwater are considered surface waters); Pomon v. Davis, 2009 R.I. Super. LEXIS 68 (June 24, 2009) (rainfall gathered outside insured house and was deposited along wall and within window well, where it would have combined with water flowing down wall from the gutter area; whether that water entered basement via window well or through the walls was of no significance because rainwater had diffused over surface of ground and did not form part of well-defined channel, lake, or pond and, therefore, constituted surface water for purposes of surface water exclusion).

111. State Farm Fire & Casualty Co. v. Paulson, 756 P.2d 764 (Wyo. 1988). *See also* Goldfarb v. Maryland Casualty Co., 311 Ill. App. 568, 37 N.E.2d 376 (1941) (rain was not surface water where there was no evidence that there was any water lying on ground); Morley v. United Servs. Auto. Ass'n, 465 P.3d 71, 77 (Colo. App. 2019). The court in *Morley* said that human-made surfaces—roofs or patios—can intercept precipitation and generate surface water, and it

The Georgia Supreme Court has held that subterranean waters that find a water table above the surface of the earth have to be classified either as bodies of water within well-defined basins, as streams flowing within their banks, or as surface water.[112]

Rainwater and subterranean water are "natural." Is water from an "artificial" source—for example, a broken water main—surface water? A number of courts have said that only water from a natural source is surface water.[113] Thus, for example, water that exits a broken water main is usually not considered surface water.[114] Conversely, a Pennsylvania federal court noted that the courts of that state have said that surface waters are commonly understood to be those on the surface of the ground, *usually* created by rain or snow, and that the word "usually" allows the surface water exclusion in a policy to

---

would be nonsensical to categorically exclude precipitation falling on a roof from the definition of surface water simply because the roof temporarily detours the water from its natural flow down grade toward the earth's surface. On the other hand, precipitation that falls or leaks into an insured building through holes in a roof does not fall within the plain meaning of the term "surface water" because it was never water "lying or flowing naturally on the earth's surface."

112. Aetna Ins. Co. v. Walker, 98 Ga. App. 456, 105 S.E.2d 917 (1958). In *Walker*, subterranean or ground waters rose to stand around the foundations and piers of the insured house and allegedly damage it. The court said that it had not been alleged that the water stood in basins of springs from which it emanated, or in any other body of water, or entered any definite stream of water, nor was there any averment that the water would eventually return to any definite body or stream of water. It was instead contended that the water would eventually return to the normal water table below the surface of the earth. That water, asserted the court, lost it identity as ground water while on the face of the earth and fit "all the definitions given of surface waters by the great weight of authority and by our Georgia courts."

113. Hatley v. Truck Ins. Exchange, 261 Ore. 622, 495 P.2d 1196 (1972) (stating that no cases had been cited to it in field of property insurance in which water from any but natural source is held to be surface water and holding that in context in which that term was used in policy, its meaning was so limited).

114. *See* Auto-Owners Ins. Co. v. United Way of E. Cent. Alabama, 497 F. Supp. 3d 1115, 1122 (N.D. Ala. 2020) (water that escapes from ruptured water main and flows across parking lot into adjacent building is not surface water); Veloz v. Foremost Ins. Co. Grand Rapids, 306 F. Supp. 3d 1271 (D. Ore. 2018) ("surface water" unambiguously refers to natural water sources, and no reasonable insured would interpret term to refer to water that escapes from human-made source such as water main); Sosa v. Massachusetts Bay Ins. Co., 458 N.J. Super. 639, 206 A.3d 1011 (2019) (surface water comes from rain, snow, or other precipitation, or underground springs, not water from broken water main); Ebbing v. State Farm Fire & Cas. Co., 67 Ark. App. 381, 1 S.W.3d 459 (1999) ("surface water" refers to water accumulating from natural causes rather than from burst water main); Ferndale Dev. Co. v. Great American Ins. Co., 34 Colo. App. 258, 527 P.2d 939 (1974) (holding that surface water, as used in policy exclusion, did not include water escaping from burst water mains). *See also* L . Safeguard Ins. Co., 1985 Me. Super. LEXIS 173 (June 21, 1985), in which a water main break occurred near the insured building and water flowed into an area behind it. The court said that the surface water exclusion refers to water on the surface of the earth of a "terranean" nature—that is, of natural origin. It did not agree that the surface water exclusion included water from an artificial source and, therefore, it did not apply.

encompass water from both natural and human-made sources.[115] The specific policy language can be critical. The Pennsylvania court highlighted the fact that the surface water exclusion applied whether the water was caused by an act of nature or "otherwise." That decision was distinguished by an Oregon court where the exclusion said it applied "whether or not there was widespread damage and whether or not it was caused by a human activity or an act of nature." The court that said "it" referred to the damage, not to water. In other words, the exclusion applied whether or not the damage to the insured property was caused by a human activity. The Oregon court said that, in contrast, in the Pennsylvania case the word "caused" was linked to the source of the water.[116]

Before they melt, ice and snow are not surface water. Thus, where ice and snow entered a basement, they were not water on the surface of the ground and the water damage caused by them once they melted was not encompassed by the water damage exclusion.[117]

[iii] Loss of Surface Water Status

When does surface water lose that status? The Nebraska Supreme Court, quoting a legal encyclopedia, said that:

> Surface waters cease to be such when they empty into and become part of a natural stream or lake, but they do not lose their character as such by reason of their flowing from the land on which they first make their appearance onto lower land in obedience to the law of gravity, or by flowing into a natural basin from which they normally disappear through evaporation or percolation.[118]

Some courts say that water may lose its status as surface water if it goes underground or is directed into a human-made trench or drainage system, preventing natural drainage.[119] For example, in a South Carolina case, the

115. Citi Gas Convenience v. Utica Mut. Ins. Co., 2016 U.S. Dist. LEXIS 15503 (E.D. Pa. Feb. 9, 2016).

116. Veloz v. Foremost Ins. Co. Grand Rapids, 306 F. Supp. 3d 1271 (D. Ore. 2018).

117. O'Neill v. State Farm Ins. Co., 1995 U.S. Dist. LEXIS 4790 (E.D. Pa. Apr. 7, 1995).

118. Lackaff v. Bogue, 158 Neb. 174, 187, 62 N.W.2d 889, 898 (1954).

119. Chateau Vill. N. Condo. Ass'n v. Am. Family Mut. Ins. Co., 170 F. Supp. 3d 1349 (D. Colo. 2016) (surface water that enters sewer system and backs up through or overflows from sewer or drain is no longer surface water); Herrington, Inc. v. City of Geneva, 2012 Ill. App. Unpub. LEXIS 2770 (2012) (water that entered insured building from a defined waterway or channel—sewer line—and was no longer surface water); Industrial Enclosure Corp. v. Northern Ins. Corp., 2000 U.S. Dist. LEXIS 11567 (N.D. Ill. July 25, 2000) (surface water, by definition, stops being surface water once it flows into drain or underground); Selective Way Ins. Co. v. Litigation Tech., Inc., 270 Ga. App. 38, 606 S.E.2d 68 (2004) (water that gathers into a deep pit and flows into a structure through the length of an underground pipe is no longer diffused and is no longer on the surface of the ground; that water has gathered into a body, and has followed a defined course through the pipe and into the building; it is no longer surface water);

state Department of Transportation installed a new underground stormwater drainage system when it widened and improved a road. However, before the installation was completed, the insured property was damaged when there was a heavy downpour and rainwater exited the incomplete drainage system. The court held that the water was surface water before it was collected in the stormwater system, but once it was deliberately contained, concentrated, and cast onto an adjoining property, it was no longer naturally flowing, diffuse water and lacked the identifiable characteristics of surface water. The court added that the water would not become surface water again for the purposes of the policy after it was discharged from a pipe or collection system.[120]

Where surface water seeped into and below the surface of the ground and entered subsurface air-conditioning and heating ducts and was circulated as vapor into the interior of a home causing humidity to damage walls, carpet, and woodwork, the loss was not caused by nor did it result from surface water.[121]

Georgetowne Square v. U.S. Fid. & Guar. Co., 3 Neb. Ct. App. 49, 523 N.W.2d 380 (1994) (where retaining wall on insured property was damaged by water and water pressure emanating from underground pipe that drained water from roof of neighboring property, that water ceased to exist as surface water or runoff once it was channeled through the pipe); Heller v. Fire Insurance Exchange, 800 P.2d 1006 (Colo. 1990) (regular path of the water from melted snow was diverted onto insured property by three parallel trenches constructed behind the property by an unknown person, and runoff lost its character as surface water when it was diverted by those trenches and therefore was not within the surface water exclusion); Transamerica Ins. Co. v. Raffkind, 521 S.W.2d 935 (Tex. Civ. App.—Amarillo 1975) (where damage was caused by or resulted from water after it had lost its status as surface water by being absorbed into ground, loss was not excluded). *See also* Central Mass Recycling, Inc. v. United Nat'l Ins. Co., 2001 Mass. Super. LEXIS 14 (Jan. 3, 2001), where water penetration apparently had resulted from thawing of snow built up outside of the insured building, which caused water to puddle at a rotted door. The court said the question was whether "trenches" created by plowing snow were "man-made trenches." It said that snow, however plowed, is not a trench and that although the snow was pushed against the exterior of the building, there was no evidence that the plowing operation intended to create any kind of trench or channel.

120. M & M Corp. v. Auto-Owners Ins. Co., 390 S.C. 255, 701 S.E.2d 33 (S.C. 2010) (water spewing in unnatural concentration from a stormwater drainage system lacks identifiable characteristics of surface water; naturally falling water that has been intentionally concentrated and cast on insured's property is not surface water for purposes of policy). A dissenting opinion contended the means of disposing of surface water did not change its character and, instead, "surface water" retains its identity until it reaches and becomes a part of a natural watercourse or body. *See also* Comley v. Auto-Owners Ins. Co., 563 S.W.3d 9 (Ky. 2018) (when water gathers into hole, flows into sewer pipe, and the enters and damages building, that water does not constitute surface water); State Farm Lloyds v. Marchetti, 962 S.W.2d 58 (Tex. App.—Houston 1st Dist. 1997) (where excessive rainfall caused sanitation sewer system to exceed its capacity and direct waters back through underground lines from street into insured home, causing non-flood water and sewage to accidently discharge or overflow from within plumbing system, exclusion did not apply even though invasion of water may have been proximately caused by excluded peril). *Compare* Front Row Theatre v. American Mfr.'s Mut. Ins. Cos., 18 F.3d 1343 (6th Cir. 1994) (water that never entered sewer system before entering building retained its character as surface water, and was excluded from policy coverage).

121. Transamerica Ins. Co. v. Raffkind, 521 S.W.2d 935 (Tex. Civ. App.—Amarillo, 1975).

There are also courts that find surface water is *not* converted into something else merely by contacting an artificial structure.[122] For example, in an Ohio case, rain fell and diffused over the surface of the ground on the properties of the insured and his neighbors. It entered a catch basin and drain pipe on the property of an adjoining neighbor of the insured, but was hampered by debris, an intersecting pipe that reduced flow, and an outlet pipe smaller than the intake pipe. Water, therefore, gushed back up from the drain pipe into the catch basin, overflowed, and reached the outside stairwell of the basement on the insured property. The water caused sliding glass doors in the basement to collapse under the pressure of the pooling water, allowing water to enter the basement. The policyholder argued the water lost its character as surface water once it entered the drain basin and drain pipe—a well-defined channel—but the court held the water was surface water that backed up from a drain and that under the policy, the loss was caused by surface water and excluded.[123] Courts have reached the same conclusion when precipitation collected in window wells,[124] in an excavation dug when an addition was being added to a home,[125] entered a "steam tunnel" that connected an athletic

---

122. Smith v. Union Auto. Indem. Co., 257 Ill. Dec. 81, 323 Ill. App. 3d 741, 752 N.E.2d 1261 (Ill. App. 2001) (surface water is not limited to water whose flow has not been altered in any way by paved surfaces, buildings, or other structures). *See also* Park Ridge Presbyterian Church v. Am. States Ins. Co., 2014 U.S. Dist. LEXIS 130492 (N.D. Ill. Sept. 17, 2014) (water that accumulated in light wells and window wells was surface water because water does not lose its character as surface water merely because its flow has been altered in some way by human-made object); Provencal, LLC v. Tower Ins. Co. of N.Y., 138 A.D.3d 732, 30 N.Y.S.3d 138 (2016) (runoff water from neighboring property that funneled into drainage basin adjacent to retaining wall, creating excessive water pressure against that wall was surface water); Legal Servs. Plan of E. Mich. v. Citizens Ins. Co. of Am., 2009 Mich. App. LEXIS 954 (Apr. 30, 2009) (rainwater that fell on street and began to pool and flow became surface water and did not cease to be surface water when it flowed into plaintiff's basement).

123. Myers v. Encompass Indem. Co., 169 Ohio App. 3d 545, 863 N.E.2d 1083 (2006). *See also* Winter Enters., LLC v. West Bend Mut. Ins. Co., 2021 U.S. Dist. LEXIS 175079 (S.D. Ohio Sept. 15, 2021) (water temporarily diverted through French drain retained its character as surface water).

124. Martinez v. Am. Family Mut. Ins. Co., 413 P.3d 201 (Colo. App. 2017) (all precipitation that fell into window wells—rain and hail—was surface water).

125. Am. Family Mut. Ins. Co. v. Schmitz, 330 Wis. 2d 263, 793 N.W.2d 111 (Wisc. App. 2010) (water that was surface water did not cease to be so when its course was affected by "trench"—space between existing crawl space and addition to home—as that trench, while humanly created, was not created for purpose of diverting water and did not create a "defined channel"). *See also* John David Angott Trust v. Great N. Ins. Co., 2006 U.S. Dist. LEXIS 29188 (E.D. Mich. May 15, 2006) (water that settled briefly into excavation, while perhaps not diffuse over large area, was of casual or vagrant character, had no substantial or permanent existence, and had not percolated, evaporated, or reached any definite watercourse or substantial body of water in which it was accustomed to flow and, thus, even as that water found its way into basement, it was surface water, and therefore excluded).

facility to a heating plant,[126] or pooled on a patio.[127] An Arizona court held that when, during heavy rains, a drainage system that was supposed to divert the water failed and the insured home flooded, that failure did not alter the water's character as surface water.[128]

As always, the specific language of the exclusion must be examined. Generally, policies do not address a change in status, but some may explicitly say that there is no coverage if damage was caused by surface water "that enters the sewer or drain system."

Because the exclusion is for damage directly or indirectly caused by surface water, a change in status may not matter. In a Texas case, rainwater flowed along the surface of the ground, into an electrical distribution basin, and through electrical conduit into the insured home. The insured contended the electrical conduit was a channel where water naturally flowed and, therefore, the water lost its character as surface water. The court said that the surface water did not co-mingle with non-surface water or change in form before entering the home. Moreover, because the exclusion was for loss caused directly or indirectly by surface water, if surface water indirectly caused damage by forcing other *non-surface* water into the home, the exclusion would apply.[129] Therefore, even assuming the status of the water as surface water

---

126. State v. North Dakota State University, 694 N.W.2d 225 (N.D. 2005) (surface water does not lose its character as surface water simply by being artificially channeled underground). *See also* Valley Forge Ins. Co. v. Hicks Thomas & Lilienstern, L.L.P, 174 S.W.3d 254 (Tex. App.—Houston 1st Dist., 2004) (heavy rains caused bayou to overflow its banks and water rushed into building, broke through interior basement wall of that building, flowed into parking garage, then into pedestrian tunnel system, and finally poured into basement of insured building causing damage; court found water flowed onward, as flood and surface water into human-made underground structures and, therefore loss was caused by a combination of flood and surface water and was excluded; distinguishing cases where water itself was altered, either by flowing into pipe and combining with sewage or by becoming vapor).

127. Boazova v. Safety Ins. Co., 462 Mass. 346, 968 N.E.2d 385 (2012) (surface water in form of rain or snow falling onto the concrete patio at the rear of house, running along surface of concrete patio to rear wall of house and then onto wood framing of the rear wall did not change its essential character as surface water). *See also* Cameron v. USAA Prop. & Cas. Ins. Co., 733 A.2d 965 (D.C. App. 1999) (where snow accumulated on uncovered outdoor patio, then melted and ran down stairwell leading to basement, water did not lose its character as surface water because it was never channeled or diverted from its natural course).

128. Anderson v. State Farm Fire & Cas. Co., 2009 U.S. Dist. LEXIS 66613 (D. Ariz. July 30, 2009). In *Anderson*, heavy rains fell on the mountainside north of the insured home, and a drainage system that was supposed to divert the water failed to do so. The rainwater flowed across the surface of the land and entered the home, causing extensive damage. The water that entered the home was surface water, and the policy did not cover the resulting damage.

129. Lapa v. Sentinel Ins. Co., 2018 Ill. App. Unpub. LEXIS 569 (Mar. 30, 2018) (where rainwater was pushed back into property from sewer main through buildings floor drains, it was surface water when it entered sewer or drain system and thus not covered as water that backs up from a sewer or drain).

changed on entering the electrical conduit, the court concluded that surface water indirectly caused the loss.[130]

[d] Waves, Tides, and Tidal Waves

[i] Waves

The word "wave" is employed in defining excluded water damage. A "wave" is "a moving ridge or swell on the surface of a liquid (as of the sea)."[131] A "'wave' does not require movement of water into an area not typically covered by it."[132] The term "wave" has been found to include those caused by natural forces and those that are human-made, for example, by passing boats.[133] It should be noted that when streets are flooded, it is not uncommon for passing cars to create waves that produce or increase damage to adjacent properties,[134] and given that the definition of "waves" includes those that are human-made, an exclusion for water damage caused by waves should apply.

[ii] Tides or Tidal Waters

Policies include either "tides" or "tidal waters," or both, in the definition of water. The word "tide" refers to the ebb and flow of the sea on the shore because of the attraction of the moon and sun.[135] A more exacting definition is "the alternate rising and falling of the surface of the ocean and of water bodies (such as gulfs and bays) connected with the ocean that occurs usually twice a day and is the result of differing gravitational forces exerted at different parts of the earth by another body (such as the moon or sun) [or] a less marked rising and falling of an inland body of water."[136] "Tidal waters" have been simply

---

130. Safeco Ins. Co. v. Moss, 2017 Tex. App. LEXIS 6117 (Tex. App.—Austin, June 29, 2017).

131. *Wave*, Merriam-Webster, https://www.merriam-webster.com/dictionary/wave. A California court gave a detailed definition. It said: "A wave is defined as a disturbance in the water when the water crests up; it is formed by the oscillation of water particles that go in a circular motion, while the surface moves in an oscillatory motion. The wave form moves through the water while the particles only go up and down. The height is measured from the crest to the trough, so that a 2-foot wave has a height of 3 to 4 feet." Allied Properties v. John A. Blume & Associates, 25 Cal. App. 3d 848, 852, 102 Cal. Rptr. 259, 261, n.9 (1972).

132. Transcon. Ins. Co. v. Rbmw, 262 Va. 502, 513, 551 S.E.2d 313, 319 (2001).

133. O'Meara v. Am. States Ins. Co., 148 Ind. App. 563, 268 N.E.2d 109, 111–12 (Ind. App. 1971) (motivating source of waves is not factor critical to definition; there are also artificial forces that may cause waves and certainly undulation on surface of water, caused by a human-made subsurface explosion would properly be designated as waves driven by artificial force). *See also* Vanderbrook v. Unitrin Preferred Ins. Co. (*In re* Katrina Canal Breaches Litig.), 495 F.3d 191, 219 (5th Cir. 2007).

134. Sher v. Lafayette Ins. Co., 988 So. 2d 186, 194, n.2 (La. 2008) (waves may be caused by cars driven in high water).

135. *Ballentine's Law Dictionary* (2010).

136. *Tides*, Merriam-Webster, https://www.merriam-webster.com/dictionary/tides.

defined as those "in which the tide ebbs and flows."[137] "It is the rise and fall of the water, and not the proportion of salt water to fresh, that determines whether a particular portion of a stream is within tide water."[138]

[iii] Tidal Waves

Standard policy language includes "tidal waves" as one of the forms of water the damage from which is excluded from coverage. Policies do not, however, define "tidal wave." A Texas court asserts that the term has a well-defined meaning but then does not deign to share that meaning.[139] A "tidal wave" is defined by one dictionary as an unusually high sea wave triggered especially by an earthquake[140] or an unusual rise of water along shore because of strong winds.[141] The first definition also describes a "tsunami."[142] The second is synonymous with "storm surge."[143] Indeed, the Fifth Circuit has said that "'storm surge' is little more than a synonym for a 'tidal wave.'"[144] A

137. *Ballentine's Law Dictionary* (2010). *See also* Commonwealth v. Vincent, 108 Mass. 441, 447 (1871) ("tide waters" are those "whether salt or fresh, wherever the ebb and flow of the tide from the sea is felt").

138. Attorney General v. Woods, 108 Mass. 436 (1871).

139. Berglund v. Hardware Dealers Mut. Fire Ins. Co., 381 S.W.2d 631, 636 (Tex. App. 1964), *rev'd*, 393 S.W.2d 309 (Tex. 1965).

140. One court has observed that tidal waves might also be caused by underwater landslides or underground nuclear testing. Sher v. Lafayette Ins. Co., 988 So. 2d 186, 194, n.2 (La. 2008) (tidal waves are caused by seismic events, such as earthquakes, underwater landslides, which may be natural or human-made, or underground nuclear testing).

141. *Tidal wave*, Merriam-Webster, https://www.merriam-webster.com/dictionary/tidal%20 wave.

142. *Tsunami*, Merriam-Webster, https://www.merriam-webster.com/dictionary/tsunami. *See also* Pararas-Carayannis v. Department of Commerce, 9 F.3d 955, 956, n.2 (Fed. Cir. 1993) (tsunami is large ocean wave usually generated by an earthquake).

143. That appears to have been the thinking of the Kentucky Supreme Court in a case in which high wind produced heavy waves that were driven against the insured buildings. The wind became more violent and the waves higher, causing the buildings to be lifted from their foundations and topple over. The policy excluded coverage for loss caused by, *inter alia*, tidal wave, high water, or overflow. The court held that the loss caused by water being driven by wind against the buildings during a flood was not embraced by the policy. Nat'l Fire Ins. Co. v. Crutchfield, 160 Ky. 802, 170 S.W. 187 (Ky. 1914). *See also* Arjen Motor Hotel Corp. v. General Acci. Fire & Life Assurance Corp., 379 F.2d 265 (5th Cir. 1967) (where waves caused portion of restaurant to collapse and policy excluded loss caused by, resulting from, contributed to, or aggravated by flood, surface water, waves, tidal water, or tidal wave, overflow of streams or other bodies of water, plain wording of exclusion effectively excluded liability for loss occasioned by collapse if it was in fact established that loss was contributed to or aggravated by waves or tidal water).

144. Tuepker v. State Farm Fire & Cas. Co., 507 F.3d 346 (5th Cir. 2007); Leonard v. Nationwide Mut. Ins. Co., 499 F.3d 419, 437 (5th Cir. 2007). *See also* New Sea Crest Healthcare Ctr., LLC v. Lexington Ins. Co., 2014 U.S. Dist. LEXIS 86585 (E.D.N.Y. June 24, 2014); Dejoie v. Republic Grp., 2009 U.S. Dist. LEXIS 149739 (E.D. La. Sept. 24, 2009) (tidal wave or storm surge is essentially massive wall of water pushed ashore by hurricane force winds).

Louisiana court more colorfully portrayed a "tidal wave" as a great body of water blown against property, a "mad fury of gargantuan waves of water."[145] Water that rises gradually without aid of the wind has been found not to be a tidal wave.[146] However, the United States Geological Survey (USGS) defines a tidal wave as "a shallow water wave caused by the gravitational interactions between the Sun, Moon, and Earth."[147]

[e] Overflow of Any Body of Water

The "overflow" of "any body of water" is an excluded cause of loss in standard property policies. Those policies typically define neither "overflow" nor "body of water." Overflow means "to cover with or as if with water (inundate)" or "to flow over the brim of."[148] A law dictionary defines it as "[t]o flow over; to flow over the bounds, over the brim; to cover with or as with water or other fluid; to spread over; to inundate: as, when one wrongfully diverts surface water and causes it to overflow another's land, causing damage."[149] One appellate judge adopted a dictionary definition of "overflow as "'to flow or run over, as rivers or water,'" "'to have the contents flowing over or spilling,'" "'flood; inundate,'" "'to flow over the edge or brim of,'" "'something that flows or runs over,'" and "'a portion crowded out of an overfilled place.'"[150]

A "body of water" is the part of the earth's surface covered with water, for example a river, lake, or ocean.[151] Courts have used the description "body

145. Ebert v. Pac. Nat. Fire Ins. Co., 40 So. 2d 40, 46 (La. App. 1949).

146. Liberty Universal Ins. Co. v. Hall, 289 So. 2d 683, 684 (Miss. 1973) (where water rose slowly over period of two to three hours and then subsided, there was no tidal wave); Grace v. Lititz Mut. Ins. Co., 257 So. 2d 217, 222 (Miss. 1972) (there was "no proof of a huge destructive tidal wave," and abundant proof of high water that arose gradually and quickly).

147. *What is the difference between a tsunami and a tidal wave?*, USGS, https://www.usgs.gov/faqs/what-difference-between-a-tsunami-and-a-tidal-wave. The USGS says that "tidal wave" was used previously to describe what is now call a tsunami.

148. *Overflow*, Merriam-Webster, https://www.merriam-webster.com/dictionary/overflow.

149. *Ballentine's Law Dictionary* (2010). *See also* Miller v. Letzerich, 49 S.W.2d 404, 121 Tex. 248 (1932).

150. Fingerle v. City of Ann Arbor, 308 Mich. App. 318, 359, 863 N.W.2d 698, 720–21 (2014) (Beckering, J., dissenting) (citing Random House *Webster's College Dictionary* (2005)), *vacated*, 498 Mich. 910, 870 N.W.2d 920 (2015). *See also* Burbridge v. Rich Properties, Inc., 365 S.W.2d 657 (Tex. App. 1963), where the court said that the word overflow means "to flow over the bounds, over the brim" but also means "to flow over; to cover with or as with water or other fluid; to spread over, to inundate."

151. *Body of water*, Fine Dictionary, http://www.finedictionary.com/body%20of%20water.html.

of water" when referring to oceans,[152] gulfs,[153] seas,[154] sounds,[155] bays,[156] lakes,[157] ponds,[158] lagoons,[159] coves,[160] pools,[161] springs,[162] impoundments,[163]

---

152. Rice v. Harken Exploration Co., 250 F.3d 264 (5th Cir. 2001).

153. Gulf Holding Corp. v. Brazoria County, 497 S.W.2d 614 (Tex. App. 1973).

154. Rockaway Park Improv. Co. v. New York, 140 A.D. 160, 124 N.Y.S. 1096 (1910).

155. United States v. La., 470 U.S. 93, 105 S. Ct. 1074, 84 L. Ed. 2d 73 (1985); Swan Island Club, Inc. v. White, 114 F. Supp. 95 (E.D.N.C. 1953).

156. Draper Mach. Works v. Dep't of Natural Res., 117 Wn. 2d 306, 815 P.2d 770 (1991); Moyer v. State, 56 Misc. 2d 549, 289 N.Y.S.2d 114 (1968); Medlock v. Galbreath, 208 Ark. 681, 187 S.W.2d 545 (1945); Ocean Industries, Inc. v. Superior Court of Santa Cruz County, 200 Cal. 235, 252 P. 722 (1927); Apalachicola Land & Development Co. v. McRae, 86 Fla. 393, 98 So. 505 (1923); Jones v. Johnson, 6 Tex. Civ. App. 262, 25 S.W. 650 (1894). *See also* Bremmer v. Shedd, 467 F. Supp. 261 (W.D. Pa. 1979); United States *ex rel.* Brown-Crummer Inv. Co. v. North Miami, 11 F. Supp. 69 (S.D. Fla. 1932); Hale v. Sengstacken, 192 F. 641 (D. Ore. 1911).

157. Sylte v. Idaho Dep't of Water Res., 165 Idaho 238, 443 P.3d 252 (2019); State *ex rel.* Swan Lake Area Wildlife Ass'n v. Nicollet County Bd. of County Comm'rs, 771 N.W.2d 529 (Minn. App. 2009); Alderson v. Fatlan, 311 Ill. Dec. 95, 372 Ill. App. 3d 300, 867 N.E.2d 1081 (Ill. App. 2007); Stone v. York Haven Power Co., 561 Pa. 189, 749 A.2d 452 (2000); Carnahan v. Moriah Prop. Owners Ass'n, 716 N.E.2d 437 (Ind. 1999); Park Dist. v. Garcia, 334 N.W.2d 824 (N.D. 1983); Lake Lotawana v. Meagher, 581 S.W.2d 105 (Mo. App. 1979); County of Darlington v. Perkins, 269 S.C. 572, 239 S.E.2d 69 (S.C. 1977); Rothrock v. Loon Island, 96 N.H. 421, 78 A.2d 512 (1951); Clear Lake Water Co. v. Superior Court of Mendocino County, 33 Cal. App. 2d 710, 92 P.2d 921 (1939); Hillebrand v. Knapp, 65 S.D. 414, 274 N.W. 821 (1937); Miami Corp. v. State, 186 La. 784, 173 So. 315 (1936); Milwaukee v. State, 193 Wis. 423, 214 N.W. 820 (1927); Lant v. Wolverton, 122 Wash. 62, 210 P. 1 (1922); Milton v. State, 144 Ark. 1, 221 S.W. 461 (1920); Hunter v. Owens, 80 Fla. 812, 86 So. 839 (1920); State *ex rel.* Cates v. W. Tenn. Land Co., 127 Tenn. 575, 158 S.W. 746 (1913); Madson v. Spokane Valley Land & Water Co., 40 Wash. 414, 82 P. 718 (1905); W. Invest. Co. v. Farmers' Nat. Bank, 35 Ore. 298, 57 P. 912 (1899); State v. Haug, 95 Iowa 413, 64 N.W. 398 (1895); Grand Rapids Ice & Coal Co. v. South Grand Rapids Ice & Coal Co., 102 Mich. 227, 60 N.W. 681 (1894); Alcorn v. Sadler, 66 Miss. 221, 5 So. 694 (1888); Smith v. Rochester, 92 N.Y. 463 (1883). *See also* Historic Aircraft Recovery Corp. v. Wrecked & Abandoned Voight F4U-1 Corsair Aircraft, 294 F. Supp. 2d 132 (D. Me. 2003).

158. Kaiser Aetna v. United States, 444 U.S. 164, 100 S. Ct. 383, 62 L. Ed. 2d 332 (1979). *See also* Comm'r of the Ind. Dep't of Envtl. Mgmt. v. Eagle Enclave Dev., LLC, 120 N.E.3d 212 (Ind. App. 2019); Reilly Constr. Co. v. Bachelder, Inc., 863 N.W.2d 302 (Iowa App. 2015); Hollenberg v. Town of Union, 918 A.2d 1214 (Me. 2007); Ind. Dep't of Envtl. Mgmt. v. Twin Eagle L.L.C., 798 N.E.2d 839 (Ind. 2003); Boxer v. Commonwealth Land Title Ins. Co., 185 A.D.2d 515, 586 N.Y.S.2d 362 (1992); Davis v. Cordova Recreation & Park Dist., 24 Cal. App. 3d 789, 101 Cal. Rptr. 358 (1972); East Orange v. Livingston, 102 N.J. Super. 512, 246 A.2d 178 (1968); McLean v. Bullard, 131 N.C. 275, 42 S.E. 609 (1902); People v. Moses, 140 N.Y. 214, 35 N.E. 499 (1893).

159. People v. Davis, 215 Ill. Dec. 289, 278 Ill. App. 3d 532, 663 N.E.2d 39 (1996); Davis v. Cordova Recreation & Park Dist., 24 Cal. App. 3d 789, 101 Cal. Rptr. 358 (1972); Henn v. State, 172 Neb. 597, 111 N.W.2d 385 (1961).

160. Groton v. Hurlburt, 22 Conn. 178 (1852); Wethersfield v. Humphrey, 20 Conn. 218 (1850); Nelson v. Butterfield, 21 Me. 220 (1842).

161. Cappaert v. United States, 426 U.S. 128, 96 S. Ct. 2062, 48 L. Ed. 2d 523 (1976).

162. Goodman v. Crystal River, 669 F. Supp. 394 (M.D. Fla. 1987).

163. Warcewicz v. Department of Environmental Protection, 410 Mass. 548, 574 N.E.2d 364 (1991) (impoundment is body of water formed by impounding water by, for example, a dam).

watercourses,[164] rivers,[165] streams,[166] creeks,[167] estuaries,[168] canals,[169] channels,[170] and harbors.[171] Courts have also said that a swimming pool,[172] "flowage,"[173] an "artisan basin,"[174] and a "resaca" or overflow basin[175] were bodies of water. A body of water can be owned publicly or privately.[176] There is disagreement about

164. State of California v. Allstate Ins. Co., 45 Cal. 4th 1008, 201 P.3d 1147, 90 Cal. Rptr. 3d 1 (2009). Note that many courts say that a "watercourse" need not flow continuously and may sometimes be dry. *See, e.g.*, Barneck v. Utah DOT, 353 P.3d 140 (Utah 2015) ("watercourse" includes channel or bed itself and does not require that bed carry running water year-round, so watercourse may be dry in times of drought and running with water at other times), *overruled on other grounds*, Scott v. Wingate Wilderness Therapy, LLC, 2021 Utah LEXIS 85 (July 9, 2021); E. Bay Sporting Club v. Miller, 118 Ohio St. 360, 161 N.E. 12 (1928); Tampa Waterworks Co. v. Cline, 37 Fla. 586, 20 So. 780 (1896); Chamberlain v. Hemingway, 27 A. 239, 63 Conn. 1 (1893). *See also* State *ex rel.* Cordray v. Helms, 192 Ohio App. 3d 426, 949 N.E.2d 522 (2011). *And see* Comley v. Auto-Owners Ins. Co., 563 S.W.3d 9, 12 (Ky. 2018) (water main line was "watercourse"); Le Brun v. Richards, 210 Cal. 308, 315, 291 P. 825, 828 (1930) (a watercourse is not errant water gathered while passing through low depression, swale, or gully, but stream in real sense, with definite channel with bed and banks, within which it flows at those times when streams of the region habitually flow).

165. Arroyo Shrimp Farm v. Hung Shrimp Farm, 927 S.W.2d 146 (Tex. App. 1996); Keener v. Sharp, 341 Mo. 1192, 111 S.W.2d 118 (1937); Board of Comm'rs v. Castetter, 7 Ind. App. 309, 33 N.E. 986 (1893); Berlin Mills Co. v. Wentworth's Location, 60 N.H. 156 (1880); Hiscox & Pearce v. Sanford, 4 R.I. 55 (1856). *See also* Sweatt v. Florida Bd. of Pilot Comm'rs, 776 F. Supp. 1538 (M.D. Fla. 1991).

166. Wilson v. Dressler, 52 Va. Cir. 410 (2000).

167. Pinckney v. Beaufort, 296 S.C. 142, 370 S.E.2d 909 (S.C. App. 1988); Department of Natural Resources v. Adams, 37 Md. App. 165, 377 A.2d 500 (1977).

168. Fla. Wildlife Fed'n Inc. v. United States Army Corps of Eng'rs, 859 F.3d 1306 (11th Cir. 2017).

169. Vanderbrook v. Unitrin Preferred Ins. Co. (*In re* Katrina Canal Breaches Litig.), 495 F.3d 191, 216 (5th Cir. 2007); United States v. The Yacona, 112 F. Supp. 863 (E.D. Pa. 1953); Harbor. Towing Corp. v. Parker (The Ruth Conway), 75 F. Supp. 514 (D. Md. 1947).

170. *In re* Everglades Island Boat Tours, LLC, 484 F. Supp. 2d 1259 (M.D. Fla. 2007); Gulliams v. Beaver Lake Club, 90 Ore. 13, 175 P. 437 (1918); Hempstead v. Lawrence, 147 A.D. 624, 132 N.Y.S. 615 (1911); San Diego v. Granniss, 77 Cal. 511, 19 P. 875 (1888). *See also* The Hokendauqua, 270 F. 270 (D.N.Y. 1919).

171. United States v. California, 447 U.S. 1, 100 S. Ct. 1994, 64 L. Ed. 2d 681 (1980); Nance v. Oyster Bay, 41 Misc. 2d 446, 244 N.Y.S.2d 916 (1963); People v. Scudder, 21 Misc. 2d 614, 191 N.Y.S.2d 511 (1959).

172. Armstrong v. Farmers Ins. Co. of Idaho, 147 Idaho 67, 70, 205 P.3d 1203, 1206, n.2 (2009). In the case, an above-ground swimming pool collapsed, resulting in water flooding a finished basement. The lower court found that the water damage exclusion applied because the phrase "body of water" unambiguously and plainly included a swimming pool. The phrase "body of water" was used by the lower court to "describe some determinable amount of water, standing or flowing, that is somehow enclosed, contained or bounded." The Idaho Supreme Court affirmed.

173. Movrich v. Lobermeier, 379 Wis. 2d 269, 905 N.W.2d 807 (2018).

174. Justesen v. Olsen, 86 Utah 158, 40 P.2d 802 (1935).

175. Associated Indem. Corp. v. CAT Contracting, 918 S.W.2d 580, 586, n.1 (Tex. App. 1996) ("resaca" is body of water created as overflow basin for Rio Grande River).

176. *See, e.g.*, Comm'r of the Ind. Dep't of Envtl. Mgmt. v. Eagle Enclave Dev., LLC, 120 N.E.3d 212 (Ind. App. 2019).

whether groundwater can be a body of water. The leading case on the issue is *Lumbermens Mut. Casualty Co. v. Plantation Pipeline Co.*[177] In that case a Georgia court said that some groundwater *may* be a "body of water," particularly major aquifers.[178] A body of water, decided the court, is "an aggregate of water having defined boundaries." It then held that because the groundwater at the site in issue was not bounded by "confining beds," although it technically was an aquifer, it was not a "body of water."[179] Other courts have simply said that ground water *is* a body of water.[180]

A few opinions have stated explicitly what is *not* a body of water. Neither a "water main nor a sink" is a body of water.[181] A drainage ditch is also not a body of water.[182]

In a very old case, the Minnesota Supreme Court said that a "hammer" or "slug" is a *body of water* driven by steam along a pipe at great velocity.[183] The case may have no application in the context of the standard water damage exclusion, but practitioners should at least be aware that it exists.

[f] Spray

Policies typically exclude losses by spray from flood, surface water, waves, tides, tidal waves, or overflow of any body of water, whether driven by wind or not.[184] They do not, however, define "spray." A dictionary definition is

---

177. Lumbermens Mut. Casualty Co. v. Plantation Pipeline Co., 214 Ga. App. 23, 447 S.E.2d 89 (1994).

178. A number of courts have said that aquifers are bodies of water. *See, e.g.*, State of South Dakota v. Kansas City Southern Indus., 880 F2d 40, 41 (8th Cir. 1989), *cert. den.*, 493 U.S. 1023, 110 S. Ct. 726, 107 L. Ed. 2d 745 (1990) (describing Madison Formation Aquifer as an "enormous, mostly subterranean body of water which exists under several states including South Dakota and Wyoming"); George v. Commonwealth, Dept. of Environmental Resources, 102 Pa. Commw. 87, 517 A2d 578, 580, n. 9 (1986) (referring to aquifer or other body of water); Mosley v. Johnson, 22 Utah 2d 348, 352, 453 P2d 149, 152 (1969) (characterizing underground water in aquiferous strata as water bodies).

179. *Accord* Aetna Cas. & Sur. Co. v. Dow Chem. Co., 28 F. Supp. 2d 440 (E.D. Mich. 1998).

180. MAPCO Alaska Petroleum v. Central Nat'l Ins. Co., 795 F. Supp. 941, 945 (D. Alaska 1991).

181. Vanderbrook v. Unitrin Preferred Ins. Co. (*In re* Katrina Canal Breaches Litig.), 495 F.3d 191, 216 (5th Cir. 2007); Sher v. Lafayette Ins. Co., 988 So. 2d 186, 194, n.3 (La. 2008).

182. Chesapeake Ship Propeller Co. v. Stickney, 820 F. Supp. 995 (E.D. Va. 1993). *See also* Northland Ice Center, Inc. v. Centennial Ins. Co., 1979 Ohio App. LEXIS 10249 (Apr. 18, 1979) (unpublished), where the insurer contended that an "intermittent stream" that served to drain water from farm land constituted a body of water. The court said that the stream was a "body of water" only when it drained water, and not when it was a dry bed.

183. Theisen v. Porter, 56 Minn. 555, 58 N.W. 265 (1894).

184. *See* ISO Form CP 10 30 06 07, § B.1.g. Under a slightly different version of the exclusion, coverage is barred for water damage, meaning flood, surface water, waves, tidal water, or overflow of a body of water. In a following sentence, the policy says the insurer does not cover spray from any of these, whether or not driven by wind. *See, e.g.*, Mayton v. Auto-Owners Ins. Co., 2006 U.S. Dist. LEXIS 28952 (E.D. Va. May 2, 2006).

"water flying in small drops or particles blown from waves or thrown up by a waterfall."[185]

[g] Wind-Driven

[i] Generally

Under the typical property coverage, an insurer will not pay for loss or damage caused directly or indirectly by water,[186] and the forms of water specified—usually flood, surface water, waves, tides, tidal waves, or overflow of any body of water—are modified by the phrase "whether driven by wind or not." Policies do not define "driven by wind." A dictionary definition of "wind" is a "natural movement of air of any velocity,"[187] and "driven" means "propelled or motivated by something."[188]

[ii] Storm Surge

One form of wind-propelled water that is a common cause of property damage is "storm surge." The National Oceanic and Atmospheric Administration's National Weather Service glossary defines it as "[a]n abnormal rise in sea level accompanying a hurricane or other intense storm, whose height is the difference between the observed level of the sea surface and the level that would have occurred in the absence of the cyclone."[189] One commentary says that storm surge happens in coastal areas that are immediately proximate to large bodies of water, such as oceans, bays, and gulfs when tropical storms push water inland as they move toward shore.[190] The commentary adds that wave action is a characteristic of storm surge and that those waves do not have to be large to cause damage; they are capable of great impact as they move farther inland, producing "sustained, repetitive, damaging force."

Because property coverage—both commercial and residential—typically does not mention "storm surge" in the water damage exclusion,[191] some

185. *Spray*, Merriam-Webster, https://www.merriam-webster.com/dictionary/spray.

186. *See, e.g.*, ISO Form CP 10 30 06 07, § B.1.g.

187. *Wind*, Merriam-Webster, https://www.merriam-webster.com/dictionary/wind.

188. *Driven*, Merriam-Webster, https://www.merriam-webster.com/dictionary/driven.

189. *Glossary S*, NOAA's National Weather Service, https://w1.weather.gov/glossary/index.php?letter=s. The definition adds that storm surge is usually estimated by subtracting the normal or astronomic tide from the observed storm tide.

190. Rimoldi, *Flooding & Storm Surge: What's the Difference?* (Aug. 24, 2021), Property Casualty360, https://www.propertycasualty360.com/2021/08/24/flooding-storm-surge-whats-the-difference/?kw=Flooding%20%26%20storm%20surge:%20What%27s%20the%20difference?&utm_campaign=claimsconnection&utm_content=20210825&utm_medium=enl&utm_source=email&utm_term=pc360.

191. There are, however, some policies that specifically define water to include "storm surge." *See, e.g.*, Silvers v. New York Prop. Ins. Underwriting Assn., 2017 N.Y. Misc. LEXIS 2444 (June 20, 2017) (quoting policy providing that "'Water' means '[f]lood, surface water, wave, including tidal wave and tsunami, tides, tidal water, overflow or any body of water or spray from any of these, all whether or not driven by wind, including storm surge'").

policyholders have argued that damage caused by storm surge is not excluded and, therefore, covered under an "all-risk" policy. Courts have not agreed. For example, the Fifth Circuit has said that storm surge is "little more than a synonym for a 'tidal wave' or 'wind-driven flood,' both of which are excluded perils" in the usual policy definition of water.[192] Courts in other jurisdictions have agreed.[193] The fact that the specific term "storm surge" is omitted from the definition of water did not, added the Fifth Circuit court, create an ambiguity and did not entitle the policyholders to recover for their "flood-induced damages."[194] The Fifth Circuit has also held that a hurricane-deductible endorsement that changed the deductible for damages during a hurricane did not expand coverage to include damages resulting from storm surge during a hurricane because it said that all other provisions of the policy applied and the water damage exclusion encompassed storm surge.[195]

Another argument advanced by insureds is that wind causes the high water of storm surge and is the proximate cause of the damage. Therefore, the water damage exclusion does not apply. The Third Circuit rejected that contention over a century ago. It considered a case in which an ocean-front home was covered by a "tornado policy." The policy excluded coverage for loss occasioned directly or indirectly by or through any tidal wave, high water, or overflow and by water or rain, whether driven by wind or not. Hurricane-force winds caused unprecedented high tides that led the house to break apart and be carried out to sea. In a subsequent suit for coverage, the plaintiff argued that the damage was caused by wind, a covered peril, and that if high water contributed to the damage, the proximate cause of the damage was not that high water, but the wind that "made the water high." The court saw no reason to discuss proximate cause as it found that perils insured against were those

---

192. Leonard v. Nationwide Mut. Ins. Co., 499 F.3d 419, 437 (5th Cir. 2007). *See also* Bilbe v. Belsom, 530 F.3d 314, 316 (5th Cir. 2008) (damage to home was caused by inundation of tidal water from lake and that was water damage within meaning of water damage exclusion, which barred coverage for damage for all flooding, whether driven by hurricane winds or not; term "flood" includes storm surges); Tuepker v. State Farm Fire & Cas. Co., 507 F.3d 346 (5th Cir. 2007) (storm surge is peril that is unambiguously excluded by water damage exclusion).

193. *See, e.g.*, AMTRAK v. Arch Specialty Ins. Co., 124 F. Supp. 3d 264, 269 (S.D.N.Y. 2015), *aff'd in part and vacated in part*, 661 Fed. Appx. 10 (2d Cir. 2016) (term "flood" unambiguously encompasses inundation of normally dry land that is caused by storm surge; storm surge pushes water beyond its usual borders and onto normally dry land); Lower Chesapeake Assocs. v. Valley Forge Ins. Co., 260 Va. 77, 532 S.E.2d 325 (2000) (no coverage for damage to docks caused by wind-driven water and gradual deterioration); Corban v. United Servs. Auto. Ass'n, 20 So. 3d 601 (Miss. 2009) ("storm surge" is plainly encompassed within "flood" or "overflow of a body of water" portions of "water damage" definition); Kitson v. National Retailers Mut. Ins. Co., 22 Pa. D. & C. 414 (1935) (wind-driven water was flood). *See also* Paulson v. Fire Ins. Exchange, 393 S.W.2d 316 (Tex. 1965) (coverage excluded where wind brought high water to insured property).

194. Leonard v. Nationwide Mut. Ins. Co., 499 F.3d 419, 438 (5th Cir. 2007). *See also* Corban v. United Servs. Auto. Ass'n, 20 So. 3d 601 (Miss. 2009).

195. Smith v. Allstate Indem. Co., 256 Fed. Appx. 694, 696 (5th Cir. 2007).

of the air and those expressly excepted were of water. The policy, noted the court, disclaimed liability for damage caused by specific water forces such as tidal wave, high water, overflow, and cloudburst and then broadly denied coverage for any loss or damage caused generally by water, even when driven by wind.[196]

In a more recent case, a Louisiana federal court was confronted with the same argument. In that case, damage to the insured property was caused by the storm surge of a hurricane. The insured pointed to part of the definition of wind—loss or damage caused when water, in any state, was carried, blown, driven, or otherwise transported by wind onto or into the insured property—and contended that, because storm surge is caused by the high winds associated with hurricanes, damage from storm surge is wind damage. The court, however, said that phrase could not be viewed in isolation. It had to be read in conjunction with language stating rising or overflow of a body of water was considered a flood whether driven by wind or not. The hurricane's storm surge was, noted the court, the rising of the Gulf of Mexico, a body of water, that was driven by wind. Therefore, it fell within the definition of "flood" and was subject to the limitations set forth in the flood coverage of the policy.[197]

The Kentucky Supreme Court reached a similar conclusion in a case where the policy excluded loss or damage directly or indirectly by or through any tidal wave, high water, overflow, or cloudburst, but it did not add whether or not driven by wind.[198] The insured buildings were flooded when the Ohio River overflowed its banks. High wind then produced heavy waves that were driven against the buildings, lifting them from their foundations and causing them to topple over. The court held the resulting damage was not covered because the policy excluded loss by water driven by wind during a flood.

[iii] Rain

A form of water that may be driven by wind and cause damage is rain.[199] When a policy is "all risk" and does not explicitly exclude losses from wind-driven

196. Newark Trust Co. v. Agricultural Ins. Co., 237 F. 788 (3d Cir. 1916). *See also* Wootton Hotel Corp. v. Northern Assurance Co., 57 F. Supp. 112 (E.D. Pa. 1944), *aff'd*, 155 F.2d 988 (3d Cir. 1946), *cert. den.*, 329 U.S. 758, 67 S. Ct. 111, 91 L. Ed. 654 (1946) (insured pier was damaged by high water driven by wind; hazard expressly excepted by terms of policy that excluded loss or damage caused directly or indirectly by tidal wave, high water, or overflow whether driven by wind or not); Palatine Ins. Co. v. Coyle, 196 S.W. 560 (Tex. Civ. App. 1917) (no coverage for damage caused by combined action of wind and water).

197. Arctic Slope Reg'l Corp. v. Affiliated FM Ins. Co., 2007 U.S. Dist. LEXIS 64850 (W.D. La. Aug. 30, 2007).

198. National Fire Ins. Co. v. Crutchfield, 160 Ky. 802, 170 S.W. 187 (1914).

199. "Wind-driven rain damage results solely from water being blown through pre-existing openings in the building." On Trading Corp. v. N.C. Ins. Underwriting Ass'n, 2009 N.C. App. LEXIS 296 (Apr. 7, 2009). *See generally* State Farm Fire & Casualty Co. v. Paulson, 756 P.2d 764 (Wyo. 1988) ("rain" is ordinarily and commonly thought of as water falling from the sky, and after it stops falling, one does not say that it is "raining," although there may still be wet

rain, courts generally hold it is a covered cause of loss.[200] That should be distinguished from rain that results in flooding.[201] Rain is not included in the typical property policy definition of water. Instead, it is usually separately excluded from coverage. Standard property policies say that loss or damage to the *interior* of any building or structure, or property inside that building or structure, caused by rain or snow, whether driven by wind or not, is not covered unless the building or structure first sustained *wind or hail* damage to its roof or walls through which the rain or snow entered.[202] Some policies say "covered cause of loss" instead of "wind or hail."[203] Others may add that there is no coverage for loss of damage caused by or that results from thawing

---

sidewalks and streets, puddles of water resulting from rain, or water running through gutters and elsewhere as a result of rain).

200. *See, e.g.*, Sunwood Condo. Ass'n v. Travelers Cas. Ins. Co. of Am., 2017 U.S. Dist. LEXIS 189892 (W.D. Wash. Nov. 16, 2017) (wind-driven rain and repeated seepage of water were covered perils under policy because they were not specifically excluded; while policy excluded loss or damage caused by "weather conditions" only when combined with earth movement, flood, or other excluded perils, it does not mention rain or repeated seepage of water); Grossberg v. Chubb Ins. Co., 2012 N.J. Super. Unpub. LEXIS 1981 (Aug. 20, 2012) (loss occasioned by wind-driven rain would be covered loss under all-risk policy, unless specifically excluded from coverage); Fidelity Southern Fire Ins. Co. v. Crow, 390 S.W.2d 788 (Tex. App. 1965) (coverage for wind-driven rain damage under all risk of physical loss endorsement). *See also* Walters Beach Condo. Ass'n v. Home-Owners Ins. Co., 2017 Mich. App. LEXIS 1810 (Nov. 16, 2017). *And see* Cochran v. Travelers Ins. Co., 606 So. 2d 22, 24 (La. App. 1992) (reference in all-risk policy exclusion to "surface water" was in context of body of water that collects and lays on surface of ground, and there was no indication that it was meant to encompass rainwater falling from sky, overflowing rooftop, and seeping into interior of building from roof, its gutters, and metal capping on roof); Wood v. Michigan Millers Mut. Fire Ins. Co., 245 N.C. 383, 96 S.E.2d 28 (1957) (finding coverage where water from torrential rain enhanced wind damage).

201. Kish v. Ins. Co. of N. Am., 125 Wn. 2d 164, 883 P.2d 308 (1994) ("flood" would encompass rain-induced flood). *See also* Bao v. Liberty Mut. Fire Ins. Co., 535 F. Supp. 2d 532 (D. Md. 2008) (pool of rainwater constitutes "surface water," which specifically falls under definition of "water damage"); State Farm Fire & Cas. Co. v. Paulson, 756 P.2d 764 (Wyo. 1988). *But see* American Surety Co. v. National Fire Ins. Co., 25 A.D.2d 734, 269 N.Y.S.2d 77 (1966) (where damage was caused by flooded street and underground pit and passageways due to unusually heavy rainstorm, and flood was defined as waves, tides, or tidal water and the rising (including overflowing or breaking of boundaries) of lakes, ponds, reservoirs, rivers, harbors, streams, and similar bodies of water, whether driven by wind or not, there was uncertainty about meaning and scope of term "flood" in exclusionary clause, and insurer was, therefore, not entitled to have issue resolved in its favor as matter of law).

202. ISO Form CP 10 20 04 02, § A.4.c. The roof or wall opening exception is discussed elsewhere. See § 3.2[4], *infra*.

203. *See, e.g.*, GBS Inv. Grp. v. United Specialty Ins. Co., 2019 U.S. Dist. LEXIS 190105 (S.D. Fla. Oct. 31, 2019) (policy excluded coverage for interior of any building or structure, or to personal property in that building or structure caused by or resulting from rain, snow, sleet, or ice, whether driven by wind or not, unless building or structure first sustained damage by covered cause of loss to its roof or walls through which rain, snow, sleet, or ice entered).

of snow, sleet, or ice on the insured building or structure.[204] Policies may also bar coverage for loss or damage caused by rain to property "in the open."[205]

[iv] Wind Driving Insured Property into Water

What is the result if covered property is deposited in water by wind? In an Oklahoma case, a house was blown off its foundation into a flooded street. The contents of the house were covered by a policy with the usual water exclusion. The court said that the wind directly damaged the property and was alone the proximate and efficient cause of the property being dropped in the flood waters where it likely was damaged further, but whatever flood damage may have resulted was "incidental." The court concluded that "[c]ommon experience and understanding suggest that when personal property of this nature is blown into a body of water, some water damage will likely result before the property can be recovered. It is fair to assume that under these facts this incidental water damage was within the terms of the policies and contracts of the parties at the time they were made."[206] Other courts have reached a similar conclusion.[207] It should be noted that none of the policies in these cases contained the broad anti-concurrent causation language found in policies today.

[v] Waves

The standard water damage exclusion includes waves in its definition of water, but what if waves do not cause the damage? In a case before the Virginia Supreme Court, there was evidence that waves during a hurricane were insignificant and did not cause damage to the insured docks and that the docks were damaged as the result of wind blowing against boats and that the boats were pitching as a result of wind and waves. The court agreed that evidence supported the trial court's finding that wind-driven water *contributed* to the damage and that was a sufficient reason to exclude coverage.[208]

---

204. *See, e.g.*, Bethany Boardwalk Grp. LLC v. Everest Sec. Ins. Co., 2020 U.S. Dist. LEXIS 225178 (D. Md. Dec. 2, 2020).

205. *See, e.g.*, Northstar Steel v. Aetna Ins. Co., 224 N.W.2d 805 (N.D. 1974) (exclusion for loss or damage to property in open caused by rain barred coverage where rain accumulated in retaining walls above ground level, which exerted pressure that bulged walls outward, caused buoyancy effect, and raised cistern tank upward, damaging attached pipes).

206. Pennsylvania Fire Ins. Co. v. Sikes, 197 Okl. 137, 140, 168 P.2d 1016, 1019 (1946).

207. *See* Gillis v. Sun Ins. Office, Ltd., 238 Cal. App. 2d 408, 47 Cal. Rptr. 868 (1965) (where gangway was blown into insured docking facility that subsided into water and was damaged, wind was cause of loss even though water and waves contributed to damage and, therefore, the loss was covered); Ebert v. Pac. Nat. Fire Ins. Co., 40 So. 2d 40 (La. App. 1949) (finding coverage where wind directly damaged property and was alone proximate and efficient cause of property being deposited in flood waters where it likely was damaged further).

208. Lower Chesapeake Assocs. v. Valley Forge Ins. Co., 260 Va. 77, 532 S.E.2d 325 (2000).

2.3 The Water Damage Exclusion: Mudslide or Mudflow

In addition to barring coverage for flood, under the standard "water" exclusion there is no coverage for loss or damage caused directly or indirectly by mudslide or mudflow.[209] In the Merriam-Webster online dictionary, a mudslide is defined as a "mudflow,"[210] which in turn is defined as "a moving mass of soil made fluid by rain or melting snow."[211] A federal court gave further definition to the terms.[212] First, it held that the exclusion for mudflows or mudslides is clear and unambiguous. Then, after citing Merriam-Webster and other dictionaries, the court said, "the plain and ordinary meaning of the word 'mudflow' is a moving mass of soil made fluid by rain or melting snow or soil made fluid by excessive water [and] of 'mudslide' would be an incline of mud or landslip of mud."

It is important to note that some policies that also exclude coverage for losses caused by earth movement define earth movement to include "mudslide" or "mudflow."[213]

The FEMA definitions of "mudslide" and "mudflow," while not binding on a court interpreting a non-FEMA policy, may, nonetheless, prove useful. The Standard Flood Insurance Policy (SFIP) defines "mudflow" as a "river of liquid and flowing mud on the surface of normally dry land areas, as when earth is carried by a current of water."[214] An agency rule defines "mudslide" not "mudflow," and suggests that the words are synonyms. The rule says a "mudslide" "describes a condition where there is a river, flow or inundation of liquid mud down a hillside usually as a result of a dual condition of loss of brush cover, and the subsequent accumulation of water on the ground preceded by a period of unusually heavy or sustained rain."[215] The definition adds that a mudslide or mudflow may be a distinct phenomenon while a landslide is in progress and will be recognized as distinct only if the mudflow, and not the landslide, is the proximate cause of any damage.

One issue that is raised is whether a mudslide or mudflow may be the product of an artificial source. Courts hold the terms apply to both natural phenomenon and those produced by human activity, especially if the policy

---

209. ISO Form CP 10 30 09 17, § B.1.g.(2).

210. *Mudslide*, Merriam-Webster, https://www.merriam-webster.com/dictionary/mudslide.

211. *Mudflow*, Merriam-Webster, https://www.merriam-webster.com/dictionary/mudflow. *See also* Monzo v. Nationwide Prop. & Cas. Ins. Co., 249 A.3d 106, 122, n.5 (Del. 2021) (citing Merriam-Webster online dictionary and saying that mudslides are associated with heavy rain).

212. West American Ins. Co. v. Red Cricket Condo. Ass'n, 2008 U.S. Dist. LEXIS 57154 (D. Idaho July 29, 2008).

213. ISO Form HO 00 02 10 00 (Exclusions), § 2.a.

214. General Property Form Standard Flood Insurance Policy, § II.C.19.

215. 44 C.F.R. § 59.1.

describes the peril as arising from natural or external forces.[216] When vegetation is obliterated in a wildfire, the danger of mudslides is increased. The Ninth Circuit has held that where, one month after a wildfire was extinguished, an insured home was destroyed by a mudslide, there was a triable issue as to whether *fire* directly caused the destruction of the home.[217] A mudslide can completely annihilate a building. One creative attorney argued before the Tenth Circuit that a mudslide caused his client's building to violently and suddenly burst apart. In other words, it exploded, bringing the damage within an explosion exception to the water exclusion. The court was not persuaded. It did not agree that "demolition by an external cascade of water, mud, and debris is an explosion."[218]

2.4 The Water Damage Exclusion: Back Up or Overflow of Water

[1] Generally

Under the standard ISO causes of loss form typically included in commercial property coverage, there is no coverage for water that backs up or overflows or is otherwise discharged *from* a sewer, drain, sump, sump pump, or related equipment.[219] The standard ISO residential policy excludes coverage for water or water-borne material that backs up *through* sewers or drains or overflows or is discharged *from* a sump, sump pump, or related equipment.[220] In some

216. Paros Props. LLC v. Colo. Cas. Ins. Co., 835 F.3d 1264 (10th Cir. 2016) (mudslide damage is excluded whether mudslide is caused by act of nature or otherwise); West American Ins. Co. v. Red Cricket Condo. Ass'n, 2008 U.S. Dist. LEXIS 57154 (D. Idaho July 29, 2008) (meaning of mudflow and mudslide does not require that they involve native soil or be naturally occurring phenomena; excavated soil placed above insured property could be source of mudslide or mudflow); Sioux City Country Club v. Cincinnati Ins. Co., 2004 U.S. Dist. LEXIS 12833 (N.D. Iowa June 22, 2004) (where damages were caused by mudslide from saturation of soil by rainwater, fact that accumulation of water was because of leaky drainage pipe does not place occurrence outside the policy exclusion for damage from earth movement and water; nothing could be more "naturally occurring" than accumulation of rainwater); State Farm Fire & Cas. Co. v. Bongen, 925 P.2d 1042 (Alaska 1996) (there was no coverage for damages from mudslide allegedly caused by construction activity above insured property because earth movement exclusion encompassed earth movement arising from natural or external forces, meaning it applied to both natural phenomena and human processes). *See also* Wilner v. Allstate Ins. Co., 99 A.D.3d 700, 953 N.Y.S.2d 49 (2012) (where mudslide caused retaining wall to collapse, it did not matter that municipal drain above that retaining wall had become clogged).

217. Stankova v. Metro. Prop. & Cas. Ins. Co., 788 F.3d 1012 (9th Cir. 2015).

218. Paros Props. LLC v. Colo. Cas. Ins. Co., 835 F.3d 1264, 1275 (10th Cir. 2016).

219. ISO Form CP 10 30 09 17, § B.1.g.(3). Some policies may not include the exclusion. *See, e.g.*, Pakmark Corp. v. Liberty Mut. Ins. Co., 943 S.W.2d 256, 259 (Mo. App. 1997) (sewage backup not *per se* excluded).

220. HO 00 03 10 00 (Exclusions), § I.A.3.b. There are other forms of the exclusion, of course. In one case, the homeowners policy proscribed coverage for loss caused by "water from

policies the exclusion applies only if it is shown on the Declarations Page.[221] Also, in some cases the exclusion may omit "overflow" and only apply to backups.[222]

Understanding the extent of a backup/overflow exclusion requires defining the terms that are its component parts, including the distinction between "from" and "through." Those definitions are discussed below.

Although the backup/overflow exclusion is very common, there are circumstances in which there is coverage for backups or overflows. The most common is when the exclusion is deleted by endorsement, a topic discussed elsewhere.[223] Secondly, some policies make it an additional coverage.[224]

[2] "From" and "Through" Defined

"From" is a preposition "used as a function word to indicate a starting point of a physical movement."[225] Citing this precise definition, one federal court held that the phrase "water that backs up or overflows *from* a sewer, drain or sump" refers only to water whose starting point, that is, its source, is a sewer, drain, or sump. Furthermore, it does not include water unable to enter a drain or sewer because of a blockage, but only water that, after having entered a drain or sewer, is diverted back up out of it.[226] For example where, because of a blockage between floors, clean water from a supply line was unable to enter a drain and simply filled a toilet bowl until it overflowed. The court said the water that overflowed never made it into a drain and because the damage was caused by water that did not "back up or overflow from a drain," the policy

---

outside the plumbing system that enters through sewers or drains, or water which enters into and overflows from within a sump pump, sump pump well or any other system designed to remove subsurface water which is drained from the foundation area." Silow v. State Farm Ins. Co., 1994 U.S. Dist. LEXIS 18192 (E.D. Pa. Dec. 19, 1994).

221. *See, e.g.*, Assurance Co. of Am., Inc. v. Jay-Mar, Inc., 38 F. Supp. 2d 349 (D.N.J. 1999) (policy excluded water that backed up or overflowed from sewer, drain or sump but *only* if "Back-Up of Sewers and Drains" was show as excluded on Declarations Page).

222. *See, e.g.*, Old Dominion Ins. Co. v. Elysee, Inc., 601 So. 2d 1243 (Fla. 1st DCA 1992) (excluding coverage for loss or damage caused directly or indirectly by water that backs up from a sewer or drain).

223. See § 3.2[6], *infra*.

224. *See, e.g.*, Spector v. USAA Cas. Ins. Co., 2019 U.S. Dist. LEXIS 57946 (E.D. La. Apr. 3, 2019); Union St. Furniture & Carpet, Inc. v. Peerless Indem. Ins. Co., 2013 Conn. Super. LEXIS 1504 (July 3, 2013); Hirschfield v. Cont'l Casualty Co., 199 Ga. App. 654, 404 S.E.2d 737 (1999).

225. *From*, Merriam-Webster, https://www.merriam-webster.com/dictionary/from.

226. 301-375 W. Onondaga St., LLC v. Liberty Mut. Fire Ins. Co., 2020 U.S. Dist. LEXIS 1228 (N.D.N.Y. Jan. 6, 2020). *See also* Front Row Theatre, Inc. v. Am. Mfr's. Mut. Ins. Companies, 18 F.3d 1343, 1348 (6th Cir. 1994) (where partial blockage in pipes may have caused water that had initially entered sewage system to be diverted back up out of lower manhole and into front doors of insured building, portion of the damage was caused by water that backed up *from* a sewer).

water exclusion did not apply and the loss was covered.[227] Similar reasoning has been employed where, because of a clogged drain, water ponded on a roof before finding its way into an insured building.[228] On the other hand, there are courts that have reached the opposite conclusion, but without considering the definition of "from."[229]

"Through" is a preposition that is "used as a function word to indicate movement into at one side or point and out at another and especially the opposite side of [or] to indicate passage from one end or boundary to another."[230] Courts interpreting insurance policies have cited this exact definition.[231] One of those courts confronted a loss caused when rainfall collecting as surface water flowed down outside stairs and gathered in a well with a clogged drain. Because the water could not enter the drain, it ran into and damaged the basement of the insured property. Reading the definitions of "back up" and "through" together, the court held that they required that there was some water in the pipe. As the water could not enter the drain, it was not possible that the water that damaged basement "backed up through the drain."[232]

---

227. Drutz v. Scottsdale Ins. Co., 2012 U.S. Dist. LEXIS 25286, at *8 (D. Md. Feb. 28, 2012) (for exclusion to properly apply, water that caused damage must have started in drain and then later exited that drain).

228. *See, e.g.*, Oak Hill Inv. IV LLC v. State Farm Fire & Cas. Co., 2017 U.S. Dist. LEXIS 158851 (N.D. Ohio Sept. 27, 2017) (where water accumulated on roof because drain was clogged, it did not necessarily back up or overflow *from* the drain and, as the exclusion is ambiguous, cause of loss was not clearly excluded from coverage and was not a basis to deny coverage); Tran v. Seneca Ins. Co., 2015 U.S. Dist. LEXIS 139527 (E.D. Pa. Oct. 14, 2015) (in response to roof bowing under weight of 2,000 gallons of standing water, firefighters cut relief holes in roof, allowing water to flow into insured building causing extensive damage, which insurer's investigator concluded was caused by obstructed drainage; court denied summary judgment to insurer, finding "back up or overflow from a drain" to be ambiguous and noting that if that phrase encompasses only water whose starting point is a sewer, drain, or sump, insured would prevail because there was no evidence that water on roof came "from" a sewer, drain, or sump).

229. *See, e.g.*, Scorpio v. Underwriters at Lloyd's, London, 2012 U.S. Dist. LEXIS 77751 (D.R.I. June 5, 2012) (tennis ball lodged in roof downspout and blocked rainwater, which accumulated on roof and entered building through access hatch; court found roof downspout was a drain, and tennis ball caused it to back up or overflow, bringing loss within exclusion for water backs up or overflows from a drain). Policies may also provide coverage for damage from water that backs up or overflows from a drain. In one such case, a drain was blocked and the court found there was coverage even though the water apparently never entered the drain. Potoff v. Chubb Indem. Ins. Co., 60 A.D.3d 477, 874 N.Y.S.2d 124 (2009) (where plastic bag clogged drain that overflowed and sent water leaking into insured apartment, court rejected insurer's argument that damage was caused by rainwater on roof that seeped or leaked into building, not water emanating "from within" drain—covered loss under policy—and affirmed summary judgment for insured).

230. *Through*, Merriam-Webster, https://www.merriam-webster.com/dictionary/through.

231. Davis v. Std. Fire Ins. Co., 2014 U.S. Dist. LEXIS 114874 (N.D.N.Y. Aug. 19, 2014).

232. Dent v. Allstate Indem. Co., 82 Va. Cir. 386 (Va. Cir. 2011) (heavy rainfall travelled as surface water across completely clogged drain as if no drain existed).

[3] "Water" Defined

Policyholders have argued for a literal interpretation of the phrase "water that backs up," which, they contend, does not include *sewage* that backs up. Generally, courts have rejected that argument and said that the word "water" as used in the exclusion is "not pure tap water or rain water," but water that backs up from sewers.[233] For example, a Minnesota trial court agreed with policyholders that coverage for damage caused by the backup of raw sewage into their basement was not barred by the exclusion because raw sewage was not explicitly written into the exclusion. The appellate court reversed. It said that water that backs up through sewers or drains includes "various compositions" of raw sewage for three specific reasons. First, the exclusion is substantially enlarged by extending coverage to losses caused *indirectly* by water backing up through sewers or drains. That, said the court, includes water that carries other substances with it. Next, the court found it reasonable that water that backs up through sewers or drains includes sewer water or water containing various levels of raw sewage. Finally, the court found it unreasonable to construe the word "water" as only pure water or water containing substances other than sewage given the implausibility of determining at what level water that contains foreign substances ceases to be water.[234] Thus, the plain and ordinary meaning of water damage exclusion included water containing raw sewage, and the insurer was successful in proving the exclusion applied. That is the majority view, supported by courts in

233. Citrano v. Hingham Mut. Fire Ins. Co., 58 Mass. App. Ct. 906, 788 N.E.2d 975 (2003). *See also* AKC, Inc. v. United Specialty Ins. Co., 2021 Ohio LEXIS 1973 (Oct. 6, 2021) (water backup exclusion plainly applies to *sewage* carried into insured property during backup or overflow); Penn-America Ins. Co. v. Mike's Tailoring, 125 Cal. App. 4th 884, 890, 22 Cal. Rptr. 3d 918, 922 (2005) (lay person reading policy would assume that backup of water from sewer would contain both water and contaminants; no reasonable person would assume that water backing up from sewer would be pure water).

234. Newberg v. Commercial Union Ins. Co., 619 N.W.2d 757 (Minn. App. 2000). The court also said that "the plain and ordinary meaning of the water-damage exclusion includes water containing raw sewage [and while the insurer] might have more explicitly addressed the types of watery substances that might back up through sewers or drains and were to be excluded from coverage . . . it does not follow that it is reasonable to read the word 'water' with a level of literalism that fails to take into account the other language in the exclusion."

California,[235] Massachusetts,[236] Missouri,[237] Oklahoma,[238] Pennsylvania,[239] and Washington.[240]

---

235. Penn-America Ins. Co. v. Mike's Tailoring, 125 Cal. App. 4th 884, 22 Cal. Rptr. 3d 918 (2005).

236. *See* Citrano v. Hingham Mut. Fire Ins. Co., 58 Mass. App. Ct. 906, 788 N.E.2d 975 (2003), in which a basement toilet backed up during heavy rains causing a two-foot flood of water-borne raw sewage. The insured homeowner argued the backup exclusion did not apply because the damage was caused by sewage, not water. The court disagreed and said that the water to which the exclusion referred was not pure tap water or rainwater, but water that backs up from sewers or drains and by common usage "sewage" implies waste borne in water. The court added that even were it to differentiate between sewer water and the sewage carried in it, and to accept the contention that the damage at issue was caused exclusively by the sewage, the loss would still be excluded because it was the water backup through the sewer line that was the vehicle by which the damaging agent—the sewage—permeated the basement. Thus, the water was at least a contributing cause of the loss, all of which, under the exclusion, was exempted from coverage.

237. *See* Rodin v. State Farm Fire & Casualty Co., 844 S.W.2d 537 (Mo. App. 1992). In *Rodin* roots in the system caused sewage to back up into the insured home. The homeowner described eight inches of effluent that entered his basement as a black liquid with solid matter floating in it that definitely was not water. He argued that the damage sustained was not caused by water but by the organisms carried into the house by the water and, therefore, the exclusion for water damage did not eliminate coverage for damage from sewage. The court said that in effect the homeowner contended the policy, when construed against the insurer, excludes only damage from pure water, not from pollutants in that water. The court responded that the homeowner had overlooked the totality of the exclusion. Whether, held the court, the loss was caused by pure water or by pollutants contained in sewage acting concurrently with water, it was excluded from coverage by clear, unambiguous policy language.

238. *See* Ellis v. State Farm Fire & Cas. Co., 322 F. App'x 594 (10th Cir. 2009) (drain or sewer line contained water and fact that it also contained waste matter did not alter fact that it was water that carried away waste). *See also* Andres v. Oklahoma Farm Bureau Mutual Insurance Co., 227 P.3d 1102 (Okla. App. 2009), *cert. den.*, 2012 Okla. LEXIS 89 (Sept. 17, 2012) (reasonable person would expect water backing up, or discharging through, the sewer or plumbing system to contain raw sewage).

239. *See* Silow v. State Farm Ins. Co., 1994 U.S. Dist. LEXIS 18192 (E.D. Pa. Dec. 19, 1994), where sewage containing both waste water and solid matter flooded the insured home to the level of 12 inches on the ground floor. The likely cause of the flood was that a municipal sewer line connected to the home's waste drain lines became clogged and when third persons attempted to remove the blockage, a surge of pressure caused the line to back up. The homeowner argued the damage that occurred was the result not of "water damage" but of fecal matter and other waste that entered her home. The court, however, agreed with the carrier that the losses at issue were the result of "water damage" as defined in the policy.

240. *See* Capelouto v. Valley Forge Ins. Co., 98 Wn. App. 7, 990 P.2d 414 (1999), where a construction company was replacing sewer pipes and installed a temporary bypass of the main sewer line near the insured property consisting of a plug on the main sewer connected to hoses and a pump. It rained, and the bypass equipment proved inadequate to handle the increased flow through the sewer line. Consequently, sewage backed up into the basement of the insured property through an overflowing toilet. The insured argued that the exclusion for water that backs up from a sewer or drain did not apply because sewage is distinct from water, and thus is not within the ordinary meaning of the exclusion. The court, however, found that interpretation was not reasonable, as the average person buying insurance would understand that water that backs up from a sewer includes sewage. In other words, that is the plain, ordinary, and popular

Other courts, most notably in Florida, have held that the exclusion is inapplicable to a backup of sewage. For example, in *Sterling v. West Palm Beach*,[241] a home was flooded with raw, untreated sewage without warning. The flood of sewage was caused by tree roots that had worked their way into the sewer lines located outside of the property. At trial, the homeowner argued unsuccessfully that the raw sewage that caused her loss was not water under any definition. On appeal, she contended there was a substantial issue of material fact regarding whether sewage was water for purposes of the exclusion. The appellate court agreed and reversed summary judgment for the insurer. The court noted there was no mention in the policy of any exclusions for damage caused by raw sewage and if the parties intended otherwise, then findings needed to be made reflecting that intention. An unreported Ohio case offers an interesting and compelling analysis.[242] In that case, a backup occurred through a sanitary sewer line, causing flooding of the lower level of an insured building. The insured argued the exclusion could apply to water, but did not apply to raw sewage, and in any event was ambiguous as it could easily refer to storm sewers or drains. The trial judge said that it seemed clear that the material that caused the damage was not water, but whatever was in the liquid that came out of the sanitary sewer. Further, "water" is not another word for "liquid" because all water is liquid but not all liquids are water. The policy, observed the judge, could have excluded damage cause by liquids or by water-borne material, but those broader terms were not used and, therefore, a distinction needed to be drawn between damage caused solely by water and that caused by those things that might be found in water.[243] The appellate court affirmed and agreed that if the exclusion was intended to encompass raw sewage backing up from sanitary sewers, it could have stated that specifically. Moreover, the court found the exclusion to be ambiguous and construed it in the light most favorable to the insured and in favor of coverage.

---

meaning attributed to sewer water, and any other interpretation ignores the clear and unequivocal meaning of the exclusion.

241. Sterling v. West Palm Beach, 595 So. 2d 284 (4th DCA 1992). *See also* Fla. Farm Bureau Ins. Co. v. Birge, 659 So. 2d 310 (Fla. 2d DCA 1994) (where sewer malfunction caused insured home to fill with raw sewage, court affirmed judgment for insured, finding language of the backup and overflow exclusion to be ambiguous; insurance company had available clear and unambiguous language that could have been used to exclude damage resulting from backup of raw sewage).

242. Fairlawn Properties, Inc. vs. Liberty Mutual Insurance Co., 1982 Ohio App. LEXIS 12282 (Dec. 8, 1982).

243. The trial court also noted that the words chosen were consistent with the well-known exemption in nearly all property insurance policies of damages caused by floods. The word "water" was used because the insurer was trying to exempt flood damage, and the damage at issue was not the kind of flood damage contemplated.

[4] "Backup"/"Back Up" Defined

[a] Generally

What is a "backup" or "back up"? The terms are generally not defined in policies and are, therefore, given their "common every day meaning."[244] The terms are easy to define, but the definitions are not so easy to apply. At its simplest, a "backup" is "'an accumulation due to stoppage.'"[245] The Merriam-Webster online dictionary says that as a verb, the word means to "to accumulate in a congested state" and as a noun it is "an accumulation caused by a stoppage in the flow."[246] An older *Webster's Dictionary* described "backup" as "an overflow or accumulation due to stoppage, malfunctioning."[247] Another older *Webster's Dictionary* defined it to mean to "rise and flow backward or overflow adjacent areas."[248]

One area of disagreement among courts is whether "back up" means "reverse flow." Some courts say a "backup" requires that water reverse its natural or intended flow within a drainage system.[249] Others say the opposite: a reversal of flow is not required.[250] For example, in a California case, a policyholder argued "back up" means to move in a "reverse direction" and because there was no evidence of water reversing its flow, a loss caused by an overflow from water backed up in a sewer line was a covered loss. The court, however, citing dictionary definitions similar to those above, found there was no coverage where a blockage in a sewer line constricted the flow of water and sewage, causing it to accumulate upstream from the obstruction and forcing the contents of the sewer line up a clean-out pipe and into the basement of the insured.[251] Another court observed that it is nearly impossible to imagine a situation—except in times of severe flooding—in which a sewer or drain would back up without a clog or obstruction, as otherwise the water or waste would flow unimpeded. Thus, if the exclusion did not apply when there has

244. Commandments, Inc. v. Penn-America Ins. Co., 2010 Phila. Ct. Com. Pl. LEXIS 394 (May 12, 2010), *aff'd*, 40 A.3d 183 (Pa. Super. 2011).

245. Fingerle v. City of Ann Arbor, 308 Mich. App. 318, 359, 863 N.W.2d 698, 721 (2014) (Beckering, J., dissenting) (quoting Random House *Webster's College Dictionary*).

246. *Backup*, Merriam-Webster, https://www.merriam-webster.com/dictionary/backup.

247. *Webster's New Universal Unabridged Dictionary* (1996).

248. *Webster's Third New International Dictionary* (1971).

249. *See, e.g.*, Thompson v. Genis Bldg. Corp., 182 Ind. App. 200, 204, 394 N.E.2d 242, 245 (1979) (plain and ordinary meaning of backing up is to rise and overflow backward).

250. Front Row Theatre, Inc. v. Am. Manufacturer's Mut. Ins. Co., 18 F.3d 1343, 1348 (6th Cir. 1994) (where policy required water back up from, rather than through, sewer or drain, water was not required to flow in direction opposite to intended and usual flow); Horizon III Real Estate v. Hartford Fire Ins. Co., 186 F. Supp. 2d 1000, 1003 (D. Minn. 2002).

251. Penn-America Ins. Co. v. Mike's Tailoring, 125 Cal. App. 4th 883–84, 894, 22 Cal. Rptr. 3d 918, 924 (2005). The court noted that another definition was to rise and flow backward or overflow adjacent areas, and that was exactly what happened in the case.

been water damage caused by a clog or obstruction in a sewer line, the "back up" exclusionary clause would be essentially void.[252]

[b] Ambiguity

Some courts find the language "water that backs up from a sewer or drain" to be ambiguous and construe it in favor of coverage. For example, one court said the phrase could be interpreted to mean a blockage in the drainage system that causes a backup producing an upward flow of water, or it could mean when surface water enters a drain, but because of excessive volume, overflows, causing a flood.[253] Many other courts, however, find no ambiguity.[254] As one court said, "[w]henever water or sewage flows into a dwelling through drains or pipes that normally carry this effluent out, the water and sewage can be seen to have 'backed up,' having gone backwards through the fixtures designed to carry it the other direction."[255] In other words, a "backup" is a "reversal of flow from the normal direction." Thus, where a sewer line cap failed and allowed water and sewage to flow directly into the basement of the insured premises, the court said the claim was not predicated on "backing up" of water and sewage within the ordinary meaning of the words, but on a "direct flow" from the sewer line into the basement, and the backup exclusion was not a bar to coverage.[256] Similarly, where a clogged drain pipe failed inside the premises and released water from the rooftop tank into the insured building, the backup exclusion did not apply.[257]

---

252. Commandments, Inc. v. Penn-America Ins. Co., 2010 Phila. Ct. Com. Pl. LEXIS 394 (May 12, 2010), *aff'd*, 40 A.3d 183 (Pa. Super. 2011) (where clog in main sewer line of insured property resulted in backup of water overflowing into premises through the toilets and drains, loss was excluded). *See also* Wandler v. Homesite Indem. Co., 2013 U.S. Dist. LEXIS 201827 (D. Wyo. Nov. 7, 2013) (ordinary and plain meaning of "backup" is water flowing out of a drain because of an obstruction and, therefore, where water from gutters ran into drainpipe, but could not escape because dirt and grass obstructed opening designed for water to escape and continued to accumulate behind obstruction, there was a backup); Jackson v. American Mutual Fire Ins. Co., 299 F. Supp. 151 (N.D.N.C. 1968), *aff'd*, 410 F.2d 395 (4th Cir. 1969) (where overflow of sewage into insured home and resulting property damage was caused by sewer line becoming surcharged with rainwater, which forced water to back up in sewer lines and on up line until it reached one connecting home's plumbing system with sewer line where it found its first outlet, thereby causing water and sewage to overflow from plumbing fixtures in house, coverage was barred by exclusion for "water which backs up through sewers or drains").

253. Somerset Indus. v. Lexington Ins. Co., 639 F. Supp. 2d 532, 540 (E.D. Pa. 2009) (exterior drain located adjacent to loading dock door was at least partially covered during rainstorm by metal plate).

254. *See, e.g.*, Motorists Mut. Ins. Co. v. Zukoff, 244 W. Va. 33, 851 S.E.2d 112 (2020).

255. Jennings v. Hartford Fire Ins. Co., 1991 U.S. Dist. LEXIS 5632 (E.D. Pa. Apr. 25, 1991).

256. Thompson v. Genis Bldg. Corp., 182 Ind. App. 200, 394 N.E.2d 242 (1979).

257. Junius Dev., Inc. v. New York Mar. & Gen. Ins. Co., 48 A.D.3d 426, 852 N.Y.S.2d 185 (2008).

[c] Necessity that Water Enter Drain[258]

Some courts have said that where water does not enter a drain, it cannot back up or overflow from it. For example, a drain between floors was blocked, which prevented clean water from the supply line entering a drain. A toilet bowl filled until it eventually overflowed. The water that overflowed the toilet never made it into the drain and therefore, said the court, could not have "backed up or overflowed from a drain." Because the damage was caused by water that did not "back up or overflow from a drain," the policy exclusion did not apply and the loss incurred by the insured was covered.[259] Similarly, a scupper drain on a roof became clogged with wind-blown debris during a rainstorm. The rainwater entered an open air-conditioning unit and flowed through ductwork to the interior of the insured building. The insured argued that because a drain was clogged, water did not overflow or back up from it, but was completely diverted. The court found the language of the exclusion to be ambiguous and the insured's interpretation to be reasonable. While water did accumulate on the roof because the drain was clogged, said the court, "it did not necessarily back up or overflow from the drain."[260]

Other courts do not require the water to enter a sewer or drain. For example, in a California case, a blockage in a sewer line approximately 20 to 40 feet away from a toilet caused the water in the toilet to overflow. The insured contended that "backs up or overflows from" means water must come out of the sewer or drain and, therefore, does not include water unable to enter an interior drain. The court noted that the operative phrase was disjunctive: the water could back up *or* it could overflow. That difference was critical said the court. It held the exclusion applied because the toilet overflowed.[261] The court

258. *See generally* Wilson, *Property Coverage for Toilet Overflows* (Nov 25, 2016), Insurance Commentary.com, https://insurancecommentary.com/property-coverage-for-toilet-overflows/.

259. Drutz v. Scottsdale Ins. Co., 2012 U.S. Dist. LEXIS 25286 (D. Md. Feb. 28, 2012) (in order for backup/overflow exclusion to apply, water that caused damage must have started in drain and then later exited that drain). *See also* Korean Cmty. Presbyterian Church v. Md. Cas. Co., 2015 U.S. Dist. LEXIS 112130 (N.D. Ga. Aug. 25, 2015) (because clog was not in drain, but in toilet, no water backed up or overflowed from a drain).

260. Oak Hill Inv. IV LLC v. State Farm Fire & Cas. Co., 2017 U.S. Dist. LEXIS 158851 (N.D. Ohio Sept. 27, 2017). Unfortunately for the insured, the court held its loss was not covered because the water that collected on the roof was surface water for which there was no coverage. *See also* Armon v. Aetna Casualty & Surety Co., 369 Pa. 465, 87 A.2d 302 (1952) (exclusion for backing up of drain did not apply where mud, stones, and pieces of wood prevented normal passage of water down through drain).

261. Cardio Diagnostic Imaging, Inc. v. Farmers Ins. Exch., 212 Cal. App. 4th 69, 150 Cal. Rptr. 3d 798 (2012). *See also* Wandler v. Homesite Indem. Co., 2013 U.S. Dist. LEXIS 201827 (D. Wyo. Nov. 7, 2013) (exclusion applied where water from gutters ran into drainpipe, but could not escape because dirt and grass obstructed opening designed for water to escape and continued to accumulate behind obstruction); Scorpio v. Underwriters at Lloyd's, London, 2012 U.S. Dist. LEXIS 77751 (D.R.I. June 5, 2012) (no coverage where, as result of blocked downspout, rainwater accumulated on roof and entered building through access hatch on roof).

noted that most of the cases cited by the insured that appeared to hold to the contrary were ones in which the policies omitted the word "overflow."

[d] Location of Blockage

For some courts, the location of any blockage does not matter. Coverage for damage caused by blockage of a sewer pipe is excluded regardless of whether the blockage occurs on or off the insured premises.[262] For example, a municipal sewer line became clogged by excess rainwater and backed-up sewer water forced its way into the insured building through drains in sinks and toilets. The court refused to engraft on the usual backup exclusion language the additional requirement that any backup had to be the result of a clog *within the insured's plumbing system*. That result, said the court, was not supported by the language of the exclusion.[263]

For other courts, location is an issue. For example, one court said that to back up means to "rise and flow backward or overflow adjacent areas" Therefore, water or waterborne material that backs up through sewers or drains, said the court, "is water or water-borne material that attempts to enter a sewer or drain, is prevented from doing so by an obstruction, and flows back to where it came from through that sewer or drain, and/or overflows into adjacent areas through that sewer or drain."[264] Thus, where waterborne material did not originate from the insured residence but from sources up the street in a municipal sewer line, the "flow backward" part of its definition did not apply, leaving only the "overflows into adjacent areas" part of the definition, and it could not be determined if the basement that flooded was an "area" that was "adjacent" to the municipal sewer line in the street. The insurer had moved for summary judgment based on the exclusion, and the court denied that motion.

262. Pichel v. Dryden Mut. Ins. Co. ,40 Misc. 3d 679, 965 N.Y.S.2d 342 (2013). *See also* Motorists Mut. Ins. Co. v. Zukoff, 244 W. Va. 33, 851 S.E.2d 112 (2020) (plain reading of policy language clearly shows that coverage for loss from clogged sewer pipe off insured premises would be excluded where water backed up and overflowed into insured premises).

263. Jennings v. Hartford Fire Ins. Co., 1991 U.S. Dist. LEXIS 5632 (E.D. Pa. Apr. 25, 1991). *See also* For Kids Only Child Dev. Ctr., Inc. v. Phila. Indem. Ins. Co., 260 S.W.3d 652 (Tex. App. 2008) (where overflow was caused by stoppage in a 12-inch city sewer main, court found policy unambiguously excluded from coverage type of drain and sewer backup insured experienced).

264. Davis v. Std. Fire Ins. Co., 2014 U.S. Dist. LEXIS 114874, at *26 (N.D.N.Y. Aug. 19, 2014). *See also* Jackson v. Am. Mut. Fire Ins. Co., 299 F. Supp. 151 (M.D.N.C. 1968), *aff'd*, 410 F.2d 395 (4th Cir. 1969) (water that backs up through sewers or drains refers to sewers or drains outside insured's plumbing system—that is, sewers or drains in the sewer system of town); Durrett v. Nationwide Prop. & Cas. Ins. Co., 2015 U.S. Dist. LEXIS 44966 (W.D. Tex. Apr. 6, 2015) (if sewage water came down from city sewer line, resulting loss was not covered).

[e] Broken Water Main

Courts have held that the exclusion does not apply when there is a water main break. For example, in a New York case,[265] the insured premises were extensively damaged by large amounts of water that entered its basement after a water main broke and water poured forth, some of it entering the rear yard and basement. The insurer contended that there was such a great amount of water that there was a backup of sewers or drains and the exclusion for damage by water that backs up through sewers or drains applied. The court did not agree. The water damage, said the court, did not occur because water backed up through sewers or drains independent of the water main break; rather the water main break itself caused the damage and as a corollary caused a backup of sewers.[266]

[5] "Overflow" Defined

As a verb, "overflow" means to cover with water—in other words, to inundate; as a noun, it means "a flowing over" or inundation.[267] A law dictionary says it means, *inter alia*, to flow over, flow over the bounds, over the brim, cover with or as with water, spread over, and to inundate.[268] One place one finds courts reciting a definition of "overflow" is in National Pollutant Discharge Elimination System (NPDES) Permits;[269] however, it is unlikely judges will find those definitions useful in construing insurance policy language. Courts are rarely called on to define the term and, because standard property policies do not provide a definition, they rely on lay dictionaries. The definitions are, therefore, similar, but with slight variations. For example:

---

265. Popkin v. Security Mut. Ins. Co., 48 A.D.2d 46, 367 N.Y.S.2d 492 (1975). *See also* Novick v. United Servs. Auto. Ass'n, 225 A.D.2d 676, 639 N.Y.S.2d 469 (1996) (where flooding of basement in house covered by homeowners insurance was caused by break in town water main underneath street, water damage exclusion did not apply).

266. *See also* Robert Dorsen, Inc. v. Aetna Casualty & Surety Co., 562 F. Supp. 495 (D.D.C. May 5, 1983) (exclusion concerns water damage from natural phenomena, not ruptured water main).

267. *Overflow*, Merriam-Webster, https://www.merriam-webster.com/dictionary/overflow. Cited by Golden Corral Corp. v. Noble Austin Apts. L.L.C., 2021 Tex. App. LEXIS 5465 (July 9, 2021). The Merriam-Webster dictionary lists "flood" as a synonym for "overflow." However, for purposes of an insurance policy exclusion for water losses, it must be presumed to be different than "flood," as otherwise it would be redundant.

268. *Ballentine's Law Dictionary* (2010).

269. *See, e.g.*, Tenn. Clean Water Network v. TVA, 206 F. Supp. 3d 1280, 1305 (M.D. Tenn. 2016) (NPDES defined "Sanitary Sewer Overflow" to mean "'discharge to land or water of wastes from any portion of the collection, transmission, or treatment system other than through permitted outfalls.'").

- "to flow over the bounds, over the brim" and "to flow over; to cover with or as with water or other fluid; to spread over, to inundate";[270]
- "[t]o flow over; to overspread or cover with water or other liquid; to flood, inundate" and "[t]o pass or spread over like a flood, so as to pervade, fill, cover, submerge, overwhelm, etc." and "[t]o flow over (the brim, banks, or sides)";[271] and
- "to flow or run over, as rivers or water" and "to have the contents flowing over or spilling"; "flood; inundate" and "to flow over the edge or brim of"; and "something that flows or runs over" and "a portion crowded out of an overfilled place."[272]

Another place to possibly find a definition is in endorsements that add backup and overflow coverage to property policies. Some endorsements will define "overflow." For example, in one case, the endorsement defined "sump pump overflow" as "'water which overflows or accidently discharges from within a sump pump, sump pump well, sump pump well discharge system or other type system designed to remove subsurface water from the foundation area of the residence premises.'"[273]

The meaning of "overflow" is said to be much broader than "overtop," which means "'[t]o rise over or above the top of; to surpass in height, surmount, tower above, top.'"[274]

[6] "Sewer" Defined

"Sewer" is not defined in the typical policy, but that does not mean the term is ambiguous.[275] A "sewer" has been defined as an "underground conduit or covered drain which carries away filth and waste matter."[276] Courts in the late

270. Miller v. Letzerich, 121 Tex. 248, 267, 49 S.W.2d 404, 414 (1932) (quoting *Webster's New International Dictionary*).

271. Vanderbrook v. Unitrin Preferred Ins. Co. (*In re* Katrina Canal Breaches Litig.), 495 F.3d 191, 214, n.19 (5th Cir. 2007) (quoting *Oxford English Dictionary*).

272. Fingerle v. City of Ann Arbor, 308 Mich. App. 318, 359, 863 N.W.2d 698, 720–21 (2014) (Beckering, J., dissenting) (quoting Random House *Webster's College Dictionary*).

273. Viscounte v. Liberty Mut. Group, 2012 U.S. Dist. LEXIS 177228 (E.D. Pa. Dec. 14, 2012).

274. Vanderbrook v. Unitrin Preferred Ins. Co. (*In re* Katrina Canal Breaches Litig.), 495 F.3d 191, 214, n.19 (5th Cir. 2007) (quoting *Oxford English Dictionary*).

275. Old Dominion Ins. Co. v. Elysee, Inc., 601 So. 2d 1243, 1245 (Fla. 1st DCA 1992).

276. *Ballentine's Law Dictionary* (2010). *See also* 301-375 W. Onondaga St., LLC v. Liberty Mut. Fire Ins. Co., 2020 U.S. Dist. LEXIS 1228 (N.D.N.Y. Jan. 6, 2020) (citing the Merriam-Webster online dictionary definition of "artificial usually subterranean conduit to carry off sewage and sometimes surface water (as from rainfall)"); Roebling v. Cincinnati, 132 N.E. 60, 64, 102 Ohio St. 460, 472–73 (1921) (sewer means large, underground passage for fluid and feculent matter by means of which this matter is carried off); Valparaiso v. Parker, 148 Ind. 379, 381, 47 N.E. 330, 331 (1897) (as generally understood in law, term "sewers" refers to underground canal or passage by means of which cities are drained).

19th century allowed that open trenches could be sewers.[277] More recently, one court has said that "[w]hile the meaning of the word 'sewer' may vary depending upon the context in which it is used . . . in the modern concept of the word . . . [it] connotes a subterranean conduit or channel to carry off water or refuse."[278] It is said that there are three types of sewers: sanitary sewers carry human and other wastes, storm sewers carry stormwater runoff, and combined sewers carry both.[279]

There is, however, disagreement over whether a facility that carries off stormwater is a sewer. Some courts say that a "storm sewer"—which they may call a drain or storm drain—is not a "sewer."[280] Others say that a sewer may be either a sanitary sewer or storm sewer.[281]

There are older cases that equate "ditches" and "sewers,"[282] while a more recent decision states unequivocally that a ditch is *not* a sewer.[283]

---

277. Aldrich v. Paine, 106 Iowa 461, 466–67, 76 N.W. 812, 814 (1898) (sewer is usually closed, but not necessarily so); Valparaiso v. Parker, 148 Ind. 379, 381, 47 N.E. 330, 331 (1897) (sewer was formerly defined to be freshwater trench artificially made, encompassed with banks on both sides to carry surface water).

278. Reutner v. Vouga, 367 S.W.2d 34, 40 (Mo. App. 1963). *See also* 301-375 W. Onondaga St., LLC v. Liberty Mut. Fire Ins. Co., 2020 U.S. Dist. LEXIS 1228 (N.D.N.Y. Jan. 6, 2020) (colloquially, sewer refers to artificial means to handle surface water and/or sewage).

279. *Bouvier Law Dictionary* (Wolters Kluwer 2012).

280. *See, e.g.*, Clinton v. Spencer, 250 Mich. 135, 148, 229 N.W. 609, 614 (1930) (sewer may serve purpose of drain, but drain may not serve as sewer); City of Sand Springs v. Hohl, 90 Okla. 124, 217, 216 P. 138, 140 (1923) (drain and sewer are not synonymous, sewer being very much more comprehensive than drain, and distinction is also to be made between sanitary sewer and storm sewer); Roebling v. Cincinnati, 132 N.E. 60, 64, 102 Ohio St. 460, 472 (1921) (applied to public improvements in streets, "sewer" and "drain" have come to have their own distinctive meanings: drain is incident to street building and is provided to prevent accumulation of water on surface of street and adjacent territory). *See also* Fuchs v. St. Louis, 167 Mo. 620, 636, 67 S.W. 610, 614 (1902) (sewers are constructed, as sanitary measures, to carry off all sewage).

281. *See, e.g.*, City of Sioux City v. Iowa Dep't of Revenue & Fin., 666 N.W.2d 587, 591 (2003) (because "sewer" is defined as artificial, usually subterranean, conduit to carry off water and certain waste matter as surface water due to rainfall, household waste, as slops waste water from sinks, baths, and excreta consisting of urine, feces, and waste water from industrial works, defining sewage services to include collecting rainwater was reasonable); Kirkham, Michael & Assocs. v. Minot, 122 N.W.2d 862, 864 (N.D. 1963) (absent anything that would indicate limitation on meaning of "sewer," it will be construed to include both storm sewers and sanitary sewers); Anselmi v. Rock Springs, 53 Wyo. 223, 233, 80 P.2d 419, 422 (1938) (court was "unable to say" that term "sewer" does not include storm sewer as well as sanitary sewer); Bennett v. New Bedford, 110 Mass. 433, 438 (1872) (structure for conducting waters of natural stream was common sewer). *See also* Medicus v. Upper Merion Township, 82 Pa. Commw. 303, 310, 475 A.2d 918, 921 (1984) ("sewer systems" encompasses "storm drains").

282. *See, e.g.*, Barton v. Drainage Dist., 174 Ark. 173, 177, 294 S.W. 418, 419 (1927) (chief difference between drains and sewers is that they are called sewers in cities and closely populated communities while they are called drains in rural and agricultural communities); Aldrich v. Paine, 106 Iowa 461, 466–67, 76 N.W. 812, 814 (1898) (word "sewer" does not seem to have meaning essentially differing from "ditch" or "drain," and what is a ditch or drain in country is called sewer in city).

283. Reutner v. Vouga, 367 S.W.2d 34, 40 (Mo. App. 1963).

[7] "Drain" Defined

"Drain" is not defined in the typical policy, but that does not mean the term is ambiguous.[284] It encompasses more than what one might at first suspect. The Merriam-Webster online dictionary defines it as "a means (such as a pipe) by which usually liquid matter is drained."[285] A law dictionary says it has been construed to include a sewer and is generally a hollow space in the ground, whether natural or artificial, in which water is collected or drained away.[286] Early cases often treated the words "drain" and "sewer" as essentially synonymous, saying sewers were found in cities and drains in the country.[287] It has also been said that "drain" has no technical or exact meaning, but generally means an artificial channel or trench through which water or sewage flows.[288]

Modern cases suggest a narrower definition. Thus, one court said a drain is a pipe used to divert water that comes from an external source, for example, surface water from rainfall.[289] In that vein, courts acknowledge that roof drains are drains within the meaning of insurance policies.[290] The word "gutter" has been said to be synonymous with "drain."[291] New York courts have differed over the status of a bathroom sink. A state panel concluded the word "drain" is unambiguous and applies to the bathroom sink drain.[292] In contrast, a New York federal court has suggested that a shower drain or a sink should not be a drain for purposes of an insurance policy.[293] On the other

---

284. Old Dominion Ins. Co. v. Elysee, Inc., 601 So. 2d 1243, 1245 (Fla. 1st DCA 1992).

285. *Drain*, Merriam-Webster, https://www.merriam-webster.com/dictionary/drain. Cited by 301-375 W. Onondaga St., LLC v. Liberty Mut. Fire Ins. Co., 2020 U.S. Dist. LEXIS 1228 (N.D.N.Y. Jan. 6, 2020); Drutz v. Scottsdale Ins. Co., 2012 U.S. Dist. LEXIS 25286 (D. Md. Feb. 28, 2012).

286. *Ballentine's Law Dictionary* (2010).

287. *See, e.g.*, Barton v. Drainage Dist., 174 Ark. 173, 177, 294 S.W. 418, 419 (1927) (chief difference between drains and sewers is that they are called sewers in cities and closely populated communities while they are called drains in rural and agricultural communities); Pioneer Real Estate Co. v. Portland, 119 Ore. 1, 247 P. 319 (1926); Aldrich v. Paine, 106 Iowa 461, 466–67, 76 N.W. 812, 814 (1898) (word "sewer" does not seem to have meaning essentially differing from "ditch" or "drain," and what is a ditch or drain in country is called sewer in city).

288. Valparaiso v. Parker, 148 Ind. 379, 381, 47 N.E. 330, 331 (1897).

289. 301-375 W. Onondaga St., LLC v. Liberty Mut. Fire Ins. Co., 2020 U.S. Dist. LEXIS 1228 (N.D.N.Y. January 6, 2020) (pipe used to transport rainwater that pooled on roof of insured building was a drain as contemplated in policy).

290. Ken Johnson Props., LLC v. Harleysville Worcester Ins. Co., 2013 U.S. Dist. LEXIS 140530 (D. Minn. Sept. 30, 2013) (open end at roof's surface connected to chute that opened onto ground on side of building one story below roof and served as channel or pipe to divert rainwater from roof, therefore qualifying as a drain); Scorpio v. Underwriters at Lloyd's, London, 2012 U.S. Dist. LEXIS 77751 (D.R.I. June 5, 2012) (roof downspout was drain).

291. St. Joseph's Condo. Ass'n, Inc. v. Pac. Ins. Co., 2008 U.S. Dist. LEXIS 86470 (E.D. La. Oct. 27, 2008).

292. Newlo Realty Co. v. U.S.F. & G. Corp., 213 A.D.2d 295, 624 N.Y.S.2d 33 (1995).

293. 301-375 W. Onondaga St., LLC v. Liberty Mut. Fire Ins. Co., 2020 U.S. Dist. LEXIS 1228 (N.D.N.Y. Jan. 6, 2020) (not even insurer argued that it was appropriate for a shower

hand, a Texas court said a floor drain was a drain because it was a conduit for draining liquid or carrying off surplus liquids.[294] Sometimes courts are compelled to state the obvious, as when a Maryland federal court stated that "common sense dictates that a toilet is not a drain."[295]

There should be no distinction between drains that are within the walls of a property and those without.[296] Nor is there anything about the common understanding of "drain," or in the policy, requiring a construction limited to *underground* pipes.[297] The way to determine the nature of a pipe is to consider its function, not its location.[298]

[8] "Sump" and "Sump Pump" Defined

A "sump" is a "a pit or reservoir serving as a drain or receptacle for liquids," such as a cesspool.[299] It has also been described as a pit or well that is constructed to collect liquids like oil or water.[300] A "sump pit" has been defined as "'a pit at the lowest point in a circulating or drainage system.'"[301] It has also been described as an artificial means to handle surface water and/or sewage.[302]

A "sump pump" is a pump—often in a basement—that removes accumulations of liquid from a sump pit.[303] It has also been defined as a pump set to

---

drain or sink to be considered a drain; where "drain" is pipe used to carry away external water, coverage would remain for leaks from clog in pipes in building's internal plumbing system, for example, bathrooms or sinks).

294. Kelley St. Assocs., LLC v. United Fire & Cas. Co., 2015 Tex. App. LEXIS 12175 (Nov. 30, 2015).

295. Drutz v. Scottsdale Ins. Co., 2012 U.S. Dist. LEXIS 25286, at *8 (D. Md. Feb. 28, 2012). *Accord* Korean Cmty. Presbyterian Church v. Md. Cas. Co., 2015 U.S. Dist. LEXIS 112130 (N.D. Ga. Aug. 25, 2015) (where policy provided sublimit for backup or overflow from sewer or drain, that sublimit did not apply because clog causing overflow was not in drain, but instead in toilet and, therefore, no water backed up or overflowed from any drain).

296. 301-375 W. Onondaga St., LLC v. Liberty Mut. Fire Ins. Co., 2020 U.S. Dist. LEXIS 1228 (N.D.N.Y. Jan. 6, 2020).

297. Newlo Realty Co. v. U.S.F. & G. Corp., 213 A.D.2d 295, 624 N.Y.S.2d 33 (1995).

298. 301-375 W. Onondaga St., LLC v. Liberty Mut. Fire Ins. Co., 2020 U.S. Dist. LEXIS 1228 (N.D.N.Y. Jan. 6, 2020).

299. *Sump*, Merriam-Webster, https://www.merriam-webster.com/dictionary/sump. Cited by the court in 301-375 W. Onondaga St., LLC v. Liberty Mut. Fire Ins. Co., 2020 U.S. Dist. LEXIS 1228 (N.D.N.Y. Jan. 6, 2020); Kokhan v. Auto Club Ins. Co., 297 So. 3d 570, 576, n.1 (Fla. 4th DCA 2020).

300. Blumenstock v. Gibson, 811 A.2d 1029, 1032, n.1 (Pa. Super. 2002,) citing *Webster's New Universal Unabridged Dictionary* (1983).

301. Pickens v. Liberty Mut. Ins. Co., 966 F. Supp. 2d 1265, 1268, n.4 (S.D. Ala. 2013), quoting *Webster's Third New International Dictionary* (1993).

302. 301-375 W. Onondaga St., LLC v. Liberty Mut. Fire Ins. Co., 2020 U.S. Dist. LEXIS 1228 (N.D.N.Y. Jan. 6, 2020) (colloquially, sump refers to artificial means to handle surface water and/or sewage).

303. *Sump pump*, Merriam-Webster, https://www.merriam-webster.com/dictionary/sump%20pump.

drain a sump[304] and as a "'pump to remove accumulations of water or other liquid from a sump pit.'"[305] A sump pump is machinery.[306]

Whether a device is a sump pump has rarely been at issue, with one apparent exception. In a case before a Florida federal court, a residence lost power in a hurricane, and the pump in the *septic system* stop functioning. Brown water backed up or overflowed into the home through a shower drain, ultimately flooding the entire house. The all-risk policy had the usual exclusion for water damage from backup or overflow, based on which the insurer determined the loss was not covered. Specifically, the company said the damage was caused by water that backed up or overflowed from a septic tank, which the insurer contended was a "sump, sump pump, or related equipment." However, the court concluded that "sump" and "sump pump" would not include a septic tank or the pump in it. The "term 'sump' and, concomitantly, 'sump pump' are," said the court, "ambiguous in the policy if they encompass a septic tank. That is because the policy in several sections states that a plumbing system or household appliance does not include a sump or sump pump, but elsewhere says that a plumbing system does include a septic tank. So at least as far as whether a septic tank is included in the definition of a sump or sump pump in the policy, those terms are ambiguous," and must be construe in favor of coverage.[307] Moreover, the court said in *dicta* that the result would be the same if the terms were not ambiguous as under the Florida Building Code definitions, a septic pump cannot be a sump pump because a sump pump is used for removal of drainage, *except raw sewage.*[308]

[9] "Related Equipment" Defined

The typical exclusion is for damage caused by water that backs up or overflows or is otherwise discharged from a sewer, drain, sump, sump pump, or *related equipment*. The phrase "related equipment" is not defined in policies,

304. Blumenstock v. Gibson, 811 A.2d 1029, 1032, n.1 (Pa. Super. 2002), citing *Webster's New Universal Unabridged Dictionary* (1983).

305. Pickens v. Liberty Mut. Ins. Co., 966 F. Supp. 2d 1265, 1268, n.4 (S.D. Ala. 2013), quoting *Webster's Third New International Dictionary* (1993).

306. State *ex rel.* Trydle v. Industrial Com., 61 Ohio Op. 2d 488, 32 Ohio St. 2d 257, 262, 291 N.E.2d 748, 752 (1972).

307. Glaser v. Geovera Specialty Ins. Co., 420 F. Supp. 3d 1287 (M.D. Fla. 2019).

308. Glaser v. Geovera Specialty Ins. Co., 420 F. Supp. 3d 1287, 1295, n.3 (M.D. Fla. 2019). The court noted that the experts appeared to agree that part of the septic system included a sump, but there was nothing in the record showing from which portion of the septic system the water backed up. The insurer, therefore, had not demonstrated that the water backed up from a sump when it showed the water came from the septic system. A fact question, therefore, existed that would prevent the court from entering summary judgment for the insurer if the terms were unambiguous.

and courts have rarely addressed it. A few cases have held that a toilet is related equipment.[309]

In one of the only cases to interpret "related equipment," there was a narrow exclusion concerning only "a sump, sump pump or related equipment." Damage to a basement was caused by water discharging from a pipe leading from a sump pump to a location outside the insured house. The court said that the term "related equipment" encompassed the piping and other related equipment needed to discharge water flowing out of the pump to a location outside the house, even though that equipment was purchased separately from the sump pump.[310]

[10] "Otherwise Discharged" Defined

There are three occurrences that trigger the usual exclusion: water that backs up, water that overflows, or water that is *otherwise discharged*. The phrase "otherwise discharged" is not defined in policies, but "captures a far broader universe of possible ways water may escape" than the other two.[311] "Otherwise" means "in a different way or manner,"[312] and "discharge" means "a flowing or issuing out."[313]

---

309. McCaughey v. Ohio Sec. Ins. Co., 2021 U.S. Dist. LEXIS 65061 (C.D. Cal. Apr. 2, 2021) (where water damage was caused by overflow from toilet tank, court concluded a straightforward reading of plain language of the exclusion for damage caused by water that backs up or overflows or is otherwise discharged from a sewer, drain, sump, sump pump, or related equipment precludes coverage for damage caused by water that overflows from a toilet; noting that insureds did not dispute that toilet's supply tank was "related equipment"); 180 Lafayette Corp. v. Wesco Ins. Co., 2021 N.Y. Misc. LEXIS 307 (Jan. 26, 2021) (damage was caused by toilet continually discharging water and causing flooding, and policy did not cover damage caused directly or indirectly by water that backed up or overflowed or was otherwise discharged from a drain or related equipment); 193 Hooper Street Condo v. Wesco Ins. Co., 2020 N.Y. Misc. LEXIS 262 (Jan. 10, 2020) (where source of the water damage for which insured sought recovery was toilet that malfunctioned and overflowed, policy exclusion applied because malfunctioning toilet constitutes at least "related equipment" within meaning of exclusion).

310. Baran v. N.J. Mfrs. Ins. Co., 2010 N.J. Super. Unpub. LEXIS 2704 (Nov. 9, 2010).

311. 301-375 W. Onondaga St., LLC v. Liberty Mut. Fire Ins. Co., 2020 U.S. Dist. LEXIS 1228 (N.D.N.Y. Jan. 6, 2020). *See also* Victoria Family LLLP v. Ohio Sec. Ins. Co., 475 F. Supp. 3d 1106 (S.D. Cal. 2020) ("otherwise discharged" serves to expand scope of exclusion).

312. *Otherwise*, Merriam-Webster, https://www.merriam-webster.com/dictionary/otherwise.

313. *Discharge*, Merriam-Webster, https://www.merriam-webster.com/dictionary/discharge. Cited by the courts in Lumbermens Mut. Casualty Co. v. S-W Indus., 39 F.3d 1324 (6th Cir. 1994); Hobson v. Indian Harbor Ins. Co., 2015 Mich. App. LEXIS 486 (Mar. 10, 2015); Bosserman Aviation Equip., Inc. v. United States Liab. Ins. Co., 183 Ohio App. 3d 29, 915 N.E.2d 687 (2009).

[11] Endorsement Deleting Exclusion

As discussed elsewhere, an endorsement may add coverage for backups and overflows.[314] Sometimes, however, an endorsement will simply delete the backup and overflow portion of the water damage exclusion.[315]

2.5 The Water Damage Exclusion: Water under the Ground Surface

Water under the ground surface can and does lead to flooding, principally in basements.[316] Another component of the standard water damage exclusion in commercial property coverage bars coverage for water under the ground surface pressing on, or flowing or seeping through, foundations; walls; floors; paved surfaces; basements, whether paved or not; or doors, windows, or other openings.[317] Residential polices generally add swimming pools[318] and specifically name sidewalks and driveways.[319] The exclusion has been held to be unambiguous.[320]

The question that arises about application of the exclusion is, "What is the meaning of 'water under the ground surface'?" The Oregon Supreme Court has said that "'water below the surface of the ground' was intended to have the general meaning of 'subterranean waters,' whether percolating waters or underground streams."[321] Following that interpretation, almost every court has

314. See § 3.3[3], *infra*.

315. *See, e.g.*, Doylestown Elec. Supply Co. v. Maryland Cas. Ins. Co., 1996 U.S. Dist. LEXIS 20599 (E.D. Pa. Dec. 30, 1996), *aff'd*, 133 F.3d 909 (3d Cir. 1997).

316. *See, e.g.*, Platek v. Town of Hamburg, 3 N.Y.S.3d 312, 24 N.Y.3d 688, 26 N.E.3d 1167 (2015). *See also* Cent. Ill. Compounding, Inc. v. Pharmacists Mut. Ins. Co., 426 Ill. Dec. 75, 115 N.E.3d 997 (Ill. App. 2018) (water service line was damaged and caused discharge of water that inundated premises above ground).

317. ISO Form CP 10 30 09 17, § B.1.g.(4).

318. *See* South Carolina Farm Bureau Mutual Insurance Co. v. Durham, 380 S.C. 506, 671 S.E.2d 610 (S.C. 2010) (where underground water pressure was at least one cause of pool floating out of its foundation after being drained, loss was excluded under water damage exclusion and anti-concurrent causation clause of policy); Jahier v. Liberty Mutual Group, 64 A.D.3d 683, 883 N.Y.S.2d 283 (N.Y. App. Div. 2009) (exclusion applied where evidence demonstrated loss was attributable to subsurface water pressure exerted on empty swimming pool, even though it was precipitated by drainage of pool and heavy rainfall).

319. HO 00 03 10 00 (Exclusions), § A.3.c.

320. Kimmel v. Nationwide Mut. Ins. Co., 1992 U.S. Dist. LEXIS 329 (E.D. Pa. Jan. 14, 1992) (exclusion was clear and unambiguous and relieved insurer of obligation to pay for damage to building caused by underground water that seeped into building through wall).

321. Hatley v. Truck Ins. Exch., 261 Ore. 622, 495 P.2d 1196 (1972). *See also* Harinderpal Ahluwalia v. Allied Prop. & Cas. Ins. Co., 2012 U.S. Dist. LEXIS 93820 (E.D. Cal. July 6, 2012) (common definition of ground water is water beneath earth's surface); Nationwide Ins. Co. v. Warren, 675 S.W.2d 402 (Ky. App. 1984) (finding exclusion inapplicable where water ran down side of house into ground next to block foundation and then turned to ice, expanded,

held that damage from water escaping an underground pipe is not excluded. That is the position of courts in Alaska,[322] California,[323] Colorado,[324] the District of Columbia,[325] Florida,[326] Maine,[327] Massachusetts,[328] Mississippi,[329]

---

and cracked foundation; water below surface of ground means underground streams, springs, or natural deposits of liquid).

322. West v. Umialik Ins. Co., 8 P.3d 1135 (Alaska 2000) (where temperature in basement dropped below freezing, causing pipe to break at well pump and allow water to infuse ground beneath house, causing settling when soil under foundation was washed away, policyholder could reasonably interpret water exclusion as referring to water from natural or external source seeping through structure and that did not describe the damage incurred).

323. Sauer v. General Ins. Co., 225 Cal. App. 2d 275, 37 Cal. Rptr. 303 (1964) (exclusion did not apply where water pipes underneath the dwelling but above ground sprung a leak and had been discharging water into ground for some time, causing earth beneath the house to become soaked and muddy and foundation piers to settle, resulting in twisting, warping, and cracking of house). *Compare* Tu v. Dongbu Ins. Co., 2018 U.S. Dist. LEXIS 151322 (N.D. Cal. Sept. 5, 2018), where the damage was caused by a broken sewer pipe under the building. The court found the exclusion applied and followed another decision in which a court relied on language in the exclusion pursuant to which the exclusion applied regardless of whether the water was naturally occurring or due to human-made or other artificial causes. The *Dongbu* court, however, did not cite any similar language.

324. Redstone Corp. v. Fire Ins. Exchange, 715 F. Supp. 300 (D. Colo. 1989) (water below surface of the ground means natural water, rather than water escaping from a water main and, thus, coverage for damage as a result of water from broken water main is not excluded); Koncilja v. Trinity Universal Ins. Co., 35 Colo. App. 27, 528 P.2d 939 (1974) (where water pipe embedded within concrete floor broke and caused water to soak into ground beneath house, causing damage, loss was covered because if insurer intended to omit from coverage plumbing system below surface of ground when it specifically insured overall plumbing system, it should have done so expressly).

325. Robert Dorsen, Inc. v. Aetna Casualty & Surety Co., 562 F. Supp. 495 (D.D.C. 1983) (finding exclusion did not apply where source of water that damaged insured goods was broken water main; exclusion concerned water damage from natural phenomena, not ruptured water main).

326. Hartford Acci. & Indem. Co. v. Phelps, 294 So. 2d 362, 363(Fla. 1st DCA 1974) (where pipe that developed leak was within and a part of plumbing system of house although it was buried in ground below, there was coverage because underground water exclusion does not refer to leaks within plumbing system; having specifically covered plumbing system leaks, insurer, if it had intended to exclude underground leaks in plumbing system, should have specifically said so). *See also* Kokhan v. Auto Club Ins. Co., 297 So. 3d 570 (Fla. 4th DCA 2020) (exclusion plainly refers to naturally flowing water exerting pressure from outside of plumbing system, not leak from within plumbing system itself).

327. L v. Safeguard Ins. Co., 1985 Me. Super. LEXIS 173 (June 21, 1985).

328. Standard Electric Supply Co. v. Norfolk & Dedham Mut. Fire Ins. Co., 1 Mass. App. Ct. 762, 307 N.E.2d 11 (1974) (finding coverage despite exclusion for water below surface of ground where damage occurred when water pipe in basement of adjacent premises burst and water escaped through foundation walls and floor, and through ground, into basement of insured premises).

329. New Hampshire Ins. Co. v. Robertson, 352 So. 2d 1307, 1311 (Miss. 1977) (where damage was caused by water from underground leak from separation of hot water line, policy had to be construed as including loss caused by leaking from plumbing system even though below surface of the earth).

Missouri,[330] New Mexico,[331] New York,[332] and Texas.[333] There are a few cases to the contrary. They are from courts in Arkansas,[334] Kansas,[335] Ohio,[336] Michigan,[337] and Pennsylvania.[338] A leading insurance treatise casts doubt on the viability of those decisions.[339]

---

330. Jones v. Columbia Mut. Ins. Co., 700 S.W.2d 187 (Mo. App. 1985) (water in pipes in house froze, and water from broken pipes ran under foundation and froze again, causing damage to carport, fireplace, and foundation; exclusion did not bar coverage because it applied only to damage resulting from natural water, or perhaps other sources).

331. King v. Travelers Ins. Co., 84 N.M. 550, 505 P.2d 1226 (1973) (where galvanized iron water line underneath concrete floor slab broke or ruptured, allowing escape and discharge of water that eroded soil and caused abnormal settling damage, loss was covered because if insurer desired to exclude from coverage plumbing system below surface of ground after specifically insuring overall plumbing system, it could have done so).

332. Cantanucci v. Reliance Ins. Co., 43 A.D.2d 622, 623, 349 N.Y.S.2d 187, 190 (1973), *aff'd*, 364 N.Y.S.2d 890, 35 N.Y.2d 890, 324 N.E.2d 360 (1974) (where water below surface of the ground escaped from ruptured sewer line buried below foundation wall and eroded the soil, causing foundation wall to sag and crack, there was coverage because exclusion should be construed as applicable to water below surface of ground as result of natural causes, and not water that happens to be found below surface as result of artificial devices such as pipes).

333. Adrian Associates, General Contractors v. National Surety Corp., 638 S.W.2d 138 (Tex. Civ. App. 1982), *aff'd*, 650 S.W.2d 67 (Tex. 1983) (because of rupture of underground water main, water escaped and migrated below surface of the ground and underneath concrete slab, causing it to subside or settle, requiring it to be reconstructed; finding coverage because phrase "water below the surface of the ground" as used in underground water exclusion in an all-risks policy did not include water from artificial source).

334. Bull v. Nationwide Mut. Fire Ins. Co., 824 F.3d 722 (8th Cir. 2016) (applying Arkansas law). *See also* Vanderburg v. Allstate Ins. Co., 2005 Ark. App. LEXIS 287 (Apr. 6, 2005) (where water came from pipe underneath slab foundation, exclusion was controlling as it was undisputed that water came from under the ground).

335. Krug v. Millers' Mut. Ins. Assoc., 209 Kan. 111, 495 P.2d 949 (1972) (no coverage because water that leaked from broken water line was water below surface of the ground within meaning of exclusion).

336. Buttelworth v. Westfield Ins. Co., 41 Ohio App. 3d 288, 535 N.E.2d 320 (1987) (water line ruptured in plumbing system of neighbor's adjacent property, and water leaking from that plumbing system ran onto insured property and caused structural damage to foundation; loss was caused by water below surface of ground that seeped through foundation, and court held exclusion clearly and unambiguously indicates that damage from any water below surface that seeps through foundation was not covered, regardless of whether the source was natural or artificial). *Accord* Shanton v. United Ohio Ins. Co., 2007 Ohio App. LEXIS 5603 (Nov. 20, 2007), *app. den.*, 117 Ohio St. 3d 1458, 884 N.E.2d 67 (2007).

337. Theater Grp. 3, LLC v. Secura Ins. Co., 2014 Mich. App. LEXIS 2165 (Nov. 13, 2014) (unpublished) (even if water originated from plumbing system, if it was under the ground surface when it entered through foundation or walls, resulting damage would not be covered under plain language of exclusion; however, there was insufficient evidence to prove that pipe or leak was actually under the ground surface).

338. Bergdoll v. York Water Co., 2008 Pa. Commw. Unpub. LEXIS 291 (Apr. 1, 2008) (exclusion applied to water damage caused by break in a high pressure water main line).

339. 5 Jeffrey E. Thomas, *New Appleman on Insurance Law Library Edition* § 43.02[3][d] (Matthew Bender 2022) (reasoning of courts finding exclusion applicable has been questioned by other courts faced with same issue, so their position is likely no longer good law).

Courts have held that the under the ground surface exclusion does not apply where water escapes on the surface and, after seeping into the ground, causes damage.[340] These courts base their decision on "water below surface of ground," meaning underground streams, springs, or percolating waters. The exclusion refers to *water* pressing on, or *flowing* or *seeping* and, therefore, courts have said, the exclusion concerns "water in liquid form, not frozen water."[341] Other courts disagree and apply the exclusion because water is still water even though it is in frozen form and exerts pressure that causes damage. Thus, the water under the ground exclusion barred coverage where rainwater ran into footings around basement walls during construction and then froze, causing the ground to heave and the walls to crack.[342]

Of course, for the exception to the exclusion to be at issue, any pipe must actually be underground.[343] If it is not, then the "water under the ground surface" exclusion will not apply, although other limitations or exclusions may still bar coverage.[344] For example, where the pipe that burst entered the insured

---

340. L v. Safeguard Ins. Co., 1985 Me. Super. LEXIS 173 (June 21, 1985) (where water main break occurred near insured building allowing water to flow into area behind that building and pond before seeping into ground and through underground air vents, into ground around, and under building where it froze, causing building to move and settle, there was coverage because underground water exclusions did not include water from artificial source); Nationwide Ins. Co. v. Warren, 675 S.W.2d 402 (Ky. App. 1984) (finding exclusion inapplicable where water ran down side of house into ground next to block foundation and then turned to ice, expanded, and cracked foundation).

341. Ariston Airline & Catering Supply Co. v. Forbes, 211 N.J. Super. 472, 511 A.2d 1278 (1986) (exclusion makes no reference to ice, although it could easily have done so). *See also* Ercolani v. Excelsior Ins. Co., 830 F.2d 31 (3d Cir. 1987) (lower court committed error in construing water damage exclusion as being applicable to collapse caused in part by freezing of ground water, which put pressure on the foundation wall; exclusion only applies to water that in its liquid state causes pressure on building, not water that has become solid and expanded due to reduction in its temperature).

342. Oak Tree, Inc. v. Commercial Union Ins. Co., 720 F. Supp. 92 (E.D. Mich. 1989). *Accord* Loretto-Utica Properties Corp. v. Douglas Co., 165 Misc. 2d 1004, 630 N.Y.S.2d 917 (1995).

343. *See* Gold v. State Farm Fire & Cas. Co., 880 F. Supp. 2d 587, 596, n.8 (E.D. Pa. 2012) (any broken utility line was alleged to be "under the floor," but not necessarily below surface of ground).

344. *See, e.g.*, Ark. Valley Drilling, Inc. v. Cont'l W. Ins. Co., 703 F. Supp. 2d 1232 (D. Colo. 2010), where there were two events. First an indoor pipe froze and burst. Next, an underground water pipe ruptured. The insured theorized that water below the surface of the ground that emanated from the frozen pipe itself froze and thawed. That exerted pressure on the underground water pipe, causing it to break, resulting in the second loss. The policy excluded loss caused by water under the ground surface regardless of any other causes or event that contributed concurrently or in any sequence to the loss. The insured argued the "water under the surface of the ground" exclusion did not apply because only one loss occurred: the rupture of the frozen water pipe was the sole cause of that loss, and it was a covered cause of loss. The court did not agree. "The rupture of the frozen indoor water pipe," said the court, "was an event that contributed concurrently and/or in sequence to the presence of water under the surface of the ground and the losses caused by water under the surface of the ground. Under the plain

house through the foundation wall and ran through artificially created gravel material that filled the area above the ground and between the foundation walls, the pipe was not below the surface of the ground and the exclusion did not apply.[345] In another case the damage was caused by a "geyser" of water from a broken water line that flooded the insured home, breaking windows and causing the ceiling to collapse. The policyholder contended that the water that caused the damage was above the ground, but the court said the exclusion applied because the water *originated* underground.[346] An Illinois court agreed that the actual loss or damage need not be below the surface of the ground as long as the water *originates* from under the ground.[347]

The specific language of the policy can yield a different result. For example, a number of cases have found no coverage where the exclusion was prefaced by a phrase like "water . . . on or below the surface of the ground, regardless of its source."[348] The same result is reached when the exclusion says it applies regardless of whether the occurrence was "caused by an act of nature or is otherwise caused" or the water is "naturally occurring or due to man-made or other artificial causes."[349]

---

meaning of the language of the concurrent or sequential cause provision . . . the losses caused by water under the surface of the ground are not covered . . . even if the rupture of the frozen indoor water pipe was the initial event or a concurrent event that contributed to the water under the surface of the ground."

345. Hudson v. Allstate Ins Co, 809 N.Y.S.2d 124, 25 A.D.3d 654 (2006) (damage was caused when water supply pipe burst and caused surrounding gravel fill to wash away).

346. Carver v. Allstate Ins. Co., 77 Ark. App. 296, 76 S.W.3d 901 (Ark. App. 2002). *Compare* Praetorian Ins. Co. v. Arabia Shrine Ctr. Houston, 2016 U.S. Dist. LEXIS 20186 (S.D. Tex. Feb. 19, 2016) (because sprinklers are not under surface of ground, any leakage from them would not be water under the ground surface); Sauer v. General Ins. Co., 225 Cal. App. 2d 275, 37 Cal. Rptr. 303 (1964) (exclusion did not apply where water pipes underneath the dwelling but above ground sprung leak).

347. Cent. Ill. Compounding, Inc. v. Pharmacists Mut. Ins. Co., 426 Ill. Dec. 75, 115 N.E.3d 997 (Ill. App. 2018).

348. Colella v. State Farm Fire & Cas. Co., 407 Fed. Appx. 616 (3d Cir. 2011); Johnson v. State Farm Fire & Cas. Co., 2021 U.S. Dist. LEXIS 59331 (D.N.J. Mar. 29, 2021); Sanko v. Allstate Ins. Co., 323 F. Supp. 3d 707 (M.D. Pa. 2018); Harden-Doss v. Country Mut. Ins. Co., 2015 U.S. Dist. LEXIS 181736 (N.D. Okla. Sept. 8, 2015); Muscutt v. Allstate Prop. & Cas. Ins. Co., 2014 U.S. Dist. LEXIS 125729 (W.D. Ky. Sept. 9, 2014); Platek v. Town of Hamburg, 3 N.Y.S.3d 312, 24 N.Y.3d 688, 26 N.E.3d 1167 (2015); Thompson v. State Farm Fire & Cas. Co., 165 P.3d 900 (Colo. App. 2007); Carver v. Allstate Ins. Co., 77 Ark. App. 296, 76 S.W.3d 901 (Ark. App. 2002). *Compare* McEwing v. Lititz Mut. Ins. Co., 77 A.3d 639 (Pa. Super. 2013) (distinguishing *Colella*).

349. Goodrich v. Garrison Prop. & Cas. Ins. Co., 526 F. Supp. 3d 789 (D. Nev. 2021) (whether intruding water was originally snowmelt or water from another source was of no consequence because exclusion encompassed losses arising from, caused by, or resulting from human or animal forces, any act of nature, or any other source); Wisteria Props. LLC v. Ohio Sec. Ins. Co., 2021 U.S. Dist. LEXIS 228135 (C.D. Cal. Nov. 17, 2021); Ruffin Rd. Venture Lot IV v. Travelers Prop. Cas. Co. of Am., 2011 U.S. Dist. LEXIS 66095 (S.D. Cal. June 20, 2011); Harleysville Ins. Co. of N.Y. v. Potamianos Props., LLC, 108 A.D.3d 1110, 969 N.Y.S.2d 342 (2013).

In one case a court found coverage where water damage was caused by a broken plumbing pipe located underneath the insured home and the policy excluded coverage for damage from water below the surface of the ground *arising from natural or external forces*. The court said water under the ground would be a spring or water that fed a well, not water from a broken plumbing pipe. The court added that the phrase "external forces" did not mean "that any losses caused by water that ends up under the ground and then causes damage are excluded from coverage . . . [r]ather . . . in this context [it] refers to the force that causes natural water under the ground to damage the dwelling."[350]

Although not common, an endorsement may add back coverage for damage caused by water under the ground surface. One should, therefore, always check for such an endorsement.[351]

2.6 The Water Damage Exclusion: Waterborne Material

Standard commercial property policies exclude coverage for loss or damage caused directly or indirectly by "waterborne material" carried or otherwise moved by flood, surface water, waves, tides, tidal water, overflow of any body of water, or spray water that backs up or overflows or is otherwise discharged from a sewer, drain, sump, sump pump or related equipment, or water under the ground surface pressing on, or flowing or seeping through foundations; walls; floors or paved surfaces; basements; or doors, windows, or other openings.[352] The exclusion also applies to material carried or otherwise moved by mudslide or mudflow. Standard homeowners policies have a similar exclusion. It proscribes coverage for a loss caused directly or indirectly by waterborne material carried or otherwise moved by flood, surface water, waves, tidal waves, tsunamis, tides, tidal water, overflow of any body of water, or spray; water that backs up through sewers or drains or overflows or is otherwise

350. Varela v. State Farm Gen. Ins. Co., 555 F. Supp. 3d 983, 991 (C.D. Cal. 2021). The court also said that policy language stating that the insurer will not cover losses associated with damage caused *directly or indirectly* is akin to an exclusion for *natural or external forces*. The words "directly or indirectly" are usually prefatory so that the typical policy says the insurer will not pay for loss or damage caused directly or indirectly by water under the ground surface. Despite the court's characterization of the terminology, the argument can be made that "directly or indirectly" refers to causation, not to the source of the water.

351. *See, e.g.*, Barking Dog v. Citizens Ins. Co. of America, 164 N.H. 80, 53 A.3d 554 (2012), where the exclusion for water under the ground surface pressing on or flowing or seeping through foundations, walls, floors, paved surfaces, basements, doors, windows, or other openings was deleted. The septic system for the insured property was damaged when ground water caused the cement risers surrounding the pump chamber to move and allow water and other materials to enter the chamber and cause its failure. The insurer argued that the terms "walls" and "floor" referred to parts of a building, not of a pump chamber. The court, however, concluded the words "walls" and "floor" could encompass the walls and floor of a pump chamber.

352. ISO Form CP 10 30 09 17, § B.1.g.(5).

discharged from a sump; sump pump or related equipment; and water below the surface of the ground, including that which exerts pressure on, or seeps, leaks, or flows through a building, sidewalk, driveway, patio, foundation, swimming pool, or other structure.[353]

"Waterborne" means "supported, carried, or transmitted by water."[354] The meaning of the term has been addressed in only a couple of federal district court cases. Both referenced lay dictionaries. In one case the parties agreed that "floated or floating upon the water" was an acceptable definition. The court applied that meaning after noting that "conveyed by water" was a second definition.[355] Another court, relying on a consensus of dictionaries, proffered three definitions: first, floating on or supported by water; second, transported or conveyed by water; and third, transmitted by water. The term could be read, said the court, to mean any of those three definitions exclusively or in any combination, but, concluded the court, its commonly understood meaning is inclusive of its primary and secondary definitions.[356] The court rejected the contention that "waterborne" was ambiguous.

These courts were not considering the "waterborne" exclusion. There appear to be only two reported decisions in which the exclusion was addressed. The first is the decision of a New York federal district court. During a hurricane, boats, driven by the storm, repeatedly struck the dock, house, and deck of the insured property. The insurer argued the boats were "waterborne material." The court began by stating that the parties had not provided it with any cases interpreting the phrase "water borne material" in an analogous context, and the court's own research had not turned up any authority. The court next, turning to the language of the exclusion, said that the qualities of "water borne material" would commonly include the capacity to enter, back up, discharge, overflow from any sewer or drain, or be located in the ground. These were processes generally associated with materials like sand, silt, or sewage.[357] Directing its attention then to dictionary definitions of "material," the court said the word refers to elements, constituents, or substances of which something is composed or can be made. The court concluded by saying that it could not imagine a boat owner inviting a friend to traverse a waterway by riding on "water borne material" and, therefore, the common definition of

353. ISO Form HO 00 03 05 11 (Exclusions), § A.3.d.

354. *Waterborne*, Merriam-Webster, https://www.merriam-webster.com/dictionary/waterborne.

355. Hartford Fire Ins. Co. v. T.A. Loving Co., 1995 U.S. Dist. LEXIS 13598 (E.D.N.C. Aug. 30, 1995), *aff'd*, 1996 U.S. App. LEXIS 15961 (4th Cir. July 2, 1996). *See also* Commercial Union Ins. Co. v. Advance Coating Co., 351 So. 2d 1183 (La. 1977) (insured contended that "waterborne" had two meanings: floated or floating on water and conveyed by water).

356. R.M.D. Corp. v. Caliber One Indem. Co., 2005 U.S. Dist. LEXIS 9615 (W.D. Ky. May 19, 2005), *rev'd on other grounds*, 194 Fed. Appx. 409 (6th Cir. 2006).

357. *See* Davis v. Standard Fire Ins. Co., 2014 U.S. Dist. LEXIS 114874 (N.D.N.Y. Aug. 19, 2014) (appearing to treat sewage as waterborne material).

"water borne material" conveyed a meaning "inapplicable to the conveyances at issue."[358]

In the other case, it appeared that the insured's home was struck and damaged by an adjacent home during a storm. The insurance company asserted that the waterborne exclusion specifically precluded coverage for damages attributed to waterborne material and that would encompass damage caused by the neighboring structure striking the insured home. The insured argued that it was unclear whether the term "material" in the exclusion included the "intact entirety" of the neighboring structure. The court did not reach that question because the insured failed to refute evidence that showed storm surge contributed to the damage to the dwelling and, therefore, pursuant to the anti-concurrent causation clause, the policy did not cover the damage.[359]

A scenario that does not appear to have reached a court is one in which an endorsement adds flood coverage but leaves the "waterborne material" exclusion in place. Borne by water, material—be it a boat, motor vehicle, building sand, or silt—forms a barrier that diverts or retains water, causing an insured property to be flooded when it would not otherwise be. Putting aside any anti-concurrent causation clause, would there be a covered loss, that is, a flood loss, or an excluded loss caused indirectly by waterborne material? If objects like boats, cars, or buildings are not "material" when waterborne, then a policyholder might succeed in getting a claim paid following the reasoning of the New York federal court. On the other hand, if the material were sand or silt, the insurer would likely prevail under the reasoning of that court.

2.7 Objects Propelled by Water

[1] Introduction

Occasionally, an object propelled by water causes damage and the question that arises is whether the water damage exclusion bars coverage. If the object is considered to be "waterborne," then, as discussed above,[360] the loss may be excluded.

[2] Boats and Docks

During a storm, it is not unusual for boats to break free of their moorings or docks to disintegrate and collided with insured property. That creates a causation conundrum: was the boat or dock blown over water to the point of

---

358. Spindler v. Great Northern Ins. Co., 2016 U.S. Dist. LEXIS 16532 (E.D.N.Y. Feb. 2, 2016), *adopted by* 2016 U.S. Dist. LEXIS 30255 (E.D.N.Y. Mar. 9, 2016).

359. Keelen v. QBE Ins. Corp., 2016 U.S. Dist. LEXIS 55895 (D.N.J. Apr. 27, 2016).

360. See § 2.6, *supra*.

collision, or did it arrive there by force of water? The riddle was addressed in post-Superstorm Sandy cases with differing results.

In a New York case,[361] two boats collided with structures and fixtures on the insured property during the hurricane. Water infiltrated the yard of the property before the boats arrived, but there was specific evidence that the property was undamaged by flood waters. The insurer contended the damage inflicted by the storm-driven vessels was from a flood and therefore excluded. The court disagreed. The damage, it said, was caused by physical collision with the watercraft, and that was a peril distinct and separate from flood. Therefore, the loss was not specifically barred by the surface water exclusion regardless of whether wind or water moved the boats.

In a New Jersey case,[362] the insureds noticed an unmoored boat in their backyard after Superstorm Sandy and believed the boat damaged their dock during the storm. The court held that the insureds were unable to recover for their dock losses because their policy excluded coverage for loss caused by the pressure or weight of water, whether driven by wind or not, to a dock and for loss caused directly or indirectly by water damage, meaning flood, surface water, waves, tidal water, or overflow of a body of water.[363] That suggests the court believed any collision of the boat with the dock was caused by the excluded peril of water whether or not the "dock exclusion" applied. The court added that the result would be unchanged if wind and rain contributed to the damage because the anti-concurrent causation clause in the policy precluded coverage for a loss caused by water damage regardless of any other cause or event contributing concurrently or in any sequence to that loss. Thus, if wind, a covered peril, combined with water to propel the boat, the loss was not covered.

In another New York case,[364] a wooden dock from another property was pushed by wind over water into the insured home, which was flooded with water. The insured argued the damage was caused solely by wind and the water exclusion did not apply. The court responded that while the dock may have been driven by wind, it was driven into the house because it had been floating on, and was also driven by, water. The policy barred coverage for damage "caused by" or "aggravated by" water whether or not it was "driven by wind." Water was certainly involved in the dock's movement, but even if wind were the main cause, it was the water on which the dock was resting

361. Spindler v. Great N. Ins. Co., 2016 U.S. Dist. LEXIS 16532 (E.D.N.Y. Feb. 2, 2016).

362. Jacobsen v. Hartford Ins. Co. Flood & Home (Sandy), 2017 U.S. Dist. LEXIS 52591 (D.N.J. Mar. 31, 2017).

363. *See also* Steve's Pier One, Inc. v. Insurance Co. of North America, 131 A.D.2d 834, 517 N.Y.S.2d 194 (1987) (only reasonable conclusion to be drawn is that proximate cause of damage was that water from Long Island Sound, driven by wind, propelled objects into damaged building and because water was proximate cause of damage, coverage was excluded).

364. Clarke v. Travco Ins. Co., 2015 U.S. Dist. LEXIS 104267 (S.D.N.Y. Aug. 7, 2015).

that at least indirectly caused or aggravated the damage. Moreover, under the anti-concurrent causation clause, coverage was excluded if the insurer could demonstrate that any of the concurrent or contributing causes were excluded by the policy.

[3] Determinative Policy Language

The specific wording of a policy can determine the outcome, as illustrated by a pair of cases reaching different results. In a Mississippi case,[365] the policy excluded coverage for both windstorm *and* water. The insured beachfront vacation home was completely destroyed during Hurricane Katrina, allegedly by a barge that broke free from its moorings and collided with the home. The insurer denied the claim because of the two exclusions, but the homeowner argued the barge was the true cause of the destruction of her home. She equated the barge with "debris," a peril not specifically excluded. The court was unmoved. The barge, asserted the court, could not have collided with the home without any other means, and it would be illogical to interpret the policy to mean that debris in a storm surge, an excluded peril, would be covered when water caused the debris to collide with the property. In a case out of the state of Washington,[366] logs and other debris in the water, allegedly propelled by waves, struck and damaged a home's foundation during a severe windstorm. Because the policy made no mention of destructive materials propelled by waves, the court found the water exclusion to be ambiguous and noted that, unlike many policies, there was no "water-borne material" exclusion that would have proscribed coverage. The insurer argued there was no distinction between water or waves and the material they contain, suggesting both parts of the exclusion applied to logs in waves. The court, however, said the average insurance purchaser would distinguish between waves and dangerous physical objects propelled by them. Waves and logs carried by waves, said the court, are factually distinguishable perils. It was the logs, and not merely the waves that propelled them, that damaged the home. Logs and waves were distinct perils; while waves may have propelled the logs, that did not transform logs and waves into a single undifferentiated peril.[367]

[4] Object Directing Water

Sometimes the water-propelled object does not itself cause damage, but allows water to enter and damage an insured building. That was the case in a flash flood in which force of the water propelled an automobile onto the sidewalk

365. Porter v. Grand Casino of Miss., Inc., 181 So. 3d 980 (Miss. 2016).

366. Johnson v. Allstate Ins. Co., 845 F. Supp. 2d 1170 (W.D. Wash. 2012).

367. The court noted that the homeowners alleged that waves had crashed into the waterfront home without incident since its construction in 1947, and that it was only in November of 2010 when waves carrying logs that struck the property that damage occurred.

in front of the insured business. The vehicle diverted flood waters against a door, causing it to break down and allow water into the building. All of the water entered through that door opening. The court found that the proximate cause of the damage was the flood water and not the vehicle because the initiating cause was the flood, which set in motion the chain of events leading to the loss. The presence of the automobile was a mere circumstantial incident controlled throughout by the flood waters.[368] The same result was reached when the operator of a boat navigating flood waters steered the boat through the front door of the insured building, allowing flood waters to enter and cause extensive damage. The insured contended the losses were caused by the boat, and the insurer said they were caused by water and were excluded. The court sided with the carrier.[369]

2.8 Miscellaneous Terms Used to Describe Water

[1] Introduction

In addition to the words used to define water damage in many policies, some policies may expand the definition to include "flash floods," "tsunamis," or "seiches." Those terms are not defined in the policies. Definitions from dictionaries and courts are provided below.

[2] Flash Flood

The Merriam-Webster online dictionary defines "flash flood" as "a local flood of short duration generally resulting from heavy rainfall in the immediate vicinity."[370] The National Oceanic and Atmospheric Administration (NOAA) describes a flash flood as:

> A rapid and extreme flow of high water into a normally dry area, or a rapid water level rise in a stream or creek above a predetermined flood level, beginning within six hours of the causative event (e.g., intense rainfall, dam failure, ice jam). However, the actual time threshold may vary in different parts of the country. Ongoing flooding can intensify to flash flooding in cases where intense rainfall results in a rapid surge of rising flood waters.[371]

---

368. Habaz v. Employers' Fire Ins. Co., 243 F.2d 784 (8th Cir. 1957).

369. Madison Block Pharmacy, Inc. v. United States Fidelity & Guaranty Co., 620 S.W.2d 343 (Mo. 1981).

370. *Flash flood*, Merriam-Webster, https://www.merriam-webster.com/dictionary/flash%20flood.

371. *Glossary F*, NOAA's National Weather Service, https://w1.weather.gov/glossary/index.php?letter=f.

One court has said that "flash flood" is a type of "flood," as evidenced by the fact it is defined in terms of a flood.[372] On the other hand, a court distinguished a "flash flood" from "extraordinary floods" and said the former do not create the widespread devastation commonly associated with the latter.[373] Nevertheless, the fact that "flash flood" is omitted from the definition of "water" in a policy is almost certainly to no avail to the owner of property damaged by one, as it is clearly a form or subset of "flood."

[3] Tsunami

A tsunami is an excluded form of water in many commercial property policies but often not in residential policies. A "tsunami" is defined as "a great sea wave produced especially by submarine earth movement or volcanic eruption."[374] The term can also be defined to include a series of waves. For example, NOAA says it is a "series of long-period waves (on the order of tens of minutes) that are usually generated by an impulsive disturbance that displaces massive amounts of water, such as an earthquake occurring on or near the sea floor," and that can also be caused by underwater volcanic eruptions and landslides.[375] Similarly, the American Geosciences Institute describes a tsunami as a series of waves "formed in a body of water by the sudden displacement of the entire water column." Undersea earthquakes, landslides, volcanic eruptions, explosions, and even meteorite impacts can, according to the institute, cause tsunami.[376] No less a jurist than William O. Douglas warned of the "awesome destructive capabilities of even a 'small' tsunami, and its

372. Horvath v. State Farm Gen. Ins. Co., 2014 Cal. App. Unpub. LEXIS 4706 (June 30, 2014).

373. Garner v. Ritzenberg, 167 A.2d 353, 354–55 (D.C. App. 1961) (expression "flash flood" is commonly used to describe accumulations of rainwater running off along natural or artificial contours of ground "but that imports no particular legal significance").

374. *Tsunami*, Merriam-Webster, https://www.merriam-webster.com/dictionary/tsunami. *See also* Pararas-Carayannis v. Department of Commerce, 9 F.3d 955, 956, n.2 (Fed. Cir. 1993) (tsunami is a large ocean wave usually generated by an earthquake).

375. *Glossary T*, NOAA's National Weather Service, https://w1.weather.gov/glossary/index.php?letter=t. NOAA says that "[w]hile traveling in the deep oceans, tsunami have extremely long wavelengths, often exceeding 50 nm, with small amplitudes (a few tens of centimeters) and negligible wave steepness, which in the open ocean would cause nothing more than a gentle rise and fall for most vessels, and possibly go unnoticed. Tsunami travel at very high speeds, sometimes in excess of 400 knots. Across the open oceans, these high-speed waves lose very little energy. As tsunami reach the shallow waters near the coast, they begin to slow down while gradually growing steeper, due to the decreasing water depth. The building walls of destruction can become extremely large in height, reaching tens of meters 30 feet or more as they reach the shoreline. The effects can be further amplified where a bay, harbor, or lagoon funnels the waves as they move inland. Large tsunami have been known to rise to over 100 feet! The amount of water and energy contained in tsunami can have devastating effects on coastal areas."

376. *Tsunamis*, American Geosciences Institute, https://www.americangeosciences.org/critical-issues/tsunamis.

ability to retain its destructive force thousands of miles from its source."[377] One insurance expert notes that every coastline on Earth is subject to a tsunami generated by a meteor strike and adds the happy thought that a major meteorite impact on the ocean could result in the extinction of most life on Earth.[378] Fortunately, that risk is extremely small.

The fact that some policies include, while others omit, "tsunami" from the definition of water will likely not aid a policyholder in arguing that a policy that omits "tsunami" is intended to cover its affects. That is because courts generally equate tsunami with tidal waves,[379] a universally excluded peril. However, scientists may not agree. The United States Geological Survey (USGS), for instance says that while a tsunami and a tidal wave are both sea waves, they "are two different and unrelated phenomena. A tidal wave is a shallow water wave caused by the gravitational interactions between the Sun, Moon, and Earth. . . . A tsunami is an ocean wave triggered by large earthquakes that occur near or under the ocean, volcanic eruptions, submarine landslides, or by onshore landslides in which large volumes of debris fall into the water."[380]

One court has said that "surface water" is not similar to "tsunami" merely because both are on a list defining water. The policy made clear, observed the court, that the unifying thread between those categories was that they all involve "'a general and temporary condition of partial or complete inundation of normally dry land.'"[381]

There are policies or endorsements that specifically state that a tsunami is *not* a flood. These are generally policies that provide flood coverage with a sublimit[382] and are, thus, not providing coverage for losses caused by a tsunami.

---

377. Committee for Nuclear Responsibility, Inc. v. Schlesinger, 404 U.S. 917, 926–27, 92 S. Ct. 242, 248, 30 L. Ed. 2d 191, 195 (1971) (Douglas, J. dissenting).

378. Merlin, *Insurance Coverage for Tsunami Floods and Earthquakes* (Mar. 11, 2011), Merlin Law Group, https://www.propertyinsurancecoveragelaw.com/2011/03/articles/insurance/insurance-coverage-for-tsunami-floods-and-earthquakes/.

379. *See, e.g.*, Hendricks v. The Tug Gordon Gill, 737 F. Supp. 1099, 1101 (D. Alaska 1989) (referring to "tsunami" as "kind of tidal wave caused by earthquakes"). *See also* Boone v. United States, 944 F.2d 1489, 1491 (9th Cir. 1991); American Sav. & Loan Assoc. v. County of Marin, 653 F.2d 364, 367 (9th Cir. 1981); Yamada v. Natural Disaster Claims Comm'n, 54 Haw. 621, 622, 513 P.2d 1001, 1002 (1973). *And see* Committee for Nuclear Responsibility, Inc. v. Schlesinger, 404 U.S. 917, 926, 92 S. Ct. 242, 247, 30 L. Ed. 2d 191, 194 (1971) (Douglas, J. dissenting) (describing seismic effect that might result from test explosion as "a tsunami, or tidal wave").

380. *What is the difference between a tsunami and a tidal wave?*, USGS, https://www.usgs.gov/faqs/what-difference-between-a-tsunami-and-a-tidal-wave.

381. Shea Props. Mgmt. Co. v. Cont'l Ins. Co., 2021 U.S. Dist. LEXIS 200557 (C.D. Cal. June 29, 2021).

382. *See, e.g.*, AMTRAK v. Arch Specialty Ins. Co., 124 F. Supp. 3d 264 (S.D.N.Y. 2015), *aff'd in part and vacated in part*, AMTRAK v. Aspen Specialty Ins. Co., 661 Fed. Appx. 10 (2d Cir. 2016); New Sea Crest Healthcare Ctr., LLC v. Lexington Ins. Co., 2014 U.S. Dist. LEXIS

Some polices define water to include a "tidal or seismic sea wave."[383] The Merriam-Webster online dictionary defines a "seismic sea wave" as "one of many gravitational water waves propagated outward in all directions from the epicenter of a submarine earthquake" and equates the term with tsunami.[384] Courts do as well.[385]

Endorsements that add coverage for earthquakes or volcanic eruptions typically state the insurer will not pay for loss or damage that is caused directly or indirectly by tidal wave or tsunami, even if attributable to an earthquake or volcanic eruption.[386]

[4] Seiche

A dictionary definition of "seiche" is "an oscillation of the surface of a landlocked body of water (such as a lake) that varies in period from a few minutes to several hours."[387] It has even been said that a seiche can last for days.[388] NOAA defines a seiche as a "standing wave oscillation of water in large lakes usually created by strong winds and/or a large barometric pressure gradient."[389] A commentary says the phenomenon "occurs when a rapid change in barometric pressure essentially pushes down on one end of a large water body causing the other end to rise. A pendulum-like movement oscillates water levels until the pressure stabilizes, causing the water's edge to move up the shore on one end of the lake and withdraw from it at the other."[390]

86585 (E.D.N.Y. June 24, 2014); PCVST-DIL LLC v. Lexington Ins. Co., 2016 N.Y. Misc. LEXIS 2031 (Apr. 21, 2016).

383. *See, e.g.*, Arctic Slope Reg'l Corp. v. Affiliated FM Ins. Co., 564 F.3d 707, 710, n.1 (5th Cir. 2009).

384. *Seismic sea wave*, Merriam-Webster, https://www.merriam-webster.com/dictionary/seismic%20sea%20wave.

385. Committee for Nuclear Responsibility, Inc. v. Schlesinger, 404 U.S. 917, 926, 92 S. Ct. 242, 247, 30 L. Ed. 2d 191, 194 (1971) (Douglas, J. dissenting) (equating tsunami and seismic sea wave); Ness v. National Indem. Co., 247 F. Supp. 944 (D. Alaska 1965) (following earthquake of tremendous force, seismic sea wave swept shore).

386. *See, e.g.*, ISO Form CP 10 45 08 99, § D.5. *See also Earthquake Volcanic Eruption and Tsunami Endorsement*, Data Polis, https://datapolis.id/database/earthquake-volcanic-eruption-and-tsunami-endorsement/.

387. *Seiche*, Merriam-Webster, https://www.merriam-webster.com/dictionary/seiche.

388. Glass v. Goeckel, 473 Mich. 667, 742, 703 N.W.2d 58, 199 (2005) (seiche can last from minutes to hours to days).

389. *Glossary S*, NOAA's National Weather Service, https://w1.weather.gov/glossary/index.php?letter=s.

390. Nelson, *The Public Trust Doctrine and the Great Lakes:* Glass v. Goeckel, 11 Alb. L. Envtl. Outlook 131, 145 (2006). *See also* Glass v. Goeckel, 473 Mich. 667, 742, 703 N.W.2d 58, 199 (2005) (seiche occurs when wind and barometric forces raise water at one end of lake, causing dip in water level at opposite end and if forces raising water on one end suddenly cease, entire lake may move in see-saw fashion, alternatively rising and falling on each end in pendulum-like movement).

Some courts identify the cause of a seiche as wind,[391] and others as barometric pressure.[392]

While others speak of seiches as occurring in landlocked lakes, the Ninth Circuit has noted that the phenomenon can occur in harbors. The court described it as an increasing of the height of the water at high tide whose extent is determined by the configuration of each particular harbor.[393] Courts have even said a seiche can happen when wind and other factors cause a *river* to flow upstream for discrete periods of time.[394] Courts have also described the phenomenon as water movements superimposed on regular tides.[395]

[5] Break, Breach, or Leak of a Levee, Dam, or Canal

[a] Introduction

Some policies include a "break, breach or leak of a levee, dam or canal" in their definition of loss by water damage.[396] In order to determine whether the exclusion applies, the terms it uses need to be defined.

[b] Break or Breach

A "break" is "a gap or opening caused or appearing as if caused by damage."[397] A "breach" is "a broken, ruptured, or torn condition or area . . . a gap . . . made by battering."[398] In both definitions, it would appear implicit that the gap or opening is the result of an unintentional occurrence. That raises the question of whether the exclusion should apply when a levee, dam, or canal is intentionally "broken" or "breached," for example, to relieve pressure. In that regard, *dicta* in a federal court opinion is interesting. The court said that "[w]hen a levee

---

391. Ispat Inland, Inc. v. Am. Commer. Barge Line Co., 2002 U.S. Dist. LEXIS 26818, at *30 (N.D. Ind. Sept. 30, 2002) (winds caused seiche which increased mean level of lake).

392. Interlake Iron Corp. v. Gartland S. S. Co., 121 F.2d 267, 269 (6th Cir. 1941) (seiche was abnormal lowering of water from variations in barometric pressure).

393. Los Angeles v. Borax Consol., Ltd., 102 F.2d 52, 57 (9th Cir. 1939), *cert. den.*, 307 U.S. 644, 59 S. Ct. 1042, 83 L. Ed. 1524 (1939) (phenomenon manifests itself as vertical movement of waters in Los Angeles Harbor, reaching its maximum and minimum in approximately 55 minutes).

394. United States v. NCR Corp., 2012 U.S. Dist. LEXIS 59089 (E.D. Wisc. Apr. 27, 2012); United States v. NCR Corp., 2011 U.S. Dist. LEXIS 40227 (E.D. Wisc. Apr. 4, 2011) (at times currents exist in river that pull water upstream as result of phenomenon, known as seiche).

395. Los Angeles v. Borax Consol., Ltd., 20 F. Supp. 69, 70 (S.D. Cal. 1937), *aff'd*, 102 F.2d 52 (9th Cir. 1939), *cert. den.*, 307 U.S. 644, 59 S. Ct. 1042, 83 L. Ed. 1524 (1939).

396. *See, e.g.*, McCrary v. Country Mut. Ins. Co., 180 F. Supp. 3d 915 (N.D. Okla. 2016); Harden-Doss v. Country Mut. Ins. Co., 2015 U.S. Dist. LEXIS 181736 (N.D. Okla. Sept. 8, 2015).

397. *Break*, Merriam-Webster, https://www.merriam-webster.com/dictionary/break.

398. *Breach*, Merriam-Webster, https://www.merriam-webster.com/dictionary/breach. *See also* Morris v. Auto-Owners Ins. Co., 2016 U.S. Dist. LEXIS 179715 (D.S.C. Dec. 29, 2016) (verb "breach" embraces idea of breaking through, or making gap in, barrier).

naturally breaks, it does so due to the strength of the existing flood waters and thus, any flood created from that break can best be described as a continuation of the original flood. However, when a breach is artificial to divert flood waters from reaching another area, any new flood resulting from that breach cannot necessarily be considered a continuation of the original flood because it is uncertain whether those new flood waters would have ever existed were it not for the intentional intervention."[399]

[c] Levee

The purpose of a levee is to protect property from flood waters.[400] The term has been defined as "a trapezoidally shaped ridge of earth built up and compacted so as to withstand the weight of water pushing against it."[401] A levee constructed in wet and swampy places to serve as a road is sometimes referred to as a "chaussee."[402] A small infield levee designed to contain water in part of a field is called a "check."[403] The Fifth Circuit, in a post-Katrina case, discussed levees and their failure. The court said:

> a levee is a flood-control structure; its very purpose is to prevent the floodwaters of a watercourse from overflowing onto certain land areas, i.e., to prevent floods from becoming more widespread. By definition, whenever a levee ruptures and fails to hold back floodwaters, the result is a more widespread flood. That a levee's failure is due to its negligent design, construction, or maintenance does not change the character of the water escaping through the levee's breach; the waters are still floodwaters, and the result is a flood (citations omitted).[404]

The term "levee" is also used to mean a landing place for vessels where freight and passengers may be loaded or unloaded.[405]

---

399. Jones v. Cornerstone Nat'l Ins. Co., 11 F. Supp. 3d 979, 986 (E.D. Mo. 2014).

400. *In re* Ingram Barge Co., 435 F. Supp. 2d 524, 530 (E.D. La. 2006).

401. Wolfsen Land & Cattle Co. v. Commissioner, 72 T.C. 1, 7 (1979). *See also* Dougan v. Rossville Drainage Dist., 270 Kan. 468, 480, 15 P.3d 338, 348 (2000) (levee is embankment or artificial mound of earth constructed along margin of river to confine stream to its natural channel or prevent inundation or overflow).

402. De Armas v. Mayor, etc. of New Orleans, 5 La 132, 152 (1833).

403. Wolfsen Land & Cattle Co. v. Commissioner, 72 T.C. 1, 7 (1979) (where land slopes downward, checks are built at low ends of fields where they act as small earth dams).

404. Vanderbrook v. Unitrin Preferred Ins. Co. (*In re* Katrina Canal Breaches Litig.), 495 F.3d 191, 214 (5th Cir. 2005).

405. Chicago, R. I. & P. R. Co. v. People, 222 Ill. 427, 427, 78 N.W. 790, 793 (1906) (space adjacent to navigable water where vessels may approach and land to unload and receive passengers and freight); St. Paul v. Chicago, M. & S. P. R. Co., 63 Minn. 330, 349, 65 N.W. 649, 651 (1896) (landing place for vessels, and for delivery of merchandise to and from those vessels). *See also* McAlpine v. Chicago G. W. R. Co., 68 Kan. 207, 212, 75 P. 73, 75 (1904) (while levee is place for the landing of boats and commerce, it is much more than that).

[d] Dam

The basic definition of a "dam" is "a barrier preventing the flow of water."[406] One court characterized a dam as "a structure, composed of wood, earth or other material, erected in and usually extending across the entire channel at right angles to the thread of the stream, and intended to retard the flow of water by the barrier or to retain it within the obstruction."[407] Other structures that might be described as dams are a "weir," which is an "obstruction in a watercourse which backs up or diverts the stream,"[408] and a "jetty," which has been described as "a kind of a dam . . . intended to deflect the current so as to deepen the channel or to form an eddy below the obstruction in which sediment may be deposited, thereby extending and protecting the bank."[409]

[e] Canal

One dictionary defines "canal" as an artificial waterway, public or private, usually used for navigation.[410] Another describes a canal as a "water-filled trench that connects two larger bodies of water."[411] In a case decided in the late 19th century, the U.S. Supreme Court said a "canal" "means a navigable public highway for the transportation of persons and property. It must not only be in a condition to hold water that can be used for navigation, but it must have in it, as part of the structure itself, the water to be navigated ready for use."[412]

2.9 The Continuous Seepage or Leakage Exclusion

[1] Generally

A common exclusion is for losses caused by continuous or repeated seepage or leakage of water over a period of time.[413] That time may be stated generally as a "period of weeks, months, or years" or specifically as "14 or more days," although there are exclusions that mention no time period at all.[414] Some

---

406. Environmental Defense Fund, Inc. v. Alexander, 467 F. Supp. 885, 912 (N.D. Miss. 1979).

407. Morton v. Oregon S. L. R. Co., 48 Ore. 444, 450, 87 P. 151, 153 (1906).

408. *Ballentine's Law Dictionary* (2010) (structure built in stream for penning fish; contrivance placed in flume to regulate amount of water passing from feeder through flume).

409. Morton v. Oregon S. L. R. Co., 48 Ore. 444, 450, 87 P. 151, 153 (1906).

410. *Ballentine's Law Dictionary* (2010).

411. *The Wolters Kluwer Bouvier Law Dictionary Desk Edition* (2012).

412. Kennedy v. City of Indianapolis, 103 U.S. 599, 604–05, 26 L. Ed. 550, 553 (1880). *See also* United States v. Sexton Cove Estates, Inc., 389 F. Supp. 602 (S.D. Fla. 1975), *rev'd on other grounds*, 526 F.2d 1293 (5th Cir. 1976).

413. ISO Form CP 10 30 04 02, § B.2.f.

414. *See, e.g.*, Gershkowit v. State Faun Gen. Ins. Co., 2021 U.S. Dist. LEXIS 252185 (C.D. Cal. Dec. 29, 2021); Freedman v. State Farm Ins. Co., 93 Cal. Rptr. 3d 296, 173 Cal. App. 4th 957 (2009).

policies cover water damage from "accidental discharge or leakage of water or steam as the direct result of the breaking apart or cracking of a plumbing, heating, air conditioning or other system or appliance," but except "continuous or repeated seepage or leakage of water, or the presence or condensation of humidity, moisture or vapor."[415] Policies may specify the source of the water, for example, plumbing or household appliances.

The word "water" in the exclusion is not limited to pure water. Water that carries away waste—sewage—is still water for purposes of the exclusion.[416] Courts generally find that the exclusion applies to foundation damage by continuous seepage or leakage underground.[417] For example, water was the cause of foundation damage to a home whether water under the foundation caused sand to wash into a drain pipe or sand was washed away by leakage.[418]

[2] "Continuous" and "Repeated" Defined

"Continuous" means "marked by uninterrupted extension in space, time, or sequence."[419] It has been defined as "extending or prolonged without interruption or cessation; unceasing."[420] "Ongoing" has been used as a synonym for continuous.[421] "Repeated" is defined as "renewed or recurring again and again."[422] The seepage or leakage may be *either* "continuous" or "repeated." Thus, it does not have to be uninterrupted.

---

415. ISO Form CP 10 30 06 07, § B.2.f. Another version of the policy language covers "sudden and accidental discharge, eruption, overflow or release of water" and says that phrase "does not include a constant or repeating gradual, intermittent or slow release of water, or the infiltration or presence of water over a period of time." Brown v. Mid-Century Ins. Co., 156 Cal. Rptr. 3d 56, 215 Cal. App. 4th 841 (2013).

416. Ellis v. State Farm Fire & Cas. Co., 322 F. App'x 594 (10th Cir. 2009). *See also* McCrary v. Country Mut. Ins. Co., 180 F. Supp. 3d 915 (N.D. Okla. 2016) (where insured home was damaged by sewer drain line failure—a leak—under slab, "seepage or leakage" exclusion applied, and fact that line also contained waste matter did not alter fact that it was water that carried away waste).

417. American Concept Ins. Co. v. Jones, 935 F. Supp. 1220, 1226 (D. Utah 1996) (no coverage where damage was caused by "sustained saturation" of soil under home because of leakage from sewer drain line undetected for two years); Mutual Redevelopment Houses v. Greater New York Mut. Ins. Co., 204 A.D.2d 145, 611 N.Y.S.2d 550 (1994) (no coverage for damage from subsidence caused by water that flowed at substantial rate out of a broken pipe joint into fill beneath building slab); Howard v. Commercial Union Ins. Co., 441 So. 2d 466 (La. App. 1983) (no coverage for structural damage to house resulting from shifting and movement of soil underlying foundation caused by leakage or seepage from damaged water pipe beneath foundation).

418. Ellis v. State Farm Fire & Cas. Co., 322 F. App'x 594 (10th Cir. 2009).

419. *Continuous*, Merriam-Webster, https://www.merriam-webster.com/dictionary/continuous.

420. Rutan v. Pasco County Sch. Bd., 435 So. 2d 399, 400 (Fla. 2d DCA 1983).

421. Tex. Friends Chabad-Lubavitch, Inc. v. Nova Cas. Co., 539 F. Supp. 3d 669, 679 (S.D. Tex. 2021).

422. *Repeated*, Merriam-Webster, https://www.merriam-webster.com/dictionary/repeated.

One court said that "in the abstract, the plain meaning of 'continuous or repeated' could be ambiguous: 'continuous' only refers to some uninterrupted period of time, so a pipe could theoretically leak for five seconds, minutes, hours, or days while being 'continuous.' Similarly, a leak could start and stop only two times while being 'repeated.' However, the language must be interpreted not in the abstract, but in the context of the policy and its intended function." The only reasonable construction, concluded the court, is that the language was clearly intended to refer to the difference in coverage between a "sudden" and a "gradual" leak, with the latter excluded.[423]

That a leak was continuous or repeated can be inferred from the size of the opening and the amount of damage. For example, a contractor remodeling a bathroom drove a nail through a pipe. Years later corrosion around the nail caused a leak. The court said that given the small size of the hole through which water leaked and the extensive water damage, the leak must have lasted a sufficient time, or stopped and started sufficiently many times, to count as "continuous" or "repeated" under any reasonable construction of those terms.[424]

Some policies use the word "constant" instead of "continuous."[425] "Constant" is defined as "invariable" and "uniform," as in a constant flow or as continually occurring or recurring.[426] Courts have defined the term as "steady, uniform,"[427] "remaining unchanged, and steady,"[428] "going on all the time; continual; persistent,"[429] "uniform, regular, constantly recurring,"[430] and "continually recurring; persistent . . . [u]nchanging in nature, value or extent; invariable."[431]

---

423. Gershkowit v. State Faun Gen. Ins. Co., 2021 U.S. Dist. LEXIS 252185 (C.D. Cal. Dec. 29, 2021).

424. Freedman v. State Farm Ins. Co., 93 Cal. Rptr. 3d 296, 173 Cal. App. 4th 957 (2009).

425. *See, e.g.*, ISO Form DP 00 02 07 14 (Perils Insured Against), § 12.b.(1).

426. *Constant*, Merriam-Webster, https://www.merriam-webster.com/dictionary/constant. *See also* Ferrill v. Union Pac. R.R., 2010 U.S. Dist. LEXIS 51686, at *15 (D. Ariz. May 24, 2010) (continually occurring or recurring); Madison v. Morovitz, 122 Conn. 208, 216, 188 A. 665 (1936) (continually recurring, regular, persistent).

427. Hale Propeller, L.L.C. v. Ryan Marine Prods. Pty., Ltd., 151 F. Supp. 2d 183, 191 (D. Conn. 2001).

428. Gross v. Johnson, 174 Neb. 273, 287, 117 N.W.2d 534, 542 (1962).

429. St. Paul Fire & Marine Ins. v. Federal Express Corp., 145 Misc. 2d 801, 805, 548 N.Y.S.2d 422, 425 (1989).

430. Domijan v. Harp, 340 S.W.2d 728, 733 (Mo. 1960).

431. Rutan v. Pasco County Sch. Bd., 435 So. 2d 399, 400 (Fla. 2d DCA 1983).

[3] "Seepage" Defined

"Seepage" is often equated with "oozing,"[432] which is defined as "to move slowly or imperceptibly."[433] It is said to contemplate the movement of fluid substances.[434] Citing a variety of dictionaries, most courts have defined "seepage" as the "act or process of seeping."[435] "Seeping" is then usually defined by courts as slowly flowing or passing through fine pores or small openings.[436] It is also described as meaning to enter, depart, or become diffused gradually,[437] or as draining off by gradual leakage.[438] Courts stress that "seepage" is a gradual process.[439] The volume of water may be evidence that there was more than

---

432. *Seepage*, Merriam-Webster, https://www.merriam-webster.com/dictionary/seepage. *See also* Landrum v. Allstate Ins. Co., 2019 U.S. Dist. LEXIS 175664, at *6 (M.D. Ga. Oct. 9, 2019) (percolation or oozing of water or fluid); Taylor Energy Co. LLC v. Underwriters at Lloyd's, 2010 U.S. Dist. LEXIS 116039 (E.D. La. Oct. 29, 2010); Hirschhorn v. Auto-Owners Ins. Co., 338 Wis. 2d 761, 782, 809 N.W.2d 529, 539 (2012) ("seepage" is defined as act or process of seeping, meaning to "ooze"); Primm v. State Farm Fire & Cas. Co., 426 So. 2d 356, 360 (La. App. 1983) ("seepage" connotes oozing or passing slowly through small openings).

433. *Oozing*, Merriam-Webster, https://www.merriam-webster.com/dictionary/oozing.

434. Mistick, Inc. v. Northwestern Nat'l Cas. Co., 806 A.2d 39, 44 (Pa. Super. 2002).

435. Firemen's Ins. Co. v. Kline & Son Cement Repair, Inc., 474 F. Supp. 2d 779, 798 (E.D. Va. 2007); Hartford Underwriter's Ins. Co. v. Estate of Turks, 206 F. Supp. 2d 968, 976 (E.D. Mo. 2002); Hirschhorn v. Auto-Owners Ins. Co., 338 Wis. 2d 761, 782, 809 N.W.2d 529, 539 (2012); Madison Constr. Co. v. Harleysville Mut. Ins. Co., 557 Pa. 595, 609, 735 A.2d 100, 108 (1999). *See also* Jamison v. Depositors Ins. Co., 2016 U.S. Dist. LEXIS 91841, at *15 (D. Neb. May 23, 2016); Hobson v. Indian Harbor Ins. Co., 2015 Mich. App. LEXIS 486 (Mar. 10, 2015). There are a few cases that defined "seepage" differently. *See, e.g.*, Landrum v. Allstate Ins. Co., 2019 U.S. Dist. LEXIS 175664, at *6 (M.D. Ga. Oct. 9, 2019) (seepage is percolation or oozing of water or fluid in which liquid flows slowly out of hole or through something); Wells v. Young, 2000 Mont. Dist. LEXIS 2526 (July 25, 2000) (seepage is defined as "natural losses of water in transit").

436. Jamison v. Depositors Ins. Co., 2016 U.S. Dist. LEXIS 91841, at *15 (D. Neb. May 23, 2016) (pass, flow, or ooze gradually, as through a porous substance); Hobson v. Indian Harbor Ins. Co., 2015 Mich. App. LEXIS 486 (Mar. 10, 2015) (pass, flow, or ooze gradually, as through a porous substance); Firemen's Ins. Co. v. Kline & Son Cement Repair, Inc., 474 F. Supp. 2d 779, 798 (E.D. Va. 2007) (slow escape of liquid or gas through porous material or small holes); Hartford Underwriter's Ins. Co. v. Estate of Turks, 206 F. Supp. 2d 968, 976 (E.D. Mo. 2002) (pass slowly through small opening or pores); Madison Constr. Co. v. Harleysville Mut. Ins. Co., 557 Pa. 595, 609, 735 A.2d 100, 108 (1999) (flowing or passing slowly through fine pores or small openings); Waldsmith v. State Farm Fire & Casualty Co., 232 Cal. App. 3d 693, 698, 283 Cal. Rptr. 607, 609, n. 4 (1991) (flow or pass slowly through fine pores or small openings).

437. Hirschhorn v. Auto-Owners Ins. Co., 338 Wis. 2d 761, 782, 809 N.W.2d 529, 539 (2012).

438. Queen City Farms, Inc. v. Central National Ins. Co., Wash. Ct. App., 64 Wash. App. 838, 883, 827 P.2d 1024, 1049 (1992).

439. Queen City Farms, Inc. v. Central National Ins. Co., Wash. Ct. App., 64 Wash. App. 838, 883, 827 P.2d 1024, 1049 (1992) (seepage generally connotes a gradual process; "seepage" cannot be both "gradual" and "sudden," but can be both "gradual" and "unexpected"). *See also* United Nuclear Corp. v. Allstate Ins. Co., 285 P.3d 644 (N.M. 2012) ("seepage" indicates gradual rather than abrupt process).

seepage.[440] It is also said that "seepage" necessarily implies some break or gap in the thing leaking.[441]

One phenomenon that has been declared not to be "seepage" is an "overflow."[442] Overflow means "a flowing over" or inundation.[443] The distinction would be between water that slowly escapes a damaged pipe or vessel—seepage—and that which arises out of an open pipe or vessel because the volume exceeds that which the pipe or vessel can contain.

[4] "Leakage" Defined

"Leakage" is "the act or process or an instance of leaking,"[444] which in turn means to enter or escape through an opening."[445] "Leakage," it is said, necessarily implies some break or gap in the thing leaking.[446] Many courts also look to the definition of "leak" and, relying on dictionaries, say it means to enter or escape through a hole usually by a fault or mistake,[447] or an unintended hole or crack through which liquid enters or escapes.[448] Some courts

---

440. Jamison v. Depositors Ins. Co., 2016 U.S. Dist. LEXIS 91841 (D. Neb. May 23, 2016).

441. Waldsmith v. State Farm Fire & Casualty Co., 283 Cal. Rptr. 607, 609, 232 Cal. App. 3d 693, 698, n. 4 (1991); Finn v. Continental Ins. Co., 267 Cal. Rptr. 22, 218 Cal. App. 3d 69 (1990).

442. Hasler v. City of San Antonio, 1986 Tex. App. LEXIS 8479, at *11 (Sept. 9, 1986).

443. *Overflow*, Merriam-Webster, https://www.merriam-webster.com/dictionary/overflow.

444. *Leakage*, Merriam-Webster, https://www.merriam-webster.com/dictionary/leakage. *See also* United States v. Coffeyville Res. Ref. & Mktg., LLC, 2022 U.S. Dist. LEXIS 58934, at *33 (D. Ka. Mar. 30, 2022); Jamison v. Depositors Ins. Co., 2016 U.S. Dist. LEXIS 91841 (D. Neb. May 23, 2016); Sam Braman & Son v. Hartford Steam Boiler Inspection & Ins. Co., 9 Ohio Misc. 203, 206, 222 N.E.2d 456, 459 (1966). *And see* Karon v. Safeco Ins. Co., 2021 U.S. Dist. LEXIS 147116, at *7 (D. Ariz. Aug. 5, 2021) ("leakage" is defined as admission or escape of water through hole in a vessel, escaping from hole or crack in pipe or container, or entering or escaping through opening usually by fault or mistake); Landrum v. Allstate Ins. Co., 2019 U.S. Dist. LEXIS 175664, at *6 (M.D. Ga. Oct. 9, 2019) ("leakage" means admission or escape of water through hole in a vessel, condition of escaping from a hole or crack in a pipe or container, or the act or process or an instance of entering or escaping through opening usually by fault or mistake).

445. *Leaking*, Merriam-Webster, https://www.merriam-webster.com/dictionary/leaking.

446. Waldsmith v. State Farm Fire & Casualty Co., 698, 283 Cal. Rptr. 607, 609, 232 Cal. App. 3d 693, n. 4 (1991); Finn v. Continental Ins. Co., 267 Cal. Rptr. 22, 218 Cal. App. 3d 69 (1990). *See also* Primm v. State Farm Fire & Cas. Co., 426 So. 2d 356, 360 (La. App. 1983) ("leakage" contemplates defect in thing that allows substance encompassed by that thing to escape).

447. *See, e.g.*, United States v. Coffeyville Res. Ref. & Mktg., LLC, 2022 U.S. Dist. LEXIS 58934, at *33 (D. Ka. Mar. 30, 2022); Queen City Farms, Inc. v. Central National Ins. Co., Wash. Ct. App., 64 Wash. App. 838, 883, 827 P.2d 1024, 1049 (1992); Waldsmith v. State Farm Fire & Casualty Co., 232 Cal. App. 3d 693, 698, 283 Cal. Rptr. 607, 609, n. 4 (1991); Sam Braman & Son v. Hartford Steam Boiler Inspection & Ins. Co., 9 Ohio Misc. 203, 206, 222 N.E.2d 456, 459 (1966).

448. *See., e.g.*, Jamison v. Depositors Ins. Co., 2016 U.S. Dist. LEXIS 91841 (D. Neb. May 23, 2016). *See also* Probus v. Allstate Ins. Co., 2021 Ky. App. Unpub. LEXIS 392 (July 2, 2021)

emphasize that all these terms describe a "gradual" or "low volume water" event.[449] However, a Nevada federal court explicitly rejected those characterizations and noted that dictionary definitions of "leakage" refer to fluid being released, but not necessarily to the volume of that release.[450] Another court said "leakage" could encompass a ruptured water line.[451] A Washington state appellate court said that it is conceivable that a temporally "sudden" event could lead to "gradual leakage."[452]

[5] Distinguishing "Seepage" from "Leakage"

Policies refer to seepage *or* leakage, implying that they are different phenomena. One distinction that has been made between the two terms is that "seepage" has a "speed" component—slow moving—and leakage does not.[453] The Eighth Circuit drew a distinction when it considered a policy that excluded continuous or repeated seepage, but not leakage, of water over a period of weeks, months, or years. The court noted that the policy used the word "leakage" in another place and said that the use of the two different terms to describe a flow of water indicated they had different meanings. The water damage at issue was from a break in a two-inch drain pipe under a basement bathroom shower stall from which water leaked whenever the shower was used. The court noted that a dictionary definition of "seepage" was to "ooze gradually," while "leakage" meant water entering or escaping through a hole or crack. The court agreed with the insured that the ordinary meaning of "leakage" more aptly described the way in which water would have flowed through the crack in the broken drain pipe. Therefore, the continuous or repeated seepage exclusion would not apply.[454]

(where water sprayed from cracked plastic nut on water supply line to toilet, damage to residence was clearly caused by leak as term is understood by ordinary people).

449. Cincinnati Ins. Co. v. Kaeding, 2017 Mich. App. LEXIS 1185 (July 20, 2017) ("leak" refers to gradual or low-volume water event); Queen City Farms, Inc. v. Central National Ins. Co., Wash. Ct. App., 64 Wash. App. 838, 883, 827 P.2d 1024, 1049 (1992) (words "leakage" and "seepage"—particularly the latter—generally connote a gradual process).

450. Danganan v. Am. Family Mut. Ins. Co., 2019 U.S. Dist. LEXIS 169806 (D. Nev. Sept. 30, 2019). *But see* Jamison v. Depositors Ins. Co., 2016 U.S. Dist. LEXIS 91841 (D. Neb. May 23, 2016) (trier of fact could find from evidence—particularly given volume of water involved—that there was an "accidental overflow or discharge of water" from the plumbing system greater than mere seepage or leakage).

451. Karon v. Safeco Ins. Co., 2021 U.S. Dist. LEXIS 147116, at *8 (D. Ariz. Aug. 5, 2021).

452. Queen City Farms, Inc. v. Central National Ins. Co., Wash. Ct. App., 64 Wash. App. 838, 883, 827 P.2d 1024, 1049 (1992).

453. Karon v. Safeco Ins. Co., 2021 U.S. Dist. LEXIS 147116, at *8 (D. Ariz. Aug. 5, 2021); Landrum v. Allstate Ins. Co., 2019 U.S. Dist. LEXIS 175664, at *7 (M.D. Ga. Oct. 9, 2019). *But see* Primm v. State Farm Fire & Cas. Co., 426 So. 2d 356, 360 (La. App. 1983) (leakage or seepage connotes gradual and slow moving event).

454. Syfco v. Encompass Indem. Co., 761 F.3d 867 (8th Cir. 2014).

[6] Temporal Requirement

Policies exclude seepage or leakage of water that occurs either over a "period of weeks, months, or years" or over "14 or more days." Some courts interpret "period of weeks" to mean 14 days or more when the number of days is not specified.[455] Where the exclusion applies to leakage or seepage over a period of *14 days or more*, some courts hold that losses occurring over the first 13 days may still be covered,[456] providing the insured can prove those losses,[457] while others find that all losses are excluded.[458] A variation of the language provides that there is no coverage for a loss caused by the "continued or repeated . . . leakage . . . over a period of time, weeks, months or years." An insurer argued "period of time" was a separate and discrete span of time. The court, however, concluded the phrase "period of time" could not "reasonably be said to refer to a separate span of time somehow distinct from 'weeks, months or years.'" Instead, under the policy language a loss was not covered if, and only if, the leakage occurred "over a period of time that may be comprised of weeks, months, or years."[459]

---

455. Wheeler v. Allstate Insurance, 687 F. App'x 757 (10th Cir. 2017). *See also* Moy v. State Farm Fire & Cas. Co., 2022 U.S. Dist. LEXIS 11105 (D. Conn. Jan. 21, 2022) (where policy excluded coverage for continuous or repeated seepage or leakage of water "which occurs over a period of time," question of whether damage occurred within first thirteen days was not relevant as that question only applied where policy limits exclusion to either period of "weeks" or "fourteen days"). *Compare* Danganan v. Am. Family Mut. Ins. Co., 2019 U.S. Dist. LEXIS 169806 (D. Nev. Sept. 30, 2019), where the insurer contended "weeks" meant an insured would be covered if he or she suffered water loss due only up until thirteen days after that loss occurred and any leaking or seeping in excess of thirteen days would not be covered because of the "weeks" provision. The court said it found nothing on the face of the policy that said anything about the number of days required for coverage. "Thirteen days" was merely an inference extrapolated from the "weeks" provision. The inferred limitation was not obvious or even reasonable, concluded the court.

456. *See, e.g.*, Hicks v. Am. Integrity Ins. Co., 241 So. 3d 925 (Fla. 5th DCA 2018) (insurance policy excluding losses caused by constant or repeated leakage or seepage over period of 14 days or more does not unambiguously exclude losses over period of 13 days or less; remanding on issue of coverage within first 13 days of leak, with extent of the losses to be determined at trial; for losses occurring after first 13 days, burden was on insurer to prove that particular loss was sustained after 13th day and was therefore not covered).

457. Landrum v. Allstate Ins. Co., 2019 U.S. Dist. LEXIS 175664 (M.D. Ga. Oct. 9, 2019) (damages estimate relied on by insured did not differentiate between damages that resulted from first 13 days of leak and those that resulted from other 12 days; absent evidence to create genuine issue of fact as to whether damages occurred from first 13 days of 25-day leak, insured could not meet her burden on summary judgment and policy excluded coverage).

458. *See, e.g.*, Gen. Star Indem. Co. v. Sherry Brooke Revocable Trust, 243 F. Supp. 2d 605 (W.D. Tex. 2001). *See also* Karon v. Safeco Ins. Co., 2021 U.S. Dist. LEXIS 147116 (D. Ariz. Aug. 5, 2021) (exclusion for seepage or leakage occurring over period of weeks, months, or years unambiguously precluded coverage for damage occurring over period of weeks, including damage occurring within first 13 days).

459. Reynolds v. Travelers Indem. Co., 233 S.W.3d 197 (Ky. App. 2007).

[7] Application of Temporal Requirement

The question of whether there has been continuous or repeated seepage or leakage is fact specific and usually must be determined by the jury, not by the court on summary judgment.[460] The burden is on the insurer to show that the terms of the exclusion apply.[461] The period of time over which the seepage or leakage occurred is an issue that is often litigated. The insurer failed to meet its burden where it did not contradict evidence presented by the insured tending to show that a theft, during which a water line was severed leading to flooding, occurred less than two weeks before it was discovered.[462] The insurer met its burden, and the exclusion applied where an expert for the insurer said a roof had been leaking for a "long time" and that damage was long-term. The expert noted there were signs in the roof and attic of advanced decay and mold. The insured claimed the roof was damaged by tree branches during a windstorm, but the court found there was no coverage.[463] In other words, once the insurer meets its burden, the insured must come forward with *sufficient* contradictory evidence.[464]

The fact that water leaked for more than the prescribed period does not necessarily bar coverage. In one case, a water line separated from the wall in an upstairs bathroom. Over a period of 27 days, a substantial amount of water flowed into the insured home. The court said that the amount of water that was released would have caused significant damage within hours or days "because the separated pipe essentially caused flooding."[465] A "leak," observed

460. Ellison v. Allstate Indem. Co., 103 F. Supp. 3d 358 (W.D.N.Y. 2015).

461. Jamison v. Depositors Ins. Co., 2016 U.S. Dist. LEXIS 91841 (D. Neb. May 23, 2016) (while insurer noted that insureds had not presented evidence showing that efflux lasted fewer than 14 days, insureds did present evidence suggesting that it *could have*, and court asserted that insured did not have to prove anything because insurer had burden to prove that exclusion applied).

462. Reynolds v. Travelers Indem. Co., 233 S.W.3d 197 (Ky. App. 2007).

463. Holliday v. Pioneer State Mut. Ins. Co., 2009 Mich. App. LEXIS 465 (Mich. App. Mar. 5, 2009). *See also* Karon v. Safeco Ins. Co., 2021 U.S. Dist. LEXIS 147116 (D. Ariz. Aug. 5, 2021); Iroquois on the Beach, Inc. v. Gen. Star Indem. Co., 2007 U.S. Dist. LEXIS 76290 (W.D. Mich. Oct. 12, 2007).

464. *See, e.g.*, Sokol v. State Farm Gen. Ins. Co., 2021 U.S. Dist. LEXIS 129489 (C.D. Cal. June 25, 2021) (insurer showed water leaked through exceptionally small hole that saturated ground, traveled through slab, and caused meaningful damage and must, therefore, have lasted sufficient length of time to qualify as continuous or repeated; insured offered insufficient evidence in opposition); Abbasid, Inc. v. Travelers Indem. Co., 2010 U.S. Dist. LEXIS 165992 (D.N.M. Mar. 10, 2010) (where insurer's evidence of leakage lasting more than 14 days consisted of statement by store manager for insured and compliant insured filed against landlord, insured had burden to put forth some evidence in dispute and could not merely assert that damage would have occurred immediately).

465. A significant volume of water suggests there was an "accidental overflow or discharge of water" from a plumbing system—typically a covered "water damage" peril—rather than mere seepage or leakage within the meaning of the exclusion. Jamison v. Depositors Ins. Co., 2016 U.S. Dist. LEXIS 91841 (D. Neb. May 23, 2016) (jury could conclude house was damaged

the court, refers to a gradual or low-volume water event. Furthermore, the time requirement of weeks, months, or years is necessary for a low-volume, gradual water leak to cause significant damage. The intent of the exclusion is to preclude coverage for losses caused by neglect, failure to maintain, and failure to occupy a home. In other words, the exclusion should apply to events that could reasonably have been discovered because of their longevity. Thus, even though the water flowed for nearly a month, the exclusion did not apply as significant damage happened almost immediately.[466] The decision may be distinguishable because the exclusion had an exception when seepage or leakage of water and the resulting damage was unknown to all insureds and was hidden within the walls or ceilings or beneath the floors or above the ceilings of a structure. Exclusions do not generally include the exception.

[8] Sudden Occurrence of Breach

That the opening through which water seeps or leaks occurs suddenly does not mean there is a "sudden and accidental discharge" of water that would make the loss covered under the standard water damage clause. The release of water, even if it commenced suddenly, may still be the type of continuous and gradual discharge that is excluded.[467]

[9] The Vermin Exclusion

Rodents can be the cause of a water leak. Policies often exclude damage by rodents. That exclusion was at issue in a case in which a visitor to the insured property discovered it was flooded and reported the situation to the owners who submitted a claim to their insurer on the same day. The insurer examined the home the next day and determined the water damage was caused by a continuous or repeated leakage of water from within a plumbing system occurring over a period of at least several weeks, if not months. The property owners hired an expert who concluded that a water line had been chewed by vermin, causing water to escape over a period of 57 to 70 days. The policy did not cover loss from continuous or repeated seepage or leakage of water occurring over a period of weeks, months, or years. It also did not cover loss resulting directly or indirectly from vermin or rodents unless the creatures caused water to escape from plumbing, in which case the policy covered loss

---

within hours or days after whatever initial breach caused flooding and, therefore, that at least some of loss was attributable to "accidental overflow or discharge of water," rather than any seepage or leakage that might have occurred during the weeks that followed).

466. Cincinnati Ins. Co. v. Kaeding, 2017 Mich. App. LEXIS 1185 (July 20, 2017).

467. Brown v. Mid-Century Ins. Co. , 156 Cal. Rptr. 3d 56, 215 Cal. App. 4th 841 (2013) (no coverage even if breach occurred within a "nanosecond"; it resulted in a "mist, stream and spray" that was constant or intermittent, and occurred over a period of at least "a month or two"). *See also* Finn v. Continental Ins. Co., 267 Cal. Rptr. 22, 218 Cal. App. 3d 69 (1990).

caused by the water. The insurer denied the claim pursuant to the "continuous or repeated seepage or leakage of water" exclusion. The court, however, found the policy was ambiguous regarding how the "leakage and seepage" clause applied to the provision that allowed for coverage of water loss caused by rodents or vermin. The court construed the policy against the insurer. It held that the policy included coverage for water damage from a continuous flow of water caused by rodents but not when the insured was aware of the leak and did not report it for weeks. As long as the insured reported water loss due to rodent chew promptly on learning of it, concluded the court, the insured would be covered up until that point for any damage caused by the water loss. In other words, the court applied the "period of weeks, months or years" language to *discovery* of the loss.[468]

[10] Rain Exclusion

Policies typically exclude coverage for loss of or damage to the interior of any building structure,[469] or to personal property in the building or structure, that is caused by or results from rain, snow, sleet, or ice, unless the building first sustains damage by a *covered cause of loss* to its roof or walls through which rain, snow, sleet, or ice enters.[470] How does that provision interact with the exclusion for "continuous or repeated seepage or leakage of water"? A Texas federal court considered that question in a post-Hurricane Harvey case. The insured in that case claimed water damage from the hurricane that lasted about four days. The policy excluded coverage for damage from continuous or repeated seepage or leakage of water occurring over a period of 14 days or more. The insured argued that the policy therefore implicitly covered damage caused by seepage or leakage that occurred over fewer than 14 days. The insurer did not dispute that the insured property experienced leakage and seepage during the hurricane, but it contended that the damage was excluded by the provision barring coverage for loss to the interior of a building caused by rain unless the building first sustains damage by a covered cause of loss to its roof or walls through which the rain enters. The court said that if leakage or seepage caused direct physical damage to covered property, that leakage or seepage would be a covered cause of loss unless it was "continuous," meaning going on for more than 14 days. Moreover, if that covered cause of loss enabled additional rainwater to enter and do further damage to the interior,

---

468. Danganan v. Am. Family Mut. Ins. Co., 2019 U.S. Dist. LEXIS 169806 (D. Nev. Sept. 30, 2019).

469. The exclusion is for damage to the *interior* of the insured building and does not apply to damage to the *exterior*. Wider v. Heritage Maintenance, Inc., 14 Misc. 3d 963, 827 N.Y.S.2d 837 (2007) (any and all damage or loss to exterior of building allegedly caused by rain would not fall under rain limitation).

470. *See* ISO Forms CP 10 30 06 07, § B.1.g.(4), HO 00 03 05 01 (Exclusions), § I.A.3..

the requirement that the building first sustain damage by a covered cause of loss through which rain enters in order for interior rain damage to be covered would be satisfied, and there would be coverage for that interior rain damage.[471]

2.10 Frozen Pipes or Equipment Exclusion

A pipe that freezes and then bursts can release hundreds of gallons of water per hour and lead to major flooding.[472] In one case, after a frozen water pipe ruptured, more than 500,000 gallons of water poured inside a home, causing extensive damage.[473] Policies often exclude coverage for a loss or damage cause by or resulting from water or other liquids that leak or flow from plumbing, heating, air conditioning, or other equipment—other than fire protective systems[474]—caused by or resulting from freezing, unless the insured either (1) "does its best" or "uses reasonable care" to maintain heat in the building or structure or (2) drains the equipment and shuts off the supply if heat is not maintained.[475] Generally, the insurer will have the burden to show the exclusion applies; however, courts may require the insured to show the exception applies. When the exception is successfully invoked, there is coverage and, therefore, the exception is discussed elsewhere.[476]

Policies do not define "freezing." The Merriam-Webster online dictionary defines the word to mean "being at or below the temperature at which water freezes" and "the temperature at which water freezes."[477] Does a pipe or appliance have to freeze solid for the freezing exclusion to apply? That is not clear either from the language of the exclusion itself or from the dictionary definition. In one case relying on a federal government tariff schedule for

471. Tex. Friends Chabad-Lubavitch, Inc. v. Nova Cas. Co., 539 F. Supp. 3d 669 (S.D. Tex. 2021).

472. *The Big Freeze: 5 Signs Your Pipes are Frozen and How to Thaw Them* (Mar. 2, 2015), Mogil Organization, https://mogil.com/the-big-freeze-5-signs-your-pipes-are-frozen-and-how-to-thaw-them/. *See, e.g.*, Wells v. State Farm Fire & Cas. Ins. Co., 447 Ill. Dec. 259, 173 N.E.3d 613 (Ill. App. 2021) (during period of below freezing weather, building's water pipes burst, and water from those pipes flooded areas of building).

473. Weber v. Farmers Ins. Co., 290 P.3d 686 (Kan. App. 2012). *See also* Dooley v. Scottsdale Ins. Co., 2015 U.S. Dist. LEXIS 19140 (D.N.J. Feb. 18, 2015) (22,000 gallons leaked into residence).

474. Anghel v. Utica Mut. Ins. Co., 127 A.D.3d 897, 7 N.Y.S.3d 390 (2015) (pipe that burst was part of automatic sprinkler system and, thus, was part of fire protective system exempted from exclusion for damages resulting from frozen pipes).

475. ISO Form CP 10 30 06 07, § B.2.g.

476. See § 3.2[3], *infra*.

477. *Freezing*, Merriam-Webster, https://www.merriam-webster.com/dictionary/freezing.

products, a court found that frozen meant "frozen throughout."[478] Courts, however, have not required insurers to show that a pipe or appliance was frozen solid. Usually, the fact that a pipe burst while temperatures were below freezing is sufficient for the freezing exclusion to bar coverage. Nonetheless, if the insured can raise doubt about freezing, it may be possible to escape application of the exclusion. There are indices that pipes are frozen—frost on pipes, odors from pipes, lack of water from faucets[479]—and if the insured can show the absence of those indices, it may be at least possible to avoid summary judgment.

Even if the insured concedes failure to take reasonable care to maintain heat in the building or shut off and drain the water supply, the burden remains on the insurer to show a pipe burst because of *freezing*.[480]

In standard residential policies,[481] freezing may be an exception to the perils covering structures unless the insured maintains heat in the building or shuts off the water supply and drains all systems and appliances of water.[482] For personal property coverage, freezing may be a covered peril but only if the insured maintains heat in the building or shuts off the water supply and drains all systems and appliances of water.[483] The difference between the coverage for structures and personal property is the burden of proof. In the former, if the court treats the "exception" as an exclusion, it will most likely place the

478. Mondiv, Div. of Lassonde Specialties Inc. v. United States, 329 F. Supp. 3d 1331, 1340 (Ct. Intl. Trade 2018) (Harmonized Tariff Schedule of the United States defines "frozen" as when product has been cooled to below its freezing point until it is frozen throughout).

479. Eberlin, *4 Signs Your Pipes Are Frozen and What to Watch For* (Aug. 4, 2019), LiveAbout, https://www.thebalancesmb.com/how-to-tell-if-your-pipes-are-frozen-2124985. *See also The Big Freeze: 5 Signs Your Pipes are Frozen and How to Thaw Them* (March 2, 2015), Mogil Organization, https://mogil.com/the-big-freeze-5-signs-your-pipes-are-frozen-and-how-to-thaw-them/.

480. ASI Lloyds v. Lytell, 781 F. Supp. 2d 326 (E.D. La. 2011) (insurer met its initial burden to show that there was no genuine dispute of fact regarding cause of burst pipe where its expert unequivocally opined that damage was completely consistent with freeze damage and provided impartial data demonstrating that nearby weather stations recorded sustained below-freezing temperatures; however, insured's expert opined that bend in copper pipe could have contributed to damage and court, therefore, was wary of choosing one expert's opinion over another on motion for summary judgment).

481. In the comparable named risk Broad Form, freezing is a named peril for both structures and personal property, but only if the insured has used reasonable care to maintain heat or shut off the water supply and drain pipes and appliances. ISO Form HO 00 02 10 00 (Perils Insured Against), § 14.

482. ISO Form HO 00 03 10 00 (Perils Insured Against; Dwelling and Other Structures), § A.2.c.(1). If the building is protected by an automatic fire protective sprinkler system, the insured is required to use reasonable care to continue the water supply and maintain heat in the building for there to be coverage. The terms "plumbing system" or "household appliance" do not include a sump, sump pump, or related equipment or a roof drain, gutter, downspout, or similar fixtures or equipment.

483. ISO Form HO 00 03 10 00 (Perils Insured Against; Personal Property), § B.14.

burden on the insurance company to show the exception applies. In the case of the latter, the insured would have the burden to show the loss or damage was caused by the covered peril of freezing.

2.11 Explosion Limitation

"Explosion" is a named peril in standard ISO broad form and commercial property policies.[484] It would also be a covered peril in an all-risk property policy unless specifically excluded. The term "explosion" is generally given a common rather than scientific meaning and is often said to mean "a bursting of something with violence, accompanied by noise."[485]

The standard current commercial policy says the coverage for explosion *does not* include loss or damage by "[r]upture or bursting due to expansion or swelling of the contents of any building or structure, caused by or resulting from water."[486] Other policies, mostly older ones, say that explosion does not include "water hammer"[487] or rupture or bursting of water pipes.[488] These limitations will generally be treated as exclusions for which the insurer has the burden of proof.[489] When they apply, coverage is properly denied.[490] Of course, if the court finds there has been no explosion, then application of the

---

484. ISO Forms CP 10 20 04 02, § A.3, HO 00 02 10 00 (Perils Insured Against), § 3.

485. 5 Jeffrey E. Thomas, *New Appleman on Insurance Law Library Edition* § 42.01A[3] (Matthew Bender 2022).

486. There do not appear to be any reported decisions interpreting this clause.

487. The "water hammer" effect "results from a sudden increase in water pressure, which can burst water mains and pipes." Sher v. Lafayette Ins. Co., 973 So. 2d 39, 58, n.7 (La. App. 2007).

488. *See, e.g.*, Pre-Cast Concrete Prods. v. Home Ins. Co., 417 F.2d 1323 (7th Cir. 1969); Louisville Gas & Electric Co. v. American Ins. Co., 412 F.2d 908 (6th Cir. 1969); Schmieder v. State Farm Fire & Casualty Co., 339 So. 2d 390 (1976 La. App. 1976); Honeymead Products Co. v. Aetna Casualty & Surety Co., 275 Minn. 182, 146 N.W.2d 522 (1966); McCreary v. Employers Mut. Fire Ins. Co., 378 S.W.2d 243 (Mo. App. 1964). Some of these older policies may add "rupture or bursting due to expansion or swelling of the contents of any building or structure, caused by or resulting from water." *See, e.g.*, Whitney Nat'l Bank v. State Farm Fire & Casualty Co., 518 F. Supp. 359, 365 (E.D. La. 1981); Rutgens Distributors, Inc. v. United States Fidelity & Guaranty Co. 50 Ill. Dec. 192, 94 Ill. App. 3d 753, 419 N.E.2d 59 (1981); Whitelegg v. Standard Accident Ins. Co., 50 Misc. 2d 702, 271 N.Y.S.2d 492 (1966).

489. Rutgens Distributors, Inc. v. United States Fidelity & Guaranty Co., 50 Ill. Dec. 192, 195, 94 Ill. App. 3d 753, 757, 419 N.E.2d 59, 63 (1981) (if insurer by terms of policy limits its coverage by excluding explosions from specified causes, burden is on insurer to prove that loss by explosion was due to a cause excepted by policy terms).

490. *See, e.g.*, Pilling v. Nationwide Mut. Fire Ins. Co., 201 W. Va. 757, 500 S.E.2d 870 (1997) (where water pipes in home ruptured, causing extensive damage, and under policy explosion did not include water hammer or rupture of water pipes, lower court erred in determining that language was ambiguous and in finding that insureds were entitled to coverage for explosion damages).

limitations is a moot point.[491] Moreover, whether or not there has been an explosion, if the policy includes a standard water damage exclusion, coverage for a flood loss may be barred.[492]

Even though a pipe may break or rupture, and the policy says a broken pipe is not an explosion, if an *explosion breaks a pipe* and causes the damage at issue, that definitional limitation does not apply and there can be coverage for the loss.[493]

Some policies may exclude all coverage for damages from explosions, but then cover resulting water damage. For example, in a Missouri case a sprinkler leakage policy excluded coverage for explosions. A "hot well" connected to a boiler broke away under pressure and ruptured water pipes in a sprinkler system. The court said that the exclusion only covered a loss suffered directly by an explosion, not by leakage of water that followed the explosion, even though that leakage was caused by the explosion.[494]

Where "water hammer" is *not* excepted from the definition of "explosion"—as is the case in modern property policies—it may be considered to be an explosion. In a case before the Fifth Circuit,[495] a fire hydrant on the sidewalk in front of the insured premises exploded, causing water to rush from the hydrant and flood the basement of the insured property. The insurer argued that there was no explosion, that an explosion changes chemical or molecular structure under heat or chemical reaction, and that neither water nor cast iron explodes. The court noted that the underground rupture of the hydrant was caused by a water hammer, an instantaneous buildup of pressure by the sudden stoppage of the flow of water. The court held there was an explosion and the loss was covered because whether energy is generated by molecular changes, breaking down of an atom, chemical reaction, or the movement of water, is immaterial. There was an explosion unless the cause was excluded, which it was not.

---

491. Travelers Fire Ins. Co. v. Tires, Inc., 153 F. Supp. 944 (W.D.S.C. 1957), *aff'd*, 253 F.2d 411 (4th Cir. 1958) (court did not need to rule on whether water hammer and bursting of water pipes limitations would prevent coverage of loss where jury found no explosion had occurred).

492. Bates v. Phenix Mut. Fire Ins. Co., 156 N.H. 719, 943 A.2d 750 (2008) (assuming without deciding that collapse of road functioning as temporary dam was an "explosion," water exclusion applied to preclude coverage where water burst through road, releasing surge of water into downstream valley that damaged insured property; it was undisputed that rain-induced flood or overflow either directly or indirectly caused damage).

493. Agric. Ins. Co. v. Ark. Power & Light Co., 235 Ark. 445, 361 S.W.2d 6 (1962) (affirming judgment for insured where jury found loss suffered was from explosion of accumulated gas or unconsumed fuel within fire box, not result of explosion or rupture in steam pipe).

494. State *ex rel.* Continental Ins. Co. v. Reynolds, 290 Mo. 362, 235 S.W. 88 (1921).

495. Commercial Union Fire Ins. Co. v. Bank of Georgia, 197 F.2d 455 (5th Cir. 1952).

2.12 Rain, Snow, Sleet, or Ice Limitation

Under a standard exclusion, insurers will not pay for any loss that is a consequence of loss or damage to the interior of any building structure—or personal property in that building or structure—caused by or resulting from rain, snow, sleet, or ice, whether driven by wind or not. There is an exception that applies when the building or structure first sustains damage by a covered cause of loss—usually wind or hail—to its roof or walls through which the precipitate enters or the loss or damage is caused by or results from thawing of snow, sleet, or ice on the building or structure.[496] This clause is characterized as a "limitation" rather than an exclusion. The exceptions to it are discussed elsewhere.[497]

2.13 Weather Conditions Exclusion

Many policies have a "weather conditions" exclusion that simply says that the insurer will not pay for loss or damage caused by or resulting from "weather conditions."[498] That is followed by a limitation pursuant to which the exclusion applies only if weather conditions contribute in any way with a specified excluded cause or event—typically, ordinance or law, earth movement, governmental action, nuclear hazard, power failure, war and military action, and *water*[499]—to produce the loss or damage. "Weather conditions" is generally not defined. One treatise characterizes it as "related to nature."[500] Rain, hail, and wind have been identified by courts as weather conditions.[501]

The scope of the weather conditions exclusion is said to be narrow. Its application is limited to "when otherwise covered weather conditions combine with other perils specifically excluded in the policy to produce damages."[502] A South Carolina federal court explained that the exclusion

---

496. ISO Form CP 10 30 09 17, § C.1.c.

497. See §§ 3.2[4], [5], *infra*.

498. *See, e.g.*, ISO Form CP 10 30 04 02, § B.3.a; ISO Form HO 00 05 05 01 (Exclusions), § B.1.

499. Other exclusions may combine with the weather conditions provision to bar coverage. *See, e.g.*, Capelouto v. Valley Forge Ins. Co., 98 Wn. App. 7, 990 P.2d 414 (1999) (rain combined with exclusion of inadequate specifications or construction).

500. Cozen, *Insuring Real Property*, § 1.06[7][d][i][D] (LexisNexis Matthew Bender 2022).

501. Julian v. Hartford Underwriters Ins. Co., 27 Cal. Rptr. 3d 648, 35 Cal. 4th 747, 110 P.3d 903 (2005) (hail, wind, or rain); Findlay v. United Pacific Ins. Co., 917 P.2d 116 (Wash. 1996) (rain and wind).

502. 5 Jeffrey E. Thomas, *New Appleman on Insurance Law Library Edition* § 43.02[12][a] (Matthew Bender 2022). *See also* Sunwood Condo. Ass'n v. Travelers Cas. Ins. Co. of Am., 2017 U.S. Dist. LEXIS 189892 (W.D. Wash. Nov. 16, 2017) (policy excluded loss or damage caused by "weather conditions," but only when combined with earth movement, flood, or other excluded perils, and it did not mention rain or repeated seepage of water that caused damage at issue). In *Legal Servs. Plan of E. Mich. v. Citizens Ins. Co. of Am.*, 2009 Mich. App. LEXIS 954 (Apr. 30, 2009), rain collected on the ground surface and flowed into a basement

makes clear that there is no coverage for property losses in cases of multiple causes where all of the causes are excluded under the policy. Moreover, [it] defines one class of excluded losses in terms of a cause, which even though it could be covered if it acted alone, is excluded because it combines with a cause of loss expressly excluded by the policy. [It] therefore has the effect of excluding losses in multi-cause situations.[503]

That being said, a Mississippi court refused to enforce the weather conditions exclusion when a policy specifically covered the weather condition of a hurricane, and the damage to the insured property was attributable in part to wind, in part to rain, and in part to storm surge. The insurer contended that the hurricane—its winds and rain—would constitute a weather condition that would relieve it of liability for damage to the insured property. The court found that the policy was ambiguous and the weather exclusion unenforceable for losses attributable to wind and rain that occurred during the hurricane.[504] In other words, even though the covered peril of a hurricane combined with the excluded peril of water to damage the property, the hurricane, though clearly a "weather condition," did not invoke the weather condition exclusion because the hurricane coverage when combined with the weather condition exclusion created ambiguity.

One standard exclusion is earth movement. Courts have found that landslides precipitated by rain,[505] or by rain and wind,[506] are not covered under the weather conditions exclusion.

---

through an opening in the wall. When the rainwater fell and began to pool and flow, the court said it became surface water and did not cease to be that when it flowed into the basement. Therefore, the water exclusion barred coverage. The court then said it agreed that the exclusion for "weather conditions" did not preclude coverage of the loss from water damage because that exclusion only applied if weather conditions contributed with certain excluded causes or events—one of which was water including surface water—to produce the loss or damage. The court concluded that none of the causes was "relevant here." The court did not clarify its meaning. It could be that it determined that rain—presumably a weather event—did not contribute to produce the loss or damage because the rain became surface water.

503. Graf v. Allstate Ins. Co., 2006 U.S. Dist. LEXIS 94908, at *8 (D.S.C. Dec. 25, 2006).

504. Buente v. Allstate Ins. Co., 422 F. Supp. 2d 690 (S.D. Miss. 2006) (policy was intended to cover damages sustained in hurricane because of effects of rain, hurricane winds, and objects that might be carried by those winds, whether or not there was also damage caused by high water).

505. Julian v. Hartford Underwriters Ins. Co., 27 Cal. Rptr. 3d 648, 35 Cal. 4th 747, 110 P.3d 903 (2005) (holding weather conditions clause excluded peril of rain inducing landslide). *But see* Palub v. Hartford Underwriters Ins. Co., 112 Cal. Rptr. 2d 270, 92 Cal. App. 4th 645 (2001).

506. Findlay v. United Pacific Ins. Co., 917 P.2d 116 (Wash. 1996) (heavy rainstorms provided initial source of water penetration into slope, high winds caused large tree roots to loosen soils, and subsequent rains penetrated the loose soils causing landslide; efficient proximate cause of loss was weather conditions, rain, and wind; loss was not covered because policy unambiguously stated it did not insure for loss caused by weather conditions if they contributed to earth movement).

The weather conditions exclusion discussed above is found in standard policies; however, there are other versions of which one needs to be aware. For example, one exclusion bars coverage for weather conditions that result in

(a) landslide or mudflow;
(b) earth sinking, rising or shifting;
(c) flood, surface waters, waves, tidal water, or spray from any of these, whether or not driven by wind;
(d) water backing up from a sewer or drain or overflowing from a sump pump well; or
(e) water below the surface of the ground, including water which exerts pressure on or seeps or leaks through a building, sidewalk, driveway, foundation, swimming pool or other structure.[507]

That, it should be noted, aligns closely with the standard water damage exclusion.

Another version states that it covers loss caused by weather conditions but will not cover them if they result in

- landslide, mudslide, or mudflow;
- mine subsidence; earth sinking, rising, or shifting (other than sinkhole collapse);
- flood, surface water, waves, tides, tidal waves, or overflow of any body of water or their spray, all whether driven by wind or not;
- water backing up from a sewer or drain; or
- water under the ground surface pressing on, or flowing or seeping through, foundations, walls, floors, or paved surfaces, basements whether paved or not, or doors, windows, or other openings.[508]

2.14 Other Exclusions

When a client presents with water damage, the attorney needs to be aware that in addition to invoking the water damage exclusion, the insurance company may raise a host of standard exclusions not related to water. For example, when an old pipe leaks or bursts, the insurer may deny coverage based on the "wear and tear" exclusion, which bars coverage for normal deterioration over time. If a newly installed plumbing system, or appliance that uses water, is the cause of water damage, there is a standard exclusion for faulty workmanship

507. Quoted in Johnson v. Allstate Ins. Co., 845 F. Supp. 2d 1170, 1172 (W.D. Wash. 2012).

508. N. Coast Enters. v. St. Paul Fire & Marine Ins. Co., 2006 U.S. Dist. LEXIS 20245, at *7–8 (W.D. Wash. Mar. 28, 2006) (policy covers loss caused by weather conditions, unless one of enumerated events was involved, while if one of those events was not present, any loss caused by weather conditions was covered). The policy adds that if loss or damage by a covered cause of loss results, the insurer will pay for that resulting loss or damage.

that may apply. A power failure can lead to flooding when a sump pump ceases to operate, in which case the standard utility services exclusion may be raised by the insurer as a basis for denying a claim. The standard earth movement exclusion is often invoked by insurers when water causes the movement or the movement causes the release of water. These exclusions are beyond the scope of this discussion but are examined in leading insurance law treatises.[509]

2.15 The Wind and Water Conundrum

When flood/water damage occurs during a windstorm, the policyholder faces a potential challenge in obtaining a recovery for any loss. In most policies, wind is a covered peril and water is an excluded peril. The insured may ascribe the loss to a single event: a tropical storm, for example.[510] However, the perils of flood and wind are categorically separate. In fact, they are often temporally separate. Tropical-force winds may impact the insured property long before a storm surge or surface water from heavy rains. In fact, by the time flood water reaches the property, the wind may have abated.[511] Thus, the perils of wind and flood often do not act concurrently.[512]

The policyholder who suffers both wind and water damage can recover for the former if the losses can be segregated. It is the burden of the insured to show the loss was caused by the covered peril.[513] If the building is still standing, experts can usually separate wind from water damage. Sometimes they cannot, and their task is all but impossible if the building is completely destroyed, perhaps even washed away. When the losses cannot be segregated by peril, most courts have traditionally allowed recovery if the insured can show that the "efficient proximate cause" of the loss was a covered peril even

---

509. *See* 5 Jeffrey E. Thomas, *New Appleman on Insurance Law Library Edition* §§ 43.02, 43.03 (Matthew Bender 2022); Cozen, *Insuring Real Property*, § 2.04 (LexisNexis Matthew Bender 2022).

510. *See, e.g.*, Berk-Cohen Assocs., LLC v. Landmark Am. Ins. Co., 2009 U.S. Dist. LEXIS 77300 (E.D. La. Aug. 27, 2009) (rejecting argument that policy covered physical loss resulting from hurricane as unitary storm resulting in both wind and flood damage; although distilling cause of damage may be difficult at times, policy differentiates between wind and flood damage and court would not treat wind and flood damage as the same when policy itself did not).

511. Appleman & Appleman, *Insurance Law and Practice*, § 192.03[H] (Matthew Bender 2011) (when house is damaged or destroyed by hurricane forces of wind and water, there is not one loss; each peril may cause damage to different parts or items of insured property, and both forces may cause damage to same item of insured property at different points in time).

512. Rossmiller, *Interpretation and Enforcement of Anti-Concurrent Policy Language in Hurricane Katrina Cases and Beyond*, New Appleman on Insurance: Current Critical Issues in Insurance Law, § IV (Oct. 2007).

513. Perito v. Northern Ins. Co., 189 Misc. 204, 69 N.Y.S.2d 611 (1947) (policyholder had to establish by fair preponderance of evidence that proximate cause of loss was windstorm; jury must not be left to mere conjecture or speculation, and bare possibility that house was damaged by wind was not sufficient).

though an excluded peril may have contributed to it.[514] The efficient proximate cause is "the moving, dominant, predominant, operative or active cause among multiple forces."[515] Not surprisingly, the efficient proximate cause doctrine is interpreted and applied differently by different courts.[516] In a few states, the courts follow a concurrent cause rule under which a loss is covered if any non-remote cause is a covered peril.[517]

The response of insurers to decisions finding coverage when a loss is caused by a covered and excluded peril is the anti-concurrent clause (ACC).[518] The typical ACC is prefatory to the list of excluded perils and states that the "loss or damage is excluded [by any of the named exclusions] regardless of any other cause or event that contributes concurrently or in any sequence to the loss."[519] Most, but not all, courts interpret the ACC language to mean that there can be no recovery for a loss caused by both a covered and excluded peril. The majority of jurisdictions that have taken a clear position have determined that ACCs are "unequivocally enforceable."[520] A handful of states prohibit enforcement of the ACC, most notably California, which has codified that prohibition.[521] The interpretation and application of ACCs has been

---

514. W. Nat'l Mut. Ins. Co. v. Univ. of N.D., 643 N.W.2d 4, 12 (N.D. 2002) (efficient proximate cause doctrine is generally recognized as universal method for resolving coverage issues involving concurrence of covered and excluded perils). *See also* 5 Jeffrey E. Thomas, *New Appleman on Insurance Law Library Edition* § 44.03[6] (Matthew Bender 2022) (when determining whether coverage exists for loss under first-party insurance when the loss is caused by combination of covered and excluded risks, loss is covered if covered risk was efficient proximate cause of loss). A few states employ the "concurrent cause rule" under which a loss is covered if any non-remote cause is a covered peril. 5 Jeffrey E. Thomas, *New Appleman on Insurance Law Library Edition* § 44.03[3] (Matthew Bender 2022).

515. Rossmiller, *Interpretation and Enforcement of Anti-Concurrent Policy Language in Hurricane Katrina Cases and Beyond*, New Appleman on Insurance: Current Critical Issues in Insurance Law, § I (Oct. 2007).

516. Varga, *When Wind and Flood Unite: The Anti-Concurrent Causation Clause*, 48 The Brief 52 (2019) (noting varied, and at times contradictory, ways in which efficient proximate cause doctrine has been interpreted and applied).

517. 5 Jeffrey E. Thomas, *New Appleman on Insurance Law Library Edition* § 44.03[3] (Matthew Bender 2022). *See* 5 Jeffrey E. Thomas, *New Appleman on Insurance Law Library Edition* § 44.04[5] (Matthew Bender 2022) for a list of states showing which rule, if any, is followed.

518. Appleman & Appleman, *Insurance Law and Practice*, § 192.03[F] (Matthew Bender 2011) (anti-concurrent cause language is designed to overturn default common law rule for analysis of multiple causes of property loss, most often referred to as efficient proximate cause rule); Rossmiller, *Interpretation and Enforcement of Anti-Concurrent Policy Language in Hurricane Katrina Cases and Beyond*, New Appleman on Insurance: Current Critical Issues in Insurance Law, § II (Oct. 2007) (anti-concurrent language overcomes efficient proximate cause).

519. ISO Form CP 10 30 09 17, § B.1.

520. Carback, *Anti-Concurrent Causation Clauses in Insurance Contracts: The State of the Law in 2017*, 19 Transactions 21, 25 (2017).

521. Cal. Ins. Code § 530. *See also* N.D. Cent. Code § 26.1-32-01.

explored in depth in treatises[522] and in scholarly articles,[523] and that discussion need not be repeated here, as this treatise is concerned with recovery for flood losses. When an insurer invokes an ACC clause, counsel has two choices. First, research the law of the pertinent jurisdiction and determine if the courts of that jurisdiction will enforce the ACC and if so, how they will interpret it.[524] Second, employ expert assistance to segregate the wind from the flood damage.[525] As a leading insurance treatise says:

> Anti-concurrent cause language addresses multiple concurrent or sequential causes of the same loss. It does not apply if the perils at work caused different damage or different losses. These would not be concurrent causes.[526]

The treatise offers a pertinent example. Hurricane winds damage the roof of a home while hurricane-induced flood waters damage its foundation. In that case, wind and flood are not concurrent causes, so the ACC does not apply.

---

522. *See* 5 Jeffrey E. Thomas, *New Appleman on Insurance Law Library Edition* § 44.04 (Matthew Bender 2022); Cozen, *Insuring Real Property*, § 48.03[3][c] (LexisNexis Matthew Bender 2022); Plitt, et al., *Couch on Insurance*, §§ 148.60, *et seq.* (Clark Boardman Callaghan 2022).

523. *See* Varga, *When Wind - and - Flood Unite: The Anti-Concurrent Causation Clause*, 48 The Brief 52 (2019); Carback, *Anti-Concurrent Causation Clauses in Insurance Contracts: The State of the Law in 2017*, 19 Transactions 21, 25 (2017); Swisher, *"Why Won't My Homeowners Insurance Cover My Loss?": Reassessing Property Insurance Concurrent Causation Coverage Disputes*, 88 Tul. L. Rev. 515 (2014); Bell, *A Concurrent Mess and a Call for Clarity in First-Party Property Insurance Coverage Analysis*, 18 Conn. Ins. L.J. 73 (2011); Altemose, *The Anti-Concurrent Clause and Its Impact on Texas Residents After Hurricane Ike*, 16 Tex. Wesleyan L. Rev. 201 (2010); Edwards, *The Wind and the Waves: The Evolution of Florida Property Insurance Law in Response to Multiple-Causation Hurricane Damage*, 34 Fla. St. U.L. Rev. 541 (2007); Rossmiller, *Interpretation and Enforcement of Anti-Concurrent Policy Language in Hurricane Katrina Cases and Beyond*, New Appleman on Insurance: Current Critical Issues in Insurance Law (Oct. 2007). *See also* Dahlquist, *Perspectives on Subsidence Exclusions and the Role of Concurrent Causation in Earth Movement Cases*, 37 Tort & Ins. L.J. 949 (2002).

524. *See* 5 Jeffrey E. Thomas, *New Appleman on Insurance Law Library Edition* § 44.04[5] (Matthew Bender 2022), for a list of states enforcing and rejecting the ACC.

525. *See* Wilson, *A Procedure for Segregating Damages from Wind and Flood Water*, 16 Tex. Tech. Admin. L. J. 141 (2014).

526. *See* 5 Jeffrey E. Thomas, *New Appleman on Insurance Law Library Edition* § 44.04[1] (Matthew Bender 2022). *See also* Corban v. United Servs. Auto. Ass'n, 20 So. 3d 601, 614 (Miss. 2009) (exclusion applies only in event that perils act in conjunction, as indivisible force, occurring at same time, to cause direct physical damage resulting in loss).

3

Recovering under Standard Property Policies

3.1 Introduction

Despite the broad water damage exclusion found in virtually all standard property polices, those same policies cover water damage, including floods, in certain narrow circumstances in the primary policy and when added by endorsement. This chapter discusses those circumstances.

3.2 Limited Water Damage Coverage

[1] Introduction: Standard Policy Language

Property policies, whether for residential or commercial properties, either name the risks they cover or cover all risks except those that are explicitly excluded. In an all-risk policy, one determines whether water damage is covered by examining the language of any pertinent exclusions.[1] The Insurance Services Organization (ISO) standard named risk policies can be "Basic" or "Broad." A Basic homeowners or commercial policy does not list water damage as a covered risk and also explicitly excludes water damage. A Broad policy lists water damage as a covered risk but explicitly excludes types of water damage. To determine coverage of water damage, one has to compare the definition of covered water damage to the exclusion.

[a] Commercial Property Policies

In the standard ISO Broad Form Commercial Property Causes of Loss, "water damage" is a covered cause of loss that is narrowly defined as "accidental discharge or leakage of water or steam as the direct result of the breaking apart or cracking of a plumbing, heating, air conditioning or other system

1. *See, e.g.*, ISO Form HO 00 03 10 00 (Homeowners 3—Special Form); ISO Form CP 10 30 06 07 (Commercial Property Causes of Loss—Special Form).

or appliance, that is located on the described premises and contains water or steam."[2] "Water damage" does *not* include the following:

- Discharge or leakage from an automatic sprinkler system, a sump, or related equipment and parts, including overflow because of sump pump failure or excessive volume of water, or roof drains, gutters, downspouts, or similar fixtures or equipment;
- The expense of repairing any defect that caused loss or damage;
- Loss or damage caused by or resulting from continuous or repeated seepage or leakage of water, or humidity, moisture or vapor, occurring over 14 days or more; or
- Loss or damage caused by or resulting from freezing, unless the insured does his or her "best"[3] to maintain heat in the building or structure or drains the equipment and shuts off the water supply if the heat is not maintained.

When the water damage coverage applies, and the building or structure containing the system or appliance is covered property, the insurer will pay the cost to tear out and replace any part of the building or structure to repair damage to the system or appliance from which the water or steam escapes, but not the cost to repair any defect that caused the loss or damage.[4]

[b] Homeowners Policies

The standard ISO Broad Form Homeowners policy insures for direct physical loss caused by "accidental discharge or overflow of water or steam," meaning discharge or overflow of water or steam from within a plumbing, heating, air conditioning, or automatic fire protective sprinkler system, or a household appliance.[5] This does not include loss

- On the "residence premises,"[6] if the dwelling has been vacant for more than 60 consecutive days immediately before the loss, but a dwelling that is being constructed is not considered vacant;
- To the system or appliance from which water or steam escaped;

---

2. ISO Form CP 10 20 04 02, § A.14.a.

3. "Best" is not defined but generally means reasonable efforts. Me. State Props., LLC v. Chubb Custom Ins. Co., 2016 U.S. Dist. LEXIS 89175 (D. Me. July 8, 2016); Auto-Owners Ins. Co. v. Hansen Hous., Inc., 604 N.W.2d 504, 512 (S.D. 2000).

4. ISO Form CP 10 20 04 02, § A.14.b.

5. ISO Form HO 00 02 10 00 (Perils Insured Against), § 12.a.

6. The term "residence premises" is defined as the property shown as the residence premises on the Declarations Page and that is the one family dwelling where the insured resides; the two-, three-, or four-family dwelling where the insured resides in at least one of those family units; or the part of any other building where the insured resides. The term includes other structures and grounds at that location. ISO Form HO 00 02 10 00 (Definitions), § 11.

- Caused by or resulting from freezing *except* freezing of a plumbing, heating, air conditioning, or automatic fire protective sprinkler system, or a household appliance if the insured has used reasonable care to maintain heat in the building or shuts off the water supply and drains all systems and appliances of water;[7]
- Caused by accidental discharge or overflow that occurs off the residence premises; or
- Caused by mold, fungus, or wet rot unless hidden within the walls or ceilings or beneath the floors or above the ceilings of a structure.[8]

A plumbing system or household appliance does not include a sump, sump pump, or related equipment or a roof drain, gutter, downspout, or similar fixtures or equipment.[9] The paragraphs of the water damage exclusion that apply to surface water[10] and water below the surface of the ground[11] do not apply to loss by water covered under this peril.

While the language found in standard ISO policies as discussed above is widely used in the industry, there are often variations that can change the coverage. One, therefore, always has to carefully examine the pertinent policy for wording that restricts or enlarges the coverage.

[2] Interpretation of Standard Policy Terminology

[a] Accidental Discharge or Leakage

Standard policies insure for direct physical loss caused by "accidental discharge or overflow of water or steam," but do not define "accidental," "discharge," or "leakage." "Accidental" is generally defined using words such as "fortuitous," "inadvertent," "unexpected," "unforeseen," and "unintentional."[12] One law dictionary defines the word as "by chance or fortuitously, without intention or design; unexpected, unusual, and unforeseen." It also says that in accident

7. *See* ISO Form HO 00 02 10 00 (Perils Insured Against), § 14.a. A plumbing system or household appliance does not include a sump, sump pump, or related equipment or a roof drain, gutter, downspout, or similar fixtures or equipment. ISO Form HO 00 02 10 00 (Perils Insured Against), § 14.b. If the insured building is protected by an automatic fire protective sprinkler system, the insured must use reasonable care to continue the water supply and maintain heat in the building for coverage to apply.

8. ISO Form HO 00 02 10 00 (Perils Insured Against), § 12.b.

9. ISO Form HO 00 02 10 00 (Perils Insured Against), § 12.c.

10. ISO Form HO 00 02 10 00 (Exclusions), § 3.a. The paragraph defines water damage to mean flood, surface water, waves, tidal water, overflow of a body of water, or spray from any of them, whether or not driven by wind.

11. ISO Form HO 00 02 10 00 (Exclusions), § 3.c. The paragraph defines water damage to mean water or water-borne material below the surface of the ground, including water that exerts pressure on, or seeps or leaks through, a building, sidewalk, driveway, foundation, swimming pool or other structure.

12. *Burton's Legal Thesaurus* (6th ed. Matthew Bender 2021).

policies it is "used in its ordinary popular sense . . . and means happening by chance, unexpectedly taking place, not according to the usual course of things, or not as expected."[13] Thus, a discharge that is part of the intended operation of an appliance is not "accidental."[14]

"Discharge" has been defined in a number of cases, almost always in the context of a pollution exclusion. Its meaning has been described as "a flowing or issuing out"[15] and to pour or send forth.[16]

"Leakage" has been tersely defined as the "escape of a liquid,"[17] and more expansively as "'admission or escape of water or other fluid,'" "the condition of 'escap[ing] from a hole or crack in a pipe or container,'" and entering or escaping "through an opening usually by a fault or mistake."[18]

[b] Plumbing Systems

Most policies do not define "plumbing" or "plumbing systems." The Merriam-Webster online dictionary defines "plumbing" as "the apparatus (such as pipes and fixtures) concerned in the distribution and use of water in a building."[19] Another dictionary says a "plumbing system" consists of "the pipes and fixtures for the distribution of water or gas in a building and for the disposal of sewage."[20] Courts sometimes cite to the definitions in building codes.[21] These definitions are broad. A code for the state of New York, for example, defines "plumbing system" as one "that includes the water distribution pipes;

---

13. *Ballentine's Law Dictionary* (LexisNexis 2010).

14. Schaber v. Allstate Ins. Co., 2007 U.S. Dist. LEXIS 92942 (N.D. Cal. Dec. 18, 2007) (no "accidental discharge" of steam because intended operation of steamer is to discharge steam).

15. Lumbermens Mut. Casualty Co. v. S-W Indus., 39 F.3d 1324, 1336 (6th Cir. 1994).

16. Hartford Underwriter's Ins. Co. v. Estate of Turks, 206 F. Supp. 2d 968, 976 (E.D. Mo. 2003); MacKinnon v. Truck Ins. Exchange, 31 Cal. 4th 635, 3 Cal. Rptr. 228, 242, 651, 7 P.3d 1205, 215 (2003); Peace v. Northwestern Nat'l Ins. Co., 228 Wis. 2d 106, 126–27, 596 N.W.2d 429, 438 (1999). *See also Burton's Legal Thesaurus* (6th ed. Matthew Bender 2021) (displacement, ejection, elimination, eviction, expulsion).

17. *Ballentine's Law Dictionary* (LexisNexis 2010).

18. Landrum v. Allstate Ins. Co., 2019 U.S. Dist. LEXIS 175664, at *3 (M.D. Ga. Oct. 9, 2019). *See also* Karon v. Safeco Ins. Co., 2021 U.S. Dist. LEXIS 147116 (D. Ariz. Aug. 5, 2021).

19. *Plumbing*, Merriam-Webster, https://www.merriam-webster.com/dictionary/plumbing. *See also* Hudson v. Allstate Ins. Co, 809 N.Y.S.2d 124; 25 A.D.3d 654 (2006) (because pipe that burst supplied water to the insured home, it was part of plumbing system).

20. *Plumbing system*, The Free Dictionary, https://www.thefreedictionary.com/plumbing+system. *See also* Ellis v. State Farm Fire & Cas. Co., 322 F. App'x 594, 597 (10th Cir. 2009) (plumbing system includes drain or sewer line). A toilet would ordinarily be considered part of a plumbing system. "Toilet" was defined as a "'bathroom fixture consisting of a bowl, usually with a detachable, hinged seat and lid, and a device for flushing with water, used for defecation and urination.'" Drutz v. Scottsdale Ins. Co., 2012 U.S. Dist. LEXIS 25286, at *8 (D. Md. Feb. 28, 2012). *See generally* Wilson, *Property Coverage for Toilet Overflows* (Nov. 25, 2016), Bill Wilson, *available at* https://insurancecommentary.com/property-coverage-for-toilet-overflows/.

21. *See, e.g.*, Purdy Lane, Inc. v. Scottsdale Ins. Co., 2021 U.S. Dist. LEXIS 27417 (S.D. Fla. Feb. 11, 2021); Holcomb v. United States Fire Ins. Co., 52 N.C. App. 474, 279 S.E.2d 50 (1981).

plumbing fixtures[22] and traps; water-treating or water-using equipment; soil, waste and vent pipes; and building drains; in addition to their respective connections, devices and appurtenances within a structure or premises; and the water service, building sewer and building storm sewer serving such structure or premises."[23]

Citing broad definitions in encyclopedias, some courts have found that gutters and roof drains are part of a plumbing system.[24] Others have said that gutters and down spouts are *not* part of a plumbing system.[25] Courts have also held that drain pipes that carry water from roof drains or downspouts are not part of a plumbing system.[26] On the other hand, underground sewer pipes[27] and water pipes[28] have been found to be a part of the plumbing system of an insured property. Water supply lines that deliver water to dishwashers or refrigerators might be considered part of a plumbing system. [29]

A patio was not a plumbing system or part of one merely because it was constructed with a grade to channel water to a driveway. A different conclusion

22. A "plumbing fixture" is a receptacle or device connected to a water supply system or that discharges to a drainage system or both.

23. 2020 Plumbing Code of the State of New York, at 14 (International Code Council and New York State Department of State 2019).

24. Holcomb v. United States Fire Ins. Co., 52 N.C. App. 474, 478, 279 S.E.2d 50, 53 (1981) (ordinary meaning of term "plumbing system" includes gutters and downspouts designed for disposal of rainwater); Schumacher v. Lumbermens Mut. Cas. Co., 154 So. 2d 637, 639 (La. App. 1963) (plumbing means fixtures for purpose of drainage and includes roof drains). *See also* J&B Trading Co., Inc. v. Leading Ins. Group Ins. Co., Ltd., 2019 N.Y. Misc. LEXIS 1704 (Apr. 8, 2019) (water damage was caused by cracked drain pipe, which could be part of plumbing system where policy did not require system to be internal, but merely required that it was located on described premises and contained water).

25. Allison v. Allstate Indem. Co., 2008 U.S. Dist. LEXIS 50684 (E.D. Pa. June 27, 2008) (because gutters and down spouts are not involved in distribution and use of water in a building, and instead conduct rainwater outside home, they do not fall within plumbing system).

26. *See, e.g.*, Cozza v. State Farm Fire & Cas. Co., 440 Fed. Appx. 73 (3d Cir. 2011) (a drain pipe running parallel to the foundation wall, four-feet underground, that carried rainwater collected from roof gutters and fed from downspouts to the main city sewer was not part of the plumbing system because it did not provide water, heat, or sanitation to the insured house, but was designed to keep rainwater outside the house). *See also* Wandler v. Homesite Indem. Co., 2013 U.S. Dist. LEXIS 201827 (D. Wyo. Nov. 7, 2013) (drainpipe, designed to carry rainwater from gutters away from home, that became obstructed by dirt and grass and backed up did not constitute plumbing system).

27. Cantanucci v. Reliance Ins. Co., 43 A.D.2d 622, 349 N.Y.S.2d 187 (1973), *aff'd*, 364 N.Y.S.2d 890, 35 N.Y.2d 890, 324 N.E.2d 360 (1974) (because broken sewer pipe was primary outlet for plaintiffs' waste pipe, it was part of plumbing system).

28. Hudson v. Allstate Ins. Co., 25 A.D.3d 654, 809 N.Y.S.2d 124 (2006) (pipe that supplied water to insured home was part of plumbing system); Bienenstock v. Federal Ins. Co., 75 Misc. 2d 745, 348 N.Y.S.2d 936 (1973) (pipe under front lawn of insured that connected street water main to interior plumbing system of residence was part of plumbing system).

29. Jamison v. Depositors Ins. Co., 2016 U.S. Dist. LEXIS 91841, at *16, n.5 (D. Neb. May 23, 2016) (refrigerator water supply line was certainly either plumbing system or household appliance).

would, agreed an appellate court, stretch the term "plumbing system" beyond its common usage.[30]

When the plumbing system is clearly not the source of the water that has caused damage, the limited water damage coverage is inapplicable. For example, where a policy covered accidental discharge, leakage, or overflow of water from a plumbing system, tanks, or pipes, and the water that did the damage accumulated on the outside of the insured building and ran under the rear door, that water never came from the plumbing system and the damage was not covered by the policy language.[31]

[c] Other Systems or Appliances

[i] Appliance

Policies do not define the words or phrases "other systems," "appliances," or "household appliances." Many courts have relied on lay dictionaries when interpreting those phrases.[32] There appears to be a consensus that an "appliance" is an apparatus, device, or thing "applied to or used as a means to an end."[33] The term has also been defined to mean "encompassing tools, instruments, devices, contrivances, machines, mechanisms, and almost anything applied for a particular purpose."[34] Apparently, an appliance need not be the property of the insured,[35] or a fixture of the insured property,[36] unless the policy language specifies otherwise.

[ii] Household Appliance

The definition of "household appliance" is slightly different. One court defined the term to mean "a tool, instrument or device adapted for a particular use in

---

30. Cameron v. USAA Prop. & Cas. Ins. Co., 733 A.2d 965 (D.C. App. 1999).

31. Schiff v. Automobile Ins. Co., 290 Mich. 457, 287 N.W. 920 (1939).

32. *See, e.g.*, J. E. Bernard & Co. v. United States, 60 Cust. Ct. 296, 282 F. Supp. 476 (1968); Murray v. Royal Indem. Co., 247 Iowa 1299, 1301, 78 N.W.2d 786, 787 (1956); Roberts v. Los Angeles, 7 Cal. 2d 477, 494, 61 P.2d 323, 330 (1936); Collinsville v. Maryland Casualty Co., 28 Ill. App. 3d 1081, 1084–85, 329 N.E.2d 832, 835 (1975).

33. Murray v. Royal Indem. Co., 247 Iowa 1299, 1301, 78 N.W.2d 786, 787 (1956); Palmer v. Great Northern Ry. Co., 119 Mont. 68, 81, 170 P.2d 768, 775 (1946); Roberts v. Los Angeles, 7 Cal. 2d 477, 494, 61 P.2d 323, 330 (1936); Cook v. Big Muddy-Carterville Mining Co., 249 Ill. 41, 47, 94 N.E. 90, 93 (1911); Honaker v. Board of Educ., 42 W. Va. 170, 174, 24 S.E. 544, 545 (1896); Collinsville v. Maryland Casualty Co., 28 Ill. App. 3d 1081, 1084–85, 329 N.E.2d 832, 835 (1975).

34. J. E. Bernard & Co. v. United States, 60 Cust. Ct. 296, 302, 282 F. Supp. 476, 480–81 (1968). *See also* Stone v. Royal Ins. Co., 211 N.J. Super. 246, 249–50, 511 A.2d 717, 719 (1986) (tool, instrument, or device adapted for particular use, and can be a fixture).

35. Schaber v. Allstate Ins. Co., 2007 U.S. Dist. LEXIS 92942 (N.D. Cal. Dec. 18, 2007) (stating in *dicta* that commercial steam floor cleaner used by contractor to clean floors of insured home was "perhaps" an appliance).

36. Stone v. Royal Ins. Co., 211 N.J. Super. 246, 249–50, 511 A.2d 717, 719 (1986) (*portable* sump pump was no less an appliance than dehumidifier or washing machine).

a house."[37] Another court said the phrase refers to "a household device that does work or performs a task, such as a washer, dryer, vacuum cleaner, or toaster."[38] A court, in *dicta*, suggested there is a difference between an "appliance" and a "household appliance," but it did not elaborate.[39] It did, however, note that the policy only covered losses caused by water or steam that escaped from a *household* appliance because of an accidental discharge or overflow.

Among the things that courts have found to be, or suggested would be, appliances are a washing machine,[40] a water heater,[41] an air conditioner,[42] cleaning apparatus,[43] a common garden hose,[44] a portable sump pump with an attached hose,[45] a refrigerator water supply line,[46] a dehumidifier,[47] and a stopcock in a supply pipe.[48] There are two opinions in which courts considered whether a waterbed was a "household appliance." A New Jersey court said "yes,"[49] and a Florida court said "no."[50]

[iii] Other System

Courts have not provided a definition for "other system." In one case, a business claimed the interior of its property had sustained water damage as the result of a recent rain storm. The policy had the typical water damage coverage provision. The insurer asserted the damage was not caused by a broken pipe or any other condition listed in the policy. Rather, the damage was caused by water that entered through a poorly constructed and maintained

---

37. Azze v. Hanover Insurance Company, 336 N.J. Super. 630, 643, 765 A.2d 1093, 1101 (2001). *See also In re* Beard, 5 B.R. 429 (S.D. Iowa 1980) (appliance connotes some useful domestic function, that is, personal, family, or household use).

38. West American Ins. Co. v. Lowrie, 600 So. 2d 34, 35 (Fla. 3d DCA 1992).

39. Schaber v. Allstate Ins. Co., 2007 U.S. Dist. LEXIS 92942 (N.D. Cal. Dec. 18, 2007) ("Although the Court is inclined to find the commercial steamer, while perhaps an 'appliance,' is not a 'household' appliance, it need not resolve that issue.").

40. Stone v. Royal Ins. Co., 211 N.J. Super. 246, 249–50, 511 A.2d 717, 719 (1986).

41. Nelson v. Allstate Ins. Co., 228 A.3d 983, 984 (R.I. 2020).

42. *In re* Beard, 5 B.R. 429 (S.D. Iowa 1980).

43. Schaber v. Allstate Ins. Co., 2007 U.S. Dist. LEXIS 92942 (N.D. Cal. Dec. 18, 2007) (commercial steamer was perhaps an "appliance").

44. Murray v. Royal Indem. Co., 247 Iowa 1299, 1301, 78 N.W.2d 786, 787 (1956) (after using common garden hose, employee of insured business did not shut off faucet, and water pressure burst hose and flooded property; court said that an appliance is "thing applied or used as a means to an end" and that "hose" seems to be exactly described as an "appliance").

45. Stone v. Royal Ins. Co., 211 N.J. Super. 246, 249–50, 511 A.2d 717, 719 (1986).

46. Jamison v. Depositors Ins. Co., 2016 U.S. Dist. LEXIS 91841, at *16, n.5 (D. Neb. May 23, 2016) (refrigerator water supply line was certainly either plumbing system or household appliance).

47. Stone v. Royal Ins. Co., 211 N.J. Super. 246, 249–50, 511 A.2d 717, 719 (1986).

48. Pullman's Palace Car Co. v. Laack, 143 Ill. 242, 32 N.E. 285 (1892).

49. Azze v. Hanover Insurance Company, 336 N.J. Super. 630, 643–44, 765 A.2d 1093, 1101–02 (2001) (electrically heated waterbed could reasonably be considered a household appliance, which is tool, instrument, or device adapted for a particular purpose).

50. West American Ins. Co. v. Lowrie, 600 So. 2d 34, 35 (Fla. 3d DCA 1992) (waterbed is item of furniture and is not a "household appliance" within ordinary meaning of that phrase).

roof. The court found that generally the policy only covered water damage from leakage from plumbing and heating components.[51] The implication was that a roof was not an "other system." Another court made clear that a "roof system" is not the same as the described systems: plumbing, heating, or air conditioning.[52]

[iv] "Any Part" of a System

Some polices may cover water damage from the accidental discharge or leakage of water or steam as the direct result of the breaking or cracking of *any part of a system* or appliance containing water or steam. The phrase "any part of" potentially broadens the coverage over language that specifies the system. Before something can be "any part of" a system, it must be a system containing water or steam. Courts have said that roofs[53] and walls[54] are not "systems as intended by the policy." An HVAC unit is a system for purposes of the coverage.[55] They have also said that "system or appliance" means the water cannot derive from a natural source.[56] Courts have implied that the system of which the thing that broke or cracked is a part need not be on the property

---

51. Dunn v. Scottsdale Ins. Co., 2013 U.S. Dist. LEXIS 107984 (M.D. Pa. Aug. 1, 2013).

52. *See also* Feenix Parkside, LLC v. Berkley N. Pac., 8 Wn. App. 2d 381, 438 P.3d 597 (2019) ("roof system" is not equivalent of plumbing, heating, or air-conditioning system, because those systems are all designed to use water or steam in their operation, while roof system serves to exclude water).

53. Silver Ridge Homeowners' Ass'n v. State Farm Fire & Cas. Co., 2022 U.S. Dist. LEXIS 46039 (D. Ore. Mar. 15, 2022), *app. dis.*, 2022 U.S. App. LEXIS 16432 (9th Cir. June 14, 2022) (system does not apply to damage sustained to roofs); Royal Surplus Lines Ins. Co. v. Brownsville Indep. Sch. Dist., 404 F. Supp. 2d 942 (S.D. Tex. 2005) (roof leaks are not necessarily discharge or leakage resulting from breaking apart or cracking of any part of a system or appliance containing water or steam, although court could envision factual scenario from which those leaks might be covered). *But see* New Orleans Assets v. Carl E. Woodward, 2002 U.S. Dist. LEXIS 25872 (E.D. La. Aug. 15, 2002) (claims for roof leaks implicate the plain language of the water damage provision defining water damage as accidental leakage from breaking apart or cracking of any part of a system containing water).

54. Silver Ridge Homeowners' Ass'n v. State Farm Fire & Cas. Co., 2022 U.S. Dist. LEXIS 46039 (D. Ore. Mar. 15, 2022), *app. dis.*, 2022 U.S. App. LEXIS 16432 (9th Cir. June 14, 2022) (system does not apply to damage sustained to siding); Caribbean I Owners' Ass'n v. Great Am. Ins. Co., 600 F. Supp. 2d 1228, 1246, n.23 (S.D. Ala. 2009) (cracking walls cannot reasonably be viewed as a "system or appliance" containing water or steam). *But see* New Orleans Assets v. Carl E. Woodward, 2002 U.S. Dist. LEXIS 25872 (E.D. La. Aug. 15, 2002) (claims for masonry leaks implicate the plain language of the water damage provision defining water damage as accidental leakage from breaking apart or cracking of any part of a system containing water).

55. New Orleans Assets v. Carl E. Woodward, 2002 U.S. Dist. LEXIS 25872 (E.D. La. Aug. 15, 2002) (leak "in coil condensation pan" that was part of HVAC was part of system).

56. Macheca Transp. Co. v. Phila. Indem. Ins. Co., 649 F.3d 661, 671 (8th Cir. 2011) ("water damage" refers to water from within human-made item rather than resulting from an element of weather). *See also* Change, Inc. v. Westfield Ins. Co., 208 W. Va. 654, 542 S.E.2d 475 (2000); Mutual Redevelopment Houses v. Greater N.Y. Mut. Ins. Co., 204 A.D.2d 145, 611 N.Y.S.2d 550 (1994), *app. den.*, 635 N.Y.S.2d 947, 86 N.Y.2d 710, 659 N.E.2d 770 (1995).

of the insured—for example, a municipal water main[57]—but must service the property.[58]

[d] Breaking Apart or Cracking

One of the differences between the language of standard commercial and homeowners policies is that the former covers water damage from the accidental discharge or leakage of water or steam as the direct result of the *breaking apart or cracking* of certain items. The latter, on the other hand, covers losses from discharge or overflow of water or steam from within one of the enumerated items, without any "breaking apart or cracking." Courts have apparently not defined "breaking apart or cracking." To break apart means to "break into parts or components or lose cohesion or unity."[59] "Cracking" means "[b]reaking or splitting without complete separation of parts."[60] The term "break" has been said to include "separation."[61] Under the language of the standard commercial policy, if a system or appliance does not "break apart" or "crack," there is no coverage.[62]

There is a phenomenon known as the "water hammer" effect. It "results from a sudden increase in water pressure, which can burst water mains and pipes."[63] In a post-Katrina case, an insurer claimed that water hammer damages were not covered under a commercial all-risk policy. The Louisiana Supreme Court replied tersely that the insurer had failed to point to an exclu-

---

57. *See* Change, Inc. v. Westfield Ins. Co., 208 W. Va. 654, 542 S.E.2d 475 (2000), where a municipal water main ruptured and damaged the insured property. In finding coverage, the court highlighted the words "any part," but did not discuss them. The implication is that "any part of a system" includes a system that is not on the insured property. The West Virginia Supreme Court also compared the accidental discharge or leakage coverage to the standard water damage exclusion. The exclusion applied to damage from water under the ground surface pressing on or flowing or seeping through foundations. It was not clear, said the court, whether the accidental discharge or leakage coverage applied to a system containing water that was wholly or partially underground. That created an ambiguity that had to be construed in favor of coverage. Therefore, applying the doctrine of *noscitur a sociis* in which the meaning of a general word may be known from the meaning of accompanying specific words, the court said the words of the exclusion—flood, waves, tides—referred to water arising from natural causes, while the accidental discharge or leakage coverage referred to human-made structures.

58. Kimmel v. Nationwide Mut. Ins. Co., 1992 U.S. Dist. LEXIS 329 (E.D. Pa. Jan. 14, 1992) (where source of water seeping into building was abandoned water line connected to water main, there was no leak in insured's water system; water main did not at any time service the insured building).

59. *Break apart*, The Free Dictionary, https://www.thefreedictionary.com/break+apart.

60. *Ballentine's Law Dictionary* (LexisNexis 2010).

61. Icarus Holdings 2, LLC v. AmGUARD Ins. Co., 2022 U.S. Dist. LEXIS 81662 (N.D. Ill. May 5, 2022).

62. *See, e.g.*, Scottsdale Ins. Co. v. Sally Group, LLC, 2012 U.S. Dist. LEXIS 47532 (S.D. Tex. Apr. 3, 2012) (no evidence that air-conditioning system leaked or broke apart; rather, cause of loss was that humidifier had been incorrectly assembled).

63. Sher v. Lafayette Ins. Co., 973 So. 2d 39, 58, n.7 (La. App. 2007).

sion that would preclude coverage for those damages and that absent a valid exclusion, it was impossible "to determine that the trial court committed error in awarding 'water hammer' damages."[64] There do not appear to be any other reported decisions in which carriers have attempted to assert a "water hammer" exclusion.

[e] Described Premises

The ISO commercial property "water damage" provision covers accidental discharge or leakage of water as the result of breaking apart or cracking of a system or appliance located on the *described premises*, meaning the premises named on the Declarations Page. The comparable homeowners policy does not cover water damage caused by accidental discharge or overflow that occurs *off the residence premises*. In both provisions, it should be noted, ownership of the system or appliance is not at issue, only its location.

Even when the policy language does not specify the location of the appliance or system, coverage may be denied where that appliance or system is not located at the insured premises. For example, there was a shack containing a toilet on the premises adjoining the insured property. A water pipe under the floor of that shack, which was part of the toilet plumbing, broke about four feet from the foundation wall of the insured building, allowing water to escape and seep through the wall into the basement of the insured property, where it damaged stored merchandise. The policy covered the accidental discharge, leakage, or overflow of water from within, *inter alia*, plumbing systems. The court agreed with the insurer that there was no coverage because all of the water damage sources covered were obviously intended to be on or in and certainly related to, the insured property.[65]

[3] Continuous or Repeated Seepage or Leakage Exception

An exception to water damage coverage is for loss or damage caused by or resulting from continuous or repeated seepage or leakage of water, or humidity,

64. Sher v. Lafayette Ins. Co., 988 So. 2d 186, 206 (La. 2008).

65. Fine v. Underwriters of Lloyd's London, 239 F.2d 362 (3d Cir. 1956). *See also* Pichel v. Dryden Mut. Ins. Co., 117 A.D.3d 1267, 1269, 986 N.Y.S.2d 268, 271 (2014) (plumbing system, as referenced in coverage provision, referred to rains on insured property). *And see* Kozlowski v. Penn Mut. Ins. Co., 295 Pa. Super. 141, 441 A.2d 388 (1982), where the policy covered "[a]ccidental discharge, leakage or overflow of water or steam from within a plumbing, heating or air conditioning system or from within a domestic appliance." A curb valve at the water main to the service line leading to a neighbor's property burst and released water that seeped into and flooded the basement at the insured property. The policyholder argued the loss was covered because "a plumbing system" meant *any* plumbing system. The court, however, found no coverage. The cause of the water leakage, it said, was a burst valve at the water main to the service line belonging to the house next door, and that line was unconnected to the insured property.

moisture, or vapor, occurring over 14 days or more. This also appears in policies as an exclusion, which is discussed elsewhere.[66]

[4] Frozen Pipes or Appliances Exception

[a] Introduction[67]

A pipe that freezes and then bursts can release hundreds of gallons of water per hour and lead to major flooding.[68] A usual exception to the limited water damage coverage for "accidental discharge or leakage of water or steam as the direct result of the breaking apart or cracking of a plumbing, heating, air conditioning or other system or appliance" "is for loss or damage caused by or resulting from *freezing*, unless the insured (1) "does its best" or "uses reasonable care" or exercises "due diligence" to maintain heat in the building or structure or (2) drains the equipment and shuts off the supply if heat is not maintained.[69] The exclusion is discussed elsewhere.[70]

A policy may also explicitly cover direct physical loss to property insured caused by freezing of a plumbing, heating or air-conditioning system or of a household appliance, unless the insured has failed to maintain heat in the building or shut off the water supply and drained the system and appliances of water.

In the case of the freezing exclusion, as with all exclusions, the general rule is that the insurance carrier bears the burden of proving the exclusion applies,[71] while the insured has the burden to prove the exception governs.[72]

---

66. See § 2.9, *supra*. See also § 3.5[6][e], *infra*, discussing application of the exclusion to water damage from an opening in a roof or wall, and § 3.10[5], regarding ensuing losses.

67. *See generally* Cozen, *Insuring Real Property*, § 4.05[4][b] (LexisNexis Matthew Bender 2022).

68. *The Big Freeze: 5 Signs Your Pipes are Frozen and How to Thaw Them* (Mar. 2, 2015), Mogil Organization, https://mogil.com/the-big-freeze-5-signs-your-pipes-are-frozen-and-how-to-thaw-them/. *See, e.g.*, Katopothis v. Windsor-Mount Joy Mut. Ins. Co., 905 F.3d 661 (D.C. App. 2018) (damage for which insured sought coverage was caused by flooding from frozen plumbing discovered when insured returned to beach home to find two inches of standing water throughout main level and additional water "gushing" from ceiling overhead); Farrell v. American Intl. Ins. Co., 2010 N.Y. Misc. LEXIS 2110 (2010) (basement flooded up to top of stairs).

69. ISO Form CP 10 20 04 02, § A.14.a.

70. See § 2.10, *supra*.

71. Van Natta v. Great Lakes Reinsurance (UK) SE, 2021 U.S. Dist. LEXIS 112637 (D. Conn. June 16, 2021). *But see* Place v. Preferred Mut. Ins. Co., 190 A.D.3d 1208, 141 N.Y.S.3d 528 (2021) (even assuming that policy covered damage to dwelling despite it not being her primary residence, plaintiff still had to prove that no exclusion precluded coverage; insured had to show that she took reasonable care to maintain heat in home while it was unoccupied, and insurer would then have to demonstrate triable issue of fact that reasonable care was not used to maintain heat in premises so that exclusion would prevent coverage).

72. Jugan v. Econ. Premier Assurance Co., 728 F. App'x 86 (3d Cir. 2018) (after insurer shows exclusion applies, burden shifts back to insured to prove exception to exclusion, such that damages claimed are covered notwithstanding exclusion); Wells v. State Farm Fire & Cas.

When the policy covers water damage from freezing incidents, the insured would generally have the burden to show coverage and the insurer has the burden then to prove exception—which is usually treated as an exclusion—is applicable.[73]

Some versions of the exclusion or exception apply only when the insured building[74] or structure is "vacant, unoccupied or being constructed." Policies that use that language almost always also provide coverage when reasonable care is exercised to maintain heat or shut off water and drain pipes. Therefore, the property doesn't have to be occupied at the time of the loss.[75]

It is important to ascertain what property is covered or excluded from coverage by a freezing clause. For example, a policy covered direct physical loss to *property insured* caused by freezing of a plumbing, heating or air-conditioning system or of a household appliance, but not a loss on the *dwelling premises* while vacant, unoccupied, or being constructed unless the insured has maintained heat in the building or shut off the water supply and drained the system and appliances of water. The insurer argued this was intended to provide coverage for a plumbing system that ruptured, but not for any damage to the house itself. The court said the plain meaning of the policy indicated otherwise. The policy provided coverage for the *insured property* against losses caused by the named perils and the *insured property* was the house. In other words, the freezing clause insured the *house* against damage caused by the freezing of a plumbing system.[76]

Even though water damage from freezing may be covered by the language of a policy, the insurer may contend that another exclusion bars coverage. For example, in a Missouri appellate case, pipes froze and broke, causing water to run under the foundation and carport of the insured home. The water then froze again, causing the foundation and carport to raise and suffer damage.

Ins. Co., 447 Ill. Dec. 259, 173 N.E.3d 613 (Ill. App. 2021) (insureds have burden to prove that exception to exclusion restores coverage).

73. Van Natta v. Great Lakes Reinsurance (UK) SE, 2021 U.S. Dist. LEXIS 112637 (D. Conn. June 16, 2021) (burden of establishing that Heat Exception to Freezing Exclusion applies is on insured). *But see* Caldwell v. Allstate Prop. Ins. Cas. Co., 2018 U.S. Dist. LEXIS 182529 (N.D. Ohio Oct. 24, 2018) (according to insurer, provision constitutes exception to an exclusion and insured, therefore, bears burden of proof, while insured claimed that entirety of provision constitutes exclusion, for which the insurer bears burden of proof; court concluded it did not need to address the issue).

74. Some policies will apply the condition when the insured building *or any living unit* within the building is vacant, unoccupied, or under construction. *See, e.g.*, Manco v. Cumberland Mut. Fire Ins. Co., 2020 U.S. Dist. LEXIS 80416 (D.N.J. May 7, 2020).

75. Hidalgo v. Mason Ins. Agency, Inc., 2005 Mich. App. LEXIS 1377 (Mich. App. 2005) (if coverage were available only if insured was using property as permanent residence at time of loss, policy would not have to limit exclusion to unheated vacant dwellings; coverage is not excluded where insured property is left temporarily vacant or unoccupied and reasonable care is made to maintain heat in building).

76. Kent v. Farm Bur. Mut. Ins. Co., 127 Idaho 776, 906 P.2d 146 (1995).

The insurer argued that there was no coverage for the damage because of the exclusion for water below the surface of the ground, including water that exerts pressure on, or seeps or leaks through a building, sidewalk, driveway, foundation, swimming pool or other structure. However, the court found that the exclusion applied only to damage resulting from "natural water," and remanded for entry of a judgment in favor of the insured.[77]

[b] Meaning of "Frozen" Pipes

Policies do not define "freezing." The Merriam-Webster online dictionary defines the word to mean "being at or below the temperature at which water freezes" and "the temperature at which water freezes."[78] Does a pipe or appliance have to freeze solid for the freezing exclusion to apply? That is not clear either from the language of policies or from the dictionary definition. In one case relying on a federal government tariff schedule for products, a court found that frozen meant "frozen throughout."[79] Courts, however, have not required a litigant to show that a pipe or appliance was frozen solid. It is usually sufficient to show that water damage was caused by freezing.

Sometimes a roof will be damaged by wind. That damage allows cold air to enter and freeze pipes. When the policy covers wind, but not water, damage, is the frozen pipe "wind damage?" In one case, for example, a policyholder claimed wind blew a hatch cover off a roof exposing adjacent water pipes to strong cold winds and that as a result, they froze and burst. Later, when the pipes thawed, water entered the insured building. In *dicta*, the court asserted that the action of wind was too remote from the actual damage to come within the policy coverage. Direct wind damage, it said, couldn't be understood as a frozen pipe. Rather "loss as direct result of wind" means damage from the strength or force of wind and, therefore, there was no coverage.[80]

---

77. Jones v. Columbia Mut. Ins. Co., 700 S.W.2d 187 (Mo. App. 1985).

78. *Freezing*, Merriam-Webster, https://www.merriam-webster.com/dictionary/freezing.

79. Mondiv, Div. of Lassonde Specialties Inc. v. United States, 329 F. Supp. 3d 1331, 1340 (Ct. Intl. Trade 2018) (Harmonized Tariff Schedule of the United States defines "frozen" as when product has been cooled to below its freezing point until it is frozen throughout).

80. Abady v. Hanover Fire Ins. Co., 266 F.2d 362, 364 (4th Cir. 1959). The policy says the insurer would be "liable for loss to the interior of the building or the property covered therein as may be caused by water, rain, snow, sand or dust entering the building through openings in the roof or walls made by direct action of wind." That raises a question about the court's reasoning. The damage to the roof according to the insured *was* caused by the force of wind blowing off the hatch cover. The freezing and thawing, on the other hand, was not the direct result of the *force* of wind. As the court said, to find coverage because the chemical or physical properties of moving air absorbing and carrying away heat and facilitating freezing would be too strained an interpretation. *See also* Williams v. Liberty Mut. Fire Ins. Co., 334 Mass. 499, 501, 135 N.E.2d 910, 911 (1956) (agreeing that when shutter over louver in building loft was ripped off during windstorm, allowing water pipe in loft to freeze and burst, causing water damage inside home, pipe was not damaged as direct result of wind and, therefore, loss was not covered). *Compare* Granchelli v. Travelers Ins. Co., 167 A.D.2d 839, 561 N.Y.S.2d 944 (1990) (windstorm was not

[c] Standards of Care

[i] "Uses Reasonable Care"

Most policies require the policyholder to "use reasonable care" to maintain heat for there to be coverage for damage from frozen pipes or appliances.[81] Courts universally agree that "reasonable care" means the care a reasonably prudent person would exercise under the same or similar circumstances.[82] Courts, however, do not agree on whether "reasonable care" is ambiguous.[83] Moreover, because coverage decisions have to be made on a case-by-case basis,[84] it has been said that it is "impossible to define what constitutes 'reasonable care' in any one situation."[85]

Whether an insured acted reasonably in maintaining heat is an objective inquiry.[86] For example, an insured homeowner moved out of the house while it was for sale. She neither maintained sufficient heating oil in the tank nor had anyone regularly check on the amount of oil in the tank between November and the following January when the oil supply was exhausted, allowing pipes to freeze and burst. The court noted that the insured was in her mid-eighties

---

too remote to be considered direct cause of loss when it blew open roof door, allowing subzero air to enter building and freeze pipe that subsequently burst, causing water damage).

81. One other standard of care found in a few policies is "necessary and ongoing care." *See, e.g.*, Manco v. Cumberland Mut. Fire Ins. Co., 2020 U.S. Dist. LEXIS 80416 (D.N.J. May 7, 2020).

82. Walker v. AMTRAK, 703 F. Supp. 2d 495, 502 (D. Md. 2010) (quoting Maryland Civil Pattern Jury Instructions); Hawbaker v. Danner, 226 F.2d 843, 847 (7th Cir. 1955); Gaston v. Parsons, 318 Ore. 247, 256, 864 P.2d 1319, 1324 (1994); Bean v. BIC Corp., 597 So. 2d 1350, 1353 (Ala. 1992) (quoting Alabama Pattern Jury Instructions); Chadwick v. Ek, 1 Wn.2d 117, 129, 95 P.2d 398, 403 (1939); Bradford v. Copleman, 11 N.J. Misc. 876, 877, 168 A. 732, 733 (N.J. 1933) (reasonable care does not mean extraordinary care); York v. Everton, 135 Mo. App. 607, 116 S.W. 490 (1909).

83. McAleavey v. Chautauqua Patrons Ins. Co., 195 A.D.3d 1551, 148 N.Y.S.3d 322 (2021) ("reasonable care" as used in policy is ambiguous inasmuch as it is susceptible of at least two reasonable interpretations); Dooley v. Scottsdale Ins. Co., 2015 U.S. Dist. LEXIS 19140 (D.N.J. Feb. 18, 2015) ("reasonable care" is unambiguous); McCartney v. Pawtucket Mut. Ins. Co., 1994 Conn. Super. LEXIS 3293 (Dec. 23, 1994) (while application of term "reasonable care" to specific factual circumstances may at times be difficult, meaning of that term is not ambiguous). *See also* Van Natta v. Great Lakes Reinsurance (UK) SE, 2021 U.S. Dist. LEXIS 112637 (D. Conn. June 16, 2021) (question of whether insured acted as reasonably prudent person would under the circumstances is highly fact specific).

84. *See* Jugan v. Econ. Premier Assurance Co., 728 F. App'x 86 (3d Cir. 2018) (issue of reasonable care very often demands fact-intensive inquiry); Van Natta v. Great Lakes Reinsurance (UK) SE, 2021 U.S. Dist. LEXIS 112637 (D. Conn. June 16, 2021) (question of whether insured acted as reasonably prudent person would under the circumstances is highly fact specific); Billitier v. Merrimack Mut. Fire Ins. Co., 777 F. Supp. 2d 488, 491 (W.D.N.Y. 2011) (in ordinary case, resolution of whether actions are "reasonable" requires sufficiently fact-intensive analysis to preclude summary judgment).

85. Dooley v. Scottsdale Ins. Co., 2015 U.S. Dist. LEXIS 19140 (D.N.J. Feb. 18, 2015).

86. Van Natta v. Great Lakes Reinsurance (UK) SE, 462 F. Supp. 3d 113, 126 (D. Conn. 2020).

and bound to a wheel chair, which undoubtedly impeded her ability to care for her property. However, said the court, the standard of reasonable care is an objective not a subjective one. The insured failed to exercise reasonable care to maintain heat and, thus, coverage for damage caused by water from the damaged pipes was excluded.[87]

Insurers sometimes attempt to apply what is in effect *res ipsa loquitor* and argue that if pipes freeze and the insured cannot present evidence of an intervening cause—for example, a power outage—then clearly the insured did not use reasonable care to maintain heat. One court rejecting that argument said that when evaluating the objective reasonableness of behavior, one must look at how an ordinary reasonable person would have acted to ensure that the temperature remained above freezing.[88] Therefore, the question is not what an expert believes to be an appropriate heat setting, but rather whether an ordinary policyholder of average intelligence would think that reasonable care has been employed.[89]

Often, there is conflicting evidence on the question of reasonable care, and a jury must determine the issue.[90] However, in other cases it can be determined as a matter of law. For example, where the insured failed to inspect the unoccupied property or take other actions to ensure it was properly heated,

---

87. McCartney v. Pawtucket Mut. Ins. Co., 1994 Conn. Super. LEXIS 3293 (Dec. 23, 1994). *See also* Ferrell v. Nationwide Mut. Ins. Co., 2011 Ohio App. LEXIS 2861 (July 7, 2011) (where insured stated that, because of health issues, she did not do anything in regard to maintenance of property, relied on her brother to take control of it, and was not aware property was vacant, finding of trial court that insured did not act with reasonable care was proper).

88. Dooley v. Scottsdale Ins. Co., 2015 U.S. Dist. LEXIS 19140 (D.N.J. Feb. 18, 2015) (if insurer intended to allow coverage for damage caused by freezing pipes only when some proven "extenuating circumstance" caused pipes to freeze, insurer should have made that explicit in policy). *Compare* Read Prop. Grp. LLC v. Hamilton Ins. Co., 2018 U.S. Dist. LEXIS 54734 (E.D.N.Y. Mar. 30, 2018) (where endorsement imposed duty on insured to keep ambient temperature throughout any covered building at or above 50 degrees, pipes freezing was evidence that insured failed to meet the requirement, and there was no coverage when insured failed to introduce contrary evidence).

89. Short v. North Pointe Ins. Co., 2013 U.S. Dist. LEXIS 61368 (S.D. Ind. Apr. 29, 2013).

90. *See, e.g.*, Cecero v. Allstate Ins. Co., 303 Fed. Appx. 111 (3d Cir. 2008) (there was ample conflicting evidence from which reasonable jury could have decided that reasonable care had not been used and, therefore, trial judge wrongfully found as matter of law that reasonable care had been used); Billitier v. Merrimack Mut. Fire Ins. Co., 777 F. Supp. 2d 488 (W.D.N.Y. 2011) (insured's actions to ensure provision and continuation of electric service to property when it was unoccupied, reasonableness of insured's reliance on statements by utility about request for power restoration, impact of failure by utility to ever notify insured that it had been unable to restore service, and reasonableness of insured's decision not to drain the plumbing or provide for an interim heat source, viewed in light of prevailing weather conditions, which were alleged to have been unseasonably warm, presented material questions of fact best reserved for jury); Place v. Preferred Mut. Ins. Co., 190 A.D.3d 1208, 141 N.Y.S.3d 528 (2021) (although insured testified that she left thermostat at 55 degrees and her mother asserted that she checked on house, insurer cited significant increase in electric usage and broken window, of which insured was aware, as evidence of frozen plumbing; neither party was entitled to summary judgment).

summary judgment for the insurer was proper.[91] Where the insured left the insured property unattended, even though he knew the electrical bills were astronomical and that the furnace's pilot light had gone out in the past, the failure of the insured to take reasonable care to maintain heat at the property was established as a matter of law.[92] On the other hand, where a recently installed heating system in a seasonal home failed, allowing pipes to freeze, but the insured regularly maintained the system, winterized the property by setting the internal temperature to approximately 50 degrees, and checked on the home approximately 15 times during the winter, the court found the efforts of the insured to maintain heat were reasonable, albeit unsuccessful.[93]

[ii] "Does Its Best"

Some policies require the policyholder "do its best" to maintain heat for there to be coverage for damage from frozen pipes or appliances. "Best" is not defined. Courts have equated "best" with "best efforts,"[94] a phrase used in many commercial contracts. It is a "heightened duty to perform an obligation

---

91. Matter of Stephenson v. Allstate Indem. Co., 160 A.D.3d 1274, 73 N.Y.S.3d 804 (2018), *app. den.*, 84 N.Y.S.3d 858, 32 N.Y.3d 904, 109 N.E.3d 1158 (2018) (insured failed, as a matter of law, to use reasonable care to maintain heat in premises while it was unoccupied for three months during winter heating season, because she did not arrange for inspection of premises or take any other action to ensure that adequate levels of heat were actually maintained during that time period). *See also* Jugan v. Econ. Premier Assurance Co., 728 F. App'x 86 (3d Cir. 2018) (insureds could not establish exercise of reasonable care by showing lack of previous freezing; summary judgment for insurer); Pazianas v. Allstate Ins. Co., 2016 U.S. Dist. LEXIS 92796 (E.D. Pa. July 18, 2016) (summary judgment for insurer because even if insured asked his daughter to inspect property, set thermostat before departing, and did not intend to be away for more than two months, no reasonable juror could find that insured used reasonable care to maintain heat in property during its vacancy); Elkin v. State Farm Ins. Co., 2013 U.S. Dist. LEXIS 92504 (D. Minn. July 2, 2013) (summary judgment for insurer where insureds' did not use reasonable care to maintain heat because they ignored warnings from utility, ignored bills showing no gas usage, and did not respond with any urgency when their realtor told them house was very cold); Brennor v. Metropolitan Prop. & Cas. Ins., 2014 N.Y. Misc. LEXIS 4888 (2014) (where insured was repeatedly warned that utility company would terminate gas and electric service if she did not pay a certain amount and she did not contact company to dispute or even address amount that was supposedly due, she failed to use reasonable care to maintain heat at premises as a matter of law); Evangelista v. Hingham Mut. Fire Ins. Co., 2005 Mass. Super. LEXIS 57 (Feb. 14, 2005) (where bills from electric company showed there was no electricity usage during winter months, given frigid temperatures, reasonable person would have been alerted to problem and would have either checked vacant summer home or asked someone to do so for them; court found insureds did not take reasonable care to maintain the heat at their unoccupied house).

92. Van Natta v. Great Lakes Reinsurance (UK) SE, 2021 U.S. Dist. LEXIS 112637 (D. Conn. June 16, 2021). *See also* Dougherty v. Allstate Prop. & Cas. Ins. Co., 185 F. Supp. 3d 585, 597 (E.D. Pa.), *aff'd*, 681 Fed. Appx. 112 (3d Cir. 2016) (summary judgment for insurer where damage from frozen plumbing could be attributed to failure of insured to sufficiently maintain furnace and insured produced insufficient evidence to contradict that conclusion).

93. McAleavey v. Chautauqua Patrons Ins. Co., 195 A.D.3d 1551, 148 N.Y.S.3d 322 (2021).

94. *See, e.g.*, Business Health Prop. v. Millers Capital Ins. Co., 2010 U.S. Dist. LEXIS 118400 (N.D. Ohio Nov. 4, 2010).

under a contract . . . [and] is more than reasonable efforts. [It requires] reasonable foresight and contingency plans to overcome obstacles to performance.[95] On the other hand, there are courts that said that "best efforts" is the equivalent of "reasonable efforts."[96] At least one court has held that "do its best" is ambiguous and when construed against in favor of the insured means "reasonable efforts."[97] Another court found that "do your best" is not ambiguous.[98]

One court has said that "[w]hile . . . 'do your best' may not preclude summary judgment where there is zero evidence of an insured doing anything which could be considered 'its best' . . . where Plaintiff has demonstrated some action and intentionality with regards to keeping heat on . . . , the question is a term of degree presenting a factual question that a jury must resolve."[99] In another case the insured used electric heat to maintain the temperature in the insured building at between 45 and 50 degrees and kept boiler pumps circulating water in the system. The loss occurred in early November, before temperatures typically became extremely cold, and the insured had been in the building shortly before the loss and had found the temperature sufficient to prevent freezing. Given that evidence, an appellate court could not say that the trial court was clearly erroneous in finding that the insured applied its *best*

---

95. *The Wolters Kluwer Bouvier Law Dictionary Desk Edition* (CCH Inc., 2012). ***But see*** Business Health Prop. v. Millers Capital Ins. Co., 2010 U.S. Dist. LEXIS 118400 (N.D. Ohio Nov. 4, 2010), where the policyholder said it was obligated to use "reasonable efforts" or "due diligence," and the court appeared to agree.

96. Wells v. State Farm Fire & Cas. Ins. Co., 447 Ill. Dec. 259, 173 N.E.3d 613 (Ill. App. 2021) (interpreting phrase "do your best" as requiring reasonable efforts to maintain heat and that reasonable efforts are to be measured in light of specific circumstances faced); Auto-Owners Ins. Co. v. Hansen Hous., Inc., 604 N.W.2d 504, 512 (S.D. 2000) (insured did its "best" if its actions were reasonable under the circumstances, and it was not required to take extraordinary measures). *See also* Me. State Props., LLC v. Chubb Custom Ins. Co., 2016 U.S. Dist. LEXIS 89175 (D. Me. July 8, 2016).

97. Sonrob Hosts, LLC v. Lafayette Insurance Co., 2012 U.S. Dist. LEXIS 154085 (W.D. Ark. Oct. 26, 2012) ("do your best" clause cannot be construed so as to mandate that policyholder go beyond exercising good business judgment to heat every room in motel at all times, regardless of whether motel is open for business and regardless of whether reasonable method is available that would maintain heat at adequate level throughout building).

98. Cont'l W. Ins. Co. v. Paul Reid, LLP, GPS, Inc., 292 Wis. 2d 674, 680–81, 715 N.W.2d 689, 692 (Wisc. App. 2006).

99. Brandy Ventures, LLC v. Mesa Underwriters Specialty Ins. Co., 2019 U.S. Dist. LEXIS 208898, at *11 (E.D. Tex. Nov. 13, 2019). The insurer in *Brandy Ventures* contended the insured did nothing to maintain heat. The damaged property was one of 48 rental properties owned and insured by the policyholder. The court found the insured sufficiently demonstrated that after a tenant evacuated the property, the utilities were transferred to the insured, construction/renovations ensued, and employees or representatives of the insured visited the property numerous times to supervise the work. Further, the insured argued that it provided a heat source at the other 47 occupied units covered by the policy, which suggested it was "doing its best" by attempting to maintain heat at all of the units, even though it failed to do so at the property issue. The policyholder characterized that failure as a "mistake amongst diligent efforts rather than a history of ignoring the issue of heat to the units."

efforts to maintain heat in the building.[100] On the other hand, where employees of the insured made visits to the unoccupied property and the insured called the gas company and requested propane service on an automatic-fill basis in which the company kept a gas tank at a certain minimum level, but the company instead provided will-call service requiring the customer to call to request gas delivery as needed, an appellate court affirmed the finding of a jury that the insured had not done its best to maintain heat.[101]

[iii] Exercised Due Diligence

A few polices exclude loss resulting from freezing unless the insured has "exercised due diligence with respect to maintaining heat" in the insured building. For the most part these are policies that were issued in the 1960s, 70s, or 80s. "Due diligence" is defined as "The customary investigation and care required in the circumstances . . . a level of inquiry and care that includes responding to known dangers, determining unknown but reasonably predictable dangers, assessing such dangers, and taking reasonable steps to cure the potential for harm each danger poses."[102] The Merriam-Webster online dictionary says it is "the care that a reasonable person exercises to avoid harm to other persons or their property."[103]

Policies that use "due diligence" as a standard of care almost always limit the freezing exclusion to buildings that are vacant, unoccupied, or under construction. If the court finds that none of those descriptors applies, "due diligence" is not at issue.[104]

[d] Maintain Heat, Shut Off Water, and Drain Pipes

The words "maintain heat" have been found not to be ambiguous.[105] One court has said that to "maintain heat, is 'to keep in an existing state'—a task that can be 'ongoing'" and that to maintain *adequate* heat means ensuring the temperature "remained above freezing."[106] The duty to maintain heat is separate from the duty to shut off the water and drain pipes—in other words, if the

---

100. Auto-Owners Ins. Co. v. Hansen Hous., Inc., 604 N.W.2d 504, 512 (S.D. 2000).

101. Cont'l W. Ins. Co. v. Paul Reid, LLP, GPS, Inc., 292 Wis. 2d 674, 715 N.W.2d 689 (Wisc. App. 2006).

102. *The Wolters Kluwer Bouvier Law Dictionary Desk Edition* (CCH Inc., 2012).

103. *Due Diligence*, Merriam-Webster, https://www.merriam-webster.com/dictionary/due%20diligence.

104. Smith v. Lumbermen's Mut. Ins. Co., 101 Mich. App. 78, 300 N.W.2d 457 (1980).

105. Manco v. Cumberland Mut. Fire Ins. Co., 2020 U.S. Dist. LEXIS 80416 (D.N.J. May 7, 2020); Dooley v. Scottsdale Ins. Co., 2015 U.S. Dist. LEXIS 19140 (D.N.J. Feb. 18, 2015). *See also* Read Prop. Grp. LLC v. Hamilton Ins. Co., 2018 U.S. Dist. LEXIS 54734 (E.D.N.Y. Mar. 30, 2018) (meaning of term "maintain" is unambiguous as used in endorsement that clearly imposes duty on insured to keep ambient temperature throughout any covered building at or above 50 degrees).

106. Manco v. Cumberland Mut. Fire Ins. Co., 2020 U.S. Dist. LEXIS 80416, at *13 (D.N.J. May 7, 2020).

insured properly shuts off the water and drains pipes, there is no requirement to maintain heat.[107] The duty to use the prescribed standard of care to turn off water and the duty to use that care in draining a system are also two different duties and require different actions.[108] The insured must fulfill both duties to obtain coverage.[109] Policies use the word "drained," which is in the past tense and, thus, requires that winterization be complete.[110] It is possible that despite the exercise of the required standard of care, a loss was unavoidable because of extremely cold temperatures and, therefore, that loss should be covered.[111]

The Massachusetts Supreme Judicial Court gave an ostensibly contradictory interpretation to the meaning of "maintain heat." The insureds consulted a licensed heating contractor who told them that their hot water heating system could not be adequately or completely drained and that the proper way to protect the system was to use a sufficient amount of anti-freeze to prevent freezing. They hired the contractor to winterize the system with anti-freeze. Despite the contractor's actions, fluid in the hot water system froze, causing pipes to burst and the home to be damaged. The court said that the reasonable implication of the contractor's advice was that with the use of anti-freeze, no heat would be required in the house and, thus, the court held the insureds exercised the prescribed standard of care for "maintaining heat." The court added that had insurer wished to exclude use of anti-freeze by a licensed heating contractor, a more explicit prohibition of that method should have been stated.[112] The problem with the court's opinion is that the use of anti-freeze is not a method of "maintaining heat"; it is a substitute for "maintaining heat," and the policy explicitly required the insured to maintain heat. Nonetheless, over 50 years later, a federal judge when presented with similar facts followed the state court and found for the insureds.[113]

---

107. Ft. Worth Lloyds Ins. Co. v. Willham, 406 S.W.2d 76 (Tex. App. 1966).

108. Weber v. Farmers Ins. Co., 290 P.3d 686 (Kan. App. 2012) (insured may have used reasonable care to shut off water, but did not use reasonable care to drain plumbing system of water).

109. Fulton v. Beacon Nat. Ins. Co., 416 S.W.3d 759, 762–63 (Ark. App. 2012) (even if there were a fact question as to whether insured appellant used reasonable care to shut off water supply, it was undisputed that he did not make any effort to drain plumbing system or appliances and use of conjunctive "and" in freezing clause makes clear that to prove coverage, insured also would have had to show that he used reasonable care to drain system and appliances of water, and it was undisputed that he took no steps to do so).

110. Manco v. Cumberland Mut. Fire Ins. Co., 2020 U.S. Dist. LEXIS 80416, at *14 (D.N.J. May 7, 2020) ("ongoing" efforts to winterize property are insufficient to trigger exception to freezing exclusion).

111. Haardt v. Farmer's Mut. Fire Ins. Co., 796 F. Supp. 804, 806 (D.N.J. 1992) (finder of fact would have to determine what actions, if any, were taken to prevent freezing and whether freezing was unavoidable despite those actions due to extremely cold temperatures).

112. Palmer v. Pawtucket Mut. Ins. Co., 352 Mass. 304, 225 N.E.2d 331 (1967).

113. *See* Certain Underwriters at Lloyd's v. Walley, 457 F. Supp. 3d 1 (D. Mass. 2020), where the insured home was heated by a propane-fired, forced hot water heating system that required electricity to operate. The home lost power during a winter storm while the insureds were away.

In an Arkansas case, a motel owner chose to maintain heat in the building by "cross heating," a commonly used system in which heaters in certain parts of the building are left on when the motel is closed to customers for the winter. The reasoning behind cross heating is that, by turning on the heat in selected rooms, that heat will cross heat rooms where the heat is turned off and maintain sufficient warmth in the building overall to prevent pipes from freezing. The court concluded that cross heating was a reasonable method to maintain heat in a building to prevent pipes from freezing and, therefore, the policyholder acted reasonably by employing the cross-heating system and did its best to maintain heat.[114]

[e] Reliance on Third Parties

Can a policyholder who is away from the property rely on a property manager, caretaker, friends, neighbors, or family to maintain heat or drain systems?

Some courts say the duty to use reasonable care or do one's best cannot be delegated. For example, one federal judge said that "[w]hen an insurance policy imposes a duty upon an insured to maintain heat in a property, the insured cannot delegate that duty to another by agreement with a third person."[115] The failure of the third party to meet the requirements of the policy can be imputed to the insured.[116] However, some courts hold that if the insured exercises the required standard of care in instructing a third party, the failure of that third party to use that care in carrying out the instructions is not imputed

---

Their professional property caretaker visited the home after the power loss, drained water from the domestic water lines, but did not drain the heating system because in the caretaker's experience it was not necessary to drain the heating system as it was charged with glycol, anti-freeze. Nonetheless, freezing caused the home to flood. The court said that "relying on an experienced caretaker's advice to use anti-freeze to avoid loss effectively constituted reasonable care under the policy to maintain heat in the building."

114. Sonrob Hosts, LLC v. Lafayette Insurance Co., 2012 U.S. Dist. LEXIS 154085 (W.D. Ark. Oct. 26, 2012). *Compare* Wells v. State Farm Fire & Cas. Ins. Co., 447 Ill. Dec. 259, 173 N.E.3d 613 (Ill. App. 2021) (finding for insurer where insured restarted water service to insured building during middle of winter knowing heating system was insufficient to keep pipes from freezing and chose to cordon off small area in building where water pipes were located and temporarily placed space heaters in that area knowing that one or more circuit breakers had tripped in past during extremely cold weather).

115. Pazianas v. Allstate Ins. Co., 2016 U.S. Dist. LEXIS 92796, at *14 (E.D. Pa. July 18, 2016). *See also* Dougherty v. Allstate Prop. & Cas. Ins. Co., 185 F. Supp. 3d 585, 597 (E.D. Pa.), *aff'd*, 681 Fed. Appx. 112 (3d Cir. 2016) (insured could not use fact that lease he once had placed responsibility of maintaining furnace on tenant as evidence that he used reasonable care to maintain his furnace because duty to use reasonable care to maintain heat is one imposed on insured pursuant to policy and cannot be delegated to others).

116. *See* Ferrell v. Nationwide Mut. Ins. Co., 2011 Ohio App. LEXIS 2861 (July 7, 2011) (brother of, and agent for, insured did not act reasonably when he took no action to maintain heat because he assumed tenant had not vacated property and utilities were still on).

to the insured.[117] On the other hand, the insured can be charged with negligence in knowingly choosing an unsuitable agent.[118] Also, the relationship between the principal and agent may determine the extent to which the former can rely on the latter.[119]

The reliance by an insured on a third party may be determined by a court to be reasonable. For example, one federal court said that "relying on an experienced caretaker's advice to use anti-freeze to avoid loss effectively constituted reasonable care under the policy to maintain heat in the building."[120] Reasonableness may also be a jury question, as it was in an Illinois case where the court said that whether it was reasonable for an insured to rely entirely on his property manager, and to not take any corrective action after

---

117. *See* International Ins. Co. v. Reid, 400 S.W.2d 939 (Tex. App. 1966), where the insured gave his ranch foreman very specific instructions for protecting an unoccupied house in extreme weather conditions including maintaining heat and draining pipes. The foreman testified that he had been given those instructions, yet he failed to exercise due diligence to maintain heat in the building and as a result it was damaged. A jury found the insured met the standard of care. On appeal, the insurer contended that although the insured may have personally exercised due diligence, failure of his employee or agent to do so would be binding on the insured and prevent recovery. The insured could not, argued the insurer, delegate the duty to maintain heat in the building without suffering the consequences of failure by the person to whom the duty was delegated to exercise due diligence. The appellate court, however, said that if it had been the intention of the insurer to require diligence of both the insured and his agent or employee, the contract of insurance could have so provided. *See also* JMB Enterprises v. Atlantic Employers Ins. Co., 228 N.J. Super. 610, 550 A.2d 764 (1988) (trial judge erred in assuming that lack of reasonable care by realtor for unoccupied dwelling was imputable to insured because realtor was its agent; if insured's own employee failed to comply with instruction to engage plumbing services to winterize property, that default would have been insured's own, but realtor was not insured's employee but an independent contractor, and if insured was reasonable in retaining services of realtor for purpose of obtaining plumbing services, it was of no consequence regarding obligation under policy, whether realtor in fact undertook that commission properly); Thomas Inv. Co. v. United States Fid. & Guar., 716 S.W.2d 395 (Mo. App. 1986) (affirming trial court holding that policy covered loss sustained when subfreezing temperatures caused rupture of plumbing pipes and radiators and water damage resulted; where units were for sale and unoccupied and owner instructed realtors to leave heat on and set thermostats at 55 degrees, but someone turned thermostats off; court implicitly found owner exercised due diligence with respect to maintaining heat by giving instruction to realtors).

118. Chow v. Merrimack Mut. Fire Ins. Co., 83 Mass. App. Ct. 622, 987 N.E.2d 1275 (2013) (if principal has actual knowledge of unsuitability of agent, principal may be held liable for his or her own negligence in selection of unsuitable agent to take action on his or her behalf).

119. *See, e.g.*, Chow v. Merrimack Mut. Fire Ins. Co., 83 Mass. App. Ct. 622, 987 N.E.2d 1275 (2013) (whether insured used reasonable care to maintain heat in building turned in part on extent to which agent's actions could be imputed to insured and whether principal may be held vicariously liable for failure of agent to use reasonable care depends on nature of their relationship; in master-servant relationship, principal may be held liable for acts of agent under doctrine of *respondeat superior*, while employer of independent contractor is not liable for harm caused to another by independent contractor's negligence, except where employer retained some control over manner in which work was performed).

120. Certain Underwriters at Lloyd's v. Walley, 457 F. Supp. 3d 1 (D. Mass. 2020). *See also* Palmer v. Pawtucket Mut. Ins. Co., 352 Mass. 304, 225 N.E.2d 331 (1967).

receiving utility bills that showed very little gas usage, was a question of fact for the jury.[121]

In a New York case, a property manager restored electric power to the insured building by removing tabs in the electric meter. The manager's rental agent testified that the electricity was on and the furnace blower was operating properly to heat the building. There was, therefore, sufficient evidence that the property manager took reasonable care to maintain heat in the building at the time the plumbing system froze, even though the actions of the property manager may have constituted theft of services. The loss caused by the frozen plumbing system was covered.[122]

[f] Vacant, Unoccupied, or Under Construction

[i] Introduction

In some policies the "water damage"[123] freezing exclusion applies when the insured building is vacant, unoccupied, or under construction *and* the insured fails to maintain heat or shut off water and drain pipes. In that case the first question is, was the insured building vacant, unoccupied, or under construction? Policies rarely define those terms. The meaning of "vacant" and "unoccupied" has been the subject of much litigation. A comprehensive analysis of that jurisprudence is beyond the scope of this treatise but is addressed extensively elsewhere.[124] The discussion below provides a basic definition of the terms and raises issues for consideration. The cases cited concern the freezing exclusion. Counsel should research the law of the pertinent jurisdiction to determine how the terms are defined and be aware that the terms may be given different meaning depending on the type of policy or when a peril or exclusion does not concern freezing.[125]

Even if the policy freezing exclusion omits any reference to vacancy, occupancy, or construction, a policy may have a separate "vacancy" exclusion under which there is no coverage for water damage when the insured property is vacant for a prescribed period of time, typically more than 60 consecutive days.

---

121. Zenk v. State Farm Fire & Cas. Co., 2018 U.S. Dist. LEXIS 241227 (N.D. Ill. Sept. 12, 2018).

122. Gallo v. Midstate Mut. Ins. Co., 45 A.D.3d 1492, 845 N.Y.S.2d 657 (2007).

123. Icarus Holdings 2, LLC v. AmGUARD Ins. Co., 2022 U.S. Dist. LEXIS 81662 (N.D. Ill. May 5, 2022) (term "water damage," although not defined in vacancy condition, is not ambiguous and means damage caused by water).

124. *See* Plitt, et al., *Couch on Insurance*, 3d, §§ 148:73–148:75 (Clark Boardman Callaghan 2022); 4af-134f *Appleman on Insurance Law & Practice Archive*, §§ 2831, *et seq.* (Matthew Bender 2011); Cozen, *Insuring Real Property*, §§ 2.04[12], 1.06[7][e][ii] (LexisNexis Matthew Bender 2022).

125. Langill v. Vt. Mut. Ins. Co., 268 F.3d 46 (1st Cir. 2001) (meaning of "vacancy" depends on type of premises and type of insurance policy); Usewick v. Safeco Ins. Co. of Am., 2013 Mich. App. LEXIS 474 (Mar. 19, 2013) (distinguishing meaning of vacancy in homeowners insurance policies from landlord protection policy).

[ii] "Vacant" Defined

Whether the word "vacant" is ambiguous is something about which courts do not agree.[126] In the Merriam-Webster online dictionary, "vacant" means "not lived in," "not put to use."[127] The definition can also be equated with "unoccupied," as in the case of a law dictionary that defines the term to mean simply "empty; not occupied."[128] Another law dictionary defines the phrase "vacant and unoccupied building" to mean a "building in which no one is living or residing and which is empty for all practical purposes."[129] One authority says the term focuses on whether personal property remains in a building, although a building does not need to be completely empty to be deemed vacant, but may contain abandoned or valueless property.[130] Courts evaluating the freezing exclusion have agreed and said that "a house is vacant when it has no contents."[131] Temporary physical absence from primary residence is generally insufficient to render house vacant,[132] but permanent absence does make the property vacant.[133]

---

126. Hemenway v. American Casualty Co., 215 F. Supp. 103 (W.D. La. 1963) (unambiguous); Smith v. Lumbermen's Mut. Ins. Co., 101 Mich. App. 78, 300 N.W.2d 457 (1980) (ambiguous).

127. *Vacant*, Merriam-Webster, https://www.merriam-webster.com/dictionary/vacant.

128. *The Law Dictionary* (Anderson Publishing Co. 2002). *See also Burton's Legal Thesaurus*, 6th Edition (Matthew Bender & Company, Inc., 2021) (not in use, not occupied, uninhabited, unoccupied, unpossessed, untenanted, unused). However, the classic definitions interpret the terms as being different, with "vacant" meaning "entirely empty" and "unoccupied" meaning lack of habitual presence of human beings. 5 Jeffrey E. Thomas, *New Appleman on Insurance Law Library Edition* § 48.03[10][a] (Matthew Bender 2022). *See also* Myers v. Merrimack Mut. Fire Ins. Co., 788 F.2d 468 (7th Cir. 1986) ("vacant" and "unoccupied" are not synonymous; former means entirely empty, meaning lack of animate or inanimate objects, while latter means lack of habitual presence of human beings).

129. *Ballentine's Law Dictionary* (LexisNexis 2010). *See also The Wolters Kluwer Bouvier Law Dictionary Desk Edition* (CCH, Inc. 2012) (condition of being without an occupant or contents; unoccupied or unused in any meaningful or profitable manner).

130. Cozen, *Insuring Real Property*, § 2.04[12] (LexisNexis Matthew Bender 2022).

131. Hemenway v. American Casualty Co., 215 F. Supp. 103, 104 (W.D. La. 1963) (home is not vacant when family is temporarily absent on ten-day business trip).

132. Monarch Ins. Co. v. Rippy, 369 P.2d 622 (Okla. 1962) (family may be absent from home, for health, pleasure, business, or convenience, for reasonable periods, and house will not, on that account, be considered as vacant); Krajenke v. Preferred Mut. Ins. Co., 68 Mich. App. 211, 242 N.W.2d 70 (1976).

133. Kent v. Farm Bur. Mut. Ins. Co., 127 Idaho 776, 906 P.2d 146 (1995) (where no one lived in house after buyers defaulted on deed of trust and moved out of insured home, house was vacant, according to plain meaning of that term, when the pipe froze).

[iii] "Unoccupied" Defined

Courts disagree over whether the word "unoccupied" is ambiguous.[134] "Unoccupied" means "not lived in; empty."[135] An "unoccupied building" has been defined as one "without animate occupants,"[136] and it is said that the word "unoccupied" is concerned with whether people use the insured building.[137] Synonyms for unoccupied include abandoned, barren, deserted, unfurnished, uninhabited, untenanted, vacant, vacated, and without contents.[138] However, the classic definition of the terms interprets them as different, with "vacant" meaning entirely empty, and "unoccupied" meaning a lack of habitual presence of human beings.[139] Storage of personal belongings does not make a premises occupied.[140]

The Texas Supreme Court said in a case involving the freezing exclusion that "the term 'occupied' has an established meaning in the law of insurance. A house is 'occupied' when human beings habitually live in it as a place of abode; a house is unoccupied when it ceases to be used for living purposes or as a customary place of human habitation. A mere temporary absence from the premises will not render the house 'unoccupied.'"[141] On the other hand,

---

134. Lee-Jordan v. Allstate Indem. Co., 2019 U.S. Dist. LEXIS 116448 (S.D.N.Y. July 12, 2019) (unambiguous); Hemenway v. American Casualty Co., 215 F. Supp. 103 (W.D. La. 1963) (unambiguous); Smith v. Lumbermen's Mut. Ins. Co., 101 Mich. App. 78, 300 N.W.2d 457 (1980) (ambiguous).

135. *Unoccupied*, Merriam-Webster, https://www.merriam-webster.com/dictionary/unoccupied.

136. *Ballentine's Law Dictionary* (LexisNexis 2010).

137. Cozen, *Insuring Real Property*, § 2.04[12] (LexisNexis Matthew Bender 2022).

138. *Burton's Legal Thesaurus*, 6th Edition (Matthew Bender & Company, Inc., 2021).

139. 5 Jeffrey E. Thomas, *New Appleman on Insurance Law Library Edition* § 48.03[10][a] (Matthew Bender 2022).

140. Lee-Jordan v. Allstate Indem. Co., 2019 U.S. Dist. LEXIS 116448 (S.D.N.Y. July 12, 2019) (occupancy requires regular presence of inhabitants, and not simply storage of personal items and belongings).

141. Samuels v. Allstate Prop. & Cas. Ins. Co., 310 F. Supp. 3d 847 (E.D. Mich. 2018) (that insured left her home, which was cold and without heat, and went to stay at her mother's house without returning for two days did not render home "unoccupied" in any meaningful sense; "unoccupied" in insurance context has been defined as lack of habitual presence of human beings); Blaylock v. American Guarantee Bank Liability Ins. Co., 632 S.W.2d 719, 721 (Tex. 1982) (where insured had occupied house as her home, left to spend the night at her son's house, and returned again the next morning, her absence was merely temporary and did not render house unoccupied for purposes of freezing exclusion). *See also* Hemenway v. American Casualty Co., 215 F. Supp. 103 (W.D. La. 1963) (home is not unoccupied when family is temporarily absent on ten-day business trip); Monarch Ins. Co. v. Rippy, 369 P.2d 622 (Okla. 1962) (to constitute occupancy of dwelling house, it is not essential that it be continuously used by family; family may be absent from home, for health, pleasure, business, or convenience, for reasonable periods, and house will not, on that account, be considered as unoccupied); Smith v. Lumbermen's Mut. Ins. Co., 101 Mich. App. 78, 300 N.W.2d 457 (1980) (mere temporary physical absence from house did not render it unoccupied); Krajenke v. Preferred Mut. Ins. Co., 68 Mich. App. 211, 242 N.W.2d 70 (1976) (temporary physical absence from primary

when there is an absence because an insured house ceases to be habitable, the house is "unoccupied," as a matter of law, within the meaning of an exclusion for frozen pipes.[142] A premises is also unoccupied when it has contents but is not dwelt or lived in.[143] A seasonal home may be considered unoccupied.[144]

While polices generally do not define "unoccupied," occasionally a policy or an endorsement will do so. For example, in one case an endorsement defined it as meaning an absence in excess of 72 hours that, the court said, "can only be reasonably read to refer to the absence of people."[145]

[iv] "Under Construction" Defined

"Under construction" simply means "being built."[146] There does not appear to be an appellate decision construing the meaning of "under construction" in the context of a freezing exclusion. The most frequent question raised about the phrase is whether it encompasses repairs, renovations, or additions to a standing building. The Seventh Circuit Court of Appeal has noted that courts generally hold that construction *does not* include repairs, maintenance, reconstruction, or renovation to an already existing structure.[147] At least one expert commentator agrees.[148] Should an insurer argue against that view, the

---

residence was insufficient to render house unoccupied). *Compare* Chow v. Merrimack Mut. Fire Ins. Co., 83 Mass. App. Ct. 622, 987 N.E.2d 1275 (2013) (approving jury instruction stating that building may be unoccupied for short periods of time, even where occupant intends to return, as in the case of vacation home, but that every time a person leave his or her house, the law would say it is unoccupied; one should evaluate whether house was being used as dwelling place at time of the loss, and whether it was occupied as such).

142. Phillips v. Pioneer State Mut. Ins. Co., 1999 Mich. App. LEXIS 1318 (Mar. 23, 1999).

143. Hemenway v. American Casualty Co., 215 F. Supp. 103 (W.D. La. 1963) (property is unoccupied when it has contents but is not dwelt or lived in).

144. *See, e.g.*, McCabe v. Allstate Ins. Co., 260 A.D.2d 850, 688 N.Y.S.2d 764 (1999) (regular presence of inhabitants makes occupancy; rejecting assertion that house was not "unoccupied" because of continuing, albeit seasonal use of premises, where no one resided at or visited house for six-month period).

145. Katopothis v. Windsor-Mount Joy Mut. Ins. Co., 905 F.3d 661 (D.C. App. 2018).

146. *Under construction*, Merriam-Webster, https://www.merriam-webster.com/dictionary/under%20construction. *See generally* Eshoo, *What Constitutes a Dwelling or Building Under Construction or Renovation for Purposes of a Vacancy Exclusion?* (Oct. 8, 2018), Merlin Law Group, https://www.propertyinsurancecoveragelaw.com/2018/10/articles/insurance/what-constitutes-a-dwelling-or-building-under-construction-or-renovation-for-purposes-of-a-vacancy-exclusion/?msclkid=4b581a92cf0e11ec9d64d1a54540a070.

147. Myers v. Merrimack Mut. Fire Ins. Co., 788 F.2d 468 (7th Cir. 1986) (interpreting "construction" in clause stating that building in process of construction would not be considered "vacant"). *But see* Lauco Llc v. Patriot Mut. Ins. Co., 2009 Me. Super. LEXIS 137 (Oct. 14, 2009) (for purposes of vacancy exclusion, construction must be interpreted to include renovation as well as new construction, although construction requires substantial continuing activity by workmen on the premises).

148. *See, e.g.*, Barlow, *Under Construction or Renovation?* (Aug. 29, 2011), PropertyCasualty360, https://www.propertycasualty360.com/2011/08/29/under-construction-or-renovation/?msclkid=4b57fc48cf0e11ec969575d73f058d02 (because dictionary definition of "construct"

insured could point out that had the carrier wanted "under construction" to include repairs, reconstruction, or renovation, it could simply have said so in the policy.

[v] Independent Vacancy Exclusion

Even though water damage caused by frozen pipes or appliances might be covered, a standard vacancy exclusion might bar that coverage. These exclusions eliminate coverage if the building or leased premises where loss or damage occurs has been "vacant" for more than 60 consecutive days. The insurer will then not pay for any loss or damage caused by, *inter alia*, water damage, even if it is a covered cause of loss. Typically, the exclusion states that buildings under *construction or renovation* are not considered "vacant." Policies may have both a vacancy exclusion and a freezing exclusion.[149] Either one may preclude coverage for a loss. Vacancy clauses have been found not to be ambiguous.[150]

Insurers include a vacancy exclusion in policies because unoccupied properties face an increased risk of loss,[151] especially from water damage from frozen pipes because if there were occupants in the insured building, they would likely notice any loss of heat before pipes froze and caused damage.[152]

The vacancy exclusion was at issue in a Michigan case in which, while a walkway removal project was underway, a pipe froze and burst, causing the entire insured facility to be flooded with approximately three inches of water. The insurer denied the claim asserting that the building was vacant at the time of the flooding incident and the walkway removal project did not constitute "construction" or "renovation" that would defeat the vacancy exclusion. The court did not agree and said that under the ordinary meaning of the policy terms, the walkway removal project qualified as "renovation."[153]

Some vacancy exclusions will limit the coverage to certain named perils effective at the "inception of any vacancy or unoccupancy," unless "prior

---

differs from that of "renovate," dwelling is under construction if it is being built from scratch; buildings being renovated already exist and, even though in one sense adding room is new construction, it really is just renovation of existing dwelling).

149. *See, e.g.*, Icarus Holdings 2, LLC v. AmGUARD Ins. Co., 2022 U.S. Dist. LEXIS 81662 (N.D. Ill. May 5, 2022); Balaji Hospitality Group v. Travelers Indem. Co. of Am., 2020 U.S. Dist. LEXIS 30575 (N.D. Ind. Feb. 20, 2020).

150. Lauco Llc v. Patriot Mut. Ins. Co., 2009 Me. Super. LEXIS 137 (Oct. 14, 2009).

151. TRB Investments Inc. v. Fireman s Fund Insurance Co., 145 P.3d 472, 474 (Cal. App. 2006).

152. Lauco Llc v. Patriot Mut. Ins. Co., 2009 Me. Super. LEXIS 137 (Oct. 14, 2009).

153. Farbman Group v. Travelers Ins. Cos., 2006 U.S. Dist. LEXIS 70199 (E.D. Mich. Sept. 28, 2006). *See also* Belich v. Westfield Insurance Co., 2000 Ohio App. LEXIS 6212 (Dec. 29, 2000) (even one day of renovation done within previous 60 days would be sufficient to overcome vacancy clause; removal of stage and some coat racks would be sufficient to constitute renovation).

approval" has been obtained from the insurer. Typically, water damage is not one of the named perils. Thus, where a pipe froze and broke after a tenant moved out of the insured premises, the court said there was no coverage because the insurer was never notified until after the loss and, therefore, never approved coverage beyond the named perils and because water damage was not one of the named perils.[154]

[g] Protective Safeguard Endorsement

A protective safeguards endorsement may be added to policies that require the policyholder to maintain a minimum temperature in the insured building.[155] Typically, the temperature required is 50 or 55 degrees. Losses caused by water damage are then excluded if the insured fails to maintain the minimum temperature.[156] Insureds have argued that they only have to exercise reasonable care, best efforts, or due diligence to maintain the minimum temperature, but courts have held that a standard of care is irrelevant when a specific minimum temperature is stated, even though the principal policy provides coverage for losses caused by frozen pipes or appliances when the insured uses reasonable care, best efforts, or due diligence to maintain heat or shut off water and drain pipes.[157] A protective safeguard provision may specifically exempt from its requirements pipes that are part of a fire protective system.[158]

[h] Evidence

Cases in which water damage from freezing pipes is at issue are especially fact-driven. Evidence that is commonly introduced includes

---

154. Kut Suen Lui v. Essex Ins. Co., 185 Wn.2d 703, 375 P.3d 596 (2016).

155. *See generally* Cozen, *Insuring Real Property*, § 2.07[17] (LexisNexis Matthew Bender 2022).

156. *See, e.g.*, Convention Plaza III, LLC v. Seneca Specialty Insurance Co., 147 A.D.3d 692, 48 N.Y.S.3d 357 (2017) (insurer submitted two expert affidavits stating that freezing water was caused by fact that the HVAC rooftop units were turned off, and the baseboard heaters alone could not keep internal temperature of premises above freezing during cold period).

157. 455 Cos., LLC v. Landmark Am. Ins. Co., 2017 U.S. Dist. LEXIS 118325 (E.D. Mich. July 28, 2017) (even though policy had exception to freezing exclusion that applied when insured had done its best to maintain heat, endorsements add condition and exclusion: coverage was conditioned on maintaining heat at 55 degrees, and losses caused by water damage were excluded to the extent insured failed to maintain heat at 55 degrees prior to loss; exclusion applied and condition was unsatisfied regardless of whether insured used "best efforts" to maintain heat). *See also* Read Prop. Grp. LLC v. Hamilton Ins. Co., 2018 U.S. Dist. LEXIS 54734 (E.D.N.Y. Mar. 30, 2018) (refusing to read "reasonable care" standard into language of endorsement, which makes it plain that existence of temperature at or above 50 degrees, not insured's efforts or attempts to obtain existence of that condition, determines whether or not there will be coverage).

158. *See, e.g.*, Anghel v. Utica Mut. Ins. Co., 127 A.D.3d 897, 7 N.Y.S.3d 390 (2015).

- The condition of the pipe or pipes that allegedly burst,[159]
- Heating days per month and use of natural gas,[160]
- Electric utility bills,[161]
- Termination of utility service,[162]
- Weather data,[163]
- Water bills,[164] and
- Business records of the insured.[165]

Expert testimony is particularly valuable. Counsel for a policyholder should anticipate that the insurance company will produce expert testimony on the cause of loss and be prepared with his or her own experts. A conflict between experts for the parties is usually sufficient for an insured to avoid

159. *See, e.g.*, Lombardi v. Allstate Ins. Co., 2011 U.S. Dist. LEXIS 157544 (W.D. Pa. Jan. 27, 2011) (expert for insured stated that failure was atypical of frozen copper pipe, which typically shows signs of deformation and/or stretching of copper material due to expansion). *See also* Geshwind v. Farm Fire & Cas. Co., 2014 N.Y. Misc. LEXIS 5936 (2014) (even if electrical service had been turned off, considering absence of bulging and deformity, there was still an issue of fact concerning whether pipe separated because of freezing temperature or because of another cause).

160. *See, e.g.*, Caldwell v. Allstate Prop. Ins. Cas. Co., 2018 U.S. Dist. LEXIS 182529 (N.D. Ohio Oct. 24, 2018). *See also* Ruiz v. Marysville Mut. Ins. Co., 393 P.3d 1058 (Kan. App. 2017) (where expert established that very little gas was used at residence around time the pipe burst as compared to previous two winters and that evidence was not controverted by insured in any "appropriate manner," lower court did not err in granting insurer's motion for summary judgment); Pazianas v. Allstate Ins. Co., 2016 U.S. Dist. LEXIS 92796 (E.D. Pa. July 18, 2016).

161. *See, e.g.*, Van Natta v. Great Lakes Reinsurance (UK) SE, 2021 U.S. Dist. LEXIS 112637 (D. Conn. June 16, 2021); Tawadros v. Allstate Ins. Co., 2020 U.S. Dist. LEXIS 114987 (N.D.N.Y. July 1, 2020); Evangelista v. Hingham Mut. Fire Ins. Co., 2005 Mass. Super. LEXIS 57 (Feb. 14, 2005).

162. *See, e.g.*, Billitier v. Merrimack Mut. Fire Ins. Co., 777 F. Supp. 2d 488 (W.D.N.Y. 2011); Geshwind v. Farm Fire & Cas. Co., 2014 N.Y. Misc. LEXIS 5936 (2014); Fulton v. Beacon Nat. Ins. Co., 416 S.W.3d 759 (Ark. App. 2012). *See also* McCabe v. Allstate Ins. Co., 260 A.D.2d 850, 852, 688 N.Y.S.2d 764, 767 (1999) (if contract for fuel delivery was terminated two years before pipes froze, that would establish lack of reasonable care if no other measures were taken).

163. *See, e.g.*, Brandy Ventures, LLC v. Mesa Underwriters Specialty Ins. Co., 2019 U.S. Dist. LEXIS 208898 (E.D. Tex. Nov. 13, 2019) (record of weather prepared by National Oceanic & Atmospheric Administration in area of insured property on days before and during day pipe burst, demonstrating freezing temperatures). *See also* Van Natta v. Great Lakes Reinsurance (UK) SE, 2021 U.S. Dist. LEXIS 112637 (D. Conn. June 16, 2021); Lombardi v. Allstate Ins. Co., 2011 U.S. Dist. LEXIS 157544 (W.D. Pa. Jan. 27, 2011); Farrell v. American Intl. Ins. Co., 2010 N.Y. Misc. LEXIS 2110 (2010).

164. *See, e.g.*, Pazianas v. Allstate Ins. Co., 2016 U.S. Dist. LEXIS 92796 (E.D. Pa. July 18, 2016); Fulton v. Beacon Nat. Ins. Co., 416 S.W.3d 759 (Ark. App. 2012).

165. Brandy Ventures, LLC v. Mesa Underwriters Specialty Ins. Co., 2019 U.S. Dist. LEXIS 208898 (E.D. Tex. Nov. 13, 2019) (insurer put forward business records as evidence, and every one indicated freeze break in pipe).

summary judgment.[166] Expert testimony on the amount of heat necessary to protect pipes may be helpful to the trier of fact but is not dispositive.[167]

Minimal evidence of reasonable care to maintain heat will suffice when it is uncontroverted by the insurer. For example, where the insured's daughter averred in an affidavit that the heat was left on at 70 degrees or more and the furnace was working when she left the insured house two weeks before pipes froze and burst, and the insurer did not challenge the affidavit, the insured established that the freezing exclusion was not applicable because reasonable care was taken to maintain heat in the home.[168]

3.3 Sprinkler Leakage

[1] Generally

The Fourth Circuit Court of Appeal has observed that the development of automatic sprinkler systems and the encouragement of their use by favorable insurance premiums created a new risk. The systems markedly reduced the danger of fire losses, but they introduced a new water hazard because sprinklers could discharge water when pipes froze or corroded.[169] In many communities, sprinklers have long been required for multistory buildings, whether residential or commercial. Thus, the standard policies issued for commercial or multistory residential buildings provide coverage for sprinkler leakage. All-risk policies do so by omitting sprinkler leakage from their water damage exclusion.[170] Named peril policies typically list sprinkler leakage as a covered cause of loss. At the same time, where a policy provides limited "water damage" coverage, it does *not* include discharge or leakage from an automatic sprinkler system.[171] "Sprinkler leakage" means leakage or discharge of a substance from an "automatic sprinkler system."[172] An underground fire-suppression pipe is

---

166. *See, e.g.*, Tawadros v. Allstate Ins. Co., 2020 U.S. Dist. LEXIS 114987 (N.D.N.Y. July 1, 2020); Manco v. Cumberland Mut. Fire Ins. Co., 2020 U.S. Dist. LEXIS 80416 (D.N.J. May 7, 2020); Badakhsh v. State Farm Ins. Co., 2015 U.S. Dist. LEXIS 200585 (C.D. Cal. Sept. 21, 2015); Lombardi v. Allstate Ins. Co., 2011 U.S. Dist. LEXIS 157544 (W.D. Pa. Jan. 27, 2011); Geshwind v. Farm Fire & Cas. Co., 2014 N.Y. Misc. LEXIS 5936 (2014); Farrell v. American Intl. Ins. Co., 2010 N.Y. Misc. LEXIS 2110 (2010).

167. Short v. North Pointe Ins. Co., 2013 U.S. Dist. LEXIS 61368 (S.D. Ind. Apr. 29, 2013).

168. Hidalgo v. Mason Ins. Agency, Inc., 2005 Mich. App. LEXIS 1377 (Mich. App. 2005).

169. Carva Food Corp. v. Equitable Fire & Marine Ins. Co., 261 F.2d 254, 257 (4th Cir. 1958).

170. The policy says that if the water described in the water exclusion results in sprinkler leakage, the insurer will pay for the loss or damage caused by that sprinkler leakage. ISO Form CP 10 30 04 02, § B.1.g.

171. ISO Form CP 10 20 04 02, § A.14.a.

172. Saiz v. Charter Oak Fire Ins. Co., 2007 U.S. Dist. LEXIS 67767 (D. Colo. Sept. 12, 2007) (coverage for sprinkler leakage is for water that accidently spills from sprinkler).

not a sprinkler and, therefore, water leaking from it does not constitute "sprinkler leakage."[173]

The standard all-risk homeowners policy omits sprinkler leakage from its water damage exclusion, but says it does *not* cover loss to a *building* caused by freezing of an automatic sprinkler system unless the policyholder maintained heat in the building or shut off the water supply, while it *does* cover loss from an *accidental discharge* of water from a sprinkler system.[174] The standard Broad Form named risk policy does not list sprinkler leakage as an exclusion and does cover accidental discharge from, or freezing of, a sprinkler system, provided that in the case of freezing, the policyholder maintained heat in the building or shut off the water supply.[175]

[2] Standard Coverage Language

The ISO Causes of Loss Broad Form specifically includes "sprinkler leakage" as a covered cause of loss. It defines "sprinkler leakage" as leakage or discharge of any substance from an automatic sprinkler system, including the collapse of a tank that is part of that system.[176] The term "automatic sprinkler system" is defined as any automatic fire protective or extinguishing system, including connected sprinklers and discharge nozzles, ducts, pipes, valves and fittings, tanks, their component parts and supports, and pumps and private fire protection mains. Additionally, when supplied from an automatic fire protective system, the term means non-automatic fire protective systems and hydrants, standpipes, and outlets.

If the building or structure that contains an automatic sprinkler system is covered property under the policy, the insurer, in addition to the loss caused by the leak, will also pay the cost to repair or replace damaged parts of the system if the damage results in sprinkler leakage or is directly caused by freezing and the cost to tear out and replace any part of the building or structure to repair damage to the system that has resulted in sprinkler leakage.

The Broad Form refers to sprinkler leakage in the clause that includes certain water damage as a covered cause of loss and in the one that excludes water damage. The coverage for water damage, meaning accidental discharge or leakage of water, does not include discharge or leakage from an automatic sprinkler system.[177] It also does not encompass loss or damage caused by or resulting from freezing, unless the insured does his or her "best" to maintain

173. Wisteria Props. LLC v. Ohio Sec. Ins. Co., 2021 U.S. Dist. LEXIS 228135 (C.D. Cal. Nov. 17, 2021). *See also* Praetorian Ins. Co. v. Arabia Shrine Ctr. Houston, 2016 U.S. Dist. LEXIS 20186 (S.D. Tex. Feb. 19, 2016) (sprinklers are not under surface of ground).

174. *See* ISO Form HO 00 03 10 00.

175. *See* ISO Form HO 00 02 10 00.

176. ISO Form CP 10 20 04 02, § A.9.

177. ISO Form CP 10 20 04 02, § A.9.a.(1).(a).

heat in the building or drains the equipment and shuts off the water supply if heat is not maintained.[178] The water damage exclusion lists four categories of water that are not covered causes of loss but says that if any of those categories of water *results* in sprinkler leakage, the insurer will pay for the loss or damage caused by that leakage.[179]

[3] Application of Sprinkler Leakage Provision

Generally, negligence by the insured will not bar the coverage.[180] A loss was covered when the attempt to fight a nearby fire affected water pressure that caused and resulted in a leak in the sprinkler system at the insured property.[181] Other exclusions may, however, preclude coverage. For example, when policies have had a "windstorm" exclusion, courts have ruled that damage to a sprinkler system caused by a windstorm is not covered.[182] If sprinkler leakage is caused by flood waters, a water/flood exclusion could bar coverage.[183]

[4] Location of Sprinkler System

Some policies may provide coverage for loss or damage caused by a leak from an automatic sprinkler system that is on the insured premises. That may preclude coverage when there is a building-wide system. For example, an insured

---

178. ISO Form CP 10 20 04 02, § A.9.a.(4).

179. ISO Form CP 10 20 04 02, § B.1.g.

180. Wertheimer-Swarts Shoe Co. v. United States Casualty Co., 172 Mo. 135, 72 S.W. 635 (1903) (negligence of employee of insured in maintaining sprinkler system did not preclude recovery).

181. *See* New York Dock Co. v. Aetna Casualty & Surety Co., 46 N.Y.S.2d 307 (1943) (pressure exerted by fire engines pumping water caused break in system, but fire was neither direct nor indirect cause of loss).

182. American Mfg. Corp. v. National Union Fire Ins. Co., 203 La. 515, 14 So. 2d 430 (1942) (finding no coverage for sprinkler leakage where section of roof to which sprinkler system feed pipe was attached was blown off by tornado or windstorm, causing water damage to insured property); Bonds-Sanders Paper Co. v. Travelers Fire Ins. Co., 12 Tenn. App. 479 (1931) (no coverage for sprinkler leakage where during windstorm chimney fell on roof of insured building, broke through roof, and damaged water pipes of sprinkler system); Maryland Casualty Co. v. Finch, 147 F. 388 (8th Cir.), *cert. den.*, 203 U.S. 592, 27 S. Ct. 780, 51 L. Ed. 331 (1906) (no coverage where cyclone broke pipes of automatic sprinkler, causing insured building to flood). *See also* Industrial Paper & Cordage Co. v. Aetna Ins. Co., 65 R.I. 357, 14 A.2d 657 (1940). *Compare* Hanover Fire Ins. Co. v. Newman's Inc., 108 F.2d 561, *cert. den.*, 309 U.S. 68, 60 S. Ct. 718, 84 L. Ed. 1024 (5th Cir. 1939) (where policy did not exclude damage from sprinkler leakage caused by extraneous force, sprinkler leakage caused by cyclone was covered).

183. *See* Alley Theatre v. Hanover Ins. Co., 436 F. Supp. 3d 938 (S.D. Tex. 2020), where flood waters filled the basement of the insured property and broke an interior concrete wall that fell and ruptured a sprinkler-system pipe. The court decided the peril of flood waters began the chain of events that proceeded in an unbroken sequence and connection. The court held that the flood was a proximate cause of the sprinkler-system rupture and leakage. Fortunately for the insured, the policy did not exclude flood coverage, but did limit covered flood losses to $3 million and that limit, held the court, applied to the loss.

occupied the second floor of a building. A broken sprinkler on the fifth floor of the building caused water damage to the insured premises. The policy covered a loss from a leak in the automatic sprinkler system "erected in or on that portion of the building occupied by the" insured. The court found that the loss insured against was leakage or discharge that occurred in the sprinkler system on the insured premises, meaning the part of the building inhabited by the policyholder. Thus, there was no coverage.[184]

[5] Vacancy Clause

Property policies often provide that, if the building where loss or damage occurs has been vacant for more than 60 consecutive days before that loss or damage, the insurer will not pay for loss or damage caused by sprinkler leakage *unless* the insured has protected the sprinkler system from freezing.[185] There may, therefore, be coverage when a sprinkler system freezes and leaks as the insured is required only to "protect" the system against freezing.[186] Indeed, if sprinkler leakage will be covered only when the insured has protected the system against freezing, the cause of any leakage is not relevant as the only question relevant to the limitation on coverage is whether insured took the requisite action.[187]

When a policy is issued to the owner or general lessee of a property, "building" means the entire building, which is then considered vacant unless at least 31 percent of its total square footage is used by its owner to conduct "customary operations."[188] Policies typically do not define the phrase "conduct customary operations."[189]

---

184. Bottomley v. Royal Ins. Co., 190 Mass. 73, 76 N.E. 463 (1906). *See also* Bonnie v. Maryland Casualty Co., 280 Ky. 568, 133 S.W.2d 904 (1939) (policy was intended to cover damage resulting from sprinkler system in building occupied by insured, not from sprinkler system in any other building). *But see* Hardin Bag & Burlap Co. v. Fidelity & Guaranty Fire Corp., 1 So. 2d 830 (La. App. 1941), *rev'd on other grounds*, 203 La. 778, 14 So. 2d 634 (1943).

185. *See* ISO Form CP 00 10 10 12, § E.6.b.(1)(b); ISO Form CP 00 17 06 07, § E.7.b.(1)(b).

186. 7th & Allen Equities v. Hartford Cas. Ins. Co., 2012 U.S. Dist. LEXIS 158081 (E.D. Pa. Nov. 2, 2012) ("protect" is undefined and could be ambiguous). *Compare* Five Star Hotels, LLC v. Ins. Co. of Greater N.Y., 2011 U.S. Dist. LEXIS 31313 (S.D.N.Y. Mar. 24, 2011) (where policy required insured to "maintain" sprinkler system, insured was only required to keep automatic sprinkler system in place on premises and was not required to ensure that water in system did not freeze).

187. Saiz v. Charter Oak Fire Ins. Co., 2007 U.S. Dist. LEXIS 67767 (D. Colo. Sept. 12, 2007).

188. *See* ISO Form CP 00 10 10 12, § E.6.a.(1)(b); ISO Form CP 00 17 06 07, § E.7.a.(1)(b).

189. An analysis of the meaning of "customary operations" is beyond the scope of this discussion. That analysis can be found elsewhere. *See* Cozen, *Insuring Real Property*, § 1.06[7][e][ii] (LexisNexis Matthew Bender 2022); Moore & Schmeeckle, *"Customary Operations" or a Vacant Building?* (June 2015), ALM, https://www.lawjournalnewsletters.com/sites/lawjournalnewsletters/2015/06/01/customary-operations-or-a-vacant-building-3/?slreturn=20220413104858.

[6] Exclusion by Endorsement

Even though a policy may initially cover loss from sprinkler leakage, an endorsement may curb or eliminate the coverage. For example, there is a standard ISO form titled "Sprinkler Leakage Exclusion" that provides a schedule of locations and then says that for the locations indicated on that schedule, sprinkler leakage is added to the exclusions section and is therefore not a covered cause of loss. It defines sprinkler leakage as "leakage or discharge of any substance from an Automatic Sprinkler System, including collapse of a tank that is part of the system."[190] The endorsement adds that if sprinkler leakage *results* in a covered cause of loss, the insurer will pay for the loss or damage caused by that loss.

3.4 Backups and Overflows

[1] Introduction

Backups and overflows of water can flood property. A sewer backup occurs when water comes up or is pushed into a building through the pipes from sewer or drainage systems. According to the Insurance Information Institute, aging sewage systems are leading to an alarming increase in sewer backups, flooded basements, and overflows.[191] Other causes are roots that find their way into sewer line cracks, combined sewage and stormwater pipelines,[192] and blockages of city sanitary mains. Water can back up into a building when gutters or rainwater pipes are blocked by debris or overwhelmed by sudden flow of water.[193] Basement flooding may not be related to sanitary sewer systems, but caused by the settling of soil adjacent to a building that allows rainwater to flow toward the building and down the outside of its foundation walls.[194] Overflows are often ordinary, everyday events: washing machines or dishwashers malfunction, clogged toilets are flushed, or bathtubs are overfilled. In coastal communities rising sea levels have brought a relatively new cause of backups: at high tide, seawater flows up storm drains and into streets.

190. CP 10 56 06 07, § A.

191. *Protect your house from sewer backups*, Insurance Information Institute, http://www.iii.org/article/sewer-backup. The article says that the Civil Engineering Research Foundation reports that the number of backed up sewers is increasing at about 3 percent annually.

192. When sewage and stormwater are combined in a single pipeline, that pipeline system can become overwhelmed during a rainstorm, causing water to back up.

193. *Protect your house from sewer backups*, Insurance Information Institute, http://www.iii.org/article/sewer-backup.

194. *Protect your house from sewer backups*, Insurance Information Institute, http://www.iii.org/article/sewer-backup. In older buildings, cracks may develop in the foundation or floor slab, allowing water to enter the basement, usually after a number of rain storms saturate the ground.

Under the standard ISO causes of loss form typically included in commercial property coverage, there is no coverage for water that backs up or overflows or is otherwise discharged *from* a sewer, drain, sump, sump pump, or related equipment.[195] The standard ISO residential policy excludes coverage for water or waterborne material that backs up *through* sewers or drains or overflows or is discharged *from* a sump, sump pump, or related equipment.[196] Because backups and overflows are not uncommon, policyholders often obtain an endorsement to add the coverage to the policy.[197] Before examining any endorsement, one should first determine whether an exclusion applies.[198] Application of the standard exclusion is discussed elsewhere.[199] Also, in the case of commercial properties, there may be a number of policies and endorsements, so it is important to determine to which of those the endorsement applies.[200]

Sometime the principal policy incorporates backup and overflow coverage. For example, in one case a policy did not provide flood protection, but did provide additional coverage for "water backup" under which the insurer would pay for direct, physical loss caused by water or waterborne material that flows into the plumbing system of the insured dwelling or other structures through sewers or drains located off the "residence premises" or water that overflows from a sump pump or sump well with a sump pump designed to drain subsurface water from the foundation area. The court said that based on the plain language of the policy, a claim for "water backup" would be based on overflow in the plumbing system of the insured's dwelling or other structures. There was no coverage because the policyholder did not claim that damage to his property was caused by water or waterborne material that flowed into the plumbing system, but that flooding was exacerbated by

195. ISO Form CP 10 30 09 17, § B.1.g.(3).

196. ISO Form HO 00 03 10 00 (Exclusions), § I.A.3.b.

197. In some cases, the endorsement may simply delete the backup/overflow exclusion. *See, e.g.*, Doylestown Elec. Supply Co. v. Maryland Cas. Ins. Co., 1996 U.S. Dist. LEXIS 20599 (E.D. Pa. Dec. 31, 1996), *aff'd*, 133 F.3d 909 (3d Cir. 1997); Montanaro v. Nationwide Ins. Co., 2003 Conn. Super. LEXIS 588 (Feb. 27, 2003).

198. There are some policies that do not exclude backups and overflows. For example, in one case, the policy excluded water that backed up or overflowed from a sewer, drain, or sump but *only* if "Back-Up of Sewers and Drains" was shown as excluded on the Declarations Page. The Declarations Page did not mention "Back-Up of Sewers and Drains" and, therefore, a loss caused by a backup was covered. Assurance Co. of Am., Inc. v. Jay-Mar, Inc., 38 F. Supp. 2d 349 (D.N.J. 1999).

199. See §§ 2.1–2.6, *supra*.

200. *See, e.g.*, McCaughey v. Ohio Sec. Ins. Co., 2021 U.S. Dist. LEXIS 65061 (C.D. Cal. Apr. 2, 2021) (insured argued water exclusion endorsement applied to "Standard Property Policy"; court found it applied to "Commercial Property Coverage Part").

negligently preformed street drainage repairs by the city. The alleged loss did not, therefore, come within the terms of the policy.[201]

When a policy covers backups or overflows, there is often a specific sublimit.[202] If it is at all possible that a loss that is apparently from a backup or overflow might be covered under a water damage provision and might exceed the sublimit, the insurer has an incentive to classify the loss as one coming under the backup or overflow coverage and to then pay up to the sublimit. Counsel for the policyholder then has to scrutinize the policy language to determine if the loss might fit under coverage for which there is no sublimit or a much higher one.

[2] Water Damage Coverage: Overflow or Discharge from a Plumbing System

The standard "water damage" exclusion proscribes coverage for water that backs up through sewers or drains. The water damage *coverage* provision often found in residential policies covers losses caused by accidental leakage, *overflow, or discharge of liquids from a plumbing system.*[203] It is important to check the specific policy language to determine whether it provides coverage for all losses or is limited only to losses to real or personal property.

Some courts say that the water damage exclusion and water damage coverage provisions, when read together, create an ambiguity about losses that result from a backup and/or overflow from sewers, drains, and/or plumbing systems.[204] Other courts say the two clauses are not contradictory. Nonetheless, most courts read the two clauses together and find that

---

201. Spector v. USAA Cas. Ins. Co., 2019 U.S. Dist. LEXIS 57946 (E.D. La. Apr. 3, 2019) (express terms of policy show that it does not provide coverage for direct or indirect damage caused by flooding, all damage was caused by flooding, and insured did not allege facts to support claim for water backup). *See also* Hirschfield v. Cont'l Casualty Co., 199 Ga. App. 654, 404 S.E.2d 737 (1999).

202. *See, e.g.*, Durrett v. Nationwide Prop. & Cas. Ins. Co., 2015 U.S. Dist. LEXIS 44966 (W.D. Tex. Apr. 6, 2015) (coverage for damage caused by water or water-borne material that backed up through sewers or drains from outside dwelling's plumbing system was limited to 5 percent of property coverage).

203. ISO Form HO 00 02 10 00 (Perils Insured Against), § 12.a. Compare that with the language of standard commercial policies that cover accidental discharge or leakage of water as the direct result of the *breaking apart or cracking* of a plumbing, heating, air conditioning, or other system or appliance, that is *located on the described premises*. ISO Form CP 10 20 04 02, § A.14.b.

204. *See, e.g.*, Andres v. Oklahoma Farm Bureau Mutual Insurance Co., 227 P.3d 1102 (Okla. App. 2009), *cert. den.*, 2012 Okla. LEXIS 89 (Sept. 17, 2012) (sewage water from city main sewer line backed up and allegedly caused extensive and permanent damage to insured home; court found sewer line was part of plumbing system of a house, and, therefore, policy both included and excluded coverage for accidental discharge or overflow of water containing sewage and construed policy in favor of coverage); United States Fid. & Guar. Co. of Miss. v. Martin, 998 So. 2d 956 (Miss. 2008) (where policy contained standard water damage exclusion and backup coverage, policy was ambiguous and would be interpreted as a whole to cover

water damage caused by a backup/overflow that originates from a pipe or clogged drain located *within* the property line of the insured comes from the insured's plumbing system and is covered,[205] while a backup/overflow from outside the property boundaries of the insured—for example, a clogged municipal sewer that forces water from *outside* the plumbing system of the insured to overflow—is not covered because of the exclusion.[206] Of course,

---

damage caused by water from sewer or drain backup, even when some damage may have resulted from flood, surface water, or overflow or any body of water).

205. *See, e.g.*, World Fire & Marine Ins. Co. v. Carolina Mills Distributing Co., 169 F.2d 826 (8th Cir. 1948) (pressure of water from overloaded city sewer in street outside insured building forced cap off of "house trap" in that building; however, had that cap not broken, pressure from the overloaded main sewer would not have forced water from that sewer high enough in plumbing system inside building to overflow from toilets, and no damage would have resulted from pressure in city's main sewer; thus, water damage insuring clause provided coverage and water damage exclusion either was in irreconcilable conflict with, and repugnant to, insuring clause or had to be so construed that its meaning would be harmonized with insuring clause); Monteleone v. Auto Club Grp., 113 F. Supp. 3d 950 (E.D. Mich. 2015) (water damage from faulty back flow preventer in plumbing waste line that extended under slab in basement was covered as discharge or overflow from within plumbing system); Cheetham v. Southern Oak Ins. Co., 114 So. 3d 257 (Fla. 3d DCA), *rev. den.*, 129 So. 3d 1069 (Fla. 2013) (water damage exclusion related to damage caused by water originating from somewhere other than plumbing system of residence and because loss was caused by deterioration of pipe within the plumbing system, which caused water or water-borne material emanating from that plumbing system to back up into residence premises, loss was covered loss under policy). *Compare* Salih v. Ohio Sec. Ins. Co., 2018 N.J. Super. Unpub. LEXIS 2647 (Dec. 3, 2018) (rejecting insured's attempt to distinguish "accidental discharge" of water in clogged toilet from sewer backup; finding endorsement that added water damage coverage for sewer backups with its sublimit of $25,000 applied).

206. Pichel v. Dryden Mut. Ins. Co., 117 A.D.3d 1267, 1269, 986 N.Y.S.2d 268, 271 (2014). *See also* Pavuk v. State Auto. Ins. Co., 1997 U.S. Dist. LEXIS 10355 (E.D. Pa. July 15, 1997), *aff'd*, 149 F.3d 1165 (3d Cir. 1998) (where water main broke and discharged water onto surrounding areas causing large sinkholes to form at insured home resulting in large cracks in basement floor and foundation walls, because water did not come from home's own plumbing system, but flowed from an outside source, loss was not covered under water damage exclusion; whether water actually entered basement was irrelevant as water from broken pipe indirectly caused damage); Jackson v. American Mut. Fire Ins. Co., 299 F. Supp. 151 (M.D.N.C. 1968), *aff'd*, 410 F.2d 395 (4th Cir. 1969) (water damage clause would cover any accidental discharge or overflow of water from within plumbing system resulting from defects in that system, for example, pipe within system clogging and thereby causing pipe to fill and overflow, but exclusion would bar coverage for loss, as here, from overflow caused by water backing up in municipal sewer lines); For Kids Only Child Dev. Ctr., Inc. v. Phila. Indem. Ins. Co., 260 S.W.3d 652 (Tex. App. 2008) (where overflow was caused by stoppage in a 12-inch city sewer main, court found policy unambiguously excluded from coverage type of drain and sewer backup insured experienced); Waldsmith v. State Farm Fire & Casualty Co., 283 Cal. Rptr. 607, 610, 232 Cal. App. 3d 693, 698 (1991) (city water main in middle of street would not be included "plumbing system"); Kozlowski v. Penn Mut. Ins. Co., 295 Pa. Super. 141, 441 A2d 388 (1982) (where curb valve at water main service line two blocks away leading to insured home burst, releasing

the specific language of any water damage insuring clause can lead to a different result.[207]

If water accidentally leaks, overflows, or is discharged, can it then become either surface or ground water? Is any damage it causes then excluded under the standard water damage exclusion? The courts do not agree. Some say the water damage exclusion applies;[208] others assert it does not.[209]

---

water that seeped into and flooded basement, there was no coverage because "plumbing systems" as used in water damage coverage clause meant system on insured premises, and not from any plumbing system; water damage exclusion did not contradict water damage coverage clause because reading policy as a whole, giving effect to all of its provisions, where cause of discharge, leakage, or overflow of water is in insured's own plumbing system, exclusion does not apply and does apply if cause is outside that system); Hallsted v. Blue Mt. Convalescent Ctr., 23 Wn. App. 349, 595 P.2d 574, *rev. den.*, 92 Wn. 2d 1023 (1979) (no coverage where sewer under street in front of insured home became clogged and sewage backed up into home; if cause of discharge is in system of insured home, exclusion does not apply, but if cause of discharge is outside that system, for example, clogged sewer pipe that forces water from outside system to overflow, then exclusion applies even though water flowed through plumbing system of insured home); Haines v. United Sec. Ins. Co., 43 Colo. App. 276, 602 P.2d 901 (1979) (where heavy rainfall entered sewer line being constructed by city near insured residences and resulting excessive pressure caused raw sewage to be discharged into basements, there was no coverage under water damage clause because cause of the flooding resulted from outside forces causing water to back up through system and, therefore, water damage exclusion controlled).

207. *See, e.g.*, 180 Lafayette Corp. v. Wesco Ins. Co., 2021 N.Y. Misc. LEXIS 307 (Jan. 26, 2021) (water damage coverage was for "covered water," and water that overflowed or was otherwise discharged from drain or related equipment was excluded by plain meaning of water exclusion and, thus, there was no conflict between provisions and no ambiguity that would require court to ignore plain terms of exclusion).

208. Krug v. Millers' Mutual Insurance Ass'n, 209 Kan. 111, 495 P.2d 949 (1972) (water leak occurred in plumbing system in pipe leading from city main, water that leaked was below surface of ground within meaning of water damage exclusion); Park v. Hanover Insurance Company, 443 S.W.2d 940 (Tex. Civ. App. 1969), *overruled*, National Surety Corp. v. Adrian Associates, 650 S.W.2d 67 (Tex. 1983) (where water line leading into home was split near point it entered house beneath foundation and water that leaked came within water damage exclusion).

209. *See, e.g.*, American Concept Ins. Co. v. Jones, 935 F. Supp. 1220 (D. Utah 1996) (specific coverage for accidental discharge of water cannot be rendered meaningless by subsequent, generic exclusion for damage caused by water below the surface); Holcomb v. United States Fire Ins. Co., 52 N.C. App. 474, 279 S.E.2d 50 (1981) (water discharged from guttering system would not become either surface water or ground water excluded from coverage); Hartford Accident and Indemnity Co. v. Phelps, 294 So. 2d 362 (Fla. 1st DCA 1974) (insured home suffered damage from underground leak in water pipe and insurer invoked underground water exclusion, but court held that exclusion did not refer to leaks within plumbing system and, having specifically covered plumbing system leaks, insurer, if it had intended to exclude underground leaks in plumbing system, should have specifically said so); King v. Travelers Insurance Company, 84 N.M. 550, 505 P.2d 1226 (1973) (where water line underneath concrete floor slab broke or ruptured, allowing escape and discharge of water, application of water below the surface of the ground exclusion would create ambiguity to be resolved in favor of insured).

[3] Endorsements Adding Coverage for Backups and Overflows

[a] Standard Residential Endorsement

Under an ISO endorsement to a standard homeowners policy, the insurer will insure up to a stated sublimit[210] loss to covered property caused by water or waterborne material that backs up through sewers or drains or overflows or is discharged from a sump, sump pump, or related equipment, even if the overflow or discharge results from mechanical breakdown.[211] However, where a basement sump pump malfunctioned, allowing the basement to flood with water that seeped through the walls, there was no coverage because the water did not emanate from an "accidental discharge or overflow."[212]

The coverage does not apply to direct physical loss of a sump pump or related equipment caused by mechanical breakdown. It also does not apply to a loss caused by the negligence of an insured.[213] The endorsement has a separate deductible for losses covered by it.[214] Policies typically exclude coverage for losses caused by mechanical breakdown, latent defect, inherent vice, or any quality in property that causes it to damage or destroy itself. The endorsement removes "mechanical breakdown" from that list.[215] Finally, the endorsement deletes the water damage exclusion in the principal policy and replaces it with one that is the same as the usual exclusion except that it defines excluded water damage to encompass water or waterborne material that backs up through sewers or drains or overflows or is discharged from a sump, sump pump, or related equipment as a *direct or indirect result of flood*.[216]

For the endorsement sublimit to apply, the loss has to be one covered by the endorsement. For example, an insured claimed her property suffered a water damage loss. The insurer concluded there was a sewer backup and

---

210. Typically, $5,000. The sublimit may be more. *See, e.g.*, Troutman v. QBE Ins. Corp., 2018 U.S. Dist. LEXIS 96115 (W.D.N.C. June 6, 2018) ($10,000); Viscounte v. Liberty Mut. Group, 2012 U.S. Dist. LEXIS 177228 (E.D. Pa. Dec. 14, 2012) ($10,000); Hartman v. Erie Ins. Co., 85 N.E.3d 454 (Ohio App. 2017) ($10,000); Myers v. Encompass Indem. Co., 169 Ohio App. 3d 545, 863 N.E.3d 1083 (2006) ($15,000).

211. In an unusual case, the insurer argued that a Sump Pump Endorsement did not cover a loss because, despite appearing within the pages of the policy, it was not, in fact, included in the policy because it provided a list of potential coverage limits, but none of them was selected and because it did not appear on the policy's Declarations Page. The court found an ambiguity in whether the parties intended to include the endorsement and construed the policy in favor of the insured. Mink v. Liberty Mut. Group, 2013 U.S. Dist. LEXIS 197148 (E.D. Pa. June 20, 2013).

212. Goodman v. Broome County Co-operative Fire Ins. Co., 135 A.D.2d 906, 521 N.Y.S.2d 898 (1987). *See also* Kelly v. U.S. Fidelity & Guar. Co., 771 P.2d 948 (Kan. App. 1989) (where sump pumps were not working and water backed up from floor drain, coverage was barred by exclusions for water that backs up through sewers or drains or water below surface of ground).

213. ISO Form HO 04 95 10 00, § A.

214. ISO Form HO 04 95 10 00, § C.

215. ISO Form HO 04 95 10 00, § B.

216. ISO Form HO 04 95 10 00, § D.

therefore, its Water Backup and Sump Discharge or Overflow endorsement with its $5,000 sublimit applied. The policyholder contended the loss was caused by a broken pipe in the plumbing system, which did not fall within the sublimit endorsement and was covered as a loss resulting from an accidental discharge or overflow of water from within a plumbing system. The court did not resolve the dispute over the cause of the loss. It denied the insurer's motion for summary judgment and said that a backup through a sewer or drain would invoke the sublimit, but a broken pipe might not.[217]

[b] Standard Commercial Endorsement

Under the commercial ISO Discharge from Sewer, Drain or Sump (Not Flood-Related) endorsement, the insurer will pay for direct physical loss or damage to covered property[218] that is caused by or results from the discharge of water or waterborne material from a sewer, drain—including a "roof drain"[219] and related fixtures[220]—or sump located on the described premises.[221] The discharge may not, however, be induced by flood or flood-related conditions.[222] The definition of flood or flood-related conditions in the endorsement parallels the language of the typical water damage exclusion.[223] The endorsement addresses the relationship between it and the water damage exclusion by saying that to the extent that that exclusion might conflict with the coverage provided by the endorsement, the exclusion does not apply to that coverage.[224] The difference between the language of the endorsement and of the water

217. Webster v. Scottsdale Ins. Co., 2021 U.S. Dist. LEXIS 54155 (S.D. Fla. Feb. 5, 2021).

218. Tu v. Dongbu Ins. Co., 2018 U.S. Dist. LEXIS 151322 (N.D. Cal. Sept. 5, 2018) (no coverage under endorsement where tenant's policy did not extend coverage to buildings, and insured tenant did not identify any other policy provision that would render damaged sewer line, subfloor, or floor covered property).

219. Even if the endorsement language does not explicitly include a roof drain within the meaning of drain, it may still be considered to be a drain. *See* Ken Johnson Props., LLC v. Harleysville Worcester Ins. Co., 2013 U.S. Dist. LEXIS 140530 (D. Minn. Sept. 30, 2013) (roof opening had open end at roof's surface connected to chute that opened onto ground on side of building; where opening and chute served as channel or pipe to divert rainwater from roof, they qualified as a drain even though pipe or channel was not to connected to plumbing system).

220. In contrast, some policies state that the word "drain" does not include a roof drain, gutter, downspout, or similar fixtures or equipment. *See* Danville Commer. Indus. Storage, LLC v. Selective Ins. Co., 442 F. Supp. 3d 921 (W.D. Va. 2020).

221. ISO Form CP 10 38 10 12, § A.

222. *See, e.g.*, *In re* Rose Ann Int'l v. Hartford Ins. Co., 2005 U.S. Dist. LEXIS 53921 (D.N.J. Aug. 4, 2005) (where rainwater ran off from elevated highways alongside of insured building onto street below and from street into sewer drains from which it backed up into building, there was no coverage under backup endorsement if backup was caused even partially by flood; insured's expert agreed that drain and sewer backup was caused by combination of water runoff and debris in drains and because endorsement defined flood as "overflow of surface water" and excluded it, there was no coverage).

223. Flood or flood-related conditions means surface water, waves—tidal and tsunami—tides, tidal water, overflow of any body of water, and storm surge.

224. ISO Form CP 10 38 10 12, § D.

damage exclusion can be critical. In a New York case, the court found that the wording of the endorsement provided broader coverage than was originally excluded, but then imposed a sublimit on those previously non-excluded losses, even though the endorsement was purportedly purchased to expand coverage. Therefore, the court concluded there was an ambiguity and decided it would interpret the endorsement "to apply only to the exact same category of losses that were originally excluded in the policy."[225]

There is no coverage if a discharge is the result of the failure of the insured to perform routine maintenance or repair that is needed to keep a sewer or drain or a sump, sump pump, or related equipment free from obstruction and in "proper working condition,"[226] or if failure of a sump pump is caused by or results from failure of power, unless the policy is endorsed to cover power failure affecting the described premises.[227] The endorsement does not define "proper working condition," but in a case in which a sump pump malfunctioned and allowed a basement to flood, the court said the phrase means "to perform maintenance and upkeep to facilitate regular functioning." The court allowed that the phrase could be read to require more rigorous maintenance, but if it was susceptible to multiple interpretations, it had to be construed against the insurer. The court then noted nothing in the record established why the sump pump failed, stated what would be required to keep a sump pump in proper working condition, or identified any tasks or maintenance the insured failed to perform. The insurer, therefore, was not entitled to summary judgment.[228]

The endorsement provides coverage for damage caused by discharge of water from a sewer, drain, or sump, but not for the cost of repairing or replacing that sewer, drain, sump, sump pump, or any related parts or equipment.[229]

If there is a "Discharge Limit for Business Interruption" entered on the endorsement schedule, the insurer will pay for business income loss and/or extra expense in accordance with the terms of the applicable Coverage Form, when the loss or expense arises out of the direct physical loss or damage specifically covered by the endorsement.[230]

The most the insurer will pay under the endorsement, for the total of *all* covered loss and expense, is the applicable discharge limit shown in the

225. 301-375 W. Onondaga St., LLC v. Liberty Mut. Fire Ins. Co., 2020 U.S. Dist. LEXIS 1228 (N.D.N.Y. Jan. 6, 2020). The endorsement replaced the water damage exclusion with one that omitted reference to sewer, drains, or sump pumps.

226. The limitation does not apply to sudden mechanical breakdown of a sump pump or its related equipment if that breakdown is not the result of negligence by the insured.

227. ISO Form CP 10 38 10 12, § C.

228. Yogi's Primopromo Llc v. Nationwide Gen. Ins. Co., 2020 U.S. Dist. LEXIS 204529 (E.D. Tenn. Aug. 17, 2020).

229. ISO Form CP 10 38 10 12, § E.

230. ISO Form CP 10 38 10 12, § B.

endorsement schedule.[231] That limit is part of, not in addition to, the limit of insurance that applies to covered property, business income, or extra expense.

If there is an "Annual Aggregate Limitation" shown on the endorsement schedule, the applicable discharge limit is an annual aggregate limit and is the most the insurer will pay for the total of all covered loss and expense caused by all occurrences in a 12-month period, regardless of the number of occurrences during that time.[232] If, therefore, the first occurrence does not exhaust the applicable discharge limit, then the balance of that limit is available for a subsequent occurrence. If an occurrence begins during one annual policy period and ends during the following one, any discharge limit that applies to the following annual policy period will not apply to that occurrence.

All provisions of the primary policy apply to the coverage provided by the endorsement unless otherwise indicated, including the deductible for direct physical loss or damage and the "period of restoration" for business income and extra expense.[233] If an occurrence results in loss payable only under the endorsement, the deductible that applies to the peril of fire will apply, but if an occurrence also causes other loss or damage that is paid under the policy, a separate deductible will not apply to the loss or damage covered under the endorsement.

Policies typically will not cover any damages that would not have occurred absent one or more of the excluded events. Thus, after Superstorm Sandy an insurer's investigator determined the damage to the insured property was caused by flooding. The policyholder asserted that the damage was from water backing up through sewers and drains and was covered by a sewer, drain, or sump endorsement. The court said that if the damages were concurrently caused by both flooding and overflow water from the premises' drainage system, there was no coverage. To establish covered damages, the insured would have to demonstrate that the backup directly, and solely, caused the damages and it failed to do so.[234]

231. ISO Form CP 10 38 10 12, § F. In commercial policies the sublimit will vary. *See, e.g.*, Covington Lodging, Inc. v. W. World Ins. Grp. (*In re* Covington Lodging Inc.), 635 B.R. 675 (N.D. Ga. 2021) ($100,000); Victoria Family LLLP v. Ohio Sec. Ins. Co., 475 F. Supp. 3d 1106 (S.D. Cal. 2020) ($25,000); 301-375 W. Onondaga St., LLC v. Liberty Mut. Fire Ins. Co., 2020 U.S. Dist. LEXIS 1228 (N.D.N.Y. Jan. 6, 2020) ($25,000); Carevel, LLC v. Aspen Am. Ins. Co., 2016 U.S. Dist. LEXIS 157919 (D.N.J. Nov. 15, 2016) ($250,000); Chateau Vill. N. Condo. Ass'n v. Am. Family Mut. Ins. Co., 170 F. Supp. 3d 1349 (D. Colo. 2016) ($300,000 per location for one occurrence); Ken Johnson Props., LLC v. Harleysville Worcester Ins. Co., 2013 U.S. Dist. LEXIS 140530 (D. Minn. Sept. 30, 2013) ($25,000); Surabian Realty Co. v. NGM Ins. Co., 462 Mass. 715, 971 N.E.2d 268 (2012) ($25,000).

232. ISO Form CP 10 38 10 12, § G.

233. ISO Form CP 10 38 10 12, § H.

234. Carevel, LLC v. Aspen Am. Ins. Co., 2016 U.S. Dist. LEXIS 157919 (D.N.J. Nov. 15, 2016).

If the policy provides coverages beyond property damage—for example, business income or extra expenses—it must be determined whether those coverages are subject to a sublimit in it. For example, an endorsement provided up to $25,000 in coverage for a loss caused by water that backed up from a sewer, drain, or sump. The insured argued that the sublimit did not apply to business income or extra expenses. The court responded that were it not for the endorsement with its sublimit, there would be no coverage at all for those losses because they arose from a backup that was not a covered loss under the policy itself.[235]

[c] Endorsement Covering "Other" Systems

Some endorsements provide coverage for water that emanates from a sump pump, sump pump well, or *other type system designed to remove subsurface water*. What is an "other system"? In one case, water coming from a joint where a sump pump connected to a discharge pipe flooded a basement. A plumber determined a broken check valve and discharge pipe on the sump pump failed and caused the flood. The policy had a sump pump endorsement that limited coverage to $10,000. The insured did not want to be subject to that limit and argued coverage should be under the main policy, not the endorsement. The issue was whether the term "system" in the endorsement was ambiguous. The insured argued that it was. The court, however, concluded that the only reasonable interpretation of "other type system" in the endorsement was that it encompassed the check valve and discharge pipe, as the valve was connected to a pipe that exclusively served the sump pump.[236]

In another case, after two tropical storms, an insured warehouse was damaged when its sump pumps were unable to keep up with the volume of water, allowing a loading bay to fill with water that then flowed through loading dock doors into the building. The insured contended the damage was covered under an endorsement for damage caused by water that entered into and overflowed from within a sump pump, sump pump well, or "other type of system designed to remove subsurface water." The entire loading bay, including the sloped concrete driveway that directed water into the sump pump was, reasoned the insured, a "system designed to remove subsurface water." The court, however, said the loading bay was not designed to remove water, but to allow for convenient loading and unloading of trucks. A sloped ramp, said the court, like a graded floor in a basement, may divert water toward a sump

235. For Kids Only Child Dev. Ctr., Inc. v. Phila. Indem. Ins. Co., 260 S.W.3d 652 (Tex. App. 2008).

236. Viscounte v. Liberty Mut. Group, 2012 U.S. Dist. LEXIS 177228 (E.D. Pa. Dec. 14, 2012).

pump or other water removal system, but that does not make it part of the system itself.[237]

[d] Source of Water

Some endorsements may emphasize the source of the water. For example, one endorsement provided coverage when the backup was caused solely by water or sewage either from outside the plumbing system of the premises that enters through a sewer or drain located *inside the interior* of the building or that enters into and overflows from within a sump pump, sump pump well, or any other system located *inside the interior* of the building.[238]

Another endorsement covered direct physical loss to covered property caused by water, or waterborne material that *originated from within* the insured dwelling and backed up through sewers or drains or overflowed or was discharged from a sump, sump pump, or related equipment. A sewer lateral in the street near the home was struck by a company installing a fiber optic network. As a result of the broken sewer lateral, a large amount of water and sewage entered the home through a downstairs toilet. The insureds wanted to avoid application of the endorsement because of its sublimit and apparently contended the water originated from the sewer lateral. The court, however, said "originates" referred to the *point of entry in the residence*, not the location of the underlying cause. The insurer, therefore, properly applied the endorsement and limited the coverage to the applicable sublimit. Moreover, the overflow at issue was, said the court, caused by an off-premises event and coverage would have been precluded by the policy water damage backup/overflow exclusion.[239]

Yet another version of a backup/overflow endorsement adds coverage for backup of water or sewage that is directly or immediately caused *solely* by water or sewage from *outside* the plumbing system of the premises that enters through a sewer or drain located *inside* the interior of the dwelling. Under that language said a court, an insured would have to show that the claimed damages were caused "solely" by water or sewage that entered through a drain in the house. In the case, the home was damaged during Superstorm Sandy.

237. Advertir Inc. v. Peerless Indem. Ins. Co., 2013 U.S. Dist. LEXIS 123450 (E.D. Pa. Aug. 29, 2013).

238. Donahue v. Burns, 2013 U.S. Dist. LEXIS 67498 (M.D. Pa. May 13, 2013).

239. Troutman v. QBE Ins. Corp., 2018 U.S. Dist. LEXIS 96115 (W.D.N.C. June 6, 2018). Arguably, there is some doubt about the water damage exclusion. It was modified twice. One endorsement only replaced the water damage exclusion itself and barred coverage for water that backed up through sewer or drains. The second endorsement was the one that added limited sewer backup coverage. It also replaced the water damage exclusion and said coverage for water that backed up through sewer or drains as a direct or indirect *result of flood* was precluded. It is unclear from the opinion which of the two replacement water damage exclusions the court would apply and in what circumstances.

An investigator for the insurer concluded that a foot of water was caused by external flooding, that three to four inches of water had backed up from drains, and that the floodwater mixed with the backup from the drains. The insureds produced no contradictory evidence, other than their own assertion that the damage was caused entirely by water overflowing from the drainage system on the property and, therefore, failed to meet their burden to show the loss was covered.[240]

[e] "Backup" Distinguished from "Overflow"

Some endorsements may cover water that *backs up through* or *overflows or is otherwise discharged from* a sewer or drain. Courts are not in agreement about the interpretation of that language. Some conclude that there is coverage when water comes up out of a sewer or drain (backs up) *and* when water spills over from a sewer or drain (overflows) because of a blockage. Others say that for the provision to apply, the water that caused the damage has to have *started* in a drain and subsequently exited that drain.[241]

[f] Damage Caused "Solely" by Backup

Some endorsements say the insurer will pay for direct loss of, or physical damage to, covered property *solely* caused by water that backs up from a sewer or drain. In that case, the insured bears the initial burden of demonstrating that another cause—flood water, for example—did not in any way contribute to the damage. Thus, even if non-flood water backed up from a drain, but the water that ultimately entered the building included an accumulation of flood water, there would be no coverage.[242]

[g] Anti-Concurrent Causation Clause in Policy Exclusion Section

It is common for the exclusion section of property policies to have a preface with an anti-concurrent causation clause (ACC). Under that clause, an excluded loss or damage is not covered regardless of any other cause or event

240. Stiso v. State Farm Fire & Cas. Co., 2015 U.S. Dist. LEXIS 155762 (D.N.J. Nov. 18, 2015).

241. *See* Ken Johnson Props., LLC v. Harleysville Worcester Ins. Co., 2013 U.S. Dist. LEXIS 140530 (D. Minn. Sept. 30, 2013), where a large amount of rain fell on an insured apartment building and, because of a clogged roof drain, the water was not diverted from the roof, but pooled and caused damage to the roof and interior ceilings. The court said that if it were to interpret the endorsement as providing coverage only for damage caused by water that *entered a drain* and backed up, then it was "certainly possible" the damage would not be covered. On the other hand, if the court found the endorsement provided coverage for damage caused by water that was *unable to enter a drain*, it was certainly possible the damage could be covered by the endorsement. In the end, the court did not reach a decision because the "Additional Coverage for Collapse" provision governed.

242. Villamil v. Sentinel Ins. Co., 356 F. Supp. 3d 418 (D.N.J. 2018).

that contributes concurrently or in any sequence to it. When a backup and overflow endorsement is added to a policy, it typically replaces the water damage exclusion by omitting backup and overflow from the list of water damages that are excluded but does not mention concurrent causation. Most courts say that the fact that the endorsement does not refer to concurrent causation does not change the fact that the ACC applies to the new language about sewer backup coverage in the endorsement. The endorsement replaces only the definition of water damage, not the prefatory ACC language.[243] Thus, where a loss is caused concurrently by an excluded cause and by backup or overflow, there is no coverage.[244] This conclusion may be strengthened when the endorsement states that the terms and conditions of the policy apply to it.[245]

A few courts believe the absence of ACC language in the endorsement to be significant. A Pennsylvania court found the endorsement and exclusion in the principal policy to be ambiguous to the extent that they failed to provide a clear indication of the continuing role of the ACC language of the exclusion. In other words, the ACC clause was in the principal policy, but it was not restated in the endorsement. That, said the court, created an ambiguity that had to be resolved in favor of the insured. It noted that the insured bought additional coverage "ostensibly to make up for deficiencies in the basic policy only to find its claim denied not by virtue of any limitation on the coverage

243. Chateau Vill. N. Condo. Ass'n v. Am. Family Mut. Ins. Co., 170 F. Supp. 3d 1349 (D. Colo. 2016) (court agreed that ACC would bar recovery if surface water and groundwater—uncovered perils—combined with sewer backup to contribute to claimed property damage; denying summary judgment to insurer because there were genuine issues of material fact regarding character of water that caused damage and whether damage was exclusively caused by sewer water backup). *See also* Doylestown Elec. Supply Co. v. Maryland Cas. Ins. Co., 1996 U.S. Dist. LEXIS 20599 (E.D. Pa. Dec. 31, 1996), *aff'd*, 133 F.3d 909 (3d Cir. 1997); Hartman v. Erie Ins. Co., 85 N.E.3d 454 (Ohio App. 2017) (although endorsement for coverage of "Loss Caused By Backup Of Sewers Or Drains" did not separately restate the water damage exclusions listed in the main policy, where damage was caused by both surface water entering home through basement windows and backup of sewer and drain, loss was excluded coverage because of anti-concurrent causation clause, which was not modified by endorsement); Surabian Realty Co. v. NGM Ins. Co., 462 Mass. 715, 971 N.E.2d 268 (2012) (endorsement deleted and replaced backup and overflow exclusion with limited coverage; by situating new coverage within structure of original policy, policy clarified that all other provisions of original policy continued to apply, including surface water exclusion and anti-concurrent cause provision and, thus, loss caused by both overflow of drain and surface water was not covered).

244. *See* Hartman v. Erie Ins. Co., 85 N.E.3d 454 (Ohio App. 2017) (backup coverage endorsement did not provide additional protection for property from damage caused by combination of covered and non-covered causes; because there was an anti-concurrent causation clause in policy, coverage was excluded when there was more than one cause for loss and one of those causes—surface water—was an excluded cause).

245. Villamil v. Sentinel Ins. Co., 356 F. Supp. 3d 418 (D.N.J. 2018) (endorsement explicitly stated that the terms and conditions of policy applied to endorsement; anti-concurrent and anti-sequential provisions are routinely enforced and function to exclude all coverage for loss occasioned by a flood, even when flood acts concurrently or sequentially with covered peril such as sewer backup).

it bought but because ancillary language in the basic policy barred coverage for another excluded loss." The court believed that no insured would pay for extra coverage expecting a claim under that coverage would be denied because the covered cause of loss—sewer and drain backup—was itself caused by an excluded cause of loss—flood—when the two would naturally happen together. The ACC clause was, therefore, unenforceable.[246]

3.5 Damage to Roof or Walls through Which Water Enters

[1] Policy Language

[a] All-Risk Policies

Commercial all-risk property policies cover losses caused by moisture in any form, including rain, snow, or sleet, entering a building through an opening in a roof or wall unless explicitly excluded or limited. The standard ISO policy language does not bar coverage for a loss caused by rain, snow, or sleet that enters a building through an opening in a roof or wall, except for water *under the ground surface* pressing on, or flowing or seeping through, *inter alia*, walls, basements, doors, windows, or "other openings."[247] There is, however, a limitation on the coverage. There is no coverage for loss of or damage to the interior of any building structure,[248] or to personal property in the building or structure, that is caused by or results from rain, snow, *sleet*, or *ice*, whether driven by wind or not. There is an exception either when the building first sustains damage by a *covered cause of loss* to its roof or walls through which rain, snow, sleet, or ice enters or when the loss or damage is caused by or results from thawing of snow, sleet, or ice that is on the building.[249] The

246. Bishops, Inc. v. Penn. Nat. Ins., 984 A.2d 982 (Pa. Super. 2009) (insured premises was damaged by water runoff that backed up through municipal drainage system and by rising flood waters that enter premises through windows, doors, and other openings, and causing additional damage). *See also* Covington Lodging, Inc. v. W. World Ins. Grp. (*In re* Covington Lodging Inc.), 635 B.R. 675 (N.D. Ga. 2021) (because ACC clause applied to excluded causes, it would not apply to damage from drain backup once that cause was no longer excluded by operation of Sewer Endorsement); Donahue v. Burns, 2013 U.S. Dist. LEXIS 67498 (M.D. Pa. May 13, 2013) (insured property was damaged by backup of sewage and insured had purchased backup of sewage endorsement, but insurer denied coverage because damage was caused by flood waters, which was specifically excluded; court found insured adequately pled bad faith cause of action by alleging insurer based denial on concurrent causes clause, which was unenforceable under state law).

247. *See* ISO Form CP 10 30 06 07, § B.1.g.(4)(a) & (c).

248. The exclusion is for damage to the *interior* of the insured building and does not apply to damage to the *exterior*. Wider v. Heritage Maintenance, Inc., 14 Misc. 3d 963, 827 N.Y.S.2d 837 (2007) (any and all damage or loss to exterior of building allegedly caused by rain would not fall under rain limitation).

249. *See* ISO Form CP 10 30 06 07, § C.1.c. Additionally, there is no coverage for a loss that is a consequence of loss or damage as described and limited in section C.

frequent cause of a roof or wall opening is wind or hail. They are not excluded and are, therefore, covered causes of loss. Many policies name them instead of using the phrase "covered cause of loss." Earth movement, on the other hand, *is excluded* by the standard ISO policy language, so if an earthquake opens a roof or wall, there is no coverage for damage caused by rain, snow, or sleet that enters through that opening.[250]

The standard ISO all-risk homeowners policy—unlike the standard commercial property policy—covers direct physical loss to an insured dwelling and other structures, but *not* for personal property.[251] On the other hand, like the commercial version, a loss to the dwelling or other structures that is caused by moisture entering through an opening in a roof or walls is covered unless specifically excluded or limited. The definition of water damage in the exclusion for that peril does not encompass damage caused by rain, snow, or sleet entering an opening in a roof or wall.[252] In the case of personal property, the policy provides coverage for *specifically named* perils or risks,[253] two of which are windstorm and hail. Coverage does not include loss to property in a building that is caused by rain, snow, or sleet unless the direct force of wind or hail damages that building causing an opening in a roof or wall through which rain, snow, or sleet enters.[254]

There is a residential policy known as the "Homeowner's Comprehensive Form." It provides all-risk coverage for direct physical loss to the dwelling, to other structures, *and* to personal property.[255] A loss to a dwelling, other structures, or personal property is then covered when caused by moisture entering a building through an opening in a roof or walls unless specifically excluded or limited, and the definition of water damage in the policy exclusion does not encompass damage from rain, snow, or sleet entering an opening in a roof or wall.[256]

[b] Named Risk Policies

Standard named risk commercial and homeowners policies generally cover losses from windstorm or hail.[257] At the same time, they typically do not cover loss to the inside of a building—or its contents—caused by rain, snow, or sleet *except when* the direct force of wind or hail damages the building and causes

---

250. *See* ISO Form CP 10 30 06 07, § B.1.b.
251. *See* ISO Form HO 00 03 05 01 (Perils Insured Against), § I.A.1.
252. *See* ISO Form HO 00 03 05 01 (Exclusions), § I.A.3.
253. *See* ISO Form HO 00 03 05 01 (Perils Insured Against), § I.B.
254. *See* ISO Form HO 00 03 05 01 (Perils Insured Against), § I.B.2.
255. *See* ISO Form HO 00 05 05 01 (Perils Insured Against), § I.A.
256. *See* ISO Form HO 00 05 05 01 (Exclusions), § I.A.3.
257. *See, e.g.*, ISO Form HO 00 02 05 01 (Perils Insured Against), § I.2; ISO Form CP 10 20 04 02, § A.4.

an opening in a roof or wall through which rain, snow, or sleet enters.[258] The two basic prerequisites to recovery are, thus, an opening created by wind or hail *and* passage of rain or snow through it.[259] Also, the opening must be caused by the *direct* force of wind or hail, which condition does not prescribe the time between the opening and the entry of rain or snow.[260] Next, the water that enters has to be in the form of *rain* or *snow*; damage from flood waters that enter a hole, no matter how it was made, are not covered under this exception.[261]

One of the standard ISO residential policies is the Homeowners Broad Coverage Liability Form. It provides coverage for *specifically named* perils or risks. It covers direct physical loss to the insured dwelling, to other structures, and to personal property from wind or hail. That does not encompass loss to the inside of a building or any property in it caused by rain, snow, or sleet *except when* the direct force of wind or hail damages the building and causes an opening in a roof or wall through which rain, snow, or sleet enters.[262] There is a water damage exclusion, but it does not include damage from rain, snow, or sleet entering an opening in a roof or wall.[263] One small difference between the standard commercial and residential policies is that the former does not mention "sleet."

[c] Non-Standard Language

The specific language of the policy at issue has to be examined meticulously for departures from standard language that may affect the coverage. Some policies may group hail and windstorm with hurricanes as named risks.[264] A policy may cover water intrusion that comes through an opening caused by wind, hail, or "other insured peril."[265] It may cover damage from water by a "covered cause of loss," which would typically not be rain itself.[266] Under some policies the rain or snow may have to be "forced" through an opening.[267]

258. ISO Form HO 00 02 05 01 (Perils Insured Against), § I.2; ISO Form CP 10 20 04 02, § A.4.c. Actually, policies usually include entry of sand or dust along with rain, snow, or sleet as a covered source of damage.

259. Bible World Christian Ctr. v. Colony Ins. Co., 2016 U.S. Dist. LEXIS 175766 (M.D. La. Dec. 20, 2016).

260. Peerless Hosiery Co. v. Northern Ins. Co., 108 F. Supp. 52, 54 (D. Conn. 1952).

261. Preis v. Lexington Ins. Co., 508 F. Supp. 2d 1061, 1074 (S.D. Ala. 2007).

262. *See* ISO Form HO 00 02 05 01 (Perils Insured Against), § I.2.

263. *See* ISO Form HO 00 02 05 01 (Exclusions), § I.3.

264. *See, e.g.*, *In re* Auto Club Indem. Co., 580 S.W.3d 852 (Tex. App.—Houston 2019).

265. *See, e.g.*, Weinberg v. Nationwide Cas. & Ins. Co., 949 F. Supp. 2d 588 (E.D. Pa. 2013).

266. Pine Island Shopping at Sunrise, LLC v. Westchester Surplus Lunes Ins. Co., 2017 U.S. Dist. LEXIS 216484 (S.D. Fla. Sept. 25, 2017).

267. *See, e.g.*, Fernandes v. Allstate Ins. Co., 305 A.D.2d 1065, 758 N.Y.S.2d 729, 730 (2003).

Others might require "actual damage" to roof or walls by direct force of wind or hail,[268] which, in the case of wind generally means damage caused by the strength or force of wind.[269] While the standard policy language speaks of an "opening" through which rain, snow, or sleet enters, some policies say entry through "damage," but whether that difference has legal consequences is not clear.[270] A policy may cover damage to the interior of a building or to personal property in it caused by or resulting from *thawing* of snow, sleet, or ice without prior damage to the roof or walls.[271]

Under an unusual version of the coverage, an insurer would pay for damage from rain or snow admitted directly to the interior of the insured building through defective roofs, leaders, or spouting. An insurer argued "defective" meant a break or leak in the structure. The Pennsylvania Supreme Court said the word "defective" was not limited to defectiveness in physical structure, but included any defect in efficient operation whereby a structure fails to function for the purpose for which it was intended. Thus, where a roof drain became clogged, allowing rainwater to pool on the roof, overtop flashing, and enter the building, the damage was the result of defective spouting—a drain pipe—and was covered.[272]

[d] Definition of Key Terms

[i] Generally

Under the language of the standard policies previously discussed, a prerequisite to application of the "opening in a roof or wall" exception to the limitation on loss by rain, snow, or sleet is that the opening be caused by hail or wind. That makes the definitions of "hail" and "wind" of critical importance. Those definitions are rarely found in policies. Also undefined is the word "opening." Similarly, policies proscribe coverage for loss or damage to the interior or contents of a *building* by rain, snow, or sleet unless the *building* first sustains wind or hail damage to its roof or walls, but do not define "building." Finally, policies refer to the "direct force" of wind or hail on roof or walls, but do not define the phrase.

---

268. *See* Abady v. Hanover Fire Ins. Co., 266 F.2d 362 (4th Cir. 1959); Commercial Carving Ins. Co. v. Manhattan Fire and Marine Ins., 191 F. Supp. 753, 759 (M.D.N.C. 1961); Granchelli v. Travelers Ins. Co., 167 A.D.2d 839, 561 N.Y.S.2d 944 (1990); Williams v. Liberty Mut. Fire Ins. Co., 334 Mass. 499, 501, 135 N.E.2d 910, 911 (1956).

269. Commercial Carving Ins. Co. v. Manhattan Fire and Marine Ins., 191 F. Supp. 753, 759 (M.D.N.C. 1961)

270. *See, e.g.*, Divine Motel Grp., LLC v. Rockhill Ins. Co., 655 Fed. Appx. 779 (11th Cir. 2016).

271. *See, e.g.*, Zaragon Holdings, Inc. v. Indian Harbor Ins. Co., 2010 U.S. Dist. LEXIS 79536 (N.D. Ill. Aug. 2, 2010).

272. Armon v. Aetna Casualty & Surety Co., 369 Pa. 465, 87 A.2d 302 (1952).

[ii] "Hail" Defined

What is hail? A dictionary definition is "precipitation in the form of small balls or lumps usually consisting of concentric layers of clear ice and compact snow."[273] That seems simple enough, but as is often the case, matters become more complicated in courtrooms where lawyers dispute the meaning of words. For example, standard ISO policies provide coverage when rain, snow, or sleet enters through an opening created by hail, suggesting sleet and hail are different. Indeed, a dictionary definition of "sleet" is "rain that freezes or partly freezes as it falls from the sky."[274] Nonetheless, the Mississippi Supreme Court said that coverage for hail includes sleet because of the "stated physical and meteorological similarities" between them.[275] On the other hand, the Eighth Circuit agreed with the refusal of a trial court to instruct the jury that the definition of "hail" includes "sleet."[276]

Given the confusion between the meaning of "hail" and "sleet," it is not surprising that a word as seemingly clear-cut to laypeople could be ambiguous to a court. A Texas court, for example, found "hail" could have more than one reasonable construction, making it ambiguous.[277]

Is there a minimum size for hail? One court agreed that the definition of the word is "ice pellets" larger than five millimeters.[278] While hail is associated with summer thunderstorms, some courts say there can be winter hail,[279] although others say there cannot.[280]

[iii] "Windstorm" Defined

The standard policy provides that there is coverage when rain, snow, or sleet enters an opening made by the direct force of *wind*. Those policies do not define "wind."

---

273. *Hail*, Merriam-Webster, https://www.merriam-webster.com/dictionary/hail.

274. *Sleet*, Merriam-Webster, https://www.merriam-webster.com/dictionary/sleet.

275. Evana Plantation, Inc. v. Yorkshire Ins. Co., 214 Miss. 321, 329, 58 So. 2d 797, 799 (1952). *See also* Southall v. Farm Bureau Mut. Ins. Co., 276 Ark. 58, 632 S.W.2d 420 (1982) (instructing jury that "hail" was to be given its everyday meaning was error; court should have, if appropriate, instructed jury that "hail" as used in policy included sleet).

276. Barton v. Columbia Mut. Casualty Ins. Co., 930 F.2d 1337, 1340 (8th Cir. 1993).

277. Commonwealth Lloyds Ins. Co. v. Downs, 853 S.W.2d 104 (Tex. Civ. App.—Fort Worth 1993) (distinguishing *Evana Plantation* and deciding that where sleet caused ice to accumulate on roof and structure to collapse from weight of ice, jury erred in finding there was covered cause of loss because, *inter alia*, there was testimony that sleet and hail are different).

278. Home Mut. Fire Ins. Co. v. Jones, 63 Ark. App. 221, 228, 977 S.W.2d 12, 15 (1998).

279. Evana Plantation, Inc. v. Yorkshire Ins. Co., 214 Miss. 321, 328, 58 So. 2d 797, 799 (1952).

280. Commonwealth Lloyds Ins. Co. v. Downs, 853 S.W.2d 104, 113 (Tex. App.—Fort Worth 1993) (hail cannot form in winter).

Insurers and courts may say an opening has to be caused by a *windstorm*, rather than just wind.[281] Courts may conclude the terms "wind" and "windstorm" are used interchangeably in policies and largely mean the same thing,[282] or they may distinguish the terms.[283] For example, a policyholder claimed the roof of the insured building was damaged in a windstorm and the interior had been damaged when rain entered through openings in the roof from the direct action of wind. The court responded that no evidence supported the claim that the roof was damaged by a *windstorm* or that rain had entered through openings caused by a *windstorm*.[284]

Insurers, understandably, want to place the emphasis on "storm" and may argue that interior damage is not covered unless the opening was created by a storm.[285] However, most policies simply refer to wind, which is defined as "a natural movement of air of any velocity."[286] Policyholders can then argue that had the insurer wanted to use the word "windstorm," it was free to have done so.[287] Unfortunately, many courts do seem to equate "wind" and "windstorm" and to make matters worse, the definition of "windstorm" is unsettled or, as one justice put it, the courts are in hopeless conflict over it.[288] Some courts define a windstorm as an "outburst of tumultuous force."[289] That begs

281. *See, e.g.*, Royale Green Condo. Ass'n v. Aspen Specialty Ins. Co., 2009 U.S. Dist. LEXIS 24349 (S.D. Fla. Mar. 24, 2009); Sun Ins. Office v. Guest Camera Store, 108 Ga. App. 339, 132 S.E.2d 851 (1963).

282. Gerhard v. Travelers Fire Ins. Co., 246 Wis. 625, 627, 18 N.W.2d 336, 337 (1945). *See also* Lumbermens Mut. Casualty Co. v. Ely, 253 Md. 254, 252 A.2d 786 (1969).

283. *See, e.g.*, Butler Prods. Co. v. Connecticut Fire Ins. Co., 1969 U.S. Dist. LEXIS 9816 (N.D. Ill. Oct. 3, 1969); General Ins. Co. of America v. Davis, 115 Ga. App. 804, 811, 156 S.E.2d 112, 116 (1967); Williams v. Detroit Fire & Marine Ins. Co., 280 Mich. 215, 217, 273 NW 452, 453 (1937) (word or expression "windstorm" is to be distinguished from word "wind").

284. Wasson v. Insurance Co. of North America, 25 Ill. App. 2d 35, 38, 165 N.E.2d 528, 530 (1960).

285. *In re* Auto Club Indem. Co., 580 S.W.3d 852, 854 (Tex. App.—Houston 2019).

286. *Wind*, Merriam-Webster, https://www.merriam-webster.com/dictionary/wind.

287. *But see* General Ins. Co. v. Davis, 115 Ga. App. 804, 810, 156 S.E.2d 112, 116 (1967), where the evidence showed only gusty wind that was capable of blowing trash and leaves, nothing tended to show wind with the force and velocity needed to meet the definition of "windstorm." The court said that contention that the policy should cover damage if there was any wind sufficient to cause it, whether or not there had been a windstorm, was without merit. That, said the court, would stretch the meaning beyond "fair interpretation" of the word.

288. Yunker v. Republic-Franklin Ins. Co., 2 Ohio App. 3d 339, 341, 442 N.E.2d 108, 111 (1982).

289. *See, e.g.*, Metropolitan Ice Cream Co. v. Union Mut. Fire Ins. Co., 210 S.W.2d 700 (Mo. App. 1948); George A. Hoagland & Co. v. Insurance Co., 131 Neb. 105, 267 N.W. 239, 241 (1936); Jordan v. Iowa Mut. Tornado Ins. Co., 151 Iowa 73, 77–78, 130 N.W. 177, 178 (1911). *See also* Butler Prods. Co. v. Connecticut Fire Ins. Co., 1969 U.S. Dist. LEXIS 9816 (N.D. Ill. Oct. 3, 1969).

the question of how much force is required and how it is measured."[290] Most courts hold that a "windstorm" is a wind that is of enough force to damage property that is in reasonable condition.[291]

[iv] "Building" Defined

Policies bar coverage for loss or damage to the interior or contents of a building by rain, snow, or sleet unless the *building* first sustains wind or hail damage to its roof or walls, but what is a building? The Merriam-Webster lay dictionary defines "building" as "a usually roofed and walled structure built for permanent use."[292] A law dictionary is similar: "A structure designed and suitable for habitation or sheltering human beings and animals, sheltering or storing property, or for use and occupation for private and public business, trade, or manufacture more broadly defined as any structure with walls and a roof."[293] One court that agreed with those definitions held that the word "building" is plain and unambiguous and means a structure with a roof and walls and, therefore, because a carport had no walls, it was not a building.[294] Nonetheless, a distinction may be drawn between the phrase "fully enclosed building"—meaning one with walls—and the word "building."[295] One court has said the term "building," without any other description, usually includes the foundation on which it rests.[296]

A Louisiana court discussed the meaning of "building" within the context of the roof or wall opening exception. In that case, an insured business alleged it had lumber stacked at its yard and the lumber was "covered or roofed." A storm unroofed the lumber. Torrential rains fell, and the lumber became

290. Pearson v. Aroostook County Patrons Mut. Fire Ins. Co., 149 Me. 313, 319, 101 A.2d 183, 186 (1953).

291. *See* Reynolds v. Shelter Mut. Ins. Co., 313 Ark. 145, 151–52, 852 S.W.2d 799, 803 (1993); Yunker v. Republic-Franklin Ins. Co., 2 Ohio App. 3d 339, 343, 442 N.E.2d 108, 112 (1982); St. Paul Fire & Marine Ins. Co. v. Central Park Mobile Homes, 22 Ariz. App. 557, 529 P.2d 711 (1974); Napanoch Realty Corp. v. Public Service Mut. Ins. Co., 39 A.D.2d 438, 440, 336 N.Y.S.2d 489, 490 (1972); Gerhard v. Travelers Fire Ins. Co., 246 Wis. 625, 627–28, 18 N.W.2d 336, 337 (1945). *See also* Rifai Props., LLC v. United Nat'l Ins. Co., 2016 U.S. Dist. LEXIS 185755 (M.D. Fla. Apr. 26, 2016) (wind of sufficient violence to be capable of damaging property either by impact of its own force or by projecting some object; winds in windstorm typically exceed 34 miles per hour).

292. *Building*, Merriam-Webster, https://www.merriam-webster.com/dictionary/building.

293. *Ballentine's Law Dictionary* (LexisNexis 2010). The definition adds that "an incomplete structure is a 'building' within the meaning of an insurance contract."

294. People's Ins. Counsel Div. v. State Farm Fire & Cas. Ins. Co., 214 Md. App. 438, 456, 76 A.3d 517, 528 (2012).

295. Herzog v. Property & Cas. Ins. Co., 2016 U.S. Dist. LEXIS 166177 (W.D. Wash. Nov. 30, 2016) (policy defined "fully enclosed building" as one with continuous walls on all sides, extending from ground level to roof, with doors and windows as necessary at various locations in the walls and including continuous roof sheltering all areas within wall perimeter).

296. Davison v. Walla Walla, 52 Wash. 453, 456, 100 P. 981, 982 (1909).

"drenched and flooded" and thereby damaged. The insurer contended there was no coverage because the lumber was not in a building but stacked in a yard. The policy, said the insurer, covered loss or damage by rain only when the insured property was in a building. The court agreed.[297]

[v] "Direct Force" Defined

The standard policy language requires an opening by the "direct force" of wind or hail. What is "direct force"? The Fourth Circuit confronted that question a number of years ago in a case in which the policyholder claimed wind blew a hatch cover off a roof, exposing adjacent water pipes to strong cold winds, and that as a result, they froze and burst. Later, when the pipes thawed, water entered the insured building. In *dicta*, the court asserted that the action of wind was too remote from the actual damage to come within the policy coverage. Direct wind damage, it said, could not be understood as a frozen pipe. Rather "loss as direct result of wind" means damage from the strength or force of wind.[298] In another case,[299] wind prevented rainwater from draining off a roof and the weight of that water caused a leak. The court found no coverage because the policyholder did not show the loss was the "direct result of windstorm."

These courts might have reached a different decision if the policy language had permitted the loss to be the *indirect* result of wind or merely the result of wind. Therefore, counsel for a policyholder should examine the precise language of the policy at issue because not every policy contains the standard language and seemingly small differences in wording can determine the coverage and the burden a policyholder has to meet to receive coverage.

---

297. Cotton Bros. v. Home Ins. Co. of N.Y., 147 La. 308, 84 So. 792 (1920).

298. Abady v. Hanover Fire Ins. Co., 266 F.2d 362, 364 (4th Cir. 1959). The policy says the insurer would be "liable for loss to the interior of the building or the property covered therein as may be caused by water, rain, snow, sand or dust entering the building through openings in the roof or walls made by direct action of wind." That raises a question about the court's reasoning. The damage to the roof according to the insured *was* caused by the force of wind blowing off the hatch cover. The freezing and thawing, on the other hand, was not the direct result of the *force* of wind. As the court said, to find coverage because the chemical or physical properties of moving air absorbing and carrying away heat and facilitating freezing would be too strained an interpretation. *See also* Williams v. Liberty Mut. Fire Ins. Co., 334 Mass. 499, 501, 135 N.E.2d 910, 911 (1956) (agreeing that when shutter over louver in building loft was ripped off during windstorm, allowing water pipe in loft to freeze and burst, causing water damage inside home, pipe was not damaged as direct result of wind and, therefore, loss was not covered). *Compare* Granchelli v. Travelers Ins. Co., 167 A.D.2d 839, 561 N.Y.S.2d 944 (1990) (windstorm was not too remote to be considered direct cause of loss when it blew open roof door allowing subzero air entered building and freeze pipe that subsequently burst, causing in water damage).

299. Sherwood Real Estate & Inv. Co. v. Old Colony Ins. Co., 234 So. 2d 445, 447 (La. App. 1970).

[vi] "Opening" Defined

Standard polices provide coverage when the direct force of wind or hail damages the building and causes an *opening* in a roof or wall through which rain, snow, or sleet enters. Policies do not define "opening." In one case the word was challenged as ambiguous. The court, however, decided the meaning was clear and meant an "open space," "gap," or "breach."[300] A dictionary definition is "something that is open" such as a breach or aperture.[301] Courts echo that definition and often add that a "hole" is an opening.[302] However, one court that interpreted the "roof or wall opening" coverage said the policyholder does not have to show wind produced a *hole* through which water entered, but rather that wind created an *opening* allowing water to enter.[303]

[2] Burden of Proof

The universally accepted rule in insurance law is that the initial burden of establishing coverage for a particular loss under a policy is on the policyholder, and the burden then shifts to the insurance carrier to prove that an exclusion or limitation on coverage applies.[304] The "roof or wall opening" clause is, in most policies, an exception to a limitation of the covered risk of windstorm or hail. That is, policies generally cover losses from windstorm or hail but limit coverage of losses inside a building caused by rain, snow, or sleet *unless* the direct force of wind or hail damages the building and causes an opening in a roof or wall through which rain, snow, or sleet enters.[305]

Not all courts treat limitations on coverage the same. Most view limitations as part of the grant of coverage and make the policyholder bear the burden of showing the limitation does not apply, while others say "limiting provisions" are functionally exclusions and place the burden on the insurance carrier to show the limitation does apply.[306] No matter how courts characterize

---

300. Dashtpeyma v. Liberty Ins. Corp., 2013 U.S. Dist. LEXIS 139015 (N.D. Ga. Sept. 27, 2013), *aff'd*, 569 Fed. Appx. 886 (11th Cir. 2014). *See also* Cappa v. Oscar C. Holmes, Inc., 25 Cal. App. 3d 978, 983, 102 Cal. Rptr. 207, 211 (1972) (place or part which is open).

301. *Opening*, Merriam-Webster, https://www.merriam-webster.com/dictionary/opening.

302. Fuji Photo Film Co. v. ITC, 386 F.3d 1095, 1098 (Fed. Cir. 2004) (hole, breach, or aperture); Burgess v. Mo., K. & T. Ry. Co of Tex., 41 S.W. 703, 704 (1897) (place which is open; a breach; an aperture; a gap, cleft, or hole).

303. Dudenhefer v. La. Citizens Prop. Ins. Corp., 280 So. 3d 771, 775 (La. App. 2019).

304. 12 Jeffrey E. Thomas, *New Appleman on Insurance Law Library Edition* § 154.05[2][a] (Matthew Bender 2022).

305. ISO Form HO 00 02 05 01 (Perils Insured Against), § I.2; ISO Form CP 10 20 04 02, § A.4.c. Actually, policies usually include entry of sand or dust along with rain, snow or sleet as a covered source of damage.

306. 12 Jeffrey E. Thomas, *New Appleman on Insurance Law Library Edition* § 154.05[2][a] (Matthew Bender 2022). Some courts even label the limitation on coverage of losses inside a building caused by rain, snow, or sleet an exclusion. Divine Motel Grp., LLC v. Rockhill Ins.

a limitation, proving an *exception* to it should be up to the insured because the exception creates coverage, and that is how courts have handled the "roof or wall opening" exception.[307]

If the policyholder has the burden of proof, what does he or she have to prove? Basically, the insured has to produce evidence that shows rain, snow, or sleet entered the insured premises through a roof or wall first damaged by wind or hail. The insured then has to show the rain, snow, or sleet caused damage.[308] Typically, the efforts of the policyholder are tested by a motion for summary judgment.[309] They have survived summary judgment in the following scenarios:

- A roofing contractor's affidavit stated that a roof was lifted as direct result of highspeed winds allowing rainwater to enter the insured home.[310]
- A public adjuster testified that damage was caused by wind.[311]

Co., 655 Fed. Appx. 779 (11th Cir. 2016); Ace Prop. & Cas. Ins. Co. v. Vegas VP, LP, 2008 U.S. Dist. LEXIS 37495 (D. Nev. May 7, 2008); Be Van Nguyen v. Atl. Cas. Ins. Co., 2008 U.S. Dist. LEXIS 28814 (E.D. La. Apr. 9, 2008); Bangor-Brewer Bowling Lanes v. Commercial Union-York Ins. Co., 2001 Me. Super. LEXIS 174 (July 3, 2001); N.H. Ins. Co. v. Carter, 359 So. 2d 52, 54 (Fla. 1st DCA 1978).

307. *See, e.g.*, Legacy Condos., Inc. v. Landmark Am. Ins. Co., 2008 U.S. Dist. LEXIS 655 (S.D. Miss. Jan. 4, 2008) (burden on insured to prove damages within exception to wind-driven rain limitation). *See also* New South Communs. v. Houston Cas. Co., 396 F. Supp. 3d 1089, 1100 (S.D. Fla. 2019); Mock v. Central Mut. Ins. Co., 158 F. Supp. 3d 1332, 1347 (S.D. Ga. 2016); Empire Pro Restoration, Inc. v. Citizens Prop. Ins. Corp., 322 So. 3d 96 (Fla. 4th DCA 2021).

308. New South Communs. v. Houston Cas. Co., 396 F. Supp. 3d 1089, 1100 (S.D. Fla. 2019); Brindley v. Firemen's Ins. Co., 35 N.J. Super. 1, 6, 113 A.2d 53, 56 (1955). *See also* Martine v. Republic Fire & Cas. Ins. Co., 2008 U.S. Dist. LEXIS 992 (E.D. La. Jan. 7, 2008) (when policies contain provision excluding loss caused by water whether driven by wind or not, unless insured property first sustains actual damage by direct force of wind, and water enters as a result of wind, the insured must prove that wind created openings and that passage of water through those openings caused damage at issue; insured need not establish that wind actually created hole but must only demonstrate that direct force of wind created opening in the buildings through which water entered).

309. The plaintiff's claim will be subject to a motion to dismiss by the insurer; however, the defendant company is unlikely to prevail on that motion because under the rules of procedure in state and federal courts, the compliant needs only to briefly state a cognizable claim. For example, in one case the compliant alleged that water entered the insured property and caused damage covered by policy. It did not say that the water entered after wind or hail damage, but it did claim that insurer wrongly denied coverage. The court denied the insurance company's motion to dismiss as it was plausible to infer that plaintiff believed wind or hail damage occurred. Hurtado USA, Inc. v. Am. Safety & Indem. Co., 2005 U.S. Dist. LEXIS 30444 (M.D.N.C. Nov. 16, 2005).

310. Berliner v. New York Prop. Ins. Underwriting Assoc., 2015 N.Y. Misc. LEXIS 4930 (May 19, 2015).

311. Allison v. Allstate Indem. Co., 2008 U.S. Dist. LEXIS 50684 (E.D. Pa. June 30, 2008).

- A public adjuster asserted that wind caused excess water to run into an open basement window, even though the policyholder offered no evidence that wind caused that window to be open.[312]
- It was unclear whether water entered through a human-made opening or an opening from wind damage.[313]
- The insureds produced evidence showing hurricane winds caused openings and cracks in the roof and walls that allowed rain to enter prior to a flood.[314]
- There was evidence of roof damage above the rooms where there was water damage to contents, and the insurance company had paid for roof damage showing that it acknowledged the roof was damaged by wind.[315]
- The policyholder stated in a deposition that she saw wind and rain and water pouring into rooms in her house and also saw the resulting water damage.[316]
- There was evidence of an ice storm accompanied by heavy winds, and the roof of the insured property dropped significantly during the storm and water entered the building.[317]
- There were genuine issues of material fact about the cause of entry of water into property.[318]

Thus, while the burden on policyholders is not great, for the coverage question to be tried, they must produce some evidence beyond conjecture or speculation.[319] Insureds have failed to meet their burden of proof and insurers were granted summary judgment in the following scenarios:

---

312. Rock-Epstein v. Allstate Ins. Co., 2008 U.S. Dist. LEXIS 76042 (E.D. Pa. Sept. 29, 2008).

313. Royale Green Condo. Ass'n v. Aspen Specialty Ins. Co., 2009 U.S. Dist. LEXIS 24349 (S.D. Fla. Mar. 24, 2009).

314. Gaffney v. State Farm Fire and Casualty Co., 2008 U.S. Dist. LEXIS 27805 (E.D. La. Apr. 7, 2008).

315. Rosen v. United Servs. Auto. Ass'n, 104 So. 3d 633 (La. App. 2012).

316. Weshifesky v. State Farm Fire & Cas. Co., 2006 N.J. Super. Unpub. LEXIS 1207 (May 4, 2006) (no requirement that insured provide expert testimony on causation to bring claim within coverage).

317. Bangor-Brewer Bowling Lanes v. Commercial Union-York Ins. Co., 2001 Me. Super. LEXIS 174 (July 3, 2001).

318. Dunn v. Scottsdale Ins. Co., 2013 U.S. Dist. LEXIS 107984 (M.D. Pa. Aug. 1, 2013).

319. Travelers Fire Ins. Co. v. Taylor, 171 F.2d 203, 205 (5th Cir. 1948) (where cause of roof collapse was not shown and could not be inferred from any evidence, water damage did not bring loss within policy terms without showing wind or hail caused opening immediately prior to entry of water); Kannatt v. Valley Forge Ins. Co., 228 A.D.2d 564, 644 N.Y.S.2d 530, *app. dis.*, 651 N.Y.S.2d 9, 88 N.Y.2d 1062, 673 N.E.2d 1236 (1996) (affirmation of insured's attorney, who had no personal knowledge of loss, that loss was caused by either wind or falling object, which pierced hole in basement door, allowing rain to fall directly through door into basement, was based on speculation and conjecture and was insufficient to defeat insurer's motion for summary judgment); Cloud v. Trinity Cos. Trinity Universal Ins. Co., 5 Kan. App. 2d

- The policyholders produced no evidence of any specific interior damage that was caused by rain entering through any openings that were made by wind.[320]
- The insured presented no evidence showing that a windstorm occurred in the area or that any windstorm caused damage to the roof or walls, and the insured's witnesses had no personal knowledge of the duration of any allegedly high winds.[321]
- The policyholder did not claim there was a hole in the roof and produced no repair records or estimates that would demonstrate that an opening in the roof had been repaired after the storm.[322]
- The property owner did not produce any evidence to support his belief the roof was damaged during a windstorm that blew branches into it, allowing wind-blown water to entering the dwelling.[323]
- The insured could not identify wind damage to the roof that was an entry point for rain that collected in the basement, but testified a part of tarpaulin had been blown off in the storm and that exterior walls had been demolished and were open to the elements.[324]
- The insured did not prove the property sustained a roof opening that allowed water to enter the building and cause interior damage.[325]
- The record merely showed some "metaphysical possibility" that a tropical storm damaged roofs.[326]

437, 439, 617 P.2d 1277, 1280 (1980) (leak in roof would not alone support inference that it was caused by wind); Sherwood Real Estate & Inv. Co. v. Old Colony Ins. Co., 234 So. 2d 445, 447 (La. App. 1970) (assertion of policyholder that strong wind caused damage was speculation where there was no evidence about wind velocity during storm, its duration, or amount of rainfall); Wasson v. Insurance Co. of North America, 25 Ill. App. 2d 35, 38, 165 N.E.2d 528, 530 (1960) (no evidence of how water entered premises or about any opening in roof or walls caused by wind); Brindley v. Firemen's Ins. Co., 35 N.J. Super. 1, 6, 113 A.2d 53, 56 (1955) (plaintiff's proof must enable fact finder to find without resort to sheer conjecture amount of particular loss ascribable to hazard assumed by carrier—that is, rain entering opening caused by wind). *See also* Petrick v. State Farm Fire & Cas. Co., 2010 N.J. Super. Unpub. LEXIS 1964 (Aug. 13, 2010) (policyholder could not argue that because water entered home, there must have been an opening and that because policy did not define "opening," evidence of water infiltration was sufficient to produce coverage).

320. New South Communs. v. Houston Cas. Co., 396 F. Supp. 3d 1089, 1100 (S.D. Fla. 2019).

321. Olivet Baptist Church v. Church Mut. Ins. Co., 2016 U.S. Dist. LEXIS 25294 (N.D. Ill. Feb. 29, 2016), *aff'd*, 672 Fed. Appx. 607 (7th Cir. 2017).

322. Petrick v. State Farm Fire & Cas. Co., 2010 N.J. Super. Unpub. LEXIS 1964 (Aug. 13, 2010).

323. Holliday v. Pioneer State Mut. Ins. Co, 2009 Mich. App. LEXIS 465 (Mich. App. Mar. 5, 2009).

324. Zions v. Essex Ins. Co., 2009 N.J. Super. Unpub. LEXIS 1318 (May 29, 2009).

325. Advanced Sleep Ctr., Inc. v. Certain Underwriters at Lloyd's, 213 So. 3d 1220, 1228 (La. App. 2017).

326. Divine Motel Grp., LLC v. Rockhill Ins. Co., 655 Fed. Appx. 779 (11th Cir. 2016).

- The report of the policyholder's expert was unsworn and, therefore, not competent to be considered by the court and, in any event, was inconclusive on the question of the cause of the alleged interior damage.[327]
- Evidence showed only a possibility that wind removed a hatch cover on the roof.[328]

Sometimes the insurance company will not dispute that wind or hail caused an opening in a roof or wall through which rain, snow, or sleet entered. The policyholder then only needs to prove causation. That is, the policyholder will have to show the rain, sleet, or snow that entered the opening caused a loss.[329] If it is clear that a loss from entry of rain, snow, or sleet through an opening that was caused by wind or hail was covered, the insurer may be liable for statutory penalties or for bad faith failure to settle.[330]

After there has been a significant storm, insurance carriers frequently argue the property damage was caused by flooding, rather than rain, snow, or sleet that entered an opening that was created by wind or hail. The company then invokes the water damage exclusion. In that case, the policyholder can meet the burden of proving coverage by showing the loss was caused by rain, snow, or sleet that entered an opening despite the fact that flood waters later damaged the property. In other words, the insured has to segregate the wind-related damages from the flood damages. For example, the Rhode Island Supreme Court said that a trial judge was wrong to say that subsequent flooding of the damaged goods absolved the insurer of liability because that in effect prevented the jury from considering a claim for damage *before* ocean waters rose and flooded the property.[331]

[3] Entry Points

[a] Windows or Doors

The standard policy language triggers coverage when rain, snow, or sleet enters an opening in a roof or wall made by wind or hail. Nonetheless, insureds have contended with success that coverage could be for damage that was caused by water that entered through *windows* that had loosened and *doors* that had

---

327. Hayden v. Westfield Ins. Co., 2013 U.S. Dist. LEXIS 153334 (W.D. Pa. Oct. 25, 2013).

328. Abady v. Hanover Fire Ins. Co., 266 F.2d 362, 364 (4th Cir. 1959) (trier of fact may not guess or speculate on mere possibilities).

329. Sullivan v. Std. Fire Ins. Co., 956 A.2d 643 (Del. 2007).

330. Best v. State Farm Fire & Cas. Co., 969 So. 2d 671 (La. App. 2007).

331. Napoletano v. Standard Fire Ins. Co., 102 R.I. 604, 608, 232 A.2d 378, 381 (1967). *See also* Parmer v. Utah Home Fire Ins. Co., 219 F. Supp. 956 (S.D. Tex. 1963) (evidence supported that greater part of damage was caused by direct wind and rain entering building through openings that were caused by direct effect of wind).

been damaged by wind.[332] For example, a basement door was blown open. Rainwater then blew in and ran down steps into a basement. The policy had the standard language referring to an opening in the roof or walls; nevertheless, the court found for the policyholder.[333] Other courts adhere to the strict language of the policy. For example, a Florida court found there was no coverage where rain entered the insured property when it was driven through window and sliding glass door openings. Because no evidence pointed to entry through openings in the roof or walls, the court said the policy clearly and unambiguously proscribed coverage for the damage suffered.[334] In a departure from the standard language, some policies include windows with roofs and walls,[335] in which case the Florida insured should have been able to recover. On the other hand, there would be no coverage when precipitation enters an *open* window.[336] In another variation, the policy in an Illinois case covered direct loss and damage caused by rain admitted directly to the interior of the insured building through defective doors. The insured contended that rain ran between two buildings, through a fire escape, and then fell directly before and through a defective door, causing the damage for which coverage was sought. The insured said the rain was not admitted directly to the interior of the building through the defective door so it was surface water, an excluded risk. The trial court found for the insured, and the appellate court affirmed.[337] It noted that there was no evidence that there was any water lying on the ground and that it is difficult to say where the line of demarcation lies between rain and surface water. The case illustrates the importance of specific facts and the inclination of courts to side with insureds on the meaning of undefined terms.

---

332. Commercial Union Ins. Co. v. Byrne, 248 So. 2d 777, 781 (Miss. 1971). *See also* Dudenhefer v. La. Citizens Prop. Ins. Corp., 280 So. 3d 771, 776 (La. App. 2019) (wind made openings by doors and windows, allowing wind-driven rain to penetrate); Napoletano v. Standard Fire Ins. Co., 102 R.I. 604, 608, 232 A.2d 378, 381 (1967) (suggesting walls and windows would be treated the same).

333. Johnson v. Kansas City Fire & Marine Insurance Co., 364 S.W.2d 68 (Mo. App. 1962) (observing that agent for insurer said policy did not cover loss "unless the door had been breached by wind"). *See also* Unobskey v. Continental Ins. Co., 147 Me. 249, 258, 86 A.2d 160, 164 (1952).

334. Fla. Windstorm Underwriting v. Gajwani, 934 So. 2d 501, 506 (Fla. 3d DCA 2005). *Compare* Tropic Sun Towers Condo. Ass'n v. Zurich Am. Ins. Co. of Illinois, 2006 U.S. Dist. LEXIS 89358 (M.D. Fla. Dec. 8, 2006) (summary judgment denied where question remained as to whether loss was caused by permanent or temporary damage to sliding glass doors that allowed water into building).

335. *See, e.g.*, Ace Prop. & Cas. Ins. Co. v. Vegas VP, LP, 2008 U.S. Dist. LEXIS 37495 (D. Nev. May 7, 2008).

336. Massmann, *"Dammed" Ice: When Ice Prevents Melting Snow from Draining Properly, Leading to Interior Leaks, Will Your Property Policy Cover the Damage?* (Jan. 30, 2012), PropertyCasualty360, https://www.propertycasualty360.com/2012/01/30/dammed-ice/.

337. Goldfarb v. Maryland Casualty Co., 311 Ill. App. 568, 37 N.E.2d 376 (1941).

[b] Rooftop Air-conditioning Units

In commercial and multistory residential buildings, air-conditioning units are often placed on a roof. In an Ohio case, roof drains became clogged with windblown debris. That permitted water to rise and to enter an air-conditioning unit. It flowed through ductwork and damaged the interior of the building. Because a clogged drain caused water to rise on the roof and because that water did not enter the building through the damaged drain but through the undamaged air-conditioning component, the court held there was no coverage.[338]

[4] Reason for the Opening

[a] Intentionally Created

An intentionally created opening does not trigger coverage: "intentionally created holes that allow water into the building are not a 'covered cause of loss.'"[339] For instance, where water overflowed a gutter and entered a building through openings in the ceiling that were part of an original building design, there was no coverage.[340] The intentionally created opening that is most often at issue occurs when a roof is repaired or replaced. Generally, courts hold that when all or part of a roof is removed to repair or replace it, there is no coverage because the building did not first sustain damage by wind or hail that caused an opening.[341] There is, of course, always the exception. In a Georgia case, a roof was under repair when water leaked through it. The court said that openings in a roof, regardless of the cause, were injuries that compromised the roof's normal function as contemplated by the policy definition of damage.[342] The problem with the court's assertion is that under the language of the policy, any opening had to be caused by a covered cause of loss.

[b] Wind-Propelled Projectiles

In the typical case, wind removes shingles or siding and allows rain, snow, or sleet to enter the insured building. Under standard policy language, there

---

338. Oak Hill Inv. IV LLC v. State Farm Fire & Cas. Co., 2017 U.S. Dist. LEXIS 158851 (N.D. Ohio Sept. 27, 2017). *See also* Royale Green Condo. Ass'n v. Aspen Specialty Ins. Co., 2009 U.S. Dist. LEXIS 24349 (S.D. Fla. Mar. 24, 2009) (where testimony about whether components were part of air-conditioning system or of roof was conflicting, summary judgment denied).

339. Christ Church of the Gospel Ministries v. Guideone Mut. Ins. Co., 2019 U.S. Dist. LEXIS 200138, at *4 (E.D. Mich. Nov. 19, 2019).

340. Bible World Christian Ctr. v. Colony Ins. Co., 2016 U.S. Dist. LEXIS 175766 (M.D. La. Dec. 20, 2016).

341. *See* Diep v. California Fair Plan Ass'n, 15 Cal. App. 4th 1205, 1209, 19 Cal. Rptr. 2d 591, 593 (1993); N.H. Ins. Co. v. Carter, 359 So. 2d 52 (Fla. 1st DCA 1978); Camden Fire Ins. Ass'n v. New Buena Vista Hotel Co., 199 Miss. 585, 24 So. 2d 848 (1946).

342. Mock v. Central Mut. Ins. Co., 158 F. Supp. 3d 1332, 1349 (S.D. Ga. 2016).

is coverage for the loss inside the building. However, what is the result when wind propels an object that then penetrates a roof or wall and produces an opening? In that case, insurance carriers have contended that the opening was not the *direct* action of wind. That argument has generally been rebuffed by courts, with one federal district court saying that insureds do not have to show that wind created a hole, but that the direct force of wind created an opening through which water entered. The court concluded that "water entering into a structure through a breach caused by the impact of a wind-blown object qualifies as damage by wind, bringing the loss under the policy coverage."[343] Following that reasoning courts have found coverage where a roof or wall was penetrated by wind-driven antenna,[344] trees or tree branches,[345] and ice.[346] The wind-driven projectile has to create an opening for there to be coverage. There was, therefore, no coverage when wind created no opening but ripped a gutter from the side of a building, allowing water to accumulate on a porch and seep into a basement.[347]

[c] Rainfall

When the policy is all-risk, rainfall itself could be considered the covered cause of loss that creates an opening.[348] In a Louisiana case, a drain on a flat roof clogged, allowing standing water to accumulate. It entered and damaged the interior of the insured premises. Coverage was denied by the insurance carrier, which contended that the water gained entry because of wear and tear and cracks in the roof, an excluded peril. An expert for the insured, however,

343. Johnson v. State Farm Fire & Cas. Co., 2008 U.S. Dist. LEXIS 122416, at *8 (E.D. La. May 19, 2008). *See also* Sun Ins. Office v. Guest Camera Store, 108 Ga. App. 339, 344, 132 S.E.2d 851, 855 (1963) (where building has roof opened either by wind lifting it or by projecting some object against it and rain enters building and damages property, that damage is caused by direct force of wind and comes within policy coverage).

344. Guest Printing Co. v. American Ins. Co., 222 Ga. 674, 151 S.E.2d 717 (1966) (finding for insured where antenna was blown down in a windstorm and made holes in roof through which water entered).

345. Amish Connection, Co. v. State Farm Fire & Cas. Co., 861 N.W.2d 230, 236 (Iowa 2015) (exception for openings caused by wind or hail would allow coverage if tornado dropped tree on roof and opening hole through which rain entered); Commercial Union Ins. Co. v. Byrne, 248 So. 2d 777 (Miss. 1971) (where branches were driven through roof in hurricane and tree made opening in roof, jury could find there was damage to the interior of the home from wind action and that substantial quantity of water entered it through openings thus created).

346. Gerhard v. Travelers Fire Ins. Co., 246 Wis. 625, 18 N.W.2d 336 (1945) (finding coverage where ice on lake was projected against insured building by force of wind).

347. Stufflebean v. Firemen's Fund Ins. Co., 710 S.W.2d 931, 933 (Mo. App. 1986).

348. Tamares Las Vegas Props., LLC v. Travelers Indem. Co., 409 F. Supp. 3d 924, 936 (D. Nev. 2019) (policy did not exclude rain as covered cause of loss, thus any water damage to building interior caused by rain was covered if rain, or any covered cause of loss, damaged roof in way that allowed rain to enter). *But see* Pine Island Shopping at Sunrise, LLC v. Westchester Surplus Lunes Ins. Co., 2017 U.S. Dist. LEXIS 216484 (S.D. Fla. Sept. 25, 2017) (rain could not be independent covered cause of loss to interior of building under all-risk policy).

asserted that existing holes in the roof were enlarged by the rainfall, leading to water intrusion. The court said that heavy rainfall would constitute a covered cause of loss, and whether that rainfall damaged the roof and allowed water to enter and damage the interior was a question of fact.[349]

[d] Temporary Roof

[i] Temporary Roof Is Still a Roof

Is a temporary roof a "roof" for purposes of the standard policy language "opening" exception? Many courts say that the durability and relative permanence of any temporary covering determines if it is a "roof" for purposes of coverage.[350] As one court noted, no roof is permanent, and if a roof is sufficiently durable to serve its function, it is still a "roof" even if not necessarily permanent.[351]

One of the leading cases on the question is a decision of the Oklahoma Supreme Court.[352] In that case an addition to a building was being constructed, requiring a part of the existing roof to be left open. The opening was protected by canvas covers that blew off in a windstorm, resulting in interior damage. The policy at issue had the standard language providing coverage if the building first suffered actual damage to the roof or walls by wind or hail. Contending the roof was not opened or breached by wind, the insurer denied a claim. The court responded that the opening was adequately protected by canvas and the loss was covered because, but for the wind, the opening was adequately closed.[353] Similarly, the Oregon Supreme Court refused to say that as a matter of law, polyethylene plastic sheeting over a plywood sublayer with staples, tacks, and wooden bats securing the components was not a roof. Further, because there was expert opinion that the temporary roof would have been adequate for as long as one or two years, it was for the jury to determine

349. La. Mid-Continent Oil & Gas Ass'n v. Peerless Ins. Co., 2019 U.S. Dist. LEXIS 45648 (M.D. La. Mar. 19, 2019). *See also* Turner Const. Co. v. Ace Prop. & Cas. Ins. Co., 429 F.3d 52, 54 (2d Cir. 2005) (where wind caused opening through which rain entered, resulting damage was caused directly by rain and only indirectly by wind; wind created opening, but only rain caused damage at issue).

350. Kunji Harrisburg, LLC v. Axis Surplus Ins. Co., 2020 U.S. Dist. LEXIS 48115 (E.D. Pa. Mar. 18, 2020).

351. Dewsnup v. Farmers Ins. Co., 349 Ore. 33, 40–41, 239 P.3d 493, 497 (2010). *See also* Michalek v. Nationwide Mut. Fire Ins. Co., 2022 U.S. Dist. LEXIS 65010 (W.D. Pa. Apr. 7, 2022) (there was insufficient evidence for court to find that tarp reinforced with wood and straps was not a roof); Camden Fire Ins. Ass'n v. New Buena Vista Hotel Co., 199 Miss. 585, 24 So. 2d 848 (1946).

352. Homestead Fire Ins. Co. v. De Witt, 206 Okla. 570, 245 P.2d 92 (1952).

353. Had the opening been boarded up or more securely closed and wind had damaged that temporary covering, the court said that it did not think it could be successfully argued that the windstorm provision did not provide coverage.

if the roof was suitable to protect the property repair.[354] Expert testimony has proven important on the question of the adequacy of a temporary roof. A federal judge refused summary judgment for an insurer, saying that whether a tarp was serving as outer layer of roof and was sufficiently secured were questions of fact and credibility where there was expert opinion on the durability of the temporary roof covering.[355] The assertions of the insured about the sufficiency of the temporary roof can also be important. Where an insured stated in an affidavit that the roof was being repaired and half of the old one had been removed and replaced with a temporary one when a storm damaged both the temporary and remaining roof, allowing wind-driven rain into building, the court said the affidavit clearly brought the damage within the policy coverage.[356]

The term "roof" is almost never defined in policies. The insured might then turn to a lay dictionary definition for support. For instance, the Merriam-Webster online dictionary defines the term simply as "the cover of a building,"[357] which could easily encompass a temporary roof cover. Indeed, a New Jersey court considered dictionary definitions and concluded the word was "fairly susceptible of two meanings" and, therefore, was ambiguous.[358] As a result, it decided a tarpaulin covering a roof opening could be a roof.[359]

[ii] Temporary Roof Is Not a Roof

Courts may think that tarps, plastic sheeting, or canvas could be a "roof," but say that a *temporary* covering is not a roof,[360] and therefore its penetration by wind or hail does not trigger coverage.[361] For example, a building's permanent roof and walls were incomplete and visqueen tarps were installed temporarily

354. Dewsnup v. Farmers Ins. Co., 349 Ore. 33, 239 P.3d 493 (2010).

355. Kunji Harrisburg, LLC v. Axis Surplus Ins. Co., 2020 U.S. Dist. LEXIS 48115 (E.D. Pa. Mar. 18, 2020) (court noted significant fact that tarp appeared to have been adequate to protect against rain many times before alleged windstorm removed it).

356. Sloan v. Allstate Ins. Co., 977 S.W.2d 72, 74 (Mo. App. 1998).

357. *Roof*, Merriam-Webster, https://www.merriam-webster.com/dictionary/roof.

358. *See also* Victory Peach Group, Inc. v. Greater New York Mut. Ins. Co., 310 N.J. Super. 82, 89, 707 A.2d 1383, 1386 (1998). *But see* Charter Oak Fire Ins. Co. v. Carteret Cty. Bd. of Comm'rs, 1996 U.S. App. LEXIS 17122 (4th Cir. July 12, 1996) ("roof" is neither ambiguous nor vague and is ordinarily thought of as permanent feature of building it covers).

359. Zions v. Essex Ins. Co., 2009 N.J. Super. Unpub. LEXIS 1318 (May 29, 2009).

360. *See, e.g.*, Ace Prop. & Cas. Ins. Co. v. Vegas VP, LP, 2008 U.S. Dist. LEXIS 37495 (D. Nev. May 7, 2008) (plain and ordinary meaning of "roof" is permanent structure covering building and temporary weather protection like visqueen tarps do not constitute roofs); Aginsky v. Farmers Ins. Exch., 409 F. Supp. 2d 1230, 1236 (D. Ore. 2005) ("roof" is permanent structure; no reasonable person would consider temporary structure of wooden framing and plastic tarp to be a "roof"); Valentino v. Harleysville Preferred Ins. Co., 120 A.3d 367 (Pa. Super. 2015) (to contend that, under insurance policy, tarpaulin was roof was "legally frivolous").

361. Camden Fire Ins. Ass'n v. New Buena Vista Hotel Co., 199 Miss. 585, 24 So. 2d 848 (1946) (felt-covered structure was not roof as contemplated by policy).

to protect the building. The court said that damage to the tarps constituted injury to a temporary weather covering, not to a roof or wall. Therefore, when rainwater entered through the wind-damaged tarp, the building had not first endured wind damage to the roof or walls.[362] Another approach taken by courts is to say that a *completed* roof has to be damaged, not one in the process of construction. In one case, for instance, a replacement roof had not been finished and a rainstorm began. Water entered and caused damage. The policy, said the court, required that the roof through which rain entered had to first be damaged. The rain went through because the roof had not been completed. Workers attempted to install the plastic tarps only after the damage had occurred. The policy clearly required a *completed* roof to be damaged, said the court. It emphasized that an uncompleted roof was in the process of being replaced, as opposed to a permanent roof in the process of improvements.[363]

Courts also question whether insurers intend to assume the increased risk of loss that temporary roof covers present.[364] The force needed to move or breach a tarpaulin, noted one court, is very unlike that which would cause a breach of a usual roof or wall.[365] For example, in a California case,[366] a section of roof of a warehouse had been removed and covered with plastic sheeting that blew open and allowed rain to enter and flood the building, damaging stored contents. The court said that if plastic sheeting were a roof, there would be coverage. However, it concluded that "roof" generally means "a permanent part of the structure it covers." Plastic sheeting was, therefore, not a roof and the policy did not cover the loss.[367] The principal case to the contrary is

---

362. Ace Prop. & Cas. Ins. Co. v. Vegas VP, LP, 2008 U.S. Dist. LEXIS 37495 (D. Nev. May 7, 2008). *See also* Charter Oak Fire Ins. Co. v. Carteret Cty. Bd. of Comm'rs, 1996 U.S. App. LEXIS 17122 (4th Cir. July 12, 1996) (where plywood and two layers of roofing felt were attached to trusses but no shingles were in place at instruction of architect who feared additional weight of shingles could potentially cause trusses to collapse, court found there was no roof "as intended by the parties under the insurance contract" and, thus, water damage to interior of building was not covered).

363. Holesapple v. Aetna Cas. & Sur. Co., 2002 Cal. App. Unpub. LEXIS 460 (Apr. 29, 2002). *Compare* Victory Peach Group, Inc. v. Greater New York Mut. Ins. Co., 310 N.J. Super. 82, 89, 707 A.2d 1383, 1386 (1998) (repairs to roof do not make it something other than a roof).

364. Aginsky v. Farmers Ins. Exch., 409 F. Supp. 2d 1230, 1236 (D. Ore. 2005) (policy language contemplates coverage of completed, permanent roof, not one under repair and temporarily covered).

365. Nooney v. Tower Group Co., 2009 N.Y. Misc. LEXIS 6466 (Sept. 23, 2009) ("roof" should be permanent part of structure).

366. Diep v. California Fair Plan Ass'n, 15 Cal. App. 4th 1205, 19 Cal. Rptr. 2d 591 (1993).

367. The court added that the parties could not have reasonably understood the word "roof" to encompass a temporary cover of plastic sheeting. It also said the policy before it was not issued specifically to insure against perils of construction. *See also* Lobell v. Graphic Arts Mut. Ins. Co., 83 A.D.3d 911, 913, 921 N.Y.S.2d 306, 308 (2011) (tarps over openings in ceiling did not come within definition "roof" as used in policy).

that of the Oklahoma Supreme Court discussed in the immediately preceding section. The California court and several others have distinguished the Oklahoma decision, arguing the policy there was specifically intended to "cover risks associated with a construction project."[368] However, that contention has flaws. First, the "roof opening" language in commercial property and builders risk policies is typically very similar. Second, temporary roofs are most often employed before a damaged roof is repaired or during a planned roof replacement. In either case, the parties would likely anticipate the risk of a temporary roof. Indeed, one federal court has said that the fact that a policy covered construction, rather than property in general, was not a critical difference.[369]

Two Nevada cases illustrate the importance of the specific facts. In the first case, the Nevada Supreme Court concluded that tarps temporarily covering a building under repair were not part of the roof, and when they were blown away, the building did not suffer damage to its roof by wind.[370] The tarps, noted the court, were installed after it had begun raining, and there had been significant damage, meaning they were not a planned replacement for a waterproof membrane that had been removed. They were not durable enough to protect the building from reasonably expected weather risks. They were thus not a roof, but even if they were, said the court, the roof did not suffer any wind damage before the damage from the entry of rain. A Nevada Federal District Court distinguished the decision of the Nevada Supreme Court. In that case, a storm was expected. A tarp and other waterproofing measures were installed on the roof before the storm hit. Were those protective measures sufficiently durable to protect the property, meaning they constituted a roof? The court said the weather conditions and whether the weatherproofing was sufficient to protect against them were questions of fact that could not be resolved on summary judgment.[371]

---

368. Interior Shutters, Inc. v. Valiant Ins. Co., 2000 U.S. App. LEXIS 33816 (10th Cir. Dec. 28, 2000) (roof opening in *Homestead* was necessary part of construction and within intent and contemplation of parties). *See also* Aginsky v. Farmers Ins. Exch., 409 F. Supp. 2d 1230, 1236 (D. Ore. 2005) (*Homestead* court focused on fact that policy expressly covered construction risks).

369. Ace Prop. & Cas. Ins. Co. v. Vegas VP, LP, 2008 U.S. Dist. LEXIS 37495 (D. Nev. May 7, 2008). The court added that in the context of a construction project, the parties could have negotiated for a limited exception to the rain exclusion providing coverage if damage to the interior was caused by rain entering through the permanent wind-damaged exterior once that exterior was complete. The building process, said the court, requires a critical decision. The builder may either complete the exterior, "drying-in" the interior, before beginning work on the interior, or begin interior work before permanently enclosing it.

370. Fourth St. Place, LLC v. Travelers Indem. Co., 127 Nev. 957, 270 P.3d 1235 (2011).

371. Tamares Las Vegas Props., LLC v. Travelers Indem. Co., 409 F. Supp. 3d 924 (D. Nev. 2019). Rainwater entered the building after the tarp was torn open by a combination of rain, wind, and hail. Those causes of loss satisfied the exception to the rain limitation providing the storm-damaged tarp was acting as a roof at the time.

[e] Contractor Negligence

California federal courts hold that an insurer cannot invoke the "Interior of Buildings Limitation" when the efficient proximate cause of the loss was a roof that was left uncovered while work was being done on the interior of a property. That failure, they assert is the most significant cause of the loss, even when it was also caused by rain.[372] In one case, for example, a contractor was repairing the roof and neglected to install a temporary covering over an open portion of the roof. Rain entered the premises and damaged the insured's property. Rain may have been the most immediate cause of the damages, but the court said that, under California law, the efficient proximate cause was the contractor's negligence. The loss would, therefore, be covered unless it was specifically excluded by the policy.

[5] Duty of Insured to Protect Property from Further Damage

Property policies typically require that the insured protect covered property from further damage.[373] Under the typical policy language, an insured has a duty after the original damage to remedy the problem within a reasonable length of time to prevent subsequent damage.[374] The requirement takes on special importance when there is an opening in a roof or siding. That is because additional damage can occur every time it rains, snows, or sleets. In a Connecticut case, for example, a windstorm blew off more than half of a roof. The water-damaged property was removed, and the opening was covered by loose boards and tarpaulins. About two weeks later another storm damaged the remaining goods. The insured, decided the court, had failed to take measures reasonably required to protect those goods after the first loss. Protecting that property was a condition precedent to the right to recover. Therefore, the court held there was no coverage.[375]

[6] Exclusions

[a] Flood or Surface Water

Even though there is an opening in the roof or walls through which precipitate may have entered, the insurer may invoke the standard "water damage"

372. Allstate Ins. Co. v. Smith, 929 F.2d 447, 451 (9th Cir. 1991) (failure of roofer to cover exposed premises was efficient proximate cause of loss); Century Theaters. Inc. v. Travelers Property Cas. Co. of America, 2006 U.S. Dist. LEXIS 15766 (N.D. Cal. Mar. 20, 2006) ("Hole in the Roof Provision" clause does, as a matter of law, not provide grounds on which insurer could deny coverage).

373. *See, e.g.*, ISO Form CP 00 10 06 07, § E.3.a.(4).

374. Travelers Indem. Co. v. Rawson, 222 So. 2d 131, 135 (Miss. 1969).

375. Peerless Hosiery Co. v. Northern Ins. Co., 108 F. Supp. 52 (D. Conn. 1952). *See also* Guideone Elite Ins. Co. v. Mount Carmel Ministries, 2015 U.S. Dist. LEXIS 163043 (S.D. Miss. Dec. 3, 2015).

exclusion that bars coverage for losses or damage by, *inter alia*, flood or surface water.[376] If the insured cannot show there was an opening created by wind or hail—or another covered cause of loss—it is difficult to avoid application of the exclusion when the insurer can point to the presence of surface water.[377]

The volume of water may support the contention of the insurance carrier that the loss was caused by surface water rather than water entering through an opening in a roof or wall. For example, hail broke a basement window, allowing hail and water to enter and damage property in the basement. The water throughout the basement was about 15 inches deep. The court noted that the parties agreed that if the damage was caused by hail and/or rain alone, the loss was covered, but not if it was caused in part by surface water. The insureds contended that there was a tremendous amount of hail but very little rain during the storm and that hail and rain exclusively caused the damage. However, the court said that no reasonable person would believe that a sufficient amount of hail could have come in through the window and caused that quantity of water. Rather, it was surface water that flooded the basement.[378]

The insured may be able to separate damage caused by flood or surface water from that caused by entry of precipitate through the roof or walls and recover for the latter unless the policy provides otherwise.[379]

---

376. *See* Bao v. Liberty Mut. Fire Ins. Co., 535 F. Supp. 2d 532 (D. Md. 2008) (even if wind broke glass door and allowed water to enter building, surface water exclusion barred coverage).

377. *See, e.g.*, Zaragon Holdings, Inc. v. Indian Harbor Ins. Co., 2010 U.S. Dist. LEXIS 79536 (N.D. Ill. Aug. 2, 2010) (where insured presented no evidence indicating that damage from covered cause of loss to sliding-glass doors or any other part of ground floor allowed driving rain to enter, summary judgment was granted insurer as damage was from standing surface water that leaked through doors to which surface water exclusion applied); Brindley v. Firemen's Ins. Co., 35 N.J. Super. 1, 113 A.2d 53 (1955) (judgment for insureds reversed for lack of evidence to support finding that wind caused openings in roof or walls, rather than that tidal or ocean water, or rain seeping through roof or walls, caused damage at issue); Unobskey v. Continental Ins. Co., 147 Me. 249, 86 A.2d 160 (1952) (during storm with high wind and heavy rain, outside door was torn open and insured basement was flooded; insured argued rainwater entered basement through opening caused by windstorm, but court concluded damage caused was by running surface water from rainstorm and melting snow, which was excluded by policy).

378. Dixon v. Commercial Union Ins. Co., 1996 Kan. App. Unpub. LEXIS 864 (Mar. 8, 1996), *aff'd*, 911 P.2d 1126 (Mar. 8, 1996). The court acknowledged that there could be situations in which hail alone could cause 15 inches of water, but here the size and placement of the hole in the window belied that possibility. The policyholders argued that "rain" was ambiguous and susceptible to two interpretations. It could, they asserted, mean falling rain or rain that hits the ground or some other object and flows into an area other than where it first fell. The court rejected that argument, saying that given that interpretation, there would be no need for the surface water exclusion except in the rarest of circumstances as most surface water occurs because of falling rain. *See also* State Farm Fire & Casualty Co. v. Paulson, 756 P.2d 764 (Wyo. 1988) (water and hail entered basement after hail broke sections of three basement windows and water completely filled basement; court found surface water exclusion applied).

379. *See, e.g.*, E.K.S., Inc. v. United States Fire Ins. Co., 1999 U.S. Dist. LEXIS 7012 (N.D. Ill. May 3, 1999) (if both flood and water that entered through roof were cause of water damage, it would have to be determine how much water damage was caused by flood and how by openings in roof).

[b] Windstorm and Hail Exclusion Endorsement

Commercial property and homeowners policies almost always cover losses from windstorms and hail. That standard coverage, however, can be eliminated by endorsement. For example, one standard ISO commercial property endorsement adds a "Windstorm or Hail" exclusion to those in the principal policy. Under that exclusion, the insurer will not pay for loss or damage caused directly or indirectly by windstorm or hail, regardless of any other cause or event contributing concurrently or in any sequence to that loss or damage, or caused by rain, snow, sand, or dust, whether driven by wind or not, if the loss or damage would not have occurred but for the windstorm or hail.[380] Pursuant to the endorsement, for there to be coverage for damage caused by the entry of rain or snow, the insured has to show that the damage to the roof or walls through which the precipitate entered was caused by a "covered cause of loss," which wind and hail no longer are.[381] If the policy is "named risk," then the insured will have to specify which of the named perils created the entry site. If it is all-risk, the insured has to show the entry point was created by a peril that is not excluded, and the endorsement adds windstorm and hail to the list of perils that *are* excluded.

There are two small discrepancies between standard named risk property polices and the standard endorsement. The former typically do not cover loss to the inside of a building—or its contents—caused by rain, snow, or *sleet* except when the direct force of *wind* or hail damages the building and causes an opening in a roof or wall through which rain, snow, or sleet enters.[382] The standard endorsement excludes loss or damage caused directly or indirectly by *windstorm*, not wind. As discussed previously, some courts distinguish between "wind" and "windstorm," and others do not.[383] An insured who has water damage caused when water entered an opening caused by wind when there was no storm could argue that by using different terms in the principal policy and the endorsement, the insurer intends a distinction and that the endorsement exclusion does not apply to damage by wind or at the very least is ambiguous. Similarly, if the precipitate that enters is sleet, the policyholder could argue that the endorsement expressly left sleet off the list entrants.

---

380. ISO Form BP 14 84 07 13, § A. There is an exception that applies if windstorm or hail results in a cause of loss other than rain, snow, sand, or dust, and that resulting cause of loss is a covered one. The endorsement explains that if, for example, windstorm or hail damages a heating system, resulting in fire, the loss or damage attributable to that fire is covered subject to any other applicable provisions in the policy.

381. GBS Inv. Grp. v. United Specialty Ins. Co., 2019 U.S. Dist. LEXIS 190105 (S.D. Fla. Oct. 31, 2019) (insured had to show water damage was *not* caused by wind-driven rain but by cause of loss covered by policy).

382. ISO Form HO 00 02 05 01 (Perils Insured Against), § I.2; ISO Form CP 10 20 04 02, § A.4.c.

383. See § 3.5[1][d][iii], *supra*.

When the exclusion is for "windstorms," the carrier bears the burden to show it applies, meaning it has to put forth evidence of the speed and/or destructive capacity of the winds.[384]

[c] Wear and Tear

Because property insurance is intended to cover an unexpected loss, not ordinary wear and tear, policies contain a "wear and tear" exclusion.[385] The insurer can successfully deny coverage by showing a loss was the result of ordinary wear and tear. Evidence of the age of a roof and its deterioration will support that defense. For example, shingles on a 30-year-old roof of a building that had suffered water intrusion had buckled and cracked. An engineering report concluded the roof had outlived its service life and that was the most likely cause of the water intrusion. The court found the carrier had met its burden of showing the wear and tear provision excluded coverage.[386] Evidence of inadequate or defective maintenance will also allow an insurance company to escape liability.[387]

[d] Faulty Workmanship

Where a loss is caused by a contractor's poor workmanship, insurers obviously want the policyholder to recover from the contractor responsible for the loss. For that reason, property policies typically have a broad exclusion for loss or damage caused by faulty, inadequate, or defective workmanship, repair, construction, renovation, or remodeling or for materials used for repair, construction, renovation, or remodeling.[388]

What exactly is "faulty workmanship"? Is it about the process or the final product, or both? This question has been discussed in several cases concerning inadequate roof covers. One court said that failure to install a temporary cover while replacing a roof was not "faulty workmanship" and that if the insurer meant for "faulty workmanship" to encompass losses resulting from flawed processes of construction, rather than "flawed quality of a

---

384. Rifai Props., LLC v. United Nat'l Ins. Co., 2016 U.S. Dist. LEXIS 185755 (M.D. Fla. Apr. 26, 2016).

385. *See, e.g.*, ISO Form CP 10 20 06 07, § B.2.d.

386. *See, e.g.*, Steven J. Inc. *ex rel.* Fenton v. Landmark Am. Ins. Co., 2015 U.S. Dist. LEXIS 80278 (M.D. Pa. June 22, 2015).

387. *See, e.g.*, Dashtpeyma v. Liberty Ins. Corp., 2013 U.S. Dist. LEXIS 139015 (N.D. Ga. Sept. 27, 2013), *aff'd*, 569 Fed. Appx. 886 (11th Cir. 2014).

388. *See, e.g.*, ISO Form CP 10 20 06 07, § B.3.c. *See* Mag-Dolphus, Inc. v. Ohio Cas. Ins. Co., 40 F. Supp. 3d 817 (S.D. Tex. 2014) (negligent workmanship exclusion barred coverage for water that entered through roof installed one year earlier); Weinberg v. Nationwide Cas. & Ins. Co., 949 F. Supp. 2d 588 (E.D. Pa. 2013) (where insured participated in class action against homebuilder and arbitrator found corrective work was warranted and damages were awarded, there was no coverage for water intrusion).

finished product," it could have said so.[389] Similarly, another court asserted that "faulty workmanship" refers to a final product. Therefore, the exclusion did not bar coverage when visqueen plastic sheeting that covered open windows and doors during a construction project blew away, allowing water to enter the insured building because the loss happened before construction was completed.[390] Of course, there are courts that take the opposite position. One described "workmanship" as a broad term referring to both a process and a finished product.[391] In that case, a roofing contractor removed a waterproof membrane from a roof. That night it began to rain and continued into the next day, during which the contractor covered the roof with tarps. Unfortunately, the tarps blew away. The insured premises suffered damage, and the court held the faulty workmanship exclusion precluded coverage.

Apparently, the exclusion can apply when the policyholder does the work. An insured who was a contractor removed wood shakes from his own roof and covered it polyethylene plastic. The covering blew away in a storm, allowing rainwater to enter the interior of the property. The court accepted that a "faulty or inadequate workmanship" exclusion could apply and held that the question of whether the workmanship was either faulty or defective was for the jury.[392]

There may be exceptions to the exclusion when damages result in a covered cause of loss,[393] there is an ensuing loss,[394] or covered and uncovered causes combined to cause the loss and the policy has no anti-concurrent cause provision.[395]

[e] Long-Term Leaks

An exclusion often found in homeowners policies or added by endorsement is for losses caused by constant or repeated seepage or leakage of water over a period of time, which may be stated generally as a "period of weeks, months, or years" or specifically as "14 or more days." Courts may interpret "period

---

389. Allstate Ins. Co. v. Smith, 929 F.2d 447, 450 (9th Cir. 1991).

390. Phila. Indem. Ins. Co. v. TL Fab, LP, 2018 U.S. Dist. LEXIS 130089 (S.D. Cal. Aug. 2, 2018).

391. Fourth St. Place, LLC v. Travelers Indem. Co., 127 Nev. 957, 270 P.3d 1235 (2011). *See also* Wider v. Heritage Maintenance, Inc., 14 Misc. 3d 963, 827 N.Y.S.2d 837 (2007).

392. Dewsnup v. Farmers Ins. Co., 349 Ore. 33, 239 P.3d 493 (2010).

393. Tamares Las Vegas Props., LLC v. Travelers Indem. Co., 409 F. Supp. 3d 924, 940 (D. Nev. 2019) (if poor planning by contractor created risk rain would enter building, exception to exclusion would apply because faulty planning resulted in covered cause of loss).

394. Rifai Props., LLC v. United Nat'l Ins. Co., 2016 U.S. Dist. LEXIS 185755 (M.D. Fla. Apr. 26, 2016) (insured could establish coverage when contractor's workmanship was faulty by proving that some or all damages fell within ensuing loss exception).

395. Key Biscayne Ambassador Condo. Ass'n v. Aspen Specialty Ins. Co., 2018 U.S. Dist. LEXIS 19440 (S.D. Fla. Feb. 5, 2018).

of weeks" to mean 14 days of more.[396] That exclusion was applied where an expert for an insurer said a roof had been leaking for a long time and that damage was long-term. The expert noted there were signs in the roof and attic of advanced decay and mold. The court found no coverage even though the insured claimed the roof was damaged by tree branches during a windstorm.[397]

Where the exclusion is for losses caused by constant or repeated leakage or seepage over a period of *14 days or more*, some courts hold that losses occurring over the first 13 days may still be covered,[398] providing the insured can prove those losses,[399] while others find that all losses are excluded.[400]

In a Texas case, the court concluded that leakage or seepage for a period of *fewer* than 14 days would be a "covered cause of loss" for purposes of coverage for damage from precipitate that enters through an opening in a roof or wall caused by a *covered cause of loss*. The court said that if leakage or seepage caused direct physical damage to covered property, the leakage or seepage would be a covered cause of loss unless it was continuous for more than 14 days. Moreover, if that covered cause of loss enabled additional rainwater to enter the property and do further damage to the interior, the requirement that interior rain damage would be covered only if the building first sustained damage by a covered cause of loss through which rain entered would be satisfied, and there would be coverage for that interior rain damage.[401]

---

396. Wheeler v. Allstate Insurance, 687 F. App'x 757 (10th Cir. 2017). *See also* Moy v. State Farm Fire & Cas. Co., 2022 U.S. Dist. LEXIS 11105 (D. Conn. Jan. 21, 2022) (where policy excluded coverage for continuous or repeated seepage or leakage of water "which occurs over a period of time," question of whether damage occurred within first 13 days was not relevant as that question only applied where policy limits exclusion to either period of "weeks" or "fourteen days").

397. Holliday v. Pioneer State Mut. Ins. Co, 2009 Mich. App. LEXIS 465 (Mich. App. Mar. 5, 2009). *See also* Karon v. Safeco Ins. Co., 2021 U.S. Dist. LEXIS 147116 (D. Ariz. Aug. 5, 2021) (exclusion for seepage or leakage occurring over period of weeks, months, or years unambiguously precluded coverage for damage occurring over period of weeks, including damage occurring within first 13 days); Iroquois on the Beach, Inc. v. Gen. Star Indem. Co., 2007 U.S. Dist. LEXIS 76290 (W.D. Mich. Oct. 12, 2007).

398. *See, e.g.*, Hicks v. Am. Integrity Ins. Co., 241 So. 3d 925 (Fla. 5th DCA 2018) (insurance policy excluding losses caused by constant or repeated leakage or seepage over period of 14 days or more does not unambiguously exclude losses over period of 13 days or less; remanding on issue of coverage within first 13 days of leak, with extent of the losses to be determined at trial; for losses occurring after first 13 days, burden was on insurer to prove that particular loss was sustained after thirteenth day and was therefore not covered).

399. Landrum v. Allstate Ins. Co., 2019 U.S. Dist. LEXIS 175664 (M.D. Ga. Oct. 9, 2019) (damages estimate relied on by insured did not differentiate between damages that resulted from first 13 days of leak and those that resulted from other 12 days; absent evidence to create genuine issue of fact as to whether damages occurred from first 13 days of 25-day leak, insured could not meet her burden on summary judgment and policy excluded coverage).

400. *See, e.g.*, Gen. Star Indem. Co. v. Sherry Brooke Revocable Trust, 243 F. Supp. 2d 605 (W.D. Tex. 2001).

401. Tex. Friends Chabad-Lubavitch, Inc. v. Nova Cas. Co., 539 F. Supp. 3d 669 (S.D. Tex. 2021).

[f] Building Upgrades

A policy may require, usually pursuant to an endorsement, that certain upgrades have to be completed and "fully operable."[402] The insurer then will not pay for loss or damage caused by or resulting from water damage originating from a roof when the policyholder has failed to comply with any building upgrade. The requirement may be that flat roofs have to be resurfaced or have been replaced within the prior 15 years and that roof drains must be kept clear of debris and maintained in operational order.[403]

3.6 Thawing of Snow, Sleet, or Ice on a Building or Structure

A standard exclusion[404] or limitation[405] in property policies is one in which insurers will not pay for any loss that is a consequence of loss or damage to the interior of any building, structure, or personal property in that building or structure that is caused by or results from rain, snow, sleet, or ice, whether driven by wind or not, unless, *inter alia*, the loss or damage is caused by or results from thawing of snow, sleet, or ice on the building or structure.

Two keys to the coverage are "thawing" and that the snow, sleet, or ice is *on* a building or structure. The Merriam-Webster online dictionary defines "thaw" as "to go from a frozen to a liquid state" and equates it with "melt."[406] Thus, a loss caused by rainwater would not be covered because it involves "no thawing of precipitates."[407] Apparently, "on the building or structure" means that the snow, sleet, or ice has to be on top of the structure, not resting against it. For example, a warehouse suffered water damage to goods stored in it. An inspection by a licensed contractor revealed roof drains that emptied onto the pavement outside the area of penetration and piles of snow plowed up against the exterior walls and around a rotted doorway. The investigator concluded that the water penetration had resulted from thawing of snow built up outside of the warehouse. The court cited, but did not address, the coverage for thawing. Instead, it said that the source of the water was the thawing snow in the doorway, or water that had flowed from the roof down the drainage pipes and onto the pavement, or both. In any event, the water was surface water and the damage was excluded under the surface water exclusion.[408]

---

402. The requirement will generally be added by endorsement.

403. *See, e.g.*, Rifai Props., LLC v. United Nat'l Ins. Co., 2016 U.S. Dist. LEXIS 185755 (M.D. Fla. Apr. 26, 2016).

404. ISO Form CP 10 30 09 17, § C.1.c.

405. *See* ISO Form HO 00 03 05 01 (Perils Insured Against), § I.B.2.

406. *Thaw*, Merriam-Webster, https://www.merriam-webster.com/dictionary/thaw.

407. Amish Connection, Co. v. State Farm Fire & Cas. Co., 861 N.W.2d 230, 236 (Iowa 2015).

408. Cent. Mass Recycling v. United Nat'l Ins. Co., 12 Mass. L. Rep. 629 (Mass. Super. 2001).

One cause of loss that is covered by the exception to the exclusion for rain, snow, sleet, or ice is "ice damming," a phenomenon in which ice forms along the edge of a roof or in gutters, preventing melting snow and ice from draining and allowing water to back up under shingles.[409] That water can leak into a building and even flood it,[410] leading to damage to the building and its contents. Insurers routinely pay for that water damage without objection.[411] However, while an insurer was required to pay any relevant costs necessary to repair the portion of an insured property damaged by ice dam loss, including costs incurred to meet ordinances, where ice dam damage did not cause building code violations, the insurer did not have to pay the cost of remedying violations discovered *after* the ice dam damage.[412]

3.7 Water Damage as a Consequence of Fire

Water used to extinguish a fire can damage the property experiencing a fire and adjacent properties. The general rule is that a policy that covers loss or damage by fire also covers loss or damage caused by water used to douse the flames because the injury is considered to be the direct result of the fire.[413] The loss is, therefore, covered as a loss by fire unless otherwise excluded. That principle has been extended to damage caused to an adjacent property that is not itself on fire but that is damaged by the water used to extinguish it. For example, there was a store on the lower story of a house. The upper story of the house caught fire and burned down, but the store and its contents

409. Massmann, *"Dammed" Ice: When Ice Prevents Melting Snow from Draining Properly, Leading to Interior Leaks, Will Your Property Policy Cover the Damage?* (Jan. 30, 2012), PropertyCasualty360, https://www.propertycasualty360.com/2012/01/30/dammed-ice/ (because ice damming occurs when snow or ice thaws, but cannot properly drain, damage would be covered under exception to exclusion).

410. *See, e.g.*, Meadows at Mainstone Farm Condo. Trust v. Strathmore Ins. Co., 2018 U.S. Dist. LEXIS 169198 (D. Mass. Sept. 28, 2018).

411. Hayley v. Allstate Ins. Co., 262 Mich. App. 571, 686 N.W.2d 273 (2004) (home sustained water damage—flooding of carpeting in two rooms—because of ice damming on roof, and insurer paid claim for that damage). *See also* Merriman v. Allstate Prop. & Cas. Ins. Co., 2021 U.S. Dist. LEXIS 118111 (E.D. Tenn. June 24, 2021); Gerber-Siggelkow v. Allstate Prop. & Cas. Ins. Co., 2021 U.S. Dist. LEXIS 92692 (D. Idaho May 11, 2021); Meadows at Mainstone Farm Condo. Trust v. Strathmore Ins. Co., 2018 U.S. Dist. LEXIS 169198 (D. Mass. Sept. 28, 2018); Zuk v. Acuity Ins. Co., 2015 Ohio Misc. LEXIS 30 (June 5, 2015); Lumbermen's Mut. Cas. Co. v. Sykes, 384 Ill. App. 3d 207, 890 N.E.2d 1086 (2008).

412. Grill v. N. Star Mut. Ins. Co., 2014 Minn. App. Unpub. LEXIS 68 (Jan. 27, 2014).

413. McManus v. Travelers Ins. Co., 360 So. 2d 207 (La. App. 1978) (fire insurer has for many years been held responsible for loss occasioned by water damage during course of fighting a fire); Fogarty v. Fidelity & Cas. Co., 122 Conn. 245, 188 A. 481 (1936) (loss that is result of *bona fide* efforts to save property, as in case of use of water to extinguish fire, is a loss by fire); Cummings v. Pennsylvania Fire Ins. Co., 153 Iowa 579, 134 N.W. 79 (1912); John Davis & Co. v. Insurance Co. of North America, 115 Mich. 382, 385, 73 N.W. 393, 394 (1897) (in general, words "loss by fire" include loss by water thrown on property to prevent its destruction by fire).

were saved. The court said the insurance company was bound by the policy to indemnify the store owner for damages to his goods from the water used to fight the fire and save them from destruction by fire.[414] In that case the premises on fire and the insured premises were in the same building, but the adjacent property need not be connected to that in which the fire occurs for there to be coverage.[415]

The water causing the damage need not have been used to fight the fire. A dress shop was in a building containing four other businesses, one of which was a butcher shop that caught fire. The fire was extinguished by the fire department without any damage to the dress shop from either fire or water. However, during the blaze, firefighters removed a skylight over the dress shop and apparently reinstalled it improperly. A few days after the fire, the dress shop proprietor arrived at the premises to find much water on the floor, on dress cases, and all through the dresses. A small space under the skylight was discovered through which water dripped down during a rainstorm. The trial court awarded the dress shop owner damages for the losses caused by the water. The insurer appealed. The Massachusetts Supreme Judicial Court said that the jury could correctly have found "a proximate causal relation between the acts of the firemen in the removal of the skylight and its condition at the time of the rain storm."[416]

When water used to extinguish a fire flows from the property that is on fire to a neighboring property, is it "surface water" for purposes of the standard water damage exclusion? That specific question does not appear to have been addressed. However, in a case before the federal First Circuit Court of Appeal, there was a fire nearby the insured premises. Firefighters used 700,000 gallons of water to extinguish the blaze. Some of that water flowed onto the land of the policyholder and damaged the insured building. The insurer conceded liability, and the court said it was correct to do so. Clearly, the insurance company did not believe the surface water exclusion applied. The court mentions that exclusion in a footnote, from which in can be inferred that the court also did not think the exclusion was applicable.[417]

Large amounts of water used to extinguish a fire can sink into the ground and cause foundation damage. That occurred in a Colorado case in which

---

414. Geisek v. Crescent Mut. Ins. Co., 19 La. Ann. 297 (1867). A court reached the same conclusion where the insured premises was a shop located in a one-story building consisting of five stores, one of the other stores caught fire, and the insured shop suffered water damage. Jiannetti v. Nat. Fire Ins. Co., 277 Mass. 434, 178 N.E. 640 (1931).

415. McDonough v. Hardware Dealers Mut. Fire Ins. Co., 448 F.2d 870 (1st Cir. 1971); Cohn v. National Fire Ins. Co., 96 Mo. App. 315, 320, 70 S.W. 259, 261 (1902) (where insured's stock of goods is damaged by water proximately caused by fire in adjacent premises, insurer is liable; insured was entitled to recover its loss by reason of water entering its premises proximately because of fire in or on adjacent premises).

416. Jiannetti v. Nat. Fire Ins. Co., 277 Mass. 434, 178 N.E. 640 (1931).

417. McDonough v. Hardware Dealers Mut. Fire Ins. Co., 448 F.2d 870 (1st Cir. 1971).

water used by firefighters entered the soil beneath the insured home, causing it to swell and damage the foundation. The insurer invoked the earth movement exclusion. The court found the exclusion applied only to naturally occurring earth movement, not human-made events like firefighting. It concluded that if the jury were to find that the earth movement responsible for the damage was caused solely by the fire and associated firefighting, it was covered.[418]

The mere fact that water damage occurs during a fire does not make it a covered loss by fire. During a fire there was an explosion that broke pipes. Water from the broken pipes flooded the premises and destroyed insured goods. The insured was unable to identify what portion of the loss was caused by the explosion, by fire, by water used to extinguish the fire, or by the flood from the broken pipes. The court said the insured failed to meet its burden to show a loss within the terms of the policy.[419]

What is the result when a flood leads to a fire? In a Sixth Circuit case, flood waters were within 60 feet of the insured location and had already entered the basement where the insured merchandise was stored, none of which had been damaged. Workers were moving those goods to higher floors when a gasoline tank was torn from its moorings by the flood waters and exploded, causing a fire to break out. The insurer contended the goods were injured solely by the rising waters and therefore the flood, not the fire, was the proximate cause of the loss. The court said that the flood waters alone damaged the goods and had that been the only cause operating, the insureds would not be entitled to recover because the insurance was against fire only. However, the fire added a new element that "rendered it impossible to control or prevent the consequences naturally following from the rising flood." Thus, the court found substantial evidence in the record that the proximate cause of the loss was the fire.[420]

3.8 Vandalism and Water Damage

[1] Introduction

Vandals cause flooding and other water damage by breaking pipes, turning on hoses, or turning off heat during freezing weather. Vandalism is typically a covered cause of loss in both commercial and residential coverages. For

418. Miller v. Am. Family Mut. Ins. Co., 104 F. Supp. 3d 1232 (D. Colo. 2015). The court also found that application of the earth movement would be contrary to public policy; however, it also said that if the earth movement was caused in part by natural causes unrelated to the fire and in part by the fire and associated firefighting efforts, the foundation damage would not be not covered because of the anti-concurrent cause clause.

419. John Davis & Co. v. Insurance Co. of North America, 115 Mich. 382, 385, 73 N.W. 393, 394 (1897).

420. Princess Garment Co. v. Fireman's Fund Ins. Co., 115 F.2d 380 (6th Cir. 1940).

example, a standard commercial property policy lists "vandalism" as a named cause of loss and defines it as "willful and malicious damage to, or destruction of, the described property."[421] That coverage is generally limited by a "vacancy" clause under which, if a building where loss or damage occurs has been vacant more than 60 consecutive days before that loss or damage, the insurer will not pay for any loss or damage caused by vandalism even if it is a covered cause of loss.[422] A comparable residential policy names "vandalism or malicious mischief" as a covered peril, but says that loss to property on the "residence premises," and any ensuing loss caused by any intentional and wrongful act committed in the course of the vandalism or malicious mischief is not included if the dwelling has been vacant for more than 60 consecutive days immediately prior to the loss.[423] Coverage for vandalism and malicious mischief has been the subject of much litigation resulting in myriad tests and results.[424] The nuances of the coverage are beyond the scope of this discussion, but are addressed at length elsewhere.[425] This discussion focuses on vandalism that causes water damage.

[2] Definition of "Vandalism"

A lay dictionary definition of vandalism is "willful or malicious destruction or defacement of public or private property."[426] Law dictionaries have defined the term as "unjustified and deliberate injury of another's property . . . the willful or deliberate destruction of or harm to property owned by another person without a legal justification"[427] and as "[w]ilful or malicious injury to, or the destruction of, property. . . . Wilful, wanton, and ruthless acts intended to damage or destroy property. . . Any unusual destruction of property wrought in the doing of a wrongful act."[428] Vandalism has been variously defined by courts as "[d]amage done for no purpose other than to destroy property for destruction's sake,"[429] "damaging something simply for the sake of damaging it,"[430] and "an act undertaken with the intent to injure that property and

421. ISO Form CP 10 20 04 02, § A.8.

422. ISO Form CP 00 10 04 02, § E.6.b.(1).(a).

423. ISO Form HO 00 02 10 00 (Perils Insured Against), § 8.

424. Burgess Farms v. New Hampshire Ins. Group, 108 Idaho 831, 833, 702 P.2d 869, 871 (1985).

425. 5 Jeffrey E. Thomas, *New Appleman on Insurance Law Library Edition* §§ 42.01A[6], 43.03[9] (Matthew Bender 2022); Cozen, *Insuring Real Property*, §§ 1.06[7][b][i][H], 2.02[1][e] (LexisNexis Matthew Bender 2022).

426. *Vandalism*, Merriam-Webster, https://www.merriam-webster.com/dictionary/vandalism.

427. *The Wolters Kluwer Bouvier Law Dictionary Desk Edition* (CCH, Inc. 2012).

428. *Ballentine's Law Dictionary* (LexisNexis 2010).

429. Certain Underwriters at Lloyds London v. Law, 570 F.3d 574, 578 (5th Cir. 2009).

430. Smith v. Shelby Ins. Co. of Shelby Ins. Group, 936 S.W.2d 261, 265 (Tenn. App. 1996).

without the intent to steal."[431] Intent and willfulness are, as noted above, usually included in polices as defining vandalism.

[3] Theft Exception

To further complicate coverage questions, many policies, especially for commercial property coverage, state that the insurer covers vandalism but "will not pay for loss or damage caused by or resulting from theft, except for building damage caused by the breaking in or exiting of burglars."[432] The theft clause has been characterized as a narrow exception to vandalism coverage, not an independent exclusion.[433] It has been frequently litigated and the result, as one commentary says, "has been a jumble of confused and conflicting judicial decisions."[434] No attempt will be made here to explore in-depth the contradictory jurisprudence. The commentary and insurance treatises cited above have done so adequately. Nonetheless, a brief discussion of two Missouri cases illustrates the muddle.

A Missouri federal court was presented with a classic water damage vandalism case. Thieves burglarized an insured building and stole copper piping and bathroom fixtures. In addition to pilfering, the culprits cut or removed water lines, which released water and damaged the property. The insured, attempting to separate vandalism from thievery, argued it was entitled to recover for the water damage caused as a result of vandalism "associated with the theft and burglary." The court rejected that dichotomy. It found the vandalism was motivated by theft and there was no coverage. The court acknowledged the perplexity the ruling posed, saying it found for the insurer reluctantly because it was "satisfied that a typical but reasonably careful layman reading the exclusion would suppose there was coverage here."[435] An earlier state court decision reached the opposite result. In that case the insured was ground floor tenant. Persons unknown entered the vacant second floor, where they tore out plumbing fixtures, broke them loose from connected water pipes, and stole them. As a result, large amounts of water flowed, leaked to the ground floor, and damaged insured property. The court said there were three events: a

---

431. Riverbend Capital, LLC v. Essex Ins. Co., 2010 U.S. Dist. LEXIS 106281 (E.D. La. Oct. 5, 2010).

432. ISO Form CP 10 20 04 02, § A.8.

433. Haas v. Audubon Indem. Co., 722 So. 2d 1022 (La. App. 1998).

434. Witus, *The Paradox of Insurance Coverage for Vandalism But Not Theft*, 56 Wayne L. Rev. 1747 (2010).

435. SSL, Inc. v. Scottsdale Ins. Co., 2017 U.S. Dist. LEXIS 218661 (W.D. Mo. Aug. 4, 2017). *Accord* Certain Underwriters at Lloyds London v. Law, 570 F.3d 574, 578 (5th Cir. 2009) (damage done in furtherance of theft or attempted theft is damage that falls within theft exception); Sjp Props., Inc. v. Mount Vernon Fire Ins. Co., 2015 U.S. Dist. LEXIS 97216 (E.D. Mo. July 27, 2015) (there is no coverage for building damage when there is vandalism in furtherance of theft).

burglary, acts of vandalism, and a theft. The loss, held the court, was directly caused by acts of vandalism, notwithstanding that burglary was an "antecedent contributing circumstance" and theft "was an independent concurring cause." Thus, the court found for the insured.[436]

When the vacancy clause applies, it may not be necessary to distinguish between vandalism and theft because the typical vacancy clause bars coverage for vandalism, theft, *and* water damage.[437]

[4] Change in Temperature Exception

Some policies that cover damage by vandalism will state that the insurer will not be liable for loss resulting from "change in temperature." When vandals have turned off heat to an insured building or broken open doors and windows, allowing the temperature to dip below freezing and causing pipes to freeze, insurers have denied coverage by invoking the change in temperature clause. They have not, however, prevailed. Courts have said that "loss resulting from change in temperature" is ambiguous. It could, for instance, be construed as a change in weather. In that case, where damage done by vandals is increased by passage of time and changes in weather, the clause excludes coverage to the extent of that increase. Thus, where vandals cause a loss of heat and expose the insured property to the existing weather conditions, courts have said there can be coverage.[438]

---

436. Beauty Supplies, Inc. v. Hanover Ins. Co., 526 S.W.2d 75 (Mo. App. 1975). *See also* Acorn Inv. Co. v. Mich. Basic Prop. Ins. Ass'n, 2009 Mich. App. LEXIS 1892 (Sept. 15, 2009) (where insured property suffered extensive flooding after someone broke off plumbing fixtures, water meter, and water supply lines and removed them, fact that evidence showed theft of removed items occurred was not material because claim was not that stolen items constitute a covered loss, but that property damage was caused by that removal; causation does not require that vandalism be last act in chain of events on which loss is based); Haas v. Audubon Indem. Co., 722 So. 2d 1022 (La. App. 1998) (vandalism does not by definition exclude taking of property but does require more than taking of property; theft exception does not exclude vandalism damage caused prior to or concurrently with theft; in view of utter destruction done to building, acts should be considered vandalism).

437. Waterstone Bank, SSB v. Am. Family Mut. Ins. Co., 348 Wis. 2d 213, 222, 832 N.W.2d 152, 156 (Wisc. App.), *rev. den.*, 352 Wis. 2d 353, 842 N.W.2d 361 (Wisc. 2013) (under vacancy clause, loss or damage sustained by reason of vandalism, water damage, or theft was not a covered risk). *See also* Saiz v. Charter Oak Fire Ins. Co., 299 Fed. Appx. 836 (10th Cir. 2008), where the insured contended that its loss might be covered as frozen sprinkler leakage and that the water damage limitation in the vacancy clause could not remove that coverage. The court responded that the issue was interesting, but the damage did not arise from freezing and, in any event, it need not determine the relationship between the two provisions because the vandalism vacancy limitation operated independently to preclude coverage.

438. Fawcett House, Inc. v. Great Central Insurance Co., 280 Minn. 325, 159 N.W.2d 268 (1968) (loss from frozen pipes was covered because it was directly caused by specifically covered risk—vandalism—even though it was indirectly and incidentally enhanced by peril of weather change expressly excluded from coverage). *See also* Kuo v. Home Ins. Co., 117 A.D.2d 320, 502 N.Y.S.2d 756 (1986) (where tenant allegedly caused damage by turning off heat, loss

[5] Vandalism and Water Damage Exclusion

When vandalism results in a loss caused by water, the water damage exclusion may serve to bar the claim. For example, a vandal removed sandbags and dirt from a levee. The levee broke, and river water flooded the insured property and destroyed buildings and personal property. The insurer invoked the water/flood exclusion. The court found there was no coverage because even if vandalism, a covered peril, was the efficient proximate cause of the loss, the policy contained an anti-concurrent cause provision that excluded coverage for water damage regardless of any other cause or event that contributed concurrently or in any sequence to the loss.[439]

Coverage was denied where someone, without the owner's permission, attached a hose to an outside spigot at the insured house and turned on the water. The water seeped into the basement, causing damage to wood paneling and carpet. The court found that water was the predominant cause of the loss, coverage for which was precluded by the water exclusion in conjunction with the anti-concurrent cause provision.[440] Without an anti-concurrent causation clause, a different result was reached. Once again, vandals turned on an outside water spigot. The homeowners were on vacation, so the spigot remained on for about two days before being discovered by a neighbor. Thousands of gallons of water poured into the ground by the foundation, ran into the ground, through the foundation walls, and into the basement, damaging inside basement walls, floor coverings, and contents. The insurer contended the water exclusion applied, but the court held the insured risk of vandalism and malicious mischief set into operation a chain of events that in unbroken sequence caused the loss. Although the last link in the chain, said the court, may have been an excluded risk, the insured peril was the proximate cause of the entire loss.[441]

---

could be covered despite "weather change" provision, but insured would have to establish that tenant threw heat switches and, if so, whether his act was one of vandalism).

439. TNT Speed & Sport Ctr. v. American States Ins. Co., 114 F.3d 731 (8th Cir. 1997).

440. Hughes v. Allstate Indem. Co., 389 Wis. 2d 625, 937 N.W.2d 305 (Wisc. App. 2019).

441. Bartholomew v. Cameron Country Mut. Ins. Co., 882 S.W.2d 173 (Mo. App. 1994). *See also* Mongar v. Windsor-Mount Joy Mut. Ins. Co., 2011 Pa. Dist. & Cnty. Dec. LEXIS 520 (Mar. 14, 2011) (where unknown persons broke into property and vandalized it by opening water faucets, which caused extensive water damage, endorsement requiring water to be shut off when property was vacant for at least 72 hours did not bar coverage because vandals set in motion uninterrupted chain of events and opening of faucets coincided with release of water, meaning two events happened at same moment, and absent anti-concurrent clause, loss was covered); Franklin Packaging Co. v. Cal. Union Ins. Co., 171 N.J. Super. 188, 408 A.2d 448 (1979) (where vandals broke into insured warehouse and drove truck into water-cooled air-conditioning unit, breaking valve and creating constant flow of water, but notwithstanding broken valve, water would have drained but for blockage in pipe caused by burlap bag left in drain on same day by plumber, court found coverage because backup blockage of the drain, excluded risk, followed sequentially insured risk of vandalism); Hatley v. Truck Insurance Exchange, 261 Or. 606, 494 P.2d 426 (1972) (unknown person moved hose adjacent to building and turned it on, causing

Many policies exclude coverage for loss or damage caused by continuous discharge of water from a plumbing system for 14 days or more. Where there was evidence of a discharge of water that was continuous for a period of 14 days or more, a claim was properly denied whether or not the cause of the leakage was vandalism.[442]

[6] Location of Vandalism

The vandalism does not necessarily have to occur on the insured property for a loss to be covered. Courts have found coverage where the insured occupies one floor of a multistory building and the vandalism occurs on another floor.[443] Similarly, the vandalism need not be directed at the insured property. For example, an earthen dike that prevented water runoff from flowing down an incline and flooding a cellar was breached by a vehicle driven through the dike and down the incline. Water entered the cellar where potatoes were stored. The potatoes were destroyed, and the insured sought coverage for an act of vandalism. The court said a jury could find that driving over the dike was a wanton act, in reckless disregard for the rights of the owner, and held the destruction of the potatoes could be covered by the vandalism and malicious mischief provision.[444]

[7] Proof and Evidence

Generally, to recover for the peril of vandalism, the insured has to show an intentional act and a malicious purpose that were the proximate cause of the damage or destruction.[445] An unintentional act will generally not support a finding of vandalism.[446] Most courts say malice may be presumed from an

---

interior of building to flood; insurer argued water that caused damage entered as excluded surface water or water below the surface of the ground, but court concluded that where vandalism consisted of turning water against building, and there was water damage as direct and immediate result, general policy exclusion for certain types of water damage did not apply).

442. Sjp Props., Inc. v. Mount Vernon Fire Ins. Co., 2015 U.S. Dist. LEXIS 97216 (E.D. Mo. July 27, 2015).

443. *See, e.g.*, Cresthill Industries, Inc. v. Providence Washington Ins. Co., 53 A.D.2d 488, 385 N.Y.S.2d 797 (1976) (finding coverage for insured first floor tenant of warehouse whose property was damaged when someone broke into unoccupied third floor, removed pipes and bathroom fixtures, and left water running from severed connections); Beauty Supplies, Inc. v. Hanover Ins. Co., 526 S.W.2d 75 (Mo. App. 1975) (vandalism on vacant second floor caused water damage to insured ground floor tenant).

444. Burgess Farms v. New Hampshire Ins. Group, 108 Idaho 831, 702 P.2d 869 (1985).

445. Burgess Farms v. New Hampshire Ins. Group, 108 Idaho 831, 833, 702 P.2d 869, 871 (1985). *See also* Grabowski v. Agricultural Ins. Co., 675 F. Supp. 279 (E.D. Pa. 1987) (to establish coverage for vandalism, insured must prove by preponderance of evidence that intentional act was done by some known or unknown person, act was done in conscious or intentional disregard of rights of others in property, and was proximate cause of damage to insured property).

446. *See, e.g.*, Peterson v. Hartland Cicero Mut. Ins. Co., 149 Wis. 2d 399, 439 N.W.2d 644 (Wisc. App. 1989) (facts did not permit court to conclude that damage was caused by

unlawful act, and no proof of personal animosity against the property owner is required.[447] The insured is not required to establish the identity of the vandal.[448]

Acts of vandalism are usually hidden from view, but not the result. Therefore, courts generally consider circumstantial evidence sufficient to prove that vandalism was the proximate cause of a loss, although mere speculation is not enough. For example, in a South Carolina case, the roof of a warehouse collapsed following a heavy rainstorm and an inspection revealed a beer can and two whiskey bottles that had been thrown on the roof, lodged in the downspout, and completely blocked drainage from the roof. The insurer contended that if throwing bottles on the roof constituted vandalism, that vandalism was not the proximate cause of the loss. The court, however, said that where an expert testified that the accumulated water on the roof would not by itself have caused the roof to collapse, the jury could find that the clogging of the downspouts was the efficient and proximate cause of the damage.[449] The case illustrates the value of experts in water damage cases.[450] That is further underscored by another case with nearly identical facts in which a Washington state

---

vandalism or malicious mischief of tenants where rental premises was tenants' home and they were short of money, had trouble paying rent, and were purchasing fuel oil in small quantities and obtained small space heaters to stay warm; only inference that could be drawn from facts was that damage was caused by pipes freezing because tenants lacked sufficient resources to maintain heat rather than deliberate decision to make house so cold pipes would freeze so as to damage building).

447. Louisville & Jefferson County Metropolitan Sewer Dist. v. Travelers Ins. Co., 753 F.2d 533, 536 (6th Cir. 1985). Another court said that property has been damaged "willfully and maliciously" if the damage results from an intentional act from which damage "manifestly would or could result." Thus, where an unknown person moved a hose next to the insured building and turned the water on, causing the interior to flood, the court decided it was obvious that some damage to the building would probably result if subjected to the full spray from the hose placed near the building at the bottom of a slope. The likelihood of some damage was enough to bring the case within the coverage. Hatley v. Truck Insurance Exchange, 261 Or. 606, 494 P.2d 426 (1972). *See also* Cresthill Industries, Inc. v. Providence Washington Ins. Co., 53 A.D.2d 488, 385 N.Y.S.2d 797 (1976); Lanza Enterprises, Inc. v. Continental Ins. Co., 142 So. 2d 580 (La. App. 1962); General Acci. Fire & Life Assurance Corp. v. Azar, 103 Ga. App. 215, 119 S.E.2d 82 (1961). *Compare* Wilcox v. Maine Mut. Fire Ins. Co., 1996 Me. Super. LEXIS 377 (Nov. 25, 1996).

448. Grabowski v. Agricultural Ins. Co., 675 F. Supp. 279, 280–81 (E.D. Pa. 1987).

449. King v. North River Ins. Co., 278 S.C. 411, 297 S.E.2d 637 (S.C. 1982). *See also* Saiz v. Charter Oak Fire Ins. Co., 299 Fed. Appx. 836 (10th Cir. 2008) (where investigator for insurer concluded cause of failure of sprinkler head was deliberate tampering resulting in physical damage to that sprinkler head, loss fit comfortably within meaning of willful or malicious destruction of property—that is, vandalism); Zaske v. Minnesota Property Ins. Placement Facility, 1992 Minn. App. LEXIS 500 (May 19, 1992) (where pipes in vacant building froze and door was open and another door was broken down, plausible cause of loss was that vandals left door open and/or turned off furnace; summary judgment for insurer was error).

450. The expert must offer more than speculation. In a case in which a cracked toilet tank led to water damage, a ceramic engineer testified that blows to the tank caused it to crack. That opinion was based on visual observance of four chips in the glaze ten months after the leak, at which time the tank was broken into a dozen pieces. The court noted that there was no direct evidence that the tank was struck with an object, of a forced or unlawful entry, or of vandalism

court reached the opposite conclusion. In that case, after prolonged heavy rains, half the roof over the insured bowling alley collapsed. The owner contended that unknown vandals had thrown cans on the roof that had washed into and plugged a downspout, causing water to back up and accumulate on the roof. The court held the collapse of the roof was not a "direct loss" from vandalism or malicious mischief, as neither the throwing of the cans nor the cans themselves was the immediate physical cause of the roof's collapse.[451]

3.9 Explosion and Water Damage[452]

An explosion can result in flooding or water damage. "Explosion" is a named peril in standard ISO broad form and commercial property policies.[453] It would also be a covered peril in an all-risk property policy unless specifically excluded. The term "explosion" is generally given a common rather than scientific meaning and is often said to mean "a bursting of something with violence, accompanied by noise."[454] Courts have found there to be an explosion where the following occurred:

- A hose became disconnected from a pipe and caused water to flood the insured store.[455]
- A fire hydrant ruptured under the buildup of pressure and flooded a basement.[456]

---

or malicious mischief. It found for the insurer. New York Underwriters Ins. Co. v. Trustees of First Baptist Church, 603 S.W.2d 378 (Tex. App. 1980).

451. Frontier Lanes v. Canadian Indem. Co., 26 Wn. App. 342, 613 P.2d 166 (1980) (loss is attributable to vandalism or malicious mischief if immediate physical cause of that loss was vandalistic or malicious act itself or instrumentality employed directly by wrongdoer to carry out that act). *Compare* Grabowski v. Agricultural Ins. Co., 675 F. Supp. 279 (E.D. Pa. 1987) (insured alleged tennis balls were actually placed in drain spout by vandals and that would, if proven, justify verdict for insured).

452. *See generally* Poli, *The Interplay Between Property Damage Caused by an Explosion and Coverage* (June 9, 2017), Merlin Law Group, https://www.propertyinsurancecoveragelaw.com/2017/06/articles/insurance/the-interplay-between-property-damage-caused-by-an-explosion-and-coverage/.

453. ISO Form CP 10 20 04 02, § A.3; ISO Form HO 00 02 10 00 (Perils Insured Against), § 3.

454. 5 Jeffrey E. Thomas, *New Appleman on Insurance Law Library Edition* § 42.01A[3] (Matthew Bender 2022).

455. Millers Mut. Fire Ins. Co. v. Schwartz, 312 S.W.2d 313 (Tex. App. 1958).

456. Commercial Union Fire Ins. Co. v. Bank of Georgia, 197 F.2d 455 (5th Cir. 1952). *Compare* Tires, Inc. v. Travelers Fire Ins. Co., 253 F.2d 411 (4th Cir. 1958) (where water main in pavement broke at or near spot where air hammer was being used and water deluged nearby insured property, court affirmed jury conclusion that there was no explosion).

- An abrupt break in a pipe connected to a hot water system flooded a home.[457]
- The rupture of the top of a sausage stuffing machine caused a part to be hurled away and strike a water pipe, flooding the premises.[458]
- Water pipes burst after they froze because of the termination of electrical service to the property, which then flooded.[459]
- Water in radiators and pipes froze and, in the process of freezing, expanded, causing pipes to burst and resulting in water damage to a home.[460]
- An oil burner was put out of operation after a leak in the furnace hot water coil allowed steam to build and blow open the furnace door, and the loss of heat caused every radiator, and some plumbing, in the house to freeze.[461]
- A break or tear in a water pipe caused by the hydraulic phenomenon known as water hammer—a surge of kinetic energy in water under pressure—resulted in water damage to merchandise in the basement of the insured premises.[462]
- The sudden rushing of hot water from a boiler into a hot-well caused a water hammer that in turn caused the hot-well to explode and break a water pipe in a sprinkler system, as a result of which the insured premises flooded.[463]

---

457. Hartford Fire Ins. Co. v. Balch, 350 P.2d 514 (Okla. 1960) (breakdown of or break in copper pipe connection resulted from excessive temperature and pressure was abrupt and in nature of an eruption or explosion, resulting from excessive pressure and failure of safety plug to blow and relieve that pressure). *Compare* Pilling v. Nationwide Mut. Fire Ins. Co., 201 W. Va. 757, 500 S.E.2d 870 (1997) (where water pipes in home ruptured, causing extensive damage and under policy, explosion did not include water hammer or rupture of water pipes, lower court erred in determining that language was ambiguous and in finding that insureds were entitled to coverage for explosion damages).

458. Royal Sausage & Meat Co. v. Aetna Casualty & Surety Co., 99 Ohio App. 77, 117 N.E.2d 207 (1954).

459. Mueller v. Frankenmuth Mut. Ins. Co., 184 Mich. App. 669, 459 N.W.2d 95 (1990). The case presents some interpretative twists. The policy covered explosions, but an explosion did not include breakage of water pipes. An extended coverage provision omitted that limitation. The court said that because the insurer specifically excluded breakage of water pipes in the principal policy, but failed to do so in the extended coverage, it intended to include breakage of water pipes within the meaning of explosion in the extended coverage.

460. Bower v. Aetna Ins. Co., 54 F. Supp. 897 (N.D. Tex. 1944).

461. Mork v. Eureka-Security Fire & Marine Ins. Co., 230 Minn. 382, 42 N.W.2d 33 (1950). *Accord* Whitelegg v. Standard Accident Ins. Co., 50 Misc. 2d 702, 271 N.Y.S.2d 492 (1966) (rupture or bursting of pipes was end result of explosion within combustion chamber of furnace).

462. L. L. Olds Seed Co. v. Commercial Union Assurance Co., 179 F.2d 472 (7th Cir. 1950).

463. American Paper Products Co. v. Continental Ins. Co., 208 Mo. App. 87, 225 S.W. 1029 (1920).

- The thermostat on a hot water heater was defective, allowing water to be brought to an excessive heat and a water pipe to be subject to great pressure and to break at its weakest point.[464]
- A ruptured washing machine hose released hot water and steam, causing substantial damage to a home,[465]

There may be limitations on the meaning that can bar coverage. These limitations are discussed elsewhere.[466] It is also possible that exclusions—including a standard water damage exclusion—may apply and override the coverage for explosions.[467]

While many courts may be generous in interpreting the meaning of "explosion," complete conjecture will not suffice to support a judgment for the insured.[468]

3.10 "Ensuing" Water Damage

[1] Introduction

Many residential policies cover certain water damage to an insured dwelling or other structure caused by prescribed, excluded causes of loss. Typically, those causes of loss are:

- Freezing of a plumbing, heating, air conditioning, or automatic fire protective sprinkler system or of a household appliance, or discharge, leakage, or overflow from within the system or appliance caused by freezing;

---

464. Daniels v. Hartford Fire Ins. Co., 110 F. Supp. 548 (S.D. Cal. 1951), *aff'd*, 201 F.2d 787 (9th Cir. 1953).

465. Gagnon v. Allstate Ins. Co., 1998 Me. Super. LEXIS 260 (Oct. 22, 1998) (affirming trial court finding of explosion, but overruling decision of lower court that majority of damage was attributable to post-explosion flow of water and steam and therefore not a "direct loss" caused by explosion).

466. See § 2.11, *supra.*

467. Bates v. Phenix Mut. Fire Ins. Co., 156 N.H. 719, 943 A.2d 750 (2008) (assuming without deciding that collapse of road functioning as temporary dam was an "explosion," water exclusion applied to preclude coverage where water burst through road, releasing surge of water into downstream valley that damaged insured property; it was undisputed that rain-induced flood or overflow either directly or indirectly caused damage).

468. *See, e.g.*, Reynolds v. Great American Ins. Co., 334 Mich. 1, 53 N.W.2d 594 (1952), where the court said that construing the evidence in the light most favorable to the insureds, the jury could have concluded that a pipe was disconnected at a slip joint because of internal pressure of steam or water expansion when the thermostat on the water heater had failed to function. That would mean it was within the realm of possibility that the damage was caused by an explosion. However, the court found scant evidence supporting that chain of events and an "utter lack of proof of explosion or showing of any facts from which an explosion could reasonably have been inferred." It said the trial court should have granted insurer's motion for a directed verdict.

- Freezing, thawing, pressure, or weight of water or ice, whether driven by wind or not, to a fence, pavement, patio or swimming pool, foundation, retaining wall, or bulkhead, or pier, wharf, or dock;
- Theft in or to a dwelling under construction, or of materials and supplies for use in the construction until the dwelling is finished and occupied;
- Vandalism and malicious mischief if the dwelling has been vacant for more than 30 consecutive days immediately before the loss;
- Wear and tear, marring, deterioration, inherent vice, latent defect, or mechanical breakdown;[469]
- Smog, rust, or other corrosion, mold,[470] or wet or dry rot;
- Smoke from agricultural smudging or industrial operations;
- Discharge, dispersal, seepage, migration, release, or escape of pollutants unless the discharge, dispersal, seepage, migration, release, or escape is itself caused by a peril insured against;
- Settling, shrinking, bulging, or expansion, including resultant cracking, of pavements, patios, foundations, walls, floors, roofs, or ceilings;
- Birds, vermin, rodents, or insects; and
- Animals owned or kept by an "insured."[471]

This list is followed by a statement that if any of the listed perils causes water damage, *not otherwise excluded*, from a plumbing, heating, air conditioning, or automatic fire protective sprinkler system or household appliance, the insurer will cover the loss caused by that water including the cost of tearing out and replacing any part of a building necessary to repair the system or appliance, but not the loss to the system or appliance from which that water escaped.[472]

---

469. *See generally* Finch & Hughes, *Exclusions from Coverage for Wear and Tear, Deterioration, Inherent Vice, Latent Defect, and Mechanical Breakdown*, 50 Tort & Ins. L.J. 49 (2014); Hecker & Goode, *Wear and Tear, Inherent Vice, Deterioration, Etc.: The Multi-Faceted All-Risk Exclusions*, 21 Tort & Ins. L.J. 634 (1986).

470. In *Fiess v. State Farm Lloyds*, 202 S.W.3d 744 (Tex. 2006), the pertinent clause covered ensuing loss caused by, *inter alia*, water damage if the loss would otherwise be covered under the policy. The policyholders sought coverage for mold stemming from small roof and window leaks. The court said the ensuing loss clause provides coverage only if a relatively common and usually minor risk, mold in this case, leads to a relatively uncommon and perhaps major loss: water damage. The court held that the policy exclusion for "mold" could not be disregarded by simply deeming all mold to be "water damage.

471. ISO Form HO 00 03 04 91 (Perils Insured Against; Dwelling and Other Structures), § 2.

472. There are other "ensuing loss" provisions that are broader than the water damage one discussed here. One common clause restores coverage even when a loss was caused by an excluded peril where the damage was caused by a "covered cause of loss." *See, e.g.*, Five Star Hotels, LLC v. Ins. Co. of Greater N.Y., 2011 U.S. Dist. LEXIS 31313 (S.D.N.Y. Mar. 24, 2011). Another clause covers ensuing loss caused by, *inter alia*, water damage if the loss would otherwise be covered under the policy. *See, e.g.*, Fiess v. State Farm Lloyds, 202 S.W.3d 744 (Tex. 2006).

This statement is known as an "ensuing loss" exception.[473] It provides coverage when four prerequisites are met: (1) a listed peril must (2) cause water damage (3) that is not otherwise excluded, (4) and the water must derive from one of the enumerated sources.

An ensuing loss has been defined as one "that occurs separate from but as a result of an excluded loss. Ensuing-loss exceptions are not applicable . . . if the ensuing loss was directly related to the original excluded risk."[474] Some policies use the phrase "resulting loss," and courts generally treat it as meaning the same as "ensuing loss."

Few reported decisions have discussed this particular ensuing loss clause, and even fewer have concerned losses that might be characterized as caused by flooding. Nevertheless, the reported cases are reviewed below to provide an outline of how courts interpret the clause.

[2] Burden of Proof

The general rule is that when the policy is all-risk, the insured has to establish that the loss appears to come within the terms of the policy and the insurer has the burden to show the risk is excluded after which the burden shifts to the insured to prove an exception to the exclusion applies.[475] The process is the same when there is a named peril policy, except that the insured has to prove that the efficient proximate cause of the loss is a named peril. Thus, because the ensuing water damage provision is an exception to a list of exclusions, the policyholder has the burden of proving its application.[476]

---

473. *See generally* Sullivan & Gordon, *A Review of Ensuing Loss Case Law: 2010 to Present*, 43 The Brief 18 (2014); French, *The "Ensuing Loss" Clause in Insurance Policies: The Forgotten and Misunderstood Antidote to Anti-Concurrent Causation Exclusions*, 13 Nev. L.J. 215 (2012); Harrington, *Lessons of the San Francisco Earthquake of 1906: Understanding Ensuing Loss in Property Insurance*, 37 The Brief 28 (2008); Chriss, *Coverage for Ensuing Water Damage under Texas Property Insurance Policies*, 46 S. Tex. L. Rev. 1247 (2005).

474. Liberty Mutual Fire Ins. Co. v. Martinez, 157 So. 3d 486, 488 (Fla. 5th DCA 2015) (citations omitted). *See also* Cooper v. Am. Fam. Mut. Ins. Co., 184 F. Supp. 2d 960, 964 (D. Ariz. 2002) (resulting or ensuing loss provision does not reinsert coverage for excluded losses, but reaffirms coverage for secondary losses ultimately caused by excluded perils); Acme Galvanizing Co., Inc. v. Fireman's Fund Ins. Co., 270 Cal. Rptr. 405, 411, 221 Cal. App. 3d 170, 179–80 (1990) (ensuing loss provision applies where there is a peril that causes a loss or injury, separate and independent, but resulting from original excluded peril, and new peril is not an excluded one, from which loss ensues).

475. 5 Jeffrey E. Thomas, *New Appleman on Insurance Law Library Edition* § 44.06[2] (Matthew Bender 2022).

476. Bodo v. GeoVera Specialty Ins. Co., 2019 U.S. Dist. LEXIS 232690 (M.D. Fla. Mar. 8, 2019) (insured has burden of proving facts that bring claim within affirmative grant of coverage); Raschkovsky v. Allstate Ins. Co., 2015 U.S. Dist. LEXIS 182040 (C.D. Calif. Dec. 21, 2015) (insured plaintiffs failed to proffer sufficient evidence from which reasonable jury could find that water damage resulted from ensuing loss and summary judgment was proper on their breach of contract claim).

[3] Direct Physical Loss

Typically, policies state that they insure against risk of *direct physical loss* to property, before they list the exclusions. When the insured seeks coverage for water damage from a damaged plumbing system, the issue is not whether there was a direct physical loss to that plumbing system, but whether there was a direct physical loss to covered property caused by the plumbing system.[477]

[4] Water Damage

There must be water damage for the exception to be triggered. For instance, a sanitary drain line located under the slab in a kitchen was broken and needed repair. There was no evidence the broken drain pipe caused any water damage to the interior of the insured home or that water seepage from that pipe caused any damage under the slab of the house. The appellate court held that the lower court erred by entering judgment against the insurer for the cost of repair and replacement of the slab necessary to reach the broken pipe. The court allowed that a different result could be reached if the homeowners came forward in the future with evidence of water damage.[478]

Water damage must cause the ensuing loss.[479] For example, in a Texas case a shower stall was constructed without a shower pan, an "inherent vice" according to the court, allowing water to leak onto wood below. Fungus developed in the dampness that rotted the floor and caused it to sink. The court said that while the water could very well have created an atmosphere that contributed to the growth of fungi that caused the rot and deterioration, it could not

---

477. Floyd v. Geovera Specialty Ins. Co., 2020 U.S. Dist. LEXIS 35346 (M.D. Fla. Mar. 2, 2020). *See also* Bodo v. GeoVera Specialty Ins. Co., 2019 U.S. Dist. LEXIS 232690 (M.D. Fla. Mar. 8, 2019) (insured failed to show direct physical loss where there was evidence of deteriorated pipe, but pipe remained operable and unblocked); Guadiana v. State Farm Fire & Cas. Co., 2012 U.S. Dist. LEXIS 136866 (D. Ariz. Sept. 25, 2012) (water damage is covered loss, not defective plumbing system).

478. Homeowners Choice Prop. & Cas. v. Maspons, 211 So. 3d 1067 (Fla. 3d DCA 2017).

479. This proposition has also been stated regarding policies that provide ensuing loss coverage when water, in any of its prescribed forms, causes fire, an explosion, or sprinkler leakage. *See, e.g.*, Bates v. Phenix Mut. Fire Ins. Co., 156 N.H. 719, 943 A.2d 750 (2008) (if water had caused fire, explosion, or sprinkler leakage on property, damage resulting from those perils would be covered, but to apply ensuing loss provision to provide coverage for what was essentially a flood would be contrary to intent of policy). *See also* Platek v. Town of Hamburg, 3 N.Y.S.3d 312, 24 N.Y.3d 688, 26 N.E.3d 1167 (2015) (where subsurface water main abutting insured property ruptured, causing water to flood into and severely damage finished basement, subsurface water did not cause "explosion" of pipe; rather, water pressure within pipe caused rupture). Some courts may say the water damage merely needs to precede the other peril. *See* Goldner v. Otsego Mut. Fire Ins. Co., 39 A.D.2d 440, 336 N.Y.S.2d 717 (1972) (for there to be loss ensuing from water damage, all that is required is that explosion follow chronologically).

be legally said that the "ensuing damage" was caused by "water damage."[480] In other words, the excluded peril of "inherent vice" may have caused the leak, but there was no water damage. The damage was caused by fungus, which, it should be noted, was itself an excluded peril.[481] Another Texas court reached a different conclusion under similar facts. A house was constructed without a shower pan beneath the shower floor, an "inherent defect" that allowed water to pass into and under the wood flooring, causing warping, cracks, rot, and deterioration. That ensuing loss, said the court, grew out of and was caused by water damage and, therefore, the ensuing loss exception applied.[482]

The distinction between the two Texas cases is that water damage caused one loss, but not the other. This dichotomy is illustrated in a Tennessee decision where water from a leaking roof pooled in crawl spaces and caused mold and fungi that rendered the home uninhabitable. The court said that it was uncontroverted that the damages claimed were a consequence of water leaking from the roof. The insurer did not claim the mold and fungi came from another source. Consequently, the loss was caused by water damage, and the exclusion for fungi and mold damage did not apply.[483] Thus, the excluded peril of inherent vice or latent defect caused the water damage that caused the ensuing loss. Some may find the distinction between the first Texas case and

---

480. Merrimack Mut. Fire Ins. Co. v. McCaffree, 486 S.W.2d 616 (Tex. App. 1972). *See also* Aetna Casualty & Surety Company v. Yates. 344 F.2d 939 (5th Cir. 1965) (finding coverage where joists, sills, and subflooring of home were almost completely rotted away and cause was that crawl space under house was inadequately vented and air trapped there, which had been chilled by air conditioning, produced condensation of moisture and consequent rotting; rot may have ensued from presence of water but not from water damage); Lundstrom v. United Servs. Auto. Ass'n—CIC, 192 S.W.3d 78 (Tex. App. 2004) (mold damage that followed rather than preceded water damage was excluded from coverage).

481. Put another way, "the water damage was not caused by the mold; instead, the mold was caused by the water damage." Fiess v. State Farm Lloyds, 2003 U.S. Dist. LEXIS 10962, at *25 (S.D. Tex. June 3, 2003) (to qualify for exception, ensuing water damage must follow from one of types of damage enumerated in exclusion; because evidence conclusively established that water damage was cause, rather than consequence, of mold, exclusion was applicable). *See also* Lundstrom v. United Servs. Auto. Ass'n—CIC, 192 S.W.3d 78 (Tex. App. 2004) (for ensuing loss exception to override exclusion for mold, mold must have caused or preceded water damage, not vice versa).

482. Employer Cas. Co. v. Holm, 393 S.W. 2d 363 (Tex. App. 1965). The insurer argued the loss was caused by an excluded inherent vice. The court responded that the inherent vice was in the shower stall, and no recovery was allowed for it. Recovery was for replacing the damaged floor, and no contention was made that there was any inherent vice in the floor, which suffered water damage. See Chriss, *Coverage for Ensuing Water Damage under Texas Property Insurance Policies*, 46 S. Tex. L. Rev. 1247 (2005), for a more in-depth discussion of Texas ensuing loss cases.

483. Home Ins. Co. v. McClain, 2000 Tex. App. LEXIS 969 (Feb. 10, 2000) (unpublished opinion).

the Tennessee decision semantical;[484] nonetheless, the Tennessee court found that the loss was *caused by water damage*, and the Texas court did not.[485]

[5] Not Otherwise Excluded

A caveat to the "ensuing loss" exception is that the "'ensuing loss' itself must not be specifically excluded elsewhere in the policy."[486] A common exclusion is for continuous or repeated seepage or leakage of water occurring over a prescribed period of time. Where an ensuing loss was caused by continuous or repeated seepage or leakage, it was "otherwise excluded" and there was no coverage.[487] Another court, however, found a policy to be ambiguous regarding how the leakage and seepage clause applied to the ensuing loss provision that allowed coverage for water loss caused by certain perils, in this case by rodents or vermin. Construing the policy against the insurer, the court held that the policy included coverage for water damage from a continuous flow of water caused by rodents, but not when the insured was aware of the leak

484. The Tennessee *McClain* decision has been criticized for construing "ensuing loss" as meaning to follow an event listed in the ensuing loss provision—water damage—rather than to follow events listed in the exclusions. Lundstrom v. United Servs. Auto. Ass'n—CIC, 192 S.W.3d 78 (Tex. App. 2004). Mold damage and whether it can be an ensuing loss is an issue over which courts are divided. Worthy, *Uncovering Mold: An Insurance Dilemma*, 10 U. Balt. J. Envtl. L. 157, 171 (2003) (courts that have analyzed policy language regarding mold are divided on whether damages from rot or mold constitute an ensuing loss).

485. Another Texas case explained that water damage is usually caused by severe storms, a bursting pipe, or broken glass that lets water inside a building and that mold is not an ensuing loss from water damage just because it is caused by water. In the case before the court, a bad roof that leaked—not water damage—caused the mold, and the policy excluded losses caused by wear and tear or deterioration to the roof. Hood v. State Farm Lloyds, 2004 U.S. Dist. LEXIS 28948 (S.D. Tex. May 13, 2004).

486. Smith v. Westfield Ins. Co., 2007 U.S. Dist. LEXIS 43996 (E.D. Pa. June 15, 2007).

487. Marsh v. Am. Family Mut. Ins. Co., 231 Ore. App. 332, 218 P.3d 573 (2009) (leak in bathroom shower allowed water to penetrate area under shower causing subfloor to sustain dry rot; court held that although under ensuing loss provision there would be coverage generally for loss caused by water, because policy contained specific exclusion for water damage caused by continuous leakage of water from plumbing system, loss was not covered, even though other types of damage caused by water were covered). *See also* Bunch v. Nationwide Mut. Ins. Co., 2014 U.S. Dist. LEXIS 5320 (W.D. Wash. Jan. 15, 2014), where water damage came from a leaky faucet and air conditioner. The policy had both a continuous or repeated seepage or leakage of water exclusion and a wear and tear, deterioration, inherent vice, latent defect, or mechanical breakdown exclusion with an ensuing water damage exception. The policyholder argued for coverage based on ambiguity created by the two exclusions. The court rejected the coverage theory and cited *Marsh*, suggesting it followed that court's reasoning when it held the former exclusion barred coverage. Unfortunately, the *Bunch* court also said that the "wear and tear, deterioration" could not create coverage. That is true, but creating coverage is exactly what an ensuing loss clause in an exclusion does. It would have been better if the court stuck to the reasoning of the *Marsh* case. While the opinion is confusing and poorly written, it is still Washington state precedent.

and did not report it for weeks. As long as the insured reported water loss due to rodent chew promptly on learning of it, concluded the court, the insured would be covered up until that point for any damage caused by the water loss.[488] Thus, the court did not disagree that a leakage and seepage clause could render ensuing water damage to be "otherwise excluded"; it simply found a way around the exclusion.

An anti-concurrent cause provision may prevent application of the ensuing loss exception. In an Arizona case, a plumbing system rupture caused water damage to the insured home. The policy excluded coverage for faulty construction or materials. It also excluded coverage for "deterioration," but if deterioration caused water damage, not otherwise excluded, from a plumbing system, the policy covered loss caused by the water including the cost to tear out and replace any part of a building necessary to repair the system. The insured sought "tear-out" coverage for the cost of accessing the entire plumbing system for replacement. The court found the plumbing pipes were defective within the meaning of either exclusion and that if the loss was excluded pursuant to either exclusion, it was not covered. It then considered the faulty construction or materials exclusion. The plain and ordinary meaning of the exclusion, said the court, was that losses caused directly or indirectly from defective pipes were not covered. Moreover, continued the court, under the anti-concurrent causation clause, where one cause may be covered but another is not, the covered one has to provide the sole basis for coverage. The court then noted that the exception to the "deterioration" exclusion only applied if the water damage is not otherwise excluded. Because the damage was "otherwise excluded" by virtue of the anti-concurrent causation clause, coverage was not "reinserted" by inclusion of the exception to the deterioration exclusion.[489]

In a Florida case, a hot water heater failed spectacularly, allowing 4,000 gallons of water to flood a home. The water caused compression or erosion—earth movement—which in turn caused structural damage for which the insured homeowner sought compensation. The court concluded that earth movement caused the loss and because it was an excluded peril, there was

488. Danganan v. Am. Family Mut. Ins. Co., 2019 U.S. Dist. LEXIS 169806 (D. Nev. Sept. 30, 2019).

489. Vasquez v. Ameriprise Ins. Co., 2021 U.S. Dist. LEXIS 63195 (D. Ariz. Mar. 30, 2021). The court also found that even if the "faulty construction or materials" exclusion did not bar coverage, a "plain and ordinary reading" of the "deterioration" exclusion would. It covered a loss caused by water including the cost of tearing out and replacing any part of a building necessary to repair the system or appliance, but the policyholder elected to replace the entire plumbing system out of a concern that leaks might recur, but the policy language specifically limits the tear out coverage to repair. *See also* Liberty Mutual Fire Ins. Co. v. Martinez, 157 So. 3d 486 (Fla. 5th DCA 2015) (damage to pool and surrounding area from subsurface water pressure, an excluded peril, was not ensuing loss).

no coverage: the loss was "otherwise excluded."[490] The same conclusion was reached where water leaked from a pipe connected to a hot water heater, causing the ground under the house to settle and the house slab to crack. Coverage for the loss was barred by an exclusion for foundation settling, cracking, shrinking, bulging, or expansion.[491]

[6] Water Damage Sublimit

After determining that the ensuing loss exception applies, it is important to examine the policy for a water damage sublimit endorsement. The language of the endorsement then has to be scrutinized to ascertain whether it applies to an ensuing loss.[492]

[7] Tear Out to Repair

[a] Plumbing System Leaks

The ensuing loss exception allows coverage for the cost of tearing out and replacing any part of a building necessary to repair the system or appliance from which that water escaped, but not the loss to the system or appliance. The exception is most often applied when water has escaped plumbing. The question then is: what, other than covered property damaged by that water, is covered? Although the standard policy language seems fairly clear, in a number of cases, courts have needed to point out that the exception does not cover the expense of repairing or replacing the damaged plumbing system itself, but does cover the cost of tearing out and repairing the portions of the property that are needed to gain access to the damaged parts of the plumbing system that caused the loss.[493] On the other hand, an Arizona federal court concluded

---

490. Hatch v. Geovera Specialty Ins. Co., 2019 U.S. Dist. LEXIS 101491 (M.D. Fla. June 18, 2019).

491. Murray v. State Farm Fire & Cas. Ins. Co., 268 Cal. Rptr. 33, 219 Cal. App. 3d 58 (1990).

492. In *Certain Interested Underwriters at Lloyd's London v. Pitu, Inc.*, 95 So. 3d 290 (Fla. 3d DCA 2012). a water pipe in the upper story of a home burst, resulting in damage the insurer estimated to be over $600,000. The court cited the exclusions for wear and tear, deterioration, inherent vice, latent defect, and mechanical breakdown and the water damage ensuing loss exception. It concluded the water damage was not excluded by the policy. Unfortunately, the court did not specify whether that was the case because none of the cited exclusions applied or because the ensuing loss exception overrode those exclusions. In any event, the court found an endorsement limiting water damage to $25,000 applied. It is not possible to determine from the opinion if the court was applying the endorsement to limit a loss covered by the water damage ensuing loss exception or a loss that was the result of a covered peril.

493. Floyd v. Geovera Specialty Ins. Co., 2020 U.S. Dist. LEXIS 35346 (M.D. Fla. Mar. 2, 2020). *See also* Colaco v. State Farm Fire & Casualty Co., 1993 U.S. App. LEXIS 10571, at *8 (9th Cir. Apr. 8, 1993) (only coverage available when pipe bursts is cost of tearing out part of building to reach that pipe and then replacing that part); Yanes v. Nat'l Specialty Ins. Co., 548 F. Supp. 3d 1307 (S.D. Fla. 2021) (no coverage for costs expended to prevent future damage);

that if the policyholder could establish that her plumbing system caused the covered water damage loss and that in order to repair that system it was necessary to replace all the pipes, the insurer was obligated to pay the tear out costs necessary to *replace all those pipes, even those not leaking*.[494]

Even though the policy may cover the cost of tearing out and replacing a part of a building as is required to repair the system or appliance from which water issued, a sublimit may apply to the water damage coverage that also applies to the tear out costs.[495]

[b] Exterior Stucco

In a Pennsylvania case, a contractor did not properly install stucco on the exterior of the insured home. Because of that faulty construction—an excluded peril—rainwater seeped into the house and damaged the flooring. Under the ensuing loss exception, the court found the policy covered the cost to replace the damaged flooring but not the stucco.[496]

[8] Sprinkler Leakage

Another version of the ensuing loss clause provides an exception to the standard water damage exclusion for loss or damage that results from sprinkler leakage. That exception was at issue in a case in which a damaged sprinkler on an adjacent property resulted in water under the ground surface—an excluded peril—seeping through basement walls into the insured property where it damaged inventory. The court said damage from seepage resulting from sprinkler leakage *elsewhere* was not covered. If the seepage *itself* caused the sprinkler system on the insured premises to leak, which in turn caused further losses, those resultant losses, said the court, would be covered. The ensuing loss exception did not provide coverage for excluded losses, but for

---

Gershkowitz v. State Farm Gen. Ins. Co., 2021 U.S. Dist. LEXIS 252185 (C.D. Cal. Dec. 29, 2021) (insurer would not have to cover cost of damage to pipe); Keenan v. Wausau Lloyds Ins. Co., 1998 Tex. App. LEXIS 5994 (Sept. 23, 1998) (where damages were from overflow of bathroom toilet, overflow formed basis of claim, not defective plumbing lines themselves, and costs to access those lines represented "incidental portion" of covered loss); Bodo v. GeoVera Specialty Ins. Co., 2019 U.S. Dist. LEXIS 232690 (M.D. Fla. Mar. 8, 2019) (no coverage where insured sought expenses of tear out to replace deteriorated pipes, rather than tear out to repair leaking pipes).

494. Guadiana v. State Farm Fire & Cas. Co., 2012 U.S. Dist. LEXIS 136866 (D. Ariz. Sept. 25, 2012) (rejecting argument by insurer that it was only required to pay tear out costs necessary to replace particular pipes that burst and that broader interpretation of tear out provision was contrary to exclusion for loss consisting of defective construction materials; finding that tea out provision applied even if repair of system that caused covered loss required complete replacement).

495. *See, e.g.*, Yanes v. Nat'l Specialty Ins. Co., 548 F. Supp. 3d 1307 (S.D. Fla. 2021).

496. Smith v. Westfield Ins. Co., 2007 U.S. Dist. LEXIS 43996 (E.D. Pa. June 15, 2007).

certain secondary losses ultimately caused by excluded perils. The damage to the inventory was due to water seeping through basement walls as a result of sprinkler leakage on another property. The water seepage did not *cause* the sprinkler leakage and, therefore, the losses were subject to the exclusion and were not covered by the ensuing loss provision.[497]

An even broader ensuing loss clause provides coverage when damage was caused by a "covered cause of loss." In a New York case the insured property was damaged by a frozen and leaking sprinkler system. The insurer invoked an exclusion for losses caused by faulty design or maintenance. The policy defined "covered cause of loss" to include leakage from fire extinguishing equipment. The court found that leakage from an automatic sprinkler system was specifically covered by the ensuing loss provision and, therefore, the faulty design or maintenance exclusion did not apply and did not bar coverage for water damage resulting from a frozen sprinkler system.[498]

---

497. Myung Sung, Inc. v. Firstline Nat. Ins. Co., 1996 U.S. Dist. LEXIS 1411 (E.D. Pa.1996).

498. Five Star Hotels, LLC v. Ins. Co. of Greater N.Y., 2011 U.S. Dist. LEXIS 31313 (S.D.N.Y. Mar. 24, 2011).

4

Recovering under a Private Flood Insurance Property Policy

4.1 Introduction

Contrary to what some believe, flood insurance is available from private insurance carriers.[1] The National Flood Insurance Program (NFIP) remains the main source of primary flood insurance coverage, but the interest among private insurers in directly underwriting flood risk has grown with advances in the analytics and data used to quantify risk.[2] In 2017, for example, the market for privately written flood insurance grew by just over 51 percent.[3] At the same time, as one federal judge observed, "flood insurance is unattractive to most insurers and often accompanied by attempts to limit the exposure it can create."[4] Thus, private insurers generally leave coverage for high flood risk properties to the NFIP, which cannot refuse coverage.[5] They most commonly

1. *See, e.g.*, Pyramid Techs., Inc. v. Hartford Cas. Ins. Co., 752 F.3d 807, 819 (9th Cir. 2014) (insurer acknowledged that flood was covered event); Burrell v. State Farm & Cas. Co., 226 F. Supp. 2d 427 (S.D.N.Y. 2002) (homeowners policy insures against all risks of loss to residence and personal property deriving from fire, flooding, and weather-related damages).

2. Horn & Webel, *Private Flood Insurance and the National Flood Insurance Program*, at 1–2 (May 7, 2019), Congressional Research Service, https://fas.org/sgp/crs/homesec/R45242.pdf.

3. Lehman, *Private Flood Insurance Market Is Getting Bigger, More Competitive, Less Profitable* (Mar. 18, 2018), Insurance Journal, https://www.insurancejournal.com/blogs/right-street/2018/03/18/483689.htm.

4. Baylor College of Med. v. Am. Guar. & Liab. Ins. Co., 2002 U.S. Dist. LEXIS 29002, at *53 (S.D. Tex. Oct. 30, 2002).

5. Horn & Webel, *Private Flood Insurance and the National Flood Insurance Program*, at 16 (May 7, 2019), Congressional Research Service, https://fas.org/sgp/crs/homesec/R45242.pdf (because NFIP cannot refuse to write policies, properties considered "undesirable" by private insurers are likely to remain in NFIP portfolio; private insurers will not compete against NFIP for policies that are inadequately priced from their perspective).

provide commercial coverage[6] or excess coverage above the NFIP maximums.[7] They limit risk by imposing sublimits or high deductibles. Their caution is well founded. Indeed, in 2017 losses exceeded premiums.[8] Nonetheless, private flood coverage exists—both primary and excess—and this chapter explores aspects of the coverage that differentiate it from standard property coverages that exclude flood losses.

4.2 Forms of Primary Coverage

[1] Introduction

The discussion below focuses on the language found in commonly used policies and endorsements. One does, however, need to be aware that for large businesses or institutions, manuscript policies, nonstandard forms drafted for a particular risk,[9] may cover flood losses.[10] One also needs to be aware that while a water damage exclusion, including flood, is nearly universal in property policies, occasionally an "all-risk" property policy will not contain that exclusion and, therefore, the policy covers flood losses even though no mention is made of flood.[11]

---

6. Focusing on commercial properties allows carriers to spread risk. *See, e.g.*, Aspen Specialty Ins. Co. v. 4 NYP Ventures LLC, 162 F. Supp. 3d 337 (S.D.N.Y. 2016) (commercial property was covered for flood by private master policy obtained by property manager that covered hundreds of properties managed by that company).

7. Horn & Webel, *Private Flood Insurance and the National Flood Insurance Program*, at 9 (May 7, 2019), Congressional Research Service, https://fas.org/sgp/crs/homesec/R45242.pdf.

8. Lehman, *Private Flood Insurance Market Is Getting Bigger, More Competitive, Less Profitable* (Mar. 18, 2018), Insurance Journal, https://www.insurancejournal.com/blogs/right-street/2018/03/18/483689.htm.

9. 1 Jeffrey E. Thomas, *New Appleman on Insurance Law Library Edition* § 1.07[9] (LexisNexis 2022).

10. *See, e.g.*, Certain Underwriters at Lloyd's, London v. Travelers Prop. Cas. Co. of Am., 161 Wn. App. 265, 256 P.3d 368 (2011) (primary all-risk property coverage provided by manuscript policy that also provided flood coverage in excess of SFIP); Cummins, Inc. v. Ace Am. Ins. Co., 2011 U.S. Dist. LEXIS 4568 (S.D. Ind. Jan. 14, 2011) (13 insurance companies provided coverage pursuant to manuscript policies "shopped" to them by insurance broker for insured; coverage included flood).

11. *See, e.g.*, Toussie v. Allstate Ins. Co., 2019 U.S. Dist. LEXIS 20309 (E.D.N.Y. Feb. 6, 2019), where a "Deluxe Plus Homeowners" insurance policy provided "all perils" coverage for scheduled personal property (SPP) and the SPP coverage did not exclude flood damage. In contrast, the policy had coverage for unscheduled personal property that was limited to certain named perils. Theft, but not flood damage, was one of those named perils. *See also* Swarzman v. AIG Prop. Cas. Co., 2017 N.Y. Misc. LEXIS 2781 (July 20, 2017) (insurer issued both homeowners policy with no flood exclusion clause and excess flood policy and insured also obtained SFIP); Omega Protein Corp. v. Lexington Ins. Co., 2007 U.S. Dist. LEXIS 98530 (W.D. La. Feb. 15, 2007) (commercial property insurance policy included per occurrence property damage limit of $7.5 million and covered all risks of direct physical loss, including flood); Amax, Inc. v. Arkwright Boston Mfrs. Mut. Ins. Co., 1978 U.S. Dist. LEXIS 7150 (S.D.N.Y. Dec. 19, 1978) (where policy listed 14 specifically excluded perils, but "liquid damage" was not among

[2] Stand Alone Policy

A "stand alone" policy is one written to cover a specific risk or peril. The Federal Emergency Management Agency (FEMA) Standard Flood Insurance Policy (SFIP) is an example of a stand alone policy. While *private primary* flood coverage may be obtained in a stand alone policy[12]—for example, an NFIP-compliant policy—it is most often secured through an endorsement to a commercial property or homeowners policy.

[3] NFIP-Compliant Policies

[a] Introduction

Under the National Flood Insurance Act (NFIA), federal agencies that regulate lending are required to adopt rules that prohibit "regulated lending institutions"[13] from making, increasing, extending, or renewing any loan secured by improved real estate or a mobile home in an area with special flood hazards in which flood insurance has been made available under the Act, unless the building or mobile home, and any personal property securing the loan, is covered for the term of the loan by flood insurance.[14] The same restriction applies to "federal agency lenders."[15] Finally, the Federal National Mortgage Association (Fannie Mae) and the Federal Home Loan Mortgage Corporation (Freddie Mac) are required by the Act to ensure that for any loan they purchase secured by improved real estate located in an area that, at the time of the origination of the loan or at any time during its term, is in an area with special flood hazards and for which flood insurance under the Act is available, the building, and any personal property securing the loan, is covered by flood insurance for the term of the loan.[16] All these lenders

---

them, insurer was liable for losses when automatic valve burst, resulting in flooding of insured property).

12. In *World Fire & Marine Ins. Co. v. Carolina Mills Dist. Co.*, 169 F.2d 826 (8th Cir.1948), a business obtained a "Water Damage Policy" that was very specialized. It covered "direct loss and damage caused solely by the accidental discharge, leakage or overflow of water or steam from within" plumbing systems, plumbing tanks, the heating system, "elevator tanks and cylinders, stand pipes for fire hose, industrial or domestic appliances, refrigerating systems, air conditioning systems, and rain or snow admitted directly to the interior of the building through defective roofs, leaders or spouting, or by open or defective doors, windows, show windows, skylights, transoms or ventilators."

13. The term "regulated lending institution" is defined as "any bank, savings and loan association, credit union, farm credit bank, Federal land bank association, production credit association, or similar institution subject to the supervision of a Federal entity for lending regulation." 42 U.S.C. § 4003(a)(10). The coverage has to be in an amount at least equal to the outstanding principal balance of the loan.

14. 42 U.S.C. § 4012a(b)(1).

15. 42 U.S.C. § 4012a(b)(2). *See also* 42 U.S.C. § 4003(a)(7) (defining "federal agency lender").

16. 42 U.S.C. § 4012a(b)(3).

are permitted to accept "private flood insurance" in satisfaction of the flood coverage requirement providing the coverage meets the prescribed statutory minimum conditions.[17]

Under the Act, a "private flood insurance" policy is required to provide coverage that is at least as broad as that of the FEMA SFIP including deductibles, exclusions, and conditions offered by the insurer.[18] The policy has to have a requirement that the insurer will give the insured and any regulated lending institution or federal agency lender 45 days' written notice of cancellation or non-renewal.[19] It has to include information about the availability of flood coverage under the Act, contain a mortgage interest clause that is similar to the one in the SFIP, and have a requirement that an insured file suit no later than one year after the date of a written denial of all or part of a claim under the policy.[20] Finally, the policy has to have cancellation provisions that are as restrictive as those in the SFIP.[21]

Any insurer issuing one of these policies has to be licensed, admitted, or otherwise approved to engage in the business of insurance in the state or jurisdiction in which the insured property is located.[22] If, however, the policy is one of difference in conditions, multiple peril, all-risk, or other blanket coverage that insures *nonresidential commercial* property, the insurer may be recognized, or not disapproved, as a surplus lines insurer by the insurance regulator of the state or jurisdiction where the property to be insured is located.[23]

In 2019, five federal regulatory agencies issued a joint final rule that provides that lending institutions may, under certain conditions, accept private flood insurance policies that do *not* meet the NFIA criteria.[24] Under what is termed "discretionary acceptance," a flood insurance policy issued by a private insurer that is not issued under the NFIP and that does not meet the definition of private flood insurance is nonetheless acceptable in satisfaction of the flood insurance purchase requirement if it meets four criteria:

1. The amount of insurance is at least equal to the lesser of the outstanding principal balance of the designated loan or the maximum limit of coverage available for the particular type of property under the NFIP.

17. If the property does not have "special flood hazards," a policy does not need to meet those requirements.
18. 42 U.S.C. § 4012a(b)(7)(B).
19. 42 U.S.C. § 4012a(b)(7)(C)(i).
20. 42 U.S.C. §§ 4012a(b)(7)(C)(ii)–(iv).
21. 42 U.S.C. § 4012a(b)(7)(D).
22. 42 U.S.C. § 4012a(b)(7)(A)(i).
23. 42 U.S.C. § 4012a(b)(7)(A)(ii).
24. Federal Reserve System, Farm Credit Administration, Federal Deposit Insurance Corporation, National Credit Union Administration, and Office of the Comptroller of the Currency, "New Rule Covers Private Flood Insurance," press release, Feb. 12, 2019, https://www.occ.gov/news-issuances/news-releases/2019/nr-ia-2019-15.html.

2. The policy is issued by an insurer that is licensed, admitted, or otherwise approved to engage in the business of insurance by the insurance regulator of the state or jurisdiction in which the property to be insured is located or, in the case of a policy of difference in conditions, multiple peril, all-risk, or other blanket coverage insuring *nonresidential commercial property*, is issued by a surplus lines insurer recognized, or not disapproved, by the insurance regulator of the state or jurisdiction where the property to be insured is located.
3. The policy covers both the mortgagor and mortgagee as loss payees, except in the case of a policy that is provided by a condominium association, cooperative, homeowners association, or other applicable group and for which the premium is paid by the association as a common expense.
4. The policy provides sufficient protection of the designated loan, consistent with general safety and soundness principles, and the lender documents its conclusion regarding sufficiency of the protection of the loan in writing.[25]

[b] Private Carrier Policies

Private insurance companies, for example, Lloyd's[26] and an AIG company,[27] offer NFIP-compliant flood policies that are almost identical to the SFIP General Property Form policy. The Lloyd's and AIG policies both say that a loss will not be denied that would have been settled under the FEMA SFIP. Each policy lists differences from the SFIP, but only one of those is significant. The SFIP states that it is governed by the NFIA, FEMA regulations, and "federal common law." In place of that, the Lloyd's and AIG policies state that they are governed by, and construed in accordance with, the law of the applicable state and that the parties agree to submit to the exclusive jurisdiction of *any competent court* within the United States. Like the SFIP policy, the private market policies say any suit brought by an insured against them has to be brought in the United States district court of the district in which the insured property was located at the time of loss. However, by statute when a claim under an SFIP is denied or the insured refuses the amount offered, exclusive jurisdiction is conferred on the United States district courts to hear and determine the action without regard to the amount in controversy.[28] Otherwise, jurisdiction

25. 12 C.F.R. § 208.25(c)(3)(iii).

26. *See Lloyd's Certificate*, TFIA, http://static1.squarespace.com/static/5258438be4b02d2a03ac168e/t/53c03906e4b06be54e6f27e4/1405106438465/Sample+General+Property+Form.pdf.

27. *See Private Market Flood Policy*, TFIA, https://static1.squarespace.com/static/5258438be4b02d2a03ac168e/t/575f52fc859fd09b4e48908e/1465864956877/Lex+General+Property+Form+15+%28revised+6.10.16%29.pdf.

28. 42 U.S.C. § 4072.

in the United States district courts is most commonly established under the "diversity" statute, which provides that those courts have "original jurisdiction of all civil actions where the matter in controversy exceeds the sum or value of $75,000, exclusive of interest and costs, and is between . . . Citizens of different States."[29] A contract could not establish jurisdiction that did not otherwise exist. Therefore, despite the language of the Lloyd's and AIG policies, an action that did not meet the jurisdictional requirements of the "diversity" statute, or invoke federal jurisdiction on some other basis, could not be brought in federal court.

[c] Advantages of NFIP-Compliant Policies

NFIP-compliant policies are governed by state law, not federal law, as is the case with a FEMA SFIP. That is an important distinction. Consumer protections, whether statutory or judicially created, do not apply to the SFIP but will apply to NFIP-compliant policies. Courts, for instance, require *strict compliance* with the proof of loss requirements in the SFIP. Insurers that act contrary to those requirements generally do not waive the right to enforce strict compliance. Generally, under state law a proof of loss may be submitted after any policy deadline so long as the insurer's rights are not prejudiced. There is no federal cause of action for bad faith refusal to settle a claim, but in most states there is some form of protection from unfair claims practices.[30] Claims that would otherwise have been paid are often, as courts have noted, barred under the law applicable to the SFIP.[31]

[4] Differences in Condition Policy

Generally, Differences in Condition (DIC) insurance is a "non-filed class of inland marine insurance."[32] Typically it is provided by surplus lines carriers, which are insurers that provide coverage for risks that are difficult to insure and may otherwise be uninsurable.[33] A DIC policy is a form of property insurance that is obtained in conjunction with an underlying commercial property

---

29. 28 U.S.C. § 1332(a)(1).

30. For example, almost all the states have adopted the NAIC Model Unfair Claims Settlement Practices Act.

31. *See, e.g.*, Charnock v. Fid. Nat'l Prop. & Cas. Ins. Co., 2014 U.S. Dist. LEXIS 1491, at *6–7 (S.D. Tex. Jan. 7, 2014) (in the "world" of NFIP any non-compliance not waived by FEMA can render unfair result). *See also* Admiralty Condo. Ass'n v. Dir., FEMA, 594 Fed. Appx. 738 (3d Cir. 2014), *cert. den.*, ___U.S.___, 135 S. Ct. 2395, 192 L. Ed. 2d 167 (2015) (court would find against policyholder even if it assumed rigid enforcement by FEMA of its regulations was disingenuous).

32. Prahl, *Difference in Conditions Coverage: What Is It and Who Needs It?* at 2 (2012), Adjusting Today, http://adjustersinternational.com/publications/adjusting-today/difference-in-conditions-coverage/0/.

33. TWBC III, Inc. v. Certain Underwriters at Lloyd's London, 323 N.J. Super. 60, 61, 731 A.2d 1228, 1230 (1999).

policy.[34] It is defined as a "special form of open-peril coverage written in conjunction with basic fire coverage and designed to provide protection against losses not reimbursed under the standard fire forms."[35] As one court said, "the purpose of a Difference in Conditions policy is to protect against a difference in conditions, in effect to protect against holes or slits in the blanket of insurance protection which a large company, of necessity, must place among many insurers, each using different fine print, or 'conditions.'"[36]

DIC policies are commonly used to provide coverage for catastrophic perils, including floods, that typically are excluded in property policies or to provide additional limits of coverage for specific perils.[37] A DIC policy may provide coverage in excess of the primary limit.[38] Although DIC coverage is usually thought of as provided by a stand alone policy that is issued by a different carrier than the one that issued the primary property policy, the primary carrier could include DIC coverage in its primary policy.[39] It also could issue a separate DIC policy.[40] Flood could be a covered peril in the main DIC policy or could be added by endorsement.[41]

There is a standard Insurance Service Organization (ISO) DIC policy.[42] It contains a list of exclusions that *does not* include "water."[43] That is why commentators say that the primary use of a DIC policy is to cover normally excluded perils such as flood.[44] When that is the purpose of a DIC policy, it is important to note that the ISO policy says that separate limits of coverage are shown on the Declarations Page for water damage.[45]

---

34. Prahl, *Difference in Conditions Coverage: What Is It and Who Needs It?* at 1 (2012), Adjusting Today, http://adjustersinternational.com/publications/adjusting-today/difference-in-conditions-coverage/0/.

35. *See Glossary D*, NAIC, http://www.naic.org/consumer_glossary.htm#D.

36. Amax, Inc. v. Arkwright Boston Mfrs. Mut. Ins. Co., 1978 U.S. Dist. LEXIS 7150, at *13–14 (S.D.N.Y. Dec. 19, 1978).

37. *Difference in Conditions Policies* (Summit Business Media, 2012).

38. Prahl, *Difference in Conditions Coverage: What Is It and Who Needs It?* at 2 (2012), Adjusting Today, http://adjustersinternational.com/publications/adjusting-today/difference-in-conditions-coverage/0/.

39. *See, e.g.*, Great Am. Ins. Co. v. Towers of Quayside No. 4 Condo. Ass'n, 2015 U.S. Dist. LEXIS 150358 (S.D. Fla. Nov. 4, 2015).

40. *See, e.g.*, Samia Cos. v. United States Fire Ins. Co., 789 So. 2d 706, 708 (La. App.), *writ den.*, 799 So. 2d 1145 (La. 2001).

41. *See, e.g.*, Tocci Bldg. Corp. v. Commonwealth Ins. Co., 22 Mass. L. Rep. 522 (Apr. 23, 2007), *aff'd*, 71 Mass. App. Ct. 1120, 885 N.E.2d 172 (2008) (Difference in Conditions policy with endorsement that included flood damage as insured-against peril with liability limited to $5 million per year and deductible of $25,000).

42. *See* ISO Form IH 00 80 09 09.

43. *See* ISO Form IH 00 80 09 09, § B.2.g.

44. Prahl, *Difference in Conditions Coverage: What Is It and Who Needs It?* at 3 (2012), Adjusting Today, http://adjustersinternational.com/publications/adjusting-today/difference-in-conditions-coverage/0/.

45. *See* ISO Form IH 00 80 09 09, § C.1.

The ISO DIC begins by covering flood loss because it is an all-risk policy that omits the usual "water" damage exclusion. It defines water damage as, *inter alia*, flood, surface water, waves, tides, tidal water, overflow of any body of water, mudslide, mudflow, and water that backs up or overflows from a sewer or drain.[46] The definition largely tracks the one in the typical commercial property policy in which the term includes flood, surface water, waves, tides, tidal waves, overflow of any body of water, mudslide or mudflow, and water that backs up or overflows from a sewer, drain, or sump.[47] If a DIC policy happens to define "flood" an as overflowing of normal boundaries of water, it should be noted that there will not be coverage for losses from surface water derived from rain or melting snow that follows no defined course as it flows over the ground.[48] Even though the language of the standard ISO DIC policy may cover flood losses, private insurers rarely agree to cover them when property is located in a high-risk zone and, therefore, an endorsement will probably be added in that case to exclude "water" damage and, most likely, will define water as does the underlying commercial property policy, with the possible exception of "water that backs up or overflows from a sewer, drain or sump." As a result, flood coverage obtained under a DIC policy will probably be for property that is *not* in a high-risk zone. Additionally, DIC policies typically contain separate limits for flood coverage.[49] The ISO DIC policy, for example, states that separate limits of coverage are shown on the Declarations Page for water damage.[50]

[5] Parametric Insurance

Parametric insurance—also called "index" or "event" based insurance—is an agreement under which an insurer consents to pay an agreed amount on the occurrence of a specified event—for example, a hurricane of specified intensity (likely based on the Saffir-Simpson scale) or a storm surge based on customized risk parameters.[51] In other words, coverage is triggered by a parameter, a metric or index that is an objective standard, rather than a verbal

---

46. *See* ISO Form IH 00 80 09 09, § G.4.

47. *See* ISO Form CP 10 30 06 07, § B.1.g.

48. *Difference in Conditions Policies* (Summit Business Media, 2012); Prahl, *Difference in Conditions Coverage: What Is It and Who Needs It?* at 5 (2012), Adjusting Today, http://adjustersinternational.com/publications/adjusting-today/difference-in-conditions-coverage/0/.

49. Prahl, *Difference in Conditions Coverage: What Is It and Who Needs It?* at 6 (2012), Adjusting Today, http://adjustersinternational.com/publications/adjusting-today/difference-in-conditions-coverage/0/.

50. *See* ISO Form IH 00 80 09 09, § C.1.

51. *Parametric Insurance*, IRMI, https://www.irmi.com/term/insurance-definitions/parametric-insurance.

description.[52] The parameters can be defined by the extent of physical damage and are typically limited to certain time periods and geographic areas.[53] Flooding, for example, might be covered based on height of the flood waters, and the set amount of coverage established at a predetermined amount based on data from prior floods and losses.[54] This avoids confusion over causation. For instance, if rainfall is a covered peril and it exceeds a specified amount, then coverage in an agreed-upon amount is triggered.[55] The insured does not have to show that rain caused particular damage or that the rain did or did not turn into "surface water" or that the damage was not caused by some other excluded peril.

Parametric solutions are not designed to be stand alone policies but instead fill protection gaps in more traditional insurance; for example, risk may be transferred with some parametric coverage when a policy has very high deductibles.[56] Although parametric insurance is becoming available for homeowners,[57] most holders of parametric flood coverage will probably be sophisticated businesses and institutions. They will likely not need the assistance of an attorney in making a claim or litigating over denial of one because the claims process is relatively straight forward.[58] There is no need for loss adjustment if the trigger or index is established.[59] Thus, claims are settled almost immediately and if the insured has coverage and there is a flood at the

---

52. Moorcraft, *What is parametric insurance?* (Oct. 29, 2018), Insurance Business America, https://www.insurancebusinessmag.com/us/news/breaking-news/what-is-parametric-insurance-114901.aspx.

53. *Parametric Insurance*, IRMI, https://www.irmi.com/term/insurance-definitions/parametric-insurance.

54. Sorrell, *What is Parametric Insurance, and Why Should We Care?* (Feb. 23, 2021), Property Casualty 360, https://www.propertycasualty360.com/2021/02/23/what-is-parametric-insurance-and-why-should-we-care/?kw=What%20is%20parametric%20insurance%2C%20and%20why%20should%20we%20care?&utm_source=email&utm_medium=enl&utm_campaign=agentbrokerinsider&utm_content=20210225&utm_term=pc360.

55. Elliott, *Rethinking the Limits of Parametric Insurance* (Sept. 24, 2019), Insurance Journal, https://www.insurancejournal.com/news/international/2019/09/24/540903.htm.

56. Moorcraft, *What is parametric insurance?* (Oct. 29, 2018), Insurance Business America, https://www.insurancebusinessmag.com/us/news/breaking-news/what-is-parametric-insurance-114901.aspx.

57. Passy, *This 'Incredibly Powerful' Home-Insurance Policy Will Make Payouts Even if Your Property Isn't Damaged* (Jan. 27, 2020), MarketWatch, https://www.marketwatch.com/story/this-powerful-home-insurance-policy-it-pays-out-even-if-your-property-isnt-damaged-2020-01-17.

58. *See generally* Stillwell, *Claims Considerations for Parametric Insurance* (Jan. 13, 2021), Property Casualty 360, https://www.propertycasualty360.com/2021/01/13/claims-considerations-for-parametric-insurance/.

59. Moorcraft, *What is parametric insurance?* (Oct. 29, 2018), Insurance Business America, https://www.insurancebusinessmag.com/us/news/breaking-news/what-is-parametric-insurance-114901.aspx.

insured premises, the insurer will pay without actual damage being established if the water level reaches the established threshold.[60] If the loss exceeds the predetermined amount of coverage, the insured bears that portion of the loss. On the other hand, the predetermined amount is generally paid even if the actual loss is less than that amount.[61]

[6] Flood Endorsements to Property Coverage

[a] Introduction

Water damage coverage, including flood, may be provided by an endorsement. The endorsement may add the coverage as a named peril, override a water damage exclusion, or delete the exclusion. However, the result may not add it for all coverages. For example, in one case an endorsement added flood as a covered peril for "physical loss or damage." The court said the endorsement added coverage "only for property damage and loss caused by flood, not interruption in business operations."[62] One also has to be alert for restrictions to the added coverage. For example, it is common for these endorsements to include a sublimit or separate deductible for flood damage. The added coverage may apply to all property insured under the policy, or only to property listed on a schedule.[63]

[b] Endorsement Adding Flood Coverage

When a policy names covered perils, and flood is not among them, an endorsement can simply add flood loss to the list of named perils.

[c] Endorsement Overriding Flood Exclusion

Almost all policies, whether all-risk or named perils, will explicitly exclude from coverage water damage including by flood. An endorsement might add back water damage coverage.[64] In that case, it is critical to determine

60. Sorrell, *What is Parametric Insurance, and Why Should We Care?* (Feb. 23, 2021), Property Casualty 360, https://www.propertycasualty360.com/2021/02/23/what-is-parametric-insurance-and-why-should-we-care/?kw=What%20is%20parametric%20insurance%2C%20and%20why%20should%20we%20care?&utm_source=email&utm_medium=enl&utm_campaign=agentbrokerinsider&utm_content=20210225&utm_term=pc360.

61. Elliott, *Rethinking the Limits of Parametric Insurance* (Sept. 24, 2019), Insurance Journal, https://www.insurancejournal.com/news/international/2019/09/24/540903.htm.

62. Protection Mutual Ins. Co. v. Mitsubishi Silicon America Corp., 164 Ore. App. 385, 395, 992 P.2d 479, 484 (1999).

63. *See, e.g.*, Terminal Ventures, Inc. v. Fireman's Fund Ins. Co., 2009 N.J. Super. Unpub. LEXIS 1793 (July 9, 2009) (covered perils included flood for any location shown on Scheduled Flood Endorsement).

64. *See, e.g.*, Alley Theatre v. Hanover Ins. Co., 436 F. Supp. 3d 938, 942 (S.D. Tex. 2020) (policy contained separate Flood Endorsement that overrode excluded peril language on flood).

how the endorsement defines terms. If the added coverage is verbatim that excluded in the policy, then the water damage exclusion is in effect overridden in *toto*. If the language is different, then one has to compare the language to determine the extent of the coverage that is added. For example, an endorsement may add back only one or more components of water damage coverage, leaving the remainder of the exclusion intact.[65] In one case, for instance, the endorsement added coverage for losses caused directly by flood/surface water, but left the rest of the water damage exclusion in the main policy in place.[66]

In another case the endorsement redefined "excluded water damage" to include only water that backed up from a sewer or drain.[67] The result was that other forms of water damage, including flood, were covered. It is important to compare the definition of any component added to coverage with the definition in the exclusion. If the definitions are identical, then the exclusion for that component is effectively overridden. If they are not, they have to be evaluated to determine the extent of the coverage added. It is also important to identify any exceptions to the coverage added back by the endorsement.[68] One common exception is a sublimit. Where a policy excluded flood and an endorsement added back coverage for all loss or damage "caused by flood" with a sublimit of $1 million, the court said the endorsement did not delete the flood exclusion from the policy. It made the flood exclusion inapplicable to the insurance specifically provided by the flood endorsement. The insurance, therefore, was limited to "the total of all loss or damage caused by Flood" and was capped by the sublimit.[69]

---

65. *See, e.g.*, Terminal Ventures, Inc. v. Fireman's Fund Ins. Co., 2009 N.J. Super. Unpub. LEXIS 1793 (July 9, 2009) (endorsement provided that covered perils included "flood" meaning flood, surface water, waves, tidal water, or overflow of body of water all whether driven by wind or not and including spray that results from any of them whether driven by wind or not).

66. McWhorter v. Bankers Std. Ins. Co., 2020 U.S. Dist. LEXIS 48668 (D. Md. Mar. 20, 2020) (endorsement stated that provisions of policy applied unless modified by the endorsement, which added coverage for losses caused by flood that were excluded by Flood or Surface Water exclusion in main policy; endorsement made clear that exclusion in main policy did not apply to extent coverage was provided in endorsement).

67. Somerset Indus. v. Lexington Ins. Co., 639 F. Supp. 2d 532, 535 (E.D. Pa. 2009) (effect of amendment was to remove exclusion for damage caused by flood, surface water, or overflow of any body of water, and maintain it for damage caused by water that backs up from sewer or drain).

68. *See, e.g.*, McWhorter v. Bankers Std. Ins. Co., 2020 U.S. Dist. LEXIS 48668 (D. Md. Mar. 20, 2020) (although endorsement added back benefits for losses caused by flood, it specifically did not cover floods already in progress or earth movement caused by a flood).

69. Certain Underwriters at Lloyd's, London v. Travelers Prop. Cas. Co. of Am., 161 Wn. App. 265, 285, 256 P.3d 368, 379 (2011).

[d] Endorsement Deleting Flood Exclusion

An endorsement may simply identify the water damage exclusion, or a part of it, and state that it is deleted.[70] Alternatively, the endorsement may delete the exclusion, state that coverage is extended to water damage, and then define water damage. If the definitions in the exclusion and the endorsement are identical, then the water damage exclusion is in effect eliminated completely. If the language is different, then one has to compare the definitions to determine the extent of the coverage added.

The endorsement may contain conditions, exceptions, or limitations. For example, a policy that provides coverage for multiple locations might exclude flood coverage for properties in certain "high risk" zones,[71] in which case the definition of "high risk zone" is critical.[72] An endorsement could specifically exclude certain properties from coverage, for instance, newly constructed or acquired buildings.[73] The most common limitation found in flood coverage endorsements is a special sublimit.[74]

An endorsement might not extend coverage to all losses. For example, an endorsement deleted flood from the list of excluded causes of loss and provided coverage for "direct physical loss or damage to Covered Property

---

70. *See, e.g.*, Gilbert/Robinson, Inc. v. Sequoia Ins. Co., 655 S.W.2d 581, 583 (Mo. App. 1983) (endorsement attached to policy removed flood damage exclusion).

71. *See, e.g.*, Lundy Enters., L.L.C. v. Wausau Underwriters Ins. Co., 2009 U.S. Dist. LEXIS 121295 (E.D. La. Dec. 29, 2009) (Flood Coverage Endorsement provided coverage for certain flood occurrences as defined in that endorsement but purported to exclude properties in certain flood zones).

72. *See* Cummins, Inc. v. Ace Am. Ins. Co., 2011 U.S. Dist. LEXIS 4568 (S.D. Ind. Jan. 14, 2011), where the endorsement defined "High Hazard Zones for Flood" as: "a) all property at a 'location' that is partially or totally situated in an area which at the time of loss or damage has been designated on a Flood Insurance Rate Map (FIRM) to be a Special Flood Hazard Area (SFHA), and/or b) all property in areas where the National Flood Insurance Program (NFIP) is not in effect, and where all property at a 'location' is partially or totally situated in an area which is within a 100 year flood plain or its worldwide equivalent, and/or c) all property at a 'location' that is partially or totally protected by dams, dikes, levees or walls which were intended to protect such property from the level of a 100 year flood or its worldwide equivalent, regardless of any Zone or Area designation or assignment by FIMA or other recognized authority having jurisdiction."

73. Baylor College of Med. v. Am. Guar. & Liab. Ins. Co., 2002 U.S. Dist. LEXIS 29002 (S.D. Tex. Oct. 30, 2002) (endorsement did not cover loss or damage to newly constructed or acquired buildings, newly acquired personal property, or unnamed premises all of which were coverage extensions under main policy).

74. *See, e.g.*, Oxford Realty Group Cedar v. Travelers Excess & Surplus Lines Co., 229 N.J. 196, 202, 160 A.3d 1263, 1267 (2017) ($1 million aggregate in any one policy year, for all losses covered occurring at insured premises resulting from flood to buildings, structures, or property in open within Flood Zone A or property in or on buildings or structures located within "such Flood Zones"); Baylor College of Med. v. Am. Guar. & Liab. Ins. Co., 2002 U.S. Dist. LEXIS 29002 (S.D. Tex. Oct. 30, 2002) (limits of insurance for all flood loss or damage could not exceed $50 million aggregate for all flood loss or damage for all premises combined in any one policy year).

caused by flood." That language limits the flood coverage in two ways. First, the coverage is only for *direct*, not indirect, loss. Second, only *physical* losses are covered. Thus, while a main policy provided extra expense coverage for a covered cause of loss, which was not flood, an endorsement did not extend extra expense coverage to flood because extra expense is not a physical loss.[75]

The need to carefully compare the endorsement to the exclusion and the remainder of the policy is demonstrated by a case in which, during a hurricane, flood water filled the basement of an insured property. The water broke an interior concrete wall that fell and ruptured a fire-suppression sprinkler pipe. The rupture released nearly a million gallons of sprinkler-system water into the basement. The policy had the usual flood exclusion except that it *did* cover a "resulting loss if fire, explosion, or sprinkler leakage results." A flood endorsement overrode the excluded peril language on flood and provided blanket flood coverage with a sublimit. The question was whether that sublimit applied to the damage from the sprinkler-system leakage. The court looked at the definitions of "flood" and "water damage." Those defined terms, it concluded, showed that sprinkler-system leakage was not the same as "flood" and, because sprinkler leakage was a covered peril separate from flood damage, the policy covered the loss. The court apparently concluded that the deletion of the flood exclusion with its exception for sprinkler leakage did not mean sprinkler leakage could not be a separate covered peril. However, in the end, the court held that because the flood from the hurricane was the proximate cause of the sprinkler-system rupture and leakage, the sublimit applied to the sprinkler-leak damage.[76]

[e] ISO Standard Flood Coverage Endorsement

[i] Generally

A standard ISO endorsement modifies commercial property coverage by adding flood to the covered perils.[77] The ISO form, or a similar one, is the most likely way policyholders will obtain primary flood coverage when they do not have a FEMA SFIP. The ISO endorsement amends standard ISO property policies that have a "Water Exclusion" rather than a more narrow exclusion just for flood. Under the endorsement, the Water Exclusion does not apply to the extent a part of it "might conflict with coverage provided" by it.[78] Thus, if the

75. Baylor College of Med. v. Am. Guar. & Liab. Ins. Co., 2002 U.S. Dist. LEXIS 29002 (S.D. Tex. Oct. 30, 2002). A loss of business income is also not a physical loss, but the policy evidently required the insurer to pay for any actual loss of business income that resulted from direct physical loss or damage to covered property caused by a covered cause of loss, *including* flood. This illustrates once again how important it is to carefully examine the language of the policy.

76. Alley Theatre v. Hanover Ins. Co., 436 F. Supp. 3d 938 (S.D. Tex. 2020).

77. ISO Form CP 10 65 10 00.

78. ISO Form CP 10 65 10 00, § D.2.

policyholder cannot fit a claim within the coverage the endorsement provides, the exclusion applies.

[ii] Definition of "Flood"

The definition of "flood" in the ISO endorsement is not the same as in the SFIP. The endorsement defines "flood" as a "general and temporary condition of partial or complete inundation of normally dry land areas" but omits "collapse or subsidence of land along the shore of a lake or similar body of water."[79] The SFIP adds that two or more acres and two or more properties, one being the insured property, have to be flooded for there to be a flood. The endorsement, like the SFIP, states that flooding may come from overflow of inland or tidal waters, unusual or rapid accumulation or runoff of surface waters, or mudflows. The endorsement provides coverage for mudflows *caused by flooding* from unusual or rapid accumulation or runoff. The SFIP and the ISO endorsement have nearly the same definition of "mudflow" except that the SFIP policy excludes "landslide, slope failure, or a saturated soil mass moving by liquidity down a slope" from the definition.

The ISO endorsement has some clauses that clarify the coverage. First, flooding in a "continuous or protracted event" is a single flood. Second, if a flood is caused by the overflow of inland or tidal waters, the flood is considered to have begun when the water *first overflowed* its banks.

[iii] Exclusions

The ISO endorsement says that the exclusions and limitations sections of the Causes of Loss Form—a standard attachment to commercial property policies—apply to coverage provided under the endorsement except as the endorsement provides otherwise.[80] Also, to the extent a tsunami causes the overflow of tidal waters, the earthquake exclusion in the Earth Movement Exclusion *does not* apply.[81] The Ordinance or Law Exclusion in the underlying policy applies to any loss under the endorsement, unless Ordinance or Law Coverage is added by endorsement.[82]

The insurer will not, under the endorsement, pay for any loss or damage caused by or resulting from a flood that begins before or within 72 hours after inception of the endorsement, and if the policyholder requests, and the insurer provides, an increase in the stated limit of insurance for flood, that increase does not apply to any flood loss or damage that begins before or within 72 hours after the request was made.[83]

79. ISO Form CP 10 65 10 00, § C.
80. ISO Form CP 10 65 10 00, § D.1.
81. ISO Form CP 10 65 10 00, § D.3.
82. ISO Form CP 10 65 10 00, § D.4.
83. ISO Form CP 10 65 10 00, § D.5.a.

Under the endorsement, the insurer does not pay for loss or damage that is caused by or results from destabilization of land that arises from accumulation of water in subsurface land areas.[84]

The endorsement explicitly bars coverage for land or the cost of excavations, grading, backfilling, or filling.[85] Therefore, there is no coverage for the cost of restoring or remediating land because of collapse or sinking caused by or resulting from a flood, but there is coverage for damage to the covered portions of a building and to covered personal property that is caused by collapse or sinking of land along the shore of a body of water as the result of erosion or undermining that is caused by waves or currents of water that exceed the cyclical levels and cause a flood.

There is no coverage for any loss or damage by a flood to personal property in the open except to the extent that coverage, if any, is specified in the Flood Coverage Schedule or in the Declarations.[86] There is also no coverage for loss or damage caused by sewer backup or overflow unless the backup or overflow results from a flood and occurs within 72 hours after the flood recedes.[87]

[iv] Debris Removal

The insurer will, under the endorsement, pay the expense to remove debris of covered property and other debris that is on the described premises, when that debris is caused by or results from a flood,[88] and will also pay the expense to remove debris of covered property that has floated or been hurled off the described premises by a flood.[89] The carrier will not, however, pay to remove deposits of mud or earth from the grounds of the described premises.[90] The debris removal coverage does not increase the applicable limit of insurance for flood, and the most the insurer, therefore, will pay for the total of debris removal and loss or damage to covered property is the limit of insurance for flood applicable to the covered property at the described premises covered under the endorsement.[91]

---

84. ISO Form CP 10 65 10 00, § D.5.b.

85. ISO Form CP 10 65 10 00, § D.5.c. *See, e.g.*, Red Lion Hotels, Inc. v. Commonwealth Ins. Co. of Am., 177 Ore. App. 58, 33 P.3d 358 (2001) (riverbank restoration project involved grading, filling, and backfilling of land with soil, earth, mineral matter, or other fill material and, therefore, fell under land exclusion, and was not covered risk).

86. ISO Form CP 10 65 10 00, § D.5.d.

87. ISO Form CP 10 65 10 00, § D.5.f.

88. ISO Form CP 10 65 10 00, § E.1.a.

89. ISO Form CP 10 65 10 00, § E.1.b.

90. ISO Form CP 10 65 10 00, § E.1.a.

91. ISO Form CP 10 65 10 00, § E.1.c.

[v] Newly Acquired or Constructed Property

The coverage extension for newly acquired or constructed property does not apply to any building or structure not fully enclosed by walls and a roof.[92] The most the insurer will pay for all loss or damage to covered newly acquired or constructed property is 10 percent of the total of all limits of insurance for flood coverage under the endorsement.[93] This coverage does not increase the limit of insurance for flood.

[vi] Limit of Insurance

The limit of insurance for flood is usually shown in the Flood Coverage Schedule or on the Declarations Page, but if it is not, then the limit applicable to fire also applies to flood.[94] The limit is the most the carrier will pay in a single occurrence of flood for loss or damage caused by that flood.[95] If there is more than one flood in a 12-month period, the most the insurer will pay for the total of all loss or damage sustained during that period caused by a flood is the amount identified as the "Annual Aggregate for Flood" shown in the Flood Coverage Schedule or on the Declarations Page. If the limit and the annual aggregate amount are the same, or if there is no amount stated as an annual aggregate, then the limit is the most that will be paid for the total of all loss or damage caused by a flood in a 12-month period, even if there is more than one occurrence of flood during that period of time. In other words, if the first flood does not exhaust the applicable limit, the balance of that limit is available for a subsequent flood. If a single flood begins during one annual policy period and ends during the following one, any limit or annual aggregate applicable to the following policy period does not apply to that flood.

If there is a covered ensuing loss—for example, loss caused by fire, explosion, and/or sprinkler leakage that results from a flood—the most that will be paid for the total of all loss or damage caused by flood, fire, explosion, and sprinkler leakage is the limit of insurance applicable to fire. In other words, the carrier will not pay the sum of the fire and flood limits.[96] The endorsement provides examples of ensuing loss where there is fire coverage under the principal policy and flood coverage under the endorsement with a limit of insurance for fire of $800,000 and for flood of $400,000 with a flood deductible of $5,000. In one example the damage from flood is $500,000 and from fire is also $500,000. The insurer would pay $400,000 for the flood loss. The payment for the fire loss would also be $400,000 because it would be capped

92. ISO Form CP 10 65 10 00, § E.2.a.
93. ISO Form CP 10 65 10 00, § E.2.b.
94. ISO Form CP 10 65 10 00, § G. The endorsement says that flood coverage may be written at a limit that is equal to or less than that which applies to other covered causes of loss.
95. ISO Form CP 10 65 10 00, § G.2.
96. ISO Form CP 10 65 10 00, § G.3.

at the difference between the basic limit of $800,000 and the flood limit of $400,000. The net proceeds to the insured would be $800,000. In the second example, the damage from flood is $800,000 and the damage from fire is $100,000. For the flood damage, the insurer would pay the limit of $400,000 and for the fire damage, the insurer would pay the limit of $100,000.

[vii] Deductible

The deductible for flood coverage provided under the endorsement is shown in the Flood Coverage Schedule or on the Declarations Page.[97] The insurer will not pay that part of the loss attributable to any deductible in an SFIP.[98] If a flood results in another covered cause of loss and if both causes of loss cause loss or damage, then only the higher deductible will be applied.[99]

[viii] Other Insurance

The endorsement has an "other insurance" clause.[100] It effectively converts the endorsement into excess coverage or establishes a large deductible. Under the endorsement, if a loss is also covered by an SFIP, or the property is *eligible to be covered*, but no SFIP is in effect, the insurer will only pay for the amount of the loss that *exceeds* the maximum limit in the SFIP, whether or not that limit is maintained or the insured can collect on any SFIP.[101] For policyholders covered, or eligible to be covered, under the SFIP General Property Form, the maximum limit is $500,000. If the other insurance clause in the endorsement is triggered and there is no SFIP, the policyholder stands to bear a large loss.

There are two exceptions to the other insurance clause. The first applies when, at the time of loss, the property is eligible for an SFIP but one is not in effect solely because of ineligibility of the property at the time the endorsement was written.[102] The second exception applies when an SFIP is not in effect because the carrier agreed to write the endorsement without underlying SFIP coverage.[103] That agreement has to be noted in a Flood Coverage Schedule or on the Declarations Page by an indication that an Underlying Insurance Waiver applies.

---

97. ISO Form CP 10 65 10 00, § H.1.
98. ISO Form CP 10 65 10 00, § H.2.
99. ISO Form CP 10 65 10 00, § H.3.
100. ISO Form CP 10 65 10 00, § I.
101. *See, e.g.*, 570 Smith St. Realty Corp. v. Seneca Ins. Co., Inc., 2019 N.Y. Misc. LEXIS 1773 (Apr. 4, 2019) (as reflected in "other insurance" provision, defendant's coverage was excess with respect to NFIP-eligible properties).
102. ISO Form CP 10 65 10 00, § I.1.a. *See* Barnett v. Fid. Nat'l Prop. & Cas. Co., 157 So. 3d 51 (La. App.), *writ den.*, 120 So. 3d 703 (La. 2013) (where property owners were ineligible for coverage under NFIP because property was located in Coastal Barrier Resource System, private coverage obtained with premium of about $3,500 and $10,000 deductible).
103. ISO Form CP 10 65 10 00, § I.1.b.

4.3 Definitions of "Flood" in Policies

In the typical property policy that *excludes* water damage, "flood" is included in the definition of "water," but "flood" is not itself defined.[104] In stand alone flood policies[105] and endorsements that add flood coverage to standard property policies, the term "flood" may be defined. Obviously, that definition is the starting point for determining the extent of the coverage and needs to be carefully scrutinized. If the loss was caused by something other than a flood, a policy providing flood coverage will not cover the loss unless it fits within some other covered cause of loss in the policy.[106]

In older policies, the definition of "flood" could be pithy, for example: "the rising of natural bodies of water."[107] The definitions in newer policies may be equally brief.[108] However, in modern policies, the definitions are usually more complex. These policy definitions almost always begin by defining "flood" as "flood."[109] That circular definition might, at first blush, appear

104. There are exceptions. For example, one policy that excluded flood coverage defined flood as "waves, tidal water or tidal wave, rising (including overflowing or breaking of boundaries) of lakes, reservoirs, rivers, streams or other bodies of water, whether driven by wind or not." E.B. Metal & Rubber Indus., Inc. v. Fed. Ins. Co., 84 A.D.2d 662, 444 N.Y.S.2d 321 (1981) (insured property was damaged when dike gave way; policyholder contended that for flood exclusion to apply, breaking of dike had to have been directly caused by rising water and that preexisting weakness in dike caused the damage, however, court found that all policy required was that there be rising waters that broke through boundaries and flowed on insured's land to constitute flood, and it was irrelevant that defect in the dike may have also contributed to break).

105. The FEMA SFIP is a stand alone policy that defines flood extensively.

106. *See, e.g.*, Mateer v. Reliance Ins. Co., 247 Md. 643, 233, A.2d 797 (1966) where the policy covered property of a shop for several perils including flood. Water blew a fitting off a pipe running to the property above the insured premises allowing to permeate and seep into the shop below and damage to articles, the premises, and equipment. The policy did not define "flood." The court said that it is common to speak of a cellar or basement being "flooded" whether the water comes from the overflow of a stream, a hard downpour, or the bursting of pipes. Thus, the court found the lower court correctly determined that there was no coverage for items on shelves and work tables damaged only by steam or drops of water, but erred in directing a verdict for the insurer regarding damaged items on the floor.

107. Sun Underwriters Ins. Co. v. Bunkley, 233 S.W.2d 153, 154 (Tex. App. 1950). Given that definition, the Texas court said it was clear the policy did not insure against any and every damage that might be caused by water, but was limited to damage caused by flood. In the case, water ran into chicken houses and caused the chickens to drown. That, said the court, could not be regarded as a flood, either under the generally accepted definitions of the term, or under the definition in the policy. Instead, the water that entered the chicken houses could be regarded only as surface waters, not as a flood, because the water was not backed up from a river, creek, or other natural watercourse.

108. *See, e.g.*, AMTRAK v. Aspen Specialty Ins. Co., 661 Fed. Appx. 10 (2d Cir. 2016) (rising and overflowing of a body of water onto normally dry land).

109. *See, e.g.*, Almah LLC v. Lexington Ins. Co., 2016 Del. Super. LEXIS 47 (Jan. 27, 2016) ("The following term(s) wherever used in this Policy means: a) Flood: Flood").

superfluous. However, it arguably incorporates common law definitions of flood as discussed elsewhere.[110]

The flood definition found in policies almost always initially includes surface waters, rising waters, waves, tide or tidal water, the release of water, and the rising, overflowing, or breaking of boundaries of natural or man-made bodies of water,[111] or the spray therefrom.[112] Some policies may add "sewer back-up resulting from any of the foregoing."[113] One common definition adds storm surge, sea surge, tsunami, and wave wash to that initial list and then modifies the entire list by the phrase "all whether driven by wind or not."[114] Another common version of the definition adds rain accumulation and run-off from natural or human-made objects to the initial list and then includes "surface waters or sewer back-up resulting from any of the" forms of flood on the list.[115] A policy may include that language but omit "surface water."[116] A common point of contention is whether a loss was caused by flooding, a named windstorm, or a weather condition. If "storm surge" or "rain" are not addressed in the definition, the insurer may argue they are the product of wind or weather and, therefore, the loss is not covered by the flood policy. A policy may, however, encompass those losses by stating that "[p]hysical loss or damage from flood associated with a storm or weather disturbance whether or not

---

110. See § 2.1[3], *supra*.

111. The definition may list the water bodies rather than refer to "natural or man-made bodies of water." *See* Seacor Holdings, Inc. v. Commonwealth Ins. Co., 635 F.3d 675, 679 (5th Cir 2011) (flood defined to mean waves, tide or tidal water, inundation, rainfall and/or resultant runoff, and rising (including overflowing or breakage of boundaries) of lakes, ponds, reservoirs, rivers, harbors, streams, or similar bodies of water whether wind-driven or not); Northrop Grumman Corp. v. Factory Mut. Ins. Co., 563 F.3d 777, 781 (9th Cir. 2009) (definition of flood included rising, overflowing, or breaking of boundaries of lakes, reservoirs, rivers, streams, or other bodies of water).

112. Some policies may omit surface water, rising water, and release of water. For example, one policy defined flood as "'waves, tides, or tidal water, the rising (including the overflowing or breaking of boundaries) of lakes, ponds, reservoirs, rivers, harbors, streams or similar bodies of water whether driven by wind or not.'" Gilbert/Robinson, Inc. v. Sequoia Ins. Co., 655 S.W.2d 581, 583 (Mo. App. 1983).

113. *See, e.g.*, Northrop Grumman Corp. v. Factory Mut. Ins. Co., 563 F.3d 777, 781 (9th Cir. 2009); New York Univ. v. Factory Mut. Ins. Co., 374 F. Supp. 3d 315 (S.D.N.Y. 2019).

114. *See, e.g.*, New York Univ. v. Factory Mut. Ins. Co., 374 F. Supp. 3d 315, 320 (S.D.N.Y. 2015); Almah LLC v. Lexington Ins. Co., 2016 Del. Super. LEXIS 47 (Jan. 27, 2016). *See also* AMTRAK v. Aspen Specialty Ins. Co., 661 Fed. Appx. 10 (2d Cir. 2016) (policy defined "flood" as surface water, flood waters, waves, tide or tidal waters, sea surge, tsunami, the release of water, the rising, overflowing, or breaking of defenses of natural or human-made bodies of water, or wind-driven water).

115. *See, e.g.*, Federal-Mogul LLC v. Ins. Co. of Pa., 780 Fed. Appx. 267 (6th Cir. 2019); Penford Corp. v. National Union Fire Ins. Co. of Pittsburgh, 2010 U.S. Dist. LEXIS 3737, at *18, n.2 (N.D. Iowa, Jan. 19, 2010).

116. *See, e.g.*, New York Univ. v. Factory Mut. Ins. Co., 374 F. Supp. 3d 315, 320 (S.D.N.Y. 2015); Almah LLC v. Lexington Ins. Co., 2016 Del. Super. LEXIS 47 (Jan. 27, 2016).

identified by name by any meteorological authority, is considered to be flood within the terms" of the policy.[117]

Some policies specifically address floods that are associated with "storms or weather disturbances." Physical loss or damage from them "is considered to be flood" regardless of whether they are named.[118] This somewhat awkward language is evidently intended to ensure coverage when, for example, there is a storm surge that is not caused by a named storm.

In some policies, the list of events considered to be a flood may be preceded by the words "a temporary condition of partial or complete inundation of normally dry land." In a case before the Second Circuit, that preamble was followed by a listing of events causing that inundation including the overflow tidal waters outside the normal watercourse or natural boundaries and the overflow, release, rising, runoff, or surge of surface water. The definition, said the court, was sufficiently broad to include an inundation of railroad tunnels by seawater driven by storm surge or a windstorm.[119]

Policy flood definitions virtually always state that they are "regardless of any other cause or event contributing concurrently or in any other sequence of loss." Some may modify "other cause or event" with "whether natural or man-made."[120] In one case that included that language, the insured contended that the flood definition did not encompass its losses to the extent they were caused by faulty workmanship that permitted flood waters to wreak havoc on the property. However, the flood definition, said the court, expressly encompassed losses from flood waters "regardless of any other cause or event, whether natural or man-made, contributing concurrently or in any other sequence of loss." Thus, the resulting losses fell within the policy definition of flood.[121]

The policy definition may provide that "direct physical damage by fire, explosion or sprinkler leakage resulting from flood is not considered to be loss by flood."[122] That should mean that fire, explosion, or sprinkler leakage that results from "flood" is not subject to any limitations the policy imposes on flood losses—for instance, a flood sublimit or deductible. It should also mean that if the policy *only* covers loss by flood, there should be no coverage.

It should be kept in mind that when the policy covers flood and defines the term, incidents that might be considered floods at common law would not generally be covered causes of loss.

---

117. New York Univ. v. Factory Mut. Ins. Co., 374 F. Supp. 3d 315 (S.D.N.Y. 2019).

118. *See* New York Univ. v. Factory Mut. Ins. Co., 374 F. Supp. 3d 315, 320 (S.D.N.Y. 2015).

119. *See, e.g.*, AMTRAK v. Aspen Specialty Ins. Co., 661 Fed. Appx. 10 (2d Cir. 2016). *See also* PCVST-DIL LLC v. Lexington Ins. Co., 2016 N.Y. Misc. LEXIS 2031 (Apr. 21, 2016). *And see* ISO Form CP 10 65 10 00, § C.

120. *See, e.g.*, New York Univ. v. Factory Mut. Ins. Co., 374 F. Supp. 3d 315, 320 (S.D.N.Y. 2015); Almah LLC v. Lexington Ins. Co., 2016 Del. Super. LEXIS 47 (Jan. 27, 2016).

121. New York Univ. v. Factory Mut. Ins. Co., 374 F. Supp. 3d 315, 328 (S.D.N.Y. 2019).

122. *See, e.g.*, New York Univ. v. Factory Mut. Ins. Co., 374 F. Supp. 3d 315, 320 (S.D.N.Y. 2015); Almah LLC v. Lexington Ins. Co., 2016 Del. Super. LEXIS 47 (Jan. 27, 2016).

4.4 Physical Loss or Damage

The policy may cover "physical loss or damage" by "flood" as it defines it. In that case, non-physical coverages—for example, loss of use—are not covered. As one court noted, the definition of flood could have included non-physical losses, but where the policy insured physical loss or damage caused by flood, the court had to read the policy by its plain terms, and by those terms of the definition of flood, it included physical loss and was silent about related non-physical coverages.[123]

4.5 Exclusions to Primary Coverage

[1] Flood Zone Exclusion

FEMA designates flood zones.[124] The high-risk flood zones begin with the letters "A" or "V" and are referred to as Special Flood Hazard Areas (SFHA).[125] Zone "A" encompasses areas subject to inundation by the 1 percent annual chance flood event.[126] Zone "V" consists of areas along coasts that are subject to inundation by the 1 percent annual chance flood event with additional hazards that are associated with storm-induced waves.[127] The mandatory flood insurance requirements of the National Flood Insurance Act apply in both zones. Private insurers generally do not provide flood coverage in them. When they do provide coverage, the policy may have a specific exclusion for property in either an "A" or "V" zone.[128] One reason for that exclusion would be that part of an insured property is in an SFHA and part is not, and another is that the policy covers more than one location. When the policy covers more than one location, it may exempt a specific property from the exclusion even though it is in a high-risk zone.[129]

There are many FEMA zones and subzones, and that can lead to confusion. For example, one policy provided for limited flood coverage but specifically excluded loss or damage to property located in zones A or V "as

123. Northrop Grumman Corp. v. Factory Mut. Ins. Co., 805 F. Supp. 2d 945, 951 (C.D. Cal. 2011).

124. *See generally Flood Zones*, FEMA, https://www.fema.gov/glossary/flood-zones.

125. 44 C.F.R. § 59.1 (definition of area of special flood hazard). There are also designations for area of special flood-related erosion hazards ("E") and of special mudslide (i.e., mudflow) hazards ("M") that are special hazard areas.

126. *Zone*, FEMA, https://www.fema.gov/glossary/zone. *See also* 44 C.F.R. § 64.3.

127. *Zone V*, FEMA, https://www.fema.gov/glossary/zone-v. See also 44 C.F.R. § 64.3.

128. *See, e.g.*, Hudson Shore Assoc., L.P. v. Praetorian Ins. Co., 172 A.D.3d 830, 831, 99 N.Y.S.3d 440, 441 (2019) (while commercial property policy provided flood insurance, it also excluded that coverage when any part of property was in SFH Zone as defined by FEMA).

129. *See, e.g.*, Penford Corp. v. National Union Fire Ins. Co. of Pittsburgh, 2010 U.S. Dist. LEXIS 3737 (N.D. Iowa, Jan. 19, 2010) (policy generally excluded flood coverage for properties located in zone A areas, but specifically exempted "Cedar Rapids, IA" from that exclusion).

defined by the Federal Emergency Management Agency (FEMA)." The insured property was located in zone AE. The insurer denied coverage, contending that AE was a subzone of zone A. Indeed, FEMA regulations say that zone A "usually is refined into" a number of zones, one of which is AE.[130] Nonetheless, the court said that "the language of FEMA's flood zone regulations raises an issue of fact rendering the insurance policy's exclusion of flood coverage ambiguous."[131]

It is possible for a policy to be issued with an exclusion for property in an SFHA after a survey shows the property for which coverage is sought is *not* in an SFHA, only to have a post-loss investigation contradict the earlier survey. In one case where that happened, the court, applying equitable estoppel, denied summary judgment to the insurer based on the exclusion. The court said that if the insurer had conducted a proper initial survey and informed the insured that its property *was* in an excluded SFHA, the insured may have opted to purchase insurance that would cover property in an SFHA that was available. It was for the jury to decide whether the insured would have purchased that coverage but for the negligently conducted survey and whether the insured reasonably relied on that survey.[132]

[2] Rain

Even though a policy may provide coverage for damage from water, and define water to include "flood" and "surface water," a rain exclusion may bar that coverage. This exclusion, discussed elsewhere,[133] bars coverage for damage to the interior of a building or the property inside it that is caused by rain, snow, sleet, or ice unless the building first sustains damage by an insured loss to its roof or walls through which that rain, snow, sleet, or ice enters.[134] Thus, if the water that causes damage is characterized as "surface water," there should be coverage, but if it is determined to be rain—and it did not enter through a breach in the roof or a wall—coverage will likely be denied.[135]

---

130. 44 C.F.R. § 59.1. The difference between zone "A" and "AE" is that the former is "without water surface elevations determined" and the latter is "with water surface elevations determined." 44 C.F.R. § 64.3.

131. Heartland Brewery Inc. v. Nova Casualty Company, 149 AD3d 522, 523, 52 N.Y.S.3d 55, 57 (2017). *Compare* Nova Cas. Co. v. Peter Thomas Roth Labs, LLC, 2018 N.Y. Misc. LEXIS 4609 (Oct. 9, 2018) (where insurer denied coverage under same exclusion for properties in AE zone, court granted summary judgment to insurer because it demonstrated that, during negotiations leading up to renewal of policy, parties were aware that insured properties were not being covered for flood damage).

132. AJT Props. v. Lexington Ins. Co., 2012 Pa. Dist. & Cnty. Dec. LEXIS 308 (July 26, 2012).

133. See § 29[10], *supra.*

134. ISO Form CP 10 30 06 07, § C.1.c.(1).

135. *See, e.g.*, Somerset Indus. v. Lexington Ins. Co., 639 F. Supp. 2d 532, 541 (E.D. Pa. 2009). In *Somerset*, the policy covered water damage including from surface water, but not

[3] Building Ordinance or Law Exclusion

Property policies generally contain an exclusion under which the insurance company will not pay for loss or damage caused directly or indirectly by enforcement of any ordinance or law regulating construction, use, or repair of any property or requiring tearing down of any property, including the cost of removing its debris.[136] The exclusion applies whether the loss results from an ordinance or law that is enforced even if the property has not been damaged or increased costs incurred to comply with an ordinance or law in the course of construction, repair, renovation, remodeling or demolition of property, or removal of its debris, following physical loss to that property.

The exclusion can be invoked after a flood when a damaged building has to be upgraded to bring it into compliance with current building code requirements.[137] To do so, the carrier has to show the expense was caused directly or indirectly by enforcement of any ordinance or law. In a Louisiana case,[138] the insurer tried to invoke the exclusion to deny coverage for the cost of asbestos abatement. A tile floor at the insured premises buckled from a flood and had to be removed. The floor tile glue contained asbestos. Asbestos abatement procedures, therefore, had to be used to properly remove the floor tile at an additional cost of approximately $25,000. The cost of the tile removal was not challenged by the insurer, but the court had to decide whether the policy covered the cost of asbestos abatement. The court said that the increased cost of construction exclusion did not proscribe coverage of the costs of asbestos abatement because it specifically excluded costs "necessitated by the enforcement of any law" and the removal was necessitated by the flood, not by

---

interior damage by rain. The court said that the limitation for rain damage did not affect recovery for *surface water* damage to the insured warehouse, and thus, the fact finder would need to determine which damage was caused by rain and which by surface water. Regarding any damage caused by rain, the court found there was a question about whether there was any damage to the roof created by a covered cause of loss and, therefore, judgment could not be granted to the insurer as to rain damage to the warehouse's interior.

136. ISO Form CP 10 30 06 07, § B.1.a.

137. *See generally* Scott G. Johnson, *Insurance Coverage for Building Code Upgrades*, 44 Tort & Ins. L.J. 1031 (2009).

138. Levitz Furniture Corp. v. Houston Cas. Co., 1997 U.S. Dist. LEXIS 5883 (E.D. La. Apr. 29, 1997). *See also* Farmers Union Mut. Ins. Co. v. Oakland, 251 Mont. 352, 355, 825 P.2d 554 (Mont. 1992), where the insured property was damaged by fire after which insured encountered additional expenses to remove materials containing asbestos. The removal was subject to regulations that increased the cost of removal and disposal over that for ordinary building materials. The insurer argued the increase was barred by the increased cost of compliance exclusion. However, the Montana Supreme Court disagreed and concluded the exclusion was clearly not applicable because the asbestos regulations did not "cause" or "result in" loss or damage. It was the fire, said the court, that caused the loss or damage. The court did, however, limit its holding to removal of fire-damaged asbestos and undamaged asbestos that had to be removed to repair damage.

enforcement of a law or ordinance. Of course, regulations governing asbestos removal would have increased the cost of that removal.

[4] Artificially Generated Electrical Currents

Under a common exclusion in property policies, the insurer will not pay for loss or damage caused by or resulting from *artificially* generated electrical, magnetic, or electromagnetic energy that damages, disturbs, disrupts, or otherwise interferes with any electrical or electronic wire, device, appliance, system or network or device, appliance, or system or network using cellular or satellite technology.[139] Electrical, magnetic, or electromagnetic energy includes electrical current, including arcing, an electrical charge produced or conducted by a magnetic or electromagnetic field, a pulse of electromagnetic energy, or electromagnetic waves or microwaves. There is usually an exception for loss or damage that ensues from an insured peril. Some policies limit that exception to the peril of fire. When water comes in contact with electricity, it can cause damage that the insurer may seek to exclude from coverage under this exclusion.

The leading case on this issue is *Continental Ins. Co. v. Arkwright Mut. Ins. Co.*[140] In that case, flood waters entered the basement of the insured building. Damage resulted when energized electrical switching panels came into contact with that water and caused "electrical arcing," which is an electrical short circuit. That in turn caused an explosion that blew large holes in switching panels. The court observed that mere seconds would have elapsed from the time the flood waters contacted the electrical equipment until the switching panels exploded. Given the absence of any significant temporal remoteness between the flood waters, the electrical arcing, and the explosion, said the court, flooding—a covered peril—proximately caused the loss, not electrical arcing.

[5] Named Storm

A policy may cover flood loss but exclude losses that result from a "named storm." That has notable significance now that winter storms are being given names, although one should check to see if the policy answers the question "named by whom?" If it does not, is the term "named storm" ambiguous?

---

139. ISO Form CP 10 30 06 07, § B.2.

140. Continental Ins. Co. v. Arkwright Mut. Ins. Co., 102 F.3d 30 (1st Cir. 1996). *See also* Davidson Hotel Co. v. St. Paul Fire & Marine Ins. Co., 136 F. Supp. 2d 901 (W.D. Tenn. 2001) where the court said the exclusion is very specific; it excludes electrical disturbances caused by electrical currents *artificially* generated. Where the electrical disturbance occurred because of water flowing onto a duct, the court found that a substantial and proximate cause of the loss was that water. Therefore, the covered peril of water, despite other factors leading to the loss that might have been excluded, rendered the insurer liable under the concurrent causation doctrine.

A named storm exclusion might broadly bar coverage for flood losses, or it could be limited in scope. For example, one policy endorsement provided a $50 million limit for the peril of flood and defined "flood" to include, *inter alia*, storm surge and a named storm. The policy also said that for the peril of flood, losses caused in a 72-hour period would be deemed one loss for purposes of that limit of liability and the deductible. It then said that a "flood" did not mean "flood" and "storm surge" *as a result of* a named storm. The court said that the "named storm" exclusion applied only to the 72-hour limitation period. The losses the insured suffered were caused by Superstorm Sandy. The court concluded that because Sandy was a "named Storm," the $50 million limit unambiguously applied to the actual losses the insured sustained in that storm. The lower court evidently applied the exclusion broadly to bar all coverage, and the appellate court reversed and held the insurer was obligated to pay the insured its proportionate share of the actual loss falling within its layer of coverage, up to the $50 million sublimit.[141] The court did not characterize the exclusion as ambiguous and then construe it against the insurer, but ambiguity would be worth raising with another court that seems disinclined to agree with the definitive interpretation of the court in this case.

[6] Land Exclusion

Property policies typically list property that is *not covered*, and the list is considered separate from the policy exclusions,[142] although courts may refer to the items on the list as exclusions.[143] That is a potentially critical difference because insurers have the burden to show an exclusion is applicable, while insureds have to show initial coverage and that would include showing that the property in question is *not* on the "property not covered" list. The list of property not covered generally includes the cost of excavations; grading; back filling, or filling, land, including land on which the property is located; bulkheads; pilings; piers; wharves; docks; and retaining walls that are not part of a building. This type of provision was applied in a case where a commercial property policy covered flood loss. The insured had built a "cofferdam"—a temporary dam—with riprap material and a plastic membrane, graded a creek channel to reroute it, made erosion and sediment control improvements, and planted trees and grasses. Snowmelt subsequently produced runoffs that flooded the creek, destroyed the cofferdam, and eroded the creek channel and embankment. The insured sought coverage for repairs to the creek channel

141. XL Ins. Am., Inc. v. Howard Hughes Corp., 154 A.D.3d 505, 61 N.Y.S.3d 497 (2017), *app. dis.*, 31 N.Y.3d 1063, 77 N.Y.S.3d 332, 101 N.E.3d 973 (2018).

142. *See, e.g.*, ISO Form CP 00 10 04 02, § A.2.

143. *See, e.g.*, Opperman v. Heritage Mut. Ins. Co., 566 N.W.2d 487 (S.D. 1997); Strand v. State Farm Ins. Co., 34 Ohio App. 3d 97, 517 N.E.2d 265 (1986).

including clearing out sediment in the stream stabilization area, repairing the cofferdam, repairing the stream stabilization area, and reseeding and repairing the eroded area adjacent to the cofferdam. The insurer denied the claim. The court agreed that the only direct physical loss of, or damage to, property from the flood was to the creek and its channel, the cofferdam, the floodplain, and the surrounding soil and plants, and each of those was either land, dams grading, or backfilling, or filling. All were expressly listed as "Property Not Covered" and the insurer, therefore, properly denied coverage.[144]

Some policies may have a true "land exclusion." For example, one policy excluded coverage for "'[L]and, land values and the cost of excavations, grading, backfilling or filling; however, to the extent included in any contract document, the cost of excavation, grading, filling or backfilling and the value of the earth to be used in the completion of the contract work is not to be excluded during the course of construction.'"[145] The property insured by the policy with that exclusion had a riverbank reinforced with large rocks—riprap—to limit erosion. The riprap was significantly eroded and destabilized by flood waters. The insured argued the exclusion did not apply to the riprap bank because it constituted an engineered structure no different from any other engineered seawall, and it was thus distinguishable from excluded bare land. The court, however, disagreed. It said that regardless of whether the riprap was "land," as contended by the insurer, the cost of remediation of the damage was excluded as the cost of grading, filling, or backfilling.[146]

---

144. Evanston Ins. Co. v. Bryan Constr., 2018 U.S. Dist. LEXIS 62172 (D. Colo. Apr. 12, 2018). *See also* 1062 Pontiac Rd., Inc. v. Axis Surplus Ins. Co., 2013 U.S. Dist. LEXIS 15084 (E.D. Pa. Feb. 5, 2013); Sioux City Country Club v. Cincinnati Ins. Co., 2004 U.S. Dist. LEXIS 12833 (N.D. Iowa June 22, 2004). In *Sioux City* rain collected on a paved parking lot, drained into an underground drainage pipe, leaked out through a hole that had rusted through that pipe, and saturated the ground. The weight of the saturated soil in a graded slope behind a retaining wall caused the wall to fail and collapse onto tennis courts. The court said that the underground drainage system fit squarely within the definition of "underground pipes, flues, and drains," and therefore was not covered property and a graded slope was "land," the repair of which would involve excavation, grading, backfilling, or filling. Therefore, the graded slope also was not covered property. Finally, the tennis courts were "paved surfaces" for purposes of the policy, and thus were not covered property.

145. Red Lion Hotels, Inc. v. Commonwealth Ins. Co. of Am., 177 Ore. App. 58, 64, 33 P.3d 358, 360 (2001).

146. Red Lion Hotels, Inc. v. Commonwealth Ins. Co. of Am., 177 Ore. App. 58, 65, 33 P.3d 358, 361 (2001). The insured also argued that even if the riverbank was not covered, a fire road, parking lot, and walkway adjacent to it fell outside the land exclusion. That issue, however, was not properly preserved for appeal.

[7] Vacancy

While a policy may cover water and/or flood losses, property insurance policies typically include a "vacancy" clause.[147] In some policies, the clause may be an exclusion. More commonly it is found among the loss conditions making it a limitation. The burden to show its application is generally on the insurer regardless of how it is characterized.[148] Additionally, many courts treat the clause as an exclusion and construe it against the insurer.[149] Water damage is of particular concern in vacant buildings. When property is unattended, a minor leak can, over time, flood the interior of a building. A trickle of water can grow and quickly flood the property. The standard clause provides that the carrier will not pay for any loss or damage caused by, *inter alia*, water damage or sprinkler leakage—unless the insured has protected the system against freezing—if the insured building has been vacant for more than 60 consecutive days before that loss or damage occurs.[150] For a loss other than ones listed, the insurer will reduce the amount it would otherwise pay by 15 percent.[151] Under the standard clause, a building is considered to be vacant unless at least 31 percent of its total square footage is used by its owner to conduct "customary operations."[152]

---

147. *See, e.g.*, ISO Form CP 00 10 04 02, § E.6. *See generally* Prahl, *Vacancy/Occupancy Clauses in Property Insurance—An Often Overlooked But Significant Limitation*, at 2 (2015), Adjusting Today, http://adjustersinternational.com/publications/adjusting-today/vacancy-occupancy-clauses-protective-safeguards-endorsements/1/.

148. *See, e.g.*, TRB Investments, Inc. v. Fireman's Fund Ins. Co., 40 Cal. 4th 19, 50 Cal. Rptr. 3d 597 (2006); Knoff v. United States Fidelity & Guaranty Co., 447 S.W.2d 497, 500–01 (Tex. Civ. App.—Houston 1st Dist., 1969).

149. *See, e.g.*, Hartford Cas. Ins. v. Mark, 2014 U.S. Dist. LEXIS 10516 (W.D. Wash. Jan. 28, 2014); Farbman Group v. Travelers Ins. Cos., 2006 U.S. Dist. LEXIS 70199 (E.D. Mich. Sept. 28, 2006).

150. ISO Form CP 00 10 04 02, § E.6.b.(1). Early policies lacked the temporal factor. For example, in *Gash v. Home Ins. Co.*, 153 Ill. App. 31 (1910), the policy said that if the premises became "vacant, unoccupied or uninhabited without written consent" of the company, the policy would be null and void. The insured residence was leased to a family. They evacuated the house at the beginning of a month because of flooding. The flood water receded and the husband returned to the house on the 18th or 19th to prepare it for the family's return. On the 20th it burned down. The court said that requiring the constant presence of someone in the house would be unreasonable and would not be in contemplation of the parties to a contract with the vacancy provision. It held that the enforced absence of the tenants under the circumstances was not a breach of the policy that would render it void, and the trial court did not err in refusing to direct a verdict for the insurer.

151. ISO Form CP 00 10 04 02, § E.6.b.(2).

152. ISO Form CP 00 10 04 02, § E.6.a.(1)(b)(ii). When the owner rents the building, it is considered vacant unless at least 31 percent of its total square footage is rented to a lessee or sub-lessee and used to conduct their "customary operations." ISO Form CP 00 10 04 02, § E.6.a.(1)(b)(i). There are, of course, other definitions for "vacant." In one policy it was defined as when either 90 percent or more of the square footage of the entire building was not rented

The vacancy clause will usually say that a building under construction or renovation is not considered vacant. For example, in a Michigan case, a one-inch pipe in the mechanical room of an insured building froze and burst. The building, which had been vacant for some time, was flooded with approximately three inches of water. The court held that because the building was under renovation at the time of the flooding, the vacancy clause did not apply.[153] The California Supreme Court construed the word "construction" broadly in a case in which a water heater or waterline ruptured and caused substantial damage to the insured vacant property. The court said that "the word 'construction' cannot reasonably be understood to be limited only to the erection of a new structure. Rather, the term contemplates all building endeavors, whether classified as new construction, renovations, or additions, which require the substantial and continuing presence of workers at the premises. This standard serves the purposes underlying the vacancy exclusion, which is premised upon the recognition that unoccupied properties face an increased risk of damage."[154]

When it appears that a vacancy clause may bar coverage, one should carefully review the policy to see if it includes a "Vacancy Permit Endorsement." These endorsements typically suspend the vacancy clause exclusions and continue coverage for a specified period of time.[155]

---

or used to conduct customary operations. A unit or suite rented or leased to a tenant did not contain enough business personal property to conduct customary operations. Farbman Group v. Travelers Ins. Cos., 2006 U.S. Dist. LEXIS 70199 (E.D. Mich. Sept. 28, 2006). "Customary operations" is generally not defined. Courts have interpreted it using a dictionary definition. *See, e.g.*, Bedford Internet Office Space, LLC v. Travelers Cas. Ins. Co., 41 F. Supp. 3d 535, 547 (N.D. Tex. 2014).

153. Farbman Group v. Travelers Ins. Cos., 2006 U.S. Dist. LEXIS 70199 (E.D. Mich. Sept. 28, 2006) (walkway removal project underway at time of flooding and undertaken pursuant to lessee's obligation to restore premises to previous condition qualified as "renovation"). *See also* Belich v. Westfield Insurance Co., 2000 Ohio App. LEXIS 6212 (Dec. 29, 2000) (hot water running from shower caused ceiling tiles to fall down, blocking drain and causing water to flood entire building while it was vacant and arguably under renovation; while under language of vacancy clause, even one day of renovation done within previous 60 days would be sufficient to overcome vacancy clause, record failed to disclose when any renovation efforts had been made, and thus did not establish that any such activities had occurred within 60 days prior to property damage).

154. TRB Investments, Inc. v. Fireman's Fund Ins. Co., 40 Cal. 4th 19, 22, 145 P.3d 472, 473, 50 Cal. Rptr. 3d 597, 599 (2006).

155. *See, e.g.*, ISO Form CP 04 50 07 88. *See generally* Prahl, *Vacancy/Occupancy Clauses in Property Insurance—An Often Overlooked But Significant Limitation*, at 4 (2015), Adjusting Today, http://adjustersinternational.com/publications/adjusting-today/vacancy-occupancy-clauses-protective-safeguards-endorsements/1/.

4.6 Limitations to Primary Coverage

[1] Introduction

While a private policy may provide coverage for damage from flood, limitations on coverage may restrict the extent of coverage. For example, there may be a separate sublimit or deductible for flood.

[2] Limits of Insurance

A "Limit of Insurance" is defined as "the most that will be paid by the insurer in the event of a covered loss under an insurance policy."[156] Standard commercial property policies say that the most the insurer will pay for loss or damage in any *one occurrence* is the applicable Limit of Insurance shown of the Declarations Page.[157] Occurrence is usually not defined in the policy.

The determination of whether there has been a single occurrence can be problematic with flooding. For example, consider two scenarios. In the first, a river rises and floods the insured property. The waters then begin to recede, only to rise and flood the property again a few days later. In the second scenario, a tropical storm pushes inland and dumps five inches of rain on a riverfront community in a few hours. The storm drainage system becomes overwhelmed, and the insured property floods. The property owner immediately begins removing debris and making repairs. Five days later the property is substantially repaired, and the remnants of the storm have stalled out over a tributary of the river. The river overflows its banks, and the property is flooded again. Is there one occurrence or two in each scenario? Some guidance can be obtained from a decision interpreting the FEMA SFIP. The court said that "a flood caused by unusually high tides associated with a storm begins with the inundation of normally dry land areas and lasts as long as the water remains. Once normally dry land areas are inundated, the flood constitutes an occurrence . . . that is ongoing and continuous at least until the water subsides and the land returns to its normally dry state."[158]

---

156. *Limit of Insurance*, IRMI, https://www.irmi.com/term/insurance-definitions/limit-of-insurance.

157. ISO Form CP 00 10 04 02, § C.

158. Miller v. Macy, 526 F. Supp. 46, 48 (D. Mass. 1981) (insureds claimed that floodwaters reached level of three feet in basement, maintained that level for a few hours, and then increased to about six feet and that sequence of events constituted two floods).

The meaning of "occurrence," when it is not defined by the policy,[159] is discussed by many court opinions in the third-party insurance context,[160] but less frequently in the relation to first-party coverages. Some of the cases involving first-party coverage are about theft or embezzlement. Most courts take the position that a scheme resulting in a series of losses is a single occurrence. For example, in a California case, the same person stole insured property from the same storage facility over the course of several days. The court held the thefts constituted a single occurrence.[161] In contrast, an Arizona court said in an unpublished opinion that when the policy does not define "occurrence," the court has to determine whether there was only one proximate, uninterrupted, and continuing cause that resulted in all of the injuries and damages. In the case, the insured received counterfeit emails in response to which it authorized three wire transfers. The result was the theft of over $350,000. The court noted that the thieves sent separate counterfeit email packages to the insured that induced it to make three wire transfers in payment of three distinct invoices. There was not, said the court, one proximate, uninterrupted, and continuing cause. Instead, each demand for payment was a distinct "causative act" that constituted a separate occurrence.[162]

Some policies define a "single occurrence of flood." For example, one policy said that each loss by flood would constitute a single occurrence if any flood occurred "within a period of the continued rising or overflow of any river(s) or stream(s) and the subsidence of same within the banks of such river(s) or stream(s) . . . or . . . any flood results from any tidal wave or series of tidal waves caused by any one disturbance."[163]

A policy might have a per occurrence limit but an annual aggregate limit for the peril of flood. For example, in a Louisiana case, a commercial property insurance policy had a *per occurrence* property damage limit of $7.5 million

---

159. Some policies do define "occurrence." For example, in *United States Fire Ins. Co. v. Safeco Ins. Co.*, 444 So. 2d 844 (Ala. 1983), the policy said that for the purpose of determining the limit of liability, all property damage arising out of continuous or repeated exposure to substantially the same general conditions would be considered as arising out of one occurrence. The insured had a problem with water leaking through the roof of the insured building because of cracks and holes. The company hired to repair the roof failed to effectively cover a portion of it, resulting in additional damage caused by rainfall. The court said that the negligence of the roofing company was a separate, intervening cause, not proximate to the cracks and holes in the other areas of the roof. The two events are easily distinguishable, and one did not cause the other; therefore, there were two occurrences.

160. *See Appleman on Insurance Law & Practice Archive* § 4891.25 (1st ed. 2011).

161. Patterson v. Am. Econ. Ins. Co., 2016 U.S. Dist. LEXIS 75538 (E.D. Cal. June 9, 2016), *aff'd*, 710 Fed. Appx. 762 (9th Cir. 2018). *See also* Ad Adver. Design Inc. v. Sentinel Ins. Co., 344 F. Supp. 3d 1175 (D. Mont. 2018); Florists' Mut. Ins. Co. v. Gradco, Inc., 2009 U.S. Dist. LEXIS 144774 (N.D. Ala. Apr. 23, 2009).

162. AIMS Ins. Program Managers, Inc. v. Nat'l Fire Ins. Co., 2021 Ariz. App. Unpub. LEXIS 123 (Feb. 4, 2021).

163. PCVST-DIL LLC v. Lexington Ins. Co., 2016 N.Y. Misc. LEXIS 2031 (Apr. 21, 2016).

and covered all risks of direct physical loss, including flood. The flood coverage, however, had an *annual aggregate* limit of $7.5 million in coverage.[164] Thus, if there were more than one clearly defined flood in a year, the most the carrier would pay would be $7.5 million, but if the insured suffered losses of $5 million each from two covered perils, whether the same or different, the insurer would pay the full $10 million if there were no other basis for limiting the payment.

[3] Sublimits

[a] "Sublimit" Defined

A "sublimit" is defined as "a limitation in an insurance policy on the amount of coverage available to cover a specific type of loss . . . [and] is part of, rather than in addition to, the limit that would otherwise apply to the loss."[165] That is, it does not apply additional coverage for a particular peril, but it imposes a cap on the amount that can be recovered that is less than the overall aggregate limit of liability.[166] When flood coverage is included in or added to a commercial property or homeowners policy, it is very common for there to be a specific flood sublimit.[167] A sublimit is not an exclusion,[168] but generally the insurer has the burden of showing policy limits,[169] just as it has the burden to show that an exclusion applies. In policies issued to large commercial ventures, the sublimit permutations can be convoluted. Anyone seeking flood

---

164. Omega Protein Corp. v. Lexington Ins. Co., 2007 U.S. Dist. LEXIS 98530 (W.D. La. Feb. 15, 2007).

165. *Sublimit*, IRMI, https://www.irmi.com/term/insurance-definitions/sublimit.

166. *See* New Jersey Transit Corp. v. Certain Underwriters at Lloyd's London, 461 N.J. Super. 440, 449, 221 A.3d 1180, 1185 (2019), *aff'd*, 245 N.J. 104, 243 A.3d 1248 (2021) (sublimit is limit within aggregate limit for certain type of risk and when sublimit applies, loss is covered only up to amount of sublimit rather than up to amount of aggregate limit); Dallas Handbag Co. v. Royal Indem. Co., 390 S.W.2d 863 (Tex. Civ. App. 1965) (sublimit did not grant coverage excluded elsewhere in policy).

167. *See, e.g.*, Evanston Ins. Co. v. Bryan Constr., 2018 U.S. Dist. LEXIS 62172 (D. Colo. Apr. 12, 2018) (commercial property policy covered flood as covered cause of loss with a limit of $500,000 per occurrence and $500,000 in aggregate); 4 NYP Ventures LLC v. Factory Mut. Ins. Co., 197 F. Supp. 3d 634 (S.D.N.Y. 2016) ($500 million all-risk policy had $20 million limit on losses related to "flood" damage because property was in flood-prone location); Protection Mutual Ins. Co. v. Mitsubishi Silicon America Corp., 164 Ore. App. 385, 992 P.2d 479 (1999) (insurer "shall not be liable under the terms of this Endorsement for more than the flood limits of liability specified elsewhere in this Policy for each occurrence and during any policy year"). *See also* Terminal Ventures, Inc. v. Fireman's Fund Ins. Co., 2009 N.J. Super. Unpub. LEXIS 1793 (July 9, 2009).

168. XL Ins. Am., Inc. v. Howard Hughes Corp., 154 A.D.3d 505, 61 N.Y.S.3d 497 (2017), *app. dis.*, 31 N.Y.3d 1063, 77 N.Y.S.3d 332, 101 N.E.3d 973 (2018) (endorsement's $50 million limit on flood coverage should not be read as an exclusion, but rather as sublimit within $150 million layer of coverage).

169. *See, e.g.*, Tunstall v. Stierwald, 809 So. 2d 916, 921 (La. 2002)

coverage under a policy issued by a private carrier has to be alert to the peculiar language of any applicable sublimit.

[b] Applicability Generally

A sublimit may simply be a lesser amount than the overall limit, or it may change a "per occurrence" limit to an "annual aggregate" limit. For example, a policy generally provided for $25 million in coverage *per occurrence*, but it also had a sublimit applicable to losses caused by flood under which there was $25 million in coverage "in the aggregate during any one policy year."[170] Another condition on a sublimit is that it may apply only when the insured property is in a "high risk" flood zone. One policy endorsement, for instance, had a $50 million sublimit for "Flood in High Hazard (100 year) Flood Zones."[171] There may also be different sublimits for flood depending on whether or not the property is located in a "high risk" zone.[172] Of course, the policy may only cover flood losses to property that is not in a "high risk" zone and apply a sublimit to those losses.[173] When more than one property is covered by a policy, there may be a specific sublimit for some, but not all, of those properties.[174] It is also important to check to see if any sublimit applies only to physical damage to property or pertains to all or some other

170. Pinnacle Entm't, Inc. v. Allianz Global Risks US Ins. Co., 2008 U.S. Dist. LEXIS 108583 (D. Nev. Mar. 26, 2008). *See also* Omega Protein Corp. v. Lexington Ins. Co., 2007 U.S. Dist. LEXIS 98530 (W.D. La. Feb. 15, 2007) (per occurrence property damage limit of $7.5 million covering all risks of direct physical loss, including flood and flood coverage had annual aggregate limit of $7.5 million in coverage).

171. Cummins, Inc. v. Ace Am. Ins. Co., 2011 U.S. Dist. LEXIS 4568 (S.D. Ind. Jan. 14, 2011). The definition of "high risk" or "high hazard" is critical. In *Cummins* the endorsement defined "High Hazard Zones for Flood" as "a) all property at a 'location' that is partially or totally situated in an area which at the time of loss or damage has been designated on a Flood Insurance Rate Map (FIRM) to be a Special Flood Hazard Area (SFHA), and/or b) all property in areas where the National Flood Insurance Program (NFIP) is not in effect, and where all property at a 'location' is partially or totally situated in an area which is within a 100 year flood plain or its worldwide equivalent, and/or c) all property at a 'location' that is partially or totally protected by dams, dikes, levees or walls which were intended to protect such property from the level of a 100 year flood or its worldwide equivalent, regardless of any Zone or Area designation or assignment by FIMA or other recognized authority having jurisdiction."

172. *See, e.g.*, Castle Oil Corp. v. ACE Am. Ins. Co., 137 A.D.3d 833, 26 N.Y.S.3d 783 (2016) (policy contained two separate annual aggregate sublimits, and for location at issue applicable sublimit was $2.5 million because property was located in one of Special Flood Hazard Areas, as defined by FEMA listed in policy).

173. *See, e.g.*, New Sea Crest Healthcare Ctr., LLC v. Lexington Ins. Co., 2014 U.S. Dist. LEXIS 86585 (E.D.N.Y. June 24, 2014) (flood sublimit limited coverage for flood damage to $1 million a year for properties outside an SFHA and did not provide flood coverage for properties inside SFHA).

174. *See* New York Univ. v. Factory Mut. Ins. Co., 374 F. Supp. 3d 315 (S.D.N.Y. 2019) ($250 million sublimit with $40 million sublimit for specifically named locations).

coverages, for example, business interruption or debris removal.[175] Where, for instance a flood endorsement with a $3 million sublimit stated that it applied to "direct physical loss to covered property," the court found that the sublimit did not apply to losses for business interruption.[176] The policy may have broad language stating that the policy's limits of liability in an occurrence apply to the total loss or damage for *all coverages* involved, in which case a flood sublimit has been held to apply to additional coverages even though they are not specifically named in the sublimit.[177] A policy may also have a sublimit that applies only to one type of flood, for example storm surge.[178]

Federal-Mogul LLC v. Ins. Co. of Pa.,[179] illustrates the complexity of flood sublimits. The commercial property policy in the case had a $200 million

---

175. *See, e.g.*, Altru Health Sys. v. American Protection Ins. Co., 238 F.3d 961, 964 (8th Cir. 2001) (where Flood Coverage Section provided that all claims for loss, damage, or expense arising out of any one flood occurrence would be adjusted as one claim and business interruption and extra expense losses arose out of flood, they as well as the property damage had to be adjusted as one claim subject to $1.5 million sublimit for flood); New Sea Crest Healthcare Ctr., LLC v. Lexington Ins. Co., 2014 U.S. Dist. LEXIS 86585 (E.D.N.Y. June 24, 2014) (all loss or damage due to flood is subject to flood sublimit and insured could not, therefore, recover beyond that sublimit for storm surge losses under additional provisions, which included debris removal, civil or military authority, demolition, ingress/egress, ordinary payroll, equipment breakdown, and service interruption). *Compare* Mark Andy, Inc. v. Hartford Fire Ins. Co., 229 F.3d 710 (8th Cir. 2000) (recovery of business-interruption losses was not capped by property-damage flood-loss limit). *See also* Oxford Realty Group Cedar v. Travelers Excess & Surplus Lines Co., 229 N.J. 196, 209, 160 A.3d 1263, 1271 (2017) (flood endorsement categorically denied any flood damage coverage in excess of $1 million and made clear that flood sublimit applied even if more than one limit applied such as limit for debris removal, and therefore, flood endorsement controlled the extent of flood coverage and it was not modified by remainder of policy terms). A thoughtful dissent in *Oxford Realty* may be of value to policyholders.

176. Alley Theatre v. Hanover Ins. Co., 436 F. Supp. 3d 938, 947 (S.D. Tex. 2020). *See also* Mark Andy, Inc. v. Hartford Fire Ins. Co., 233 F.3d 1090 (8th Cir. 2000); Victory Container Corp. v. Sphere Ins. Co., 448 F. Supp. 1043 (S.D.N.Y. 1978). *And see* Penford Corp. v. National Union Fire Ins. Co. of Pittsburgh, 2010 U.S. Dist. LEXIS 3737 (N.D. Iowa, Jan. 19, 2010) (distinguishing *Mark Andy* because policy contained clause regarding sublimits that could make flood sublimit applicable to all losses, including business interruption, but finding ambiguity that could only be resolved by extrinsic evidence that had to be considered by jury).

177. New York Univ. v. Factory Mut. Ins. Co., 374 F. Supp. 3d 315 (S.D.N.Y. 2019).

178. Orient Overseas Assoc. v. XL Ins. Am., Inc., 2016 N.Y. Misc. LEXIS 2048 (May 11, 2016). In *Orient Overseas*, several insurers issued separate policies covering a fixed percentage of the coverage with an overall flood sublimit of $5 million. The policies were largely the same, but one company added a $5 million sublimit for losses from storm surge. The court said that storm surge is a type of flood, and, therefore, losses caused by storm surge were treated as if the loss was caused by flood. That meant that the flood sublimit applied across the board. It was the maximum the insurers collectively would pay for a flood loss, with each paying its percentage share. However, two buildings were governed by the policies, and the court found each was entitled to coverage for flood loss up to the sublimit. The storm surge sublimit, on the other hand, was not broken down by property. The two buildings, therefore, were entitled only to the collective pro rata share of that insurer's contribution, with each building receiving one-half of that amount.

179. Federal-Mogul LLC v. Ins. Co. of Pa., 780 Fed. Appx. 267 (6th Cir. 2019).

"Flood Aggregate Limit of Liability" for all locations combined in any one policy year. There were then three sublimits: $70 million annual aggregate for flood in Moderate Hazard Zones; $30 million annual aggregate for flood in High Hazard Zones; and $5 million for flood for, *inter alia*, coverages for contingent time element and service interruption property damage and time element combined. Flooding damaged one of the policyholder's facilities, and it suffered a loss of $64,500,000, which included $39,406,467 for property damage and $25,093,533 of "time element" loss. The insurer, applying the "High Hazard Zones" sublimit, paid $30 million. The insured argued the sublimit applied only to physical loss or damage caused by the flood, not to time element loss. The district court looked at the sublimit for contingent time element and service interruption and said that there was no similar inclusion of any type of time element loss in the High Hazard flood sublimit. It concluded that "[t]he explicit inclusion of certain types of time element loss in a flood-related sublimit supports a finding that the High Hazard sublimit does not implicitly include time element loss."[180] The United States Court of Appeal for the Sixth Circuit, however, did not agree. It held that the "High Hazard Zones" sublimit applied to both the property and time element losses.

[c] Statement of Values

In a Florida case the policy provided flood coverage with a sublimit of $10 million. The policy also had a Statement of Values. Under it the policyholder could claim up to $2 million for damage to its marina and $1 million for business interruption and rental income loss related to the marina. The policy also listed coverage amounts for other property, bringing the total to $12.5 million. After a hurricane, the policyholder sought coverage for damage to the marina. The insurer paid $3 million, but the insured argued it was entitled to a payment up to the sublimit of $10 million. The court did not agree. It said that reading the policy as a whole, the flood coverage was not to be interpreted as separate or additional coverage. The flood coverage was, therefore, subject to the same limitations as the rest of the policy, including the Statement of Values.[181]

[d] Ensuing Loss Clause and Sublimits

A policy may provide that even if the peril of flood for which there is a sublimit is the predominant cause of loss or damage, any ensuing loss or damage not otherwise excluded by the policy will not be subject to any sublimits. In

180. Federal-Mogul Corp. v. Ins. Co., 2015 U.S. Dist. LEXIS 137394 (E.D. Mich. Oct. 8, 2015).

181. Aligned Bayshore Holdings, LLC v. Westchester Surplus Lines Ins. Co., 385 F. Supp. 3d 1295 (S.D. Fla. 2019).

applying that language, courts may bar coverage for an ensuing loss directly related to the original excluded or sublimited risk. For example, corrosion of metal components in railroad tunnels was a large source of damages after the tunnels were flooded in Superstorm Sandy. The policyholder argued that the corrosion was caused by chloride from the combination of seawater residue with oxygen in the air, and thus was an ensuing loss that was not subject to the flood sublimit in the policy. The chloride attack on the metal components was, said the insured, a covered peril that was separate from the flood because the accelerated corrosion began only after the seawater was pumped out of the tunnels, meaning the corrosion was not contemporaneous with the flood. The court demurred. It found that the corrosion could not be meaningfully separated from water damage that was plainly subject to the flood sublimit, nor could it be attributed to a distinct covered peril, arising from the original, sublimited peril of flood. Thus, the policy sublimit applied.[182]

[e] Direct Physical Loss or Damage

In *Baylor College of Med. v. Am. Guar. & Liab. Ins. Co.*,[183] there was an endorsement adding flood coverage with a $50 million sublimit for all direct physical loss or damage to covered property by flood in any one policy year. The policy also contained various coverage extensions including a Research and Development Extension of Coverage subject to a $50 million sublimit for business income.[184] Flooding during a tropical storm caused Baylor College to suffer damage to real and personal property and to its research and development projects. It claimed the flooding caused more than $300 million in losses, but the insurer would only pay $50 million, contending all the losses were subject to the flood endorsement sublimit. The court noted that the policy said the Extensions of Coverage Limits of Insurance applied in addition to endorsement sublimits. The court concluded that the business income and the extensions of coverage each had their own applicable limits of insurance, and the flood endorsement did not exclude those coverages or make their limits subject to the flood sublimit. It especially took note of the fact that the flood endorsement sublimit did not apply to losses or damage

---

182. AMTRAK v. Aspen Specialty Ins. Co., 661 Fed. Appx. 10 (2d Cir. 2016) ($125 million flood sublimit).

183. Baylor College of Med. v. Am. Guar. & Liab. Ins. Co., 2002 U.S. Dist. LEXIS 29002 (S.D. Tex. Oct. 30, 2002).

184. In its opinion, the court said that by stating that the Research and Development Extension of Coverage Limit of Insurance was "included" in business income, it provided that compensation for Research and Development losses would apply against the $50 million sublimit for business income. It found that losses recovered under the Research and Development Extension of Coverage reduced the $50 million business income sublimit, but applied in addition to the flood endorsement sublimit.

that were outside *direct physical loss or damage* to covered property caused by flood. The business income limit, rather than the flood sublimit, would apply to business income losses because of suspended operations from direct physical loss or damage to covered property due to flood. The *Baylor* court's observation about the phrase "direct physical loss or damage" is emphasized in a California case that found a flood sublimit containing that wording was only applicable to "physical loss or damage," and not to business interruption/ time element damages.[185]

[f] Loss Caused by Windstorm

A flood sublimit has been held not to apply to losses from "storm surge" in cases where there was no reference to storm surge in the applicable flood definition. For example, the storm surge initiated by Superstorm Sandy inundated and damaged the property of a company that provides electricity. As a result of the damage it suffered, the company made an insurance claim. Under its primary and excess policies, it had a total amount of coverage available of $1 billion, but there was a $250 million submit for losses caused by "flood." The insurer argued a storm surge was a type of "flood," and the flood sublimit applied. The court, however, decided that wind caused the storm surge, wind was a covered peril other than flood, and the storm surge was, therefore, not subject to the flood sublimits.[186] Similarly, the Fifth Circuit has held that damage from rain and flood that was caused directly by a hurricane could not trigger a flood liability limit because those losses were not caused by the peril of flood.[187] A New Jersey court followed the Fifth Circuit in a

185. Northrop Grumman Corp. v. Factory Mut. Ins. Co., 805 F. Supp. 2d 945, 949 (C.D. Cal. 2011) (finding it significant that flood sublimit only referred to "physical loss or damage," and not to loss *caused* by physical loss or damage, as it did in defining business interruption loss).

186. Public Serv. Enter. Grp., Inc. v. Ace Am. Ins. Co., 2015 N.J. Super. Unpub. LEXIS 620 (Mar. 23, 2015). *See also* Pinnacle Entm't, Inc. v. Allianz Global Risks US Ins. Co., 2008 U.S. Dist. LEXIS 108583 (D. Nev. Mar. 26, 2008) (where excess policies incorporated definition of flood as general and temporary condition of partial or complete inundation of normally dry land areas from overflow of inland or tidal waters, definition did not expressly exclude wind-driven inundations of water and, thus, did not sufficiently communicate exclusion for storm surge, which is a specific type of flood). In a Ninth Circuit case the lower court held a flood exclusion was limited to floods that were *not* caused by wind, but the appellate court reversed the judgment for the insured and specifically said it disagreed with *Pinnacle*. Northrop Grumman Corp. v. Factory Mut. Ins. Co., 563 F.3d 777, 787, n.8 (9th Cir. 2009).

187. Seacor Holdings, Inc. v. Commonwealth Ins. Co., 635 F.3d 675, 683 (5th Cir 2011) (rejecting insurer's argument that inclusion of "whether wind-driven or not" in flood definition would be meaningless if flood limit of liability did not apply when windstorms caused flooding because while water driven by wind may be a flood, if wind-driven flood is caused by another covered peril, for example, named storm, then only liability limit for named windstorm would not be flood sublimit). *Compare* Northrop Grumman Corp. v. Factory Mut. Ins. Co., 563 F.3d

case of damage from Sandy. The policy language defined "named windstorm" to *include* wind-driven water, storm surge, and flood associated with, or that occurs in conjunction with, a named windstorm. The court said that wording provided that water damage resulting from a storm surge associated with a named windstorm did not fall within the definition of "flood" and, therefore, the water damage that occurred during the storm was not subject to the flood sublimit.[188]

The Fifth Circuit reached a different conclusion in a case in which a New Orleans theme park was damaged from flooding associated with Hurricane Katrina.[189] The policy had a flood sublimit that applied "per occurrence." It also defined "Weather Cat Occurrence" as "all loss occurring during a 72-hour period caused by or resulting from, *inter alia*, Flood, wind, hail, sleet, tornadoes, hurricane, or lightening, associated with or occurring in conjunction with a storm or weather disturbance named by the National Weather Service." The court held that because flood is a weather phenomenon within that definition, the flood sublimit applied one time per occurrence to limit loss and damage as respected that flood.

[g] Multiple Insurers and Quota Share Programs

In coverage for large commercial ventures, there may be multiple insurers, each of whom issues a separate policy covering a fixed percentage of the coverage, a quota share program. The language of the policies will dictate application of any sublimit. For example, where each policy stated that the total amount to be indemnified, for any loss occurrence, would not exceed the sublimit applicable to the loss, subject to the pro-rata participation, there was a single flood sublimit of $5 million. Each carrier was responsible for paying its percentage share of a flood loss, and the total amount paid could not exceed the sublimit.[190]

777, 786 (9th Cir. 2009) (absence of phrase "whether wind-driven or not" did not render exclusion ambiguous and allow coverage for damages from storm surge).

188. New Jersey Transit Corp. v. Certain Underwriters at Lloyd's London, 461 N.J. Super. 440, 449, 221 A.3d 1180, 1185 (2019), *aff'd*, 245 N.J. 104, 243 A.3d 1248 (2021). The court also said that although the definition of "flood" included "surge," the definition of "named windstorm" more specifically encompassed the wind-driven water or associated storm surge and when two provisions of a policy address the same subject, the more specific provision controls over the more general. Moreover, had the parties intended that damage from a storm surge would be subject to the flood sublimit, that would have been stated in plain language.

189. Six Flags, Inc. v. Westchester Surplus Lines Ins. Co., 565 F.3d 948 (5th Cir 2009).

190. Orient Overseas Assoc. v. XL Ins. Am., Inc., 2016 N.Y. Misc. LEXIS 2048 (May 11, 2016).

[4] Deductibles

[a] Generally

Deductibles that apply specifically to flood losses are common in policies that cover those losses.[191] Some policies will have a "percentage" deductible. These can be tricky to untangle. For example, in a New York case,[192] the insured suffered a flood loss of nearly $2.3 million. There was a flood sublimit of $2.5 million. The deductible was 2 percent of the total insurable value at risk, subject to a minimum of $250,000. On a "Schedule of Locations Endorsement" the total value listed for the property was just under $125 million. The question was whether the value at risk was the sublimit or the amount on the "Schedule of Locations Endorsement." The court decided that it was the latter.[193] That meant the deductible was 2 percent of the total value listed, or just less than $2.5 million. In other words, the deductible exceeded the loss. The insured argued that the coverage was then illusory as the deductible almost equaled the sublimit. The court did not agree. It said, in effect, that the insured could recover for a loss in excess of the deductible *up to* the sublimit. In a Nevada case,[194] the court quoted a clause under which for each occurrence of flood, the deductible was 5 percent of the 100 percent combined physical and time element value at all locations where physical loss or damage occurs. There was also a minimum deductible of $500,000, plus 2 percent of the 100 percent combined physical and time element value at all locations where physical loss or damage occurred. All this was modified by a puzzling maze of conditions. It leads the reader to agree with a New Jersey Supreme Court justice who said that "[d]eciphering an insurance contract should not be comparable to breaking the Enigma code."[195]

A deductible is subtracted from the adjusted loss "for any one occurrence."[196] That raises the question of the meaning of "occurrence" in the case of floods, a topic discussed above.[197]

---

191. *See, e.g.*, Evanston Ins. Co. v. Bryan Constr., 2018 U.S. Dist. LEXIS 62172 (D. Colo. Apr. 12, 2018) ($25,000 deductible per occurrence).

192. Castle Oil Corp. v. ACE Am. Ins. Co., 137 A.D.3d 833, 26 N.Y.S.3d 783 (2016).

193. In *Landscapes Unlimited, LLC v. Lexington Ins. Co.*, 2006 U.S. Dist. LEXIS 84465 (D. Neb. Nov. 20, 2006), the court took the opposite position. It found that "value at risk" meant value at risk to the *insurer*, as opposed to the value of the property. That amount was the sublimit. The 5 percent deductible should, said the court, be applied to that amount. The opinion was subsequently vacated. Landscapes Unlimited, LLC v. Lexington Ins. Co., 2006 U.S. Dist. LEXIS 101482 (D. Neb., Dec. 18, 2006).

194. Pinnacle Entm't, Inc. v. Allianz Global Risks US Ins. Co., 2008 U.S. Dist. LEXIS 108583 (D. Nev. Mar. 26, 2008).

195. Oxford Realty Group Cedar v. Travelers Excess & Surplus Lines Co., 229 N.J. 196, 212, 160 A.3d 1263, 1273 (2017) (Albin, J. dissenting).

196. *See, e.g.*, ISO Form CP 00 10 04 02, § D.

197. *See* § 4.6[2], *supra*.

[b] Applicability of Windstorm Deductible

A policy that includes both windstorm and flood coverages may have a separate deductible for each. The question of how to apply those deductibles then arises. In a post-Katrina case, an insurer argued the hurricane was a "multiperil occurrence" requiring use of deductibles for both flood and named windstorm. The Court of Appeals for the Fifth Circuit initially decided that Katrina was a named windstorm for purposes of application of the named windstorm deductible. The insurer then asserted that water damages could not be covered under that deductible because the definition of named windstorm did not include flooding. However, the court said that a hurricane could include losses caused by heavy rains. It noted that most policies specifically exclude coverage for "water-related events" that often accompany windstorms, but the policy before it did not. Rather it contained separate deductibles for the perils of named windstorm and flood, without indicating when, if ever, multiple deductibles would apply. If the damage caused by rain and flood was "caused directly" by the hurricane, opined the court, then it could be covered under the named windstorm deductible. Turning to state law, the court said that state appellate courts had found that windstorm policies may cover damage from affiliated heavy rains, if the wind was the proximate cause of the damages. It followed that Katrina's winds were the proximate cause of the water-related damages, and the court, therefore, held that under the policy, Katrina was a single event that required only the named windstorm deductible, even if the storm included multiple acts of rain and wind.[198]

The Fifth Circuit reached the same conclusion in a case in which there was a relatively small flood deductible and a large windstorm deductible. The insured property was damaged by Hurricane Harvey. If the windstorm deductible were applied to the claim for loss, the insured would recover nothing. That deductible explicitly applied to flood losses caused by a named storm. Thus, the court found for the insurer and said the result was even more inescapable than in the earlier case. Moreover, the policy had an anti-stacking provision under which if multiple deductibles could apply to a single occurrence, the largest deductible would be applied.[199]

The Fifth Circuit has also held that a windstorm deductible does not enlarge the coverage. It said that "[a]s a mechanism for shifting risk from the insurer to the insured, a deductible clause can only logically be applied after a covered loss has been established, and it is unnatural to interpret a deductible clause as a mechanism that increases the risk of the insurer by expanding the scope of coverage."[200] The policy at issue was an all-risk property policy

198. Seacor Holdings, Inc. v. Commonwealth Ins. Co., 635 F.3d 675 (5th Cir. 2011).

199. Pan Am Equities, Inc. v. Lexington Ins. Co., 959 F.3d 671 (5th Cir. 2020).

200. Penthouse Owners Association, Inc. v. Certain Underwriters at Lloyds, London, 612 F.3d 383, 387 (5th Cir. 2010). *See also* Alley Theatre v. Hanover Ins. Co., 436 F. Supp. 3d 938

that had a typical flood exclusion with an anti-concurrent causation clause. An endorsement added a Windstorm or Hail Deductible. The insured building was completely destroyed by Hurricane Katrina. Nothing was left but a slab. The insured recovered the policy limit from its flood insurer; however, the property insurer denied coverage, citing the flood exclusion and the anti-concurrent causation clause. The policyholder argued the loss was caused completely by the wind that preceded the hurricane's storm surge. The trial court noted that the Windstorm Deductible applied to loss or damage caused directly or indirectly by windstorm, "regardless of any other cause or event that contributed concurrently or in any sequence to the loss or damage." That language tracked exactly the language of the anti-concurrent causation clause in the flood exclusion. Thus, the lower court concluded that the deductible endorsement operated as a reverse anti-concurrent cause clause. In other words, the deductible did not serve to limit coverage, but expanded it to include any damage caused "concurrently or in any sequence to" windstorm, even if the damage otherwise would not have been covered pursuant to the flood exclusion. The appellate court reversed. It said the Windstorm Deductible applied only when it was being decided whether to apply it to a loss, *after* it is determined that there is coverage for the loss under the policy. The court acknowledged that there was a possibility that explicit words of coverage in a deductible, interpreted in the context of the policy as a whole, could establish coverage or an ambiguity, but that exception was not the case before it.[201]

[c] Buyback Deductible

A deductible may be reduced or removed from a policy by paying an additional premium.[202] A policyholder may also purchase a "Deductible Buy-Back Policy" from another insurer that pays some portion of the deductible in the primary policy.[203] Buybacks are often employed to counter the high deduct-

---

(S.D. Tex. 2020), where a flood coverage endorsement had a $3 million sublimit. The policy also had a Named Storm Deductible Endorsement. The insured argued that because the policy provided for a separate deductible in the event of a named storm, the flood limitation did not apply to damages resulting from a named storm. The insurer responded that the named storm endorsement did not create independent coverage for named storm events separate from wind, rain, or flood perils, but rather created an additional deductible. The court agreed. Nothing in the endorsement, it said, created a new covered peril for a "named storm," separate from other covered perils, such as flood.

201. *See* Madelaine Chocolate Novelties v. Great Northern Ins. Co., 399 F. Supp. 3d 3 (E.D.N.Y. 2019) (finding ambiguity in policy with flood exclusion containing anti-concurrent causation clause and windstorm endorsement also with anti-concurrent causation clause; refusing to resolve ambiguity in favor of insured and finding triable issue of fact as to intent of parties).

202. *Buyback Deductible*, IMRI, https://www.irmi.com/term/insurance-definitions/buyback-deductible.

203. *Deductible Buy-Back Policies*, Law Insider, https://www.lawinsider.com/clause/deductible-buy-back-policies.

ibles applied to windstorm or named storm coverage.[204] These deductibles are commonly stated as a percentage of the insured value and can range from 1 to 5 percent, and occasionally higher.[205]

In a case after Hurricane Harvey hit Texas in 2017, the insured had a deductible buyback policy that stated the covered perils as "Windstorm or Hail associated with a Named Storm." The court found that Hurricane Harvey fell within the definition of "windstorm," meaning that there was coverage if there was "direct physical loss or damage" that was "caused by" Harvey. The insurer sought to deny coverage for flood damage that was clearly associated with Harvey. It argued that the policy did not cover damage caused by rising flood waters, while it would cover water damage that resulted from high winds, for example, if there was roof or structural damage that allowed rainwater to enter the building. The court, however, responded that the policy made no such distinction as to either the type of damage covered or the manner in which that damage occurred. Therefore, the insurer was not entitled to a declaration that because the loss was caused by the peril of flood, not by the perils of windstorm or hail, there was no deductible buyback coverage under the policy for the insured's Hurricane Harvey claim.[206]

4.7 Additional Coverages

[1] Introduction

Standard commercial property policies contain additional coverages, several of which are of particular importance to flooding: debris removal, preservation of property,[207] pollutant clean-up and removal, and increased cost of construction.[208] Coverage may also be added for business interruption losses, extra expenses, and expediting expenses. These are discussed elsewhere.[209]

[2] Increased Cost of Compliance

Flooding is a peril that can cause extensive damage to property. In most communities, when a building is destroyed, or damaged beyond a prescribed percentage, the reconstruction has to meet requirements adopted after the building

204. *See, e.g.*, ISO Form CP 03 25 10 06 (Commercial Property: Named Storm Percentage Deductible endorsement).

205. *See, e.g.*, St. Joseph's Condo. Ass'n v. Pac. Ins. Co., 2008 U.S. Dist. LEXIS 86470 (E.D. La. Oct. 24, 2008) (deductible of 10 percent of total value of insured property).

206. Landmark Am. Ins. Co. v. SCD Mem'l Place II, LLC, 2020 U.S. Dist. LEXIS 126983 (S.D. Tex. Apr. 14, 2020). This recommendation by a magistrate judge was adopted by the court. Landmark Am. Ins. Co. v. SCD Mem'l Place II, LLC, 2020 U.S. Dist. LEXIS 126451 (S.D. Tex. July 17, 2020).

207. Preservation of property coverage is discussed in § 6.5, *infra*.

208. *See, e.g.*, ISO Form CP 00 10 04 02, § A.4.

209. *See* §§ 6.2, 6.3, and 6.4, *infra*.

was initially constructed, and the cost to meet those requirements can be enormous. They may prescribe standards for construction materials, plumbing, electrical wiring, setback of structures from property lines, and maximum floor area ratios.[210] For the most part, laws that affect building construction are local ordinances,[211] but state law may also apply, and in some cases federal law may govern construction. For example, the Americans with Disabilities Act (ADA)[212] may mandate property upgrades to undamaged premises. Increased cost of construction incurred to comply with enforcement of an ordinance or law can be included by additional coverage commonly found in commercial property policies and sometimes called "Ordinance and Law."[213] The same policies usually have an "Ordinance and Law" or "Civil Authority" exclusion, but the *additional* coverage for increased cost of construction is not subject to that exclusion to the extent it would conflict with the provisions of the increased cost of construction coverage.[214] The additional coverage generally provides that in the event of damage by a *covered cause of loss* to a building that is covered property, the insurer will pay the increased costs of complying with enforcement of an ordinance or law in the course of repair, rebuilding, or replacement of *damaged* parts of that property.[215] Because the coverage is limited to loss by a covered cause of loss, the policy also has to cover the peril of flood.[216]

The principal limitation on the coverage is that there be a causal connection between the loss and the enforcement. Where evidence showed an inspection occurred only because of the incident that gave rise to liability and the thoroughness of the inspection was also a result of the incident, the court found that the proximate cause of the inspection was the infiltration of water into a duct in an electrical room that resulted in an electrical disturbance that in turn activated the sprinkler system, leading to water damage. It held, therefore, that the insurer was liable for costs associated with code compliance.[217]

---

210. Expensive retrofitting may be required: hurricane impact windows or construction techniques to mitigate flood or earthquake damage.

211. *See generally* Scott G. Johnson, *Insurance Coverage for Building Code Upgrades*, 44 Tort & Ins. L.J. 1031 (2009).

212. 42 U.S.C. §§ 12101, *et seq.*

213. *See, e.g.*, ISO Form CP 00 10 04 02, § A.4.e.

214. *See, e.g.*, ISO Form CP 00 10 04 02, § A.4.e.(8).

215. *See, e.g.*, ISO Form CP 00 10 04 02, § A.4.e.(2).

216. *See, e.g.*, JAW The Pointe, L.L.C. v. Lexington Ins. Co., 460 S.W.3d 597 (Tex. 2015), where the property damage that triggered the ordinances resulted from both wind, a covered cause of loss, and flooding, an excluded peril. The policy's anti-concurrent causation clause excluded coverage for loss or damage caused directly or indirectly by flooding, regardless of any other cause contributing concurrently or in any sequence to the loss. Therefore, because flood damage triggered the enforcement of the city ordinances, the policy excluded coverage regardless of the fact that wind damage contributed concurrently or in any sequence to the loss.

217. Davidson Hotel Co. v. St. Paul Fire & Marine Ins. Co., 136 F. Supp. 2d 901, 911 (W.D. Tenn. 2001).

On the other hand, a court said that "the necessity of a relationship between the damage and the code enforcement work is not satisfied by the fact that the covered work cannot be completed until the code-compliant repairs are performed." Thus, there was no coverage for the increased cost of compliance where an inspection after a flood revealed a condition in violation of the building code that existed *before* the flood.[218]

Conflict can arise over the meaning of "enforcement." For example, does "enforcement" require a written directive? [219] If a building official conveys the requirements of an ordinance orally, does that constitute enforcement? The issue is illustrated by a case in which the basement of a hospital flooded during a tropical storm. The hospital lost power from damage to its electrical switchgear. The hospital had an electrical contractor repair or replace refurbished distributors. It then made a claim for reconstruction that included the cost to replace refurbished distributors it contended did not meet code requirements with new distributors. The policy had a typical increased cost of compliance provision. Under it, the insurer would pay the reasonable and necessary costs to satisfy the minimum requirements of the *enforcement of a law* that regulated repair as long as the law was in force when the insured loss occurred, enforcement of that law was a direct result of the insured loss, and the law was not one with which the hospital would have to comply had the insured loss not occurred. As evidence of enforcement, the hospital produced a letter in which the health department putatively advised it to comply with the current building code. The court said that "enforcement of law" focused not on what the code technically said but on what building officials actually required. In this case, no positive action was undertaken by city officials and the hospital was not sanctioned for alleged non-compliance. The insurer did not have to pay to replace the repaired equipment with new equipment.[220]

---

218. St. George Tower v. Insurance Co. of Greater N.Y., 139 A.D.3d 200, 206, 30 N.Y.S.3d 60, 64 (2016). In *St. George*, pressure testing of a pump resulted in a flood that caused mold to develop, making it necessary to remove internal finishes. During the course of the remediation, it was discovered that concrete slabs were in a distressed and deteriorated condition and in violation of the building code that required repair before the water damage remediation could be completed. The latent problem that was uncovered by inspection necessitated by the covered damage was, said the court, not a problem related to the covered damage. The condition of the concrete slabs bore no relationship to the covered loss, the water damage. The court concluded the ordinance or law endorsement could not be triggered by discovery, in the course of an inspection necessitated by a covered event, of structural problems that were code violations. The court specifically declined to adopt the reasoning of *Davidson Hotel*.

219. *See, e.g.*, Bischel v. Fire Ins. Exchange, 1 Cal. App. 4th 1168, 177, 2 Cal. Rptr. 2d 575, 581 (Cal. App. 1991) ("enforcement" means carrying out mandate or command, which is accomplished by implementing building standards and withholding permits for construction in violation of those standards).

220. St. Luke's Episcopal Health Sys. Corp. v. Factory Mut. Ins. Co., 2007 U.S. Dist. LEXIS 101038 (S.D. Tex. Apr. 24, 2007).

[3] Debris Removal

[a] Introduction

Besides the damage they do to property, floods often deposit debris on the grounds of the insured property and sometimes inside an insured building. It is usually critically important to remove debris after a flood because often reconstruction cannot begin until the debris is cleared away. Generally, under a Debris Removal clause, an insurer will pay the expenses incurred by the policyholder to remove "debris of covered property"[221] that is caused by or results from a covered cause of loss occurring during the policy period, but only if it is reported to the insurer *in writing* within 180 days of the date of the direct physical loss or damage.[222] One commentary says that under the typical policy language, expenses have to be reported, but not necessarily incurred, within that 180 days and, therefore, a contractor's estimate given to the insurer for uncompleted work should fulfill the reporting requirement, although insurers have been known to insist that the work has to have been completed within 180 days for coverage to apply.[223] Therefore, if the 180-day deadline is approaching and debris removal cannot be completed, the insured should ask for an extension, which, given a good reason for the delay, insurers may grant.

Demolition associated with debris removal is not covered,[224] but the cost to repair property that is damaged in removing debris may be covered.[225]

---

221. In other words, the debris itself has to be "of covered property." *See, e.g.*, Harbor Cmtys., LLC v. Landmark Am. Ins. Co., 2008 U.S. Dist. LEXIS 59179 (S.D. Fla. Aug. 4, 2008). *See also* W.H. Breshears, Inc. v. Federated Mut. Ins. Co., 832 F. Supp. 288 (E.D. Cal. 1993), *aff'd*, 38 F.3d 1219 (9th Cir. 1994) (where vandals caused gasoline to be released from storage tank on and into ground, debris removal coverage did not cover cost of extracting pollutants from land or water or to remove, restore, or replace polluted land or water as policy covered debris of covered property).

222. *See, e.g.*, ISO Form CP 00 10 04 02, § A.4.a.(1). *See* Dudey & Malecki, *Debris Removal and Pollution Damage: How These Additional Costs Impact the Property Claim* (2015), Adjusting Today, http://adjustersinternational.com/publications/adjusting-today/debris-removal-and-pollution-damage/ for a history of coverage for debris removal and an analysis of policy language.

223. Dudey & Malecki, *Debris Removal and Pollution Damage: How These Additional Costs Impact the Property Claim* at 4 (2015), Adjusting Today, http://adjustersinternational.com/publications/adjusting-today/debris-removal-and-pollution-damage/.

224. Harbor Cmtys., LLC v. Landmark Am. Ins. Co., 2008 U.S. Dist. LEXIS 59179 (S.D. Fla. Aug. 4, 2008) (debris removal coverage does not include demolition costs because they entail act of destroying or wrecking, neither of which is within meaning of removal).

225. Manduca Datsun, Inc. v. Universal Underwriters Ins. Co., 106 Idaho 163, 168, 676 P.2d 1274, 1279 (Idaho App. 1984). In *Manduca Datsun* the court said that damage to asphalt would be recoverable under a Debris Removal clause where the most cost-effective way to remove debris would be using heavy equipment that would necessarily produce asphalt damage. The economic purpose of insurance coverage would be partly or wholly defeated, said the court, if it did not pay for damage that was necessarily caused by the debris removal process itself.

Policy language usually does not specify that any debris be removed from the premises of the insured for expenses of removal to be covered. Courts have, therefore, held that there is coverage for removing damaged covered property that is not located on the insured premises.[226] "Covered property," it should be noted, is not necessarily property owned by the insured. Typically, property policies cover personal property of others that is in the care, custody, or control of the insured.[227]

Debris removal coverage is not often litigated. One case in which it was is *Greenspoint Investors, Ltd. v. Travelers Lloyds Ins. Co.*[228] In *Greenspoint*, a hurricane damaged the roof, a skylight, and some windows at the insured premises and allowed significant amounts of water to enter the building. The policy provided the insurer would pay the cost to remove debris of covered property caused by a covered cause of loss, but if the total direct physical damage *and* debris removal expense exceeded the limit of insurance, it would pay up to an additional $25,000 in any one occurrence. The insured argued that the debris removal provision was triggered when the limit of insurance had been exhausted. The insurer countered that the provision was an absolute limit of $25,000 on the cost allowed for debris removal. The court determined the policy covered the expense to remove demolition material and other trash or construction detritus from the structure for a covered loss up to the policy limits. The court also found that the policy unambiguously intended to provide an additional amount of up to $25,000 past the limit of insurance for debris removal expenses. Debris removal expenses were included in the limit, and the allowance of an additional amount for debris removal expense clearly meant that the additional amount of coverage was triggered once the limit of insurance had been reached by a combination of direct physical damage and debris removal expenses. However, the condition precedent that the policy limits be exhausted before additional debris removal coverage was triggered, when coupled with the use of the phrases "we will pay for your expense" and "up to an additional $25,000," meant that the additional debris removal expense was payable up to $25,000 for expenses *actually incurred* and could not be included in a hypothetical replacement cost component of actual cost value.

---

226. Mont. Rail Link v. Lexington Ins. Co., 175 F. Supp. 2d 1248, 1250 (D. Mont. 2001) (where rail cars derailed and spilled their contents into river, cost of removing that debris was covered as policy provided no basis for insurer's assumption that debris removal had to be linked with covered real property or premises of insured). *See also* Stadium Lincoln-Mercury v. Heritage Transp., 160 Ohio App. 3d 128, 826 N.E.2d 332 (Ohio App. 2005) (expense of towing damaged vehicles from accident scene covered by debris removal clause).

227. *See, e.g.*, ISO Form CP 00 10 04 02, § A.1.c. *See also* Mont. Rail Link v. Lexington Ins. Co., 175 F. Supp. 2d 1248 (D. Mont. 2001).

228. Greenspoint Investors, Ltd. v. Travelers Lloyds Ins. Co., 2015 U.S. Dist. LEXIS 25301 (S.D. Tex. Mar. 3, 2015).

[b] "Debris" Defined

"Debris" is not defined in policies. Courts describe it as waste material that results from the destruction of something.[229] They have determined that debris removal includes cleanup costs and can encompass employee wages and benefits paid to accomplish a cleanup.[230] However, debris removal is not synonymous with demolition costs.[231] Courts find debris removal coverage for the cost of extracting from the ground fuel that escaped from storage tanks[232] and property in transit that is damaged in an accident.[233]

[c] Limits of Coverage

Under the standard debris coverage, the most a carrier will pay for the total of direct physical loss or damage together with the debris removal expense is the limit of insurance that applies to the covered property that has sustained loss or damage.[234] In addition, the amount it will pay for debris removal is limited to 25 percent of the sum of the deductible and the amount it pays for direct physical loss or damage to covered property that has sustained loss or damage.[235]

Insurance companies will, under the standard coverage, pay up to an additional $10,000 for debris removal expense, for each location, in any one occurrence of physical loss or damage to covered property, provided the total of the actual debris removal cost and the amount the company pays for direct physical loss or damage exceeds the limit of insurance on the covered property that has sustained loss or damage and/or the actual debris removal cost exceeds 25 percent of the total of the deductible and the amount the carrier pays for direct physical loss or damage to the covered property that has sustained

229. Stadium Lincoln-Mercury v. Heritage Transp., 160 Ohio App. 3d 128, 137, 826 N.E.2d 332, 339 (Ohio App. 2005); Lexington Ins. Co. v. Ryder System, Inc., 142 Ga. App. 36, 37, 234 S.E.2d 839 (1977).

230. Interstate Gourmet Coffee Roasters, Inc. v. Seaco Ins. Co., 59 Mass. App. Ct. 78, 794 N.E.2d 607 (2003).

231. *See* Greenspoint Investors, Ltd. v. Travelers Lloyds Ins. Co., 2015 U.S. Dist. LEXIS 25301 (S.D. Tex. Mar. 3, 2015), where the court appeared to accept expert testimony that debris removal is the process of gathering and moving of debris or demolition material and then disposing of it off-premises. Debris removal costs, said the expert, generally consist of dumpster costs, general labor, and a small percentage of supervisory labor. Another expert distinguished between demolition of damaged drywall and its disposal/removal from the structure. The court agreed that demolition and debris removal are distinct.

232. Lexington Ins. Co. v. Ryder System, Inc., 142 Ga. App. 36, 37, 234 S.E.2d 839, 840 (1977).

233. Mont. Rail Link v. Lexington Ins. Co., 175 F. Supp. 2d 1248 (D. Mont. 2001); Stadium Lincoln-Mercury v. Heritage Transp., 160 Ohio App. 3d 128, 826 N.E.2d 332 (Ohio App. 2005).

234. *See, e.g.*, ISO Form CP 00 10 04 02, § A.4.a.(3).(a).

235. *See, e.g.*, ISO Form CP 00 10 04 02, § A.4.a.(3).(b).

loss or damage.[236] Therefore, if one or both of the contingencies applies, the insurer's total payment for direct physical loss or damage and debris removal expense may reach, but will never exceed, the limit of insurance on the covered property that has sustained loss or damage, plus $10,000.[237]

Limits can be quite recondite, requiring careful review as illustrated by a New Jersey case.[238] The policy there provided coverage for debris removal. The insurer agreed to pay the necessary and reasonable expense incurred to remove the debris of covered property caused by or resulting from a covered cause of loss. The amount it would pay was up to 25 percent of the amount it paid for direct physical loss or damage to covered property plus the deductible that was applicable to that direct physical loss or damage. That limit was part of, and not in addition to, the limit that applied to the lost or damaged covered property. However, if the sum of direct physical loss or damage and debris removal expense exceeded that limit or the debris removal expense exceeded the 25 percent limitation *and* the amount specified in the Supplemental Coverage Declarations for Debris Removal (additional)—$500,000 in any one occurrence—the insurer would also pay an additional amount, up to that $500,000. The policy also said that payments under the Debris Removal coverage would not increase the applicable covered property limit, but if a limit was specified in the Supplemental Coverage Declarations, that limit—$500,000 in any one occurrence—would apply in addition to the applicable covered property limit. The insured property suffered significant flood damage from Superstorm Sandy. The property owner removed debris that resulted from repair construction and from damage caused by the flood. It submitted a claim for flood damage in excess of $1,000,000 and for debris removal in excess of $200,000. It sought to recover debris removal costs as an amount due over and above the $1,000,000 of flood coverage provided under the flood endorsement. The insurer, however, contended all damage caused by the flood was subject to the $1,000,000 flood limitation for a flood occurrence and paid that amount. The court agreed with the insurer. The flood endorsement, it said, categorically denied any flood damage coverage in excess of $1,000,000. The court added that the endorsement also clarified that the $1,000,000 ceiling would apply even if more than one limit, such as that for

---

236. *See, e.g.*, ISO Form CP 00 10 04 02, § A.4.a.(4).

237. The ISO Form CP 00 11 04 02, § A.4.a.(5) provides examples of how the debris removal coverage is calculated where there is no coinsurance penalty. One expert notes the possibility of ambiguity in the policy language and, to avoid potential disagreement with the carrier over a claim amount, recommends determining the meaning of the coverage language before any need arises. Hayman, *Hurricanes and Windstorm Coverage: Case Studies and Coverages* at 4 (2011), Adjusting Today, http://adjustersinternational.com/publications/adjusting-today/hurricanes-and-windstorm-coverage/0/.

238. Oxford Realty Group Cedar v. Travelers Excess & Surplus Lines Co., 229 N.J. 196, 160 A.3d 1263 (2017).

debris removal, applied. Therefore, the court held that the flood endorsement controlled the extent of flood coverage and was not modified by the rest of the policy terms.

[d] Exception for "Pollutants"

Debris removal coverage does not include the expense of extracting "pollutants" from land or water or of removing, restoring, or replacing polluted land or water.[239] The usual definition of "pollutants" is any "solid, liquid, gaseous or thermal irritant or contaminant, including smoke, vapor, soot, fumes, acids, alkalis, chemicals and waste."[240] Given the fact that flood waters can carry all manner of chemicals and other pollutants, one might expect to find a number of cases in which the exception has been litigated, but that is not the case.

One case that discussed the pollution exception to debris removal coverage is a decision by a Louisiana federal court.[241] In the case, flood waters caused a tile floor to buckle. The tiles had to be removed, and the floor tile glue contained asbestos requiring asbestos abatement procedures to properly remove the tile. The policy covered debris removal but excluded coverage for the "clean-up or the removal of debris of pollutants." The court said that provision was "not likely triggered" because the insured removed the debris of the flood, the damaged floor tile, not the debris of a pollutant. Had actions been instituted to remove the debris of a pollutant, the costs incurred would not have been covered.

In a case out of Hawaii,[242] water carried arsenic into a concrete slab. The accumulation of arsenic posed a health risk requiring abatement. A debris removal clause was not at issue, but a pollution exclusion was. The insurer argued the damage was excluded because pollution, an excluded peril, was one of the causes of the loss and, therefore, the damage was not covered, pursuant to anti-concurrent language in the policy, even if other covered perils—for instance, moisture infiltration—also caused the damage. The pollution exclusion said that:

> [the policy did] not insure against loss or damage caused directly or indirectly by [t]he actual, alleged or threatened discharge, dispersal, seepage, migration, release or escape of pollutants. But, if the same is the direct result of a covered cause of loss, we do insure direct physical loss or damage to covered property caused by the actual contact of the covered property with the pollutants.

---

239. *See, e.g.*, ISO Form CP 00 10 04 02, § A.4.a.(2).

240. *See, e.g.*, ISO Form CP 00 10 04 02, § H.2. "Waste" includes materials to be recycled, reconditioned, or reclaimed.

241. Levitz Furniture Corp. v. Houston Cas. Co., 1997 U.S. Dist. LEXIS 5883 (E.D. La. Apr. 29, 1997).

242. Ass'n of Apt. Owners of Imperial Plaza v. Fireman's Fund Ins. Co., 939 F. Supp. 2d 1059 (D. Haw. 2013).

The court held that the arsenic was caused by a covered cause of loss and therefore fell within the exception when pollution is the "direct result of a covered cause of loss." The case does not address the pollution exception to debris removal coverage, but it could have involved flood waters rather than merely moisture and, therefore, illustrates how carefully one must parse the language of an exclusion or exception.

[4] Loss of Residential Use Coverage

Homeowner policies pay for living expenses if the policyholder has to vacate his or her residence under certain circumstances.[243] The standard ISO policy provides that if a covered cause of loss makes the policyholder's residence not fit to live in,[244] the insurer will cover any necessary increase in living expenses incurred so that the household of the insured can maintain its normal standard of living.[245] The insurer will pay for the shortest time that is required to repair or replace the damage or, if the insured permanently relocates, the shortest time required for the household of the insured to settle elsewhere. The same applies when a civil authority prohibits the insured from use of the residence premises because of direct damage to neighboring premises by a peril that the policy insures against.[246]

Unfortunately, flood is an excluded peril in standard ISO homeowner policies. Thus, there will only be coverage in the rare circumstance that an endorsement adds flood as a peril. Moreover, the FEMA SFIP does not provide loss of use coverage. If, however, the insured has private flood coverage, loss of use is optional coverage.[247] If the insured has elected that coverage, it may be as little as $5,000[248] or as much as $50,000.[249]

243. *See generally* Cozen, *Insuring Real Property*, §4.11 (LexisNexis Matthew Bender 2022) for a discussion of "loss of use" coverage.

244. "Tenantability" is generally defined by a reasonable person standard under which "an untenantable home is one which cannot be used for the purposes for which it is intended and cannot be restored, using ordinary repairs, without unreasonable interruption of the occupancy." Flores v. Allstate Tex. Lloyd's Co., 229 F. Supp. 2d 697, 700 (S.D. Tex. 2002).

245. ISO Form HO 00 03 05 11, § I.D.1.

246. ISO Form HO 00 03 05 11, § I.D.1.

247. Private market flood policy generally provides additional living expenses up to $25,000. *Why do I need additional living expenses on my flood insurance?*, Flood Insurance Guru, https://www.floodinsuranceguru.com/blog/why-do-i-need-additional-living-expenses-on-my-flood-insurance.

248. The Aon Edge policy provides the option for $5,000 in additional living expenses coverage plus $500 for food spoilage.

249. Zurich's Residential Property Flood Insurance policy provides loss of use coverage in the amount of 20 percent of building coverage up to a maximum of $50,000.

[5] Claim Preparation Expenses

Given the potential complexity of flood claims, expenses of preparing a claim can be considerable. Some policies cover certain costs incurred in preparing a claim. An example of a coverage clause is one quoted in a North Carolina case that provided the policy covered:

> Expenses incurred by the Insured or by the Insured's representative including Auditors, Accountants, Appraisers, Lawyers, Consultants, Architects, Engineers or other such professionals in order to arrive at the loss payable under this policy in the event of a claim. This provision does not cover expenses incurred for the services of any public adjuster.[250]

The insurer argued that the only lawyers' expenses included in that coverage were those incurred in preparing the claim, not in suing on the policy. The court, however, said that the claim preparation expenses covered lawyer fees incurred in arriving at the "loss payable" and the proceedings before the court concerning the disputed meaning of ingress/egress and its relation to business interruption loss were necessary to determine the loss payable. The insurer also attempted to avoid paying the expenses of an officer of a risk management and employee benefits consulting firm who assisted the insured by claiming he was actually a public adjuster. The insured noted that the consultant was not a public adjuster because he was not licensed as one in the state and because he did not perform the services of a public adjuster. The insurer countered that the consultant performed all the services of a public adjuster. The court disagreed. It said that the consultant did not independently investigate the loss as would a public adjuster, but rather evaluated information given to him and, therefore, his fees as a consultant were covered expenses under the policy.

4.8 Excess Flood Insurance

[1] Introduction

[a] Inadequacy of the Standard Flood Insurance Policy

For most property owners, if they have flood insurance, they obtained it in a FEMA SFIP. The maximum coverage under an SFIP, however, is $250,000 for a single-family home and $500,000 for business real property. At the end of 2021, the *average* home price in the United States was $382,890.[251] One does not need to be a commercial real estate agent to know that a great many commercial properties are valued at far above $500,000. Moreover, for businesses,

---

250. Fountain Powerboat Indus. v. Reliance Ins. Co., 119 F. Supp. 2d 552, 559–60 (E.D.N.C. 2000).

251. *United States Housing Market*, Redfin, https://www.redfin.com/us-housing-market.

the maximum contents coverage is also $500,000, an amount that may be satisfactory for many small businesses, but is wholly inadequate for larger ones. Thus, the SFIP is insufficient coverage for many property owners. The gap between the value of the property and the SFIP coverage can be filled by what is called "excess" insurance.

FEMA does not offer excess coverage; therefore, by definition, it is private flood insurance. Once the limits of the SFIP have been exhausted, the excess policy will pay, ordinarily without an additional deductible,[252] up to the policy limits. Those limits will vary with the carrier, but they may add as little as an additional $500,000 in building coverage and $100,000 in contents coverage, combined limits of up to $15 million, or perhaps more,[253] depending on the carrier. A primary policy that provides flood coverage may serve as excess coverage to an SFIP.[254] Sometimes, the excess coverage will be provided as part of a Differences of Conditions (DIC) policy.[255] A DIC policy covers gaps left in a commercial property policy.[256]

When the value of property exceeds the SFIP limits of coverage, excess insurance may be mandated by a lender.[257] A lender may even force-place excess coverage when it believes the primary policy is inadequate to protect its interest.[258]

252. Note that an excess policy may have its own deductible.

253. Price, *Excess Flood Insurance: Why NFIP Isn't Enough* (May 20, 2009), Property Casualty 360, http://www.propertycasualty360.com/2009/05/20/excess-flood-insurance-why-nfip-isnt-enough (good excess policy will provide combined limits up to $15 million).

254. *See, e.g.*, Seahorn Invs., LLC v. Fed. Ins. Co., 2014 U.S. Dist. LEXIS 133522 (S.D. Miss. Sept. 23, 2014) (apartment project had first tier excess to SFIP in form of primary property policy that provided flood coverage, second tier excess insurance policy providing up to $5 million in excess of the primary policy, and third tier excess policies with policy limits of $7.5 million each).

255. *See, e.g.*, Samia Cos. v. United States Fire Ins. Co., 789 So. 2d 706 (La. App.), *writ. den.*, 799 So. 2d 1145 (La. 2001).

256. Price, *Excess Flood Insurance: Why NFIP Isn't Enough* (May 20, 2009), Property Casualty 360, http://www.propertycasualty360.com/2009/05/20/excess-flood-insurance-why-nfip-isnt-enough.

257. *See* DeZube, *What You Need to Know about Excess Flood Insurance: Pricey, Private-Sector Excess Flood Insurance Covers You When a Federal Flood Policy Isn't Enough*, Houselogic, https://www.houselogic.com/finances-taxes/home-insurance/what-you-need-know-about-excess-flood-insurance/. *See also* Henley v. Love Ins. Group, LLC, 2017 U.S. Dist. LEXIS 26244 (N.D. Tex. Feb. 24, 2017) ($975,000 of $1.2 million price to purchase apartment complex was financed and lender, as condition of loan, required property owner to obtain and carry $975,000 in flood insurance, including $475,000 excess coverage). *And see* Aspen Specialty Ins. Co. v. 4 NYP Ventures LLC, 162 F. Supp. 3d 337 (S.D.N.Y. 2016) (lender required $100 million in flood loss coverage for commercial property).

258. *See, e.g.*, Melinder v. Tex. Farmers Ins. Co., 2014 U.S. Dist. LEXIS 5103 (S.D. Tex. Jan. 15, 2014): (property owner purchased SFIP providing $152,000 for structural coverage, but lender determined that policy was inadequate and secured lender-placed excess flood insurance policy in amount of $98,000). *See also* Markey v. La. Citizens Fair Plan, 2008 U.S. Dist. LEXIS 63066 (E.D. La. Aug. 19, 2008) (creditor-placed excess residential property policy).

[b] Excess Insurance Defined

Excess insurance, a comparatively recent type of coverage,[259] is secondary or supplemental.[260] Basic insurance—a commercial property policy, for example—is written on a "primary" basis,[261] meaning it provides the first layer of coverage.[262] A primary property insurer has to indemnify a policyholder when a claim for a covered loss is submitted. The liability of an excess insurance only arises after a specified amount of the primary coverage is exhausted.[263] In other words, the liability of an excess insurer is not triggered until the underlying primary policy limits have been paid or, under some excess policies, admitted by the primary insurer.[264] A mere claim for the policy limits of the primary coverage does not trigger the liability of the excess insurer.[265] Excess insurance, therefore, affords specific coverage over the underlying limit of the primary policy.[266] By definition, there can be no excess coverage without primary coverage.[267]

---

259. Michael F. Aylward, *Excess: The New Frontier, New Appleman on Insurance: Current Critical Issues in Insurance Law* § II (July 2008).

260. Richmond, *Rights and Responsibilities of Excess Insurers*, 78 Denv. U.L. Rev. 29, 30 (2000). Attorneys should be aware that the insurance industry has enacted seven "Guiding Principles for Insurers of Primary and Excess Coverages." The principles address the relationship between the insurers and are not law. They are primarily concerned with liability coverages. The principles are quoted and discussed in Horowitz, *Relationship and Duties Among Primary and Excess Carriers*, 14 Fid. L.J. 223, 225–26 (2008).

261. Marick, *Excess Insurance: An Overview of General Principles and Current Issues*, 24 Tort & Ins. L.J. 715 (1989).

262. 1 Jeffrey E. Thomas, *New Appleman on Insurance Law Library Edition* § 1.06[7] (Matthew Bender 2022). *See also* Archer-Daniels-Midland Co. v. Phoenix Assur. Co., 975 F. Supp. 1129 (S.D. Ill.1997) (primary policy provides "first dollar" coverage up to limits of policy).

263. Seaman & Kittredge, *Excess Liability Insurance: Law and Litigation*, 32 Tort & Ins. L.J. 653 (1997).

264. *See, e.g.*, ARM Props. Mgmt. Group v. RSUI Indem. Co., 2008 U.S. Dist. LEXIS 108624 (W.D. Tex. Aug. 22, 2008) (under excess policy, liability arose for excess carrier only after primary insurer either paid or admitted liability for full amount of underlying coverage). *See also* Allmerica Financial Corp. v. Certain Underwriters at Lloyd's, London, 449 Mass. 621, 630, 871 N.E.2d 418, 426 (2007) (insurance program involving primary policy and one or more excess policies divides risk into distinct units and insures each unit individually; individual insurers do not, absent specific provision, act as coinsurers of entirety of risk; rather, each insurer contracts with insured individually to cover particular portion of risk).

265. Gunter v. Farmers Ins. Co., 2012 U.S. Dist. LEXIS 193969 (E.D. Ark. Sept. 19, 2012), *aff'd*, 736 F.3d 768 (8th Cir. 2013) (rejecting contention of insureds that exhaustion of policy does not mean that insurer has paid out policy limits and that obligation of excess insurer is triggered by their claim to recover policy limits from primary carrier; common-sense application of principles of exhaustion warrants finding that primary policy had not been exhausted and that obligations of excess insurer had not been triggered).

266. Richmond, *Rights and Responsibilities of Excess Insurers*, 78 Denv. U.L. Rev. 29, 30 (2000).

267. Westview Assocs. v. Guar. Nat'l Ins. Co., 717 N.Y.S.2d 75, 740 N.E.2d 220, 95 N.Y.2d 334 (2000) (by definition, excess coverage covers same types of claims as primary policy, but for additional amounts).

By their nature, primary and excess policies do not insure the same risk.[268] The policy language determines when the liability of the primary insurer is "exhausted."[269] Generally, excess policies require an insured to maintain a prescribed underlying layer of primary coverage.[270] It is important to be aware of the relationship between the parties. The insured has a contractual relationship with both the primary and excess insurers, but the two insurers have no contractual relationship with each other.[271]

In the case of flood coverage, an insurer may provide the primary property insurance for perils *other than* flood and be excess to an SFIP. That insurer is, therefore, the excess insurer *solely* for flood coverage.[272]

A deductible can in effect create excess coverage. For example, a policyholder had two primary all-risk property policies with a combined limit of $75 million. A third policy afforded up to $100 million in covered property loss, subject to a $75 million deductible. The court said that policy "principally served as excess" all-risk to the other policies.[273]

Sometimes, it is not immediately clear whether a policy is excess or a stand alone policy. In a Pennsylvania case,[274] the insured had an SFIP policy with one carrier and a policy with another carrier, the defendant, that had a flood endorsement. The endorsement said that the insured was permitted to purchase insurance in excess of the amount provided for by the endorsement and could also use insurance under the policy as excess coverage over another policy. The defendant claimed its coverage was excess because under it the insured could have another policy subject to the same plan, terms, conditions, and provisions as the defendant's policy, in which case the defendant would pay its share of the covered loss, which the policy defined as the proportion that the applicable limit under the defendant's policy bore to the limit of all policies covering on the same basis. The court rejected the defendant's argument because of a sentence in the defendant's policy that stated: "Such excess or other insurance shall not be considered in applying Insurance Under More Than One Policy nor shall it be considered in the application of any pro

268. Exec. Risk Indem., Inc. v. Charleston Area Med. Ctr., Inc., 681 F. Supp. 2d 694, 709 (S.D.W.V. 2009). *See also* Ferguson v. State Farm Ins. Co., 2007 U.S. Dist. LEXIS 34030 (E.D. La. May 4, 2007) (flood policy was not excess insurance, as it covered a loss not covered by homeowners policy).

269. ARM Props. Mgmt. Group v. RSUI Indem. Co., 2008 U.S. Dist. LEXIS 108624 (W.D. Tex. Aug. 22, 2008).

270. 1 Jeffrey E. Thomas, *New Appleman on Insurance Law Library Edition* § 1.06[7] (Matthew Bender 2022).

271. Marick, *Excess Insurance: An Overview of General Principles and Current Issues*, 24 Tort & Ins. L.J. 715 (1989).

272. *See, e.g.*, Certain Underwriters at Lloyd's, London v. Travelers Prop. Cas. Co. of Am., 161 Wn. App. 265, 256 P.3d 368 (2011).

273. Continental Ins. Co. v. Arkwright Mut. Ins. Co., 102 F.3d 30, 32 (1st Cir. 1996).

274. Pine Grove Manufactured Homes v. Ind. Lumbermens Mut. Ins. Co., 2010 U.S. Dist. LEXIS 112188 (M.D. Pa. Oct. 21, 2010).

rata or apportionment provision." The court concluded that under the plain language of the contract, the insured held a policy for excess coverage with the defendant.

[c] Layered Coverage

Homeowners and small businesses are often unaware of the existence of excess flood coverage. It is most often purchased by large organizations. Because of the risk that flooding will cause substantial losses, excess insurers often will only agree to insure a portion of the risk above the primary coverage. The layers of excess coverage above the first are sometimes referred to as "catastrophe coverage" because they protect against an unusual but calamitous event.[275] The coverage of a New Orleans theme park company illustrates multilayered coverage.[276] The company obtained $450 million in combined limits. The policies provided four separate layers of coverage: (1) primary coverage with $25 million in limits, (2) a first excess layer with $50 million in limits, (3) a second excess layer with $125 million in limits, and (4) a third excess layer with $250 million in limits. Typically, the coverage in a multilayered policy program is "ground-up," meaning a given layer of coverage is not triggered until the layer beneath it is totally exhausted.[277]

[d] Umbrella Coverage Distinguished from Excess Coverage

Umbrella coverage is sometimes confused with excess coverage. True excess insurance does not expand the scope of coverage but only increases the amount of coverage for the same perils insured by the underlying primary policy.[278] An umbrella policy provides "first dollar" coverage for risks that may not be insured by the primary policy.[279] It may provide the initial layer of coverage for a peril not covered by either a primary policy or excess policy.[280] An umbrella policy, however, often affords first layer and excess coverage.[281] That is, it can be a hybrid that combines aspects of primary and excess cover-

---

275. Seaman & Kittredge, *Excess Liability Insurance: Law and Litigation*, 32 Tort & Ins. L.J. 653 (1997).

276. Six Flags, Inc. v. Westchester Surplus Lines Ins. Co., 565 F.3d 948 (5th Cir 2009).

277. New Jersey Transit Corp. v. Certain Underwriters at Lloyd's London, 461 N.J. Super. 440, 449, 221 A.3d 1180, 1185 (2019), *aff'd*, 245 N.J. 104, 243 A.3d 1248 (2021).

278. 1 Jeffrey E. Thomas, *New Appleman on Insurance Law Library Edition* § 1.06[7] (Matthew Bender 2022). *See also* Douglas R. Richmond, *The Tiresome Problem of Exhaustion in Excess Insurance, New Appleman on Insurance: Current Critical Issues in Insurance Law* § II.A (Spring 2014) (true excess policy does not broaden underlying coverage; it increases amount of coverage available to compensate for loss, but does not increase scope of coverage).

279. Michael F. Aylward, *Excess: The New Frontier, New Appleman on Insurance: Current Critical Issues in Insurance Law* § III.C (July 2008).

280. 5 Jeffrey E. Thomas, *New Appleman on Insurance Law Library Edition* § 41.02[3][b] (Matthew Bender 2022)

281. Treesdale, Inc. v. TIG Ins. Co., 681 F. Supp. 2d 611 (W.D. Penn. 2009).

age.[282] An umbrella policy may provide coverage that exceeds the limits of a primary policy as well as coverage for perils that are not insured against in the primary policy. This "gap-filler" coverage differentiates true excess insurance from umbrella insurance.[283]

Umbrella policies are most commonly found in liability coverages, not property insurance. "Difference in Conditions" (DIC) policies are one form of umbrella property insurance. They are a "special form of open-peril coverage written in conjunction with basic fire coverage and designed to provide protection against losses not reimbursed under the standard fire forms."[284] One use for DIC policies is to provide coverage for catastrophic risks—floods or earthquakes, for example—that are usually excluded risks in property policies.[285] However, primary flood coverage in a DIC policy is only likely to be available when the property has a low risk of flooding. A DIC policy can also provide excess coverage for losses covered by a primary policy.[286]

[2] Stand Alone or Follow Form

Excess coverage can be acquired in a "stand alone" policy. That means the policy has its own insuring agreement, conditions, definitions, and exclusions that provide and restrict the coverage.[287] The coverage is determined by the terms set forth in the *excess* policy.[288]

In the alternative, the excess policy may "follow form." That means it covers the peril or perils insured under the primary policy and on the same basis.[289] "Follow form" language may be brief and straightforward. For example:

> The insurance afforded by this policy shall be subject to the same terms and conditions (except as regards premiums, limits of liability and the following conditions) as the Primary Insurer: ____________

---

282. Marick, *Excess Insurance: An Overview of General Principles and Current Issues*, 24 Tort & Ins. L.J. 715 (1989).

283. 5 Jeffrey E. Thomas, *New Appleman on Insurance Law Library Edition* § 41.02[3][b] (Matthew Bender 2022)

284. *See Glossary D*, NAIC, http://www.naic.org/consumer_glossary.htm#D.

285. *See Difference-in-Conditions (DIC) Insurance*, IRMI, https://www.irmi.com/online/insurance-glossary/terms/d/difference-in-conditions-dic-insurance.aspx.

286. *Difference in Conditions Policies* (Summit Business Media, 2012).

287. Richmond, *Rights and Responsibilities of Excess Insurers*, 78 Denv. U.L. Rev. 29, 30 (2000). It is important to be aware that a primary policy could be all-risk *without* an exclusion for flood, while the excess policy could be all-risk but *with* an exclusion for flood. *See, e.g.*, Omega Protein Corp. v. Lexington Ins. Co., 2007 U.S. Dist. LEXIS 98530 (W.D. La. Feb. 15, 2007).

288. 5 Jeffrey E. Thomas, *New Appleman on Insurance Law Library Edition* § 41.02[3][b] (Matthew Bender 2022).

289. Michael F. Aylward, *Excess: The New Frontier, New Appleman on Insurance: Current Critical Issues in Insurance Law* § III.A.2 (July 2008). This is commonly called "specific" excess coverage. Marick, *Excess Insurance: An Overview of General Principles and Current Issues*, 24 Tort & Ins. L.J. 715 (1989).

Insurance Company, Policy Number __________, (hereinafter referred to as the Primary Coverage).[290]

The clause may be a bit more in depth. A very common "follow form" clause for instance states:

> In respect of the perils hereby insured against, this Policy is subject to the same warranties, terms and conditions (except as regards the premium, the amount and limits of liability other than the deductible or self-insurance provision where applicable, and the renewal agreement, if any; and EXCEPT AS OTHERWISE PROVIDED HEREIN) as are contained in or as may be added to the policy/ies of the primary insurer(s) prior to the happening of a loss for which claim is made hereunder, and should any alteration be made in the premium for the policy/ies of the primary insurer(s), then the premium hereon shall be adjusted accordingly.[291]

In either event, the effect of the language is to bind the excess insurer to the terms of the primary policy.[292] As a consequence, any ambiguity in the primary policy is transmitted into the excess policy.[293] Coverage issues then turn only on interpretation of the primary policy.[294] The terms of the primary policy are incorporated unless *explicitly* excepted.[295] Thus, a primary policy excluded damages caused by water including "water that backs up from a sewer or drain." An excess policy had a definition of flood that did not include that type of water damage. The court found that definition in no way negated or contradicted the water exclusion in primary policy. Therefore, as the excess policy was subject to the same terms and conditions as the primary one, the

290. Ace Am. Ins. Co. v. Adm'rs of the Tulane Educ. Fund, 2008 U.S. Dist. LEXIS 66299 (E.D. La. Aug. 28, 2008).

291. Wentwood Woodside I LP v. GMAC Commer. Mortg. Corp., 419 F.3d 310 (5th Cir. 2005).

292. Haering v. Topa Ins. Co., 244 Cal. App. 4th 725, 734, 198 Cal. Rptr. 3d 291, 296 (2016); Royal Indem. Co. v. Chi. Hosp. Risk Pooling Program, 309 Ill. Dec. 954, 959, 372 Ill. App. 3d 104, 108, 865 N.E.2d 317, 322 (2007).

293. *See, e.g.*, Pinnacle Entm't, Inc. v. Allianz Global Risks US Ins. Co., 2008 U.S. Dist. LEXIS 108583 (D. Nev. Mar. 26, 2008) (where policyholder's property suffered damage from storm surge and excess policies excluded from coverage damage and loss caused by flood, but it was unclear whether definition of "flood" in primary policy included storm surge, ambiguous language was construed in favor of coverage by excess carriers). *Compare* Northrop Grumman Corp. v. Factory Mut. Ins. Co., 563 F.3d 777 (9th Cir. 2009) (though primary policy must be consulted in interpreting excess policy, court refused to treat those two documents as only one contract and found no ambiguity in excess policy based on labels placed on certain types of damages in *primary* policy).

294. Houbigant, Inc. v. Fed. Ins. Co., 374 F.3d 192, 203 (3d Cir 2004).

295. Michael F. Aylward, *Excess: The New Frontier, New Appleman on Insurance: Current Critical Issues in Insurance Law* § III.A.2 (July 2008).

former excluded damages caused by water that backed up through a sewer or drain.[296]

The excess carrier is, of course, allowed to provide any exceptions to the coverage in the primary policy that it wishes.[297] If the express terms of the excess policy and any of those in the primary policy conflict, the terms in the primary policy that conflict are not incorporated into the excess coverage.[298] That means that any inconsistency or conflict between the policies is resolved by applying the terms of the excess policy.[299] These conflicts can be subtle. In one case a homeowner purchased an SFIP and an excess flood policy with $100,000 in coverage. SFIPs provide increased cost of compliance coverage. The insured home was damaged in a flood. After receiving the full amount of coverage under the SFIP, the policyholder claimed $100,000 for increased cost of compliance under the excess policy. The claim was denied. The excess insurer argued its policy provided no increased cost of compliance coverage. That policy, observed the court, covered "direct physical loss by or from flood" as defined in the SFIP. The SFIP defined flood to require "evidence of physical changes to the property." The court held that there was no increased cost of compliance coverage in the excess policy because those expenses were not physical losses.[300]

Thus, follow form is not as simple and straightforward as it might initially appear. As one federal judge asserted: "it could be said that following . . . form is akin to singing along with Mitch Miller—the bouncing ball may at once exclude coverage, then provide it, then take it away again, only to give it back, all within the same form of the policy and without a change in font."[301]

While an excess policy may be "follow form" and bind the excess carrier to the contents of the primary policy, that does not mean that excess insurer is bound by the interpretation the primary insurer places on its policy language.[302] Excess and primary carriers can have very different understandings

296. Ace Am. Ins. Co. v. Adm'rs of the Tulane Educ. Fund, 2008 U.S. Dist. LEXIS 66299 (E.D. La. Aug. 28, 2008).

297. Orleans Parish Sch. Bd. v. Lexington Ins. Co., 95 So. 3d 1205 (La. App. 2012).

298. Home Ins. Co. v. American Home Prods. Corp., 902 F.2d 1111, 1133 (2d Cir. 1990).

299. Haering v. Topa Ins. Co., 244 Cal. App. 4th 725, 734, 198 Cal. Rptr. 3d 291, 296 (2016).

300. Thomas v. Std. Fire Ins. Co., 414 F. Supp. 2d 567 (E.D. Va. 2006).

301. Premier Entm't Biloxi, LLC v. James River Ins. Co., 2007 U.S. Dist. LEXIS 74099, at *14 (S.D. Miss. Oct. 3, 2007).

302. Michael F. Aylward, *Excess: The New Frontier, New Appleman on Insurance: Current Critical Issues in Insurance Law* § III.A.2 (July 2008) ("follow form" clause binds excess insurer to terms of lower layer policy, not to underlying insurer's interpretation of those terms). Douglas R. Richmond, *The Tiresome Problem of Exhaustion in Excess Insurance, New Appleman on Insurance: Current Critical Issues in Insurance Law* § II.B (Spring 2014) (excess carrier may rightfully deny coverage where primary carrier pays uncovered loss by mistake or as business accommodation to key policyholder). *But see* ARM Props. Mgmt. Group v. RSUI Indem.

of the meaning of the primary policy.[303] Indeed, the voluminous insurance case law is replete with disputes between insurance companies over the meaning of their policies. Moreover, the excess policy generally follows the wording of the underlying insurance at the time the policies were issued,[304] although courts have held that a change in the scope of the primary insurance that results from an action for reformation binds the excess carrier as it reflects the parties' intent at the time of contracting.[305]

It is possible, though unusual, for a second layer excess carrier to issue a policy that follows the form of the first layer carrier. For example, an insurance company provided all-risk *primary* property coverage for perils other than flood. The policyholder had primary *flood* coverage in an SFIP. The company that provided the other primary property coverage was also excess to the SFIP. There was a second layer of excess coverage, and that policy followed the form of the non-SFIP policy.[306]

[3] Coincidental Excess Insurance

Property insurance policies typically contain an "other insurance" clause. These clauses define the extent to which the policy applies if any other policy applies to the same loss.[307] The clause discourages "over-insuring" and reduces moral hazard.[308] There are three common types of other insurance clauses: pro rata, excess, and escape.[309] Under an excess other insurance clause the carrier attempts to limit its liability to the amount of loss that exceeds all other

---

Co., 2008 U.S. Dist. LEXIS 108624 (W.D. Tex. Aug. 22, 2008) (where excess carrier argued underlying insurers may have paid policy limits, but failed to take advantage of exceptions in their coverage or otherwise overpaid, court said that was not relevant to the issue of whether excess insurer's liability had attached; that both underlying insurers paid their policy limits as defined in excess insurance contract was sufficient to trigger duties of excess carrier).

303. Aspen Specialty Ins. Co. v. 4 NYP Ventures LLC, 162 F. Supp. 3d 337 (S.D.N.Y. 2016) (excess insurer with "follow the form" policy is bound by language of underlying policy, but that does not mean insurer will have same interpretation of that language as primary insurer).

304. The excess policy could, of course, incorporate changes to the underlying policy. *See, e.g.*, Stewart Enters. v. RSUI Indem. Co., 614 F.3d 117, 120, n.8 (5th Cir. 2010) (excess policy was subject to same warranties, terms, and conditions as "contained in or as may be added to" primary policy prior to loss for which claim is made).

305. Michael F. Aylward, *Excess: The New Frontier, New Appleman on Insurance: Current Critical Issues in Insurance Law* § III.A.2 (July 2008).

306. Certain Underwriters at Lloyd's, London v. Travelers Prop. Cas. Co. of Am., 161 Wn. App. 265, 256 P.3d 368 (2011).

307. 5 Jeffrey E. Thomas, *New Appleman on Insurance Law Library Edition* § 41.02[4][b] (Matthew Bender 2022).

308. Richmond, *Issues and Problems in "Other Insurance," Multiple Insurance, and Self-Insurance*, 22 Pepp. L. Rev. 1373, 1379 (1995). *See also* 5 Jeffrey E. Thomas, *New Appleman on Insurance Law Library Edition* § 41.02[4][b] (Matthew Bender 2022) (standard commercial property forms include other insurance clause to preclude possibility of redundant coverage).

309. 5 Jeffrey E. Thomas, *New Appleman on Insurance Law Library Edition* § 47.12[3][c] (Matthew Bender 2022).

"valid and collectible insurance," up to the policy limits.[310] "Valid" normally means enforceable—if, for example, the other insurance is subject to rescission because of a misrepresentation, it would not generally be regarded as valid—and in general "collectible" means the insurer is solvent and the aggregate policy limits have not been exhausted.[311] When an excess other insurance clause renders an otherwise primary policy excess, it is a "coincidental" excess policy or "excess by coincidence."[312]

Other insurance clauses raise a host of thorny questions.[313] In the case of conflicting excess other insurance clauses, courts generally ignore them and prorate the loss among the carriers.[314] Courts almost always hold that a primary policy that is coincidentally excess as a result of an "other insurance" clause has to pay before a *true excess policy* written over other primary insurance.[315] However, the questions raised by coincidental excess insurance are largely academic in the case of flood insurance for two reasons. First, excess other insurance clauses are mainly found in liability, not property, policies.

---

310. Richmond, *Issues and Problems in "Other Insurance," Multiple Insurance, and Self-Insurance*, 22 Pepp. L. Rev. 1373, 1385 (1995) ("typical excess clause might read: 'This insurance shall apply only as excess insurance over any other valid and collectible insurance which would apply in the absence of this policy, except insurance written specifically to cover as excess over the limits of liability applicable to . . . this policy.'").

311. Stanovich, *Other Insurance and the CGL Policy* (Apr. 2009), IRMI, https://www.irmi.com/articles/expert-commentary/other-insurance-and-the-cgl-policy.

312. Michael F. Aylward, *Excess: The New Frontier, New Appleman on Insurance: Current Critical Issues in Insurance Law* § III.A.2 (July 2008) (primary insurers may characterize their policies as "excess" based on terms of "other insurance" clauses, making primary policy coincidentally excess by reason of "other insurance" language); Marick, *Excess Insurance: An Overview of General Principles and Current Issues*, 24 Tort & Ins. L.J. 715 (1989) (excess coverage arises by "coincidence" when interpretation of "other insurance" clauses contained within two policies applying to same property renders one policy excess). *See also* Guaranty Nat'l Ins. Co. v. American Motorists Ins. Co., 981 F.2d 1108, 1109 (9th Cir. 1992) (where two carriers had each issued primary policy, coverage of one policy became excess to coverage afforded by other in what could be called "excess by coincidence").

313. *See* 5 Jeffrey E. Thomas, *New Appleman on Insurance Law Library Edition* § 47.12[1] (Matthew Bender 2022) (case law regarding conflicting "other insurance" clauses has not evolved in consistent, logical, and coherent way); Godfrey, *Insurance—"Other Insurance" Clauses—Conflict between Escape Clauses and Excess Clauses*, 27 La. L. Rev. 114 (1966).

314. 5 Jeffrey E. Thomas, *New Appleman on Insurance Law Library Edition* § 47.12[3][d] (Matthew Bender 2022). *See also* State Farm Fire & Cas. Co. v. LiMauro, 492 N.Y.S.2d 534, 65 N.Y.2d 369, 482 N.E.2d 13, (1985); Mission Ins. Co. v. United States Fire Ins. Co., 401 Mass. 492, 496, 498, 517 N.E.2d 463, 466, n.4 (1988) (where policies each contain excess or escape clauses, they are declared mutually repugnant, and each insurer is required to contribute to loss, as giving effect to both clauses would result in no coverage for insured).

315. Michael F. Aylward, *Excess: The New Frontier, New Appleman on Insurance: Current Critical Issues in Insurance Law* § III.B (July 2008). *See also* Markey v. La. Citizens Fair Plan, 2007 U.S. Dist. LEXIS 48390 (E.D. La. July 3, 2007) (other insurance clause made clear that policy would only come into effect as primary coverage if there were no other "valid or collectible insurance" and that otherwise, it would be considered excess and only go into effect if other primary policy limits were exhausted).

Second, almost every type of property policy—whether commercial property or homeowners[316]—explicitly excludes flood losses from coverage. Therefore, it would be quite unlikely to find a property policy from a private insurer that covered flood at all, let alone made its coverage excess to other insurance covering flood loss by virtue of an excess other insurance clause. Interestingly, the FEMA SFIP may address that circumstance. The policy provides that when a loss that it covers is also covered by other insurance that includes flood coverage not issued under the NFIA, and the other policy has a provision stating that it is excess insurance, the SFIP is primary.[317] The SFIP is undoubtedly referring to a policy that is explicitly excess, but does an excess "other insurance" clause in effect state that the policy "is excess insurance"? Once again, the question is largely academic, as a primary property policy that did not exclude flood losses and had an excess "other insurance" clause would be rare.

[4] SFIP as Excess Insurance

One example of a primary flood policy with an excess "other insurance" clause is the Dwelling Form of the FEMA SFIP. It states in the "other insurance" clause that if there is other insurance in the name of a condominium association covering the same property as that covered by the policy of a unit owner, that unit owner's policy is excess to the association policy.[318] The policy issued to a condominium association is called a Residential Condominium Building Association Policy (RCBAP). In a Texas case, an association had flood coverage under an RCBAP. After a flood loss, it received over $185,000 under that policy. A couple that owned a unit had their own Dwelling Form SFIP, and the insurer administering the policy determined they suffered just under $30,000 in flood damage, but did not pay. The unit owners sued the insurer. The court said that under the language of the Dwelling Form policy, it acted as an excess flood policy to the association RCBAP. The RCBAP, said the court, was the primary policy, and its coverage was not exhausted by the flood damage. The court concluded that if the unit owners had a claim, it was against the association, not the excess insurer.[319]

As the Texas court said, for a unit owner to recover under a Dwelling Form SFIP as excess insurance, the limits of the associations RCBAP SFIP

316. Even very specialized forms of property insurance like equipment breakdown insurance exclude coverage for floods. *See, e.g.*, HSB Freestyle Policy Form 6671 (10/2002) § B.1.f; ISO Form BM 00 20 07 01, § B.3.

317. FEMA General Property Form—Standard Flood Insurance Policy, § VII.C.b. (June 2014).

318. FEMA Dwelling Form—Standard Flood Insurance Policy, § VII.C.2 (June 2014).

319. Orlando v. State Farm Fire & Cas. Co., 2011 U.S. Dist. LEXIS 14497 (S.D. Tex. Feb. 14, 2011).

have to be exhausted. For example, in a Florida case, the RCBAP had coverage limits up to $846,000. In a storm surge, the condominium building and a unit owner's dwelling unit were completely flooded. Both the building and the unit were a total loss and were eventually razed. The association's insurer paid it about $50,000 less than the coverage limits. The unit owners were denied coverage under their Dwelling Form SFIP policy. Their insurer concluded the RCBAP policy limits had not been exhausted. The court found that under the "other insurance" clause, the RCBAP policy was the primary coverage, and the unit owner's policy was excess coverage. The coverage of an excess policy is not triggered until the damages exhaust the limits of the primary policy; therefore, concluded the court, because the payment under the RCBAP policy failed to reach the limits of the policy, there was no basis for a claim by the unit owners.[320]

[5] Maintenance of Underlying Insurance Clause

Because an excess policy by definition supplements primary coverage, purchase of an underlying layer of primary coverage is a prerequisite to issuing a follow form excess policy.[321] Moreover, excess policies typically require the policyholder to maintain primary insurance "in full force and effect" in the amount stated in a Schedule of Underlying Insurance.[322] An example of a "maintenance clause" reads:

> It is a condition precedent to recovery under this Policy that the Policy(ies) and Limit(s) of the Primary . . . Insurer(s) set forth in . . . the Schedule be maintained in full force and effect, except for any reduction or exhaustion of any underlying aggregate Limits of Liability contained therein, solely by the amount of loss(es) paid or admitted during the policy year.[323]

---

320. Conley v. Fla. Family Ins. Co., 2010 U.S. Dist. LEXIS 87907 (N.D. Fla. Aug. 26, 2010). *See also* King v. Casa Grande Condo. Ass'n, 416 Fed. Appx. 363 (5th Cir. Jan. 28, 2011) (unit owners were entitled to payments under SFIP issued to them only after the primary coverage of condominium association was exhausted).

321. Marick, *Excess Insurance: An Overview of General Principles and Current Issues*, 24 Tort & Ins. L.J. 715 (1989).

322. *See, e.g.*, LES Realty Trust 'A' v. Landmark Am. Ins. Co., 82 Mass. App. Ct. 694, 977 N.E.2d 566 (2012) (excess policy required that primary policy be maintained in full effect). *See generally* Michael F. Aylward, *Excess: The New Frontier, New Appleman on Insurance: Current Critical Issues in Insurance Law* § III.A.3 (July 2008) (excess policies typically contain "maintenance of underlying insurance" clauses that mandate insured maintain underlying insurance in amounts warranted in Schedule of Underlying Insurance).

323. Stewart Enters. v. RSUI Indem. Co., 614 F.3d 117, 120, n.8 (5th Cir. 2010).

Failure to comply with the maintenance clause can result in the loss of excess coverage,[324] although the policy may simply limit the liability of the excess insurer.[325]

[6] Available Excess Coverage

[a] Generally

Few insurance companies offer excess flood coverage. It is available from two of the world's largest insurers: AIG and Lloyd's of London.[326] Even companies that write excess coverage may not do so for properties at a high risk for flooding.[327] The carrier may require the property to have the maximum coverage available under an SFIP.

Excess flood coverage can be acquired with an endorsement to an existing property policy.[328] It can also be obtained in a stand alone policy providing excess either flood coverage alone or for some or all risks covered by the primary policy. A policy could both include primary property coverage and also flood coverage in excess of a FEMA SFIP.[329]

---

324. Marick, *Excess Insurance: An Overview of General Principles and Current Issues*, 24 Tort & Ins. L.J. 715 (1989).

325. Michael F. Aylward, *Excess: The New Frontier, New Appleman on Insurance: Current Critical Issues in Insurance Law* § III.A.3 (July 2008) (policy may state that if insured fails to maintain any required underlying insurance in force, excess policy applies only in same manner as it would have applied had underlying insurance been maintained in force). *See also* Marick, *Excess Insurance: An Overview of General Principles and Current Issues*, 24 Tort & Ins. L.J. 715 (1989) (where policy provides that failure to comply with maintenance clause results in excess insurer only being liable to extent it would have been had insured complied, excess insurer should provide coverage subject to uninsured "gap" in amount of primary coverage that insured was supposed to have purchased).

326. DeZube, *What You Need to Know about Excess Flood Insurance* (Aug. 22, 2013), Houselogic, http://www.houselogic.com/home-advice/disaster-insurance/what-you-need-know-about-excess-flood-insurance/.

327. Wells, *Excess Flood Insurance—When the Federal Plan Isn't Sufficient* (Aug. 7, 2006), Insurance Journal, http://www.insurancejournal.com/magazines/features/2006/08/07/72126.htm. If an insurer will cover high-risk properties, it may charge an additional premium. *See, e.g.*, Wentwood Woodside I LP v. GMAC Commer. Mortg. Corp., 419 F.3d 310 (5th Cir. 2005), where the insurer's standard excess property policy covered flood loss but excluded coverage for a property in a high-risk zone. It allowed an exception to the exclusion to be purchased for an additional premium.

328. *See, e.g.*, Ace Am. Ins. Co. v. Adm'rs of the Tulane Educ. Fund, 2008 U.S. Dist. LEXIS 66299 (E.D. La. Aug. 28, 2008) (excess property policy contained flood exclusions but also had "Flood and Water Damage Endorsement" that provided up to $75 million for flood or water damage per occurrence); Premier Entm't Biloxi, LLC v. James River Ins. Co., 2007 U.S. Dist. LEXIS 74099 (S.D. Miss. Oct. 3, 2007).

329. *See, e.g.*, Certain Underwriters at Lloyd's, London v. Travelers Prop. Cas. Co. of Am., 161 Wn. App. 265, 256 P.3d 368 (2011), where the primary policy excluded flood, but the insured obtained an endorsement adding back coverage for all loss or damage caused by flooding. That flood coverage was excess to an SFIP. The primary policy was the *initial layer* of coverage for losses caused by other perils.

The ISO standard excess flood insurance endorsement and two stand alone polices are discussed below. The purpose of the discussion is to alert the reader to key provisions affecting the scope of coverage.

[b] Standard Excess Flood Insurance Endorsement

A standard ISO endorsement[330] can be used to provide coverage that is excess to an NFIP policy.[331] One of the first things to note about the endorsement is that it modifies standard ISO property policies that have a "Water Exclusion" rather than a more narrow exclusion just for flood. The endorsement provides that the Water Exclusion does not apply to the extent a part of it "might conflict with coverage provided" by the endorsement. That means that if the insured fails to fit a claim within the coverage provided by the endorsement, the exclusion applies.

The coverage under the ISO endorsement is somewhat different from that offered by the NFIP. For example, the definition of "flood" is not the same. The endorsement defines a flood as a "general and temporary condition of partial or complete inundation of normally dry land areas" but omits "collapse or subsidence of land along the shore of a lake or similar body of water." The NFIP policy adds that two or more acres and two or more properties, one being the insured property, have to be flooded for there to be a flood. The endorsement, like the NFIP policy, says the flooding may derive from overflow of inland or tidal waters, unusual or rapid accumulation or runoff of surface waters, or mudflows. The endorsement states specifically that it covers mudflows *caused by flooding* from unusual or rapid accumulation or runoff. The definition of "mudflow" in the two policies is virtually identical except that the NFIP policy excludes from the definition "landslide, slope failure, or a saturated soil mass moving by liquidity down a slope."

The endorsement contains a couple of clauses that help clarify the coverage. First, flooding in a "continuous or protracted event" constitutes a single flood; second, if a flood is caused by overflow of inland or tidal waters, it is considered to begin when the water *first overflows* its banks.

The policy does not cover land or the cost of excavations, grading, backfilling, or filling.[332] It also does not cover any building or structure not *fully enclosed* by walls and a roof. In contrast, the NFIP policy covers buildings with *two or more* outside rigid walls and a fully secured roof.

330. ISO Form CP 10 65 10 00.

331. Koehler, *Flood: Understanding and Recovering from One of Nature's Worst Disasters*, at 3 (2010), Adjusting Today, http://adjustersinternational.com/publications/adjusting-today/flood-understanding-and-recovering/0/.

332. *See, e.g.*, Red Lion Hotels, Inc. v. Commonwealth Ins. Co. of Am., 177 Ore. App. 58, 33 P.3d 358 (2001) (riverbank restoration project involved grading, filling, and backfilling of land with soil, earth, mineral matter, or other fill material and, therefore, fell under land exclusion and was not covered risk).

The endorsement contains an "other insurance" clause that in effect converts the policy into excess coverage or creates a huge deductible. It provides that if the loss is also covered by an NFIP policy, or the property is *eligible to be covered*, but no NFIP policy is in effect, then the insurer will only pay for the amount of the loss that exceeds the maximum limit in the NFIP policy, whether or not that limit is maintained or the insured can collect on any NFIP policy.[333]

There are two exceptions to the other insurance clause. The first is invoked when, at the time of the loss, the property is eligible for NFIP coverage, but an NFIP policy is not in effect solely because of ineligibility of the property at the time the endorsement was written. The second exception is when an NFIP policy is not in effect because the insurer agreed to write the endorsement without underlying NFIP coverage. The existence of that agreement must be memorialized in a Flood Coverage Schedule or the Declarations Page by an indication that an Underlying Insurance Waiver applies. There is actually a third exception that is implicit in the other insurance clause. That is that the clause does not apply whenever the property is *ineligible* for an NFIP policy.[334]

[c] Pacific Specialty Insurance Company Excess Flood Coverage

Pacific Specialty Insurance Company provides excess flood insurance, which it explains in an Agent's Manual.[335] Unlike the Lloyds policy, the Pacific Specialty coverage is only for residential buildings. To be eligible for coverage, a property has to be covered by an SFIP at the maximum limits of $250,000 building and $100,000 contents. Buildings must be walled, roofed, principally above ground, and permanently affixed to a site. In addition to exclusions found in the SFIP, coverage is not available for boathouses, manufactured prefabricated, mobile homes, or any structure not on a permanent or fixed foundation, buildings entirely over water, buildings under construction, and frame dwellings in "V" zones that are not built on driven pilings.

Properties that have experienced a building flood loss in excess of $150,000 or a contents flood loss in excess of $50,000 within the prior five years are not eligible for coverage. The building coverage limit is $250,000 for Standard and Preferred Residential Dwellings for a total combined building limit of $500,000. Coverage has to be equal to 80 percent or more of current

---

333. *See, e.g.*, 570 Smith St. Realty Corp. v. Seneca Ins. Co., Inc., 2019 N.Y. Misc. LEXIS 1773 (Apr. 4, 2019) (as reflected in "other insurance" provision, defendant's coverage was excess with respect to NFIP-eligible properties).

334. *See, e.g.*, Barnett v. Fid. Nat'l Prop. & Cas. Co., 157 So. 3d 51 (La. App.), *writ den.*, 120 So. 3d 703 (La. 2013) (where property owners were ineligible for coverage under NFIP because property was located in Coastal Barrier Resource System, private coverage obtained with premium of about $3,500 and $10,000 deductible).

335. Pacific Specialty Insurance Company Excess Flood Insurance Program Agent's Manual, *available at* https://willow.psic-onespot.com/forms/XSF-MAN(I)_Ed.1.0.pdf.

replacement value or to the maximum limits if 80 percent is greater than them. The policy does not insure against any loss caused directly or indirectly by enforcement of any ordinance or law regulating the use, construction, repair, or demolition of property, including debris removal expense. A policy will not be issued to cover more than one building described in the application.

[7] Policy Contents

[a] Definitions Follow Form

When the excess policy follows form, the definitions in the primary policy apply to the excess policy unless it states otherwise. The definition of "flood" can be critical to the liability of the excess carrier. During Hurricane Katrina, a Louisiana casino barge was detached from its moorings and carried across an interstate highway. The primary policy defined flood as "[a] general and temporary condition of partial or complete inundation of normally dry land areas from . . . the overflow of inland or tidal waters." Two excess carriers issued policies with exclusions for flood. They argued the loss was caused by storm surge, which was an excluded flood. The court, however, found that the definition in the primary policy did not expressly exclude wind-driven inundations of water and was not, therefore, sufficient to communicate an exclusion for storm surge, which is a specific type of flood. The ambiguity was construed in favor of coverage.[336]

[b] Exclusions Follow Form

Unless the excess policy provides otherwise, the exclusions in the primary policy apply to the excess coverage. For example, where a primary policy contained a water damage exclusion that defined water to include that which backed up from a sewer or drain and the excess carrier's policy did not, the court found that because the excess policy in no way negated or contradicted the water exclusion in the primary policy, the exclusion in the primary policy applied.[337]

At the same time, an excess insurer cannot have the benefit of an interpretation of an exclusion that would not apply to the primary policy. For example, during a storm, a portion of a bluff on which an insured residence sat collapsed into the ocean. Two days later the home was condemned. The primary policy was an SFIP that covered erosion and collapse as a "flood," but not *gradual* erosion, which was specifically excluded. The primary insurer paid the policy limit. The excess carrier, however, invoked the gradual erosion

336. Pinnacle Entm't, Inc. v. Allianz Global Risks US Ins. Co., 2008 U.S. Dist. LEXIS 108583 (D. Nev. Mar. 26, 2008).

337. Ace Am. Ins. Co. v. Adm'rs of the Tulane Educ. Fund, 2008 U.S. Dist. LEXIS 66299 (E.D. La. Aug. 28, 2008).

exclusion. The court denied summary judgment to the excess carrier because it found that, viewed in favor of the insureds, a fact-finder could reasonably find that the loss after the storm was not from "gradual erosion," but from a covered collapse.[338]

An excess policy can both follow form *and* contain a broad exclusion that swallows limited coverage in the primary policy. A Louisiana case illustrates this principle.[339] In the case, the primary policy provided some flood coverage. The follow the form excess policy had an endorsement excluding coverage for "electronic data," but an exception to that exclusion stated it did not apply to loss or damage caused by or resulting from the perils of flood if and to the extent flood was "already covered by this or by an underlying policy." The insureds contended the excess policy, therefore, offered flood coverage for electronic data or electronic media as a follow form policy because the primary policy offered some flood coverage. The court, however, noted that the excess policy had an unambiguous flood exclusion, and it refused to create flood coverage out of an exception to another exclusion.

[c] Deductibles Follow Form

Unless the excess policy provides otherwise,[340] the deductible is determined by the primary policy. For example, in a New York case,[341] the insured had $20 million in primary flood loss coverage and $40 million in excess flood loss coverage. The question before the court was what was the applicable deductible for flood coverage under the primary policy and, therefore, the threshold level of losses at which the excess carriers were liable under their policies? Under the primary policy, if the property was located in a high hazard flood zone, the deductible was 5 percent of the property's replacement cost value subject to a $100,000 minimum. The insured had a claim of over $100 million, and the primary insurer paid $20 million. The first-layer excess insurers paid their limit of $30 million, and the second-layer excess insurers paid $29.5 million of their $50 million in coverage. The insured sought the remaining $20.5 million from the second-layer excess insurers arguing the deductible was the minimum $100,000. The court, however, held that the quote to which

338. Furrow v. Wright Nat'l Flood Ins. Co., 2016 U.S. Dist. LEXIS 159547 (D. Mass. Nov. 17, 2016).

339. Orleans Parish Sch. Bd. v. Lexington Ins. Co., 95 So. 3d 1205 (La. App. 2012).

340. *See* Axis Surplus Ins. Co. v. Innisfree Hotels, Inc., 2006 U.S. Dist. LEXIS 73230 (S.D. Ala. Oct. 5, 2006), where the underlying policies covered flood loss, but the excess policy specifically excluded it. The excess policy also stated that only losses that would have been payable under the excess policy would contribute to the satisfaction, reduction, or exhaustion of underlying limits. Thus, if a certain category of loss—in this case flood—was not subject to payment under the excess policy, then losses within that category, even if paid by underlying insurers, would not count toward the threshold that had to be satisfied before coverage was triggered under the excess policy.

341. Aspen Specialty Ins. Co. v. 4 NYP Ventures LLC, 162 F. Supp. 3d 337 (S.D.N.Y. 2016).

the insured agreed provided for a combined property value of $384.2 million, making the deductible $19.2 million. While the minimum flood deductible was $100,000, the high hazard flood zone deductible in the primary policy applied to the excess policies.

[d] Special Deductibles

Special deductibles in an excess policy can be at issue. For example, an excess policy had a general deductible of $75 million. It also had Special Deductible Endorsement providing that loss or damage from mechanical or electrical breakdown would be subject to a $50,000 deductible in lieu of any other policy deductible amounts *except* those for flood. In a flood, the property suffered a loss to electrical switching panels allegedly caused by electrical arcing. The underlying insurers paid for the loss, but the excess carrier denied coverage, contending it had been caused by, or resulted directly from, flooding and therefore the $50,000 deductible in the endorsement *did not* displace the $75 million deductible in the policy. The court agreed. The endorsement, averred the court, unambiguously provided that the $50,000 deductible did not apply if another deductible for flooding damage did. Damage to mechanical or electrical equipment proximately caused by flooding came within the exception to the $50,000 Special Deductible Endorsement and, therefore, the $75 million deductible applied.[342]

[e] Sublimits[343]

An excess policy may have a specific flood sublimit. In that event, despite the fact that the excess policy may be "all-risk" and covers all perils not specifically excluded, the sublimit may serve to reduce the excess insurer's liability for flood losses.[344] A sublimit may apply to all losses, to all flood losses, or to all flood losses when a property is located in a prescribed flood zone.[345]

[f] Limits of Liability

The excess insurer's limit of liability is usually specifically excepted from following form. In most cases, that limit will be a stated amount that can be determined easily from the face of the policy. However, one needs to be alert to complex limit formulations. For example, one excess policy provided that

---

342. Continental Ins. Co. v. Arkwright Mut. Ins. Co., 102 F.3d 30, 32 (1st Cir. 1996).

343. See § 4.6[3], *supra* on sublimits generally.

344. *See, e.g.*, Dillard Univ. v. Lexington Ins. Co., 2009 U.S. Dist. LEXIS 46785 (E.D. La. June 3, 2009).

345. *See, e.g.*, Certain Underwriters at Lloyd's, London v. Travelers Prop. Cas. Co. of Am., 161 Wn. App. 265, 256 P.3d 368 (2011), where a flood endorsement had $1 million sublimit for properties located in Flood Zone A.

in the event of loss the carrier's liability would be limited, in any one "occurrence," to the *least* of:

- The actual adjusted amount of the loss, less applicable deductibles and primary and underlying excess limits;
- 115 percent of the individually stated value for each scheduled item of property insured at the location that had the loss as shown on the latest Statement of Values, less applicable deductibles and primary and underlying excess limits; and
- The limit of liability shown on the Declarations Page of the policy or as endorsed to the policy.

The coverage was for nine different properties, all of which were damaged by Hurricane Katrina. An "occurrence" was defined as an event causing a loss or series of losses and, in the case of a hurricane-related occurrence, the policy covered all hurricane-related losses occurring within a 72-hour period. Therefore, said the court, the properties were damaged in a single occurrence and the limit of liability formula applied. The insurer contended it could choose a different measure for each property, and the insured responded that only one of the three measurements should apply to all the properties. The court agreed with the insured. "The policy definitions of 'loss' and 'occurrence'" said the court, "both contemplate a series of losses subject to the Limit of Liability clause. Therefore, the valuation method should be applied uniformly to all the losses in a series."[346]

[8] Exhaustion of Primary Coverage

[a] Generally

The point of excess insurance is to cover a loss that exceeds the limit of the underlying primary policy. Therefore, the excess carrier should have no liability until the coverage provided by that underlying policy is exhausted. Of course, with insurance nothing is ever that simple. How the excess insurance policy defines "exhaustion" determines the carrier's liability. Courts, interpreting policy language, may require "actual exhaustion" or "functional exhaustion."

The discussion below generally assumes that there is a primary and single excess policy so that the issue is the exhaustion of the limits of the primary policy. However, there are often layers of excess coverage, in which case there may be an issue of whether a layer of coverage has been exhausted, triggering coverage by the next layer. As a general rule, the principles outlined below apply when there are multiple layers of excess coverage.

---

346. ARM Props. Mgmt. Group v. RSUI Indem. Co., 2008 U.S. Dist. LEXIS 108624 (W.D. Tex. Aug. 22, 2008).

[b] Functional Exhaustion

The leading case on "functional exhaustion" is almost a century old.[347] In that case, a dressmaker purchased property insurance totaling $15,000 in coverage and an excess policy. His property was burglarized, and he lost more than $15,000 in property. He filed claims for $15,000 under the primary coverage but settled for $6,000. Because the losses exceeded $15,000, he also filed a claim under the excess policy. He argued the excess policy was triggered even though he settled the primary claim for less than face value.[348] The First Circuit said that the insured should have been allowed to prove the amount of his loss, and, if it was greater than the amount of the expressed limits of the primary insurance, then he was entitled to recover from the excess carrier to the extent of the policy. That policy provided for exhaustion in payment of claims "to the full amount of the expressed limits." Claims are paid to the full amount of the policies, said the court, if they are settled and discharged, thereby exhausting the coverage of the primary insurance. "Payment" should not be interpreted only to mean payment in cash, as the word is often used to mean the satisfaction of a claim by compromise, or in other ways. The court acknowledged that there were decisions holding that "exhausted in the payment of claims" required collection from the primary policy as a condition precedent to recover excess insurance, but could see nothing in the policy before it to require "a construction so burdensome."

The majority of courts have agreed with the First Circuit.[349] Another federal circuit court explained that settlement with a primary insurer *functionally* exhausts primary coverage and triggers an excess policy, although by settling, the policyholder loses any right to coverage of the difference between the settlement amount and the limits of the primary insurance, and thus the excess carrier cannot be made liable for any part of that difference because it would not have agreed to pay for losses below the limits of the underlying primary coverage.[350] Courts, therefore, have not required excess insurers to cover the difference between any settlement amount and the limits of the primary insurance.[351]

---

347. Zeig v. Mass. Bonding & Ins. Co., 23 F.2d 665 (2d Cir. 1928).

348. The *Zeig* court did not relate the facts of the case, but a more recent opinion by that court did. *See* Mehdi Ali v. Fed. Ins. Co., 719 F.3d 83, 93 (2d Cir. 2013).

349. O'Connor, *Insurance Coverage Settlements and the Rights of Excess Insurers*, 62 Md. L. Rev. 30, 52 (2003) (vast majority of courts considering below-limits settlements have adopted analysis in *Zeig*).

350. Koppers Co. v. Aetna Cas. & Sur. Co., 98 F.3d 1440, 1454 (3d Cir. 1996). The court said that rule encourages settlement and allows an insured to obtain the benefit of its bargain with the excess insurer, while preventing the insured from obtaining a double recovery.

351. Douglas R. Richmond, *The Tiresome Problem of Exhaustion in Excess Insurance, New Appleman on Insurance: Current Critical Issues in Insurance Law* § III.D (Spring 2014) (as long as excess insurer's attachment point is not lowered—and no court that has recognized

A Minnesota federal court followed that reasoning in a flood case.[352] The plaintiff policyholder sued its insurance broker for failure to procure the excess coverage the plaintiff requested. It had flood coverage of $50 million in two layers but suffered flood losses in excess of $100 million. It settled with its insurer for $34.5 million and agreed to absorb the loss between that amount and the limit of the policies. The plaintiff alleged its broker was at fault for procuring an excess policy that was worded too narrowly to encompass its losses and sought $50 million in damages from the broker, the amount of excess coverage it claimed it asked the broker to obtain. The broker moved to dismiss because the plaintiff had not alleged that it collected or received a judgment entitling it to the entire of underlying insurance coverage. It argued that because the plaintiff settled with the underlying insurers, it had not exhausted the limit of those underlying policies and an excess policy could not have attached. The court disagreed and denied the motion. The court held that the plaintiff had exhausted the limits of its underlying policies by agreeing to settle with the carriers and choosing to absorb the losses between that sum and the limits of those policies. If the allegations in the complaint were proven true, said the court, the broker's alleged failure to procure adequate excess insurance coverage at the $50 million layer could have caused substantial harm to the plaintiff.

[c] Actual Exhaustion

Commentators agree that courts are increasingly less likely to find "functional exhaustion" and more likely to hold that an excess insurer has no obligation to pay anything on a claim if the policyholder settled with the underlying insurer without obtaining payment of the full policy limits.[353] That, however, is not necessarily because they disagree with the reasoning of earlier decisions that impose liability under "functional exhaustion," but because of changing policy language.[354] As one observer has said, ". . . courts are increasingly

---

functional exhaustion has required excess insurer to drop down—its indemnity obligation is unchanged).

352. Archer Daniels Midland v. Aon Risk Servs., Inc., 1999 U.S. Dist. LEXIS 23527 (D. Minn. Feb. 25, 1999). *See also* Underwood v. Nationwide Mut. Fire Ins. Co., 2008 U.S. Dist. LEXIS 134850 (N.D. Fla. July 16, 2008) (policy was silent about whether full amount of primary coverage needed to be collected or actually paid out before excess coverage was triggered).

353. One caveat is that the vast majority of cases rejecting "functional exhaustion" have interpreted excess *liability* policies, not first-party property polices. There are reasons for treating them differently. For one, the former generally require the insurer to defend the insured in an underlying suit as well as indemnify the insured for any judgment against it. *See* Mehdi Ali v. Fed. Ins. Co., 719 F.3d 83, 93 (2d Cir. 2013) (nothing is inherently errant or unusual about interpreting exhaustion clause in excess liability insurance policy differently than similarly written clause in first-party property insurance policy).

354. *See, e.g.*, O'Connor, *Caveat Settlor: Insurance Coverage Settlements and the Triumph of Policy Language over Precedent*, 79 Alb. L. Rev. 101, 102 (2015) (shift away from "functional exhaustion" is not result of change in judicial philosophy, but because policy language

willing to require actual exhaustion of primary policies to trigger excess coverage where the terms of excess . . . policies plainly require it."[355]

The American Law Institute, in a comment to its Restatement, says that "functional exhaustion" can be avoided by excess carriers simply by including a policy provision similar to "[l]iability under this excess policy shall attach only after the underlying insurers have paid the full amount of the underlying limits" or "[c]overage under this policy shall attach only after the full amount of the underlying limits has been paid by the underlying insurers."[356] In one of the leading cases on actual exhaustion, the excess policy contained an "exhaustion clause" that provided that the excess insurer would be liable only after the insurers under each underlying policy had paid or *had been held liable to pay* the full amount of the underlying limit.[357] The Fifth Circuit in a single opinion examined the language of four different excess policies. The pertinent language in each policy stated as follows:

- Coverage attached only after all underlying carriers had paid in cash the full amount of their respective liabilities, the full amount of the underlying policies had been collected by the plaintiffs, the insureds or the insureds' counsel, and all underlying insurance had been exhausted.
- The insurer would only be liable to make payment under the excess policy after the total amount of the underlying limit of liability had been paid in legal currency by the insurers of the underlying insurance as covered loss thereunder.
- Excess coverage attached only after any insurer subscribing to any underlying policy had agreed to pay or had been held liable to pay the full amount of its respective limits of liability.[358]

---

they are being asked to construe has changed; cases where courts have held that below-limits settlements render excess coverage inaccessible invariably involve unambiguous policy language that permits no other result).

355. Douglas R. Richmond, *The Tiresome Problem of Exhaustion in Excess Insurance, New Appleman on Insurance: Current Critical Issues in Insurance Law* § III.C (Spring 2014). *See also* Stempel, *An Analytic "Gap": The Perils of Relentless Enforcement of Payment-by-Underlying-Insurer-Only Language in Excess Insurance Policies*, 52 Tort & Ins. L.J. 807 (2017) (more recent decisions have been receptive to enforcing policy language requiring that underlying limit may be satisfied *only* through payment by underlying insurer); Michael F. Aylward, *Excess: The New Frontier, New Appleman on Insurance: Current Critical Issues in Insurance Law* § V.A.1 (July 2008).

356. Restatement of the Law of Liability Insurance § 39 cmt. d (ALI 2019).

357. Qualcomm, Inc. v. Certain Underwriters at Lloyd's, London, 73 Cal. Rptr. 3d 770, 774, 161 Cal. App. 4th 184, 189 (2008).

358. Note that this wording does require that payment has been made, only that the primary carrier has agreed or been ordered to pay. That raises the question of whether a mere commitment to pay the limit of the primary policy should be treated as actual payment in determining if the underlying limit has been exhausted. Michael F. Aylward, *Excess: The New Frontier, New Appleman on Insurance: Current Critical Issues in Insurance Law* § V.A.4 (July 2008).

- Excess coverage attached in the event of exhaustion of all of the limit(s) of liability of the underlying insurance solely as a result of payment of loss thereunder.

In each case, the Fifth Circuit found that "the plain language of the policies dictate that the primary insurer pays the full amount of its limits of liability before excess coverage is triggered."[359] As one commentator noted, "The more specific an excess policy is in requiring actual payment of the underlying limits of primary insurance or lower-level excess insurance, obviously, the stronger the excess insurer's argument for actual exhaustion."[360] The burden, as discussed below, is on the insured to show ambiguity that should be construed against the excess insurer, and the more specific the policy language, the less likely a court will find any ambiguity.

The triggering language may be specific enough for a court to find exhaustion in the face of the excess carrier's claims that the underlying insurers paid claims they should not have. For example, in one case,[361] the policy said the excess insurer's liability attached only after the primary and underlying excess insurers had paid, or had admitted liability, for the full amount of their respective ultimate net loss liability as set forth in a schedule. The underlying insurers paid their limits, but the excess insurer argued they failed to take advantage of exceptions in their coverage or otherwise overpaid. The court, however said that was not relevant to the issue of whether the excess insurer's liability had attached. The simple fact that both underlying insurers paid their policy limits as defined in the excess insurance contract was sufficient to trigger the duties of the excess carrier.

[d] Payment by Primary Insurer Must Be for Flood Loss

Generally, for the exhaustion requirement to be met, the losses that exceed the primary limit have to be attributable to a peril actually covered under the primary policy.[362] It is possible that flood is only one of the perils covered by the primary policy. In the case of an excess flood policy then, the loss that exhausts the limit of the primary policy must be a flood loss. That can be

---

359. Citigroup Inc. v. Fed. Ins. Co., 649 F.3d 367, 372 (5th Cir. 2011).

360. Douglas R. Richmond, *The Tiresome Problem of Exhaustion in Excess Insurance, New Appleman on Insurance: Current Critical Issues in Insurance Law* § III.A (Spring 2014). *See also* Aylward, *Paying to Play: What Does It Mean to "Exhaust" Underlying Insurance?* (May 2012), For the Defense, https://www.morrisonmahoney.com/writable/resources/documents/underlyinginsurance-aylward.pdf (courts generally apply "actual exhaustion" when policies explicitly require actual payment of limits, but when policies do not mention exhaustion requirements or insuring language reads ambiguously, courts are more likely to side with insureds).

361. ARM Props. Mgmt. Group v. RSUI Indem. Co., 2008 U.S. Dist. LEXIS 108624 (W.D. Tex. Aug. 22, 2008).

362. Michael F. Aylward, *Excess: The New Frontier, New Appleman on Insurance: Current Critical Issues in Insurance Law* § V.A.3 (July 2008).

complicated by the fact that the primary policy likely has a flood sublimit. For example, consider a property owner who obtains an all-risk commercial property policy with a $5 million aggregate limit and a $1 million sublimit for flood. The property owner also procures an excess flood policy. The property is damaged in a storm by both the waters of a storm surge and rainwater that enters the building when the roof is torn open by wind, both covered perils under the primary policy. The insured claims losses of $2 million. The primary insurer pays $1.25 million for the losses it determines were caused by covered perils, but does not segregate those losses according to perils even though it may have estimated that the flooding resulted in approximately $750,000 of the damage.[363] If the insured submits a claim to the excess insurer, that carrier will almost certainly deny it on the grounds that the insured has not proven that the flood losses exceeded the sublimit of the primary policy. To succeed, either with the excess carrier or in court, the insured will need to have the damage investigated and establish that it had *flood* losses that exceeded $1 million.[364] Of course, had there been no sublimit, the insured would have had no possibility of recovery from the excess carrier as the losses it claimed did not exceed the aggregate limit. Even if it claimed losses exceeding that limit, it could only recover from the excess flood insurer losses for flood that exceed the limit. Thus, if the primary carrier paid $4.5 million for non-flood losses and $500,000 for flood losses, but the insured claimed $1 million in flood losses, it could seek recovery from the excess flood carrier.

The hypothetical above assumes that the excess policy follows form, but not all excess policies do. For example, in one case,[365] the excess policy said first that "in determining the amount of any one loss, disaster, or casualty for which this policy is excess, the total loss for all coverages caused by any combination of perils, one or more of which is insured against under the primary

363. Whether the primary insurer segregates losses by peril can be enormously important to the insured. *See, e.g.*, Stewart Enters. v. RSUI Indem. Co., 614 F.3d 117, 124 (5th Cir. 2010), where the court presents a hypothetical in which if the underlying insurers allocated all losses to flood and paid the limits of the policies, the insured would receive $25 million less from the second layer excess carrier than if the underlying insurers allocated all losses to wind.

364. The insured has the burden of segregating covered perils from non-covered ones. Ace Am. Ins. Co. v. Adm'rs of the Tulane Educ. Fund, 2008 U.S. Dist. LEXIS 66299 (E.D. La. Aug. 28, 2008). The importance of having an expert investigate the damage and prepare a report on its causes and cost is illustrated in *Markey v. La. Citizens Fair Plan*, 2008 U.S. Dist. LEXIS 16773 (E.D. La. Mar. 5, 2008), where the court initially found that the cost of wind damage did not exceed the limit of the primary policy and, therefore, the excess wind insurer had no liability and the court granted summary judgement to it. The policyholders moved for reconsideration and submitted an expert's report showing that the wind-related damage could exceed the primary policy limit. The court granted the motion for reconsideration because there had been no showing that policyholder exercised anything other than due diligence in obtaining the new information about the wind claim, and the evidence was material and controlling and clearly would have produced a different result if present with the original motion.

365. Archer-Daniels-Midland Co. v. Phoenix Assur. Co., 975 F. Supp. 1129 (S.D. Ill. 1997).

policy, shall be used even though all such perils or coverages are not insured against under this excess policy." That was followed by a clause reading: "any recoveries made under the primary policy shall be considered as first applying to those perils and/or coverages not insured against by this policy. Upon exhaustion of the primary policy limits, this policy shall drop down and be liable for the loss in excess of the amount attributed to the primary policy as respects those perils and/or coverages insured hereunder subject to the limit of this policy." Under the hypothetical, if the $1.25 million recovery is applied first to the peril not insured against by the excess policy—rainwater that entered the building through the damaged roof—then the flood sublimit is not applicable and the $5 million aggregate limit of the primary policy has not been exhausted. It will avail the insured nothing to segregate the loss by perils.

[e] Coverage for an "Occurrence"

Whether losses are from a single occurrence or not may determine whether the liability of an excess insurer is triggered. For example, in an Alabama case,[366] a primary property policy provided $100,000 for each occurrence, and the excess policy covered each occurrence that exceeded that amount. The roof of the insured building leaked, causing merchandise in it to be damaged. A roofing company was hired to repair the roof, and its failure to effectively cover a portion of the roof on which it was working resulted in additional damage caused by rainfall. The damages exceeded $100,000, and the two insurance companies disputed whether the losses were from one or two occurrences. The excess insurer of course argued that there were two occurrences because if the limit was not exceeded in either occurrence, its coverage was not triggered. The court sided with the excess carrier and found there were two occurrences. Evidently the primary insurer attempted to convince the court to apply case law based on the NFIA definition of occurrence. The court, however, said it was not persuaded by cases addressing the application of occurrence clauses in insurance policies to claims for flood damage because federal law on what constitutes a single occurrence from flood water "is very specialized and has little application to the case at hand."

The Alabama case is merely illustrative. The number of occurrences is determined by reference to the definition of "occurrence" in the policy and by the courts. Many commercial property policies do not define the term, but the general rule is that "an occurrence is determined by the cause or causes of the resulting injury" and the focus is on the "underlying cause of the injury, not the injury or claim itself."[367] The law of the pertinent jurisdiction and the distinctive facts surrounding an event will be determinative.

---

366. United States Fire Ins. Co. v. Safeco Ins. Co., 444 So. 2d 844 (Ala. 1983).

367. Camerlengo, *The Timeless Question of "How Many Occurrences?,"* 50 The Brief 50, 51 (2021). *See also* Eyerly, Carmel & Aldama, *Determining the Number of Occurrences and*

The definition of "occurrence" may refer to an excluded peril, but that does not eliminate the exclusion. For example, where the definition included hurricanes and ensuing water damage, it did not obviate a flood exclusion because the purpose of the definition was simply to state the number of times that the excess insurer might potentially be liable for the policy limits in a particular situation.[368]

[f] Application of Sublimit

In a case decided by a Washington State appellate court,[369] the policy provided $10 million ordinance and law coverage and added flood coverage by endorsement with a sublimit of $1 million. The insured property was flooded and had a flood-related claim including costs for repair of physical damage and for compliance with applicable building codes. The excess insurer argued the underlying coverage was not exhausted until $10 million was paid. The underlying carrier agreed it owed $1 million and asserted its coverage was then exhausted. The court found that underlying policy provided a maximum of $1 million coverage for *all* flood loss and that the excess carrier offered nothing to rebut that conclusion.

[g] Burden of Proof

Exhaustion of the underlying policy is a condition of coverage by an excess policy. Generally, the policyholder bears the burden of proof for all conditions precedent to coverage.[370] Thus, the burden is on the policyholder to prove exhaustion.[371] That, however, begs the question: what exactly does the policyholder have to prove? In one case, the court found the policyholder had failed to properly plead exhaustion of the directly underlying insurance. However, the court granted leave to amend to properly plead exhaustion and added that the policyholder would not be required to show actual exhaustion of the underlying policy in the form of payment to it because to require the insured

---

Its Effect on Coverage, ABA Coverage J. (Winter 2016); Maloney, *The Application of "Per-Occurrence" Deductible Provisions in First-Party Property Claims*, 37 Tort & Ins. L.J. 921 (2002) (discussing three prevailing theories for determining number of occurrences).

368. Ace Am. Ins. Co. v. Adm'rs of the Tulane Educ. Fund, 2008 U.S. Dist. LEXIS 66299 (E.D. La. Aug. 28, 2008).

369. Certain Underwriters at Lloyd's, London v. Travelers Prop. Cas. Co. of Am., 161 Wn. App. 265, 256 P.3d 368 (2011).

370. Scottsdale Ins. Co. v. Byrne, 913 F.3d 221, 228, n.6 (1st Cir. 2019); W. Alliance Ins. Co. v. N. Ins. Co., 176 F.3d 825, 831 (5th Cir. 1999).

371. National Elec. Mfrs. Ass'n v. Gulf Underwriters Ins. Co., 162 F.3d 821, 826 (4th Cir. 1998) (burden was on insured to establish compliance with all policy conditions, and it failed to demonstrate that it has exhausted its primary or other excess insurance); General Refractories Co. v. Allstate Ins. Co., 1994 U.S. Dist. LEXIS 7561 (E.D. Pa. June 8, 1994) (condition precedent to excess insurer's liability is exhaustion of primary insurance and, thus, insured has to establish that it has exhausted limits of each primary policy).

to actually to collect the full amount of the primary coverage to exhaust that insurance would be "unnecessarily stringent."[372]

The issue may be whether a loss is covered or excluded because, of course, if a loss is caused by an excluded peril, it does not apply to determining whether the primary coverage has been exhausted. The insurer always bears the burden of proving an exclusion applies, but after that, the insured bears the burden of segregating the amount of covered losses from excluded losses.[373]

[9] Insolvency of Primary Insurer

Counsel seeking to recover from an excess insurer on behalf of a client needs to be aware of the consequences of the insolvency of the primary insurer.[374] This is a complex topic that is thoroughly discussed elsewhere,[375] so it is raised here merely to alert counsel to pertinent issues. Moreover, it will only arise when the primary coverage is provided by a private insurer, not by a FEMA SFIP because, while the National Flood Insurance Program is deeply in debt,[376] it borrows from the Department of the Treasury, which presumably cannot become insolvent.

The question from the insured when the primary insurer is insolvent and unable to pay the claim at issue is: will the excess insurer "drop down" to provide coverage the primary insurer would otherwise have paid?[377] The general rule is that the answer to the question is to be found in the excess coverage policy. When an excess policy defines its coverage as in excess of "the limits of the underlying insurance" or by referring to "the amounts specified" in the primary policy, the excess carrier has not been required to drop down to afford coverage below the amount stated.[378] Some courts have held that when

372. Fisher Sci. Co., L.L.C. v. AIU Ins. Co., 2008 Pa. Dist. & Cnty. Dec. LEXIS 185 (Jan. 22, 2008).

373. Ace Am. Ins. Co. v. Adm'rs of the Tulane Educ. Fund, 2008 U.S. Dist. LEXIS 66299 (E.D. La. Aug. 28, 2008).

374. When a primary carrier becomes insolvent, the insured may be able to recover at least a portion of a claim from a state Guaranty Fund. *See* 9 Jeffrey E. Thomas, *New Appleman on Insurance Law Library Edition* §§ 106,01, *et seq.* (Matthew Bender 2022) for a discussion of this abstruse area of law.

375. *See* 9 Jeffrey E. Thomas, *New Appleman on Insurance Law Library Edition* § 102.03 (Matthew Bender 2022); Stempel, *An Analytic "Gap": The Perils of Relentless Enforcement of Payment-by-Underlying-Insurer-Only Language in Excess Insurance Policies*, 52 Tort & Ins. L.J. 807 (2017); Richmond, *Rights and Responsibilities of Excess Insurers*, 78 Denv. U.L. Rev. 29, 86–92 (2000).

376. "As of August 2020, FEMA's debt was $20.5 billion despite Congress having canceled $16 billion in debt in October 2017." National Flood Insurance Program, U.S. GAO, https://www.gao.gov/highrisk/national-flood-insurance-program.

377. 9 Jeffrey E. Thomas, *New Appleman on Insurance Law Library Edition* § 102.03[1] (Matthew Bender 2022).

378. Michael F. Aylward, *Excess: The New Frontier, New Appleman on Insurance: Current Critical Issues in Insurance Law* § IV.B.1 (July 2008).

the excess policy language says the coverage is excess to "collectible" or "valid and collectible" insurance, an excess insurer must drop down to substitute coverage for the insolvent primary insurer.[379] Other policy language that may result in coverage by an excess insurer includes "loss payable" clauses[380] and statements that coverage is in excess of the amounts "recoverable" from the primary insurer or that the excess coverage applies when the underlying limits of the primary policy have been "reduced or exhausted."[381]

[10] Service of Suit Clause

Lloyd's of London writes many excess insurance policies in the United States.[382] Those policies may contain a "service of suit" clause reading:

> It is agreed that in the event of the failure of Underwriters hereon to pay any amount claimed to be due hereunder, Underwriters hereon, at the request of the Assured will submit to the jurisdiction of any court of competent jurisdiction within the United States and will comply with all requirements necessary to give such Court jurisdiction and all matters arising hereunder shall be determined in accordance with the law and practice of such court.[383]

Generally, in a service of suit clause an insurance company agrees to submit to the jurisdiction of the court in which a policyholder has filed a coverage action, but the clause is not considered a "choice of law" provision.[384] However, there are courts that have construed the words "law and practice" as referring to the substantive law or conflict of law rules of the forum.[385] Therefore, counsel bringing suit against an excess insurer should carefully review the language of any service of suit clause in the policy.

---

379. 9 Jeffrey E. Thomas, *New Appleman on Insurance Law Library Edition* § 102.03[3][a][ii] (Matthew Bender 2022).

380. 9 Jeffrey E. Thomas, *New Appleman on Insurance Law Library Edition* § 102.03[3][a][iii] (Matthew Bender 2022).

381. 9 Jeffrey E. Thomas, *New Appleman on Insurance Law Library Edition* § 102.03[3][a][iv] (Matthew Bender 2022).

382. Marick, *Excess Insurance: An Overview of General Principles and Current Issues*, 24 Tort & Ins. L.J. 715 (1989).

383. McDermott International, Inc. v. Lloyds Underwriters of London, 944 F.2d 1199 (5th Cir. 1991).

384. 1 Jeffrey E. Thomas, *New Appleman on Insurance Law Library Edition* § 7.07[2][b] (Matthew Bender 2022).

385. 1 Jeffrey E. Thomas, *New Appleman on Insurance Law Library Edition* § 6.07[2][b] (Matthew Bender 2022).

5

Recovering under a FEMA Standard Flood Insurance Policy

5.1 Introduction

[1] The National Flood Insurance Program

The National Flood Insurance Act (NFIA) was enacted in 1968.[1] It was intended to share the risk of flood loss through affordable insurance for property owners at a time when premiums charged by private insurers were seen as prohibitively expensive.[2] The Act created the National Flood Insurance Program (NFIP) to implement its provisions.[3] From its inception until 1979, the NFIP was administered by the United States Department of Housing and Urban Development. After that, the Federal Insurance and Mitigation Administration (FIMA) of the Federal Emergency Management Agency (FEMA) began administering the program.[4] In 2003, FEMA became part of the Department of Homeland Security (DHS).

[2] The "Write Your Own" Program

In 1983, FEMA adopted regulations that established the "Write Your Own" (WYO) Program.[5] Under the program, private insurers—called WYO

1. *National Flood Insurance Program Flood Insurance Manual*, at 1-1 (FEMA Apr. 2021).

2. Majmudar, *The National Flood Insurance Program: Maintaining Its Head Above Water*, 16 U. Miami Int'l & Comp. L. Rev. 183, 188–89 (2009); Richards, *The National Flood Insurance Program: A "Flood" of Controversy*, 82 Fla. Bar J. 8 (2008); Pham, *The Future of The National Flood Insurance Program in the Aftermath of Hurricane Katrina*, 12 Conn. Ins. L.J. 629 (2005/2006).

3. Herke, *Teething Pains at Age 25: Developing Meaningful Enforcement of the National Flood Insurance Program*, 7 Tul. Envtl. L.J. 165, 169 (1993).

4. *National Flood Insurance Program Flood Insurance Manual*, at 1-1 (FEMA Apr. 2021).

5. *National Flood Insurance Program Flood Insurance Manual*, at 1-1 (FEMA Apr. 2021).

companies[6]—may sell NFIP flood insurance policies—called a Standard Flood Insurance Policy (SFIP)—and adjust and pay claims arising under those policies.[7] They may market NFIP flood coverage packaged with their typical property insurance policies.[8] Under the program, applications and administration are the responsibility of the private insurers, while the federal government guarantees coverage for flood losses and funds the indemnity when there is a claim.[9] In other words, the government serves as the guarantor for the WYO insurers,[10] but those insurers write and service the SFIP under their own names.[11] The insurers act as fiscal agents but not as general ones.[12] They issue the policy, collect the premium, and pay the claims.[13] A 2011 United States Senate report stated that approximately 85 percent of SFIPs were sold through WYO insurers, while the rest were sold through the NFIP by private insurance agents.[14]

WYO insurers may sell FEMA flood insurance to policyholders they insure under their own property business lines and may sell coverage in any state in which they are authorized to do business.[15] Generally, the insurer employs its own customary standards, staff, and independent contractor resources.[16] Insurers participating in the program have to encourage their property insurance policyholders to obtain flood insurance through the program.[17] If a WYO carrier rejects an application from an agent or producer, it has to notify that agent or producer of the rejection so the business can be placed through the NFIP Servicing Agent or another WYO carrier.[18] The coverage is issued on a

---

6. 44 C.F.R. § 62.23(b). The term includes intergovernmental risk-sharing pools for covering public entity structures.

7. 44 C.F.R. §§ 62.23(c), (d).

8. Pham, *The Future of The National Flood Insurance Program in the Aftermath of Hurricane Katrina*, 12 Conn. Ins. L.J. 629, 632 (2005/2006).

9. 44 C.F.R. § 62.23(f) (federal government is guarantor, and primary relationship between WYO insurer and government is "of a fiduciary nature"). *See also* Senate Report 112-98 on Flood Insurance Reform and Modernization Act of 2011 at 2 (Dec. 5, 2011).

10. Pham, *The Future of The National Flood Insurance Program in the Aftermath of Hurricane Katrina*, 12 Conn. Ins. L.J. 629, 632 (2005/2006).

11. Senate Report 112-98 on Flood Insurance Reform and Modernization Act of 2011 at 2 (Dec. 5, 2011).

12. 44 C.F.R. § 62.23(g).

13. French, *Insuring Floods: The Most Common and Devastating Natural Catastrophes in America*, 60 Vill. L. Rev. 53, 66 (2015). The WYO carriers are paid 1.5 percent of the amount paid to the insured as a fee for handling the claim. Niles v. Tex. Farmers Ins. Co., 2021 U.S. Dist. LEXIS 125851 (S.D. Tex. Apr. 27, 2021).

14. Senate Report 112-98 on Flood Insurance Reform and Modernization Act of 2011 at 2 (Dec. 5, 2011).

15. 44 C.F.R. § 62.23(a).

16. 44 C.F.R. § 62.23(e).

17. 44 C.F.R. § 62.23(h)(1).

18. 44 C.F.R. § 62.23(h)(5).

separate SFIP form, rather than added by endorsement to another policy.[19] When adjusting a claim, a WYO insurer uses its general company standards, guided by the NFIP claims manuals.[20]

[3] The Standard Flood Insurance Policy

[a] Generally

The SFIP comes in three forms: the Dwelling Form, the General Property Form, and the Residential Condominium Building Association Policy (RCBAP) form. The forms are nearly identical, although there are small differences. The main distinction between them is not their contents but the types of property they cover. Throughout this chapter, when the SFIP is discussed, the General Property Form will be cited except where there are differences between it and the other two forms.

By rule, the SFIP is authorized only under terms and conditions established by federal statute, the program regulations, the Federal Insurance Administrator's interpretations, and the express terms of the policy and, therefore, representations about the extent and scope of coverage that are not consistent with that federal statute, the program regulations, the Federal Insurance Administrator's interpretations, and the express terms of the policy are void.[21] There are policies in which the insured and the insurer agree on the value of the property insured, and that amount is then payable in the event of a total loss. These are called "valued policies." The SFIP is *not* a valued policy.[22]

Under the policy, if an insured has paid the full amount due of any applicable premiums, surcharges, and fees; has complied with all terms and conditions of the policy; and has furnished accurate information and statements, the insurer will pay for *direct physical loss* by or from flood to the insured property.[23]

[b] Insurable Interest

It is a fundamental precept of insurance that to obtain coverage, one must have an interest in the subject matter of the policy, which is known as an "insurable interest." FEMA defines "insurable interest" as "an interest in property to the extent that the owner of the interest derives a benefit from the preservation of the property and will suffer a loss from its destruction."[24] Determining insurable interest for a property is a fact-specific inquiry. Complex questions

19. 44 C.F.R. § 62.23(h)(6).
20. 44 C.F.R. § 62.23(i)(1).
21. 44 C.F.R. § 61.13(e).
22. General Property Form Standard Flood Insurance Policy, § II.C.30.
23. General Property Form Standard Flood Insurance Policy, § I.C.
24. *National Flood Insurance Program Claims Manual*, at 251 (Oct. 2021).

of insurable interest can arise with mixed-use buildings and buildings under multiple ownership. The NFIP can cover those buildings under either a single policy or multiple policies, depending in part on whether a single policy form or multiple forms apply. FEMA recommends that under those circumstances, adjusters contact the insurer for assistance, in which case the adjuster may be required to submit underwriting referrals. The adjuster is required to follow the insurer's underwriting reporting procedures.

FEMA provides examples of insurable interests. A mortgagee has an insurable interest in mortgaged property. A shareholder with an insurable interest in a non-residential property—for example, a building with cooperative form of ownership—may obtain an SFIP to protect its financial interest in the property from loss. An individual listed as an owner of an LLC that owns a residential building and who resides in that building may obtain an SFIP to protect his or her financial interest in the property from loss. An individual or entity with a financial interest in an estate that holds insurable property may obtain an SFIP to protect that interest from loss. If a tenant has sufficient interest in property under a rent-to-own agreement, the landlord and the tenant both have an insurable interest, and each may be named insureds under the SFIP.[25] In the case of a "capital lease," the leaseholder has an insurable interest in the leased property item, which he or she can claim under a loss, even if the property is not solely owned by the policyholder.

Where there is a question about insurable interest, the policyholder must provide the documentation in force at the time of the loss that indicates the names of all owners of the property in question; all owners and the policyholder must disclose and verify all lienholders for the property, including personal property contents; and the policyholder must provide the documentation in force at the time of the loss that indicates the vested financial interest that legally connects the policyholder to the other entities.[26] For an insurer to issue payment, it has to obtain a signed and sworn declaration (affidavit) by all owners and the policyholder that attests that no other interest owns the property in question and no other interest has a lien on the property. The insurer will, says FEMA, want all owning interests and the policyholder to sign a hold harmless agreement relieving the insurer of any claims made against the insurer for damage to property insured on the claimed date of loss from liability to any other entity, individual, or lienholder whose interest in the property was not disclosed to the insurer. Furthermore, FEMA states that it has to verify that no other SFIP is in force at the same location. The insurer

25. If a lease agreement requires a tenant to purchase building coverage, the building owner must be named on the policy but the tenant may also be named although the tenant does not have an insurable interest. Coverage for contents owned by the tenant must be written on a separate policy in the name of the tenant only, and generally tenants may not purchase building coverage if the owner or another party has purchased it on the same building.

26. *National Flood Insurance Program Claims Manual*, at 252 (Oct. 2021).

has to immediately endorse the policy with the names of all owners, individuals, and entities, with applicable lienholders for the respective property as declared.

[c] Dwelling Form

The Dwelling Form is issued to homeowners, residential renters, or owners of a residential building containing one to four units.[27] The policy provides building and/or contents coverage for

- Single-family, non-condominium residences with incidental occupancy limited to less than 50 percent of the total floor area;
- Two- to four-family, non-condominium buildings with incidental occupancy limited to less than 25 percent of the total floor area;
- Units in residential condominium buildings;
- Residential townhouses or rowhouses; and
- Personal contents in a non-residential building.

The maximum amount of building coverage is $250,000, and the maximum contents coverage is $100,000.[28]

[d] General Property Form

The General Property Form is issued to an owner or lessee of a non-residential business or other non-residential buildings or units.[29] The policy provides coverage for

- Hotels or motels;
- Licensed bed-and-breakfast inns;
- Retail shops, restaurants, or other businesses;
- Mercantile buildings;
- Grain bins, silos, or other farm buildings;
- Agricultural or industrial processing facilities;
- Factories;
- Warehouses;
- Pool houses, clubhouses, or other recreational buildings;
- Houses of worship;
- Schools;
- Nursing homes;
- Non-residential condominiums;
- Condominium buildings with less than 75 percent of total floor area in residential use;

27. *National Flood Insurance Program Flood Insurance Manual*, at 2-1 (FEMA Apr. 2021).
28. *National Flood Insurance Program Flood Insurance Manual*, at 3-3 (FEMA Apr. 2021).
29. *National Flood Insurance Program Flood Insurance Manual*, at 2-1 (FEMA Apr. 2021).

- Detached garages;
- Sheds;
- Stock, inventory, or other commercial contents; and
- Similar non-residential risks.

Additionally, the General Property Form is issued to an owner of a residential building with five or more units.[30] It provides coverage for apartment buildings, residential cooperative buildings, dormitories, assisted-living facilities, and hotels, motels, tourist homes, and rooming houses that have five or more units where the normal guest occupancy/stay is six months or more.

The maximum amount of building coverage is $500,000, and the maximum contents coverage is also $500,000.[31]

[e] Residential Condominium Building Association Policy

The Residential Condominium Building Association Policy (RCBAP) is issued to a residential condominium association on behalf of association and unit owners and provides building coverage and, if desired, coverage of commonly owned contents for a residential condominium building with 75 percent or more of its total floor area in residential use.[32] The policy insures against direct physical loss by or from flood to the residential condominium building described on the Declarations Page at the described location, including all units within the building and improvements within those units.[33]

The policy defines "condominium" as the form of "ownership of one or more buildings in which each unit owner has an undivided interest in common elements."[34] A "condominium building" is a type of building in which each unit owner has an undivided interest in common elements of the building.[35] A residential condominium building contains one or more family units in which at least 75 percent of the floor area is residential.[36] A "unit" is a single-family residential space in a residential condominium building.[37] Finally, a "condominium association" is an entity made up of unit owners responsible for maintenance and operation of common elements owned in undivided shares by unit owners and other buildings in which unit owners have use rights, where membership in the entity is a required condition of ownership.[38]

---

30. *National Flood Insurance Program Flood Insurance Manual*, at 2-2 (FEMA Apr. 2021).
31. *National Flood Insurance Program Flood Insurance Manual*, at 3-3 (FEMA Apr. 2021).
32. *National Flood Insurance Program Flood Insurance Manual*, at 2-2 (FEMA Apr. 2021).
33. Residential Condominium Building Association Standard Flood Insurance Policy, III.A.1.
34. Residential Condominium Building Association Standard Flood Insurance Policy, II.C.8.
35. Residential Condominium Building Association Standard Flood Insurance Policy, II.C.10.
36. Residential Condominium Building Association Standard Flood Insurance Policy, II.C.26.
37. Residential Condominium Building Association Standard Flood Insurance Policy, II.C.28.
38. Residential Condominium Building Association Standard Flood Insurance Policy, II.C.9.

The NFIP does not allow multiple building policies on a single building, but there is an exception is for residential condominium buildings.[39] A Dwelling Form policy with building coverage may be issued to a unit owner in a condominium building that is also insured under a RCBAP; however, no more than $250,000 may be paid in combined benefits for a single unit under the Dwelling Form and the RCBAP.[40] The insurer will only pay for damage once, so items of damage paid for under the RCBAP cannot also be claimed under the Dwelling Form policy.

[f] Scheduled Building Policy

The NFIP allows for a "Scheduled Building Policy" that provides a group of policies for buildings with the same ownership and the same location.[41] The properties where the buildings are located have to be contiguous. A single policy may cover anywhere from two to ten buildings and will require the insured to designate a specific amount of insurance for each building.

[g] Judicial Interpretation of the SFIP

The policy forms are all incorporated into the Code of Federal Regulations as appendices to FEMA rules. The policy states that it "and all disputes arising from the insurer's policy issuance, policy administration, or the handling of any claim under the policy are governed exclusively by the flood insurance regulations issued by FEMA, the National Flood Insurance Act of 1968, as amended . . . and Federal common law."[42] Therefore, courts hold that state insurance regulations do not apply to the policy or to insurers' actions.[43] Moreover, because the policy forms are found in the Code of Federal Regulations, they are law and policyholders have constructive knowledge of their contents. For that reason, courts say that ambiguity in the policy is not, as is usually the case, construed in favor of the insured.[44] They also generally refuse

39. *National Flood Insurance Program Flood Insurance Manual*, at 2-14 (FEMA Apr. 2021).

40. Residential Condominium Building Association Standard Flood Insurance Policy, § I.G.

41. *National Flood Insurance Program Flood Insurance Manual*, at 2-10 (FEMA Apr. 2021).

42. General Property Form Standard Flood Insurance Policy, § X. The term "federal common law" does not create new law to resolve disputes arising from claims under a FEMA flood policy. Easterling v. S. Farm Bureau Cas. Ins. Co., 2020 U.S. Dist. LEXIS 222148 (S.D. Miss. June 24, 2020).

43. Residences at Bay Point Condo. Ass'n v. Std. Fire Ins. Co., 41 F. Supp. 3d 427, 429 (D.N.J. 2014); Greer v. Owners Ins. Co., 434 F. Supp. 2d 1267, 1275 (N.D. Fla. 2006).

44. McGair v. Am. Bankers Ins. Co., 693 F.3d 94, 101 (1st Cir. 2012). *See also* Abbott, *Floods, Flood Insurance, Litigation, Politics—and Catastrophe: The National Flood Insurance Program*, 1 Sea Grant L. & Pol'y J. 129, 146 (2008). The doctrine of *contra proferentem* is, however, apparently not wholly inapplicable. It is occasionally applied in SFIP cases. *See, e.g.*, Krauss v. Aetna Casualty & Surety Flood Ins. Program, 1991 U.S. Dist. LEXIS 6712 (E.D. Pa. May 17, 1991).

to allow extra-contractual causes of action under the guise of "federal common law."[45] They do not, for example, recognize a federal cause of action for bad faith,[46]

Finally, the Appropriations Clause of the United States Constitution states that money may not be drawn from the Treasury of the United States except by an appropriation made by law.[47] Payment of a claim on an SFIP is a direct charge on the Treasury,[48] and, therefore, courts hold that claimants have to strictly comply with the NFIP requirements.[49]

[4] Manuals and Handbooks

FEMA offers many publications that explain aspects of the NFIP and the SFIP.[50] Some of the publications are directed to insurers and claims professionals, but there are also many for policyholders, in English and Spanish.[51] The most important of the publications are FEMA's two manuals and a handbook on claims.

The *Flood Insurance Manual* is over 500 pages. It is used primarily by insurers and agents selling and servicing NFIP flood insurance. It may be of use to policyholders and their counsel in understanding the coverage, and it is especially valuable when questions arise about the effective date, renewal, or cancellation of policies. FEMA cautions that the manual represents current guidance on the topics it covers, but it "is not a substitute for applicable legal requirements, nor is it itself a rule. It is not intended to, nor does it impose, legally-binding requirements on any party, except where parties

45. Sutor v. Fed. Emergency Mgmt. Agency, 2009 U.S. Dist. LEXIS 59152 (E.D. Pa. July 9, 2009).

46. Boggs v. Imperial Fire & Cas. Ins. Co., 2018 U.S. Dist. LEXIS 139551 (S.D.W. Va. Aug. 17, 2018); Surfsand Resort, LLC v. Nationwide Mut. Fire Ins. Co., 2017 U.S. Dist. LEXIS 171548 (D. Or. Oct. 16, 2017); Baker v. Allstate Ins. Co., 2007 U.S. Dist. LEXIS 61029 (E.D. La. Aug. 20, 2007).

47. U.S. Const. art I, § 9, cl. 7.

48. Howell v. State Farm Ins. Cos., 540 F. Supp. 2d 621 (D. Md. 2008).

49. Bleecker v. Std. Fire Ins. Co., 130 F. Supp. 2d 726 (E.D.N.C. 2000). For example, the "constructive total loss" doctrine does not apply to the SFIP because coverage is limited to damage sustained directly as a result of flooding. Hampton v. First Protective Ins., 461 F. Supp. 3d 265 (D.S.C. 2020); Moffett v. Computer Scis. Corp., 2011 U.S. Dist. LEXIS 4147 (D. Md. Jan. 13, 2011). The doctrine allows an insured to recover the policy limits when a building is condemned and ordered to be razed, is beyond repair, or the cost of repair exceeds the value of the building.

50. *See Insurance Outreach Publications and Resources*, FEMA, https://www.fema.gov/flood-insurance/outreach-resources.

51. The agency also offers a great many forms for both adjusters and policyholders. *See Find an Insurance Form*, FEMA, https://www.fema.gov/flood-insurance/find-form.

have voluntarily entered into an agreement requiring compliance with FEMA guidance."[52]

The *Claims Manual* replaced a publication called the *Adjuster Claims Manual*. Like its predecessor, the current manual is directed to adjusters and claims examiners; however, it has a wealth of information that policyholders or their counsel can use in preparing a claim or litigating one. The manual is intended "to improve clarity of claims guidance to WYOs, vendors, adjusters, and examiners so that policyholders experience consistent and reliable service."[53] In addition, policyholders and their lawyers may find it useful in preparing or litigating claims. Like the *Flood Insurance Manual*, however, the *Claims Manual* "is not a substitute for applicable legal requirements, nor is it itself a rule."

The *Claims Handbook* is specifically for policyholders.[54] The handbook "provides step-by-step guidance" on the things a policyholder needs to know about filing a flood claim and explains what to do when a policyholder is not satisfied with the result of a claim.[55] The handbook does not contain the same disclaimer found in the manuals but warns that "[f]ederal laws and regulations supersede information in this handbook where conflicts exist."[56]

The FEMA disclaimers raise a question about the import of the manuals and the handbook. In general, courts defer to the interpretation an agency, including FEMA, gives to its regulations as long as that interpretation is not inconsistent with the regulations or plainly erroneous.[57] The United States Supreme Court has said that, because they are not created through formal adjudication or rulemaking, interpretations in policy statements, agency manuals, and enforcement guidelines are not entitled to the same deference.[58] Courts have, therefore, refused to follow the *Flood Insurance Manual* and its bulletins.[59] The *Claims Manual*, however, may be different. By regulation,

52. *National Flood Insurance Program Flood Insurance Manual*, at TOC i (FEMA Apr. 2021).

53. *National Flood Insurance Program Claims Manual*, at 1 (Oct. 2021).

54. Another useful publication for policyholders is *Answers to Questions about the NFIP* (Feb. 17, 2021), FEMA, https://agents.floodsmart.gov/sites/default/files/fema-answers-to-questions-about-the-NFIP.pdf.

55. *National Flood Insurance Program Claims Handbook* (Oct. 2017).

56. *National Flood Insurance Program Claims Handbook*, at 11 (Oct. 2017).

57. Criger v. Becton, 902 F.2d 1348, 1351 (8th Cir. 1990).

58. Christensen v. Harris Cnty., 529 U.S. 576, 120 S. Ct. 1655, 146 L. Ed. 2d 621 (2000). *See also* Davis v. Nationwide Mut. Fire Ins. Co., 811 F. Supp. 2d 1240, 1248 (E.D. Va. 2011) (stating that FEMA guidance on SFIP provisions should not be treated as regulatory interpretation entitled to controlling weight).

59. Podgorski v. Liberty Mut. Grp. Inc., 2016 U.S. Dist. LEXIS 171209 (N.D. Ill. Dec. 12, 2016); Fernandez v. Fid. Nat'l Prop. & Cas. Ins. Co., 2015 U.S. Dist. LEXIS 98030 (S.D. Tex. July 28, 2015); Lombardi's Cucina, Inc. v. Harleysville Ins. Co., 2010 U.S. Dist. LEXIS 84277 (W.D. Wash. Aug. 17, 2010). *But see* Prastos v. Travelers Ins. Cos., 2015 U.S. Dist. LEXIS 28767

WYO insurers are to adjust claims in accordance with their general company standards, "guided by NFIP Claims manuals."[60] In response, some courts have held the *Claims Manual* is incorporated by reference into FEMA regulations, making it binding.[61] For example, a Louisiana court reasoned that it was "entirely appropriate (indeed, mandatory) for [a policyholder] to support her interpretation of the SFIP with reference to the *Claims Manual*. FEMA's regulations dictate the terms and conditions of the SFIP, and the same regulations incorporate the *Claims Manual* by reference."[62]

[5] The Role of Private Attorneys in SFIP Claims

A great many attorneys whose specialty is insurance law do not accept cases in which a claim against an SFIP for flood loss has been denied. There are numerous reasons for this reluctance, including the following:

- Potential clients rarely seek out counsel before the deadline for submitting a complete and proper proof of loss has passed. That deadline is virtually absolute, and failure to meet it is a permissible basis for denial of the claim.[63]
- There is virtually no basis for obtaining attorney's fees under the policy,[64] and state law extra-contractual claims that may provide an opportunity for fees, or a sufficient recovery that the client can pay fees, are preempted.[65]
- The possible recovery is limited because the maximum coverage under the SFIP is relatively small.[66]

In other words, there is little potential for reasonable remuneration in litigation. Attorneys might be able to both be of valuable assistance to a client and earn a fee in preparing a proof of loss. As explained elsewhere,[67] the proof of loss required by the SFIP is complicated and involves accompanying documents. Much of the work can probably be performed by a clerk or paralegal with only a few hours of the attorney's time required. If an attorney chooses to make this part of his or her practice, it is imperative that a way be

---

(D.N.J. Mar. 10, 2015) (stating that a FEMA bulletin should be given "controlling weight" unless plainly erroneous or inconsistent with an applicable regulation).

60. 44 C.F.R. § 62.23(i)(1).

61. Suopys v. Omaha Prop. & Cas., 404 F.3d 805, 811 (3d Cir. 2005); White Hall On MS River, LLC v. Hartford Ins. Co., 2015 U.S. Dist. LEXIS 45294 (S.D. Miss. Apr. 7, 2015); Residences at Bay Point Condo. Ass'n v. Std. Fire Ins. Co., 41 F. Supp. 3d 427, 437 (D.N.J. 2014).

62. Nguyen v. Hartford Underwriters Ins. Co., 2021 U.S. Dist. LEXIS 11657, at *12 (M.D. La. Jan. 21, 2021).

63. See § 5.06, *infra*.

64. See § 5.09[3][k], *infra*.

65. See § 5.09[3][i], *infra*.

66. See § 5.01[3], *supra*.

67. See § 5.06, *infra*.

found to begin the work almost immediately after a client has suffered a flood loss because the proof of loss usually has to be submitted within 60 days of that loss.

5.2 The Definition of Flood

[1] Generally

[a] Statutory Definition

The National Flood Insurance Act says that the term "flood" has the meaning prescribed in FEMA regulations and *may* include "inundation from rising waters or from the overflow of streams, rivers, or other bodies of water, or from tidal surges, abnormally high tidal water, tidal waves, tsunamis, hurricanes, or other severe storms or deluge."[68] Secondly, the Act provides that the term "flood" also includes inundation from mudslides proximately caused by accumulations of water on or under the ground.[69] Finally, under the Act, "flood" includes the collapse or subsidence of land along the shore of a lake or other body of water as a result of erosion or undermining caused by waves or currents of water exceeding anticipated cyclical levels.[70] Courts rarely cite to the statutory definition.

[b] FEMA Rule Definition

The FEMA rules define "flood" or "flooding" to mean:

> (a) A general and temporary condition of partial or complete inundation of normally dry land areas from:
>
> (1) The overflow of inland or tidal waters.
>
> (2) The unusual and rapid accumulation or runoff of surface waters from any source.
>
> (3) Mudslides (i.e., mudflows) which are proximately caused by flooding as defined in paragraph (a)(2) of this definition and are

---

68. 42 U.S.C § 4121(a)(1).

69. 42 U.S.C § 4121(b). All of the provisions of title 42 of the United States Code apply with respect to mudslides in the same manner and to the same extent as to floods described in 42 U.S.C § 4121(a)(1), subject to and in accordance with FEMA regulations, modifying the provisions of title 42, including those relating to land management and use, to the extent necessary to insure that they can be effectively applied, as the Administrator may prescribe to achieve the purposes of title 42 and the objectives of the National Flood Insurance Program.

70. 42 U.S.C § 4121(c). All of the provisions of title 42 of the United States Code apply with respect to collapse or subsidence in the same manner and to the same extent as to floods described in 42 U.S.C § 4121(a)(1), subject to and in accordance with FEMA regulations, modifying the provisions of title 42, including those relating to land management and use, to the extent necessary to insure that they can be effectively applied, as the Administrator may prescribe to achieve the purposes of title 42 and the objectives of the National Flood Insurance Program.

akin to a river of liquid and flowing mud on the surfaces of normally dry land areas, as when earth is carried by a current of water and deposited along the path of the current.

(b) The collapse or subsidence of land along the shore of a lake or other body of water as a result of erosion or undermining caused by waves or currents of water exceeding anticipated cyclical levels or suddenly caused by an unusually high water level in a natural body of water, accompanied by a severe storm, or by an unanticipated force of nature, such as flash flood or an abnormal tidal surge, or by some similarly unusual and unforeseeable event which results in flooding as defined in paragraph (a)(1) of this definition.[71]

[c] Policy Definition

Curiously, the policy definition is somewhat different from that in the FEMA rule. The policy first defines "flood" to mean a general and temporary condition of partial or complete inundation of two or more acres of "normally dry land"[72] area or of two or more properties—one of which is the property of the policyholder—from overflow of inland or tidal waters, unusual and rapid accumulation, or runoff of surface waters from any source,[73] or mudflow.[74] Under the policy the second definition is a collapse or subsidence of land along the shore of a lake or similar body of water that is the result of erosion or undermining caused by waves or currents of water exceeding anticipated cyclical levels that result in a flood as described in the first definition.[75] Claimants are bound by both the terms of the policy and the applicable FEMA rules.[76] Neither definition requires that there be a "disaster" in order for there to be coverage.[77] Flood waters may ebb and flow before finally receding. Is

71. 44 C.F.R. § 59.1.

72. Few cases have interpreted the phrase "normally dry land." One that has is *Mason v. National Flood Insurers Ass'n*, 361 F. Supp. 939, 941 (D. Haw. 1973), where the court said: "The area in which the seawall, and particularly the seawall footing, was located certainly cannot be considered 'normally dry land area.' Portions of the seawall were regularly submerged with rise in the tides as well as with washing of the waves against the wall." In another case, water entered upper floors of a building by seeping from balconies to the interior. The court said that as the "flood waters" did not rise from the ground floor to reach those upper floors, the water that affected the upper floors did not emanate from the "inundation of normally dry land areas." Cross Queen, Inc. v. Director, Federal Emergency Management Agency, 516 F. Supp. 806, 807–08 (D.V.I. 1980).

73. *See, e.g.*, Segal v. Great American Ins. Co., 390 F. Supp. 1074, 1077 (E.D.N.Y. 1974) (local rainstorm and resulting runoff of surface waters may produce "flood").

74. General Property Form Standard Flood Insurance Policy, § II.B.1.

75. General Property Form Standard Flood Insurance Policy, § II.B.2.

76. Sanchez v. Selective Ins. Co. of the Southeast, 2015 U.S. Dist. LEXIS 105978 (S.D. Fla. Aug. 12, 2015); Global Equities I Ltd. Pshp. v. Omaha Property & Cas., 1997 U.S. Dist. LEXIS 17954 (E.D. La. Nov. 10, 1997).

77. *See* Hooper v. National Flood Insurers Ass'n, 1977 U.S. Dist. LEXIS 12566 (E.D. Mich. Dec. 5, 1977).

there then one or several foods? A "flood which reaches several crests over a relatively short period is a continuous occurrence," one court has said, "even when the floodwaters temporarily recede in the interim."[78]

[2] Proof of Flood

[a] Burden on Policyholder to Show a Flood

The general rule in insurance law is that the policyholder has the burden to show coverage.[79] Thus, to recover, those insured under a FEMA SFIP must show not only that their property was flooded but also that there was a general and temporary condition of partial or complete inundation of two or more acres of normally dry land area. It is not sufficient for a policyholder to show that there was substantial flooding in the community in which their property is located.[80] For example, in a Florida case, the insured introduced into evidence a *Miami Herald* newspaper article stating that the Miami area experienced a record amount of rain on the date the insured home was claimed to have been flooded. There was testimony that there was water in the home and that the street in front of the home was under water. The court said that to determine whether there was a *general condition* of flooding, the focus has to be on the immediate neighborhood of the insured property, rather than the Miami area. Obviously, said the court, uniform amounts of rain do not fall over an area, and differences in topography can create wide differences in flooding potential. Here, the insureds failed to demonstrate that a *general condition* of flooding existed. Their burden of proof was to establish that there was a general condition of flooding, which meant they had to demonstrate that the flooding was not substantially confined to the insured premises, or to properties immediately adjacent to it.[81]

78. Miller v. Macy, 526 F. Supp. 46 (D. Mass. 1981) (flood is continuous until water recedes and land returns to normally dry state). Federal law regarding what constitutes a single occurrence from flood water has been characterized as "very specialized." United States Fire Ins. Co. v. Safeco Ins. Co., 444 So. 2d 844, 847 (Ala. 1983).

79. Bull's Corner Rest., Inc. v. FEMA, 759 F.2d 500, 503 (5th Cir. 1985) (burden of proof was on insured to establish that there had been general flooding); Pecarovich v. Allstate Ins. Co., 80 F. Supp. 2d 1094, 1098 (C.D. Cal. 2000), *rev'd on other grounds*, 2002 U.S. App. LEXIS 27854 (9th Cir. Oct. 31, 2002) (insured has burden of proof of establishing that flood, as defined by SFIP, caused loss).

80. Shaw v. Am. Bankers Ins. Co., 2021 U.S. Dist. LEXIS 76602 (S.D. Tex. Apr. 21, 2021) (where insurer entered into evidence letter sent to insured stating that inspector found no visible signs of covered flood damage to insured structure and/or contents, and insured failed to present or pointed to any record evidence in response other than that hurricane brought substantial flooding to Houston, that did not satisfy burden of raising factual dispute as to whether property was flooded).

81. Mussoline v. Morris, 692 F. Supp. 1306, 1316 (S.D. Fla. 1987). *See also* Donahue v. Am. Family Mut. Ins. Co., 2006 U.S. Dist. LEXIS 9501 (D. Minn. Mar. 6, 2006) (noting that the conditions that caused damage were substantially confined to dwelling of insured, and thus excluded by policy; there was no evidence that the conditions that caused damages extended

[b] Evidence of Flood

Without a flood, there may be a loss,[82] but there can be no *flood* loss. How does the policyholder prove there was a flood? What evidence must the insured produce? Evidence of flooding in the immediate geographical area of the insured property, as opposed to an entire community, can be helpful because topography can create wide differences in flooding potential.[83] The insured, however, still has to show that his or her property flooded. Thus, although Hurricane Harvey brought substantial flooding to the city of Houston, that fact did not satisfy the burden on the insureds to raise a factual dispute as to whether their Houston area home was flooded.[84] Records of local authorities may prove useful but can also undermine the insured's case.[85]

[3] Aspects of "Flood"

[a] Mudflow

"Mudflow" is specifically named as a form of flood in the policy definition of the term.[86] More specifically, the policy says that a "flood" is a general and temporary condition of partial or complete inundation of two or more acres of normally dry land area or of two or more properties from mudflow. A "mudflow" is a "river of liquid and flowing mud on the surface of normally dry land areas, as when earth is carried by a current of water."[87] Shortly after the Ninth Circuit held that the phrase "liquid and flowing mud" denoted "nothing more than saturated soil mass moving by liquidity down a slope,"[88]

---

beyond insured property or street was submerged in water or that water entered any other home on block).

82. *See, e.g.*, Winkler v. Great American Insurance Co., 447 F. Supp. 135 (E.D.N.Y. 1978) (finding no evidence that any flood had occurred, or that flood occasioned loss where property experienced beach erosion during winter in which one neighboring house disappeared and another had porch damage; court considered meteorological evidence indicating that in five years prior to "loss year," there were 18 storms as great or greater than particular one alleged to have been cause of the loss).

83. Bull's Corner Restaurant, Inc. v. Director of FEMA, 759 F.2d 500, 503 (5th Cir. 1985).

84. Shaw v. Am. Bankers Ins. Co., 2021 U.S. Dist. LEXIS 76602 (S.D. Tex. Apr. 21, 2021). *See also* Mussoline v. Morris, 692 F. Supp. 1306, 1316 (S.D. Fla. 1987) (explaining that the focus must be on the plaintiffs' immediate neighborhood, not entire city).

85. McAlister v. Director, Federal Emergency Management Agency, 544 F. Supp. 15 (D. Vt. 1982) (evidence on which court relied to determine loss was not caused by a "flood" included that no entry was made in local flood records, rainfall at time of alleged loss was no higher than that occurring frequently throughout the year, stream did not rise beyond its normal cyclical levels, and flood alarm that was located three-quarters of a mile away from insured's property was not triggered).

86. General Property Form Standard Flood Insurance Policy, § II.B.1.c.

87. General Property Form Standard Flood Insurance Policy, § II.C.19.

88. McHugh v. United Serv. Auto. Ass'n, 164 F.3d 451, 455 (9th Cir. 1999).

FEMA excepted from the definition of "mudflow" landslides, slope failures, or saturated soil masses moving by liquidity down a slope.[89]

The FEMA rules define "mudslide" not "mudflow," and suggest that the words are synonyms. The rule definition says a "mudslide" "describes a condition where there is a river, flow or inundation of liquid mud down a hillside usually as a result of a dual condition of loss of brush cover, and the subsequent accumulation of water on the ground preceded by a period of unusually heavy or sustained rain."[90] The definition adds that a mudslide or mudflow may be a distinct phenomenon while a landslide is in progress, and will be recognized as distinct only if the mudflow, and not the landslide, is the proximate cause of any damage.

For a "mudflow" or "mudslide" to constitute a flood, there must be "inundation." For example, after substantial rainfall, the slope behind an insured home began to slip away. The foundation of the home was gradually exposed. There were cracks in the foundation wall. The court reasoned that there had not been a covered event because the property had never been inundated with either water or mud. According to the court, coverage required an occurrence in which mud caused damage in a way similar to that of clear water—that is, by entering or covering the structure or forcefully striking against it.[91]

[b] Inundation

The NFIA statute, the FEMA rule, and the policy all use the term "inundation," but none defines it. One law dictionary defines it as synonymous with "flood."[92] The Merriam-Webster online dictionary defines "inundate" as to "overwhelm" or "cover with a flood."[93] Courts have said the term commonly means the rising and spreading of water over land that is not usually submerged.[94] Thus, where rainwater collected on the balconies on upper floors of a multi-story hotel and seeped into the rooms, there was no "inundation."[95] One court decided that without knowing the depth of standing water, it was unclear whether water "inundated" property. And, where a policyholder acknowledged that the area in question was a swale between her house and her neighbor's house, she could not establish that the existence of standing

89. *See* 65 Fed. Reg. 60758 (Oct. 12, 2000).

90. 44 C.F.R. § 59.1.

91. Beck v. Dir., Fed. Emergency Mgmt. Agency, 534 F. Supp. 516 (N.D. Ohio 1982).

92. *Ballentine's Law Dictionary* (LexisNexis 2010).

93. *Inundate*, Merriam-Webster, https://www.merriam-webster.com/dictionary/inundate.

94. Mathews v. Farmers Ins. Co., 2005 U.S. Dist. LEXIS 39848 (D. Or. June 27, 2005). *See also* Donahue v. Am. Fam. Mut. Ins. Co., 2006 U.S. Dist. LEXIS 9501 (D. Minn. Mar. 6, 2006); Beck v. Dir., Fed. Emergency Mgmt. Agency, 534 F. Supp. 516, 518 (N.D. Ohio 1982).

95. Cross Queen v. Dir., 516 F. Supp. 806, 807–08 (V.V.I. 1980) (where flood waters did not rise from ground floor to reach upper floors, but collected on balconies and seeped inside, water that affected upper floors did not emanate from inundation of normally dry land areas).

water in the swale revealed a partial inundation because water is expected to collect in a swale even if it is normally dry.[96] A California federal court found that "inundation" within the meaning of the policy had occurred when water produced by severe rainstorms thoroughly infiltrated the ground beneath the home of the insured and caused destabilization of the home's foundation.[97]

[c] Surface Water

The policy definition of flood includes the phrase "unusual and rapid accumulation or runoff of surface waters," but the policy does not define "surface waters." Courts hold the term is not ambiguous[98] and that they may consider its common meaning,[99] which, according to *Black's Law Dictionary*, is water lying on the surface of the earth but not part of a lake or watercourse. It has also been described as rain diffused over the surface of the earth.[100] Surface water, therefore, does not include water from a burst pipe.[101] Some courts say it also does not include water that emanates from a human-made structure;[102] however, the majority view appears to be that water that lands on artificial surfaces is "surface water."[103]

[d] Two or More Acres or Properties

It is not clear why the FEMA policy limits the definition of flood to inundation of two or more acres of normally dry land area or of two or more properties.[104] If an insured property is at the lowest point in the vicinity, it

---

96. Donahue v. Am. Fam. Mut. Ins. Co., 2006 U.S. Dist. LEXIS 9501 (D. Minn. Mar. 6, 2006).

97. Wagner v. Dir., Fed. Emergency Mgmt. Agency, 658 F. Supp. 1530, 1536 (C.D.C. 1987), *rev'd on other grounds*, 847 F.2d 515 (9th Cir. 1988).

98. Cross Queen, Inc. v. Dir., Fed. Emergency Mgmt. Agency, 516 F. Supp. 806 (D.V.I. 1980).

99. Hernandez-Rodriguez v. A1 Sun Prot., Inc., 2010 U.S. Dist. LEXIS 32508 (S.D. Fla. Mar. 17, 2010).

100. Cross Queen, Inc. v. Dir., Fed. Emergency Mgmt. Agency, 516 F. Supp. 806, 808 (D.V.I. 1980).

101. Hernandez-Rodriguez v. A1 Sun Prot., Inc., 2010 U.S. Dist. LEXIS 32508 (S.D. Fla. Mar. 17, 2010).

102. Cross Queen, Inc. v. Dir., Fed. Emergency Mgmt. Agency, 516 F. Supp. 806, 808 (D.V.I. 1980) (when rain collected on balconies of multi-story hotel and seeped into rooms, damage was not caused by "surface waters"). *See also* Flamingo S. Beach I Condo. Ass'n, Inc. v. Selective Ins. Co. of Southeast, 492 F. App'x 16, 19 (11th Cir. 2012) (where rains caused water to pool on elevated deck several feet above ground and flow into building lobby, water did not pool on *ground* and was not, therefore, "surface water").

103. *See, e.g.*, Fid. Coop. Bank v. Nova Cas. Co., 726 F.3d 31 (1st Cir. 2013). *See also* Oak Hill Inv. IV LLC v. State Farm Fire & Cas. Co., 2017 U.S. Dist. LEXIS 158851 (N.D. Ohio Sept. 27, 2017).

104. Arguably, the restriction is based on the congressional finding that "flood disasters have created personal hardships and economic distress which have required unforeseen disaster relief measures and have placed an increasing burden on the Nation's resources." 42 U.S.C. § 4001(a).

could suffer severe flood damage even though it is the only property in the area that is flooded. Yet, unless the inundated property exceeds two acres in area, there has not been a "flood" and, therefore, the policy does not cover the loss. For there to be a flood, however, there does not have to be flood damage. If, for example, the property of the policyholder who makes a claim and another property are both flooded, but the other property suffers no damage from the flood, the policy condition is met and there is coverage.[105] A pool of standing water that straddles a property line demonstrates a general condition of flood.[106] One of the parcels of land can be public property, for example, a roadway.[107]

There are a number of cases that discuss the "general condition of inundation" before the modifying language of "two or more acres or properties" was added to the policy. Some of them were decided when the SFIP had an exclusion for a flood confined to the premises on which the insured property was located *unless* that flood was displaced over two acres of the premises. These cases can be helpful in understanding the "general condition" restriction but may be of limited precedential value given the current policy wording.

One particularly noteworthy case is *Pecarovich v. Allstate Ins. Co.*[108] In that case, the district court said there was evidence to support the proposition that the loss was caused by settling of ground underneath the insured property caused by saturation from the rain, runoff, and accumulation of water. However, said the court, there was no evidence that showed that the immediate neighborhood suffered from partial or complete inundation of normally dry land area. At most, the rain and runoff inundated the backyard area directly behind the insured home, but did not affect any of adjacent neighbors and did not affect an area larger than two acres on the insured property. Thus, the policyholder failed to show that a "flood" as defined by the policy affected the property. The Ninth Circuit reversed. It noted that a portion of the backyard of the insured property was flooded when stormwater ran down hills behind the home. When, said the appellate court, the lower court applied the "two acre" limitation to exclude coverage, it failed to give weight to the declaration

105. Caracci v. Parish of Jefferson, 1979 U.S. Dist. LEXIS 10629 (E.D. La. Aug. 2, 1979) (policy does not require damage to neighboring houses, but merely "inundation" of normally dry land areas; nowhere does policy state that entrance of water into residences is prerequisite for coverage). *See also* Hooper v. Nat'l Flood Insurers Ass'n, 1977 U.S. Dist. LEXIS 12566 (E.D. Mich. Dec. 5, 1977) (*damage* in immediate area was substantially limited to property of plaintiff policyholder, but flooding in general area of plaintiffs' home was severe and generalized, and extensive use of sandbags and dykes in immediate area clearly demonstrated that flooding was not substantially limited to plaintiffs' property).

106. Conrad v. Omaha Property & Cas. Ins. Co., 1995 U.S. Dist. LEXIS 7907 (E.D. Pa. June 7, 1995).

107. *National Flood Insurance Program Claims Manual*, at 87 (Oct. 2021).

108. Pecarovich v. Allstate Ins. Co., 80 F. Supp. 2d 1094 (C.D. Cal. 2000), *rev'd*, 2002 U.S. App. LEXIS 27854 (9th Cir. Oct. 31, 2002).

of a neighbor whose property was adjacent to and above the insured property. That neighbor stated that during the storm, an enormous amount of water ran off the hills into his backyard and flowed across his property, damaging a retaining wall. Both the neighbor and the insured, therefore, experienced flood conditions on their properties. That conclusion was not negated by the fact that the stormwater, which derived from the same source, took different paths to reach the two properties.[109]

An earlier case suggested that additional properties had to be adjacent to that of the policyholder seeking coverage. In that case, there was evidence that "undefined" flooding occurred nearby the property of the policyholder, but the immediately adjacent properties were not flooded. The court held that the insured had not made out a case for coverage because the flooding was not shared by more than one property and its adjacent properties.[110] However, neither the current nor the prior policy language use the word "adjacent" or a synonym for it. The present wording defines a flood as inundation of two or more acres of normally dry land area or of two or more properties, one of which is that of the policyholder. That would seem to allow coverage where the property of the claimant is surrounded by higher ground that is in turn bordered by lower ground. If after a rainstorm, the claimant's property and nearby, but not adjacent, property floods, there should be coverage for the claimant's loss. However, FEMA nonetheless says that the "reference to 'partial or complete inundation of two or more acres of normally dry land area or of two or more properties' requires that the two or more acres must be continuous acres, and that the two or more inundated parcels of land must touch."[111]

[e] Collapse or Subsidence

The policy says that a collapse or subsidence of land along the shore of a lake or similar body of water resulting from erosion or undermining by waves or currents of water exceeding anticipated cyclical levels can cause a flood. A FEMA rule expands on the policy. It says a flood can be defined as the collapse or subsidence of land along the shore of a lake or other body of water as a result of erosion or undermining caused by waves or currents of water exceeding anticipated cyclical levels or suddenly caused by an unusually high water level in a natural body of water, accompanied by a severe storm, or by an unanticipated force of nature, such as flash flood or an abnormal tidal surge, or by some similarly unusual and unforeseeable event that results in

109. Pecarovich v. Allstate Ins. Co., 2002 U.S. App. LEXIS 27854 (9th Cir. Oct. 31, 2002).

110. Segal v. Great Am. Ins. Co., 390 F. Supp. 1074 (E.D.N.Y. 1974) (whether or not particular rain caused flooding nearby, it did not give rise to covered flood condition at plaintiff's property).

111. *National Flood Insurance Program Claims Manual*, at 87 (Oct. 2021).

flooding.[112] In a South Carolina case the policyholder asserted that the rule had a "more inclusive" definition of land subsidence flooding than did the policy. The court, however, found that the policy definition prevailed over the one in the rule.[113]

There is a statutory definition that merely says the term "flood" includes "the collapse or subsidence of land along the shore of a lake or other body of water as a result of erosion or undermining caused by waves or currents of water exceeding anticipated cyclical levels."[114] If possible, FEMA regulations and NFIA statutes have to be harmonized. If they cannot be, however, courts uphold the statute.[115]

[f] Erosion

There is no coverage for loss to property caused *directly* by earth movement even if that movement is caused by flood, except for losses from mudflow and land subsidence that are the result of *erosion* that is specifically insured under the policy definition of flood.[116] Under the policy, the definition of "flood" includes the collapse or subsidence of land along the shore of a lake or similar body of water that is the result of erosion or undermining caused by waves or currents of water exceeding anticipated cyclical levels.[117] "Erosion means the process of the gradual wearing away of land masses."[118]

A New Jersey federal court adopted four elements that a policyholder has to show to demonstrate flood-related erosion: "(1) collapse or subsidence of land, (2) the land is along the shore of a lake or similar body of water, (3) the collapse or subsidence resulted from erosion or undermining caused by waves or currents of water exceeding anticipated cyclical levels, and (4) the waves or currents resulted in a flood as defined in" the policy.[119] That definition requires an inundation from the overflow of inland or tidal waters, unusual and rapid accumulation or runoff of surface waters from any source, or mudflow. Thus, there was no flood where a river did not overflow its banks but removed a

---

112. 44 C.F.R. § 59.1.

113. Dippel v. S.C. Farm Bureau Mut. Ins. Co., 2019 U.S. Dist. LEXIS 145686, at *10, n.10 (D.S.C. Aug. 26, 2019).

114. 42 U.S.C. § 4121(c). Dippel v. S.C. Farm Bureau Mut. Ins. Co., 2019 U.S. Dist. LEXIS 145686 (D.S.C. Aug. 26, 2019) (insured has to show that collapse or subsidence of land along shore of natural body of water was result of erosion or undermining caused by waves or currents of water exceeding anticipated cyclical levels at time of alleged damage for land subsidence definition of flooding to apply).

115. Berger v. Pierce, 933 F.2d 393, 397 (6th Cir. 1991).

116. General Property Form Standard Flood Insurance Policy, § V.C.

117. General Property Form Standard Flood Insurance Policy, § II.B.2.

118. 44 C.F.R. § 59.1.

119. Elwell v. Selective Ins. Co. of Am., 2016 U.S. Dist. LEXIS 140515 (D.N.J. Oct. 11, 2016).

revetment protecting the land on which the insured building sat and continued to remove dirt from the banks until the land supporting the building collapsed into the river. While the third element—collapse from erosion by currents of water—was met, the fourth was not, as the changing course and altered banks of the river were an "overflow" of inland water resulting in an inundation.[120] In comparison, there was coverage when water *overflowed* a riverbank causing a bluff supporting an insured home to slide.[121]

To date, no court has explicitly employed the four elements embraced in the New Jersey decision; however, other courts have considered the factors when evaluating whether a loss resulted from flood-related erosion.[122]

[4] Direct Physical Loss

[a] Generally

The policy pays for *direct physical loss* by or from flood to insured property.[123] "Direct physical loss by or from flood" means loss or damage to insured property directly caused by a flood and requires evidence of *physical changes* to the property.[124] FEMA emphasizes that the phrase "directly caused by a flood" means that a flood is the immediate cause of loss, damage, or change to insured property, with no intervening cause or factor after the flood leading to damage. There must be evidence of physical changes to the property and, says FEMA, the phrase "evidence of physical changes to the property" means there has to be visible evidence showing the flood ruined, damaged, or changed the property.[125] For example, part of an air-conditioning system was damaged by flooding after which the system would function only if it were completely replaced. The insured, therefore, claimed coverage for the cost of replacing compressors that were an essential part of the system but that were not damaged by flood waters. The insurer argued there was no coverage for the compressors because the policy covered only direct physical loss by or from flood and the compressors were not damaged by flood waters. The court concurred.[126]

---

120. Mathews v. Farmers Ins. Co., 2005 U.S. Dist. LEXIS 39848 (D. Or. June 27, 2005). *See also* McAlister v. Director, Federal Emergency Management Agency, 544 F. Supp. 15 (D. Vt. 1982) (no coverage for loss from gradual erosion of stream bank).

121. Zumbrun v. United Services Auto. Ass'n, 719 F. Supp. 890 (E.D. Cal. 1989).

122. *See, e.g.*, Chesapeake Ship Propeller Co. v. Stickney, 820 F. Supp. 995, 999–1001 (E.D. Va. 1993); McAlister v. Dir., Fed. Emergency Mgmt. Agency, 544 F. Supp. 15 (D. Vt. 1982).

123. General Property Form Standard Flood Insurance Policy, § I.C.

124. General Property Form Standard Flood Insurance Policy, § II.C.14.

125. *National Flood Insurance Program Claims Manual*, at 91 (Oct. 2021).

126. Ruth v. Selective Ins. Co. of Am., 2017 U.S. Dist. LEXIS 20534 (D.N.J. Feb. 14, 2017). *See also* Atlas Pallet, Inc. v. Gallagher, 725 F.2d 131, 137 (1st Cir. 1984) (river flooding caused collapse of milldam, which produced malfunctioning of sprinkler system because it lost positive

[b] Exposure to Moisture

Notwithstanding FEMA's assertion that flood waters have to physically contact insured property for there to be coverage, courts have found for policyholders when moisture caused by a flood-damaged insured property. For example, a policyholder claimed several items of personal property inside an insured residence were damaged during a hurricane by a flood. The insurer denied coverage, contending the policyholder had not shown that flood waters entered the residence and damaged the property. The policyholder responded that the personal property was destroyed by significant amounts of moisture following the storm at a time the policyholder was unable to access the home to mitigate the moisture problem. The court decided that damage from prolonged exposure to moisture during and after a flood constitutes direct physical loss by or from flood.[127] Other courts have reached a similar conclusion.[128]

[c] Structural Damage Related to Flooding

A building can suffer structural damage from flooding without flood waters touching the building. Despite FEMA's insistence that flood waters must physically contact insured property for there to be coverage, a number of courts have sided with policyholders in these cases. *Quesada v. Director, Federal Emergency Management Agency*[129] is a prominent case in point. The insured home in that case was damaged by settling or compacting of the fill underneath the foundation. That was the result of the saturation of the fill by waters that did not enter the home. When the saturated fill compacted, the floor slab beneath the home shifted, causing extensive cracking of the floors and walls. FEMA contended that the water had to physically enter the house for there

---

head of water and failure of sprinkler system was not caused directly by flood, but by collapse of dam).

127. Hampton v. First Protective Ins., 461 F. Supp. 3d 265, 279 (D.S.C. 2020).

128. Stevens v. Bankers Ins. Co., 970 F. Supp. 769 (N.D. Cal. 1997) (where, although flood water did not touch inventory, it was damaged by moisture in the air, court held there was coverage as flood water in form of ambient moisture destroyed inventory); Krauss v. Aetna Casualty & Surety Flood Ins. Program, 1991 U.S. Dist. LEXIS 6712 (E.D. Pa. May 17, 1991) (where flood waters entered basement but not residence, summary judgment was denied regarding claims for damage to items and structural repairs on first floor as policy could be read to cover humidity/mildew damage; words "directly and proximately caused by a flood" include damage that results from occurrence of flood, although not from immersion in flood water).

129. Quesada v. Director, Federal Emergency Management Agency, 753 F.2d 1011 (11th Cir. 1985). *See also* Woodson v. Allstate Ins. Co., 186 F. Supp. 3d 510, 517 (E.D.N.C. 2016), *rev'd on other grounds*, 855 F.3d 628 (4th Cir. 2017) (where erosion flood, storm surge, and waves undermined ground floor slab, but did not actually enter building, loss was covered because flood waters do not necessarily have to touch area of house for it to be damaged by flooding); Graham v. Republic Fire & Casual Ins. Co., 2018 U.S. Dist. LEXIS 166057 (M.D. La. Sept. 26, 2018) (where floors were allegedly damaged by flooding underneath raised home, policyholders stated plausible claim that flooding caused direct damage to floors).

to be coverage. The court disagreed. It said there was no question that the water thoroughly inundated the foundation of the home, and it could discern "no sound reason why coverage should be denied solely because the water did not rise so high as to actually enter the living area of [the] home." In a subsequent case, the Seventh Circuit reached the same conclusion. In that case, flood waters washed away a retaining wall and soil, leading to cracks in the foundation and causing an exterior wall that bore the weight of the second story to tilt outward. The policyholder sought coverage for the cost to prevent further movement of the wall, which could cause a collapse. The insurer paid to fix the cracks in the house but refused to pay to render the house stable and safe for occupancy. The lower court found for the policyholder, and the appellate court affirmed. It noted that the insurer did not contend that the physical changes to the house were not symptomatic of physical damage or that the flood was not a proximate cause of that damage. The court asked, "[i]f there is physical damage to the house, and that damage was caused by a flood, how can the policy not provide coverage?"[130]

It is important to be aware that when soil is washed away from under a building or a building shifts from soil saturation, many courts say that the damage that results is "earth movement," which is a specifically excluded peril.[131]

5.3 Coverage

[1] Building Coverage

[a] Building and Additions

The SFIP insures against direct physical loss by or from flood for the building described on the Declarations Page at the described location.[132] Generally, a "building" is defined by the policy as a "structure with two or more outside rigid walls and a fully secured roof that is affixed to a permanent site."[133] FEMA explains that "affixed by weight" does not mean affixed to a permanent site for purposes of the SFIP definition of building.[134] Thus, a home that

130. Downey v. State Farm Fire & Cas. Co., 266 F.3d 675 (7th Cir. 2001).

131. See § 5.03[8][c], *infra*.

132. General Property Form Standard Flood Insurance Policy, § III.A.1.

133. General Property Form Standard Flood Insurance Policy, § II.C.6.a. *See, e.g.*, Suburbia Garden Nursery, Inc. v. Dir., Fed. Emergency Mgmt. Agency, 637 F. Supp. 56 (E.D. Mo. 1986) ("shade shelter" was not "building"); Jackson v. Nat'l Flood Insurers Ass'n, 398 F. Supp. 1383 (S.D. Tex. 1974) (concrete that covered entire area beneath beach house was building).

134. *National Flood Insurance Program Claims Manual*, at 90 (Oct. 2021). The manual says that a building meets the criteria of "affixed to a permanent site" if, for example, it is mechanically anchored to the ground or its foundation is installed in the ground. A structure or its foundation placed on top of the ground, without excavation, or being mechanically secured, does not meet the definition of "building."

was merely resting on piers was not a building under the policy and was not covered for a loss.[135]

The term "building" does not mean a gas or liquid storage tank, a shipping container, or a recreational vehicle, park trailer, or similar vehicle. A building is a "structure," but the policy does not define "structure." A FEMA rule, however, defines "structure" to mean a "building with two or more outside rigid walls and a fully secured roof, that is affixed to a permanent site."[136] An enclosure below the lowest elevated floor is not a building under the building coverage and, thus, enclosed ground floors below the required base-flood elevation were not covered.[137]

When the building is a "condominium"—meaning one or more buildings in which each unit owner has an undivided interest in common elements[138]—and the named insured is the "condominium association,"[139] the building coverage includes all units within the building and the improvements within the units, provided the units are owned in common by all unit owners.

The policy also covers additions and extensions that are attached to, and in contact with, the building by a rigid exterior wall, a solid load-bearing interior wall, a stairway, an elevated walkway, or a roof.[140] The insured has the option to separately insure any of these additions and extensions, but additions and extensions attached to, and in contact with, the building by a common interior wall that is *not* a solid loadbearing wall are considered part of the building and *cannot* be separately insured.

---

135. Niles v. Tex. Farmers Ins. Co., 2021 U.S. Dist. LEXIS 125851 (S.D. Tex. Apr. 27, 2021). The insured argued that the requirement that a building be affixed to a permanent site was ambiguous and that here could reasonably be interpreted as affixed because it was permanently attached to its site by its plumbing and water system and because its A/C unit and ductwork also mechanically attach the home directly to the ground. The court did not agree.

136. 44 C.F.R. § 59.1. The rule adds that structure also means a manufactured home or travel trailer without wheels, built on a chassis and affixed to a permanent foundation, that is regulated under the community's floodplain management and building ordinances or laws. It does not mean a recreational vehicle or a park trailer or other similar vehicle or a gas or liquid storage tank. One court has found the definitions of "building" and "structure" to be circular and ambiguous. Dean Blanchard Seafood, Inc. v. Acadian Ins. Servs., 616 F. Supp. 2d 612, 621 (E.D. La. 2008).

137. Carneiro Da Cunha v. Std. Fire Ins. Co./Aetna Flood Ins. Program, 129 F.3d 581 (11th Cir. 1997). *See also* Keshwani v. Am. Bankers Ins. Co., 2020 U.S. Dist. LEXIS 101685 (S.D. Tex. June 10, 2020).

138. General Property Form Standard Flood Insurance Policy, § II.C.8.

139. A condominium association is an entity made up of unit owners responsible for maintenance and operation of common elements owned in undivided shares by unit owners and other buildings in which unit owners have use rights where membership in the entity is a required condition of unit ownership. General Property Form Standard Flood Insurance Policy, § II.C.9.

140. General Property Form Standard Flood Insurance Policy, § III.A.3.

[b] Fixtures, Machinery, and Equipment

Under the building coverage, the FEMA policy insures against direct physical loss by or from flood for certain prescribed fixtures, machinery, and equipment.[141] These include awnings and canopies; blinds; carpet permanently installed over unfinished flooring; central air conditioners; elevator equipment; fire extinguishing apparatus; fire sprinkler systems; walk-in freezers; furnaces; light fixtures; outdoor antennas and aerials attached to buildings; permanently installed cupboards, bookcases, paneling, and wallpaper; pumps and machinery for operating pumps; ventilating equipment; and wall mirrors that are permanently installed. Additionally, in units within the building, the policy covers built-in dishwashers; built-in microwave ovens; garbage disposal units; hot water heaters, including solar water heaters; kitchen cabinets; plumbing fixtures; radiators; ranges; refrigerators; and stoves.

[c] Construction Materials

Materials and supplies to be used for construction, alteration, or repair of the insured building are covered while they are stored in a fully enclosed building at the described location or on an adjacent property.[142]

[d] Building Under Construction

There is coverage under the SFIP for a building under construction, alteration, or repair at the described location. If the structure is not yet walled or roofed, then coverage applies only while the work is in progress or, if the work is halted, only for a period of up to 90 continuous days thereafter.[143] However, there is no coverage until the building is walled and roofed if the lowest floor, including the basement floor, of a non-elevated building or the lowest elevated floor of an "elevated building"[144] is either below the base flood elevation in certain "A" flood zones or below the base flood elevation adjusted to include the effect of wave action in certain "V" flood zones.[145] The lowest floor level is based on the bottom of the lowest horizontal structural member of the floor in those "V" zones or the top of the floor in those "A" zones.

[e] Manufactured Home or Travel Trailer

A manufactured or mobile home is a structure that is built on a permanent chassis, is transported to its site in one or more sections, and is affixed to a

141. General Property Form Standard Flood Insurance Policy, § III.A.4.

142. General Property Form Standard Flood Insurance Policy, § III.A.5.

143. General Property Form Standard Flood Insurance Policy, § III.A.6.a.

144. An "elevated building" is one that has no basement and that has its lowest elevated floor raised above ground level by foundation walls, shear walls, posts, piers, pilings, or columns. General Property Form Standard Flood Insurance Policy, § II.C.15.

145. General Property Form Standard Flood Insurance Policy, § III.A.6.b.

permanent foundation.[146] A travel trailer does not have wheels, is built on a chassis and is affixed to a permanent foundation, and is regulated under the community's floodplain management and building ordinances or laws.[147] Manufactured homes and travel trailers are buildings within the policy definition, but recreational vehicles, park trailers, or other similar vehicles are not. If a manufactured home or travel trailer is in a special flood hazard area,[148] it has to be anchored at the time of the loss in one of three ways prescribed by the policy.[149] It may be anchored by over-the-top or frame ties to ground anchors, in accordance with the manufacturer's specifications, or in compliance with the community's floodplain management requirements, unless it has been continuously insured by the National Flood Insurance Program at the same described location since September 30, 1982.

FEMA says the SFIP only insures a manufactured home, mobile home, or travel trailer affixed to a permanent foundation.[150] When located in a Special Flood Hazard Area (SFHA), manufactured homes, mobile homes, and travel trailers have to be secured to resist flotation. If anchor straps or tie-downs are not installed, the building must be installed based on the local community's regulations or manufacturer's specification. If the manufactured home, mobile home, or travel trailer has site-built additions greater than its original square foot area, the adjustor is required to look up and obtain the entire property card on the community assessor's web page and provide it along with the Preliminary Report.

The wheels of a travel trailer have to be removed. If wheels are attached to axles at the time of the loss, a travel trailer is not eligible for coverage. A travel trailer in a recreational camping park outside the regulations of the local community is also not eligible for coverage

FEMA requires adjusters to locate and photograph the data plate on the manufactured home or mobile home or, in the case of a travel trailer for which a data plate may not be available, the adjuster should locate and photograph the metal tag on the trailer's metal chassis frame.[151] FEMA specifies the pro-

146. General Property Form Standard Flood Insurance Policy, § II.C.6.b. FEMA says a manufactured home is a legal term created on June 15, 1976, by the U.S. Department of Housing and Urban Development. A mobile home is a structure built before June 15, 1976. Manufactured and mobile homes are not modular homes. *National Flood Insurance Program Claims Manual*, at 255 (Oct. 2021).

147. General Property Form Standard Flood Insurance Policy, § II.C.6.c.

148. A "Special Flood Hazard Area" (SFHA) is one that has special flood or mudflow, and/or flood-related erosion hazards, and is shown on a Flood Hazard Boundary Map or Flood Insurance Rate Map as Zone A, AO, A1–A30, AE, A99, AH, AR, AR/A, AR/AE, AR/AH, AR/AO, AR/A1–A30, V1–V30, VE, or V. General Property Form Standard Flood Insurance Policy, § II.C.27.

149. General Property Form Standard Flood Insurance Policy, § III.A.7.

150. *National Flood Insurance Program Claims Manual*, at 256 (Oct. 2021).

151. If the data tag is not available or in case of a travel trailer, FEMA says the adjuster should obtain a copy of property title or the property card from the internet, and one of the

cess for building valuation,[152] damage estimation,[153] and loss settlement[154] for manufactured homes, mobile homes, and travel trailers.

[f] Property below Lowest Elevated Floor in Some Buildings

[i] Covered Property

The policy enumerates property that is covered if it is below the lowest elevated floor of an "elevated"[155] "post-FIRM" building and located in certain "A" or "V" zones or is in a basement regardless of the zone.[156] A "post-FIRM" building is one for which construction or substantial improvement occurred after December 31, 1974, or on or after the effective date of an initial Flood Insurance Rate Map (FIRM), whichever is later.[157] A "basement" is any area of a building, including any sunken room or sunken portion of a room, that has its floor below ground level on all sides.[158]

According to FEMA, the policy definition of a basement means the floor level of a room, or any area of a floor level in a building, is below the ground level on all sides. The agency acknowledges that the definition may differ from what policyholders consider as their "basement."[159] However, says FEMA, the policy considers a sunken room, or sunken portion of a room, to be a basement if the floor level is below the ground level on all sides.[160] The entire below-ground-floor-level area, including walls and the ceiling that may extend above grade, adds FEMA, is subject to basement coverage limitations. The agency says "ground-level" is the surface of the ground immediately along the perimeter of the building. If an exterior area of egress out of a building is

---

following to document the full description of the building: bill of sale, the manufacturer's build sheet, or the homeowners insurance appraisal.

152. *National Flood Insurance Program Claims Manual*, at 258 (Oct. 2021).

153. *National Flood Insurance Program Claims Manual*, at 258 (Oct. 2021).

154. *National Flood Insurance Program Claims Manual*, at 258–60 (Oct. 2021).

155. An "elevated building" is one with "no basement and that has its lowest elevated floor raised above ground level by foundation walls, shear walls, posts, piers, pilings, or columns." General Property Form Standard Flood Insurance Policy, § II.C.15. Whether a building is elevated may be stated on the Declarations Page. For example, in *Keshwani v. Am. Bankers Ins. Co.*, 2020 U.S. Dist. LEXIS 101685 (S.D. Tex. June 10, 2020), the Declarations Page said the insurer would provide coverage for an "elevated" building. The court said that supported a conclusion that the home was an elevated building despite the fact that the ground floor had one side on ground level.

156. General Property Form Standard Flood Insurance Policy, § III.A.8.

157. General Property Form Standard Flood Insurance Policy, § II.C.23.

158. General Property Form Standard Flood Insurance Policy, § II.C.5. Courts have found the definition to be clear. *See, e.g.*, Linder & Assocs. v. Aetna Cas. & Sur. Co., 166 F.3d 547 (3d Cir. 1999); Nelson v. Becton, 929 F.2d 1287, 1289 (8th Cir. 1991).

159. *National Flood Insurance Program Claims Manual*, at 88 (Oct. 2021).

160. *National Flood Insurance Program Claims Manual*, at 88 (Oct. 2021).

below the ground level on all sides, it is a basement. Finally, sump wells, says the agency, are not basements because they are not a floor level.

The coverage is for property installed in its functioning location and, if necessary for operation, connected to a power source.[161] The property provided coverage is

- Central air conditioners;
- Cisterns and the water in them;
- Drywall for walls and ceilings in a basement and the cost of labor to nail it, unfinished and unfloated and not taped, to the framing;
- Electrical junction and circuit breaker boxes;
- Electrical outlets and switches;
- Elevators, dumbwaiters, and related equipment, except for related equipment installed below the base flood elevation after September 30, 1987;[162]
- Fuel tanks and the fuel in them;
- Furnaces and hot water heaters;
- Heat pumps;
- Non-flammable insulation in a basement;
- Pumps and tanks used in solar energy systems;
- Stairways and staircases attached to the building, not separated from it by elevated walkways;
- Sump pumps;
- Water softeners and the chemicals in them, water filters, and faucets installed as an integral part of the plumbing system;
- Well water tanks and pumps;
- Required utility connections for any item on the list; and
- Footings, foundations, posts, pilings, piers, or other foundation walls and anchorage systems required to support a building.

The cost to remove property that is not on this list in order to repair covered structural damage to the insured building may be covered, but not the cost to repair or replace them for damage they suffer during flooding.[163]

"Clean-up" is also included in this part of the coverage.[164] The policy does not define "clean-up." It has been held to mean removal of dirt and

161. General Property Form Standard Flood Insurance Policy, § III.A.8.a.

162. *See, e.g.*, Chesapeake Motel & Villas, Inc. v. Wright Nat'l Flood Ins. Co., 2019 U.S. Dist. LEXIS 223296 (S.D. Fla. Nov. 22, 2019) (hoisting machinery was "related equipment" necessary to make elevator operational and because it was installed below base flood elevation after September 30, 1987, there was no coverage).

163. Hampton v. First Protective Ins., 461 F. Supp. 3d 265, 274 (D.S.C. 2020).

164. General Property Form Standard Flood Insurance Policy, § III.A.8.b.

extraneous matter that is deposited by flood waters,[165] but not removal of non-owned debris.[166]

[ii] Below Ground Level

In determining whether a space is a basement, the key phrase is "below ground level."[167] FEMA says "ground-level" is the surface of the ground immediately along the perimeter of the building. If an exterior area of egress out of a building is below the ground level on all sides, it is a basement.[168] Courts have been clear about the meaning of "ground level." If, when leaving a lower level, a person has to step up, even a single inch, the level is *below* ground level.[169] "Ground level" is determined at the time of a flood, not fixed when a space is constructed.[170] A "basement" can, therefore, be "created" when soil is added around a building.[171] In one case, for instance, a lower level was below ground level on three sides and became a basement when gravel was dumped into an alley. The gravel raised the surface level of the alley to the height of the entry threshold that was above the level of the floor.[172]

[2] Personal Property

[a] Generally

If the insured has purchased personal property coverage, the policy insures against direct physical loss by or from flood to personal property inside the fully *enclosed*[173] insured building owned solely by the insured or, in the case of a condominium, owned solely by the condominium association and used exclusively in the conduct of the business affairs of the condominium association or owned in common by the unit owners of the condominium association.[174] When the policy insures personal property, the coverage will be for either household personal property or other than household personal property,

165. Davis v. Nationwide Mut. Fire Ins. Co., 811 F. Supp. 2d 1240, 1258–59 (E.D. Va. 2011). *See also* Weisbecker v. Szalkowski, 2016 U.S. Dist. LEXIS 84128 (D.N.J. June 29, 2016) (coverage for removal of sand from crawl space located within perimeter of building).

166. Torre v. Liberty Mut. Fire Ins. Co., 781 F.3d 651, 655 (3d Cir. 2015).

167. Matusevich v. Middlesex Mut. Assur. Co., 782 F.3d 56 (1st Cir. 2015).

168. *National Flood Insurance Program Claims Manual*, at 88 (Oct. 2021).

169. *See, e.g.*, Linder & Assocs. v. Aetna Cas. & Sur. Co., 166 F.3d 547, 550 (3d Cir. 1999); Nelson v. Becton, 929 F.2d 1287 (8th Cir. 1991). *See also* Unger v. Liberty Mut. Ins. Co., 849 F. Supp. 839, 846 (E.D.N.Y. 1994) ("ground level" is area close and adjacent to lower level door, not that of sidewalk and street substantial distance away from lower level).

170. Linder & Assocs. v. Aetna Cas. & Sur. Co., 166 F.3d 547, 551 (3d Cir. 1999).

171. Destefanis v. Fugate, 2013 U.S. Dist. LEXIS 179878 (E.D.N.Y. Dec. 19, 2013).

172. Linder & Assocs. v. Aetna Cas. & Sur. Co., 166 F.3d 547 (3d Cir. 1999).

173. Property stored in an "umbrella building" that had no walls, just a roof supported by columns, was not covered because it was not located in an enclosed building. Riverside Bldg. Supply, Inc. v. Federal Emergency Management Agency, 723 F.2d 1159 (4th Cir. 1983).

174. General Property Form Standard Flood Insurance Policy, § III.B.1.

while within the insured building, but not both.[175] If the policy insures household personal property, it will insure property usual to a living quarters that belongs to the insured or a member of the household of the insured, or at option of the insured, a domestic worker or guest or property for which the insured may be legally liable.[176] If the policy insures other than household personal property, it will insure the furniture, fixtures, machinery, equipment, and stock[177] of the insured and, except for property listed in the policy as not insured, other personal property owned by the insured and used in the business of the insured.[178] The policy lists property that is only insured under the personal property section of the coverage. That property is

- Air-conditioning units, portable or window type;
- Carpets, not permanently installed, over unfinished flooring;
- Carpets over finished flooring;
- Clothes washers and dryers;
- "Cook-out" grills;
- Food freezers, other than walk-in, and food in any freezer;
- Outdoor equipment and furniture stored inside the insured building;
- Ovens and the like; and
- Portable microwave ovens and portable dishwashers.

[b] Property below Lowest Elevated Floor in Some Buildings

The policy enumerates property that is covered if it is below the lowest elevated floor of an elevated post-FIRM building and located in certain "A" or "V" zones or is in a basement regardless of the zone.[179] A "post-FIRM" building is one for which construction or substantial improvement occurred after December 31, 1974, or on or after the effective date of an initial Flood Insurance Rate Map (FIRM), whichever is later.[180] A "basement" is any area of a building, including any sunken room or sunken portion of a room, that has its floor below ground level on all sides.[181] The coverage is for property installed in its functioning location and, if necessary for operation, connected to a power source. The property provided coverage is air-conditioning units,

175. General Property Form Standard Flood Insurance Policy, § III.B.3.
176. General Property Form Standard Flood Insurance Policy, § III.B.3.a.
177. Stock is "merchandise held in storage or for sale, raw materials, and in process or finished goods, including supplies used in their packing or shipping." It does not include any property that is classified as not insured under the policy except parts and equipment for self-propelled vehicles, furnishings and equipment for watercraft, spas and hot-tubs, including their equipment, and swimming pool equipment. General Property Form Standard Flood Insurance Policy, § II.C.28.
178. General Property Form Standard Flood Insurance Policy, § III.B.3.b.
179. General Property Form Standard Flood Insurance Policy, § III.B.5.
180. General Property Form Standard Flood Insurance Policy, § II.C.23.
181. General Property Form Standard Flood Insurance Policy, § II.C.5.

portable or window type; clothes washers and dryers; and food freezers, other than walk-in, and food in any freezer.

[c] Special Limits

For certain items of personal property, the policy limits coverage to no more than $2,500 for any loss to one or more of them.[182] These are artwork; photographs; collectibles or memorabilia, including but not limited to porcelain or other figures, and sports cards, rare books, or autographed items; jewelry; watches; precious and semiprecious stones; articles of gold, silver, or platinum; furs; or any article containing fur that represents its principal value. Additionally, the policy will pay only for the *functional value* of antiques.[183]

[d] Tenants and Condominium Unit Owners

The personal property of a tenant has to be inside the fully enclosed building.[184] A tenant may apply up to 10 percent of the personal property limit to improvements that have been made a part of the building the tenant occupies and that the tenant acquired, or made at the tenant's expense, even though the tenant cannot legally remove them. The coverage does not increase the amount of insurance that applies to insured personal property.[185]

A condominium unit owner may apply up to 10 percent of the personal property limit to cover loss to interior walls, floors, and ceilings that are not insured under a policy issued to the condominium association that insures the condominium building.[186] The coverage does not increase the amount of insurance that applies to insured personal property.

[3] Debris Removal

Under the policy, the insurer will pay the expense to remove *non-owned* debris that is on or in insured property and debris of *insured property anywhere*.[187] The policy does not define "insured property," but land is not covered property.[188] Therefore, the cost to remove debris that is not owned by the insured from the land of the insured is not covered.[189] FEMA explains that "insured

182. General Property Form Standard Flood Insurance Policy, § III.B.6.
183. General Property Form Standard Flood Insurance Policy, § III.B.7.
184. General Property Form Standard Flood Insurance Policy, § III.B.10.
185. General Property Form Standard Flood Insurance Policy, § III.B.8.
186. General Property Form Standard Flood Insurance Policy, § III.B.9.
187. General Property Form Standard Flood Insurance Policy, § III.C.1.a.
188. General Property Form Standard Flood Insurance Policy, § IV.6.
189. Torre v. Liberty Mut. Fire Ins. Co., 781 F.3d 651 (3d Cir. 2015); Jacobsen v. Hartford Ins. Co. Flood & Home (Sandy), 2017 U.S. Dist. LEXIS 52591 (D.N.J. Mar. 31, 2017) (debris from unmoored boat located on lawn of insured). *See also* Keating v. State Farm Fire & Cas. Co., 2002 U.S. Dist. LEXIS 11644 (E.D. Pa. Mar. 14, 2002). *But see* Dickson v. Am. Bankers

property" means the insured building and insured personal property and that the policy does not pay for removal of non-insured debris owned by the policyholder anywhere, for example, non-insured damaged property or debris that is located in the yard or driveway or on another parcel of land.[190] The policy also does not cover non-insured items of property, even if their removal facilitates cleanup of covered building repairs. For example, says FEMA, there is no coverage for removal of carpet installed inside a basement, or of plants, shrubs, or trees along the perimeter of the building to access foundation or siding repairs.

If the insured, or a member of the household of the insured, performs the removal work, the value of that work will be based on the federal minimum wage.[191] This coverage does not increase the limits for building or personal property coverage.[192]

[4] Loss Avoidance Measures

[a] Sandbags, Supplies, and Labor

Pursuant to the policy, an insurer will pay up to $1,000 for costs incurred to protect the insured building from a flood or imminent danger of flood, for reasonable expenses to buy sandbags, including sand to fill them, fill for temporary levees, pumps, and plastic sheeting and lumber used in connection with those items as well as the value of work, at the federal minimum wage, that the insured performs.[193] This coverage only applies if damage to insured property by or from flood is imminent and the threat of flood damage is apparent enough to lead a person of common prudence to anticipate flood damage,[194] for example, an approaching tropical storm or hurricane.[195] There has to be either a general and temporary condition of flooding in the area near the described location, even if the flood does not reach the building or an evacuation order or other civil order has been issued by a legally authorized official for the community in which the building is located calling for measures to preserve life and property from the peril of flood. Damage to property during preventive action is likely not covered.[196] The coverage does not increase the limit for building or property coverage.

Ins. Co., 2013 U.S. Dist. LEXIS 183163 (D.N.D. Mar. 18, 2013), *rev'd on other grounds*, 739 F.3d 397 (8th Cir. 2014).

190. *National Flood Insurance Program Claims Manual*, at 109 (Oct. 2021).
191. General Property Form Standard Flood Insurance Policy, § III.C.1.b.
192. General Property Form Standard Flood Insurance Policy, § III.C.1.c.
193. General Property Form Standard Flood Insurance Policy, § III.C.2.a.(1).
194. General Property Form Standard Flood Insurance Policy, § III.C.2.a.(2).
195. Slater v. Hartford Ins. Co., 2015 U.S. Dist. LEXIS 36824 (M.D. Fla. Mar. 24, 2015).
196. Ono v. Becton, 1988 U.S. Dist. LEXIS 4774 (N.D. Ill. May 18, 1988).

[b] Property Removed to Safety

An insurer will pay up to $1,000 for the reasonable expenses incurred to move insured property to a place other than the described location that contains the property to protect it from flood or the imminent danger of flood.[197] The policy says that reasonable expenses include the value of work, at the federal minimum wage, the insured or a member of the household of the insured performs. If insured property is moved to another location to protect it from flood or the imminent danger of flood, the policy will cover that property while at that location for 45 consecutive days from the date the insured begins to move it there.[198] The property moved may either be property insured under the building or personal property coverages.[199] The personal property that is moved has to be placed in a fully enclosed building or otherwise "reasonably" protected from the elements. Any property removed, including a "moveable home,"[200] must be placed above ground level or outside of the special flood hazard area.[201] This coverage does not increase the limits of building or personal property coverage.[202]

[5] Pollution Damage

The policy covers damage caused by pollutants to insured property if the discharge, seepage, migration, release, or escape of those pollutants is caused by or results from flood, but $10,000 is the most the insurer will pay.[203] This coverage does not increase the limits of the building or personal property coverages. Any payment when combined with all other payments for the same loss cannot exceed the replacement cost or actual cash value, as appropriate, of the insured property. The coverage does not include testing for or monitoring of pollutants unless required by law or ordinance.

[6] Increased Cost of Compliance

[a] Generally

The policy pays the insured to comply with a state or local floodplain management law or ordinance that affects repair or reconstruction of a building

197. General Property Form Standard Flood Insurance Policy, § III.C.2.b.(1).
198. General Property Form Standard Flood Insurance Policy, § III.C.2.b.(2).
199. General Property Form Standard Flood Insurance Policy, § III.A.2 (coverage for building property located at another location for period of 45 days at another location, as set forth in coverage for "Property Removed to Safety" clause); General Property Form Standard Flood Insurance Policy, § III.B.2 (coverage for personal property for 45 days while stored at temporary location, as set forth in "Property Removed to Safety" clause).
200. *See* General Property Form Standard Flood Insurance Policy, § II.C.6.
201. General Property Form Standard Flood Insurance Policy, § III.C.2.b.(3).
202. General Property Form Standard Flood Insurance Policy, § III.C.2.b.(4).
203. General Property Form Standard Flood Insurance Policy, § III.C.3.

suffering flood damage.[204] Eligible compliance activities are elevation, floodproofing, relocation,[205] or demolition, or any combination of them, of the building. Eligible floodproofing activities are limited to non-residential buildings and residential buildings with basements that satisfy FEMA's standards published in the Code of Federal Regulations.[206] Relocating a well or septic system to bring them into compliance with current floodplain management rules has been held not to be covered.[207] Note that all conditions and provisions of the policy apply to this specialized coverage.[208]

[b] Limits of Coverage

Under the policy, the insurer will pay up to $30,000 for increased cost of compliance, which only applies to policies with building coverage.[209] Payment of claims under this coverage is in addition to the amount of coverage that appears on the Declarations Page; however, the most the insured can collect for both building property and increased cost of compliance cannot exceed the maximum coverage permitted. There is no separate deductible for a claim under increased cost of compliance coverage.

[c] Eligibility

The policy requires that a building insured under the building property clause that sustains a loss caused by a flood must meet one of two criteria. First, it has to be a building that has had flood damage[210] in which the cost to repair equals or exceeds 50 percent of the market value of the building at the time of the flood and the state or community has to have a substantial damage provision in its floodplain management law or ordinance that is being enforced against the building.[211] Second, and alternatively, the building has to be a "repetitive loss building."[212] That means it is insured by a FEMA flood insurance policy; has suffered flood damage on two occasions during a ten-year period ending on the date of the second loss; the cost to repair the flood

204. General Property Form Standard Flood Insurance Policy, § III.D.1.

205. The coverage is for a required, not a voluntary, relocation. Nixon v. Nationwide Mut. Ins. Co., 244 F. Supp. 3d 1245 (N.D. Ala. 2017) (no coverage for relocation not required to comply with state or local law).

206. *See* 44 C.F.R. §§ 60.6(b), (c)

207. Bevis v. State Farm Fire & Cas. Co., 2008 U.S. Dist. LEXIS 102271 (D.N.H. Dec. 2, 2008).

208. General Property Form Standard Flood Insurance Policy, § III.D.6.

209. General Property Form Standard Flood Insurance Policy, § III.D.2.

210. Flood damage does not mean *covered* flood damage. Damages not covered under the policy can be factored into the calculation to determine whether the cost to repair equals or exceeds 50 percent of the market value of the building. Hampton v. First Protective Ins., 461 F. Supp. 3d 265, 278 (D.S.C. 2020)

211. General Property Form Standard Flood Insurance Policy, § III.D.3.a.(2).

212. General Property Form Standard Flood Insurance Policy, § III.D.3.a.(1).

damage, on average, equaled or exceeded 25 percent of the market value of the building at the time of each flood loss; and, in addition to the current claim, the previous qualifying claim has to have been paid and the state or community has to have a cumulative, substantial damage provision or repetitive loss provision in its floodplain management law or ordinance that is being enforced against the building.

Increased cost of compliance coverage pays the insured to comply with state or local floodplain management laws or ordinances that meet the minimum FEMA standards as set forth in its regulations.[213] The insurer will pay for compliance activities that exceed those standards under conditions the policy prescribes. The coverage will pay for the incremental cost, after demolition or relocation, of elevating or floodproofing a building during its rebuilding at the same or another site to meet state or local floodplain management laws or ordinances, subject to the exclusion for compliance activities needed to bring additions or improvements made after the loss occurred into compliance.[214] The insurer will also pay to bring a flood-damaged building into compliance with state or local floodplain management laws or ordinances even if that building had received a variance before the present loss from the applicable floodplain management requirements.[215]

[d] Conditions

When a building insured under building property coverage sustains a flood loss, payment for the loss under the increased cost of compliance coverage will be for the increased cost to elevate, floodproof, relocate, or demolish, or any combination of them, caused by the enforcement of current state or local floodplain management ordinances or laws.[216] Payment for eligible demolition activities will be for the cost to demolish and clear the site of the building debris or a portion of it, caused by the enforcement of current state or local floodplain management ordinances or laws. Eligible activities for the cost of clearing the site include those necessary to discontinue utility service to the site and ensure proper abandonment of onsite utilities. When the building is repaired or rebuilt, it must be intended for the same occupancy as the present building unless otherwise required by current floodplain management ordinances or laws.[217]

---

213. General Property Form Standard Flood Insurance Policy, § III.D.3.b. *See* 44 C.F.R. § 60.3. Under the minimum criteria of 44 C.F.R. § 60.3(b)(4), states and communities have to require the elevation or floodproofing of buildings in unnumbered A zones to the base flood elevation where elevation data is obtained from a federal, state, or other source. These compliance activities are also eligible for coverage.

214. General Property Form Standard Flood Insurance Policy, § III.D.3.d.

215. General Property Form Standard Flood Insurance Policy, § III.D.3.e.

216. General Property Form Standard Flood Insurance Policy, § III.D.4.a.

217. General Property Form Standard Flood Insurance Policy, § III.D.4.b.

[e] Exclusions

There are a dozen exclusions that apply specifically to increased cost of compliance coverage.[218] They are

- The cost to comply with any floodplain management law or ordinance in communities participating in the Emergency Program;
- The cost associated with enforcement of any ordinance or law that requires any insured or others to test for, monitor, clean up, remove, contain, treat, detoxify or neutralize, or in any way respond to, or assess the effects of pollutants;
- The loss in value to any insured building because of the requirements of any ordinance or law;
- The loss in residual value of the undamaged portion of a building demolished as a consequence of enforcement of any state or local floodplain management law or ordinance;
- Any increased cost of compliance until the building is elevated, floodproofed, demolished, or relocated on the same or to another premises and unless the building is elevated, floodproofed, demolished, or relocated as soon as reasonably possible after the loss, not to exceed two years;
- Any code upgrade requirements, for example, plumbing or electrical wiring, not specifically related to the state or local floodplain management law or ordinance;
- Any compliance activities needed to bring additions or improvements made after the loss occurred into compliance with state or local floodplain management laws or ordinances;
- Loss because of any ordinance or law with which the insured was required to comply before the current loss;
- Any rebuilding activity to standards that do not meet the FEMA minimum requirements, including where the insured has received a variance in connection with the current flood loss to rebuild the property to an elevation below the base flood elevation;
- Increased cost of compliance for a garage or carport;
- Any building insured under a FEMA Group Flood Insurance Policy; and
- Assessments made by a condominium association on individual condominium unit owners to pay increased costs of repairing commonly owned buildings after a flood in compliance with state or local floodplain management ordinances or laws.

218. *See* General Property Form Standard Flood Insurance Policy, §§ III.D.5.a-l.

[7] Property Not Covered

The policy lists 17 types of property that are not covered.[219] The policy does not insure

- Personal property that is not inside the fully enclosed building;
- A building, and the personal property in it, located entirely in, on, or over water or seaward of mean high tide if it was constructed or substantially improved after September 30, 1982;
- Open structures, including a building used as a boathouse or any structure or building into which boats are floated, and personal property located in, on, or over water;
- Recreational vehicles, other than travel trailers as defined by the policy,[220] whether affixed to a permanent foundation or on wheels;
- Self-propelled vehicles or machines, including their parts and equipment; however, there is coverage for those self-propelled vehicles or machines that are not licensed for use on public roads and are used mainly to service the described location or designed and used to assist handicapped persons, while the vehicles or machines are inside a building at the described location;
- Land, land values, lawns, trees, shrubs, plants, growing crops, or animals;
- Accounts, bills, coins, currency, deeds, evidences of debt, medals, money, scrip, stored value cards, postage stamps, securities, bullion, manuscripts, or other valuable papers;
- Underground structures and equipment, including wells, septic tanks, and septic systems;
- Those portions of walks, walkways, decks, driveways, patios, and other surfaces, all whether protected by a roof or not, located outside the perimeter, exterior walls of the insured building;
- Containers, including related equipment, for example, tanks containing gases or liquids;
- Buildings or units and all their contents if more than 49 percent of the actual cash value of the building is below ground, unless the lowest level is at or above the base flood elevation and is below ground by reason of earth having been used as insulation material in conjunction with energy-efficient building techniques;
- Fences, retaining walls, seawalls, bulkheads, wharves, piers, bridges, and docks;
- Aircraft or watercraft, or their furnishings and equipment;

219. General Property Form Standard Flood Insurance Policy, § IV.
220. General Property Form Standard Flood Insurance Policy, § II.C.6.c.

- Hot tubs and spas that are not bathroom fixtures, and swimming pools, and their equipment, for example, heaters, filters, pumps, and pipes, wherever located;
- Property not eligible for flood insurance pursuant to the provisions of the Coastal Barrier Resources Act and the Coastal Barrier Improvement Act;
- Personal property owned by or in the care, custody, or control of a unit owner, except for property of the type and under the circumstances set forth in the personal property provision of the policy; and
- A residential condominium building located in a Regular Program community.

[8] Exclusions

[a] Losses That Are Not Direct Physical Loss By or From Flood

Under the policy, the insurer will only pay for "direct physical loss by or from flood." Thus, there is no coverage for loss of revenue or profits; loss of access to the insured property or described location; loss of use of the insured property or described location; loss from interruption of business or production; any additional living expenses incurred while the insured building is being repaired or is unable to be occupied for any reason; the cost of complying with any ordinance or law requiring or regulating the construction, demolition, remodeling, renovation, or repair of property, including removal of any resulting debris, except for losses covered under the increased cost of compliance coverage; and any other economic loss suffered by the insured.[221]

The policy also excludes coverage for an alteration of the insured property that significantly increases the risk of flooding,[222] and for anything the insured or any member of household of the insured does or conspires to do to deliberately cause loss by flood.[223]

[b] Flood in Progress

There is a "flood in progress" exclusion in the policy. Should the policy become effective as of the time of a loan closing,[224] the insurer will not pay for a loss caused by a flood that is a continuation of one that existed prior to the coverage becoming effective.[225] In all other circumstances, the insurer will not pay for a loss caused by a flood that is a continuation of one that existed on or

221. General Property Form Standard Flood Insurance Policy, § V.A.
222. General Property Form Standard Flood Insurance Policy, § V.D.10.
223. General Property Form Standard Flood Insurance Policy, § V.D.9.
224. *See* 44 C.F.R. § 61.11(b).
225. General Property Form Standard Flood Insurance Policy, § V.B.

before the day the insured submitted the application for coverage and the correct premium. The date of application is determined by rule.[226]

FEMA guidance to adjusters for claims for which the flood-in-progress exclusion may be helpful in understanding how the agency views the exclusion. FEMA says that damage from a flood that begins on or before the date the policyholder submitted the application for coverage and the correct premium is not insured, even if the flood event does not damage the insured property until *after* the policy's first term begins.[227] When a policyholder asks to add coverage to an existing policy and a flood is already in progress, any damage that occurs to insured property from that same flood event on or before the date the policyholder submitted a request for additional coverage and the correct premium of any increased coverage will only be insured at the prior policy limits. Whether a flood is in progress for a claim, says FEMA, is evaluated on an individual basis.

Evidence that a flood may be in progress may include a recent flood in the community where the insured building is located caused by the same source of flooding as the one on the insured property or an event initiating a flood that causes damage, for example, a spillway opening, a levee breaching, a dam releasing water, or water escaping from the banks of a stream, river, creek, or other waterway.[228] Additionally, sometimes FEMA will determine the date of a flood in a given geographic area, and although that may not be the date a particular policyholder experiences flooding, courts have deferred to the agency determination.[229]

FEMA will apply the exclusion regardless of individual property, city, county, or parish boundaries and does not interpret it as triggered only when flood waters physically touch the insured building.[230] Additionally, it applies regardless of any waiting period provision.[231]

226. *See* 44 C.F.R. § 61.11(f).

227. *National Flood Insurance Program Claims Manual*, at 236 (Oct. 2021).

228. *National Flood Insurance Program Claims Manual*, at 237 (Oct. 2021).

229. In *Roden v. Nationwide Mutual Fire Insurance Co.*, 2014 U.S. Dist. LEXIS 138306 (N.D. Miss. Sept. 30, 2014), FEMA issued a bulletin containing a start date of a flood of April 25. The policyholders sustained flood damage on May 10 and alleged that on April 25 the nearest gauge recorded a depth of almost four feet below flood stage. The insurer denied the policyholders' claim asserting the flood to be in progress given the date set by FEMA. The policyholders argued the "in progress" date was selected in an arbitrary and capricious manner and was inaccurate. The court said that FEMA sets forth guidelines regarding how the flood-in-progress date is established and that Congress has delegated authority to FEMA to issue that guidance and to determine that denial is proper if a flood is deemed to be in progress at a policy's effective date. The court therefore deferred to the agency's interpretation and refused to disturb the determination of the flood-in-progress date.

230. *National Flood Insurance Program Claims Manual*, at 237 (Oct. 2021).

231. *See* 44 C.F.R. § 61.11. FEMA says a policy may be purchased without the 30-day waiting period, but that does not mean that the exclusion does not apply.

When a loss occurs on or before the date the waiting period for coverage began or when there is evidence that a flood may have been in progress on or before the date the policyholder submitted a request for additional coverage, FEMA says that adjusters should identify and investigate the following:

- The date the policy was purchased;
- The date the policy or additional coverage went into effect;
- The date the flooding as defined by the policy began;
- Evidence of flood prevention prior to the effective date of the policy, for example, temporary levees, sandbagging, constructed berms, and pumps; and
- Data sources, including the National Oceanic and Atmospheric Administration (NOAA) for data on river and lake levels, news reports and social media or other sources that may help to determine when flooding was first reported, and community or other officials for assistance in determining lake or river levels.[232]

Adjusters, states FEMA, should interview the policyholder and conduct a neighborhood canvass to determine the location of any flood waters in relation to the insured property location at the time the policy became effective. They are required by FEMA to detail in a narrative their process and evidence used for recommending coverage or denial of it. If they need assistance in confirming when a flood began, they are advised to notify the insurer.[233]

A flood may be in progress, but an intervening event that had not started at the time the policy went into effect could generate a separate, independent flood that is not excluded.[234] FEMA says that if a different flood caused by another source damages the insured property, insurers have to determine if a separate flood-in-progress applies to the loss that invokes the exclusion.[235] Insurers are to consider the date the policyholder submitted the application for coverage or a request for additional coverage under the policy, and the correct premium, and compare it to the start date of this other flood. Insurers may request assistance from FEMA to determine whether a flood began before the policy term or additional coverage became effective, and they are required to report each claim to FEMA in which they apply the flood-in-progress exclusion.

232. *National Flood Insurance Program Claims Manual*, at 237 (Oct. 2021).

233. *National Flood Insurance Program Claims Manual*, at 238 (Oct. 2021).

234. *See, e.g.*, Jones v. Cornerstone Nat'l Ins. Co., 2015 U.S. Dist. LEXIS 22436 (E.D. Mo. Feb. 25, 2015).

235. *National Flood Insurance Program Claims Manual*, at 238 (Oct. 2021).

[c] Earth Movement

The FEMA policy has an "earth movement" exclusion that has been found not to be ambiguous.[236] Under it, there is no coverage for loss to property caused *directly* by earth movement even if that movement is caused by flood.[237] The policy gives as examples of earth movement earthquakes, landslides, land subsidence, sinkholes, destabilization or movement of land that results from accumulation of water in subsurface land areas, and gradual erosion. There is, however, coverage for losses from mudflow and land subsidence that are the result of erosion that are specifically insured under the policy definition of flood. In the early case of *West v. Harris*, the Fifth Circuit said that the policy "provides that the *only* earth movement covered is a mudslide caused or precipitated by accumulation of water on or under the ground."[238] Subsequently the policy was amended to add coverage for losses due to erosion caused by flooding.[239] Courts, therefore, generally say that coverage is limited to earth movement caused by flood-related erosion or mudslide.[240]

In *West*, the insured home was built on reclaimed swamp land, and the soil expanded when wet and contracted when dry. The area received a 12- to 14-inch rainfall that caused flooding in front of the home, but no flood waters entered it. Almost immediately, the homeowners noticed damage to the home. There were small cracks in the walls that steadily grew. A jury found that the damage was a direct loss by flood, and the appellate court said there was sufficient testimony to support that finding; however, the proof also brought into effect the earth movement exclusion. While most courts have followed *West*,[241] others have refused to do so. For example, in an Eleventh Circuit case, a tropical storm produced torrential rain. The area surrounding the insured home flooded, but the home itself did not. It did, however, sustain damage due to the

236. *See, e.g.*, Dippel v. S.C. Farm Bureau Mut. Ins. Co., 2019 U.S. Dist. LEXIS 145686 (D.S.C. Aug. 26, 2019).

237. General Property Form Standard Flood Insurance Policy, § V.C.

238. West v. Harris, 573 F.2d 873, 877 (5th Cir. 1978), *cert. den.*, 440 U.S. 946, 99 S. Ct. 1424, 59 L. Ed. 2d 635 (1979). *See also* Jaskierny v. Mut. of Omaha Ins. Co., 1996 U.S. Dist. LEXIS 19139 (E.D. La. Dec. 17, 1996) (earth movement in SFIP exclusion appears to codify *West*).

239. Quesada v. Dir., Fed. Emergency Mgmt. Agency, 753 F.2d 1011 (11th Cir. 1985).

240. *See, e.g.*, Sodowski v. Nat'l Flood Ins. Program of Fed. Emergency Mgmt. Agency, 834 F.2d 653 (7th Cir. 1987); Plywood Prop. Assocs. v. Nat'l Flood Ins. Program, 928 F. Supp. 500 (D.N.J. 1996); Chesapeake Ship Propeller Co. v. Stickney, 820 F. Supp. 995, 1000 (E.D. Va. 1993); *In re* Stenersen Corp., 61 B.R. 702 (D. Md. 1986).

241. *See, e.g.*, Wagner v. Dir., Fed. Emergency Mgmt. Agency, 847 F.2d 515, 522 (9th Cir. 1988) (courts have all but universally held that FEMA policy does not cover losses stemming from water-caused earth movements and, therefore, there was no coverage where flood waters did not damage insured properties directly and all losses were caused by shifting of the earth beneath them; coverage determined by earth movement exclusion, which expressly precludes coverage for losses caused by landslides).

settling or compacting of the fill beneath the foundation as a result of saturation of the fill by water from the storm. When the saturated fill compacted, the floor slab shifted, fracturing the floors and walls. The appellate court held that the earth movement exclusion did not apply. It distinguished *West* principally because the home in that case was built on reclaimed swampland, which was supported by soil that expanded and contracted with normal changes in the soil moisture.[242]

[d] Water

There is no coverage for direct physical loss caused directly or indirectly by perils that are related to water.[243] For example, there is no coverage for direct physical loss caused directly or indirectly by the pressure or weight of ice, freezing or thawing, and rain, snow, sleet, hail, or water spray.

There is also no coverage for direct physical loss caused directly or indirectly by water, moisture,[244] mildew,[245] or mold damage that results primarily from any condition substantially confined to the insured building or that is within the control of the insured including, but not limited to, design, structural, or mechanical defects; failures, stoppages, or breakage of water or sewer lines, drains, pumps, fixtures, or equipment; or failure to inspect and maintain the property after a flood recedes.[246]

---

242. Quesada v. Dir., Fed. Emergency Mgmt. Agency, 753 F.2d 1011 (11th Cir. 1985). *See also* Woodson v. Allstate Ins. Co., 186 F. Supp. 3d 510, 516 (E.D.N.C. 2016), *rev'd on other grounds*, 855 F.3d 628 (4th Cir. 2017) (damage to ground floor slab caused by subsidence of land along shore of body of water brought about by waves and unusually high water level in natural body of water was covered); Elwell v. Selective Ins. Co. of Am., 2016 U.S. Dist. LEXIS 140515 (D.N.J. Oct. 11, 2016) (policy does not provide that flood-related erosion cannot entail soil settlement or other earth movement, and flood-related erosion may involve some movement of earth).

243. General Property Form Standard Flood Insurance Policy, § V.D.

244. *But see* Hampton v. First Protective Ins., 461 F. Supp. 3d 265, 279 (D.S.C. 2020) (damage from prolonged exposure to moisture during and after a flood constitutes direct physical loss by or from flood); Stevens v. Bankers Ins. Co., 970 F. Supp. 769 (N.D. Cal. 1997) (where, although flood water did not touch inventory, it was damaged by moisture in the air, court held there was coverage as flood water in form of ambient moisture destroyed inventory).

245. *But see* Krauss v. Aetna Cas. & Sur. Flood Ins. Program, 1991 U.S. Dist. LEXIS 6712 (E.D. Pa. May 17, 1991) (where flood waters entered basement but not residence, summary judgment was denied regarding claims for damage to items and structural repairs on first floor as policy could be read to cover humidity/mildew damage; words "directly and proximately caused by a flood" include damage that results from occurrence of flood, although not from immersion in flood water).

246. General Property Form Standard Flood Insurance Policy, § V.D.4. *See, e.g.*, Dippel v. S.C. Farm Bureau Mut. Ins. Co., 2020 U.S. Dist. LEXIS 188335 (D.S.C. June 26, 2020) (policy bars coverage for mold damage that occurs because insured fails to inspect and maintain property after prior flood); Shearer v. State Farm Fire & Cas. Co., 2018 U.S. Dist. LEXIS 6298 (E.D.N.C. Jan. 16, 2018) (no coverage for water, moisture, mildew, or mold damage resulting from failure to inspect and maintain property after flood receded).

The policy does not cover damage caused by long-term exposure to moisture, water, rot, and insect infestation including damage from the lack of climate control inside a building when repairs do not include the timely repair of an HVAC system. The policy also does not cover preexisting damage to structural building components, for example, damage caused by rot, or for any resulting damage to non-structural finished building material. The agency does, however, say that when local authorities restrict, or prolonged inundation of flood water prevents, access, thus blocking the efforts of the insured to promptly remove wet building and personal property items, and the delay directly results in water, moisture, mildew, or mold damage to property not in physical contact with surface flood water, the damage may be covered.[247] FEMA says that for these claims, the claim file must include proper documentation. That includes photographs, an acceptable explanation by the adjuster, or a signed statement by the policyholder or by a community official supporting payment for property damages. Where the damage is substantially confined to the building or within the policyholder's control, the file should include information documenting the failure of the policyholder to inspect and maintain the insured property or take reasonable measures to reduce damage when it was feasible to do so. The SFIP, says FEMA, does not cover damage caused by long-term exposure to moisture, water, rot, and insect infestation including damage from the lack of climate control inside a building when the approach to repair does not include timely repair to the building HVAC system.

The policy also excludes direct physical loss caused directly or indirectly by water or water-borne material that backs up through sewers or drains, discharges or overflows from a sump, sump pump, or related equipment, or seeps or leaks on or through the insured property, unless there is a flood in the area and the flood is the proximate cause of the sewer or drain backup, sump pump discharge or overflow, or seepage of water.[248] Also excluded are direct physical losses caused directly or indirectly by the pressure or weight of water unless there is a flood in the area and the flood is the proximate cause of the damage from the pressure or weight of water.[249] For the exceptions, the adjuster has to document that a flood occurred in the area that was the proximate cause of the backup of the sewer or drain, overflow of the sump pump, pump failure, seepage of water, or damage from the pressure or weight of water.[250] When paying a loss from a flood in the area proximately causing

247. *National Flood Insurance Program Claims Manual*, at 125 (Oct. 2021).

248. General Property Form Standard Flood Insurance Policy, § V.D.5. *See* Donahue v. Am. Family Mut. Ins. Co., 2006 U.S. Dist. LEXIS 9501 (D. Minn. Mar. 6, 2006) (no coverage for sump pump overflow). *Compare* Conrad v. Omaha Prop. & Cas. Ins. Co., 1995 U.S. Dist. LEXIS 7907 (E.D. Pa. June 7, 1995) (no exclusion for seepage from general condition of flood).

249. General Property Form Standard Flood Insurance Policy, § V.D.6.

250. *National Flood Insurance Program Claims Manual*, at 126 (Oct. 2021).

discharge or overflow of water or water-borne material from a sump, sump pump, or related equipment, the insurer has to document the claim file showing that a property policy endorsement or policy rider did not also cover that loss.[251] If coverage is provided by a property policy, payment under the SFIP has to apply a proportional loss distribution.[252] FEMA says that while a flood is two or more parcels of partial or complete inundation of normally dry land, or two or more continuous acres of normally dry land, for purposes of coverage under the exception to the exclusion, the flood does not have to be on the parcel of land described at the location, but may be within the proximate area.

[e] Losses That May Be Covered by Other Insurance

Direct physical losses caused directly or indirectly by power, heating, or cooling failure are not covered unless the failure results from direct physical loss by or from flood to power, heating, or cooling equipment on the described location.[253] There is also an exclusion for the perils of theft, fire, explosion, wind, or windstorm.[254]

[f] Property Located on Land Leased from the Federal Government

The policy does not insure for loss to any building or personal property located on land leased from the federal government, arising from or incident to flooding of that land by the federal government, where the lease expressly holds the federal government harmless under flood insurance issued under any federal government program.[255]

---

251. *National Flood Insurance Program Claims Manual*, at 126 (Oct. 2021). If any property policy does provide coverage, the SFIP payment has to apply a proportional loss distribution.

252. *See* General Property Form Standard Flood Insurance Policy, § VII.B.

253. FEMA explains that the policy does not cover damage to insured property caused by a power surge or outage that originates from failure or shutting down of equipment not located at the described location, *even if the reason is a direct result of a flood.* For example, if a utility shuts down a section of the electrical grid to avoid system damage from a flood, when power returns, the initial surge of electricity can damage insured property, but that damage is not covered. The policy does cover damage to any covered building or personal property item, for example a building's main service, home security system, plugged-in television, or HVAC system, when a flood *physically* damages related system equipment installed at the described location. For example, if a flood damages power equipment at the described location and that damage creates an electrical short within the power system resulting in damage to another item of property part of or connected to the power system, the damage to the item is covered, even though it was not physically touched by flood water. *National Flood Insurance Program Claims Manual*, at 126 (Oct. 2021).

254. General Property Form Standard Flood Insurance Policy, § V.D.8.

255. General Property Form Standard Flood Insurance Policy, § V.E.

5.4 Notice of Loss

[1] Requirement to Give Notice of Loss

The notice of loss from the policyholder is, says FEMA, the first step in the claims process.[256] The FEMA flood insurance policy says that in the case of a flood loss to insured property, the policyholder must give prompt written notice to the insurer.[257] The *Claims Manual* reiterates the requirement.[258] The policy does not define "prompt," and a policyholder brochure says a policyholder should *immediately* report any flood loss to the insurance company or agent who wrote the policy.[259] There is a FEMA form entitled "First Notice of Loss" that the agency says policyholders use to give prompt written notice of a flood loss to their insurer.[260]

[2] The Meaning of "Prompt" Notice

Courts have provided little guidance on the meaning of "prompt" in the FEMA policy. It is not even clear how the notice period is measured. FEMA says notice has to be given "in case of a flood loss to insured property." So, the notice period begins at the time of loss. However, the time of loss may not be easy to determine in a flood. For example, if a property owner evacuates, he or she likely does not know precisely when a loss occurred. Floods may last days, weeks, or even months,[261] making it difficult to establish the date of a loss. Moreover, flood waters may rise, recede, and then rise again.[262] When those fluctuations happen over several months, a policyholder may not know at what point his or her loss transpired. Different losses may happen at different times. For instance, flood waters may initially only damage the exterior of an insured building, but later enter it and damage its contents. A building might be damaged initially on one day and totally destroyed a week later. It may not matter when in fact a flood loss occurred, because FEMA sometimes establishes a "legal" date of loss, usually because of a major flood event.[263]

256. *National Flood Insurance Program Claims Manual*, at 263 (Oct. 2021).

257. General Property Form Standard Flood Insurance Policy, § VII.G.1.

258. *National Flood Insurance Program Claims Manual*, at 263 (Oct. 2021) (SFIP requires policyholder to give prompt written notice of loss to insurer).

259. *Answers to Questions about the NFIP*, at 29 (Feb. 17, 2021), FEMA, https://agents.floodsmart.gov/sites/default/files/fema-answers-to-questions-about-the-NFIP.pdf.

260. *See First Notice of Loss*, FEMA, https://www.fema.gov/sites/default/files/documents/FEMA-form_206-FY-21-110_notice-of-loss_2021.pdf.

261. Floods may even last years. *See, e.g.*, Hooper v. Nat'l Flood Insurers Ass'n, 1977 U.S. Dist. LEXIS 12566 (E.D. Mich. Dec. 5, 1977) (flooding along lake shoreline occurred over two-year period).

262. *See, e.g.*, Presley v. Nat'l Flood Insurers Ass'n, 399 F. Supp. 1242 (E.D. Mo. 1975).

263. *See, e.g.*, www.nfipiservice.com/Stakeholder/pdf/bulletin/w-13008.pdf in which FEMA established a date of loss for New York residents after Hurricane Sandy.

Notice has been considered late when submitted 37 days,[264] 51 days,[265] five months,[266] and seven months after the loss.[267] One court seems to have concluded that a notice of loss has to be submitted within 72 hours "of the flood,"[268] but it did not offer any basis for the 72-hour limit or explain whether the clock should start with the beginning of a flood or its termination.

Curiously, in a case before the Ninth Circuit in which the notice was given 56 days after the loss, the insurer apparently did not challenge the notice as the majority did not discuss it and a dissent characterized the notice as "timely."[269]

Whether notice is "prompt" may well be fact driven as illustrated by an Ohio case in which homeowners noticed problems in their home after two substantial February rainfalls. They did not provide notice of their loss until late June, eight days after a professional engineer advised them that the problems were caused by a flood. The court decided the homeowners had fulfilled notice requirement of the FEMA policy when they promptly contacted their insurance agent after receiving information about the nature and cause of their loss.[270]

[3] Justified Delays

FEMA says that when a policyholder delays a notice of loss, the adjuster for the insurance company should ask questions in order to understand the circumstances and reasons for the delay.[271] The agency explains that the concern is that if an *avoidable* delay caused damage to undamaged property or increased damage from salvageable to non-salvageable property, the policy may not provide coverage. A "justified delay," according to FEMA, could be an order issued by local authorities or a prolonged inundation that prevented the policyholder from gaining prompt access to the property. The agency says there may be other justified delays, but that it is important that an adjuster determines if the delay prejudiced the rights of the insurer to confirm the loss and the amount of insured damage. There is considerable ambiguity in FEMA's

---

264. Galt Ocean Manor Condo. Ass'n, Inc. v. First Cmty. Ins. Co., 2014 U.S. Dist. LEXIS 188209 (S.D. Fla. Mar. 19, 2014).

265. Allender v. Farmers Ins. Exch., 2005 U.S. Dist. LEXIS 27530 (W.D. Wash. Nov. 4, 2005).

266. Ibarra v. Tex. Farmers Ins. Co., 2020 U.S. Dist. LEXIS 10205 (S.D. Tex. Jan. 22, 2020).

267. Jacobson v. Metro. Prop. & Cas. Ins. Co., 672 F.3d 171 (2d Cir. 2012).

268. Arcell v. Kennedy, 1998 U.S. Dist. LEXIS 8157 (E.D. La. May 22, 1998). The property was evidently flooded on May 8. The court noted that there was no proof that the insureds notified the insurer of flood damage within 72 hours of the flood. The records of the insurer showed it was first notified on May 13, which was, as the court said, "more than 72 hours after the receding of the flood waters."

269. Flick v. Liberty Mut. Fire Ins. Co., 205 F.3d 386, 389 (9th Cir.), *cert. den.*, 531 U.S. 927, 121 S. Ct. 305, 148 L. Ed. 2d 245 (2000).

270. Beck v. Director, 1981 U.S. Dist. LEXIS 17307 (N.D. Ohio Nov. 4, 1981).

271. *National Flood Insurance Program Claims Manual*, at 263 (Oct. 2021).

statement about justified delays. Most importantly, it does not explicitly state that a justified delay excuses late notice. It also does not explain how an adjuster for an insurer would be in contact with a policyholder and able to ask questions about the delay *before* any notice when adjusters are not assigned to a claim until notice is given. Indeed, the insurer does not know there is a claim until it receives notice of the loss.

[4] Notice-Prejudice Rule

In most jurisdictions, a late notice would be evaluated pursuant to the "notice-prejudice" rule. Under the rule, a late notice does not defeat a claim unless the insurer is prejudiced by the delay.[272] However, courts do not apply the rule to the FEMA policy. As one court explained, "The standards governing insurance programs administered by private insurers are different from the standards governing insurance programs administered by the federal government. Unlike state courts which typically apply a 'notice-prejudice' or substantial compliance rule, federal courts do not allow policyholders who give late notice of losses to recover under federal flood insurance policies even if the government is not prejudiced by the late notice."[273]

[5] Notice to Insurance Agent

The FEMA policy says the insured must give prompt written notice to the *insurer*. Notice to an *agent of the insured* is not notice to the insurer.[274] On the other hand, notice to the local agent of the insurer meets the notice requirement.[275] Effective October 1, 2021, a FEMA rule states that "[t]he duly licensed property or casualty agent acts for the policyholder and does not act as agent for the Federal Government, the Federal Emergency Management Agency, the Write Your Own (WYO) program participating insurance company . . . or the NFIP servicing agent."[276] Presumably by "licensed property or casualty agent," FEMA does not mean an employee of a WYO carrier or an exclusive agent of the carrier, but that is not completely clear.

---

272. *See* 1 Jeffery E. Thomas, *New Appleman on Insurance Law Library Edition* § 4.04[4][d] (LexisNexis 2022).

273. Bleecker v. Std. Fire Ins. Co., 130 F. Supp. 2d 726, 731 (E.D.N.C. 2000).

274. *See, e.g.*, Briggs & Stratton Corp. v. Royal Globe Ins. Co., 64 F. Supp. 2d 1346 (M.D. Ga. 1999) (notice to independent insurance agent or broker who is agent of insured does not constitute notice to insurer).

275. *See, e.g.*, Nixon v. Nationwide Mut. Ins. Co., 244 F. Supp. 3d 1245 (N.D. Ala. 2017).

276. 44 C.F.R. § 61.13(f).

5.5 Claims Adjustment

[1] Generally

Claim adjustment is the "ascertainment of the amount that an insured should recover from a loss."[277] It is an analysis and valuation of a loss and settling of the amount of the payment the underwriting insurer is required to pay to the insured under the policy. This section focuses especially on the role of the independent insurance adjuster as prescribed by FEMA. The agency's advice and requirements for adjusters can be valuable to claimants. First, it forewarns them of what to expect in the adjustment process. Second, it alerts them to the type of information for which the adjuster will look. Next, it educates claimants, allowing them to ask questions that may help them obtain a favorable settlement of their claim. Finally, it can help claimants better prepare to contest any offer made by the insurer that they consider to be unsatisfactory.

[2] Claims Adjusters

[a] Generally

An adjuster is assigned to investigate a claim after the insured has given written notice of a loss. Adjusters may be either "independent" or an employee of the insurer—that is, a staff adjuster.[278] Independent adjusters must register with the National Flood Insurance Program to be able to adjust flood losses for NFIP insurers, and they have to possess an active Flood Control Number (FCN).[279] FEMA specifies the necessary qualifications. The Adjuster Registration Application contains five registration categories. They are residential, manufactured home/travel trailer, small commercial, large commercial, and condominium.[280] Adjusters may register for any or all categories if they meet the FEMA adjuster qualification requirements. The fact that an adjuster does not meet FEMA requirements does not relieve the insured of duties under the policy including filing a complete and timely proof of loss.[281]

---

277. *The Wolters Kluwer Bouvier Law Dictionary Desk Edition* (2012). *See also Insurance Operations—Claim Procedures and the Claim Adjustment Process*, Frank Thompson, https://sites.uni.edu/thompsona/Claims%20Settlement.pdf (claims adjusting is process of determining coverage, legal liability, and settling claim).

278. The WYO insurers that process claims often contract with a company that employs independent adjusters. These independent adjusters travel to areas where there have been storms and floods. They are, therefore, sometimes called "storm troopers." Koehler, *Flood: Understanding and Recovering from One of Nature's Worst Disasters*, at 3 (2008), Adjusting Today, https://icma.org/documents/flood-understanding-and-recovering-one-natures-worst-disasters.

279. *National Flood Insurance Program Claims Manual*, at 12 (Oct. 2021).

280. *National Flood Insurance Program Claims Manual*, at 13 (Oct. 2021).

281. Touchton v. Fid. Nat'l Prop. & Cas. Ins. Co., 911 F. Supp. 2d 505 (E.D. Mich. 2012). The adjuster assigned to investigate the claim in *Touchton* never inspected the property, but

At one time, FEMA said that an adjuster would *generally* contact the insured within 24 to 48 hours after receiving a notice of loss.[282] The agency conceded that "depending on local conditions and the severity of flooding, it may take more time."[283] Today, FEMA tells insureds that an adjuster should contact them within a "few days" of starting the claim and that if they do not hear from an adjuster, they can contact their insurance agent or the company again.[284] On the other hand, the agency tells adjusters that they *must* contact a policyholder within 24 to 48 hours of the *claim assignment*, "or as soon as reasonably possible depending size and scope of the storm."[285] All that notwithstanding, there have been instances in which adjusters completed their work without ever contacting the insured.[286]

FEMA says the initial contact will *preferably* be by telephone; however, if that is not possible, the adjuster *will* send the policyholder or designated agent an electronic message, postcard, or letter that acknowledges the assignment and provides the adjuster's telephone number and any other means of contact.

As if there were not enough ambiguity already, the SFIP has a "claims guidelines" section at the end of the policy. It instructs insureds to "[i]dentify the claims adjuster assigned to your claim and contact him or her if you have not been contacted within 24 hours after you reported the claim to your insurance representative."

[b] Adjuster Conduct

FEMA "expects" claims professionals to adopt the agency's "core values" of compassion, fairness, integrity, and respect.[287] Its expectations include that claims professionals will do the following:

- Know the unique reporting requirements of the NFIP;
- Communicate the coverage and limitations to policyholders during an inspection;

---

sent an assistant who was not a licensed insurance adjuster. The adjuster prepared two proofs of loss that the insureds said were inaccurate. The failure of the licensed adjuster to inspect the property and to prepare accurate proofs of loss did not help the insureds in their subsequent litigation. The insurer prevailed because insureds never submitted a proof of loss.

282. *Flood Insurance Claims Handbook*, at 5 (FEMA, Aug. 2014).

283. It can take weeks before an adjuster *inspects* the insured property. *See, e.g.*, Azoulay v. Allstate Ins. Co., 2014 U.S. Dist. LEXIS 159177 (D. Conn. Nov. 12, 2014) (insured submitted claim in late August 27 and adjuster inspected property on September 21).

284. *Starting Your Recovery: FEMA's Flood Insurance Claims Process*, at 1 (FEMA Sept. 22, 2020).

285. *National Flood Insurance Claims Manual*, at 269 (Oct. 2021).

286. *See* Darouiche v. Fid. Nat'l Ins. Co., 415 Fed. Appx. 548 (5th Cir. 2011) (before insured learned of damage to property, insurer opened claim and assigned it to independent adjuster who determined amount due).

287. *National Flood Insurance Program Claims Manual*, at 9 (Oct. 2021). "Diversity" was listed as a core FEMA value in the prior edition of the manual but was removed from the current edition, meaning, evidently, that diversity is no longer a FEMA value.

- Adjust all claims in compliance with the SFIP, the *Claims Manual*, and any applicable bulletin issued by FEMA;
- Help the policyholder document his or her loss as completely and accurately as reasonably possible;
- Respond promptly to all inquiries, be available to answer questions, update the policyholder about the status of a claim, and present clear and correct information about the claim;
- Include all allowances payable in the policy in the estimate and, because NFIP coverage differs from other policies, spend additional time if needed addressing differences with the policyholder;
- Explain coverage early in the claim process in a clear manner;[288]
- Set reasonable expectations with policyholders and ensure that they understand what is required to complete adjustment of their claim; and
- Be considerate of the policyholder's time, keep appointments, and honor their commitments.[289]

FEMA asserts that all individuals handling claims *will* maintain the "highest standards of honesty, impartiality, character, and conduct."[290] The agency says it does not accept any professional conflict of interest. Any independent adjuster or adjusting firm performing work on behalf of the NFIP or registered in the Flood Adjuster Capacity Program (FACP) may not work in any capacity providing support, inspections, consulting, or estimating for or as a public adjuster (licensed or not), or provide representation adverse to the NFIP. Adjusters cannot accept any money from a third party to steer business to a specific firm or individual, nor may they accept monetary or nonmonetary incentives from policyholders. When FEMA receives a complaint asserting a violation of its Code of Conduct, it will investigate to confirm the validity of the complaint. When an insurer or adjusting firm learns of a violation, it has to conduct an internal investigation and immediately notify FEMA if the violation is confirmed.[291] If FEMA determines that there was a violation of the Code of Conduct, it will act to revoke the FCN for a period of one year or longer and provide notification to the adjuster.

Despite FEMA's ostensible commitment to the "highest standards," insureds have accused adjusters of intimidation and misconduct.[292] However,

288. For example, says the agency, post-FIRM elevated building and basement coverage can confuse the policyholder and require additional explanation.

289. *National Flood Insurance Program Claims Manual*, at 10 (Oct. 2021).

290. *National Flood Insurance Program Claims Manual*, at 14 (Oct. 2021).

291. *National Flood Insurance Program Claims Manual*, at 15 (Oct. 2021).

292. *See, e.g.*, McGair v. Am. Bankers Ins. Co., 693 F.3d 94 (1st Cir. 2012) (insured alleged adjuster attempted to intimidate her by telling her that she had no coverage and encouraged her to misrepresent claim as one for drywall, which was covered, instead of wood paneling, which was not); Baker v. Allstate Ins. Co., 2007 U.S. Dist. LEXIS 61029 (E.D. La. Aug. 20, 2007) (insured alleged insurer instructed its adjusters to undervalue damages, delay processing of claims, and engage in multiple, time-consuming valuations of claims).

the majority rule is that independent adjusters do not owe a general duty of care to an insured.[293] If a policyholder *knows* the independent adjuster is working for the insurer, that adjuster is generally not liable for any misconduct that injures the policyholder.[294]

[c] Adjuster Authority

FEMA says it expects adjusters to understand, and to communicate to a policyholder, that they do not have the authority to approve or deny a claim.[295] Adjustments are only recommendations and subject to review by the insurer. An adjuster should, says FEMA, follow the insurer's guidelines; however, any questions that require clarification should be forwarded through the internal chain of command.

[d] Inspection of Property

The prior *Adjuster Claims Manual* said the adjuster was *required* to inspect the property within 48 hours of *receiving the loss assignment.*[296] Currently, FEMA simply says that an adjuster who cannot inspect "within a reasonable timeframe" should promptly submit a status report explaining the cause for the delay.[297] FEMA adds that an adjuster should *avoid* visiting the insured without an appointment.

The FEMA *Claims Manual* imposes a few obligations on adjusters making a site visit. Adjusters must provide a policyholder with a copy of the *Flood Insurance Claims Handbook*[298] and Increased Cost of Compliance (ICC) Brochure. An adjuster has to spend time reviewing these documents with the policyholder and discuss with the policyholder flood coverage and non-coverage issues, and how they apply to the loss. The adjuster, however, may not say whether the insurer will approve or deny the claim. The adjuster also has to confirm that any mortgagee is correct and identify all parties to the contract.

---

293. Plitt & Sandstrom, *Evaluating the Relationship between Independent Insurance Adjusters and Insureds: The Case against Imposing an Independent Duty of Care*, 48 Creighton L. Rev. 245, 261 (2015).

294. Stempel, *The "Other" Intermediaries: The Increasingly Anachronistic Immunity of Managing General Agents and Independent Claims Adjusters*, 15 Conn. Ins. L.J. 599, 608 (2009). *See* Marzen, *The Personal Liability of Insurance Claims Adjusters for Insurance Bad Faith*, 118 W. Va. L. Rev. 411 (2015), for a discussion of the liability of adjusters who are employees of the insurer.

295. *National Flood Insurance Program Claims Manual*, at 11 (Oct. 2021).

296. *Adjuster Claims Manual*, at II-4 (FEMA, Sept. 2013).

297. *National Flood Insurance Program Claims Manual*, at 251 (Oct. 2021). The manual also says the adjuster should address inspection delays caused by the policyholder, or representatives of the policyholder, including failure to set a reasonable time and date to conduct the inspection.

298. Presumably this means the "National Flood Insurance Claims Manual," as there is no handbook.

Additionally, FEMA says the adjuster *should* present his or her FCN card and any government-issued photo ID to the policyholder at the beginning of the inspection.[299]

A FEMA fact sheet describes what policyholders should expect from the adjuster at the inspection.[300] It says that the adjuster should do the following:

- Explain the NFIP flood claims process;
- Inspect the property, and during the inspection scope the loss by taking measurements and photos;
- Explain what an advance payment is and how to receive one;
- Discuss the policy coverage and provide information about how to present the loss to the insurance company;
- Ask for a current mailing address and phone number if the insured has been displaced;
- Discuss eligibility for Increased Cost of Compliance;
- Help present the claim to the insurer by submitting all the necessary documents to support the loss;
- Provide a repair estimate of the damage;
- Provide a proof of loss for signature if required; and
- Answer questions about the claim.

FEMA warns insureds that the adjuster should never ask them for money, collect the deductible amount, or charge a fee for his or her services.

[e] Remote Claims Adjusting

[i] Generally

FEMA authorizes remote adjusting when appropriate.[301] Remote adjusting requires the agreement and cooperation of the policyholder. Remote adjusting does not constitute a waiver of any documentation requirements of the SFIP nor shift any responsibilities under the SFIP. FEMA warns that remote adjusting is only appropriate in certain circumstances.[302] Every loss is unique and, therefore, adjusters should evaluate each claim on a case-by-case basis to determine if remote adjustment is appropriate.[303] FEMA say remote adjustment is not the best option in the following scenarios:

---

299. *National Flood Insurance Program Claims Manual*, at 250 (Oct. 2021).

300. *See Starting Your Recovery: FEMA's Flood Insurance Claims Process* (FEMA Sept. 22, 2020).

301. *National Flood Insurance Program Claims Manual*, at 278 (Oct. 2021). FEMA limits remote adjusting to adjusters with an active flood control number (FCN) registered for the claim type they are handling. Adjuster trainees or mentored adjusters may not remotely adjust claims.

302. *National Flood Insurance Program Claims Manual*, at 279 (Oct. 2021).

303. FEMA says adjusters should discuss with the adjusting firm if remote adjustment is appropriate for a specific claim and explain the decision to remote adjust the loss in the narrative report.

- The policyholder lacks necessary technical equipment, for example a smart phone, internet, or cell service;
- The policyholder is not able to access the damaged property;
- The policyholder requests a physical inspection;
- The level of detail required to support a payment recommendation is high, and the time required from the policyholder would be unreasonable or burdensome;
- There is a need for a subject matter expert;
- The cause of loss is in question or may require neighborhood canvassing to confirm general condition of flood;
- The adjuster is unable to confirm the building description or there are underwriting questions;
- There is substantial damage to the property;
- There is a third party representing the policyholder;
- There is damage from other perils; and
- The adjuster is not able to substantiate prior loss repairs.[304]

[ii] Adjuster Responsibilities When Remote Claim Adjusting

FEMA says adjusters must use the methods approved by the flood insurer to remotely survey the damage with the policyholder or review photos that the policyholder provides to remotely adjust the loss.[305] Adjusters are required to communicate directly with policyholders and devote a sufficient amount of time to confirm the proper rating and coverage, instruct the policyholder on what is needed to document the loss, assist the policyholder in securing the visual documentation necessary to support scope, secure measurements, and verify the extent of damage. When an adjuster remotely adjusts a claim, the adjuster must provide the policyholder with a copy of the NFIP *Claims Handbook* by mail or email, and place extra emphasis on protecting the policyholder by using encryption and password-protected documents, conducting communications with the policyholder from a non-public location, and not sharing information with third parties without the express permission of the policyholder.

[iii] Release of Claim File Information to Policyholders

In a remote adjustment, the adjuster is required to do the following:

- Ensure files contain the photographs or other documentation provided by the policyholder to support a general condition of flood and direct physical damage by or from flood and the loss, with photographs clearly depicting water lines and damages;

---

304. *National Flood Insurance Program Claims Manual*, at 279–80 (Oct. 2021).

305. *National Flood Insurance Program Claims Manual*, at 278 (Oct. 2021). FEMA notes that each flood insurer may already have existing apps, web portals, or other technology to remotely survey policyholder damage.

- Determine building valuation based on reasonably available information to confirm insurance to value; and
- Maximize the use of trusted digital signature methods to complete the proof of loss.[306]

[iv] Best Practices for Remote Adjusting
FEMA says that when a claim is remotely adjusted, clear and concise communication is imperative because the policyholder becomes the eyes of the adjuster.[307] Adjusters, at a minimum, have to explain to a policyholder their role in the remote adjustment process and supply directions describing the following:

- How to document a general and temporary condition of flood, the process used to make this determination, and locate and measure interior and exterior water lines;
- Why room measurements are necessary and how to aid in obtaining the measurements;
- How to frame and capture damage in a photo;
- The importance of exterior and interior photos, including damaged and undamaged building and contents;
- Building equipment and contents claim requirements such as capturing in photographs the make, model, and serial numbers of major appliances, electronics, and items of exceptional value; and
- The need to keep swatches of carpet, drapes, and upholstery of unrepairable contents when removing debris to show the adjuster if necessary, and the need to carefully photograph all materials that must be removed.

The adjuster's narrative in a remote adjustment has to confirm that a general and temporary condition of flood existed and explain evidence of direct physical damage by or from flood, how like kind and quality of replaced items were identified, how room measurements were documented, and additional methods used to verify measurements, for example, tax records, realty sites, and prior losses.

[v] Insurer Responsibilities
FEMA says that when remotely adjusting a loss, insurers must ensure that coverage is confirmed; that cause, extent of damage, and direct physical damage by or from flood are clearly documented and supported; and that files contain all required documentation prior to payment.[308] FEMA warns that it may conduct a quality review on claims that are remote adjusted.

306. *National Flood Insurance Program Claims Manual*, at 278–79 (Oct. 2021). FEMA says the trusted method could be a digital signature or a photograph of the signed proof of loss, which is still due 60 days from the date of loss.

307. *National Flood Insurance Program Claims Manual*, at 279 (Oct. 2021).

308. *National Flood Insurance Program Claims Manual*, at 280 (Oct. 2021).

[f] Claims Adjustment Guidance for Adjusters

[i] Determining Cause of Loss

FEMA says that adjusters have to confirm on every claim that a general and temporary condition of flooding occurred, as defined in the policy, and that may require canvassing the neighborhood to identify if other properties flooded, interviewing neighbors, or reviewing news articles or videos documenting the flood.[309] Sometimes, FEMA advises, contacting the nearest police or fire department may help confirm a general and temporary condition of flood. The adjuster is required to document when the flooding began, the source of the water, and whether the flood caused direct physical loss to covered property.[310]

FEMA recommends that during the claims process, adjusters consider using information provided by FEMA—for example, Geographic Information Systems (GIS) products—information provided by state or county government websites, publicly available information like online real estate listings, or open-source map products that show the property in its pre-disaster condition.

[ii] Building Scope and Estimate

Before adjusting losses, adjusters have to ensure that related software is properly calibrated for the geographic area where the loss occurred and accounts for post-disaster pricing factors and property-specific issues. [311] They have to consistently document all state and local sales tax on applicable goods or services, subject to applicable depreciation. They have to document the scope of loss and provide notations for scope, quantity, and quality. Adjusters have to take or obtain "meaningful" photographs of the loss that clearly document damaged and non-damaged items and support the recommendation for payment or non-payment of the claim, or any portion of the claim. They have to identify covered flood-damaged building components and estimate the reasonable and necessary cost of repair or replacement of the damaged property. FEMA says the scope of damage includes room measurements, preliminary damage findings, and photographs that document and describe the quantity, quality, and extent of damage to covered property. The agency says adjusters should account for conditions unique to the loss or location and factors, for example, exceptional quantities, craftmanship, or assemblies, that may require an adjustment to the scope and price to repair. These adjustments should be documented by the adjuster with a notation in the estimate under the applicable line item. The adjuster should determine if damaged items are salvageable, requiring cleaning, refinishing, or repair, or if the damages are non-salvageable and require replacement. In the estimate of loss, the adjuster should include

309. *National Flood Insurance Program Claims Manual*, at 222 (Oct. 2021).
310. *National Flood Insurance Program Claims Manual*, at 222 (Oct. 2021).
311. *National Flood Insurance Program Claims Manual*, at 224 (Oct. 2021).

the itemized listing of all damaged property items, organized room by room, in the unit-cost style of estimating. The unit pricing should include all costs related to labor, material, and equipment use, and only include the expense that restores the property with like kind and quality material and labor. The pricing should be reasonable and customary to the loss and location. FEMA says that once a policyholder obtains a signed agreement with a contractor, if differences exist with the insurance estimate, it may be necessary for the adjuster, supervising adjuster, or claim examiner to communicate with the policyholder and the contractor to understand the pricing differences or explain coverage issues to reach a claim settlement.[312]

Note that FEMA has a form that it says is used by adjusters to list potentially substantial damaged structures in preparation for a possible increased cost of compliance (ICC) claim.[313]

[iii] Personal Property/Contents

FEMA says adjusters are expected to list, document, and value the *entire* contents loss and to provide that list to the policyholder for review.[314] If a policyholder chooses to complete the inventory, then adjusters are expected to start it and ensure the policyholder understands how to document the remaining contents. Adjusters have to include documentation that supports the claimed loss by photographing the extent of damages, quantities, qualities, and value and have to ensure coverage and depreciation are appropriately applied to their recommendation. They also have to explain their judgment on recommending repair instead of replacement when it may not be apparent to the policyholder or the claims examiner. The contents inventory should include notations specific to the applicable line item that address descriptions of quality, make, model and serial number when applicable, quantity, age, special limit item, and cost to replace with like kind and quality at current pricing.[315] Damages should be listed room by room, be priced individually with like kind and quality, and include all costs related to applicable tax, removal, shipping, and assembly. Each replaced item has to individually include a fair and reasonable rate of depreciation that represents the age or physical condition of the item at the time of loss. FEMA says adjusters should address any salvage or buyback opportunity with the policyholder or with a third party, promptly, and provide an explanation in the interim or narrative report. When a policyholder agrees to buyback items, that should be fully disclosed in the content loss as a credit under the applicable property line item.

---

312. *National Flood Insurance Program Claims Manual*, at 225 (Oct. 2021).

313. *Adjuster's Preliminary Flood Damage Assessment* (FEMA Form 086-0-20), FEMA, https://www.fema.gov/sites/default/files/documents/FEMA-Form_086-0-20_preliminary-damage-assessment.pdf.

314. *National Flood Insurance Program Claims Manual*, at 225 (Oct. 2021).

315. *National Flood Insurance Program Claims Manual*, at 226 (Oct. 2021).

[iv] Special Limits

Adjusters have to apply the $2,500 special limit in their recommendation to the aggregate actual cash value (ACV) of all applicable contents described in the policy, for example, jewelry, furs, and contents used in business.[316] They should add documentation to the claim file to support the recommended payment. FEMA reminds adjusters that the aggregate ACV is subject to the policy deductible, and any excess loss to items subject to the $2,500 special limits cannot be applied to the contents deductible.

[v] Depreciation

Adjusters, says FEMA, should apply depreciation based on the age and physical condition of each item replaced in the building and the personal property estimates.[317] Application of the same rate of depreciation (lump-sum) to all building and personal property items is not an acceptable practice because items of property come in a variety of materials, are purchased or installed on different dates, are used for different purposes, and have differing life expectancies. FEMA says the adjuster should apply depreciation to the material, labor, and equipment usage, including overhead and profit and sales tax, on all claimed replacement items of property. All claimed replacement items have to reflect depreciation, regardless of whether the loss qualifies for replacement cost or ACV loss settlement. Adjusters, says FEMA, should document the claim file to support the rate of depreciation or the lack of depreciation. If an adjuster applies minimal or no depreciation, the narrative should include the underlying rationale. When considering the rate of depreciation for any replaced item of property, the agency says, the adjuster should take into account previous repairs or modifications that may have extended the life of the item beyond its original condition.

[vi] Progress Notes

FEMA requires adjusters to note certain information in the claim file. That includes information that adequately reflects the progress of the claim and communications with the policyholder. An adjuster also has to note the scope of damage, calculations of replacement cost and actual cash value, and a diagram of the insured building with measurements. The file has to include information that confirms receipt of documents or information provided by the policyholder.[318]

---

316. *National Flood Insurance Program Claims Manual*, at 226 (Oct. 2021).
317. *National Flood Insurance Program Claims Manual*, at 226 (Oct. 2021).
318. *National Flood Insurance Program Claims Manual*, at 227 (Oct. 2021).

[vii] Flood-in-Progress Exclusion

When a flood claim is reported, an insurer has to determine when it started and if the flood-in-progress exclusion applies.[319] The adjuster is required to investigate if a flood is already in progress on or before the date the policyholder submitted the application for coverage under the SFIP and paid the correct premium. FEMA explains that the policy excludes a loss directly or indirectly caused by a flood that is already in progress on or before the date the policyholder submitted the application for coverage. Thus, damage from a flood that begins on or before the date the policyholder submitted the application is not insured, even if the flood event does not damage the insured property until after the first term of the policy begins. When, at the request of the policyholder, coverage is added to an existing policy and a flood is already in progress, damage to insured property from that same flood event on or before the date the policyholder submitted a request for additional coverage and the correct premium of any increased coverage will only be insured at the prior policy limits.

Whether a flood is in progress for a claim is evaluated on an individual basis.[320] FEMA says that evidence that a flood may be in progress on or before the date the policyholder submitted the application for coverage or request for additional coverage may include either a flood in the area where the insured building is located caused by the same source of flooding as the flood on the insured property or an event initiating a flood that causes damage, for instance, a spillway opening, a levee breach, a dam releasing water, or water escaping from the banks of a waterway. FEMA asserts that it will apply the flood-in-progress exclusion regardless of individual property, city, county, or parish boundaries and does not interpret it as triggered only when flood waters *physically* touch the insured building.

When a loss occurs on or before the date the waiting period for coverage began or when there is evidence that a flood may have been in progress on or before the date the policyholder submitted a request for additional coverage, FEMA says the adjuster should identify and investigate the following:

- The date the policy was purchased;
- The date the policy or additional coverage went into effect;
- The date the flooding began;
- Evidence of flood prevention prior to the effective date of the policy, for example temporary levees, sandbagging, constructed berms, or pumps; and

319. *National Flood Insurance Program Claims Manual*, at 236 (Oct. 2021).
320. *National Flood Insurance Program Claims Manual*, at 237 (Oct. 2021).

- Data sources, including the NOAA for data on river and lake levels, news reports, and social media or other sources that may help to determine when flooding was first reported, and officials for assistance in determining lake or river levels.

FEMA also says adjusters should interview the policyholder and conduct a neighborhood canvass to determine the location of the flood waters in relation to the insured property at the time the policy became effective. In the narrative, the adjuster is required to detail the process followed and evidence used for recommending coverage or denial. If the adjuster needs assistance in confirming when a flood began, FEMA says he or she should notify the insurer.

Insurers may request assistance from FEMA in determining whether a flood began before the policy term or additional coverage became effective and are required to report each claim to FEMA to which an insurer applies the flood-in-progress exclusion.[321]

[viii] Lowest Elevated Floor Determination

Determining the lowest elevated floor is critical. Full coverage for post-FIRM elevated buildings in an SFHA begins at the lowest elevated floor, which is the lowest floor raised above ground, even if pilings extend beyond it.[322] False floors and raised floors that appear to be elevated do not qualify as the lowest elevated floor. A "hanging floor"[323] would qualify as a lowest elevated floor for the purposes of full coverage. Full coverage in a "non-V zone"[324] starts at the top of the floor.

FEMA says that if an elevated floor is constructed over a crawlspace and the crawlspace is below the ground level on all sides, the building is not elevated and its lowest floor is the below-ground-level crawlspace floor, meeting the policy definition of a basement.[325] If the building is rated elevated, it will require correction. An elevated building with an attached garage that has been converted to living space is considered a non-elevated building.

[ix] Overhead and Profit

FEMA says that overhead and profit (OHP) is added to an estimate when the complexity of the repairs requires coordination by a general contractor at a typical industry standard of 10 percent overhead and 10 percent profit.[326] Adjusters should evaluate each claim, says the agency, and document support of their decision in the file.

321. *National Flood Insurance Program Claims Manual*, at 238 (Oct. 2021).
322. *National Flood Insurance Program Claims Manual*, at 254 (Oct. 2021).
323. The *Claims Manual* provides an example of a "hanging floor."
324. A "V zone" is a coastal area with an increased chance of flooding.
325. *National Flood Insurance Program Claims Manual*, at 255 (Oct. 2021).
326. *National Flood Insurance Program Claims Manual*, at 263 (Oct. 2021).

Overhead expenses are the ongoing costs associated with running a business and are typically categorized as indirect (general) or direct. Indirect overhead costs are fees that a contractor pays on a regular basis that are not specific to a particular job, for example, salaries and benefits for office personnel who may not work on the site, office rent, utilities, supplies, phone and internet lines, business insurance and licenses, and various ongoing expenses like marketing, advertising, travel costs, and legal fees. Direct overhead costs are typically those ongoing costs for a particular job, for example, short-term office structures like trailers, architect's stations, and leased office space; project-specific salaries for foremen, schedulers, engineers, and job superintendents; job-specific equipment rental; and short-term water and sanitation facilities.

When a policyholder performs the duties of a general contractor on some trades or repairs, the policyholder is entitled to a fair overhead allowance, but not profit, for the time spent hiring, scheduling, and overseeing repair performance. The allowance is limited to 5 percent. The adjuster, says FEMA, has to fully justify a higher percentage.

FEMA says it typically omits general contractor OHP on adjuster-estimated allowances for cleanup, treatment against mold and mildew, building dry-out, HVAC, kitchen appliances, carpet and padding, and contractor receipts or quotes. These "Non-OHP trades," says the agency, are mostly performed by the policyholder or outside services hired by the policyholder.[327] If the general contractor estimates or repairs include "Non-OHP trades," FEMA says the adjuster should ensure justification, note the file, and apply OHP accordingly.

[x] Coverage and Controlled Substances

FEMA prohibits issuance of a policy to a person or entity that acknowledges that the property is used in violation of the federal law on "maintaining drug-involved premises."[328] Use of property to grow or dispense marijuana violates that law. A policy will be voided and a claim denied where it is discovered that the insured property is *likely* in violation of that law because it is used primarily and principally for the manufacture or distribution of a controlled substance. FEMA says a flood insurance policy has to be voided and coverage denied where it is determined after a claim has been filed that it is *more likely than not* that the primary or principal use of the insured structure has been manufacture or distribution of a controlled substance. When there is a question of coverage, adjusters are required to conduct a "reasonable investigation" to confirm the use of the property and report the information to the insurer to confirm coverage.

327. *National Flood Insurance Program Claims Manual*, at 264 (Oct. 2021).

328. *National Flood Insurance Program Claims Manual*, at 261 (Oct. 2021). *See* 21 U.S.C. § 856.

[xi] Remediation, Drying, and Emergency Service Contractors
FEMA says that when a loss is covered, there are five ways an adjuster can include the cost to structurally dry salvageable building materials.[329] First, the cost can be calculated by square footage. Under this method, the allowance represents the estimated cost and time to structurally dry the building based on the time and equipment of the owner, including the building HVAC system. FEMA says an increased allowance for treating against mold and mildew may be required on longer drying efforts. An average base unit price can be derived, says the agency, by adding the estimated allowances for an average loss and then dividing the sum by the square foot for an average-size dwelling. The unit price may then be adjusted based on the facts of the loss. Adjusters may also list each allowance in the estimate without converting them to a square foot unit price.

When professional drying or rental equipment is used, but there is no properly completed "drying log,"[330] the number of dehumidifiers and air movers and the number of days of drying are based on the length of time flood water remained inside the building; the reasonable period unsalvageable materials remained installed; and the length of time after removal of unsalvageable building items, building cleanup, and sanitizing was performed, to the start of mechanical drying. FEMA warns that the scope and costs have to be reasonable and in line with water mitigation costs.

If professional drying services are performed and a properly completed drying log is provided along with the itemized invoice, then FEMA says the claim payment should consider the number and type of equipment for the duration of time validated by the drying log and again, the scope and costs have to be reasonable and in line with water mitigation costs.

FEMA says Personal Protective Equipment (PPE) is covered, but the cost is considered included in the unit price for material removal, cleaning, or mildewcide application. The adjuster has the responsibility of discussing and negotiating the mitigation estimate with the mitigation company and has to verify what the contractor estimate line items contain. The adjuster may only include in the estimate what is insured by the SFIP and must not allow a duplication of those items.

Finally, FEMA says the majority of the work performed to mitigate water damage can be addressed using line-item unit cost pricing, including labor

329. *National Flood Insurance Program Claims Manual*, at 277 (Oct. 2021).

330. A drying log is a record of daily temperature and relative humidity readings of both indoor and outdoor air, moisture readings and the recorded location of affected and unaffected building materials, the drying goal, and dry standard for the affected materials. The properly completed log, an industry standard, should also include a moisture map, the daily operating status of the building's HVAC system, and all instruments and equipment used by the technician. *National Flood Insurance Program Claims Manual*, at 277 (Oct. 2021).

and profit.[331] Lump-sum, unexplained charges, and charges based on time and expense should be investigated and documented to identify the charge and to prevent duplication of charges. Ancillary charges of travel, food, and lodging by the water mitigation company are not payable.

FEMA recommends that for more information, adjusters consult either the Structural Drying bulletin, which is appendix F to the *Claims Manual*, or the *Standard and Reference Guide for Professional Water Damage Restoration* (2021) published by the Institute of Inspection Cleaning and Restoration Certification (IICRC). The guide is available for purchase online.[332]

[g] Non-Waiver Agreements and Reservation of Rights Letters

A non-waiver agreement allows the adjuster to investigate a loss where a potential coverage concern exists without waiving the rights of the National Flood Insurance Program. FEMA says insurers may require use of a reservation of rights or non-waiver agreement in accordance with their standard business practices. A non-waiver agreement or reservation of rights may, says the agency, be the most effective way of communicating that late filing of a claim may prejudice the rights of the insurer to fully investigate it.[333] To the extent possible, the adjuster is to include all known reasons for the non-waiver agreement. If the policyholder will not sign the non-waiver agreement, the adjuster is to contact the insurer to send a reservation of rights letter.

[h] Guidance to Adjusters on Claims for Specific Property

[i] Generally

The FEMA *Claims Manual* provides guidance to adjusters on how to evaluate claims for some specific losses. Understanding this guidance allows a claimant and his or her representatives to be better prepared to make the case for coverage. The manual also provides advice to policyholders that can be invaluable in obtaining coverage.

[ii] Countertops

FEMA provides extensive direction on the adjustment of claims for countertops. Note that the agency says its documentation requirements apply to any "countertop, sink, toilet, vanity top, bathtub, shower stall, or other such fixture."[334]

FEMA has developed guidelines for adjusters about the various types of materials used for countertops and precautions for removing and resetting

331. *National Flood Insurance Program Claims Manual*, at 277 (Oct. 2021)
332. *See* https://iicrc.org/s500/.
333. *National Flood Insurance Program Claims Manual*, at 263 (Oct. 2021).
334. *National Flood Insurance Program Claims Manual*, at 235 (Oct. 2021).

them. The guidance addresses countertops that are post-form, roll-top laminated; job-built, laid flat, or self-edge laminated; formed concrete and ceramic tile; natural or human-made stone materials; and Corian and other solid surfaces.[335]

FEMA says it is aware of unique instances in which a countertop can be damaged beyond repair directly by or from the flood; when an adjuster recommends replacement of a countertop, the claim file has to include documentation that explains and supports the judgment to replace, rather than remove and reset.[336]

FEMA says that at the initial loss inspection, the adjuster should examine, photograph, and document the condition of the surface, edge, and underside of the countertop in a report.[337] The adjuster should note the number of adjoining seams, material thickness, and substrate material covering any cabinet framing located underneath the countertop.

Policyholders should expect the adjuster discuss removal and re-installation of countertops at the initial loss inspection because that is what FEMA tells them they should do. For that reason, it is advisable for the policyholder to have a contractor at the inspection so that any disagreement over completely replacing the countertop is addressed at the outset. FEMA tells adjusters they should "set the expectation" that any countertop, sink, toilet, vanity top, bathtub, shower stall, or other similar items can be salvaged for re-use. The agency says adjusters should inform policyholders that they should notify the adjuster immediately if damage occurs during removal and provide photographs "when necessary." It also says that a policyholder has to retain any items damaged during removal. FEMA notes that policy does not cover *avoidable* damage. Therefore, when removal irreparably damages a previously undamaged item, the removal effort has to support a finding that the damage was unavoidable. FEMA says a policyholder can best support a request for payment when unavoidable damage occurs by providing clear photographs of the damage at the time of its occurrence and a signed statement from the contractor.[338] The statement has to explain the action taken to remove the item, state how the damage occurred, and address salvage.

FEMA says adjusters should factor in the additional time and labor required to safely remove and reset salvageable items and should apply the "appropriate" credit reflecting any previously estimated allowance to reinstall. If an adjuster recommends no payment, he or she should include an explanation in the estimate and narrative report.

335. *National Flood Insurance Program Claims Manual*, at 233–34 (Oct. 2021).
336. *National Flood Insurance Program Claims Manual*, at 234 (Oct. 2021).
337. *National Flood Insurance Program Claims Manual*, at 235 (Oct. 2021).
338. *National Flood Insurance Program Claims Manual*, at 235 (Oct. 2021).

[iii] HVAC Equipment and Heating Machinery

The policy provides coverage for damage to HVAC equipment components, including air-conditioning compressors in the open, connected to, and servicing the building, when a component or the entire system suffers direct physical loss by or from flood.[339] Heating machinery installed in a detached building at the described location is covered if it services the insured building.[340] Direct physical loss by or from flood is defined as "loss or damage to insured property, directly caused by a flood. There must be evidence of physical changes to the property." Elevated platforms attached to the building are covered.

If a new HVAC component replaces one damaged by flood and is not compatible with the existing undamaged HVAC component, FEMA says the system may not function properly or at all because of a different type of refrigerant or a different Seasonal Energy Efficiency Ratio (SEER) rating. A retrofit of the existing undamaged component could solve the issue of component incompatibility, but that, says FEMA, is not covered by the policy.[341] There is also no coverage for the cost to upgrade an HVAC system required by law, regulation, or ordinance. Additionally, there is no coverage for an undamaged component as the policy only provides coverage for the fair proportion of the total value of a pair or set that the lost, damaged, or destroyed article bears to the pair or set.

Note the claim file has to include identifying information—manufacturer, model and serial number, and whenever possible capacity—for major building equipment, for example, furnaces and central air-conditioning units. The adjuster has to provide available identifying information on all insured flood-damaged appliances to include the make, model number, and serial number, and a photograph of any identifying tags or labeling. If that information is not accessible or available, FEMA says the adjuster should document the items with a detailed description and explanation in the narrative report.

[iv] Perimeter Wall Sheathing

In the prior version of the *Claims Manual*, there was extensive guidance on coverage for perimeter wall sheathing damage, which it said was covered when caused by a direct physical loss by or from flood.[342] The most recent version of the manual removed the guidance specific to sheathing. FEMA explains that

339. *National Flood Insurance Program Claims Manual*, at 245 (Oct. 2021).

340. *National Flood Insurance Program Claims Manual*, at 246 (Oct. 2021).

341. *National Flood Insurance Program Claims Manual*, at 246 (Oct. 2021).

342. *National Flood Insurance Program Claims Manual*, at 251 (May 2020). "Exterior sheathing," one court explained, "is building material that is nailed or screwed to the exterior frame of a house—essentially, the home's external shell. It comes in different forms—some more resistant to water damage than others—and rarely attracts attention because typically it is covered from view with siding or some other exterior wall finish." Nguyen v. Hartford Underwriters Ins. Co., 2021 U.S. Dist. LEXIS 11657, at *2 (M.D. La. Jan. 21, 2021).

the "SFIP requires direct physical loss by or from flood, and there must be evidence of physical changes to the property for coverage. The adjuster should document damage caused by flood; determine whether any damage was pre-existing or from a cause other than flood (e.g., insect, wet/dry rot, improper installation, construction defect); and include the appropriate scope of repair for covered damage. As this approach mirrors general NFIP claim handling guidance, FEMA no longer believes a separate section addressing sheathing is warranted."[343] Some will find this opaque "justification" for the agency's action less than useful.

[v] Cisterns, Water Softeners, and Well Water Pumps

FEMA says that cisterns, their components, and the water in them are covered when installed or located within the insured building, an eligible detached garage, or an enclosed porch, including within an enclosure or basement, but not when they are installed or located outside of those areas.[344] Cisterns installed underground are not covered. A water softener, and the chemicals in it, that is installed in a building at the described location, connected to and servicing the insured building, is covered.[345] Well water pumps and related components are insured when located inside the insured building, including underneath it, inside an attached utility shed, attached pump house, or an eligible detached garage. The equipment has to be installed at or above ground level. Pumps and related components for building water supply or landscaping are eligible property. There is no coverage for well water pumps or related components below ground level or installed inside a detached pump house or inside another building or structure that is not insured property or for pumps or related equipment used for hot tubs, spas, or swimming pools.

[vi] Porches

FEMA notes that a porch may be original to the building or an attached addition. It can be fully or partially enclosed, screened, or open and built on the ground or elevated. A covered porch is not a covered deck or a covered patio. Porches are an addition or extension attached to and in contact with the insured building and are covered under the policy when attached to and in contact with the insured building by means of a rigid exterior wall, a solid load-bearing interior wall, a stairway, an elevated walkway, or a roof.[346] The

343. *NFIP Claims Manual Table of Changes*, at 29, FEMA, *available at* https://www.fema.gov/sites/default/files/documents/fema_table-of-changes-nfip-claims-manual_2021.pdf.

344. *National Flood Insurance Program Claims Manual*, at 222 (Oct. 2021).

345. *National Flood Insurance Program Claims Manual*, at 223 (Oct. 2021).

346. *National Flood Insurance Program Claims Manual*, at 268 (Oct. 2021). However, the porch cannot be constructed in a manner subject to certain limitations. See General Property Form Standard Flood Insurance Policy, § IV.9, which provides that portions of walks, walkways, decks, driveways, patios, and other surfaces—all whether protected by a roof or

agency advises adjusters that building materials used to construct a porch, as well as common porch furniture, are exterior rated and generally resist inundation damage from flood water. The adjuster should consider if repair and refinishing is the extent of the loss, but if replacement is recommended, that must be documented in the claim file.

[vii] Solar Panels, Generators, Compressors, and Transformers

Air-conditioning condensers and solar panels are insured, even if set apart from the insured building, but the SFIP does not cover other equipment, for example, electrical supply generators, air compressors, and substation transformers owned by the policyholder that may service the insured building, unless that equipment is hard-wired and in an insured building or a building physically attached to the insured structure by means of a qualifying addition or extension. Generators stored in a building at the described location are considered personal property, and generators or other such equipment in a basement are not insured.[347]

[i] Direction on Identification of Certain Property

Adjusters are required to provide identifying information—manufacturer, model and serial number, and whenever possible capacity—on major building equipment, for example, furnaces, central air-conditioning units, and major appliances like refrigerators, washers, dryers, and televisions.[348] They have to include a photograph of any identifying tags or labeling. If the required information is not available or accessible, adjusters should document the items with a detailed description and explanation in their narrative report.

[j] Preliminary Report

The initial report by an adjuster is the "Preliminary Report Form." [349] A copy of the two-page form is available at the FEMA website.[350] FEMA says it prefers that the report be submitted the same day as the inspection, but it has to be submitted no later than 15 calendar days after the assignment. If the initial inspection is delayed, FEMA says the adjuster should *immediately* submit a narrative that documents the insurer's claim file with the reason for the *unavoidable* delay, and the report detailing the delay has to be submitted no later than the 15th day after the assignment.

---

not—located outside the perimeter, exterior walls of the insured building are property that is not insured.

347. *National Flood Insurance Program Claims Manual*, at 247 (Oct. 2021).

348. *National Flood Insurance Program Claims Manual*, at 246–47 (Oct. 2021).

349. *National Flood Insurance Program Claims Manual*, at 281 (Oct. 2021).

350. *See Preliminary Report*, FEMA, https://www.fema.gov/sites/default/files/documents/FEMA-Form_086-0-13_preliminary-report.pdf.

FEMA says adjusters should complete the entire Preliminary Report Form, giving special attention to reserve amounts, building foundation components, and measurement of waterlines.

The agency says adjusters are required to recommend reserves in the Preliminary Report based on the initial inspection and to provide updated reserves as the claim progresses.[351] The reserve is the adjuster's best approximation of the amount of damage to the covered building and personal property at the time of, and prior to, an estimate being prepared.

For the portion of the report regarding building foundation components, FEMA says a building that has walls installed over top of a concrete slab is non-elevated, and has either a slab-on-grade, raised slab-on-grade, or raised slab-on-stem wall foundation.[352] A building that has a floor installed above the ground level, supported by foundation walls, shear walls, posts, piers, pilings, or columns, is, says FEMA, an elevated building. If a concrete slab is installed within the foundation's perimeter, that slab is not considered structural to the foundation, unless it is six inches thick and reinforced with "re-bar" driven into the building's foundation.[353] If an elevated floor is constructed over a crawlspace that is below ground level on all sides, the building is not considered elevated, and its lowest floor is the below-ground-level crawlspace floor, meeting the policy definition of a basement.

The adjuster is required to record in the Preliminary report the highest waterline on the exterior and interior of the building.[354] FEMA says the recorded interior waterline should not be higher than the exterior one. Adjusters should, says the agency, look for an exterior debris line on all buildings and provide measurements, and it is advisable for them to have a photograph of a tape measure against the exterior and interior walls that clearly shows the waterline measurement. Because plantings and shrubbery may retain debris, adjusters should photograph and report that measurement. If an adjuster is unable to identify a debris line, that should be addressed in the narrative report. Waterlines have to be recorded in inches. To collect accurate data of areas damaged, FEMA says it is necessary that adjusters use either negative or positive numbers. A negative number indicates that flood water was found only in the basement, while in elevated buildings a negative number indicates that flood water did not enter above the floor used for rating.

Exterior waterlines are always recorded using a positive number, and the adjuster should measure the exterior water depth from the lowest point of the land immediately outside the building. For basements, the interior waterline

351. *National Flood Insurance Program Claims Manual*, at 281 (Oct. 2021).

352. *National Flood Insurance Program Claims Manual*, at 281 (Oct. 2021).

353. *National Flood Insurance Program Claims Manual*, at 282 (Oct. 2021). A structural concrete floor of this type does not change an elevated building into a non-elevated one.

354. *National Flood Insurance Program Claims Manual*, at 282 (Oct. 2021).

is measured from the floor above the basement down and the value recorded on the Preliminary Report with a negative sign in front of the recorded inches. If water enters the main living area, that is the floor above the basement, the measurement is to be from that floor up and is shown as a positive number. FEMA asks adjusters to note the height of the basement ceiling. In elevated buildings adjusters are to measure the interior water height in a crawlspace or enclosure from the lowest floor.[355]

When special issues arise from the inspection, the adjuster should add a narrative memo to the Preliminary Report.[356] There is a FEMA form titled "Adjuster's Narrative Report."[357]

[k] Policyholder Representatives

[i] Generally

FEMA says that when an adjuster becomes aware that a policyholder has a representative—typically a public adjuster, attorney, relative, or translator—the adjuster should notify the insurer promptly.[358] The notification should be forwarded with the Preliminary Report or as an interim status report and include any documents received related to the representation.

In a publication for policyholders, FEMA subtly discourages them from employing an attorney or public adjuster.[359] In response to the question "Do policyholders need to hire a representative?" FEMA says it is committed to paying the full amount due on every flood insurance claim and that it provides "several free, non-adversarial dispute resolution processes to make sure policyholders get every penny they are entitled to under their food insurance policy." Most people, concludes the agency, do not feel that it is necessary to incur the expenses of hiring an attorney or public adjuster to handle a claim. That may be true of "most people," but hundreds of claimants bring suit each year over what they consider to be an unsatisfactory resolution of their claims.

The agency reminds the parties that, because FEMA flood insurance is a federal program, all stakeholders, including FEMA itself, have to adhere to federal privacy law.[360] Whenever a policyholder authorizes a party to speak with a National Flood Insurance Program stakeholder, including FEMA, about

---

355. FEMA says that in non-V zones, the reference point of the lowest floor is the top of the floor while in V zones, the reference point of the lowest floor is the lowest horizontal structural member. When the water depth is below the lowest floor, the number of inches should, says FEMA, be represented by a negative number.

356. *National Flood Insurance Program Claims Manual*, at 283 (Oct. 2021).

357. *See Narrative*, FEMA, https://www.fema.gov/sites/default/files/documents/FEMA-Form_086-0-15_narrative.pdf.

358. *National Flood Insurance Program Claims Manual*, at 230 (Oct. 2021).

359. *Answers to Questions about the NFIP*, at 34 (Feb. 17, 2021), FEMA, https://agents.floodsmart.gov/sites/default/files/fema-answers-to-questions-about-the-NFIP.pdf.

360. *See* 5 U.S.C. § 552a; 6 C.F.R. §§ 5.20, *et seq.*

his or her claim, the policyholder has to do so in writing in a document known as a letter of representation. The stakeholder has to obtain the authorization to protect the privacy of the policyholder. Additionally, the policyholder also has to submit documentation that includes the full names, addresses, dates, and places of birth of all named policyholders, the names of representatives, and the policyholder's signature. The document has to be notarized or state: "I declare under penalty of perjury that the foregoing is true and correct." The date the statement is executed and the signature of the policyholder must appear on that document.[361]

[ii] Attorney Representation

FEMA says that when a policyholder becomes represented by an attorney, and the proper letter of representation and privacy release signed by the policyholder is obtained, claims adjusters and examiners have to ensure all verbal and written communications are held directly with the attorney, unless the attorney approves direct communication with the policyholder.[362]

[iii] Public Adjusters[363]

Public adjusters are licensed professionals. They are independent claims adjusters who represent policyholders instead of insurance companies.[364] They negotiate settlement of claims with an insurer's claim representative and typically are compensated with a percentage of the payable loss secured for the client.[365] FEMA recommends that when a policyholder is represented by a public adjuster, and the proper letter of representation and privacy release signed by the policyholder is obtained, the claims adjuster and examiner send all written communications, including the insurer-adjuster-prepared proofs of loss, to *both* the public adjuster *and* the policyholder. The agency says that, after verbally communicating with the public adjuster during an inspection or over the telephone, a "best practice" is for representatives of the insurer to follow up with a written correspondence or email to the public adjuster, with a copy to the policyholder.[366] FEMA reminds the parties that before a public adjuster may communicate with insurer representatives about a claim, the public adjuster has to be licensed and in good standing in the state and have a signed contract with the policyholder.

---

361. *National Flood Insurance Program Claims Manual*, at 230 (Oct. 2021). *See also National Flood Insurance Program Claims Manual*, at 276 (Oct. 2021).

362. *National Flood Insurance Program Claims Manual*, at 230 (Oct. 2021).

363. *See generally* National Association of Public Insurance Adjusters, http://www.napia.com/; *Making the Best Choice When Hiring a Public Adjuster*, United Policyholders, http://www.uphelp.org/pubs/making-best-choice-when-hiring-public-adjuster.

364. *Glossary P*, NAIC, http://naic.org/consumer_glossary.htm#P.

365. *Public Adjuster*, IRMI, https://www.irmi.com/online/insurance-glossary/terms/p/public-adjuster.aspx.

366. *National Flood Insurance Program Claims Manual*, at 231 (Oct. 2021).

[l] Closing and Interim Reports

An adjuster's closing report is due 30 days after the Preliminary Report is submitted.[367] FEMA states that adjusters should conclude a claim within 45 days after the Preliminary Report, but if a claim cannot be concluded within that time, they should file an interim report every 30 days until the claim is concluded or as directed by the claims examiner. It is important, warns FEMA, for an adjuster to inform the insurer of the reason a claim remains open more than 45 days after the assignment. The report can be a brief memo that notifies the insurer of the claim handling status or a copy of correspondence from the adjuster to the policyholder that requests additional information or serves as a reminder of previously requested information discussed at the date of the inspection.[368] Interim reports are also required anytime issues arise of which the insurer should be aware.[369]

Closing reports include the narrative, summary of coverage, interests, claim activities, adjustment decisions, estimate, settlement recommendations, and all other relevant documents to support the claim.[370] Adjusters, says FEMA, may need to provide multiple narrative reports when the circumstances are unusual, challenging, or complicated, and additional explanation is appropriate. Reports are only to include facts, and FEMA says a narrative should outline relevant information based on facts that address who, what, where, when, how, and why. Adjusters should also provide specific details in the narrative report when the adjuster applies judgment to any part of the loss adjustment.

[m] Proof of Loss

The role of the adjuster in preparing a proof of loss is a bit unclear. It is quite common for independent adjusters to complete a proof of loss and request the policyholder to sign it. Indeed, there is a FEMA form the agency says can be used when the adjuster prepares the proof of loss.[371] FEMA explains that the adjuster provides the proof of loss as a courtesy to the policyholder who then reviews and verifies the accuracy of the information and amounts. The policy itself says that the adjuster who investigates the claim may furnish the policyholder with a proof of loss form, and may help the policyholder complete it; however, that is "a matter of courtesy only," and the policyholder still has to send the insurer a proof of loss within 60 days after the loss even if the adjuster does not furnish the form or help the policyholder complete it.[372] On

367. *National Flood Insurance Program Claims Manual*, at 280 (Oct. 2021).

368. *National Flood Insurance Program Claims Manual*, at 284 (Oct. 2021).

369. *National Flood Insurance Program Claims Manual*, at 283 (Oct. 2021).

370. *National Flood Insurance Program Claims Manual*, at 284 (Oct. 2021).

371. *Proof of Loss - Building & Contents (Adjuster-Prepared)* (FEMA Form 206-FY-21-112), FEMA, https://www.fema.gov/sites/default/files/documents/FEMA-form_206-FY-21-112_adjuster-proof-of-loss_2021.pdf.

372. General Property Form Standard Flood Insurance Policy, § VII.G.7.

the other hand, FEMA says that the adjuster should provide a proof of loss for signature if required,[373] and that it expects adjusters to "proactively assist" policyholders with the proof of loss.[374]

[3] Use of Outside Professional Services

[a] Generally

FEMA says that insurers may only rely on outside professionals who perform work in accordance with all applicable laws regarding professional licensure and conduct.[375] It is important for policyholders and their counsel to know that insurers have to keep all professional reports in the claim file and, when requested by the policyholder, provide a complete copy of the requested report.

Insurers and their retained service providers may not assert that they are exempt from state licensing laws because they are federal employees or federal contractors or are performing work for the federal government unless FEMA expressly authorizes an exemption in writing.

FEMA says it will not pre-authorize an assignment to an expert or expert fees.[376] Insurers have to obtain FEMA approval to pay the expense regardless of the dollar amount. Only an insurer, or WYO vendor if authorized by the insurer, can request outside professional services. When making an assignment, an insurer has to verify the entity and that the individual from whom services are sought is qualified and licensed in good standing with the state where the insured property is located before authorizing an inspection. When making an assignment for a professional service, the insurer has to specify the type of service needed including the covered property to be inspected[377] and secure a pre-inspection expense cost estimate to confirm expenses are fair and responsible before authorizing the inspection.[378]

373. *See Starting Your Recovery: FEMA's Flood Insurance Claims Process* (FEMA Sept. 22, 2020).

374. *National Flood Insurance Program Claims Manual*, at 11 (Oct. 2021).

375. *National Flood Insurance Program Claims Manual*, at 242 (Oct. 2021). Insurers are responsible for making sure the professional services they hire are familiar and compliant with state licensing requirements and rules that regulate the profession. When a report from a professional service is used to support the decision of the insurer, the report has to disclose that it complies with state rules regulating licensure and professional conduct. If a report does not meet the state's requirement, the claim decision may become invalid.

376. *National Flood Insurance Program Claims Manual*, at 244 (Oct. 2021).

377. The assignment should be clear, says FEMA, that non-covered property is not part of the assignment unless it involves such determination. The agency will not authorize expenses incurred to inspect or evaluate non-covered property, for example, pools, pool decks, sidewalks, retaining walls that are not an integral part of the foundation, bulkheads, and non-covered buildings.

378. FEMA says it will not authorize payment for any expense that exceeds the original quoted fee unless the engineer can document pre-approval from the insurer or authorized vendor prior to incurring the expense.

A Building Structural Evaluation can be requested when the cause of the damage is uncertain, the extent of the damage is unknown, there is a need to discern the cost-effective method of repair, or the policyholder contests the recommended loss settlement because of structural issues or issues of causation with certain building items.[379] Adjusters do not have the authority to assign an expert. FEMA says they should submit a request to the insurer to have the building's structure evaluated as soon as the need is identified.

FEMA considers a final report from a professional as a normal component of a claim file and, thus, whenever an insurer retains professional services to investigate a claim, the insurer has to keep all reports in the claim file and, when requested by the policyholder, provide a complete copy of the requested report.[380]

FEMA says insurers and their representatives may not adopt any practice that may influence the opinions or recommendations of a professional.[381] Insurers may not request changes to reports; however, when insurers or their representatives have a question that requires a written response, they may request that the professional prepare an addendum to the final report in response.

[b] Engineers

FEMA says it will not pay for multiple engineers to conduct an inspection unless pre-approval was received from the insurer with a detailed explanation that the inspection requires different expertise or disciplines to evaluate the damage, for example, a structural and electrical engineer. Any co-signer of a report holding him- or herself out as a professional engineer (PE) has to have a current license in the inspection state and include the engineer license number on the report. Engineer travel expenses have to be fair and reasonable and conform with U.S. General Services Administration travel rates. FEMA will not pay for lodging within the contiguous United States, food expenses, or photos.[382]

The invoices of engineers have to be itemized by time and expense (no lump sums), separately report inspection and travel time, and provide all applicable receipts for air travel, vehicle rental, hotel, tolls, and parking.

Insurers and their representatives may not adopt any practice that may influence the opinions or recommendations of a professional service. Insurers may not request changes to reports. When, however, insurers or representatives have a question that requires a written response, they may request that the professional service prepare an addendum to the closing report in response. Insurers have to keep the entire expert report in the claim file and provide a copy of the final expert report and any addendums to the policyholder.

---

379. *National Flood Insurance Program Claims Manual*, at 241 (Oct. 2021).
380. *See* 44 C.F.R. § 62.23(i)(10).
381. *National Flood Insurance Program Claims Manual*, at 243 (Oct. 2021).
382. *National Flood Insurance Program Claims Manual*, at 245 (Oct. 2021).

When making a claims decision, an insurer should, states FEMA, only rely on final reports that meet the proper disclosures and reporting standards for the report type involved. They have to use reports in context with all other relevant information and data gathered throughout the claim investigation process when making a claim determination. When a report involves a structural evaluation of the building, the professional should disclose and report at least the following:

- Date of inspection;
- The individual who performed the inspection;
- Building description and foundation type—all components;
- Site observations supported with annotated photographs, analytical discussion, and conclusion;
- Cost-effective method to repair, when applicable;
- Signature of the engineer of record with professional seal or state license number; and
- Name and curriculum *vitae* of all persons who assisted with the technical content of the report.

The engineer, says FEMA, should not interpret policy terms and conditions or discuss coverage.

[c] Financial Accounting Professionals

FEMA says a commercial loss involving damage to a significant quantity, value, or specialized type of business contents may require the services of a CPA to provide a detailed report of findings.[383] The role of a CPA is to help promptly document and certify the quantity and value of damaged inventory, goods in process, or raw materials. The question of financial recovery through a buyback by the policyholder, says the agency, or salvage through the involvement of a third party can also be addressed. The CPA can also help inform the policyholder what documentation is needed and how it can be presented to best support the loss of his or her commercial contents quickly. A detailed report of findings is required when a financial accounting professional is engaged.

[4] Payment of Claim

[a] Payment and Paying the Undisputed Loss

The SFIP says that a loss is payable 60 days after the insurer receives the policyholder's proof of loss or within 90 days after the adjuster files his or her report signed and sworn to by the policyholder, once the insurer reaches

383. *National Flood Insurance Program Claims Manual*, at 242 (Oct. 2021).

an agreement with the policyholder, there is an entry of a final judgment, or there is a filing of a valid appraisal award.[384] FEMA advises claims examiners that if the insurer receives a proof of loss that is not supported or agreed to, the insurer should pay the undisputed claim and issue a partial proof of loss rejection letter. A lienholder, FEMA notes, is not required on payments under the personal property coverage unless there is a loan specific to the coverage.

[b] Claim Closed without Payment Reasons

FEMA says the claims examiner should carefully review the adjuster's report for claims that are to be closed without payment.[385]

[c] Requests for Additional Payment

[i] Generally

FEMA says it expects policyholders to ask adjusters at the time of the loss what happens if the estimate does not fully cover the costs to recover from their flood loss.[386] The agency says the adjuster should help the policyholder understand what steps may be necessary if a request for additional payment (RAP) is needed and explain the FEMA procedures.

A request for a RAP is not a *claim* for additional payment; there is only one claim per flood loss. The insurer may not deny a RAP solely because the policyholder has not completed repairs or because the policyholder has not exhausted all monies paid on repairs. After an initial loss settlement, it remains the duty of a policyholder to prove a loss for any RAP. Policyholders must submit a completed proof of loss and documentation to support the amount requested initially and completed proofs of loss for any additional payment requests to the insurer within 60 days after the date of loss or within any extension of that deadline granted by FEMA.[387]

[ii] RAP for Omission

If a RAP is on an omitted item or an omission of quality, and there is no dispute on the facts documented in the claim file, the insurer should pay without documenting the remaining damage and repair. For example, a front door was omitted from the original estimate, and photos from the claim file show that the door experienced direct physical loss by or from flood. The adjuster is to notate the claim file, obtain the proof of loss and any necessary waiver,

384. General Property Form Standard Flood Insurance Policy, § VII.J.

385. *National Flood Insurance Program Claims Manual*, at 226 (Oct. 2021). Examiners must use the correct "Closed Without Payment" (CWOP) reason code to ensure the appropriate expense payment is issued.

386. *National Flood Insurance Program Claims Manual*, at 285 (Oct. 2021).

387. *National Flood Insurance Program Claims Manual*, at 135 (Oct. 2021).

and make the payment. FEMA says the RAP omission procedure is improper where the only difference is one of price. In that event, the policyholder must prove actual repairs for the pricing difference.[388]

[iii] RAP for Items Previously Included in Loss Settlement

When a policyholder submits a RAP, the request should document the remaining loss, if any and all repairs. For repaired damages, FEMA says, the policyholder should provide all documentation related to the repairs, which may include copies of a contractor estimate with corresponding proof of repair—credit card invoices, cancelled checks, debit entry on bank account registry for cash payments—contractor repair receipts, new material purchase invoices, or other evidence that the policyholder has obligated or expended payment, in addition to photographs of all repaired damages.

If a policyholder has undertaken some or all repairs independently, or without hiring a third party, that policyholder should submit documentation for material costs and any inventory of his or her labor hours, plus photographs. FEMA says that any documentation related to flood-damage tearout, flood cleanup, treatment, and building dry-out should also be provided by the policyholder to the insurer.

For unrepaired damages the policyholder should provide copies of the contractor- and policyholder-signed repair agreement with the corresponding estimate to repair and material purchase orders, plus photographs of all nonrepaired damage. FEMA warns that an unsigned estimate or proposal is not sufficient as a basis for a RAP, because the policyholder is under no obligation to pay the estimated amount until he or she has a contract in place for repairs. FEMA tells insurers to follow their same procedures to consider a RAP as they would with the initial loss. The procedures may require the insurer to mandate an on-site inspection of the property, hire any necessary experts, or invoke any of the other options after a loss provided by the SFIP.

FEMA says the insurer agrees to pay the policyholder for insured property damaged by flood with materials of like kind and quality and like use, but may not pay the policyholder for the increased cost to repair due to betterments or improvements in materials or workmanship, changes related to other renovations, repairs that are not for flood damage on the claimed date of loss, or code upgrades.[389]

For a pricing RAP only, provided there is no item of omission or quality, FEMA says the insurer may issue additional payment provided the documented loss and repair exceeds the sum of all building claim payments, plus the deductible and any withheld depreciation.

388. *National Flood Insurance Program Claims Manual*, at 286 (Oct. 2021).

389. *National Flood Insurance Program Claims Manual*, at 287 (Oct. 2021).

When a RAP is based only on an estimate of damage from a third party—for example, a public adjuster or attorney—the agency says the claim handling should at minimum ensure the full and proper scope of damage and repair is accounted for in the insurance estimate. A RAP based on increases in unit pricing without proper documentation or justification is not substantiated. The insurance estimate should account for pricing that is reasonable and customary to the loss and location.

[5] Claims Examiners

FEMA says that examiners are the claims administrators for the insurer.[390] They have the authority to pay claims, to make and confirm coverage determinations, and to deny coverage when appropriate. They should provide guidance to adjusters as needed. FEMA says it expects every examiner handling NFIP flood losses to do the following:

- Understand their first obligation to a policyholder is to identify coverage under the SFIP,
- Seek comprehensive reports from adjusters allowing the examiner to resolve claims with accuracy and efficiency, and
- Understand their payment decisions must be in accordance with the SFIP.

FEMA says the responsibilities of a claims examiner include the following:

- Adjuster assignment;
- Managing the claim file, including issuing advance payments, resolving rating issues and coverage issues with their underwriting department, overseeing adjusters to ensure timely reporting of settlement recommendations, recommending and hiring experts, and issuing proper payments;
- Claims reporting and forms management; and
- Communicating with policyholders, including partial and full denial letters and other communications, as necessary.

FEMA also expects claims examiners to know the provisions of the SFIP, to know the content of the *Claims Manual*, to communicate coverage and limitations to policyholders, and to oversee all flood claims in compliance with the manual.

390. *National Flood Insurance Program Claims Manual*, at 16 (Oct. 2021).

[6] Direction to Policyholders on Documenting Claims

A FEMA fact sheet says the adjuster for the insurance company will help the policyholder document the flood damage.[391] It advises policyholders to provide photos and videos of the flood loss to the adjuster and notes it can be helpful to organize them by room. FEMA counsels insureds to keep documents—for example, receipts, bank statements, and contractor's invoices—that show how flood-damaged items were repaired or replaced and to provide these documents to the adjuster. When the policyholder receives the estimate of the flood loss from the adjuster, FEMA says he or she should carefully review the detailed estimate to ensure it is complete.

[7] Advance Payments

[a] Generally

FEMA says that in a large flooding event, it will generally authorize advance payments to policyholders.[392] In that event, FEMA says the proof of loss requirement will be conditionally waived. When advance payments are authorized, an adjuster should notify the policyholder that adjusters may request an advance payment.

There is a FEMA form titled "Advance Payment Request—Building & Contents,"[393] which the agency says can be use by policyholders to request an advance payment of the total claim for flood damage to eligible insured building property and personal property.

[b] Advance Payments before and after Inspection

[i] Pre-inspection

FEMA says that during major flood events, insurers may offer policyholders an advance payment even before their adjuster inspects the property.[394] The agency allows a payment of up to $5,000 on building and contents losses combined less deductibles. The insurer has to obtain and verify the certain prescribed information before the payment is issued. A proper notice of loss has to have been made, and there has to be an active flood insurance policy covering the property and confirming current coverage terms, amounts, and deductibles. The insurer has to obtain verbal or written statements from the policyholder.[395] The adjuster or examiner has to confirm that a flood, as

---

391. *See Starting Your Recovery: FEMA's Flood Insurance Claims Process* (FEMA Sept. 22, 2020).

392. *National Flood Insurance Program Claims Manual*, at 216 (Oct. 2021).

393. *See Advanced Payment Building*, FEMA, https://www.fema.gov/sites/default/files/documents/FEMA-form_206-FY-21-113_advanced-payment-bldg_2021.pdf.

394. *National Flood Insurance Program Claims Manual*, at 216 (Oct. 2021).

395. *National Flood Insurance Program Claims Manual*, at 217 (Oct. 2021).

defined by policy, directly damaged the insured property, identify the source of the flood, describe how the flood occurred, with supporting documentation from an official weather bureau or reputable news media as necessary, and explain other effects from the flood to support that the loss is in excess of the advanced amount. The adjuster or examiner also has to provide the approximate depth of flood water on the exterior of the building and inside the interior floor level; state whether the extent of damage is limited to an area subject to coverage limitations, for example, a basement or lower enclosure, or state the extent of damage is in a ground-level floor or elevated floor level; describe damage to the building and personal property; and address any prior loss to avoid a duplication of payment of non-repaired property items.

There is also a pre-inspection advance of up to $20,000 that is only available when it is authorized by FEMA. For the policyholder to receive this larger advance, FEMA says the insurer should, in addition to the information for the usual advance, also obtain photographs depicting flood water depths and damage to the building and personal property and verify out-of-pocket expenses related to the repair or replacement of covered property.[396]

[ii] Post-inspection

Once the adjuster inspects the property, FEMA allows insurers to issue an advance payment of up to 25 percent of the reserve amount indicated on the Preliminary Report for *building or contents* less the applicable deductibles.[397] The insurer can issue the payment after the adjuster submits the Preliminary Report and any other applicable documentation normally submitted or required with the Preliminary Report, including photographs, a policyholder-signed Advance Payment Request form, any underwriting memorandum, a preliminary damage assessment (APDA),[398] and an adjuster narrative addressing any prior paid loss.

An insurer may issue a larger advance payment amount when it obtains more substantive documentation. The NFIP allows a payment of up to 50 percent of the reserve amount indicated on the Preliminary Report for *building* coverage less the deductible.[399] In addition to obtaining and verifying the information required for a 25 percent advance payment, FEMA says the insurer should also obtain a signed contract between the policyholder and a

396. Verification of expenses could be by paid receipts, invoices, or estimates with canceled checks, or an estimate signed by a contractor on letterhead itemizing the repair or the facilitation of repairs, to covered property.

397. *National Flood Insurance Program Claims Manual*, at 218 (Oct. 2021).

398. FEMA provides considerable information about preliminary damage assessments at https://www.fema.gov/disasters/how-declared/preliminary-damage-assessments. The applicable form is available at https://www.fema.gov/sites/default/files/documents/FEMA-Form_086-0-20_preliminary-damage-assessment.pdf.

399. *National Flood Insurance Program Claims Manual*, at 218 (Oct. 2021).

contractor together with an estimate of repair. The estimate should itemize the repair and cost to covered property.

Insurers may also issue a post-inspection advance payment based on the FEMA-authorized Building Valuation Loss Assessment (BVLA) advance payment method. In addition to the Preliminary Report and any other applicable documentation that is normally submitted or required with the Preliminary Report, the adjuster also has to submit a properly completed BVLA worksheet to the insurer. The insurer may also issue post-inspection advance payments based on their own proprietary estimation approach, but may not broaden or change any coverage term in the FEMA policy.[400] The insurer has to document any deviations from normal FEMA processes and include a reference to the proprietary process in the claim file. A claim payment under the insurer's own proprietary estimation approach is subject to all standard FEMA claim documentation and payment standards.

[c] Advance or Partial Payment for Increased Cost of Compliance

The FEMA policy provides Increased Cost of Compliance (ICC) coverage of up to $30,000 toward the cost to repair or rebuild a flood-damaged structure in compliance with state or local floodplain management ordinances or laws.[401] Policyholders may request an advance or partial payment from the insurer to help cover the cost of the eligible compliance measures subject to approval by the insurer after supporting documentation and a signed ICC proof of loss signed Advance Payment form for ICC have been submitted.[402] There is a form titled "Advance Payment Request Increased Cost of Compliance (ICC)" that can be used to request an advance payment of the total benefits payable under ICC coverage.[403] FEMA authorizes advance payments of up to 50 percent of the available ICC limits.[404] Insurers may advance up to that amount to an eligible policyholder meeting two conditions. First, the policyholder has to sign a written agreement that the funds will be used only for eligible ICC work. Second, the policyholder has to sign a written agreement that if all or part of the advanced funds are not used within the permitted time limits for completing the eligible work, or any extensions that may be granted, he or she agrees that the amounts not spent on eligible work will be returned. If the policyholder does not agree to the conditions, no ICC benefits will be paid until after completion of eligible work.

---

400. *National Flood Insurance Program Claims Manual*, at 219 (Oct. 2021).

401. *National Flood Insurance Program Flood Insurance Manual*, at 2–10 (FEMA Apr. 2021).

402. *National Flood Insurance Program Claims Manual*, at 300 (Oct. 2021).

403. *See Advanced Payment ICC*, FEMA, https://www.fema.gov/sites/default/files/documents/FEMA-form_206-FY-21-114_advanced-payment-icc_2021.pdf.

404. *National Flood Insurance Program Claims Manual*, at 301 (Oct. 2021).

FEMA says a policyholder that does not return ICC funds after failing to complete the ICC eligible work within the authorized time will be subject to any available administrative, civil, or criminal remedies including, but not limited to, a determination that the policy is void, a federal debt collection action, and legal actions under either state or federal laws.[405]

If an insurer issues payment in accordance with FEMA's terms and conditions and properly documents ICC advance partial payments, FEMA will apply the standards stated in its *Claims Manual* in all reviews or audits of files, including any reviews under the Arrangement or the Improper Payment Information Act.[406] However, if a payment is incorrectly made to an insured, if a claim is not properly documented, if an insurer omits an additional named insured, or if an insurer fails to act in compliance with the obligations set forth in the arrangement or applicable law, that insurer will be responsible for the erroneous payment.[407]

[d] Procedure for Issuing Advance Payment

FEMA says insurers may offer an advance payment on the written, verbal, or electronic request of a policyholder. With an advance payment, the insurer has to include a written notice that conditions the payment on the acknowledgment of the policyholder that:

- The payment is not intended to provide reimbursement to the policyholder for non-insured expenses.[408]
- Issuance and acceptance of the payment does not prejudice or waive any claim or defense available to either the policyholder or insurer and does not constitute an admission of coverage under the policy.
- The insured property has suffered a covered loss.
- If the insurer determines the claim is not a covered loss or if the payment exceeds the amount of the covered loss, the policyholder is ineligible for payment and will have to repay the amount that exceeds the covered loss.

---

405. Under a FEMA rule—44 C.F.R. § 11.1—the general standards and procedures that govern the collection, compromise, termination, and referral to the Department of Justice of claims for money and property that are prescribed in regulations issued jointly by the Government Accountability Office and the Department of Justice apply to the administrative claim collection activities of FEMA. Unfortunately, regulation cited in the rule—4 C.F.R. part 101, *et seq.*—no longer appears in the Code of Federal Regulations. *See generally* 31 U.S.C. § 3711 on collection and compromise of claims of the United States government.

406. *See* 33 U.S.C. § 3321.

407. *National Flood Insurance Program Claims Manual*, at 302 (Oct. 2021).

408. For example, costs related to evacuation, temporary housing while the property is uninhabitable, a rental car to cover the loss of a personal vehicle, or any other expense not covered by the FEMA policy.

- Acceptance of the payment does not affect the policyholder's right to seek additional payment under the terms and conditions of the policy.
- After the claim is settled, the insurer will reduce the final payment by the amount of any advance payments that were made.
- In the case of building coverage, the insurer has to include as co-payee any mortgagee shown on the Declarations Page of the policy or any known mortgagee on any advance payment.
- To finalize the claim, the claimant has to execute a proof of loss that meets the policy requirements for all amounts received, including the amount of the advance payment, except as may otherwise be authorized by FEMA under any applicable waiver.[409]

[e] Payment Exceeding Loss

FEMA says that claims adjusters and examiners have to make sure they avoid recommending and issuing advance payments that exceed the final total claim payment.[410] To avoid issuing an advance payment in excess of the covered loss, they should account for six factors when determining the amount of the payment. Those factors are the amount of the deductible; the interior water depth; non-flood-related damage; the pre-loss condition and actual cash value (ACV) of damaged property, especially if a prior flood payment was issued; the scope of damage, for example, damage limited to a basement or lower enclosure with a post-FIRM elevated building subject to coverage limitations; and the use of flood avoidance measures, for example, sandbags or removal of property to safety.

If an insurer issues an advance payment that exceeds the covered loss, it has to attempt to recoup the funds. FEMA prescribes the minimum steps the insurer has to take.[411] First, the insurer has to send a letter by certified mail or equivalent trackable delivery service to the policyholder that states the amount due; describes the charges; describes the remedies available to FEMA on failure of the policyholder to repay the amount due by the deadline, including, but not limited to federal debt collection procedures;[412] states the deadline for either submitting payment or disputing the validity of an

409. *National Flood Insurance Program Claims Manual*, at 219 (Oct. 2021).

410. *National Flood Insurance Program Claims Manual*, at 219 (Oct. 2021).

411. *National Flood Insurance Program Claims Manual*, at 220 (Oct. 2021).

412. Under a FEMA rule—44 C.F.R. § 11.1—the general standards and procedures that govern the collection, compromise, termination, and referral to the Department of Justice of claims for money and property that are prescribed in regulations issued jointly by the Government Accountability Office and the Department of Justice apply to the administrative claim collection activities of FEMA. Unfortunately, regulation cited in the rule—4 C.F.R. part 101, *et seq.*—no longer appears in the Code of Federal Regulations. *See generally* 31 U.S.C. § 3711 on collection and compromise of claims of the United States government.

overpayment, which must be at least 30 days from the date of the letter; and provides contact information for an individual representing the insurer that the policyholder can contact directly to dispute the validity of the overpayment or seek more information. Next, if the policyholder does not pay the amount due by the stated deadline, the insurer has to attempt to contact the policyholder by telephone and then send a follow-up letter by certified mail or equivalent trackable delivery service to the policyholder's last known address.

If an insurer is unable to recoup the overpayment after making its best efforts, it has to provide FEMA with a narrative explaining the basis of the overpayment determination and identifying the insurer's efforts to recoup the funds, copies of all written correspondence with the policyholder about the overpayment, and a copy of the claim file.

[8] Subrogation

When an adjuster or policyholder identifies a potential cause or contribution for the flood loss, in addition to a weather event, that may entitle the policyholder to recovery from a third party for the loss, FEMA says the adjuster should complete a "Cause of Loss and Subrogation Report."[413] The adjuster should provide available factual information about the cause or contributing factors for the loss. Claim handling, review, and payment should, says FEMA, proceed as normal. The insurer should provide the information to its internal reviewers if it will handle the potential subrogation claim itself or, if it chooses to refer the matter to FEMA, the entire claim file and subrogation forms should be forwarded to FEMA for potential pursuit.

5.6 Proof of Loss

[1] Generally

Probably the greatest hurdle an insured faces in obtaining compensation for a flood loss is submitting an acceptable, timely proof of loss. FEMA describes a proof of loss as a policyholder's "signed and sworn statement of loss with documentation to support the dollar amount requested."[414] The agency says a proof of loss is not the claim and it is not "just a form."

---

413. *National Flood Insurance Program Claims Manual*, at 290–91 (Oct. 2021). The Cause of Loss and Subrogation Report is FEMA Form 086-0-16, *available at* https://omb.report/icr/202007-1660-003/doc/103289200. There is also an Adjuster's Subrogation Referral—FF-206-FY-21-148—which FEMA says adjusters use to identify potentially responsible third parties and their actions that may have caused worsened flood damage. *See Subrogation Referral*, FEMA, https://www.fema.gov/sites/default/files/documents/FEMA-Form_206-FY-21-148_subrogation-referral.pdf.

414. *National Flood Insurance Program Claims Manual*, at 284 (Oct. 2021).

A proof of loss form has to be sent to the insurer within 60 days after a loss.[415] That means it has to be sent to the WYO insurer or FEMA, depending on who issued the policy, not to another party, for example, the independent adjuster.[416]

There is an exception to the requirement that the policyholder submit a proof of loss. At the option of an insurer, it may accept the adjuster's report of the loss instead of the insured's proof of loss.[417]

[2] FEMA Proof of Loss Form

There is a specific FEMA form described as "Proof of Loss—Building & Contents (Policyholder-Prepared)."[418] FEMA "encourages" policyholders to use the FEMA proof of loss form when complying with the policy requirements in case of a loss, but warns that completing and signing the form alone does not meet all the policy requirements and that policyholders have to provide documentation to support the loss and dollar amount declared on the form.[419] There is no requirement that policyholders use the form, and courts have said the policy does not require that a proof of loss be presented in any certain form.[420] Indeed, the agency has sometimes told claimants that they can submit a proof of loss in a letter.[421] However, the agency also says that a fully completed FEMA proof of loss form, signed by the policyholder with the required documentation, is required on *every claim on which the adjuster recommends payment*.[422]

Neither FEMA nor a WYO insurer is required to provide a policyholder with a proof of loss form. Indeed, where a state law required insurers to provide proof of loss forms to policyholders, that law was preempted and no claim for its violation could be brought against a WYO carrier.[423]

---

415. General Property Form Standard Flood Insurance Policy, § VII.G.4.

416. Garcia-Pedrosa v. FEMA, 2020 U.S. Dist. LEXIS 3010 (S.D. Fla. Jan. 7, 2020) (form sent to company that employed independent adjuster that was not "Direct Servicing Agent" for FEMA was not sent to FEMA and was insufficient).

417. General Property Form Standard Flood Insurance Policy, § VII.G.9. The policy says the adjuster's report will include information about the loss and the damages sustained and the policyholder has to sign that report. The insurer may also require the policyholder to swear to the report.

418. *See Proof of Loss*, FEMA, https://www.fema.gov/sites/default/files/documents/FEMA-form_206-FY-21-108_proof-of-loss_2021.pdf.

419. *National Flood Insurance Program Claims Manual*, at 284 (Oct. 2021).

420. Decosta v. Allstate Ins. Co., 730 F.3d 76 (1st Cir. 2013); Mancini v. Redland Ins. Co., 248 F.3d 729 (8th Cir. 2001).

421. Georgia Pacific Corp. v. National Flood Ins. Program, 1989 U.S. Dist. LEXIS 18142 (E.D. Mo. Apr. 5, 1989).

422. *National Flood Insurance Program Claims Manual*, at 284 (Oct. 2021).

423. Dodson v. Wright Nat'l Flood Ins. Co., 2021 U.S. Dist. LEXIS 96808 (S.D. Ala. May 20, 2021).

When an insured has an increased cost of compliance (ICC) claim, there is an entirely separate proof of loss form provided by FEMA.[424] The agency says the form supports calculations to determine the amount of insurance benefits for mitigation activities and that policyholders use it to state the amount for an increased cost of compliance claim with sworn details of loss. A signed ICC proof of loss is required on valid ICC claims.[425]

While adjusters may assist the policyholder in completing a proof of loss, FEMA says that assistance is only a courtesy and policyholders are required to use their own judgment regarding the amount of the loss and must justify that amount.[426] Thus, where a proof of loss was prepared by the policyholder's attorneys and their experts for use in litigation and the policyholder had no knowledge of the contents of the form, the court ruled that he failed to comply with the SFIP requirement that a proof of loss be based on the insured's "own judgment."[427]

[3] Sworn, Signed, and Notarized

[a] Sworn

A proof of loss is a *sworn* statement of loss.[428] The policy does not explain the meaning of "sworn," and neither does FEMA. Under federal law, if any federal law—or any rule, regulation, order, or requirement made pursuant to federal law—requires or permits something to be supported, evidenced, established, or proved by sworn declaration, verification, certificate, statement, oath, or affidavit, in writing, the matter may be supported, evidenced, established, or proved by the unsworn declaration, certificate, verification, or statement, in writing subscribed as true under penalty of perjury, and dated, in substantially the following form: "I declare (or certify, verify, or state) under penalty of perjury that the foregoing is true and correct. Executed on (date)."[429] The

---

424. *See Proof of Loss - Increased Cost of Compliance (ICC)* (FEMA Form 206-FY-21-109), FEMA, https://www.fema.gov/sites/default/files/documents/FEMA-form_206-FY-21-109_icc-proof-of-loss_2021.pdf.

425. *National Flood Insurance Program Claims Manual*, at 302 (Oct. 2021). FEMA says that after all required ICC documents are received, an insurer sends the policyholder an ICC proof of loss form for final payment. It has to be signed, dated, and returned to the insurer for processing.

426. *National Flood Insurance Program Claims Manual*, at 284 (Oct. 2021). *See also* General Property Form Standard Flood Insurance Policy, § VII.G.7. *See also* Beggs v. Am. Bankers Ins. Co., 2019 U.S. Dist. LEXIS 230394, at *14, n.11 (E.D. Va. July 25, 2019) (even if insurer *intentionally* undervalued insured property in courtesy proof of loss forms, insureds were obligated to exercise their own judgment in completing their proofs of loss).

427. Loolara v. Nat'l Flood Ins. Program, 2021 U.S. Dist. LEXIS 140968 (M.D. La. July 28, 2021).

428. *National Flood Insurance Program Claims Manual*, at 284 (Oct. 2021).

429. 28 U.S.C. § 1746.

statute applies to FEMA flood policies.[430] The key phrase is "under penalty of perjury." The proof of loss has to acknowledge the penalty of perjury.[431] A proof of loss that provided, "I hereby declare and attest that the information contained in this letter is true and correct to the best of my knowledge" did meet the requirement that the statement be "sworn."[432] Where a proof of loss bore a title stating it was "sworn" and the insurer did not challenge the description, it was not a sworn document.[433]

[b] Signed

[i] Signed by Policyholder

The policy says the proof of loss has to be signed and sworn to by "you,"[434] and "you" means the named insured or insureds shown on the Declarations Page of the policy.[435] Thus, most courts say an attorney for the insured cannot sign a proof of loss for his or her client.[436]

[ii] Electronic Signature

FEMA says that electronic signatures are acceptable.[437] Indeed, the agency says it encourages the use of electronic signatures on proofs of loss and other submissions,[438] and will not deny the legal effect, validity, or enforceability of a signature solely because it is in electronic form.[439] It adds that insurers *should* accept electronic signatures "in accordance with their general business

---

430. Clark v. Wright Nat'l Flood Ins. Co., 380 F. Supp. 3d 523, 530 (E.D. La. 2019), *aff'd*, 821 F. App'x 342 (5th Cir. Aug. 4, 2020).

431. Hagstotz v. Nationwide Mut. Ins. Co., 2018 U.S. Dist. LEXIS 177218 (D.N.J. Oct. 16, 2018).

432. Clark v. Wright Nat'l Flood Ins. Co., 380 F. Supp. 3d 523, 530 (E.D. La. 2019), *aff'd*, 821 Fed. Appx. 342 (5th Cir. Aug. 4, 2020).

433. Knutson v. Selective Ins. Co., 2017 U.S. Dist. LEXIS 29322 (D.N.J. Mar. 1, 2017).

434. General Property Form Standard Flood Insurance Policy, § VII.G.4.

435. General Property Form Standard Flood Insurance Policy, § II.A.

436. Abel v. Wright Nat'l Flood Ins. Co., 2019 U.S. Dist. LEXIS 226466 (S.D. Tex. Dec. 2, 2019); Johnson v. Imperial Fire & Cas. Ins. Co., 2008 U.S. Dist. LEXIS 59503 (E.D. La. July 28, 2008); Deverant v. Selective Ins. Co., 2003 U.S. Dist. LEXIS 1304 (E.D. Pa. Jan. 7, 2003). *But see* Mitchell v. Nat'l Flood Ins. Program, 2008 U.S. Dist. LEXIS 9937 (E.D. La. Feb. 8, 2008) (denying summary judgment for defendant where proof of loss signed by attorney for insured who first obtained verbal power of attorney and was sworn). *See also* Persohn v. Integon Nat'l Ins. Co., 2021 U.S. Dist. LEXIS 32211 (S.D. Tex. Jan. 14, 2021), *app. dis.*, 2021 U.S. App. LEXIS 24741 (5th Cir. June 4, 2021), where the only document received by the insurer was a demand letter from the attorney for the insureds, which they argued constituted a proof of loss. The court said that assuming the attorney had authority to file a proof of loss for the clients, it was deficient because it was not sworn.

437. *National Flood Insurance Program Claims Manual*, at 236 (Oct. 2021).

438. FEMA says it is approving and encouraging the use of electronic signatures to improve the policyholder's experience and to reduce administrative burdens. *National Flood Insurance Program Claims Manual*, at 236 (Oct. 2021).

439. *National Flood Insurance Program Claims Manual*, at 236 (Oct. 2021).

practices and applicable laws." FEMA requires signers to use an acceptable electronic form of signature, the signature to be executed or adopted by a person with the intent to sign the electronic document, the signature to be attached to or associated with the electronic document being signed, a means to identify and authenticate a particular person as the signer, and a means to preserve the integrity of the signed document. Despite FEMA's acceptance of electronic signatures, they present potential legal problems of which the parties should be aware.[440]

[c] Notarization

FEMA says that proof of loss forms do not require a notary.[441] At least one federal court has said specifically that notarization is not required.[442] Nonetheless, the agency cautions policyholders that WYO insurers or NFIP Direct may require the forms to be affirmed by a public notary.[443] Some courts have said proofs of loss have to notarized.[444] Others say that the proof of loss has to contain "something beyond just a signature."[445] A Louisiana federal court said that while a sworn statement has to be made in front of a notary, a statement under penalty of perjury asserting that the facts contained in the proof of loss are true and correct does not have to be notarized.[446] Obviously, the policyholder should ask the insurer whether notarization is required before submitting a proof of loss and, when in doubt, have it notarized.

---

440. *See* Ennis & Green, *Electronic Signatures: Not So Fast* (ABA Dec. 17, 2019).

441. *National Flood Insurance Program Claims Manual*, at 285 (Oct. 2021). *See also* Bullard v. Connor, 716 F. Supp. 1081 (N.D. Ill. 1989) (FEMA directly issued policy and told insured that notarization was not necessary).

442. Brouner v. Farmers Ins. Co. of Wash., Inc., 2011 U.S. Dist. LEXIS 9695 (W.D. Wash. Feb. 1, 2011).

443. *Answers to Questions about the NFIP*, at 30 (Feb. 17, 2021), FEMA, https://agents.floodsmart.gov/sites/default/files/fema-answers-to-questions-about-the-NFIP.pdf. *See, e.g.*, Mancini v. Redland Ins. Co., 248 F.3d 729 (8th Cir. 2001); Touchton v. Fid. Nat'l Prop. & Cas. Ins. Co., 911 F. Supp. 2d 505 (E.D. Mich. 2012) (insurer clearly informed plaintiffs that they had to both sign and notarize proof of loss).

444. *See, e.g.*, Azoulay v. Allstate Ins. Co., 2014 U.S. Dist. LEXIS 159177 (D. Conn. Nov. 12, 2014) (because policyholder did not submit signed and notarized proof of loss for all of damages claimed, he failed to strictly comply with terms of SFIP); Debartolo v. Capitol Preferred Ins. Co., 2014 U.S. Dist. LEXIS 147769 (M.D. Fla. Oct. 15, 2014) ("sworn" requires notarization, and signature does not suffice).

445. *See, e.g.*, Hagstotz v. Nationwide Mut. Ins. Co., 2018 U.S. Dist. LEXIS 177218 (D.N.J. Oct. 16, 2018) (because supplemental proof of loss was not sworn by virtue of being notarized, and it did not satisfy unsworn statutory declaration requirements, it failed to contain "something beyond just a signature" satisfying "signed and sworn" requirement); Uddoh v. Selective Ins. Co., 2014 U.S. Dist. LEXIS 178249 (D.N.J. Dec. 29, 2014) (although SFIP does not define "sworn," many courts have interpreted it to require notarization or "something beyond just a signature").

446. Clark v. Wright Nat'l Flood Ins. Co., 380 F. Supp. 3d 523, 530 (E.D. La. 2019), *aff'd*, 821 Fed. Appx. 342 (5th Cir. Aug. 4, 2020).

[4] Timeliness

[a] Generally

FEMA says in its *Claims Manual* that policyholders have to "submit" a proof of loss *within 60 days of the date of loss* or within any extension granted by the Federal Insurance Administrator.[447] The policy states that the policyholder has to "send" the insurer a proof of loss *within 60 days after the loss.*[448] Despite the fact that the policy uses the word "send," at least one court has said the insurer has to *receive* the proof of loss within the time limit in order for it to be timely.[449]

It would be helpful if FEMA would clarify the timeliness requirement first by using either "submit" and "send" in the *Claims Manual* and policy and second by stating whether the proof of loss has to be submitted/sent or received within the time limit. However, the agency has not seen fit to do so even though it updated the *Claims Manual* in 2021 and amended the policy in 2021.

Because a "proof of loss" is the document described in the policy, meaning it includes more than just the proof of loss form, the deadline applies to all information the policy says has to be furnished, which includes specifications of damaged buildings, detailed repair estimates, and an inventory of damaged personal property. The policyholder may not submit a proof of loss form and later supplement it with the required information after expiration of the deadline.[450]

The deadline for an increased cost of compliance (ICC) claim is different. FEMA says a policyholder has to file a request for ICC within 60 days from the substantial damage notice from the community and that it makes decisions about claims filed after 60 days on a case-by-case basis.[451] Additionally, the deadline to provide an ICC Proof of Loss *and* complete the chosen and approved mitigation activities is six years from the date of the flood loss.

---

447. *National Flood Insurance Program Claims Manual*, at 284 (Oct. 2021).

448. General Property Form Standard Flood Insurance Policy, § VII.G.4.

449. *See* Seahorse Oceanside Apts. Condo. Ass'n v. Homesite Ins. Co., 446 F. Supp. 3d 1097 (S.D. Fla. 2020), where the policyholder sent a proof of loss using an incorrect zip code. The insurer never received it. The court held that the proof of loss requirement had not been met and noted that while insured may have "sent" a proof of loss, the form was not sent to the insurer at the address listed in the contract.

450. Morgan v. Tex. Farmers Ins. Co., 2020 U.S. Dist. LEXIS 17495 (S.D. Tex. Feb. 4, 2020).

451. *National Flood Insurance Program Claims Handbook*, § 2.4.1 (FEMA, Oct. 2017). FEMA advises policyholders that to file an ICC claim, they are to notify their insurer's claims representative immediately on receiving the letter from the community and they are to provide a copy of the letter to the insurance company. FEMA says the claims representative will provide additional information to help the insured complete the ICC claim. It says the insured has to sign a separate Increased Cost of Compliance Proof of Loss to receive payment.

[b] Notice-Prejudice Rule

Many states have adopted the "notice-prejudice rule" by either statute or court ruling. Under the rule, an untimely proof of loss would not necessarily block a claim unless the insurer was prejudiced by the delay. Under another general rule, the conduct of an insurer can waive a late proof of loss. These rules do not apply to the FEMA flood policy. A late proof of loss bars a claim.[452] The policyholder bears the burden of showing compliance with the proof of loss requirement.

[c] Meaning of "Date of Loss"

The policy says the policyholder has to send the insurer a proof of loss within 60 days *after the loss*.[453] The proof of loss has to state the date and time of the loss.[454] It does not, however, explain how to determine that date. For example, when policyholders evacuate in anticipation of flooding, they may not know when flood waters actually caused their loss. Nonetheless, the 60 days begins to run. Thus, a policyholder who did not return to the insured property and discover the damage to it until 60 days after the loss was found to have failed to file a timely proof of loss.[455]

Sometimes, FEMA will declare a "legal" date of loss for a flood. That date may or may not be the actual date of loss for any particular claimant. In a major flood event, FEMA typically establishes a range of dates of loss. For example, in 2019 after torrential rain in the Midwest produced widespread flood damage in Iowa, Nebraska, and Wisconsin, the agency issued a bulletin stating the dates of loss for the event. It said the date of loss in Iowa was from March 12, 2019, to April 12, 2019, while in Nebraska it was from March 12, 2019, to April 4, 2019.[456]

When FEMA declares a range, the actual date of loss still governs; the insured does not receive the benefit of the most favorable date within the range.[457]

---

452. *See, e.g.*, Slater v. Hartford Ins. Co., 26 F. Supp. 3d 1239 (M.D. Fla. 2014); Bruinsma v. State Farm Fire & Cas. Co., 410 F. Supp. 2d 628 (W.D. Mich. 2006). *See also* Rossetti v. Selective Ins. Co. of Am., 2017 U.S. Dist. LEXIS 10670 (D.N.J. Jan. 25, 2017) (even "extraordinary circumstances" would not relieve insured of obligation to submit timely proof of loss). It is possible, of course, that the insurer will pay the claim even if the proof of loss is late. *See, e.g.*, Surfsand Resort, LLC v. Nationwide Mut. Fire Ins. Co., 785 Fed. Appx. 384 (9th Cir. Nov. 18, 2019) (insurer paid claim even though proof of loss was submitted subsequent to 60-day deadline).

453. General Property Form Standard Flood Insurance Policy, § VII.G.4.

454. General Property Form Standard Flood Insurance Policy, § VII.G.4.a.

455. O'Kane v. Hartford Fire Ins. Co., 2005 U.S. Dist. LEXIS 28907 (D.N.J. Nov. 17, 2005).

456. *See* https://nfipservices.floodsmart.gov/sites/default/files/w-19006.pdf.

457. Slater v. Hartford Ins. Co., 26 F. Supp. 3d 1239, 1251, n.15 (M.D. Fla. 2014).

[d] Calculation of 60-Day Period

Neither the policy nor FEMA explain how to calculate 60 days. What happens if, for example, the 60th day falls on a holiday or weekend? Under the Federal Rules of Civil Procedure, the day of an event that triggers a period is omitted and the last day of the period is included,[458] unless it is a Saturday, Sunday, or legal holiday, in which case the period continues to run until the end of the next day that is not a Saturday, Sunday, or legal holiday.[459] At least one court has applied the rule to the proof of loss deadline.[460]

[5] Amount of Claim

The SFIP says the proof of loss is the insured's statement of the amount he or she is claiming under the policy.[461] Thus, courts have said that for the proof of loss to be sufficient, it has to state the amount claimed.[462] Some courts say a proof of loss cannot simply state that the amount is "undetermined."[463] It also cannot say that the amount is "to be determined" and follow that with specific figures.[464] It is not sufficient to state that a claim is "at least" a specific amount or to state more than one amount without identifying the amount sought.[465] A "placeholder" claim, in which the insured claims the full amount of the coverage for purposes of preserving the claim, is not acceptable.[466]

The amount claimed has to be stated in the proof of loss, not an attachment to it.[467] Thus, an invoice attached to a proof of loss is not a statement of the amount of the claim.[468]

There are courts that have been more lenient. For example, one said that if a definitive amount can be determined from the proof of loss, the insured has

458. *See, e.g.*, Moran v. Am. Bankers Ins. Co. of Florida, 2019 U.S. Dist. LEXIS 119426 (E.D. La. July 18, 2019) (where property was damaged on August 5, deadline was October 4).

459. Fed. R. Civ. P. 6(a)(1).

460. Slater v. Hartford Ins. Co., 26 F. Supp. 3d 1239, 1251 (M.D. Fla. 2014).

461. General Property Form Standard Flood Insurance Policy, § VII.G.4.

462. Mancini v. Redland Ins. Co., 248 F.3d 729, 734–35 (8th Cir. 2001); Howell v. State Farm Ins. Cos., 540 F. Supp. 2d 621, 628 (D. Md. 2008).

463. Williams v. Am. Strategic Ins. Corp., 2014 U.S. Dist. LEXIS 40225 (E.D. La. Mar. 26, 2014). *But see* Smith v. Am. Bankers Ins. Co., 2014 U.S. Dist. LEXIS 70371 (E.D. La. May 22, 2014); Portnoy v. Dir., Fed. Emergency Mgmt. Agency-Nat'l Flood Ins. Program, 2003 U.S. Dist. LEXIS 1291 (E.D. Pa. Jan. 17, 2003).

464. Palagruto v. Director, 1999 U.S. Dist. LEXIS 1915 (E.D. Pa. Feb. 24, 1999).

465. Uddoh v. Selective Ins. Co. of Am., 772 F. App'x 29 (3d Cir. May 13, 2019); Deverant v. Selective Ins. Co., 2003 U.S. Dist. LEXIS 1304 (E.D. Pa. Jan. 7, 2003).

466. Admiralty Condo. Ass'n v. Dir., FEMA, 594 Fed. Appx. 738 (3d Cir. 2014), *cert. den.*, ___U.S.___, 135 S. Ct. 2395, 192 L. Ed. 2d 167 (2015).

467. Cummings v. Fid. Nat. Indem. Ins. Co., 636 Fed. Appx. 221, 224 (5th Cir. 2016).

468. Clark v. Wright Nat'l Flood Ins. Co., 2019 U.S. Dist. LEXIS 11231 (E.D. La. Jan. 23, 2019).

satisfied the policy requirement.[469] Others have allowed an approximation of damages.[470]

[6] Documents to be Submitted with Proof of Loss

[a] Building Repair Estimate

The policy says that the proof of loss has to include "[s]pecifications of damaged buildings and detailed repair estimates."[471] An estimate can be submitted after the proof of loss but must be submitted within the 60-day deadline or any extension.[472]

The policy does not explain the meaning of a "detailed repair estimate." Courts say it may be the insured's estimation of the expense of repair founded on either personal knowledge or research.[473] Indeed, the policy says that "[i]n completing the proof of loss, you must use your own judgment concerning the amount of loss and justify that amount."[474] It is more usual, however, for the requirement to be met with a contractor's repair estimate.[475]

An estimate to rebuild an insured property is not the estimate of repairs required by the policy[476] and ordinarily does not satisfy the requirement that the proof of loss include a detailed repair estimate of the flood damage.[477] That may not be the case, however, where the insured building is completely destroyed and can only be repaired by rebuilding it.[478]

---

469. Thalheim v. Allstate Ins. Co., 2003 U.S. Dist. LEXIS 12417 (E.D. La. July 11, 2003).

470. *See, e.g.*, Slater v. Hartford Ins. Co., 2015 U.S. Dist. LEXIS 36824 (M.D. Fla. Mar. 24, 2015); Copeland v. FEMA, 2004 U.S. Dist. LEXIS 2460 (E.D. La. Feb. 17, 2004).

471. General Property Form Standard Flood Insurance Policy, § VII.G.4.f. *See also* Jackson v. Fid. Nat'l Ins. Co., 2015 U.S. Dist. LEXIS 66589 (E.D. La. May 20, 2015); Cardon Prop. No. 4, LLC v. Fid. Nat'l Indem. Ins. Co., 58 F. Supp. 3d 645 (E.D. La. 2014); Ottallah v. State Farm Fire & Cas. Co., 2008 U.S. Dist. LEXIS 58375 (E.D. La. July 31, 2008).

472. Reaves v. Tex. Farmers Ins. Co., 2020 U.S. Dist. LEXIS 69055 (S.D. Tex. Jan. 27, 2020) (where estimate was submitted four days after proof of loss deadline, insured did not present timely proof of loss). *See also* Trosclair v. State Farm Fire & Cas. Co., 2008 U.S. Dist. LEXIS 102930 (E.D. La. Dec. 9, 2008) (estimates, receipts, or invoices provided after suit has been initiated do not satisfy requirement for detailed estimate of repairs); Wells v. Fid. Nat'l Ins. Co., 2008 U.S. Dist. LEXIS 58140 (E.D. La. July 14, 2008) (estimate submitted after filing proof of loss cannot be considered in determining whether insured complied with proof of loss requirement).

473. *See, e.g.*, Sun Ray Vill. Owners Ass'n v. Old Dominion Ins. Co., 546 F. Supp. 2d 1283, 1292 (N.D. Fla. 2008).

474. General Property Form Standard Flood Insurance Policy, § VII.G.5.

475. *See, e.g.*, Aylward v. Fed. Emergency Mgmt. Agency, 781 F. Supp. 2d 272, 277 (W.D.N.C. 2011). *See also* Bercier v. Bernard, 2010 U.S. Dist. LEXIS 126414 (W.D. La. Nov. 29, 2010).

476. McDowell v. USAA Gen. Indem. Co., 2017 U.S. Dist. LEXIS 101978 (D.N.J. June 30, 2017).

477. Monistere v. State Farm Fire & Cas. Co., 559 F.3d 390 (5th Cir. 2009).

478. Strickland v. Am. Strategic Ins. Corp., 2020 U.S. Dist. LEXIS 172687 (N.D. Fla. July 31, 2020).

How much detail is required in a repair estimate is unclear; however, a simple statement that the costs will exceed a stated amount is insufficient.[479] The general rule is that the insured must enable the insurer to verify the amount claimed and evaluate the merits of the claim.[480] The policy refers to "detailed repair estimates." One court concluded that a "substantial damage" letter from a local government, various contractor estimates, and engineering reports regarding the nature, scope, and cause of damages could not be construed to constitute "detailed repair estimates."[481] FEMA has a building property worksheet that it says policyholders can use to provide specifications of the damaged building and a detailed repair estimate, including an inventory of the of flood-damaged building property showing the quantity, description, actual cash value, and amount of loss.[482]

The adjuster assigned by the insurer is required to identify covered flood-damaged building components and estimate the reasonable and necessary cost of repair or replacement of the damaged property.[483] FEMA says the policyholder will receive a copy of the estimate.[484] The adjuster, says the agency, uses his or her understanding of the extent, type, and location of the damage along with knowledge gained from visits to complete the detailed estimate of the flood-related damage. The agency advises policyholders to review the estimate and to speak with the adjuster about any questions. It also says that the estimate serves as a guide when obtaining bids from licensed professional contractors for repair work. All that notwithstanding, the adjuster's estimate does not relieve the insured of the obligation to provide documentation that supports his or her claim.[485]

[b] Inventory of Damaged Personal Property

[i] Generally

The policy requires the insured to "[p]repare an inventory of damaged property showing the quantity, description, actual cash value, and amount of loss."[486] It instructs the insured to "[a]ttach all bills, receipts, and related documents."

479. Graham v. Republic Fire & Cas. Ins. Co., 2019 U.S. Dist. LEXIS 141737 (M.D. La. Aug. 20, 2019).

480. *See, e.g.*, Sun Ray Vill. Owners Ass'n v. Old Dominion Ins. Co., 546 F. Supp. 2d 1283, 1292 (N.D. Fla. 2008).

481. McDowell v. USAA Gen. Indem. Co., 2017 U.S. Dist. LEXIS 101978 (D.N.J. June 30, 2017).

482. *Building Property Worksheet* (FEMA Form 206-FY-21-107), FEMA, https://www.fema.gov/sites/default/files/documents/FEMA-form_206-FY-21-107_building-property-worksheet_2021.pdf.

483. See § 5.05[2][e][ii], *supra*.

484. *National Flood Insurance Program Claims Handbook*, § 2.2.3 (Oct. 2017).

485. Constr. Funding, LLC v. Fid. Nat'l Indem. Ins. Co, 2014 U.S. Dist. LEXIS 161414 (E.D. La. Nov. 17, 2014).

486. General Property Form Standard Flood Insurance Policy, § VII.G.3.

It further requires the proof of loss to include that "inventory of damaged personal property."[487] "A generic line-item list of estimated, unsubstantiated damages falls short of the required inventory."[488]

One court has said that the inventory requirement applies even if the insured does not have contents coverage.[489] However, FEMA advises policyholders *who purchased personal property coverage* to make a list of damaged personal property, to include any related details or documents, and to be sure to note the quantity of each item, description, brand name, where the item was purchased, approximate age, purchase price, model and serial number, and the amount it will cost to replace the item with like kind and quality at current pricing.[490]

After a flood, personal property may be missing or need to be discarded. While the policy does not require photographs to accompany an inventory, they are a way of showing that missing property existed.[491] FEMA recommends that policyholders not discard anything before an adjuster sees it, unless local law requires otherwise or the damaged property presents a health hazard. The agency further advises policyholders who discard property to first take photographs of it and to keep samples for the adjuster to see.[492]

While the policy directs claimants to attach all bills, receipts, and related documents to the inventory, these papers are often destroyed or lost in the flood. The mandate that claimants attach bills and receipts to the inventory can only apply, say courts, when they exist.[493] Thus, courts have been willing to look to other support for a claim, including an inventory with price verification found online.[494]

487. General Property Form Standard Flood Insurance Policy, § VII.G.4.i. *See also* Garcia v. Foremost Ins. Co. of Grand Rapids, Mich., 2020 U.S. Dist. LEXIS 79682 (E.D. Tex. Apr. 10, 2020).

488. Paul v. Liberty Mut. Fire Ins. Corp., 2020 U.S. Dist. LEXIS 98190, at *15 (E.D. Tex. May 18, 2020).

489. McDowell v. USAA Gen. Indem. Co., 2017 U.S. Dist. LEXIS 101978 (D.N.J. June 30, 2017).

490. *National Flood Insurance Program Claims Handbook*, § 2.1 (Oct. 2017). Commentaries have noted that the inventory has to list the identity, quantity, replacement cost, estimated depreciation, and resulting current value for each damaged item. Maligno & Rajotte, *Trial by Water: Reflections on Superstorm Sandy*, 26 Fordham Envtl. Law Rev. 345, 376 (2015); Ballard, Howard-Gibbon, Furnish & Scheinwald, *Natural Disasters, Access to Justice, and Legal Services*, 17 N.Y. City L. Rev. 1, 15 (2014).

491. Tuircuit v. Wright Nat'l Flood Ins. Co., 2014 U.S. Dist. LEXIS 156386 (E.D. La. Nov. 4, 2014).

492. *National Flood Insurance Program Claims Handbook*, § 2.1 (Oct. 2017).

493. Robins v. Nationwide Mut. Ins. Co., 2013 U.S. Dist. LEXIS 168286 (M.D. Pa. Nov. 26, 2013); Provenza v. State Farm Fire & Cas. Ins. Co., 2007 U.S. Dist. LEXIS 41284 (E.D. La. June 6, 2007).

494. Tuircuit v. Wright Nat'l Flood Ins. Co., 2014 U.S. Dist. LEXIS 156386 (E.D. La. Nov. 4, 2014).

[ii] Personal Property (Contents) Worksheet

FEMA has a personal property worksheet that it says policyholders can use to list the inventory of flood-damaged personal property, which includes the quantity, description, actual cash value, and amount of loss.[495] Adjusters have been known to give the worksheet to policyholders to assist them in making an accurate inventory of personal property,[496] but policyholders can download a copy of the form for themselves at the FEMA website.

[iii] Actual Cash Value Determination

The policy requires the insured to prepare an inventory of damaged property showing *actual cash value*.[497] It defines "actual cash value" as "[t]he cost to replace an insured item of property at the time of loss, less the value of its physical depreciation."[498] The FEMA *Claims Manual* explains depreciation to *adjusters*. It says that adjusters should apply depreciation based on the age[499] and physical condition of each item in the personal property estimate.[500] An insured can use this information in determining how to compute depreciation. Failure to determine actual cash value, meaning depreciated value, defeats the claim.[501]

[iv] Prior Flood Damage

The SFIP says the insurer may request, in writing, that the insured furnish a complete inventory of the lost, damaged, or destroyed property, including evidence that prior flood damage has been repaired.[502] According to one court, the policy language is not a coverage exclusion for prior unrepaired damages, and, therefore, evidence of repair is not a condition to recovery under the

495. *Personal Property (Contents) Worksheet* (FEMA Form 206-FY-21-106), FEMA, https://www.fema.gov/sites/default/files/documents/FEMA-form_206-FY-21-106_personal-property-claims_2021.pdf.

496. Robins v. Nationwide Mut. Ins. Co., 2013 U.S. Dist. LEXIS 168286 (M.D. Pa. Nov. 26, 2013).

497. General Property Form Standard Flood Insurance Policy, § VII.G.3.

498. General Property Form Standard Flood Insurance Policy, § II.C.2.

499. Statement of the age of property in the claimant's inventory is critical. *See* Jacobsen v. Hartford Ins. Co. Flood & Home (Sandy), 2017 U.S. Dist. LEXIS 52591 (D.N.J. Mar. 31, 2017) (claimants made no attempt to estimate age for most of claimed items, but merely stated that most property was purchased sometime between 2005 and 2011).

500. *National Flood Insurance Program Claims Manual*, at 226 (Oct. 2021). The manual adds that application of the same rate of depreciation to personal property items throughout an adjustment or estimate, despite many differences in material type, age, and use, is not acceptable.

501. Unger v. Liberty Mut. Ins. Co., 849 F. Supp. 839 (E.D.N.Y. 1994). *See also* Paul v. Liberty Mut. Fire Ins. Corp., 2020 U.S. Dist. LEXIS 98190 (E.D. Tex. May 18, 2020), where a generic line-item list of estimated, unsubstantiated damages was found not to satisfy the requirement of an inventory including actual cash value, amount of loss, and specifications.

502. General Property Form Standard Flood Insurance Policy, § VII.H.2.e.

policy.[503] At the same time, the policy does not cover damage to insured property that occurred prior to the covered loss, and that includes unrepaired damage from a previous flood.[504] Therefore, FEMA says an insurer has to verify that damages from any previous loss have been repaired before the subject loss occurred and exclude any unrepaired previous damages from the adjustment. If a claimant does not provide enough evidence to show that property damaged in a prior flood has been repaired or replaced, an insurer's decision to deny coverage is not subject to appraisal.[505]

[7] Multiple and Supplemental Proofs of Loss

The policy does not address supplemental proofs of loss, but it also does not proscribe them.[506] FEMA says that submitting a proof of loss "does not prevent the policyholder from submitting an additional proof of loss, such as an amended proof of loss for additional payment."[507] The agency says that when a claimant sees additional damage after submitting a proof of loss, he or she may file a request for an additional flood payment.[508] The policyholder then has to repeat the documentation and filing process including a proof of loss for the newly discovered damage.[509] The additional request has to be completed within the 60-day limit, or within any time extensions granted by FEMA.[510] The proof of loss has to be submitted to the insurer, but FEMA instructs insureds to present the completed proof of loss and documentation to the adjuster.

[8] Substantial Compliance with Proof of Loss Requirement

Policyholders whose claims have been denied for failure to submit an appropriate proof of loss frequently contend that they have "substantially complied"

---

503. Westmoreland v. Fid. Nat'l Indem. Ins. Co., 2015 U.S. Dist. LEXIS 69417 (M.D. La. May 29, 2015) (policy provides insurer option to request evidence of repair).

504. *National Flood Insurance Program Claims Manual*, at 268 (Oct. 2021).

505. Reef Enters. v. Wright Nat'l Flood Ins. Co., 2017 U.S. Dist. LEXIS 30317 (S.D. Miss. Mar. 3, 2017).

506. Miller v. Selective Ins. Co. of Am., 2009 U.S. Dist. LEXIS 116332, at *13, n.5 (D.N.J. Dec. 15, 2009); Petersen v. Nat'l Flood Ins. Program, 200 F. Supp. 2d 499, 505 (E.D. Pa. 2002).

507. *National Flood Insurance Program Claims Manual*, at 285 (Oct. 2021). *See also* Young v. Imperial Fire & Cas. Ins. Co., 2014 U.S. Dist. LEXIS 51863 (E.D. La. Apr. 15, 2014) (several timely proofs of loss combined with other documents may be considered sufficient).

508. *National Flood Insurance Program Claims Handbook*, § 2.4 (FEMA, Oct. 2017).

509. Courts have also said that a specific proof of loss is required for supplemental claims. Barros v. Wright Nat'l Flood Ins. Co., 2019 U.S. Dist. LEXIS 206091 (S.D. Fla. Nov. 26, 2019); Ravasio v. Fid. Nat'l Prop. & Cas. Ins. Co., 81 F. Supp. 3d 274 (E.D.N.Y. 2015); Howell-Douglas v. Fid. Nat'l Indem. Ins. Co., 24 F. Supp. 3d 579, 582–83 (E.D. La. 2014); Howell v. State Farm Insurance Co., 540 F. Supp. 2d 621, 627 (D. Md. 2008).

510. *National Flood Insurance Program Claims Handbook*, § 2.4 (FEMA, Oct. 2017). *See also* Roussell v. Allstate Ins. Co., 26 F. Supp. 3d 552 (E.D. La. 2014) (supplemental claims generally may not "piggyback" on initial timely proof of loss).

with the policy requirements and that should be sufficient. While some courts have agreed,[511] most courts hold substantial compliance is not enough; claimants have to "strictly follow the rules."[512] Circuit courts have said that the proof of loss mandate is a regulatory limit on disbursement of federal funds that has to be strictly construed.[513] As the Third Circuit said, "Even if we assume that FEMA's resort to rigid enforcement of its regulations was disingenuous, this case is controlled by the rule that participants in federal insurance programs can expect no indulgence when it comes to procedure."[514] Policyholders are charged with knowledge of terms of the policy and of the agency rules.[515]

[9] Waivers and Extensions

[a] Waiver

The policy provides that it cannot be changed and none of its provisions can be waived "without the express written consent of the Federal Insurance Administrator."[516] It adds that no action that the insurer takes under the terms of the policy can constitute a waiver of any of its rights.[517] Thus, insureds have to submit a proper and timely proof of loss unless they are given

511. These courts interpret the policy to require enough information to provide an insurer with the capability of evaluating the merits of the claim. *See, e.g.*, Mitchell v. Nat'l Flood Ins. Program, 2008 U.S. Dist. LEXIS 9937 (E.D. La. Feb. 8, 2008); Conrad v. Omaha Prop. & Cas. Ins. Co., 1995 U.S. Dist. LEXIS 7907 (E.D. Pa. June 7, 1995); Dixie Warehouse v. Fed. Emergency Mgmt. Agency, 547 F. Supp. 81 (M.D.N.C. 1982); Brennan v. Fed. Emergency Mgmt. Agency, 1981 U.S. Dist. LEXIS 10848 (D. Mass. Feb. 13, 1981).

512. *See, e.g.*, Mancini v. Redland Ins. Co., 248 F.3d 729, 733 (8th Cir. 2001); Gowland v. Aetna, 143 F.3d 951 (5th Cir. 1998); Scharr v. Selective Ins. Co., 2017 U.S. Dist. LEXIS 175222 (W.D.N.Y. Oct. 23, 2017); Sun Ray Vill. Owners Ass'n v. Old Dominion Ins. Co., 546 F. Supp. 2d 1283, 1289 (N.D. Fla. 2008); Bruinsma v. State Farm Fire & Cas. Co., 410 F. Supp. 2d 628, 634 (W.D. Mich. 2006).

513. Admiralty Condo. Ass'n v. Dir., FEMA, 594 Fed. Appx. 738 (3d Cir. 2014), *cert. den.*, 575 U.S. 1038, 135 S. Ct. 2395, 192 L. Ed. 2d 167 (2015); Gunter v. Farmers Ins. Co., 736 F.3d 768, 773 (8th Cir. 2013); Jacobson v. Metro. Prop. & Cas. Ins. Co., 672 F.3d 171, 175 (2d Cir. 2012); Flick v. Liberty Mut. Fire Ins. Co., 205 F.3d 386, 392 (9th Cir.), *cert. den.*, 531 U.S. 927, 121 S. Ct. 305, 148 L. Ed. 2d 245 (2000).

514. Admiralty Condo. Ass'n v. Dir., FEMA, 594 Fed. Appx. 738, 742 (3d Cir. 2014), *cert. den.*, 575 U.S. 1038, 135 S. Ct. 2395, 192 L. Ed. 2d 167 (2015).

515. Collins v. Encompass Ins. Co., 2009 U.S. Dist. LEXIS 97974 (E.D. La. Oct. 14, 2009); Kehoe v. Travelers Ins. Co., 2009 U.S. Dist. LEXIS 1585 (N.D.N.Y Jan. 12, 2009); Oaks v. Allstate Ins. Co., 2006 U.S. Dist. LEXIS 83652 (E.D. Ky. Nov. 14, 2006).

516. General Property Form Standard Flood Insurance Policy, § VII.C.

517. *See also* Carney v. Metro. Prop. & Cas. Ins. Co., 2020 U.S. Dist. LEXIS 64038 (D. Mass. Apr. 9, 2020) (even if insurer said it would send insured proof of loss form, but did not, claim was properly denied as it was obligation of insured to submit timely proof of loss); Beggs v. Am. Bankers Ins. Co., 2019 U.S. Dist. LEXIS 230394, at *14, n.11 (E.D. Va. July 25, 2019) (even if insurer *intentionally* undervalued insured property in courtesy proof of loss forms, insureds were obligated to exercise their own judgment in completing their proofs of loss); Psychiatric Solutions, Inc. v. FEMA, 2015 U.S. Dist. LEXIS 41297 (E.D. Pa. Mar. 31, 2015) (actions or inactions of a WYO company are all but irrelevant).

a written waiver.[518] They cannot be relieved of that policy obligation through waiver by implication or estoppel.[519] There can be no implied waiver, even by FEMA.[520] A breach of contract by the insurance company will not even relieve the insured of the policy mandate.[521] However, courts are split over the question of whether an *anticipatory* breach or repudiation will excuse a policyholder from submitting a proof of loss.[522] For example, the Fourth Circuit has suggested that the doctrine of anticipatory repudiation, which frees the non-repudiating party from the contract obligations, applies to a FEMA flood policy.[523] The Second Circuit, on the other hand, has said that because the doctrine rests on notions of waiver and estoppel, its application to an SFIP is "dubious."[524]

[b] Extensions of Deadline

[i] Blanket Extension

After a major flood event, it is common for FEMA to extend the deadline for filing proofs of loss. The extension may be as little as an additional 60 days or as much as two years, and additional extensions may also be granted. Extensions are announced by bulletin to WYO companies, WYO vendors, NFIP direct servicing agents, and independent adjusting firms.[525] Policyholders can access the bulletins by visiting the pertinent FEMA web page[526] and clicking on "WYO Company Bulletins."

---

518. Stoner v. S. Farm Bureau Cas. Ins. Co., 758 F.3d 991 (8th Cir. 2014); Sanz v. United States Sec. Ins. Co., 328 F.3d 1314, 1318 (11th Cir. 2003); Neuser v. Hocker, 246 F.3d 508 (6th Cir. 2001). In rare instances, WYO insurers have offered to accept a proof of loss after the deadline; however, because the insurer is not authorized to waive the deadline, a policyholder cannot rely on that offer. Suopys v. Omaha Prop. & Cas., 404 F.3d 805, 808 (3d Cir. 2005).

519. *See, e.g.*, Phelps v. Fed. Emergency Mgmt. Agency, 785 F.2d 13 (1st Cir. 1986); Miller v. Am. Strategic Ins. Corp., 2016 U.S. App. LEXIS 21731 (5th Cir. Dec. 6, 2016); Zumpano v. Am. Bankers Ins. Co., 2019 U.S. Dist. LEXIS 121000 (S.D. Fla. July 18, 2019); West Monroe, LLC v. United States, 2018 U.S. Dist. LEXIS 116677 (W.D. La. July 12, 2018).

520. Ekeler v. Fed. Emergency Mgmt. Agency, 2021 U.S. Dist. LEXIS 138065 (D. Neb. July 23, 2021) (implied waiver is not allowed under SFIP or under law, and fact that FEMA paid out part of untimely proof of loss was not express consent to waive 60-day requirement for any other untimely claims).

521. Howell v. State Farm Ins. Cos., 540 F. Supp. 2d 621, 629–30 (D. Md. 2008).

522. Gunter v. Farmers Ins. Co., 736 F.3d 768, 775 (8th Cir. 2013) (noting split of authority between circuits). There does not, however, appear to be any disagreement that a simple *denial* of a claim is not a repudiation of the policy. Evanoff v. Std. Fire Ins. Co., 534 F.3d 516, 521 (6th Cir. 2008).

523. Studio Frames v. Std. Fire Ins. Co., 369 F.3d 376, 381 (4th Cir. 2004).

524. Jacobson v. Metro. Prop. & Cas. Ins. Co., 672 F.3d 171 (2d Cir. 2012).

525. *See, e.g.*, https://nfipservices.floodsmart.gov/sites/default/files/w-19018_0.pdf (Tropical Storm Imelda extension announcement).

526. *See The Write Your Own (WYO) Program*, FEMA, https://nfipservices.floodsmart.gov/write-your-own-program.

Bulletins that declare an extension of the proof of loss deadline have to be read carefully because there are usually limitations on the extension. Typically, a bulletin will *waive* proofs of loss when the independent adjuster and the insured agree on the loss,[527] and it will *extend* the proof of loss deadline when they do not agree. There may be geographical limitations. For example, a hurricane or tropical storm may affect several states, but the extension will probably apply to fewer than all the states affected and may even limit the extension to specific counties in a state. There may be a temporal limitation, confining the extension to losses occurring on specific dates.[528] Thus, if an insured property avoided flood damage during a hurricane or tropical storm, but suffered a loss a week later during a localized cloud burst, the extension probably does not apply.

[ii] Individual Extension

By rule, FEMA has the authority to waive provisions of policy.[529] However, the agency has not put forward any process or prescribed criteria for obtaining a waiver to extend the proof of loss deadline. The *Claims Manual* states that if an examiner *receives* a proof of loss after 60 days from the date of loss, or any extension granted by FEMA, the examiner has to submit a waiver request through the NFIP system, which is called "PIVOT," and obtain approval of a waiver before issuing payment.[530] However, FEMA has granted applications for extensions made directly to it on behalf of an insured.[531]

A request for a waiver may have to be supported by documentation of the claim for which it is requested.[532] It is possible for more than one waiver to be granted for losses that are related to a single flood.[533] There does not appear to be any basis for the deadline to be tolled while FEMA considers a request for waiver.

---

527. *See, e.g.*, Baltazor, Inc. v. Fid. Nat'l Ins. Program, 544 F. Supp. 2d 516, 521 (E.D. La. 2008) (proof of loss waived entirely if insured accepted settlement of claim).

528. For example, after Tropical Storm Imelda hit Texas, a limited extension was granted for all claims associated with Flood Insurance Claims Office (FICO) Number 379, which was identified as "Texas, September 17, 2019, through September 27, 2019." https://nfipservices.floodsmart.gov/sites/default/files/w-19018_0.pdf.

529. 44 C.F.R. § 61.13(d). The rule says: "The Standard Flood Insurance Policy and required endorsements must be used in the Flood Insurance Program, and no provision of the said documents shall be altered, varied, or waived other than by the express written consent of the Federal Insurance Administrator through the issuance of an appropriate amendatory endorsement, approved by the Federal Insurance Administrator as to form and substance for uniform use."

530. *National Flood Insurance Program Claims Manual*, at 270 (Oct. 2021).

531. *See, e.g.*, Surfsand Resort, LLC v. Nationwide Mut. Fire Ins. Co., 2018 U.S. Dist. LEXIS 108873 (D. Ore. June 28, 2018); Diamond v. Fed. Emergency Mgmt. Agency, 689 F. Supp. 163 (E.D.N.Y. 1988).

532. Psychiatric Sols., Inc. v. FEMA, 2015 U.S. Dist. LEXIS 41297 (E.D. Pa. Mar. 31, 2015).

533. *See, e.g.*, Schubert v. Chertoff, 2009 U.S. Dist. LEXIS 75835 (E.D. La. Aug. 26, 2009).

In a rather dramatic confrontation, a federal court asked FEMA what criteria it uses to determine which claims might be considered after the proof of loss deadline. The court reported that "FEMA was not able at first to articulate the criteria . . . [but later] advised the Court of the criteria, effectively conceding that they had not theretofore been published."[534] The criteria FEMA revealed to the court included the following:

- Severity of flood damages,
- Whether damage required expert evaluation,
- Whether salvage was involved that delayed adjustment,
- Whether the policyholder had difficulty listing all flood-damaged items,
- Whether there were settlement disputes that could have delayed adjustments,
- Whether the insured required additional time because of health,
- Whether there were prior losses for which repairs and replacement of personal property had to be documented, and
- Whether the insured demonstrates additional covered damage for which supplemental payment would be appropriate.

The criteria have not been codified, and since stating them, FEMA has denied a waiver where an insured repaired damages before the property was inspected.[535] Repair prior to inspection was not one of the stated criteria. On the other hand, the agency allowed a waiver where a WYO insurer submitted a request and explained that the proof of loss was late mainly because of the length of time it took for the insured to provide documentation that damages from a prior flood had been repaired.[536] Thus, the agency applied one of the explicit criteria it identified.

[10] Rejected Proof of Loss

The claims examiner reviews the proof of loss to confirm accuracy, that the policyholder properly supported the claim for damage on the form, and that values match the amount to be paid.[537] When the proof of loss fails to meet the prescribed standards, it will be rejected and the rejection may be effective even if not received by the policyholder.[538] FEMA, however, says that when a proof

---

534. Moffett v. Computer. Scis. Corp., 647 F. Supp. 2d 517, 519–20 (D. Md. 2009).

535. Reynolds v. S. Farm Bureau Cas. Ins. Co., 2008 U.S. Dist. LEXIS 20006, at *5 (W.D. Tex. Mar. 13, 2008).

536. Reef Enters. v. Wright Nat'l Flood Ins. Co., 2017 U.S. Dist. LEXIS 30317 (S.D. Miss. Mar. 3, 2017).

537. *National Flood Insurance Program Claims Manual*, at 285 (Oct. 2021).

538. Cohen v. Allstate Ins. Co., 2018 U.S. Dist. LEXIS 34236 (S.D. Tex. Mar. 2, 2018), *aff'd*, 924 F.3d 776 (5th Cir. 2019) (although neither insured nor insured's public adjuster received letters rejecting proof of loss, critical fact was mailing, not receipt).

of loss is not compliant in content or form, the examiner should reject it and *communicate the decision directly to the policyholder*.[539] When the examiner can support payment of a *portion* of the claim, FEMA says the examiner is to issue a partial rejection of the proof of loss and pay the undisputed amount. The examiner should, says FEMA, provide *written notification* of the rejection to the policyholder, explain all issues, and request documentation required to resolve those issues.

If a policyholder brings suit in response to the rejection, that rejection may constitute a denial of the claim because, by filing suit, the insured has treated the rejection as a written denial of his or her claim.[540]

5.7 Denial of Claim

Under the FEMA regulations, WYO insurers generally employ their own "customary standards."[541] However, the agency tells policyholders that "[a]n insurer will mail a denial letter to [them], in which the insurer will formally reject part or all of the claim and explain why based on the specific policy provisions."[542] The policy does not authorize adjusters to approve or disapprove claims, or to tell policyholders whether the insurer will approve a claim.[543] Adjusters, says FEMA, may answer general flood insurance coverage questions in an effort to provide good customer service, but they should also tell policyholders that the insurer provides the final claim decision.

FEMA prescribes the contents of the denial letter.[544] Each letter has to include seven elements:

- The date of the denial letter;[545]
- The name(s) of the policyholder(s), the mailing address, and the loss location;
- The date of loss;
- The date(s) the policyholder submitted a request for payment, including an advance payment, or failed to comply with a material term of the policy;

539. *National Flood Insurance Program Claims Manual*, at 285 (Oct. 2021).

540. Migliaro v. Fidelity Nat'l Ins. Co., 880 F.3d 660, 664–65 (3d Cir. 2018).

541. 44 C.F.R. § 62.23(e).

542. .*Answers to Questions about the NFIP*, at 32 (Feb. 17, 2021), FEMA, https://agents.floodsmart.gov/sites/default/files/fema-answers-to-questions-about-the-NFIP.pdf.

543. General Property Form Standard Flood Insurance Policy, § VII.G.8.

544. *See National Flood Insurance Program Claims Manual*, at 317–18 (Oct. 2021).

545. FEMA notes that the date of the initial denial letter begins the one-year period from which the policyholder may file suit and the 60-day period to file an appeal with the agency. *National Flood Insurance Program Claims Manual*, at 315, 317 (Oct. 2021).

- The item(s) denied with the corresponding dollar amount denied, whenever applicable;[546]
- A plain-language explanation for the non-payment or non-coverage;[547] and
- Citations to the relevant sections of the policy and a web link to it.

The agency says that an insurer has to include with every denial an attachment that explains the rights of the policyholder after a whole or partial denial.[548] FEMA has a document called "Policyholder Rights" that insurers can use for this purpose and can modify to include brand identity or contact information. FEMA says that it intends for the Policyholder Rights document to replace previous standard paragraphs in denial letters about appeals and litigation.[549]

When the reasons given in the denial letter do not agree with the facts of the claim, or if the policy citation referenced does not fully support the denial decision, FEMA says the letter may be faulty and result in a premature or ineligible appeal, in which case the agency will forward the letter to the insurer and request that the insurer deal directly with the policyholder to resolve the matter by making a final determination and sending an adequate denial letter.[550]

5.8 Claim File

[1] Generally

FEMA says that insurers may *only rely* on documentation contained within a claim file when making a claim determination.[551] Thus, when a claim is denied in whole or part, the contents of the claim file are critical if an attorney representing a policyholder intends to challenge the decision of the insurer. Also, a review of the file may reveal that important documents are missing. An insured, for example, maintained that supplemental proofs of loss had been submitted directly to FEMA. However, it denied ever receiving them. FEMA observed that the insured had obtained the claims file about nine months after the supplemental proofs of loss were purportedly executed, and yet the file

546. FEMA says denial letters should avoid general terms, for example, "various items" or "finished items in a basement," and instead list the items not covered by the policy.

547. Rather than quote the policy at length, FEMA says the denial letter should explain why the policy does not provide coverage.

548. *See National Flood Insurance Program Claims Manual*, at 318 (Oct. 2021).

549. The document, notes the agency, provides policyholders with the option to submit flood insurance appeals by email.

550. *National Flood Insurance Program Claims Manual*, at 318 (Oct. 2021).

551. *National Flood Insurance Program Claims Manual*, at 275 (Oct. 2021).

did not include them.[552] Obviously, the insured would have been in a stronger position if the file had been reviewed immediately on receipt and FEMA had been notified of the omission.

[2] Contents of Claim Files

FEMA says insurers have to guarantee that claim files contain all documentation in their possession that is directly related to the adjustment, investigation, and payment of an individual claim.[553] The documentation includes the Declarations Page or verifications of coverage applicable on the date of loss; copies of claim payment checks; correspondence to or from the insurer and policyholder about the claim at issue or underwriting issues relevant to the claim at issue; communications between insurer, claims examiner, adjuster, and other insurer employees and contractors; adjuster reports and supporting materials, including preliminary reports, final reports, estimates, log notes, and photographs; materials submitted by the policyholder, including estimates or supporting documents and prior losses provided by the policyholder or policyholder representative; proofs of loss and other requests for additional payment; claim decision letters; denial letters; and expert reports. Insurers are not required to obtain drafts of these documents, but they have to maintain and disclose them if acquired during the adjustment, investigation, or payment of a claim. FEMA adds that insurers should include electronic mail or other electronic communications in the file

FEMA says carriers have to ensure that individual claim files do not contain materials unrelated to the claim. If, for example, an insurer receives communications pertaining to multiple policyholders, it has to remove the personally identifiable information of other policyholders who are not part of the claim file in question before including the communication in the file. Insurers are allowed to redact any privileged communications from a claim file before disclosure; however, privileged communications are limited to privileges that the insurer anticipates will be asserted to preclude disclosure in court, for instance, the attorney-client privilege.

[3] Release of Claim File Information to Policyholders

Policyholders may obtain a copy of their claim file.[554] To do so, they have to submit a signed request to their insurer. At a minimum, the request has to include the policyholder's full name, current address, and date and place of

552. LCP West Monroe, LLC v. United States, 2018 U.S. Dist. LEXIS 116677 (W.D. La. July 12, 2018).
553. *National Flood Insurance Program Claims Manual*, at 275 (Oct. 2021).
554. *National Flood Insurance Program Claims Manual*, at 276 (Oct. 2021).

birth. The signature of the policyholder has to be either notarized or submitted with the following statement:

> I declare (or certify, verify, or state) under penalty of perjury that the foregoing is true and correct. Executed on (date).
>
> (Signature)[555]

Despite the assertion by FEMA that insureds may request their claim file, evidently there are no consequences for insurers who fail to comply with a request for a file. For instance, an insured requested the file, but he did not receive it. He said that he also did not receive a denial of his claim. If the insurer had given him the file, he argued it would have contained the denial. Moreover, he contended the statute of limitations had not started to run because he had not received a denial. However, the court found that failure to provide the claim file was not a basis for invoking estoppel and barring the insurer's statute of limitations defense.[556]

[4] Representative of Policyholder Obtaining Claim File

If a representative of a policyholder, for example, an attorney or public adjuster, requests a copy of a claim file on behalf of his or her client, he or she also has to provide a letter of representation that meets the requirements of FEMA.[557] Insurers may not disclose a policyholder's information to a representative or allow a representative to act on behalf of a policyholder without obtaining a letter of representation. The letter has to be signed by all policyholders named on the policy. At minimum, a letter has to include the policyholder's full name, current address, and date and place of birth; the name of the third-party representative; a statement from the policyholder authorizing the representative to act on his or her behalf; and a request that the insurer release records to the representative. The policyholder's signature must be either notarized or submitted with the following statement:

> I declare (or certify, verify, or state) under penalty of perjury that the foregoing is true and correct. Executed on (date).
>
> (Signature)[558]

---

555. *See* 28 U.S.C. § 1746.

556. Hampson v. Wright Nat'l Flood Ins. Co., 2020 U.S. Dist. LEXIS 175993 (S.D. Fla. Sept. 23, 2020).

557. *National Flood Insurance Program Claims Manual*, at 276 (Oct. 2021).

558. *See* 28 U.S.C. § 1746.

5.9 Dispute Resolution

[1] Appraisal

[a] Generally[559]

FEMA says the SFIP provides both the policyholder and insurer the option to demand appraisal.[560] The parties may, but are not required to, invoke appraisal.[561] Claims professionals, the agency cautions, should only use appraisal to resolve disputes that involve the amount to pay for flood damages. Appraisal cannot be used to determine the scope, coverage, or causation of damage. FEMA encourages policyholders and insurers to exhaust all other avenues available to determine the fair price of the agreed loss before invoking appraisal. For example, before appraisal, FEMA says a policyholder should provide the insurer with contractors' estimates, receipts, invoices, photographs, and any other relevant documentation or a written explanation to support his or her claim.

When one of the parties demands appraisal, each then chooses a "competent and impartial appraiser" within 20 days after receiving a written request from the other party.[562] The two appraisers choose an umpire, and if they cannot agree on an umpire within 15 days, either party may request that the choice be made by a judge in the state where the insured property is located. The appraisers separately state the actual cash value, replacement cost, and amount of loss to each item. If they submit a written report of an agreement to the insurer, the amount agreed on will be the amount of loss. If they fail to agree, they submit their differences to the umpire. A decision agreed to by any two sets the amount of actual cash value and loss, or, if it applies, the

559. *See generally* Smith, *Property Insurance Appraisal: Is Determining Causation Essential to Evaluating the Amount of Loss?*, 2012 J. Disp. Resol. 591, 593 (2012); Law & Starinovich, *What Is It Worth? A Critical Analysis of Insurance Appraisal*, 13 Conn. Ins. L.J. 291, 294 (2006/2007).

560. *National Flood Insurance Program Claims Manual*, at 221 (Oct. 2021). *See* General Property Form Standard Flood Insurance Policy, § VII.M.

561. Dwyer v. Fid. Nat'l Prop. & Cas. Ins. Co., 2007 U.S. Dist. LEXIS 26517 (E.D. La. Apr. 3, 2007) (appraisal provision is permissive, not mandatory).

562. General Property Form Standard Flood Insurance Policy, § VII.M. FEMA says that appraisers and umpires cannot profit from a higher claim payment made to a policyholder and that if a policyholder hires a public adjuster or attorney, and the basis of their fee is securing a higher claims payment for the policyholder, no one employed, affiliated with, or related to that public adjuster or attorney may serve as the appraiser or the umpire. No one employed, affiliated with, or related to the adjuster or owner of the adjusting company who receives a fee based on the policyholder receiving a higher payment can serve as an appraiser or umpire. Appraisers chosen by insurers have to be similarly impartial. To avoid a conflict of interest, no one employed, affiliated with, or related to the adjuster or owner of the adjusting company who receives a fee based upon the policyholder receiving a higher payment can serve as an appraiser or umpire. *National Flood Insurance Program Claims Manual*, at 221 (Oct. 2021).

replacement cost and loss. Each party pays its own appraiser and bears the other expenses of the appraisal and umpire equally.

Appraisal is not arbitration. Therefore, it is not subject to the Federal Arbitration Act.[563] If the policy is issued by a private carrier on behalf of FEMA, the agency is not a proper party to the appraisal as it was not a party to the policy.[564] Before appraisal is invoked, there has to be agreement on the scope of loss.[565] Other disputes, including the scope of coverage,[566] cannot be resolved by appraisal.[567] FEMA adds that appraisal should only be used to resolve disputes over the amount to pay for flood damages. [568] A Florida federal court has explained that there are three disputes that may possibly be subject to appraisal.[569] The first is where the parties agree on the property damaged and its severity, but not on actual value. The second arises when the parties agree on the property that was damaged but not on how to repair or replace it.[570] Finally, the court said appraisal might appear appropriate when the parties disputed which property was actually damaged by flooding, but concluded that was a coverage dispute and not subject to appraisal.

[b] Pre-Conditions to Appraisal

FEMA prescribes certain pre-conditions to the employment of appraisal.[571] When a pricing dispute remains, the SFIP allows appraisal under the following conditions:

- The policyholder and the insurer have to agree on the scope of loss, and there has to be an agreed list of insured items damaged by flood.

---

563. Dwyer v. Fid. Nat'l Prop. & Cas. Ins. Co., 565 F.3d 284, 286–87 (5th Cir. 2009).

564. *See* 44 C.F.R. § 62.23(g).

565. Sharpe v. Am. Nat'l Prop. & Cas. Co., 2014 U.S. Dist. LEXIS 76088 (E.D. La. June 3, 2014).

566. *See, e.g.*, Caivano v. Allstate Ins. Co., 2017 U.S. Dist. LEXIS 50490 (D.N.J. Mar. 31, 2017) (motion to compel appraisal denied where insurer denied claim for benefits for foundational damage and, therefore, parties disagreed about scope of coverage); Sharpe v. Am. Nat'l Prop. & Cas. Co., 2014 U.S. Dist. LEXIS 76088 (E.D. La. June 3, 2014) (because parties did not agree on scope of coverage under policy, invocation of appraisal clause was improper); Apple v. Allstate Ins. Co., 2010 U.S. Dist. LEXIS 68848 (M.D. Fla. June 18, 2010) (appraisal could not be invoked where parties appeared to dispute whether items such as painting ceiling, bringing slab up to level, repairing drywall in ceiling, and packing and storing of contents of residence were covered).

567. Appraisal may not be used to determine the scope, coverage, or causation of damage. *National Flood Insurance Program Claims Manual*, at 221 (Oct. 2021).

568. *National Flood Insurance Program Claims Manual*, at 221 (Oct. 2021).

569. De La Cruz v. Bankers Ins. Co., 237 F. Supp. 2d 1370, 1374 (S.D. Fla. 2002).

570. This dispute would be subject to appraisal, said the court, because the same analysis required to fix value would lend itself to determining whether property could be returned to its original value and the means to achieve that result. *But see* Sam v. Nat'l Lloyds Ins. Co., 2011 U.S. Dist. LEXIS 118216 (S.D. Tex. Oct. 13, 2011) (where parties disagreed about severity of damage and whether property needed to be repaired or replaced, appraisal was not proper).

571. *National Flood Insurance Program Claims Manual*, at 221 (Oct. 2021).

- The parties cannot use appraisal if the policyholder submits an appeal to FEMA or initiates litigation. Appraisal has to result in a complete resolution of the entire claim.
- The policyholder has to submit a timely and completed proof of loss with supporting documentation for the items subject to appraisal.[572]
- A proof of loss, signed by the policyholder, that includes adequate documentation to justify the increased unit costs and pricing is a condition precedent to appraisal. An estimate, not supported by any other information, for example, from a public adjuster or contractor, is not adequate and appraisal is then not proper.
- If a policyholder invokes appraisal and then attempts to resolve issues regarding eligibility, coverage, or scoping of loss, then the policyholder did not properly invoke appraisal, rendering the process, including any award, invalid. If the WYO inappropriately issues payment to the policyholder or if the WYO inappropriately used appraisal, the WYO is responsible to FEMA for any erroneous payments, including fees.[573]

[c] Appeals or Litigation

Insurers cannot employ appraisal if a policyholder submits an appeal to FEMA or initiates litigation.[574] If the insurer invokes a policyholder's request for appraisal, the policyholder may not later file an appeal with FEMA on the same items or the same dispute reason.[575] If the parties are in litigation, a court cannot order an appraisal that would not resolve all the policyholder's claims and result in dismissal. [576]

Generally, SFIP policy provisions cannot be waived without express written consent of FEMA; however, it has been held that, by its actions, a party may waive the right to demand appraisal.[577] The appraisal clause in the policy does not prescribe a time limit for invoking appraisal, and a party may, therefore, invoke the clause after filing suit,[578] so long as the failure to invoke appraisal does not constitute waiver.[579] Any suit, of course, has to be filed within the one-year limitation.[580]

---

572. If the policyholder submitted a signed and sworn proof of loss and the insurer paid the amount in full, FEMA notes that there is no dispute regarding pricing and no need for appraisal.

573. *National Flood Insurance Program Claims Manual*, at 221 (Oct. 2021).

574. *National Flood Insurance Program Claims Manual*, at 221 (Oct. 2021).

575. *Answers to Questions about the NFIP*, at 32 (Feb. 17, 2021), FEMA, https://agents.floodsmart.gov/sites/default/files/fema-answers-to-questions-about-the-NFIP.pdf (if policyholder completes appraisal, he or she cannot also file an appeal).

576. Prastos v. Travelers Ins. Cos., 2015 U.S. Dist. LEXIS 28767 (D.N.J. Mar. 10, 2015).

577. Dwyer v. Fid. Nat'l Prop. & Cas. Ins. Co., 565 F.3d 284 (5th Cir. 2009).

578. Mahood v. Omaha Prop. & Cas., 174 F. Supp. 2d 284, 291 (E.D. Pa. 2001).

579. Dwyer v. Fid. Nat'l Prop. & Cas. Ins. Co., 565 F.3d 284, 288 (5th Cir. 2009).

580. Reef Enters. v. Wright Nat'l Flood Ins. Co., 2017 U.S. Dist. LEXIS 30317 (S.D. Miss. Mar. 3, 2017).

By rule, on refusal of a claimant to accept the amount allowed on any claim after appraisal, the claimant may bring an action against the insurer.[581] Appraisal, however, is not a pre-condition to filing suit because as one court has said, it is a dispute resolution method that either party may invoke.[582] Furthermore, the claimant policyholder is not bound by the completed appraisal.[583]

[2] Appeal

[a] Generally

By regulation, a policyholder, whether insured by a participating insurer or directly by FEMA, may appeal a decision, including a determination of any insurance agent, adjuster, insurance carrier, or any FEMA employee or contractor regarding a claim, a proof of loss, or loss estimate.[584] Because this administrative appeal provides an adequate remedy, courts hold that a policyholder may not invoke the federal Administrative Procedures Act (APA).[585]

To file an appeal, the insured has to comply with all requirements set out in the policy. The appeal is available after the insurer issues a "final claim determination." A final claim determination is a written denial, in whole or in part, of the claim. After a final claim determination is issued, an insured may appeal any action taken by the insurer, a FEMA employee, a FEMA contractor, an insurance adjuster, or an insurance agent. However, FEMA says a policyholder may "only appeal what the insurance company denied in the denial letter."[586]

FEMA says that there is no filing fee for an appeal and that policyholders do not need to be represented by a third party.[587] If a policyholder is represented by a third party, FEMA will not pay for any costs incurred for that representation. The agency recommends that, before filing an appeal, a policyholder work with the adjuster and submit supporting documentation to justify his or her position and that if the policyholder is unable to agree with the adjuster, he or she should first contact the adjusting firm and the adjuster's supervisor and then, if no agreement can be reached, the insurance company's claims department.

581. 44 C.F.R. § 62.22(a).

582. Dwyer v. Fid. Nat'l Prop. & Cas. Ins. Co., 565 F.3d 284 (5th Cir. 2009).

583. Dwyer v. Fid. Nat'l Prop. & Cas. Ins. Co., 2007 U.S. Dist. LEXIS 26517 (E.D. La. Apr. 3, 2007).

584. 44 C.F.R. § 62.20(b).

585. Muse v. Nat'l Flood Ins. Program, 2019 U.S. Dist. LEXIS 32097 (E.D. La. Feb. 28, 2019); Clutter v. Long, 2018 U.S. Dist. LEXIS 171038 (E.D.N.Y. Sept. 28, 2018).

586. Appealing Your Flood Insurance Claim, at 1 (FEMA Oct. 20, 2015).

587. *Answers to Questions about the NFIP*, at 33 (Feb. 17, 2021), FEMA, https://agents.floodsmart.gov/sites/default/files/fema-answers-to-questions-about-the-NFIP.pdf.

[b] Limitations on Appeal

The appeals process is intended to resolve claim issues, not to grant coverage or limits that are not provided by the policy.[588] That has been interpreted to mean that the appeal is not a claim determination, but merely a review of the final decision of the insurer for errors.[589] Filing an appeal does not waive any of the requirements for perfecting a claim under the policy or extend any of its time limitations. Disputes that are, or have been, subject to appraisal cannot be appealed.[590] Moreover, when a policyholder files an appeal on any issue, that issue can no longer be resolved by appraisal or other pre-litigation remedies. [591] A policyholder who files suit against an insurer on a flood insurance claim issue is barred from filing an appeal, and all appeals submitted for decision but not yet resolved will be terminated on notice of the commencement of litigation about the claim.[592]

[c] Procedures

To pursue an appeal a policyholder has to submit a written appeal to FEMA within 60 days from the date of the decision;[593] provide a copy of the written denial, in whole or in part, of the claim; identify relevant policy and claim information and state the basis for the appeal; and submit relevant documentation to support the appeal.[594] Note that FEMA says appeals can be submitted by email and that it receives *and processes* appeals that are emailed more quickly than those sent by regular mail or express delivery.[595] The agency says that it calculates the 60-day time frame by counting the day after the date on the denial letter and then counts every Saturday, Sunday, and legal holiday.[596] If the 60th day is a Saturday, Sunday, or legal holiday, it then extends the period to the next day that is not a Saturday, Sunday, or legal holiday. FEMA says it considers an email electronic time stamp, U.S. Mail postmark, or express carrier acceptance date as the time of submission to it.

---

588. 44 C.F.R. § 62.20(c).

589. Clutter v. Long, 2018 U.S. Dist. LEXIS 171038 (E.D.N.Y. Sept. 28, 2018); Fowl, Inc. v. Fid. Nat'l Prop. & Cas. Ins. Co., 2012 U.S. Dist. LEXIS 71883 (E.D. La. May 23, 2012); Mertz v. FEMA, 2011 U.S. Dist. LEXIS 94267 (D. Or. Feb. 14, 2011).

590. 44 C.F.R. § 62.20(c)(1).

591. 44 C.F.R. § 62.20(c)(2).

592. 44 C.F.R. § 62.20(d). *See also Appealing Your Flood Insurance Claim*, at 1 (FEMA Oct. 20, 2015) (appeals process is unavailable to any policyholder who files lawsuit against their insurance company or enters appraisal process to determine value of their claim).

593. FEMA says policyholders should send their appeals package to FEMA, 400 C Street SW, 6th Floor SW, Washington, D.C. 20472-3010, or FEMA-NFIP-Appeals@fema.dhs.gov. *Appealing Your Flood Insurance Claim*, at 1 (FEMA Oct. 20, 2015).

594. 44 C.F.R. § 62.20(e).

595. *Appealing Your Flood Insurance Claim*, at 1 (FEMA Oct. 20, 2015). The agency also says that cybersecurity requirements do not permit FEMA to access file sharing sites, CDs, DVDs, or any electronic storage device.

596. *National Flood Insurance Program Claims Manual*, at 315 (Oct. 2021).

The regulation governing appeals says that a policyholder should submit only the documentation that pertains to the claim. It then provides a lengthy list of examples of the kinds of documentation that FEMA will require to adjudicate the appeal. Those documents are:

- A copy of the proof of loss submitted to the insurer;
- Room-by-room itemized estimates from the adjuster, including contractors' estimates, detailing unit cost and quantities for the items requiring repair or replacement;
- Replacement cost proofs of loss;
- Preliminary Report;
- Final Report;
- Detailed damaged personal property inventories that include the approximate age of the items;
- Completed Mobile Home Worksheet;
- Mobile Home Title, including Salvage Titles;
- Real estate appraisals that exclude land values;
- Advance payment information;
- Clear exterior and interior photographs confirming that damage resulted from direct physical loss by or from flood;
- Proof of prior repair;
- Evidence of insurance and policy information, including the Declarations Page;
- Elevation Certificate, if the risk is an elevated building;
- Any community determination made regarding substantial damage;
- Information about substantial improvement;
- Zone determinations;
- Pre-loss and post-loss inventories;
- Financial statements;
- Tax records;
- Lease agreements;
- Sales contracts, settlement papers, and deeds;
- Emergency (911) address change information;
- Salvage information;
- Condominium association bylaws;
- Proof of other insurance, including homeowners or wind policies, and any claim information submitted to the other companies;
- Waiver, Letter of Map Revision (LOMR), or Letter of Map Amendment (LOMA) information;
- Paid receipts and invoices including cancelled checks that support out-of-pocket expenses pertaining to the claim;
- Underwriting decisions;
- Architectural plans and drawings;
- Death certificates;

- Wills;
- Divorce decrees;
- Powers of attorney;
- Current lienholder information;
- Current loss payee information;
- Paid receipts and invoices documenting damaged stock;
- Detailed engineering reports specifically addressing flood-related damage and preexisting damage;
- Engineering surveys;
- Market values;
- Documentation of Flood Insurance Rate Maps (FIRM) dates;
- Documentation reflecting dates of construction and substantial improvement;
- Loan documents including closings;
- Evidence of insurability as a Residential Condominium Association;
- Franchise Agreements;
- Letters of representation, including those from attorneys and public adjusters;
- Any assignment of interest in a claim; and
- Any other pertinent information that FEMA may request in processing a claim.

FEMA adds to the list credit card statements and properly completed drying logs.[597] Additionally, the agency says that when an appeal is submitted by a representative of the policyholder, that representative should indicate his or her relationship to the policyholder and provide documents that verify and authorize the relationship, including a waiver allowing access to personal information.[598] Finally, FEMA "encourages policyholders to provide as much detail and documentation as needed to support their position in the initial appeal."[599]

[d] Resolution of Appeal

Under the pertinent regulation, FEMA has to acknowledge in writing receipt of an appeal from a policyholder and include with the acknowledgment contact information for a FEMA point of contact who can advise the policyholder

597. *Answers to Questions about the NFIP*, at 33 (Feb. 17, 2021), FEMA, https://agents.floodsmart.gov/sites/default/files/fema-answers-to-questions-about-the-NFIP.pdf.

598. *Appealing Your Flood Insurance Claim*, at 1 (FEMA Oct. 20, 2015). The waiver is pursuant to 5 U.S.C. § 552a.

599. *National Flood Insurance Program Claims Manual*, at 316-17 (Oct. 2021).

about the status of the claim.[600] The agency adds that it will request the claim file from the insurance company.[601]

During the appeal process, if the insurer can resolve the issues in favor of the policyholder under the terms and conditions of the policy, FEMA encourages them to do so.[602]

The Federal Insurance Administrator will review the documents submitted and may notify the policyholder in writing that additional information is required.[603] A request for additional information has to include the date by which it has to be provided, which has to be in no case less than 14 calendar days. Failure to provide the requested information in full, or to request an extension by the due date, can result in dismissal of the appeal. A re-inspection of the property may be conducted at the discretion of the Federal Insurance Administrator. The administrator is to ensure that all information necessary to rule on the appeal has been provided before making an appeal decision.

The Federal Insurance Administrator will review the appeal documents, including any reinspection report, and will provide specific information on the grounds on which the claim was denied initially.[604] After the review, the administrator will determine if the insurance company correctly denied the claim.[605] While the appeal is supposedly only a review for errors in the insurer's final decision,[606] in practice, it is not so limited. For example, in a case decided by the Second Circuit, the insurer denied a claim for lack of a complete proof of loss. The court noted that the subsequent appeal was rejected, but the basis of the decision was not the proof of loss, but three separate grounds: failure to provide prompt notice, the damage was a consequence of prior floods, and that land subsidence was the proximate cause of the damage.[607]

The administrator will provide an appeal decision in writing to the policyholder and insurer within 90 days from the date that all information has been submitted by the policyholder and include specific information for the resolution of the appeal. The pertinent regulation says that "[n]o further administrative review will be provided to the insured."[608]

600. 44 C.F.R. § 62.20(f)(1).

601. *Appealing Your Flood Insurance Claim*, at 1 (FEMA Oct. 20, 2015).

602. *National Flood Insurance Program Claims Manual*, at 316 (Oct. 2021).

603. 44 C.F.R. § 62.20(f)(2).

604. 44 C.F.R. § 62.20(f)(3).

605. *Appealing Your Flood Insurance Claim*, at 1 (FEMA Oct. 20, 2015).

606. Mertz v. FEMA, 2011 U.S. Dist. LEXIS 94267 (D. Or. Feb. 14, 2011).

607. Jacobson v. Metro. Prop. & Cas. Ins. Co., 672 F.3d 171, 173 (2d Cir. 2012).

608. FEMA says it will provide an appeal decision in writing with specific information concerning resolution of the appeal and that the letter constituting that writing "will end the appeals process." *Appealing Your Flood Insurance Claim*, at 2 (FEMA Oct. 20, 2015).

FEMA says that at the conclusion of the appeal, it will provide its decision in writing to both the policyholder and the insurer, with specific information about resolution of the appeal.[609]

FEMA may overturn the denial and inform both the policyholder and the insurer of its determination and recommend the most appropriate action to the insurer when the agency agrees with the policyholder. It also may concur in the denial and explain its decision in plain language with references to the policy and other relevant publications. It may also suggest actions the policyholder can take to achieve a different outcome.

[e] Judicial Review

The pertinent regulation refers a policyholder who does not agree with a FEMA appeal decision to the subsection of the policy addressing suit against the insurer.[610] That subsection says that a suit has to be commenced within one year of the date of a written denial of all or part of the claim.[611] The regulation says that the one-year period to file suit commences with the written denial from the insurer and is *not extended* by the appeals process.[612] That lack of extension is contrary to what many might expect,[613] especially as in the aftermath of a major flood, appeals may not be promptly resolved. That can put insureds in an untenable situation. Either they file suit before the appeal is resolved, in which case the appeal is terminated, or they wait and risk having the limitations period run out. Nonetheless, equitable estoppel generally is not available against the government to escape the consequences of the one-year limitation.[614]

[3] Litigation

[a] Right to File Suit

By rule, on disallowance of any claim on grounds *other than failure to file a proof of loss*, or on refusal of the claimant to accept the amount allowed on

609. *National Flood Insurance Program Claims Manual*, at 317 (Oct. 2021).

610. 44 C.F.R. § 62.20(f)(4).

611. General Property Form Standard Flood Insurance Policy, § VII.O.

612. Texas courts have suggested the possible application of equitable tolling. *See* Batie v. S. Farm Bureau Prop. & Cas. Co., 2015 U.S. Dist. LEXIS 98028 (S.D. Tex. July 28, 2015); Altman v. Napolitano, 2013 U.S. Dist. LEXIS 28260 (S.D. Tex. Mar. 1, 2013); Wolfe v. Am. Bankers Ins. Co., 2013 U.S. Dist. LEXIS 28258 (S.D. Tex. Mar. 1, 2013).

613. *See The Flood Insurance Claims Process in Communities after Sandy: Lessons Learned and Potential Improvements*: Hearing before the Subcomm. on Housing, Transportation, and Community Development, 113th Cong., 2d Sess. (July 30, 2014) (statement of chmn. Robert Mendez) (laypersons will likely assume they should or have to wait for appeal to be completed before filing suit).

614. Brower v. Nat'l Flood Ins. Program, 1988 U.S. Dist. LEXIS 17689 (W.D. Mich. July 27, 1988).

any claim after appraisal, the claimant may institute an action on the claim against the insurer.[615] The rule bars judicial review when a claim is denied solely for failure to file a proof of loss.[616] The rule, however, does not prevent the defendant from raising the lack of a proof of loss as a defense providing the claim has been denied on some other ground.[617] The judicial review *statute* provides that on the disallowance of any claims for proved and approved losses covered by flood insurance, or on the refusal of the claimant to accept the amount allowed on a claim, the claimant may bring an action on that claim.[618] It does not mention disallowance of claims on grounds other than failure to file a proof of loss. However, as discussed immediately below, a policyholder has to file a complete proof of loss as a condition of bringing suit under the policy.

There is no requirement in the policy that an insured has to give a 60-day "post-proof-of-loss cushion" before bringing suit.[619]

[b] Burden of Proof

In any insurance litigation, when a policyholder sues an insurer for breach of contract for failure to pay a claim, the insured has the burden of bringing the alleged loss within the coverage of the policy. For claims under the SFIP, that means the plaintiff insured has to allege more than that the insured property was damaged and there was flooding in the community in which the property is located. For example, the city of Houston suffered widespread and catastrophic flooding during Hurricane Harvey. However, that well-known fact did not relieve a Houston area property owner of the burden to raise factual dispute as to whether *the insured property* was flooded.[620]

[c] Compliance with Policy as Pre-Condition to Suit

The SFIP says that an insured may not bring suit to recover money under the policy unless he or she has complied with all the requirements of the policy.[621] This is a condition precedent to waiver of sovereign immunity by the federal government and thus is a condition of the jurisdiction of the courts.[622] An insured cannot, therefore, bring an action seeking policy benefits without

---

615. 44 C.F.R. § 62.22(a).

616. *See, e.g.*, Howard v. Dir., Federal Emergency Mgmt. Agency, 960 F. Supp. 1095 (S.D. Miss. 1996).

617. Schumitzki v. Dir., Fed. Emergency Mgmt. Agency, 656 F. Supp. 430, 433 (D.N.J. 1987).

618. 42 U.S.C. § 4072.

619. Seahorse Oceanside Apts. Condo. Ass'n v. Homesite Ins. Co., 446 F. Supp. 3d 1097, 1108 (S.D. Fla. 2020).

620. Shaw v. Am. Bankers Ins. Co., 2021 U.S. Dist. LEXIS 76602 (S.D. Tex. Apr. 21, 2021).

621. General Property Form Standard Flood Insurance Policy, § VII.O.

622. Wagner v. Director, Fed. Emergency Mgmt. Agency, 847 F.2d 515, 518 (9th Cir. 1988).

showing compliance with all policy requirements.[623] That includes submitting a complete,[624] sworn proof of loss even if suit is filed prior to expiration of the time for filing a proof of loss.[625] A court may allow a policyholder to take a voluntary dismissal without prejudice and to refile after submitting the proof of loss.[626]

The Dwelling Form policy says that any action for coverage has to commence *after the date of the written denial*.[627] Therefore, where an insurer issued a written denial one month after the insureds *initiated* litigation, the action was dismissed for failure to satisfy the prerequisites to suit in the SFIP.[628] Interestingly, the language of the General Form SFIP is different. It says the insured has to start a suit within one year *of the date* of the written denial.[629]

The written denial must be of the claim that is being litigated. Thus, where the insurer sent a letter with an advance payment for a building claim and informed the insured that there was no coverage for additional living expenses, the court said the letter was not a written denial of the insured's supplemental building coverage claim and could not, therefore, serve as a basis for triggering the court's jurisdiction.[630]

[d] Claim Limited to Breach of Contract

Courts assert that the National Flood Insurance Act neither explicitly nor implicitly permits extra-contractual claims against an insurer.[631] An insured, therefore, has but one remedy under the FEMA policy for non-payment of a claim: an action for breach of contract.[632]

---

623. *See, e.g.*, Bruinsma v. State Farm Fire & Cas. Co., 410 F. Supp. 2d 628, 633 (W.D. Mich. 2006).

624. Trosclair v. State Farm Fire & Cas. Co., 2008 U.S. Dist. LEXIS 102930 (E.D. La. Dec. 9, 2008) (if proof of loss is not complete, insured has failed to comply with pre-condition to bringing suit).

625. Marseilles Homeowners Condo. Ass'n v. Fid. Nat'l Ins. Co., 542 F.3d 1053 (5th Cir. 2008); Seahorse Oceanside Apts. Condo. Ass'n v. Homesite Ins. Co., 446 F. Supp. 3d 1097 (S.D. Fla. 2020).

626. Morales v. Am. Strategic Ins. Corp., 2020 U.S. Dist. LEXIS 27918 (N.D. Fla. Feb. 19, 2020) (noting court could condition dismissal on payment of some or all of a defendant's costs, including attorney's fees).

627. Dwelling Form Standard Flood Insurance Policy, § VII.O.

628. Castleberry v. Am. Strategic Ins. Corp., 2021 U.S. Dist. LEXIS 157059 (M.D. La. Aug. 19, 2021).

629. General Property Form Standard Flood Insurance Policy, § VII.O.

630. Nichols v. Liberty Mut. Ins. Co., 2021 U.S. Dist. LEXIS 224233 (M.D. La. Nov. 19, 2021).

631. *See* Wright v. Allstate Ins. Co., 500 F.3d 390 (5th Cir. 2007). *See also* Melanson v. United States Forensic, LLC, 183 F. Supp. 3d 376 (E.D.N.Y. 2016); Psychiatric Sols., Inc. v. FEMA, 101 F. Supp. 3d 490 (E.D. Pa. 2015); Howell-Douglas v. Fid. Nat'l Indem. Ins. Co., 24 F. Supp. 3d 579 (E.D. La. 2014).

632. Howell-Douglas v. Fid. Nat'l Indem. Ins. Co., 24 F. Supp. 3d 579, 583 (E.D. La. 2014).

[e] Limitation Period

[i] Generally

The SFIP states that if a policyholder sues, the suit has to be initiated within one year of the date of the *written denial* of all or part of the claim.[633] A statute provides that on disallowance of a claim—or on refusal of the claimant policyholder to accept the amount allowed on a claim—the claimant may institute an action on the claim within one year after the *date of mailing of the notice* of disallowance or partial disallowance of that claim.[634] A FEMA rule also refers to the date of mailing.[635] Courts appear to agree that the limitation does not run from the date the denial is *received*,[636] but they do not agree on whether it begins on the date of the written denial or of its mailing. Some courts state that it is the former,[637] while most say it is the latter.[638] One court noted that discrepancy, saying "the time for filing suit pursuant to the SFIP is calculated by the date of the denial letter, and pursuant to the statute

---

633. General Property Form Standard Flood Insurance Policy, § VII.O. If a claim is based strictly on a state law tort, however, the NFIP statute of limitations should not apply and the pertinent state statute of limitations should instead apply. Spence v. Omaha Indem. Ins. Co., 996 F.2d 793, 796 (5th Cir. 1993).

634. 42 U.S.C. § 4072. The statute refers to actions by, and suits against, "the Administrator," but applies when an SFIP is issued and administered by a private insurer on behalf of FEMA. Brusco v. Harleysville Ins. Co., 2014 U.S. Dist. LEXIS 86794 (D.N.J. June 26, 2014); Miller v. American Bankers Ins. Group, 85 F. Supp. 2d 1297 (S.D. Fla. 1999); Parsons Footwear v. Omaha Prop. & Cas. Co., 19 F. Supp. 2d 588, 591 (N.D. W. Va. 1998).

635. 44 C.F.R. § 62.22(a) (on disallowance of any claim on grounds other than failure to file proof of loss, or on refusal of claimant to accept amount allowed on any claim after appraisal, claimant within one year after date of mailing of notice of disallowance or partial disallowance of claim may, pursuant to 42 U.S.C. § 4072, institute an action on that claim). Note that neither the policy nor the statute mentions denial "other than for failure to file a proof of loss." In *Green v. Beers*, 2014 U.S. Dist. LEXIS 180986 (E.D. La. Jan. 22, 2014), the court said it was not apparent from the record that the denial was based on a claim that included a sworn proof of loss. The court then decided that "given that the statute of limitations begins to run as of the date Defendant denied Plaintiff's claim that is based upon her sworn proof of loss, not from the date Defendant denied a claim based upon an adjuster's report," it could not conclude that the action had been filed after the statute of limitations had expired.

636. Hampson v. Wright Nat'l Flood Ins. Co., 2020 U.S. Dist. LEXIS 175993 (S.D. Fla. Sept. 23, 2020); Chatelain v. United States Dep't of Homeland Sec., 2019 U.S. Dist. LEXIS 123879 (E.D. La. July 25, 2019).

637. *See, e.g.*, Hampson v. Wright Nat'l Flood Ins. Co., 2020 U.S. Dist. LEXIS 175993 (S.D. Fla. Sept. 23, 2020) ("statute of limitations is triggered by the date of the Notice of Partial Denial and receipt of the Notice of Partial Denial is not a material fact").

638. SH Marathon, Ltd. v. Homesite Ins. Co., 2021 U.S. Dist. LEXIS 67047 (S.D. Fla. Apr. 7, 2021) (federal law requires claimant to bring suit within one year of mailing of denial of claim); Cholankeril v. Selective Ins. Co. of Am., 2016 U.S. Dist. LEXIS 91457 (D.N.J. July 14, 2016) (statute states on its face that mailing of notice triggers limitations period). *See also* Phillips v. Am. Strategic Ins. Corp., 2020 U.S. Dist. LEXIS 5423 (S.D. Fla. Jan. 10, 2020); Migliaro v. Fid. Nat'l Indem. Ins. Co., 2017 U.S. Dist. LEXIS 15497 (D.N.J. Feb. 2, 2017); Smith v. Nat'l Flood Ins. Program of the Fed. Emergency Mgmt. Agency, 156 F. Supp. 2d 520 (E.D. Pa. 2001).

by the date the denial letter is mailed" but found it unnecessary to resolve the inconsistency.[639]

The termination of the limitations period is determined using the Federal Rules of Civil Procedure.[640] Under the rules when a period is stated in days it is computed by excluding the day of the event that triggers the period, counting every day, including intermediate Saturdays, Sundays, and legal holidays, and including the last day of the period unless the last day is a Saturday, Sunday, or legal holiday, in which case the period continues to run until the end of the next day that is not a Saturday, Sunday, or legal holiday.[641]

FEMA cannot extend the one-year statute of limitations to file suit.[642] The limitation is codified in both the National Flood Insurance Act and the Code of Federal Regulations. Policyholders are, therefore, charged with knowledge of it, as they are with any law, and are bound by it even if they were never provided a copy of the policy.[643]

[ii] Triggering the Limitations Period: Denial of the Claim

[A] Generally

The policy says a policyholder has to initiate suit within one year of the date of the written *denial* of *all or part* of the claim.[644] Therefore, it is critical to determine when there has been a denial. The determination becomes challenging when the denial is partial, conditional, or ambiguous. Before that, of course, there has to be a claim. If there is no claim, just an inquiry into the scope of coverage, a response explaining the coverage is not a denial and, therefore, does not trigger the limitation period.[645]

[B] Rejection of Proof of Loss

The Third Circuit has rejected the argument that rejection of a proof of loss is *per se* a denial of a claim. It has, however, held that "written rejection of a proof of loss constitutes a denial of the claim if, based on it, the policyholder

---

639. Linblad v. Nationwide Mut. Ins. Co., 2014 U.S. Dist. LEXIS 168444 (D.N.J. Dec. 4, 2014).

640. Smith v. Nat'l Flood Ins. Program of the Fed. Emergency Mgmt. Agency, 156 F. Supp. 2d 520 (E.D. Pa. 2001).

641. Fed. R. Civ. P. 6(a).

642. *National Flood Insurance Program Claims Manual*, at 289 (Oct. 2021). *But see* Gaffney v. State Farm Ins. Co., 1997 U.S. Dist. LEXIS 4092 (E.D. La. Mar. 31, 1997) (insurer granted extension to statute of limitations).

643. Miller v. Am. Bankers Ins. Group, 85 F. Supp. 2d 1297, 1301 (S.D. Fla. 1999). *See also* Lang v. USAA Gen. Indem. Co., 2011 U.S. Dist. LEXIS 166572 (S.D. Tex. Aug. 8, 2011). *But see* Royal Inn v. Courtier, 1996 U.S. Dist. LEXIS 11038 (E.D. La. July 31, 1996) (rejecting as unreasonable argument that "unsophisticated purchaser of insurance" received adequate notice of policy contents through publication of policy in Code of Federal Regulations).

644. General Property Form Standard Flood Insurance Policy, § VII.O.

645. Bevis v. State Farm Fire & Cas. Co., 2008 U.S. Dist. LEXIS 102271 (D.N.H. Dec. 2, 2008).

files suit . . . thereby accepting the written rejection of a proof of loss as a written denial of the claim."[646]

[C] Partial Denial

Partial disallowance of a claim triggers the limitations period.[647] A letter to the insured stating that some part of the claim is being denied is sufficient.[648] For example, a policyholder claimed damages to two buildings, a restaurant and a house. The insurer sent a letter denying the claim for the house because it was not covered by the policy, but it stated a check would be sent to cover the damages to the restaurant. The letter said that because a portion of the claim was denied, the policyholder had one year within which to file suit. The court said, therefore, that it was irrelevant whether a single claim or separate claims for each building were filed. Each claim sought benefits for damages arising from a single flooding event under a single policy, and the letter triggered the statute of limitations.[649]

A denial letter can approve the great majority of the claim, include a check, and deny one small portion of it.[650] It can offer partial settlement of the claim on a "take it or leave it" basis.[651] On the other hand, a letter from FEMA that offered less than the claimant sought was found not to be a denial because it said that if the insured accepted payment, no rights to seek additional payment would be waived and additional payment could be sought by submitting a proof of loss.[652]

---

646. Migliaro v. Fid. Nat'l Indem. Ins. Co., 880 F.3d 660, 665 (3d Cir. 2018).

647. The statute and policy refer to partial disallowance, not partial acceptance. *See* Price v. Fugate, 2015 U.S. Dist. LEXIS 84498 (W.D. Tex. June 30, 2015) (partial acceptance of claims has no bearing on jurisdictional statute of limitations).

648. *See* Ekhlassi v. Nat'l Lloyds Ins. Co., 295 F. Supp. 3d 750, 755–56 (S.D. Tex. 2018) (letter to policyholder stated claim could not be processed without proof of loss and that coverage was being denied for other damages; because letter made clear insurer was denying the majority of claim, court found that statute of limitations had begun to run); St. Germain Place Owners Ass'n v. Tex. Farmers Ins. Co., 2012 U.S. Dist. LEXIS 90740 (S.D. Tex. June 29, 2012) (letter informed insured that its claim was being allowed only in the amount of $93,475.22 and that the remainder of claim, $259,409.99, was being rejected).

649. Lionheart Holding Grp v. Phila Contributionship Ins. Co, 368 Fed. Appx. 282 (3d Cir. 2010).

650. Stone v. Franklin Homeowners Assur., 2014 U.S. Dist. LEXIS 85411 (M.D. Pa. June 23, 2014) (insureds received letter informing them that insured had approved majority of their claim, included check for $32,142.43, and denied claim of $827.56 for replacement of basement light fixtures, which insurer concluded were not covered). *See also* Brusco v. Harleysville Ins. Co., 2014 U.S. Dist. LEXIS 86794 (D.N.J. June 26, 2014) (letter with check enclosed paying portion of claim and explaining why part of remainder of claim was not being paid together with statement that letter was decision to deny claim triggered statute of limitations).

651. State Bank of Coloma v. National Flood Ins. Program, 851 F.2d 817 (6th Cir. 1988) (letter offering 50 percent compromise of claim was partial denial because it was clear that it categorically rejected part of the claim and only remaining issue was whether claimant would accept payment offered and claimant was given 15 days to accept payment or insurer would "close the file").

652. Garcia-Pedrosa v. FEMA, 2020 U.S. Dist. LEXIS 3010 (S.D. Fla. Jan. 7, 2020).

[D] Conditional Denial or Reconsideration after Denial

A conditional denial, for example, one providing merely advice as to a possible or likely future negative determination, does not begin the running of the limitations period.[653] When an insurer gave notice that it denied a claim "pending documentation of replacement from [a] prior flood loss," it was an express written denial of part of the claim, not just a request for evidence. The letter started the limitations period.[654] A denial of a claim that expresses a willingness to reconsider on receipt of additional documents is still a written denial even though the insurer continues to process the claim.[655] Where a claim is denied, reconsideration of that claim and a subsequent offer of settlement does not reset the limitations clock.[656]

[E] Confusing Denials

Insurance language is abstruse, and laypersons are often baffled by communications from insurers. The confusion can be compounded when the policy is a FEMA SFIP. For example, an insurer sent a policyholder a letter rejecting a proof of loss and stating the letter was *not* a denial of the claim. More than one year later, the policyholder sued the insurer. The court found that the letter, despite denying that it was a rejection of a claim, was indeed a written denial of a claim that triggered the running of the limitations period. The court said that representations made by an insurer cannot change the SFIP without express written consent of FEMA.[657] To further muddle matters, on appeal, the Third Circuit affirmed and said that in effect, by filing suit, the insured accepted that the written rejection of the proof of loss was a written denial of the claim.[658]

In another case, the insurer denied the claim based on an inspection of the wrong property. The independent adjuster found no damage at that property and recommended no payment. Several days later, after discovering the error, the adjuster visited the correct property with the insured's public adjuster. The next day, while the claim was being adjusted, the insurer denied it for lack of damage. About one year later, the insurer received the insured's request for additional payment, and a year after that the insurer finally paid the claim, but based on the estimate of its adjuster. The insured brought suit a few weeks

653. Wing Bldg. Holding Co. LLC v. Std. Fire Ins. Co., 2015 U.S. Dist. LEXIS 17761 (N.D.N.Y Feb. 13, 2015).

654. Cohen v. Allstate Ins. Co., 2018 U.S. Dist. LEXIS 67681 (S.D. Tex. Apr. 23, 2018).

655. Cohen v. Allstate Ins. Co., 924 F.3d 776 (5th Cir. 2019).

656. Nabhan v. National Con-Serv, 1 F. Supp. 2d 91, 96 (D. Mass. 1998).

657. Migliaro v. Fid. Nat'l Indem. Ins. Co., 2017 U.S. Dist. LEXIS 15497 (D.N.J. Feb. 2, 2017).

658. Migliaro v. Fid. Nat'l Indem. Ins. Co., 880 F.3d 660, 665 (3d Cir. 2018).

later, but the court said it was time barred because even though the first denial was based on mistaken information, it still triggered the limitations period.[659]

Apparently, a denial does not have to come from the insurer for it to trigger the limitation. An insured received a denial letter on the letterhead of the insurer's parent company, an organization with which the insured was not in privity. The court, however, held the letter triggered the limitations period. It said that under federal law, causes of action accrue when the plaintiff has enough facts about the harm he or she has suffered that reasonable inquiry will reveal the cause of action.[660]

When an insured receives more than one written denial, which one governs? An insured received an initial letter stating the claim was being denied because, *inter alia*, the insured had failed to provide prompt notice of the loss. In response, the insured submitted proof that prompt notice of the loss had been given and then asked for the claim to be reopened. The carrier agreed to reconsider the claim. It then sent a second letter that confirmed its denial. The first letter of disallowance, said the court, was superseded by the second notice, and the second notice was controlling for purposes of applying the period of limitations.[661] That decision can be contrasted with one by the Ninth Circuit which said that once the limitations period is initiated by a denial, neither reconsideration of the denial nor responding to further inquiries has an effect on the limitations period.[662] For example, an insurer denied a claim in December 2014. It later accepted a new proof of loss and sent a check to cover some of the claimed damages in January 2016. By sending that check, contended the insured, the company revoked its initial denial. That, in turn, restarted the limitations period. The court, however, disagreed, observing that the Ninth Circuit had held that a new limitations period on a subsequent denial of a claim only begins if *FEMA* sets aside the previous denial. Moreover, the insurer's decision to pay some claims after first denying them all should not, said the court, be construed as reopening the claims and extending the limitations period. When the carrier denied the claims, the policyholder was on notice that a suit would have to be filed within one year.[663]

---

659. SH Marathon, Ltd. v. Homesite Ins. Co., 2021 U.S. Dist. LEXIS 67047 (S.D. Fla. Apr. 7, 2021).

660. Battle v. Seibels Bruce Ins. Co., 288 F.3d 596, 604 (4th Cir. 2002).

661. Horeftis v. National Flood Insurers Ass'n, 437 F. Supp. 794 (E.D. Mich. 1977).

662. Wagner v. Director, Fed. Emergency Mgmt. Agency, 847 F.2d 515, 521 (9th Cir. 1988). *Accord* SH Marathon, Ltd. v. Homesite Ins. Co., 2021 U.S. Dist. LEXIS 67047 (S.D. Fla. Apr. 7, 2021); Clutter v. Long, 2018 U.S. Dist. LEXIS 171038 (E.D.N.Y. Sept. 28, 2018); Steelcraft, Inc. v. Bankers & Shippers Ins. Co., 979 F. Supp. 60, 62 (D. Mass. 1997).

663. Apatow v. Am. Bankers Ins. Co., 2016 U.S. Dist. LEXIS 180529 (C.D. Cal. Dec. 21, 2016). The court allowed that if an insured receives new denials of claims previously unknown to him or her, then there could be a basis for extending the limitations period.

[F] Timely Denial

The policy says losses are payable 60 days after the insurer receives the proof of loss or within 90 days after the insurance adjuster files an adjuster's report signed and sworn to by the policyholder in lieu of a proof of loss.[664] If the insurer fails to pay or deny the claim within the time limit, is that considered to be a denial? One court has said that if the failure to pay a claim within 60 days is not viewed as denial of the claim, an insurer could prevent the policyholder from bringing suit indefinitely simply by taking no action on the claim.[665] However, subsequent decisions have held the loss-payment clause in the policy does not require insurers to make a determination on a claim within 60 days after they receive a proof of loss.[666] Failure to pay a claim within 60 days after a proof of loss does not, therefore, represent denial of a claim.

[iii] Equitable Tolling

In certain narrow circumstances, equitable tolling might apply to the SFIP limitations period.[667] By FEMA rule, however, "[t]he one-year period to file suit commences with the written denial from the insurer and is not extended by the appeals process."[668] Thus, some courts hold that equitable tolling does not apply while FEMA entertains an administrative appeal.[669] There are, however, several cases from the federal Southern District of Texas that suggest otherwise.[670]

[iv] Consequences of Initially Filing in State Court

It is very common in insurance litigation for a policyholder to file suit in a state court and for the insurer to then remove the action to federal court pursuant to diversity jurisdiction. The FEMA policy, however, says the insured has to file any suit "in the United States District Court of the district in which

---

664. General Property Form Standard Flood Insurance Policy, § VII.J.1.

665. Altman v. Napolitano, 2013 U.S. Dist. LEXIS 28260 (S.D. Tex. Mar. 1, 2013).

666. Poirrier v. Fed. Emergency Mgmt. Agency, 2020 U.S. Dist. LEXIS 4586 (M.D. La. Jan. 10, 2020) (noting policy describes several events—the parties reach agreement, there is an entry of a final judgment, or there is a filing of an appraisal award—one of which has to occur before loss is payable); Lockhart v. Fed. Emergency Mgmt. Agency, 2019 U.S. Dist. LEXIS 233193 (M.D. La. Dec. 20, 2019).

667. Cholankeril v. Selective Ins. Co. of Am., 2016 U.S. Dist. LEXIS 91457, at *10, n.8 (D.N.J. July 14, 2016) (equitable tolling may relax strict application of limitations where defendant actively misled plaintiff in way relevant to limitations period and caused failure to comply with limitation).

668. 44 C.F.R. § 62.20(f)(4).

669. Buck v. Std. Fire Ins. Co., 2016 U.S. Dist. LEXIS 193364 (N.D.N.Y. Sept. 6, 2016); Abend Family L.P. v. NGM Ins. Co., 2014 U.S. Dist. LEXIS 160574 (D. Vt. Nov. 13, 2014); Jokumsen v. Fed. Emergency Mgmt., 2013 U.S. Dist. LEXIS 97556 (D. Neb. July 11, 2013).

670. *See* Batie v. S. Farm Bureau Prop. & Cas. Co., 2015 U.S. Dist. LEXIS 98028 (S.D. Tex. July 28, 2015); Altman v. Napolitano, 2013 U.S. Dist. LEXIS 28260 (S.D. Tex. Mar. 1, 2013); Wolfe v. Am. Bankers Ins. Co., 2013 U.S. Dist. LEXIS 28258 (S.D. Tex. Mar. 1, 2013).

the insured property was located at the time of loss."[671] The statutory limitation states that a claimant may institute an action in "the United States district court for the district in which the insured property or the major part thereof shall have been situated" within one year after the mailing of notice of disallowance or partial disallowance.[672] While insureds often initiate an action on an SFIP in state court,[673] under the policy and statute, exclusive jurisdiction rests with the federal courts. Thus, because a state tribunal lacks jurisdiction, filing an action in state court *does not* toll the limitations period.[674] Instead, the limitations period runs until the case is filed in the proper federal court.[675]

[f] Exhaustion of Administrative Remedies

By rule, a policyholder *may* appeal a "decision" about a claim, proof of loss, or loss estimate to FEMA.[676] The rule is permissive and does not require policyholders to appeal as a pre-condition to filing a suit. The policy does not mention the appeal and does not state that an appeal to FEMA is a condition precedent to filing suit.[677] Is there then a requirement that policyholders exhaust the administrative remedy of a FEMA appeal? The pertinent rule states that if an insured files suit on a flood claim, that insured is prohibited from filing an appeal with FEMA,[678] a prohibition that would be superfluous if there were an exhaustion requirement. Moreover, the agency asserts that the appeals process does not eliminate or replace the right to bring an action in court.[679] Generally, therefore, courts have determined that the agency administrative appeal is merely an option.[680] Nonetheless, some courts have stated

---

671. General Property Form Standard Flood Insurance Policy, § VII.O.

672. 42 U.S.C. § 4072.

673. *See, e.g.*, Castro v. Fid. Nat'l Ins. Co., 2007 U.S. Dist. LEXIS 28792 (S.D. Fla. Apr. 18, 2007).

674. Ekhlassi v. Nat'l Lloyds Ins. Co., 926 F.3d 130 (5th Cir. 2019), *cert. den.*, ___U.S.___, 140 S. Ct. 857, 205 L. Ed. 2d 457 (2020); Woodson v. Allstate Ins. Co., 855 F.3d 628 (4th Cir. 2017); Gibson v. Am. Bankers Ins. Co., 289 F.3d 943 (6th Cir. 2002); Hairston v. Travelers Cas. & Sur. Co., 232 F.3d 1348 (11th Cir. 2000).

675. Gunvordahl v. Selective Ins. Co., 2020 U.S. Dist. LEXIS 220983 (D.S.D. Nov. 24, 2020); Apatow v. Am. Bankers Ins. Co., 2016 U.S. Dist. LEXIS 180529 (C.D. Cal. Dec. 21, 2016); Parsons Footwear v. Omaha Prop. & Cas. Co., 19 F. Supp. 2d 588, 592 (N.D. W. Va. 1998).

676. 44 C.F.R. § 62.20(b).

677. Buck v. Std. Fire Ins. Co., 2016 U.S. Dist. LEXIS 193364 (N.D.N.Y. Sept. 6, 2016).

678. 44 C.F.R. § 62.20(d).

679. *See* Bruno v. Paulison, 2009 U.S. Dist. LEXIS 13910, at *19, n.4 (D. Md. Feb. 12, 2009).

680. *See, e.g.*, McDowell v. USAA Gen. Indem. Co., 2017 U.S. Dist. LEXIS 101978 (D.N.J. June 30, 2017); Slater v. Hartford Ins. Co., 26 F. Supp. 3d 1239, 1246 (M.D. Fla. 2014); Jokumsen v. Fed. Emergency Mgmt., 2013 U.S. Dist. LEXIS 97556 (D. Neb. July 11, 2013); Mertz v. FEMA, 2011 U.S. Dist. LEXIS 94267 (D. Or. Feb. 14, 2011). *See also* Clutter v. Long, 2018 U.S. Dist. LEXIS 151205 (E.D.N.Y. Aug. 31, 2018) (describing appeal process as "discretionary intermediate review").

or suggested there is an exhaustion requirement.[681] Under the Federal Tort Claims Act (FTCA),[682] prior to bringing a tort claim against the United States, a party has to present the claim to the appropriate federal agency and obtain a final written denial.[683] Some courts have said that a plaintiff policyholder has to exhaust the administrative remedies under the FTCA.[684] The FTCA, however, should not arise in an action on an SFIP because the claim would be for breach of contract, not for a tort, and tort claims are preempted by the National Flood Insurance Act.[685]

[g] Service, Jurisdiction, and Venue

[i] Service of Process

Under the Federal Rules of Civil Procedure, to sue an agency of the United States, the plaintiff has to serve the United States and send a copy of the summons and complaint by registered or certified mail to the agency.[686] The plaintiff serves the United States by delivering a copy of the summons and complaint to the United States attorney for the district where the action is brought and sending a copy of each by registered or certified mail to the Attorney General of the United States at Washington, D.C.[687]

[ii] Jurisdiction

[A] Generally

By statute, original and exclusive jurisdiction is conferred on the United States district court for the district "in which the insured property or the major part thereof shall have been situated" to hear and decide actions on claims under a FEMA flood policy, regardless of the amount in controversy.[688] The

681. *See, e.g.*, Surfsand Resort, LLC v. Nationwide Mut. Fire Ins. Co., 2017 U.S. Dist. LEXIS 171548 (D. Or. Oct. 16, 2017) (policyholder appealed denial of coverage to FEMA *as required* by SFIP); Roussell v. Allstate Ins. Co., 26 F. Supp. 3d 552, 554 (E.D. La. 2014) (insured filed appeal with FEMA *as is required* before bringing suit). *See also* Admiralty Condo. Ass'n v. Dir., FEMA, 594 Fed. Appx. 738, 740 (3d Cir. 2014), *cert. den.*, ___U.S.___, 135 S. Ct. 2395, 192 L. Ed. 2d 167 (2015) (after exhausting its administrative remedies, policyholder sued FEMA); Treasure Bay Gaming & Resorts, Inc. v. Omaha Prop. & Cas. Co., 2002 U.S. Dist. LEXIS 28158 (S.D. Miss. Mar. 18, 2002).

682. 28 U.S.C. §§ 2671, *et seq.*

683. 28 U.S.C. § 2675(a).

684. Oppenheim v. Dir. Fed. Emergency Mgmt. Agency, 1988 U.S. App. LEXIS 22395 (9th Cir. June 22, 1988); Foster v. FEMA, 128 F. Supp. 3d 717 (E.D.N.Y. 2015); Holeman v. Director, Federal Emergency Mgmt. Agency, 699 F. Supp. 98 (N.D. Tex. 1988), *cert. den.*, 89 U.S. 1012, 109 S. Ct. 1123, 103 L. Ed. 2d 185 (1989); Kolner v. Director, 1983 U.S. Dist. LEXIS 17596 (N.D. Ill. Apr. 19, 1983).

685. See § 5.09[3][i], *infra*.

686. Fed. R. Civ. P. 4(i)(2).

687. Fed. R. Civ. P. 4(i)(1). *See also* Evanicky v. FEMA, 2019 U.S. Dist. LEXIS 142392 (S.D. Tex. Aug. 21, 2019).

688. 42 U.S.C. § 4072.

statute applies to "actions against the Administrator." The "administrator" is the head of FEMA.[689] Of course, the vast majority of FEMA flood policies are not issued by the agency but by private insurers—WYO companies—on its behalf. Those insurers make the initial determination of whether a claim will be paid. Does the statute confer jurisdiction over them? The Third Circuit has held that it "vests district courts with original exclusive jurisdiction over suits by claimants against WYO companies based on partial or total disallowance of claims for insurance arising out of the National Flood Insurance Act."[690] Those companies are fiscal agents for the federal government, and a suit against them is a suit against FEMA.[691] The Second,[692] Fifth,[693] and Sixth[694] Circuits agree. In the Fourth[695] and Eleventh[696] Circuits, the jurisdiction question remains unresolved. The Seventh Circuit has refused to ignore the fact that the statute is limited to suits against the "Director."[697]

[B] Federal Question Jurisdiction

The federal district courts have "original jurisdiction of all civil actions arising under the Constitution, laws, or treaties of the United States."[698] This is commonly referred to as "federal question" jurisdiction. It is invoked when federal law establishes the asserted cause of action or when a federal issue is necessarily raised, actually disputed, substantial, and capable of being resolved in federal courts without disturbing the federal-state balance Congress has approved.[699] Federal question jurisdiction can apply to suits over the FEMA flood policy.[700] Thus, when the federal jurisdiction conferred for actions on

---

689. 42 U.S.C. § 4004(3).

690. Van Holt v. Liberty Mut. Fire Ins. Co., 163 F.3d 161, 167 (3d Cir. 1998). The court explained that a suit against a WYO insurer is the "functional equivalent of a suit against FEMA" because the insurer is a fiscal agent for the federal government.

691. Ekhlassi v. Nat'l Lloyds Ins. Co., 926 F.3d 130 (5th Cir. 2019), *cert. den.*, __U.S.__, 140 S. Ct. 857, 205 L. Ed. 2d 457 (2020).

692. Palmieri v. Allstate Ins. Co., 445 F.3d 179, 185 (2d Cir. 2006).

693. Eaker v. State Farm Fire & Cas. Ins. Co., 216 F. Supp. 2d 606 (S.D. Miss. 2001).

694. Gibson v. Am. Bankers Ins. Co., 289 F.3d 943, 947 (6th Cir. 2002).

695. Studio Frames v. Std. Fire Ins. Co., 369 F.3d 376, 379–80 (4th Cir. 2004) (noting there is substantial disagreement among circuits regarding whether statute establishes original exclusive jurisdiction over claims brought by insured against WYO carrier and declining to decide that question).

696. Newton v. Capital Assur. Co., 245 F.3d 1306 (11th Cir. 2001) (declining to decide if statute provides basis for jurisdiction against WYO companies while noting that on its face statute provides only for suits against FEMA).

697. Downey v. State Farm Fire & Cas. Co., 266 F.3d 675 (7th Cir. 2001).

698. 28 U.S.C. § 1331.

699. Gunn v. Minton, 568 U.S. 251, 257, 133 S. Ct. 1059, 185 L. Ed. 2d 72 (2013); Grable & Sons Metal Prods., Inc. v. Darue Eng'g & Mfg., 545 U.S. 308, 314, 125 S. Ct. 2363, 162 L. Ed. 2d 257 (2005).

700. *See* Newton v. Capital Assur. Co., 245 F.3d 1306 (11th Cir. 2001); Borden v. Allstate Ins. Co., 589 F.3d 168 (5th Cir. 2009); Van Holt v. Liberty Mut. Fire Ins. Co., 163 F.3d 161 (3d Cir. 1998). *See also* Monticello Rd., LLC v. Auto-Owners Ins., 2017 U.S. Dist. LEXIS 118698

claims under a FEMA flood policy does not apply, there may still be federal question jurisdiction.[701]

[C] Supplemental Jurisdiction

Generally, in any civil action over which federal district courts have original jurisdiction, they have "supplemental jurisdiction" over all other claims that are so related to claims in the action within their original jurisdiction that they "form part of the same case or controversy."[702] Thus, if the insured sues both its WYO insurer and its insurance agent, courts have exercised supplemental jurisdiction over the claim against the agent.[703]

The court may decline to exercise supplemental jurisdiction over a claim if it raises a novel or complex issue of state law, if it substantially predominates over the claim or claims over which the district court has original jurisdiction, if the district court has dismissed all claims over which it has original jurisdiction,[704] or if there are other compelling reasons for declining jurisdiction.[705] Federal court *may not* exercise supplemental jurisdiction against a non-consenting state agency, for example, a state-sponsored insurer of last resort.[706]

(D.S.C. July 28, 2017) (removal proper under federal question jurisdiction where insureds sued insurer for bad faith failure to pay claim; although plaintiffs relied solely on state common law, resolution of claim was based on SFIP and necessarily depended on interpretation of substantial question of federal law). *Compare* Breen v. Ivantage Select Agency, Inc., 2019 U.S. Dist. LEXIS 123012 (D.S.C. July 24, 2019) (where policyholder sued for common law negligence and violation of Unfair Trade Practices Act, federal court remanded to state court because state law causes of action did not necessarily raise federal issues and plaintiff could establish all required elements of claims independently of federal law).

701. McGair v. Am. Bankers Ins. Co., 693 F.3d 94 (1st Cir. 2012); Studio Frames v. Std. Fire Ins. Co., 369 F.3d 376, 380 (4th Cir. 2004); Battle v. Seibels Bruce Ins. Co., 288 F.3d 596 (4th Cir. 2002); Downey v. State Farm Fire & Cas. Co., 266 F.3d 675 (7th Cir. 2001).

702. 28 U.S. Code § 1367(a). *See, e.g.*, Graveran v. Allstate Ins. Co., 2019 U.S. Dist. LEXIS 65611 (S.D. Fla. Apr. 17, 2019); Winkler v. State Farm Fire & Cas. Co., 266 F. Supp. 2d 509 (S.D. Miss. 2003).

703. Smith v. Nat'l Flood Ins. Program and Martin, 796 F.2d 90 (5th Cir. 1986); Nicol v. Auto-Owners Ins. Co., 2006 U.S. Dist. LEXIS 9502 (D. Minn. Mar. 8, 2006).

704. *See, e.g.*, Garcia v. Nationwide Ins. Co., 2020 U.S. Dist. LEXIS 128899 (S.D. Tex. July 22, 2020); Goff v. Allstate Ins. Co., 2018 U.S. Dist. LEXIS 179302 (M.D. La. Sept. 28, 2018); Smith v. Keer & Heyer, Inc., 2018 U.S. Dist. LEXIS 125887 (D.N.J. July 27, 2018).

705. 28 U.S. Code § 1367(c).

706. *See* McGuire v. Citizens Prop. Ins. Corp., 2017 U.S. Dist. LEXIS 52907 (M.D. Fla. Apr. 6, 2017), where the policyholder invoked federal jurisdiction against the WYO insurer and supplemental jurisdiction against the state-sponsored insurer. The court said that the Eleventh Amendment bars federal courts from exercising supplemental jurisdiction against non-consenting state agencies. It remanded the state law claims against the state-sponsored insurer and WYO insurer. It also allowed the insured to amend the complaint against the WYO carrier to state claims against it under federal law.

[D] Federal Tucker Act

The Tucker Act constitutes a general waiver of sovereign immunity by the federal government.[707] Under the law, the United States Court of Federal Claims has jurisdiction to render a judgment on any claim against the United States that is founded on either "any express or implied contract with the United States" or for "liquidated or unliquidated damages in cases that do not sound in tort."[708] When a claim exceeds $10,000, that court has exclusive jurisdiction.[709] Where policyholders sued FEMA for allegedly breaching a settlement agreement and sought approximately $56,000, a federal district court ruled that under the Tucker Act the Court of Federal Claims had sole jurisdiction.[710]

[iii] Venue

By statute, on disallowance of a claim or refusal of a claimant to accept the amount allowed, the claimant may institute an action in the "United States district court for the district in which the insured property or the major part thereof shall have been situated."[711] This venue directive is not permissive. A claim has to be filed in the district court that presides over the geographical region where the insured property is situated.[712] That is true regardless of whether the defendant is FEMA or an insurance company.[713]

[h] Proper Defendant

By statute, when a claim under the FEMA flood policy is denied, or the policyholder refuses an offer of settlement, any action has to be initiated against the Administrator of FEMA, not the agency itself.[714] If a WYO insurer denies a claim, FEMA is not a proper defendant,[715] because the statutory waiver of sovereign immunity that allows the FEMA Administrator to be sued only applies to actions concerning denial *by FEMA* of a claim.[716] Thus, when a

707. 28 U.S.C. § 1491.

708. 28 U.S.C. § 1491(a)(1).

709. 28 U.S.C. § 1346(a)(2).

710. Flammia v. Nat'l Flood Ins. Program, 2020 U.S. Dist. LEXIS 170471 (D.N.J. Sept. 16, 2020).

711. 42 U.S.C. § 4072.

712. Deland v. Wright Flood Ins. Co., 2018 U.S. Dist. LEXIS 142870 (E.D. La. Aug. 10, 2018).

713. Gulf Coast Vacation Props., LLC v. Gulfstream Prop. & Cas. Ins. Co., 2020 U.S. Dist. LEXIS 5962 (M.D. Fla. Jan. 14, 2020); Iwachiw v. Travelers, 2014 U.S. Dist. LEXIS 130576 (S.D.N.Y. Sept. 16, 2014).

714. 42 USCS § 4072.

715. Hutten v. Serv. Ins. Co., 2020 U.S. Dist. LEXIS 229769 (E.D.N.C. Dec. 8, 2020); Flammia v. Nat'l Flood Ins. Program, 2020 U.S. Dist. LEXIS 170471 (D.N.J. Sept. 16, 2020).

716. 42 U.S.C. § 4072. Note that if a WYO insurer denies a claim and the insured appeals to FEMA, the limited waiver does not apply and the court has no jurisdiction over the agency. Clutter v. Long, 2018 U.S. Dist. LEXIS 171038 (E.D.N.Y. Sept. 28, 2018).

private insurance company acting as a WYO carrier issues the policy and denies the claim, the proper defendant is that insurer.[717]

[i] Jury Trial

In an action against the federal government, there is no right to a trial by jury unless Congress expressly grants the authority by statute.[718] There is no such grant in the National Flood Insurance Act.[719] Moreover, there is no right to a jury trial against WYO insurers when federal funds are involved, which there will be in a claim under a flood policy because claims are paid by the United States Treasury.[720] However, in a state law tort action in which no federal funds are at stake, an insured may be entitled to a jury trial.[721]

An insurer may in effect waive any objection to a jury trial. For example, an insurer initially agreed to a jury trial in a proposed pre-trial order and then, four years later, moved to strike the demand for a jury trial. The court denied the motion, noting that the plaintiff insured went through all of discovery and a significant part of trial preparation assuming there would be a trial by jury.[722]

Under the Federal Rules of Civil Procedure, courts may try an issue with an "advisory jury" even though the matter is not triable by a jury of right.[723] In at least one flood insurance case, a federal court agreed to an advisory jury.[724]

[j] Preemption

One of the most confused and oft-litigated aspects of coverage under the FEMA SFIP is preemption of extra-contractual claims, a topic beyond the

---

717. Bax v. Allstate Ins. Co., 2019 U.S. Dist. LEXIS 158015 (D.S.C. Sept. 17, 2019). *See also* Felix v. United States AG, 2018 U.S. Dist. LEXIS 185225 (E.D.N.C. Oct. 30, 2018) (action for failure to pay claim cannot be brought against current insurer when it did not provide coverage in effect when loss occurred).

718. Gunter v. Farmers Ins. Co., 736 F.3d 768, 773 (8th Cir. 2013).

719. M&K Rest. LLC v. Farmers Ins. Co., 29 F. Supp. 3d 1204 (E.D. Ark. 2014); Reeder v. Nationwide Mut. Fire Ins. Co., 419 F. Supp. 2d 750 (D. MD. 2006); Latz v. Gallagher, 550 F. Supp. 257 (W.D. Mich. 1982); Kolner v. Director, Federal Emergency Management Agency, 547 F. Supp. 828 (N.D. Ill. 1982). *See also* Thompson v. Wright Nat'l Flood Ins. Co., 2019 U.S. Dist. LEXIS 234746 (D.S.C. July 2, 2019).

720. Grissom v. Liberty Mut. Fire Ins. Co., 678 F.3d 397, 402 (5th Cir. 2012). *See also* Greenberg v. Wright Nat'l Flood Ins. Co., 2016 U.S. Dist. LEXIS 134194 (N.D. Tex. Sept. 29, 2016) (unless FEMA notifies of intent not to defend or indemnify WYO insurer, there is no right to trial by jury).

721. *See, e.g.*, M&K Rest. LLC v. Farmers Ins. Co., 29 F. Supp. 3d 1204 (E.D. Ark. 2014); Reeder v. Nationwide Mut. Fire Ins. Co., 419 F. Supp. 2d 750 (D. Md. 2006); Bleecker v. Standard Fire Ins. Co., 130 F. Supp. 2d 726, 737 (E.D.N.C. 2000).

722. Long Beach Rd. Holdings, LLC v. Foremost Ins. Co., 2019 U.S. Dist. LEXIS 58379 (E.D.N.Y. Apr. 4, 2019).

723. Fed. R. Civ. P. 39(c).

724. Virgil v. Horace Mann Ins. Co., 2008 U.S. Dist. LEXIS 65595 (E.D. La. Aug. 15, 2008).

scope of this discussion.[725] The SFIP says that the "policy and all disputes arising from the insurer's policy issuance, policy administration, or the handling of any claim under the policy are governed exclusively by the flood insurance regulations issued by FEMA, the National Flood Insurance Act of 1968, as amended . . . and Federal common law."[726] Courts have interpreted that language as a broad ban on extracontractual claims.[727] They have, thus, barred a plethora of state claims including for bad faith breach of contract,[728] negligence,[729] fraud and misrepresentation,[730] and breach of the covenants of good faith and fair dealing.[731] Courts have also found claims based on violation of a state statute to be preempted.[732]

There is disagreement over whether actions concerning mistakes in assessing premiums are preempted.[733] However, the greatest conflict has arisen over whether claims about procurement of a policy are preempted.

Policy procurement litigation may be about failure to obtain the coverage sought or failure to obtain coverage at all. Some courts say that, because preemption is based on the language of the policy, if no policy was issued,

---

725. See 5 Jeffery E. Thomas, *New Appleman on Insurance Law Library Edition* § 57.27[8] (LexisNexis 2022) for a comprehensive discussion of preemption.

726. General Property Form Standard Flood Insurance Policy, § X.

727. *See* Gunter v. Farmers Ins. Co., 736 F.3d 768, 772 (8th Cir. 2013); Shuford v. Fid. Nat'l Prop. & Cas. Ins. Co., 508 F.3d 1337, 1343 (11th Cir. 2007); Gallup v. Omaha Prop. & Cas. Ins. Co., 434 F.3d 341 (5th Cir. 2005); Wright v. Allstate Ins. Co., 415 F.3d 384, 390 (5th Cir. 2005); Gibson v. Am. Bankers Ins. Co., 289 F.3d 943 (6th Cir. 2002). *See also* TAF, L.L.C. v. Hartford Fire Ins. Co., 549 F. Supp. 2d 1282, 1289 (D. Colo. 2008); Baltazor, Inc. v. Fid. Nat'l Ins. Program, 544 F. Supp. 2d 516, 522 (E.D. La. 2008); Moffett v. Computer Scis. Corp., 457 F. Supp. 2d 571 (D. Md. 2006); Peal v. N.C. Farm Bureau Mut. Ins. Co., 212 F. Supp. 2d 508 (E.D.N.C. 2002); Neill v. State Farm Fire & Cas. Co., 159 F. Supp. 2d 770 (E.D. Pa. 2000); Bianchi v. State Farm Fire & Cas. Co., 120 F. Supp. 2d 837 (N.D. Cal. 2000); Mason v. Witt, 74 F. Supp. 2d 955 (E.D. Cal. 1999); Stapleton v. State Farm Fire & Cas. Co., 11 F. Supp. 2d 1344 (M.D. Fla. 1998).

728. Knapp v. Hartford Ins. Co., 2020 U.S. Dist. LEXIS 18291 (D.S.C. Jan. 31, 2020).

729. Surfsand Resort, LLC v. Nationwide Mut. Fire Ins. Co., 2017 U.S. Dist. LEXIS 171548 (D. Or. Oct. 16, 2017).

730. Miranda v. Selective Ins. Co. of the SE, 2017 U.S. Dist. LEXIS 37796 (E.D. La. Mar. 16, 2017).

731. Ling v. Farmers Ins. Grp., 2017 U.S. Dist. LEXIS 14882 (S.D. Tex. Feb. 2, 2017).

732. *See, e.g.*, Dodson v. Wright Nat'l Flood Ins. Co., 2021 U.S. Dist. LEXIS 96808 (S.D. Ala. May 20, 2021) (claim based on state statute requiring insurer to provide insured with proof of loss form barred); Greer v. Owners Ins. Co., 434 F. Supp. 2d 1267 (N.D. Fla. 2006) (claim based on Florida "Valued Policy" statute preempted).

733. Powers v. Autin-Gettys-Cohen Ins. Agency, Inc., 2000 U.S. Dist. LEXIS 15924 (E.D. La. Oct. 24, 2000) (finding no preemption of claim based on overcharging for premiums). *But see* Grissom v. Liberty Mut. Fire Ins. Co., 678 F.3d 397 (5th Cir. 2012) (where insurer allegedly failed to inform policyholder that he was eligible for less expensive policy, suit for negligent misrepresentation was preempted); Podgorski v. Liberty Mut. Group Inc., 2016 U.S. Dist. LEXIS 171209 (N.D. Ill. Dec. 12, 2016) (where insurer failed to notify insured of redesignation of property to lower-risk zone for which premiums were lower, action seeking refund of excess premium payments and punitive damages was preempted).

there can be no preemption of an action for failure to issue a policy.[734] Most procurement litigation, however, is about the extent of the coverage that is obtained. Many courts have said that state law claims about failure to procure flood insurance are not preempted.[735] FEMA has objected to these decisions. In 2009 it released a bulletin that said the agency intended for state law claims that relate to policy formation, renewal, and administration to be preempted.[736] Some courts have agreed with the agency's position,[737] while others have not.[738] Effective October 1, 2021, FEMA changed the language of the policy. Previously the preemption language referred to "all disputes arising from the handling of any claim under the policy," but now says "all disputes arising *from the insurer's policy issuance, policy administration*, or the handling of any claim." This wording is apparently intended to bar procurement claims. It remains to be seen how courts will respond.

[k] Damages

[i] Consequential Damages

Because the FEMA flood policy provides coverage for "direct physical loss," consequential damages cannot be recovered.[739] Courts have, therefore, denied recovery for a variety of consequential damages.[740] The policy, moreover,

---

734. *See, e.g.*, Smith v. Keer & Heyer, Inc., 2018 U.S. Dist. LEXIS 125887 (D.N.J. July 27, 2018); Star Spa Servs. v. Robert G. Turano Ins. Agency, Inc., 595 F. Supp. 2d 519 (M.D. Pa. 2009); Roybal v. Los Alamos Nat'l Bank, 375 F. Supp. 2d 1324 (D.N.M. 2005). The same reasoning may apply when a policy has lapsed because at that point the relationship the plaintiff has with the defendant is that of a potential future policyholder. Norris v. Allstate Ins. Co., 2018 U.S. Dist. LEXIS 211771 (S.D. Tex. Dec. 17, 2018).

735. Harris v. Nationwide Mut. Fire Ins. Co., 832 F.3d 593 (6th Cir. 2016); Campo v. Allstate Ins. Co., 562 F.3d 751 (5th Cir. 2009); Packard v. Farmers Ins. of Columbus, Inc., 672 F. Supp. 2d 817 (S.D. Ohio 2009); Padalino v. Std. Fire Ins. Co., 616 F. Supp. 2d 538, 546 (E.D. Pa. 2008); TAF, L.L.C. v. Hartford Fire Ins. Co., 549 F. Supp. 2d 1282 (D. Colo. 2008); Reeder v. Nationwide Mut. Fire Ins. Co., 419 F. Supp. 2d 750 (D. Md. 2006); Waltrip v. Brooks Agency, Inc., 417 F. Supp. 2d 768 (E.D. Va. 2006); Jamal v. Travelers Lloyds of Tex. Ins. Co., 129 F. Supp. 2d 1024 (S.D. Tex. 2001).

736. "Notice of FEMA's intent to Adopt, by Regulation, a Clarification of the Express Preemption Clause of the Standard Flood Insurance Policy." The bulletin was available at http://www.nfipiservice.com/stakeholder/pdf/bulletin/w-09038.pdf, but no longer appears at the agency web page.

737. *See, e.g.*, Parker v. Miss. Farm Bureau Cas. Ins. Co., 997 F. Supp. 2d 481 (S.D. Miss. 2014); Davis v. Nationwide Mut. Fire Ins. Co., 783 F. Supp. 2d 825 (E.D. Va. 2011).

738. *See, e.g.*, Henderson v. Nationwide Mut. Fire Ins. Co., 2017 U.S. Dist. LEXIS 17926 (W.D.N.C. Feb. 8, 2017).

739. Batchelor v. Wright Nat'l Flood Ins. Co., 2019 U.S. Dist. LEXIS 141079 (S.D. Fla. Aug. 19, 2019); Linblad v. Nationwide Mut. Ins. Co., 2014 U.S. Dist. LEXIS 168444 (D.N.J. Dec. 4, 2014); Perdido Sun Condo. Ass'n v. Nationwide Mut. Ins. Co., 2007 U.S. Dist. LEXIS 64571 (N.D. Fla. Aug. 30, 2007); Scritchfield v. Mut. of Omaha Ins. Co., 341 F. Supp. 2d 675 (E.D. Tex. 2004).

740. Martin v. CSAA Ins. Exch., 300 F. Supp. 3d 1067 (N.D. Cal. 2018) (mental distress); Linblad v. Nationwide Mut. Ins. Co., 2014 U.S. Dist. LEXIS 168444 (D.N.J. Dec. 4, 2014)

explicitly excludes coverage for loss of revenue or profits, loss of access to the insured property, loss of use of the property, loss from interruption of business or production, additional living expenses, and any other economic loss suffered.[741]

[ii] Punitive Damages

Neither penalties nor punitive damages may be awarded under the National Flood Insurance Act.[742] The proscription applies to litigation under the Act and, therefore, pertains whether the defendant is a WYO insurer or FEMA.[743]

[I] Fees, Costs, and Interest

[i] Attorney's Fees Generally

Under the "American rule," parties to litigation bear their own attorney's fees absent a contractual agreement to pay fees or a statute providing for the payment of fees. Neither the National Flood Insurance Act nor the FEMA flood policy provides for the award of attorney's fees. Courts, therefore, hold a policyholder cannot recover attorney's fees in a breach of contract action against FEMA or a WYO insurer.[744]

[ii] Attorney's Fees and Federal Equal Access to Justice Act

It may be possible for a policyholder to obtain attorney's fees under the federal Equal Access to Justice Act (EAJA).[745] It provides that in a civil action—other than an action sounding in tort—including one for judicial review of agency action, that is brought by or against the United States, the court *shall* award to a prevailing party, other than the government, fees and other expenses,

---

(economic damages); Moffett v. Computer Scis. Corp., 457 F. Supp. 2d 571, 589 (D. Md. 2006) (delay damages); Bianchi v. State Farm Fire & Cas. Co., 120 F. Supp. 2d 837, 841 (N.D. Cal. 2000) (mental distress).

741. General Property Form Standard Flood Insurance Policy, § V.A *See also In re* Estate of Lee, 812 F.2d 253, 257–58 (5th Cir. 1987) (policy unambiguously excludes coverage for consequential damages); Moffett v. Computer Scis. Corp., 457 F. Supp. 2d 571, 589 (D. Md. 2006).

742. West v. Harris, 573 F.2d 873 (5th Cir. 1978), *cert. den.*, 440 U.S. 946, 99 S. Ct. 1424, 59 L. Ed. 2d 635 (1979); Jamal v. Travelers Lloyds of Tex. Ins. Co., 129 F. Supp. 2d 1024 (S.D. Tex. 2001); Bianchi v. State Farm Fire & Cas. Co., 120 F. Supp. 2d 837, 842 (N.D. Cal. 2000). *See also* 3608 Sounds Ave. Condo. Ass'n v. South Carolina Ins. Co., 58 F. Supp. 2d 499, 502 (D.N.J. 1999) (punitive damages discourage insurers from arbitrarily denying legitimate claims, but WYO insurer has no pecuniary incentive to deny claims because all are paid by federal government); Durkin v. State Farm Mut. Ins. Co., 3 F. Supp. 2d 724, 729 (E.D. La. 1997) (allowing recovery of punitive damages would defeat the purpose of providing affordable insurance).

743. Eaker v. State Farm Fire & Cas. Ins. Co., 216 F. Supp. 2d 606 (S.D. Miss. 2001).

744. *See, e.g.*, West v. Harris, 573 F.2d 873 (5th Cir. 1978), *cert. den.*, 440 U.S. 946, 99 S. Ct. 1424, 59 L. Ed. 2d 635 (1979); Jamal v. Travelers Lloyds of Tex. Ins. Co., 129 F. Supp. 2d 1024, 1031 (S.D. Tex. 2001); Bianchi v. State Farm Fire & Cas. Co., 120 F. Supp. 2d 837, 842 (N.D. Cal. 2000); 3608 Sounds Ave. Condo. Ass'n v. South Carolina Ins. Co., 58 F. Supp. 2d 499, 502 (D.N.J. 1999); House v. Bankers Ins. Co., 43 F. Supp. 2d 1329 (M.D. Fla. 1999); Durkin v. State Farm Mut. Ins. Co., 3 F. Supp. 2d 724, 729 (E.D. La. 1997).

745. 28 U.S.C. § 2412.

including reasonable expert witness and attorney's fees.[746] The party seeking fees has the burden of proving that the government's position was not substantially justified.[747] If the court finds that the position of the government was "substantially justified"—or that "special circumstances" make an award unjust—the Act does not apply.[748] Clearly the EAJA applies when FEMA is a party.[749] There has been, however, considerable debate about whether the EAJA door is open when a WYO insurer is a party to an action, with courts coming down on both sides.[750] The Fifth Circuit probably slammed the door shut, however, in an opinion that other circuits will likely find persuasive. The court said that WYO insurers are not the United States and they are not officials of the United States. Furthermore, serving as a fiscal agent of the government and participating in a heavily regulated federal program does not transform a private entity into a federal agency.[751]

[iii] Costs

Under the Federal Rules of Civil Procedure, unless a federal statute, the rules, or a court order provides otherwise, costs, other than attorney's fees, *should* be allowed to the prevailing party; however, costs against the United States, its officers, or its agencies may be imposed only to the extent allowed by law.[752] Nothing in the National Flood Insurance Act or FEMA rules authorizes awarding costs against the agency.

A few courts have refused to strike the request of a policyholder for costs against a WYO insurer.[753] On the other hand, another court said that any claim

---

746. 28 U.S.C. § 2412(d).

747. 28 U.S.C. § 2412(d)(1)(B).

748. Even if an insured successfully leaps that hurdle, the EAJA defines a party as an individual whose net worth did not exceed $2 million at the time the action was filed or an owner of an unincorporated business, or any partnership, corporation, association, or organization the net worth of which did not exceed $7 million at that time. 28 U.S.C. § 2412(d)(2)(B).

749. Dwyer v. Fid. Nat'l Prop. & Cas. Ins. Co., 565 F.3d 284, 290 (5th Cir. 2009). When the decision of a WYO insurer is appealed to FEMA and the agency supports denial of a claim, its role in the administrative process does not convert it into the party subject to suit. Jokumsen v. Fed. Emergency Mgmt., 2013 U.S. Dist. LEXIS 97556 (D. Neb. July 11, 2013); Gottlandsini, LLC v. Fugate, 2012 U.S. Dist. LEXIS 125427 (D. Mass. Sept. 5, 2012); Bruno v. Paulison, 2009 U.S. Dist. LEXIS 13910 (D. Md. Feb. 12, 2009).

750. *See, e.g.*, Island Club Condo., Inc. v. Wright Nat'l Flood Ins. Co., 2019 U.S. Dist. LEXIS 80342 (S.D. Fla. May 9, 2019) (WYO insurer is not an agency of United States as required for recovery under EAJA); St. Claude Bywater Props., L.L.C. v. Fid. Nat'l Ins. Co., 2008 U.S. Dist. LEXIS 7690 (Feb. 1, 2008) (WYO insurers represent FEMA in federal court when lawsuits are brought, and therefore act as entity of executive branch and, thus, are potentially subject to EAJA attorney's fee awards).

751. Dwyer v. Fid. Nat'l Prop. & Cas. Ins. Co., 565 F.3d 284, 288 (5th Cir. 2009).

752. Fed. R. Civ. P. § 54(d)(1).

753. Collier v. Wright Nat'l Flood Ins. Co., 2019 U.S. Dist. LEXIS 61017 (S.D. Fla. Apr. 9, 2019); Lovers Lane, LLC v. Wright Nat'l Flood Ins. Co., 2019 U.S. Dist. LEXIS 3234 (M.D. Fla. Jan. 8, 2019).

against a WYO carrier "for taxable litigation costs [was for] state law damages not contemplated by the National Flood Insurance Act and . . . preempted by federal law."[754]

[iv] Interest

There is broad agreement among the courts that interest, whether pre-judgment or post-judgment, is not available in an action under an SFIP.[755]

[4] Declaratory Judgment Actions

The National Flood Insurance Act does not provide for declaratory relief.[756] Many courts hold, however, that a policyholder may bring an action under the federal Declaratory Judgment Act,[757] because it "merely serves as the procedural vehicle by which a plaintiff may seek a declaration clarifying" his or her rights under the policy.[758] Nonetheless, most actions for declaratory relief are dismissed as redundant with a breach of contract claim.[759]

754. Feltman v. Wright Nat'l Flood Ins. Co., 2018 U.S. Dist. LEXIS 207204 (S.D. Fla. Dec. 6, 2018). *See also* Rodriguez v. Wright Nat'l Flood Ins. Co., 2018 U.S. Dist. LEXIS 138157 (S.D. Fla. Aug. 14, 2018) (recovery of costs is barred under NFIA because Act only covers losses cause directly by flood); Ravasio v. Fid. Nat'l Prop. & Cas. Ins. Co., 81 F. Supp. 3d 274 (E.D.N.Y. 2015).

755. Newton v. Capital Assur. Co., 245 F.3d 1306 (11th Cir. 2001); Studio Frames, Ltd. v. Std. Fire Ins. Co., 483 F.3d 239, 253 (4th Cir. 2007); Sandia Oil Co. v. Beckton, 889 F.2d 258 (10th Cir. 1989); *In re* Estate of Lee, 812 F.2d 253 (5th Cir. 1987). *See also* Ravasio v. Fid. Nat'l Prop. & Cas. Ins. Co., 81 F. Supp. 3d 274 (E.D.N.Y. 2015); Moffett v. Computer Scis. Corp., 457 F. Supp. 2d 571, 589 (D. Md. 2006).

756. Jones v. Wright Nat'l Flood Ins. Co., 2019 U.S. Dist. LEXIS 31103 (M.D. Fla. Feb. 6, 2019) (plaintiff not entitled to declaratory relief because it is not expressly permitted in SFIP or NFIA statute). *See also* Batchelor v. Wright Nat'l Flood Ins. Co., 2019 U.S. Dist. LEXIS 141079 (S.D. Fla. Aug. 19, 2019); Shearer v. State Farm Fire & Cas. Co., 2018 U.S. Dist. LEXIS 6298 (E.D.N.C. Jan. 16, 2018); Scritchfield v. Mut. of Omaha Ins. Co., 341 F. Supp. 2d 675, 682 (E.D. Tex. 2004).

757. 28 U.S.C. §§ 2201, *et seq.*

758. Fisher v. Beers, 2014 U.S. Dist. LEXIS 95379 (E.D. La. July 14, 2014). *See also* Jakubowski v. Fed. Emergency Mgmt. Agency, 2013 U.S. Dist. LEXIS 43789 (D.N.J. Mar. 27, 2013); Perdido Sun Condo. Ass'n v. Nationwide Mut. Ins. Co., 2007 U.S. Dist. LEXIS 64571 (N.D. Fla. Aug. 30, 2007).

759. Raffell v. Scottsdale Ins. Co., 2020 U.S. Dist. LEXIS 106188 (S.D. Fla. June 16, 2020); Jones v. Wright Nat'l Flood Ins. Co., 2019 U.S. Dist. LEXIS 31103 (M.D. Fla. Feb. 6, 2019); Fisher v. Beers, 2014 U.S. Dist. LEXIS 95379 (E.D. La. July 14, 2014).

6

Recovering under Business Interruption and Related Coverages

6.1 Introduction

Business interruption losses caused by natural disasters[1]—wide spread flooding, for example—can be enormous,[2] but even a small, localized event—for instance a burst water pipe—can be costly and threaten the continued existence of a business. A business may also have expenses required to continue its operations that it would not normally incur, such as renting temporary facilities or expediting the repair of property. For these reasons, many businesses purchase insurance coverage for business interruptions and for what are called "extra expenses" and "expediting expenses." This chapter discusses the applicability of these coverages to flood losses.

6.2 Business Interruption Coverage

[1] Introduction

Business interruption coverage—also commonly referred to as "business income coverage"[3] or "time element" loss[4]—has been available for over 100

1. *See generally* Kornfeld, *Insurance Coverage for Droughts, Due to Climate Change: The Case for "Loss of Business Income" and "Loss of Use,"* 10 Ariz. J. Envtl. L. & Pol'y 151 (2019); Millikan, *Practice Tips: Time Element Losses during Catastrophes*, 31 The Brief 52 (2002).

2. French, *The Aftermath of Catastrophes: Valuing Business Interruption Insurance Losses*, 30 Ga. St. U.L. Rev. 461, 463 (2014). *See also* Optical Works & Logistics, LLC v. Sentinel Ins. Co., 2020 U.S. Dist. LEXIS 53987 (D.R.I. Mar. 26, 2020) (business interruption insurance is particularly useful when a natural disaster occurs because many businesses otherwise lack resources to continue business operations).

3. *Business Income Coverage*, IRMI, https://www.irmi.com/term/insurance-definitions/business-income-coverage.

4. *See, e.g.*, Almah LLC v. Lexington Ins. Co., 2016 Del. Super. LEXIS 47 (Jan. 27, 2016) (coverage for service interruption time element losses).

years and was first called "use and occupancy" insurance before being renamed "business interruption" in the 1940s.[5] It is "commercial property insurance covering loss of income suffered by a business when damage to its premises by a covered cause of loss causes a slowdown or suspension of its operations."[6] Its purpose is to "do for the insured during the period of business interruption what the business would have done had no interruption occurred."[7]

The coverage comes in many forms. Property policies often include it as a coverage within the form.[8] It can be added to a property insurance policy by endorsement.[9] As one court observed, "[f]ew generalizations about business interruption endorsements can be made . . . because the nature of the coverage

---

5. Ainslie et al., *Business Insurance Law and Practice Guide* § 16.02[1] (Matthew Bender 2020). *See generally* Morrison, Miller & Paris, *Business Interruption Insurance: Its Theory and Practice* (National Underwriter 1986), which is out of print, but remains available. Even though it has been three decades since it was published, it is still considered by many to be the authoritative work on the subject. A more recent work is Pastor & Insua, *Business Income Coverage Guide* (National Underwriter Co. 2015).

6. *Business Income Coverage*, IRMI, https://www.irmi.com/term/insurance-definitions/business-income-coverage. *See also* Associated Photographers, Inc. v. Aetna Cas. & Sur. Co., 677 F.2d 1251, 1253 (8th Cir. 1982) (business interruption insurance recognizes and protects insurable interest in earnings).

7. 5 Jeffrey E. Thomas, *New Appleman on Insurance Law Library Edition* § 46.03[1] (LexisNexis 2020). *See also* Polytech, Inc. v. Affiliated FM Ins. Co., 21 F.3d 271, 274 (8th Cir. 1994) (protecting against business interruption loss is similar to protecting going concern value of business, which is treated as property interest similar to goodwill); Yount v. Lafayette Ins. Co., 4 So. 3d 162, 171 (La. App. 2009) (general purpose of business interruption insurance is to protect earnings insured would have enjoyed had no interruption or suspension occurred); Howard v. Foremost Ins. Co., 82 A.D.2d 398, 400, 441 N.Y.S.2d 674, 676 (1981) (goal of business interruption coverage is to preserve continuity of insured's earnings).

8. French, *Covid-19 Business Interruption Insurance Losses: The Cases for and Against Coverage*, 27 Conn. Ins. L.J. 1, 6 (2020) (typically, business interruption insurance is purchased as part of "all risk" property policy). *See also* Rouse, *Eight Key Concepts to Understand in Business Interruption Coverage*, available at https://www.marsh.com/us/services/property-risk-management/insights/business-insurance.html. *See, e.g.*, Kelaher, Connell & Conner, P.C. v. Auto-Owners Ins. Co., 440 F. Supp. 3d 520, 523 (D.S.C. 2020) (Business Owners Insurance Policy included business interruption insurance); United Fire & Cas. Co. v. Arkwright Mut. Ins. Co., 53 F. Supp. 2d 632 (S.D.N.Y. 1999) (all-risk property insurance policy covered property damage and business interruption loss caused by any insured peril, including fire, windstorm, vandalism, earthquake, and flood); American States Ins. Co. v. Creative Walking, 16 F. Supp. 2d 1062 (E.D. Mo. 1998) (business owners commercial property insurance policy provided coverage for damage to business personal property and loss of business income); Almah LLC v. Lexington Ins. Co., 2016 Del. Super. LEXIS 47 (Jan. 27, 2016).

9. Ainslie et al., *Business Insurance Law and Practice Guide* § 16.01 (Matthew Bender 2020). *See, e.g.*, Altru Health System v. American Protection Insurance Co., 238 F.3d 961 (8th Cir. 2001); Cargill, Inc. v. Appalachian Ins. Co., 1983 U.S. Dist. LEXIS 20156 (D. Minn. Jan. 24, 1983). The title of the endorsement may vary from carrier to carrier. For example, some insurers called it a "Gross Earnings Endorsement." *See, e.g.*, Protection Mutual Ins. Co. v. Mitsubishi Silicon America Corp., 164 Ore. App. 385, 992 P.2d 479 (1999), *rev. den.*, 330 Ore. 331, 6 P.3d 1100 (2000); Victory Container Corp. v. Sphere Ins. Co., 448 F. Supp. 1043, 1045 (S.D.N.Y. 1978).

varies widely."[10] Whether incorporated into a property policy or added by endorsement, "business interruption and property damage represent distinct forms of coverage."[11]

Business interruption coverage is also available in a freestanding policy. For example, the Insurance Services Office (ISO) has a standard "Business Income (and Extra Expense) Coverage Form."[12] The discussion below is based on the language of that form.[13]

The coverage also might be included in a "Difference in Conditions" (DIC) policy.[14] "DIC coverage" is defined as a "special form of open-peril coverage written in conjunction with basic fire coverage and designed to provide protection against losses not reimbursed under the standard fire forms."[15] Generally, DIC insurance is a "non-filed class of inland marine insurance," typically provided by surplus lines carriers,[16] which are subject to less regulation than licensed, admitted carriers.[17]

Business interruption insurance is also available in "Highly Protected Risk" (HPR) Forms. These policies provide broad, flexible coverage and often high limits.[18] They are typically not issued to ordinary insureds but are generally offered to large businesses that meet prescribed loss-prevention-and-reduction criteria.[19]

---

10. Protection Mutual Ins. Co. v. Mitsubishi Silicon America Corp., 164 Ore. App. 385, 389, 992 P.2d 479, 481 (1999), *rev. den.*, 330 Ore. 331, 6 P.3d 1100 (2000). The court added that the particular terms and conditions of a policy have to be examined to determine whether a specific business interruption loss falls within the scope of coverage.

11. Victory Container Corp. v. Sphere Ins. Co., 448 F. Supp. 1043, 1045 (S.D.N.Y. 1978). *See also* Baylor College of Med. v. Am. Guar. & Liab. Ins. Co., 2002 U.S. Dist. LEXIS 29002, at *23, n.4 (S.D. Tex. Oct. 30, 2002) (courts have long recognized distinctions between business interruption coverage and property damage coverage).

12. ISO Form CP 00 30 10 12. There is also a form without extra expense coverage. *See* CP 00 32 10 12.

13. While the ISO policy is discussed here, attorneys should be aware that unlike policy language used in other lines of insurance drafted by ISO, policy language in business interruption policies can vary from insurer to insurer. French, *Covid-19 Business Interruption Insurance Losses: The Cases for and Against Coverage*, 27 Conn. Ins. L.J. 1, 7 (2020).

14. *See, e.g.*, Archer Daniels Midland Co. v. Aon Risk Services, Inc. of Minnesota, 356 F.3d 850 (8th Cir. 2004); Archer-Daniels-Midland Co. v. Phoenix Assur. Co., 936 F. Supp. 534 (S.D. Ill. 1996); Tocci Bldg. Corp. v. Commonwealth Ins. Co., 22 Mass. L. Rep. 522 (Apr. 23, 2007), *aff'd*, 71 Mass. App. Ct. 1120, 885 N.E.2d 172 (2008).

15. *See Glossary D*, NAIC, http://www.naic.org/consumer_glossary.htm#D.

16. Prahl, *Difference in Conditions Coverage: What Is It and Who Needs It?* at 2 (2012), Adjusting Today, *available at* http://adjustersinternational.com/publications/adjusting-today/difference-in-conditions-coverage/0/.

17. 1 Jeffrey E. Thomas, *New Appleman on Insurance Law Library Edition* § 1.06[8] (LexisNexis, 2020).

18. *HPR Insurance*, Allianz, https://www.agcs.allianz.com/solutions/sme-insurance/highly-protected-risk-insurance.html.

19. 5 Jeffrey E. Thomas, *New Appleman on Insurance Law Library Edition* § 46.02[3] (LexisNexis 2020). *See generally* DiPrato, *Highly Protected Risk: What Does It Mean Today?*

In some cases, manuscript policies, which are non-standard forms drafted for a particular risk,[20] are produced to meet the needs of individual policyholders or a class of similar risks.[21] Additionally, because policyholders are often large businesses in a position, unlike ordinary consumers, to negotiate with an insurer, a policy may be based on standard language but contain changes the parties agreed to include.[22] The fact that sophisticated parties negotiated the terms of the contract will likely mean a court will not construe the policy against the insurance company as the one who drafted it.

Because of the wide variety of forms in which business interruption coverage can be found, the language can vary considerably from policy to policy. As one commentator has observed, a "comprehensive analysis of the terms and conditions of a particular policy is essential to determine the insurer's obligations with respect to covered perils and any applicable policy exclusions or limitations, as well as the proper methodology to compute the insured's business interruption losses."[23] It is also important to be aware that the interpretation courts place on business interruption coverage language is not consistent.[24]

When trying to determine whether business interruption coverage applies to losses caused by flood, it is important to determine whether flood is a covered cause of loss under that policy or is specifically excluded, as it often is.[25] For instance, in one case, the insured had policies covering both flood and wind damage; however, only the latter provided for a loss resulting from business interruption.[26]

(Sept. 20, 2016), Property Casualty 360, https://www.propertycasualty360.com/2016/09/20/highly-protected-risk-what-does-it-mean-today/#:~:text=Highly%20Protected%20Risk%20(HPR)%20at%20one%20time%20was,lower%20rating%20structure%20than%20the%20other%20standard%20insurers.

20. 1 Jeffrey E. Thomas, *New Appleman on Insurance Law Library Edition* § 1.07[9] (LexisNexis 2020).

21. 5 Jeffrey E. Thomas, *New Appleman on Insurance Law Library Edition* § 46.02[4] (LexisNexis 2020). *See also* Borghesi, *Business Interruption Insurance: A Business Perspective*, 17 Nova L. Rev. 1147, 1152 (1993) (manuscript business interruption policy may offer broader coverage and address perils specific to business of policyholder).

22. Cargill, Inc. v. Appalachian Ins. Co., 1983 U.S. Dist. LEXIS 20156 (D. Minn. Jan. 24, 1983) (while policy contained terms and conditions that were standard in insurance industry, through negotiations, some changes were made).

23. Cot, *Insurance Coverage for Business Interruption Claims in the Aftermath of Hurricanes Katrina and Rita*, 53 LA Bar J. 368, 369 (2006).

24. French, *The Aftermath of Catastrophes: Valuing Business Interruption Insurance Losses*, 30 Ga. St. U.L. Rev. 461, 473 (2014).

25. See § 6.02[3][a], *infra*.

26. La Louisiane Bakery Co. v. Lafayette Ins. Co., 61 So. 3d 17 (La. App. 2011).

Business interruption insurance covers the right to use or occupy property and, therefore, there is generally an insurable whether the policyholder owns or leases or has some other contractual interest in the insured property.[27]

[2] Coverage

[a] Standard Policy Language

[i] Generally

Business interruption coverage comes in one of two forms: (1) gross earnings and (2) net profit plus continuing expenses. The "gross earnings" form calculates loss by subtracting direct costs not incurred from the amount of lost sales.[28] The "net profit plus continuing expenses" is more common. For example, the ISO Business Income (and Extra Expense) Coverage Form defines "business income" to mean net income that would have been earned and continuing normal operating expenses incurred, including payroll.[29] Additionally, for manufacturing risks,[30] net income includes the net sales value of production. Coverage is provided in three varieties: business income including rental value, business income other than rental value, and simply rental value. "Rental Value" is defined as business income consisting of net income that would have been earned or incurred as rental income from tenant occupancy of the premises that is described in the Declarations as furnished and equipped

---

27. Ainslie et al., *Business Insurance Law and Practice Guide* § 16.02[1] (Matthew Bender 2020). Actually, in some circumstances, the insured need not have any present interest in the property to recover. For example, a policyholder claimed business interruption losses when it had to shut down its hotel after the property was severely damaged in a hurricane. Instead of reopening the hotel, the insured sold it about nine months after the storm. The insurer denied business interruption coverage for losses stemming from any time after the hotel was sold. The court, however, said that to limit the indemnity period to the date of that sale would shortchange the insured if the hotel could not have been restored by that date. If the recovery was reduced because of the sale of the hotel during the period of interruption, it would defeat the very purpose for which the insured purchased business interruption insurance: to return to it that amount of profit that it would have earned during the period of interruption had a casualty not occurred. B A Properties, Inc. v. Aetna Cas. & Sur. Co., 221 F. Supp. 2d 592, 598 (D.V.I. 2002).

28. Borghesi, *Business Interruption Insurance: A Business Perspective*, 17 Nova L. Rev. 1147, 1150 (1993).

29. ISO Form CP 00 30 10 12.A.1. *See, e.g.*, Finger Furniture Co. v. Commonwealth Ins. Co., 404 F.3d 312, 314 (5th Cir. 2005) (insurer "shall be liable for the ACTUAL LOSS SUSTAINED by insured resulting directly from such interruption of business, but not exceeding the reduction in gross earnings less charges and expenses which do not necessarily continue during the interruption of business").

30. *See* Borghesi, *Business Interruption Insurance: A Business Perspective*, 17 Nova L. Rev. 1147, 1149 (1993), where the author explains that the insurance industry has traditionally characterized business entities as manufacturing or mercantile. For the former, coverage is premised on loss capacity for production, while for the latter, it is premised on lost sales or revenues.

by the insured, including fair rental value of any portion of those premises occupied by the insured,[31] and continuing normal operating expenses incurred in connection with that premises, including payroll and the amount of charges that are the legal obligation of the tenant but would otherwise be the obligation of the insured.[32] The type of coverage is determined by examining the Declarations and finding for which of the three types of coverage a limit of insurance is shown. If limits of insurance are shown under more than one of the three options, the provisions of the coverage apply separately to each.

While business interruption losses sustained because of the inability to collect rent from a commercial tenant may be covered under the terms of a policy,[33] operating expenses on any leased property beyond the date on which a lease was terminated cannot be obtained.[34]

Some insureds will be nonprofit entities. How are donations to a nonprofit characterized for purposes of determining "income"? A Texas federal court noted that a nonprofit may obtain revenue simultaneously from operations and from charitable donations and said that donations are considered revenue for a nonprofit organization.[35]

31. This language has been interpreted to mean that the potential rent the insured could have earned for the space it occupied, regardless of whether it had any intention or expectation of receiving that rent, may be recovered as long as it can show a loss of rental value that was caused by direct physical damage to the insured location. Imperial Trading Co. v. Travelers Prop. Cas. Co. of Am., 2009 U.S. Dist. LEXIS 64010 (E.D. La. July 24, 2009). In *Imperial Trading*, the insured was a tenant who was required by its lease to pay rent on property it leased even though the premises had been damaged in a hurricane. It sought to recover the rent it paid to the landlord during the time that building was uninhabitable. The court found the policy language to be ambiguous and construed it in favor of coverage. Thus, the insured tenant could recover the amount it could have earned from subleasing the space. However, the court also said that fair rental value has to be calculated on the date of the casualty, not during the highly unusual market conditions following a hurricane. Moreover, the insured could not simply recover the rent it paid to the landlord. That amount had been set forth in the lease five years earlier. While it could be some evidence of fair market value, it did not, without more, demonstrate the fair rental value of the property at the time of the hurricane.

32. ISO Form CP 00 30 10 12, § F.5.

33. 1626 2nd Ave LLC v. National Specialty Ins. Co., Inc., 148 A.D.3d 529, 48 N.Y.S.3d 596 (2017). *See also* Chalmette Retail Ctr., LLC v. Lafayette Ins. Co., 21 So. 3d 485 (La. App. 2009) (choice to use date that each tenant actually reopened in calculating separate period for each retail space was not unreasonable in light of evidence that some spaces became usable faster than others).

34. Lundy Enters., LLC v. Indus. Risk Insurers, 2009 U.S. Dist. LEXIS 81359 (E.D. La. Sept. 8, 2009).

35. Alley Theatre v. Hanover Ins. Co., 2020 U.S. Dist. LEXIS 52393 (S.D. Tex. Mar. 26, 2020).

[ii] Actual Loss

The ISO policy provides that the insurer will pay for the *actual loss* of business income the insured suffers because of the necessary "suspension" of its "operations" during the "period of restoration."[36] Under that language, where an insured had not begun repairs, it had not incurred an *actual loss* of business income and its claim was properly denied.[37] Where an insured's business income for its period of restoration was more than double that of the prior 13 months, a court said it had no *actual loss* of business income.[38] Payments an insurer makes to indemnify its insured for damaged inventory can be considered in calculating liability for loss from business interruption. Thus, an insurer's liability for loss from business interruption can be offset by payments made to indemnify its insured for damaged inventory.[39]

After being closed by a fire, a restaurant business did not pay rent or payroll and yet sought recovery for business interruption. The insurer noted that under the terms of the restaurant's lease, it did not have to pay rent and that the only employees were the two owners of the business. The court said that because there was no evidence that when the business was interrupted it sustained any actual loss through payment of rent or salaries, it could not recover.

[iii] Direct Physical Loss

The suspension of business operations has to be caused by *direct physical loss of or damage to* property at "premises"[40] described in the Declarations and

---

36. That period may also be referred to as the "due diligence and dispatch period" or "period of indemnity." Schirle, *Time Element Coverages in Business Interruption Insurance*, 37 The Brief 32 (2007).

37. Tamares Las Vegas Props., LLC v. Travelers Indem. Co., 409 F. Supp. 3d 924, 942 (D. Nev. 2019) (policy provides coverage only for lost profits actually incurred by suspending operations as result of covered cause of loss, not prospective loss). *But see* Georgia-Pacific Corp. v. Allianz Ins. Co., 977 F.2d 459 (8th Cir. 1992) (rejecting insurer's argument that there was no actual loss when insured, rather than repair damaged machinery, replaced it with refurbished machinery and decided to eventually purchase new machinery). *See also* Cont'l Cas. Co. v. F-Star Prop. Mgmt., 2011 U.S. Dist. LEXIS 76921 (W.D. Tex. July 15, 2011) (that repairs have commenced does not establish that policyholder has incurred business interruption losses).

38. B.F. Carvin Constr. Co. v. CNA Ins. Co., 2008 U.S. Dist. LEXIS 53678 (E.D. La. July 14, 2008). *Compare* Orrill, Cordell, & Beary, L.L.C. v. CNA Ins. Co., 2009 U.S. Dist. LEXIS 20867 (D.D. La. Mar. 16, 2009), where the insured law firm suffered a loss of contingency fees after Hurricane Katrina, but an increase in profit in its hourly fees. Because there were no allegations that the firm's net profit increased because of an increase in the volume of business conditions caused by the hurricane, recovery for the decrease in contingency fees was not precluded.

39. Baxter Int'l, Inc. v. Am. Guar. & Liab. Ins. Co., 308 Ill. Dec. 198, 861 N.E.2d 263, 369 Ill. App. 3d 700 (2006) (indemnification payment for damaged inventory was a "sale" and could be considered in calculating lost profit or "reduction in gross earnings" under policy).

40. For loss of or damage to personal property in the open or in a vehicle, the described premises include the area within 100 feet of those premises.

for which a business income limit of insurance is shown in the Declarations.[41] Generally, direct physical damage to property of the insured is required to trigger coverage.[42] However, that generally does not require the insured to have made a claim for any physical damage.[43]

One expert notes that the term "damage" and the phrase "direct physical loss of or damage" are not defined in policies, and concludes "there is no basis in the policy language itself to conclude that tangible, physical damage is required in order to trigger coverage."[44] However, the phrase "direct physical loss or damage" generally means that an event had a direct impact and proximately caused a loss that is related to the physical matter of the property.[45] Thus, even though flood is a covered cause of loss, if flooding does not cause *physical damage*, there should be no coverage.[46]

---

41. *See, e.g.*, Peerless Dyeing Co. v. Industrial Risk Insurers, 392 Pa. Super. 434, 573 A.2d 541 (1990) (coverage only available if there is property damage). *See generally* Downs & Hungerford, *Business Interruption Coverage: A Primer on the Physical Loss Requirements*, 12 Nevada Lawyer 12 (2004).

42. Aztar Corp. v. U.S. Fire Ins. Co., 223 Ariz. 463, 476, 224 P.3d 960, 973 (Ariz. App. 2010) (damaged property must be covered to trigger business interruption coverage); Roundabout Theatre Co. v. Cont'l Cas. Co., 302 A.D.2d 1, 751 N.Y.S.2d 4 (2002) (policy clearly and unambiguously provided coverage only where insured's property suffered direct physical damage). *But see* Datatab, Inc. v. St. Paul Fire and Marine Ins. Co., 347 F. Supp. 36 (S.D.N.Y. 1972), where a water main broke in the basement of the building in which the insured rented the 5th and 6th floors. Several water pumps were thereby damaged, rendering the air-conditioning system inoperative. That, in turn, forced a shutdown of the insured's computers and data processing equipment. The insured had no property in the basement, and water did not reach its offices. The insurer denied coverage because there was no physical damage to the insured's premises. The court, however, agreed with the insured that "premises" referred to the building as a whole.

43. 5 Jeffrey E. Thomas, *New Appleman on Insurance Law Library Edition* § 46.03[5] (LexisNexis 2020).

44. French, *Covid-19 Business Interruption Insurance Losses: The Cases For and Against Coverage*, 27 Conn. Ins. L.J. 1, 8 (2020).

45. Newman Myers Kreines Gross, P.C. v. Great Northern Ins. Co., 17 F. Supp. 3d 323, 331 (S.D.N.Y. 2014) (phrase "direct physical loss or damage" unambiguously requires some form of actual, physical damage to insured premises to trigger loss of business income coverage); Ass'n of Apt. Owners of Imperial Plaza v. Fireman's Fund Ins. Co., 939 F. Supp. 2d 1059, 1070 (D. Haw. 2013); St. Paul Mercury Ins. Co. v. Magnolia Lady, Inc., 1999 U.S. Dist. LEXIS 17895 (N.D. Miss. Nov. 4, 1999) (no business interruption coverage could be claimed where no physical loss or damage occurred to insured property). *See also* U.S. Specialty Ins. Co. v. Atl. Biologicals Corp., 2020 U.S. Dist. LEXIS 128007 (S.D. Fla. June 1, 2020) (traditional black letter rule of insurance law is that physical loss is prerequisite to any claim by insured for derivative damages such as business interruption).

46. *See, e.g.*, Cargill, Inc. v. Appalachian Ins. Co., 1983 U.S. Dist. LEXIS 20156 (D. Minn. Jan. 24, 1983), where flood and high water were perils insured against. The use of the insured's property was impeded by high water that blocked access to a portion of that property. However, under the policy, business interruption coverage was only provided when a flood caused property damage and that damage resulted in the interruption of business. There was no coverage because the high water did not damage that portion of the property; it only blocked access to it.

[iv] "Operations"

Coverage is triggered by necessary "suspension" of "operations." "Operations" is defined as the business activities of the insured that occur at the described premises.[47] In one case, a company that sold, serviced, leased, and installed slot machines in casinos argued that its "operations" included its interrelated workings and the casinos that were its customers. Those casinos were closed after a hurricane. The insured contended that until the damaged casinos were back in business, its operations were not restored and it was entitled to business interruption coverage. The court did not agree. It relied on the policy definition of "operations" and said that while the insured no doubt enjoyed a symbiotic business relationship with the casinos, the notion that this business relationship somehow made the casino industry part of the operations of the insured for purposes of coverage was without contract language support.[48]

Some policies do not use the word "operations" but instead state that the policy insures against loss resulting from necessary interruption of "business." An Arizona court concluded that "business" is broader than use of the premises.[49] The case concerned the collapse of an expansion of a casino and resort. The existing casino and hotel did not sustain any physical damage from the collapse and remained fully operational except for temporary access closures ordered by state authorities. There was, however, a significant decrease in patronage. The court, referring to "mutual dependency," said that the collapse of the expansion interrupted the business and the loss would fall within that term. It rejected the conclusion of the trial court that claims could not fall within the business interruption coverage because the hotel and casino still had the same operational capacity.

[v] Suspension of Operations

"Suspension" is defined in the ISO policy to mean either the slowdown or cessation of business activities of the insured or that a part or all of the described premises is rendered untenantable when the coverage includes rental value.[50] If a policy does not define suspension, many courts hold that "necessary suspension" refers only to a *total cessation* of business activity,[51] not a mere

47. ISO Form CP 00 30 10 12, § F.2.

48. Wms Indus. v. Fed. Ins. Co., 2009 U.S. Dist. LEXIS 68678 (S.D. Miss. Aug. 4, 2009).

49. Aztar Corp. v. U.S. Fire Ins. Co., 223 Ariz. 463, 224 P.3d 960 (Ariz. App. 2010). *See also* Pacific Coast Engineering Co. v. St. Paul Fire & Marine Ins. Co., 9 Cal. App. 3d 270, 274, 88 Cal. Rptr. 122, 124 (1970) (business interruption insurance provides coverage only for losses resulting directly from interruption of insured's business).

50. ISO Form CP 00 30 10 12, § F.6.

51. *See generally* Schirle, *Time Element Coverages in Business Interruption Insurance*, 37 The Brief 32, 36 (2007) (historically, courts have overwhelmingly required complete cessation of operations to trigger business interruption coverage).

slowdown,[52] although there is some support for the contrary position,[53] and some policies may specifically define "suspension" to include a slowdown of business activity.[54] Additionally, a policy may base coverage on an "interruption" of business.[55]

Has the insured experience a "necessary suspension" of its operations if it continues its business at an alternate location? A number of courts have said that business interruption insurance covers losses sustained because of the inability to continue to use *specified* premises.[56] In a case decided by the Third Circuit,[57] the insured quickly restored a portion of its operations at another location. The lower court, noting that coverage ceased under the policy when

---

52. American States Ins. Co. v. Creative Walking, 16 F. Supp. 2d 1062, 1065 (E.D. Mo. 1998). The court also said that if an insured is able to continue business operations at a temporary facility, it has not suffered a "necessary suspension" of operations. *See also* Madison Maidens, Inc. v. Am. Mfrs. Mut. Ins. Co., 2006 U.S. Dist. LEXIS 39633 (S.D.N.Y. June 15, 2006) (complete cessation of activity, even a temporary one, was required); Royal Indemnity Insurance Co. v. Mikob Properties, Inc., 940 F. Supp. 155, 160 (S.D. Tex. 1996) (if insured premises are still operating, business interruption insurance does not cover decrease in income); Home Indem. Co. v. Hyplains Beef, L.C., 893 F. Supp. 987, 992 (D. Kan. 1995) (term "suspension" connotes temporary, but complete, cessation of activity, and therefore the policy did not provide coverage for slowdown or reduction in operations); Buxbaum v. Aetna Life & Casualty Co., 103 Cal. App. 4th 434, 126 Cal. Rptr. 2d 682 (2002) (where water pipe broke and law firm's premises was flooded, business interruption coverage did not apply because firm did not "suspend" operations, it did not assert that water damage prevented attorneys from working at those premises, or any other place, and time sheets showed that there were billable hours on each day in question); Keetch v. Mut. of Enumclaw Ins. Co., 66 Wash. App. 208, 831 P.2d 784 (1992). *See generally* Taylor, Park & O'Brien, *Unique Coverage Issues in Flood Losses*, 48 Tort & Ins. L.J. 619 (2013) (phrase "necessary suspension of operations" is generally understood to mean total cessation of business activity, so that complete shutdown or cessation of insured business is required for recovery of lost business income).

53. Manta & Shultz, *Y2K: Liability and Coverage Issues*, 18 Temp. Envtl. L. & Tech. J. 27, 42 (1999) (regarding whether there has to be complete cessation of business to qualify for business interruption coverage when policy requires "necessary suspension of your operations," or whether slow down or loss of efficiency is sufficient, majority rule is that word suspension connotes temporary, but complete, cessation of activity, while minority rule implies that coverage might exist if business continues at slow rate).

54. *See, e.g.*, Cincinnati Ins. Co. v. Washer & Refrigeration Supply Co., 2008 U.S. Dist. LEXIS 112464 (D. Ala. Aug. 8, 2008).

55. 5 Jeffrey E. Thomas, *New Appleman on Insurance Law Library Edition* § 46.03[7][a] (LexisNexis 2020).

56. *See, e.g.*, Keetch v. Mut. of Enumclaw Ins. Co., 66 Wn. App. 208, 211, 831 P.2d 784, 786 (1992) (business interruption coverage indemnifies insured for losses sustained because of his or her inability to continue to use *specified* premises); Linnton Plywood Ass'n v. Protection Mut. Ins. Co., 760 F. Supp. 170, 172 (D. Ore. 1991) (business interruption insurance is to indemnify insured for any loss sustained because of inability to continue to use *specified* premises as result of destruction of those premises or parts of them); Pacific Coast Engineering Co. v. St. Paul Fire & Marine Ins. Co., 9 Cal. App. 3d 270, 275, 88 Cal. Rptr. 122, 125 (1970) (business interruption insurance is to indemnify insured against losses arising from loss sustained by inability to continue to use *specified* premises).

57. Am. Med. Imaging Corp. v. St. Paul Fire & Marine Ins. Co., 949 F.2d 690 (3d Cir. 1991).

the insured resumed "normal business operations," agreed with the insurer that there was no coverage. The appellate court, however, said that under the construction of the policy put forward by the lower court, the insured would have no motivation to mitigate losses and continuing business at any level would bar recovery.[58] The appellate court refused to accept that interpretation of a policy. That, the court observed, would impose an *affirmative duty* on the insured to mitigate losses.[59] On the other hand, an Arizona federal court said that if a policyholder is able to continue activities at another temporary location, it has not suffered a "necessary suspension" of its operations.[60] That ruling is consistent with the usual definition of "operations." "Operations" is defined as the business activities of the insured that occur at the described premises *and* the "tenantability" of the described premises, if coverage included rental value.[61] Note, however, that the phrase "business activities of the insured that occur at the described premises" describes the type of activities, not their location.

The loss or damage has to be caused by or result from a covered cause of loss.[62] Thus, if the insured voluntarily suspends operations, there is no coverage.[63]

[vi] Period of Restoration

The "period of restoration"—which may be called a "period of recovery" in some policies—begins under the ISO policy 72 hours after the time of direct physical loss or damage for business income coverage caused by or resulting

58. *Compare* Home Indem. Co. v. Hyplains Beef, L.C., 893 F. Supp. 987, 993 (D. Kan. 1995) (distinguishing *Am. Med.* and declining to apply its reasoning).

59. *See also* Evans v. Lafayette Ins. Co., 2007 U.S. Dist. LEXIS 92885 (E.D. La. Dec. 18, 2007) (where law firm had numerous offices and New Orleans office was closed after Hurricane Katrina, total cessation of business occurred at that office because work did not occur in it for period of time following hurricane, and fact that employees of that office worked from remote locations did not prevent complete cessation of business from occurring in Louisiana; insured had obligation to mitigate damages and did so by having employees work at other locations while New Orleans office could not be occupied).

60. Alon v. State Farm Fire & Cas. Co., 2013 U.S. Dist. LEXIS 202822 (D. Ariz. Feb. 25, 2013) (insured moved home-based business after water line burst and flooded home office).

61. ISO Form CP 00 30 10 12, § F.2.

62. Bethany Boardwalk Grp. LLC v. Everest Sec. Ins. Co., 2020 U.S. Dist. LEXIS 38427 (D. Md. Mar. 5, 2020) (water that entered building through defective roof that peeled back during storm was covered cause of loss).

63. *See, e.g.*, Yar-Lo, Inc. v. Travelers Indem. Co., 14 N.Y.S.3d 577, 578, 130 A.D.3d 1402, 1403 (2015) (under terms of policy, insured was entitled to compensation for lost business income only if it was forced to suspend its operations because of a hazard against which it was insured; insurer presented *prima facie* evidence that insured was never forced to close as result of sewage flood and that insured decided to terminate its lease and vacate premises, while insured failed to present any evidence to demonstrate that its actions were a result of covered loss).

from any covered cause of loss at the described premises.[64] It ends on the earlier of the date when the property at the described premises should be repaired, rebuilt, or replaced with reasonable speed and similar quality,[65] or the date when business is resumed at a new permanent location.[66] "Resuming" operations "does not require that the business be as prosperous as before, just that the business is operating again."[67]

Some policies may not have a "72-hour" provision.[68] Others may limit the period of suspension or restoration to a prescribed period of time, often 12 months.[69] However, the expiration date of the policy does not cut the period of restoration short.

The term "period of restoration" does not include any increased period that is required because of enforcement of, or compliance with, any ordinance or law that regulates construction, use, or repair, or requires tearing down of any property or that requires any insured or others to test for, monitor, clean up, remove, contain, treat, detoxify or neutralize, or in any way respond to or assess the effects of pollutants.[70] It also generally does not include any additional time required for improvements or modifications.[71] Some policies may not require direct physical loss. For example, one policy provided in part that

---

64. ISO Form CP 00 30 10 12, § F.3.a. One court described the 72-hour clause as a deductible and held that, where the insured business was closed for only four hours each time it rained and flooded the building's basement, those brief closures never came close to meeting the required 72-hour period, so the claim for lost business income failed. Stevens v. Zurich Am. Ins. Co., 2015 U.S. Dist. LEXIS 120117 (N.D. Cal. Sept. 9, 2015).

65. The insured often cannot begin repairs until it receives payment for the physical damage. Thus, if the insurer delays making that payment, the period of restoration may include that delay. United Land Investors, Inc. v. N. Ins. Co., 476 So. 2d 432 (La. App. 1985) (although insured received advance from insurer, it could not commence repairs until it received money to complete the work).

66. ISO Form CP 00 30 10 12, § F.3.b. *See, e.g.*, Cincinnati Ins. Co. v. Washer & Refrigeration Supply Co., 2008 U.S. Dist. LEXIS 112464 (D. Ala. Aug. 8, 2008) (where insured recommenced business at new permanent location within 60 days of Hurricane Katrina, period of restoration ended within 60 days of Katrina).

67. Cincinnati Ins. Co. v. Washer & Refrigeration Supply Co., 2008 U.S. Dist. LEXIS 112464 (D. Ala. Aug. 8, 2008). *See also* Dictiomatic, Inc. v. U.S. Fid. & Guar. Co., 958 F. Supp. 594, 602 (S.D. Fla. 1997) (period of restoration ended on date on which insured was back on premises and "up and running").

68. *See, e.g.*, Dictiomatic, Inc. v. U.S. Fid. & Guar. Co., 958 F. Supp. 594, 602 (S.D. Fla. 1997) (concluding as matter of law that period of restoration began on date of direct physical loss or damage caused by hurricane).

69. Borghesi, *Business Interruption Insurance: A Business Perspective*, 17 Nova L. Rev. 1147, 1157 (1993).

70. The term "pollutants" is defined to mean any solid, liquid, gaseous, or thermal irritant or contaminant, including smoke, vapor, soot, fumes, acids, alkalis, chemicals, and waste, and "waste" includes materials to be recycled, reconditioned or reclaimed. ISO Form CP 00 30 10 12, § F.4.

71. Borghesi, *Business Interruption Insurance: A Business Perspective*, 17 Nova L. Rev. 1147, 1156 (1993).

the "period of recovery included time to restore the business to the condition that would have existed had no loss occurred, beginning on the later of the date on which the liability of the insurer for loss or damage would otherwise terminate or the date on which repair, replacement, or rebuilding of the damaged portion of the property has actually been completed. A federal court said that under that policy language, an interruption did not end when access to the insured facility was restored, but rather when the business was restored "to the condition that would have existed had no loss occurred."[72]

The period of restoration is tied to the operations of the insured, not those of its customers.[73] Thus, if the insured resumes its operations, the fact that its customers remain closed does not extend the period of restoration.

[vii] Extended Business Income Provision

When determining the period of coverage, one should be alert to any "Extended Business Income" provisions. Typically, the Declarations Page will state the length of the "Extended Period of Indemnity" that applies to business income losses.[74] The policy will provide that the insurer will pay for the actual loss of business income incurred during the extended coverage period. It is important to be alert to any limitations on the provision.[75]

[b] The Meaning of "Direct Physical Loss or Damage"[76]

The usual definition of "physical damage" is "a distinct, demonstrable, and physical alteration" of the structure of the property.[77] The Fifth Circuit has said that "[t]he language 'physical loss or damage' strongly implies that there was an initial satisfactory state that was changed by some external event into an unsatisfactory state—for example, the car was undamaged before the collision dented the bumper."[78] The Third Circuit has added that "[f]ire, water, smoke and impact from another object are typical examples of physical damage from

72. Fountain Powerboat Indus. v. Reliance Ins. Co., 119 F. Supp. 2d 552, 558 (E.D.N.C. 2000).

73. Wms Indus. v. Fed. Ins. Co., 2009 U.S. Dist. LEXIS 68678 (S.D. Miss. Aug. 4, 2009).

74. *See, e.g.*, Island Concepts, LLC v. Certain Underwriters at Lloyd's, 2014 U.S. Dist. LEXIS 155494 (E.D. La. Oct. 31, 2014) (Declarations Page provided that insured purchased "Extended Period of Indemnity" of 90 days for business income losses).

75. *See, e.g.*, Cincinnati Ins. Co. v. Washer & Refrigeration Supply Co., 2008 U.S. Dist. LEXIS 112464 (D. Ala. Aug. 8, 2008) (coverage for "extended business income" did not apply when loss of business income was incurred as result of unfavorable business conditions caused by impact of covered cause of loss in area where described premises were located).

76. *See generally* 5 Jeffrey E. Thomas, *New Appleman on Insurance Law Library Edition* § 46.03[2] (LexisNexis 2020).

77. *See, e.g.*, MRI Healthcare Ctr. of Glendale, Inc. v. State Farm Gen. Ins. Co., 187 Cal. App. 4th 766, 115 Cal. Rptr. 3d 27 (Cal. Ct. App. 2010); AFLAC Inc. v. Chubb & Sons, Inc., 260 Ga. App. 306, 581 S.E.2d 317 (2003).

78. Trinity Indus. Inc. v. Ins. Co. of N. Am., 916 F.2d 267, 270–71 (5th Cir. 1990).

an outside source that may demonstrably alter the components of a building and trigger coverage."[79] For example, in a case where a plumbing joint failed, causing water damage to the insured property, the court said the joints did not sustain direct physical loss or damage from an insured peril. Most of them had been properly installed, and those that were not never reached an initial satisfactory state and, therefore, there was no external event that changed them into an unsatisfactory state and coverage was not triggered.[80]

"Direct" means "immediate" or "proximate," as distinguished from "remote" or "incidental."[81] A direct loss has to be shown before the insured can recover. For example, a vacant rental property was flooded after the water meter, copper piping, and other fixtures were removed, apparently by thieves. The insured sought coverage under the covered risk of vandalism, and the appellate court agreed the peril applied to the loss; however, it said that because there was no evidence of "direct physical loss" to the particular items for which the insured sought to recover, it could not conclude that either party was entitled to summary judgment.[82]

Under a business interruption coverage requirement that there be "direct physical loss or damage," even if flood is a covered peril, there will generally be no coverage if the insured property is not immediately altered by flooding.

[3] Covered Causes of Loss and the Flood Exclusion

[a] Coverages and Flood Exclusion

To determine the covered causes of loss, the exclusions, and the limitations on coverage under the ISO policy, one has to look to the Declarations where the applicable Causes of Loss form will be listed.[83] There are three standard causes

---

79. Port Auth. of N.Y. & N.J. v. Affiliated FM Ins. Co., 311 F.3d 226, 235 (3d Cir. 2002) (physical damage to building as entity by sources unnoticeable to naked eye has to meet higher threshold).

80. W2001Z/15 CPW Realty, LLC v. Lexington Ins. Co., 2014 N.Y. Misc. LEXIS 349 (Jan. 22, 2014). *See also* Universal Image Prods., Inc. v. Chubb Corp., 703 F. Supp. 2d 705, 709 (E.D. Mich. 2010) (insured contended that water seepage into insured building caused direct physical loss in form of pervasive odor, mold, and bacterial contamination, but court found that insured property had not suffered any structural or tangible damage). *Compare* Bethany Boardwalk Grp. LLC v. Everest Sec. Ins. Co., 2020 U.S. Dist. LEXIS 38427 (D. Md. Mar. 5, 2020) (property suffered water damage, which constituted physical damage when rainwater entered through roof that had been improperly installed).

81. Travelers Indem. Co. v. Jarrett, 369 S.W.2d 653, 655 (Tex. App. 1963). *See also* Sullivan v. Std. Fire Ins. Co., 956 A.2d 643 (Del. 2008); Roundabout Theatre Co v. Continental Cas Co, 302 A.D.2d 1, 7, 751 N.Y.S.2d 4, 8 (2002) (plain meaning of words "direct" and "physical" narrows scope of coverage and mandates conclusion that losses resulting from off-site property damage do not constitute covered perils).

82. Acorn Inv. Co. v. Mich. Basic Prop. Ins. Ass'n, 2009 Mich. App. LEXIS 1892 (Sept. 15, 2009).

83. ISO Form CP 00 30 10 12, § A.3.

of loss forms: Basic,[84] Broad,[85] and Special.[86] The first two name specific perils.[87] Both include "sprinkler leakage,"[88] which can result in "flooding." The Broad form adds "water damage" as a cause of loss.[89] The ISO Special Form provides all-perils or all-risk, which would cover a loss by flood or water; however, it and the other two forms exclude coverage for water damage including flood. Under the exclusion, the carrier will not pay for loss or damage caused directly or indirectly by "water."[90] It defines water to include:

- Flood, surface water, waves including tidal wave and tsunami, tides, tidal water, overflow of any body of water, or spray from any of them, and all whether or not driven by wind, including storm surge;
- Mudslide or mudflow;

---

84. ISO Form CP 10 10 10 12.

85. ISO Form CP 10 20 10 12.

86. ISO Form CP 10 30 10 12. Typically, one of these forms would be used with the ISO Business Income (and Extra Expense) Coverage Form. *See, e.g.*, Pel Hughes Printing, L.L.C. v. Hanover Ins. Group, Inc., 2008 U.S. Dist. LEXIS 31224 (E.D. La. Apr. 16, 2008) (CP 00 30 06 95 form use in conjunction with CP 10 30 06 95 listing causes of loss).

87. The Basic Form provides coverage for fire, lightning, explosion, smoke, windstorm, hail, riot, civil commotion, aircraft, vehicles, vandalism, sprinkler leakage, sinkhole collapse, and volcanic action. *Basic Causes of Loss Form*, IRMI, https://www.irmi.com/term/insurance-definitions/basic-causes-of-loss-form. The Broad Form adds falling objects; weight of snow, ice, or sleet; and water damage. *Broad Causes of Loss Form*, IRMI, https://www.irmi.com/term/insurance-definitions/broad-causes-of-loss-form.

88. ISO Form CP 10 10 10 12, § A.9; ISO Form CP 10 20 10 12 § A.9. "Sprinkler leakage" is defined to mean leakage or discharge of *any substance* from an automatic sprinkler system and includes the collapse of a tank that is part of the system.

89. ISO Form CP 10 20 10 12 § A.14. The form defines "water damage" narrowly as the accidental discharge or leakage of water or steam as the direct result of the breaking apart or cracking of a plumbing, heating, air-conditioning, or other system or appliance located on the described premises and that contains water or steam. "Water damage" does not include discharge or leakage from an automatic sprinkler system, a sump, or related equipment and parts, including overflow because of sump pump failure or excessive volume of water, or roof drains, gutters, downspouts, or similar fixtures or equipment. It also does not include the cost to repair any defect that caused the loss or damage or loss or damage caused by or resulting from continuous or repeated seepage or leakage of water, or the presence or condensation of humidity, moisture, or vapor, occurring over 14 days or more. Finally, water damage does not include loss or damage caused by or resulting from freezing, unless the insured does his or her best to maintain heat in the building or structure or drains the equipment and shuts off the water supply if heat is not maintained.

90. *See, e.g.*, ISO Form CP 10 30 10 12, § B.1.g. *See also* Five Towns Nissan, LLC v. Universal Underwriters Insurance Co., 125 A.D.3d 580, 581, 5 N.Y.S.3d 35, 36 (2015) (under Special Form Cause of Loss policy terms excluded losses due to flooding, and there was no coverage for loss of business income). Other standard policies will also exclude flood coverage. *See., e.g.*, Newman Myers Kreines Gross, P.C. v. Great Northern Ins. Co., 17 F. Supp. 3d 323 (S.D.N.Y. 2014) ("Business Income with Extra Expense Insurance for Law Firms" policy excluded loss or damage caused by flood); Valley Forge Insurance Co. v. Hicks Thomas & Lilienstern, L.L.P., 174 S.W.3d 254, 258 (Tex. App. 2004) (loss of business income not covered as it resulted from flood or surface water).

- Water that backs up or overflows or is otherwise discharged from a sewer, drain, sump, sump pump, or related equipment;
- Water under the ground surface pressing on or flowing or seeping through foundations, walls, floors or paved surfaces, basements, whether paved or not, or doors, windows, or other openings; and
- Waterborne material carried or otherwise moved by water or material carried or otherwise moved by mudslide or mudflow.

The exclusion applies regardless of whether any water, mudslide, or mudflow is caused by an act of nature or otherwise.[91] However, if those events result in fire, explosion, or sprinkler leakage, the insurer will pay for the loss or damage caused by that fire, explosion, or sprinkler leakage. In the case of sprinkler leakage, it must be a covered cause of loss.

As obvious as it may seem, the covered cause of loss has to be found in the policy at issue, not another one. For example, an insured argued that even though its business interruption policy may have excluded flood damage, it had flood insurance with a different insurer where flood was a covered cause of loss. The court responded that "covered cause of loss" is a contractual term between these parties, and their agreement did not reasonably allow the business interruption policy to be read to include "any force consisting in whole or part of a listed exclusion."[92]

The exclusion is invoked when loss or damage is caused *indirectly* by water. Thus, a claim for loss of income during a storm was not covered. The loss was caused by interruption of normal business because rising water over the access road eliminated entry to the insured premises and the damages, therefore, were caused by an excluded peril.[93] The same result was reached where the substation supplying power to the insured premises was damaged by flooding from Superstorm Sandy, which resulted in a power interruption that caused business interruption losses.[94] Similarly, where hurricanes were a covered cause of loss, but not flooding, business losses under a Civil Authority Clause were not covered because a condition of coverage was that the damage to property other than the premises of the insured that precipitated the civil authority action be caused by or result from a covered cause of loss and the civil authority actions in prohibiting road travel and closing the insured facility resulted from hurricane *and* flood. The court held that when the damage to

---

91. For example, if a dam, levee, seawall, or other boundary or containment system fails in whole or in part, for *any reason*, to contain the water in it, the exclusion applies.

92. Narricot Indus. v. Fireman's Fund Ins. Co., 2002 U.S. Dist. LEXIS 19074, at *21, n.9 (E.D. Pa. Sept. 30, 2002).

93. Constitution State Ins. Co. v. Werner Enterprises, Inc., 1987 U.S. Dist. LEXIS 6023 (E.D. La. June 26, 1987).

94. La Casa Di Arturo, Inc. v. Tower Group, Inc., 26 N.Y.S.3d 725 (2015).

other property resulted from a covered risk as well as an excluded one, there was no covered cause of loss.[95]

A New York court ruled that there was no coverage where a loss of business income was the result of an off-premises power failure caused by severe tidal flooding at a substation. The policyholder argued that its loss was not caused by a flood but by the power failure. There was no flood at the insured premises, noted the insured, and the flood damage exclusion did not apply to premises that were not part of the policy. The policy, responded the court, clearly excluded from the definition of a covered cause of loss losses caused "indirectly" by flood, and the fact that the flood occurred at a utility substation facility did not render the exclusion inapplicable.[96]

[b] Avoiding the Flood Exclusion

When flooding is accompanied by a windstorm, the question of which peril is the cause of loss arises. The determination is fact driven, and it is critical that counsel for the insured assemble those facts. For example, in a case following Hurricane Katrina, a New Orleans physician sought business interruption coverage after her landlord permanently closed her office. The office was on the second floor of a multi-story building that, as a result of the storm, sustained extensive wind damage. Because of breaches in the levee protection system, the first floor was inundated with seven to eight feet of water for about two weeks. The insurer denied coverage. It contended that losses were flood related stemming from a lack of access to the building because of the water on the first floor. Because flood waters were expressly excluded as a "covered peril" under the policy, the insurer decided there was no business interruption coverage. The insured, however, produced extensive testimony about the entry of rainwater through the ceiling, walls, and broken windows. The court found that the office sustained direct physical loss and damage as a result of wind and rain, not from direct contact with flood waters and that those losses and damages alone caused the suspension in the medical practice of the insured. It held that an award of insurance proceeds under the business interruption coverage was appropriate under the facts.[97]

---

95. Narricot Indus. v. Fireman's Fund Ins. Co., 2002 U.S. Dist. LEXIS 19074 (E.D. Pa. Sept. 30, 2002) (policy terms, read together, showed that conjunction of covered peril and excluded peril was not a "covered cause of loss" and, although hurricane caused damage to other property, because flood also caused that damage, it was not caused by covered cause of loss whether hurricane caused floods that in sequence damaged property or floods came concurrently with hurricane to damage that property).

96. Northern Spy Food Co., LLC v. Tower Natl. Ins., 2016 N.Y. Misc. LEXIS 1033 (Mar. 22, 2016) (flood exclusion applied regardless of location of flood).

97. Yount v. Lafayette Ins. Co., 4 So. 3d 162, 171 (La. App. 2009).

In another post-Katrina case, the owner of a large New Orleans apartment complex claimed business income losses based on an asserted increase in rental value of 40 percent because of an increase in demand after the hurricane. The Fifth Circuit Court of Appeals said that, "[a]lthough flood-related damages . . . [were] excluded, stimulated demand as a result of flood damage to other structures is a proper consideration in calculating lost income." The insurer attempted to invoke the flood exclusion, but that, the court responded would extend the flood exclusion beyond its function. The exclusion, said the court, applied to "all coverage parts" of the policy. If coverage was permissible, and the insurer did not deny that the policy covered wind damage, then the flood exclusion had "nothing further to say, and the only remaining issue is calculation of damages." The policy expressly allowed that calculation to consider favorable business conditions, and the court declined to use a limitation on coverage to change the calculation for a covered loss.[98]

The exclusion may be avoided where the loss is caused by *anticipated* flooding. For example, a law firm was unable to access its offices when the utility company preemptively shut off power in anticipation of Superstorm Sandy and the flooding it was expected to bring. The law firm sought business interruption coverage, but the insurer invoked the flood exclusion. In *dicta*, a federal court said that the power outage was not directly caused by flood and the insurer could not meet the burden of proving that the losses would not be covered.[99]

[4] Policies Covering Flood Loss

Some policies may cover flood losses,[100] but it is more likely that an endorsement to the policy will add flood coverage[101] or override a flood exclusion and add back coverage.[102] The endorsement might simply void the exclusion,[103] or

98. Berk-Cohen Assocs., L.L.C. v. Landmark Am. Ins. Co., 433 Fed. Appx. 268 (5th Cir. July 20, 2011).

99. Newman Myers Kreines Gross, P.C. v. Great Northern Ins. Co., 17 F. Supp. 3d 323, 333–34 (S.D.N.Y. 2014).

100. *See, e.g.*, United Fire & Cas. Co. v. Arkwright Mut. Ins. Co., 53 F. Supp. 2d 632 (S.D.N.Y. 1999) (all-risk property insurance policy covered property damage and business interruption loss caused by any insured peril, including fire, windstorm, vandalism, earthquake, and flood). *See also* Simkins Industries, Inc. v. Lexington Ins. Co., 42 Md. App. 396, 401 A.2d 181 (1979) (boiler and machinery policy excluded loss from flood unless accident ensued in which case insurer would be liable only for any loss from ensuing accident); Almah LLC v. Lexington Ins. Co., 2016 Del. Super. LEXIS 47 (Jan. 27, 2016).

101. *See, e.g.*, Lundy Enters., LLC v. Indus. Risk Insurers, 2009 U.S. Dist. LEXIS 81359 (E.D. La. Sept. 8, 2009) (flood coverage endorsement stated that flood was added to covered causes of loss).

102. *See, e.g.*, Gilbert/Robinson, Inc. v. Sequoia Ins. Co., 655 S.W.2d 581, 583 (Mo. App. 1983) (endorsement attached to policy that, by its terms, removed flood damage exclusion).

103. *See, e.g.*, Dream Spa, Inc. v. Fireman's Fund Ins., 2008 U.S. Dist. LEXIS 8933 (S.D.N.Y. Feb. 6, 2008). In *Dream Spa* the property policy provided business interruption coverage for

it could contain specific conditions and/or limitations on flood coverage. Also, proceeds under an endorsement may be limited to a loss in excess of coverage under a Federal Emergency Management Agency (FEMA) Standard Flood Insurance Policy (SFIP).[104] However, the SFIP does not cover business income, civil authority, or dependent property losses.[105]

It is important to determine whether the coverage specifically applies to business interruption. For example, in one case the policy provided coverage for damage to *property* and for actual loss of business income caused by covered causes of loss. Sewer backups, under the policy language, were not covered causes of loss; however, the exclusion did not bar coverage of up to $50,000 for loss or damage to *covered property* caused by water that backed up from a sewer or drain. The court concluded that the policy provided coverage for *property damage* caused by a sewer backup, but not for *business income* loss as loss of income was covered only when it was the result of a covered cause of loss and that did not include a loss caused by a sewer backup.[106] A different result was reached in a case where water runoff backed up through a municipal drainage system during torrential rains of a hurricane. The primary policy excluded flood and sewer and drain backup as covered perils. An endorsement removed the exclusion as a bar to coverage for damage caused by sewer and drain backup, with a sublimit of $5,000 for physical damage. Another endorsement provided business interruption coverage. The court found that once the exclusion for sewer and drain backup was removed, that peril was covered for business interruption losses *and* the much higher sublimit of the business interruption endorsement applied, not that of the endorsement removing the exclusion.[107]

When coverage is added by a "flood endorsement," that endorsement may include a sublimit for flood coverage. It is important then to determine if

---

suspensions from a covered cause of loss It also stated that "water damage"—as that term is commonly defined—was *not* a covered cause of loss. However, a Water Damage Endorsement (WDE) was added that eliminated from the definition water that backs up from a sewer or drain or that is underground. The insured suffered a loss from a sewer backup, and the insurer contended that was not a covered cause of loss for purposes of the business interruption coverage. The court, however, said that the WDE deleted sewer backups from the exclusions list as if it were never there and, therefore, it would read the policy as if the causes listed in the WDE were never listed as exclusions.

104. *See, e.g.*, Lundy Enters., LLC v. Indus. Risk Insurers, 2009 U.S. Dist. LEXIS 81359 (E.D. La. Sept. 8, 2009) (proceeds under endorsement were limited and triggered by damages in excess of coverage limits of National Flood Insurance Program; once insurer paid policy limits, flood did not become excluded peril, but rather one for which policy limits had been paid).

105. Taylor, Park & O'Brien, *Unique Coverage Issues in Flood Losses*, 48 Tort & Ins. L.J. 619 (2013).

106. 1335 Piccard LLC v. Nat'l Fire Ins. Co. of Hartford, 171 Fed. Appx. 993 (4th Cir. 2006).

107. Bishops, Inc. v. Penn Nat'l Ins., 984 A.2d 982 (Pa. Super. 2009) (language removing exclusion did not restate language that barred coverage on ground of concurrent causation by another excluded cause of loss, one of which was flood).

the sublimit applies to the business interruption coverage. In one case, for example, the court found that the business interruption coverage had its own applicable limits of insurance, and the flood endorsement did not exclude it or make its limits of insurance subject to the endorsement sublimit. The court noted that business interruption and property damage coverage are distinct and that the policy reflected the distinction between direct physical loss or damage to covered property from a covered cause of loss and reduction in business income that results from suspension of operations during the covered property's restoration.[108] The holding is based on an exacting review of the entire policy and the endorsements and may, therefore, be of limited precedent as the wording of the policies and endorsements in other cases may well be different. The case illustrates the need to carefully parse policy language when a flood sublimit is at issue.

[5] Other Exclusions

[a] Ordinance or Law Exclusion

Generally, the insurer is liable for business interruption that results from enforcement of a building code.[109] Many policies, however, exclude business interruption coverage for any *increase* of loss that results from enforcement of a local or state ordinance or law that regulates construction, repair, or demolition of the insured property. The exclusion is found in standard ISO Causes of Loss forms.[110] It applies when a loss results from an ordinance or law that is enforced.[111]

Application of the exclusion is illustrated by a case in which the insured contracted with a builder to construct a hotel on its property. After the builder completed a retaining wall, but before completion of the hotel, there was a rainstorm in which rainwater flowed from the parking lot into the earth behind the retaining wall, weakening it and causing a portion of it to collapse. The town deemed the wall unsafe and issued a stop work order and then required the entire wall to be rebuilt. That delayed opening of the hotel for

108. Baylor College of Med. v. Am. Guar. & Liab. Ins. Co., 2002 U.S. Dist. LEXIS 29002 (S.D. Tex. Oct. 30, 2002). *See also* Alley Theatre v. Hanover Ins. Co., 436 F. Supp. 3d 938, 948 (S.D. Tex. 2020) ($3 million Flood Endorsement Limit did not apply to lost-business income that resulted from flood damage and instead, $5 million Income Coverage Limit applied).

109. Davidson Hotel Co. v. St. Paul Fire & Marine Ins. Co., 136 F. Supp. 2d 901, 912 (W.D. Tenn. 2001) (absent express exclusion of business interruption coverage for costs associated with ordinance enforcement, there is coverage; business interruption provision did not expressly exclude coverage).

110. *See, e.g.*, ISO Form CP 10 30 06 07, § B.1.a (eliminates coverage of costs for enforcement of any ordinance or law regulating construction, use, or repair of any property or tearing down any property including cost of removing its debris).

111. *See, e.g.*, Reichert v. State Farm General Ins. Co., 212 Cal. App. 4th 1543, 152 Cal. Rptr. 3d 6 (2012) (exclusion applied where insured property was demolished pursuant to flood plain regulation).

over 100 days. The insured sought business interruption coverage. The insurer paid for only two weeks of business losses, and the insured sued. The court said that the delay was not the result of storm damage, but the town's requirement that the retaining wall be brought into compliance with local ordinances. The policy covered business interruption losses resulting from direct physical loss, damage, or destruction caused by an insured peril and excluded coverage for increased losses that resulted from enforcement of ordinances and laws regulating construction, repair, or demolition of the insured property. Therefore, the insurer was only required to compensate the insured for one week of business interruption, as the builder admitted that repairs to the damaged portion of the retaining wall would have been completed in one week had not the town required it to be rebuilt.[112]

[b] Idle Periods Clause/Exclusion

A policy may include an "idle periods clause." An example would be a clause that reads the insurer will not be liable for a loss "with respect to any period during which goods would not have been produced or business operations or services maintained had no fire or other peril insured against occurred."[113] A more detailed clause reads that the policy does not insure against "[a]ny loss during any idle period, including but not limited to when production, operation, service or delivery or receipt of goods would cease, or would not have taken place or would have been prevented due to: 1) physical loss or damage not insured by this Policy on or off of the Insured Location; 2) planned or rescheduled shutdown; 3) strikes or other work stoppage; 4) any other reason other than physical loss or damage insured by this Policy."[114] These clauses, whether or not denominated as such, are in effect exclusions.[115] They provide "an exemption for business interruption liability where there is a period when for reasons other than insured property damage, production or operations would not have been maintained."[116] The Ninth Circuit has said that, under the clause, if "there was a period when goods would not have been produced

112. Tocci Bldg. Corp. v. Commonwealth Ins. Co., 22 Mass. L. Rep. 522 (Apr. 23, 2007), *aff'd*, 71 Mass. App. Ct. 1120, 885 N.E.2d 172 (2008). The court noted that the builder actually repaired the damaged wall in three days and, therefore, when the insurer compensated the plaintiffs for two weeks of business interruption, it actually exceeded its requirements under the policy.

113. Quoted by the court in *Manufacturers Mutual Fire Ins. Co. v. Royal Indemnity Co.*, 501 F.2d 299, 300 (9th Cir. 1974).

114. Quoted by the court in *J.L. French Auto. Castings, Inc. v. Factory Mut. Ins. Co.*, 2004 U.S. Dist. LEXIS 25932 (N.D. Ill. Dec. 21, 2004).

115. Whether a court views a provision as an exclusion can matter very much, as the general rule in insurance law is that the insured bears the burden of bringing the loss under coverage while the insurer has the burden to show an exclusion applies.

116. Cargill, Inc. v. Appalachian Ins. Co., 1983 U.S. Dist. LEXIS 20156 (D. Minn. Jan. 24, 1983).

or operations and services maintained, then, as to that hypothetically 'idle' period there was no liability."[117] If an interruption of business is caused by a peril that is covered *and also* by one that is *not* covered, according to a leading treatise, the idle periods exclusion bars coverage for the period of interruption that is attributed to the peril that is not covered.[118]

[c] Cancellation of Contracts Exclusion

Some policies may contain a "cancellation of contracts"[119] exclusion. For example, one policy provided that the insurer would not "cover any increase in loss that's caused by the suspension, lapse or cancellation of any lease, license, contract or order. However, if the suspension, lapse or cancellation results directly from the interruption of [the insured's] business, [the insurer would] cover any increase in a covered loss that affects . . . earnings. But [the insurer would] only pay for such increase during the period of restoration."[120] A federal court, in *dicta*, said that this exclusion may have prohibited recovery where prior to Hurricane Katrine, the insured had a single public works project contract that was cancelled after the storm.[121]

[d] Acts and Decisions

Some polices may have an "acts and decisions" exclusion under which the insurer will not pay for loss or damage caused by or resulting from any acts or decisions, including the failure to act or decide, of any person, group, organization, or government body. However, as discussed below,[122] "civil authority" is standard additional coverage for losses when a civil authority bars access to the insured property. The "acts and decisions" exclusion was found inapplicable to a business interruption claim in a case after Superstorm Sandy in which a utility preemptively shut down distribution of electricity for a few hours before flood waters damaged the utility network and prevented power from being immediately restored. The court said that the insurer could not invoke the exclusion to relieve it of the obligation to insure the policyholder for the business interruption losses that followed those initial few hours of

117. Manufacturers Mutual Fire Ins. Co. v. Royal Indemnity Co., 501 F.2d 299, 301 (9th Cir. 1974).

118. 5 Jeffrey E. Thomas, *New Appleman on Insurance Law Library Edition* § 46.06[2][b] (LexisNexis 2020).

119. *See generally* 5 Jeffrey E. Thomas, *New Appleman on Insurance Law Library Edition* § 46.06[7][b] (LexisNexis 2020).

120. Am. Med. Imaging Corp. v. St. Paul Fire & Marine Ins. Co., 949 F.2d 690, 694, n.2 (3d Cir. 1991).

121. B.F. Carvin Constr. Co. v. CNA Ins. Co., 2008 U.S. Dist. LEXIS 53678 (E.D. La. July 14, 2008).

122. See § 6.02[6][a], *infra*.

the storm. The electrical service loss that followed that short period, said the court, was proximately caused by the damage to the network resulting from the hurricane.[123]

[6] Additional Coverages

[a] Civil Authority[124]

The ISO Business Income (and Extra Expense) Coverage Form specifically provides that when a *covered cause of loss* causes damage to property other than property at the described premises,[125] the insurer will pay for actual loss of business income sustained by the insured caused by action of a "civil authority" that prohibits access to the described premises.[126] The policy only requires an "action" by a civil authority, not a "formal order."[127] One court has said that where law enforcement and local government officials were "asking" and "encouraging" residents to stay off the streets because of an impending hurricane landfall, those advisories could be considered an "action of civil authority" that would not have been given but for the hurricane, as the civil authority clause in question did not require a formal order to be issued by civil authorities.[128] The phrase "civil authority" "includes civil officers in whom a portion of the sovereignty is vested and in whom the enforcement of municipal regulations or the control of the general interest of society is confided" and encompasses police officers and firefighters.[129]

---

123. Johnson Gallagher Magliery, LLC v. Charter Oak Fire Ins. Co., 2014 U.S. Dist. LEXIS 35548 (S.D.N.Y. Mar. 18, 2014).

124. *See generally* Schirle, *Civil Authority and Ingress/Egress Coverage Claiming Lost Income after Hurricanes and Other Catastrophic Events*, 47 The Brief 61 (2018).

125. French, *Covid-19 Business Interruption Insurance Losses: The Cases For and Against Coverage*, 27 Conn. Ins. L.J. 1, 8 (2020) (coverage is triggered if civil authority prevents policyholder from doing business because of damage to someone else's property).

126. ISO Form CP 00 30 10 12, § A.5.a. *See also* Taylor, Park & O'Brien, *Unique Coverage Issues in Flood Losses*, 48 Tort & Ins. L.J. 619 (2013) (civil authority clause is triggered only if (1) there is loss of earnings by insured (2) access to business is specifically prohibited (3) by action of civil authority (4) as result of direct physical loss to property other than covered location (5) that was caused by covered loss).

127. *See, e.g.*, Narricot Indus. v. Fireman's Fund Ins. Co., 2002 U.S. Dist. LEXIS 19074 (E.D. Pa. Sept. 30, 2002) (Civil Authority Clause did not require formal or written order and, in fact, did not mention an order at all, but rather an action that could be instructing businesses to halt operations; if insurer wanted to be more exacting about what type of behavior qualified as "actions," it could have been). Some policies, however, may require an "order." *See, e.g.*, Altru Health System v. American Protection Insurance Company, 238 F.3d 961, 963 (8th Cir. 2001) (coverage for actual loss sustained by insured, resulting directly from interruption of business when, as direct result of damage to, or destruction of, property within 1,000 feet of insured premises, access is *specifically prohibited by order* of civil authority).

128. Kean, Miller, Hawthorne, D'Armond McCowan & Jarman, L.L.P. v. Nat'l Fire Ins. Co., 2007 U.S. Dist. LEXIS 64849 (M.D. La. Aug. 2, 2007).

129. Princess Garment Co. v. Fireman's Fund Ins. Co., 115 F.2d 380, 382 (6th Cir. 1940).

There are two conditions that have to be met for the ISO civil authority coverage to apply. First, access to the area immediately surrounding the damaged property has to be "prohibited"[130] by a civil authority as a result of that damage, and the described premises have to be within that are, but *not more than one mile* from the damaged property.[131] Note that most, but not all, policies contain a geographical limitation, while others may have a "dependent locations" extension.[132] Second, the action of the civil authority has to be taken in response to dangerous physical conditions that result from the damage or continuation of the covered cause of loss that caused the damage, or the action has to be taken to enable a civil authority to have unimpeded access to the damaged property.[133]

A third implied condition is that there must be a nexus between the damage to property other than the insured premises and the action by the civil authority. For example, there was no coverage where the insured could not show a link between any property damage and issuance of an evacuation order in anticipation of the landfall of a hurricane.[134] A South Carolina federal court agreed and said that where a policy required the order of civil authority to be "because of" damage or destruction to adjacent property, there had to be property damage or destruction at the time the civil authority order was issued. Thus, there was no coverage when the governor issued an evacuation order in anticipation of a hurricane.[135] That appears to be the majority, but

---

130. Generally, coverage under a civil authority provision is only available when a civil authority prevents the property from being accessed at all. Taylor, Park & O'Brien, *Unique Coverage Issues in Flood Losses*, 48 Tort & Ins. L.J. 619 (2013). *See, e.g.*, Kean, Miller, Hawthorne, D'Armond McCowan & Jarman, L.L.P. v. Nat'l Fire Ins. Co., 2007 U.S. Dist. LEXIS 64849 (M.D. La. Aug. 2, 2007) (advisories and recommendations did not actually prohibit access to insured premises, but merely recommended or encouraged residents to remain off streets if possible and insured did not offer any evidence that its employees, or any other residents, were specifically prohibited from driving on streets and/or traveling to and entering its business premises); St. Paul Mercury Ins. Co. v. Magnolia Lady, Inc., 1999 U.S. Dist. LEXIS 17895 (N.D. Miss. Nov. 4, 1999) (no coverage where authorities closed bridge for repair, but there was no denial of access to insured property and business continued operating and accepting customers); 54th St. Ltd. Partners, L.P. v. Fid. & Guar. Ins. Co., 306 A.D.2d 67, 763 N.Y.S.2d 243 (2003) (civil authority coverage limited to loss of income while access to premises was barred, not when subsequently traffic in area was diverted and access was not denied).

131. ISO Form CP 00 30 10 12.A, § 5.a.(1).

132. Typically, under a "Dependent Locations" clause, coverage is extended to losses incurred during a "restoration period" when the insured business is interrupted by direct physical loss or damage, caused by a covered peril, to property at a dependent location that is described on a schedule. *See, e.g.*, Evanston Ins. Co. v. Amspec Holding Corp., 2020 U.S. Dist. LEXIS 193902 (S.D. Tex. Oct. 20, 2020).

133. ISO Form CP 00 30 10 12.A, § 5.a.(2).

134. Dickie Brennan & Co. v. Lexington Ins. Co., 636 F.3d 683, 684 (5th Cir. 2011) (evidence failed to demonstrate required nexus between evacuation order and damage to property "other than at the described premises").

135. Kelaher, Connell & Conner, P.C. v. Auto-Owners Ins. Co., 440 F. Supp. 3d 520 (D.S.C. 2020). *See also* Evanston Ins. Co. v. Amspec Holding Corp., 2020 U.S. Dist. LEXIS 193902

not universal, view.[136] In a case out of the Southern District of New York where the policy provided coverage for the actual loss of business income when access to the premises was prohibited by order of a civil authority as the direct result of a covered cause of loss to property in the immediate area, the court said in *dicta* that the insured could seek to recover lost business income resulting from an initial evacuation order because it was preemptive and based on the risk of future flood damage and power outages.[137] It is possible that the extension of an evacuation order after a hurricane has struck and caused property damage may provide the required nexus for coverage.[138]

Where the insured can show a connection between property damage and the action of a civil authority, there will be coverage. For instance, a county government issued an evacuation order. The county attorney said that the fact that an approaching storm had been causing damage as it moved toward the county was the reason for the order. The insured closed its business in response to the order, and the insurer rejected a claim for coverage because it said the evacuation order had been issued because of the *threat* of property damage, not because of actual property damage as required by the policy. The appellate court, however, found that the insured had presented evidence that actual damage to property other than the insured premises had been a basis for the evacuation order.[139] A Texas federal court distinguished that decision. It said that where the "only relevance of prior damage to other property in

---

(S.D. Tex. Oct. 20, 2020) (finding no business interruption coverage where there was no evidence that hurricane damaged any property before Coast Guard began issuing precautionary port closures orders that resulted in loss of business for insured).

136. *See, e.g.*, Dickie Brennan & Co., Inc. v. Lexington Insurance Co., 636 F.3d 683, 684 (5th Cir. 2011) (where no nexus was shown between evacuation order and damage to property, other than at insured premises, trial court properly granted summary judgment for insurer); Jones, Walker, Waechter, Poitevent, Carrere & Denegre, LLP v. Chubb Corp., 2010 U.S. Dist. LEXIS 109055 (E.D. La. Oct. 12, 2010) (policy did not insure against impairment of operations that occurred simply because civil authority prohibited access unless there was nexus between order and certain physical damage; direct nexus between damage sustained and order that policy requires suggested that policy was designed to address situation in which damage occurs and civil authority subsequently prohibits access).

137. Bamundo, Zwal & Schermerhorn, LLP v. Sentinel Ins. Co., Ltd., 2015 U.S. Dist. LEXIS 39409 (S.D.N.Y. Mar. 27, 2015). The court noted, however, that any claim for damages incurred between the initial order on October 28 and a subsequent one on October 31 would fail because the policy provided that coverage under the Civil Authority provision would begin 72 hours after the order of a civil authority.

138. Jones v. Chubb Corp., 2010 U.S. Dist. LEXIS 109055 (E.D. La. Oct. 12, 2010) (initial evacuation order did not trigger coverage because although it prohibited access, it did not do so based on property damage; however, order extending mandatory evacuation was arguably one that could trigger civil authority coverage because it prohibited access to premises and did so in light of damage sustained throughout city).

139. Assurance Co. of America v. BBB Service Co., Inc., 265 Ga. App. 35, 593 S.E.2d 7 (2003). The damage mentioned in the case was on islands, including in the Bahamas, and to the south of Florida. Thus, it would appear that if a hurricane damages property far away from the insured premises, there may be coverage unless the policy prescribes that the "other property"

deciding whether to issue a civil authority order that would preclude access to the insured's property is to provide a basis for fearing future damage to the area where the insured property is located, the causal link between the prior damage and the civil authority order is missing."[140] Thus, the business interruption losses suffered by the insured were not covered by its policy when a mandatory evacuation order was issued for the Texas county in which the insured property was located because of the anticipated threat of damage to that county, and not because of property damage that had occurred in Florida and the Gulf of Mexico, which the official who issued the order took into account.[141]

Under the ISO policy, the civil authority coverage for business income begins 72 hours after the time of the first action of the civil authority that prohibits access to the described premises and applies for up to four consecutive weeks from the date on which the coverage began.[142]

The action of the civil authority has to be taken in response to dangerous physical conditions that result from the damage of a *covered cause of loss*. For example, the mayor of New York City, in anticipation of the landfall of Superstorm Sandy and the expected heavy flooding and power outages, issued an evacuation order for the area in which the insured had its offices. After the storm hit and there was significant flooding, the mayor continued the order for approximately two months, prohibiting the insured from reoccupying its office even though the property did not itself suffer any flood damage. The court found that there was no business interruption coverage because it was clear that flooding directly caused the mayor to issue the evacuation orders

---

be near or adjacent to the insured premises. Note that the ISO policy requires the damage to be within one mile of the insured premises.

140. S. Tex. Med. Clinics, P.A. v. CNA Fin. Corp., 2008 U.S. Dist. LEXIS 11460, at *31 (S.D. Tex. Feb. 15, 2008). *See also* Dickie Brennan & Co. v. Lexington Ins. Co., 636 F.3d 683, 684 (5th Cir. 2011) (where evacuation order by Louisiana officials did not refer to any property damage and nothing in record, including order itself, showed issuance of order was "due to" physical damage to property, either distant property in Caribbean or property in Louisiana, insureds failed to demonstrate nexus between any prior property damage and evacuation order).

141. The order requiring evacuation was issued by an official who said he feared that the hurricane would strike nearby. That fear was based in part on the fact it had previously damaged property thousands of miles to the east as it crossed Florida and entered the Gulf of Mexico. However, the order was not issued "due to" actual physical damage that occurred in Florida and on oil rigs in the Gulf. Although official stated in his affidavit that his decision to order a mandatory evacuation was due in part to the fact that the hurricane had already damaged that property, his affidavit made clear that the damage in Florida and in the Gulf was relevant only as a basis for anticipating the harm that could result if the hurricane made landfall near the county over which he had jurisdiction.

142. ISO Form CP 00 30 10 12, § A.5.a.

and "covered cause of loss" was defined in the policy to exclude loss due to flooding.[143]

A flood can set in motion events leading a civil authority to close a business. For example, in a Pennsylvania decision, flood waters broke and destroyed municipal water mains, leaving the city defenseless against fire for several days. The mayor declared a state of emergency and ordered all stores to close because of the serious fire danger and, as a result of the prohibition, the plaintiff insured had no access to its business premises for four days. It sought business interruption coverage under a policy that insured against the risks of fire and lightning. The court found that there was no coverage because the loss was not caused by a fire. The policy did not cover "prohibition of access because of apprehension of either the possibility or probability of a fire which never occurred."[144] The policy did not insure against flood loss, but if it had, would there have been business interruption coverage? The New York case discussed previously suggests there might have been, while under the holding of the Pennsylvania court the answer would be no.

[b] Alterations and New Buildings

The ISO policy provides that the insurer will pay for the actual loss of business income sustained by the insured because of direct physical loss or damage at the described premises caused by or resulting from any covered cause of loss to new buildings or structures, whether complete or under construction, alterations or additions to existing buildings or structures, and machinery, equipment, supplies, or building materials located on or within 100 feet of the described premises and used in the construction, alterations, or additions or incidental to the occupancy of new buildings.[145] If the direct physical loss or damage postpones the start of operations,[146] the "period of restoration" for business income coverage begins on the date operations would have begun had the direct physical loss or damage not occurred.

---

143. Bamundo, Zwal & Schermerhorn, LLP v. Sentinel Ins. Co., Ltd., 2015 U.S. Dist. LEXIS 39409 (S.D.N.Y. Mar. 27, 2015).

144. Cleland Simpson Co. v. Firemen's Ins. Co., 11 Pa. D. & C.2d 607 (1957), *aff'd*, 392 Pa. 67, 140 A.2d 41 (1958). *Compare* Narricot Indus. v. Fireman's Fund Ins. Co., 2002 U.S. Dist. LEXIS 19074 (E.D. Pa. Sept. 30, 2002) (while town suspended industry to ration drinking water made limited by flooding and to stop industrial waste from overwhelming flooded waste water treatment plant, those measures were not "preventative" as they did not prevent a covered cause of loss, i.e., a hurricane or flood; regardless of whether town took those measures to prevent hurricane and flood damage or alleviate perils caused by hurricane and flood damage, measures still resulted from hurricane and flood).

145. ISO Form CP 00 30 10 12, § A.5.b.

146. "Operations" is defined as the business activities of the insured that occur at the described premises *and* the "tenantability" of the described premises, if coverage included rental value. ISO Form CP 00 30 10 12, § F.2.

[c] Extended Business Income

Under the ISO policy, if the necessary suspension of the insured's operations produces a business income loss payable under the policy, the insurer will pay for the actual loss of business income incurred beginning on the date property (except "finished stock")[147] is actually repaired, rebuilt, or replaced and operations are resumed and ending the earlier of the date the insured could restore its operations, with speed, to the level that would generate the business income amount that would have existed if no direct physical loss or damage had occurred or 60 consecutive days after the beginning date.[148] This extended business income coverage, however, does not apply to loss of business income incurred as a result of unfavorable business conditions caused by the effect of the covered cause of loss in the area where the described premises are located. Loss of business income has to be caused by direct physical loss or damage at the described premises caused by or resulting from any covered cause of loss.

When the necessary suspension of the insured's operations produces a rental value loss payable under the policy, the insurer will pay for the actual loss of rental value incurred beginning on the date property is actually repaired, rebuilt, or replaced and tenantability is restored and ending on the earlier of the date the insured could restore tenant occupancy, with reasonable speed, to the level that would generate the rental value that would have existed if no direct physical loss or damage had occurred or 60 consecutive days after the beginning date.[149] Extended business income coverage, however, does not apply to loss of rental value incurred as a result of unfavorable business conditions caused by the effect of the covered cause of loss in the area where the described premises are located. Loss of rental value has to be caused by direct physical loss or damage at the described premises caused by or resulting from any covered cause of loss.

[d] Utility Services

Business interruption losses are often caused by the loss of utility services, but policies usually do not cover those losses.[150] The coverage may be added

---

147. The term "finished stock" is defined as stock the insured has manufactured and includes whiskey and alcoholic products being aged, unless there is a coinsurance percentage shown for business income in the Declarations, but does not include stock the insured has manufactured that is held for sale on the premises of any retail outlet insured under the policy. ISO Form CP 00 30 10 12, § F.1.

148. ISO Form CP 00 30 10 12, § A.5.c.(1).

149. ISO Form CP 00 30 10 12, § A.5.c.(2).

150. 5 Jeffrey E. Thomas, *New Appleman on Insurance Law Library Edition* § 46.05[1][d] (LexisNexis 2020). *See, e.g.*, Cincinnati Ins. Co. v. Washer & Refrigeration Supply Co., 2008 U.S. Dist. LEXIS 112464 (D. Ala. Aug. 8, 2008) (special exclusion applicable to business income coverage for any loss caused directly or indirectly by failure of power or other utility service

by endorsement. The language of these endorsements can vary greatly,[151] so they have to be carefully examined to determine the extent of coverage. For example, is the coverage limited to losses that result from damage or destruction of utility equipment within a certain distance of the insured property? What utility services are encompassed: electric, gas, water, telephone?

A standard ISO endorsement intended to modify the ISO Business Income (and Extra Expense) Coverage Form says that the business income coverage is extended to apply to a suspension of operations at the described premises that is caused by an interruption in utility service to it provided that the interruption results from direct physical loss or damage[152] by a covered cause of loss to specified utility properties.[153] The endorsement includes a schedule that indicates which utility services are included. These may include water supply including pumping stations and water mains, wastewater removal, communication supply including telephone, radio, microwave or television services and power supply including electricity, steam or gas and their utility generating plants, switching stations, substations, transformers, and transmission lines.[154]

Because the coverage only applies to interruption in utility service that results from direct physical loss or damage by a *covered cause of loss*, the utility service endorsement can be nullified by a flood exclusion.[155] For example, a New York law firm sought business interruption coverage after it lost power for a prolonged period after Superstorm Sandy. However, the policy had the typical water damage exclusion that includes flood and, said the court, water caused "direct physical loss or damage" to the utility network and that was

---

supplied to described premises). *See also* Bonner, *Utility Interruption Coverage* (May 20, 2019), The Balance, https://www.thebalancesmb.com/utility-interruption-coverage-462359.

151. *See Utility Service Interruption Coverage*, IRMI, https://www.irmi.com/term/insurance-definitions/utility-service-interruption-coverage.

152. In a post-Superstorm Sandy case, an insurer argued that because the electric utility preemptively shut down service before the storm, there was no direct physical loss or damage to electrical service. The court, however, noted that the storm did cause direct physical damage to the utility company property and, therefore, the insurer was only entitled to summary judgment regarding the time between the preemptive shutdown and the arrival of the storm and its invading flood tide. Johnson Gallagher Magliery, LLC v. Charter Oak Fire Ins. Co., 2014 U.S. Dist. LEXIS 35548 (S.D.N.Y. Mar. 18, 2014).

153. ISO Form CP 15 45 09 17, § A.

154. ISO Form CP 15 45 09 17, § E.

155. *See, e.g.*, Protection Mutual Ins. Co. v. Mitsubishi Silicon Am. Corp., 164 Ore. App. 385, 992 P.2d 479 (1999), *rev. den.*, 330 Ore. 331, 6 P.3d 1100 (2000), where the court found that the policy did not cover business interruption caused when a utility service was halted or was not useable because of flooding at the *utility site*. An endorsement eliminated the flood exclusion in the main policy and in effect added coverage for physical damage to the covered property. It covered property damage and loss caused by flood, not interruption in the insured's business operations.

an excluded cause of loss.[156] The exclusion may also be found in the endorsement itself.[157]

[e] Contingent Business Interruption Coverage[158]

Contingent business interruption insurance is relatively new and, therefore, there is not a great deal of case law interpreting it.[159] This coverage may also be called "Dependent Business Premises" insurance.[160] It protects against losses caused by the inability of a "supplier"[161] or a customer to do business with the policyholder because of physical loss or damage at the property of that supplier or customer.[162] Another version of the coverage applies when a neighboring business is needed to attract customer traffic to the insured business, for example an anchor store in a shopping center or mall.[163] A "contributing property" is one presently in operation or production and adding to the business of the insured when the loss occurs, and depending on the language of the policy may include property of the insured.[164]

---

156. Johnson Gallagher Magliery, LLC v. Charter Oak Fire Ins. Co., 2014 U.S. Dist. LEXIS 35548 (S.D.N.Y. Mar. 18, 2014). *See also* La Casa Di Arturo, Inc. v. Tower Group, Inc., 26 N.Y.S.3d 725 (2015).

157. *See, e.g.*, Protection Mutual Ins. Co. v. Mitsubishi Silicon America Corp., 164 Ore. App. 385, 992 P.2d 479 (1999), *rev. den.*, 330 Ore. 331, 6 P.3d 1100 (2000) (Service Interruption Endorsement extended business interruption coverage to losses sustained because of interruption of, *inter alia*, water service; however, where water service was cut off because of flood, flood exclusion in endorsement barred coverage).

158. *See generally* Mascali, *Contingent Business Interruption Coverage*, 41 Tort Trial & Ins. Prac. L.J. 843 (2006).

159. Zurich Am. Ins. Co. v. ABM Indus., Inc., 397 F.3d 158, 168 (2d Cir. 2005). *See also* 5 Jeffrey E. Thomas, *New Appleman on Insurance Law Library Edition* § 46.05[1][e] (LexisNexis 2020) (contingent business interruption insurance can present challenging causation questions when flood damages both insured's property and contingent property).

160. *See, e.g.*, Wms Indus. v. Fed. Ins. Co., 2009 U.S. Dist. LEXIS 68678 (S.D. Miss. Aug. 4, 2009).

161. The policy may not define "supplier." In one case, the court held that the policy language did not limit coverage to those suppliers in direct contractual privity with the insured. Archer-Daniels-Midland Co. v. Phoenix Assur. Co., 936 F. Supp. 534, 544 (S.D. Ill. 1996).

162. French, *Covid-19 Business Interruption Insurance Losses: The Cases For and Against Coverage*, 27 Conn. Ins. L.J. 1, 8–9 (2020). *See generally* Ainslie et al., *Business Insurance Law and Practice Guide* § 16.03 (Matthew Bender 2020); Bowman & Hayden, *A Practical Guide to Evaluating Contingent Business Interruption Losses, New Appleman on Insurance*, Current Critical Issues in Insurance Law 49 (Dec. 2008).

163. Ainslie et al., *Business Insurance Law and Practice Guide* § 16.03[2] (Matthew Bender 2020).

164. Aztar Corp. v. U.S. Fire Ins. Co., 223 Ariz. 463, 475, 224 P.3d 960, 972 (Ariz. App. 2010). In *Aztar* the allegedly "contributing property" was an expansion of the existing business that collapsed before completion. The court said that the collapsed expansion was never completed and was, therefore, not "contributing." There is a question of whether a property that is to become a part of the insured business is "contributing" as that term is generally used in policies. However, the policy at issue referred to "contributing or recipient properties" of the insured.

Typically, the coverage requires physical damage to the contingent property that is caused by a peril covered by the policy.[165] There is, however, a great deal of variety in the wording of contingent business interruption coverage. A provision may state that the insurer will pay for the actual loss of business income the insured sustains because of physical loss or damage at the premises of a "dependent property" or "secondary dependent property" caused by or resulting from any covered cause of loss.[166] Some language limits coverage to loss of income arising from damage to scheduled properties, while other covers losses that arise from damage to the property of "suppliers" or "customers," terms that may or may not be defined.[167] Generally, there is no requirement that there be a total shutdown at the contingent property.[168]

[f] Loss of Ingress or Egress[169]

Some polices may specifically provide coverage for loss of ingress or egress. For example, in one case the policy covered a "loss sustained during the period of time when, as a direct result of a peril not excluded, ingress to or egress from real and personal property not excluded hereunder, is thereby prevented."[170] The insured business manufactured boats at its facility in eastern North Carolina. It was struck by Hurricane Floyd. The storm dumped heavy, record-setting rainfall. The only roads leading to the insured property were flooded for days. Because of the poor road conditions, production at the insured facility fell to 33 percent of full capacity. The insured sought coverage under the provision for loss of ingress or egress. The insurer denied the claim because it contended only physical loss or damage could trigger coverage. The court did not agree. The policy, it said, was exceedingly clear: a loss sustained because of the inability to access the facility was a covered event without physical damage to the property. Flooding because of a hurricane was "exactly the type of peril this business interruption loss was drafted to insure against."

---

165. 5 Jeffrey E. Thomas, *New Appleman on Insurance Law Library Edition* § 46.05[1][b] (LexisNexis 2020). *See also* Ainslie et al., *Business Insurance Law and Practice Guide* § 16.03[2] (Matthew Bender 2020) (business interruption loss occurs when there is damage or destruction of real or personal property, covered by peril insured against in direct damage policy form, during policy term, on premises described in policy itself and not operated by insured, that wholly or partially prevents delivery of materials to insured or to others for account of insured, resulting directly in interruption of insured's business).

166. French, *Covid-19 Business Interruption Insurance Losses: The Cases for and Against Coverage*, 27 Conn. Ins. L.J. 1, 8–9 (2020).

167. 5 Jeffrey E. Thomas, *New Appleman on Insurance Law Library Edition* § 46.05[1][b] (LexisNexis 2020).

168. Ainslie et al., *Business Insurance Law and Practice Guide* § 16.03[2] (Matthew Bender 2020).

169. *See generally* Schirle, *Civil Authority and Ingress/Egress Coverage Claiming Lost Income after Hurricanes and Other Catastrophic Events*, 47 The Brief 61 (2018).

170. Fountain Powerboat Indus. v. Reliance Ins. Co., 119 F. Supp. 2d 552, 556 (E.D.N.C. 2000).

Some policies contain a loss of ingress or egress clause that specifically does not require physical loss or damage to the insured premises[171] but requires physical loss or damage to some other property. For example, one policy provided that it covered "Actual Loss Sustained . . . by the insured due to the necessary interruption of the Insured's business due to the prevention of ingress to or egress from an Insured Location, whether or not the premises or property of the Insured is damaged, provided that such prevention is a direct result of physical damage of the type insured by this Policy, to the kind of property not excluded by this Policy."[172]

[7] Limits of Insurance

[a] Generally

The ISO Business Income (and Extra Expense) Coverage Form states that the most the insurer will pay for loss in any one occurrence is the applicable Limit of Insurance shown in the Declarations.[173] Payments under coverage for alterations and new buildings, civil authority, extra expense, or extended business income will not increase the applicable Limit of Insurance.

[b] Sublimits

Policies may have a sublimit that applies to flood losses. Sublimits are often found in complex commercial property policies that have many coverages and endorsements. Application of the sublimit can be unclear. For example, the policy may not specifically state whether a sublimit applies to a business interruption loss as well as property damage.[174]

The sublimit may have layers. For example, one policy had a $250 million annual aggregate for flood losses but a $50,000 annual aggregate for certain identified coverages, for instance, Off-Premises Service Interruption.[175] Sublimits can vary a great deal, and the policy language needs to be examined carefully to determine the applicable limit of coverage. For example, in a case after Superstorm Sandy, the parties disputed whether a $25 million sublimit for flood applied to "time element"—meaning business interruption—losses.

---

171. *See generally* 5 Jeffrey E. Thomas, *New Appleman on Insurance Law Library Edition* § 46.05[3][c] (LexisNexis 2020).

172. County of Clark v. Factory Mut. Ins. Co., 2005 U.S. Dist. LEXIS 47574, at *7–8 (D. Nev. Mar. 28, 2005). *See also* Newman Myers Kreines Gross, P.C. v. Great Northern Ins. Co., 17 F. Supp. 3d 323, 329 (S.D.N.Y. 2014) (coverage for business income loss because of impairment of business operations when existing ingress to or egress from premises is prevented by direct physical loss or damage by a covered peril to property at location *contiguous* to premises).

173. ISO Form CP 00 30 10 12, § B.

174. *See, e.g.*, Penford Corp. v. Nat'l Union Fire Ins. Co., 2010 U.S. Dist. LEXIS 3737 (N.D. Iowa Jan. 19, 2010).

175. David S. Brown Enters. v. Affiliated FM Ins. Co., 2020 U.S. Dist. LEXIS 239208 (D. Md. Dec. 18, 2020).

The court found that while different sublimits applied to other types of losses, the $25 million flood sublimit applied to both physical damage and time element losses.[176] In other cases, a sublimit may only apply to the property portion of the coverage.[177]

It is important to determine whether a flood sublimit in a property policy to which business interruption is added by endorsement also applies to the business interruption coverage. For example, in a New York case, a $250 million flood limit in a commercial property policy was found to apply to property damage but not to a business interruption loss covered under an endorsement.[178] In a Texas case, an insured premises was flooded when sewage overflowed floor drains. The policy had the usual exclusion for loss from water that backs up or overflows from a sewer or drain. An endorsement added business interruption coverage with a sublimit for sewer backup. The court agreed with the insurer that the endorsement superseded the exclusion for sewer and drain backups found in the main policy but provided for limited recovery for those events.[179]

Two cases decided by the Eighth Circuit demonstrate how critical the specific policy language is to the outcome. In the first case, the policy had an endorsement adding flood coverage with a $5 million sublimit. It also had an "All Other Perils (AOP) Sublimit" of $38 million. The court agreed with the policyholder that the sublimit in the flood endorsement applied only to direct property damage[180] and that once flood was no longer an excluded cause of loss, the AOP sublimit applied to flood just as it did to any other cause of loss. The court noted that the flood endorsement did not mention business interruption coverage and concluded that at best, the policy was ambiguous on the question of business interruption losses caused by a flood and had to be construed against the insurer.[181] In a subsequent case, the same court reached a different conclusion.[182] In that case a hospital parking lot was flooded, and the state health department ordered the hospital to evacuate its patients. The

176. Almah LLC v. Lexington Ins. Co., 2016 Del. Super. LEXIS 47 (Jan. 27, 2016).

177. *See, e.g.*, Dream Spa, Inc. v. Fireman's Fund Ins., 2008 U.S. Dist. LEXIS 8933 (S.D.N.Y. Feb. 6, 2008).

178. Victory Container Corp. v. Sphere Ins. Co., 448 F. Supp. 1043 (S.D.N.Y. 1978). *Compare* New York Univ. v. Factory Mut. Ins. Co., 374 F. Supp. 3d 315 (S.D.N.Y. 2019) (where recovery for time element loss was governed by applicable limit of liability that applied to insured physical loss or damage, time element claims were subject to limit of liability for flood, as well as its sublimit).

179. For Kids Only Child Dev. Ctr., Inc. v. Phila. Indem. Ins. Co., 260 S.W.3d 652 (Tex. App. 2008).

180. *See also* Alley Theatre v. Hanover Ins. Co., 436 F. Supp. 3d 938, 948 (S.D. Tex. 2020) ($3 million Flood Endorsement Limit did not apply to lost-business income that resulted from flood damage and instead, $5 million Income Coverage Limit applied).

181. Mark Andy, Inc. v. Hartford Fire Ins. Co., 233 F.3d 1090 (8th Cir. 2000).

182. Altru Health System v. American Protection Insurance Co., 238 F.3d 961 (8th Cir. 2001).

hospital submitted a claim to its insurer for damage to the parking lot and for business interruption. The insurer contended its liability was reduced by the flood sublimit of $1.5 million. The hospital countered that the sublimit did not apply to its business interruption claim. The court noted that the policy provided that all liability for loss or expense for any one occurrence would not exceed the smallest of any applicable sublimit. The $1.5 million sublimit was found in an endorsement to the policy that added the flood coverage. Therefore, it was "any applicable sublimit" and applied to the entire claim, including the one for business interruption. Additionally, the policy stated that all claims for loss, damage, or expense arising out of any one flood occurrence had to be adjusted as one claim. The business interruption losses and property damage arose out of the flood and had to be adjusted as one claim, all subject to the sublimit.

What the cases illustrate is that the specific policy language is paramount.[183] Counsel for a policyholder has to examine it through a microscope.

[c] The Meaning of "Occurrence"

Whatever limit applies, it is the maximum amount the insurer will pay for "any one occurrence." The meaning of the word "occurrence" is, therefore, potentially critical to the amount the insured can recover. The term is one that has been subject to much discussion and judicial interpretation. One law dictionary defines "occurrence" as simply a "happening; an event."[184] Another is more specific and says that it is "any event that gives rise to liability for the assured under an insurance contract. The occurrence includes all of the logically related actions and events that result from the initial occurrence, as well as the damages that result."[185]

[8] Loss Conditions

[a] Appraisal

The ISO Business Income (and Extra Expense) Coverage Form provides that if the insurer and insured disagree on the amount of net income and operating expense or the amount of loss, either one may make written demand for an appraisal of the loss.[186] The policy then outlines the usual procedure found

183. *See, e.g.*, Penford Corp. v. Nat'l Union Fire Ins. Co., 2010 U.S. Dist. LEXIS 3737 (N.D. Iowa Jan. 19, 2010), finding that the policy before it was somewhere between that considered in *Altru* and *Mark Andy*. It did not, as in *Altru*, clearly subject all loss from flood to a single sublimit. However, said the court, the policy in *Mark Andy* did not contain language like that of the limits provision in the case before it. The court decided extrinsic evidence would be required to determine the intent of the parties and that interpretation of the policy in light of that evidence was a question of fact reserved for a jury.

184. *Ballentine's Law Dictionary* (2010).

185. *The Wolters Kluwer Bouvier Law Dictionary Desk Edition* (2012).

186. ISO Form CP 00 30 10 12, § C.1.

in standard commercial property policies. Each party selects a competent and impartial appraiser who in turn selects an umpire or, if they cannot agree, either one may request that the umpire be selected by a judge. The appraisers state separately the amount of net income and operating expense or amount of loss and, if they fail to agree, they submit their differences to the umpire. A decision agreed to by any two is binding. Each party pays its chosen appraiser and bears the other expenses of the appraisal and umpire equally. The insurer retains the right to deny the claim if there is an appraisal.

[b] Duties in the Event of Loss

The duties of the insured in the case of a loss are generally those found in commercial property policies. For example, the insured has to:

- Notify the police if a law may have been broken.
- Give the insurer prompt notice of the direct physical loss or damage including a description of the property involved.
- As soon as possible, give the insurer a description of how, when, and where the direct physical loss or damage occurred.
- Take all reasonable steps to protect the covered property from further damage,[187] and keep a record of the expenses required to protect that property, for consideration in the settlement of the claim, and if feasible, set the damaged property aside and in the best possible order for examination.[188]
- Allow the insurer to inspect the property proving the loss or damage and to examine the books and records of the insured as often as may be reasonably required; allow the insurer to take samples of damaged and undamaged property for inspection, testing, and analysis; and permit the insurer to make copies from the insured's books and records.
- Submit a signed, sworn proof of loss containing the information request by the insurer to investigate the claim within 60 days after the request of the insurer.[189]

---

187. Insureds have a general obligation to mitigate their losses. Expenditures in mitigation of damages have to be made in the reasonable expectation of reducing the recovery below the amount of the loss and expenditures that result in an increase in the loss cannot be justified. Howard v. Foremost Ins. Co., 82 A.D.2d 398, 441 N.Y.S.2d 674 (1981), *aff'd*, 453 N.Y.S.2d 682, 439 N.E.2d 397 (1982).

188. The policy says this will not increase the limit of insurance, but that the insurer will not pay for any subsequent loss or damage resulting from a cause of loss that is not a covered cause of loss.

189. The timeliness of the proof of loss may be affected by the nature of the business. For example, in one case, documentation for a business interruption loss could not be supplied until after the time period provided under the contract had expired because of the nature of the business. The proof of loss was submitted almost one year after a sump pump burned out, causing water to back up into portions of the lower level of the insured property. A company representative was on the premises within one day of the flood and witnessed the inability to

- Cooperate with the insurer in the investigation or settlement of the claim.[190]

An additional requirement is that if the insured intends to continue its business, it has to resume all or part of its operations as "quickly as possible."[191]

As is the case in almost every commercial property policy, the insurer reserves the right to examine any insured under oath, while not in the presence of any other insured and at times that may be reasonably required, about any matter relating to the insurance or the claim, including the books and records of the insured.[192]

[c] Amount of Loss[193]

[i] Generally

The most important thing to know about loss valuation for business interruption coverage is that the judicial decisions about how business interruption losses should be valued are not consistent.[194] Counsel for policyholders litigating claims have to prepare thoroughly and carefully research the precedents in their jurisdiction. Policy language has to be scrutinized, as small differences in wording can render those precedents unavailing and the policy more or less favorable to the insured.

Some business interruption coverage is "valued," which means the parties have agreed on the value of the loss in advance; however, most policies require proof of the actual loss of business the insured has sustained.[195] The burden, then, is on the insured to establish the extent of the damage caused by an interruption and the applicability of the policy.[196] It can be important, therefore, to retain a forensic accountant to prepare an independent review of the loss, evaluate the claim, and assess relevant business factors.[197] The assistance of an expert is particularly important when records are missing.

---

conduct business for a time. That placed the insurer on constructive notice that the business was not operational for a period of time following the flood. The court concluded that was enough to raise a material issue of fact about the absence of prejudice to the insurer by the late proof of loss sufficient to defeat its motion for summary judgment. International Design Center v. Federal Ins. Co., 1992 Conn. Super. LEXIS 2106 (July 10, 1992).

190. ISO Form CP 00 30 10 12, § C.2.a.

191. ISO Form CP 00 30 10 12, § C.2.a.(8).

192. ISO Form CP 00 30 10 12, § C.2.b.

193. *See generally* 5 Jeffrey E. Thomas, *New Appleman on Insurance Law Library Edition* §46.08 (LexisNexis 2020).

194. French, *The Aftermath of Catastrophes: Valuing Business Interruption Insurance Losses*, 30 Ga. St. U.L. Rev. 461, 473 (2014).

195. Cot, *Insurance Coverage for Business Interruption Claims in the Aftermath of Hurricanes Katrina and Rita*, 53 LA Bar J. 368, 369 (2006).

196. Howard v. Foremost Ins. Co., 82 A.D.2d 398, 401, 441 N.Y.S.2d 674, 676 (1981), *aff'd*, 453 N.Y.S.2d 682, 439 N.E.2d 397 (1982).

197. Mohn, *Determining Business Interruption Losses after Hurricane Harvey* (Aug. 30, 2017), Property Casualty 360, http://www.propertycasualty360.com/2017/08/30/determining

The ISO policy sets forth the method by which the amount of the business income loss will be determined.[198] The determination is based on:

- The net income of the business before the direct physical loss or damage occurred;[199]
- The likely net income if no physical loss or damage had occurred, but not including any net income that would likely have been earned as a result of an increase in the volume of business because of favorable business conditions caused by the effect of the covered cause of loss on customers or on other businesses;
- The operating expenses, including payroll expenses, required to resume operations with the same quality of service that existed just before the direct physical loss or damage; and
- Other relevant sources of information, including the insured's financial records and accounting procedures, bills, invoices and other vouchers, and deeds, liens, or contracts.[200]

Business income includes "continuing normal operating expenses incurred." Some expenses will continue, and others will diminish after a loss.[201] As one commentary notes, if a retail store loses sales when its business is interrupted, "non-continuing" expenses could include the cost of purchasing the goods, any sales commissions, and supplies or materials related to sales, for example packaging.[202]

-business-interruption-losses-after-hur?eNL=59a70783160ba0ad15229578&utm_source=PC360_Daily&utm_medium=EMC-Email_editorial&utm_campaign=08302017&page_all=1.

198. ISO Form CP 00 30 10 12.C.3.a. *See generally* Miller & Jean, *Effect of Post-Loss Economic Factors in Measuring Business Interruption Losses: An Insured's and Insurer's Perspectives*, Current Critical Issues in Insurance Law 25 (Winter 2010).

199. *See, e.g.*, Travelers Indem. Co. v. P1 Group, 2020 U.S. Dist. LEXIS 38113 (D. Kan. Mar. 5, 2020) (where burst drain line flooded hospital property and hospital then discharged all patients, insurer calculated business interruption damages by averaging income hospital received on daily basis for prior month and then comparing that to income actually received on first three days after resuming business).

200. Some policies say that due consideration will be given to the experience of the business before the damage or destruction and to the probable experience after it had no loss occurred. One commentary asks why insurers use the phrase "probable experience after it had no loss occurred" if they really mean that only the prior experience of the business should be used to value the loss. It would be simple enough for policies to say that when a loss is valued, "'only the historical performance of the policyholder shall be considered.'" French, *The Aftermath of Catastrophes: Valuing Business Interruption Insurance Losses*, 30 Ga. St. U.L. Rev. 461, 499 (2014).

201. *See* United Land Investors, Inc. v. N. Ins. Co., 476 So. 2d 432 (La. App. 1985) (amount of non-continuing expenses deducted from total earnings).

202. Borghesi, *Business Interruption Insurance: A Business Perspective*, 17 Nova L. Rev. 1147, 1161 (1993).

[ii] Proof of Loss

The burden is on the insured to prove its entitlement to business interruption proceeds under the policy and the amount of those proceeds.[203] The attorney for the insured will need to carefully consider potential evidence of the loss. One commentator identifies the information needed to review the insured's position as revenue or sales documents, expense documents, profit and loss statements, inventory reports, business plans, budgets and/or forecasts, business history, changes and milestone events, and business environment and community factors.[204] For a company that has been growing rapidly, prior sales may not accurately reflect the income that would have been earned had no loss occurred. In that case, business income can be supplemented with market trends.[205]

Unique aspects of a loss—for example, a seasonal business cycle or a new competitor—need to be considered.[206] Suspension of a retailer's business during the holiday season should result in a larger reimbursement from the insurer than a suspension during slower retail months, but the insured has to be able to prove the increase in sales would have occurred, making it all the more important to have yearly records proving the amount of income that would have been earned.[207] In a post-Katrina case, a food service company resumed operations ten days after the storm and was the only company of its kind doing business in the area. It lost sales because many of its customers were not able to resume business but also acquired new business during the period of restoration because of entities that came into the area and because its competitors were unable to resume operations immediately following the storm. The court upheld an award of the net profit that the insured would have earned if the damage to its property had not occurred reduced by the net profit that *was earned* by the resumption of operations.[208]

Business interruption losses can be difficult to prove, but they only need to be proved with reasonable certainty and the proof only needs to be as

203. Dictiomatic, Inc. v. U.S. Fid. & Guar. Co., 958 F. Supp. 594, 603 (S.D. Fla. 1997).

204. Mohn, *Determining Business Interruption Losses after Hurricane Harvey* (Aug. 30, 2017), Property Casualty 360, http://www.propertycasualty360.com/2017/08/30/determining-business-interruption-losses-after-hur?eNL=59a70783160ba0ad15229578&utm_source=PC360_Daily&utm_medium=EMC-Email_editorial&utm_campaign=08302017&page_all=1.

205. Carter & Weiant, *The Ice Storm of 1998: Can Business Interruption Insurance Save Your Bottom Line?*, 24 Ver. B. J. & L. Dig. 37, 38 (1998).

206. Mohn, *Determining Business Interruption Losses after Hurricane Harvey* (Aug. 30, 2017), Property Casualty 360, http://www.propertycasualty360.com/2017/08/30/determining-business-interruption-losses-after-hur?eNL=59a70783160ba0ad15229578&utm_source=PC360_Daily&utm_medium=EMC-Email_editorial&utm_campaign=08302017&page_all=1.

207. Carter & Weiant, *The Ice Storm of 1998: Can Business Interruption Insurance Save Your Bottom Line?*, 24 Ver. B. J. & L. Dig. 37, 38 (1998).

208. Consolidated Cos., Inc. v. Lexington Ins. Co., 2009 U.S. Dist. LEXIS 8542 (E.D. La. Jan. 23, 2009).

precise as circumstances in a particular situation permit.[209] "Broad latitude is given in proving lost profits . . . and mathematical certainty or precision is not required."[210] On the other hand, the loss cannot be merely speculative.[211] Unfortunately, calculating lost profits is almost inherently speculative. That, says one expert observer "has caused the courts some consternation when trying to apply traditional evidentiary standards of proof to such claims."[212] As one commentary says, "Calculating lost income is considerably more conceptual and theoretical than evaluating and determining replacement or repair of damaged property. Business interruption evaluation often involves theoretical calculations that require significant and difficult projections such as a projection of the period of interruption and of the business that would have been conducted during the period of interruption."[213] For example, a store suffered water damage to its goods, and the owner made a business decision to divert merchandise intended for two other stores to replace those damaged goods. After that, the three stores had total sales that were lower than projected. The court said the policy was not intended to include business interruption to the other stores where no physical damage occurred, and in any event any reason asserted for the lower-than-projected sales was pure speculation.[214]

When there is widespread flooding in the area in which a business is located, an insurer may take the position that the insured did not actually suffer any business interruption loss because, as a result of extensive destruction,

209. Dictiomatic, Inc. v. U.S. Fid. & Guar. Co., 958 F. Supp. 594, 605 (S.D. Fla. 1997) (claim for lost profits must be shown with reasonable degree of certainty); Citadel Broad. Corp. v. Axis U.S. Ins. Co., 162 So. 3d 470 (La. App. 2015). *See* Buffman Inc. v. Lafayette Ins. Co., 36 So. 3d 1004 (La. App. 2010), for a case in which an appellate court meticulously examined the evidence of business income loss considered by the jury in the trial court.

210. Malcolm v. Marathon Oil Co., 642 F.2d 845, 864 (5th Cir. 1981) (relaxation of standards of proof particularly appropriate where finder of fact has to estimate lost future profits); Citadel Broad. Corp. v. Axis U.S. Ins. Co., 162 So. 3d 470, 475 (La. App. 2015). *See also* Graphic Prods. Distribs. v. Itek Corp., 717 F.2d 1560 (11th Cir. 1983).

211. Pyramid Techs., Inc. v. Hartford Cas. Ins. Co., 752 F.3d 807, 822 (9th Cir. 2014) (insured failed to show that there were material issues of fact that it actually lost business of potential customer as result of flood; whether customer would have contracted with insured if there was no flood, and for what amount, was too speculative to support claim); Polytech, Inc. v. Affiliated FM Ins. Co., 21 F.3d 271, 276 (8th Cir. 1994) (to obtain award for lost profits under Missouri law, insured has to produce evidence providing adequate basis for estimating lost profits with reasonable certainty and prove actual facts that present basis for rational estimate of damages without resorting to speculation); Am. Med. Imaging Corp. v. St. Paul Fire & Marine Ins. Co., 949 F.2d 690 (3d Cir. 1991) (no rule requires that evidence of lost earnings identify particular customers and hypothetical transactions that would have produced revenues but for covered loss).

212. French, *The Aftermath of Catastrophes: Valuing Business Interruption Insurance Losses*, 30 Ga. St. U.L. Rev. 461, 488 (2014).

213. Bowman & Hayden, *A Practical Guide to Evaluating Contingent Business Interruption Losses, New Appleman on Insurance*, Current Critical Issues in Insurance Law, 49, 50 (December 2008).

214. Howard v. Foremost Ins. Co., 82 A.D.2d 398, 441 N.Y.S.2d 674 (1981).

few customers or clients would have visited the business after the disaster, even if it had not itself been affected.[215]

The cases addressing proof of loss demonstrate that the attorney representing a client seeking lost profits has to carefully research the law of the applicable jurisdiction, employ experts, and be prepared to put forward inventive arguments on the client's behalf.

[iii] Insureds Operating at a Loss[216]

Recovery is made more complicated when the insured is "in the red." The ISO Business Income (and Extra Expense) Coverage Form provides that the insurer will pay for the *actual loss* of business income the insured suffers and defines "business income" to mean net income that would have been earned and continuing normal operating expenses incurred, including payroll.[217] A number of courts have concluded that there can be recovery under business interruption coverage even though a business is operating at a loss.[218] One specific question that arises is whether projected "net income" and "continuing operating expenses" are added together to determine the recoverable loss or are "continuing operating expenses" recoverable regardless of whether the amount of "net income" is positive or negative?[219]

In a California case,[220] an insured premises was flooded when a water heater on the second floor broke. At the time of the incident, the company, which had previously done well, was losing money. It sought coverage for "normal operating expenses" during the period its business operations had

215. French, *The Aftermath of Catastrophes: Valuing Business Interruption Insurance Losses*, 30 Ga. St. U.L. Rev. 461, 464 (2014).

216. *See generally* Miller & Jean, *Effect of Post-Loss Economic Factors in Measuring Business Interruption Losses: An Insured's and Insurer's Perspectives*, Current Critical Issues in Insurance Law 25 (Winter 2010).

217. ISO Form CP 00 30 10 12, § A.1.

218. *See, e.g.*, Cosmetics Plus Group, Ltd. v. Am. Int'l Group, Inc. (*In re* Cosmetics Plus Group, Ltd.), 379 B.R. 464, 470 (S.D.N.Y. 2007) (that net income before loss was negative was not dispositive; it was also necessary to look at what net income would have been if no loss had occurred); Liberty Mut. Ins. Co. v. Sexton Foods Co., 42 Ark. App. 102, 106–07, 854 S.W.2d 365 (1993) (rejecting insurer's argument that recovery is completely barred when insured business is not operating at a profit). *See also* Prudential LMI v. Colleton Enterprises, Inc., 1992 U.S. App. LEXIS 25719 (4th Cir. Oct. 5, 1992), where the insurer argued that it need not indemnify for lost profits because the insured motel had recorded losses during the preceding 32-month period. While the court ultimately denied recovery for lost profits, it rejected the insurer's premise. The court said an insured may rely on evidence that, without regard to what it had been doing, and even if it had been doing badly and losing money, it nevertheless would have earned a profit during the period of interruption had it not occurred. For example, said the court, the insured might show that a general economic upturn for the business had been imminent or that a specific event had created a profit opportunity that had been thwarted.

219. French, *The Aftermath of Catastrophes: Valuing Business Interruption Insurance Losses*, 30 Ga. St. U.L. Rev. 461, 482 (2014).

220. Amerigraphics, Inc. v. Mercury Casualty Co., 182 Cal. App. 4th 1538, 107 Cal. Rptr. 3d 307 (2010).

been interrupted by the flooding. The insurer denied the claim, noting that during the loss period the insured had an actual operating loss that was less than its projected operating loss. The insured pointed to the policy language under which "business income" meant net income *and* continuing normal operating expenses. The court agreed with the insured that the conjunction "and" in that definition meant that the insurer would pay an insured for any lost income and would also pay its continuing normal business expenses during the period of business suspension. To the extent there is no lost income, said the court, the amount paid for lost income would be zero, but the insured could still be paid for its operating expenses. Thus, the insured was allowed to recover continuing fixed expenses even though it would have had a loss if its business operations had not been interrupted.[221] On the other hand, the Tennessee Supreme Court has said that:

> [the] amount of "business income" under the insurance policy . . . should be determined by adding the amount of "net income" and the amount of "continuing normal operating expenses" [and] if "net income" is a positive number (which will occur whenever there are net profits), the amount of "business income" will be the sum of two positive numbers, and the insured will be entitled to recover that amount. If, however, "net income" is a negative number (which will occur whenever there is a net loss), the amount of "business income" will be the amount of "continuing normal operating expenses" reduced by the amount of the net loss [and if] the amount of the net loss that would have been incurred had there been no business interruption exceeds the amount of normal operating expenses actually incurred, the resulting number is a negative number, and there can be no recovery for an "actual loss of business income."[222]

221. The court said that there is nothing in the policy language to suggest that if a business is not earning a profit, it should not expect coverage for its continuing expenses during the period that it cannot operate. *See also* Koken v. Lexington Ins. Co., 2006 U.S. Dist. LEXIS 9198 (E.D. Pa. Feb. 1, 2006). In *Koken*, the insured was in financial distress at the time of the September 11 terrorist attack. The premises of the insured were subject to an evacuation order. The insured sought to collect for continuing payroll expenses during its closure. The insurer argued that the insured suffered no actual loss because it experienced no reduction of *net profit* earned during the interruption period. The court interpreted the phrase in the policy "net profit which is thereby prevented from being earned" to mean revenue the insured was earning minus operating expenses. It noted that the insured would only be prevented from *earning* positive revenue. The insured could recover, therefore, *necessary* payroll expenses. If, because of the insolvency of the insured, the policy were construed to avoid coverage for those expenses, the insured would have to pay its ordinary payroll expenses during the business interruption without receiving any accompanying benefit of the reasonable value of the services of its employees. *See also* United Land Investors, Inc. v. N. Ins. Co., 476 So. 2d 432 (La. App. 1985) (finding business had not "earned" all its operating expenses because it had operated at a loss and loss was therefore properly deducted from amount of total operating expenses to determine "earnings").

222. Continental Ins. Co. v. DNE Corp., 834 S.W.2d 930, 934–35 (Tenn. 1992). *See also* Island Concepts, LLC v. Certain Underwriters at Lloyd's, 2014 U.S. Dist. LEXIS 155494 (E.D.

The California case discussed previously noted that it is not unusual for business income to fluctuate from year to year. The court said a business should not have to worry that if it does poorly for a year or two, it will not be paid anything under its "business income" coverage if it has a covered catastrophic loss when its business is down.[223] One commentary argues that under the policy interpretation of the Tennessee court, "an insurer may be engaging in a form of fraud by selling business interruption insurance to a policyholder whose business is operating at a loss. If the policy does not cover the continuing operating expenses of a business that is losing money when its operations are interrupted by a covered loss, then what value does the policyholder receive in exchange for the premium it pays for business interruption coverage?"[224]

What if a business is closing and will, therefore, have no future earnings? In a New York case in which the insured was going out of business, there were not demonstrable probable future earnings, and the court therefore ruled that there could be no recovery for business interruption losses beyond the conclusion of the going out of business sale.[225]

As always, despite the holdings of courts on the question of recovery when an insured is losing money before a business interruption, the specific language of the policy at issue can render any precedents inapplicable.

[iv] Increased Revenues after a Flood[226]

It is possible that a business might both be damaged by a flood and experience increased consumer demand as a result of it. For example, a hardware store in a flooded area might see demand increase as homeowners and other businesses make repairs. How that will affect the store's business interruption coverage depends on the policy language and the interpretations courts give it.[227] In one post-Katrina case, the insured's business income for its period of

---

La. Oct. 31, 2014); Dictiomatic, Inc. v. U.S. Fid. & Guar. Co., 958 F. Supp. 594, 605 (S.D. Fla. 1997) (if amount of net loss that would have been incurred had there been no business interruption exceeds amount of normal operating expenses actually incurred, resulting number is negative number and there can be no recovery for "actual loss" of business income); Liberty Mut. Ins. Co. v. Sexton Foods Co., 42 Ark. App. 102, 854 S.W.2d 365 (1993) (recovery may be had even though business is operating at a loss; proper way to calculate amount due is to reduce sum of net profit and continuing expenses by amount of non-continuing expenses).

223. Amerigraphics, Inc. v. Mercury Casualty Co., 182 Cal. App. 4th 1538, 1554, 107 Cal. Rptr. 3d 307, 320 (2010).

224. French, *The Aftermath of Catastrophes: Valuing Business Interruption Insurance Losses*, 30 Ga. St. U.L. Rev. 461, 484 (2014).

225. Cosmetics Plus Group, Ltd. v. Am. Int'l Group, Inc. (*In re* Cosmetics Plus Group, Ltd.), 379 B.R. 464 (S.D.N.Y. 2007).

226. *See generally* Miller & Jean, *Effect of Post-Loss Economic Factors in Measuring Business Interruption Losses: An Insured's and Insurer's Perspectives*, Current Critical Issues in Insurance Law 25 (Winter 2010).

227. *See generally* Chattman & Miller, *Measuring Business Interruption Loss in Wide-Impact Catastrophes: Insurance Against Catastrophes or Only Against Insured Damage from Catastrophes?* 19 Coverage 1 (Jul./Aug. 2009).

restoration was more than double that of the prior 13 months. The court said it had no actual loss of business income as required by the policy.[228] The more difficult question is whether the insured can recover the increased revenues it would have realized but for the flood. That hardware store that remained open, for example, saw an increase in sales, while its unfortunate competitor that had to close did not receive the benefit of the increase in demand. Is its business loss measured by its historical sales or by what its sales would have been if it too had remained open? Consideration of post-loss conditions can work for or against an insured.[229]

Where policy language provides that the calculation of loss can take into account past performance, probable future performance, and performance that would have been experienced had no interruption occurred, the insurer is likely not limited to calculating interruption loss earnings based on the *actual period* of closure. A Louisiana federal court said that the calculations were not limited to the actual period of business closure but could include a lengthier period, possibly encompassing high sales figures for the first days after reopening during which the insured might recoup some of its claimed interruption losses. The policy provided coverage for earnings "had no interruption" occurred. That language, said the court, did not exclude profit opportunities that arose because of increased consumer demand *created* by the flood. Therefore, the court held that business interruption loss earnings could include sales the insured "would have made in the aftermath of the flood had it been open for business during that period."[230] Similarly, the Louisiana Supreme Court allowed a business interruption loss to include rental value *after* a hurricane when rent had doubled.[231]

In contrast to the Louisiana decisions, the Fifth Circuit has usually taken the position that only the insured's historical financial data should be considered when calculating business interruption losses. In *Finger Furniture Co., Inc. v. Commonwealth Ins. Co.*,[232] furniture stores owned by a Texas company were closed after a tropical storm caused the area to flood. The insurer, relying on language in the policy that directed consideration of the "probable experience" after an event "had no loss occurred," contended that because

---

228. B.F. Carvin Constr. Co. v. CNA Ins. Co., 2008 U.S. Dist. LEXIS 53678 (E.D. La. July 14, 2008).

229. *See, e.g.*, Fireman's Fund Ins. Co. v. Holland Am. Line-Westours, Inc., 25 Fed. App'x 602, 603 (9th Cir. 2002) (post-loss make-up sales deducted from amount of loss).

230. Levitz Furniture Corp. v. Houston Cas. Co., 1997 U.S. Dist. LEXIS 5883 (E.D. La. Apr. 29, 1997). Under that ruling, it may be that if the business had been partially opened, it could recover losses based on the earnings it would have enjoyed had it been fully opened. *See also* Stamen v. Cigna Prop. & Cas. Ins. Co., 1994 U.S. Dist. LEXIS 21905 (S.D. Fla. June 13, 1994) (lost profits should be measured, at least in part, by increased profits that would have resulted had stores owned by insured been open immediately after hurricane).

231. Sher v. Lafayette Ins. Co., 988 So. 2d 186 (La. 2008).

232. Finger Furniture Co., Inc. v. Commonwealth Ins. Co., 404 F.3d 312 (5th Cir. 2005).

demand for furniture increased after the flood, the insured quickly made up any lost sales and did not, therefore, experience a business interruption loss. The court, however, held that only historical sales numbers could be used to calculate the insured's loss.[233] In a subsequent Mississippi case, when a casino reopened after a hurricane, its revenues were much greater because many nearby casinos remained closed and customers had limited choices. The insured contended that post-hurricane sales *should* be taken into account to show that losses were greater than the pre-hurricane numbers would indicate. The Fifth Circuit, however, agreed with the insurer that recovery should be based on net profits the casino would probably have earned if the hurricane had not struck and damaged its facilities.[234] An earlier unreported Fourth Circuit case reached a similar conclusion. In that case, a South Carolina motel was damaged by Hurricane Hugo. The lower court held that the loss should include profits the motel would have realized had it been able to accommodate the influx of repair persons and construction workers to the area during the months after the hurricane. In reversing, the appellate court said that the premise for assessing *profit expectancies* during a business interruption is that the precipitating event had not occurred. In this case, had Hugo not struck, the claimed earnings source would not have come into being and to allow the recovery granted by the lower court would be to confer a windfall on the insured "rather than merely to put it in the earnings position it would have been in had the insured peril not occurred."[235]

A potentially key phrase in a policy is consideration of "favorable business conditions." In a post-Katrina federal case, for example, the owner of a large New Orleans apartment complex claimed business income losses based on an asserted increase in rental value of 40 percent because of an increase in demand after the hurricane. The insurer, however, would only pay based on occupancy rates and rental values before the storm. The policy said, as does the standard ISO policy, that the amount of lost business income would be determined based on, *inter alia*, likely net income if no physical loss or damage had occurred, but not including any net income that would likely have been earned as a result of an increase in the volume of business because of favorable business conditions caused by the impact of the *covered cause of loss*. This clause, said the court meant that the insured could not prove business income using evidence of likely net income that was earned as a result of an increase in the volume of business caused by the impact of the covered cause of loss at issue. The insured noted that flooding was not a *cause* of its loss. The court said that the policy did not intend to exclude from the determination of

233. *Accord* Alley Theatre v. Hanover Ins. Co., 2020 U.S. Dist. LEXIS 52393 (S.D. Tex. Mar. 26, 2020).

234. Catlin Syndicate Ltd. v. Imperial Palace of Miss., Inc., 600 F.3d 511 (5th Cir. 2010).

235. Prudential LMI v. Colleton Enterprises, Inc., 1992 U.S. App. LEXIS 25719 (4th Cir. Oct. 5, 1992).

loss favorable business conditions that resulted from losses that were not covered under the policy, for example, flood. Thus, the court held that the policy allowed the insured to recover for favorable market conditions resulting from flooding.[236] The decision was appealed to the Fifth Circuit, which affirmed.[237] "Although flood-related damages . . . are themselves excluded," said the court, "stimulated demand as a result of flood damage to other structures is a proper consideration in calculating lost income." The insurer attempted to invoke the flood exclusion, but the court responded that would extend the flood exclusion beyond its function. The exclusion, said the court, applied to "all coverage parts" of the policy. If coverage was permissible, and the insurer did not deny that the policy covered wind damage, then the flood exclusion had "nothing further to say, and the only remaining issue is calculation of damages." The policy expressly allowed that calculation to consider favorable business conditions, and the court declined to use a limitation on coverage to change the calculation for a covered loss. Interestingly, the court never mentioned the Mississippi and Texas cases discussed earlier. The lower court distinguished them based on the "increase in the volume of business because of favorable business conditions" language.

The cases do not reveal a bright line test.[238] Insurance is intended to make the insured whole, not to bestow a windfall.[239] Equity, therefore, appears to play a role in the decisions. Courts, it would seem, do not want insureds to receive more than a fair amount for their losses and also do not want insurers to avoid paying just compensation for those losses.[240] It is incumbent,

---

236. Berk-Cohen Assocs., LLC v. Landmark Am. Ins. Co., 2009 U.S. Dist. LEXIS 77300 (E.D. La. Aug. 27, 2009).

237. Berk-Cohen Assocs., L.L.C. v. Landmark Am. Ins. Co., 433 Fed. Appx. 268 (5th Cir. July 20, 2011).

238. One commentary says that there are not enough decisions to "proclaim that any particular school of thought is the majority position." French, *The Aftermath of Catastrophes: Valuing Business Interruption Insurance Losses*, 30 Ga. St. U.L. Rev. 461, 477 (2014).

239. Taylor, Park & O'Brien, *Unique Coverage Issues in Flood Losses*, 48 Tort & Ins. L.J. 619 (2013) (business interruption coverage is aimed at protecting insured, but it is also designed to prevent insured from being placed in better position than if no loss or interruption of business had occurred).

240. *See, e.g.*, Consolidated Companies Inc. v. Lexington Ins. Co., 616 F.3d 422 (5th Cir. 2010) (in light of the goal of making insured whole, only reasonable reading of policy is that it required reduction of "actual loss" by income earned during partial resumption of operations); Am. Auto Ins. v. Fisherman's Paradise, 1994 U.S. Dist. LEXIS 21068 (S.D. Fla. Oct. 3, 1994) (because windfall profits were not within scope of policy, it was unnecessary to determine sufficiency of evidence supporting lost profits); Stamen v. Cigna Prop. & Cas. Ins. Co., 1994 U.S. Dist. LEXIS 21905 (S.D. Fla. June 13, 1994) (fact that stores would have reaped greater profits in aftermath of hurricane and that insurer, therefore, would have to pay higher business interruption losses "is not accurately described as a windfall"); Lyon Metal Prods., L.L.C. v. Prot. Mut. Ins. Co., 254 Ill. Dec. 455, 467, 321 Ill. App. 3d 330, 344, 747 N.E.2d 495, 507 (2001) (business interruption insurance, like all insurance, should comport with public policy of indemnifying insured for loss, but not providing windfall profit).

therefore, on counsel for an insured to make the case to the court that it would be unfair for the insured not to realize the profit it would have earned—and that its more fortunate competitors did realize—had it not lost that opportunity through no fault of its own.

[v] Reductions in Amount of Recovery

The ISO policy provides that the insurer will reduce the amount of the business income loss, other than extra expense, to the extent the insured *can* resume its operations,[241] in whole or in part, by using damaged or undamaged property (including merchandise or stock) at the described premises or elsewhere.[242] Other policies may provide that the insurer can reduce the amount it pays to the extent a reduction in the volume of business income from an "affected channel" is offset by an increase in the volume of business from "other income channels." In a post-Katrina case, the insured provided engineering, accounting, and consulting services. The specific nature of its services changed after the storm, but it remained engineering and consulting, and it had a significant growth in income from those services. The increase in business volume from these "other income channels" more than offset any decline in its pre-storm business income. The court found that the insurer properly refused to pay the insured's claim for business interruption losses first because the insured suffered no actual loss that triggered coverage, and second because even if coverage had been triggered, the amount of pre-storm business income loss was properly offset by income generated by post-storm business operations.[243]

Under the ISO policy, if the insured does not resume operations, or does not resume them as quickly as possible, the insurer will pay based on the length of time it would have taken to resume operations as quickly as possible.[244]

When there is enough inventory to meet the insured's projected sales for a period of interruption, there is no loss of earnings, but what if the inventory is damaged and the insurer pays for that damage under property loss coverage? Payment for damaged inventory then has to be considered in calculating the business interruption loss.[245] That is because policies generally provide that

---

241. One court explained that regardless of whether operations *are* resumed, if the policyholder is capable of resuming operations, the business income is reduced based on the level to which operations *could have* been resumed. If the insured does resume operations, the reduction is fully offset by revenue earned by any operations; however, if operations are not resumed, the insured receives reduced benefits and does not earn any revenue to offset the reduction. Polymer Plastics Corp. v. Hartford Cas. Ins. Co., 2006 U.S. Dist. LEXIS 103077 (D. Nev. Sept. 26, 2006).

242. ISO Form CP 00 30 10 12, § C.3.c.(1).

243. Rimkus Consulting Group, Inc. v. Hartford Cas. Ins. Co., 552 F. Supp. 2d 637, 645–46 (S.D. Tex. 2007).

244. ISO Form CP 00 30 10 12, § C.3.d.

245. Lyon Metal Prods., L.L.C. v. Prot. Mut. Ins. Co., 254 Ill. Dec. 455, 464, 321 Ill. App. 3d 330, 340, 747 N.E.2d 495, 504 (2001)

the insurer will pay for the *actual loss* of business income. If the insurer, in effect, purchases the damaged inventory, there has been no actual loss.[246]

[vi] Prompt Payment

Under the ISO policy, the insurer will pay for covered losses within 30 days after it receives the sworn proof of loss, if the insured has complied with all of the terms of the policy and the parties have reached agreement on the amount of loss or an appraisal award has been made.[247]

6.3 Extra Expense Coverage

[1] Introduction

A coverage related to business interruption is called "extra expense." In the ISO policy, extra expense coverage is included; however, sometimes it is not included along with business interruption coverage but is added by endorsement. Extra expense insurance provides funds that are necessary, but would not ordinarily be expended, to continue the operations of a business.[248] As one court explained, it is coverage "that makes it possible for the insured to maintain business operations that otherwise would have been interrupted pending permanent repair/restoration of the insured's property."[249]

[2] Coverage

[a] Standard Policy Language

[i] Definition and Coverage

The ISO Business Income (and Extra Expense) Coverage Form defines "extra expenses" as those "necessary"[250] expenses an insured incurs during a "period

---

246. Note that a policy may include an endorsement under which the determination of net sales includes any amount recovered under property damage policies for loss or damage to or destruction of merchandise as though the merchandise had been sold to the insured's regular customers.

247. ISO Form CP 00 30 10 12, § C.4.

248. Ainslie et al., *Business Insurance Law and Practice Guide* § 16.04[1] (Matthew Bender 2020); 5 Jeffrey E. Thomas, *New Appleman on Insurance Law Library Edition* § 47.10[5][e] (LexisNexis 2020); Erickson & Henlin, *Understanding Extra Expense*, 45 Tort & Ins. L.J. 1 (2009) (intent of extra expense clauses is to provide coverage for those necessary additional expenses that commercial insured incurs to operate its business during period of restoration following direct physical loss). *See, e.g.*, Detroit Edison Co. v. Protection Mut. Ins. Co., 134 F.3d 790, 792, n.3 (6th Cir. 1998) (coverage includes expenses incurred to maintain business operations).

249. Chalmette Retail Ctr., LLC v. Lafayette Ins. Co., 21 So. 3d 485, 498 (La. App. 2009).

250. Policies generally do not define "necessary." Courts have interpreted it to mean "essential." Nonetheless, what is necessary depends on the facts of a particular case, and the insured may be required to show that the expense was contractually required or needed to continue the business or reduce a loss. Erickson & Henlin, *Understanding Extra Expense*, 45 Tort &

of restoration"[251] that the insured would not have incurred had there been no direct physical loss or damage to property caused by or resulting from a cause of loss covered under the policy.[252] Flood, of course, is likely not a covered cause of loss.[253] Other policies may define the coverage as the excess of total costs sustained during the period of restoration over those that would have been experienced in the normal course of business.[254] As with all insurance coverage, it is critical to examine the specific policy language, as it can vary from policy to policy or endorsement to endorsement. For example, a sewage backup caused substantial property damage and expenses to the insured, and it claimed, *inter alia*, extra expense coverage. The pertinent endorsement provided that coverage without reference to "covered causes of loss" and stated that the insurer would pay for extra expenses resulting from any loss or damage covered by the policy. While the principal policy excluded coverage for sewer backups, the endorsement provided it with a sublimit and the court concluded that extra expenses that resulted from the sewer backup were independently covered under the endorsement.[255]

The ISO policy provides extra expense coverage if the Declarations Page shows that business income coverage applies at that insured premises.[256] In that case, the insurer will pay the expense, other than to repair or replace property, to avoid or minimize a "suspension"[257] of business and to continue

---

Ins. L.J. 1 (2009). *See also* Chatham Corp. v. Dann Ins., 285 Ill. Dec. 663, 669, 351 Ill. App. 3d 353, 359, 812 N.E.2d 483, 489 (2004) ("necessary" does not encompass expenses that insureds may have wanted to incur on gratuitous or voluntary basis, which would have been opposite of necessary).

251. Generally, for there to be extra expense coverage, there has to be a period of restoration. Erickson & Henlin, *Understanding Extra Expense*, 45 Tort & Ins. L.J. 1 (2009). For extra expense coverage under the ISO policy, the period of restoration begins immediately after the time of direct physical loss or damage. ISO Form CP 00 30 10 12, § F.3.a.(2). This definition differs from that in the policy's business interruption coverage. There are, however, policies in which the definition is the same. Cozen, *Insuring Real Property* § 3.04[1][c] (LexisNexis Matthew Bender 2020).

252. ISO Form CP 00 30 10 12, § A.2.b. *See, e.g.*, Millville Quarry, Inc. v. Liberty Mut. Fire Ins. Co., 31 Fed. Appx. 116 (4th Cir. Mar. 19, 2002) (expenses of operation of additional pumps, construction of pump barges, water inflow investigations, and grouting of underground conduits were not covered as extra expenses as all would have been required even if four permanent pumps had not been rendered inoperable by flood).

253. *See, e.g.*, For Kids Only Child Dev. Ctr., Inc. v. Philadelphia Indem. Ins. Co., 260 S.W.3d 652 (Tex. App. 2008) (extra expense provision did not provide coverage for drain and sewer backup because costs did not arise from covered cause of loss; loss or damage caused directly or indirectly by water that backed up or overflowed from sewer, drain, or sump was specifically excluded).

254. Erickson & Henlin, *Understanding Extra Expense*, 45 Tort & Ins. L.J. 1 (2009).

255. Wichita Realty v. Cont'l W. Ins. Co., 118 P.3d 715 (Kan. App. 2005), affirming 2005 Kan. App. Unpub. LEXIS 417 (Ka. App. Sept. 2, 2005) without a written opinion.

256. ISO Form CP 00 30 10 12, § A.2.a.

257. "Suspension" is defined in the ISO policy to mean either the slowdown or cessation of business activities of the insured or that a part or all of the described premises is rendered

"operations"[258] at the described premises[259] or at a replacement or temporary location.[260] It will also pay relocation expenses and the costs to equip and operate any replacement or temporary location. It will pay the expense to minimize the "suspension" of business if the insured cannot continue operations and to repair or replace property, but only to the extent that reduces the amount of loss that would have been payable otherwise under the policy.[261]

Generally, extra expense insurance is intended to cover the insured for temporary expenses that are related to continued business operations. Normal ongoing expenses are not necessary extra expenses, and loss of revenue is not an expense at all.[262] Additional rent that an insured has to pay at a new *permanent* location is not a temporary expense and is not a covered extra expense.[263] On the other hand, when damage from wind, rain, and water intrusion forced a school to *temporarily* rent facilities in which to hold classes, that rent was a covered extra expense.[264]

When a loss claimed as an extra expense could also be claimed under the covered property provisions of a commercial property policy, is the extra expense claim barred? In one case, a building was severely damaged

---

untenantable when the coverage includes rental value. ISO Form CP 00 30 10 12, § F.6. Where a policy provided coverage only when there was a "necessary suspension," a court held the phrase referred to a total cessation of business activity. American States Ins. Co. v. Creative Walking, 16 F. Supp. 2d 1062, 1065 (E.D. Mo. 1998). On the other hand, where the term "extra expense" clearly included expenses necessary to carry on business operations, the court said the definition of the term would not make any sense if the policy were interpreted to cover only those extra expenses incurred as a result of a complete cessation of business. The insurer's argument that the policy only covered extra expenses if business operations were stopped was, in the view of the court, inconsistent with the terms of the policy. Archer Daniels Midland Co. v. Aon Risk Services, Inc. of Minnesota, 356 F.3d 850, 856 (8th Cir. 2004).

258. "Operations" is defined as the business activities of the insured that occur at the described premises *and* the "tenantability" of the described premises, if coverage includes rental value. ISO Form CP 00 30 10 12, § F.2.

259. Generally, extra expense coverage applies when there is damage to the insured premises. However, damage at another premises on which the insurer is dependent may be the source of a loss for the insured. Some policies, therefore, provide "contingent extra expense coverage" covering those losses. Cozen, *Insuring Real Property* § 3.04[2] (LexisNexis Matthew Bender 2020).

260. ISO Form CP 00 30 10 12, § A.2.b.(1).

261. ISO Form CP 00 30 10 12, § A.2.b.(2).

262. *See* Stevens v. Zurich Am. Ins. Co., 2015 U.S. Dist. LEXIS 120117 (N.D. Cal. Sept. 9, 2015) (payroll and rent expenses were normal ongoing expenses, not necessary ones that would not have been incurred if there had been no direct physical loss or damage, and lost revenue was an income loss, not an expense). *See also* GBP Partners, Ltd. v. Md. Cas. Co., 2013 U.S. Dist. LEXIS 84177 (S.D. Tex. June 14, 2013) (where landlord decided to abate its tenants' rents, reducing its revenue to extent that tenants may have actually paid lower rent, it did not incur any cost or expense; foregoing rent is not an expenditure of money).

263. Rimkus Consulting Group, Inc. v. Hartford Cas. Ins. Co., 552 F. Supp. 2d 637 (S.D. Tex. 2007).

264. Kiln Underwriting Ltd. v. Jesuit High Sch. of New Orleans, 2008 U.S. Dist. LEXIS 86286 (E.D. La. Oct. 24, 2008).

by a tornado. The insured relocated machinery and replaced equipment and claimed the costs as extra expenses because it incurred them to minimize the slowdown of business and to continue business activities previously performed. The insurer countered that the expenditures were not covered as extra expenses because they were subject to primary coverage under the covered property provision of the policy. The court sided with the insured. It noted that the policy language did not specifically prohibit coverage for an extra expense if it could also be reimbursed as covered property. Additionally, the policy defined "extra expenses" to include the costs for which the insured sought reimbursement. The insurer could have excluded recovery for extra expenses when they were reimbursable under the covered property coverage but did not. The court concluded that either the insured correctly interpreted the policy to cover its claim as an extra expense or the policy was ambiguous and had to be construed in favor of the insured.[265] The decision has significance for flood claim losses because the covered property portion of a policy could be subject to either a flood sublimit or an outright exclusion for flood losses while the extra expense coverage may not.

While an insured may be able to recover under either the covered property or extra expense provisions of a commercial property policy, when the policy explicitly states that property is not covered, the insured cannot make an "end-run" around that policy limitation by characterizing a cost as an extra expense.[266] For example, floods can be caused by damaged pipes, but policies typically state that "covered property" does not include underground pipes, flues, or drains or cost of excavations, grading, backfilling, or filling. Thus, the cost of replacing a pipe that has caused flooding is usually not covered. For example, after raw sewage was discharged into the insured restaurant, the policyholder sought coverage for the cost of digging up and replacing the broken sewage line that caused the discharge. The insured argued that replacement of the sewage pipe was an extra expense incurred to allow it to continue its business operations. The court, however, concluded that there was no getting around the clear language of the policy under which an underground pipe was not covered property.[267]

[ii] Amount of Coverage

The amount of coverage will be based on all expenses that exceed normal operating expenses the insured would have incurred by "operations" during

---

265. Midwest Reg'l Allergy, Asthma, Arthritis & Osteoporosis, P.C. v. Cincinnati Ins. Co., 2013 U.S. Dist. LEXIS 115388 (W.D. Mo. Aug. 15, 2013), *aff'd*, 795 F.3d 853 (8th Cir. 2015).

266. Note that some policies may specifically define "extra expense" as one "not otherwise excluded." *See, e.g.*, Formosa Plastics Corp., U.S.A. v. ACE Am. Ins. Co., 2010 U.S. Dist. LEXIS 119382 (D.N.J. Nov. 9, 2010).

267. 1062 Pontiac Rd., Inc. v. Axis Surplus Ins. Co., 2013 U.S. Dist. LEXIS 15084 (E.D. Pa. Feb. 5, 2013).

the "period of restoration" if no direct physical loss or damage had occurred.[268] From that amount, the insurer will deduct the salvage value remaining of any property bought for temporary use during the "period of restoration," after "operations" begin again, and any expense paid for by *other insurance*, except for insurance written subject to the same plan, terms, conditions, and provisions as the ISO policy. The amount of extra expense is also determined based on necessary expenses that reduce any business income loss that would have otherwise been incurred.[269] The insurer will reduce the amount of an extra expense loss to the extent the insured can return its "operations" to normal and discontinue the expense.[270] Some courts say that there is no requirement that the extra expenses be in excess of normal operating expenses.[271] Other courts, looking to policies that say an extra expense has to reduce the amount of loss that otherwise would have been payable, conclude that the insured has to show that the extra expenses claimed exceed what it would have normally cost to operate the business had no loss occurred.[272] Extra expenses are payable only if the expense was actually incurred by the insured.[273] They have to be incurred during the period of restoration.[274]

---

268. ISO Form CP 00 30 10 12, § C.3.b.(1).

269. ISO Form CP 00 30 10 12, § C.3.b.(2).

270. ISO Form CP 00 30 10 12, § C.3.c.(2).

271. Dillard Univ. v. Lexington Ins. Co., 2009 U.S. Dist. LEXIS 46785 (D.D. La. June 3, 2009). In *Dillard*, the plaintiff could not reoccupy its campus after Hurricane Katrina and temporarily moved its operations to another location. The insurer argued that for the insured to recover excess expenses, its actual operating expenses for the temporary arrangement had to be in excess of the costs that would normally have been incurred to conduct the business had no loss or damage occurred. The court characterized that interpretation as "nonsensical" because the services provided under the temporary arrangement were not the same services normally provided. It would be a coincidence, averred the court, if the temporary services costs were more when fewer services were being provided under the temporary arrangement. Because the insured would not normally have incurred any of the cost of a temporary operation, the full amount was "over and above" or "in excess of" the insured's total cost of normal operations.

272. *See, e.g.*, Travelers Indem. Co. v. Pollard Friendly Ford Co., 512 S.W.2d 375 (Tex. Civ. App.—Amarillo 1974). *See also* Formosa Plastics Corp., U.S.A. v. ACE Am. Ins. Co., 2010 U.S. Dist. LEXIS 119382 (D.N.J. Nov. 9, 2010) (while expenses claimed may have exceeded normal costs of portion of insured business, additional expenses were not covered as extra expenses unless post-loss expenses exceeded normal total operating expenses for entire business); Nassau Gallery, Inc. v. Nationwide Mut. Fire Ins. Co., 2003 Del. Super. LEXIS 487 (Apr. 17, 2003); Irving v. St. Paul Fire & Marine Ins. Co., 1995 Conn. Super. LEXIS 1742 (June 6, 1995) (extra expenses incurred after insured premises and its contents sustained water damage not recoverable where policy provided insurer would cover extra expenses to extent that they exceeded what it would have normally cost insureds to conduct their business had no loss occurred and normal operating costs for relevant period would have been over $20,000 more than amount of claimed extra expense).

273. Greenspoint Investors, Ltd. v. Travelers Lloyds Ins. Co., 2015 U.S. Dist. LEXIS 25301 (S.D. Tex. Mar. 3, 2015). *See also* 5 Star Tech v. Am. Guar. & Liab. Ins. Co., 2020 U.S. Dist. LEXIS 117327 (W.D. Tex. Apr. 28, 2020).

274. Alon v. State Farm Fire & Cas. Co., 2013 U.S. Dist. LEXIS 202822 (D. Ariz. Feb. 25, 2013). *See generally* Erickson & Henlin, *Understanding Extra Expense*, 45 Tort & Ins. L.J. 1

The burden will be on the insured to prove any extra expenses. In a Louisiana case, an appellate court found there to be a lack of any evidence in the record to support a jury finding of extra expenses. The court concluded the jury finding was "manifestly erroneous" and, therefore, reversed the award of extra expenses.[275] Similarly, when a loss is the result of both a covered and a non-covered peril, the insured has the burden of showing the portion of the loss that is attributable to the covered cause of loss. Where an insured made no attempt to allocate extra expense cost between covered and non-covered causes of loss, the trial court did not err when it granted an insurer's motion for judgment n.o.v.[276]

The amount of loss covered may not be limited by the expiration of the policy. In *Archer-Daniels-Midland Co. v. Phoenix Assur. Co.*,[277] the insured incurred substantial extra expenses and losses of income because of increases in transportation and raw material costs after unprecedented river flooding. The costs were incurred from June 1993 through June 1994. The insurer refused to pay for the costs incurred after October 1, 1993, the date the policy expired. The court, however, said that under the policy, the *period of restoration* was not to be limited by the date of expiration of the policy.

Coverage ends with the termination of the period of restoration. Under the ISO policy, the period of restoration ends on the earlier of the date when the damaged property should be repaired, rebuilt, or replaced with reasonable speed and similar quality or when the business of the insured is resumed at a new permanent location.[278] Actual repair is not necessary to end the period of restoration.[279] An unreported Fourth Circuit case discussed the ending of the period of restoration. In the case, a quarry operator had water pumps designed to remove natural accumulations of water from the quarry. They were rendered inoperable when the quarry flooded. It was months before substitute pumps were able to remove enough water for the quarry to resume operations. The court held that the period of recovery did not end when the quarry resumed operations but on the date when the permanent pumps should have been repaired, rebuilt, or replaced with reasonable speed and similar quality and that was the date when adequate temporary replacement pumps were installed.[280]

(2009) (when expense is incurred is often as important as fact it is incurred at all as grant of coverage expressly states that extra expense is limited to costs actually incurred by the insured during period of restoration).

275. Chalmette Retail Ctr., LLC v. Lafayette Ins. Co., 21 So. 3d 485 (La. App. 2009).

276. St. Joseph Light & Power Co. v. Zurich Ins. Co., 698 F.2d 1351 (8th Cir. 1983).

277. Archer-Daniels-Midland Co. v. Phoenix Assur. Co., 975 F. Supp. 1124 (S.D. Ill. 1997).

278. ISO Form CP 00 30 10 12, § F.3.b.

279. Erickson & Henlin, *Understanding Extra Expense*, 45 Tort & Ins. L.J. 1 (2009).

280. Millville Quarry, Inc. v. Liberty Mut. Fire Ins. Co., 31 Fed. Appx. 116 (4th Cir. Mar. 19, 2002).

As with other forms of coverage, there may be sublimits to extra expense coverage,[281] and it is important to determine whether there are any sublimits for flood-related losses that apply to extra expense coverage.[282]

[iii] Additional Coverages

The ISO Business Income (and Extra Expense) Coverage Form provides that if a covered cause of loss causes damage to property other than that at the described premises, the insurer will pay for the necessary extra expense caused by action of civil authority that prohibits access to that premises.[283] Generally, the conditions on coverage are the same as those for business interruption claims, as discussed previously.[284] The ISO policy adds that civil authority coverage for extra expense begins immediately after the first action of a civil authority prohibiting access to the premises and ends four consecutive weeks after the date of that action or when the insured's civil authority coverage for business income ends, whichever is later.

The additional coverage for "alterations and new buildings" in the ISO policy includes extra expenses.[285]

[iv] Contingent Extra Expense Coverage

Under contingent extra expense insurance, an insured is covered for an extra expense loss resulting from physical damage by an insured peril on premises that are *not operated* by the policyholder.[286] This coverage is usually not found in extra expense coverage and has to be added by endorsement. The coverage operates much like that of contingent business interruption coverage.[287] It can present challenging causation questions when a flood damages both the insured's property and the contingent property.[288]

---

281. *See, e.g.*, Piankatank River Golf Club, Inc. v. Selective Way Ins. Co., 2009 U.S. Dist. LEXIS 40027 (E.D. Va. May 11, 2009) (extra expense coverage capped at $50,000).

282. *See, e.g.*, Altru Health Sys. v. American Protection Ins. Co., 238 F.3d 961 (8th Cir. 2001) ($1,500,000 sublimit for flood losses applied to extra expense claim); Kiln Underwriting Ltd. v. Jesuit High Sch. of New Orleans, 2008 U.S. Dist. LEXIS 86286 (E.D. La. Oct. 24, 2008) (recovery for flood damage limited to $250,000 per year); Pel Hughes Printing, L.L.C. v. Hanover Ins. Group, Inc., 2008 U.S. Dist. LEXIS 31224 (E.D. La. Apr. 16, 2008) ($250,000 limit for business income loss and extra expenses applied).

283. ISO Form CP 00 30 10 12, § A.5.a.

284. See § 6.02[6][a], *supra.*

285. ISO Form CP 00 30 10 12, § A.5.b.

286. Ainslie et al., *Business Insurance Law and Practice Guide* § 16.04[2] (Matthew Bender 2020).

287. See § 6.02[6][e], *infra.*

288. 5 Jeffrey E. Thomas, *New Appleman on Insurance Law Library Edition* § 46.05[1][e] (LexisNexis 2020).

[b] Flood as a Covered Cause of Loss

The ISO policy covers "extra expenses" the insured would not have incurred had there been no direct physical loss or damage to property caused by or resulting from a *cause of loss covered under the policy*.[289] Typically, of course, flood damage will be excluded and, therefore, not a covered cause of loss.[290] Some coverage may, however, be added back by an endorsement. For example, in an Ohio case,[291] a commercial property policy with extra expense coverage included the usual water exclusion barring coverage for losses caused, *inter alia*, by flood and water backing up or overflowing from a sewer or drain. During a torrential rainfall, rainwater flowing into storm sewers backed up through drains inside the building housing the insured business. It had to cease all business operations for several weeks. The insured had purchased coverage for "Water Back-up and Sump Overflow" through an endorsement to the policy and argued the water backup was, therefore, a covered cause of loss and that she was entitled to payment for extra expenses. The insurer, however, countered that the endorsement applied only to direct physical damage to her property and did not extend to extra expense coverage. The court found for the business owner. It noted that pursuant to the endorsement, water backup was no longer excluded from the definition of a covered cause of loss in the main policy. The policy as modified applied to all coverages including extra expense. The court concluded that the policy did not clearly and unambiguously exclude coverage for the claimed extra expenses that arose from the damage from water backup, and the insurer had failed to meet its burden to show clear application of the exclusion.

[c] Direct Physical Loss or Damage

Policies cover extra expenses the insured would not have incurred had there been no *direct physical loss or damage to property* caused by or resulting from covered cause of loss.[292] Thus, courts generally hold that an insured has to suffer "direct physical loss or damage" to trigger the extra expense clause.[293]

289. ISO Form CP 00 30 10 12, § A.2.b.

290. *See, e.g.*, Valley Forge Ins. Co. v. Hicks Thomas & Lilienstern, L.L.P, 174 S.W.3d 254, 258 (Tex. App. 2004) (extra expense not covered under policy because of exclusion for loss resulting from flood or surface water).

291. Trautman v. Union Ins. Co., 2010 Ohio App. LEXIS 1255 (Apr. 5, 2010).

292. ISO Form CP 00 30 10 12, § A.2.b. *See* Erickson & Henlin, *Understanding Extra Expense*, 45 Tort & Ins. L.J. 1 (2009) (policies typically require "direct physical loss"—physical loss of or damage to insured property—as condition precedent to coverage).

293. Newman Myers Kreines Gross, P.C. v. Great Northern Ins. Co., 17 F. Supp. 3d 323, 331 (S.D.N.Y. 2014) (phrase "direct physical loss or damage" unambiguously requires some form of actual, physical damage to insured premises to trigger extra expense coverage).

In *Phoenix Ins. Co. v. Infogroup, Inc.*,[294] the insured had to relocate its business because of the threat of a flood. It sought compensation for its relocation costs and associated expenses. The court said that loss of use as the result of the *threat* of flooding did not meet the requirement for physical loss. The claimed cause of the loss of use was the mere risk of flood, and while that risk was real, it did not prevent the insured from using the facility. More importantly, mere loss of use did not constitute physical loss or damage under the extra expense clause.

The damage may not have to occur at the insured property for extra expenses to be covered. For example, widespread flooding of the Mississippi River and its tributaries caused disruption of river, road, and rail transportation. Archer Daniels Midland Company, which processes farm products, incurred substantial extra expenses because of increases in costs of transportation and raw materials. The insurer argued that the extra expense coverage in its policy was limited to situations in which the described property of the insured was damaged. The court, however, concluded that property damage did not have to occur at a scheduled location for there to be coverage. The insurer, noted the court, could have explicitly limited coverage to extra expense incurred as a result of damage to property at scheduled locations—a limitation that occurred in several other parts of the policy—but it did not. Thus, the court found that the policy language was unambiguous and did not require that the "direct physical damage" be to property insured under the property damage coverage or be to property at scheduled locations.[295] Of course, a different result could be reached where a policy requires that the cost of extra expenses incurred is due to direct physical loss to the insured property.[296]

294. Phoenix Ins. Co. v. Infogroup, Inc., 147 F. Supp. 3d 815 (S.D. Iowa 2015).

295. Archer-Daniels-Midland Co. v. Phoenix Assur. Co., 936 F. Supp. 534 (S.D. Ill. 1996).

296. *See, e.g.*, Imperial Trading Co. v. Travelers Prop. Cas. Co. of Am., 2009 U.S. Dist. LEXIS 64010 (E.D. La. July 24, 2009), where the policy unambiguously stated that extra expenses had to be reasonable and necessary, and would be paid only if they were sustained due to direct physical loss of or damage to property at the premises described in the Declarations. Therefore, said the court, expenses sustained because of damage to other premises, or no premises at all, would not fall under the contractual definition of "extra expenses." For example, the insured claimed that it was forced to make incentive payments to employees to keep them from leaving the area. However, observed the court, there was no apparent connection between the incentive payments and the physical damage to the insured property. The payments were made because of general hurricane devastation, not because of damage to the building. Similarly, where the insured employer provided temporary housing for its employees, the expenses were undertaken because of damage done to the homes of those employees, not to the insured building. They were not, therefore, recoverable extra expenses.

[d] Disaster Relief and Insurance Recovery

After a major flood event, insureds may be eligible for governmental assistance. If they receive disaster relief funds, is the amount of extra expense recovery offset by the amount of the federal funds? In a post-Katrina case, an insured parochial school sought extra expense coverage but had applied to FEMA for a Public Assistance Grant to cover those same expenses. The insurer argued its liability should be offset by any amount the school received from FEMA. The court, however, noted that federal law limits duplication of federal disaster benefits: FEMA does not provide assistance for damages covered by insurance. Federal law prevents covered parties and insurers from failing to seek or provide coverage to prevent them from treating the federal government as a primary insurer. Federal disaster relief programs, said the court, provide a "safety net." Insurers bears the primary responsibility for any covered loss. Thus, the court refused to offset the amount owed by the insurer.[297]

[e] Covered Extra Expenses

[i] Generally[298]

There are a great many costs that may qualify as covered extra expenses. Generally, these include expenses to continue or resume operations at the damaged insured premises or to equip and operate at a replacement or temporary location.[299] In the example of a country club with a golf course, covered extra expenses might include the cost of renting temporary buildings and facilities—for example, portable buildings for office use and portable toilets—during the time the clubhouse building is uninhabitable.[300] A finance charge on a line of credit used for rebuilding might also be considered an extra expense.[301] Temporary stabilization of the premises on which the insured property sits could be an extra expense.[302] After Hurricane Katrina, a business had to temporarily relocate a considerable distance away, and it rented out hotel rooms and apartments for its employees. The court found that to be a necessary extra

---

297. Kiln Underwriting Ltd. v. Jesuit High Sch. of New Orleans, 2008 U.S. Dist. LEXIS 86286 (E.D. La. Oct. 24, 2008).

298. *See generally When Does a Commercial Policy Provide Insurance Coverage for Extra Expenses?* (Mar. 22, 2017), Property Casualty 360, http://www.propertycasualty360.com/2017/03/22/when-does-a-commercial-policy-provide-insurance-co?ref=related-embedded.

299. 5 Jeffrey E. Thomas, *New Appleman on Insurance Law Library Edition* § 46.04[3][a] (LexisNexis 2020).

300. *See* Olde Colonial Vill. v. Millers Mut. Ins., 2002 Del. Super. LEXIS 341 (Del. Super. Ct. May 17, 2002) (stating in *dicta* that "extra expense" of renting temporary office while association building was rendered uninhabitable would be covered).

301. Seward Park Hous. Corp. v. Greater N.Y. Mut. Ins. Co., 43 A.D.3d 23, 28–29, 836 N.Y.S.2d 99, 102 (2007) (line of credit allowed insured to rebuild garage and resume receiving rental income).

302. Tastee Treats, Inc. v. United States Fid. & Guar. Co., 2010 U.S. Dist. LEXIS 125499 (S.D. W. Va. Nov. 29, 2010), *aff'd*, 474 Fed. Appx. 101 (4th Cir. June 6, 2012).

expense of staffing the temporary offices.[303] Advertising used to inform the public that a business remains open is a compensable extra expense.[304] Where a building was damaged and its doors could not be locked and windows were open, making tools and parts susceptible to loss by theft, watch protection was reasonably necessary and a recoverable expense.

A Texas court offered several examples of extra expenses, which it described as costs necessary to allow a business to keep its doors open despite damage.[305] The court said that if a flood destroys a bakery's ovens, it has to buy new ones or it will have to close its doors. A restaurant with broken sewage pipes has to rent portable toilets or it cannot serve food to patrons. A company whose office is damaged in a hurricane has to rent a trailer until repairs are finished. These businesses, said the court, would be unable to operate if they did not spend that money and, therefore, the expenditures are extra expenses.

[ii] Protection from Additional Water Damage

Expenses related to protecting an insured building from further water inundation and damage fell under extra expense coverage.[306] These expenses included covering a roof over a holiday weekend, boarding up windows with plastic sheathing, parachuting a ceiling with plastic, building a retaining pool to catch rainwater, and emergency/temporary electric services. The court noted that these expenses would also fall under the property coverage. At the same time, they were necessary to mitigate further damage and would fall within the extra expense provision because protecting the building from further water inundation through the roof, windows, and floor and providing emergency electrical services were all necessary to minimize the suspension of business and continue operations. The court also found that pumping out water as it made its way into the building during the period of restoration and clearing debris were covered extra expenses as well.

[iii] Costs of Employees

Operating expenses like regularly scheduled wages of hourly employees accrued during a period of suspension or earnings and added vacation time for the salaried employees are generally not recoverable as added expenses as

---

303. Rimkus Consulting Group, Inc. v. Hartford Cas. Ins. Co., 552 F. Supp. 2d 637 (S.D. Tex. 2007). *Compare* Imperial Trading Co. v. Travelers Prop. Cas. Co. of Am., 2009 U.S. Dist. LEXIS 64010 (E.D. La. July 24, 2009) (expense of temporary on-site housing not covered as it was incurred because of damage done by hurricane to employees' homes).

304. Nassau Gallery, Inc. v. Nationwide Mut. Fire Ins. Co. 2003 Del. Super. LEXIS 487 (Apr. 17, 2003) (publicity was related to normal conduct of business and allowed insured to operate during its restoration period).

305. GBP Partners, Ltd. v. Md. Cas. Co., 2013 U.S. Dist. LEXIS 84177 (S.D. Tex. June 14, 2013).

306. Demers Bros. Trucking, Inc. v. Certain Underwriters, 600 F. Supp. 2d 265, 279 (D. Mass. 2009).

the insured would have been liable for them in the ordinary course of its business.[307] However, compensatory vacation time an insured offered to its salaried employees who worked beyond their normally scheduled hours during a suspension period was a compensable extra expense because the employer would not have made that vacation time available to its salaried employees had the accident not happened, and because it was offered to avoid or minimize the suspension of business.[308] After Hurricane Katrina, a company hired additional employees and sought to recover their costs as an extra expense. These employees served to address inefficient conditions at the warehouse—for example, debris removal, refrigeration problems, and destruction of an inventory tracking system. The court found the expenses were recoverable.[309] After a tornado damaged the property of an automobile dealership, some of its employees were required to work up to 18 hours a day. Exiting and entering the property was difficult and time-consuming, so the company purchased meals for the employees to reduce the time they spent away from the jobsite. The court found the extra compensation and meals to be proper extra expenses.[310]

[iv] Cleanup Costs

After a flood, cleaning up the premises is important for the insured to be able to return to business. Hourly workers who expend time over and above what they are ordinarily scheduled in order to perform tasks that minimize damage and restore regular operations may be an extra expense.[311] However, a court denied a claim for extra expenses based on payroll costs for employees of the insured who were paid to clean up debris and damage after a hurricane. The court said the evidence did not support a determination that those were "extra expenses," expenses the insureds would not have incurred had there been no direct physical loss or damage. While no one disputed the employees were paid to clean up debris, there was no evidence to show the insured incurred

307. *But see* Travelers Indem. Co. v. Pollard Friendly Ford Co., 512 S.W.2d 375 (Tex. Civ. App.—Amarillo 1974), where employees watched over a building after tornado damage prevented it from being locked up. The court found the expenses incurred by paying employees whose ordinary incomes were operating expenses rather than fixed expenses were recoverable as their incomes would not have been expenses to the insured during a time when it was not doing business. The expenses, said the court, were in addition to normal ones and incurred as a result of direct damage to the property.

308. Interstate Gourmet Coffee Roasters, Inc. v. Travelers Indem. Co., 2018 U.S. Dist. LEXIS 131293 (D. Mass. Aug. 6, 2018) (policy language did not suggest coverage for employees whose normal schedules were disrupted or inconvenienced because of occurrence.)

309. Consolidated Cos., Inc. v. Lexington Ins. Co., 2009 U.S. Dist. LEXIS 8542 (E.D. La. Jan. 23, 2009).

310. Travelers Indem. Co. v. Pollard Friendly Ford Co., 512 S.W.2d 375 (Tex. Civ. App.—Amarillo 1974).

311. Interstate Gourmet Coffee Roasters, Inc. v. Travelers Indem. Co., 2018 U.S. Dist. LEXIS 131293 (D. Mass. Aug. 6, 2018).

extra payroll costs, that the insured paid employees more than they would have paid absent the physical damage to the insured property.[312]

Services to remove and dry water that resulted from fire-suppression efforts were not an extra expense but rather were covered under the property coverage.[313]

[v] Repair, Restoration, or Replacement

Under the ISO policy, the insurer will pay the expense, *other than to repair or replace property*, to avoid or minimize a suspension of business and to continue operations.[314] That language reflects the view of courts that repair or restoration of property is not an extra expense as typically defined. For example, in a Wisconsin case, the insured property was a supermarket that operated in a building that the insureds rented. After the building was destroyed, the landlord decided not to rebuild it and the insureds built their own building in which to continue the business. They sought the costs of building the new structure and of equipment and fixtures destroyed in the old building as extra expenses. The court, however, found that the items for which the insureds sought coverage were either those they had previously owned or those that their landlord owned, and those were not covered under the extra expense insurance.[315] Other courts agree and note that repairing or restoring property should be covered by the primary provisions of a commercial property policy, not by extra expense coverage.[316] Note, however, that some policies provide extra expense coverage for expenses incurred to repair or replace property to the extent it reduces the amount of loss that otherwise would have been payable.[317]

[vi] Costs of Compliance with Duties after Loss

The duties of the insured after a loss under the ISO policy were discussed earlier.[318] The insured will incur expenses in complying with those duties. Generally, courts hold that costs of investigating, cooperating with the insurers' investigation, and complying with the duties under the policy after a loss are

312. Imperial Trading Co. v. Travelers Prop. Cas. Co. of Am., 2009 U.S. Dist. LEXIS 64010 (E.D. La. July 24, 2009).

313. Demers Bros. Trucking, Inc. v. Certain Underwriters, 600 F. Supp. 2d 265, 278 (D. Mass. 2009).

314. ISO Form CP 00 30 10 12, § A.2.b.(1).

315. Thompson v. Threshermen's Mut. Ins. Co., 172 Wis. 2d 275, 493 N.W.2d 734 (Wis. App. 1992).

316. *See, e.g.*, Nassau Gallery, Inc. v. Nationwide Mut. Fire Ins. Co. 2003 Del. Super. LEXIS 487 (Apr. 17, 2003) (reconstruction expenditures are related to primary coverage, not extra expense provisions).

317. *See, e.g.*, Interstate Gourmet Coffee Roasters, Inc. v. Travelers Indem. Co., 2018 U.S. Dist. LEXIS 131293 (D. Mass. Aug. 6, 2018); Nassau Gallery, Inc. v. Nationwide Mut. Fire Ins. Co. 2003 Del. Super. LEXIS 487 (Apr. 17, 2003).

318. See § 6.02[8], *supra*.

not incurred to avoid suspension of the insured's business operations and are not recoverable.[319]

6.4 Expediting Expense

An "expediting expense" is defined as the cost "to complete repairs to put the insured back in business as rapidly as possible, even if a temporary arrangement."[320] The coverage may be found in a variety of property policies and pays for temporary repairs to speed up permanent repair or replacement of covered property or equipment.[321] For example, the ISO Contractors Equipment Coverage Form,[322] Builder's Risk Coverage Form,[323] and Inland Marine Installation Coverage Form[324] all contain an "Expediting Expense" clause. The clauses are identical and provide that, for loss or damage to covered property from a covered cause of loss, the insurer will pay for the extra cost the insured necessarily incurs to make temporary repairs and to expedite permanent repairs or replacement of the damaged property.[325] Unless a different limit of insurance is shown on the Declarations Page, the most the insurer will pay is $25,000 per occurrence.[326]

Some clauses may more specifically define the covered expenses. For example, a policy may provide that it covers the "reasonable extra cost of temporary repairs and of expediting the repair of property damaged by an insured peril, including overtime and the extra cost of express or other rapid means of

---

319. Cozen, *Insuring Real Property* § 3.04[1][d] (LexisNexis Matthew Bender 2020).

320. *Expediting Expense*, IRMI, https://www.irmi.com/term/insurance-definitions/expediting-expense. *See* 5 Jeffrey E. Thomas, *New Appleman on Insurance Law Library Edition* § 46.04[2] (LexisNexis 2020) (some policy forms distinguish between "extra expense" and "expediting expense" and have separate sublimits of liability for each type of coverage).

321. *Expediting Expense Coverage*, IRMI, https://www.irmi.com/term/insurance-definitions/expediting-expense-coverage.

322. ISO Form IH 00 68 05 17 § A.5.c.

323. ISO Form IH 00 70 05 17 § A.5.d.

324. ISO Form IH 00 73 05 17 § A.5.b.

325. There are other slightly different versions of expediting expense coverage. For example, one policy provided that "In the event of direct physical loss of or damage to Covered Property caused by or resulting from a Covered Cause of Loss, [the insurer would] pay for the reasonable and necessary additional expenses [the insured incurred] to make temporary repairs, expedite permanent repairs, or expedite permanent replacement, at the premises sustaining loss or damage." Quoted in *Greenspoint Investors, Ltd. v. Travelers Lloyds Ins. Co.*, 2015 U.S. Dist. LEXIS 25301 (S.D. Tex. Mar. 3, 2015).

326. *See, e.g.*, Pepper Mill Condo. Ass'n v. Hartford Fire Ins. Co., 71 Pa. D. & C. 4th 54 (2005), where the insured sought coverage for the cost of constructing a temporary parking lot to replace a collapsed parking deck. The insurer paid the $25,000 limit for expediting expense and argued it was not required to pay the full cost of temporary parking. The court agreed. The insurer was obligated, it said, to pay for construction of a new structure to replace the damaged one, but any loss suffered by the insured to construct temporary parking spaces was not compensable under the policy.

transportation to the extent such costs are not otherwise recoverable." Under that language, a court decided the reasonable expenses incurred to accelerate or expedite repair or replacement of damaged property were covered as part of the full replacement cost.[327]

Another version of the expediting clause covers the reasonable extra cost to make *temporary repairs* and to expedite the *permanent repair or replacement* of property damage by an insured peril. That language has been held to limit coverage to "temporary repairs" as opposed to "temporary replacements," which are not covered.[328]

The expediting expense coverage is for expenses *actually incurred*.[329] The fact that repairs have commenced does not establish that the policyholder has *incurred* expediting expenses.[330] Note that expediting clauses do not typically refer to expenses incurred during a particular period, specifically the "period of restoration" that is usually referenced in business interruption coverage. Thus, a California appellate court upheld an award of expediting expenses despite the objection of the insurer that the award should be limited to expenses incurred by the policyholder from the time that it acquired title to the property to the end of the period of restoration. The court responded that the insurer had failed to explain *why* recoverable expenses for temporary repairs should be limited to those incurred during the period of restoration. It noted that the expediting expense clause did not expressly limit recoverable expenses to those incurred during the period of restoration and, in fact, did not mention the period of restoration.[331] Recovery of expediting expenses may be limited by the policy language to the extent that the expenses actually reduce the loss.[332]

327. Weitz Co. LLC v. Lloyd's of London, 2010 U.S. Dist. LEXIS 148065 (S.D. Iowa Dec. 20, 2010).

328. Detroit Edison Co. v. Protection Mutual Insurance Co., 134 F.3d 790, 795 (6th Cir. 1998). *See also* Cincinnati Gas & Elec. Co. v. Hartford Steam Boiler Inspection & Ins. Co., 2008 U.S. Dist. LEXIS 29569 (S.D. Ohio Apr. 10, 2008). *Compare* R.D. Offutt Co. v. Lexington Ins. Co., 494 F.3d 668 (8th Cir. 2007) (finding coverage where policy covered reasonable extra cost of temporary repair and/or replacement of insured property).

329. Greenspoint Investors, Ltd. v. Travelers Lloyds Ins. Co., 2015 U.S. Dist. LEXIS 25301 (S.D. Tex. Mar. 3, 2015).

330. Cont'l Cas. Co. v. F-Star Prop. Mgmt., 2011 U.S. Dist. LEXIS 76921 (W.D. Tex. July 15, 2011).

331. Daimlerchrysler Servs. North America LLC v. Zurich American Ins. Co., 2005 Cal. App. Unpub. LEXIS 5385 (June 22, 2005).

332. *Expediting Expense Coverage*, IRMI, https://www.irmi.com/term/insurance-definitions/expediting-expense-coverage. *See also* Morrison, Miller & Paris, *Business Interruption Insurance: Its Theory and Practice* (National Underwriter 1986) (for expediting expenses, hindsight has to be used because only after the fact is it possible to determine whether or not there was any actual savings and the amount).

6.5 Preservation of Property Clause

When a business anticipates the possibility of flood damage to covered property, it may incur expenses in moving that property to safety or suffer a loss when the property is damaged in transit. There may be coverage for those expenses under a "preservation of property" clause. This is a standard provision in commercial property policies but is easily overlooked. Under the ISO Building and Personal Property Coverage Form version of the clause, the insurer will pay for any direct physical loss or damage to covered property when it is necessary to move it from the insured premises to preserve it from loss or damage by a covered cause of loss.[333] Because flood damage or loss is typically an excluded cause of loss, the coverage usually will not apply when the insured moves property to protect it from flood waters. One, therefore, needs to determine if the policy is one that provides flood coverage or if it has been added by endorsement. There are two other conditions on the coverage in the ISO clause. First, the coverage is only for direct physical loss or damage to covered property while it is being moved or temporarily stored at another location.[334] Second, it only applies if the loss or damage occurs within 30 days after the covered property is first moved.[335]

Some policies have broader coverage than does the ISO Building and Personal Property Coverage Form. For example, insurers may pay the cost to *remove* covered property from the insured premises in addition to paying for direct physical loss or damage to it.[336] An Iowa federal court examined a policy with removal coverage and decided that "preserve" meant keeping the property safe from "injury, harm, or destruction."[337] It then noted that the clause covered property, not operations. The policy, therefore, was not intended to cover any costs associated with suspension of operations or their re-establishment. The insured, however, was entitled to be reimbursed for the necessary expense of removing property, including its data. The question of whether certain costs were "necessary" could not, said the court, be resolved on summary judgment.

The "Preservation of Property" clause needs to be distinguished from the "Protection of Property" clause, which is generally found in the "Loss Conditions" portion of the policy.[338] It requires the insured to take reasonable steps

---

333. ISO Form CP 00 10 10 12 § A.4.b. *See generally* Cozen, *Insuring Real Property*, § 1.06[4][i] (Matthew Bender & Co., 2020) (Preservation of Property clause provides coverage for property removed from insured premises to protect it from covered peril).

334. ISO Form CP 00 10 10 12 § A.4.b.(1).

335. ISO Form CP 00 10 10 12 § A.4.b.(2).

336. The coverage ended when the property was returned to the original location.

337. Phoenix Ins. Co. v. Infogroup, Inc., 147 F. Supp. 3d 815 (S.D. Iowa 2015).

338. *See, e.g.*, ISO Form CP 00 10 10 12 § E.3.a.(4). *See also* Phoenix Ins. Co. v. Infogroup, Inc., 147 F. Supp. 3d 815 (S.D. Iowa 2015) (Protection of Property clause is not itself a source

to protect covered property from further damage. It applies to property that is already damaged, not to property the insured seeks to preserve from being damaged. The insurer will, under both common law and standard policy language, pay the costs of these "mitigation" efforts.[339]

---

of coverage, but it is a duty that insureds have to perform in the event of loss or damage to covered property).

339. *See* 5 Jeffrey E. Thomas, *New Appleman on Insurance Law Library Edition* § 45.02[1] (LexisNexis 2020).

7

Recovering under Builder's Risk Insurance

7.1 Introduction

Water damage including flooding is a matter of particular concern for construction projects. As one expert commentary observes, there can be many causes: human error, for example, an ill-fitted plumbing connection; an accident that triggers a sprinkler system; a local water main break; a region-wide heavy rain with or without storm surge.[1] Losses include property damage, costs of cleanup, and costly delays in construction. The parties to a construction project—whether a home renovation or a major commercial project—generally acquire "builder's risk" insurance to cover water damage among other causes of loss. The coverage comes in a variety of forms and will often initially exclude water or flood damage. However, as discussed next,[2] most *construction contracts* require flood coverage. Additionally, construction lenders will generally require flood coverage as a condition of making a loan,[3] so a builder's risk policy that lacks flood coverage will generally have the coverage added by endorsement.

1. Gadaire & Szczucki, *Builders' Risk: Water Damage or Flood? Addressing the Risks, Understanding the Coverage for Damage and Mitigating the Exposures*, at 2 (May 2016), *available at* https://www.chubb.com/US-EN/_Assets/doc/2016-05-Builders-Risk--Water-Damage-or-Flood.pdf. The authors add that water may infiltrate a building through unfinished areas during construction and through defects once the project is complete. For example, rain can enter through open windows, doors, and unprotected/yet-to-be-completed openings or interior plumbing and fire-suppression systems may leak because of defects or installation mistakes.

2. See § 7.05, *infra.*

3. *See, e.g.*, https://www.bankersonline.com, a website offering information to banking professionals. It sponsors topic forums, and one of them advises that when making construction loans, lenders have two options concerning purchase of flood insurance: require it before closing the loan, or delay its purchase until a slab is poured or an elevation certificate is issued. *Flood Insurance on New Construction*, Bankers Online, https://www.bankersonline.com/forum/ubbthreads.php/ubb/printthread/Board/90/main/243914/type/thread#:~:text=Flood%20Insurance%20%26%20Construction%20Loans.%20When%20it%20comes,is%20poured%20or%20an%20elevation%20certificate%20is%20issued.

"Builder's risk insurance"—also called "Course of Construction" insurance[4]—is "first-party" property insurance.[5] It "is a unique form of property insurance that typically covers only projects under construction, renovation, or repair and insures against accidental losses, damages or destruction of property for which the insured has an insurable interest."[6] Builder's risk coverage "protects the contractor insured against loss even without contractor error."[7] It compensates the insured for loss from physical damage or destruction caused to the construction project itself.[8] It is distinguished from commercial general liability insurance on a construction project, which protects the insured against loss to *others* from the contractor's errors.[9] Builder's risk insurance is often required to comply with government regulations or as a condition to meet lending or other contractual agreements.[10]

A builder's risk policy insures against damage to the work and property of contractors occurring during construction.[11] Generally, the policy extends coverage until the property is occupied or abandoned.[12] Despite the fact that these policies are called "builder's risk," the insured under a policy may

---

4. Rodriguez, *Understanding Builder's Risk Insurance; When to Have a Builder's Risk Policy* (Mar. 8, 2018), LiveAbout, https://www.thebalance.com/understanding-builders-risk-insurance-844798. Insurers may have other names for the coverage, for example: "Contractor's and Owner's Property Protection Insurance Policy." N. Coast Enters. v. St. Paul Fire & Marine Ins. Co., 2006 U.S. Dist. LEXIS 20245 (W.D. Wash. Mar. 28, 2006).

5. Stover, *A Guide to Builder's Risk Insurance*, 53 Tort & Ins. L.J. 819 (2018).

6. Fireman's Fund v. Structural Sys. Tech., Inc., 426 F. Supp. 2d 1009, 1025 (D. Neb. 2006).

7. Estrin Const. Co. v. Aetna Cas. & Sur. Co., 612 S.W.2d 413, 427 (Mo. App. 1981).

8. Southern California Edison Co. v. Harbor Ins. Co., 83 Cal. App. 3d 747, 757, 148 Cal. Rptr. 106, 111 (1978). *See also* Fireman's Fund v. Structural Sys. Tech., Inc., 426 F. Supp. 2d 1009, 1025 (D. Neb. 2006). Physical damage may simply mean that the property does not function properly. For example, in one case, the insured was constructing a siphon culvert. The rising waters of a flash flood filled the culvert with mud, dirt, and other debris so that it was completely blocked. The insured sought the expense of clearing the blockage. The insurer refused coverage because the structure of the culvert was not damaged. The court, however, said that the culvert was rendered useless by the blockage and entirely ineffective for the only purpose for which it was being built. Before the insured could complete the project, the culvert had to be cleared and, held the court, the insured was entitled to the cost of clearing it. Morrison-Knudsen Co. v. Phoenix Insurance Co. of Hartford, 172 F.2d 124 (8th Cir. 1949).

9. Estrin Const. Co. v. Aetna Cas. & Sur. Co., 612 S.W.2d 413, 427 (Mo. App. 1981). *See also* Southern California Edison Co. v. Harbor Ins. Co., 83 Cal. App. 3d 747, 756, 148 Cal. Rptr. 106, 111 (1978) (liability insurance indemnifies contractor to third parties).

10. *From Groundbreaking to Remodeling: Builders Risk 101 Guide*, at 2, *available at* https://go.usassure.com/rs/381-ISO-510/images/From%20Groundbreaking%20to%20Renovating%20A%20Builders%20Risk%20101%20Guide.pdf.

11. Cozen, *Insuring Real Property*, § 6.01 (LexisNexis Matthew Bender 2020). *See also* Stover, *A Guide to Builder's Risk Insurance*, 53 Tort & Ins. L.J. 819 (2018) (builder's risk covers building during construction, before it becomes insurable as completed structure, while materials and components are being moved on-site, assembled, and put in place).

12. Farm Bureau Mut. Ins. Co. v. McAndrews Livestock Co., 2010 Iowa App. LEXIS 1177 (Oct. 6, 2010).

include the ultimate owner of the construction project and lending institutions as well as contractors performing the work and architects or engineers,[13] but typically not suppliers of materials.[14] Indeed, the named insured under the policy will typically be either the property owner or the general contractor.[15] A neighboring property owner would have no insurable interest in a building under construction and would not, therefore, be eligible to be added on to a builder's risk policy.[16]

Builder's risk coverage is incorporated into standard commercial building and personal property coverage.[17] Those policies cover direct physical loss of or damage to covered property caused by or resulting from a covered cause of loss. Covered property includes, if not covered by other insurance, additions under construction, alterations, and repairs to the insured building,[18] and materials, equipment, supplies, and temporary structures used for making those additions, alterations, or repairs.[19] There is also coverage for new buildings while being built at the insured premises, which may be capped at $250,000.[20] Experts recommend against use of a commercial building and personal property policy for builder's risk coverage because of its limitations.[21]

---

13. Prahl, *Course of Construction Insurance: Some Important Considerations* (Dec. 2001), *available at* http://roughnotes.com/rnmagazine/2001/december01/12p46.htm.

14. Malecki, *Builder's Risk Insurance: Specialized Coverage for Construction Projects*, Adjusting Today, *available at* https://adjustersinternational.com/publications/adjusting-today/builders-risk-insurance/0/.

15. Stover, *A Guide to Builder's Risk Insurance*, 53 Tort & Ins. L.J. 819 (2018). Note that there can be coverage in certain circumstances for a loss suffered by a party that is not a named insured. *See* El-Ad 250 West LLC v. Zurich Am. Ins. Co., 2016 N.Y. Misc. LEXIS 1239 (Mar. 30, 2016) (although developer of project was only named insured, losses by its affiliates, who also bore risk of delay in completion damages, could be recovered where it could be shown parties intended to cover those affiliates).

16. 145 W. 21st Realty LLC v. First W. 21st St. LLC, 2016 N.Y. Misc. LEXIS 275 (Jan. 22, 2016).

17. *See, e.g.*, ISO Form CP 00 10 04 02. *See generally* Meislik, *Is It Enough To Write: "X Must Also Carry Builder's Risk Insurance"?—A Rhetorical Question* (Apr. 5, 2015), Ruminations, http://www.retailrealestatelaw.com/archives/2809 (some of special risks encountered during new construction or renovations can be covered by a basic Building and Personal Property Coverage Form); Austin, *Builders Risk Insurance: Is It Always Necessary?* (Nov. 2012), IRMI, https://www.irmi.com/articles/expert-commentary/is-builders-risk-insurance-necessary (some property policy forms provide coverage for builder's risk exposure equal to that provided by builder's risk policies).

18. ISO Form CP 00 10 04 02, § A.1.a.(5).(a).

19. ISO Form CP 00 10 04 02, § A.1.a.(5).(b).

20. ISO Form CP 00 10 04 02, § A.5.a.(1).(a).

21. Meislik, *Is It Enough To Write: "X Must Also Carry Builder's Risk Insurance"?—A Rhetorical Question* (Apr. 5, 2015), Ruminations, http://www.retailrealestatelaw.com/archives/2809 (ISO building and personal property coverage form, if used at all, should be limited to small projects; policy has many exclusions and does not afford appropriate coverage to contractors and subcontractors, sufficiently cover materials off-premises or in transit, or provide contractors and subcontractors with direct coverage). *See also* Prahl, *Course of Construction*

One of those limitations is that under the Causes of Loss form that is typically incorporated into the policy, water damage, including flood, is excluded.[22] Flood coverage will, therefore, have to be found in an endorsement.

Builder's risk coverage may be found in an "inland marine" policy.[23] Inland marine insurance is not easy to define. The glossary prepared by the National Association of Insurance Commissioners describes it in part as "coverage for property that may be in transit, held by a bailee, at a fixed location, a movable good that is often at different locations (e.g., off road constructions equipment), or scheduled property."[24] Generally, inland marine insurance covers products, materials, and equipment when they are transported over land or while they are temporarily warehoused by a third party.[25] It is used to fill in gaps for property that is difficult to value, has a fluctuating value, or is capable of changing locations.[26] Property insured under a builder's risk policy presents those challenges. Equipment and material may move to and from a site during construction, and the value of structures will fluctuate as they are built, repaired, or renovated. Forms and rates of inland marine builder's risk policies are not subject to the requirement of filing with state insurance regulators, allowing carriers to create their own coverage provisions and rates, which can be tailored to the particular risk exposure.[27]

While property owners, contractors, and lenders may look to a builder's risk policy to recover for a loss, it is important to be aware that subcontractors—for example, electricians, plumbers, and heating, ventilating, and air-conditioning (HVAC) installers—may be separately insured by a policy

---

Insurance: Some Important Considerations (Dec. 2001), *available at* http://roughnotes.com/rnmagazine/2001/december01/12p46.htm (builder's risk provides considerably broader coverage than in standard commercial property policy).

22. *See* ISO Form CP 10 30 06 07, § B.1.g.

23. *See, e.g.*, Fireman's Fund v. Structural Sys. Tech., Inc., 426 F. Supp. 2d 1009 (D. Neb. 2006). The insurer provided inland marine coverages including for materials, supplies, machinery, equipment, and fixtures for which the insured had assumed liability and contracted to install or erect. The insurance carrier denied the coverage was builder's risk. The court disagreed and found that a reasonable insured would understand the policy to provide builder's risk coverage for the damage in question. *See also* RK Mech., Inc. v. Travelers Prop. Cas. Co. of Am., 944 F. Supp. 2d 1013 (D. Colo. 2011).

24. *Glossary I*, NAIC, https://content.naic.org/consumer_glossary.htm#I.

25. *Understanding Inland Marine Insurance*, Insurance Information Institute, https://www.iii.org/article/understanding-inland-marine-insurance. *See also* Malecki, *Builder's Risk Insurance: Specialized Coverage for Construction Projects*, Adjusting Today, *available at* https://adjustersinternational.com/publications/adjusting-today/builders-risk-insurance/0/ (inland marine builder's risk policy necessary to cover materials and equipment in storage awaiting transit to job site and while in transit).

26. 5 Jeffrey E. Thomas, *New Appleman on Insurance Law Library Edition* § 52.01[1][a] (LexisNexis 2020).

27. Prahl, *Course of Construction Insurance: Some Important Considerations* (Dec. 2001), *available at* http://roughnotes.com/rnmagazine/2001/december01/12p46.htm.

known as an "installation floater."[28] That is in effect a builder's risk policy written to cover only a specific type of property during installation.[29]

7.2 Insurable Interest

The concept of an insurable interest takes on added meaning in a builder's risk policy. A party seeking to recover for a flood loss at a construction site needs to be prepared to identify the insurable interest in the property at issue because it is an issue the insurer may raise. The general rule is that one may not recover on a policy in the event of loss without an insurable interest in the subject matter.[30] An insurable interest in property has been described as any interest in which a party would profit from or gain some advantage by its continued existence and suffer some loss or disadvantage by its destruction.[31] In some states the insurable interest doctrine has been codified. New York, for example, has a statute providing that:

> No contract or policy of insurance on property made or issued in this state, or made or issued upon any property in this state, shall be enforceable except for the benefit of some person having an insurable interest in the property insured. In this article, "insurable interest" shall include any lawful and substantial economic interest in the safety or preservation of property from loss, destruction or pecuniary damage.[32]

The "substantial economic interest" may be fee ownership but need not be. Other interests are considered substantial economic ones.[33] For example, a mortgagor or construction lender has an economic interest in the property securing the debt.[34] In a builder's risk policy there are a number of parties that

---

28. Austin, *Builders Risk Insurance: Is It Always Necessary?* (Nov. 2012), IRMI, https://www.irmi.com/articles/expert-commentary/is-builders-risk-insurance-necessary.

29. Fireman's Fund v. Structural Sys. Tech., Inc., 426 F. Supp. 2d 1009 (D. Neb. 2006). 5 Jeffrey E. Thomas, *New Appleman on Insurance Law Library Edition* § 50.01[3][d][iii] (LexisNexis 2020).

30. *See, e.g.*, Commonwealth v. Rodebaugh, 519 A.2d 555, 563 (Pa. Commw. 1986).

31. Adams v. Allstate Ins., 723 F. Supp. 111, 115 (D. Ark. 1989).

32. NY CLS Ins. § 3401. *See also* Rev. Code Wash. § 48.18.040(2) ("insurable interest . . . means any lawful and substantial economic interest in the safety or preservation of the subject of the insurance free from loss, destruction, or pecuniary damage). *Compare* Cal. Ins. Code § 281 ("Every interest in property, or any relation thereto, or liability in respect thereof, of such a nature that a contemplated peril might directly damnify the insured, is an insurable interest.").

33. *See* Cassadei v. Nationwide Mut. Fire Ins. Co., 21 A.D.3d 681, 799 N.Y.S.2d 687 (2005) (ownership not required to create insurable interest); Boston Ins. Co. v. Beckett, 91 Idaho 220, 419 P.2d 475 (1966) (mere right to use property may constitute insurable interest).

34. Sotelo v. Washington Mut. Ins. Co., 734 A.2d 421, 423 (Pa. Super. 1999); CLS Mtg., Inc. v. Bruno, 86 Wn. App. 390, 937 P.2d 1106 (1997) (mortgagee's insurable interest is initially presumed to be the value mortgaged, and because the mortgagee's insurable interest cannot

may be insureds but not have an insurable interest when there is a loss. These would include architects,[35] engineers, and tenants of a building under repair or renovation.[36] Contractors are generally insured under a builder's risk policy, and while they usually have no ownership interest in the property, they have a financial stake in the continued existence of projects under construction and, therefore, generally are held to have an insurable interest in the subject property during construction.[37] Of course, when the covered property under the policy includes machinery and equipment and temporary structures like scaffolding, the contractor's interest is clear. The policy may provide that coverage is for the interest of a contractor in the property *to the extent* the insured property owner has assumed liability. In one case in which that was the language of the policy, heavy rainfall caused a two-month delay in a construction project, and the contractor suffered financial loss that it sought to recover from the insurer. The court examined the underlying agreement between the owner and contractor and found that the former was not obligated to insure the interests of the contractor beyond the "replacement cost" of the project. Therefore, said the court, the contractor could not recover damages in excess of the full replacement cost of the damaged property, as those interests were not insured.[38]

7.3 Builder's Risk Policies: Coverages and Flood Exclusions

[1] Introduction

It is always important to review the exact language of a policy, but this is especially true of builder's risk policies. That is because there can be significant variation from one policy to another in coverages and exclusions,[39] and

exceed value of property subject to mortgage, its ability to recover is limited to extent of debt secured by the property).

35. *See* Dyson & Co. v. Flood Engineers, Architects, Planners, Inc., 523 So. 2d 756, 759 (Fla. 1st DCA 1988) (company hired to design and engineer specifications for construction project had insurable interest because where potential risk to be insured under builder's risk policy is one of liability for damages to construction project, that risk will constitute "insurable interest").

36. Tenants may have an insurable interest in property. *See, e.g.*, Sigola Mfg., Inc. v. Dairyland Ins. Co., 124 A.D.2d 654, 508 N.Y.S.2d 38 (1986).

37. Cozen, *Insuring Real Property*, § 6.02[3][a] (LexisNexis Matthew Bender 2020). *See, e.g.*, Homestead Fire Ins. Co. v. De Witt, 206 Okla. 570, 572, 245 P.2d 92, 94 (1952) (in so far as it was necessary for contractor to alter or disturb condition of roof of existing building, it had insurable interest in that building).

38. Weitz Co. LLC v. Lloyd's of London, 2010 U.S. Dist. LEXIS 148065 (S.D. Iowa Dec. 20, 2010).

39. Stover, *A Guide to Builder's Risk Insurance*, 53 Tort & Ins. L.J. 819 (2018).

there are a wide variety of policies available.[40] Unlike more common forms of coverage—for example, commercial general liability or homeowner's policies—many insurance companies do not use standard polices for builder's risk insurance.[41] Also, manuscript policies—non-standard forms drafted for a particular risk[42]—are not uncommon.[43] Typically, the policy would be issued by a single carrier, but it is important to be aware that for large projects, there may be several carriers sharing a percentage of the risk.[44] This section provides an overview of the coverage found in policies from the Insurance Service Organization, the American Association of Insurance Services, and an individual insurance carrier.

Builder's risk policies typically cover the structure, building materials, supplies, equipment, and machinery that are intended to become a permanent part of a covered building or structure; temporary structures constructed and used on the job site, including construction forms and scaffolding and "falsework";[45] and generally materials in transit and in temporary storage

40. Cozen, *Insuring Real Property*, § 6.01 (LexisNexis Matthew Bender 2020). *See also From Groundbreaking to Remodeling: Builders Risk 101 Guide*, at 7 (coverage forms are not standard in marketplace and vary by insurance provider), *available at* https://go.usassure.com/rs/381-ISO-510/images/From%20Groundbreaking%20to%20Renovating%20A%20Builders%20Risk%20101%20Guide.pdf.

41. Malecki, *Builder's Risk Insurance: Specialized Coverage for Construction Projects*, Adjusting Today, *available at* https://adjustersinternational.com/publications/adjusting-today/builders-risk-insurance/0/ (contrary to general belief, provisions of builder's risk policies do not follow those of Insurance Services Office).

42. 1 Jeffrey E. Thomas, *New Appleman on Insurance Law Library Edition* § 1.07[9] (LexisNexis 2020).

43. Cozen, *Insuring Real Property*, § 6.01 (LexisNexis Matthew Bender 2020) (specially manuscripted coverage may be available under certain circumstances); Meeder & Chivilo, *Builder's Risk Insurance: Resurrecting the Project after the Storm: Best Practices for Securing Coverage for Project and Claim Costs after Major Loss Events* (Sept. 14, 2017), Holland, & Knight, https://www.hklaw.com/publications/Builders-Risk-Insurance-Resurrecting-the-Project-After-the-Storm-09-14-2017/ (general practice is for insurance companies to issue builder's risk insurance on their own manuscripted forms). *See also* Indianapolis Airport Auth. v. Travelers Prop. Cas. Co. of Am., 849 F.3d 355 (7th Cir. 2017) (commercial inland marine policy was not boilerplate contract of adhesion but instead customized policy negotiated by parties); Residential Constructors, LLC v. Ace Prop. & Cas. Ins. Co., 2006 U.S. Dist. LEXIS 80403 (D. Nev. Nov. 1, 2006) (insurer stated that from time to time it issues manuscript policies drafted for specific customer whose terms and conditions are subject to specific negotiation between insurer and insured).

44. Meeder & Chivilo, *Builder's Risk Insurance: Resurrecting the Project after the Storm: Best Practices for Securing Coverage for Project and Claim Costs after Major Loss Events* (Sept. 14, 2017), Holland & Knight, https://www.hklaw.com/publications/Builders-Risk-Insurance-Resurrecting-the-Project-After-the-Storm-09-14-2017/ (large-value builder's risk coverage is usually underwritten through syndicated policy in which there may be several different companies with an agreed percentage of risk; when insured has a claim, it is important to identify all syndicated carriers and to place them on notice of it as early as possible).

45. "Falsework" is a temporary structure serving as support for part of the permanent structure. Prahl, *Course of Construction Insurance: Some Important Considerations* (Dec. 2001), *available at* http://roughnotes.com/rnmagazine/2001/december01/12p46.htm.

away from the job site.[46] The policies cover "direct physical loss of or damage to covered property." Generally, that means some physical change.[47] Builder's risk policies will state a total completed value, but the value of the property increases as construction proceeds.[48] A policy, therefore, may state that the value of covered property will be determined "as of the time of loss or damage."[49]

The discussion of policy language illustrates key areas addressed by builder's risk policies. These are covered property, property *not* covered, water damage exclusions, and debris removal coverage. The last is of particular importance because flooding can deposit much debris that has to be removed, often at considerable cost, before a construction project can resume.

[2] Insurance Service Organization Policies

[a] Introduction

The Insurance Services Office (ISO) collects statistical data, promulgates rating information, develops standard policy forms, and files information with state regulators on behalf of insurance companies.[50] It has been a leading source

---

46. Stover, *A Guide to Builder's Risk Insurance*, 53 Tort & Ins. L.J. 819 (2018). *See, e.g.*, Oceanside Pier View, L.P. v. Travelers Prop. Cas. Co. of Am., 2008 U.S. Dist. LEXIS 37755 (S.D. Cal. May 6, 2008) (coverage for property that would become permanent part of buildings or structures at job site while in transit to job site or temporary storage locations and while at job site or at temporary storage location). However, where precast concrete panels awaiting delivery were destroyed at the manufacturing plant where they were made, they were not in storage. 151 First Side Assocs., L.P. v. Peerless Ins. Co., 2010 U.S. Dist. LEXIS 23093 (W.D. Pa. Mar. 11, 2010) (for facility to fit within plain meaning of "storage location," it must be space or place used for putting or keeping things for future use; manufacturing plant was production site, not storage facility).

47. Sierra Pac. Power Co. v. Hartford Steam Boiler Inspection & Ins. Co., 665 F.3d 1166, 1172 (9th Cir. 2012) (direct physical loss contemplates actual change in insured property); AFLAC Inc. v. Chubb & Sons, Inc., 260 Ga. App. 306, 308, 581 S.E.2d 317, 319 (2003) (direct physical loss or damage contemplates actual change in insured property then in satisfactory state, causing it to become unsatisfactory for future use or requiring that repairs be made). *See also* One Place Condo., LLC v. Travelers Prop. Cas. Co. of Am., 2015 U.S. Dist. LEXIS 56565 (N.D. Ill. Apr. 22, 2015) (requirement that loss be physical is widely held to exclude alleged losses that are intangible or incorporeal). *See generally* Stover, *A Guide to Builder's Risk Insurance*, 53 Tort & Ins. L.J. 819 (2018) (it is generally held that "physical loss" requires some physical change in the condition of the covered property).

48. One Place Condo., LLC v. Travelers Prop. Cas. Co. of Am., 2015 U.S. Dist. LEXIS 56565 (N.D. Ill. Apr. 22, 2015).

49. *See, e.g.*, ISO Form CP 00 20 10 12, § E.6. *See generally* Cozen, *Insuring Real Property*, § 6.02[4] (LexisNexis Matthew Bender 2020) (builder's risk policies may provide for recovery of cost to repair or replace damaged property, value of property at time of loss, or lesser of the two); Garaffa & Raschke, *The Valuation of Losses under Builder's Risk Policies*, 40 The Brief 50 (American Bar Association, Fall 2010).

50. *Insurance Services Office Inc. (ISO)*, IRMI, https://www.irmi.com/online/insurance-glossary/terms/i/insurance-services-office-inc.-iso.aspx. Verisk Analytics is a data analytics provider

of information about property/casualty insurance risk since 1971.[51] It is the recognized leader in creating standard policies for many types of coverage.[52] Most property or general liability policies are written on ISO forms.[53] Some insurance carriers issue policies using ISO forms and endorsements without any changes, while others employ the ISO language as a basis for drafting their own forms. Many policies and endorsements contain an amalgam of ISO standard wording and an insurer's proprietary language.[54] Even though builder's risk policies are less likely than other types of insurance to be drafted by ISO,[55] ISO language is still important because of its similarity to that found in other policies.

[b] ISO Commercial Property Builder's Risk Coverage Form

Under the ISO Commercial Property Builder's Risk Coverage Form, the insurer will pay for direct physical loss of or damage[56] to covered property at the premises described in the Declarations that is caused by or results from any covered cause of loss.[57] The causes of loss are set forth in one of three separate forms: Basic,[58] Broad,[59] and Special.[60] The first two name specific perils. Both include "sprinkler leakage,"[61] which can result in "flooding." It is defined to

---

serving customers in insurance, natural resources, and financial services. *About Verisk*, Verisk, http://www.verisk.com/about.html.

51. *Access Our Products*, Verisk, http://www.verisk.com/iso.html.

52. https://www.verisk.com/insurance/capabilities/insurance-policy-programs/.

53. Stempel, *The Insurance Policy as Statute*, 41 McGeorge L. Rev. 203, 207 (2010). Yu, *Let's Get Physical: Loss of Use of Tangible Property as Coverage in Cyber Insurance*, 40 Rutgers Computer & Tech. L.J. 229, 238 (2014) (ISO commercial general liability policy language has become industry standard).

54. Bonner, *Insurance Services Office (ISO)* (May 16, 2019), The Balance, https://www.thebalance.com/insurance-services-office-iso-462706.

55. Malecki, *Builder's Risk Insurance: Specialized Coverage for Construction Projects*, Adjusting Today, *available at* https://adjustersinternational.com/publications/adjusting-today/builders-risk-insurance/0/.

56. Sierra Pac. Power Co. v. Hartford Steam Boiler Inspection & Ins. Co., 665 F.3d 1166, 1172 (9th Cir. 2012) (direct physical loss contemplates actual change in insured property); AFLAC Inc. v. Chubb & Sons, Inc., 260 Ga. App. 306, 308, 581 S.E.2d 317, 319 (2003) (direct physical loss or damage contemplates actual change in insured property then in satisfactory state, causing it to become unsatisfactory for future use or requiring that repairs be made). *See also* One Place Condo., LLC v. Travelers Prop. Cas. Co. of Am., 2015 U.S. Dist. LEXIS 56565 (N.D. Ill. Apr. 22, 2015) (requirement that loss be physical is widely held to exclude alleged losses that are intangible or incorporeal).

57. ISO Form CP 00 20 10 12, § A.

58. ISO Form CP 10 10 10 12.

59. ISO Form CP 10 20 10 12.

60. ISO Form CP 10 30 10 12.

61. ISO Form CP 10 10 10 12, § A.9; ISO Form CP 10 20 10 12 § A.9. If the building or structure containing the system is covered property, the insurer will pay the cost to repair or replace damaged parts of the system if the damage results in sprinkler leakage or is directly caused by freezing. It will also pay to tear out and replace any part of the building or structure to repair damage to the system that has resulted in sprinkler leakage.

mean leakage or discharge of *any substance* from an automatic sprinkler system and includes the collapse of a tank that is part of the system. The Broad form adds "water damage" as a cause of loss,[62] but defines it narrowly as the accidental discharge or leakage of water or steam as the direct result of the breaking apart or cracking of a plumbing, heating, air-conditioning, or other system or appliance located on the described premises and that contains water or steam. "Water damage" does not include discharge or leakage from an automatic sprinkler system, a sump, or related equipment and parts, including overflow because of sump pump failure or excessive volume of water, or roof drains, gutters, downspouts, or similar fixtures or equipment. It also does not include the cost to repair any defect that caused the loss or damage or loss or damage caused by or resulting from continuous or repeated seepage or leakage of water, or the presence or condensation of humidity, moisture, or vapor, occurring over 14 days or more. Finally, water damage does not include loss or damage caused by or resulting from freezing, unless the insured does his or her best to maintain heat in the building or structure or drains the equipment and shuts off the water supply if heat is not maintained.[63]

Most builder's risk policies are written on an all-perils or all-risks basis.[64] That is the coverage provided by the ISO Special Form. Therefore, it covers a loss by flood or water unless excluded. All three causes of loss forms exclude coverage for water damage including flood.

Under the exclusion, the carrier will not pay for loss or damage caused directly or indirectly by "water."[65] It defines water to include the following:

- Flood; surface water; waves, including tidal wave and tsunami; tides; tidal water; overflow of any body of water; or spray from any of them, and all whether or not driven by wind, including storm surge;
- Mudslide or mudflow;
- Water that backs up or overflows or is otherwise discharged from a sewer, drain, sump, sump pump, or related equipment;[66]
- Water under the ground surface pressing on or flowing or seeping through foundations; walls; floors or paved surfaces; basements, whether paved or not; or doors, windows, or other openings; and

62. ISO Form CP 10 20 10 12 § A.14.

63. If this coverage applies and the building or structure containing the system or appliance is covered property, the carrier will pay the cost to tear out and replace any part of the building or structure to repair damage to the system or appliance from which the water or steam escaped, but it will not pay the cost to repair any defect that caused the loss or damage.

64. Malecki, *Builder's Risk Insurance: Specialized Coverage for Construction Projects*, Adjusting Today, *available at* https://adjustersinternational.com/publications/adjusting-today/builders-risk-insurance/0/.

65. *See, e.g.*, ISO Form CP 10 30 10 12, § B.1.g.

66. *But see* Rodriguez, *Understanding Builder's Risk Insurance; When to Have a Builder's Risk Policy* (Mar. 8, 2018), LiveAbout, https://www.thebalance.com/understanding-builders-risk-insurance-844798 (water damage from backup of sewers and drains is usually covered).

- Waterborne material carried or otherwise moved by water or material carried or otherwise moved by mudslide or mudflow.

The exclusion applies regardless of whether any water, mudslide, or mudflow is caused by an act of nature or otherwise.[67] However, if they result in fire, explosion, or sprinkler leakage, the insurer will pay for the loss or damage caused by that fire, explosion, or sprinkler leakage. In the case of sprinkler leakage, it must be a covered cause of loss.

The property covered by the policy is the "building under construction." That means the building or structure[68] described in the Declarations while it is in the course of construction. It includes foundations, fixtures and machinery, equipment used to service the building;[69] and building materials and supplies of the insured used for construction, provided the property is intended to be permanently located in or on the building or structure described in the Declarations or within 100 feet of the premises.[70] Additionally, temporary structures built or assembled on site, including cribbing, scaffolding, and construction forms, are covered property if not covered by other insurance.[71] Covered property does not include land or water and, when outside of buildings, lawns, trees, shrubs or plants other than part of a vegetated roof, radio or television antennas and their lead-in wiring, masts or towers, or signs other than those attached to buildings.[72]

An additional coverage under the policy is debris removal.[73] Unfortunately, under this additional coverage, the insurer will only pay the expense to remove debris on the described premises when it is caused by or results from a

67. For example, if a dam, levee, seawall, or other boundary or containment system fails in whole or in part, for *any reason*, to contain the water in it, the exclusion applies.

68. When a policy describes covered property as "buildings or structures in the course of construction," it should be remembered that although a building is a structure, not all structures are buildings. Malecki, *Builder's Risk Insurance: Specialized Coverage for Construction Projects*, Adjusting Today, *available at* https://adjustersinternational.com/publications/adjusting-today/builders-risk-insurance/0/.

69. If contractor's equipment, for example, bulldozers or ditch diggers, are not covered, a contractor's equipment floater would be recommended. Malecki, *Builder's Risk Insurance: Specialized Coverage for Construction Projects*, Adjusting Today, *available at* https://adjustersinternational.com/publications/adjusting-today/builders-risk-insurance/0/.

70. ISO Form CP 00 20 10 12, § A.1. Property damaged when it is not at the job site is not covered. 151 First Side Assocs., L.P. v. Peerless Ins. Co., 2010 U.S. Dist. LEXIS 23093 (W.D. Pa. Mar. 11, 2010) (precast concrete panels awaiting delivery were destroyed by fire at manufacturing plant where they were made).

71. ISO Form CP 00 20 10 12, § A.1.c. In some policies, scaffolding, temporary structures, construction forms, and cribbing will be subject to a sublimit or their values may be added to the policy limit. Malecki, *Builder's Risk Insurance: Specialized Coverage for Construction Projects*, Adjusting Today, *available at* https://adjustersinternational.com/publications/adjusting-today/builders-risk-insurance/0/.

72. ISO Form CP 00 20 10 12, § A.2.

73. ISO Form CP 00 20 10 12, § A.4.

covered cause of loss that occurs during the policy period.[74] Even when debris removal is covered, it does not apply to

- Removing debris of property of the insured that is not insured under the policy, or that is in the possession of the insured but is not covered property;
- Removing debris of property owned by or leased to the landlord of the building where the described premises are located, unless the insured has a contractual responsibility to insure that property and it is insured under the policy;
- Removing any property that is "property not covered," including property addressed under the "Sod, Trees, Shrubs and Plants Coverage Extension";
- Removing property of others of a type that would not be covered property under the policy;
- Removing deposits of mud or earth from the grounds of the described premises;
- Extract "pollutants" from land or water; or
- Removing, restoring, or replacing polluted land or water.

[c] ISO Commercial Inland Marine Builder's Risk Coverage Form

The ISO commercial inland marine builder's risk policy will pay for direct physical loss of or damage[75] to covered property from any of the covered causes of loss,[76] which are all causes of loss that are not excluded.[77] Covered property means property intended to be permanently in or on the building or structure described in the Declarations that is the insured's building materials and supplies used for construction, fixtures and machinery, and equipment used to service the building.[78] Covered property also includes foundations

74. Additionally, the expenses will be paid only if they are reported to the carrier in writing within 180 days of the date of direct physical loss or damage.

75. Sierra Pac. Power Co. v. Hartford Steam Boiler Inspection & Ins. Co., 665 F.3d 1166, 1172 (9th Cir. 2012) (direct physical loss contemplates actual change in insured property); AFLAC Inc. v. Chubb & Sons, Inc., 260 Ga. App. 306, 308, 581 S.E.2d 317, 319 (2003) (direct physical loss or damage contemplates actual change in insured property then in satisfactory state, causing it to become unsatisfactory for future use or requiring that repairs be made). *See also* One Place Condo., LLC v. Travelers Prop. Cas. Co. of Am., 2015 U.S. Dist. LEXIS 56565 (N.D. Ill. Apr. 22, 2015) (requirement that loss be physical is widely held to exclude alleged losses that are intangible or incorporeal).

76. ISO Form IH 00 70 04 11, § A.

77. ISO Form IH 00 70 04 11, § A.3. (covered causes of loss defined as direct physical loss or damage to covered property except those causes of loss listed in exclusions).

78. ISO Form IH 00 70 04 11, § A.1.(1). Fixtures, machinery, and equipment used to service the building include legal liability of the insured for similar property belonging to others. Generally, property damaged when it is not at the job site is not covered. 151 First Side Assocs., L.P. v. Peerless Ins. Co., 2010 U.S. Dist. LEXIS 23093 (W.D. Pa. Mar. 11, 2010) (precast concrete panels awaiting delivery were destroyed by fire at manufacturing plant where they were made).

of a building or structure described in the Declarations while in the course of construction[79] and temporary structures that are built or assembled on site, including cribbing, scaffolding, and construction forms.[80] The policy does not cover existing buildings or structures to which improvements, alterations, repairs, or additions are being made, land or water, or lawns, trees, shrubs, or plants.[81]

There are additional coverages that are noteworthy. First, the insurer will pay for loss or damage that is caused by or results from a covered cause of loss to building materials and supplies that are owned by others, in care, custody, or control of the insured, and located in or on the building described in the Declarations, or within 100 feet of its premises.[82] Next, the insurer will pay the cost to remove debris of covered property caused by or resulting from a covered cause of loss occurring during the policy period, but only if reported to the insurer in writing within 180 days of the date of the direct physical loss or damage.[83] Finally, the policy provides limited coverage for loss or damage to covered property by fungi, or wet or dry rot if they are the result of one or more of the covered causes of loss.[84]

The policy includes a water damage exclusion. Under it, the insurer will not pay for loss or damage caused directly or indirectly by water.[85] Water means flood, surface water, waves—including tidal wave and tsunami—tides, tidal water, overflow of any body of water, or spray from any of them, all whether or not driven by wind.[86] It also means waterborne material carried or otherwise moved by any of those waters.[87] The exclusion applies regardless of whether the water is caused by an act of nature or otherwise. For example, the exclusion applies if a dam, levee, seawall, or other boundary or containment system fails in whole or in part, for any reason, to contain the water. If, however, water results in fire, explosion, or theft, the insurer will pay for the direct loss or damage caused by them if they would be covered under the policy. Note that the insurer also will not pay for loss or damage caused by or resulting from "weather conditions," unless the loss or damage is the result of a covered cause of loss.[88] The exclusion only applies if weather conditions contribute in any way with one of the primary excluded causes or events—one

79. ISO Form IH 00 70 04 11, § A.1.(2).

80. ISO Form IH 00 70 04 11, § A.1.(3).

81. ISO Form IH 00 70 04 11, § A.2.

82. ISO Form IH 00 70 04 11, § A.4.a.

83. ISO Form IH 00 70 04 11, § A.4.b.(1). This coverage does not apply to costs to extract "pollutants" from land or water or to remove, restore, or replace polluted land or water.

84. ISO Form IH 00 70 04 11, § A.4.g.

85. ISO Form IH 00 70 04 11, § B.1.f. Note that the exclusion applies whether or not the loss event results in widespread damage or affects a substantial area.

86. ISO Form IH 00 70 04 11, § B.1.f.(1).

87. ISO Form IH 00 70 04 11, § B.1.f.(2).

88. ISO Form IH 00 70 04 11, § B.3.a.

of which is water—to produce the loss or damage. The water exclusion is subject to deletion. If a limit of insurance for water damage is shown in the Declarations, the exclusion is deleted.[89]

[3] American Association of Insurance Services Builder's Risk Coverage Scheduled Jobsite Form

The American Association of Insurance Services (AAIS) is a national not-for-profit advisory organization governed by its member insurance companies that serves the property casualty insurance industry by, among other services, providing insurance forms.[90] Its builder's risk insurance forms are a part of its *Inland Marine Guide*.[91] These forms are used by many insurers and meet the various needs of those confronted with course-of-construction loss exposures.[92] The coverage of a typical AAIS builder's risk policy is illustrated here by the 2004 Builders' Risk Coverage Scheduled Jobsite Form.[93] It is an "all-risk" policy covering risks of direct physical loss[94] unless limited or excluded.[95] It covers loss to buildings and structures while in the course of construction, erection, or fabrication, but is limited to materials and supplies that will become a permanent part of the buildings or structures, foundations, excavations, grading, filling, attachments, permanent fencing, and other permanent fixtures, scaffolding, construction forms, or temporary fencing at the "jobsite," and temporary structures at that site.[96] It also covers the cost to remove the debris of covered property caused by a covered peril.[97]

---

89. ISO Form IH 00 70 04 11, § A.5.b. The coverage option is included within the limits of insurance applicable to the covered property at the premises where the loss occurred.

90. *Our Role in Insurance*, AAIS, https://www.aaisonline.com/web/guest/our-role-in-insurance.

91. *Inland Marine Guide*, AAIS, https://www.aaisonline.com/web/guest/inland-marine-guide.

92. Malecki, *Builder's Risk Insurance: Specialized Coverage for Construction Projects*, Adjusting Today, *available at* https://adjustersinternational.com/publications/adjusting-today/builders-risk-insurance/0/.

93. *See* http://www.btisinc.com/QBRN/Forms/NICForms/IM%207051%2004%2004%20BUILDERS%20RISK%20COVERAGE%20SCHEDULED%20JOBSITE%20FORM.pdf.

94. Sierra Pac. Power Co. v. Hartford Steam Boiler Inspection & Ins. Co., 665 F.3d 1166, 1172 (9th Cir. 2012) (direct physical loss contemplates actual change in insured property); AFLAC Inc. v. Chubb & Sons, Inc., 260 Ga. App. 306, 308, 581 S.E.2d 317, 319 (2003) (direct physical loss or damage contemplates actual change in insured property then in satisfactory state, causing it to become unsatisfactory for future use or requiring that repairs be made). *See also* One Place Condo., LLC v. Travelers Prop. Cas. Co. of Am., 2015 U.S. Dist. LEXIS 56565 (N.D. Ill. Apr. 22, 2015) (requirement that loss be physical is widely held to exclude alleged losses that are intangible or incorporeal).

95. AAIS Form IM 7051 04 04, Additional Coverage Limitation, Perils Covered.

96. AAIS Form IM 7051 04 04, Course of Construction § 1.

97. AAIS Form IM 7051 04 04, Coverage Extensions § 1.a. The coverage does not include costs to remove, restore, or replace polluted land or water. AAIS Form IM 7051 04 04, Coverage Extensions § 1.b.(2).

The policy does not cover land.[98] It also does not cover a "standing building or structure," part of one, or one to which additions, alterations, improvements, or repairs are being made.[99]

The policy covers direct loss by fire, explosion, or sprinkler leakage that results from a "flood," but does not otherwise cover a loss caused by "flood."[100] The term "flood" is defined as "flood, surface water, waves, tidal water, or the overflow of a body of water, all whether driven by wind or not" and includes spray that results from any of them whether or not wind driven.[101] There is also an exclusion for sewer backups and water below the surface.[102] The policy does not cover water that backs up through a sewer or drain or below the surface of the ground, including water that exerts pressure on or flows, seeps, or leaks through or into a covered building or structure.[103] There are two other exclusions related to water. First, the policy does not cover loss caused by water that leaks or flows from plumbing, heating, air-conditioning systems, or appliances other than fire protective systems caused by freezing; however, the exclusion does not apply if the insured uses reasonable care to maintain heat in the building or structure or drains the equipment and turns off the supply if heat is not maintained.[104] Finally, the insurer will not pay for a loss caused by or resulting from rain, snow, ice, or sleet to property *in the open* that is not part of the permanent building or structure.[105]

[4] Progressive Insurance Contractors' All-Risks Policy Form

Progressive Insurance Company has an all-risk policy that provides both first- and third-party coverages.[106] Under the first-party coverage, the insurer will indemnify the insured for any unforeseen and sudden physical loss or damage

98. AAIS Form IM 7051 04 04, Course Property Not Covered § 3.

99. AAIS Form IM 7051 04 04, Course Property Not Covered § 5. The policy defines "standing building or structure" as any building or structure that has been wholly or partially constructed, erected, or fabricated as well as one that is in the process of construction, erection, or fabrication at the inception of the policy.

100. AAIS Form IM 7051 04 04, Perils Excluded § 1.c. The exclusion does not apply to covered property while in transit.

101. AAIS Form IM 7051 04 04, Definitions § 4.

102. *But see* Rodriguez, *Understanding Builder's Risk Insurance; When to Have a Builder's Risk Policy* (Mar. 8, 2018), LiveAbout, https://www.thebalance.com/understanding-builders-risk-insurance-844798 (water damage from backup of sewers and drains is usually covered).

103. AAIS Form IM 7051 04 04, Perils Excluded § 1.h. The policy does cover direct loss by fire, explosion, or theft resulting from either water that backs up through a sewer or drain or below the surface of the ground. The exclusion does not apply to covered property while in transit.

104. AAIS Form IM 7051 04 04, Perils Excluded § 2.f.

105. AAIS Form IM 7051 04 04, Perils Excluded § 2.l.

106. Progressive Insurance BHD Contractors' All Risks Policy Form 19002-P. *See* https://www.progressiveinsurance.com.my/pdf/pw_contractors_allrisks_en.pdf.

from any cause, other than those specifically excluded, that requires repair or replacement.[107] The insurer has the option of paying for the loss or for repair or replacement of the damaged property. The insurer will also reimburse the insured for the cost of clearing debris following any event giving rise to a claim. Under the third-party coverage, the insurer will indemnify the insured for sums the insured becomes legally liable to pay as damages for, *inter alia*, accidental loss of or damage to property that belongs to third parties and occurs in direct connection with the construction or erection of the items insured under the policy and happening on or in the immediate vicinity of the site during the period of coverage.[108]

There is a standard endorsement entitled "Special Conditions Concerning Safety Measures with Respect to Precipitation, Flood and Inundation."[109] Under it, the insurer will only indemnify the insured for loss, damage, or liability caused directly or indirectly by precipitation, flood, or inundation if adequate safety measures have been taken in designing and executing the project. "Adequate safety measures" means that, "at all times throughout the policy period, allowance is made for precipitation, flood and inundation up to a return period of 20 years for the location insured on the basis of the statistics prepared by the meteorological agencies." The insurer will not pay for loss, damage, or liability resulting from the failure of the insured to immediately remove obstructions—for example, sand or trees—from watercourses within the construction site, whether carrying water or not, to maintain free waterflow.

Another standard endorsement is called "Special Conditions for Laying Water Supply and Sewer Pipes."[110] It provides that the insurer will indemnify the insured for any loss, damage, or liability because of the flooding or silting of pipes, trenches, or shafts. The insurer is only liable if the pipes, immediately after laying, have been secured in a manner by backfilling that they cannot be displaced if the trench is flooded and they have been closed to prevent water, silt, or the like from penetrating, and the trenches of tested pipe sections have been backfilled immediately on completion of the pressure test.

---

107. Progressive Insurance BHD Contractors' All Risks Policy Form 19002-P § 1.

108. Progressive Insurance BHD Contractors' All Risks Policy Form 19002-P § 2.

109. Progressive Insurance BHD Contractors' All Risks Policy Form 19002-P, Endorsement 110.

110. Progressive Insurance BHD Contractors' All Risks Policy Form 19002-P, Endorsement 117.

7.4 Water Damage/Flood Exclusion and Added Coverage

As can be seen from the policies, water damage or flood is nearly always excluded from a basic builder's risk insurance policy.[111] It is critically important to examine the language of the exclusion to determine if it applies to a particular loss. For example, a builder's risk policy excluded losses caused by or resulting from "flood," which it defined as "waves, surface water, run-off, tides or tidal water, and the rising out of or overflowing of any body of water, whether or not driven by wind." A retaining wall on the insured property was damaged by water and water pressure from an underground pipe that drained water from the roof of a neighboring building. The court said there was doubt that the rainwater and snowmelt that flowed off the roof of the structure on the adjoining property was runoff, and the damage it caused would have been excluded, but because the water causing the damage ceased to exist as runoff once it was channeled through a pipe, the loss was covered.[112]

Water damage/flood coverage almost always has to be added by endorsement, which is generally available.[113] However, in a high-risk zone it may be difficult to obtain or very expensive in the private market. Private market insurers may also apply a low sublimit of coverage or a high deductible. Another way flood coverage can be added is with a Difference in Conditions (DIC) policy. Indeed, DIC coverage is generally acquired to obtain additional causes of loss coverage over a high deductible for risks like flood.[114]

111. Rodriguez, *Understanding Builder's Risk Insurance; When to Have a Builder's Risk Policy* (Mar. 8, 2018), LiveAbout, https://www.thebalance.com/understanding-builders-risk-insurance-844798 (standard exclusions include water damage); Stover, *A Guide to Builder's Risk Insurance*, 53 Tort & Ins. L.J. 819 (2018) (some of the more typical exclusions found in builder's risk policy form include water). Even if it is included in the main policy, an endorsement may exclude flood coverage. *See, e.g.*, Fireman's Fund v. Structural Sys. Tech., Inc., 426 F. Supp. 2d 1009 (D. Neb. 2006) (endorsement excluded loss or damage caused by or resulting from or to flood for property situated in Flood Zone A or B as defined by Army Corp. of Engineers).

112. Georgetowne Square v. United States Fidelity & Guar. Co., 3 Neb. App. 49, 523 N.W.2d 380 (1994). The policy had an exception to the exclusion for a loss because of the collapse of a building or structure caused by the weight of rain, snow, ice, or sleet. The court said that the damage at issue, as stipulated by the parties, was from the build-up of water underground and water pressure underground that emanated from an underground drainage pipe. That was not damage caused by the weight of water.

113. Malecki, *Builder's Risk Insurance: Specialized Coverage for Construction Projects*, Adjusting Today, *available at* https://adjustersinternational.com/publications/adjusting-today/builders-risk-insurance/0/ (flood coverage generally available by endorsement); *From Groundbreaking to Remodeling: Builders Risk 101 Guide*, at 7 (depending on coverage form, project type, and total completed value, endorsements, including flood, may be purchased), *available at* https://go.usassure.com/rs/381-ISO-510/images/From%20Groundbreaking%20to%20Renovating%20A%20Builders%20Risk%20101%20Guide.pdf.

114. Malecki, *Builder's Risk Insurance: Specialized Coverage for Construction Projects*, Adjusting Today, *available at* https://adjustersinternational.com/publications/adjusting-today

No matter the source of flood coverage, the coverage language has to be examined carefully. Some endorsements will simply delete the exclusion for "flood" in the main policy.[115] That policy then has to be reviewed to determine the extent of coverage. The language may provide coverage for "water damage" while excluding "flood, surface water, waves, tides, tidal waves, overflow of any body of water."[116] Other endorsements will add coverage for flood, but not other water damage, and define "flood."[117] That definition can vary.[118] An ISO endorsement that can be added to a commercial property policy has a fairly typical definition: a general and temporary condition of partial or complete inundation of normally dry land areas because of overflow of inland or tidal waters, unusual or rapid accumulation or runoff of surface waters from any source, or mudslides or mudflows caused by unusual or rapid accumulation or runoff of surface waters from any source.[119] It is important to be aware of any time limitations. For example, some endorsements may limit the occurrence of a flood to 72 hours, in which case a flood that lasts longer may be subject to a second deductible.[120] On the other hand, the ISO endorsement says that flooding in a continuous or protracted event constitutes a single flood, but it also says that if there is more than one flood in a 12-month period, the most the insurer will pay for the total of all flood loss or damage

---

/builders-risk-insurance/0/ (noting that insurers of a builder's risk policy may not provide DIC coverage, even when construction contract requires it). A DIC policy presents a potential coverage gap because of the deductible and the interaction with a FEMA SFIP. *See* Boggs, *Flood, Flood or Flood! Who Responds: AAIS, ISO or NFIP? – Part III*, Insurance Journal, https://www.insurancejournal.com/blogs/academy-journal/2015/05/13/367509.htm.

115. *See, e.g.*, AAIS Form CO 1223 04 02.

116. *See., e.g.*, Gateway II LLC v. Hartford Fire Ins. Co., 2016 N.Y. Misc. LEXIS 1325 (Apr. 5, 2016).

117. *See, e.g.*, AXIS Surplus Ins. Co. v. Lake CDA Dev. LLC, 2008 U.S. Dist. LEXIS 69020 (D. Idaho Sept. 10, 2008) (policy had water exclusion barring coverage for loss caused directly or indirectly by water, but also had Flood Endorsement); Mission Nat'l Ins. Co. v. Coachella Valley Water Dist., 258 Cal. Rptr. 639, 210 Cal. App. 3d 484 (1989) (endorsement stated that it was "understood and agreed that the peril of flood" was included in the policy and defined "flood").

118. Gadaire & Szczucki, *Builders' Risk: Water Damage or Flood? Addressing the Risks, Understanding the Coverage for Damage and Mitigating the Exposures*, at 3(May 2016), *available at* https://www.chubb.com/US-EN/_Assets/doc/2016-05-Builders-Risk--Water-Damage-or-Flood.pdf.

119. ISO Form CP 10 65 10 00, § C. See Boggs, *Flood, Flood or Flood! Who Responds: AAIS, ISO or NFIP?—Part III*, Insurance Journal, https://www.insurancejournal.com/blogs/academy-journal/2015/05/13/367509.htm, for a discussion of the practical differences between the AAIS and ISO endorsements.

120. Gadaire & Szczucki, *Builders' Risk: Water Damage or Flood? Addressing the Risks, Understanding the Coverage for Damage and Mitigating the Exposures*, at 4 (May 2016), *available at* https://www.chubb.com/US-EN/_Assets/doc/2016-05-Builders-Risk--Water-Damage-or-Flood.pdf.

sustained during that period is the amount identified as the annual aggregate for flood.[121]

When coverage is unavailable in the private market, it is usually available in the Federal Emergency Management Agency (FEMA) Standard Flood Insurance Policy (SFIP). That policy does not cover loss from backup of sewers and drains,[122] it but does include coverage for a building under construction, alteration, or repair,[123] and for materials and supplies to be used for construction, alteration, or repair of an insured building.[124] Unfortunately, the building coverage is limited to $250,000 for a residential building and $500,000 for a commercial building. For that reason, the SFIP may be supplemented by an excess policy. When a construction site is in a flood zone, insurers may require the maximum amount of coverage available through the SFIP, and indeed it is unlikely a builder's risk carrier will provide flood coverage without requiring purchase of an SFIP policy when a project is located in a flood zone.[125]

7.5 Contractual Requirement for Coverage

Construction contracts generally require builder's risk insurance.[126] One of the most commonly used documents in the construction industry is the General Conditions of the Contract for Construction—form A201—from the

121. ISO Form CP 10 65 10 00, § G.2.

122. 5 Jeffrey E. Thomas, *New Appleman on Insurance Law Library Edition* § 50.02[3][f] (LexisNexis 2020) (SFIP does not apply to loss from backup of sewers and drains, or to consequential loss, and that coverage would have to be found in builder's risk or DIC policy).

123. The SFIP provides coverage for a building under construction, alteration, or repair; however, if the structure is not yet walled or roofed, coverage applies only while the work is in progress or if the work is halted, only for a period of up to 90 continuous days thereafter. Standard Flood Insurance Policy § III.A.6. (2015). Note that coverage does not apply until the building is walled and roofed if the lowest floor, including the basement floor, of a non-elevated building or the lowest elevated floor of an elevated building is below the base flood elevation in prescribed zones or below the base flood elevation adjusted to include the effect of wave action in prescribed zones.

124. The SFIP covers materials and supplies to be used for construction, alteration, or repair of an insured building while they are stored in a fully enclosed building at the described location or on an adjacent property. Standard Flood Insurance Policy § III.A.5. (2015).

125. 5 Jeffrey E. Thomas, *New Appleman on Insurance Law Library Edition* § 50.02[3][f] (LexisNexis 2020).

126. *See, e.g.*, Roost Project, LLC v. Andersen Contr. Co., 437 F. Supp. 3d 808 (D. Idaho 2020) (under contract, contractor agreed to purchase and maintain property insurance in builder's risk "all-risk" or equivalent policy form with commercially reasonable deductibles covering perils of windstorm or hail, water damage, weight of rain, snow, ice, or sleet); Modern Builders, Inc. v. Alden-Conger Pub. Sch. Dist. # 242, 2005 U.S. Dist. LEXIS 18736 (D. Minn. Aug. 30, 2005) (contract required builder to procure all-risk property insurance for project including coverage for flood); John S. Clark Co. v. United Nat'l Ins. Co., 304 F. Supp. 2d 758 (M.D.N.C. 2004) (under Design-Build Agreement property owner agreed to obtain all-risk insurance to cover construction project for physical loss or damage including coverage for flood).

American Institute of Architects (AIA).[127] Under an exhibit to that document, the property owner is required to obtain property insurance on a builder's risk form unless the parties shift that obligation to the contractor.[128] The required insurance *must* provide coverage for direct physical loss or damage and *may not* exclude the risk of flood.[129] Thus, if the party required to obtain builder's risk insurance with flood coverage fails to so and the other party suffers a flood loss that would have been covered, the injured party should be able to recover for that loss in a breach of contract action.[130]

7.6 Deductibles

Although occasionally a builder's risk policy will carry no deductible,[131] most do and a variety of types of may be employed. There may be a specific dollar amount. It could be as little as $1,000[132] or $5,000,[133] and range up to $10,000,[134] $25,000,[135] $100,000,[136] or higher.[137]

Percentage deductibles are also used in builder's risk insurance. Those deductibles can be based on the value of the project at the time of loss under what is called a "value-at-risk-at-time-of-loss" (VARTOL) clause.[138] That

127. *See* https://help.aiacontracts.org/public/wp-content/uploads/2020/05/Preview_A201-2017.pdf. *See generally* Maloney, *Five Key Changes in the 2017 AIA A201 General Conditions for Construction Contracts* (Mar. 30, 2020), Jimerson Birr, https://www.jimersonfirm.com/blog/2020/03/five-key-changes-2017-aia-a201-general-conditions-construction-contracts/.

128. AIA Document A101-2017 Exhibit A, § A.2.3.1. *See* https://help.aiacontracts.org/public/wp-content/uploads/2020/05/Preview_A101ExhibitA_2017.pdf.

129. AIA Document A101-2017 Exhibit A, § A.2.3.1.1. *See* https://help.aiacontracts.org/public/wp-content/uploads/2020/05/Preview_A101ExhibitA_2017.pdf.

130. *See, e.g.*, Frank Coluccio Constr. Co. v. King County, 136 Wn. App. 751, 150 P.3d 1147, (2007).

131. *See, e.g.*, Ajax Bldg. Corp. v. Hartford Fire Ins. Co., 2002 U.S. Dist. LEXIS 28550 (Aug. 14, 2002).

132. *See, e.g.*, Great Am. Ins. Co. v. W. States Fire Prot. Co., 730 F. Supp. 2d 1308 (D. N. Mex. 2009); Hacienda Construction, Inc. v. Veals, 2008 U.S. Dist. LEXIS 44529 (E.D. La. June 5, 2008); South Tippecanoe School Bldg. Corp. v. Shambaugh & Son, Inc., 182 Ind. App. 350, 395 N.E.2d 320 (1979).

133. *See, e.g.*, Spring St. Apts Waco, LLC v. Phila. Indem. Ins. Co., 2017 U.S. Dist. LEXIS 217120 (W.D. Tex. Apr. 5, 2017).

134. *See, e.g.*, James F. Campenella Constr. Co. v. Great Am. Ins. Co., 2010 U.S. Dist. LEXIS 125098 (E.D. Pa. Nov. 24, 2010).

135. *See, e.g.*, St. Paul Fire & Marine Ins. Co. v. L.E.S. Subsurface Plumbing Co., 266 A.D.2d 139, 699 N.Y.S.2d 31 (1999).

136. *See, e.g.*, OPI Int'l, Inc. v. Gan Minster Ins. Co., 1997 U.S. Dist. LEXIS 24846 (S.D. Tex. Jan. 23, 1997).

137. *See, e.g.*, Garden City Apts., LLC v. Xcel Plumbing of N.Y., Inc., 233 F. Supp. 3d 346 (E.D.N.Y. 2017) (deductible of over $250,000); Niagara Mohawk Power Corp. v. S. J. Groves & Sons Co., 134 A.D.2d 822, 522 N.Y.S.2d 38 (1987) ($250,000).

138. Gadaire & Szczucki, *Builders' Risk: Water Damage or Flood? Addressing the Risks, Understanding the Coverage for Damage and Mitigating the Exposures*, at 4 (May 2016), *available at* https://www.chubb.com/US-EN/_Assets/doc/2016-05-Builders-Risk--Water-Damage-or

means that a percentage is applied based on the value of the portion of the project that has been completed at the time of the loss. For example, if at the time of loss, the value of the improvements is $1 million and the percentage is 5, the deductible is $50,000. A deductible of 5 percent is common.[139]

Water damage or flood coverage often has a separate deductible that is different from the one that applies to losses generally.[140] The deductible may be a specific dollar amount or a percentage, or a combination.[141] For example, in a Louisiana case,[142] the general deductible was $25,000. The deductible for water damage *other than flood* was $50,000, and the flood deductible was 5 percent of the total insured values at risk at the time and place of loss subject to a $500,000 minimum.[143] The insured project was a hotel renovation. A heavy rain caused flooding and extensive physical damage during the construction. The insured argued that the deductible was $500,000. The insurer countered that it was nearly $3.5 million, a figure it arrived at by multiplying the value of the project at the time of loss by 5 percent. The trial court found that the policy language was clear and unambiguous and sided with the insurer. The appellate court, however, held that the policy language was ambiguous. It reversed and remanded. It said that on remand the trial court should determine whether extrinsic evidence resolved that ambiguity and whether the presumption in favor of coverage in the case of an ambiguity applied, noting that under the pertinent state law the presumption in favor of an insured does not apply where the insured is a sophisticated commercial entity that itself drafts or uses its agents to secure desired policy provisions.[144]

When there is a percentage deductible and a sublimit for a specific peril, is the deductible calculated by multiplying the percentage by the total insured value at risk or the sublimit? A Florida court held that a percentage deductible clause was ambiguous in that situation and construed it in favor of the insured. It held that the maximum deductible was determined by multiplying

-Flood.pdf. The value at the time of loss can be computed by multiplying the total insured values at risk at the time of loss by the percentage of completion. *See., e.g.*, McDonnel Grp., L.L.C. v. Starr Surplus Lines Ins. Co., 15 F.4th 343 (5th Cir. 2021).

139. *See., e.g.*, El-Ad 250 West LLC v. Zurich Am. Ins. Co., 2016 N.Y. Misc. LEXIS 1239 (Mar. 30, 2016).

140. *See, e.g.*, Gateway II LLC v. Hartford Fire Ins. Co., 2014 N.Y. Misc. LEXIS 4234 (Sept. 22, 2014) ($5,000 deductible generally, water damage/flood deductible of $25,000).

141. Malecki, *Builder's Risk Insurance: Specialized Coverage for Construction Projects*, Adjusting Today, *available at* https://adjustersinternational.com/publications/adjusting-today/builders-risk-insurance/0/.

142. The McDonnel Grp., LLC v. Starr Surplus Lines Ins. Co., 2020 U.S. Dist. LEXIS 23123 (E.D. La. Feb. 11, 2020).

143. *See also* Terra-Adi Int'l Dadeland, LLC v. Zurich Am. Ins. Co., 2007 U.S. Dist. LEXIS 14620 (S.D. Fla. Mar. 1, 2007) (deductible for flood of 5 percent of the total insured values at risk at time and place of loss subject to minimum deduction of $250,000).

144. McDonnel Grp., L.L.C. v. Starr Surplus Lines Ins. Co., 15 F.4th 343 (5th Cir. 2021).

the percentage by the sublimit, but noted that the insured value at risk at the time of loss could be less than the total sublimit.[145]

It is very possible that a policy will have different deductibles for different perils.[146] For example, the deductible for a windstorm may exceed the value of the loss, but that for flood or rain, sleet, ice, or snow may not.[147]

Builder's risk polices may cover "soft costs," usually by endorsement. As discussed below,[148] a soft costs deductible is typically stated in the number of days the delay must exceed to trigger coverage.

7.7 Covered Property

The most basic question to ask when seeking to bring a claim within a builder's risk policy is: was the damaged property covered by the policy? Are, for example, preexisting buildings covered? One needs to look to the specific policy language to make that determination. The policy may explicitly cover the buildings and structures at the designated site,[149] it may limit coverage to improvements or alterations at the site, or it may not plainly address the issue.[150]

In an Oklahoma case the insured contracted to construct an addition to a school building. While the roof for the addition was being attached to the roof of the existing building, an opening had to be left in the roof of the exiting building. Canvas covers were placed over the opening, but a sudden windstorm blew them off and rainwater entered and damaged the interior of the existing structure. The contractor sought to recover the cost of necessary repairs. The insurer contended the policy covered only the new addition. The policy described the covered property as a "one story composition roof masonry building, while in course of construction, including foundations (except as hereinafter excluded), additions, attachments, and all permanent fixtures belonging to and constituting a part of said building." The court said

145. Terra-Adi Int'l Dadeland, LLC v. Zurich Am. Ins. Co., 2007 U.S. Dist. LEXIS 14620 (S.D. Fla. Mar. 1, 2007).

146. *See, e.g.*, 550 Seabreeze Dev., LLC v. Ill. Union Ins. Co., 2020 U.S. Dist. LEXIS 14514 (S.D. Fla. Jan. 29, 2020) (Rain, Sleet, Ice, or Snow endorsement had $250,000 deductible, while Named Windstorm deductible was $1,500,000).

147. Who has the burden of proving the applicable cause of loss when there are different deductibles for different causes of loss? As a general rule, the insured has burden to show that a claim falls within the coverage of the policy. State Farm Fire & Cas. Co. v. Estate of Mehlman, 589 F.3d 105 (3d Cir. 2009).

148. See § 7.09, *infra*.

149. *See, e.g.*, WHP 9, Inc. v. Centennial Ins. Co., 2007 N.J. Super. Unpub. LEXIS 611 (Oct. 23, 2007) (where policy defined "covered property" as buildings or structures as described in Declarations while under construction, erection, or fabrication, damaged sewer pipe was existing structure that was not included in completed value of the project and was not being constructed, erected, or fabricated and was not, therefore, covered property).

150. Cozen, *Insuring Real Property*, § 6.02[3][b][i] (LexisNexis Matthew Bender 2020).

that the parties to the policy contemplated that it would cover all risks incurred in the construction of the addition, that it would be necessary to attach the roof of the new building to that of the old one, and that, therefore, it was a necessary part of the work to be done. Thus, concluded the court, the parties intended the policy to protect the contractor in attaching the roof as well as in the actual erection of the walls and other portions of the new building.[151]

7.8 Coverage Limit

When a builder's risk policy provides flood coverage, it is important to determine if there is a limit on the coverage that is different from the limit that applies generally to the coverage.[152]

7.9 Soft Cost Coverage

[1] Introduction

When a construction site is flooded, it delays the progress of the project for some period of time. There are costs associated with a delay that, in the construction industry, are known as "soft costs."[153] They are generally not covered in a main builder's risk policy[154] but are often added by an endorsement to the policy.[155] The document may be called a "soft cost" or a "delayed completion

151. Homestead Fire Ins. Co. v. DeWitt, 206 Okla. 570, 245 P.2d 92 (1952). *Accord* Thompson v. Trinity Universal Ins. Co., 708 S.W.2d 45 (Tex. App. 1986).

152. *See, e.g.*, McDonnel Grp., L.L.C. v. Starr Surplus Lines Ins. Co., 15 F.4th 343 (5th Cir. 2021) (coverage limitation of $10,000,000 for peril of flood).

153. 5 Jeffrey E. Thomas, *New Appleman on Insurance Law Library Edition* § 50.03[7][a] (LexisNexis 2020) (term "soft costs" has long been used by construction professionals to describe costs associated with construction project other than labor and materials, which are referred to as "hard costs").

154. Malecki, *Builder's Risk Insurance: Specialized Coverage for Construction Projects*, Adjusting Today, *available at* https://adjustersinternational.com/publications/adjusting-today/builders-risk-insurance/0/ (generally delay in completion and resulting loss of business income, loss of rents, extra expense, interest on loans, and other consequential losses incurred after insured property loss are not covered by the basic builder's risk policy although some insurers automatically include soft costs coverage, which is activated by designating the limit on the policy Declarations). *See also* Hunt Constr. Group, Inc. v. Allianz Global Risks United States Ins. Co., 2007 U.S. Dist. LEXIS 57799 (S.D. Ind. Aug. 7, 2007) (normally, coverage for soft costs must be added by endorsement to builder's risk insurance; insurance contract unambiguously lacked coverage for soft costs and because no endorsement added coverage for those costs, additional insurance premiums were not covered by policy as they were soft costs).

155. Austin, *Builders Risk Insurance: Is It Always Necessary?* (Nov. 2012), IRMI, https://www.irmi.com/articles/expert-commentary/is-builders-risk-insurance-necessary (while soft costs can be insured, they may need to be added by specific endorsement to whatever property insurance policy is used to insure builder's risk exposure); *Soft Costs* (Inland Marine Underwriters Association 2001) (soft cost coverage is generally provided by endorsement or extension to builder's risk policies), *available at* https://www.imua.org/Files/reports/Soft_Costs.html.

coverage" endorsement.[156] The language of the coverage has to be examined carefully because it varies from insurer to insurer and because there are several possible contingencies.[157] It is important to be aware that there has to be an underlying physical loss or damage to covered property by a covered cause of loss for delay coverage to apply.[158] Also, the loss or damage must delay *completion* of the project.[159] If there is a delay before the original completion date and the entire project is still finished prior to that date, insurers will take the position that there has been no delay.[160]

[2] Definition of "Soft Costs"

Expert commentaries agree that defining soft costs is problematic.[161] They disagree on what the definition is. One commentary, for example, provides a fairly brief list of potentially covered soft costs: architect and engineering fees, building inspection fees, construction loan fees, insurance premiums, interest expenses, legal fees, lost tax credits, advertising costs, and leasing expenses including renegotiation costs.[162] Another provides a more extensive list that

---

156. 5 Jeffrey E. Thomas, *New Appleman on Insurance Law Library Edition* § 50.03[7][a] (LexisNexis 2020) (other names are delayed opening coverage, delayed start-up coverage, or time element coverage).

157. *Builders Risk Coverage: Navigating Hard and Soft Costs, Delay in Opening Expenses and Construction Delay: Measurement Strategies for Contractors and Insurers to Resolve Recurring and Costly Disputes*, at 19 (Nov. 18, 2015), *available at* http://media.straffordpub.com/products/builders-risk-coverage-navigating-hard-and-soft-costs-delay-in-opening-expenses-and-construction-delay-measurement-2015-11-18/presentation.pdf.

158. 5 Jeffrey E. Thomas, *New Appleman on Insurance Law Library Edition* § 50.03[7][a] (LexisNexis 2020) (delay coverage is subject to conditions, and exclusions in builder's risk policy). *See also Builders Risk Coverage: Navigating Hard and Soft Costs, Delay in Opening Expenses and Construction Delay: Measurement Strategies for Contractors and Insurers to Resolve Recurring and Costly Disputes*, at 19 (Nov. 18, 2015), *available at* http://media.straffordpub.com/products/builders-risk-coverage-navigating-hard-and-soft-costs-delay-in-opening-expenses-and-construction-delay-measurement-2015-11-18/presentation.pdf (delayed completion insurance only pays if loss is because of occurrence of peril covered under policy, which usually means physical loss or damage; policy usually will not respond when job is late simply because contractor had difficulty making completed project perform as guaranteed).

159. James F. Campenella Constr. Co. v. Great Am. Ins. Co., 2010 U.S. Dist. LEXIS 125098 (E.D. Pa. Nov. 24, 2010) (insured could only recover for soft costs by showing that water leak caused delay in completion of entire construction project).

160. Malecki, *Builder's Risk Insurance: Specialized Coverage for Construction Projects*, Adjusting Today, *available at* https://adjustersinternational.com/publications/adjusting-today/builders-risk-insurance/0/.

161. 5 Jeffrey E. Thomas, *New Appleman on Insurance Law Library Edition* § 50.03[7][a] (LexisNexis 2020) (incorporation of term "soft costs" into insurance policies has not strictly adhered to definition used in construction industry, and resulting lack of consistency has caused considerable confusion about coverage for losses associated with costs other than labor and materials).

162. *Builders Risk Coverage: Navigating Hard and Soft Costs, Delay in Opening Expenses and Construction Delay: Measurement Strategies for Contractors and Insurers to Resolve*

adds real estate or property taxes, additional expenses for extension or renewal of financing, bond interest payments, fees paid to help rearrange financing, refunds of deposits made by prospective occupants, and storage costs.[163]

The point is not that there is a "correct" or "exhaustive list" of soft costs, but that the claimant must identify all the losses that might be covered and then think creatively about how they might fit into the definitional language of the endorsement. That is easier said than done because that language varies widely. The definition might not even appear in the endorsement, but instead be found on the Declarations Page.[164] It may also be on a schedule.[165] Many forms provide a list from which the insured must select by "checking" the boxes.[166] Others automatically provide coverage for the costs shown.

The list of covered soft costs might be quite narrow: "actual and necessary business costs in excess of . . . budgeted amount for the 'project' consisting only of type shown in the Declarations," which are interest on money borrowed to finance construction, advertising expenses, realty taxes and other assessments, and costs resulting from the renegotiation of leases or construction loans.[167] It might be more extensive: advertising and promotional expenses; architect, engineer, designer, and consultant fees; costs resulting from renegotiation of a sales contract, leases, or construction loans; general overhead and administrative expenses, other than legal, accounting, and professional fees; insurance premiums; interest on money borrowed to finance construction; legal and accounting fees and other costs to renegotiate and prepare revised contracts

---

Recurring and Costly Disputes, at 17 (Nov. 18, 2015), *available at* http://media.straffordpub.com/products/builders-risk-coverage-navigating-hard-and-soft-costs-delay-in-opening-expenses-and-construction-delay-measurement-2015-11-18/presentation.pdf.

163. *Soft Costs* (Inland Marine Underwriters Association 2001), *available at* https://www.imua.org/Files/reports/Soft_Costs.html.

164. *See, e.g.*, One Place Condo., LLC v. Travelers Prop. Cas. Co. of Am., 2014 U.S. Dist. LEXIS 33974 (N.D. Ill. Mar. 17, 2014); Oceanside Pier View, L.P. v. Travelers Prop. Cas. Co. of Am., 2008 U.S. Dist. LEXIS 37755 (S.D. Cal. May 6, 2008).

165. *See, e.g.*, 151 First Side Assocs., L.P. v. Peerless Ins. Co., 2010 U.S. Dist. LEXIS 23093 (W.D. Pa. Mar. 11, 2010).

166. 5 Jeffrey E. Thomas, *New Appleman on Insurance Law Library Edition* § 50.03[7][a] (LexisNexis 2020).

167. One Place Condo., LLC v. Travelers Prop. Cas. Co. of Am., 2014 U.S. Dist. LEXIS 33974 (N.D. Ill. Mar. 17, 2014); Oceanside Pier View, L.P. v. Travelers Prop. Cas. Co. of Am., 2008 U.S. Dist. LEXIS 37755 (S.D. Cal. May 6, 2008). The "in excess of the budgeted amount for the project" language can be critical. For example, in one case the soft costs claimed by the insured, said the court, would have fallen under the enumerated soft costs. Nevertheless, because the amount claimed exceeded the sublimit, most of them would be excluded. However, the parties agreed that those costs did not exceed "the budgeted amount for the project." Therefore, decided the court, the amounts claimed were not excluded. HB Constr., Inc. v. Travelers Prop. Cas. Co. of Am., 2019 U.S. Dist. LEXIS 129666 (D. N. Mex. Aug. 1, 2019). *See also* Indianapolis Airport Auth. v. Travelers Prop. Cas. Co. of Am., 849 F.3d 355 (7th Cir. 2017), for a case interpreting "budgeted amount for the project."

and other documents; permit and inspection fees; and realty taxes and realty assessments.[168] The list might add survey fees and storage costs.[169]

One source for determining soft costs on a project is lenders providing project financing, which may have a section in the lending information on anticipated events and their financial impact.[170]

[3] Limitations

Soft costs coverage is usually limited to "actual and necessary" expenses during the "period of delay" that are a direct result of delay in the completion of operations.[171] The endorsement typically defines "period of delay" as beginning on the date the project would have been completed, had no loss occurred, following any waiting period, and ending on the actual date when the intended occupancy or operations for the project can commence.[172] The phrase "actual and necessary" is not defined in policies, but actual "is something real or actually existing as opposed to something merely possible"[173] and necessary is "something indispensable and which cannot be disregarded or omitted."[174]

There is usually a dollar limitation on the amount of soft costs the insurer will cover.[175] This is a sublimit that is less than the limit of coverage for the entire policy. The limitation may be an amount per occurrence and/or per month, sometimes with a *per diem* limit.[176]

---

168. *See, e.g.*, HB Constr., Inc. v. Travelers Prop. Cas. Co. of Am., 2019 U.S. Dist. LEXIS 129666 (D. N. Mex. Aug. 1, 2019).

169. *See* ISO Form IH 99 15 05 17, § F.3 ("soft costs" means additional interest expense on money borrowed to finance construction or reconstruction; real estate or property taxes; advertising and promotional expense; insurance expenses; commissions, legal and accounting costs and fees and administrative expenses incurred as result of necessary renegotiating of lease or leases; architectural fees, building inspection and permit fees, and charges; storage charges; and survey costs).

170. *Soft Costs* (Inland Marine Underwriters Association 2001), *available at* https://www.imua.org/Files/reports/Soft_Costs.html.

171. ISO Form IH 99 15 05 17, § A.1.

172. ISO Form IH 99 15 05 17, § F.2. The expiration date of the policy does not cut the period of delay short.

173. Steen v. Modern Woodmen of America, 296 Ill. 104, 110, 129 N.E. 546, 549 (1920).

174. Abraham v. Insurance Co. of N. Am., 117 Vt. 75, 80, 84 A.2d 670, 673 (1951) ("necessary" is a word susceptible of various meanings).

175. *See, e.g.*, Indianapolis Airport Auth. v. Travelers Prop. Cas. Co. of Am., 849 F.3d 355 (7th Cir. 2017) (soft cost coverage limited to $100 million); HB Constr., Inc. v. Travelers Prop. Cas. Co. of Am., 2019 U.S. Dist. LEXIS 129666 (D. N. Mex. Aug. 1, 2019) (Declarations specified limit of $100,000 for soft costs); One Place Condo., LLC v. Travelers Prop. Cas. Co. of Am., 2015 U.S. Dist. LEXIS 56565 (N.D. Ill. Apr. 22, 2015) (soft costs and special time element with a limit of $3,300,000); Oceanside Pier View, L.P. v. Travelers Prop. Cas. Co. of Am., 2008 U.S. Dist. LEXIS 37755 (S.D. Cal. May 6, 2008) (policy with total completed value and soft costs limit of $3,073,407); Gateway II LLC v. Hartford Fire Ins. Co., 2014 N.Y. Misc. LEXIS 4234 (Sept. 22, 2014) (soft costs coverage limited to $1 million).

176. *Soft Costs* (Inland Marine Underwriters Association 2001), *available at* https://www.imua.org/Files/reports/Soft_Costs.html.

If there are separate sublimits for delay in completion and for flood losses, which one applies? A New York court confronted that question. The main policy covered losses caused by a flood with a $5 million annual aggregate limit. Delay in completion coverage was added by an endorsement that had a $7 million sublimit. The endorsement stated that all other terms and conditions of the policy to which it was attached remain unchanged. The court found the flood sublimit applied when delay in completion losses were caused by a flood. Had the cause of loss been something other than a flood, the $7 million sublimit for delay in completion would have applied, but where the cause of the loss had its own, lower aggregate limit, that lower limit applied.[177]

[4] Deductible

Soft cost deductibles are usually stated in days.[178] The number may be as few as five days[179] or as many as 90 days.[180] Typically, the insurer will not pay soft costs until the deductible period expires and then only those incurred in excess of the deductible, up to the limit of insurance. Soft costs are generally paid for losses sustained during the "period of delay" in completion.[181] Thus, where the period of delay began on the "planned completion date" and ended on the date the project should have been completed "using reasonable speed and similar materials and workmanship," the 90-day deductible period ran from September 28, the date the project was originally scheduled to open for operations, until December 27. After the loss incident, the new planned opening date was February 22 of the following year. Thus, the court decided the insured could recover soft costs it incurred between December 27 and February 22.[182]

177. El-Ad 250 W. LLC v. Zurich Am. Ins. Co., 44 Misc.3d 633, 988 N.Y.S.2d 462 (2014), *aff'd*, 130 A.D.3d 459, 13 N.Y.S.3d 68 (2015). The court noted that the definition of flood losses in the policy included *all losses*, not just *physical property* damage, but that other policies define flood losses to include only physical damage.

178. *But see* El-Ad 250 W. LLC v. Zurich Am. Ins. Co., 44 Misc.3d 633, 988 N.Y.S.2d 462 (2014), *aff'd*, 130 A.D.3d 459, 13 N.Y.S.3d 68 (2015) (flood deductible of greater of either $250,000 or 5 percent of loss applied to both physical loss and delay losses).

179. *See, e.g.*, Gateway II LLC v. Hartford Fire Ins. Co., 2014 N.Y. Misc. LEXIS 4234 (Sept. 22, 2014) (five days under one policy and 14 days under another).

180. Indianapolis Airport Auth. v. Travelers Prop. Cas. Co. of Am., 178 F. Supp. 3d 745 (S.D. Ind. 2016), *aff'd in part, rev'd in part*, 849 F.3d 355 (7th Cir. 2017) (deductible period for soft costs was 90 days, meaning period of delay had to exceed 90 days to trigger coverage).

181. ISO Form IH 99 15 05 17, § A.1. The definition of period of delay will be critical. An ISO endorsement defines "period of delay" to mean the period of time that begins on the date the project would have been completed, had no loss occurred, following any waiting period, and ends on the actual date when the intended occupancy or operations of the building or structure for the project can commence. ISO Form IH 99 15 05 17, § F.2.

182. Indianapolis Airport Auth. v. Travelers Prop. Cas. Co. of Am., 849 F.3d 355 (7th Cir. 2017).

There may be a separate deductible, also stated in days, for flood loss. A Florida case illustrates the confusion that can occur with that separate deductible. The deductible for physical property damage was 5 percent, and the insured argued only that deductible applied. The deductible period for flood was 60 days. The latter, determined the court, operated independently of the former, and the insured was subject to both. The court then had to decide whether two deductible periods applied because the project was delayed by two different hurricanes. The court found the policy to be ambiguous as to whether the delays at issue were subject to a single 60-day deductible period or a 120-day period, as the insurer contended. The court sided with the insured.[183]

[5] Covered Cause of Loss

Soft cost endorsements require that the delay be directly caused by loss or damage covered under the main policy.[184] Thus, if a delay is caused by flood or other water damage, the claimant must show that is a loss covered under the policy,[185] which in the case of an all-risk policy means it is not explicitly excluded. For example, two inches of rain falling over two days caused damage to portions of the interior of a building under construction. The property owner claimed soft costs for project delay. The insurer denied coverage because there was an exclusion for loss caused by rain, whether driven by wind or not, to the interior of any building or structure, or the property inside, unless the building or structure first sustained windstorm or hail damage to its roof, windows, or walls through which the rain entered. The court found that the exclusion applied, and there was no coverage for soft costs.[186]

[6] Exclusions

The standard ISO soft costs endorsement has a couple of its own exclusions. First, there is no coverage for a soft cost expense caused by or resulting from delay because of interference at the location by strikers or others charged with rebuilding, repairing, or replacing the damaged property.[187] Next, there is no coverage when the delay is because of the suspension, lapse, or cancellation

183. Terra-Adi Int'l Dadeland, LLC v. Zurich Am. Ins. Co., 2007 U.S. Dist. LEXIS 14620 (S.D. Fla. Mar. 1, 2007).

184. ISO Form IH 99 15 05 17, § A.1. That underlying peril must generally be to covered property.

185. 5 Jeffrey E. Thomas, *New Appleman on Insurance Law Library Edition* § 50.03[7][a] (LexisNexis 2020) (delay coverage is subject to conditions and exclusions in builder's risk policy itself and, therefore, is contingent on there being a covered loss to covered property).

186. Ace Prop. & Cas. Ins. Co. v. Vegas VP, LP, 2008 U.S. Dist. LEXIS 37495 (D. Nev. May 7, 2008).

187. ISO Form IH 99 15 05 17, § C.1.a.

of any license, lease, or contract unless the suspension, lapse, or cancellation results from a delay in completion of operations by a covered cause of loss.[188] The insurer also will not pay the costs to test for, monitor, or assess the existence, concentration, or effects of "pollutants."[189] Finally, there is no coverage for any other "indirect loss or damage."[190]

Other potential exclusions of which to be aware are

- Improvements or betterments necessary to correct original construction deficiencies;
- Delay in opening because of adverse weather conditions;
- Penalties for failure to complete the described project or failure to complete it on time;
- Non-compliance with the contract;
- Delay beyond the time it should take to rebuild or replace property that has incurred loss; and
- Enforcement of any ordinance or law that either regulates construction, use, or repair or requires the demolition of any property.[191]

[7] Civil Authority Coverage

The endorsement may include "civil authority coverage." Under it, when a covered cause of loss causes damage to property other than that at the described job sites, the insurer will pay for "actual and necessary" soft cost expenses, loss of business income, and loss of rental value sustained by the action of a civil authority that prohibits access to the described job site.[192] There are two conditions that have to be met. First, access must be prohibited by a civil authority to the area immediately surrounding the damaged property as a result of the damage, and the described job site is within that area, but not more than one mile from the damaged property. Second, the action of the civil authority has to be taken in response to dangerous physical conditions that result from the damage or continuation of the covered cause of loss that caused the damage, or the action was taken to enable the civil authority to have unimpeded access to the damaged property. The coverage applies for up to four consecutive weeks from the date of the action by the civil authority. This coverage can be of great value after a flood in the vicinity of the construction site even if flood waters do not enter the site, providing the underlying policy covers floods. For example, if a flood washes away much of a nearby

188. ISO Form IH 99 15 05 17, § C.1.b.
189. ISO Form IH 99 15 05 17, § C.1.c.
190. ISO Form IH 99 15 05 17, § C.2.
191. *Soft Costs* (Inland Marine Underwriters Association 2001), *available at* https://www.imua.org/Files/reports/Soft_Costs.html.
192. ISO Form IH 99 15 05 17, § B.2.

road or bridge and the authorities bar access in the interests of public safety, losses associated with the inability to continue construction should be covered even though the construction site itself was not flooded.

[8] The Means for Determining the Amount of Loss

Obviously, no claim can be paid and no final adjudication can be rendered until the amount of the loss can be determined. The soft costs endorsement may address that determination specifically. For example, the standard ISO endorsement provides that the amount of any soft costs is to be determined "based on relevant sources of information." Those sources include

- The insured's financial records and accounting procedures;
- Bills, invoices, and other vouchers;
- Deeds, liens, or contracts; and
- Construction records and project progress reports.[193]

The endorsement also sets forth information required to establish the amount of loss in business income and rental value.[194]

7.10 Expediting Expense

An "expediting expense" is defined as the cost "to complete repairs to put the insured back in business as rapidly as possible, even if a temporary arrangement."[195] The coverage may be found in some builder's risk policies and pays for temporary repairs to speed up permanent repair or replacement of covered property or equipment.[196] For example, one ISO Builder's Risk Coverage Form contains an "Expediting Expense" clause.[197] The clause provides that, for loss or damage to covered property from a covered cause of loss, the insurer will pay for the extra cost the insured necessarily incurs to make temporary repairs and to expedite permanent repairs or replacement of the damaged property. Unless a different limit of insurance is shown on the Declarations Page, the most the insurer will pay is $25,000 per occurrence. While expediting expenses might be a relatively small portion of an overall claim, they are important to identify because they will contribute to making the insured whole.

193. ISO Form IH 99 15 05 17, § E.2.a.

194. ISO Form IH 99 15 05 17, § E.2.b.

195. *Expediting Expense*, IRMI, https://www.irmi.com/term/insurance-definitions/expediting-expense.

196. *Expediting Expense Coverage*, IRMI, https://www.irmi.com/term/insurance-definitions/expediting-expense-coverage.

197. ISO Form IH 00 70 05 17 § A.5.d.

7.11 Faulty Workmanship Exclusion

Even though water may be the apparent cause of loss, another excluded peril may be the *proximate cause* of loss. When water enters a building under construction and causes damage, carriers frequently raise the "faulty workmanship" exclusion.

In a case several decades ago, the Ninth Circuit held that the faulty workmanship exclusion was ambiguous.[198] In that case, which did not involve a builder's risk policy, a contractor removed most of a roof from the insured property but did not install a temporary cover, and when it rained, office equipment and improvements were damaged. The insurer invoked the faulty workmanship exclusion. The insured argued the exclusion could mean a flawed product or flawed process. Failing to put a temporary cover over the roof would not be a flawed product but would be a flawed process. The court found that the exclusion was ambiguous and construed it to mean a flawed product. The insurer next contended that rain, an excluded risk, caused the property damage, not the contractor's failure. The court, however, decided that although rain operated more immediately to produce the loss, it was the contractor's failure to cover the premises that set in motion the chain of events leading to the loss. The failure to cover the roof was the efficient proximate cause of the loss, and the insurer was liable. The court's interpretation of the faulty workmanship exclusion has been called an "outlier," and a number of courts have criticized it.[199] Nonetheless, there are courts that have followed the reasoning of the Ninth Circuit in cases with similar facts and where the coverage was under a builder's risk policy.[200]

---

198. Allstate v. Smith. 929 F.2d 447 (9th Cir. 1991).

199. *See, e.g.*, James McHugh Constr. Co. v. Travelers Prop. Cas. Co. of Am., 223 F. Supp. 3d 462, 469 (D. Md. 2016), citing decisions that disagree with the analysis of the Ninth Circuit.

200. *See, e.g.*, Phila. Indem. Ins. Co. v. TL Fab, LP, 2018 U.S. Dist. LEXIS 130089 (S.D. Cal. Aug. 2, 2018) (where insured installed plastic sheeting over open windows and doors, but high winds damaged or destroyed it and rain entered buildings, court found faulty workmanship exclusion inapplicable); Century Theaters, Inc. v. Travelers Prop. Cas. Co. of Am., 2006 U.S. Dist. LEXIS 15766 (N.D. Cal. Mar. 20, 2006) (where contractor did not install temporary protective covering to prevent water intrusion, despite incomplete waterproofing system and unsealed penetrations and during heavy rainstorm water to enter interior of building, court found faulty workmanship exclusion was ambiguous and did not, as matter of law, justify denial of coverage); M.A. Mortenson Co. v. Indem. Ins. Co. of N. Am., 1999 U.S. Dist. LEXIS 22641 (D. Minn. Dec. 23, 1999) (where contractor installed protective devices at construction site to guard against damage caused by rainfall, but those measures were overwhelmed by heavy rainfall that resulted in flooding, court held faulty workmanship exclusion did not apply because alleged failure of contractor to complete work before onset of the rainy season was failure of process, not a flawed product).

In a more recent decision, the Ninth Circuit found the exclusion could apply.[201] The contractor in that case had not placed enough ballast water in an underground fuel storage tank to prevent it from floating in an excavation hole during rainy weather before complete installation of the tank. The tank was damaged, delaying the project. The lower court held that the faulty workmanship exclusion did not apply because damages did not occur from a flaw in the "product," that is, the underground storage tank. The appellate court noted that exclusion was not only for faulty workmanship but also for faulty construction. It reversed and said that "construction" could be interpreted as referring to the "process" in completing the covered project. The court did not decide the exclusion applied, but rather said that further proceedings before the lower court were necessary to resolve whether the losses were, in fact, caused by or resulted from faulty, inadequate, or defective construction, in which case the exclusion would apply.

In a case out of Washington state,[202] a building under construction was damaged during several days of a violent rainstorm by water that penetrated through unfinished openings and migrated through the building, causing significant damage to its interior. The policy covered losses caused by some weather conditions and excluded those caused by others. The insurer denied coverage, asserting that the loss was caused by faulty workmanship and investigations of the extent of those defects during a process called "flood testing." The insurer pointed to an exclusion for defective construction under which the policy did not cover losses caused by faulty, inadequate, or defective design, specifications, workmanship, repair, construction, renovation, remodeling, grading, or compaction. The court denied a motion by the insured for summary judgment on the scope of coverage and left questions of the exclusions to the trier of fact. The case is a reminder that even though a policy may cover losses from floods, the peril proximately causing the loss may be excluded.

7.12 Exclusions for Extremes of Temperature or Freezing

One problem faced at construction sites is that pipes may be exposed to the elements and unprotected. They may freeze and cause water damage or even flooding to the property. Some policies may anticipate that peril by excluding from coverage loss or damage caused by or resulting from extremes of temperature or caused by freezing. Those exclusions were invoked in a case in which, on Christmas Eve, a sprinkler head froze and ruptured, causing water to fill a subbasement of a building under construction. The flooding damaged

201. Engineered Structures, Inc. v. Travelers Prop. Cas. Co. of Am., 2020 U.S. App. LEXIS 25994 (9th Cir. Aug. 17, 2020).

202. N. Coast Enters. v. St. Paul Fire & Marine Ins. Co., 2006 U.S. Dist. LEXIS 20245 (W.D. Wash. Mar. 28, 2006).

mechanical and electrical equipment in the subbasement and caused some structural damage to the building. The court first noted "extremes of temperature" was an ambiguous term and that freezing temperatures might not be considered extreme in December. It then rejected the argument that freezing was the proximate, efficient, and dominant cause of the flooding and water damage. It concluded that a reasonable insured would not consider a loss caused by freezing to incorporate a loss "visibly occasioned by water damage by virtue of the mere fact that the presence of water can best be explained by the rupturing of a sprinkler head" that had frozen. The loss, found the court, was caused by water damage, and judgment should be for the insured.[203]

7.13 Ensuing Loss

Builder's risk policies usually contain an "ensuing loss" provision.[204] Generally, an ensuing loss is one that follows from a loss caused by an excluded peril.[205] An "ensuing loss" clause is "intended to preserve coverage for losses caused, in part, by an excluded peril if a loss follows (or 'ensues') from a covered peril."[206] The clause, unfortunately, is the subject of much misunderstanding and conflicting interpretation.[207] It can come into play when a builder's risk policy covers water damage and that damage follows faulty workmanship, an excluded peril. Some courts find in those cases that water damage resulting from faulty workmanship is excluded.[208] Other courts do not. For example, in a Florida case, the insured claimed water intrusion occurred because of faulty workmanship and caused damage to the exterior and interior of the insured building. The court said that the loss for which the insured was seeking coverage resulted from water intrusion, and that was separate from repair of the faulty construction. In response, the insurer said that the ensuing loss

---

203. Album Realty Corp. v. Am. Home Assur. Co., 80 N.Y.2d 1008, 607 N.E.2d 804, 592 N.Y.S.2d 657 (1992).

204. Stover, *A Guide to Builder's Risk Insurance*, 53 Tort & Ins. L.J. 819 (2018).

205. 5 Jeffrey E. Thomas, *New Appleman on Insurance Law Library Edition* § 44.05[1] (LexisNexis 2020).

206. French, *The "Ensuing Loss" Clause in Insurance Policies: The Forgotten and Misunderstood Antidote to Anti-Concurrent Causation Exclusions*, 13 Nev. L.J. 215, 219 (2012) (purpose of clause is to clarify that the exclusions should not swallow basic coverage provided by policy).

207. 5 Jeffrey E. Thomas, *New Appleman on Insurance Law Library Edition* § 44.05[1] (LexisNexis 2020).

208. *See, e.g.*, Gateway II LLC v. Hartford Fire Ins. Co., 2016 N.Y. Misc. LEXIS 1325 (Apr. 5, 2016), where the faulty workmanship exclusion said the insurer would not pay for loss or damage caused by or resulting from faulty workmanship, but if loss or damage by a covered cause of loss resulted, it would pay for loss or damage caused by that covered cause of loss. Water damage was a covered loss. The insured claimed water damage and argued that because of the exception, the insurer should be liable under the water damage coverage. The court disagreed. There is no coverage, it said, when the causing loss is directly related to the original excluded risk.

exception was not applicable when the ensuing loss is directly related to the original excluded one. However, the court said that "if the faulty workmanship resulted in water intrusion that subsequently resulted in ensuing losses, the cost to repair the faulty workmanship is excluded but the ensuing losses from the water intrusion are covered."[209] Note that although in the builder's risk context, the faulty workmanship exclusion is generally the one invoked, another exclusion could also be at issue.

7.14 Termination of Coverage

While some policies may terminate on a specific date,[210] builder's risk is intended to provide coverage during construction and therefore, unlike other types of insurance, it does not necessarily terminate on a certain date.[211] Typically, coverage ends when an event specified in the policy occurs. In the ISO policy these events are:

- The policy expires or is cancelled.
- The property is accepted by the purchaser.[212]
- The interest of the named insured in the property ends.
- The named insured abandons the construction with no intent to complete it.
- 90 days after construction is complete or 60 days after any building described in the Declarations is occupied in whole or in part or put to its intended use.[213]

---

209. The Bartram, LLC v. Landmark Am. Ins. Co., 864 F. Supp. 2d 1229, 1235 (N.D. Fla. 2012). *See also* Selective Way Ins. Co. v. Nat'l Fire Ins. Co., 988 F. Supp. 2d 530 (D. Md. 2013), where a subcontractor installed a water supply line that leaked and caused water damage to the finishes in the building. The court found that the damage was a covered loss despite the faulty workmanship exclusion because the ensuing loss clause applied.

210. Stover, *A Guide to Builder's Risk Insurance*, 53 Tort & Ins. L.J. 819 (2018) (some policies will specify date certain for termination of the coverage).

211. Malecki, *Builder's Risk Insurance: Specialized Coverage for Construction Projects*, Adjusting Today, *available at* https://adjustersinternational.com/publications/adjusting-today/builders-risk-insurance/0/ (builder's risk policies are intended to terminate when work has been completed and property is ready for use or occupancy, even though some minor finishing work might remain).

212. *See, e.g.*, Shamrock Homebuilders, Inc. v. Cherokee Ins. Co., 225 Tenn. 236, 466 S.W.2d 204 (1971) (purchasers of new home executed documents required for closing of transaction, deed and deed of trust were filed for record, but when they entered house they found that water pipes had frozen and burst and house was flooded and seriously damaged, and they then demanded transaction be rescinded; court found sale of property had not been completed and builder's risk coverage had not terminated). A variation on the termination event is installation or erection of the property is completed and accepted as *satisfactory*. Fireman's Fund v. Structural Sys. Tech., Inc., 426 F. Supp. 2d 1009 (D. Neb. 2006).

213. ISO Form CP 00 20 10 12, § F.4. *See* Great Am. Ins. Co. v. Jefferson County Comm'n, 776 F. Supp. 2d 1252 (N.D. Ala. 2010) (phrase "put to its intended use" means to bring into particular service or end for which structure was designed); AXIS Surplus Ins. Co. v. Lake CDA

The AAIS policy omits the occupancy or intended use contingencies.[214] Other policies may provide for termination when any other insurance covers the property as a completed building or structure.[215]

Determining whether the policy was in effect at the time of an alleged flood is obviously critical and, because it is subject to interpretation, a matter over which the parties may disagree. For example, in *Great Am. Ins. Co. v. Jefferson County Comm'n*,[216] the county hired a contractor to expand and upgrade existing facilities at its sewage treatment plant. A control system installed by a subcontractor improperly took pumps out of service, causing a flood at a pumping facility. The insurer contended that the facility was put to its intended use the day the pumps began running on a continuous basis, while the general contractor argued the facility was not yet put to its intended use because certain features were not installed and others were still being tested. The court agreed with the general contractor and noted that although the pumps were installed and functioning, there was a long list of components that were not installed and employees of the contractor were onsite working on a number of remaining items.

The termination of coverage question is complex and one that is beyond the scope of this treatise. It is discussed at length in a number of important cases[217] and in expert commentaries.[218] The *Jefferson County* case is discussed here to illustrate the importance of the issue and that it is one insurance companies are likely to raise.

Dev. LLC, 2008 U.S. Dist. LEXIS 69020 (D. Idaho Sept. 10, 2008) (because language referred to "property" as opposed to structure or some other specific component of entire project, it was unclear whether "coverage ends" section of policy applied to structure—retaining wall—or entire property); McCarty v. Maryland Casualty Co., 429 F. Supp. 112, 116 (D. Ark. 1976) (building would be occupied when used for purpose within contemplation of parties, provided use was not to test building for defects and provided it was not transient or trivial). *See generally* Stover, *A Guide to Builder's Risk Insurance*, 53 Tort & Ins. L.J. 819 (2018) (absent specified termination date, coverage typically ceases when project is considered to be "completed," and date of completion will generally be defined by policy as being when owner accepts structure as complete, when a certificate of occupancy is issued by the local building authority, or when structure is put to its intended use).

214. *See, e.g.*, AAIS Form IM 7051 04 04, Additional Coverage Limitation § 2.

215. Great Am. Ins. Co. v. Jefferson County Comm'n, 776 F. Supp. 2d 1252, 1264 (N.D. Ala. 2010).

216. Great Am. Ins. Co. v. Jefferson County Comm'n, 776 F. Supp. 2d 1252 (N.D. Ala. 2010).

217. *See, e.g.*, Fireman's Fund Ins. Co. v. Millers' Mutual Ins. Ass'n., 451 F.2d 1140 (10th Cir. 1971); Hendrix v. New Amsterdam Cas. Co., 390 F.2d 299 (10th Cir. 1968); Reliance Ins. Co. v. Jones, 296 F.2d 71 (10th Cir. 1961); Commercial Standard Co. v. Rhode Island, 193 F.2d 375 (5th Cir. 1952); McCarty v. Md. Cas. Co., 429 F. Supp. 112 (D. Ark. 1976); Cuthrell v. Milwaukee Mechanics Insurance Co. of Milwaukee, Wisconsin, 234 N.C. 137, 66 S.E.2d 649 (N.C. 1951).

218. *See* 5 Jeffrey E. Thomas, *New Appleman on Insurance Law Library Edition* § 50.01[4] (LexisNexis 2020); Cozen, *Insuring Real Property*, § 6.03[2] (LexisNexis Matthew Bender 2020).

8

Recovering under Boiler and Machinery or Equipment Breakdown Insurance

8.1 Introduction

Boiler and Machinery (B&M) insurance is a form of coverage that has existed for over 150 years.[1] It was created in response to the dangers of steam power in the mid-19th century.[2] B&M insurance has undergone enormous change and in fact, it is today more commonly called "equipment breakdown" insurance,[3] although it is still often referred to as B&M for short. Policies now cover far more than boilers.[4] Among the equipment usually covered today are generators, engines, pumps, compressors, and turbines and refrigeration and air-conditioning equipment as well as boilers.[5] Policies may also cover elevators, sprinklers, security systems, and electronic business equipment like fax machines, copiers, and telephone systems.[6]

1. Malecki, *Equipment Breakdown Coverage: This Oft-Misunderstood Coverage Is a Necessity for Many Clients*, *available at* http://www.roughnotes.com/rnmagazine/2008/march 08/03p114.htm. In 1866 the Hartford Steam Boiler Inspection and Insurance Company (HSB) was founded. *History*, HSB, http://www.munichre.com/HSB/hsb-history/index.html.

2. Explosions were occurring at the rate of almost one every four days. *History*, HSB, http://www.munichre.com/HSB/hsb-history/index.html.

3. Malecki, *Equipment Breakdown Insurance: Too Important to Ignore!*, at 1 (2009), Adjusting Today, *available at* http://adjustersinternational.com/publications/adjusting-today /equipment-breakdown-insurance/1/.

4. Tapia, *Equipment Breakdown Coverage: Not Your Father's Boiler & Machinery Insurance* (2000), Insurance Journal, http://www.insurancejournal.com/magazines/features/2000/11/27/21 234.htm (modern equipment breakdown coverage was traditionally called boiler and machinery insurance).

5. O'Connor, *Construction Law: Recent Issues in Property Coverage*, 34 Wm. Mitchell L. Rev. 177, 202 (2007). *See, e.g.*, New York Underwriters Ins. Co. v. Coffman, 540 S.W.2d 445 (Tex. Civ. App.—Fort Worth, 1976) (breakdown of air-conditioning compressor covered).

6. Tapia, *Equipment Breakdown Coverage: Not Your Father's Boiler & Machinery Insurance* (2000), Insurance Journal, http://www.insurancejournal.com/magazines/features/2000/11/27/2 1234.htm. *See also Equipment Breakdown Insurance FAQ*, Allen Financial Insurance Group, http://eqgroup.com/Equipment-Breakdown.htm.

Equipment breakdown insurance is a very specialized form of property insurance.[7] A limited number of insurance carriers offer it.[8] It is not widely understood.[9] It is a form of property insurance that covers named perils, instead of all risks.[10] The typical coverage is for losses to "covered equipment," consequential damage to other property, and losses that are "related" to breakdown to covered equipment including, for example, business losses and the expense to recover from a breakdown. Policy language can vary considerably, however, and endorsements may change the language.

Policyholders may be able to recover flood-related losses under a B&M policy. These policies do not cover direct loss from a flood but may cover the consequential loss when the failure of covered equipment results in flooding. Also, flooding may initiate events that lead to an accident to covered equipment.

8.2 Covering a Property Insurance "Gap"

Equipment breakdown insurance is a form of "gap" coverage.[11] The equipment it covers is also covered by standard commercial property policies as contents or, if permanently affixed, as part of the insured building. The coverage, however, is for losses that are caused by an external event, for example,

---

7. O'Connor, *Construction Law: Recent Issues in Property Coverage*, 34 Wm. Mitchell L. Rev. 177, 202 (2007).

8. Tapia, *Equipment Breakdown Coverage: Not Your Father's Boiler & Machinery Insurance* (2000), Insurance Journal, http://www.insurancejournal.com/magazines/features/2000/11/27/21234.htm (noting that over 200 companies offer equipment breakdown coverage).

9. Austin, *Equipment Breakdown—More Than Just Boiler and Machinery* (2011), IRMI, http://www.irmi.com/articles/expert-commentary/equipment-breakdown; Malecki, *Equipment Breakdown Insurance: Too Important to Ignore!* at 6 (2009), Adjusting Today, *available at* http://adjustersinternational.com/publications/adjusting-today/equipment-breakdown-insurance/1/ (equipment breakdown insurance ranks high among more frequently misunderstood property coverages); Malecki, *Equipment Breakdown Coverage: This Oft-Misunderstood Coverage Is a Necessity for Many Clients, available at* http://www.roughnotes.com/rnmagazine/2008/march08/03p114.htm; Tapia, *Equipment Breakdown Coverage: Not Your Father's Boiler & Machinery Insurance* (2000), Insurance Journal, http://www.insurancejournal.com/magazines/features/2000/11/27/21234.htm (many agents and brokers may not understand equipment breakdown insurance).

10. Stone Container Corp. v. Hartford Steam Boiler Inspection & Ins. Co., 165 F.3d 1157, 1161 (7th Cir. 1999). *See also* Austin, *Equipment Breakdown—More Than Just Boiler and Machinery* (2011), IRMI, http://www.irmi.com/articles/expert-commentary/equipment-breakdown.

11. As a general rule, insurers are not required to fill the gap in coverage. For example, in *Commonwealth Ins. Co. v. Stone Container Corp.*, 351 F.3d 774 (7th Cir. 2003), the insured argued the insurer misrepresented its coverage and failed to disclose the gap. However, the court held the insurer did not have a duty to disclose the gap in coverage; instead, the insured was required to know the contents of its policies. Non-disclosure, concluded the court, provide no basis for holding the insurer liable.

fire, vandalism, or windstorm.[12] Additionally, standard commercial property policies explicitly exclude coverage for mechanical breakdown. The exclusion is typically for rupture or bursting that is caused by centrifugal force,[13] and explosion of steam boilers, steam pipes, steam engines, or steam turbines that are owned or leased by the policyholder.[14] There are, however, exceptions as some comprehensive all-risk commercial property policies incorporate equipment breakdown coverage.[15] When they do not, a B&M policy covers the "gap."

While commercial property policies usually exclude coverage for mechanical breakdown, they often do not define "mechanical breakdown." Courts have interpreted the phrase to mean "a functional defect in the moving parts of the equipment which causes the latter to cease functioning or to function improperly."[16] The phrase is part of an exclusion and will, therefore, be narrowly construed. Courts have restricted it to losses that arise from "internal or inherent" deficiency or defect, as opposed to those from any *external* cause.[17]

8.3 Policy Forms

At one time equipment breakdown coverage could only be obtained in a stand alone policy covering losses excluded by a commercial property policy. These policies continue to be available.[18] Today, however, many carriers offer the

---

12. Austin, *Equipment Breakdown—More Than Just Boiler and Machinery* (2011), IRMI, http://www.irmi.com/articles/expert-commentary/equipment-breakdown. *See also Equipment Breakdown Insurance FAQ*, Allen Financial Insurance Group, http://eqgroup.com/Equipment-Breakdown.htm ("all risk" property coverage is not designed to pay for equipment accidents, while equipment breakdown coverage is intended to pay for damage caused by risks like short circuits, centrifugal force, and mechanical breakdown).

13. *See, e.g.*, ISO Form CP 10 10 04 02, § B.2.e.

14. *See, e.g.*, ISO Form CP 10 10 04 02, § B.2.d. *See generally* Boggs, *Three Commercial Property Endorsements Every Client Should Have* (July 27, 2009), My New Markets, http://www.mynewmarkets.com/articles/102464/three-commercial-property-endorsements-every-client-should-have (equipment breakdown insurance fills gaps in causes of loss in commercial property policy, for example, losses to equipment caused by power surge). *See also* Continental Ins. Co. v. Acadia Ins. Co., 974 F. Supp. 371, 374 (D. Vt. 1997) (hazards of boilers and production machinery are often not included in general insurance policies).

15. 5 Jeffery E. Thomas, *New Appleman on Insurance Law Library Edition* § 51.01[2][c][i] (LexisNexis 2020). Equipment breakdown coverage may also be added by endorsement to a comprehensive property policy. *See, e.g.*, St. Mary's Area Water Auth. v. St. Paul Fire & Marine Ins. Co., 2007 U.S. Dist. LEXIS 34814 (M.D. Pa. May 11, 2007).

16. National Investors Fire & Casualty Co. v. Preddy, 248 Ark. 320, 322, 451 S.W.2d 457, 458 (Ark. 1970). *See also* Lake Charles Harbor & Terminal Dist. v. Imperial Casualty & Indem. Co., 670 F. Supp. 189 (W.D. La. 1987); Standard Structural Steel Co. v. Bethlehem Steel Corp., 597 F. Supp. 164 (D. Conn. 1984).

17. Caldwell v. Transportation Ins. Co., 234 Va. 639, 644, 364 S.E.2d 1, 3 (1988).

18. *See* Malecki, *Equipment Breakdown Insurance: Too Important to Ignore!*, at 2 (2009), Adjusting Today, *available at* http://adjustersinternational.com/publications/adjusting-today

coverage as an endorsement to their commercial property policy,[19] or as part of a comprehensive property coverage package.[20]

To determine whether a client has equipment breakdown coverage, one should first look for a separate policy. It may be called "equipment breakdown," boiler and machinery," or something else. The coverage may be embedded in a property policy. One then has to refer to the Declarations Page to determine the coverage and any applicable sublimits. When the Declarations Page is not clear, one has to read the policy to determine if coverage is found in the policy or is added by an endorsement. Typically, an endorsement removes an exclusion for equipment breakdown and "adds back" the coverage.[21] If coverage is added by endorsement, it is important to be aware that other exclusions in the main policy usually still apply unless the endorsement specifically deletes them.[22]

8.4 Declarations Page

The Declarations Page is important for determining the extent of coverage. Policies often cross-reference it.[23] Some list the covered equipment, or

---

/equipment-breakdown-insurance/1/ (commonly, B&M coverage is written under separate policy).

19. *See, e.g.*, McCaughey v. Ohio Sec. Ins. Co., 2021 U.S. Dist. LEXIS 65061 (C.D. Cal. Apr. 2, 2021) (Equipment Breakdown Enhancement Endorsement modified Causes of Loss—Special Form removing exclusion for mechanical breakdowns); Nat'l Union Fire Ins. Co. v. Travelers Indem. Co., 210 F. Supp. 2d 479 (S.D.N.Y. 2002) (all-risk property policy with Boiler and Machinery Endorsement); Litho Color, Inc. v. Pacific Emplrs. Ins. Co., 98 Wn. App. 286, 289, 991 P.2d 638, 640 (1999) (Boiler and Machinery endorsement to commercial property insurance policy); Rorer Group v. Insurance Co. of N. Am., 440 Pa. Super. 69, 655 A.2d 123 (1995) (Boiler and Machinery Endorsement to all-risk policy). *See also* Scottsdale Ins. Co. v. Sally Group, LLC, 2012 U.S. Dist. LEXIS 47532 (S.D. Tex. Apr. 3, 2012) (Commercial Property Conditions Form with Equipment Breakdown Coverage Endorsement).

20. *See, e.g.*, Commonwealth Ins. Co. v. Stone Container Corp., 351 F.3d 774, 776 (7th Cir. 2003) (all-risk policy included B&M insurance); Detroit Edison Co. v. Protection Mut. Ins. Co., 134 F.3d 790, 793 (6th Cir. 1998). *See generally* Austin, *Equipment Breakdown—More Than Just Boiler and Machinery* (2011), IRMI, http://www.irmi.com/articles/expert-commentary/equipment-breakdown (equipment breakdown coverage may be found in property policy when it is imbedded in policy form); Tapia, *Equipment Breakdown Coverage: Not Your Father's Boiler & Machinery Insurance* (2000), Insurance Journal, http://www.insurancejournal.com/magazines/features/2000/11/27/21234.htm (perhaps only a dozen companies offer equipment breakdown coverage on monoline basis).

21. Austin, *Equipment Breakdown—More Than Just Boiler and Machinery* (2011), IRMI, http://www.irmi.com/articles/expert-commentary/equipment-breakdown.

22. *See, e.g.*, Rorer Group v. Insurance Co. of N. Am., 440 Pa. Super. 69, 73–74, 655 A.2d 123, 125 (1995), where an endorsement extended coverage and removed exclusions for explosion, mechanical breakdown, electrical injury, and rupture or bursting. It also added cracking, a coverage not previously excluded. The endorsement, however, did not address policy exclusions for corrosion or latent defects. It could not, therefore, abrogate or modify them.

23. *See* Malecki, *Equipment Breakdown Insurance: Too Important to Ignore!* at 6 (2009), Adjusting Today, *available at* http://adjustersinternational.com/publications/adjusting-today/eq

"objects," on the Declarations Page.[24] Other policies, however, will define "covered equipment" in the policy itself.[25] Some have "schedules" that are attached to the policy and list covered equipment.[26] The coverage is based on an accident or breakdown to covered equipment or objects, making it critical to determine the meaning of those terms.[27]

The Declarations Page lists the available coverage. It will usually include limits for a coverage based on monetary amounts[28] or a time period. If nothing is shown for a particular coverage, then that coverage is not provided. The ISO Equipment Breakdown Protection Coverage Form provides the listed coverages that are provided if either a limit or the word "included" is shown for that coverage.[29] A Travelers company policy says that coverage is provided if a limit, the word "included," or an *other coverage indicator* is shown on the Declarations Page.[30] When a coverage is "included," the limit for it is part of the base limit or total limit per breakdown.[31]

There is a standard ISO "Equipment Breakdown Protection Coverage Form Declarations" that one can employ to understand the contents and importance

uipment-breakdown-insurance/1/ (equipment breakdown Declarations Page is important part of policy, and data on it should be checked carefully to make sure it is correct and complete, as there are references to data shown on it throughout other portions of policy and any errors or omissions on it can be damaging to intended coverage).

24. *See, e.g.*, Pioneer Chlor Alkali Co. v. Royal Indem. Co., 879 S.W.2d 920, 925, n.1 (Tex. App.—Houston 14th Dist., 1994) ("object" was equipment shown on Declarations Page). *See also* ISO Form BM 00 25 02 91, § F.2 ("object" means equipment shown in Declarations). The policy adds that a full description of specific object categories is found in the "Object Definitions endorsement" attached to the coverage form.

25. *See, e.g.*, ISO Form BM 00 20 07 01; HSB Freestyle Policy Form 6671 (10/2002).

26. *See, e.g.*, Foote Mineral Co. v. Maryland Casualty Co., 173 F. Supp. 925 (D. Tenn. 1959), *aff'd*, 277 F.2d 452 (6th Cir. 1960), *cert. den.*, 364 U.S. 818, 81 S. Ct. 49, 5 L. Ed. 2d 48 (1960) (policy provided coverage against loss by accident of objects described in detail on two schedules); Good Canning Co. v. London Guarantee & Acci. Co., 128 F. Supp. 778, 781 (D. Ark. 1955); Enosburg Falls v. Hartford Steam Boiler Inspection & Ins. Co., 117 Vt. 114, 85 A.2d 577 (1952) (objects were set forth in separate schedules each describing different items of equipment, and many types of accidents were provided for in coverage); Senn Products Corp. v. Hartford Steam Boiler Inspection & Ins. Co., 180 Misc. 675, 41 N.Y.S.2d 133 (1943) ("objects" insured were described in schedules attached to policy).

27. *See, e.g.*, Hartford Steam Boiler Inspection & Ins. Co. v. Kleinman, 293 S.W. 894 (Tex. App. 1927) (fire box and chimney were parts of heating plant but were not parts of boiler described in policy as covered equipment; where explosions occurred in fire box and chimney, resulting damage was not covered under policy).

28. *Boiler and Machinery Coverage Form* (Summit Business Media, 2013).

29. ISO Form BM 00 20 07 01, § A.2.

30. Travelers EnergyMax 21, § A.2.

31. Malecki, *Equipment Breakdown Insurance: Too Important to Ignore!* at 5 (2009), Adjusting Today, *available at* http://adjustersinternational.com/publications/adjusting-today/equipment-breakdown-insurance/1/ (if $500,000 base limit is selected and other coverages are designated in Declarations as being included, coverage will hinge on how much is left after paying for damage to property named insured owns or has in its care, custody, or control).

of these forms.[32]The ISO form lists coverage limits for ammonia contamination, consequential loss, data and media, hazardous substance, and water damage. The form also provides for recording a business income report date, business income annual value, and business income coinsurance percentage. The listed deductibles on the ISO form follow an explanation that a deductible will apply only when an amount, hours, days, or the word "included" is shown for a particular coverage. In that case, the deductible for *that* coverage is a part of the "combined deductible." Deductibles usually apply separately for each coverage. However, if one is shown as "combined," the insurer will subtract the combined deductible amount from the total amount of any loss to which that combined deductible is applicable.[33] On the ISO form, deductibles for property damage and spoilage are listed in dollar amounts, while those for business income,[34] extra expense, and utility interruption are stated in terms of hours or days. Finally, the ISO Declarations form provides for recording additional insureds, mortgage holders, loss payees, and their addresses.

8.5 Coverage

[1] Generally

Boiler and Machinery or Equipment Breakdown insurance covers damage to *covered items* from an accident or breakdown and damage to the *other property* of the insured that is caused by an accident to covered items.[35] Disputes over whether a loss is within the policy coverage are for a jury to resolve.[36]

[2] Covered Equipment

To understand the extent of coverage, one needs to determine what equipment is covered. That is because a covered cause of loss is generally defined as an "accident" causing direct physical damage to "covered equipment" or to an "object." Covered equipment or objects may be listed on the Declarations Page.[37] Policies may specify which equipment that is not otherwise identified

32. ISO Form BM DS 07 07 01.
33. ISO Form BM 00 20 07 01, § D.1.a.
34. *See* Austin, *Equipment Breakdown—More Than Just Boiler and Machinery* (2011), IRMI, http://www.irmi.com/articles/expert-commentary/equipment-breakdown (business income coverage may be subject to average daily value (ADV) deductible based on number of days business income would have been earned during period of interruption had no accident occurred).
35. *Boiler & Machinery Insurance/Equipment Breakdown Insurance*, Brunswick Companies, http://www.brunswickcompanies.com/ci-boiler-machinery-equipment-breakdown-insurance.html.
36. Welders Supply, Inc. v. American Employers' Ins. Co., 342 F.2d 972, 974 (6th Cir. 1965).
37. ISO Form BM 00 25 02 91, § F.2 (objects are equipment shown on Declarations Page).

on the Declarations Page is "covered equipment."[38] Policies also often prescribe which equipment *is not* covered equipment. An example that has potential consequences for water or flood damage claims is "'sewer piping, any underground vessels or piping, any piping forming a part of a sprinkler system or water piping other than boiler feedwater piping, boiler condensate return piping or water piping forming a part of a refrigerating or air conditioning system.'"[39]

[3] "Accident" as Covered Cause of Loss

[a] Generally

In most B&M policies, the covered cause of loss is an "accident." The word "accident" has been used in insurance policies for many years and has been construed by countless courts; however, the specific manner in which it is defined in a policy is critical to the coverage. For example, in one policy "accident" was defined as sudden and accidental tearing asunder of the object caused by *pressure of contents therein.* Ammonia gas escaped through a hole in the shell of a refrigeration system after a short of electricity in a coil. The loss, argued the insurer, was not caused by pressure from within. The court agreed. It concluded the predominant efficient cause of the loss was electrical arcing, not "sudden accidental tearing asunder" of any part of the refrigeration system that was a result of the pressure of the contents in it.[40] Because policies generally require the equipment malfunction to result from an accident, chronic failures of equipment that are attributable to age are not covered.[41] For the same reason, losses caused by design, construction, or installation defects are not covered.[42]

Losses that are not proximately caused by the "accident" are not covered, and causation is often the critical issue. For example, in a Massachusetts case wastewater flooded the basement of a sewage treatment facility after a pump

38. HSB Freestyle Policy Form 6671 (10/2002) § A.1.b.(1) (covered equipment not specified on Declarations Page is equipment that generates, transmits, or uses energy, including electronic communications and data processing equipment, or that, during normal usage, operates under vacuum or pressure, other than weight of its contents).

39. *See* Snohomish Cty. Pub. Hosp. Dist. No. 1 v. Hartford Fire Ins. Co., 2018 U.S. Dist. LEXIS 82861, at *3 (W.D. Wash. May 15, 2018) (quoting policy). The court held that where only part of a hydraulic cylinder was in a hole extending below ground, it was not an underground vessel. Additionally, although the cylinder held a liquid—hydraulic fluid—it did so not because its purpose was to hold a liquid, but because it required that liquid to operate.

40. Rueckert Meat Co. v. Hartford Steam Boiler, Inspection & Ins. Co., 368 S.W.2d 914 (Mo. App. 1963).

41. O'Connor, *Construction Law: Recent Issues in Property Coverage*, 34 Wm. Mitchell L. Rev. 177, 202 (2007).

42. Scottsdale Ins. Co. v. Sally Group, LLC, 2012 U.S. Dist. LEXIS 47532 (S.D. Tex. Apr. 3, 2012).

failed. At the time, the flow of wastewater coming into the facility was unusually high because of infiltration of rainwater, snowmelt, and tidal surges. The court found that the insured failed to prove the incident was caused by an accident because it had not demonstrated that the breakdown of the pump was the efficient proximate cause that set in motion the train of events that brought about the damage without intervention of any other force.[43] On the other hand, the insurer had not shown that the insureds could not prove that the failure of the pump was the efficient proximate cause of the loss. Both parties had moved for summary judgment, and the court ruled that with discovery yet to be completed, it was an open question whether the mechanical breakdown of the pump set in motion the train of events leading to the catastrophic damage to the facility.

The definition of "accident" might specifically refer to flood. For example, an insured bowling alley suffered water damage when rain entered the building while the roof was being replaced. A California court found no coverage under the commercial property policy because the damage did not result from rain entering through a damaged roof—a covered cause of loss—but from rain entering through an *uncompleted* roof. The insureds then attempted to bring the loss within the coverage of a B&M endorsement. The policy added to the typical definition of accident that if covered electrical equipment required drying out as a result of a *flood*, the drying would be considered an "accident." The court said that if the only damage was that equipment got wet, then under the endorsement the only form of "drying out" that qualified as an "accident" was when it was the "result of flood," not rain.[44]

[b] Typical Policy Language

[i] ISO Boiler and Machinery Coverage Form

The ISO Boiler and Machinery Coverage Form states that a covered cause of loss is an "accident" to an "object" listed on the Declarations Page.[45] The policy defines "object" as equipment shown on the Declarations Page.[46] The policy adds that a full description of specific object categories is found in

43. Hull Permanent Sewer Comm'n v. Artford Steam Boiler Insp. & Ins. Co., 2017 U.S. Dist. LEXIS 50595 (D. Mass. Mar. 31, 2017).

44. Holesapple v. Aetna Cas. & Sur. Co., 2002 Cal. App. Unpub. LEXIS 460 (Apr. 29, 2002).

45. ISO Form BM 00 25 02 91, § A.2.

46. ISO Form BM 00 25 02 91, § F.2. *See* Malecki, *Equipment Breakdown Insurance: Too Important to Ignore!*, at 2 (2009), Adjusting Today, *available at* http://adjustersinternational.com/publications/adjusting-today/equipment-breakdown-insurance/1/ ("object" refers to general category of equipment covered and defined in more precise terms of what "object" included). The policy definition of a specific object can determine the coverage. In *Norfolk & W. R. Co. v. Royal Indemnity Co.*, 257 F. 849 (D. Pa. 1919), for example, the word "boiler" encompassed "'all connecting pipes and fittings up to and including the valve nearest the boiler.'" A "whistle pipe," which was beyond the whistle valve, ruptured. The court concluded the rupture happened beyond the physical limits of what the insurer undertook to cover against steam pressure.

the "Object Definitions endorsement" attached to the coverage form.[47] "Accident" is defined as a "sudden and accidental breakdown"[48] of an object, or part of one.[49] That "breakdown" need not be shown by direct physical evidence. An inference may support a determination that there was an accident.[50] The question of whether there has been an "accident" is generally one for the jury.[51] Because the word "sudden" is part of the definition of "accident," that is, a coverage term, the insured has the burden to show that the alleged accident was sudden.[52]

Under the ISO Boiler and Machinery Coverage Form, a breakdown has to be *manifested* by physical damage to the object and the damage has to require repair or replacement.[53] "Manifest" does not mean, one court has said, *discovered* by the insured.[54] A thing manifests when there are "observable signs of

---

47. Some policies may define "object" rather than cross-reference the Declarations Page. The definition may be ambiguous and construed in favor of the insured. *See* Lakeshore Marine, Inc. v. Hartford Acc. & Indem. Co., 164 Ga. App. 417, 296 S.E.2d 418 (1982).

48. Can a breakdown be the result of an external cause, for example, a power surge? *See* Nat'l Union Fire Ins. Co. v. Travelers Indem. Co., 210 F. Supp. 2d 479 (S.D.N.Y. 2002) (damage to insured's property from power surge allegedly caused by vandalism to off-premises transformer owned by utility company constituted "breakdown" as used in definition of "accident" as term should be construed broadly to include internal damage resulting from *external* causes).

49. *See generally* Hoey, *The Meaning of "Accident" in Boiler and Machinery Insurance and New Developments in Underwriting*, 19 Forum 467 (1984) (boiler and machinery policies once had varying definitions of "accident" depending on type of object insured, but in the early 1960s a uniform and concise definition of "accident" was adopted by many insurers).

50. *See, e.g.*, Commercial Union Ins. Co. v. F.R.P. Co., 172 Ga. App. 244, 249–50, 322 S.E.2d 915, 920 (1984) (where cooling system malfunctioned allegedly because of defective "O" ring, but there was no physical evidence any defect, fact that system worked "perfectly" after ring was replaced allowed inference that ring was defective).

51. Food Source, Inc. v. Zurich Ins. Co., 751 S.W.2d 596, 598 (Tex. App.—Dallas 1988).

52. Fairhaven Power Co. v. Hartford Steam Boiler Inspection & Ins. Co., 1995 U.S. Dist. LEXIS 21733 (N.D. Cal. June 2, 1995).

53. ISO Form BM 00 25 02 91, § F.1. *See* Hoey, *The Meaning of "Accident" in Boiler and Machinery Insurance and New Developments in Underwriting*, 19 Forum 467, 468 (1984) (if "accident" is defined to mean sudden and accidental damage requiring repair or replacement, only damage rather than breakdown of object is required). *See also* Good Canning Co. v. London Guarantee & Acci. Co., 128 F. Supp. 778, 788 (D. Ark. 1955) (that brick wall was moved approximately six inches was almost conclusive proof that damage was caused by pressure of steam or water in boiler and resulted from sudden occurrence).

54. Zurich Am. Ins. v. Emplrs Ins. Co., 2005 U.S. Dist. LEXIS 47947 (W.D. Wash. July 25, 2005). In the case, coverage was triggered because a crack was manifesting by operational and maintenance problems during the policy period, although insured was unaware of them. The court noted that the policy required that any breakdown manifest itself, but did not say to whom or require that insured understand the connection between any breakdown and evidence of it. The crack progressed for over a year before the equipment seized and failed. The failure occurred after the policy terminated. Nonetheless, the court found coverage. It concluded, in effect, that the breakdown was the crack that had previously "manifested." *Compare* New England Gas & Electric Ass'n v. Ocean Acc. & Guarantee Corp., 330 Mass. 640, 656, 116 N.E.2d 671, 681 (1953) (injury that arose from use of property during policy term was not removed from coverage merely because condition that caused injury *antedated* policy).

an underlying event or causative factor." The observer does not have to understand or comprehend the causative connections. An insured may, therefore, be aware of problems with covered equipment but unaware of the manifestation of physical damage requiring repair or replacement.

One aspect of the definition of "accident" that is often overlooked is the requirement that any damage compel "repair or replacement." Just because equipment has ceased to function does not mean it requires repair or replacement. Where, for instance, a fan iced over and ceased working, the insurer contended there had been no accident because the fan only needed to be defrosted; it did not require repair.[55]

Under the ISO policy an object has to be "in use" or "connected ready for use" at the location specified in the policy at the time of the accident.[56] "In use" has been construed to mean the object is "being used for the purpose for which it was designed."[57]

[ii] Hartford Steam Boiler Policy

One widely used form is the Hartford Steam Boiler (HSB) policy. It states that a covered cause of loss is an "accident" and that without an accident, there is no equipment breakdown coverage.[58] The policy then defines "accident" as a "fortuitous event" that causes direct[59] physical damage to "covered equipment."[60] Unless otherwise specified on the Declarations Page, "covered equipment" is equipment that either generates, transmits, or uses energy, including electronic communications and data processing equipment, or, during normal usage, operates under vacuum or pressure, other than the weight of its contents.[61] The equipment generally has to be at a location described on the Declarations Page and owned or leased by the named insured or operated under the control of the named insured.[62] Unlike the ISO policy, however, the HSB policy does not require that the equipment be "in use."[63]

---

55. Associated Freezers v. Fireman's Fund Ins. Co., 1996 Tex. App. LEXIS 98 (Tex. App.—Houston 1st Dist., Jan. 11, 1996).

56. ISO Form BM 00 25 02 91, § A.2.

57. Foote Mineral Co. v. Maryland Casualty Co., 173 F. Supp. 925, 930 (D. Tenn. 1959), *aff'd*, 277 F.2d 452 (6th Cir. 1960), *cert. den.*, 364 U.S. 818, 81 S. Ct. 49, 5 L. Ed. 2d 48 (1960) (generator under repair and not producing direct current was not in use).

58. HSB Freestyle Policy Form 6671 (10/2002) § A.1.

59. *See* Dixie Pine Products Co. v. Maryland Casualty Co., 133 F.2d 583, 585 (5th Cir. 1943) (it is well settled that "direct cause" is ordinarily synonymous in legal intendment with "proximate cause"); Central Louisiana Electric Co. v. Westinghouse Electric Corp., 579 So. 2d 981, 985, n.8 (La. 1991) ("direct" as used in contract insuring against direct loss or damages means immediate or proximate as distinguished from remote).

60. HSB Freestyle Policy Form 6671 (10/2002) § A.1.a.

61. HSB Freestyle Policy Form 6671 (10/2002) § A.1.b.(1).

62. HSB Freestyle Policy Form 6671 (10/2002) § A.1.b.(2).

63. Thirteen items are explicitly excepted from the definition of "covered equipment." These include buried vessels or piping, waste, drainage or sewer piping, valves or fittings forming part of a sprinkler or fire-suppression system, and water piping not part of a closed loop used to

The HSB policy is based on the ISO form, but it adds that an accident has to be one of six events:

- Mechanical breakdown, including rupture[64] or bursting caused by centrifugal force;
- Artificially generated electrical current, including electrical arcing, damaging electrical devices, appliances, or wires;
- Explosion, but not a combustion explosion, of steam boilers, piping, engines, or turbines;
- An event inside steam boilers, pipes, engines, or turbines that damages them;
- An event inside a hot water boiler or other water heating equipment that damages them; or
- Bursting, cracking,[65] or splitting.[66]

This list of "perils" can be a starting point for determining equipment breakdown exposure. As one authority notes, an insured may not have a "boiler and machinery" exposure but may still have insurable equipment breakdown exposures: electrical arcing or mechanical breakdown of HVAC or refrigeration equipment.[67]

[c] Occurrences That Are *Not* Accidents

Policies may define some occurrences *not* to be accidents. In the ISO policy, for instance, seven occurrences are defined not to be accidents. These include depletion, deterioration,[68] corrosion,[69] erosion, wear and tear, and breakdown

---

conduct heat or cooling from a boiler or refrigeration or air-conditioning system. HSB Freestyle Policy Form 6671 (10/2002) §§ G.8.b.(5)–(8).

64. *See* Cleveland Drop Forge Co. v. Travelers' Indem. Co., 114 Ohio St. 549, 151 N.E. 671 (1926) (breaking apart of boiler head constituted "rupture"); Louisville College of Dentistry v. Hartford Steam Boiler Inspection & Ins. Co., 185 Ky. 778, 215 S.W. 941 (1919). *See also* Travellers Indem. Co. v. B & B Ice & Coal Co., 248 Ky. 443, 446, 58 S.W.2d 640, 641 (1933) (sudden rupture need not be accompanied by extremely loud noise).

65. *See* Sam Braman & Son v. Hartford Steam Boiler Inspection & Ins. Co., 9 Ohio Misc. 203, 222 N.E.2d 456 (Ohio C.P. 1966), where the court said that the original meaning of "crack" was "break." The court conclude that in context of the policy before the court, the term meant incomplete separation or fissuring caused by concealed or inherent defects in material, or negligence in operation of machinery, or both together. The court found that it would be unreasonable to extend coverage to negligent opening of a valve, not in course of operation.

66. HSB Freestyle Policy Form 6671 (10/2002) §§ A.1.a.(1)–(6).

67. Austin, *Equipment Breakdown—More Than Just Boiler and Machinery* (2011), IRMI, http://www.irmi.com/articles/expert-commentary/equipment-breakdown.

68. *See, e.g.*, 515 Assocs. LLC v. Travelers Indem. Co., 160 Fed. Appx. 147 (3d Cir. 2005) (when old and deteriorating condition of elevators was cause of breakdown, there was no coverage); Foods v. Western Nat'l Mut. Ins. Co., 508 N.W.2d 231 (Minn. App. 1993) (failure caused by deterioration or leakage was not covered).

69. *See, e.g.*, Central Louisiana Electric Co. v. Westinghouse Electric Corp., 579 So. 2d 981 (La. 1991) (corrosion pitting that formed gradually was not sudden and accidental occurrence).

of electronic computer or electronic data processing equipment.[70] The HSB policy has a similar list. It includes depletion, deterioration, rust, corrosion, erosion, settling, wear and tear, any gradually developing condition, and any defect, programming error, programming limitation, computer virus, malicious code, loss of "data," loss of access, loss of use, loss of functionality, or other condition within or involving "data" or "media."[71]

"Corrosion" or "wear and tear" may result in water damage that will not be covered. For example, where the accidental discharge of water from a sprinkler system was from deterioration of materials because of corrosion or wear and tear, the loss was not covered.[72]

The triggering of a safety or protective device is not an accident under some policies.[73] That one of these devices is triggered or employed does not necessarily preclude finding that there was an accident. There remains a question of causation.[74]

Even though a named occurrence is not considered an accident, an accident can result from one of those occurrences. As the Louisiana Supreme Court explained, if corrosion, which is defined not to be an accident, directly causes a sudden and accidental event that directly causes damage, that damage would be covered because its proximate cause was a covered risk, an accident.[75] Corrosion, said the court, was only an indirect cause. A hypothetical posed by the court may have implications for a flood loss. If, said the court, a turbine generator blade fractured as a result of corrosion, there would be no coverage if corrosion were excluded from the definition of accident, because corrosion would be the direct cause of the fracture. Any "downstream damage" that occurred to adjacent machinery, however, would be covered, said the court. That would be because the damage would be directly caused by the fracturing of the blade, which *would* be an accident, and not by the corrosion,

70. ISO Form BM 00 25 02 91, §§ F.1.a, b & e.

71. HSB Freestyle Policy Form 6671 (10/2002) § G.1.1.b.(1)–(3). The policy says these occurrences are not accidents no matter how they are caused and regardless of whether the condition or event is normal and expected or unusual and unexpected.

72. *See, e.g.*, Louis Meyers & Son, Inc. v. Affiliated F M Ins. Co., 424 F.2d 471 (2d Cir. 1970).

73. 515 Assocs. LLC v. Travelers Indem. Co., 160 Fed. Appx. 147 (3d Cir. 2005); Simkins Industries, Inc. v. Lexington Ins. Co., 42 Md. App. 396, 401 A.2d 181 (1979).

74. Commercial Union Ins. Co. v. F.R.P. Co., 172 Ga. App. 244, 322 S.E.2d 915 (1984) (loss caused by malfunction of cooling system; that chemicals were removed from reaction tank by safety device did not change cause of their loss).

75. Central Louisiana Electric Co. v. Westinghouse Electric Corp., 579 So. 2d 981, 987 (La. 1991). *See also* Pioneer Chlor Alkali Co. v. Royal Indem. Co., 879 S.W.2d 920 (Tex. App.—Houston 14th Dist., 1994) (agreeing that while policy definition of accident excluded corrosion, it did not exclude sudden and accidental breakdown caused by corrosion); Riefflin v. Hartford Steam Boiler Inspection & Ins. Co., 164 Mont. 287, 293, 521 P.2d 675, 678 (Mont. 1974) (internal boiler scaling problem was not an accident under usual meaning of term as defined in policy; however, cracking of boiler sections caused by scale build-up was accident covered by policy).

which would be the remote indirect cause. Applying that hypothetical to a water pump, if corrosion caused it to fail, the damage to the pump would not be covered. However, if water escaped and damaged other covered equipment, that damage could be covered if the pump failure were considered an accident.

The list of occurrences defined to not be accidents may be modified in some policies by a statement that they are not accidents "unless a sudden and accidental breakdown ensues." This modification was interpreted by one court to mean that the presence of deterioration "does not bar a claim if an unrelated unexpected and unintended breakdown occurs, and that a breakdown due to natural deterioration cannot be 'unexpected' from the insured's perspective."[76]

[d] "Flood" as an Accident

A plaintiff operated a dam, power house, and plant on a river. The river overflowed its banks during a heavy rainfall and inundated the plant and the machinery in it, including a generator. The insurer contended the flood was not an accident and, therefore, there was no coverage. The court said that "flood" would come within the broad and general definition of the term "accident," but the policy defined "accident" as "sudden and accidental breaking, deforming, burning out or rupturing." The generator and the other damaged equipment were submerged, and there "certainly was no breaking, deforming, burning out or rupturing" of any of them. For example, separator wedges in the generator were found to be softened and swollen when the generator was taken apart. That swelling, said the court, was the result of the 60-hour submersion in water and could not be regarded as sudden or accidental, even if it might be regarded as a deforming.[77]

[4] "Breakdown" as the Covered Cause of Loss

Not all policies use the word "accident" to define a covered cause of loss. The ISO Equipment Breakdown Protection Coverage Form, for example, says that a covered cause of loss is a "breakdown" to covered equipment.[78] "Breakdown" means a prescribed direct physical loss that causes damage to covered equipment and requires its repair or replacement.[79] One court has stated that

76. 515 Assocs. LLC v. Travelers Indem. Co., 160 Fed. Appx. 147, 151 (3d Cir. 2005).

77. Cornell Wood Prods. Co. v. Hartford Steam Boiler Inspection & Ins. Co., 62 F. Supp. 303 (N.D. Ill. 1945).

78. ISO Form BM 00 20 07 01, § A.1.

79. ISO Form BM 00 20 07 01, § F.1. *See also* Connie's Constr. Co. v. Continental Western Ins. Co., 227 N.W.2d 204 (Iowa 1975) (mechanical breakdown is functional defect in moving parts causing equipment to either operate improperly or cease operating). Not all policies will define "breakdown." *See, e.g.*, Zurich Am. Ins. v. Emplrs Ins. Co., 2005 U.S. Dist. LEXIS 47947 (W.D. Wash. July 25, 2005) (construing undefined term of "breakdown" to encompasses any defect in or failure of equipment causing it to stop functioning or function improperly);

it is not necessarily true that a mechanical breakdown can only result from an internal cause.[80] "Covered equipment" is defined by both inclusion and exclusion.[81] The term includes equipment built to operate under internal pressure or vacuum, electrical or mechanical equipment used in generation, transmission, or use of energy, communication, and computer equipment, and any of that equipment owned by a utility and used solely to supply utility services to the premises of the named insured.[82] With the exception of that utility equipment, covered equipment is required to be located at a premises described on the Declarations Page and also to be owned, leased, or operated under the control of the named insured.[83] The policy contains a lengthy and technical list of items that are specifically excluded from the definition of covered equipment definition.[84] Counsel needs to carefully compare that list with the damaged items.

A Travelers policy that tracks the ISO language identifies three malfunctions that constitute breakdowns: failure of pressure or vacuum equipment; mechanical failure, including rupture[85] or bursting caused by centrifugal force; and electrical failure, including arcing.[86] A policy may define "breakdown" in a manner similar to that of "accident." In one case, for example, the term was defined to mean sudden and accidental direct physical loss to covered equipment that was manifested by physical damage that required repair or replacement.[87] While a dictionary definition of "breakdown" includes being rendered inoperative by breakage or wear, or wearing out,[88] as one commentary notes,

---

Fairhaven Power Co. v. Hartford Steam Boiler Inspection & Ins. Co., 1995 U.S. Dist. LEXIS 21733 (N.D. Cal. June 2, 1995) (undefined term "breakdown" was ambiguous and construed in favor of insured).

80. St. Mary's Area Water Auth. v. St. Paul Fire & Marine Ins. Co., 472 F. Supp. 2d 630 (M.D. Pa. 2007).

81. ISO Form BM 00 20 07 01, § F.6.

82. ISO Form BM 00 20 07 01, § F.6.a. Note that if the policy provides utility interruption coverage, utility equipment supplying services to the premises of the named insured is *not* encompassed by the definition of covered equipment.

83. The exception does not apply to certain coverages as provided in the policy.

84. ISO Form BM 00 20 07 01, § F.6.b. By way of example, one exception is for vessels, piping, and other equipment buried below ground. ISO Form BM 00 20 07 01, § F.6.b.(6). Another exception is for vehicles, aircraft, self-propelled equipment, or floating vessels. ISO Form BM 00 20 07 01, § F.6.b.(8).

85. Cases have defined "rupture" in particular situations. *See* Cleveland Drop Forge Co. v. Travelers' Indem. Co., 114 Ohio St. 549, 151 N.E. 671 (1926); Louisville College of Dentistry v. Hartford Steam Boiler Inspection & Ins. Co., 185 Ky. 778, 215 S.W. 941 (1919).

86. Travelers EnergyMax 21, § F.1.

87. Cowiche Growers, Inc. v. Cont'l Cas. Co., 2010 U.S. Dist. LEXIS 113140 (E.D. Wash. Oct. 25, 2010).

88. *See, e.g.*, *Webster's New Universal Unabridged Dictionary* at 257 (Random House, 1966).

if the reason for a breakdown is wear, policyholders should not expect the loss to be covered.[89]

[5] Coverage

[a] Property Damage

The typical B&M policy states that the insurer will pay for direct or physical damage to "covered property" located at the premises that is described on the Declarations Page at the time of the accident or breakdown.[90] Payment for damage to covered *property* is only afforded when there is a covered cause of loss that is a breakdown to covered *equipment*.[91] To determine which *equipment* is covered, one has to examine the particular language of the policy.

Generally, "covered property" is defined as property owned by the named insured or in the "care, custody or control" of the named insured and for which the named insured is legally liable.[92] Thus, the definition extends coverage to property in the "care, custody or control" of the named insured as lessee, or perhaps bailor. Some policies will have a more specific definition of covered property. For example, one policy defined it to include *permanently installed* machinery and equipment in the building or structure.[93]

[b] Business Interruption[94]

Business interruption—also called business income or time element insurance—is "commercial property insurance covering loss of income suffered by a business when damage to its premises by a covered cause of loss causes a slowdown or

89. Malecki, *Equipment Breakdown Coverage: This Oft-Misunderstood Coverage Is a Necessity for Many Clients, available at* http://www.roughnotes.com/rnmagazine/2008/march08/03p114.htm (if equipment stops functioning from wear and tear or corrosion, no coverage should be expected).

90. *See* ISO Form BM 00 20 07 01, § A.2.a; HSB Freestyle Policy Form 6671 (10/2002) § A.2.a.

91. *See* ISO Form BM 00 20 07 01, §§ A.1, A.2.a; Travelers EnergyMax 21, § A.1. *See, e.g.*, Hartford Steam Boiler Inspection & Ins. Co. v. Kleinman, 293 S.W. 894 (Tex. App. 1927) (fire box and chimney, while part of heating plant, were not part of boiler described in policy as covered equipment and, therefore, there was no coverage for damage from explosion caused by gas accumulation in fire box and chimney).

92. ISO Form BM 00 25 02 91, § A.1; HSB Freestyle Policy Form 6671 (10/2002) § G.9.a. An insured could be "legally liable" by express agreement or by implication.

93. Bay Colony Condo. Assoc. v. Scottsdale Ins. Co., 2012 U.S. Dist. LEXIS 182016 (D.N.J. Dec. 26, 2012).

94. Business interruption coverage is found in other policies besides B&M. It is discussed extensively in § 6.02, *supra*.

suspension of its operations."[95] Basically, it pays for lost earnings.[96] Losses for business interruption can greatly exceed those for the cost of repairing damaged equipment.[97] Therefore, the insured will want to bring flood-related losses within the business interruption coverage of the policy and, despite the flood exclusion typically found in B&M policies, it is possible to do so.[98]

"Business income" is generally defined as the aggregate of net income—net profit or loss before income taxes—that would have been earned or incurred as well as continuing normal operating expenses incurred, including employee payroll.[99] Many policies pay for "actual loss" of business income during what is called a "period of restoration" that results directly from the necessary total or partial interruption of the business,[100] and any "necessary expenses" incurred during that period to reduce the loss to the extent they do not exceed the amount of loss that otherwise would have been payable.[101] Generally, policyholders have the burden to prove their loss with reasonable certainty,[102] and also that the interruption was necessary.[103]

In the HSB policy, "period of restoration" means the period of time that begins with the "accident" and continues until the earlier of the date the physical damage to covered equipment has been repaired or replaced or on which that damage could have been repaired or replaced in the exercise of "due diligence and dispatch," plus the number of days, if any, shown on the Declarations Page for Extended Period of Restoration.[104] The ISO Equipment Breakdown Protection Coverage Form defines the term differently. It says the

95. *Business Income Coverage*, IRMI, https://www.irmi.com/term/insurance-definitions/business-income-coverage. *See also* Associated Photographers, Inc. v. Aetna Cas. & Sur. Co., 677 F.2d 1251, 1253 (8th Cir. 1982) (business interruption insurance recognizes and protects insurable interest in earnings).

96. *See, e.g.*, Detroit Edison Co. v. Protection Mut. Ins. Co., 134 F.3d 790, 792, n.3 (6th Cir. 1998) (business interruption insurance covers loss of earnings caused by lost sales or production).

97. Tapia, *Equipment Breakdown Coverage: Not Your Father's Boiler & Machinery Insurance* (2000), Insurance Journal, http://www.insurancejournal.com/magazines/features/2000/11/27/21234.htm. *See also* Austin, *Equipment Breakdown—More Than Just Boiler and Machinery* (I2011), IRMI, http://www.irmi.com/articles/expert-commentary/equipment-breakdown.

98. *See* §§ 6.02[3], [4], *supra*.

99. HSB Freestyle Policy Form 6671 (10/2002) § G.5; ISO Form BM 00 20 07 01, § F.2.

100. HSB Freestyle Policy Form 6671 (10/2002) § A.2.c.(1).

101. *See, e.g.*, HSB Freestyle Policy Form 6671 (10/2002) § A.2.c.(2); ISO Form BM 00 20 07 01, § A.2.c. Some policies provide "valued coverage." Under it, the insured receives a specified amount whether or not there is an actual loss of earnings. Cozen, *Insuring Real Property*, § 5.07[1] (Matthew Bender & Co., 2020).

102. Jacobs Press v. Hartford Steam Boiler Inspection & Ins. Co., 1997 U.S. App. LEXIS 3769 (4th Cir. Mar. 4, 1997).

103. *See* Anderson & Middleton Lumber Co. v. Lumbermen's Mut. Cas. Co., 53 Wn.2d 404, 410, 333 P.2d 938, 942 (1959) (insured had burden to show that, with use of diligence and dispatch, it was necessary for its business to remain closed for time period claimed).

104. HSB Freestyle Policy Form 6671 (10/2002) § G.19.

"period of restoration" begins at the time of the breakdown, or 24 hours before the insurer receives notice of it, whichever is later, and ends 5 consecutive days after the date when the damaged property is repaired or replaced with "reasonable speed and similar quality."[105]

[c] Extra Expense[106]

Extra expense coverage provides funds that are necessary, but would not ordinarily be expended, to continue the operations of a business.[107] As one court explained, it is coverage "that makes it possible for the insured to maintain business operations that otherwise would have been interrupted pending permanent repair/restoration of the insured's property."[108]

Under the HSB policy, the carrier will pay the reasonable and necessary "extra expense" to operate the insured business during the "period of restoration."[109] "Extra expense" is defined as the additional cost incurred to operate the business over and above the cost that normally would have been incurred during the same period had no "accident" occurred.[110] The "period of restoration" begins at the time of the "accident" and continues until the earlier of the date that the physical damage to the "covered equipment" is repaired or replaced or on which the damage could have been repaired or replaced in the exercise of due diligence and dispatch, plus any number of days shown on the Declarations Page for "Extended Period of Restoration."[111] The HSB policy provides what is called "pure extra expense insurance."[112] Generally, it is coverage obtained by businesses—for example, hospitals or banks—that have to continue to operate after an accident or mechanical breakdown.

---

105. ISO Form BM 00 20 07 01, § F.13.

106. Extra expense coverage is discussed extensively in § 6.03, *supra*.

107. Ainslie et al, *Business Insurance Law and Practice Guide* § 16.04[1] (Matthew Bender 2020); 5 Jeffrey E. Thomas, *New Appleman on Insurance Law Library Edition* § 47.10[5][e] (LexisNexis 2020); Erickson & Henlin, *Understanding Extra Expense*, 45 Tort & Ins. L.J. 1 (2009) (intent of extra expense clauses is to provide coverage for those necessary additional expenses that commercial insured incurs to operate its business during period of restoration following direct physical loss). *See, e.g.*, Detroit Edison Co. v. Protection Mut. Ins. Co., 134 F.3d 790, 792, n.3 (6th Cir. 1998) (coverage includes expenses incurred to maintain business operations).

108. Chalmette Retail Ctr., LLC v. Lafayette Ins. Co., 21 So. 3d 485, 498 (La. App. 2009).

109. HSB Freestyle Policy Form 6671 (10/2002) § A.2.d. *See also* ISO Form BM 00 20 07 01, § A.2.c (Business Income and Extra Expense—Extra Expense Only). *And see* ISO Form BM 15 34 09 88 (Boiler and Machinery Extra Expense Values Worksheet). The worksheet provides the insurer with information about estimated extra expenses that will be needed over and above normal if alternate facilities or equipment are used.

110. HSB Freestyle Policy Form 6671 (10/2002) § G.12.

111. HSB Freestyle Policy Form 6671 (10/2002) § G.19.

112. Malecki, *Equipment Breakdown Insurance: Too Important to Ignore!* at 10 (2009), Adjusting Today, *available at* http://adjustersinternational.com/publications/adjusting-today/equipment-breakdown-insurance/1/.

What might be called "expense to reduce loss" is another type of extra expense coverage. It is only available when business interruption coverage is not accompanied by extra expense coverage.[113] It pays necessary expenses incurred to reduce the business income loss, but only to the extent those expenses reduce the business income loss.

[d] Expediting Expense[114]

Expediting and extra expense coverage can easily be confused.[115] Extra expense coverage is broader than expediting expense coverage and covers expenses "incurred to maintain business operations beyond normal coverage."[116] Under expediting expense coverage—also called "mitigating cost"—the insurer pays the "reasonable" extra cost to make temporary repairs and expedite permanent repairs or permanent replacement of damaged property for damaged *covered* property, meaning property owned by the named insured or in the care, custody, or control of the named insured and for which the named insured is legally liable.[117] A temporary *replacement* is not covered under that language, as the coverage is for *repair*, and temporarily replacing damaged property is not the same as repairing it temporarily.[118]

[e] Ordinance and Law

Ordinance and law coverage protects against the increased cost of complying with building requirements. The coverage applies when an "accident" damages a building that is "covered property"—meaning property owned by the named insured or in the care, custody, or control of the named insured and for which the named insured is legally liable—and the loss is increased by an ordinance or law regulating construction or repair of buildings.[119] The ordinance or law has to be in force at the time of the "accident." The loss cannot be

113. Malecki, *Equipment Breakdown Insurance: Too Important to Ignore!* at 10 (2009), Adjusting Today, *available at* http://adjustersinternational.com/publications/adjusting-today/equipment-breakdown-insurance/1/.

114. Expediting expense coverage is discussed in § 6.04, *supra.*

115. Malecki, *Equipment Breakdown Insurance: Too Important to Ignore!* at 10 (2009), Adjusting Today, *available at* http://adjustersinternational.com/publications/adjusting-today/equipment-breakdown-insurance/1/.

116. Detroit Edison Co. v. Protection Mut. Ins. Co., 134 F.3d 790, 792, n.3 (6th Cir. 1998).

117. *See* ISO Form BM 00 20 07 01, § A.2.b; HSB Freestyle Policy Form 6671 (10/2002) § A.2.k. *See also* Hartford Steam Boiler Insp. & Ins. Co. v. Menada, Inc., 2018 U.S. Dist. LEXIS 59897 (S.D. Fla. Apr. 6, 2018) (where insured hired company to inspect equipment that was not functioning, cost to dismantle and service equipment was covered expediting expense).

118. Detroit Edison Co. v. Protection Mut. Ins. Co., 134 F.3d 790 (6th Cir. 1998).

119. HSB Freestyle Policy Form 6671 (10/2002) § A.2.j.(1). *See also* ISO Form BM 00 20 07 01, A.3.g. The ISO policy also has an ordinance and law exclusion. ISO Form BM 00 20 07 01, § B.1.

addressed under any demolition or hazardous substances coverage. Typically, the insurer will pay for the actual and necessary cost to repair or reconstruct the damaged portions of a building and also will pay to bring *undamaged* portions into compliance with the ordinance or law.[120]

Policies usually pay two types of "additional costs" to comply with an ordinance or law. They pay the actual and necessary cost to demolish and clear the site of the undamaged parts of the building, and they pay to reconstruct the undamaged parts of the building.[121] Additional costs are those that are beyond what would have been payable under the policy had no applicable ordinance or law been in effect at the time of the accident.[122]

Policies may have both an ordinance and law coverage clause and an ordinance and law exclusion clause. The clauses obviously need to be read together to determine the extent of coverage. The coverage clause may say it applies notwithstanding the exclusion.[123]

There may be limitations on the coverage. For example, a Travelers Equipment Breakdown policy says the carrier will not pay for demolition or site clearing until *undamaged* portions of the building or structures are actually demolished.[124] The insurer will not pay for any increase in loss until the damaged or destroyed buildings are actually either rebuilt or replaced and approved by the pertinent regulatory agency. An increase in loss exceeding the amount required to meet the minimum requirement of any ordinance, law, rule, regulation, or ruling at the time of the breakdown is not covered.[125] An increase in loss resulting from a substance declared by a governmental agency to be hazardous to health or the environment—for example, removal of asbestos—is not covered.[126] Also, under the Travelers policy, if the building or structure is damaged by a breakdown covered by the policy while there is also other uncovered physical damage, and the building damage in its *entirety* results in enforcement of an ordinance or law, the insurer will not pay the total amount of the loss. It will only pay the proportion that the covered breakdown loss bears to the total physical loss.[127]

---

120. HSB Freestyle Policy Form 6671 (10/2002) § A.2.j.(2).

121. HSB Freestyle Policy Form 6671 (10/2002) § A.2.i.(2).

122. HSB Freestyle Policy Form 6671 (10/2002) § A.2.i.(3).

123. *See e.g.*, ISO Form BM 00 20 07 01, § A.2.g; Travelers EnergyMax 21, § A.2.k. *See also* Malecki, *Equipment Breakdown Insurance: Too Important to Ignore!* at 4 (2009), Adjusting Today, *available at* http://adjustersinternational.com/publications/adjusting-today/equipment-breakdown-insurance/1/.

124. Travelers EnergyMax 21, § A.2.k.(2).

125. Thus, if the policyholder goes beyond the minimum requirements, it does so at its own expense. *Boiler and Machinery Coverage Form* (Summit Business Media, 2012).

126. There may, however, be coverage under a commercial property policy.

127. Travelers EnergyMax 21, § A.2.k.(3).

[f] Demolition

Demolition coverage may be either separately listed or included within "Ordinance and Law" coverage.[128] The coverage generally applies if an "accident" damages a building that is "covered property"—meaning property owned by the named insured or in the care, custody, or control of the named insured and for which the named insured is legally liable—and the loss is increased by an ordinance or law requiring demolition of a building that could otherwise be repaired.[129] The ordinance or law has to be in force at the time of the accident and cannot be not addressed under any Hazardous Substances coverage.

The actual and necessary cost to demolish and clear the site of the undamaged parts of the building and the cost to reconstruct the undamaged parts of the building may be covered as an "additional cost" to comply with an ordinance or law.[130]

[g] Utility Interruption

Some policies provide "utility interruption" coverage. If a policyholder has coverage for business interruption, extra expense, or spoilage damage, the utility interruption clause extends to include losses that result from interruption of utility services.[131] There are conditions on the coverage extension. For example, a Travelers policy requires the following:

- The interruption has to be the direct result of a breakdown—as defined by the policy—to covered equipment—also as defined by the policy—that is owned, operated, or controlled by the local utility.
- The equipment has to be located more than 500 feet from the insured premises.
- The equipment has to be used to supply air conditioning, communication services, electric power, gas, heating, refrigeration, steam, water, or waste treatment to the insured premises.
- The interruption to the insured premises has to last at least the length of time shown on the Declarations Page—often 12 or 24 hours—before the coverage commences.[132]

There is also a specific exclusion applicable to utility interruption coverage in the Travelers policy. It bars coverage for any loss that results from aircraft; civil commotion; collapse; freezing caused by cold weather; impact of aircraft, missiles, or vehicles; lightning; molten material; objects falling from aircraft or missiles; riot; smoke; vandalism; vehicles; weight of snow, ice, or

128. Travelers EnergyMax 21, § A.2.k.
129. HSB Freestyle Policy Form 6671 (10/2002) § A.2.i.(1).
130. HSB Freestyle Policy Form 6671 (10/2002) § A.2.i.(2).
131. *See, e.g.*, ISO Form BM 00 20 07 01, § A.2.e.
132. Travelers EnergyMax 21, § A.2.d.

sleet; acts of sabotage, or deliberate acts of load shedding by the supplying or distributing utility whether or not coverage for that cause of loss is provided by another policy or a self-insurance risk retention plan.[133]

[h] Errors and Omissions

An errors and omission clause restores coverage that would have been in effect but for an error or omission—an unintentional, honest mistake—by the policyholder. For example, under the ISO Equipment Breakdown Protection Coverage Form, the carrier will pay for a loss or damage that it would not have paid because of any error or unintentional omission in the description or location of the insured property, or in any subsequent amendments, any failure by error to include any premises owned or occupied by the insured at the inception date, or any error or unintentional omission by the insured that results in cancellation of any insured premises.[134] The insured has to report any errors or omissions when it discovers them for the clause to apply. The clause does not extend coverage where the insured fails to obtain coverage it desired or fails to provide information related to coverage that renders it ineffective.[135]

[i] Consequential Loss

B&M policies pay not only for repair or replacement of covered equipment, but also for other loss or damage—consequential loss or damages—that is a direct result of an accident to covered property. The insured has to show the direct result. That is, if the consequential loss or damage does not result from an accident to, or breakdown of, an object or covered equipment, there is no coverage.[136] If the consequential loss does result from such an accident or breakdown, the insured may be able to recover for a flood-related loss. For example, an insured sought recovery of the cost to open up a turbine, take it apart, clean it, and reassemble it after sand and silt was found in it. A steam line that ran from the turbine across a river had, according to the insured, broken off during a flood. The sand and silt entered the turbine through that broken pipe. The court concluded that there was sufficient evidence from which a jury could find that the turbine damage was the direct result of the accident that broke the steam pipes and allowed the mud or debris to enter.[137]

---

133. Travelers EnergyMax 21, § B.18. The exclusion applies to all resulting direct or indirect loss.

134. ISO Form BM 00 20 07 01, § A.2.h.

135. *See Boiler and Machinery Coverage Form* (Summit Business Media, 2012).

136. Withington Co. v. Maryland Casualty Co., 75 R.I. 297, 65 A.2d 710 (1949).

137. Simkins Industries, Inc. v. Lexington Ins. Co., 42 Md. App. 396, 412, 401 A.2d 181, 190 (1979). *Compare* Cafritz Co. v. Employers Commercial Union Ins. Co., 309 A.2d 302 (D.C. 1973) (air-conditioning unit was covered equipment and terminal board had to be replaced to

In another case, a boiler exploded and released steam that melted sprinkler heads, allowing water to escape and damage merchandise that belonged to the insured. The insurer conceded liability for the consequential losses caused by steam but denied coverage for those caused by the water that escaped from the sprinklers. It argued that the damage caused by that water was immediately and directly due to an "independent agency" and only remotely to the explosion of the boiler, the covered equipment. The court did not agree. The policy provided coverage for the damage because the active and efficient cause that released the water was clearly heat from the explosion, and not intervention of any new and independent agency. The court noted that the insurer knew of the automatic sprinklers at the time it issued the policy, and "the outpouring of the water from the sprinklers was the inevitable consequence of the explosion of the boiler."[138] While the case is about proximate cause, it also illustrates how water or flood damage can be covered as a consequential loss.

8.6 Exclusions

[1] Generally

B&M policies typically exclude the same perils that are barred from coverage in commercial property policies: earth movement, water, nuclear hazard, war or military action, and mold.[139] There are also usually exclusions that are unique to equipment breakdown coverage. These include an accident to covered equipment while being tested; lack of or excess of power, light, heat, steam, or refrigeration; and breakdown caused directly or indirectly by hail or windstorm, and deliberate acts, for example, vandalism, malicious mischief, and sabotage. As is generally the case, the insured first has to show that the policy provides coverage and then the burden shifts to the insurer to show that the specific language of the policy excludes it.[140]

The prefatory language to an exclusion is often critical. For example, the ISO Equipment Breakdown Protection Coverage Form says the insurer will not pay for loss or damage caused directly or indirectly by any excluded peril, that the loss or damage is excluded regardless of any other cause or event that contributes concurrently or in any sequence to it, and that the exclusions apply

return it to working order, but because there was no evidence terminal board was damaged by accident, there was no coverage for cost of its replacement).

138. Hartford Steam Boiler Inspection & Ins. Co. v. Sonneborn, 96 Md. 616, 54 A. 610 (1903).

139. Malecki, *Equipment Breakdown Insurance: Too Important to Ignore!* at 5 (2009), Adjusting Today, *available at* http://adjustersinternational.com/publications/adjusting-today/equipment-breakdown-insurance/1/. Windstorm or hail, smoke, aircraft or vehicles, riot or civil commotion, and vandalism can be added to the list of exclusions by a standard endorsement. ISO Form BM 99 39 07 90.

140. Leprino Foods Co. v. Factory Mut. Ins. Co., 453 F.3d 1281, 1287 (10th Cir. 2006); Fire Ins. Exch. & Farmers Ins. Exch. v. Pring-Wilson, 831 F. Supp. 2d 493, 506 (D. Mass. 2011).

whether or not widespread damage results or a substantial area is affected.[141] The HSB policy states that the insurer will not pay for any excluded loss, damage, or expense, even though any other cause or event contributes concurrently or in any sequence, or caused directly or indirectly by any of the excluded perils whether or not caused by or resulting from an "accident."[142]

The "efficient proximate cause" doctrine as applied to property coverage provides that when a loss is caused by both covered and excluded perils, the loss is covered if the covered peril is the efficient proximate cause of the loss.[143] To counter the doctrine, insurers add "anti-concurrent cause" language to policies and thus defeat operation of the efficient proximate cause rule.[144] An example of that language is the "concurrently or in any sequence" wording that is found in both the ISO and HSB policies as noted above. In most states, that language will negate the "efficient proximate cause" doctrine.[145] However, in some states, most notably California and North Dakota, courts hold that, based on applicable statutes, an insurer may not contractually bar coverage when the efficient proximate cause of a loss is a covered peril.[146] The concurrent causation clause does not apply at all where there was no "concurrent" or other "contributing" cause of the loss at issue.[147]

[2] Water/Flood

[a] Generally

Some B&M policies exclude "flood" losses but do not define flood.[148] Most exclude "water" and define it to include flood.[149] Typically, coverage is barred for three categories of water:

141. ISO Form BM 00 20 07 01, § B. *See* Hartford Steam Boiler Inspection & Ins. Co. v. Quantum Chem. Corp., 1996 U.S. Dist. LEXIS 17551 (N.D. Ill. Nov. 12, 1996).

142. HSB Freestyle Policy Form 6671 (10/2002) § B.

143. *See generally* Bell, *A Concurrent Mess and a Call for Clarity in First-Party Property Insurance Coverage Analysis*, 18 Conn. Ins. L.J. 73 (2011/2012). *See also* Kelly v. Farmers Ins. Co., 281 F. Supp. 2d 1290, 1296 (W.D. Okla. 2003); Murray v. State Farm Fire & Cas. Co., 203 W. Va. 477, 487, 509 S.E.2d 1, 11 (1998).

144. *See, e.g.*, St. Mary's Area Water Auth. v. St. Paul Fire & Marine Ins. Co., 472 F. Supp. 2d 630, 636 (M.D. Pa. 2007).

145. *See, e.g.*, Preferred Mut. Ins. Co. v. Travelers Cos., 955 F. Supp. 9, 11–12 (D. Mass. 1997) (under "chain of events" rule, insured would recover for otherwise excluded loss if efficient proximate cause of that loss was covered; however, where preamble provided policy did not apply to losses resulting directly or indirectly from particular proximate cause, chain of events rule was avoided and liability was effectively excluded without regard to efficient proximate cause).

146. *See, e.g.*, W. Nat'l Mut. Ins. Co. v. Univ. of N.D., 643 N.W.2d 4 (N.D. 2002).

147. Hartford Steam Boiler Inspection & Ins. Co. v. Quantum Chem. Corp., 1996 U.S. Dist. LEXIS 17551 (N.D. Ill. Nov. 12, 1996).

148. ISO Form BM 00 25 02 91, § B.4.g.

149. *See, e.g.*, HSB Freestyle Policy Form 6671 (10/2002) § B.1.f; ISO Form BM 00 20 07 01, § B.3; Travelers EnergyMax 21, § B.3.

- Flood, surface water, waves, tides, tidal waves, overflow of any body of water, or spray from any of them, and all whether or not driven by wind;[150]
- Mudslides or mudflow; and
- Water damage from backup of sewer,[151] drains, or drainage piping.[152]

Some policies add another peril to the list: water damage that is caused by discharge from, or leakage of, sprinkler systems or domestic water piping.[153] Frequently, there is a separate exclusion for water or other means employed to extinguish a fire, even when the attempt is unsuccessful.[154] When fire damage is covered, a loss is not necessarily excluded because there was also water damage caused by endeavors to extinguish the fire.[155]

There may be an anti-concurrent causation clause in the exclusion. When damage arises from multiple causes, these clauses may operate to bar coverage.[156] Typical language will state that the insurer will not pay for any excluded loss, damage, or expense, even if any other cause or event contributes concurrently or in any sequence to the loss, damage, or expense.

There may be exceptions to a water/flood exclusion. The HSB policy, for example, will pay for the amount actually spent to dry out electrical "covered equipment," subject to any applicable deductible.[157] The insurer, however, will not pay more than the actual cash value,[158] nor will it pay to replace the equipment or for any other loss, damage, or expense. The ISO Boiler and

---

150. A Travelers policy adds "tsunami." Travelers EnergyMax 21, § B.3.

151. If this exclusion is omitted, there may be coverage. *See, e.g.*, W. Nat'l Mut. Ins. Co. v. Univ. of N.D., 643 N.W.2d 4 (N.D. 2002) (as B&M policy did not explicitly exclude coverage for sewer backup, insurer conceded coverage was provided).

152. The HSB policy excludes water that backs up or overflows from a sewer, drain, or sump. HSB Freestyle Policy Form 6671 (10/2002) § B.1.f.(3).

153. ISO Form BM 00 20 07 01, § B.3.d. A Travelers policy adds sewer piping. Travelers EnergyMax 21, § B.3.d. *See* Bergquist v. Auto-Owners Ins. Co., 2020 U.S. Dist. LEXIS 6885 (W.D. Wisc. Jan. 13, 2020). In *Bergquist*, there was water damage caused by an underground water pipe connected to a fire hydrant that had degraded and ruptured. The policy defined equipment breakdown to mean physical loss or damage both originating within, *inter alia*, any water piping other than boiler feed water piping between the feed pump and boiler, boiler condensate return piping, or water piping forming part of a refrigerating or air-conditioning system. The court read this as an exclusion and, as none of three exceptions applied, it held that coverage was excluded for damage that originated in water piping, which was the source of the damage to the insured's property.

154. *See, e.g.*, ISO Form BM 00 25 02 91, § B.4.e; Travelers EnergyMax 21, § B.10.

155. Jacobs Press v. Hartford Steam Boiler Inspection & Ins. Co., 1997 U.S. App. LEXIS 3769 (4th Cir. Mar. 4, 1997).

156. Hull Permanent Sewer Comm'n v. Artford Steam Boiler Insp. & Ins. Co., 2017 U.S. Dist. LEXIS 50595 (D. Mass. Mar. 31, 2017).

157. HSB Freestyle Policy Form 6671 (10/2002) § B.1.f.

158. *See* Travellers Indem. Co. v. B & B Ice & Coal Co., 248 Ky. 448, 446, 58 S.W.2d 640, 642 (1933) ("cash value" means price property would bring when offered for sale by one who desires, but is not compelled, to sell, and is purchased by one who desires, but is not compelled, to buy).

Machinery Coverage Form says that if an "accident" results from a flood, the insurer will pay for "direct damage"[159] to covered property caused by that accident.[160] For example, flooding swept trees downstream. The trees struck and broke pipes that belonged to the insured. The breaking of the pipes was, agreed the insurer, an accident within the meaning of the policy even though caused by flooding.[161]

[b] FEMA Standard Flood Insurance Policy

Flood damage for equipment is covered under the FEMA Standard Flood Insurance Policy (SFIP). The building portion of the SFIP policy covers central air conditioners, elevator equipment, fire extinguishing apparatus, fire sprinkler systems, walk-in freezers, furnaces pumps and machinery for operating pumps, and ventilating equipment.[162] Although the policy largely excludes coverage for lower levels or basements, it still specifically covers the following:

- Central air conditioners;
- Electrical junction and circuit breaker boxes;
- Elevators, dumbwaiters, and related equipment, except for related equipment installed below the base flood elevation after September 30, 1987;
- Fuel tanks and the fuel in them;
- Furnaces and hot water heaters;
- Heat pumps;
- Pumps and tanks used in solar energy systems;
- Sump pumps; and
- Well water tanks and pumps.

There is a comparable list in Coverage B for personal property. Reading the two lists together, one can determine which items are insured as fixtures, machinery, and equipment under Coverage A and which ones are insured as personal property under Coverage B.[163] Personal property coverage has to be purchased separately and basically covers personal property inside a fully enclosed insured building[164] against direct physical loss by or from flood.[165]

159. *See* Preferred Mut. Ins. Co. v. Travelers Cos., 955 F. Supp. 9, 11 (D. Mass. 1997) (noting lack of definition of "direct damage").

160. ISO Form BM 00 25 02 91, § B.4.g.

161. Simkins Industries, Inc. v. Lexington Ins. Co., 42 Md. App. 396, 401 A.2d 181 (1979) ("direct damage" occurred when silt and sand entered turbines through broken pipes).

162. General Property Form Standard Flood Insurance Policy, § III.A.4 (Oct. 2015).

163. Studio Frames, Ltd. v. Std. Fire Ins. Co., 483 F.3d 239, 246 (4th Cir. 2007).

164. *See* Riverside Bldg. Supply, Inc. v. Federal Emergency Management Agency, 723 F.2d 1159 (4th Cir. 1983) (property stored in "umbrella building" lacking walls and consisting of roof supported by columns was not covered because it was not located in enclosed building).

165. General Property Form Standard Flood Insurance Policy, § III.B (Oct. 15).

Under the General Property Form SFIP, personal property has to be owned solely by the insured.[166]

[c] Backup or Overflow of Sewer, Drains, or Drainage Piping

The backup or overflow portion of the water damage exclusion may be avoided in some cases. For example, wastewater flooded the basement of a sewage treatment facility after a pump failed. At the time, the flow of wastewater coming into the facility was unusually high because of infiltration of rainwater, snowmelt, and tidal surges. The insurer argued the exclusion applied because the loss was caused by water that "overflowed" from a "sewer." Either an interceptor pipe bringing wastewater into the facility overflowed, said the insurer, or the facility itself is part of a sewer system and, therefore, part of a sewer. The court rejected those arguments. It said that the interceptor pipe leading into the facility did not overflow; it just brought wastewater into the facility as it was intended to do. It also concluded that the term "sewer" did not apply to an entire facility that treated wastewater.[167]

Can the backup or overflow of a sewer, drain, or pipe be the result of "a mechanical breakdown" covered by a B&M policy? In one case, water damage was caused by the overflow from a toilet caused in turn by a supply tank valve being stuck in the "on" position. The insured argued that its losses were caused by a mechanical breakdown of the toilet's trip lever failing to close the flush valve when it got stuck in the on position. The insurer countered that there was no mechanical breakdown because no mechanical part of the toilet broke down. Instead, there was merely a "malfunction." The court, however, noted that the policy did not define "mechanical breakdown" and said that a malfunction can be construed to be within the ordinary and popular definition of "breakdown." Unfortunately, the court also said that the water exclusion absolutely barred coverage for water that overflowed from a sewer, drain, or related equipment. While an endorsement removed an exclusion of coverage for "mechanical breakdowns," the effect of the water exclusion, said the court, was not vitiated simply because the B&M endorsement allowed for recovery for "mechanical breakdowns." Even if the overflow was caused by a mechanical breakdown, the water exclusion still applied.[168] It can be inferred that had there been no exclusion, there would have been coverage.

---

166. *See* Cardon Prop. No. 4, LLC v. Fid. Nat'l Indem. Ins. Co., 58 F. Supp. 3d 645, 655 (E.D. La. 2014) (if insured did not own personal property at time of loss, it cannot recover for that loss).

167. Hull Permanent Sewer Comm'n v. Artford Steam Boiler Insp. & Ins. Co., 2017 U.S. Dist. LEXIS 50595 (D. Mass. Mar. 31, 2017).

168. McCaughey v. Ohio Sec. Ins. Co., 2021 U.S. Dist. LEXIS 65061 (C.D. Cal. Apr. 2, 2021) (water exclusion precluded coverage for damage caused by water overflowing from sewers, drains, or "related equipment" and toilet's supply tank was "related equipment").

[3] Explosion

The initial purpose of boiler and machinery insurance was to protect from the risk that a boiler would explode, a then not uncommon occurrence, or suffer a catastrophic failure.[169] It may, therefore, seem remarkable that the modern version of the coverage, equipment breakdown insurance, contains an explosion *exclusion*. However, these exclusions limit coverage for explosions, rather than totally exclude it. One purpose of the exclusion is to avoid an overlap in coverage with a commercial property policy.

The HSB policy bars coverage for damage or expense caused directly or indirectly by a "combustion explosion," or any other explosion, whether or not caused by or resulting from an "accident."[170] There is an exception for steam boilers, steam piping, steam engines, or steam turbines.[171]

Under a Travelers policy, coverage for explosion is generally excluded.[172] However, the insurer will pay for direct loss or damage by an explosion of a steam boiler, electric steam generator, steam piping, steam turbine, steam engine, gas turbine, or any other moving or rotating machinery when an explosion is caused by centrifugal force or mechanical breakdown, unless the loss or damage is otherwise excluded. There are two additional exclusions. The first excludes "combustion explosions," including those that result in a breakdown, that occur at the same time as a breakdown, or ensue from a breakdown.[173] "Breakdown" is defined as the failure of pressure or vacuum equipment, mechanical failure, including rupture[174] or bursting caused by centrifugal force, and electrical failure, including arcing, resulting in physical damage requiring repair or replacement.[175] An explosion within the furnace of a chemical recovery boiler or the gas passages from the furnace to the atmosphere is also excluded from coverage.[176]

A loss caused by or resulting from an explosion is generally excluded by the ISO Boiler and Machinery Coverage Form, although the policy does cover losses caused by or resulting from an explosion of a *covered object*.[177] The

169. 5 Jeffery E. Thomas, *New Appleman on Insurance Law Library Edition* § 51.01[2][a] (LexisNexis 2020).

170. HSB Freestyle Policy Form 6671 (10/2002) § B.1.a.

171. *See, e.g.*, Stone Container Corp. v. Hartford Steam Boiler Inspection & Ins. Co., 165 F.3d 1157, 1161 (7th Cir. 1999) (distinguishing between fired and unfired pressure vessels).

172. Travelers EnergyMax 21, § B.6.

173. Travelers EnergyMax 21, § B.7.

174. *See* Cleveland Drop Forge Co. v. Travelers' Indem. Co., 114 Ohio St. 549, 151 N.E. 671 (1926) (breaking apart of boiler head constituted "rupture"); Louisville College of Dentistry v. Hartford Steam Boiler Inspection & Ins. Co., 185 Ky. 778, 215 S.W. 941 (1919) (irregular, semicircular opening developed in casting on front of boiler evidenced rupture).

175. Travelers EnergyMax 21, § F.1.

176. Travelers EnergyMax 21, § B.8.

177. ISO Form BM 00 25 02 91, § B.4.a. The exclusion can be modified by endorsement. *See* ISO Form BM 99 40 06 95. The endorsement provides the insurer will pay for direct loss

policy also excludes coverage for an explosion occurring at the same time as an accident or that ensues from an accident,[178] or that is of gas or unconsumed fuel within the furnace of a boiler or fired vessel or within the passages from that furnace to the atmosphere.[179]

Even though explosion exclusions are common in equipment breakdown policies, those policies usually do not define the term. Courts have found the term to be difficult to define.[180] They try to give the word its "ordinary-language meaning."[181] Often they say it is a violent bursting, or expansion, with noise, following the sudden creation of great pressure.[182]

[4] Fire

Because all commercial property policies cover fire losses, equipment breakdown policies exclude coverage for fire. The exclusion may be short[183] and may bar coverage for a fire that occurs at the same time as an *accident* or that ensues from an accident.[184] The exclusion generally does not apply unless a fire is hostile, and a fire that happens at the same time as an accident is considered a "hostile fire."[185] A fire required for operation of equipment and that is the ordinary fire required for its operation is not hostile.[186] Therefore, the fire exclusion applies to fires that begin *outside* the covered equipment.

---

or damage caused by an explosion of one of the "objects" specified in the endorsement if it is covered by the policy and described on an "object definitions" endorsement that is a part of the policy and that is not otherwise excluded.

178. ISO Form BM 00 25 02 91, § B.4.b.

179. ISO Form BM 00 25 02 91, § B.4.c.

180. *See, e.g.*, Julius Hyman & Co. v. American Motorists Ins. Co., 136 F. Supp. 830, 833–34 (D. Colo. 1955); Bower v. Aetna Ins. Co., 54 F. Supp. 897, 898 (D. Tex. 1944); Crombie & Co. v. Employers' Fire Ins. Co., 250 S.W.2d 472, 474 (Tex. App. 1952). *But see* Hartford Steam Boiler Inspection & Ins. Co. v. Quantum Chem. Corp., 1996 U.S. Dist. LEXIS 17551 (N.D. Ill. Nov. 12, 1996) (rejecting contention that "explosion" has no generally accepted meaning).

181. *See, e.g.*, Stone Container Corp. v. Hartford Steam Boiler Inspection & Ins. Co., 165 F.3d 1157, 1160 (7th Cir. 1999); Hartford Steam Boiler Inspection & Ins. Co. v. Quantum Chem. Corp., 1996 U.S. Dist. LEXIS 17551 (N.D. Ill. Nov. 12, 1996).

182. Hartford Fire Ins. Co. v. Empire Coal Min. Co., 30 F.2d 794, 798 (8th Cir. 1929) (characteristics of explosion are sudden and rapid combustion, great expansion of air, and sharp noise or report). *See also* Pre-Cast Concrete Products, Inc. v. Home Ins. Co., 417 F.2d 1323, 1326 (7th Cir. 1969); Bower v. Aetna Ins. Co., 54 F. Supp. 897, 898 (D. Tex. 1944).

183. *See, e.g.*, Travelers EnergyMax 21, § B.7.

184. ISO Form BM 00 25 02 91, § B.4.b. *See* Associated Electric Cooperative v. Mutual Boiler & Machinery Ins. Co., 492 F. Supp. 410 (W.D. Mo. 1980) (exclusion did not necessitate that each piece of equipment be damaged by fire, but only that fire ensue).

185. *See, e.g.*, Good Canning Co. v. London Guarantee & Acci. Co., 128 F. Supp. 778, 788 (D. Ark. 1955); First Nat'l Bank v. Royal Indem. Co., 193 Iowa 221, 186 N.W. 934 (1922).

186. *See, e.g.*, Dixie Pine Products Co. v. Maryland Casualty Co., 133 F.2d 583, 585 (5th Cir. 1943); Holmes v. Employers' Liability Assurance Corp., 70 Ohio App. 239, 259, 43 N.E.2d 746, 754 (1941); St. John v. American Mut. Fire & Marine Ins. Co., 11 N.Y. 516, 518 (1854).

[5] Deterioration, Corrosion, and Wear and Tear

While some policies preclude coverage for deterioration, corrosion, erosion, and wear and tear by excepting them from the definition of "accident,"[187] others explicitly exclude them.[188] Typically, the exclusion will be preceded by a statement that the insurer will not pay for loss or damage *caused* directly or indirectly by one of the excluded perils. The exclusion can serve to bar a claim for water damage even if the object that failed was covered equipment.[189]

The insurer seeking to invoke the exclusion has to show the excepted condition caused damage, whether directly or indirectly.[190] While the insurer will not pay for a loss caused by an excepted condition, the policy may provide that if a breakdown occurs, the carrier will pay the resulting loss or damage.[191]

"Deterioration," "corrosion," "erosion," and "wear and tear" are generally not defined in policies but have often been construed by courts. For example, a Pennsylvania federal court said that the "terms 'depletion,' 'deterioration,' 'corrosion' and 'erosion' . . . in common understanding can mean no more than the action of normally expected elements of stress, friction, and the daily traumas of its life to the object during its normal life expectancy."[192] The court characterized "wear and tear" as the "ordinary and natural deterioration or abrasion" of an object by expected contact between its component parts and outside objects during its natural life expectancy.[193]

---

187. *See, e.g.*, HSB Freestyle Policy Form 6671 (10/2002) § B.1.b.(1) (depletion, deterioration, rust, corrosion, erosion, settling, and wear and tear are not accidents).

188. *See, e.g.*, ISO Form BM 00 20 07 01, § B.11. (coverage for depletion, deterioration, corrosion, erosion, or wear and tear excluded); Travelers EnergyMax 21, § B.12 (coverage for depletion, deterioration, corrosion, erosion, wear and tear, rust, fungus, decay, wet or dry rot, and mold excluded). *See also* Snohomish Cty. Pub. Hosp. Dist. No. 1 v. Hartford Fire Ins. Co., 2018 U.S. Dist. LEXIS 82861 (W.D. Wash. May 15, 2018) (corrosion exclusion stated insurer would not pay for loss or damage caused by or resulting from wear and tear, or change in color, texture, or finish or rust, corrosion, decay, or deterioration).

189. *See, e.g.*, Bergquist v. Auto-Owners Ins. Co., 2020 U.S. Dist. LEXIS 6885 (W.D. Wisc. Jan. 13, 2020) (policy expressly excluded damage resulting from rust, corrosion, or decay, which was original cause of rupture of water pipe that caused water damage).

190. J.O.B. Invs., LLC v. Gootee Servs., LLC, 908 F. Supp. 2d 771 (E.D. La. 2012) (not enough for insurer to produce evidence that air-conditioning unit was corroded, as exclusion was triggered only if corrosion caused damage, whether directly or indirectly).

191. ISO Form BM 00 20 07 01, § B.11. *See also* Travelers EnergyMax 21, § B.12 (if "breakdown" ensues, insurer pays ensuing loss or damage not otherwise excluded).

192. Cyclops Corp. v. Home Ins. Co., 352 F. Supp. 931, 936 (W.D. Pa. 1973). *See also* Arkwright-Boston Mfrs. Mut. Ins. Co. v. Wausau Paper Mills Co., 818 F.2d 591 (7th Cir. 1987) (chemical action of sulfuric acid causing holes to appear in steel characterized as corrosion); Lakeshore Marine, Inc. v. Hartford Acc. & Indem. Co., 164 Ga. App. 417, 296 S.E.2d 418 (1982) (corrosion is gradual wearing away or disintegration by chemical process, for example, rusting of iron).

193. Cyclops Corp. v. Home Ins. Co., 352 F. Supp. 931, 936 (W.D. Pa. 1973).

[6] Earth Movement

B&M policies almost always exclude coverage for "earth movement." For example, the ISO Boiler and Machinery Coverage Form precludes coverage for accidents that are caused directly or indirectly by earth movement, *including but not limited to* earthquakes, landslides, mudslides, subsidence, or volcanic eruptions.[194] A commentary says it is unclear whether this wording only applies to "natural movement" or includes "human movement."[195] Under the HSB policy, coverage is barred for loss or damage that is caused directly or indirectly by earth movement, whether natural or human-made, *including but not limited to* earthquakes, shocks, tremors, subsidence, landslides, rock falls, earth sinking, sinkhole collapse, or *tsunamis*.[196] Note that the ISO policy does not include tsunamis among the "earth movements" that are excluded. Both the HSB and ISO policies state that the exclusion is not limited to the specifically named earth movements.

Some policies may provide that the breakdown of any structure or foundation that supports a covered object or any part of it is not an accident, and therefore not covered. That language was found in the policy covering a plant that stood on the waterfront of a bay. An earthquake caused massive submarine slides, and the plant dropped into the bay. The lower court found that the damage was caused by an "earthslide" that preceded the seismic wave and, therefore, there was no coverage. The appellate court affirmed.[197]

[7] Ordinance or Law

An Ordinance or Law exclusion is intended to prevent the insured from obtaining a windfall: property made more valuable than that which was damaged or destroyed as a result of complying with the requirements of an ordinance or law.[198] Policies may both provide some ordinance or law coverage and limit it by exclusion, while others just exclude it. For example, the ISO Boiler and Machinery Coverage Form says that the insurer will not pay for any "increase in loss" that is caused by, or results from, the enforcement of any ordinance, law, regulation, rule, or ruling that regulates or restricts repair, replacement,

194. ISO Form BM 00 25 02 91, § B.4.i.

195. Malecki, *Equipment Breakdown Insurance: Too Important to Ignore!* at 5 (2009), Adjusting Today, *available at* http://adjustersinternational.com/publications/adjusting-today/equipment-breakdown-insurance/1/.

196. HSB Freestyle Policy Form 6671 (10/2002) § B.1.c.

197. Fidelity & Casualty Co. v. Halibut Producers Cooperative, 73 Wn.2d 153, 154, 437 P.2d 182, 183 (1968).

198. Wood, *The Insurance Fallout Following Hurricane Andrew: Whether Insurance Companies Are Legally Obligated to Pay for Building Code Upgrades Despite the "Ordinance or Law" Exclusion Contained in Most Homeowners Policies*, 48 U. Miami L. Rev. 949, 951 (1994).

alteration, use, operation, construction, or installation.[199] After a flood, property owners often incur cleanup costs; therefore, it is significant that ordinance or law exclusions may apply to the cost of cleanup or disposal of covered property.[200] The exclusion may extend to the cost of any study required by a governmental entity as a prerequisite to returning to operations.[201]

[8] Perils Covered by Other Insurance

Equipment breakdown policies typically exclude coverage caused by certain causes of loss when coverage for that cause of loss is provided by another policy whether or not collectible. The exclusion may even apply if there is a self-insurance risk retention plan.[202] Under the HSB policy, the exclusion applies whether or not any other policy provides the same coverage or scope of coverage.[203] The prescribed excluded causes of loss in the ISO Equipment Breakdown Protection Coverage Form are breakdowns caused by aircraft or vehicles; freezing from cold weather; lightning; sinkhole collapse; smoke; riot; civil commotion or vandalism; or the weight of snow, ice, or sleet.[204] Under a Travelers policy, the exclusion is for breakdowns caused directly or indirectly by aircraft; civil commotion; collapse; freezing caused by cold weather; impact by a missile, aircraft, or vehicle; lightning; molten material; objects falling from aircraft or missiles; riot; smoke; vandalism; vehicles; and the weight of snow, ice, or sleet.[205] The HSB policy states that the insurer will not pay for an accident caused by or resulting from, *inter alia*, *water damage*, meaning discharge or leakage of water or steam as the direct result of breaking apart or cracking of any part of a system or appliance containing water or steam.[206] However, if any of the excluded perils happens at a location not described on the Declarations Page and causes an electrical surge or other "electrical disturbance," the exclusion may not apply.[207]

---

199. ISO Form BM 00 25 02 91, § B.1. *See also* HSB Freestyle Policy Form 6671 (10/2002) § B.1.b (carrier will not pay for loss, damage, or expense caused directly or indirectly by enforcement of, or change in, any ordinance, law, regulation, rule, or ruling regulating or restricting repair, replacement, alteration, use, operation, construction, or installation, except as specifically provided otherwise in coverage section of policy). Usually nothing in ordinance or law exclusions limits them to laws or rulings of authorities that relate to the permitting process for replacement of damaged property. Hartford Steam Boiler Inspection & Ins. Co. v. Quantum Chem. Corp., 1996 U.S. Dist. LEXIS 17551 (N.D. Ill. Nov. 12, 1996).

200. Travelers EnergyMax 21, § B.1.

201. Hartford Steam Boiler Inspection & Ins. Co. v. Quantum Chem. Corp., 1996 U.S. Dist. LEXIS 17551 (N.D. Ill. Nov. 12, 1996).

202. Travelers EnergyMax 21, § B.14.

203. HSB Freestyle Policy Form 6671 (10/2002) § B.3.

204. ISO Form BM 00 20 07 01, § B.12.

205. Travelers EnergyMax 21, § B.14.

206. HSB Freestyle Policy Form 6671 (10/2002) § B.3.

207. HSB Freestyle Policy Form 6671 (10/2002) § B.4. The surge or disturbance has to have been transmitted through utility service transmission lines to a described location. At that

[9] Neglect

A policy may require an insured to protect its covered property by excluding coverage if the insured fails or neglects to use all "reasonable" means to protect or to save and preserve that property from damage after an "accident"[208] or at and after the time of the loss.[209] It has been held that the exclusion does not apply where the evidence is of negligence before the accident.[210]

[10] Equipment Being Repaired or Tested

Coverage may be excluded when covered equipment is being tested or repaired. The exclusion may specify particular types of testing[211] or may refer generally to testing.[212]

[11] Lack of Power

Coverage may be excluded for loss or damage that is caused directly or indirectly by lack of, or excess of, power, light, heat, steam, or refrigeration except as provided by business income, extra expense, or utility interruption and/or spoilage damage coverage.[213] Courts have found these exclusions to be unambiguous and to apply to the consequences of a loss of power. In one case, a power failure of four hours resulted in three compressors being exposed to snow and freezing temperatures. They were damaged beyond repair. According to the insured, the immediate and proximate cause of the loss was the freezing temperatures. The policy, argued the insured, provided coverage because damage from freezing was not expressly excluded. However, the court decided the policy excluded damage from loss of power and heat, and it can reasonably be

---

location, the surge or disturbance has to have resulted in an "accident" to "covered equipment" owned or operated under the control of the insured or the landlord of the insured. Finally, the loss, damage, or expense caused by the surge or disturbance cannot be a covered cause of loss under another coverage part or policy of insurance, whether collectible or not, and without regard to whether or not that other coverage part or policy provides the same coverage or scope of coverage.

208. HSB Freestyle Policy Form 6671 (10/2002) § B.1.g. *See* Cornell Wood Prods. Co. v. Hartford Steam Boiler Inspection & Ins. Co., 62 F. Supp. 303 (N.D. Ill. 1945) (insurer contended submersion of insured objects was result of insured's deliberate and intentional act of permitting water to accumulate by ceasing efforts to eject and control flood waters, but court found insured took all reasonable precautions to protect insured objects from flood waters and abandoned its efforts only when, in the exercise of sound discretion, it seemed necessary to do so in order not to endanger human life).

209. ISO Form BM 00 20 07 01, § B.19; Travelers EnergyMax 21, § B.20.

210. Maryland Casualty Co. v. Neiman-Marcus Co., 186 F.2d 140, 142 (5th Cir. 1951).

211. *See* ISO Form BM 00 20 07 01, § B.9 (excluding damage to covered equipment undergoing pressure or electrical test).

212. *See* ISO Form BM 00 25 02 91, § B.4.h (excluding accident to any object while being tested).

213. *See, e.g.*, Travelers EnergyMax 21, § B.17.

assumed the exclusion extended to what would follow if power and heat were lost in freezing weather.[214]

8.7 Limits of Insurance

Policies have a section on the limits of the insurance. A limitation that is common to all B&M policies states that the insurer will pay no more for one accident or one breakdown than the amount shown as the limit on the Declarations Page.[215] The limitation is determined by the definition of "one accident" or "one breakdown." The ISO Boiler and Machinery Coverage Form provides that if an initial "accident" or "breakdown" causes other "accidents" or "breakdowns," all of them are considered to be one "accident" or "breakdown."[216] All "accidents" or "breakdowns" at any single location that manifest at the same time and are the result—or, in the case of policies called equipment breakdown protection, the direct result[217]—of the same cause are considered to be one "accident" or "breakdown." The HSB policy is similar. Under it, "one accident" is all "accidents" that occur at the same time from the same event, and if an "accident" causes other "accidents," then all of them are considered to be "one accident."[218]

Under many policies, including the HSB policy, the limit of insurance for each individual coverage—for example, property damage or expediting expense—from loss, damage, or expense that arises from any "one accident" is the amount indicated *for that coverage* on the Declarations Page. Those limits, says the HSB policy, "are a part of, and not in addition to, the Equipment Breakdown Limit."[219] The amount of the limit per breakdown, then, is the maximum the carrier will pay for any one breakdown, even if the various coverage parts are greater than the limit, while at the same time, the chosen limit for any specific coverage is the maximum the carrier will pay in any one breakdown for that loss.[220] When a coverage is shown as "included" on the

214. Sawyer Fruit & Vegetable Co-operative Corp. v. Lumbermens Mut. Casualty Co., 73 Ill. Dec. 1, 117 Ill. App. 3d 407, 453 N.E.2d 826 (Ill. App. 1983).

215. *See, e.g.*, ISO Form BM 00 25 02 91, § C.1; HSB Freestyle Policy Form 6671 (10/2002) § C.1. A commentary says that under the ISO Equipment Breakdown Protection Coverage Form, the amount of the limit per breakdown selected by the insured is the maximum the carrier will pay for any one breakdown, despite the fact that the various coverage parts purchased exceed that limit. At the same time, the limit selected for any specific coverage is the maximum the carrier will pay in any one breakdown for that loss. *Boiler and Machinery Coverage Form* (Summit Business Media, 2013).

216. ISO Form BM 00 25 02 91, § F.3.

217. ISO Form BM 00 20 07 01, § F.12. *See also* Travelers EnergyMax 21, § F.14.

218. HSB Freestyle Policy Form 6671 (10/2002) § F.17.

219. HSB Freestyle Policy Form 6671 (10/2002) § C.2.a. When an amount of time is shown, the coverage continues for no more than the amount of time that *immediately* follows the "accident."

220. *Boiler and Machinery Coverage Form* (Summit Business Media, 2013).

Declarations Page, it is provided *up to the remaining amount* of the Equipment Breakdown Limit, and if no limit is shown for a coverage,[221] or a coverage is shown as "Excluded," it is considered to have a $0 limit.[222] When two or more coverage limits apply to the same loss or portion of a loss, the insurance company will only pay the smallest of the applicable limits. Thus, when there is a loss under a specific individual coverage and all or part of it is not covered because the applicable coverage is excluded or has a limit that is less than the amount of the loss, the insurer will not pay the *remaining amount* of that loss under any other coverage.[223]

The ISO Boiler and Machinery Coverage Form, it should be noted, references direct damage[224] to *covered property* that results from one accident while other policies limit payment to one accident or one breakdown and then define accident or breakdown as a physical loss to covered *equipment*.

8.8 Deductibles

The amount of the deductible is stated on the Declarations Page. It may be a stated amount or a percentage of loss. There may be a single deductible or different deductible amounts that apply to different causes of loss. The deductible clause can be succinct. The ISO Boiler and Machinery Coverage Form, for instance, simply states that the insurer will not pay for any loss or damage that results from any "one accident" until it exceeds the stated deductible.[225] If an initial "accident" causes others, the policy provides they are all considered to be "one accident," and all accidents at any single location that manifest at the same time and result from the same cause are considered to be one accident.[226] The meaning of "one accident" can be critical to determining whether losses will be covered. If the insurer treats a series of breakdowns as separate events and applies the deductible to each, the insured may recover little if anything, whereas if the deductible is applied once, the recovery may be considerable.[227]

---

221. *See, e.g.*, Malecki, *Equipment Breakdown Insurance: Too Important to Ignore!* at 5 (2009), Adjusting Today, *available at* http://adjustersinternational.com/publications/adjusting-today/equipment-breakdown-insurance/1/, where the author explains that if a $500,000 base limit is chosen and other coverages are designated as "included," the coverage will depend on how much is left after paying for damage to property the named insured owns or has in its care, custody, or control.

222. HSB Freestyle Policy Form 6671 (10/2002) § C.2.a.

223. HSB Freestyle Policy Form 6671 (10/2002) § C.2.b.

224. *See* Preferred Mut. Ins. Co. v. Travelers Cos., 955 F. Supp. 9, 11 (D. Mass. 1997) (taking note that policy did not define "direct damage").

225. ISO Form BM 00 25 02 91, § D.

226. ISO Form BM 00 25 02 91, § F.3.

227. *See, e.g.*, Me. Woods Pellet Co., LLC v. W. World Ins. Co., 2021 U.S. Dist. LEXIS 61699 (D. Me. Mar. 31, 2021) (finding single deductible should apply to three events that insurer had treated separately).

When the amount of loss or damage exceeds the deductible, the insurer will pay up to the applicable limit of insurance. If, however, more than one "object"—which means the equipment shown on the Declarations Page[228]—is involved in one accident, only the highest deductible will apply.[229]

The deductible clause in the ISO Equipment Breakdown Protection Coverage Form has two subsections and is more complex.[230] The first subsection discusses the application of deductibles and the second their determination. Under the former, the insurer will not pay for loss or damage that results from any "one breakdown"[231] until the amount of covered loss or damage exceeds the deductible for each applicable coverage, after which the insurer will pay the amount of covered loss or damage that exceeds the deductible, up to the pertinent limit of insurance.[232] Also, deductibles apply separately for each applicable coverage with two exceptions. The first exception applies when the deductible is shown on the Declarations Page as combined for any of the coverages, in which case the insurer will initially subtract the combined deductible amount from the total amount of any loss to which the combined deductible applies.[233] Second, if more than one piece of "covered equipment" is involved in one breakdown, only one deductible, that being the highest, applies for each of the applicable coverages.[234]

The second subsection explains how the various types of deductibles are applied.[235] The Declarations Page states the type of deductible. Typically, there is more than one type, with different types applying to different coverages. The types are dollar, time, multiple of daily value, percentage of loss, and maximum or minimum.[236] "Dollar" deductible means a specific stated dollar amount. It will likely apply to property damage. If the Declarations Page shows a dollar deductible, the insurer first subtracts the deductible amount from any loss it would otherwise pay.[237] "Time deductibles" are often applied to business income or extra expense coverage. They are stated in hours—most often 24—or days. They cause the insured to bear the full loss for that stated

228. ISO Form BM 00 25 02 91, § F.2.

229. ISO Form BM 00 25 02 91, § D.

230. *See generally* Malecki, *Equipment Breakdown Insurance: Too Important to Ignore!* at 7 (2009), Adjusting Today, *available at* http://adjustersinternational.com/publications/adjusting-today/equipment-breakdown-insurance/1/.

231. A "breakdown" is a prescribed direct physical loss that causes damage to covered equipment. ISO Form BM 00 20 07 01, § F.1. "One breakdown" means that if an initial breakdown causes other breakdowns, all will be considered one breakdown. Additionally, all breakdowns at any one premises that manifest themselves at the same time and are the direct result of the same cause are considered to be one breakdown. ISO Form BM 00 20 07 01, § F.12.

232. ISO Form BM 00 20 07 01, § D.1.

233. ISO Form BM 00 20 07 01, § D.1.a.

234. ISO Form BM 00 20 07 01, § D.1.a.

235. ISO Form BM 00 20 07 01, § D.2.

236. Another type of deductible is "multiple per unit." *See* Travelers EnergyMax 21, § D.2.b.

237. ISO Form BM 00 20 07 01, § D.2.a.

period. When there is a time deductible, the policy says the insurer will not be liable for any loss under the coverage to which the time deductible applies that occurs during that specified time period *immediately following* a breakdown.[238] When a deductible is stated as a percentage of loss, the insurer will not be liable for that stated percentage of the gross amount of loss or damage—before the applicable deductible or coinsurance—that is insured under the applicable coverage.[239]

Generally, a deductible applies to damages or loss associated with a specific accident or breakdown. Where the same object or covered equipment experiences a series of accidents or breakdowns, the deductible applies to each of them.[240]

8.9 Conditions

[1] Generally

Boiler and machinery policies contain many conditions. Some are unique to the form of coverage. The conditions commonly included address abandonment; additional insureds; appraisal; bankruptcy; coinsurance; concealment, misrepresentation, or fraud; defense of the insured; duties in the event of loss or damage; insurance under two or more coverages; joint or disputed loss; legal actions against the carrier; liberalization; loss payable; mortgage holders; bailees; other insurance; policy period and coverage territory; insurer's privilege to adjust with the owner; reducing the loss; suspension; transfer of rights of recovery against others to the insurer; and valuation.

Supplementing the conditions found in the policy will be a "Common Policy Conditions" form. It addresses cancellation,[241] changes to the policy,[242] examination of the books and records of the named insured,[243] inspections

238. ISO Form BM 00 20 07 01, § D.2.b. *See also* Austin, *Equipment Breakdown—More Than Just Boiler and Machinery* (2011), IRMI, http://www.irmi.com/articles/expert-commentary/equipment-breakdown (business income may be subject to an ADV deductible based on number of days business income would have been earned during period of interruption had no accident occurred; amount can be significant and likely much greater than direct damage deductible).

239. ISO Form BM 00 20 07 01, § D.2.d.

240. *See, e.g.*, Community Federal Sav. & Loan Ass'n v. Hartford Steam Boiler Inspection & Ins. Co., 580 F. Supp. 1170, 1173 (E.D. Mo. 1984) (where covered air-conditioning unit suffered series of failures and repairs over six months, deductible applied to each failure).

241. *See, e.g.*, ISO Form IL 00 17 11 98, § A.

242. *See, e.g.*, ISO Form IL 00 17 11 98, B.

243. *See, e.g.*, ISO Form IL 00 17 11 98, C. The clause allows the insurer to examine and audit the named insured's books and records at any time during the policy period and up to three years after it.

and surveys by the insurer,[244] premiums,[245] and the transfer by the named insured of its rights and duties under the policy.[246] The Travelers Common Policy Conditions form adds that, when there is any doubt, the term "equipment breakdown" means boiler and machinery and *vice versa*.[247]

[2] Duties in the Event of Loss or Damage

Equipment breakdown policies typically require insureds to assure that certain steps are taken in the event of loss or damage to covered property.[248] These are:

- Give prompt notice to the insurer of the loss or damage, including a description of the property.[249]
- Act, if possible, to reduce the loss, damage, or expense.[250]

---

244. *See, e.g.*, ISO Form IL 00 17 11 98, D. The inspections and surveys clause gives the insurer the right to make inspections and surveys at any time. The insurer can also give reports to the named insured on the conditions it finds and recommend changes. It does not *require* the insurer to make any inspections, surveys, reports, or recommendations. The clause makes clear that the insurer does not make safety inspections and does not warrant that conditions are safe, healthful, or in compliance with laws, regulations, codes, or standards. There is an exception for any inspections, surveys, reports, or recommendations the insurer may make about certification under state or municipal statutes, ordinances, or regulations of boilers, pressure vessels, or elevators. *See* Clarendon Am. Ins. Co. v. Bayside Rest., LLC, 567 F. Supp. 2d 1379, 1388 (M.D. Fla. 2008) (insured may not to rely on inspection conducted by third party at request of insurer).

245. *See, e.g.*, ISO Form IL 00 17 11 98, E.

246. *See, e.g.*, ISO Form IL 00 17 11 98, F. The condition prohibits the insured from transferring its rights and duties under the policy without written consent of the insurer. Courts do not agree on the question of whether the condition prohibits assignment of claims. The majority rule is that an anti-assignment clause "is unenforceable once an insured occurrence takes place because at that point the insured is entitled to recovery under the policy; that right is a chose in action; a chose in action is a form of personal property; the anti-assignment provision amounts to a restraint upon the alienation of this property right; and, a restraint upon the alienation of property is in opposition to public policy." Wehr Constructors, Inc. v. Assur. Co. of Am., 384 S.W.3d 680, 682–83 (Ky. 2012). The minority rule is that no assignments are allowed without the consent of the insurer. *See* Keller Founds., Inc. v. Wausau Underwriters Ins. Co., 626 F.3d 871, 875 (5th Cir. 2010). *See also* Bambrick, *In re Katrina Canal Breaches Litigation: The Louisiana Supreme Court Defies the Majority in Upholding Prohibitions on Postloss Assignments of Insurance Policies*, 86 Tul. L. Rev. 1345 (2012).

247. Travelers Form IL T0 01 01 07, § G.

248. HSB Freestyle Policy Form 6671 (10/2002) § E.6; Travelers EnergyMax 21, § E.1.d.

249. HSB Freestyle Policy Form 6671 (10/2002) § E.6.a. Specific notice requirements are often modified by state law. *See, e.g.*, New York Underwriters Ins. Co. v. Coffman, 540 S.W.2d 445 (Tex. Civ. App.—Fort Worth, 1976) (requirement that notice be given to certain office was void and unenforceable as in violation of state statute).

250. HSB Freestyle Policy Form 6671 (10/2002) § E.6.b. The insured has to protect property from further damage; resume its business, partially or completely at the location of loss or at another location; make up lost business within a reasonable amount of time; use merchandise or other property available; use property or services of others; and salvage the damaged property.

- Allow a reasonable time and opportunity for the insurer to examine the property and premises before repair or replacement or before physical evidence of the accident is removed, while taking necessary measures to protect the property from further damage.[251]
- Do not make any statement that will assume any obligation or admit any liability, for any loss, damage, or expense for which the insurer may be liable without the insurer's consent.[252]
- Promptly send any legal papers or notices received regarding the loss, damage, or expense to the insurer.[253]
- Allow the insurer to inspect the property, premises, and records of the insured as often as may be reasonably required, to take samples of damaged and undamaged property for inspection, testing, and analysis, and to make copies from the books and records of the insured.[254]
- Allow the insurer, if it so requests, to examine under oath the insured and any of its agents, employees, and representatives.[255]
- Within 60 days after the insurer requests it, send the insurer a signed, sworn proof of loss containing the information it requests.[256]
- Cooperate with the insurer in the investigation and settlement of the claim.[257]

Additionally, under the HSB policy, the insured has responsibility to provide the insurer with documentation that demonstrates that the loss, damage, or expense was the result of an "accident" that is covered under the policy and to calculate the dollar amount of the loss, damage, and expense the insured maintains is covered.[258] The insured has to do these things at its expense. If an insured fails to comply with the duties set forth in the policy after loss or damage, the insurer may be able to deny the claim.[259]

251. HSB Freestyle Policy Form 6671 (10/2002) § E.6.c.

252. HSB Freestyle Policy Form 6671 (10/2002) § E.6.d.

253. HSB Freestyle Policy Form 6671 (10/2002) § E.6.e.

254. HSB Freestyle Policy Form 6671 (10/2002) § E.6.f.

255. HSB Freestyle Policy Form 6671 (10/2002) § E.6.g. The policy says the carrier may examine any insured under oath while not in the presence of any other insured and that the examination may be at any time reasonably required; may be about any matter relating to the insurance, the loss, damage or expense, or claim, including, but not limited to, the books and records of the insured; and may be recorded by any methods chosen by the carrier.

256. HSB Freestyle Policy Form 6671 (10/2002) § E.6.h.

257. HSB Freestyle Policy Form 6671 (10/2002) § E.6.i.

258. HSB Freestyle Policy Form 6671 (10/2002) § E.8. The duty of the insured to show that any loss, damage, or expense was the result of a covered "accident" applies whether or not the possible "accident" occurred at the insured's premises or involved the insured's equipment.

259. *See, e.g.*, Riefflin v. Hartford Steam Boiler Inspection & Ins. Co., 164 Mont. 287, 293, 521 P.2d 675, 678 (Mont. 1974) (failure to submit notice of accident and proof of loss as soon as practicable precluded payment of claims).

[3] Reducing Loss

After a breakdown or accident, certain obligations are imposed on the insured.[260] Among these are resuming business partially or completely, making up for lost business within a reasonable period of time, and using every reasonable means to reduce or avert loss, including using property or services of others.[261] Sometimes, these duties are found in the clause on the duties of the insured in the event of loss or damage.[262]

The obligation to use every reasonable means to reduce or avert loss does not mean that damaged equipment can be replaced with upgraded, more expensive equipment at the insurer's expense, even though that may be the quickest way to return safely to normal operations.[263]

[4] Valuation

All B&M policies contain a valuation clause, although their specificity varies. The purpose of the clause is to determine how the insurer will respond to any loss. Usually, a policy provides that for damaged covered property, the insurer will pay the lesser of the cost to repair the damaged property,[264] the cost to replace it,[265] or the amount actually spent that was necessary to repair or replace it.[266] The standard ISO policy, for instance, says the insurer will

---

260. *See* Anderson & Middleton Lumber Co. v. Lumbermen's Mut. Cas. Co., 53 Wn.2d 404, 333 P.2d 938 (1959), where the insured had a duty under the policy to use "diligence and dispatch and all reasonable means" to resume business. The insured then had the burden, said the court, to show that, with use of diligence and dispatch, it was required to have its business shut down for the period of time claimed.

261. Travelers EnergyMax 21, § E.1.i. *See also* ISO Form BM 00 20 07 01, § E.1.j.

262. *See, e.g.*, HSB Freestyle Policy Form 6671 (10/2002) § E.6.b. The clause requires the insured to protect property from further damage; resume business, partially or completely at the location of loss or at another location; make up lost business within a reasonable amount of time; use merchandise or other property available; use property or services of others; and salvage any damaged property.

263. Hartford Steam Boiler Inspection & Ins. Co. v. Quantum Chem. Corp., 1996 U.S. Dist. LEXIS 17551 (N.D. Ill. Nov. 12, 1996).

264. If the insurer initially directs the insured to repair rather than replace covered equipment, it may subsequently have to pay to replace it if there is another covered cause of loss. Community Federal Sav. & Loan Ass'n v. Hartford Steam Boiler Inspection & Ins. Co., 580 F. Supp. 1170 (E.D. Mo. 1984).

265. *Consider* Va. Apple Storage, Inc. v. Ins. Ctr. of Winchester, Inc., 1997 Va. Cir. LEXIS 740 (Apr. 11, 1997) (not every loss embraced by coverage terms of boiler and machinery policy occurs for item of property for which there is established market in which to determine replacement costs at time of loss; character of damaged property determines appropriate method of evaluation used to determine replacement costs, and appraisers frequently testify based on market, cost, or income method of valuation).

266. *See, e.g.*, HSB Freestyle Policy Form 6671 (10/2002) § E.10.a. The policy says the insurer will pay the amount the insured spent to repair or replace covered property directly or indirectly damaged by a breakdown to covered equipment, but that payment will be the lesser of the three options. Travelers EnergyMax 21, § E.1.l.(1).

determine the value of covered property based on the cost to repair, rebuild, or replace the damaged property with property of same kind, capacity, size, or quality on the same or another site, whichever is the less costly, or the cost actually and necessarily spent to repair, rebuild, or replace on the same or another site, whichever is the less costly; however, the insurer will not pay for damaged property that is obsolete and useless to the insured.[267] The HSB policy adds to that. It states that the amount of payment will be based on the most cost-effective way to replace the function, capacity, and remaining useful life of the damaged property.[268] "Most cost-effective" may include the use of generic, used, or reconditioned parts, equipment, or property. Use of the phrase "most cost-effective" has been interpreted to mean that the insurance company does not have "unfettered discretion" to arrive at the valuation. The valuation, instead, has to take into consideration the function, capacity, and remaining useful life of the damaged property and that, as one court has said, would "seem to necessitate consideration of estimates and opinions produced by the insured."[269]

If a policy says the insurer will pay the cost to repair or replace, whichever is less, and the repair costs are less, the insured cannot recover the replacement cost by contending repair was impractical.[270]

Policies often discuss payment for replacing *covered equipment* with more efficient equipment. The HSB policy, for instance, states that generally the insured has to pay any extra expense to replace damaged *property* with property of a better kind or quality or of a different size or capacity.[271] If, however, covered *equipment* has to be replaced because of an "accident," then the insurer will pay the additional cost of replacement providing it agrees the replacement is better for the environment, safer for people, or more energy efficient than the equipment that was replaced.[272] Nonetheless, the insurer will

---

267. ISO Form BM 00 20 07 01, § E.1.l. The policy, notes a commentary, provides for replacement cost recovery of damaged property and if replacement cost is not wanted, an endorsement must be added to eliminate the policy's property damage valuation clause. *Boiler and Machinery Coverage Form* (Summit Business Media, 2013). The endorsement is ISO Form BM 99 59 07 01 (Equipment Breakdown: Actual Cash Value). Under the endorsement, the insurer will pay the amount spent to repair or replace covered property directly damaged by any breakdown.

268. HSB Freestyle Policy Form 6671 (10/2002) § E.10.b.

269. Hartford Steam Boiler Insp. & Ins. Co. v. Menada, Inc., 2018 U.S. Dist. LEXIS 59897, at *12 (S.D. Fla. Apr. 6, 2018).

270. New York Underwriters Ins. Co. v. Coffman, 540 S.W.2d 445 (Tex. Civ. App.—Fort Worth, 1976).

271. *See, e.g.*, HSB Freestyle Policy Form 6671 (10/2002) § E.10.c. *See also* Hartford Steam Boiler Inspection & Ins. Co. v. Quantum Chem. Corp., 1996 U.S. Dist. LEXIS 17551 (N.D. Ill. Nov. 12, 1996) (whether physical differences between damaged equipment and replacement equipment caused latter not to be of "like kind" was question of fact).

272. *See, e.g.*, HSB Freestyle Policy Form 6671 (10/2002) § E.10.d. The replacement provision only applies to property damage coverage, to any property valued on an Actual Cash Value basis, or to replacement of component parts. Also, it does not increase any applicable limits.

not pay more than 125 percent of what the cost would have been to replace the equipment with that of like kind and quality, and it will not pay to increase the size or capacity of that equipment. A similar purpose is served by the "new generation coverage clause" in a Travelers policy. While the policy does not define "new generation," the policy affords "up to 125% of replacement value of unrepairable equipment for upgrades to state-of-the-art technologies."[273] If covered *equipment* cannot be repaired, or the cost of repair is greater than the cost of replacement, and the damage is equal to or greater than 100 percent of actual cash value, the insured has the option to choose to replace the damaged covered equipment with "newer generation covered equipment" of the "same capacity." In that case, the insurer will pay up to 25 percent more than for covered equipment of like kind, quality, and capacity.[274] Except for the new generation coverage, the insured has to pay any extra cost to replace damaged property with that of a better kind or quality or larger capacity.[275] If, however, no replacement equipment of like kind is on the market, the insurer may have to pay the cost to acquire the available equipment that is most nearly similar to the equipment being replaced even though the result is that the insured receives an "upgrade and the policy has no "new generation" clause.[276]

The HSB policy lists the property that will be valued on an actual cash value basis, a figure that includes deductions for depreciation.[277] Those properties are *any property* not currently serving a useful or necessary function for the insured,[278] any *covered property* not repaired or replaced by the insured 24 months after the "accident," and any *covered property* for which the actual cash value coverage is stated on the Declarations Page. Generally, policies do not define "actual cash value."[279]

Under circumstances spelled out in policies,[280] property that is held for sale by the insured is valued at the sales price as if no loss or damage had

273. https://www.travelers.com/iw-documents/business-insurance/boiler-machinery-EnergyMax21-CP-6943.pdf.

274. Travelers EnergyMax 21, § E.1.l.(3). The 25 percent is measured by the cost at the time of the breakdown.

275. Travelers EnergyMax 21, § E.1.l.(4).

276. *See* Hartford Steam Boiler Inspection & Ins. Co. v. Quantum Chem. Corp., 1996 U.S. Dist. LEXIS 17551 (N.D. Ill. Nov. 12, 1996).

277. HSB Freestyle Policy Form 6671 (10/2002) § E.10.e.

278. *Compare* Malecki, *Equipment Breakdown Insurance: Too Important to Ignore!* at 8 (2009), Adjusting Today, *available at* http://adjustersinternational.com/publications/adjusting-today/equipment-breakdown-insurance/1/ (insurers do not pay for damaged property that is considered obsolete and useless to insured).

279. *See* Travellers Indem. Co. v. B & B Ice & Coal Co., 248 Ky. 448, 446, 58 S.W.2d 640, 642 (1933) (term "cash value" means price boiler would bring when offered for sale by one who desires to sell, but is not compelled to do so, and is bought by one who desires to purchase, but is not compelled to do so).

280. For example, one condition is generally that the property was manufactured by the insured.

occurred.[281] Any discounts or expenses that would have applied are subtracted from that amount.

A recovery is typically reduced by the salvage value of the damaged property,[282] and policies may address salvage value.[283]

B&M policies usually contain an "anti-stacking" clause. Under it, if two or more coverages apply to the same loss or damage, the insurer will only pay the *actual* amount of the loss or damage.[284] Thus, if the insured chooses more than one coverage that could apply to the loss, the insured cannot stack two or more coverage amounts so that it is paid more than the *actual* amount of the suffered loss.[285]

[5] Appraisal

Many B&M policies have an appraisal clause.[286] An appraisal clause typically states that if the parties do not agree on the value of the property or the amount of loss, either of them may make written demand for an appraisal of the loss. If there is an appraisal, the insurer still has the right to deny the claim.[287]

[6] Coinsurance

A "coinsurance" clause limits the amount an insurer will pay on a claim. Coverages subject to the clause are listed on the Declarations Page. The HSB policy says that when the clause applies, the insurer will not pay the full amount of any loss if the value of the property that is subject to the coverage at the time of the accident multiplied by the coinsurance percentage on the Declarations Page is greater than the applicable limit.[288] The most the insurer will pay in that case is calculated by a mathematical formula outlined in detail in the policy.

The HSB policy also has a business income coverage coinsurance clause. It applies unless the Declarations Page states otherwise.[289] Under it, the insurer

---

281. *See, e.g.*, HSB Freestyle Policy Form 6671 (10/2002) § E.10.f; Travelers EnergyMax 21, § E.1.l.(7).

282. Jacobs Press v. Hartford Steam Boiler Inspection & Ins. Co., 1997 U.S. App. LEXIS 3769 (4th Cir. Mar. 4, 1997) (any verdict for damage to covered equipment would have to give credit for salvage value).

283. *See, e.g.*, Travelers EnergyMax 21, § E.9.

284. BM 00 20 07 01, § E.1.e.

285. *Boiler and Machinery Coverage Form* (Summit Business Media, 2013).

286. *But see* ISO Form BM 00 25 02 91; HSB Freestyle Policy Form 6671 (10/2002).

287. ISO Form BM 00 20 07 01, § E.1.b.

288. HSB Freestyle Policy Form 6671 (10/2002) § E.4.a.

289. HSB Freestyle Policy Form 6671 (10/2002) § E.3. *See also* ISO Form BM 00 20 07 01, § E.1.m; Travelers EnergyMax 21, § E.1.n. *And see* Austin, *Equipment Breakdown—More*

will not pay the full amount of a business income loss when the "business income actual annual value"[290] is more than the "business income estimated annual value"[291] at the time of the "accident." The most the insurer will pay then is determined by a mathematical formula stated in the policy.

[7] Joint or Disputed Loss

[a] Generally

Although insurers try to make the exclusions in commercial property policies dovetail with the equipment breakdown coverage, they do not always succeed.[292] A loss could, therefore, trigger, or at least appear to trigger, both the commercial property and B&M policies.[293] Payment to the insured will probably be held up if there is a dispute between the insurers.[294] For that reason, a policy may have a "Joint or Disputed Loss" or loss adjustment clause.[295] It facilitates payment for a loss when there are both commercial property and equipment breakdown policies in effect, damage occurs to covered property that is covered by both policies, and the insurance companies disagree over liability.[296] Once the provisions of the policies are met, the insurers are required

---

Than Just Boiler and Machinery (2011), IRMI, http://www.irmi.com/articles/expert-commentary/equipment-breakdown (due diligence is required to make sure proper values have been submitted, as business income coverage may be subject to coinsurance clause).

290. The phrase "business income actual annual value" is defined to mean business income that would have been earned in the current fiscal year if the accident had not occurred. The carrier will, in its calculations, consider the actual experience of the business prior to the accident and the likely experience the insured would have had without that accident. HSB Freestyle Policy Form 6671 (10/2002) § G.6.

291. "Business income estimated annual value" means the anticipated income reported to the insurer and shown on the Declarations Page. When no value is shown, it will be the most recent report of anticipated business income values on file with the insurer. HSB Freestyle Policy Form 6671 (10/2002) § G.7.

292. Austin, *Equipment Breakdown—More Than Just Boiler and Machinery* (2011), IRMI, http://www.irmi.com/articles/expert-commentary/equipment-breakdown.

293. Boggs, *Three Commercial Property Endorsements Every Client Should Have* (July 27, 2009), My New Markets, http://www.mynewmarkets.com/articles/102464/three-commercial-property-endorsements-every-client-should-have.

294. Austin, *Equipment Breakdown—More Than Just Boiler and Machinery* (2011), IRMI, http://www.irmi.com/articles/expert-commentary/equipment-breakdown; Boggs, *Three Commercial Property Endorsements Every Client Should Have* (July 27, 2009), My New Markets, http://www.mynewmarkets.com/articles/102464/three-commercial-property-endorsements-every-client-should-have.

295. *See* Ark. Power & Light Co. v. Hartford Steam Boiler Inspection & Ins. Co., 257 F.3d 853, 855 (8th Cir. 2001); Hartford Steam Boiler Inspection & Ins. Co. v. Underwriters at Lloyd's & Cos. Collective, 271 Conn. 474, 857 A.2d 893 (2004), *cert. den.*, 544 U.S. 974, 125 S. Ct. 1826, 161 L. Ed. 2d 723 (2005); Arcadian Corp. v. Olin Corp., 698 So. 2d 9 (La. App. 1997), *writ. den.*, 827 So. 2d 1174 (La. 2002).

296. Travelers EnergyMax 21, § E.3.a.

to pay the insured for the disputed loss and may not "hold the insured hostage" while they contest their respective amounts of liability for the loss.[297]

These clauses are standard for many B&M policies, but they may be added by endorsement.[298] Whether the clause is added by endorsement or found in the main policy, the commercial property policy has to have comparable language for the insured to receive its benefit.

[b] Clause Contents

A Joint or Disputed Loss clause does not apply if the carriers do not admit to any liability and neither one maintains that coverage applies under the policy of the other.[299] Under a Travelers policy, the clause applies when the commercial property policy that insures the covered property has a similar clause at the time of loss with substantially similar requirements, procedures, and conditions and the damage was caused by a loss for which both insurers admit to some liability or there is disagreement between them about whether the damage was caused by a covered cause of loss in their policies or over the extent of participation of the policies in a loss insured against partially or wholly by any or both policies.[300] When those conditions are met, each insurer will, after a written request from the insured, pay the entire amount of loss that they have agreed is covered by their respective policies as well as half of the amount in dispute.[301] There are some additional conditions in the Travelers policy. The insurer, for instance, will not pay a share of the amount in dispute that exceeds the amount payable under the equivalent specification of the commercial property policy. The insurer also will not pay more than the amount it would have paid had there been no commercial property policy in effect at the time of loss. In no event will the insurer pay more than the limit of insurance on the Declarations Page.

There may be more than one commercial property carrier. For example, one company may provide primary coverage[302] while another is responsible

297. Boggs, *Three Commercial Property Endorsements Every Client Should Have* (July 27, 2009), My New Markets, http://www.mynewmarkets.com/articles/102464/three-commercial-property-endorsements-every-client-should-have. *See also* Ark. Power & Light Co. v. Hartford Steam Boiler Inspection & Ins. Co., 257 F.3d 853, 855 (8th Cir. 2001) (insured receives prompt payment when insurers with potentially overlapping coverages disagree about cause of loss).

298. *See, e.g.*, ISO Form BM 99 42 02 91; ISO Form BM 99 43 09 96. *See also* Ark. Power & Light Co. v. Hartford Steam Boiler Inspection & Ins. Co., 257 F.3d 853, 855 (8th Cir. 2001); Arcadian Corp. v. Olin Corp., 698 So. 2d 9 (La. App. 1997), *writ. den.*, 827 So. 2d 1174 (La. 2002).

299. Travelers EnergyMax 21, § E.3.b; ISO Form BM 00 20 07 01, § E.3.b.

300. Travelers EnergyMax 21, § E.3.c.

301. Travelers EnergyMax 21, § E.3.d.

302. There also may be more than one commercial property insurance carrier. *See, e.g.*, Ark. Power & Light Co. v. Hartford Steam Boiler Inspection & Ins. Co., 257 F.3d 853 (8th Cir. 2001) (insured had one boiler and machinery policy, but its property insurance was provided by six carriers).

for excess coverage.[303] Those insurers will share responsibility for half of the disputed amount. A clause may say the disputed amount has to be reduced by the amount of the highest deductible in any of the policies.[304]

If an insured accepts proceeds paid pursuant to a Joint or Disputed Loss clause, it does not waive any other rights against the company that issued the equipment breakdown policy.[305] When the insurers pay the claim and the insured accepts the payment, an agreement arises between the insurers to proceed with arbitration, in which the insured agrees to participate but not intervene.[306] Under the ISO Equipment Breakdown Protection Coverage Form, the carrier that is determined to be responsible for the larger percentage of the ultimate loss has to return the excess contribution to the other insurer, and the former has to pay liquidated damages to the latter on the amount of that insurer's excess contribution.[307]

Arguably, a suit by the insurers against a third party to which they are subrogated should not be brought until after the arbitration because the apportionment will ultimately determine the loss of each insurer, and if the whole loss is borne by one insurer, the other has no interest in pursuing the claim against the third party. However, where no evidence was presented that any court had ordered arbitration, a Louisiana appellate court ruled a suit against a third party could proceed.[308]

[c] Comparable Clause in Commercial Property Policy

B&M policies routinely incorporate a Joint or Disputed Loss clause, but commercial property policies usually do not.[309] Both policies have to include the provision for the insured to benefit.[310] Unless the general commercial property and B&M coverage is provided by the same company,[311] the agreement has

---

303. If the excess policy is "follow the form," it would be deemed to include the Joint or Disputed Loss clause. If it is not, the excess policy would need to have its own clause.

304. *See, e.g.*, Arcadian Corp. v. Olin Corp., 698 So. 2d 9 (La. App. 1997), *writ. den.*, 827 So. 2d 1174 (La. 2002) (where all-risk property policies had deductibles of $500,000 and boiler and machinery had deductible of $1,750,000, latter applied). *Accord* Ark. Power & Light Co. v. Hartford Steam Boiler Inspection & Ins. Co., 257 F.3d 853 (8th Cir. 2001).

305. Travelers EnergyMax 21, § E.3.d.(6).

306. Travelers EnergyMax 21, § E.3.e.

307. ISO Form BM 00 20 07 01, § E.3.f.

308. Arcadian Corp. v. Olin Corp., 698 So. 2d 9 (La. App. 1997), *writ. den.*, 827 So. 2d 1174 (La. 2002).

309. Austin, *Equipment Breakdown—More Than Just Boiler and Machinery* (2011), IRMI, http://www.irmi.com/articles/expert-commentary/equipment-breakdown.

310. Boggs, *Three Commercial Property Endorsements Every Client Should Have* (July 27, 2009), My New Markets, http://www.mynewmarkets.com/articles/102464/three-commercial-property-endorsements-every-client-should-have.

311. That can happen when there is a combined commercial property/equipment breakdown policy. Boggs, *Three Commercial Property Endorsements Every Client Should Have* (July 27, 2009), My New Markets, http://www.mynewmarkets.com/articles/102464/three-commercial-property-endorsements-every-client-should-have. *See also* Malecki, *Equipment Breakdown*

to be appended to the commercial property policy by endorsement. ISO has a standard endorsement form for commercial property policies.

[d] ISO Endorsement

An ISO endorsement modifies commercial property policies.[312] It states that it is intended to facilitate payment of insurance proceeds when both boiler and machinery and commercial property policies are in effect, damage occurs to covered property that is insured by both policies, and there is dispute between the insurers over whether there is coverage or the amount of loss to be paid, if any, by each of them under their respective policies.[313]

The endorsement does not apply when neither insurer admits to any liability and neither one maintains that coverage applies under the other policy.[314] Also, it only applies if the B&M policy has a similar provision at the time of the loss or damage, containing substantially the same requirements, procedures, and conditions, the damage to the covered property was caused by a loss for which both insurers acknowledge some liability, and the total amount of loss is agreed to by the insured and the insurers.[315]

When the endorsement does apply, the insurers will pay, after a written request from the insured, the entire amount of loss each agrees is covered, if any, by its policy and one-half the amount of the loss in dispute.[316] If the insured accepts the payments, it does not alter, waive, or surrender any other rights against the commercial property carrier.[317]

Arbitration is provided for under the endorsement. If both companies acknowledge some liability under their respective policies and agree to submit the differences to arbitration, they will determine the amount each will pay, and then pay the insured within 90 days.[318] Otherwise, they agree to submit their dispute to arbitration within 90 days after payment.[319] By the terms of the endorsement, the policyholder agrees to cooperate with any arbitration procedures.[320] The insurer that is found responsible for the larger percentage of the ultimate loss has to return the excess contribution to the other insurer, and the former has to pay liquidated damages to the latter on the amount of the excess contribution of that insurer.[321]

Insurance: Too Important to Ignore! at 8 (2009), Adjusting Today, *available at* http://adjustersinternational.com/publications/adjusting-today/equipment-breakdown-insurance/1/.

312. ISO Form CP 12 70 09 96.
313. ISO Form CP 12 70 09 96, § A.
314. ISO Form CP 12 70 09 96, § B.
315. ISO Form CP 12 70 09 96, § C.
316. ISO Form CP 12 70 09 96, § D.
317. ISO Form CP 12 70 09 96, § D.6.
318. ISO Form CP 12 70 09 96, § E.1.
319. ISO Form CP 12 70 09 96, § E.2.
320. ISO Form CP 12 70 09 96, § E.3.
321. ISO Form CP 12 70 09 96, § F.

[8] Privilege of Insurer to Adjust with Owner

There is usually a condition regarding property of third parties that is in the care, custody, or control of the insured. Typically, in the event of loss, damage, or expense involving that property, the insurer has the right to settle with the *owner* of the property, and settlement satisfies any claim the insured has against the insurer.[322]

[9] Defense of Insured

Generally, the insurer has the right to defend its insured at its expense against suits that arise from claims of owners of property in the care, custody, or control of the insured, but the insurer is not obligated to do so.[323] Under a Travelers Equipment Breakdown policy, the insurer has the right *and duty* to defend the insured when there is damage to property of another that is in the care, custody, or control of the insured for which the insured is legally liable and that was caused by a breakdown to covered equipment.[324] If a claim or suit is brought against the insured that alleges it is liable, the Travelers policy says the company may either settle the claim or suit or defend it while reserving the right to settle at any time.[325]

[10] Transfer of Rights of Recovery against Others to Insurer

A "subrogation clause" is standard in B&M policies. The clause concerns transfer of rights of recovery to the insurance company.[326] A basic version of the clause is found in the ISO Boiler and Machinery Coverage Form. Under it, if any person or organization to or for whom the insurer makes payment has rights to recover damages from another, the rights are transferred to the insurer to the extent of its payment.[327] The HSB policy adds that before an accident, an insured may waive its rights against another party in writing, but after it the insured may only waive those rights if at the time of the accident the other party was someone insured under the policy or was a business firm owned or controlled by the insured or that owns or controls the insured.[328]

---

322. HSB Freestyle Policy Form 6671 (10/2002) § F.12; ISO Form BM 00 20 07 01, § E.1.i.

323. HSB Freestyle Policy Form 6671 (10/2002) § E.5; ISO Form BM 00 20 07 01, § E.1.c. *See generally Boiler and Machinery Coverage Form* (Summit Business Media, 2013) (defense condition is placed in policy because property of others for which insured is legally liable is considered covered property, and breakdown of covered equipment of insured could easily damage property of others and lead to lawsuit against insured).

324. Travelers EnergyMax 21, § E.1.c.(1).

325. Travelers EnergyMax 21, § E.1.c.(2).

326. *Boiler and Machinery Coverage Form* (Summit Business Media, 2013).

327. ISO Form BM 00 25 02 91, § E.1.f. The person or organization is then required do everything necessary to secure the rights of the insurer and is prohibited from doing anything after a loss to impair those rights.

328. HSB Freestyle Policy Form 6671 (10/2002) § F.14.

[11] Suspension

A suspension clause applies when covered equipment is found to be in a "dangerous condition" or exposed to one. Unfortunately, "dangerous condition" is usually not defined in policies. Whenever a "dangerous condition" is found, any representative of the insurer can suspend the coverage against loss from a "breakdown" to that "covered equipment."[329] Usually the suspension is initiated by delivering or mailing a written notice to the last known address of the insured or the address where the covered equipment is located.[330] Once there is a suspension, coverage can only be reinstated by an endorsement for the covered equipment at issue.[331]

8.10 Endorsements

Endorsements can add to, subtract from, or modify a policy. One endorsement for B&M policies may be titled either "Actual Cash Value" or a "Repair or Replacement." It eliminates the standard property damage valuation clause and replaces it with language that states the insurer will pay the amount the insured spends to repair or replace covered property directly damaged by a breakdown and that valuation will be as of the time of the breakdown.[332] The insurer will not, however, pay for damaged property that is obsolete and useless to the insured.

In many states there are statutes or regulations imposing requirements on insurers, and an endorsement is automatically added to a policy to conform its contents to those requirements. An endorsement may govern time limits on contractual performance, for example, extending the time period for submitting a proof of loss when there is a declared disaster.[333] Other endorsements may require insurers to provide a written estimate of damages to real property on request.[334] There are state-specific endorsements that add a Joint or Disputed Loss Agreement to a policy.[335]

---

329. ISO Form BM 00 20 07 01, § E.2.i.
330. HSB Freestyle Policy Form 6671 (10/2002) § F.13.
331. ISO Form BM 00 20 07 01, § E.2.i.
332. ISO Form BM 99 59 07 01. *Consider* Cafritz Co. v. Employers Commercial Union Ins. Co., 309 A.2d 302 (D.C. 1973) (endorsement providing loss meant amount actually expended by insured to repair or replace property shifted ultimate burden of persuasion to insurer, it being at most sufficient to establish, *prima facie*, extent of loss).
333. ISO Form BM 01 01 07 01.
334. ISO Form BM 01 37 05 02.
335. *See, e.g.*, ISO Form BM 01 29 12 97 (Rhode Island changes—Joint or Disputed Loss Agreement); ISO Form BM 01 32 12 98 (Texas changes—Joint or Disputed Loss Agreement).

8.11 Successive Insurers

It is possible that covered equipment will experience an initial accident or breakdown and then, after repair, undergo subsequent accidents or breakdowns. If the insured changes insurers, which company is responsible during a series of equipment failures? In one case the motor of an air-conditioning unit chiller had a mechanical breakdown that was a covered loss. Two days after the loss, the insured cancelled the policy and acquired coverage from a different insurer. The previous insurer accepted liability and instructed the insured to repair the motor. Less than a month later, the motor failed again. It failed two more times in the months following. The court said that even assuming the subsequent breakdowns were proximately caused by ineffective repair, they happened when the first policy was no longer in effect. Thus, the first insurer was not liable for the later losses.[336]

Which policy provides coverage is not always apparent, and insureds do not always retain expired policies. The insured has the burden to show coverage.[337] That generally means proving that there is a policy covering the loss.[338] Many courts say that the policy has to be attached to the complaint in an action against an insurer.[339] If the policy cannot be produced, however, courts usually allow evidence of its contents to be introduced.[340] While a court may accept a sample policy of the type apparently issued by the insurer at the time the policy in question was issued,[341] that will not provide critical information found on the Declarations Page, for example, specific limits of insurance or endorsements that were added to the policy.

---

336. Community Federal Sav. & Loan Ass'n v. Hartford Steam Boiler Inspection & Ins. Co., 580 F. Supp. 1170 (E.D. Mo. 1984) (replacement insurer covered subsequent failures as each mechanical breakdown was sudden and accidental). *See also* Resorts International, Inc. v. American Home Assurance Co., 311 So. 2d 806 (Fla. 3d DCA 1975).

337. *See, e.g.*, Borough of Sayreville v. Bellefonte Ins. Co., 320 N.J. Super. 598, 605, 728 A.2d 225, 228 (1998).

338. Gold Fields Am. Corp. v. Aetna Cas. & Sur. Co., 173 Misc. 2d 901, 904, 661 N.Y.S.2d 948, 950 (1997).

339. *See, e.g.*, Karaskiewicz v. Allstate Ins. Co. (*In re* Am. Arbitration Ass'n Arbitration), 109 Ill. App. 2d 370, 372, 248 N.E.2d 756, 758 (1969); State Farm Mut. Auto. Ins. Co. v. Jones, 98 Ga. App. 46, 56, 104 S.E.2d 725, 733 (1958).

340. *See, e.g.*, Rubenstein v. Royal Ins. Co. of Am., 44 Mass. App. Ct. 842, 846, 694 N.E.2d 381, 384 (1998); Borough of Sayreville v. Bellefonte Ins. Co., 320 N.J. Super. 598, 605, 728 A.2d 225, 228 (1998); Fraser v. Metropolitan Life Ins. Co., 165 Wash. 667, 669, 5 P.2d 978, 980 (1931). *See generally* Jones, *No Policy, No Problem? How Insureds are Finding Coverage Even Though They Can't Find Their Policies*, 50 Drake L. Rev. 611 (2002).

341. *See, e.g.*, Gold Fields Am. Corp. v. Aetna Cas. & Sur. Co., 173 Misc. 2d 901, 906, 661 N.Y.S.2d 948, 951 (1997).

9

Recovering under Commercial General Liability Insurance

9.1 Introduction

Commercial general liability insurance—sometimes referred to as "public liability"—is known by the acronym "CGL." Most CGL insurance is written on standardized forms developed by the Insurances Services Office, Inc. (ISO).[1] Indeed, because of the uniformity of language in CGL policies, courts cite and find particularly persuasive decisions from courts in other jurisdictions.[2]

CGL insurance covers damages a court might award in litigation against the insured as well as the costs of defending the insured in any suit. The duty of the insurer to defend is an obligation that is independent from the duty to pay claims under the policy.[3] Often, the duty to defend is the most important part of the coverage because the insured party may prevail in a legal action and still incur substantial expenses in its defense.[4] In fact, when an insured

1. Cypress Point Condo. Ass'n v. Adria Towers, L.L.C., 226 N.J. 403, 417, 143 A.3d 273, 281 (2016) (although not required to do so, most insurers prepare their CGL policies based on ISO's standard forms); Am. Family Mut. Ins. Co. v. Am. Girl, Inc., 268 Wis. 2d 16, 33, 673 N.W.2d 65, 74 (2004).

2. Am. Home Assur. Co. v. AGM Marine Contractors, Inc., 467 F.3d 810, 812 (1st Cir. 2006) (absent state precedent, decisions elsewhere construing standard CGL language may be useful); R.N. Thompson & Assocs., Inc. v. Monroe Guar. Ins. Co., 686 N.E.2d 160, 162 (Ind. App. 1997) (because of uniformity of language in CGL policies, factually similar decisions from courts elsewhere are particularly persuasive).

3. Henning v. Contl. Cas. Co., 254 F.3d 1291, 1295 (11th Cir. 2001). *See also* Morgan Int'l Realty v. Dade Underwriters Ins. Agency, 617 So. 2d 455, 457 (Fla. 3d DCA 1993) (duty to defend is distinct from and broader than duty to indemnify).

4. Jerry, *The Insurer's Right to Reimbursement of Defense Costs*, 42 Ariz. L. Rev. 13 (2000) (as percentage of total claims costs, expense of providing defenses to insureds is considerable and according to industry data, approximately 14 percent of expenditures on claims is attributable to defense costs).

loses a case, the defense costs may be considerably greater than the damages awarded.[5]

Standard CGL policies provide three coverages: bodily injury and property damage (Coverage A), personal and advertising injury (Coverage B), and medical payments (Coverage C). The property damage portion of Coverage A does not cover damage to the property of the insured.[6] Instead, its purpose is to insure against *liability* for damage to the property of others for which the insured is responsible. This coverage can apply when the insured is alleged to be responsible for water damage to the property of another. This can happen in several circumstances:

- The insured caused water on its property to enter the property of a third party.[7]
- The insured caused water over which it had control to enter the property of a third party.[8]

---

5. Pine Cone Harbour Condo. Ass'n v. Nationwide Mut. Ins. Co., 1993 U.S. Dist. LEXIS 21429 (W.D. Va. Oct. 19, 1993), *aff'd*, 30 F.3d 130 (4th Cir. 1994) (underlying suit against association was settled for relatively small amount; however, association incurred substantial legal fees in its defense of action for which insurer disclaimed liability and refused to defend).

6. *See* State Farm Fire & Cas. Co. v. Metro. Mgmt., 2007 U.S. Dist. LEXIS 99406 (D. Haw. Oct. 31, 2007) (clearly, purpose of owned property exclusion is to prevent liability coverage designed to protect an insured from third-party claims from being turned into first-party property coverage for losses to insured's own property); Porter v. Clarendon Nat'l Ins. Co., 76 Mass. App. Ct. 655, 660, 925 N.E.2d 58, 62, *rev. den.*, 457 Mass. 1103, 928 N.E.2d 950 (2010) ("own, rent, or occupy" exclusion is common to commercial general liability policies and prevents insured from using general liability policy as property insurance); State Farm v. English Cove Assocs., 121 Wn. App. 358, 360–61, 88 P.3d 986, 988 (2004) (owned property exclusion is intended to prevent general liability policy from providing first-party benefits to insured).

7. *See, e.g.*, Grinnell Mut. Reinsurance Co. v. Hubbs, 370 Ill. Dec. 563, 988 N.E.2d 761 (Ill. App. 2013) (plaintiff in underlying action alleged damage to cropland after insureds altered flow and level of surface and groundwater by constructing dam and holding pond on insured property); Lone Star Steakhouse & Saloon, Inc. v. Liberty Mut. Ins. Group, 343 F. Supp. 2d 989 (D. Kan. 2004) (as part of construction of its restaurant, insured built and maintained storage basin on its property to handle stormwater runoff and adjacent property owner alleged that overflow from that water basin damaged its property).

8. *See, e.g.*, Essex Ins. Co. v. H & H Land Dev. Corp., 525 F. Supp. 2d 1344 (M.D. Ga. 2007) (property owners sued insured alleging that development by insured of adjacent subdivision artificially increased surface water runoff causing their properties to be damaged by excess stormwater and silt, sediment, and debris that accompanied it); Home Depot U.S.A., Inc. v. Nat'l Fire Ins. Co., 2007 U.S. Dist. LEXIS 20032 (N.D. Tex. Mar. 21, 2007) (plaintiff in underlying suit alleged excavation for Home Depot site caused water runoff that resulted in loss of lateral support for, and damage to, its apartment buildings and real property); Great Northern Ins. Co. v. Interior Constr. Corp., 823 N.Y.S.2d 765, 7 N.Y.3d 412, 857 N.E.2d 60 (2006) (subcontractor worked on existing sprinkler system for tenant and failed to drain pipes properly before beginning work and flood occurred, causing property damage to premises of tenant on floor below); Bituminous Casualty Corp. v. Burns, 200 So. 2d 612 (Fla. 3d DCA 1967), *cert. den.*, 204 So. 2d 326 (Fla. 1967) (insured, while constructing storm sewer, closed off canal end of local storm sewer but did not remove dam from outfall during hurricane and in heavy rains incident to storm, water backed up in area and inundated property of third party); Vappi & Co. v. Aetna Casualty & Surety Co., 348 Mass. 427, 204 N.E.2d 273 (1965) (insured builder was

- The insured caused water to damage the property of a third party while performing work on the property of that party.[9]
- The insured caused the flow of water in a watercourse not on its property to be impeded and enter the property of a third party.[10]
- The activities of the insured exacerbated a flood.[11]
- The insured failed to disclose to a buyer or tenant that property was flood prone when the insured had a duty to do so.[12]
- There was negligent planning and preparation for anticipated flooding by an insured landlord or managing agent.[13]

9.2 The Underlying Claim

The underlying action for water damage against the insured will often be for negligence, although trespass and nuisance are also possible causes of action.[14] The viability of these actions will depend on the law of the pertinent jurisdiction, a topic beyond the scope of this discussion.[15]

Generally, as set forth in the Restatement, one is subject to liability for a private nuisance if his or her conduct is a legal cause of an invasion of another's interest in the private use and enjoyment of land, and the invasion is

---

sued by neighboring property owner who sought to recover for negligent diversion of surface water onto her premises from raising grade of property where work took place).

9. *See, e.g.*, Kenneth Cole Prods. v. Mid-Continent Cas. Co., 763 F. Supp. 2d 1331 (S.D. Fla. 2010) (during construction project employee of insured caused damage to property by negligently striking fire sprinkler, which then dispersed water and caused flood that resulted in $141,000 worth of water damage).

10. *See, e.g.*, Travelers Indem. Co. v. Holman, 330 F.2d 142 (5th Cir. 1964): (heavy rains caused surface water that in turn caused loose dirt fill on property of insured to slip down into creek, damming it up and resulting in overflow onto property of claimants).

11. *See, e.g.*, Saden v. Kirby, 759 So. 2d 921 (La. App. 2000) (Sewerage & Water Board found negligent for failing to timely repair electrical feeder line that supplied power to two of three pumps at drainage pumping station, resulting in 2.5 inches of additional flood waters and prolongation of period of flooding); Columbia Casualty Co. v. United States Fidelity & Guar. Co., 178 Ariz. 104, 870 P.2d 1200 (Ariz. App. 1994) (landowners adjacent and downstream from insured asserted that activities by the insured on river banks increased flood damage to their property).

12. *See, e.g.*, Thompson v. Best, 478 N.E.2d 79 (Ind. App. 1985) (in response to buyer's question, seller denied home had water problems, but basement flooded shortly after sale and did so periodically; court found buyer established elements of fraud).

13. *See, e.g.*, Hernandez-Ortiz v. 2 Gold, LLC, 2017 N.Y. Misc. LEXIS 3685 (Sept. 27, 2017) (tenants' property damaged in Hurricane Sandy).

14. Clayman, *After Me, the Flood: Liability and Damages for Water Run-Off* at 7, Eagle Law, *available at* available at: www.eagle-law.com/wp-content/uploads/Paper-Clayman.pdf.

15. *See* Dobbs, Hayden, & Bublick, *Dobbs' Law of Torts*, §§ 53, 121, 398, 403, 441 (2d ed. Thompson West 2021) for a general discussion of water damage and actions for negligence, nuisance, and trespass. Note that trespass or nuisance might not be covered under a CGL policy as "property damage" but could be covered under the "personal and advertising injury" coverage.

either intentional and unreasonable or unintentional and otherwise actionable under the rules on liability for negligent or reckless conduct, or for abnormally dangerous conditions or activities.[16] The Restatement specifically says that an invasion of an interest in the use and enjoyment of land that results from interference with the flow of surface water may constitute a nuisance.[17] Nuisance actions have been brought where water from the common areas of a homeowners association flooded the basements of individual homes,[18] water poured over the gutter and onto the front of the plaintiff's building,[19] and construction of a swimming pool altered the flow of surface water onto a neighboring property, diminishing its value.[20]

One is subject to liability for trespass, according to the Restatement, if he or she intentionally enters land in the possession of another, or causes a thing or a third person to do so, or fails to remove from the land a thing that he or she is under a duty to remove.[21] Additionally, one who recklessly or negligently enters land in the possession of another or causes a thing or third person to enter is subject to liability to the possessor if his or her presence or the presence of the thing or the third person on the land causes harm to the land, to the possessor, or to a thing or a third person in whose security the possessor has a legally protected interest.[22] One court has stated that if someone without the permission of the person in possession of land pours a bucket of water on it, he or she commits a trespass.[23] A trespass action was brought when a surface water drainage system was installed that caused all of the surface water from the area to be collected into drains and then to be discharged on the plaintiff's land.[24] A trespass action was also brought where an electric company built a dam across a stream, causing the water from that stream to back up, over, and around the lands of the plaintiff.[25]

When a claim concerns *surface water*, liability depends on the drainage law doctrine adopted in a particular state.[26] Some states follow the "common

16. Restatement (Second) of Torts, § 822 (1979).

17. Restatement (Second) of Torts, § 833 (1979).

18. Shadow Group v. Heather Hills Home Owners Ass'n, 156 N.C. App. 197, 579 S.E.2d 285 (2003) (water from common areas of association flowed into basements of various townhouses and constituted nuisance).

19. Sixty-Eight Devonshire, Inc. v. Shapiro, 348 Mass. 177, 202 N.E.2d 811 (1964).

20. Angeles v. Larson, 249 S.W.3d 278 (Mo. App. 2008).

21. Restatement (Second) of Torts, § 158 (1979).

22. Restatement (Second) of Torts, § 165 (1979). This definition of "trespass" includes entry as a result of an abnormally dangerous activity.

23. Snow v. Columbia, 305 S.C. 544, 409 S.E.2d 797 (S.C. App. 1991).

24. Chesarone v. Pinewood Builders, Inc., 345 Mass. 236, 186 N.E.2d 712 (1962).

25. Scheurich v. Empire Dist. Elec. Co., 188 S.W. 114 (Mo. 1916).

26. This topic is beyond the scope of this discussion. There are entire treatises focused on it. *See, e.g.*, Beck & Kelley, *Waters and Water Rights* (Matthew Bender, 2021); Tarlock & Robison, *Law of Water Rights and Resources* (Clark Boardman Callaghan, 2021). There are also state-specific books. *See, e.g.*, Slater, *California Water Law and Policy* (Matthew Bender, 2021);

enemy" rule under which one may control the flow of surface water over his or her own premises, without any obligation to neighboring properties.[27] That rule has been subject to many exceptions and limitations.[28] In many jurisdictions the rule is one of "reasonable use" under which liability arises when the defendant's conduct is either intentional and unreasonable or negligent, reckless, or in the course of an abnormally dangerous activity.[29]

9.3 Definition of "Property Damage"

There are two parts to the definition of "property damage." First, it means *physical injury* to "tangible property,"[30] including any resulting loss of its use.[31] The Illinois Supreme Court explained that tangible property suffers a *physical* injury when it is "altered in appearance, shape, color or in other material dimension,"[32] but it does not experience *physical* injury if it suffers intangible damage, for example, diminution in value as a result of the failure of a component.[33] The standard commercial general liability policy does not

---

Brown, Bryan & McElyea, *Montana Water Law* (Rocky Mtn. Mineral Law Found. 2021); Ciliberto & Zilis, *Colorado Water Law Benchbook* (CBA-CLE 2019).

27. Morrison v. Bucksport & Bangor R.R. Co., 67 Me. 353, 355 (1877).

28. *See* Gerrard, *Environmental Law Practice Guide* § 21.02[1][c] (Matthew Bender 2021) for an overview of the "modified common enemy" rule. *See also* Elliott, *Diffused Surface Water in Wyoming: Ascertaining Property Owners' Rights and Settling Disputes*, 11 Wyo. L. Rev. 409, 414–15 (2011).

29. Heins Implement Co. v. Missouri Highway & Transp. Comm'n, 859 S.W.2d 681, 689 (Mo. 1993).

30. *See* Mid-Continent Cas. Co. v. Acad. Dev., Inc., 2010 U.S. Dist. LEXIS 87637 (S.D. Tex. Aug. 24, 2010) (no requirement that tangible property belong to plaintiffs in underlying action).

31. *See, e.g.*, ISO Form CG 00 01 12 07, § V.17.a. All loss of use is deemed to occur at the time of the physical injury that caused it. Loss of use is "property damage" and, therefore, physical injury to the property is not required under the clear language of the standard CGL policy. Frankenmuth Mut. Ins. Co. v. Mitch Harris Bldg. Co., 2012 Mich. App. LEXIS 194 (Mich. App. Jan. 31, 2012).

32. The first evidence of water damage is often stained ceilings or walls. In *Emplrs. Mut. Cas. Co. v. Kenny Hayes Custom Homes, LLC*, 2016 U.S. Dist. LEXIS 15340 (S.D. Ala. Feb. 9, 2016), the insurer argued there was no "property damage" where walls in a home were stained. The change in color, contended the insurer, did not alter the material substance of the wall and the damage was, therefore, not a physical injury. The court did not agree. While damage to the exterior of the walls might seem small, it was damage to physical property and the court found that even if only the alleged exterior damage to the walls was considered, before the walls were opened for inspection, there was a physical injury to the property.

33. Traveler's Ins. Co. v. Eljer Mfg., 258 Ill. Dec. 792, 197 Ill. 2d 278, 301–02, 757 N.E.2d 481, 496 (2001) (term "physical" limits word "injury" in policy definition of "property damage," and phrase "physical injury" does not include intangible damage to property, such as economic loss and, therefore, diminution in value of whole, resulting from failure of component to perform as promised, does not constitute physical injury). *See also* Phibro Animal Health Corp. v. National Union Fire Ins. Co., 446 N.J. Super. 419,437, 142 A.3d 761, 771 (2016); Cunningham v. Universal Underwriters, 98 Cal. App. 4th 1141, 1155, 120 Cal. Rptr. 2d 162, 173 (2002) (coverage for claims alleging damage to or loss of use of *tangible* property means there is no coverage for loss of use of intangible property rights and tangible property refers to things

define "tangible property," but courts have said it is "that which is capable of being handled, touched, or physically possessed."[34] The limitation of property damage to physical injury to tangible property generally means the basic coverage does not apply to purely economic losses, meaning lost profits, goodwill, or loss of investment.[35] The second meaning of property damage is loss of use of tangible property not physically injured.[36] An Oregon appellate court explained this portion of the coverage. The owner of a building alleged that inadequate window assemblies caused a delay in completion and occupancy of its building, with resulting loss of rental income. The court said the delay in completion and occupancy was an injury that constituted loss of use of tangible property that had not been physically injured or destroyed, and that was property damage for which coverage clearly applied.[37]

When water leaks into a newly constructed building, an insurer may argue that correcting faulty workmanship is not covered because faulty workmanship does not constitute "property damage." Courts would agree, but they distinguish the faulty workmanship from the damage caused by it, for example, damage to the interior of a building caused by the water.[38]

9.4 Known Loss

The "known loss" rule has been called a cousin of the fortuity doctrine.[39] The latter, often viewed as an "implied exclusion," is the fundamental principal that insurance does not cover a loss that is not "fortuitous."[40] The idea behind

---

that can be touched, seen, and smelled and as matter of law interference with non-possessory interest in land of another does not satisfy that definition).

34. Lamar Truck Plaza, Inc. v. Sentry Ins., 757 P.2d 1143, 1144 (Colo. App. 1988) (purely economic losses—lost profits or investment—are not included in definition of "tangible property). *See also* Graber v. State Farm Fire & Casualty Co., 244 Mont. 265, 269, 797 P.2d 214, 216 (Mont. 1990). *But see* Dietrich v. Travelers Ins. Co., 551 So. 2d 64, 66 (La. App. 1989) (Louisiana Supreme Court equates "tangible property" with "corporeal property," and thus, although right to benefits payable under health and disability policy may be intangible, actual benefits that would have been payable constitute tangible property, that is, money).

35. Johnson, *The Practical Art: On the Archaeology and Architecture of Liability Insurance Contracts*, 78 Def. Couns. J. 143, 162 (2011). *Consider* Land v. Auto-Owners Ins. Co., 511 Fed. Appx. 795 (10th Cir. 2013) (conclusory allegations of property damage in underlying complaint alleging physical injury to or loss of use of tangible property insufficient; insured failed to show that underlying suit challenging propriety of assessment of, and attempts to collect, homeowners fees, alleged property damage).

36. *See, e.g.*, ISO Form CG 00 01 12 07, § V.17.b. These losses of use are deemed to occur at the time of the occurrence that caused them.

37. Milgard Mfg., Inc. v. Continental Ins. Co., 92 Ore. App. 609, 613, 759 P.2d 1111, 1112 (1988) (injury, however, came squarely within policy exclusion).

38. *See, e.g.*, Travelers Indem. Co. v. Miller Bldg. Corp., 97 Fed. Appx. 431 (4th Cir. 2004).

39. Martinez, *A Unified Theory of Insurance Risk*, 74 U. Pitt. L. Rev. 713, 742 (2013).

40. *See, e.g.*, Easy Corner, Inc. v. State Nat'l Ins. Co., 154 F. Supp. 3d 151 (E.D. Pa. 2016) (implied "fortuity exclusion" precludes coverage for losses arising from non-fortuitous events). *See generally* Cozen & Bennett, *Fortuity: The Unnamed Exclusion*, 20 Forum 222 (1985).

the fortuity doctrine is that "insurance is intended to cover losses that occur by chance."[41] The "known loss" rule is basically that a policyholder cannot buy an insurance policy to obtain coverage for a loss that he or she knows has already occurred.[42] The standard commercial general liability policy reflects the rule as it provides that it applies to property damage only if prior to the policy period, no insured and no employee authorized by the named insured to give or receive notice of an occurrence or claim knew that the property damage had occurred, in whole or part.[43] The rule is illustrated in a Georgia case in which the plaintiff property owners sued the insured alleging the insured's development of an adjacent subdivision artificially increased surface water runoff and caused their properties to be damaged by the excess stormwater, silt, sediment, and debris. The insurer denied coverage because the damage was a known loss that was not subject to coverage. The court rejected application of the known loss rule because the insurer presented no evidence that the insured ever reported the alleged property damage to any insurer or received a demand or claim for damages from the plaintiffs.[44]

9.5 Coverage for an "Occurrence"[45]

[1] Introduction

Under a commercial general liability policy, the carrier will pay sums the insured is legally obligated to pay as damages to which the coverage applies.[46] Coverage applies only if the property damage is caused by an "occurrence."[47] The occurrence has to take place in the "coverage territory"[48] and during the

41. Martinez, *A Unified Theory of Insurance Risk*, 74 U. Pitt. L. Rev. 713, 742 (2013).

42. Holley, *The "Fortuity Doctrine": Misapplying the Known Loss Rule to Liability Insurance Policies*, 41 Tex. Tech. L. Rev. 529, 531 (2009).

43. ISO Form CG 00 01 12 07, § I.A.1.b.(3).

44. Essex Ins. Co. v. H & H Land Dev. Corp., 525 F. Supp. 2d 1344 (M.D. Ga. 2007). Note that the policy had a "known loss" endorsement under which it only provided coverage for property damage when prior to the policy period, no insured knew the property damage had occurred, in whole or in part. The court said that under the endorsement, a loss that was known to have occurred before the policy period was not covered. Note that the language of the endorsement is nearly identical to that of ISO Form CG 00 01 12 07, § I.A.1.b.(3).

45. *See generally* Dykes, *Occurrences, Accidents, and Expectations: A Primer of These (and Some Other) Insurance-Law Concepts*, 2003 Utah L. Rev. 831 (2003).

46. *See, e.g.*, ISO Form CG 00 01 12 07, § I.A.1.a.

47. *See, e.g.*, ISO Form CG 00 01 12 07, § I.A.1.b.(1).

48. The basic coverage territory is the United States and its territories and possessions, Puerto Rico, and Canada. *See, e.g.*, CG 00 01 12 07, § V.4.a. The coverage territory includes international waters or airspace, but only if the injury or damage occurs during travel or transportation between the United States and its territories and possessions, Puerto Rico, or Canada. *See, e.g.*, CG 00 01 12 07, § V.4.b. The coverage territory also includes any other part of the world if the injury or damage arises out of goods or products made or sold by the insured in the United States and its territories and possessions, Puerto Rico, or Canada, activities of a person

policy period.[49] Additionally, the coverage applies only if, prior to the policy period, no insured[50] and no employee[51] authorized by the named insured to give or receive notice of an occurrence or claim, knew that the property damage had occurred, in whole or in part.[52]

Generally, when occurrence is defined in terms of property damage and property damage is physical injury, there is no occurrence until there is an injury.[53] However, what if there is more than one injured party and injuries to the first cause subsequent injuries to the second? That was the case in the Chicago flood of 1992. The insured contracted to replace pilings at bridges on the Chicago River. The city owned an underground tunnel system beneath the river that was damaged in the fall of 1991 by the negligence of the insured while driving pilings. The following spring, because of the progression of the tunnel damage, water flooded the tunnel system and damaged buildings not owned by the city. One of the insurers argued that the only party injured during the period of its policy was the city. The court refused to limit coverage to the damages suffered by the city. It said it would not impose an interpretation in which a claimant must suffer his or her property damage during the policy period, rather than suffering property damage *caused by or arising out of* property damage during the policy period. Thus, the policy was triggered by

---

whose home is in the United States and its territories and possessions, Puerto Rico, or Canada, but is away for a short time on the business of the insured, or a personal and advertising injury offense that take place through the internet or similar electronic means of communication, provided the responsibility of the insured to pay damages is determined in a suit on the merits, in the United States and its territories and possessions, Puerto Rico, or Canada or in a settlement to which the carrier agrees. *See, e.g.*, CG 00 01 12 07, § V.4.c.

49. *See, e.g.*, ISO Form CG 00 01 12 07, §§ I.A.1.b.(1) & (2). *See also* Fireman's Fund Ins. Co. v. Hartford Fire Ins. Co., 73 F.3d 811 (8th Cir. 1996) (no occurrence within policy period); Porter v. Clarendon Nat'l Ins. Co., 76 Mass. App. Ct. 655, 659, 925 N.E.2d 58, 62, *rev. den.*, 457 Mass. 1103, 928 N.E.2d 950 (2010) (where condominium association built retaining wall and paved two parking spaces on abutting property some time before 2000 and retaining wall and parking spaces remained on that property until abutter sued in 2004, trespass occurred continuously, for duration policies in effect from October 1, 2000, to October 1, 2003); Heather Hill Villas Condo. Ass'n v. Am. Equity Ins. Co., 816 So. 2d 250 (Fla. 2d DCA 2002) (where in underlying action by association against unit owner, unit owner counterclaimed for alleged damages from excessive moisture in her condominium unit, dates in counterclaim were clearly outside term of coverage, and lower court correctly determined there was no coverage).

50. "Insured" means anyone listed in § II.1 of the policy.

51. Employee includes a leased worker—meaning a person leased to the named insured by a labor leasing firm under an agreement to perform duties related to the conduct of the business of the named insured—but not a temporary one. *See, e.g.*, CG 00 01 12 07, § V.5 & 10.

52. *See, e.g.*, ISO Form CG 00 01 12 07, § I.A.1.b.(3). If an insured or authorized employee knew, prior to the policy period, that the property damage occurred, then any continuation, change, or resumption of that damage during or after the policy period is deemed to have been known prior to the policy period.

53. *See, e.g.*, Fireman's Fund Ins. Co. v. Hartford Fire Ins. Co., 73 F.3d 811 (8th Cir. 1996) (gradual deterioration of standpipe's support system was not property damage; subsequent separation of pipe at joint coupling that caused flooding of water was actual injury).

the damage to the tunnel in autumn and covered the resulting flood damage in spring sustained by the building owners.[54]

[a] "Occurrence" as an "Accident"

Commercial general liability policies cover an "occurrence," typically defined as an "accident."[55] They add that an accident includes continuous or repeated exposure to "substantially the same general harmful conditions."[56] They do not, however, define "accident." Generally, common law determines what is, or is not, an accident for purposes of triggering coverage.[57] The meaning of the word has been the subject of countless court opinions and analyzed by the leading treatises on insurance law.[58] In general, an accident is an unforeseen event.[59] As a rule, the determination by a court of whether an event is an accident is based not on whether an act was intended, but whether the injury

---

54. Great Lakes Dredge & Dock Co. v. Commercial Union Assur. Co., 57 F. Supp. 2d 525 (N.D. Ill. 1999).

55. *See, e.g.*, ISO Form CG 00 01 12 07, § V.13.

56. *See* Great Lakes Dredge & Dock Co. v. Commercial Union Assur. Co., 57 F. Supp. 2d 525 (N.D. Ill. 1999) (where tunnel was damaged and damage worsened until six months later, water flooded the tunnel, flooding resulted from "exposure to substantially the same general conditions"). *See also* Admiral Indem. Co. v. 899 Plymouth Court Condo. Ass'n, 2017 U.S. Dist. LEXIS 9803 (Jan. 24, 2017) (repeated leakage of water from pool that caused damage met definition of occurrence as "continuous or repeated exposure").

57. *Accident*, IRMI, https://www.irmi.com/online/insurance-glossary/terms/a/accident.aspx (noting that occasionally "accident" is defined in policy).

58. *See* 3 Jeffrey E. Thomas, *New Appleman on Insurance Law Library Edition* § 18.02[6] (Matthew Bender 2022); Steven Plitt et al., *Couch on Insurance* § 129.3 (3d ed. Supp. 2015). *Consider* Willing v. Cmty. Ass'n Underwriters of Am., Inc., 2007 U.S. Dist. LEXIS 48543 (W.D. Wash. July 5, 2007), where the underlying suit was brought against developers who also served on the board of a condominium association. The association sued them as developers for construction defects and as directors for breach of fiduciary duty based on a conflict of interest in their dual roles. The insurer for the association argued the underlying litigation did not allege "property damage caused by an occurrence" against the developers in their capacity of directors. The court, however, concluded there was evidence property damaged occurred because the defendant failed to maintain and repair the condominium, in violation of their fiduciary duties. There was sufficient evidence to show the association sued for conduct covered by the policy, thereby triggering the duty to defend.

59. *See, e.g.*, Am. Family Mut. Ins. Co. v. Am. Girl, Inc., 268 Wis. 2d 16, 673 N.W.2d 65 (2004) (accident means event that takes place without one's foresight or expectation); Utica Mut. Ins. Co. v. Travelers Indem. Co., 223 Va. 145, 147, 286 S.E.2d 225, 226 (Va. 1982) (incident unexpected from viewpoint of insured); Hauenstein v. St. Paul-Mercury Indem. Co., 242 Minn. 354, 358–59, 65 N.W.2d 122, 126 (1954) (accident is unexpected, unforeseen, or undesigned happening or consequence from either known or unknown cause). *See also* General Cas. Co. v. Image Builders, Inc., 2010 U.S. Dist. LEXIS 115631 (W.D.N.C. Oct. 29, 2010) (where insured contractor allegedly failed to place water drainage pipes properly and to compact and/or grade dirt, resulting in front half of property separating and sliding down face of mountain during heavy rain, property owners maintained "heavy rain" constituted "occurrence"; however, court found that slope failure is natural consequence of faulty site preparation, and purpose of compaction of constructed slope and installation of slope drainage is to prevent heavy rains from destroying that slope and, as result, heavy rain was not separate cause of slope

was intended.[60] However, courts may infer intent to injure where the harm is obvious, for example, battery.[61] When the insured intends to injure another, there is no accident, even though the insured did not foresee the extent of the injury.[62]

These general principles apply regardless of the type of injury at issue including water damage. Thus, unforeseen, unexpected, and unintended property damage will be considered to have been caused by accident.[63] An intentional act, negligently performed, resulting in unintended consequences can be an accident.[64] Although, the distinction between an accidental occurrence

---

failure, but rather means by which faulty construction of slope was brought to its unfortunate fruition).

60. *See, e.g.*, Gruetzmacher v. Acuity, 393 F. Supp. 2d 860, 866 (D. Minn. 2005) (coverage is for unexpected injury even where there was an intent to act). *See also* Lexington Ins. Co. v. Va. Sur. Co., 2013 U.S. Dist. LEXIS 199153 (C.D. Cal. Feb. 26, 2013) (construction of freeway and channel that allegedly resulted in flooding was much more like scenario where occurrence resulting in injury would be deemed an accident especially absent evidence of intent to flood-damaged property).

61. *See generally* Monteleone, *Coverage Issues under Commercial General Liability and Directors' and Officers' Liability Policies*, 18 W. New Eng. L. Rev. 47, 51–57 (1996). The court apparently inferred intent in Cambridge Mut. Fire Ins. Co. v. 1347–49 N. Sedgwick Condo. Ass'n, 2013 U.S. Dist. LEXIS 9750 (N.D. Ill. Jan. 23, 2013). In that case, the owner of a commercial unit in a condominium building asked the association to address a raw sewage backup problem. The association employed a plumber to address the problem, but the sewage backup was not solved. The owner employed a plumber to determine the cause of the backup, and submitted a report and estimate of the needed repairs, but the association did not respond and over the following year the unit flooded with raw sewage on several occasions, including twice in one week. The court granted Judgment on the Pleadings to the association's insurer because the underlying complaint in the action by the unit owner against the association did not allege an occurrence.

62. *See, e.g.*, Hartford Fire Ins. Co. v. Spreen, 343 So. 2d 649, 651 (Fla. 3d DCA 1977) (where insured swung at another, fact that he did not foresee or intend extent of harm inflicted did not convert admitted assault and battery into an accident). *See also* Frankenmuth Mut. Ins. Co. v. Mitch Harris Bldg. Co., 2012 Mich. App. LEXIS 194 (Mich. App. Jan. 31, 2012), where the purchaser of a condominium unit in community developed by the insured claimed her property began to be inundated with flood waters because of defects and deficiencies in the common elements of the community. She alleged numerous defects and deficiencies to the drainage system for her property and the roadways of the development. She contended the insured made material representations about the land including that it was not in a floodplain and/or not subject to flooding and that the roads and drainage system in the community would be adequate for her unit. The insurer responded that claims for fraud and misrepresentation and fraud in the inducement required an intentional act and, therefore, it had no duty to defend or indemnify. The court agreed. It said the claims did not satisfy the "occurrence" requirement under the policy to trigger coverage because they all require an intentional or reckless act and, thus, were not, by definition, accidental in nature.

63. Bundy Tubing Co. v. Royal Indem. Co., 298 F.2d 151 (6th Cir. 1962) (alleged negligent manufacture of tubing causing it to fail and leak was unforeseen, unexpected, and unintended as it occurred in relatively short time and damage to property was therefore caused by accident).

64. *See* Am. Empire Surplus Lines Ins. Co. v. Hathaway Dev. Co., 288 Ga. 749, 707 S.E.2d 369 (2011) (deliberate act, performed negligently, is accident if effect is not the intended or expected result); McGroarty v. Great American Ins. Co., 43 A.D.2d 368, 351 N.Y.S.2d 428

and an intentional or expected event can prove to be extremely subtle.[65] What is the role of negligence? Courts have said that the term "accident" does not exclude "human fault called negligence,"[66] nor can it be held that negligence is synonymous with accident.[67]

[b] Intentional Act, Accidental Injury

Some courts hold that there is no covered occurrence when an injury is accidentally caused by intentional acts. For instance, in a case before a Georgia federal court, a homeowners association claimed that the developer of a nearby property allowed silt, sediment, and stormwater runoff to leave the property it was developing and damage a lake on the association's property.

(1974), *aff'd*, 368 N.Y.S.2d 485, 36 N.Y.2d 358, 329 N.E.2d 172 (1975) (where insured's construction activities on its property damaged neighbor's property, forewarnings in forms of cracks and water inflow through walls served only to demonstrate negligence of insured in failing either to cease adding burdens on adjoining land or to take precautions against those additions worsening damage already resulting from what had been done up to that point); Vappi & Co. v. Aetna Casualty & Surety Co., 348 Mass. 427, 204 N.E.2d 273 (1965) (neighboring property owner sued insured builder who diverted surface water onto her premises by raising grade of property where work took place for negligence in failing to take precautions to prevent that diversion and harmful results; court found general allegations in underlying complaint would allow proof of injuries that could be regarded as caused by accident because unintended or unforeseen consequences of reckless or negligent acts, and even of intentional acts, at least if not undertaken "with malice or intent to injure" may be within definition of "accident"); Wolk v. Royal Indem. Co., 27 Misc. 2d 478, 210 N.Y.S.2d 677 (1961) (insured in constructing golf course changed contour of land causing neighboring property to flood; damage was an accident as insured did not intend to inflict damage; whether act of insured be negligent, wanton, willful or even violative of criminal statute, if result of that act was not intended then it is accidental). *See also* Purity Spring Resort v. TIG Insurance Co., 2000 U.S. Dist. LEXIS 10918 (D.N.H. July 18, 2000) (where insured had no reason to anticipate property damage from intentionally releasing water from lake, flooding was an accident within meaning of "occurrence" in policy); Baker v. American Ins. Co., 212 F. Supp. 353 (D.S.C.), *aff'd*, 324 F.2d 748 (4th Cir. 1963) (where contractor building shopping center removed all vegetation and unprecedented rain over 5-month period resulted in water damage to adjacent landowners when surface water from construction site crossed street and flowed downhill onto those adjacent properties, losses sustained were completely unexpected, unforeseeable, extraordinary and not intentional). *Compare* Hutchinson Water Co. v. United States Fidelity & G. Co., 250 F.2d 892 (10th Cir. 1957) (where insured water company failed to maintain adequate pressure for fire-fighting purposes and unexpected and unpredicted lightning caused fire that damaged property, those damages could not be said to have been caused by accident as they were natural and probable consequences of negligent act).

65. Essex Ins. Co. v. H & H Land Dev. Corp., 525 F. Supp. 2d 1344, 1349 (M.D. Ga. 2007).

66. United States Fidelity & Guaranty Co. v. Armstrong, 479 So. 2d 1164 (Ala. 1985). *See also* Albuquerque Gravel Products Co. v. American Employers Ins. Co., 282 F.2d 218 (10th Cir. 1960) (suit alleged insured's negligent construction of loading ramp across natural watercourse caused flooding; court found that assuming negligence in construction of ramp, results of floods were not accidental); Iowa Mut. Ins. Co. v. Fred M. Simmons, Inc., 258 N.C. 69, 128 S.E.2d 19 (1962) ("accident," considered in its usual, ordinary, and popular sense does not necessarily exclude human fault called negligence).

67. C. Y. Thomason Co. v. Lumbermens Mut. Casualty Co., 183 F.2d 729 (4th Cir. 1950) (not correct to say that there may not be an accident as result of negligence).

The insurer for the developer argued there was no accident and, therefore, no occurrence. The developer countered that the unintended consequences of its intentional conduct should be considered an accident. The court agreed with the insurance company. It said that the policy only covered injuries from accidental acts, not those accidentally caused by intentional acts. The fact that the builder anticipated damage would result from its activities and unsuccessfully attempted to prevent it did not render its intentional conduct accidental. The court held that because the damage was the result of intentional construction activities, it was not caused by an "occurrence" and thus was not covered.[68] The court, in a subsequent case, acknowledged the holding could create an "awkward environment for commercial parties seeking to offset their risk with insurance" as almost every conceivable accident for which an insured could be held liable would involve some intentional act.[69]

In contrast, many courts will find there to be a covered accident when the insured *intentionally* causes water to enter the property of another but intends no harm to that property. For example, the Alabama Supreme Court found there was an accident where the insured acted intentionally. In that case the insured, while constructing a new sewer system, intentionally crushed an existing sewer line to allow work to proceed on the new line. As a result, sewage

---

68. Owners Ins. Co. v. Chadd's Lake Homeowners Ass'n, 2004 U.S. Dist. LEXIS 30675 (N.D. Ga. Dec. 28, 2004). *See also* Hartford Fire Ins. Co. v. Gandy Dancer, LLC, 864 F. Supp. 2d 1157 (D.N.M. 2012) (where allegation of plaintiff in underlying action was that system, which defendants designed, deposited water on plaintiff's land, resulting water damage was natural consequence of diverting water and not an accident); Monticello Insurance Co. v. Wil-Freds Construction, Inc., 214 Ill. Dec. 597, 277 Ill. App. 3d 697, 705, 661 N.E.2d 451 (1996) (where plaintiff in underlying action sued construction contractor for leaking in parking garage, water damage to lobby of the office building and basement underneath that lobby, and interior water damage caused by water penetration of roof; court held that construction defects set forth in complaint were natural and ordinary consequences of the improper construction techniques and, thus, did not constitute an occurrence). *Compare* Essex Ins. Co. v. H & H Land Dev. Corp., 525 F. Supp. 2d 1344 (M.D. Ga. 2007) where property owners sued alleging that development by the insured of an adjacent subdivision artificially increased surface water runoff from the development site causing their properties to be damaged by excess stormwater and the silt, sediment, and debris that accompanied it. The questions, said the court, were whether the property damage resulted from the unintentional runoff or from the intentional construction activity and at what stage in a chain of causation does intent come into play? Although the construction work was intentional, the runoff was not and it was the runoff, not the intentional construction, that caused injury to the neighboring property owners. Even though the construction activity was clearly intentional, the insured intended to prevent an increase in surface water runoff and failure of that attempt could be found to have been unintentional.

69. *See* Travelers Indem. Co. v. Douglasville Dev., LLC, 2008 U.S. Dist. LEXIS 71956 (N.D. Ga. September 19, 2008) where the claimants in the underlying action alleged that because of land-clearing and earthwork by the insured on adjacent property, an increased volume of water at an increased velocity carrying silt and sediment flowed across their properties. They contended this increased water was the result of negligent design and implementation of a stormwater drainage system and erosion and sediment control plan. The court said that the language of the insured's business liability insurance policy only provided coverage of "random events that involve no element of intent or conscious action."

backed up in the line and overflowed through a manhole onto a nearby property. The insurance company contended that all of the acts that caused the sewage overflow were intended, that the resulting overflow should have been expected and, therefore, that there was no covered occurrence. The court said the legal standard for determining whether an injury was expected or intended is purely subjective: the insured had to have possessed *specific intent* to inflict the damage, and there was no evidence to suggest that the insured specifically intended to discharge raw sewage onto the damaged property.[70] Similarly, in a Florida case, an insured intentionally filled in a watercourse and raised its elevation. That, as the insured knew, blocked the flow of water. The owner of a neighboring property sued the insured alleging that by blocking the flow of water and failing to provide adequate drainage, the insured caused water to back up and flood the plaintiff's property. In the insured's action against the insurer, the court noted that there were no allegations in the underlying complaint that the insured intended to flood the neighboring property or otherwise intentionally cause damage to it or that the insured knew or intended that filling in the watercourse would necessarily cause that property across the street to flood and be damaged in rainstorms. The intentional filling of the watercourse was not an accident, but the unintentional flooding and damage resulting from the negligent failure to provide adequate drainage facilities was an accident as it was neither expected nor intended.[71]

[c] Prior Experience

In a New Hampshire case, the insured, against the urgings of a state agency, released dammed water from its lake and that water flooded a neighboring property on two successive years. The insurer contended that the flooding and resulting damage the second year were not an accident because the insured intentionally released the water when it knew from the prior year that the released water would flood nearby properties. The court responded that because the owner of the damaged property claimed negligence, and the allegations in the complaint would permit an inference that at least in the first year, the insured had no reason to anticipate property damage from releasing

70. United States Fidelity & Guaranty Co. v. Armstrong, 479 So. 2d 1164 (Ala. 1985). *See also* Bituminous Casualty Corp. v. Burns, 200 So. 2d 612 (Fla. 3d DCA 1967), *cert. den.*, 204 So. 2d 326 (Fla. 1967) where the insured was constructing a storm sewer and closed off the canal end of a local storm sewer to prevent water from entering the construction area. It employed pumps to remove water from the site. A hurricane threatened the area and the insured apparently evacuated the site without removing the dam from the outfall into the canal. In the heavy rains incident to the storm, water backed up and inundated a nearby property. The insurance carrier argued there was no coverage because an intended result, or a result that would naturally be expected to follow, would not be an accident. The court did not agree. It concluded that it could not be said as a matter of law that the insured intended, knew, or should have known, that the result of its dam would be the flooding of the neighboring property.

71. Grissom v. Commercial Union Ins. Co., 610 So. 2d 1299 (Fla. 1st DCA 1992).

the water, the earlier flooding was an accident within the meaning of "occurrence" in the policy and, at a minimum, the claims based on earlier flooding would fall within the occurrence language of the policy, triggering coverage.[72]

As the insurer in the New Hampshire case argued, knowledge by the insured of the consequences of its actions in a prior event can preclude a finding of an accident. A Florida court articulated this proposition in a case in which a construction company built a dam in a drainage ditch in close proximity to a neighboring property. After a heavy rain, and as a direct result of the dam, the neighboring property was inundated and damaged. The construction company then removed the dam only to later reconstruct it. The neighboring property was again flooded after another rainstorm. In a suit against the construction company, the owner of the neighboring property contended the company knew that re-erecting the dam would probably result in the flooding of its property. The court said the allegations in the complaint "effectively eliminate" the idea of the "unexpected," which is an important element in a legal definition of the term "accident."[73] A similar conclusion was reached by the Eighth Circuit Court in a case in which a city sewage pump overloaded, shut off, backed up, and flooded a residence. The flooding was repeated five times before the city installed an alarm system to protect against more backups. The court held that the first backup was an "occurrence" but that the city expected the five subsequent backups and, therefore, they were not covered occurrences.[74] Of course, there may still be an accident, an unforeseen event, if there is a reasonable basis for believing there was another cause for the second incident.[75]

---

72. Purity Spring Resort v. TIG Insurance Co., 2000 U.S. Dist. LEXIS 10918 (D.N.H. July 18, 2000). Note that the damage in Purity Spring was bacterial contamination of surface springs caused by the flood waters.

73. Bennett v. Fidelity & Casualty Co., 132 So. 2d 788 (Fla. 1st DCA 1961).

74. Carter Lake v. Aetna Casualty & Surety Co., 604 F.2d 1052 (8th Cir. 1979) (city took calculated risk that backup would not occur, and elected to continue operations without correcting its methods; once city was alerted to problem, its cause, and likelihood of reoccurrence, it could not ignore problem and then look to its insurer to reimburse it for liability incurred by reason of its inaction).

75. *See* Lone Star Steakhouse & Saloon, Inc. v. Liberty Mut. Ins. Group, 343 F. Supp. 2d 989 (D. Kan. 2004) where the insured operated a restaurant with a storage basin on its property to handle stormwater runoff. Its neighbor sued alleging that overflow from that water basin damaged its property. The case was settled and the neighbor paid by the insurer for its damages. Subsequently, the neighbor filed a second action against the insured alleging additional flooding incidents. The insurer argued its insured was aware of the inadequacy of its drainage system but failed to take steps to stop the ongoing flooding of the neighboring property. There was no "occurrence" within the meaning of the policy, contended the insurer, because an insured who is alerted to a problem of ongoing property damage, its cause, and the likelihood of recurrence, cannot just ignore the problem and then claim that any resulting future damage is an "accident" for which its insurer is liable. The court, however, said that damage from a known recurring condition may still be considered an "accident" when the insured took remedial steps designed to prevent the damage from reoccurring. The insured was aware that the basin had overflowed

[d] Rainfall

Often, rainfall is the sole or partial source of the water at issue. How does that fact affect the determination of whether there has been an "accident"? Two federal circuit courts have addressed that question. In one case, an insured local government operated a pump at a sewage system lift station. A combination of heavy rainfall and the operation of the pump caused sewage and water to back up from the main into several residences. The Tenth Circuit Court of Appeal said that in general, a loss that is the natural and probable consequence of a negligent act is not caused by accident although a negligently caused loss may be accidental if in fact an immediate or concurrent cause of the loss is an *unprecedented or unforeseeable* event. That loss is not the natural and probable consequence of the negligent act and is, therefore, caused by an accident. In the case before the court, although the heavy rainfall undoubtedly combined with negligent operation of the pump to bring about the harmful backup, the rainfall was not unusual or unprecedented for the season of the year and the asserted loss was not caused by accident, within the meaning of the CGL policy.[76] In a case before the Fourth Circuit Court, a property owner alleged that when the insured contractor built an underpass adjacent to his property, a ditch was dug and earth was left piled up for more than a year. As a result. during periods of heavy rain, the property owner's building was inundated with water to the depth of one foot. The court said that neither the means nor the result was accidental, because the acts that caused the damage were persistently and continuously done and the results were the normal consequences of those acts.[77]

[e] Expected or Intended from the Standpoint of the Insured

Some policies define "occurrence" to mean an accident that results in "property damage neither expected nor intended from the standpoint of the insured."[78] In a case with that definition, the Alabama Supreme Court said that where an underlying complaint alleged the defendant knowingly built and sold homes that would flood, the insured was charged with intentional acts that were not an occurrence and, therefore, not covered by the policy.[79]

---

and prior settlement put it on notice that the basin had caused flooding damages, however, the court found the insurer ignored conflicting evidence available to the insured from which it could have reasonably believed that the subsequent flooding or claimed damages resulted not from the basin, but from problems on property of the neighbor.

76. Aurora v. Trinity Universal Ins. Co., 326 F.2d 905 (10th Cir. 1964).

77. C. Y. Thomason Co. v. Lumbermens Mut. Casualty Co., 183 F.2d 729 (4th Cir. 1950).

78. Some say that "from the standpoint of the insured" means the standpoint of the "objective" insured and others that it means the standpoint of the actual insured whose conduct is at issue. Dykes, *Occurrences, Accidents, and Expectations: A Primer of These (and Some Other) Insurance-Law Concepts*, 2003 Utah L. Rev. 831, 832 (2003).

79. Ladner & Co. v. Southern Guaranty Ins. Co., 347 So. 2d 100 (Ala. 1977).

Polices that omit the phrase "expected nor intended from the standpoint of the insured" have an exclusion for property damage that is expected or intended from the standpoint of the insured.[80] This exclusion is discussed below.[81]

[2] Construction Defects as an Occurrence

One of the most litigated insurance law questions in the twenty-first century has been whether a construction defect is an occurrence under a commercial general liability policy.[82] A "construction defect" is defined as a problem with a structure's design or construction that is the result of the failure to design or construct it in a reasonable workmanlike manner.[83] A comprehensive analysis of the case law addressing the question of whether construction defects are occurrences for purposes of CGL coverage is beyond the scope of this discussion. Fortunately, there are a number of scholarly journal articles[84] and at least one treatise[85] devoted exclusively to the topic.

Construction defect cases rarely involve a "flood" as the term is defined in insurance law or even the large amounts of water that might loosely be referred to as "flooding." Typically, the cases concern flaws to the construction

80. *See, e.g.*, ISO Form CG 00 01 12 07, § I.A.2.a.

81. *See* § 9.07[2], *supra*.

82. Wielinski, *Construction Defect and Occurrence: Still Crazy After All These Years* (2014), IRMI, https://www.irmi.com/articles/expert-commentary/construction-defect-and-occurrence-still-crazy-after-all-these-years (issue of whether defective workmanship constitutes "occurrence" for purposes of coverage for associated property damage under CGL policies has been subject of considerable litigation for many years); French, *Construction Defects: Are They "Occurrences?"* 47 Gonz. L. Rev. 1, 3 (2011) (one of most litigated issues in insurance law in recent years has been whether construction defects constitute "occurrences" under CGL policies); Friedlander, *Construction Defect Litigation: Courts Fragmented Rationales Regarding Coverage for Contractors Faulty Workmanship*, 11 Suffolk J. Trial & App. Adv. 119, 120 (2006) (coverage disputes about construction defects constitute rapidly growing area of controversy in insurance industry).

83. Kealy, *Construction Defect Analysis for Occurrence and Manifestation Occurrence Form Policies* (Sept. 21, 2015), Insurance Journal, https://www.insurancejournal.com/magazines/mag-features/2015/09/21/381748.htm.

84. *See, e.g.*, French, *Revisiting Construction Defects as "Occurrences" under CGL Insurance Policies*, 19 U. Pa. J. Bus. L. 101 (2016); French, *Construction Defects: Are They "Occurrences?"* 47 Gonz. L. Rev. 1 (2011); Friedlander, *Construction Defect Litigation: Courts Fragmented Rationales Regarding Coverage for Contractors Faulty Workmanship*, 11 Suffolk J. Trial & App. Adv. 119 (2006); Franco, *Insurance Coverage for Faulty Workmanship Claims under Commercial General Liability Policies*, 30 Tort & Ins. L.J. 785 (Spring 1995); Henderson, *Insurance Protection for Products Liability and Completed Operations—What Every Lawyer Should Know*, 50 Neb. L. Rev. 415 (1971).

85. Wielinski, *Insurance for Defective Construction* (4th ed. IRMI 2015). *See also* Shean & Patin, *Construction Insurance: Coverages and Disputes* § 6.4[d][2] (Matthew Bender 2017).

or installation of a roof, siding,[86] plumbing,[87] windows,[88] or doors[89] that allow moisture to enter and lead to water damage or mold. The case law merits attention here because the same defects that allow small amounts of water to enter and damage a structure *could* allow the larger amounts that policyholders would describe as a "flood."[90]

The events that bring about construction defect litigation are usually mundane and happen every day. For example, several months after having a new roof installed, a homeowner discovers the roof is leaking and she has extensive damage to her walls and floors. She sues the contractor, who submits a claim to his insurer. The insurer denies the claim. A CGL policy, says the insurer, only covers "accidents." A leaking roof is not an accident "because it is reasonably foreseeable that a contractor who does defective work will be legally required to either fix the faulty workmanship or pay for it."[91] The incredulous contractor counters that he did not intend to install a flawed roof so the deficiency

---

86. *See, e.g.*, Amerisure Ins. Co. v. C-Cure Corp., 2004 U.S. Dist. LEXIS 30689 (S.D. Tex. Aug. 17, 2004) (in two underlying lawsuits plaintiffs claimed there was water infiltration from allegedly defective exterior home siding). *See also* Cincinnati Ins. Cos. v. Collier Landholdings, LLC, 614 F. Supp. 2d 960 (W.D. Ark. 2009) (after substantial completion of building and occupancy by tenants, water infiltrated building through ceiling, walls, and floor).

87. *See, e.g.*, Pekin Ins. Co. v. Richard Marker Assocs., 224 Ill. Dec. 801, 289 Ill. App. 3d 819, 682 N.E.2d 362, *app. den.*, 228 Ill. Dec. 719, 175 Ill. 2d 531, 689 N.E.2d 1140 (1997) (failure of insured to design proper location and insulation of plumbing pipes and failure to insulate exterior facing areas caused water pipes to burst, causing damage to furniture, clothing, and antiques).

88. *See, e.g.*, Pella Corp. v. Liberty Mut. Ins. Co., 246 F. Supp. 3d 1247 (S.D. Iowa 2017) (plaintiffs in underlying action alleged insured's windows were defectively designed, manufactured, or installed, and allowed water intrusion to buildings that resulted in third-party property damage).

89. *See, e.g.*, Am. Family Mut. Ins. Co. v. Spectre W. Builders Corp., 2011 U.S. Dist. LEXIS 11328 (D. Ariz. Feb. 4, 2011) (plaintiff in underlying action alleged sliding glass door system failure, which resulted in water intrusion causing damage to structural components, exterior and interior finishes).

90. *See* Reggie Constr., Ltd. v. Westfield Ins. Co., 2014 Ohio App. LEXIS 3703 (Ohio App. Sept. 2, 2014) (homeowner sued insured builder of new home alleging it allowed home to remain open through winter season and as result structure flooded, causing home to be severely impacted by mold).

91. French, *Revisiting Construction Defects as "Occurrences" under CGL Insurance Policies*, 19 U. Pa. J. Bus. L. 101, 103 (2016). *See also* Corbett, *Listen to What the Insurance Policy Says: Construing Commercial General Liability Exclusions without Preconceptions* (2017), National Law Review, *available at* https://www.natlawreview.com/article/listen-to-what-insurance-policy-says-construing-commercial-general-liability (insurance companies have long contended that CGL policies do not cover property damage involving alleged deficient workmanship by insured). *See, e.g.*, State Auto Prop. & Cas. Ins. Co. v. Miller, 2013 U.S. Dist. LEXIS 39645 (E.D. Pa. Mar. 22, 2013) (faulty workmanship and resulting property damage from leaking roof lack requisite fortuity of an accident to be considered an occurrence).

was an accident and, moreover, if a construction defect claim is not covered under the policy, why would he even buy CGL insurance?[92]

The response to the arguments put forward has not been consistent and has created confusion.[93] However, in recent years, the trend has been for the courts to agree with policyholders and conclude that a construction defect can be an accident and, therefore, an occurrence.[94] Differences remain, however, with three principal consequences:

- One must carefully analyze the law of the jurisdiction in question and do so with particular attention to the fact that this is an area of law in which precedents are being overturned by courts and legislatures.[95]
- Parties frequently offer precedent from other jurisdictions to support their position,[96] and courts appear to give that extraterritorial case law due consideration.
- Because what is an occurrence in one state may not be one just across the border in another state, choice of law is critical, particularly for contractors doing business in more than one jurisdiction.[97]

---

92. French, *Construction Defects: Are They "Occurrences?"* 47 Gonz. L. Rev. 1 (2011).

93. Wielinski, *Construction Defect and Occurrence: Still Crazy after All These Years* (2014), IRMI, https://www.irmi.com/articles/expert-commentary/construction-defect-and-occurrence-still-crazy-after-all-these-years (application of laws of various states continues to result in differing, and usually confusing, results, making it difficult for insureds to predict whether there will be coverage for claims involving construction defects); Friedlander, *Construction Defect Litigation: Courts Fragmented Rationales Regarding Coverage for Contractors Faulty Workmanship*, 11 Suffolk J. Trial & App. Adv. 119, 134 (2006) (given differing rationales among courts, uncertainty exists about extent of construction defect coverage available under CGL policies).

94. Corbett, *Listen to What the Insurance Policy Says: Construing Commercial General Liability Exclusions without Preconceptions* (2017), National Law Review, *available at* https://www.natlawreview.com/article/listen-to-what-insurance-policy-says-construing-commercial-general-liability (trend has moved decisively toward treating deficient workmanship as occurrence that can trigger coverage of resulting property damage); French, *Revisiting Construction Defects as "Occurrences" under CGL Insurance Policies*, 19 U. Pa. J. Bus. L. 101, 122–23 (2016) (in past five years there has been near unanimity by courts that construction defects can constitute occurrences).

95. *See General Liability Insurance Coverage: Key Issues in Every State* § 12.01 (Matthew Bender 2015) (50-State Survey: Is Faulty Workmanship an "Occurrence"?) for an overview of state law. Note that Arkansas, Colorado, Hawaii, and South Carolina have statutes that in effect provide that construction defects are occurrences. French, *Revisiting Construction Defects as "Occurrences" under CGL Insurance Policies*, 19 U. Pa. J. Bus. L. 101, 125–26 (2016).

96. Friedlander, *Construction Defect Litigation: Courts Fragmented Rationales Regarding Coverage for Contractors Faulty Workmanship*, 11 Suffolk J. Trial & App. Adv. 119, 120 (2006).

97. Wielinski, *Construction Defect and Occurrence: Still Crazy after All These Years* (2014), IRMI, https://www.irmi.com/articles/expert-commentary/construction-defect-and-occurrence-still-crazy-after-all-these-years.

The positions taken by courts fall into one of three categories.[98] First, those in a few states continue to hold that defective work is not an occurrence.[99] These courts ask if the damage was the result of an "intentional act"[100] and, because they generally consider construction to be an intentional act, find there was no accident.[101] Other courts conclude that if the damage is the unintended result of faulty workmanship,[102] then it is accidental and an occurrence.[103]

---

98. Kealy, *Construction Defect Analysis for Occurrence and Manifestation Occurrence Form Policies* (Sept. 21, 2015), Insurance Journal, https://www.insurancejournal.com/magazines/mag-features/2015/09/21/381748.htm; Wielinski, *Construction Defect and Occurrence: Still Crazy after All These Years* (2014), IRMI, https://www.irmi.com/articles/expert-commentary/construction-defect-and-occurrence-still-crazy-after-all-these-years.

99. French, *Revisiting Construction Defects as "Occurrences" under CGL Insurance Policies*, 19 U. Pa. J. Bus. L. 101, 135 (2016) (minority position adopted by supreme courts of Arkansas, Kentucky, and Pennsylvania is that construction defects cannot be "accidents" and thus, they should not be viewed as occurrences under terms of CGL policies).

100. Note that earlier versions of the CGL policy included "expected or intended" language in the definition of "occurrence." In current standard CGL policies, that language has been moved to the exclusions section of the policy where there is an exclusion that bars coverage for property damage expected or intended from the standpoint of the insured. When applying the "expected or intended" language, one has to examine the state of mind of the insured to determine whether the property damage was caused by an accident or whether the insured expected or intended to cause the damage at issue and while courts do not agree if the test should be whether the insured subjectively expected or intended to cause the damage or objectively should have expected or intended to cause the damage, the majority of courts that have addressed the issue have adopted a subjective standard. French, *Construction Defects: Are They "Occurrences?"* 47 Gonz. L. Rev. 1, 7, 17 (2011).

101. Kealy, *Construction Defect Analysis for Occurrence and Manifestation Occurrence Form Policies* (Sept. 21, 2015), Insurance Journal, https://www.insurancejournal.com/magazines/mag-features/2015/09/21/381748.htm (some courts hold that if damage resulted from intentional act of construction, it is not an occurrence).

102. The Tennessee Supreme Court explained that the determination of whether there has been an "accident" requires the court to establish whether damages would have been foreseeable if the insured had completed the work properly. In a case where water penetration resulting from faulty window installation was at issue, the court said that assuming that the windows would be installed properly, the insured could not have foreseen water penetration; therefore, the water penetration was both an "accident" and an "occurrence" for which there was coverage. Travelers Indem. Co. of Am. v. Moore & Assocs., 216 S.W.3d 302 (Tenn. 2007).

103. Kealy, *Construction Defect Analysis for Occurrence and Manifestation Occurrence Form Policies* (Sept. 21, 2015), Insurance Journal, https://www.insurancejournal.com/magazines/mag-features/2015/09/21/381748.htm; Wielinski, *Construction Defect and Occurrence: Still Crazy after All These Years* (2014), IRMI, https://www.irmi.com/articles/expert-commentary/construction-defect-and-occurrence-still-crazy-after-all-these-years. *See, e.g.*, Cypress Point Condo. Ass'n v. Adria Towers, L.L.C., 226 N.J. 403, 143 A.3d 273 (2016) (where condominium association sued its developer/general contractor for damage to interior structure, residential units, and common areas of condominium complex from roof leaks and water infiltration at interior window jambs and sills, which were allegedly result of defective work performed by subcontractors, court held consequential damages caused by faulty workmanship constituted "property damage," and event resulting in that damage—water from rain flowing into the interior of property—was "occurrence" under the plain language of standard CGL policy). *And see* Auto-Owners Ins. Co. v. Wier-Wright Enters., 2017 U.S. Dist. LEXIS 37477 (N.D. Ala. Mar.

Finally, for some courts the question of whether there was an occurrence turns on what property is damaged. When the damage is to a property other than to the work of the contractor, there is an occurrence, but if the damage is to the contractor's own work, then there is not an occurrence.[104] This position is based on the meaning of the term "property damage" as used in CGL policies, which is "physical injury to tangible property." One commentator who has written extensively and cogently on the issue of insurance for construction defects, notes that the definition does not distinguish between property created by a contractor and separate property owned by a third party, and that courts holding that defective work itself cannot be viewed as property damage have not offered a satisfying explanation for their position.[105]

It is important to recognize that the fact that a jurisdiction takes the position that the damage in a particular case meets its definition of an occurrence does not mean the insurer will concede liability. As more and more courts have found some or all construction defects to be occurrences, insurers have retreated to a backup position, claiming that a loss that arises out of deficient workmanship falls within the scope of at least one of the exclusions in standard CGL policies.[106]

16, 2017) (under Alabama law contractor's faulty work is generally not considered an accident, but when faulty work creates condition that in turn damages property, conduct is considered an accident under Alabama law; thus, generally faulty workmanship would not be an accident but damage to home and personal property from leaky roof could be); Emplrs. Mut. Cas. Co. v. Kenny Hayes Custom Homes, LLC, 2016 U.S. Dist. LEXIS 15340 (S.D. Ala. Feb. 9, 2016) (courts have found that faulty workmanship that causes a leak can, at least in some circumstances, result in occurrence); Potomac Ins. of Ill. v. Jonson Huang, 2002 U.S. Dist. LEXIS 4710 (D. Kan. Mar. 1, 2002) (faulty workmanship—negligence—may not be an accident, but it may cause one when, for example, it leads to actual physical act of windows leaking).

104. French, *Revisiting Construction Defects as "Occurrences" under CGL Insurance Policies*, 19 U. Pa. J. Bus. L. 101, 126 (2016) (construction defects are considered occurrences to extent property other than work performed by policyholder is damaged). *See also* Kealy, *Construction Defect Analysis for Occurrence and Manifestation Occurrence Form Policies* (Sept. 21, 2015), Insurance Journal, https://www.insurancejournal.com/magazines/mag-features/2015/09/21/381748.htm. *And see* Pekin Ins. Co. v. Richard Marker Assocs., 224 Ill. Dec. 801, 804, 289 Ill. App. 3d 819, 822, 682 N.E.2d 362, 365, *app. den.*, 228 Ill. Dec. 719, 175 Ill. 2d 531, 689 N.E.2d 1140 (1997) (CGL policies are intended to provide coverage for injury or damage to person or property of others, but not to pay the costs associated with repairing or replacing insured's defective work and products).

105. French, *Revisiting Construction Defects as "Occurrences" under CGL Insurance Policies*, 19 U. Pa. J. Bus. L. 101, 105, 134 (2016) (courts holding that defective work itself cannot be viewed as property damage have not offered satisfying explanation why non-defective work that has been damaged and needs to be repaired or replaced because of defective workmanship constitutes property damage but defective work itself that also needs to be repaired or replaced does not constitute property damage).

106. Corbett, *Listen to What the Insurance Policy Says: Construing Commercial General Liability Exclusions without Preconceptions* (2017), National Law Review, https://www.natlawreview.com/article/listen-to-what-insurance-policy-says-construing-commercial-general-liability.

[3] An Occurrence during Roof Repairs

When a roofing company repairs or replaces a roof, will its commercial general liability policy cover water damage to the interior of the building from rainwater? This is a question that is often litigated. The heart of the question is whether there has been an accident. There are cases in which the roofer failed to cover an opening and others where an attempt to do so was unsuccessful.

The most basic question is whether when a roof is left exposed to the elements, water enters the building by accident. The Alabama Supreme Court considered that issue in a typical case. The insured contracted to re-roof a home. While the work was being done, it rained almost every day, and the roof was uncovered much of the time. The homeowner sued to recover for the resulting interior damage. The court noted that the roofer had taken steps to prevent damage, evidencing a lack of intent to cause damage. The court concluded that after the "repeated exposure to conditions," the roof leaked and there was, therefore, an "occurrence" under the policy.[107] Similarly, in a New York case, an insurer argued there was no accident where property damage was the result of a roofing company "half doing the roofing job and leaving it exposed to the elements." The court, however, said it had no doubt that the average person would consider the event an accident in the "common conception" of the word.[108] The North Carolina Supreme Court allowed that interior damage could be an accident when water seeped into a building

107. Moss v. Champion Ins. Co., 442 So. 2d 26 (Ala. 1983).

108. Rex Roofing Co. v. Lumber Mut. Casualty Ins. Co., 280 A.D. 665, 116 N.Y.S.2d 876 (1952), *app. den.*, 281 A.D. 744, 118 N.Y.S.2d 732 (1953) (roof was flat surface and snow-covered, and rainwater was unable to drain off and collected on roof and backed up under felts, leaking down into interior of building, and insurer argued damage was caused by faulty workmanship). *Compare* Midland Constr. Co. v. United States Casualty Co., 214 F.2d 665 (10th Cir. 1954) (distinguishing *Rex Roofing* by saying court was not persuaded that ordinary afternoon shower was an accident); Christ v. Progressive Fire Ins. Co., 101 So. 2d 821 (Fla. 2d DCA 1958) (disagreeing with reasoning in *Rex Roofing* that would require court to hold that ordinary afternoon shower is accident within meaning of insurance policy). *And see* Iowa Mut. Ins. Co. v. Fred M. Simmons, Inc., 258 N.C. 69, 128 S.E.2d 19 (1962) (where water seeping into building under covering roofing contractor placed over exposed opening of roof, court found that *Midland* and *Christ* were factually distinguishable; to adopt narrow view that "accident" in liability policies necessarily excludes negligence would mean that in most, if not all, cases insurer would be free of coverage and policy would be rendered meaningless). In *Employers Ins. Co. v. Alabama Roofing & Siding Co.*, 271 Ala. 394, 124 So. 2d 261 (1960), a roofing contractor began work about noon, and there was a rainstorm after work stopped for the day but before the project was completed. Water entered the building, damaging the ceiling and walls and inventory. The insurance company disclaimed liability under the policy because the damage was not caused by an accident. The Alabama Supreme Court asserted it did not subscribe to the view that "accident" necessarily excludes human fault, that is, negligence. It said it understood *Christ* and *Midland Const. Co.* to hold, in effect, that if damage was the result of negligence, it necessarily precluded finding the damage resulted from an accident. However, the Alabama court followed *Rex Roofing* and found there was an accident for which the insurer was liable.

under the covering a roofing contractor had placed over the exposed opening of the roof.[109]

Roofing cases often turn judges into meteorologists, as one issue is whether the rain was unexpected. The New Mexico Supreme Court held that because the rainfall that entered a home being re-roofed occurred in October, "ordinarily a fairly dry month," it was unexpected and could be considered accidental. The insurer was, therefore, obligated to defend against any claim and pay any judgment rendered.[110] In contrast, in a federal case, by the time workers began closing an opening in a roof, it had begun to rain and water entered the building below damaging merchandise. The court said that an unprecedented, torrential downpour might under certain conditions be considered an accident, but afternoon showers happen frequently and are not unusual or unexpected. There was no accident.[111] A court in Florida, where sudden "torrential downpours" are common in summer, agreed. In the case, a roofing contractor began work on a July day but suspended operations for the weekend. On Sunday rainwater seeped through the top of the building into storerooms on the ground floor. The court said that a contractor who proceeds to repair a roof but then leaves the work unfinished over a weekend without taking proper precautions to protect against rain while having every reason to anticipate showers are likely in the Florida "rainy season"—a matter of common knowledge—cannot claim that there was an accident.[112] A subsequent Florida case is a reminder that, as the court said, each case turns on "a factual determination as to the unexpected nature of the rainfall." A hotel sued a roofer alleging it suffered property damage because a "sudden, unusual and unexpected rainstorm" developed while a portion of the hotel's

---

109. Iowa Mut. Ins. Co. v. Fred M. Simmons, Inc., 258 N.C. 69, 128 S.E.2d 19 (1962). *See also* Oak Creek Apartments LLC v. Garcia, 2013 Mich. App. LEXIS 550 (Mar. 21, 2013) (damages to building resulting from roofer's failure to adequately or properly secure open roof area, which allegedly led to rainwater intrusion, were, excluding repair or replacement costs of roof, but including costs to bring the building into compliance with the municipal code, caused by "occurrence" under CGL policy).

110. O'Rourke v. New Amsterdam Casualty Co., 68 N.M. 409, 362 P.2d 790 (1961) (distinguishing cases in which occurrence was in summertime or "rainy season").

111. Midland Constr. Co. v. United States Casualty Co., 214 F.2d 665 (10th Cir. 1954).

112. Christ v. Progressive Fire Ins. Co., 101 So. 2d 821 (Fla. 2d DCA 1958) (ordinary afternoon shower is not an accident within meaning of insurance policy). *See also* Michigan Mut. Liability Co. v. G. & L. Roofing Co., 123 So. 2d 300 (Fla. 3d DCA 1960), where the insured roofing business contracted to put a new roof on a residence in June. When rain clouds appeared, the workers attempted to seal the paper already laid, but rain fell before the sealing could be completed. Water entered and damaged the interior of the residence. The rain was heavy but of short duration. The court said that afternoon showers are not unusual or unexpected, but happen frequently and are of common occurrence. This was a rapid developing, heavy summer shower—certainly not unusual for South Florida during the summer—and not an accident.

roof had no protective covering. The trial court found there was no accident and, therefore, no coverage under the roofer's liability policy. The appellate court reversed and said that Florida law did not support the proposition that rainfall cannot, as a matter of law, constitute an accident or occurrence under a liability insurance policy.[113]

Insurance companies attempt to limit their liability for claims against roofing contractors by adding an endorsement to commercial general liability policies that requires the insured to cover an open roof with "suitable waterproof material." These endorsements are often called a Roofing Limitation Endorsement (RLE)[114] but may be known by other names, for example, Open Roof and Heating Equipment Coverage Limitation Endorsement. An endorsement might provide that its coverage does not apply to "property damage" arising directly or indirectly out of an "open roof" and then state that the exclusion does not apply if an "open roof" is covered with suitable waterproof material at the time of the loss and that suitable waterproof material has been secured to the structure.[115] The definition of "open roof" is important. It might be defined as any roof, or section of a roof, for which the protective covering—shingles, tar, felt paper—has been removed, leaving the shell of the structure exposed. Another version of endorsement might say there is no coverage for a loss due to property damage that arises out of rain, snow, hail, or any combination of them if a suitable waterproof temporary covering that can withstand the "normal elements" and that is large enough to cover the area being worked on has not been *properly secured* in place. It may then require the cover to be in place whenever the insured leaves the job site and state that tar paper and/or felt paper are suitable covering in roofing work.

A South Carolina federal court considered the application of an RLE.[116] In the underlying action, a homeowner alleged that rainwater entered her home after the insured roofer removed the shingles and left the building exposed to heavy rains. Interestingly, the insurer did not contest that there had been an occurrence under the policy. Instead, it invoked the endorsement. The question before the court was whether a "suitable waterproof temporary covering" had been properly secured on the roof. Because the policy did not define "suitable," and there was no judicially determined definition, the court found there was a genuine issue of material fact regarding whether the RLE barred coverage.

---

113. Adams v. Kent Ins. Co., 431 So. 2d 335 (Fla. 4th DCA 1983).

114. *See, e.g.*, Cont'l Ins. Co. v. Atl. Cas. Ins. Co., 603 F.3d 169, 172, (2d Cir. 2010); Atl. Cas. Ins. Co. v. Sealtite Roofing & Constr. Co., 73 F. Supp. 3d 953, 956 (N.D. Ill. 2014).

115. *See generally* https://www.k2constructionins.com/wp-content/uploads/2021/07/FSIC-CG-08-00-06-21-EXCLUSION-OPEN-ROOF-AND-HEAT-PROCESSING.pdf.

116. Williford Roofing, Inc. v. Endurance Am. Specialty Ins. Co., 2017 U.S. Dist. LEXIS 16033 (D.S.C. Feb. 6, 2017).

[4] Multiple or Single Occurrence

[a] Introduction

Standard CGL policies have an "aggregate" and "each occurrence" limit. The amount of the limit is shown on the Declarations Page. These limits are the most the insurer will pay regardless of the number of claims made or suits brought or the number of persons or organizations making claims or bringing suits.[117] The aggregate limit is the most the insurer will pay during the policy period for the sum of covered medical expenses, bodily injury or property damage, and personal and advertising injury.[118] The aggregate limit applies regardless of the number of occurrences. The "each occurrence" limit is the most the insurer will pay for the sum of bodily injury or property damage and medical expenses because of all bodily injury and property damage arising out of any one "occurrence."[119] "Occurrence" is defined as "an accident, including continuous or repeated exposure to substantially the same general harmful conditions."[120] The phrase "continuous or repeated exposure to substantially the same general harmful conditions" is meant to include exposure to a condition that could continue for days, weeks, months, or even years.[121] The amount of the limits will vary.

[b] Multiple Events

More than one event can cause damage to the same property. A classic example is found in an Alabama case in which the property of a tenant was damaged by a leaky roof. The tenant suffered additional damage when workers for the company repairing the roof failed to adequately cover the portion

117. ISO Form CG 00 01 12 07, § III.1.
118. ISO Form CG 00 01 12 07, § III.2.
119. ISO Form CG 00 01 12 07, § III.5.
120. ISO Form CG 00 01 12 07, § V.13.
121. 3 Jeffrey E. Thomas, *New Appleman on Insurance Law Library Edition* § 18.02[6][a] (Matthew Bender 2022). *See, e.g.*, Emplrs Mut. Cas. Co. v. Arbella Prot. Ins. Co., 24 A.3d 544 (R.I. 2011) (where water from quarry flowed onto neighboring property "over the years," from time to time, on numerous occasions, and several occasions, those characterizations did not convey sense that alleged flooding constituted continuous or repeated exposure to substantially the same general harmful conditions so that it could be determined as matter of law that alleged flooding damage was result of one occurrence); Nationwide Mut. Ins. Co. v. Gibson, 2009 U.S. Dist. LEXIS 139138 (N.D. Ill. Sept. 1, 2009) (water damage caused by faulty construction was single occurrence over years); Carpenter Plastering Co. v. Puritan Ins. Co., 1988 U.S. Dist. LEXIS 16422 (N.D. Tex. Aug. 23, 1988) (where building suffered water damage because of cracks in the wall panels constructed by insured and continued to experience water damage after apparently successful repair, there was a single occurrence that was result of continuous or repeated exposure).

of it on which they were working. The court found there were two separate occurrences.[122]

[c] Multiple Injuries

The number of occurrences can determine the amount available to compensate injured parties. For example, the negligence of the insured causes a levee to be breached. Flood waters inundate a small subdivision of 20 homes. Each suffers $100,000 in damages. The total loss is $2 million. If there is a single occurrence and the "each occurrence" limit is $1 million, then each homeowner can receive only $50,000. If, however, there are 20 occurrences, and the aggregate limit is $2 million, then each homeowner can be fully compensated. The majority view looks to the cause.[123] If a single cause, the breaching of the levee, is the source of multiple losses, there was only one occurrence. The minority approach is to consider the effect: how many individual claims or injuries resulted from an event?[124] Generally, under that analysis, the levee breach would be found to have resulted in 20 occurrences. The law of the pertinent jurisdiction must be examined to determine which test is applicable.[125]

The Eleventh Circuit has illustrated the majority position. The surface water drainage system of the city of Mobile, Alabama, was allegedly negligently planned, constructed, operated, and maintained. As a consequence, over 200 property owners sued the city. Their properties suffered flood damage when, following major rains, overflows occurred at various points in the drainage system. The insurer contended that as there were three separate rainfalls that resulted in flooding, it was liable for only three "occurrences." In opposition, the city and the flood victims maintained that each incident of flooding to the property of each individual property owner was an occurrence. The court disagreed with all the parties. The rainfall and flooding, said the court, were not occurrences at all, but acts of God for which the city was not liable. It was, rather, the intervening negligence of the city in maintaining its water drainage system that created liability. Further, occurrence did not refer to the flooding damages suffered by each individual property, because that interpretation would improperly focus on the effects of the events leading

---

122. United States Fire Ins. Co. v. Safeco Ins. Co., 444 So. 2d 844 (Ala. 1983) (initial water damage was caused by occurrence of leaky roof, and later damage was caused by occurrence of roofing crew negligence in failing to adequately cover exposed portion of roof).

123. 3 Jeffrey E. Thomas, *New Appleman on Insurance Law Library Edition* § 16.09[3][a][iv] (Matthew Bender 2022).

124. *General Liability Insurance Coverage: Key Issues in Every State* § 9.01 (Matthew Bender, 2022).

125. *See General Liability Insurance Coverage: Key Issues in Every State* §9.02 (Matthew Bender, 2022), which surveys the law of all 50 states and the District of Columbia.

to liability, rather than on the *cause* of those events. The court then held that "each discrete act or omission, or series of acts or omissions [by the city] which caused water to flood and damage properties instead of draining properly [was] a single 'occurrence.'" For example, if because of the city's negligence a drain on one street was blocked, causing water to flood ten houses on that street, that would be a single occurrence while if at some other location, a storm sewer spilled over or broke open because of the city's negligence and water flooded a house, that would be another occurrence.[126]

In an Iowa decision the court took a different approach. The underlying claims in the case were by many customers of the insured window manufacturer. Generally, they alleged that the insured's windows were defectively designed, manufactured, or installed, and allowed water intrusion to buildings. The insured sought a declaration that each claim presented one occurrence, because each presented unique underlying circumstances. The court said the definition of occurrence did not address whether unintended water intrusion in different places, at different times, and caused by defects in different products constituted a single occurrence merely because the damage-causing instances were of the same type or could be described in the same manner. Given that ambiguity, the court found that each claim presented one occurrence.[127]

9.6 Act of God Defense

The standard commercial general liability policy provides that the insurer will pay sums the insured becomes "legally obligated to pay as damages" because of property damage to which the policy applies.[128] Thus, if the insured cannot be "legally obligated to pay" because the event that caused the damage at issue

126. Home Indem. Co. v. City of Mobile, 749 F.2d 659 (11th Cir. 1984). *See also* United Nat'l Ins. Co. v. Assurance Co. of Am., 2015 U.S. Dist. LEXIS 153822 (D. Nev. Nov. 12, 2015) (where the insured contractor worked on four phases of subdivision and in each phase negligently graded and paved leading to ponding and drainage problems, and moisture intrusion, court found there were four occurrences as each phase suffered damages from work done in that phase); Twin City Fire Ins. Co. v. Ill. Nat'l Ins. Co., 2012 U.S. Dist. LEXIS 197629 (W. D. Tex. Mar. 12, 2012) (three automobile accidents occurred in which plaintiffs alleged that because of contractor's defective work on road project, water did not drain properly from road and increased risk of hydroplaning; court concluded three accidents were a single occurrence); Arthur A. Johnson Corp. v. Indemnity Ins. Co., 6 A.D.2d 97, 175 N.Y.S.2d 414 (1958) (insured, while working on subway platform, opened basement vaults of two buildings and constructed temporary walls that were unable to withstand water pressure when sewer overflowed during rainstorm; court found that laying open vaults of each building and erecting temporary but inadequate walls were distinct and separate acts giving rise to separate accidents and liabilities; coincidence that buildings were adjacent to one another was of no import). *Compare* Great Lakes Dredge & Dock Co. v. City of Chicago, 260 F.3d 789 (7th Cir. 2001) (where tunnel was damaged by negligence of insure and it subsequently collapsed and caused a flood, there was a single occurrence).

127. Pella Corp. v. Liberty Mut. Ins. Co., 246 F. Supp. 3d 1247 (S.D. Iowa 2017).

128. ISO Form CG 00 01 12 07, § I.A.1.a.

was an "act of God," there should be no coverage. However, the "act of God" defense is exceedingly narrow.[129] In the case of flooding, it generally has to be shown that the flood was extraordinary and the damage would have occurred regardless of any negligence by the party accused of causing it.[130]

For example, the North Dakota Supreme Court considered a case in which the defendant property owner drained ponds, allegedly causing water to flood neighboring land. The defendant argued the neighboring land would have flooded without the additional water drained from his land because it was a period of "unusually high rainfall and runoff," an act of God. The court said that for the defendant to prevail on that defense, he had to establish that the rainfall, runoff, and flooding were unprecedented and extraordinary, could not have been reasonably anticipated, could not have been reasonably provided against, and were the sole proximate cause of the damage. The court found that the snowmelt, rain, and resulting runoff were not unpredictable or extraordinary, were foreseeable, and could have been reasonably anticipated. It added that if the defendant's negligence combined with an act of God to cause the damages, then the defendant would be liable.[131]

In an earlier from Massachusetts case, the defense was successfully invoked. The defendant owned a hydroelectric plant and in conjunction with it operated a dike. During a hurricane, the dike overflowed and flooded the property of the plaintiffs, who alleged the damage was the result of negligent maintenance. The torrential rains and flood that accompanied the hurricane were, said the court, wholly without precedent in the state. The plaintiffs responded that a hurricane two years earlier provided a warning of the flood potential. The court, however, said that hurricane—and resulting flood—was itself unprecedented, and "no one could foresee that it would be repeated." The plaintiffs then argued the defendant should be strictly liable under *Rylands v. Fletcher*. The court said the rule of that case did not apply where there was an act of God and the flood at issue "was plainly beyond the capacity of any one to anticipate, and was clearly an act of God." The defendant was not, therefore, liable.[132]

---

129. Binder, *Act of God? or Act of Man?: A Reappraisal of the Act of God Defense in Tort Law*, 15 Rev. Litig. 1, 14 (1996). *See also* Fraley, *Re-examining Acts of God*, 27 Pace Envtl. L. Rev. 669, 673–74 (2010) (while many courts emphasize ability to anticipate disastrous event, very heart of act of God doctrine rests on strict interpretation of human-nature separation and within doctrine, act of God occurs only when event in question is caused exclusively by forces of nature without any human action or interference). *See generally* Villa, *Is the "Act of God" Dead?*, 7 Wash. J. Envtl. L. & Pol'y 320 (2017); Kristl, *Diminishing the Divine: Climate Change and the Act of God Defense*, 15 Widener L. Rev. 325 (2010).

130. Clayman, *After Me, the Flood: Liability and Damages for Water Run-Off* at 8, Eagle Law, *available at* www.eagle-law.com/wp-content/uploads/Paper-Clayman.pdf.

131. Lang v. Wonnenberg, 455 N.W.2d 832 (N.D. 1990).

132. Golden v. Amory, 329 Mass. 484, 109 N.E.2d 131 (1952). *Compare* Binder, *Act of God? or Act of Man?: A Reappraisal of the Act of God Defense in Tort Law*, 15 Rev. Litig. 1,

One of the cases in which a CGL insurer raised the act of God defense involved a dramatic "domino-effect" flood. A snow storm caused a tree or limb to strike a power line, which fell and caused electricity to arc and the insured's water pipe to burst. A million gallons of water escaped, flooding an adjacent road and washing sand into a nearby wetland. The insurer argued it was not liable because the incident was caused by an act of God and the insured was never legally obligated to pay for the loss. However, it was determined that the insured was strictly liable for the damage to the wetland and, therefore, the insurer had a legal obligation to pay for their remediation. Regarding the other damages, the insured had no legal obligation to pay because the incident was the consequence of an act of God and the insured could not be liable for that. The insurer, therefore, was also not liable.[133]

It should be remembered that coverage in liability policies includes two facets: the duty of the insurer to defend its insured when the insured is a defendant in a lawsuit and its duty to indemnify the insured if damages are ultimately assessed in that lawsuit.[134] The duty to defend is an obligation that is independent from the duty to pay claims under the policy.[135] Thus, insurers generally have to provide a defense to their insureds even though the insured may not ultimately be liable. Thus, the fact that there is an "act of God" defense does not mean the insurer is relieved of the obligation to *defend*.

15–17 (1996). The author says the modern interpretation of the act of God defense is very narrow and the harm has to happen by direct, immediate, and exclusive operations of the forces of nature. Moreover, if the event occurred in the past, then it could recur and be anticipated. If the damage caused by a flood could have been avoided or prevented by prudence, foresight, and care reasonably expected, but not exercised, liability exists. Finally, the test is not subjective, but objective: what would a reasonable person under similar circumstances have known, or reasonably should have known?

133. Indus. Park Water Co. v. Nat'l Fire Ins. Co., 2006 R.I. Super. LEXIS 43 (Apr. 25, 2006). *See also* Indus. Park Water Co. v. Nat'l Fire Ins. Co., 2005 R.I. Super. LEXIS 16 (Feb. 9, 2005) (because insured could not be held legally responsible for consequences of snowstorm, it was not legally obligated to pay for resulting damages and as policy implicitly excluded coverage for damages to property for which insured was not legally obligated to pay, insurer was justified in denying claim for moneys paid for those damages).

134. Morgan Int'l Realty v. Dade Underwriters Ins. Agency, 617 So. 2d 455, 457 (Fla. 3d DCA 1993). *See also* Monteleone, *Coverage Issues under Commercial General Liability and Directors' and Officers' Liability Policies*, 18 W. New Eng. L. Rev. 47, 58 (1996) (insurer's obligation under typical CGL policy is two-fold: to defend insured in any lawsuit or proceeding alleging covered claim and indemnify insured for any insurable damages arising from covered claim).

135. Henning v. Contl Cas. Co., 254 F.3d 1291, 1295 (11th Cir. 2001). *See also* Morgan Int'l Realty v. Dade Underwriters Ins. Agency, 617 So. 2d 455, 457 (Fla. 3d DCA 1993) (duty to defend is distinct from and broader than duty to indemnify).

9.7 Standard CGL Policy Exclusions

[1] Introduction

The standard commercial general liability policy contains 17 exclusions from coverage for bodily injury or property damage. These exclusions are expected or intended injury; contractual liability; liquor liability; workers' compensation and similar laws; employer's liability; pollution; aircraft, auto, or watercraft; mobile equipment; war; damage to property; damage to your product; damage to your work; damage to impaired property or property not physically injured; recall of products, work, or impaired property; personal and advertising injury; electronic data; and distribution of material in violation of statutes. Some of these, for example, employer's liability, apply only to bodily injury. Those that apply to property damage and have been raised in water damage cases are discussed below.

[2] Expected or Intended Injury

The first exclusion is for "expected or intended injury," and it bars coverage for property damage that is expected or intended from the standpoint of the insured.[136] In an underlying suit, the plaintiff may allege both knowing and negligent conduct, in which case there is the possibility of coverage despite the exclusion.[137]

The application of this exclusion has been the subject of extensive and complex litigation. Discussion of those cases is beyond the scope of this treatise; however, the exclusion has been examined in depth by leading insurance law treatises[138] and by scholarly articles.[139]

[3] Contractual Liability

The "Contractual Liability" exclusion applies the fortuity concept of insurance by barring coverage of any agreements by an insured to become liable

---

136. *See, e.g.*, ISO Form CG 00 01 12 07, § I.A.2.a.

137. Admiral Indem. Co. v. 899 Plymouth Court Condo. Ass'n, 2017 U.S. Dist. LEXIS 9803 (Jan. 24, 2017) (in action concerning leaking pool, plaintiffs made allegations of knowing conduct by insured and also alleged negligence; therefore, there was a duty on part of insurer to defend).

138. *See* 3 Jeffrey E. Thomas, *New Appleman on Insurance Law Library Edition* § 18.03[2] (Matthew Bender 2022).

139. *See, e.g.*, French, *Debunking the Myth That Insurance Coverage Is Not Available or Allowed for Intentional Torts or Damages*, 8 Hastings Bus. L.J. 65 (2012); Ingram, *The Expected or Intended Exclusion in Liability Insurance: What about Self-Defense?*, 42 Creighton L. Rev. 123 (2009); Ingram, *The "Expected or Intended" Exclusion Clause in Liability Insurance Policies: What Should It Exclude?*, 13 Whittier L. Rev. 713 (1992).

after the policy is in force and the liability is a certainty.[140] It excludes coverage for property damage for which the insured is obligated to pay damages because of an assumption of liability in a contract or agreement.[141] Obviously, the specific language of the contract at issue is critical.[142] Many courts find that the exclusion does not bar coverage for all contract liability, but only liability assumed in a hold harmless or indemnification agreement.[143] Commentators generally concur.[144]

Not all courts, however, agree that the exclusion is limited to hold harmless or indemnification agreements. In a Texas federal court case, for example, the Dallas Area Rapid Transit (DART) Authority contracted with the insured as general contractor to construct a light rail system. The contract required the insured to protect the work site and surrounding property from damage and to repair any damage. During the construction project, unusually heavy rains caused water damage to a building adjacent to the construction site, and the owner of the building sued DART and its contractors, alleging that the construction activities were the cause of the damage. In the suit against the general contractor, the building owner alleged the general contractor assumed

---

140. Am. Family Mut. Ins. Co. v. Am. Girl, Inc., 268 Wis. 2d 16, 673 N.W.2d 65 (2004).

141. *See, e.g.*, ISO Form CG 00 01 12 07, § I.A.2.b.

142. *See* W. Bend Mut. Ins. Co. v. Cleland Homes, Inc., 2016 U.S. Dist. LEXIS 108030 (N.D. Ind. Aug. 16, 2016), where homeowners sued their builder claiming that negligence in building their homes caused water intrusion into or under their basements. The insurer invoked the Contractual Liability exclusion, arguing that but for obligations the builder assumed under its sales contracts, it would not have any liability. The court, however, said the insurer had not provided copies of any sales contracts. What the builder agreed to do or not to do was unknown. Without the contracts to examine, the court said it had difficulty concluding that a contract to build and sell a particular home would have provisions ensuring that the entire subdivision was not designed negligently.

143. *See* Am. Family Mut. Ins. Co. v. Am. Girl, Inc., 268 Wis. 2d 16, 48, 673 N.W.2d 65, 81 (2004) (contractually assumed liability exclusion applies where insured has contractually assumed liability of third party—as in indemnification or hold harmless agreements—and does not exclude coverage for any and all liabilities to which insured is exposed under terms of contracts it makes generally); Olympic, Inc. v. Providence Wash. Ins. Co., 648 P.2d 1008, 1011 (Alaska 1982) (liability assumed by insured under contract refers to liability incurred when one promises to indemnify or hold harmless another, and does not refer to liability that results from breach of contract). *See generally* Stanovich, *Contractual Liability and the CGL Policy* (2002), IRMI, https://www.irmi.com/articles/expert-commentary/contractual-liability-and-the-cgl-policy (in indemnity or hold harmless agreement, one party—indemnitor—promises to reimburse, and in some cases defend, other party—indemnitee—against claims or suits brought against indemnitee by a third party; purpose of these agreements is to transfer risk of financial loss from indemnitee to indemnitor; agreement does not relieve indemnitee from liability to third party, but instead gives the indemnitee legal right to collect from indemnitor).

144. *See* 3 Jeffrey E. Thomas, *New Appleman on Insurance Law Library Edition* § 18.03[3][a] (Matthew Bender 2022) (exclusion on its face might appear to bar all contract liability, but actually is limited to contracts in which insured assumed liability of another, that is, hold harmless or indemnification agreements); 2 *New Appleman Law of Liability Insurance* § 9.05[2] (Matthew Bender 2022).

liability for the damage under its contract with DART. The insurer invoked the Contractual Liability clause of its CGL policy, noting that the insured had settled, and at the time it did so, the trial court had already granted summary judgment on all statutory and tort claims. Thus, the only remaining basis for liability was breach of contractual obligations the insured assumed in its contract with DART. The insured general contractor responded that the contractual liability exclusion did not apply because its liability arose from its own breach of contract and not from liability of another that it assumed. The contractual liability exclusion, said the insured, applies only when an insured has assumed the liability of another such as in hold-harmless or indemnity agreements. It relied on the word "assumption" and argued that to give meaning to that word in the exclusion, the liability assumed has to be that of another party. The court first noted that there was a difference of opinion about the exclusion among courts, both state and federal. It answered the contention of the insured by saying that had the exclusion been intended to be so narrow as to apply only to an agreement in which the insured assumes liability of another by an indemnity or hold-harmless agreement, "it would have been simple to have said so." The court went on to observe that in its contract with DART, the insured undertook a legal obligation to protect property adjacent to the construction site, and to repair or pay for damage to that property. The breach of contract claim against the insured was, therefore, based on an obligation or liability *contractually assumed* by the insured within the meaning of the exclusion.[145]

The exclusion does not apply to liability for damages the insured would have had even without the contract or agreement assuming liability. In other words, if the insured would have been liable to a third party had there been no indemnification agreement, the exclusion is inapplicable.[146] The exclusion also

145. Gilbert Tex. Constr., L.P. v. Underwriters at Lloyd's London, 327 S.W.3d 118 (2010). *See also* State Farm Fire & Cas. Co. v. Metro. Mgmt., 2007 U.S. Dist. LEXIS 99406 (D. Haw. Oct. 31, 2007) (where association sued its property manager and property manager claimed status as insured under association policy, court found that exclusion for coverage for liability for which insured is obligated to pay damages by reason of assumption of liability in contract or agreement applied because all claims by association arose, if at all, from manager's performance or non-performance of its obligations under its management contract with association). The holdings of these courts would appear to ignore a distinction between assuming the liability of another—agreeing to be responsible for the legal obligation of another—and assuming a duty to others, an obligation that exists because of the agreement.

146. 3 Jeffrey E. Thomas, *New Appleman on Insurance Law Library Edition* § 18.03[3][b] (Matthew Bender 2022). *See also* W. Bend Mut. Ins. Co. v. Cleland Homes, Inc., 2016 U.S. Dist. LEXIS 108030 (N.D. Ind. Aug. 16, 2016) (allegation that grading subdivision, creating drainage paths and retention areas altered flow of surface water so as to increase runoff onto plaintiff's lots, and causing concurrent rise in groundwater level of those lots sounded like typical tort claim that would exist independent of any sales contracts); Gilbert Tex. Constr., L.P. v. Underwriters at Lloyd's London, 327 S.W.3d 118 (2010) (when liability of insured is result of

was not applied in a case in which the insured landlord was obligated by lease to keep its roof in serviceable condition and repair. Failure to do so caused the lease premises to be flooded during rainstorms on four occasions. The court noted that although the liability of the insured was based on its performance of its duties under the lease, the occurrence alleged to have caused the property damage was a flood and the underlying complaint sought damages for the destruction of that property, not for the cost of repairing or replacing the inadequate roof.[147]

The exclusion also does not apply to liability for damages the insured assumed in a contract or agreement that is an "insured contract," when the damage happens after execution of that contract or agreement.[148] "Insured contract" is defined to include a contract for a lease of premises,[149] a side track agreement,[150] an easement or license agreement,[151] an obligation required by ordinance to indemnify a municipality, an elevator maintenance agreement, and the part of a contract or agreement pertaining to the business of the named insured—including indemnification of a municipality for work performed for it—pursuant to which the named insured assumes the *tort liability* of another to pay for property damage to a third person or organization.[152] There are

---

otherwise covered basis in addition to its contractually assumed liability, exception brings claim back into coverage).

147. Pa. Mfrs. Indemnity Co. v. Pottstown Indus. Complex, L.P., 215 A.3d 1010 (Pa. Super. 2019) (that underlying action asserted only breach of contract cause of action did not change conclusion that it alleges occurrence potentially within scope of coverage; contract exclusion was limited to claims for which insured was obligated to pay damages by reason of assumption of liability in contract or agreement).

148. For the purposes of liability assumed in an insured contract, reasonable attorney fees and necessary litigation expenses are considered damages.

149. The portion of a lease contract that indemnifies any person or organization for damage by fire to the leased premises while rented to or temporarily occupied by the named insured with permission of the owner is, however, not an insured contract.

150. A "sidetrack agreement" is one "between a railroad and a business in which the railroad agrees to build a siding on the property of the business, and the business will hold the railroad harmless for certain liability arising out of the use of the sidetrack. *Railroad Sidetrack Agreement*, IRMI, https://www.irmi.com/term/insurance-definitions/railroad-sidetrack-agreement.

151. There is an exception for easements or licenses in connection with construction or demolition operations on or within 50 feet of a railroad.

152. *See* ISO Form CG 00 01 12 07, § V.9. *See, e.g.*, Duininck Bros., Inc. v. Howe Precast, Inc., 2008 U.S. Dist. LEXIS 70938 (E.D. Tex. Sept. 19, 2008) (underlying suits were brought against contractor by victims of accidents that occurred in the area as a result of standing water on the freeway because of concrete barriers installed while contractors worked on roadway; subcontractor's agreement to indemnify contractor was an "insured contract" because it was an agreement pertaining to subcontractor's business under which it undertook another party's tort liability to a third party). Tort liability means liability that would be imposed by law absent any contract or agreement. Stanovich, *Contractual Liability and the CGL Policy* (2002), IRMI, https://www.irmi.com/articles/expert-commentary/contractual-liability-and-the-cgl-policy (coverage applies only to particular type of assumed liability, that which arises from breach

three circumstances in which an agreement to assume tort liability is not an insured contract. These are any contract or agreement that does the following:

- Indemnifies a railroad for property damage that arises out of construction or demolition operations, within 50 feet of any railroad property, and affects a railroad bridge or trestle, tracks, roadbeds, tunnel, underpass, or crossing;
- Indemnifies an architect, engineer, or surveyor for damage that arises out of preparing, approving, or failing to prepare or approve maps, shop drawings, opinions, reports, surveys, field orders, change orders, or drawings and specifications, or giving directions or instructions, or failing to give them, if that is the primary cause of the or damage; and
- Provides that an insured who is an architect, engineer, or surveyor assumes liability for damage that arises out of rendering or failure to render professional services, including preparing, approving, or failing to prepare or approve maps, shop drawings, opinions, reports, surveys, field orders, change orders, or drawings and specifications, or giving directions or instructions, or failing to give them, and supervisory, inspection, architectural, or engineering activities.

The purpose of the "insured contract" exception to the exclusion is to provide coverage when a party with which the insured has contracted invokes an indemnification clause in that agreement.

The Contractual Liability exclusion is nuanced and subject to recondite exceptions—and exceptions to the exceptions—that have been much litigated. When an insurer raises the exclusion to deny coverage for a water damage claim, the party seeking coverage needs the counsel of an attorney with extensive experience in commercial general liability insurance.

---

of duty and that exists independent of any contractual relationship indemnitee may have with injured party). Some policies may narrow the definition by eliminating agreements pertaining to the business of the named insured from the definition. *See, e.g.*, Western Heritage Ins. Co. v. Jacobs Dev. Corp., 2013 U.S. Dist. LEXIS 184369 (E.D.N.Y. Dec. 16, 2013), where a passerby tripped and fell on a sidewalk in front of multi-story residential building and sued the building owner, which filed a third-party complaint against the company that had provided concrete installation at the site. The building owner contended it was entitled to full contractual indemnity from that company based on a Subcontract Agreement Rider between the parties in which the company was required to defend, indemnify, and hold harmless the building owner, at its own expense, against all liability or claimed liability for bodily injury. The insurer for the company invoked the contractual liability exclusion, which omitted from the definition of "insured contract" an agreement pertaining to the business of the named insured. The court found that the Subcontract Agreement Rider did not meet the definition of an insured contract and, thus, did not fall within the exception to the exclusion. Therefore, the exclusion for contractual liability applied to the underlying claims against the insured company for contractual liability.

[4] Pollution

The lengthiest exclusion in the standard commercial general liability policy is for property damage arising out of actual,[153] alleged, or threatened discharge, dispersal, seepage, migration, release, or escape of pollutants.[154] A "pollutant" is any solid, liquid, gaseous, or thermal irritant or contaminant and includes smoke, vapor, soot, fumes, acids, alkalis, chemicals, and waste.[155] Under the exclusion, there is no coverage for discharge, dispersal, seepage, migration, release, or escape of pollutants *at or from* any premises, site, or location that is, or was at any time, owned or occupied by, or rented or loaned to, any insured.[156] There is an exception for property damage for which the named insured may be held liable, if the named insured is a contractor and the owner or lessee of the premises, site, or location has been added to the policy as an additional insured with respect to the ongoing operations of the named insured performed for that additional insured at that premises, site, or location and the premises, site, or location is not and never was owned or occupied by, or rented or loaned to, any insured, other than the additional insured.[157] Also under the exclusion, there is no coverage for discharge, dispersal, seepage, migration, release, or escape of pollutants at or from any premises, site, or location that is, or was at any time, used by or for any insured or others for handling, storage, disposal, processing, or treatment of waste.[158] Finally, there is no coverage for any loss, cost, or expense related to testing, monitoring, cleaning up, or removing the effects of pollutants.[159]

---

153. *See* Nat'l Fire Ins. Co. v. Martinelli, 2008 U.S. Dist. LEXIS 52911 (E.D. Cal. July 10, 2008) (where levee broke and enormous amount of wastewater stored in process pond flooded out onto neighboring property, there was quite literally unintentional "freedom from containment, and under California law there was no question this constituted *actual* discharge, dispersal, release, or escape).

154. *See, e.g.*, ISO Form CG 00 01 12 07, § I.A.2.f. It is important to be aware that the exclusion has evolved over the years. In a long tail claim, counsel may encounter an earlier version and needs to be prepared to address the differences to the particular facts of the client's case.

155. *See, e.g.*, ISO Form CG 00 01 12 07, § V.15. Waste includes materials that are to be recycled, reconditioned, or reclaimed.

156. *See* ISO Form CG 00 01 12 07, § I.A.2.f.(1).(a).

157. *See* ISO Form CG 00 01 12 07, § I.A.2.f.(1).(a).(i).

158. *See* ISO Form CG 00 01 12 07, § I.A.2.f.(1).(b). There is also no coverage for discharge, dispersal, seepage, migration, release, or escape of pollutants that are or were at any time transported, handled, stored, treated, disposed of, or processed as waste by or for any insured or any person or organization for whom the named insured may be legally responsible or at or from any premises, site, or location on which any insured or any contractors or subcontractors working directly or indirectly on the behalf of any insured are performing operations if pollutants are brought on or to the premises, site, or location in connection with those operations by that insured, contractor, or subcontractor. ISO Form CG 00 01 12 07, §§ I.A.2.f.(1).(c) & (d). There are three exceptions that would likely not apply to water damage claims.

159. *See* ISO Form CG 00 01 12 07, § I.A.2.f.(2). The actual language is more detailed but is not related to water damage.

As can be seen, the Pollution exclusion is complex web of interrelated provisions and exceptions. A detailed analysis of its application is beyond the scope of this treatise; however, it is examined in great length by the leading insurance law treatises[160] and by scholarly articles.[161]

One way to understand the scope of the Pollution exclusion is to forget about "pollution" in the usual sense. As one expert in the insurance field explains, the easiest way to think of the Pollution exclusion is that it can apply to a *contaminant* and, therefore, if there is something that could contaminate something else, the pollution exclusion could apply.[162] When insurers invoke the exclusion and the underlying claim is for water damage, they almost always assert that the water, or a substance in it, is a contaminant. Courts have found the exclusion applicable to claims for water damage when the water contained sediment and silt,[163] alkaline,[164] fly ash,[165] or salt-water/

---

160. *See* 3 Jeffrey E. Thomas, *New Appleman on Insurance Law Library Edition* § 18.03[6] (Matthew Bender, 2022); Steven Plitt et al., *Couch on Insurance* §§ 127.14–.15 (3d ed. Supp. 2015)

161. *See, e.g.*, Meeks, *The Pollution Delusion: A Proposal for a Uniform Interpretation of Pollution in General Liability Absolute Pollution Exclusions*, 77 Geo. Wash. L. Rev. 824 (2009); Guiliano, *The Sudden and Accidental Exception to the Pollution Exclusion Solution?*, 13 Temp. Envtl. L. & Tech. J. 261 (1994).

162. Connelly, *How Much Do You Know about Pollution Exclusions?* (February 2015), Independent Agent, https://www.iamagazine.com/markets/how-much-do-you-know-about-pollution-exclusions.

163. *See* Builders Mut. Ins. Co. v. Half Court Press, L.L.C., 2010 U.S. Dist. LEXIS 78727 (W.D. Va. Aug. 3, 2010) (runoff sediment could be found to constitute pollutants for purpose of Total Pollution Exclusion); Essex Ins. Co. v. H & H Land Dev. Corp., 525 F. Supp. 2d 1344 (M.D. Ga. 2007) (stormwater runoff and resulting sediment deposits are, under the plain language of policy, contaminants excluded by terms of pollution exclusion); Clarendon Am. Ins. Co. v. Bay Inc., 10 F. Supp. 2d 736, 743 (S.D. Tex. 1998) (sand, gravel, cement, and silica are pollutants within total pollution exclusion); Pa. Nat'l Mut. Cas. Ins. Co. v. Triangle Paving, Inc., 973 F. Supp. 560 (W.D.N.C. 1996) (because sedimentation is not excluded as type of pollutant, issue becomes whether reasonable person in position of defendant would understand pollution exclusion to encompass sedimentation contamination, and exhaustive legislation treating sedimentation as environmentally dangerous offers compelling evidence that sedimentation is commonly understood to be solid contaminant and, thus, pollutant). *See also* Centro Dev. Corp. v. Cent. Mut. Ins. Co., 2017 U.S. Dist. LEXIS 151622 (N.D. Ga. June 10, 2017) (where plaintiff in underlying action alleged insured caused stormwater, siltation, and debris to come onto and damage her property, court said that stormwater whether contaminated or uncontaminated unambiguously qualified as pollutant for purposes of exclusion). *But see* Molton, Allen and Williams, Inc. v. St. Paul Fire and Marine Ins. Co., 347 So. 2d 95, 98 (Ala. 1977) (pollution exclusion did not bar coverage for unintentional washing of sand from rainfall into plaintiffs' lakes; court accepted argument that exclusion was intended to cover only industrial pollution).

164. City of Salina v. Md. Cas. Co., 856 F. Supp. 1467 (D. Kan. 1994) (wastewater contained concentrated sodium hydroxide cleaning solution, an alkali with high pH, which is hazardous to those who came into contact with it and to vegetation, aquatic life, and wildlife and is clearly a pollutant; noting that definition of pollutant clearly and explicitly lists "alkalis" as a specific type of covered irritant or contaminant).

165. Fly ash is a non-hazardous industrial waste byproduct generated by burning of coal in a coal generation plant. In one case fly ash was disposed of in a ravine on the property of

brine.[166] Courts disagree about whether sewage is a pollutant. Many say yes, it is.[167] Others, find it is not, especially when the sewage is waterborne.[168]

---

insured, and during a flash flood, it and other waste materials washed and migrated onto a neighbor's property, damaging their five-acre lake. The court said that despite efforts to categorize fly ash as a benign substance, it clearly constituted "waste" and fell within the policy definition of pollution. Therefore, coverage for the incident was barred. Grain Dealers Mut. Ins. Co. v. Farmers Alliance Mut. Ins. Co., 2001 U.S. Dist. LEXIS 24299 (W.D. Okla. May 14, 2001), *aff'd*, 298 F.3d 1178 (10th Cir. 2002).

166. *See* Century Sur. Co. v. Dewey Bellows Operating Co., 2009 U.S. Dist. LEXIS 78295 (S.D. Tex. Sept. 2, 2009) (Texas courts have consistently held that saltwater is pollutant); Am. Equity Ins. Co. v. Castlemane Farms, Inc., 220 F. Supp. 2d 809 (S.D. Tex. 2002) (insured landscape and gardening company that had been hired by state agency to landscape right-of-way to highway adjacent to damaged property allegedly damaged saltwater disposal pipeline and it discharged onto that adjacent land; court found that it was reasonable to conclude that saltwater was contaminant when introduced, accidentally, onto property that is not meant to receive it and granted summary judgment to insurer under pollution exclusion). *Compare* Milliken v. Fidelity & Casualty Co., 338 F.2d 35 (10th Cir. 1964) (where saltwater escaped from disposal system, court found insurer had duty to defend). *See also* Nat'l Fire Ins. Co. v. Martinelli, 2008 U.S. Dist. LEXIS 52911 (E.D. Cal. July 10, 2008). In *Martinelli*, a levee of a process pond containing saltwater/brine wastewater failed and neighboring property was flooded and olive trees and grape vines on the property were killed. The dispositive question, said the court, was whether the pollution exclusion applied to exclude the damage. The court began by observing that it is possible to "conceive of many situations in which saltwater is not commonly thought of as pollution"; in other words, the court appears to suggest that natural saltwater would not be a pollutant. However, the court held that widespread flooding of a substantial amount of saltwater/brine from a commercial process pond onto adjacent agricultural land was decidedly what is commonly thought of as pollution and, therefore, the damage caused by it was excluded from coverage by the pollution exclusion.

167. *See, e.g.*, Royal Ins. Co. v. Bithell, 868 F. Supp. 878 (E.D. Mich. 1993) (where raw sewage from sewer line beneath insured home entered it, court found sewage was clearly a contaminant or pollutant excluded from coverage); City of Grosse Pointe Park v. Mich. Mun. Liab. & Prop. Pool, 473 Mich. 188, 702 N.W.2d 106 (2005) (insured city had practice of discharging sewage into nearby creek when its sewer system became overtaxed during heavy periods of rain, and as a result nearby residents sued city; court held pollution exclusion was not ambiguous and that discharges fell within scope of that exclusion; "waste," pollutant under exclusion, is commonly understood to include sewage).

168. *See, e.g.*, Fla. Farm Bureau Ins. Co. v. Birge, 659 So. 2d 310 (Fla. 2d DCA 1994) (finding homeowners insurance policy containing pollution exclusion did not unambiguously exclude from coverage damage to insured home caused by sewer malfunction that flooded home with raw sewage); Minerva Enters. v. Bituminous Cas. Corp., 312 Ark. 128, 851 S.W.2d 403 (1993) (where tenant of mobile home park found her mobile home flooded with solid and liquid sewage and claimed insured landlord had failed to exercise ordinary care in maintaining its septic system, insurer refused to defend or to indemnify based on pollution exclusion; court found exclusion ambiguous and agreed that "waste" as used in exclusion was intended to exclude industrial wastes, not common household wastes); United States Fidelity & Guaranty Co. v. Armstrong, 479 So. 2d 1164 (Ala. 1985) (where, during construction of new sewer system, raw sewage flowed onto adjacent land whose owner sued insured, insurer contended pollution exclusion excluded coverage, but court observed it had held exclusion was intended to cover only industrial pollution and contamination; court said it "should not be understood" to hold that raw sewage could *never* be pollutant, only that policy clause, under facts of case before it, did not eliminate coverage). *See also* Evanston Ins. Co. v. J&J Cable Constr., LLC,

Courts also say that damage from water containing sewage may be caused by the water, in which case the exclusion should not apply.[169]

Courts may also decide that regardless of whether sewage is a pollutant, if the damage at issue is caused by the force of the water, then the pollution exclusion is inapplicable. For example, in a New York case,[170] a city sewer main ruptured and discharged a flood of water and sewage into many homes. The homeowners sued the city for property damage. The insurer disclaimed coverage based on the total pollution exclusion. The court said that assuming, without deciding, that raw sewage unambiguously constitutes a "contaminant" for purposes of the exclusion, in the underlying complaints at least some of the damages incurred were arguably attributable to the force of the rushing of water and it could not be said that the erosion and structural damage alleged—shifted foundations and cracked interior walls—would not have occurred "but for" the presence of raw sewage.[171] Thus, insurer had a duty to defend, although the issue of its duty to indemnify would await the proof at trial.

2016 U.S. Dist. LEXIS 129371 (M.D. Ala. Sept. 22, 2016) (sewage is not pollutant within terms of policy absolute pollution exclusion).

169. Guenther v. City of Onalaska, 223 Wis. 2d 206, 588 N.W.2d 375 (Wisc. App. 1998) (finding it possible that exclusion for contamination by pollutants could be read not to apply to occurrence "as routine as a domestic sewer backup," which caused at least some damages unrelated to any toxic nature of the sewage); Incorporated Village of Cedarhurst v. Hanover Insurance Co., 89 N.Y.2d 293, 653 N.Y.S.2d 68, 675 N.E.2d 822 (1996) (because any risk of liability faced by insured allegedly arose from flood-like nature of the discharge of water and sewage rather than its polluting character, insurer was obligated to defend, but trial was necessary before any determination on indemnification could be made).

170. City of Kingston v. Harco Nat'l Ins. Co., 46 A.D.3d 1320, 848 N.Y.S.2d 455 (2007), *app. dis.*, 858 N.Y.S.2d 648, 10 N.Y.3d 822, 888 N.E.2d 389 (2008). *See also* Incorporated Village of Cedarhurst v. Hanover Ins. Co., 653 N.Y.S.2d 68, 89 N.Y.2d 293, 675 N.E.2d 822 (1996), where the issue was whether the insurer was required to defend the insured village for property damage allegedly caused by a discharge or overflow of raw sewage from its sewer system. The insurer disclaimed coverage pursuant to the pollution exclusion in its policy. The court noted that the allegations in the underlying complaint were about damage from a "flood-like event," not an injury from the "polluting," irritating, or contaminating nature of the sewage. The pollution exclusion did not apply, said the court, when the complaint did not allege that the discharge actually resulted in pollution. Thus, the pollution exclusion did not relieve the insurer of its obligation to defend, although evidence of pollution-related injuries could develop at trial and absolve the insurer of its duty to indemnify. A vigorous dissent argued to no avail that there was no conceptual way to differentiate between damage *arising out of* flooding with the hazardous contaminant of sewage and any other invasion of sewage into a human habitat. Incorporated Village of Cedarhurst v. Hanover Ins. Co., 653 N.Y.S.2d 68, 73, 89 N.Y.2d 293, 303, 675 N.E.2d 822, 827 (1996) (Levine, J., dissenting).

171. *See also* Commodore Plaza Condo. Ass'n v. QBE Ins. Corp., 2013 U.S. Dist. LEXIS 192675 (S.D. Fla. May 20, 2013) (where underlying complaint alleged association failed to install roof tarps in timely and proper manner resulting in additional water and mold damage and workers it hired were removing asbestos containing materials improperly and without the proper qualifications, pollution exclusion was inapplicable because complaint did not allege damages were caused by fungus, bacteria, or asbestos).

Water alone has been held not to be a pollutant.[172] For example, each spring, when the water rose, the owner of a lake raised flood gates and released some of the water. The water flowed into an area of surface springs that then experienced bacterial contamination. The owner of the surface springs sued. The insurer for the lake owner denied coverage based on the pollution exclusion. The court noted that the plaintiff in the underlying action did not allege that water from the lake was polluted or contaminated, but that flooding caused by the release of water from the lake resulted in contamination of the springs with surface bacteria the origin of which was not alleged. Because the lake water was not alleged to be a pollutant, release of it did not constitute release of a pollutant within the meaning of the pollution exclusion.[173] In contrast, Georgia courts have held that stormwater unambiguously qualifies as a pollutant.[174] That appears to be because stormwater runoff invariably carries sediment or silt with it, and they can be considered pollutants,[175] although not all courts agree.[176]

[5] Property Damage Exclusions

Two property damage exclusions that are standard in CGL policies—known as "Ongoing Operations" and "Your Work"—are often raised, frequently together, in construction defect cases where there has been water damage. When both exclusions are raised by the insurer, it is important to be aware of both the differences and similarities between them.

[a] Ongoing Operations Exclusion

Under the Ongoing Operations Exclusion, there is no coverage for property damage to "that particular part" of *real property* on which the named insured

---

172. Builders Mut. Ins. Co. v. Half Court Press, L.L.C., 2010 U.S. Dist. LEXIS 78727 (W.D. Va. Aug. 3, 2010) (water is not pollutant under exclusion, and damage from water does not fall under exclusion); State Auto Property and Cas. Ins. Co. v. Gorsuch, 323 F. Supp. 2d 746 (W.D. Va. 2004) (uncontaminated water has not been treated as a pollutant under plain and ordinary meaning of that term in a pollution exclusion clause).

173. Purity Spring Resort v. TIG Insurance Co., 2000 U.S. Dist. LEXIS 10918 (D.N.H. July 18, 2000). *Compare* Liberty Mut. Fire Ins. Co. v. Copart of Conn., Inc., 2021 U.S. Dist. LEXIS 157457 (N.D. Tex. Aug. 20, 2021) (pollution exclusion applied to stormwater runoff containing aluminum, lead, titanium, arsenic, and copper).

174. Centro Dev. Corp. v. Cent. Mut. Ins. Co., 2017 U.S. Dist. LEXIS 151622 (N.D. Ga. June 10, 2017).

175. *See, e.g.*, Owners Ins. Co. v. Chadd's Lake Homeowners Ass'n, 2004 U.S. Dist. LEXIS 30675 (N.D. Ga. Dec. 28, 2004) (damage alleged was caused by discharge of silt, sediment, and stormwater runoff that, when discharged into lake, altered content, appearance, and purity of lake water, affecting its cleanliness and its benefit as an amenity; pollution exclusion applied because silt, sediment, and stormwater runoff constitute pollutants).

176. *See* Nationwide Mut. Ins. Co. v. Boyd Corp., 2010 U.S. Dist. LEXIS 5438 (E.D. Va. Jan. 25, 2010) (pollution exclusion inapplicable where underling complaint alleged damage from excess water flow, stormwater runoff, and sediments).

or any contractors or subcontractors working directly or indirectly on behalf of the named insured *are* performing operations, if that property damage arises out of those operations.[177] There are several things of which to take note in the exclusion. The first is the awkward phrase "that particular part." It is not defined in the standard CGL policy. Generally, courts interpret it to mean that damage to the part of real property on which the insured has contracted to work is excluded, but not consequential damage caused by faulty construction.[178] For example, if a roofer contracts to repair a roof, damage to the roof is not covered, but damage to other parts of the property as a consequence of the work on the roof is usually covered.[179] Of course, few things are simple when insurance policy language is being interpreted. Take, for instance, cases in which insured pool painters were claimed to be responsible for the pools popping out of the ground while empty. In a New Jersey case, not only was the pool cracked and beyond repaired, but also the incident caused considerable damage to the adjacent decking and landscaping. The insurer conceded the Ongoing Operations exclusion did not bar coverage for the damages to the decking and landscaping, but it denied any coverage for the pool based on the exclusion. The trial court said the pool was not the subject of the faulty workmanship as the insured did not sell or install it or repair it. The insured's task was to paint the pool, and its negligence led to its damage. That damage was consequential to the negligence of the insured's acts and omissions and, therefore, covered under the policy. The appellate court reversed. It concluded that draining the pool was the first step in painting it, which was the work the insured was hired to perform, and thus, the property damage arose out of those operations and occurred while the insured was performing operations.[180] Does that mean, to return to the roofing example, that if the roofer is hired to replace several shingles on the front of the

177. ISO Form CG 00 01 12 07, § I.A.2.j.(5).

178. *See, e.g.*, Emplrs. Mut. Cas. Co. v. Kenny Hayes Custom Homes, LLC, 2016 U.S. Dist. LEXIS 15340 (S.D. Ala. Feb. 9, 2016) (where alleged water damage did not arise from work being performed on property that was damaged but instead caused damage to otherwise non-defective portion of property, exclusion did not apply); Century Sur. Co. v. Dewey Bellows Operating Co., 2009 U.S. Dist. LEXIS 78295 (S.D. Tex. Sept. 2, 2009) (where insured operated a saltwater injection well on leased two-acre facility and was alleged to have discharged significant amount onto real property, damage fell under exclusion because allegations in underlying suit all included property damage to two-acre area on which insured operated disposal facility as result of those operations).

179. *See, e.g.*, Builders Mut. Ins. Co. v. Mitchell, 210 N.C. App. 657, 709 S.E.2d 528 (2011) (exclusion does not apply to previously undamaged property that is not part of insured's work product).

180. Ohio Cas. Ins. Co. v. Island Pool & Spa, Inc., 418 N.J. Super. 162, 12 A.3d 719 (2011). *Accord* Pekin Ins. Co. v. Willett, 235 Ill. Dec. 350, 301 Ill. App. 3d 1034, 704 N.E.2d 923 (1998). *See also* Camelot Dev. Group, LLC v. Jim Karrels Trucking Sand & Gravel, Inc., 322 Wis. 2d 736, 778 N.W.2d 172 (Wisc. App. 2009), where the insured, while grading a property, hit a drain tile causing flooding to the property, the insured argued there should be coverage because he was not "performing operations" on the drain tile when he struck it. However, the court said that the exclusion bars coverage for property damage to "that particular part" of the

roof and damages the back of it while gaining access to the front, there is no coverage? Apparently so.

The next aspect of the exclusion of which to take note is that it applies to "real property," another term the standard CGL policy does not define. Obviously, the phrase "real property" is used to draw a distinction with "personal property," but that still does not define the former. *Black's Law Dictionary* defines "real property" as a term applied to land and immovable property on land such as buildings.[181] Another dictionary defines a "building" as a "structure designed and suitable for habitation or sheltering human beings and animals, sheltering or storing property, or for use and occupation for private and public business, trade, or manufacture."[182] It adds that a foundation is a part of a building.

Finally, the exclusion has a temporal aspect. It applies to *real property* on which the named insured or any contractors or subcontractors *are* performing operations. Thus, commentators generally agree that, for the exclusion to apply, the property damage at issue has to have occurred while the operations of the insured were ongoing, that is, while the work is being performed.[183] What does it mean for the work to be "ongoing"? The Fifth Circuit Court of Appeals considered a case in which water intrusion occurred during a time in which the insured's construction activities building a five-unit condominium project were suspended. Arguably, the insured was performing operations at the time of the damage because the project had not yet been completed. The court, however, said that the ordinary meaning of "performing operations" is the active performance of work and prolonged, open-ended, and complete suspension of construction activities pending purchase of the condominium units did not fall within the ordinary meaning of "performing operations."

---

property being worked on and the drain tile was intrinsically tied to "that particular part" of the property being worked on.

181. *Real Property*, Black's Law Dictionary: Free Online Legal Dictionary 2d Ed., https://thelawdictionary.org/real-property/.

182. *Ballentine's Law Dictionary* (LexisNexis, 2010).

183. Grinnell Mut. Reinsurance Co. v. Ripley, 2009 Minn. App. Unpub. LEXIS 1349 (Minn. App. Dec. 29, 2009). In *Grinnell* homeowners sued their contractor after their yard flooded and water seeped into their home's basement. They sought money damages for re-construction and installation of surface water drainage improvements to prevent future flooding. The court noted that although the underlying complaint described a flood, it did not attribute its claim to costs resulting from the flood, but rather alleged that costly alterations were necessary because the house was defectively constructed, not as a result of the flood. The flood occurred after construction operations had ceased, but the property damage at issue was defective construction that necessarily occurred while construction operations were ongoing. That damage was excluded from coverage. *Compare* Am. Family Mut. Ins. Co. v. Wilkinson Family, 2012 U.S. Dist. LEXIS 191141 (D. Ariz. June 1, 2012) (homeowners hired insured to add extension to their home, which required tying into existing sewer lines and subsequently when all sewer lines were filled with water to test them, they leaked under slab; exclusion for operations of insured did not apply because insured was not performing ongoing work at the time of occurrence).

There was not, the court noted, a brief, temporary halt of work, as might occur at the conclusion of each workday or during several days of inclement weather, but rather a total cessation of active construction work for the foreseeable future. Although the insured intended to eventually complete construction work once the units were sold, an insured is not actively performing a task, said the court, simply because he or she has not yet completed it, but plans to do so some time in the future.[184]

[b] "Your Work" Exclusion

There is no coverage under the standard commercial general liability policy for property damage to "that particular part" of any property that has to be repaired or replaced because "your work"—meaning the work of the named insured—was incorrectly performed on it.[185] "Your work" is defined as work or operations performed by the named insured or on behalf of the named insured and materials, parts, or equipment furnished in connection with that work or those operations.[186] The exclusion is often invoked by insurers when the underlying action is for construction defects. As discussed earlier,[187] insurers routinely argue that construction defects are not accidental and, therefore, not an occurrence covered under a CGL policy. Thus, the "Your Work" exclusion is an alternative policy defense for insurance carriers.

The exclusion is often at issue when the underlying claim is for water damage. For example, the owners of an apartment building claimed that while replacing the roof, the roofer failed to protect the building from rainstorms that caused extensive water damage to the interior of the building. The court said that generally the "Your Work" exclusion is construed to exclude coverage when the damage is to the property on which the insured has contracted to perform operations,[188] but not to exclude coverage when the damage is

---

184. Mid-Continent Cas. Co. v. JHP Dev., Inc., 557 F.3d 207 (5th Cir. 2009) (noting that cases cited by insurer were consistent with interpretation that exclusion j(5) applies only to damage caused during active physical construction activities and none of those cases holds or suggests that exclusion applies to damage caused during prolonged suspension of active construction work).

185. ISO Form CG 00 01 12 07, § I.A.2.j.(6).

186. ISO Form CG 00 01 12 07, § V.22.a. It also includes warranties or representations with respect to the fitness, quality, durability, performance, or use of the work of the named insured and providing, or failing to provide, warnings or instructions. ISO Form CG 00 01 12 07, § V.22.b.

187. See § 9.07[7], *supra*.

188. *See, e.g.*, Oak Creek Apartments LLC v. Garcia, 2013 Mich. App. LEXIS 550 (Mar. 21, 2013) (where contractor's workmanship is faulty, exclusion unambiguously proscribes coverage for damage to particular part of property with regard to which workmanship was faulty, but not damages to other property); General Cas. Co. v. Image Builders, Inc., 2010 U.S. Dist. LEXIS 115631 (W.D.N.C. Oct. 29, 2010) (where insured contractor allegedly failed to place water drainage pipes properly and to compact and or grade dirt, resulting in front half of

to property on which the insured was not performing operations. Thus, the court concluded the roof was the "particular part" of the property on which the work was incorrectly performed and any damages for repair or replacement of the defective roof were excluded from coverage, but damages to the interior of the building were not the "particular part" of any property as used in the exclusion. Those damages were not subject to the exclusion and were covered.[189] In a case decided by the Fifth Circuit Court of Appeal, the insured failed to properly water-seal the exterior finishes and retaining walls of a condominium project, and large quantities of water penetrated the interior of the structure through ceilings and walls and under doors, damaging interior drywall, stud framing, electrical wiring, and wood flooring. The federal court said that the plain meaning of the exclusion is that "property damage only to parts of the property that were themselves the subjects of the defective work is excluded." The exclusion, said the court, did not bar coverage for damage to parts of the property that were the subject of only non-defective work by the insured and were damaged by defective work on other parts of the property

---

property separating and sliding down face of mountain during heavy rain, faulty workmanship in construction of that slope was part of work of named insured and excluded from coverage); Camelot Dev. Group, LLC v. Jim Karrels Trucking Sand & Gravel, Inc., 322 Wis. 2d 736, 778 N.W.2d 172 (Wisc. App. 2009) (insured, while grading property, hit drain tile causing flooding to that property; insured argued exclusion did not apply because it bars coverage only for damage occurring when "your work was incorrectly performed on it" and he was not performing work on drain tile, but on land, but court held that drain tile buried on property was so associated with that property that insured was not working on something different when he damaged drain tile, he was working on property itself).

189. ACUITY v. Burd & Smith Constr., Inc., 721 N.W.2d 33 (ND 2006), *overruled on other grounds*, K & L Homes, Inc. v. Am. Family Mut. Ins. Co., 829 N.W.2d 724, 736 (N.D. 2013). *See also* Builders Mut. Ins. Co. v. Mitchell, 210 N.C. App. 657, 709 S.E.2d 528 (2011) (where water intrusion that damaged interior components of home was result of alleged faulty workmanship on roof and gutter system, exclusion did not apply to previously undamaged property that was not part of insured's work product); United States Fidelity & Guaranty Co. v. Bonitz Insulation Co., 424 So. 2d 569 (Ala. 1982) (where insured contracted for construction of roofing and insulation on gymnasium and roof began to leak almost immediately and was entirely replaced about six years later, exclusion applied to remove liability for damage to roof itself from coverage; however, there were also claims for damage to ceilings, walls, carpets, and gym floor, and court concluded there could be no doubt that if there was damage to some other property than the insured's work, liability for that damage would become liability of insurer under policy). *And see* Breezewood of Wilmington Condos. Homeowners' Ass'n v. Amerisure Mut. Ins. Co., 335 Fed. Appx. 268 (4th Cir. July 1, 2009) (insured served as general contractor for condominium development and was sued by association for defects in construction and design of buildings including excessive moisture introduced into wood products that necessitated repairs and reconstruction of major portions of property; issue before court was whether "property damage" was caused by "occurrence," as North Carolina courts have consistently held that "property damage" in context of commercial general liability policies means damage to property that was previously undamaged and does not include expense of repairing property or completing project that was not done correctly; court noted its conclusion was consistent with policy, read as whole, which contained "Your Work" exclusion).

and, therefore, did not exclude coverage for the water damage to the interior portions of the condominiums.[190]

The exclusion is for work or operations performed by the named insured or *on its behalf*. Therefore, the work or operations of a subcontractor for the insured fall within the exclusion.

There is an exception to the "Your Work" exclusion for "property damage" that is included in the "products completed operations hazard" (PCOH). That phrase is defined in the standard CGL policy to mean property damage that occurs *away from premises* the named insured owns or rents,[191] and arising out of "your work" or "your product" after the work is completed.[192] PCOH is confusing and not clearly identified in the standard CGL policy.[193] The coverage is

---

190. Mid-Continent Cas. Co. v. JHP Dev., Inc., 557 F.3d 207 (5th Cir. 2009). *Compare* Century Indemnity Co. v. Golden Hills Builders, Inc., 348 S.C. 559, 561 S.E.2d 355 (S.C. 2002) (where homeowners alleged their home was defective because synthetic stucco exterior allowed moisture damage to properly constructed substrate and framing and argued "Your Work" exclusion should be interpreted to mean that only work incorrectly performed—exterior stucco—was excluded and repairs to other parts of the property where the work was correctly performed—substrate and substructure—were not; however, court held coverage for repair and/or replacement of substrate and substructure was excluded). *See also* Pulte Homes of N.M., Inc. v. Ind. Lumbermens Ins. Co., 367 P.3d 869 (N.M. App. 2015) (where all of damage claimed is damage to work of insured, "your work" exclusion applies to preclude coverage, but where windows and sliding glass doors installed by insured caused damage to other property, namely stucco around windows, exclusion did not apply); Pa. Mfrs. Indemnity Co. v. Pottstown Indus. Complex, L.P., 215 A.3d 1010 (Pa. Super. 2019) (where underlying claims allege that insured's faulty work caused event that damaged other property, there was an occurrence and insurer had duty to defend).

191. Stanovich, *The Hazards of Products and Completed Operations: Understanding the Fundamentals* (2006), IRMI, https://www.irmi.com/articles/expert-commentary/the-hazards-of-products-and-completed-operations (bodily injury or property damage that takes place on named insured premises is not within products-completed operations hazard, although that can be amended by endorsement called "Products-Completed Operations Hazard Redefined"—ISO Form CG 24 07—which changes definition by removing requirement that bodily injury or property damage take place away from premises of named insured for claim to be included within products-completed operations hazard).

192. *See, e.g.*, ISO Form CG 00 01 12 07, § V.16. There are exceptions for products still in the physical possession of the named insured and work abandoned or not yet completed. Work that may need service, maintenance, correction, repair, or replacement, but is otherwise complete, is treated as completed. Products-completed operations hazard does not include bodily injury or property damage that arises out of transportation of property, unless injury or damage arises out of a condition in or on a vehicle not owned or operated by the named insured, and that condition was created by loading or unloading of that vehicle by any insured. It also does not include injury arising out of the existence of tools, uninstalled equipment, or abandoned or unused materials. A final exception is for products or operations for which the classification, listed on the Declarations Page or in a policy schedule, states that products-completed operations are subject to the general aggregate limit. *See* Goodwin v. Wright, 100 Wn. App. 631, 635–36, 6 P.3d 1, 4 (2000) (purpose of products-completed operations hazard coverage is to insure against the risk that the product or work, if defective, may cause bodily injury or damage to property of others after it leaves hands of insured).

193. Stanovich, *The Hazards of Products and Completed Operations: Understanding the Fundamentals* (2006), IRMI, https://www.irmi.com/articles/expert-commentary/the-hazards-of

not found in a single section of the policy.[194] To discover it, one first has to look at the Declarations Page, which typically has a box labeled "Limits of Insurance." In that box, there will be a row that reads "products-completed operations aggregate limit."[195] Next to it will be a line that, if products-completed operations hazard coverage applies, will be filled in with the word "included." If it is, the "Your Work" exclusion is nullified,[196] and PCOH is a part of the policy coverage.[197] One leading insurance treatise asserts that the exception has the effect of limiting the exclusion to property damage that happened before the work of the insured was complete.[198] There is then coverage for occurrences during the policy term.[199] However, as discussed below, there is a standard exclusion for property damage to completed work.[200]

-products-and-completed-operations (any type of coherent explanation as to how PCOH coverage actually works is usually lacking).

194. Kneisel & Cooke, *The Products-Completed Operations Hazard: When Coverage Exists, Just What Is Covered?*, 2009 Construction Law Update § 6.02 (Aspen Publishers, Inc. 2009).

195. The PCOH aggregate limit shown on the Declarations Page is the most the carrier will pay for damages because of bodily injury and property damage included in the products-completed operations hazard. CG 00 01 12 07, § III.3.

196. Owners Ins. Co. v. Jim Carr Homebuilder, LLC, 157 So. 3d 148 (Ala. 2014) (if Declarations Page shows coverage for "products-completed operations," then "Your work" exclusion does not apply and here insured bargained and paid for up to total of $4 million in coverage for its "products-completed operations," which nullifies and renders inapplicable "Your Work" exclusion). *See also* Am. Family Mut. Ins. Co. v. Wilkinson Family, 2012 U.S. Dist. LEXIS 191141 (D. Ariz. June 1, 2012) (where insured added extension to home, requiring tying into existing sewer lines, and subsequently sewer lines when filled with water to test them, leaked under slab, "Your Work" exclusion, by its terms, did not apply to "property damage" included in "products-completed operations hazard"; as property damage occurred on property of homeowner, which was not owned or rented by insured and insured's work had ceased, "products-completed operations hazard" applied, and exclusion was inapplicable).

197. *See* Am. Home Assur. Co. v. AGM Marine Contractors, Inc., 379 F. Supp. 2d 134, 137 (D. Mass. 2005), *aff'd*, 467 F.3d 810 (1st Cir. 2006) (PCOH, when properly construed as subpart of entire policy, describes coverage within policy for same type of injuries or damages covered by rest of policy; nothing in PCOH provision dispenses with requirement that occurrence cause damage).

198. 3 Jeffrey E. Thomas, *New Appleman on Insurance Law Library Edition* § 18.03[10][i][iv] (Matthew Bender 2022).

199. Products and completed operations coverage is only for occurrences that happen during the term of the CGL policy and for it to continue year-to-year after completion of the work, the named insured has to purchase completed operations coverage either year-to-year after the original policy term or for a specified term after completion of the work, with the project scheduled as covered and endorsed to include the owner as an additional insured under ISO CG 20 37 04 13. Coverage can also be obtained under a project-specific policy written for the term of construction plus an extended coverage period negotiated by the parties. Locke & Comiskey, *A Dozen Things You Wish You Had Known about Commercial Project Insurance* at 15 (2013), *available at* www.gdhm.com/wp-content/uploads/2016/08/whl-a-dozen-things-you-wish-you-had-known-acrel-vancouver-fall-2013.pdf.

200. See § 9.07[5][d], *infra*.

[c] Damage to Your Product Exclusion

There is a standard exclusion for property damage to the product of the insured "arising out of it or any part of it."[201] A court found this exclusion applied in a case in which the plaintiff in the underlying action sued a construction contractor for, *inter alia*, leaking in a parking garage, water damage to a lobby of an office building and basement underneath that lobby, and interior water damage caused by water penetration of a roof, all constructed by the defendant.[202] Another court applied the exclusion where an improperly installed waterproofing membrane on a plaza deck leaked and the owner sued for the cost of repairing the deck.[203] That court added that a building, or building addition, falls within the meaning of "product."

[d] Your Completed Work Exclusion

There is an exclusion to coverage for property damage to the work of the named insured arising out of the work, or any part of it, *and included* in the products-completed operations hazard.[204] Thus, for the exclusion to apply, the damage has to not only be to "your work"—that is, the work of the named insured—but also be included in the products-completed operations hazard.[205]

PCOH is defined in the standard CGL policy to mean property damage that occurs *away from premises* the named insured owns or rents,[206] and

201. ISO Form CG 00 01 12 07, § I.A.2.k. *See generally* Henderson, *Insurance Protection for Products Liability & Completed Operations—What Every Lawyer Should Know*, 50 Neb. L. Rev. 415 (1971).

202. Monticello Insurance Co. v. Wil-Freds Construction, Inc., 214 Ill. Dec. 597, 277 Ill. App. 3d 697, 705, 661 N.E.2d 451 (1996).

203. Wm. C. Vick Constr. Co. v. Pa. Nat'l Mut. Cas. Ins. Co., 52 F. Supp. 2d 569 (E.D.N.C. 1999).

204. *See, e.g.*, ISO Form CG 00 01 12 07, § I.2.l. *See generally* Henderson, *Insurance Protection for Products Liability & Completed Operations—What Every Lawyer Should Know*, 50 Neb. L. Rev. 415 (1971).

205. Owners Ins. Co. v. Jim Carr Homebuilder, LLC, 157 So. 3d 148, 156–57 (Ala. 2014).

206. *See* Central Trust Co., N.A. v. Hartford Ins. Group, 1985 Ohio App. LEXIS 8651 (Sept. 4, 1985) (where two separate floods related to sewer and culvert system occurred and damaged properties, property owners filed civil actions against insured; court found it was at least arguable that claims did not fall within exclusion as culvert system extended throughout tract of land owned by insured, and it was at least arguable that damage did not occur "away from premises owned by or rented to" named insured). *See also* Stanovich, *The Hazards of Products and Completed Operations: Understanding the Fundamentals* (2006), IRMI, https://www.irmi.com/articles/expert-commentary/the-hazards-of-products-and-completed-operations (bodily injury or property damage that takes place on named insured premises is not within products-completed operations hazard, although that can be amended by endorsement called "Products-Completed Operations Hazard Redefined"—ISO Form CG 24 07—which changes definition by removing requirement that bodily injury or property damage take place away from premises of named insured for claim to be included within products-completed operations hazard).

arising out of "your work" or "your product" *after the work is completed*.[207] The definition is designed to ensure the policy covers accidents occurring while construction is under way, but not property damage that is caused by poor workmanship in a completed building.[208]

The exclusion is sometimes referred to as the "Your Work" exclusion, which can cause it to be confused with another exclusion known by the same name. That exclusion applies to property damage that occurred before the work was completed.[209] This exclusion applies *after the work is completed* and might better be called the "Your Completed Work" exclusion.[210]

PCOH is confusing and not clearly identified in the standard CGL policy.[211] The coverage is not found in a single section of the policy.[212] To discover it, one first has to look at the Declarations Page, which typically has a box labeled

---

207. *See, e.g.*, ISO Form CG 00 01 12 07, § V.16. There are exceptions for products still in the physical possession of the named insured and work abandoned or not yet completed. Work that may need service, maintenance, correction, repair, or replacement, but is otherwise complete, is treated as completed. Products-completed operations hazard does not include bodily injury or property damage that arises out of transportation of property, unless injury or damage arises out of a condition in or on a vehicle not owned or operated by the named insured, and that condition was created by loading or unloading of that vehicle by any insured. It also does not include injury arising out of the existence of tools, uninstalled equipment, or abandoned or unused materials. A final exception is for products or operations for which the classification, listed on the Declarations Page or in a policy schedule, states that products-completed operations are subject to the general aggregate limit. *See* Goodwin v. Wright, 100 Wn. App. 631, 635–36, 6 P.3d 1, 4 (2000) (purpose of products-completed operations hazard coverage is to insure against the risk that the product or work, if defective, may cause bodily injury or damage to property of others after it leaves hands of insured).

208. Westfield Ins. Co. v. Sheehan Constr. Co., 564 F.3d 817, 819 (7th Cir. 2009) ("products-completed operations hazard" definition is designed to ensure that policy covers accidents that occur while construction is under way, but not property damage caused by poor workmanship in completed building).

209. 3 Jeffrey E. Thomas, *New Appleman on Insurance Law Library Edition* § 18.03[10][i][iv] (Matthew Bender 2022).

210. *See* Liberty Mut. Fire Ins. Co. v. E.E. Cruz & Co., 475 F. Supp. 2d 400 (S.D.N.Y. 2007) (property damage alleged did not fall within scope of exclusion, because at time of occurrence work under contract had not yet been completed). *Consider* Flori v. Allstate Ins. Co., 120 R.I. 511, 388 A.2d 25 (1978), where a property owner contracted for renovation of the downstairs area of a dwelling. After foundation and concrete work was begun, the premises were flooded. The property owner sued, but the allegations in the underlying complaint failed to specify whether the alleged negligence of the insured occurred before or after his operations would be deemed completed under the policy. The pleadings, therefore, left in doubt whether the completed operations exclusion was applicable. That doubt had to be resolved against the insurer, which was, therefore, required to defend.

211. Stanovich, *The Hazards of Products and Completed Operations: Understanding the Fundamentals* (2006), IRMI, https://www.irmi.com/articles/expert-commentary/the-hazards-of-products-and-completed-operations (any type of coherent explanation as to how PCOH coverage actually works is usually lacking).

212. Kneisel & Cooke, *The Products-Completed Operations Hazard: When Coverage Exists, Just What Is Covered?*, 2009 Construction Law Update § 6.02 (Aspen Publishers, Inc. 2009).

"Limits of Insurance." In that box, there will be a row that reads "products-completed operations aggregate limit."[213] Next to it will be a line that, if products-completed operations hazard coverage applies, will be filled in with the word "included." If it is, PCOH is a part of the policy coverage.[214]

There is an important exception to the exclusion. It does not apply if the damaged work, or the work out of which the damage arises, was performed by a subcontractor on behalf of the named insured. The exception did not appear in the 1973 version of the standard CGL policy. It was added by ISO in 1986. Courts enforce the exception. As the New Jersey Supreme Court noted, if an insurer does not want to insure the risk of the damage described in the exception, it can amend the policy by endorsement.[215] Indeed, there are standard ISO endorsements that do exactly that. One retains the basic exclusionary language and simply omits any reference to subcontractors.[216] Another includes a schedule for describing designated sites or operations and provides that with respect to the sites or operations designated in that schedule, there is no coverage for property damage to the work of the named insured that arises out of it, or any part of it, and is included in the products-completed operations hazard.[217] It omits any mention of subcontractors. Thus, the exception for work performed by a subcontractor on behalf of the named insured applies unless the work is listed in the schedule.

The subcontractor exception is sometimes at issue. For example, homeowners claimed a builder was negligent in building their homes and that as a result, there was water intrusion into or under their basements. The insurer contended the property damage—erosion under the foundations and diminishment of the

---

213. The PCOH aggregate limit shown on the Declarations Page is the most the carrier will pay for damages because of bodily injury and property damage included in the products-completed operations hazard. CG 00 01 12 07, § III.3.

214. *See* Am. Home Assur. Co. v. AGM Marine Contractors, Inc., 379 F. Supp. 2d 134, 137 (D. Mass. 2005), *aff'd*, 467 F.3d 810 (1st Cir. 2006) (PCOH, when properly construed as subpart of entire policy, describes coverage within policy for same type of injuries or damages covered by rest of policy; nothing in PCOH provision dispenses with requirement that occurrence causes damage).

215. Cypress Point Condo. Ass'n v. Adria Towers, L.L.C., 226 N.J. 403, 431, 143 A.3d 273, 289 (2016) (insurers chose not to negotiate away subcontractor exception and instead issued series of 1986 ISO standard form CGL policies that explicitly provide coverage for property damage caused by subcontractor's defective performance). *See also* Travelers Indem. Co. of Am. v. Moore & Assocs., 216 S.W.3d 302 (Tenn. 2007) (damages resulting from subcontractors' faulty installation of windows not excluded from coverage, even if those damages affected contractor's work); Kalchthaler v. Keller Constr. Co., 224 Wis. 2d 387, 591 N.W.2d 169 (1999) (exception to exclusion stating it did not apply to work done by subcontractors of insured meant coverage for damage to completed work caused by work of subcontractor was restored and there was, therefore, coverage for building leak causing water damage to interior).

216. ISO Form CG 22 94 10 01 (Exclusion—Damage to Work Performed by Subcontractors on Your Behalf).

217. ISO Form CG 22 95 10 01 (Exclusion—Damage to Work Performed by Subcontractors on Your Behalf—Designated Sites or Operations).

value of the homes—was expressly excluded by the plain language of the exclusion. The homeowners countered that the concrete basement/foundations for their houses were poured by a subcontractor and, therefore, the exception to the exclusion was applicable and the damage was covered by the policy. The court did not agree. It said that if the homeowners claimed that defective performance by the subcontractor—for example, that the subcontractor dug the foundations too deep or used defective concrete that was porous and crumbling—caused their problems, then the subcontractor exception would apply. That, however, was not what they claimed. Instead, they were alleging the subdivision was designed with a negligent drainage plan and that their homes were improperly sited on lots with a water table that was too high to allow basements to be constructed, so the exclusion applied.[218]

9.8 Non-Standard Exclusions

[1] Water Damage Liability Exclusion

There is an endorsement that can be added to commercial general liability policies that excludes water damage liability. One version broadly bars coverage for property damage—occurring *on or from* premises owned or leased by any insured—to buildings or contents that arise out of the following:

- Discharge, leakage, or overflow of water from plumbing, heating, refrigeration, or air-conditioning systems; standpipes for fire hoses; or automatic sprinkler systems;
- Collapse or fall of tanks or component parts or supports of automatic sprinklers;[219] and
- Leakage or overflow of water from *any external source* including roofs, gutters, downspouts, and foundations.[220]

Similar language was examined in a case before the Massachusetts Supreme Judicial Court. In the case, an employee of the insured, while moving stock, accidently struck a sprinkler pipe and head, causing water to escape and seep to the floor below. The water damaged property of the occupant of that floor who sued the insured. The insurer denied coverage because the damage

218. W. Bend Mut. Ins. Co. v. Cleland Homes, Inc., 2016 U.S. Dist. LEXIS 108030 (N.D. Ind. Aug. 16, 2016). *See also* Wilshire Ins. Co. v. RJT Constr., LLC, 581 F.3d 222 (5th Cir. 2009) (where homeowner alleged negligent work on foundation by insured contractor, and foundation was work of contractor, not that of subcontractor to the insured, exclusion applied to preclude coverage for repairing foundation).

219. The exclusion does not apply to "property damage" due to fire.

220. *See* AGL04450611 (Commercial General Liability Water Damage Liability Exclusion Endorsement). *See generally* Centraal Stikstof Verkoopkanter, N. v. Walsh Stevedoring Co., 380 F.2d 523 (5th Cir. 1967); Public Service Mut. Ins. Co. v. Hudson Properties, Inc., 15 Misc. 2d 963, 182 N.Y.S.2d 710 (1959).

emanated from an automatic sprinkler system. The insured argued the exclusion should not apply because the injury was not caused by discharge of water from an automatic sprinkler system but by the negligent act of its employee. The discharge from the sprinkler was, the insured averred, an indirect cause at best. In other parts of the policy the term "cause" was modified by the words "direct" or "indirect" and, therefore, had the insurance company intended to exclude indirect or remote causes in the exclusion, said the insured, it could have used words similar to "directly" or "indirectly." The court, however, concluded the omission of those words from the exclusion was not important, as they could infuse "no additional meaning in the clear contract statement of the intent to exclude damage caused by discharge from the sprinkler system."[221]

Two New York cases illustrate how the specific language of the endorsement can be critical to the outcome. In the first, a property was damaged after a leak in a standpipe at the adjacent insured premises. The commercial general liability policy had an exclusion for water that was prefaced with the statement that it applied to discharges, leakages, or overflows of water that occurred "on or from premises owned by or rented to the named insured and injure or destroy buildings or property *therein*." The majority said that it appeared that the damage was caused by a leak on the insured premises. The property affected was not "therein," but located in the adjoining building. A dissenting opinion responded that the only reasonable construction that could be placed on the exclusion was that it was broad enough to include all property damaged wherever located and was not confined to damage only to property located on the insured premises.[222] A few years later, another New York court distinguished the earlier decision. In that case, water leaked from the insured premises, a loft, and damaged goods located at a premises below. The policy had an exclusion for discharge, leakage, or overflow of water on or from premises owned by or rented to the named insured. The court rejected the argument that the exclusion only applied when the damaged property was located on the premises of the insured. It said it found it impossible to believe that the policy would exclude water flowing out from the premises, but only damage from that flow while the water was still in the premises. The phrase

221. Boston Camping Distributor Co. v. Lumbermens Mut. Casualty Co., 361 Mass. 769, 772, 282 N.E.2d 374, 376 (1972).

222. B & H Management Corp. v. Hardware Mut. Casualty Co., 9 A.D.2d 533, 196 N.Y.S.2d 452 (1960), *aff'd*, 212 N.Y.S.2d 412, 9 N.Y.2d 674, 173 N.E.2d 234 (1961). *See also* Leathermode Sportswear, Inc. v. Liberty Mut. Ins. Co., 150 Conn. 63, 186 A.2d 79 (1962), where the insured leased the fifth floor of a building. Another party had possession of the fourth floor and stored personal property there. Water from toilets leaked from the fifth floor and damaged the property on the floor below. A water damage clause barred coverage for discharge, leakage, or overflow of water "insofar as any of them occur on or from premises owned by or rented to the named insured and injure or destroy buildings or property therein." The court said that the damage was to property stored off the insured premises by water negligently allowed to seep from that premises. Thus, the situation contemplated by the exclusion did not exist.

"on or from premises," held the court, means that a leak "emanates from the insured's premises and passes out from there."[223] The Oregon Supreme Court said it would favor the construction of the later New York case; however, the exclusion was "not a model of clarity," and the fact of differing results reached by courts strongly indicates an ambiguity. Thus, it construed the exclusion against the insurer and found coverage where the insured's property accidentally flooded and the water damaged the ceiling, carpets, and merchandise of the occupant of the property below.[224]

[2] Weather-Related Damage to Work in Progress

An exclusion that may be found in a policy issued to a company involved in construction work bars coverage for weather-related damage to work in progress. The exclusion is for claims that arise out of property damage to any building or structure or to any property within that building or structure before the work of the insured is completed resulting from, caused by, or arising out of water—meaning rain, hail, sleet, or snow—entering through an opening created during the course of the work. There is an exception. The exclusion does not apply if the insured checked and documented weather reports on the day work was being done to make sure that adverse weather was not predicted and installed an appropriate waterproof covering of any opening left unfinished prior to leaving the work site.[225]

In a Florida case, an insured roofing contractor removed all the mortar and tile from an entire roof area, leaving openings and penetrations that would allow rainwater to enter the building. It then allegedly failed to cover the openings, holes, and penetrations in the roof deck. Subsequently, on several occasions, substantial amounts of rainwater entered the building, causing severe damage to ceilings, walls, floors, furniture, fixtures, appliances, and other personal property. In order to avoid application of the weather-related

---

223. El-Mel Realty Corp. v. Empire Mut. Ins. Co., 24 A.D.2d 141, 264 N.Y.S.2d 559 (1965), *aff'd*, 271 N.Y.S.2d 998, 17 N.Y.2d 901, 218 N.E.2d 704 (1966). *But see* Allied Grand Doll Mfg. Co. v. Globe Indem. Co., 215 N.Y.S.2d 945, 28 Misc. 2d 1048 (1961) (faucet left open over weekend on premises leased by insured on sixth floor of building caused flooding and water seepage throughout building; exclusion for discharge, leakage, or overflow of water on or from premises owned by or rented to named insured did not apply because "premises" did not refer to entire building including portions not rented or controlled by insured).

224. Jones v. Insurance Co. of North America, 264 Ore. 276, 504 P.2d 130 (1972). The court noted that the exclusion applied to water leakage that occurred "on or from" the insured's premises, which seemed to mean the policy did not cover damage caused by water originating on that premises and escaping elsewhere. However, said the court, the clause went on to provide that the water leakage excluded was that which injured or destroyed "buildings or property therein," and the disagreement was about the antecedent of "therein."

225. An appropriate waterproof covering is one properly installed and that is consistent with what is customarily used within the industry as a best practice to avoid weather-related water damage.

damage exclusion, the argument was put forth that the underlying complaint alleged rainwater intrusion through both openings and penetrations in the building and the exclusion applied only to damage from water entering through openings. The court rejected any distinction between "penetrations" and "openings" and said that dictionary definitions suggest that penetrations are a subset of openings. The exclusion, therefore, applied.[226]

[3] Interference with Natural Drainage Exclusion

In what a court described as a "farm insurance policy," there was an exclusion for "property damage resulting from diversion or obstruction of streams or surface water, or from interference with the natural drainage to or from the land of others." While this exclusion was not in a commercial general liability policy, the same or a similar exclusion could be added by endorsement to a standard CGL policy, so it is worth considering how a court interpreted it. In an Illinois case, the insured constructed a dam and holding pond. Subsequently, the owner of a neighboring property alleged he suffered damage to his cropland by the insured's alteration of the flow and level of surface and groundwater. The insurer invoked the exclusion. The insured argued the flooding was caused by subsurface water and the term "drainage" did not include *subsurface* drainage. The court did not agree. It said that, as a matter of law, the word "drainage" in the exclusion had to be read to include both surface and subsurface drainage. It affirmed summary judgment for the insurer, saying that construction of the dam and retention pond interfered with the natural drainage on the adjacent property and resulted in damage to that property.[227]

[4] Residential Construction Work Exclusion

Water damage claims associated with residential construction may be barred from coverage by a commercial general liability policy under an endorsement often called a "Residential Construction Exclusion," although it may carry another title.[228] This exclusion is not standard.[229] It can vary greatly from one

---

226. Century Sur. Co. v. Diversified Constr. & Restoration, Inc., 2013 U.S. Dist. LEXIS 192076 (S.D. Fla. Sept. 13, 2013) (although underlying complaint indicates that at one point roofer installed temporary covering on roof, no allegation suggests that covering was appropriate and met industry best practices or that roofer checked and documented weather reports to make sure that adverse weather was not predicted).

227. Grinnell Mut. Reinsurance Co. v. Hubbs, 370 Ill. Dec. 563, 988 N.E.2d 761 (Ill. App. 2013).

228. Hickman, *Construction Defect Crisis Produces Coverage-Restricting Endorsements* (Aug. 2003), IRMI, https://www.irmi.com/articles/expert-commentary/construction-defect-crisis-produces-coverage-restricting-endorsements (residential construction exclusion endorsements may vary and carry variety of titles).

229. Hickman, *Construction Defect Crisis Produces Coverage-Restricting Endorsements* (Aug. 2003), IRMI, https://www.irmi.com/articles/expert-commentary/construction-defect

insurer to the next. Its purpose is to remove coverage for operations in connection with property intended for habitation.[230] An example of the exclusion reads that the policy does not apply to property damage that "in whole or in part, directly or indirectly, arises out of or is related to any past, present, continuing or future 'residential construction work' performed by or on behalf of an 'insured,' or by or on behalf of any other person or entity, on 'residential property.'"[231] A key component of the exclusion is the definition of "residential construction work." The definition may include single-family homes, apartments, town homes, condominiums, and even assisted living facilities, hotels, and college dormitories or may exclude from the definition specific types of construction, for example, apartment buildings.[232] The definition may be very specific, for instance, "any place of habitation designed or intended for occupancy as a dwelling place by a natural person or a group of natural persons constituting a family."[233] Some endorsements may only apply to new construction, while others may encompass renovation work as well.[234] Other endorsements are state specific.[235]

The exclusion has rarely been construed by courts. It has, however, been examined in at least two Massachusetts cases concerning water damage. One of those cases was before a federal court. In it an additional insured under a commercial general liability policy sought a defense for two lawsuits that arose from flood damage to neighboring property. The damage occurred

-crisis-produces-coverage-restricting-endorsements.

230. Hickman, *Construction Defect Crisis Produces Coverage-Restricting Endorsements* (Aug. 2003), IRMI, https://www.irmi.com/articles/expert-commentary/construction-defect-crisis-produces-coverage-restricting-endorsements.

231. CWC Builders, Inc. v. United Specialty Ins. Co., 134 F. Supp. 3d 589, 598 (D. Mass. 2015). *See also* First Mercury Ins. Co. v. Waterside Condo. Ass'n, 2013 U.S. Dist. LEXIS 171542 (D. Ore. Dec. 5, 2013) (exclusion provided that policy did not apply to property damage arising out of residential construction work regardless of whether those operations were conducted by named insured or on behalf of named insured or whether those operations were conducted for named insured or for others).

232. Hickman, *Construction Defect Crisis Produces Coverage-Restricting Endorsements* (Aug. 2003), IRMI, https://www.irmi.com/articles/expert-commentary/construction-defect-crisis-produces-coverage-restricting-endorsements.

233. *See* FSS Automatic Sprinkler Corp. v. Tudor Ins. Co., 2010 Mass. App. Unpub. LEXIS 1054 (Sept. 21, 2010). First Mercury Ins. Co. v. Waterside Condo. Ass'n, 2013 U.S. Dist. LEXIS 171542 (D. Ore. Dec. 5, 2013) illustrates how specific the language of the exclusion can be. The exclusion in that case defined "residential construction work" as "Design, supervision, project management, construction of, or work performed by you or on your behalf on the construction of a single family dwelling, a multi-family dwelling (other than an apartment building), condominium or town home, or. . . . Design, supervision, project management, construction of, or work performed by you or on your behalf on the conversion of apartments to condominiums."

234. Hickman, *Construction Defect Crisis Produces Coverage-Restricting Endorsements* (Aug. 2003), IRMI, https://www.irmi.com/articles/expert-commentary/construction-defect-crisis-produces-coverage-restricting-endorsements.

235. *See, e.g.*, First Mercury Ins. Co. v. Waterside Condo. Ass'n, 2013 U.S. Dist. LEXIS 171542 (D. Ore. Dec. 5, 2013).

during demolition of a building. Fire hoses were placed in the basement of the building and turned on to control dust. The flooding of the neighboring property was believed to have occurred when the hoses were left on. The insurer argued it was entitled to summary judgment because the residential construction work exclusion in its policy barred coverage for all claims that arose out of work on the project. There was no question that the project was for residential construction as defined in the policy, and the court found the exclusion to be applicable.[236] The other opinion is an unpublished state appellate court decision. The insured in that case was in the business of installing and maintaining fire protection sprinkler systems. It contracted to install a sprinkler system in a building that was being converted from a jail into luxury condominium units. A sprinkler pipe leaked and caused water damage in the building. The insurer, citing a "Exclusion for Residential Construction Work," denied coverage. The insured argued the exclusion was ambiguous because it purported to exclude all residential construction, while it includes construction of apartment buildings, which arguably are very similar to condominium buildings. The court agreed that the exclusion was ambiguous and construed it against the insurer and in favor of coverage.[237]

[5] Contractor's Professional Liability Exclusion

An exclusion that is often added by endorsement to a CGL policy issued to a contractor is a "Professional Liability Exclusion."[238] There are two standard ISO endorsements that are widely used by insurers.[239]

The first endorsement provides that the policy does not apply to property damage[240] that arises out of the rendering of, or failure to render, any professional services by the insured or on behalf of the insured.[241] It only applies to the provision of engineering, architectural, or surveying services to others in the insured's capacity as an engineer, architect, or surveyor and provision or hiring independent professionals to provide engineering, architectural, or surveying services in connection with construction work the insured performs. The endorsement defines "professional services" to include preparing, approving, or failing to prepare or approve maps, shop drawings, opinions, reports, surveys, field orders, change orders, or drawings and specifications and supervision or inspection performed as part of any related architectural

---

236. CWC Builders, Inc. v. United Specialty Ins. Co., 134 F. Supp. 3d 589 (D. Mass. 2015).

237. FSS Automatic Sprinkler Corp. v. Tudor Ins. Co., 2010 Mass. App. Unpub. LEXIS 1054 (Sept. 21, 2010).

238. 3 *New Appleman Law of Liability Insurance* § 28.05[2] (Matthew Bender, 2022).

239. Stanovich, *The CGL and the Professional Liability Exclusion* (Apr. 2014), IRMI, https://www.irmi.com/articles/expert-commentary/the-cgl-and-the-professional-liability-exclusion.

240. The endorsement also encompasses bodily injury and personal and advertising injury.

241. ISO Form CG 22 79 01 96, § 1.

or engineering activities.[242] "Professional services" do not include those within construction means, methods, techniques, sequences, and procedures employed by the insured in connection with the operations in the capacity of the insured as a construction contractor.[243] That means that allegations of faulty construction would not be excluded, to the extent they are construction "means and methods."[244] For example, in an underlying action, plaintiffs sued a builder for water intrusion to a newly constructed home. The insurer contended that the claims in that action were barred by the professional liability exclusion because they arose out of the builder's rendering, or failure to render, professional services. However, said the court, the exclusion stated that professional services did not include those within construction means, methods, techniques, sequences, and procedures employed in connection with the operations of the insured in its capacity as a construction contractor. The insurer had not shown that the actions complained of in the underlying case fell outside that language and had not, therefore, demonstrated that the covered damages were excluded by the professional liability exclusion.[245]

The second standard endorsement is entitled "limited." It excludes property damage[246] that arises out of rendering of, or failure to render, any professional services by the insured, but only with respect to engineering, architectural, or surveying services provided in the capacity of the insured as an engineer, architect, or surveyor.[247] It defines "professional services" to include preparing, approving, or failing to prepare or approve maps, shop drawings, opinions, reports, surveys, field orders, change orders, or drawings and specifications and supervision and inspection performed as part of any related architectural or engineering activities. The exclusion applies even if a claim against any insured alleges negligence or other wrongdoing in the supervision, hiring, employment, training, or monitoring of others by that insured, if the occurrence that causes property damage involved rendering of, or failure to render, any professional services by the insured with respect to providing engineering, architectural, or surveying services in the insured's capacity as an engineer, architect, or surveyor. Finally, the exclusion does not apply to the operations of the insured in connection with construction work performed by the insured or on behalf of the insured. This endorsement is intended for design-build contractors—that is, those who both design and build a project. It does not exclude design work done as part of the construction work of the

242. ISO Form CG 22 79 01 96, § 2.

243. ISO Form CG 22 79 01 96, § 3.

244. Stanovich, *The CGL and the Professional Liability Exclusion* (Apr. 2014), IRMI, https://www.irmi.com/articles/expert-commentary/the-cgl-and-the-professional-liability-exclusion.

245. Emplrs. Mut. Cas. Co. v. Kenny Hayes Custom Homes, LLC, 2016 U.S. Dist. LEXIS 15340 (S.D. Ala. Feb. 9, 2016).

246. The endorsement also encompasses bodily injury and personal and advertising injury.

247. ISO Form CG 22 80 04 13.

named insured, including construction work done on behalf of the named insured.[248]

Whether an action involves "professional services" is an issue that is litigated when there is a professional liability exclusion.[249] For example, in an underlying action a property owner sued after raw sewage flowed onto her land during construction of a new sewer system. The insurer of the defendant brought a declaratory judgment action to determine its liability and contended there was no coverage because of a "professional services exclusion." The court said that in matching the allegations of the underlying complaint with the terms of the policy, it could find no allegation as to "the rendering of or the failure to render any professional services." Therefore, the insurer had a duty to defend its insured.[250]

Other endorsements may negate the professional services exclusion. For example, the Texas Department of Transportation contracted for the construction of a road. A suit was brought against the agency because the project allegedly expanded the floodplain and caused the plaintiffs' properties to flood. The agency was an additional insured under the contractor's insurance policy for injury or damaged that resulted from general supervision by it of the contractor's work. The policy also had a professional services exclusion, which the insurer invoked to avoid coverage. The court, however, said that the additional insured endorsement specifically said that it broadened coverage, and it could not understand how the policy coverage can be broadened to specifically include supervision that is then excluded as a "professional service."[251]

---

248. Stanovich, *The CGL and the Professional Liability Exclusion* (Apr. 2014), IRMI, https://www.irmi.com/articles/expert-commentary/the-cgl-and-the-professional-liability-exclusion.

249. See 3 *New Appleman Law of Liability Insurance* § 28.05[2] (Matthew Bender, 2022) for a discussion of how courts have interpreted "professional services."

250. United States Fidelity & Guaranty Co. v. Armstrong, 479 So. 2d 1164 (Ala. 1985).

251. St. Paul Ins. Co. v. Texas DOT, 999 S.W.2d 881 (Tex. App. 1999).

10

Recovering under Directors and Officers Insurance

10.1 Introduction

It is possible for corporate officers and directors to be personally liable for acts performed in their official capacity.[1] That includes acts that lead to flood damage. For example, in *Wicks v. Milzoco Builders, Inc.*,[2] the corporate defendant was sued by individuals who purchased homes in a neighborhood the defendant developed. The homeowners contended that excessive surface water runoff from higher elevations periodically flooded their yards and basements and rendered their homes uninhabitable. One cause of action they brought was for trespass. That claim was brought not only against the corporation but also against three of its officers. The complaint alleged that the defendants were aware, or could be imputed to have been aware, that the proposed development would be built on a slope and that natural drainage would concentrate much of the water and sewage on approximately a half dozen of the proposed lots and that despite that knowledge, the defendants did not order or perform adequate soil testing of the site and failed to provide for any special drainage considerations in the grading and landscaping of the property. The lower courts held that the complaint did not state a cause of action against those officers individually and apart from their capacities as corporate officers. The

1. Discussion of the liability of corporate officers and directors is beyond the scope of this treatise. There are excellent resources available on the topic. *See, e.g.*, Colombo, *Law of Corporate Officers and Directors: Rights, Duties, and Liabilities* (Clark Boardman Callaghan 2020); Knepper & Bailey, *Liability of Corporate Officers and Directors* (Matthew Bender 2019); Bradenburg, *You're the Problem, Officer: Whether Executive Officers Should Be Subjected to the Same Standards of Liability as Directors under Current Corporate Governance Law*, 89 U. Cin. L. Rev. 710 (2021); Petrin, *The Curious Case of Directors' and Officers' Liability for Supervision and Management: Exploring the Intersection of Corporate and Tort Law*, 59 Am. U.L. Rev. 1661 (2010).

2. Wicks v. Milzoco Builders, Inc., 503 Pa. 614, 470 A.2d 86 (1983).

Pennsylvania Supreme Court, however, said that an officer of a corporation who takes part in the commission of a tort by the corporation can be personally liable and, therefore, corporate officers may be held liable for misfeasance. The court acknowledged that the mere averment that a corporate officer should have known the consequences of the liability-creating corporate act is insufficient to impose liability, but in the case before it, the complaint could be read to say that the individual appellees actually knew that the location of the proposed development created, at least, an unreasonable risk of the drainage problems that occurred and that they deliberately ordered the work to proceed. The court held that the personal participation of the officers in the alleged negligent, injury-producing actions of which the plaintiffs complained had been sufficiently pleaded to withstand a motion to dismiss.

The injured plaintiff may, therefore, be able to recover flood-related losses from officers and directors as well as the corporation in a tort action. In the case of individual officers and directors the question is, will the company's Directors & Officers insurance policy cover the losses? The answer is maybe, if the needle of the property damage exclusion is threaded.

10.2 Directors & Officers Insurance Generally

Directors & Officers (D&O) Liability Insurance protects directors and officers and the corporation that has to indemnify them from losses that arise out of claims made by "outsiders."[3] Because it is a relatively new form of coverage,[4] appellate decisions interpreting it are relatively few,[5] and practitioners, therefore, need to be aware that courts in their states may rely on decisions handed down in other jurisdictions more than they ordinarily would.[6]

There is no standard policy form for D&O insurance.[7] For other types of coverage, for example, commercial general liability insurance, there are

3. Mount Hawley Ins. Co. v. FSLIC, 695 F. Supp. 469, 484 (C.D. Cal. 1987). *See generally* Monteleone & Conca, *Directors and Officers Indemnification and Liability Insurance: An Overview of Legal and Practical Issues*, 51 Bus. Law. 573 (1996).

4. Dobiac, *I Came, I Saw, I Underwrote: D & O Liability Insurance's Past Underwriting Practices and Potential Future Directions*, 14 Conn. Ins. L.J. 487, 518 (2008); Johnston, *Corporate Indemnification and Liability Insurance for Directors and Officers*, 33 Bus. Law. 1993, 2012 (1978).

5. Kokinda, *D&O Liability Insurance: There Are Exclusions, and Then There Are Exclusions*, 28-10 ABIJ 46 (2010); Romano, *What Went Wrong with Directors' and Officers' Liability Insurance?*, 14 Del. J. Corp. L. 1, 29 (1989).

6. *See, e.g.*, Oak Park Calabasas Condominium Assn. v. State Farm Fire & Casualty Co., 137 Cal. App. 4th 557, 564, 40 Cal. Rptr. 3d 263, 267 (2006).

7. *Director and Officer Indemnification and Insurance—Issues for Public Companies to Consider* at 8 (July 15, 2013) (D&O policies are "off the shelf" products); Kokinda, *D&O Liability Insurance: There Are Exclusions, and Then There Are Exclusions*, 28-10 ABIJ 46

standard Insurance Service Office (ISO) policies that almost all insurers use. D&O policies, on the other hand, are different with each insurer although there are common elements.[8] Also, insurance companies have drafted specific policies to meet the needs of specific types of policyholders, for example, non-profit entities.[9] In 2019, the ISO did adopt a D&O policy for *privately* held companies,[10] and it is cited here. The Travelers Non-Profit Management and Organization Liability Insurance Policy (NPMOLIP) is also cited.[11]

D&O coverage is generally in two parts. "Side A" coverage reimburses individual directors and officers for "un-indemnified payments."[12] "Side B" coverage reimburses the corporation for indemnification payments it has made to directors and officers for covered losses,[13] not for its own misconduct.[14] Coverage is triggered when an obligation to indemnify is incurred.[15] There is also "Side C" coverage that is not standard[16] but that applies to claims against the company itself.[17] Usually, it is effectively excess coverage, and in publicly held corporations it is often limited to securities claims.[18]

(2010) (D&O policies are not as standardized); Monteleone, *Coverage Issues under Commercial General Liability and Directors' and Officers' Liability Policies*, 18 W. New Eng. L. Rev. 47, 62 (1996).

8. Kokinda, *D&O Liability Insurance: There Are Exclusions, and Then There Are Exclusions*, 28-10 ABIJ 46 (2010).

9. *Director and Officer Indemnification and Insurance—Issues for Public Companies to Consider* at 8 (July 15, 2013).

10. ISO Form ML 00 02 01 19.

11. Travelers Non-Profit Management and Organization Liability Insurance Policy, CIRI 72001.

12. Romano, *What Went Wrong with Directors' and Officers' Liability Insurance?*, 14 Del. J. Corp. L. 1, 9 (1989).

13. *Id.*

14. Baker & Griffith, *The Missing Monitor in Corporate Governance: The Directors' & Officers' Liability Insurer*, 95 Geo. L.J. 1795, 1802 (2007); Quinn & Levin, *Directors and Officers Liability Insurance: Probable Directions in Texas Law*, 20 Rev. Litig. 381, 416 (2001).

15. Griffith, *Uncovering a Gatekeeper: Why the SEC Should Mandate Disclosure of Details Concerning Directors' and Officers' Liability Insurance Policies*, 154 U. Pa. L. Rev. 1147, 1165 (2006).

16. Dobiac, *I Came, I Saw, I Underwrote: D & O Liability Insurance's Past Underwriting Practices and Potential Future Directions*, 14 Conn. Ins. L.J. 487, 491 (2008).

17. Skilling, *Coverage for Ill-Gotten Gains?: Discussing the (Un)Insurability of Restitution and Disgorgement*, 72 Wash & Lee L. Rev. 1077, 1084 (2015); Baker & Griffith, *The Missing Monitor in Corporate Governance: The Directors' & Officers' Liability Insurer*, 95 Geo. L.J. 1795, 1802 (2007).

18. 4 Jeffery E. Thomas, *New Appleman on Insurance Law Library Edition* § 26.05[1] (Matthew Bender, Rev. Ed. 2020).

10.3 Coverage

[1] Insuring Agreement

Usually, D&O policies provide "all-risk" coverage, meaning they cover all claims for wrongful acts not specifically excluded.[19] Typically, the insuring agreement for Side A coverage states that the insurer will pay any loss an insured person becomes "legally obligated to pay" as the result of a claim first made during the policy period, or any extended reporting or discovery period, for a wrongful act.[20] For Side B coverage, the insuring agreement may say the insurer will pay on behalf of the organization all loss for which it has indemnified any insured person that the person was legally obligated to pay for each covered claim first made against insured persons during the policy period or any extended reporting or discovery period, alleging a wrongful act that first occurred before the end of the policy period and was reported to the insurance company.[21] "Pay on behalf" means the insurer has to pay a covered loss once the insured becomes legally obligated to pay it, rather than after the insured has paid it.[22] Interpreting the coverage requires definitions for four words: "loss," "claim," "insured," and "wrongful," which are discussed below.

[2] Loss

The definition of "loss" varies among policies. All will have inclusions and exclusions. Generally, they define "loss" to include damages, judgments, settlements, and defense costs.[23] Damages may be limited to "compensatory" damages.[24] Policies often define loss to require a claim for "wrongful acts." Some policies limit the definition to claims against certain persons.[25] Others apply to claims against *any* insured.[26] For example, in one policy loss means the total amount *any insured* becomes legally obligated to pay, and "insured" means both the insured organization and the insured persons.[27]

---

19. 4 Jeffery E. Thomas, *New Appleman on Insurance Law Library Edition* § 26.05[2] (Matthew Bender, Rev. Ed. 2020).
20. Non-Profit Management and Organization Liability Insurance Policy § I.A.
21. ISO Form ML 00 02 01 19, § I.B.
22. 4 Jeffery E. Thomas, *New Appleman on Insurance Law Library Edition* § 26.05[3] (Matthew Bender, Rev. Ed. 2020).
23. 4 Jeffery E. Thomas, *New Appleman on Insurance Law Library Edition* § 26.06[5] (Matthew Bender, Rev. Ed. 2020).
24. *See* ISO Form BP 17 24 01 10, § H.7.
25. MGIC Indem. Corp. v. Home State Sav. Ass'n, 797 F.2d 285 (6th Cir. Ohio 1986) (claim or claims made against directors and officers).
26. Non-Profit Management and Organization Liability Insurance Policy § II(J).
27. Non-Profit Management and Organization Liability Insurance Policy § II(G).

[3] Claim

Even though the language of D&O policies differs widely, the definition of "claim" is often similar from policy to policy.[28] Almost all of them include four actions in the definition.[29] They are:

- A written demand for monetary damages;[30]
- A civil proceeding commenced by service of a complaint or similar pleading;
- A criminal proceeding commenced by return of an indictment; and
- A formal administrative or regulatory proceeding commenced by filing of a notice of charges, formal investigative order, or similar document.

One of these actions has to occur. That an insured is aware of an alleged injury is insufficient to meet the definition of "claim."[31] When an injured party is seeking to recover for a flood-related loss, only the first two actions will be at issue.

What is a "written demand"? Courts have found that a letter from an attorney that suggests his or her client is considering bringing a lawsuit, a threat to bring a suit,[32] or a claim that a wrongful act has occurred are not claims because they are not written demands for monetary damages.[33] A claim that a wrongful act has occurred, said one federal court, is not the same as a claim for payment *on account of* a wrongful act because the definition does not refer to a claim that wrongdoing occurred but to a demand for an amount of money owed to the claimant because of the alleged wrongdoing.[34]

---

28. However, one respected treatise says that there is no "standard" definition of "claim" and, therefore, one must closely examine the term when evaluating D&O policies. 3 *New Appleman Law of Liability Insurance* § 22.05[7] (Matthew Bender, Rev. Ed. 2020).

29. *See generally* Quinn & Levin, *Directors and Officers Liability Insurance: Probable Directions in Texas Law*, 20 Rev. Litig. 381, 462 (2001).

30. Some policies also include a written demand for "non-monetary" relief. *See, e.g.*, ISO Form ML 00 02 01 19, § V.A.1 (written demand, other than shareholder derivative demand, for monetary damages or nonmonetary relief, including injunctive relief). *See also* 3 *New Appleman Law of Liability Insurance* § 22.05[7] (Matthew Bender, Rev. Ed. 2020).

31. Titan Indem. Co. v. Williams, 743 So. 2d 1020 (Miss. App. 1999).

32. *But see* Deer Oaks Office Park Owners Ass'n v. State Farm Lloyds, 2012 U.S. Dist. LEXIS 19240 (W.D. Tex. Feb. 15, 2012) (where letter from attorney used word "demand," it placed insured on notice that party asserted a right and where it further warned that attorney had been asked to pursue litigation if satisfactory settlement could not be reached and concluded by stating that if attorney had not received response by specified date, client has instructed attorney to file suit, letter constituted claim).

33. Quinn & Levin, *Directors and Officers Liability Insurance: Probable Directions in Texas Law*, 20 Rev. Litig. 381, 460 (2001). *See, e.g.*, Hyde v. Fidelity & Deposit Co. of Am., 23 F. Supp. 2d 630, 633 (D. Md. 1998) (claim must be something more than notice).

34. MGIC Indem. Corp. v. Home State Sav. Ass'n, 797 F.2d 285 (6th Cir. Ohio 1986). *See also* Mt. Hood, LLC v. Travelers Cas. & Sur. Co. of Am., 2009 U.S. Dist. LEXIS 16775 (D. Or. Mar. 3, 2009) (demand for monetary relief before initiation of suit constituted claim).

Claimants have to pursue their own claims. If an insured is told by a person that someone else *may* make a claim, that is not a claim.[35]

In some policies, actions may only meet the definition of a claim if brought against "insured persons."[36] Where an underlying suit was brought against a corporation and the policy required that a claim be "made against" an insured person, a court concluded that a D&O policy was not implicated because, regardless of the conduct described in the complaint, it was not a claim "made against" any director or officer who was an "insured person."[37]

[4] Insured Person

The phrase "insured person" is often defined to mean former, present, or future directors, officers, trustees, employees, or managers.[38] Some policies modify the words "directors and officers" with the phrase "while acting within the scope of their duties."[39] Many D&O policies require an insured person to be "duly elected or appointed."[40] Unfortunately, they do not define "duly." One federal court has said that "duly elected" means through "regular and proper channels" of corporate governance.[41]

D&O policies may extend coverage, sometimes by endorsement, to estates, heirs, and marital estates, meaning spouses. This is because directors and officers named in a suit may shield assets by transferring them to spouses,

35. Quinn & Levin, *Directors and Officers Liability Insurance: Probable Directions in Texas Law*, 20 Rev. Litig. 381 (2001).

36. *See, e.g.*, ISO Form BP 17 24 01 10 § H(1)(b) limiting the definition of "claim" to a written demand for monetary damages or civil, criminal, or administrative proceedings against any "insured person."

37. Medical Mut. Ins. Co. v. Indian Harbor Ins. Co., 583 F.3d 57 (1st Cir. 2009). *See also* Am. Sec. Bank & Trust Co. v. Progressive Cas. Ins. Co., 2011 U.S. Dist. LEXIS 68231 (M.D. Tenn. June 24, 2011).

38. *See, e.g.*, Non-Profit Management and Organization Liability Insurance Policy § IV(2)(I) (definition includes persons who were, now are, or will become duly elected or appointed directors, trustees, or officers of any insured organization or employees, committee members, or volunteers of any insured organization that is a non-profit entity); ISO Form ML 00 02 01 19, §§ V.D, F, H ("insured person" means any "executive" or "employee," and "executive" means any natural person who was, is now, or will be duly elected or appointed director, officer, trustee, or "manager," and "manager" is any natural person who was, is now, or will be member of Board of Managers or equivalent position of organization that is a limited liability company).

39. *See* N. Sec. Ins. Co. v. Sandpiper Vill. Condo. Trust, 24 Mass. L. Rep. 500 (Mass. Super. Ct. 2008). That the defendant has to have been acting within the scope of corporate duties may be implied. *See* International Ins. Co. v. St. Paul Fire & Marine Ins. Co., 1988 U.S. Dist. LEXIS 12215 (E.D. Pa. Oct. 25, 1988).

40. *See, e.g.*, Non-Profit Management and Organization Liability Insurance Policy § II(G).

41. Sphinx Int'l, Inc. v. Nat'l Union Fire Ins. Co., 412 F.3d 1224, 1228 (11th Cir. 2005). *See also* Wojtunik v. Kealy, 2011 U.S. Dist. LEXIS 36229 (D. Ariz. Mar. 31, 2011); Julio & Sons Co. v. Travelers Cas. & Sur. Co. of Am., 684 F. Supp. 2d 330, 337 (S.D.N.Y. 2010) (violation of company bylaws would be one indication that person has not been duly elected or appointed).

and plaintiffs' attorneys may name them in suit papers.[42] The spouse of an "insured person" is then protected when a suit is brought against community property or property held jointly.[43]

[5] Wrongful Act

Generally, D&O policies pay only those claims that arise out of a *wrongful act* by an insured in his or her official capacity.[44] A typical policy definition of "wrongful act" is:

> "any actual or alleged error, misstatement, misleading statement, act or omission or neglect or breach of duty by the Directors or Officers in the discharge of their duties solely in their capacity as Directors or Officers of the Association, individually or collectively, or any matter claimed against them solely by reason of their being Directors or Officers of the Association."[45]

The phrase "solely by reason of their being directors or officers" is intended to encompass situations in which a director or officer is sued simply because of his or her office as opposed to for specific conduct.[46] Note that the definition includes "alleged" errors, misstatements, misleading statements, acts, or omissions. Some policies will define "wrongful act" to include acts or omissions "committed or attempted or allegedly committed or attempted."[47]

Policies may omit the word "negligent" in the definition of "wrongful act" or employ it to modify "act, error, and omission." When "negligent" modifies "act, error, and omission," courts hold the definition does not include intentional or other non-negligent wrongdoing.[48]

---

42. *Spousal Coverage*, IRMI, https://www.irmi.com/online/insurance-glossary/terms/s/spousal-coverage.aspx.

43. *Executive Risk/Directors' and Officers' Insurance*, Scott Simmonds, http://www.scottsimmonds.com/bank-insurance-coverage/executive-riskdirectors-officers-insurance/.

44. Hollingsworth v. Landing Condos. of Waukesha Ass'n, 353 Wis. 2d 553, 846 N.W.2d 34 (2014).

45. As quoted in *MGIC Indem. Corp. v. Home State Sav. Ass'n*, 797 F.2d 285, 287 (6th Cir. Ohio 1986).

46. Johnston, *Corporate Indemnification and Liability Insurance for Directors and Officers*, 33 Bus. Law. 1993, 2017 (1978). *See also* 3 *New Appleman Law of Liability Insurance* § 22.05[9][a] (Matthew Bender, Rev. Ed. 2020).

47. Non-Profit Management and Organization Liability Insurance Policy § II.S.

48. 4 Jeffery E. Thomas, *New Appleman on Insurance Law Library Edition* § 26.06[3] (Matthew Bender, Rev. Ed. 2020). *See, e.g.*, Cambridge Mut. Fire Ins. Co. v. 1347-49 N. Sedgwick Condo. Ass'n, 2013 U.S. Dist. LEXIS 9750 (Jan. 23, 2013); Sova v. Cove Homeowner's Ass'n, 102 So. 3d 863, 874 (La. App. 2012).

10.4 Exclusions

[1] Generally

The language that precedes an exclusion can be critical.[49] It may only bar coverage of losses for a specified peril, or it may preclude all losses that are based on, arise out of, or in any way relate to the named peril.[50] Generally, courts construe the phrase "arising out of" very broadly,[51] requiring only a slight connection or incidental relationship between the injury and the excluded risk.[52] Thus, in the case of flood damage, loss of income because of the inability to use flood-damaged property could be said to arise out of the flood.

[2] Dishonesty/Intentional Conduct

Almost all D&O policies preclude coverage for fraud, dishonesty, and deliberate criminality.[53] For example, one widely used policy says the insurer will not be liable to pay for a loss in connection with a claim made against any insureds brought about, or contributed to, by any "deliberately fraudulent or dishonest act or omission or any purposeful violation of any statute or regulation" by the insured.[54] Not all policies will include an intent requirement,[55] but when a modifier like "deliberate" is used, it will generally be more difficult for an insurer to successfully deny coverage.[56] Note that some polices will defend up until a criminal act is proven.[57]

Language like "purposeful violation of any statute or regulation" may be especially important in the case of flood damage. There are many statutes, ordinances, and regulations intended to prevent flooding that an insured

---

49. Monteleone & Conca, *Directors and Officers Indemnification and Liability Insurance: An Overview of Legal and Practical Issues*, 51 Bus. Law 573, 607 (1996).

50. *D&O Insurance Policy Exclusions*, Conner Strong & Buckelew, *available at* https://www.connerstrong.com/resources/site1/news/1414CSB%20ER%20Policy%20Exclusions-2.pdf.

51. *See* Windt, *Insurance Claims & Disputes: Representation of Insurance Companies and Insureds*, § 11:22A (5th ed. West 2012).

52. VierraMoore, Inc. v. Cont'l Cas. Co., 940 F. Supp. 2d 1270, 1281 (E.D. Cal. 2013).

53. Quinn & Levin, *Directors and Officers Liability Insurance: Probable Directions in Texas Law*, 20 Rev. Litig. 381, 432 (2001). *See also* Kokinda, *D&O Liability Insurance: There Are Exclusions, and Then There Are Exclusions*, 28-10 ABIJ 46, 67 (2010).

54. Non-Profit Management and Organization Liability Insurance Policy § IV(10).

55. 3 *New Appleman Law of Liability Insurance* § 22.06[2][b][i] (Matthew Bender, Rev. Ed. 2020).

56. Kokinda, *D&O Liability Insurance: There Are Exclusions, and Then There Are Exclusions*, 28-10 ABIJ 46, 67 (2010).

57. Iannucci, *The ABCs of D&O: Insuring Your Board's Decisions*, at 25 (Cooperator 2011), IHG, *available at* https://www.ihginsurance.com/getmedia/dcac9491-6c5b-4cbb-a4b6-060cedc11ae9/ABCs_of_DO_Cooperator.pdf.

might violate. For example, officers or directors might approve construction plans knowing they do not conform to local floodplain zoning ordinances or to requirements for stormwater runoff retention.

An underlying complaint might allege both dishonest and negligent acts. Thus, some claims may fit within a dishonesty exclusion while others that can be proved by demonstrating negligence would not be excluded.[58] However, the fact that directors claim to have been merely negligent is not conclusive.[59]

Policies may require a judgment or some final adjudication that determines that the conduct at issue actually happened. For example, in one policy the dishonesty exclusion does not apply unless a "judgment or other final adjudication" adverse to the insured demonstrates a "deliberately fraudulent or dishonest act or omission or purposeful violation."[60] If a policy bars coverage when an insured is "adjudged guilty of criminal acts," a trial or some other adjudication is required. The insurance company cannot decide for itself that an insured has committed a crime.[61]

[3] Construction

D&O policies may have a "design or construction" exclusion. For example, in one case an exclusion barred coverage for claims for wrongful acts based on, arising out of, directly or indirectly resulting from, in consequence of, or in any way involving development, planning, or landscaping of any real property; the exercise of any development rights with respect to any real property; any actual or alleged violation of any federal, state, local, or common law rule, law, regulation or ordinance respecting the environment or environmental conservation, in connection with any development, planning, or landscaping of real property; or the design, construction, renovation, or rehabilitation of any building, structure, or other improvement on any real property.[62] Clearly, this exclusion could be implicated when a change to real property causes another property to flood.

58. Hotel Des Artistes v. Transamerica Ins. Co., 1994 U.S. Dist. LEXIS 7800 (S.D.N.Y. June 10, 1994).

59. State Farm Fire & Cas. Co. v. Anderson, 2013 U.S. Dist. LEXIS 57837 (S.D. Miss. Apr. 23, 2013).

60. Non-Profit Management and Organization Liability Insurance Policy § IV.10.

61. Quinn & Levin, *Directors and Officers Liability Insurance: Probable Directions in Texas Law*, 20 Rev. Litig. 381, 434 (2001).

62. Marquez Knolls Property Owners Assn., Inc. v. Executive Risk Indemnity, Inc., 153 Cal. App. 4th 228, 62 Cal. Rptr. 3d 510 (2007).

[4] Property Damage

D&O policies are intended to cover financial losses, not property damage.[63] Thus, all of them exclude property damage.[64] This eliminates any overlapping of coverage between them and general or homeowners liability policies.[65] Property damage exclusions can be rather narrow. For example, an exclusion might state that the insurer will not be liable to make any payment for loss in connection with any claim made against any of the insureds for any damage to or destruction of any tangible property.[66] A broader exclusion is that the insurer will not be "liable for 'loss' or obligated to defend any 'claim' made against any 'insured' . . . [b]ased upon, arising out of or attributable to physical injury to tangible property, including all resulting loss of use of that property or loss of use of tangible property that is not physically injured."[67]

Whether narrow or broad, D&O policies generally do not define "property damage." Commercial General Liability (CGL) policies, however, do typically define the term and can be looked to for its meaning. There are usually two parts to the definition. First, it is physical injury to "tangible property"[68] including any resulting loss of its use.[69] Tangible property is said to suffer *physical* injury when it is "altered in appearance, shape, color or in other material dimension," but not if it has intangible damage. That is because the term "physical" limits "injury," and the phrase "physical injury" does not include intangible damage, for example, economic loss and, therefore, a diminution in value does not constitute physical injury.[70] The second meaning of the term is *loss of use* of tangible property that is not physically injured.[71] D&O coverage may be added by an endorsement to a CGL policy. In that case, the property damage definition in the CGL policy will probably apply.[72] The reason for the property damage exclusion is that D&O policies cover *claims against an*

---

63. Quinn & Levin, *Directors and Officers Liability Insurance: Probable Directions in Texas Law*, 20 Rev. Litig. 381, 427 (2001).

64. 4 *New Appleman on Insurance Law Library Edition* § 26.07[3][c] (Matthew Bender, Rev. Ed. 2020).

65. Quinn & Levin, *Directors and Officers Liability Insurance: Probable Directions in Texas Law*, 20 Rev. Litig. 381, 433 (2001).

66. Non-Profit Management and Organization Liability Insurance Policy § IV.1.

67. ISO Form ML 00 02 01 19, § A.3.b.

68. "Tangible property" is usually not defined in policies, but many courts say it is "that which is capable of being handled, touched, or physically possessed" and, therefore, does not include purely economic losses. Graber v. State Farm Fire & Casualty Co., 244 Mont. 265, 269, 797 P.2d 214, 216 (Mont. 1990); Lamar Truck Plaza, Inc. v. Sentry Ins., 757 P.2d 1143, 1144 (Colo. App. 1988).

69. *See, e.g.*, ISO Form CG 00 01 12 07, § V.17.a.

70. Traveler's Ins. Co. v. Eljer Mfg., 258 Ill. Dec. 792, 197 Ill. 2d 278, 301–02, 757 N.E.2d 481, 496 (2001).

71. *See, e.g.*, ISO Form CG 00 01 12 07, § V.17.b.

72. *See, e.g.*, Oak Ford Owners Ass'n v. Auto-Owners Ins. Co., 510 F. Supp. 2d 812 (M.D. Fla. 2007), where the policy included CGL coverage covering property damage, and a D&O

insured, not property damage, and the exclusion bars *claims related* to property damage.

A great many courts find that business or economic losses are not property damage when interpreting the definition of "property damage" in CGL policies.[73] One of those decisions is *County of Monroe v. Travelers Ins. Cos.*[74] In that case, a company contracted with a local government to construct a sewer project partially beneath an existing canal. While the tunnel under the canal was being dug, the canal bottom collapsed, causing extensive flooding. The contractor sued the local government for, *inter alia*, negligence for failure to investigate and advise the contractor of actual site conditions and for inadequate and incorrect design and construction plans. It sought damages for work completed but not paid for, loss of profits, and delay and performance of extra work not contemplated by the terms and conditions of the contract. Although a notice of claim by the contractor said it was injured by flooding causing substantial damage to its property, there was no mention of property damage in the actual complaint. Lost profits, delay, and performance of extra work are not, said the court, encompassed within the term *property damage* as defined in the local government's liability policy. Those losses were intangibles in contrast to the policy requirement of damage to tangible property.

There is no coverage if the allegations of the underlying complaint are solely and entirely within the property damage exclusion.[75] When the exclusion contains "arising out of" language, some courts interpret it broadly and

---

endorsement excluding coverage for property damage. The court examined the definition of property damage in the CGL policy to interpret the exclusion.

73. SLA Property Management v. Angelina Casualty Co., 856 F.2d 69, 73 (8th Cir.1988) (lost profits are not physical, tangible property damages and thus not within scope of coverage); Lassen Canyon Nursery, Inc. v. Royal Ins. Co. of Am., 720 F.2d 1016, 1018 (9th Cir. 1983) (economic losses, for example, lost profits or good will, are not property damage); Lucker Mfg. v. Home Ins. Co., 818 F. Supp. 821, 828 (E.D. Pa. 1993) (insurer contracted to defend and indemnify insured for damages resulting from loss of use of tangible property only, and business reputation, profits, and other business and economic losses were intangibles and not covered under policy); Lazzara Oil Co. v. Columbia Casualty Co., 683 F. Supp. 777, 780–81 (M.D. Fla. 1988) (all damages claimed had to do with loss of profits and fact that part of claimed lost profits represented losses on sale of tangible property did not alter fact that damages sought were for economic losses, not property damage), *aff'd*, 868 F.2d 1274 (11th Cir. 1989); Lowenstein Dyes & Cosmetics, Inc. v. Aetna Life & Cas. Co., 524 F. Supp. 574, 577 (E.D.N.Y. 1981), *aff'd*, 742 F.2d 1437 (2d Cir. 1983) (business losses were not "property" covered by policy that only insured against injury to or loss of use of another's "tangible property"); Liberty Mut. Ins. Co. v. Consolidated Milk Producers' Ass'n, 354 F. Supp. 879, 882 (D.N.H. 1973) (property damage does not include business losses such as cost of replacing spoiled product, and loss of profits and goodwill). *See also* Travelers Indem. Co. v. Kinney, 1994 U.S. App. LEXIS 15154 (4th Cir. June 20, 1994) (claims for negligence and breach of fiduciary duty against board member of savings and loan association for having approved high-risk loans were not barred by property damage exclusion). *See generally* Vasichek, *Liability Coverage for "Damages Because of Property Damage" under the Comprehensive General Liability Policy*, 68 Minn. L. Rev. 795 (1984).

74. County of Monroe v. Travelers Ins. Cos., 100 Misc. 2d 417, 419 N.Y.S.2d 410 (1979).

75. Scharf v. Federal Ins. Co., 261 A.D.2d 257, 690 N.Y.S.2d 265 (1999).

others do not. Courts may view the underlying cause of action as one that "owes its very existence to the" property damage and, therefore, hold it is barred.[76] Similarly, many courts hold that "arising out of" language encompasses claims that *emanate* from property damage.[77] Other courts say they will consider whether the underlying claim *could have arisen* independent of the excluded event or cause even though it would likely not have arisen but for property damage.[78] Thus, claims that are only *tangentially* related to property damage may not be excluded.[79] For example, if an employee of the company causes property damage, but the underlying cause of action against officers or directors is for negligent hiring, supervision, or entrustment, the "arising out of" language may not bar coverage.[80]

---

76. *See, e.g.*, Employers Ins. of Wausau v. Duplan Corp., 899 F. Supp. 1112 (S.D.N.Y. 1995), in which an insurer moved to dismiss a cross-claim against it that sought payment of defense costs and indemnification of certain of its officers and directors under a D&O policy. The underlying action was for a breach of fiduciary duty based on method to disburse funds to cover payment of claims for pollution damage. The insurer argued that the exclusions for property damage and pollution barred coverage. The insured responded the claim was not for the damage, but for the breach of duty. The court, however, said that examination of the substance of the fiduciary duty claim demonstrated that it arose from, and was inextricably intertwined with, the damage claim. The allegations challenging the exercise of fiduciary duty did not, said the court, convert what was fundamentally a pollution damage claim into a one triggering the duty to defend. It was "no mere coincidence" that the fiduciary duty claim was asserted in an action seeking recovery for pollution damage. "Quite the contrary," said the court, "the fiduciary duty claim owes its very existence to the pollution damage claim."

77. *See, e.g.*, Commodore Plaza Condo. Ass'n v. QBE Ins. Corp., 2013 U.S. Dist. LEXIS 5195 (S.D. Fla. Jan. 14, 2013).

78. Landing Council of Co-Owners v. Fed. Ins. Co., 247 F. Supp. 3d 802 (S.D. Tex. 2017). In the case, a condominium association board of directors made a number of decisions, including to terminate the condominium regime and sell the property after the property was damaged by a hurricane. Unit owners sued the board alleging, *inter alia*, breach of fiduciary duty, negligence, tortious interference with contract, and slander of title. The court found that many of the claims were not barred because they appeared to have arisen independently of the hurricane property damage. While that may be true, the board would probably never have acted as it did, had there not been hurricane damage to the property. *Compare* Board of Managers of Yardarm Condo. II v. Federal Ins. Co., 669 N.Y.S.2d 332, 247 A.D.2d 499 (1998), where the plaintiff in the underlying action was a condominium unit owner in a building damaged by a fire. She sued the condominium board alleging, *inter alia*, that it was negligent in failing to rebuild in a timely manner. The insurer disclaimed coverage based on the property damage exclusion in the policy, which provided it would not cover any claim that was directly or indirectly, based on or attributable to, arising out of, resulting from, or in any manner related to property damage. The court found the insurer had no duty to defend or indemnify because the underlying claim was indirectly, if not directly, related to the property damage caused by the fire.

79. *See, e.g.*, Admiral Indem. Co. v. Travelers Cas. & Sur. Co. of Am., 881 F. Supp. 2d 570, 577, n.5 (S.D.N.Y. 2012); Pulliam v. Travelers Indem. Co., 403 S.C. 332, 342, 743 S.E.2d 117, 122 (Ct. App. 2013).

80. Somerset Med. Ctr. v. Exec. Risk Indem., Inc., 2010 N.J. Super. Unpub. LEXIS 605 (Mar. 22, 2010) (interpreting parallel bodily injury portion of exclusion).

It is possible for an underlying claimant to suffer flood-related losses without having any property damage.[81] For example, flood waters may block access to the claimant's property. If that claimant is a retailer, it may lose sales because customers cannot enter the property. If the claimant is a manufacturer, it may not be able to ship its products to its customers. As discussed above, courts generally hold that those economic losses are not property damage. However, the question that could arise in those circumstances, and which apparently has not been addressed by any appellate court, is whether coverage is barred because there has been a "loss of use of tangible property that is not physically injured" for which the particular policy proscribes coverage. It could be argued that the inability to access property means it cannot be *used*. On the other hand, it could be contended that the property is being *used* to safely store the goods or products of the underlying claimant.

10.5 Other Insurance

An "other insurance" clause is especially important to D&O coverage because an insured entity that maintains it will almost certainly have commercial general liability and likely crime/fidelity policies that may be subject to it. Typically in D&O policies, the other insurance provision is an "excess clause."[82] For example, one commonly used policy says that if a loss that would otherwise be covered under it is insured under any other valid and collectible policy or policies, then the D&O coverage applies only in excess of the amount of any deductibles, retentions, and limits of liability under that other insurance, whether the other insurance is said to be primary, contributory excess, contingent, or otherwise except when that other policy is written specifically as excess of the D&O policy by reference to the policy number of the D&O

81. What if there is property damage, but not to the property of the underlying claimant? For example, the property of that claimant cannot be accessed because a roadway or bridge not on the claimant's property is washed out. Some courts have said that the property at issue is that of the claimant. County of Monroe v. Travelers Ins. Cos., 100 Misc. 2d 417, 419 N.Y.S.2d 410 (1979) (it is manifest that damage that commercial general liability policies required was property damage sustained by complaining party). However, when the policy excludes coverage for a claim "[b]ased upon, arising out of or attributable to physical injury to tangible property," it can be argued that it refers to *any* property.

82. Quinn & Levin, *Directors and Officers Liability Insurance: Probable Directions in Texas Law*, 20 Rev. Litig. 381, 471 (2001). The "other insurance" clause could also say that the D&O policy is null and void, or inapplicable, up to the limits of the other policy or that the coverage it provides is "complementary" and each insurer would share any loss on a *pro rata* basis up to its respective limit of liability. 3 *New Appleman Law of Liability Insurance* § 22.08[4] (Matthew Bender, Rev. Ed. 2020).

policy.[83] In other words, when there is other insurance, that other policy is the first to defend and pay.[84]

The other policies may have "other insurance" clauses, and those clauses may have language that is nearly identical to that in the D&O policy. Generally, courts try to give effect to the language of all the policies except when they are inconsistent. For example, a D&O and CGL policy may both state that they are excess over any other policy. In that case, the general rule is that the provisions are mutually repugnant.[85] The "other insurance" clauses are then ignored, and losses are prorated among the insurers.[86]

10.6 No Action Clause

Insurance policies almost always addresses legal actions against the insurer. A provision that does so is called a "no action" clause. It will typically say that no action will lie against the insurer unless, as a condition precedent, the insured has complied with the terms of the policy.[87] The clause also usually says that no action may be brought against the insurance carrier unless the amount of the insured's obligation to pay has been finally determined by a judgment against an insured after an actual trial or by the written agreement of the insured, the claimant, and the carrier. This precondition is generally rather strictly enforced by courts.[88] Some court may, however, permit a declaratory judgment action to determine coverage.[89]

---

83. Non-Profit Management and Organization Liability Insurance Policy § V.K.

84. Quinn & Levin, *Directors and Officers Liability Insurance: Probable Directions in Texas Law*, 20 Rev. Litig. 381, 471 (2001). *See, e.g.*, Fieldston Prop. Owners Ass'n, Inc. v. Hermitage Ins. Co., Inc., 920 N.Y.S.2d 763, 16 N.Y.3d 257, 945 N.E.2d 1013 (N.Y. 2011), where a CGL policy said it was primary, but pursuant to the other insurance clause in D&O policy, it was excess. The CGL insurer had the primary duty to defend.

85. Monteleone & Conca, *Directors and Officers Indemnification and Liability Insurance: An Overview of Legal and Practical Issues*, 51 Bus. Law 573, 603 (1996).

86. 3 *New Appleman Law of Liability Insurance* § 22.08[4] (Matthew Bender, Rev. Ed. 2020).

87. Non-Profit Management and Organization Liability Insurance Policy § V.H. This no action clause may prevent an insured from suing the insurance company when the insured has settled a claim without the consent of the company in violation of the policy. LaCroix, *D&O Insurance: Insured That Settled Underlying Claim without Insurer's Consent Cannot Sue the Insurer for Breach of Contract or Bad Faith* (2015), The D&O Diary, http://www.dandodiary.com/2015/04/articles/d-o-insurance/do-insurance-insured-that-settled-underlying-claim-without-insurers-consent-cannot-sue-the-insurer-for-breach-of-contract-or-bad-faith/.

88. *See, e.g.*, Haxton v. CNA Financial Corp., 1990 U.S. App. LEXIS 19764 (6th Cir. Nov. 2, 1990); S & S Healthcare, Inc. v. Virginia Sur. Co., 1998 U.S. Dist. LEXIS 21810 (W.D. Va. Dec. 21, 1998).

89. *See, e.g.*, Eureka Federal Sav. & Loan Ass'n v. American Casualty Co., 873 F.2d 229, 233 (9th Cir. 1989); Wilbanks Secs., Inc. v. Scottsdale Ins. Co., 215 F. Supp. 3d 1196 (W.D. Okla. 2016). *But see* Zaborac v. American Casualty Co., 663 F. Supp. 330, 333 (C.D. Ill. 1987) (declaratory judgment action barred by no action clause).

No action clauses may also say that no one has a right under the policy to join the insurance company as a party to any action against the insureds to determine its liability and that the company may not be impleaded by the insureds or their legal representatives.

10.7 Conclusion

Coverage for a flood-related loss under a D&O policy is problematic. The most formidable obstacle to coverage is the property damage exclusion. Nonetheless, the practitioner seeking to recover a client's flood-related losses should at least consider whether a D&O policy provides one of the coverages that could be implicated.

11

Recovering under an Automobile Policy

11.1 Introduction

A source of funds to pay for a flood loss that is sometimes overlooked is policies insuring motor vehicles. Most of these policies allow the insured to obtain coverage specifically for flood or water damage. However, even if that coverage does not apply, a loss arguably may be covered because the insured vehicle "collided" with water.

11.2 Policy Language

Automobile flood damage may be covered when the client's policy includes first-party physical damage coverage. Automobile physical damage coverage is required by lenders or by dealerships when they sell or lease vehicles, so clients may only have it if they have an outstanding automobile loan or leased the vehicle. Approximately three-quarters of drivers carry the coverage.[1] Physical damage coverage is of two components: collision and "other than collision," more commonly referred to as "comprehensive."

Although insurers may draft their own policies, many use standard forms created by the Insurance Services Organization (ISO) either in whole or in part.[2] The ISO has written a personal auto policy (PAP) and a business auto policy (BAP) that are in common use. The PAP says the insurer will pay for "direct and accidental loss" to the insured's covered auto caused by "other than collision" if the Declarations indicate that coverage and "collision" if the Declarations indicate that coverage.[3] "Collision" is defined as an "upset"[4] of

1. Linkov & Bartlett, *Why Flooded-Out Cars Are Likely Total Losses* (July 8, 2021), Consumer Reports, *available at* https://www.consumerreports.org/car-insurance/why-flooded-out-cars-are-likely-total-losses/.

2. 6 Jeffrey E. Thomas, *New Appleman on Insurance Law Library Edition* § 62.01[3][b] (LexisNexis 2021).

3. ISO Form PP 00 01 09 18, Part D § A.

4. See 6 Jeffrey E. Thomas, *New Appleman on Insurance Law Library Edition* § 62.02[2][a] (LexisNexis 2021), for a discussion of the meaning of the words "upset" and "overturn."

the automobile "or its impact with another vehicle or object."[5] The policy lists certain perils, one of which is "water or flood," and says that a loss caused by one of them *is considered* "other than collision."[6] One commentary says that the language introducing the enumerated perils does not clearly limit coverage to those perils and that the phrase "is considered" is "hardly clear and unambiguous" and could have been clearer if the intent was to limit coverage to the enumerated perils.[7]

The language of the ISO BAP is different. It lists comprehensive, specified causes of loss and collision as coverages. Comprehensive and specified causes of loss are alternatives. The insured may purchase one or the other. First, the BAP says the insurer will pay for loss to a covered auto under "comprehensive" coverage from any cause except its collision with another object or its "overturn."[8] Under "specified causes of loss" coverage, the insurer will pay for a loss caused by an enumerated peril, one of which is "flood,"[9] and another of which is the sinking of any conveyance transporting the covered vehicle.[10] Finally, under "collision" coverage, the insurer will pay for a loss caused by the covered auto's collision with another object or its "overturn."

11.3 "Direct" and "Accidental" Loss

Under the standard policy language, the insurer will pay for direct and accidental loss to the insured vehicle. "Direct" means there is a causal relationship in which the harm flows from an immediate or proximate cause rather than a remote one—in other words, the efficient and proximate cause.[11] Determining the definition of "accidental" can be challenging; however, in the case of physical damage coverage, courts have long said that an accidental loss is one that was "unusual and unexpected."[12] Damage caused by an "act of God" can

5. ISO Form PP 00 01 09 18, Part D § B.

6. ISO Form PP 00 01 09 18, Part D § B.6.

7. 6 Jeffrey E. Thomas, *New Appleman on Insurance Law Library Edition* § 62.03[3] (LexisNexis 2021).

8. ISO Form CA 00 01 11 20, § A.1.a. See 6 Jeffrey E. Thomas, *New Appleman on Insurance Law Library Edition* § 62.02[2][a] (LexisNexis 2021), for a discussion of the meaning of the words "upset" and "overturn."

9. ISO Form CA 00 01 11 20, § A.1.b.(4).

10. ISO Form CA 00 01 11 20, § A.1.b.(6).

11. 6 Jeffrey E. Thomas, *New Appleman on Insurance Law Library Edition* § 62.05[2] (LexisNexis 2021).

12. *See, e.g.*, United Servs. Auto. Ass'n v. Speed, 179 Wn. App. 184, 197, 317 P.3d 532, 539 (2014) ("accident" is unusual, unexpected, and unforeseen happening); Overton v. Progressive Ins. Co., 585 So. 2d 445 (Fla. 4th DCA 1991) ("accident" means that which happens by chance or fortuitously, without intention or design, and which is unexpected, unusual, and unforeseen); Kirkley v. Merrimack Mut. Fire Ins. Co., 232 N.C. 292, 294, 59 S.E.2d 629, 631 (1950) ("accidental" is that which is unintended, unexpected, unforeseen, and fortuitous).

be an accident.[13] That may be significant in flooding cases, as the source of the flood waters is usually nature.

The question of whether there was an "accident" arose in an odd case tried in a Louisiana federal court. The insured contended that as the result of an unusually heavy rainstorm, a large amount of rainwater landed on the roof of his home and ran off the roof into the *vertical* exhaust pipe of a recreational vehicle parked along the side of the house and then into the vehicle's exhaust manifold. Evidence of this was that rusty water escaped from exhaust pipes when he attempted to run the engine. The court said that for the loss to be direct and accidental, the damage would have to be the product of an unexpected or unforeseen event. A normal rain storm, said the court, would likely not qualify as a direct and accidental loss because it would be expected to occur in the usual course of things. Because the insured had failed to prove that heavy rains fell on the date that he said the damage occurred, his claim was properly denied.[14] In an unpublished decision, the Fifth Circuit sidestepped the question of whether a "normal rain storm" could be direct and accidental and simply said that a "loss due to a severe rain event qualifies as a 'direct and accidental loss.'" The appellate court affirmed based on the fact that the insured could not produce sufficient evidence to show that water from a severe rain event actually caused the damage for which he sought coverage.[15] The distinction drawn by the lower court between normal and severe rainstorms seems to fall apart on examination. Would it not be even more unforeseen for an ordinary rainstorm to cause the damage the insured claimed than an extraordinary one? If, during a normal rainfall, the bank of a stream eroded, carrying clay and vegetation downstream to partially block a culvert, would the resulting flood not be unforeseen? Would it not be just as unforeseen as a flood that occurred when a heavy rainstorm caused the volume of water in that stream to overwhelm the culvert?

11.4 "Colliding" with Flood Waters

Policies define collision as impact with another vehicle or *object*. The first question, then, when a policyholder seeks coverage for a "collision" with water, is whether water is an object. The consensus of the courts, going back

---

13. Royal Indem. Co. v. McClatchey, 101 Ga. App. 507, 509, 114 S.E.2d 394, 396 (1960). *But see* Ness v. National Indem. Co., 247 F. Supp. 944 (D. Alaska Dec. 13, 1965) (losses due to natural catastrophe—earthquake—were not caused by accident); Manard Molasses Co. v. Sun Ins. Office, Ltd., 170 So. 2d 691 (La. App. 1965) (collision or upset is generally held to include any occurrence resulting in violent meeting of any object, whether mobile or immobile, that causes meeting or contact with insured vehicle, except those occurrences considered to be acts of God).

14. Rosenthal v. Allstate Prop. & Cas. Ins. Co., 2017 U.S. Dist. LEXIS 59564 (E.D. La. Apr. 19, 2017).

15. Rosenthal v. Allstate Prop. & Cas. Ins. Co., 712 Fed. Appx. 401 (5th Cir. 2017).

over a century, is that water is an object.[16] In the most notable exception, the policy covered collision "with any other automobile, vehicle or object," and the Wisconsin Supreme Court, applying the doctrine of *ejusdem generis*, said that any collision has to have been with another automobile, vehicle, or *somewhat similar object* and in the case before it, the insured vehicle was damaged when it ran off the road, down a bank, and into a river.[17]

The next question is whether there is a collision when the insured vehicle is damaged by striking—that is, colliding with—water. One commentary opines that if a vehicle drives head-on into flood waters and becomes incapacitated, there is a collision because of the striking together of water and the insured vehicle.[18] In a case decided by the North Carolina Supreme Court, the insured automobile rolled into a canal and struck the water in it. The court held that this constituted a collision, and the insured was entitled to recover for loss by collision with another object.[19] In another case, the court found that the force of a collision with a puddle of water bent a tie rod, causing the driver to lose control and bringing about an accident.[20]

---

16. Tuten v. First of Georgia Ins. Co., 117 Ga. App. 409, 160 S.E.2d 903 (1968) (water in river was object); Morton v. Blue Ridge Ins. Co., 255 N.C. 360, 121 S.E.2d 716 (1961) (water in canal was object); Washington Fire & Marine Ins. Co. v. Ryburn, 228 Ark. 930, 311 S.W.2d 302 (Ark. 1958) (water in ditch was object); Harris v. Allstate Ins. Co., 309 N.Y. 72, 127 N.E.2d 816 (1955) (water was tangible body or object); Providence Washington Ins. Co. v. Proffitt, 150 Tex. 207, 211, 239 S.W.2d 379, 381 (1951) (flood waters constitute object); Long v. Royal Ins. Co., 180 Wash. 360, 40 P.2d 132 (1935) (water is tangible object); Ringo v. Automobile Ins. Co., 143 Ore. 420, 22 P.2d 887 (1933) (coming into contact with water and bed of stream constituted collision with another object); Columbia Ins. Co. v. Chatterjee, 93 Okla. 249, 250, 219 P. 102, 103 (1923) (water and land are objects within meaning of law of accident insurance policies, and automobile that runs into either or both collides with an object); Harris v. American Casualty Co., 83 N.J.L. 641, 85 A. 194 (1912) (water and land are objects). *See also* Gans v. Columbia Ins. Co., 99 N.J.L. 44, 123 Atl. 240 (1924) (policy providing coverage for aircraft).

17. Wettengel v. United States Lloyds, 157 Wis. 433, 147 N.W. 360 (1914).

18. Smith, *Auto Damage after a Hurricane: Comp or Collision?* (Sept. 26, 2018), Property Casualty 360, https://www.propertycasualty360.com/2018/09/26/auto-damage-after-a-hurricane-comp-or-collision-2/?kw=Auto%20damage%20after%20a%20hurricane:%20comp%20or%20collision?&et=editorial&bu=PC360&cn=20180927&src=EMC-Email&pt=AgentBrokerInsider.

19. Morton v. Blue Ridge Ins. Co., 255 N.C. 360, 121 S.E.2d 716 (1961). *See also* Tuten v. First of Georgia Ins. Co., 117 Ga. App. 409, 160 S.E.2d 903 (1968) (loss was caused by collision of insured automobile with water in river); Bolduc v. New York Fire Ins. Co., 244 Minn. 192, 199, 69 N.W.2d 660, 665 (1955) (striking of water surface may be considered within coverage of collision policy). *But see* Allison v. Iowa Mut. Ins. Co., 43 N.C. App. 200, 258 S.E.2d 489 (1979), *cert. den.*, 298 N.C. 805, 262 S.E.2d 1 (1979) (collapse of bridge on which insured truck was being operated, resulting in truck sliding down into river or creek underneath bridge and thereby being damaged, was not a collision).

20. Harris v. Allstate Ins. Co., 309 N.Y. 72, 127 N.E.2d 816 (1955). In *Harris*, the driver of an insured vehicle ran into a puddle of water and lost control of the car, which mounted an embankment and turned over. Evidently the driver lost control because the impact with the water bent the tie rod. The court said that any damage to the tie rod resulting from contact with the puddle was caused not by any destructive action of the water, but solely by reason of the impact or *collision* of the fast-moving car with that body of water.

Sometimes, a vehicle is not damaged by the initial contact with water.[21] The injury is caused by the force of the water sweeping the vehicle away or by entry of water into the engine and interior of the vehicle. One question then presented is whether the water has to be moving for there to be a collision, or is any contact a collision? Some policies provide coverage for collision with any *moving or stationary* object, but most do not include those modifiers.

Some courts have seemed to suggest the water should be moving. For example, in a case before the Texas Supreme Court, a car was being driven over a causeway when it hit water. It came to a halt in an inclining position with water on one side up to the running board and on the other up to the door handle, but with no damage to it at that point. The driver was unable to extricate the automobile, and the force of river flood waters washed it from the causeway into the river. An effort to pull the automobile out with a wrecker failed and it was damaged beyond repair by the water. The court held that the force of the flood waters against the vehicle was a collision. There was coverage, said the court, even though the vehicle had come to rest after the original collision with the water, only to be then washed from the causeway by the force of flood waters. "The collision of the water with the automobile set in motion the series of events which, unbroken by the intervention of any new and independent cause, led to the destruction of the automobile."[22]

The Washington Supreme Court agreed in a case in which the plaintiff drove his truck into water that had overflowed a river onto the highway on which he was driving. The truck stalled and later was swept away by the swiftly flowing water. It was never recovered. The insurer argued that there was no collision when the truck became bogged down in the water or when it was swept into the river and no upset when it was carried into the river. The proximate cause of the loss according to the insurer was the action of flood waters that carried the truck into the river channel, a peril not covered by the policy. The court said that the sole question was whether the action of the water was a collision within the terms of the policy. It stated that water is a tangible object and that its contact, *when moving*, with a stationary object

---

21. One commentary asserts that if a driver hydroplanes because of water on a road and crashes the vehicle, the loss is because of an impact with an object, and it is proper to file a collision claim. Smith, *Auto Damage after a Hurricane: Comp or Collision?* (Sept. 26, 2018), Property Casualty 360, https://www.propertycasualty360.com/2018/09/26/auto-damage-after-a-hurricane-comp-or-collision-2/?kw=Auto%20damage%20after%20a%20hurricane:%20comp%20or%20collision?&et=editorial&bu=PC360&cn=20180927&src=EMC-Email&pt=AgentBrokerInsider. However, is the water the "object"? It would seem that the object would be what the vehicle struck and that caused any damage.

22. Providence Washington Ins. Co. v. Proffitt, 150 Tex. 207, 239 S.W.2d 379 (1951). Interestingly, the author of the opinion later said that he had "stretched automobile collision insurance coverage to the breaking point" by holding it covered a collision with rushing flood waters. Scott, *In Memoriam: Robert Wilburn Calvert, The Prudentialist*, 26 St. Mary's L. J. 905, 911 (1995).

would be a collision. If that contact was not a collision, the court was "at a loss for words by which it may be properly described." Therefore, the loss of the truck was because of an accidental collision with another object under the terms of the policy.[23]

Obviously, for there to be a collision, one body has to be moving. However, both bodies, as courts acknowledge, do not need to be in motion for there to be a collision.[24] And, neither the Texas nor Washington court said that *only* contact with moving water could be a collision. In the Texas case, it is not even clear whether the damage was by the force of the water striking the vehicle or hurling it against other objects or entry of water into the engine and interior. In the Washington case, on the other hand, it could be said that the loss was caused by the force of the water because the vehicle was carried away and never found.

Courts often say that "collision" means a striking together, violent contact.[25] Can entry of water into an engine without force invoke collision coverage? In a Florida case, an insured was driving on a beach whose surface was not sufficiently firm to withstand the weight and gave way under the car, causing it to sink into the soft sand and become stuck. It was damaged while partially submerged by the incoming tide before it could be extricated. The court focused on the collapse of the "road bed" and said that was not a collision and there was, therefore, no coverage. The court did not address whether entry of rising water into the vehicle was a collision. On the other hand, the Arkansas Supreme Court appears to have allowed that damage caused by entry of water into a motor without force could come under collision coverage. In the case, the driver of a truck lost control of the vehicle on a slick roadway. It careened off the road and down an embankment, where it plunged into a ditch filled with water. The left front fender, front bumper, and radiator were all damaged, and the motor was "soaked and almost completely ruined." The court held that the damages to the truck were caused by a collision with the water in the ditch.[26] Note that damages to the fender, bumper, and radiator were most

23. Long v. Royal Ins. Co., 180 Wash. 360, 40 P.2d 132 (1935).

24. Bolduc v. New York Fire Ins. Co., 244 Minn. 192, 198, 69 N.W.2d 660, 665 (1955) (it is not necessary to collision between two objects that both should be in motion); Harris v. American Casualty Co., 83 N.J.L. 641, 85 A. 194 (1912).

25. *See, e.g.*, Allison v. Iowa Mut. Ins. Co., 43 N.C. App. 200, 258 S.E.2d 489 (1979), *cert. den.*, 298 N.C. 805, 262 S.E.2d 1 (1979); Aetna Casualty & Surety Co. v. Cartmel, 87 Fla. 495, 100 So. 802 (1924); Universal Service Co. v. American Ins. Co., 213 Mich. 523, 181 N.W. 1007 (1921); Harris v. American Casualty Co., 83 N.J.L. 641, 85 A. 194 (1912). *See also* Bolduc v. New York Fire Ins. Co., 244 Minn. 192, 199, 69 N.W.2d 660, 665 (1955) (collision means act of colliding, and imports striking together).

26. Washington Fire & Marine Ins. Co. v. Ryburn, 228 Ark. 930, 311 S.W.2d 302 (1958). *See also* Ringo v. Automobile Ins. Co., 143 Ore. 420, 22 P.2d 887 (1933) (where insurer argued that damage caused to automobile by being plunged into river and remaining there some hours did not come within policy coverage, court said that *coming into contact with water* and bed of stream constituted collision with another object).

likely caused by the impact of the truck hitting the water, but the "soaking" of the motor would have happened after the truck came to rest in the ditch.

There are cases in which vehicles are damaged when they fall into water while entering or exiting a ferry. These cases are usually decided based on policy language providing that "while [the insured vehicle is] being transported in any conveyance by land or water, the stranding, sinking, collision, burning or derailment of such conveyance" is a peril insured against. Some courts conclude that "stranding, sinking, collision, burning or derailment" applies to the insured vehicle as well as the conveyance, the ferry.[27] Other courts say that "stranding, sinking, burning, collision, or derailment" refer to the conveyance, not to the automobile that was being transported.[28] In one case, the court allowed that had the policy only provided collision coverage, it could be that the "plunging of the car into the water and finally striking and resting upon the bottom of the stream was a collision"; however, the policy also had a "stranding, sinking, collision, burning or derailment" clause under which the court found there was coverage.[29]

A case that stands out from the other water collision cases was decided by the Federal District Court for Alaska. The insured vehicle was parked near a dock. Following an earthquake, a seismic sea wave swept the area including the dock, and the vehicle was found approximately 1,000 feet from where it had been parked. It was upside down and substantially damaged. The court said that collision coverage is, in the minds of policyholders, intended to insure against losses due to "accidents," not against those due to natural catastrophes. The action of the wave that damaged the vehicle was precipitated by the earthquake that in turn was caused by the elements of nature, not by the hand of man and, therefore, the damage was not caused by collision.[30] It is no doubt true that when a consumer obtains collision coverage on a vehicle, he or she assumes its purpose is to protect against a loss caused by collision with another vehicle. However, the limited imagination of the average consumer does not change the usual policy language defining collision: impact with another vehicle *or object*. In the Alaska case, there was an impact with an object, the wave of water. That, under the consensus of the courts, was a collision no matter the expectations of the consumer who purchased the policy.

---

27. *See* Liverpool & London & Globe Ins. Co. v. Jones, 207 Ark. 237, 180 S.W.2d 519 (1944); Importers' & Exporters' Ins. Co. v. Jones, 166 Ark. 370, 266 S.W. 286 (1924); Wheeler v. Globe & Rutgers Fire Ins. Co., 125 S.C. 320, 118 S.E. 609 (S.C. 1923).

28. Johnson v. Glens Falls Ins. Co., 131 S.C. 253, 127 S.E. 14 (S.C. 1925). In *Johnson*, the automobile was aboard the ferry and still in gear. It suddenly and swiftly moved forward and plunged over the far end of the ferry into the river. The court said that it was perfectly clear that the sole cause of the accident was the improper handling of the car by the plaintiff who was at the wheel and in absolute control of the vehicle.

29. Liverpool & London & Globe Ins. Co. v. Jones, 207 Ark. 237, 180 S.W.2d 519 (1944).

30. Ness v. National Indem. Co., 247 F. Supp. 944 (D. Alaska 1965).

11.5 Loss Caused by Water or Flood

[1] Generally

When a policyholder has comprehensive coverage, it typically covers a loss caused by flood or water. In that event, it will not matter that there was not a collision. For example, one commentator posits that if a vehicle is parked on the side of a road and flood waters rise to submerge the engine block, the loss would be considered a comprehensive one.[31] If the comprehensive coverage only applies to "flood" losses, the coverage issue becomes problematic.

[2] Loss Caused by Water or Flood

Water is a broad term encompassing water in its natural states—oceans, seas, lakes, ponds, rivers, streams, brooks, and even puddles—as surface water or as water released from a broken pipe or water main, and damage caused by water is not limited to resting, flowing, or escaping water.[32] Thus, when a policy covers loss by water or flood, there is no need to determine whether there has been a flood when that damage was caused by water.

Under loss by water or flood, coverage may be so obvious that the insurer does not deny liability. For example, a car was in a garage awaiting repairs when a flash flood occurred. Muddy flood water reached a height of 18 inches on the automobile. All of the car's underside mechanical parts were submerged, and water got inside the car. The comprehensive coverage included loss by water or flood, and the insurer did not dispute that the loss was an insured event.[33] In another case, the insured automobile was damaged by flood water sweeping down on it while it was being driven across a gully. The court said the insurer was liable to the insured for damage to his automobile that the evidence showed he sustained as a result of the flood.[34]

For there to be coverage, the loss has to be caused by the properties of water. For example, in a New York case, the driver of an insured vehicle ran into a puddle of water and lost control of the car, which mounted an embankment and turned over. Evidently the driver lost control because the impact with the water bent the tie rod. The court said that any damage to the tie rod resulting from contact with the puddle was caused, not by any destructive

31. Smith, *Auto Damage after a Hurricane: Comp or Collision?* (Sept. 26, 2018), Property Casualty 360, https://www.propertycasualty360.com/2018/09/26/auto-damage-after-a-hurricane-comp-or-collision-2/?kw=Auto%20damage%20after%20a%20hurricane:%20comp%20or%20collision?&et=editorial&bu=PC360&cn=20180927&src=EMC-Email&pt=AgentBrokerInsider.

32. 6 Jeffrey E. Thomas, *New Appleman on Insurance Law Library Edition* § 62.03[4][f] (LexisNexis 2021).

33. Foley v. United Service Auto. Ass'n, 187 Kan. 405, 357 P.2d 824 (Kan. 1960).

34. Lumbermen's Ins. Co. v. Heiner, 74 Ariz. 152, 245 P.2d 415 (Ariz. 1952).

action of the water, but solely by reason of the impact or *collision* of the fast-moving car with that body of water. Because the policy covered loss caused by water but excluded damage caused by "collision," the insurer was not liable. The court said that "loss caused by water" meant the policy covered "only hazards naturally associated with water's distinctive and peculiar properties and engendered by the destructive power of water as such, as in cases of submersion, inundation or leakage."[35]

[3] Loss Caused by Flood

When coverage is sought under a policy covering a loss by flood, but not water, the insured has to prove the loss was occasioned by an event meeting the definition of flood. As discussed in the next subsection, at one time there were policies that defined "flood" as "rising waters." Contemporary policies, however, rarely define the term. A relatively recent exception can be found in a North Carolina case where the policy defined "flood" as "the overflow of a river, stream or other body of water." The insured claimed coverage for an incident in which the insured vehicle became mired in mud and water from a retention pond that seeped around the vehicle, surrounded it, and damaged the engine. The complaint, however, did not allege that any river, creek, or other body of water *overflowed*, and the appellate court concluded that the allegations failed to state a claim for coverage under the policy. In its appellate brief, the insured argued that the water overtopped the retention pond and covered the site where the vehicle was located. The court said that this allegation was not in the complaint and was not properly asserted on appeal.[36]

When a policy covers flood but not water damage, judges are met with the large body of law interpreting the word "flood."[37] As one respected treatise observes, courts have struggled when policies cover only flood damage, but when the twin perils of water and flood are found in comprehensive coverage, courts do not need to decide whether there has been a flood. When a vehicle is damaged by surface water or water discharged from a pipe or a water main, it is covered by the water peril.[38]

35. Harris v. Allstate Ins. Co., 309 N.Y. 72, 76, 127 N.E.2d 816, 818 (1955) (loss caused by water must be taken to comprehend only damaging effect of water when it operates as active agent in moving against or falling on automobile, and not when its role is merely that of object that vehicle itself moves against or strikes).

36. N.C. Concrete Finishers, Inc. v. N.C. Farm Bureau Mut. Ins. Co., 202 N.C. App. 334, 688 S.E.2d 534 (2010).

37. See § 2.01[3], *supra*, for a discussion of the meaning of "flood."

38. 6 Jeffrey E. Thomas, *New Appleman on Insurance Law Library Edition* § 62.03[4][f] (LexisNexis 2021).

[4] Loss Caused by Flood Meaning Rising Waters

At one time, there were policies, not all for automobiles, that defined "flood" to mean "rising waters."[39] Some policies narrowed the definition to rising waters in lakes, streams, or rivers.[40] In the case of a policy with the broader definition, an insured tractor was being operated on a beach and became stuck in the sand. It was then submerged by the ocean tide. The insurer argued there was no coverage because "flood" meant an inundation of water over land that is not usually covered by it. The insured countered that the policy was intended to cover loss by the rising of tidal waters. The Oregon Supreme Court said the insurer could have limited its risk by, for example, excepting tidal waters from the meaning of flood. The insurer did not limit the coverage, and the court held for the insured.[41]

[5] Loss Caused by Flood Meaning Rising Streams or Navigable Waters

Policies may define "flood" as the "rising of streams or navigable waters." The South Carolina Supreme Court said that the phrase was intended to limit, not enlarge, the meaning of "flood." Flood did not mean the ordinary rising of the tide because the word "rising" contemplates that which is abnormal or unusual.[42] A Texas court said that under that language, "navigable waters" did not include a branch that was dry except when it rained.[43]

[6] Loss Caused by Flood or Rising Waters

Some policies provide coverage for loss caused by flood *or* rising waters. In a case in which an automobile became stuck at a public landing on a river and then was covered by rising tide water before it could be freed, the South Carolina Supreme Court found there was coverage. Simply put, the phrase "flood or rising waters" provided coverage for a loss caused by a "flood" or caused by "rising waters."[44]

---

39. *See, e.g.*, Roberts v. Union Ins. Soc., 215 Ore. 183, 332 P.2d 600 (1958); Carl Ingalls, Inc. v. Hartford Fire Ins. Co., 137 Cal. App. 741, 31 P.2d 414 (1934); Home Ins. Co. v. Wheatley, 6 Tenn. App. 580 (1926).

40. *See* Monte Christo Drilling Corp. v. Universal Ins. Co., 376 F.2d 61 (5th Cir. 1967) (coverage for flood "meaning rising waters in lakes, streams or rivers").

41. Roberts v. Union Ins. Soc., 215 Ore. 183, 332 P.2d 600 (1958).

42. Long Motor Lines, Inc. v. Home Fire & Marine Ins. Co., 220 S.C. 335, 340–41, 67 S.E.2d 512, 515 (S.C. 1951) (moving van became stuck on beach, and loss was caused by rising tide).

43. St. Paul Fire & Marine Ins. Co. v. Carroll, 106 S.W.2d 757 (Tex. Civ. App. 1937) (finding no ambiguity in words "rising of streams or navigable waters"). The court subsequently distinguished *Long Motor Lines* in a case in which the policy covered loss caused by caused by flood *or* rising waters. *See* Myers v. Calvert Fire Ins. Co., 246 S.C. 46, 142 S.E.2d 704 (S.C. 1965) (flood is rising water, but all rising water is not flood; flood does not include ordinary rising of tide that occurs at regular intervals capable of exact determination).

44. Myers v. Calvert Fire Ins. Co., 246 S.C. 46, 142 S.E.2d 704 (S.C. 1965).

[7] Loss Caused by Water but Not Caused by Rain, Sleet, Snow, or Flood

A policy provided coverage for an automobile from the perils of tornado, cyclone, windstorm, hail, earthquake, explosion, and accidental and external discharge or leakage of water; it excluded damage caused by rain, sleet, snow, or flood. A severe rainstorm dropped over two inches of rain in a little less than two hours. Two feet of rainwater filled streets and then broke the windows of a basement garage where the insured car was kept and caused damage to the car. The court held the damage was covered because the water that damaged the car was neither rain nor flood waters but surface water.[45]

In a Texas case, the insured automobile dealer paid for coverage for loss by external discharge or leakage of water except loss resulting from rain, snow, or sleet. The dealer declined parallel coverage that specifically included "flood or rising waters" as a covered peril. Unprecedented rain fell and caused a river to overflow its banks, and its water engulfed a lot where the dealership stored cars. Seven of the cars were submerged, and the dealership claimed the resulting damage was caused by an "external discharge or leakage of water." The insurer argued that the water that damaged the automobiles was flood water and that because the coverage the insured had accepted and paid for did not insure against flood waters, whereas coverage that was not taken and paid for did insure against flood waters, the policy expressly failed to cover the damages for which the insured sued. The court agreed. The coverage against external discharge or leakage of water did not include, and was not meant to include, said the court, an unprecedented overflow of a river, and that was made clear by reference to the coverage the insured declined that offered to insure not only against external discharge or leakage of water but also against flood or rising water as well. Because the dealership did not accept and pay for that coverage, the policy expressly failed to cover the damage for which the dealership sued, and it could not recover.[46]

[8] Loss Caused by External Discharge or Leakage of Water

Some policies provide coverage for a loss caused by *external discharge or leakage of water*.[47] Often, these policies exclude from that phrase "damage caused by rain, sleet, snow, flood." One court found that "external discharge or leakage of water" meant losses sustained when a vehicle has been subjected to damage from water coming from an outside source, other than rain, which

45. Poole v. Sun Underwriters Ins. Co., 65 S.D. 422, 274 N.W. 658 (1937).

46. Glens Falls Ins. Co. v. McCown, 149 Tex. 587, 236 S.W.2d 108 (Tex. Civ. App. 1951). *Accord* Henry v. Dubuque Fire & Marine Ins. Co., 185 S.W.2d 658 (Mo. App. 1945).

47. *See, e.g.*, Pennsylvania Fire Ins. Co. v. Sikes, 197 Okl. 137, 168 P.2d 1016 (1946); Henry v. Dubuque Fire & Marine Ins. Co., 185 S.W.2d 658 (Mo. App. 1945).

was expressly excluded.[48] In another case, the court held that there was no coverage because the waters of a storm surge constituted a flood. The flood was the proximate cause of the loss, not the wind that caused the storm surge.[49]

A policy may cover loss by "external discharge or leakage of water," but not flood. For example, a truck owner purchased coverage for direct and accidental loss or damage caused by external discharge or leakage of water except loss resulting from rain, snow, or sleet. The insured declined comprehensive coverage, which included loss by water or flood. The truck owner, evidently anticipating a flood, placed the truck on high ground and chained it to a sturdy pole. Nonetheless, the truck was washed away by the force of flood waters. The court found no coverage. It said that "external discharge or leakage of water" was "recognized by the policy as a separate and distinct coverage from that pertaining to 'flood or rising waters.'" Looking at the policy as a whole, it was clear that "external discharge or leakage of water" was not intended to be synonymous with "flood or rising waters."[50]

11.6 Exclusions

The ISO personal auto policy has a number of exclusions that may be pertinent to a flood loss claim. First, the policy will not pay for a loss that occurs while the vehicle is being used as a public or livery conveyance, including any period of time it is being used by any person who is logged into a "transportation network platform" as a driver, whether or not a passenger is "occupying" the vehicle.[51] A "public or livery conveyance" is a vehicle carrying passengers or goods for compensation.[52] A "transportation network platform" is an online-enabled application or digital network used to connect passengers with drivers who use vehicles to provide prearranged transportation services for compensation.[53] There is also no coverage for loss to any electronic equipment that reproduces, receives, or transmits audio, visual, or data signals including radios and stereos, tape decks, compact disc systems, navigation systems, internet access systems, personal computers, video entertainment systems, telephones, televisions, two-way mobile radios, scanners, or citizens band radios.[54] However, the exclusion does not apply to electronic equipment

48. A. B. Veirs, Inc. v. Myers, 19 Md. App. 330, 311 A.2d 448 (1973). The court rejected the argument that the language of the policy was ambiguous and should be interpreted to include water flowing from within the insured vehicle's radiator.

49. Kitson v. National Retailers Mut. Ins. Co., 22 Pa. D. & C. 414 (1935).

50. Saul v. St. Paul Mercury Indem. Co., 173 Kan. 679, 250 P.2d 819 (1952).

51. ISO Form PP 00 01 09 18, Part D, Exclusion 1.

52. *See Ballentine's Law Dictionary*, 3rd Edition.

53. ISO Form PP 00 01 09 18, Definition § L.

54. ISO Form PP 00 01 09 18, Part D, Exclusion 4. Loss to tapes, records, discs or other media used with any of the electronic equipment is also not covered. ISO Form PP 00 01 09 18, Part D, Exclusion 5.

permanently installed in the vehicle. Finally, there is no coverage for loss to any "custom equipment" in or on the vehicle above $1,500.[55] "Custom equipment" is equipment, furnishings, and parts in or on any vehicle other than original manufacturer equipment, furnishings, or parts or replacements of original manufacturer equipment, furnishings, or parts with other equipment, furnishings, or parts of like kind and quality.[56]

It is important to take note of the limits of liability in the ISO personal auto policy. First, the most the insurer will pay under the policy is the lesser of the actual cash value of the damaged property or amount required to repair or replace the property with other property of like kind and quality.[57] Second, the most the company will pay for a loss to a non-owned vehicle that is a trailer or for custom equipment is $1,500. For electronic equipment that reproduces, receives, or transmits audio, visual, or data signals and that is permanently installed in the auto in locations not used by the auto manufacturer for installation of that equipment, the most the insurer will pay is $1,000.

If a repair or replacement results in better than like kind or quality, the insurer will not pay for the amount of the betterment.[58] In the event of a total loss, an adjustment for depreciation and physical condition will be made in determining actual cash value.[59] This limitation is of particular importance when the loss is the result of flooding because the chief mechanic for *Consumer Reports* says when a car has been in a flood, it may be simply too expensive to repair.[60]

The business auto policy also has exclusions of which to be aware. The insurer will not pay for a loss to tapes, records, discs, or other similar audio, visual, or data electronic devices designed for use with audio, visual, or data electronic equipment.[61] There is no coverage for any device designed or used to detect speed-measuring equipment—for instance, radar or laser detectors, and any jamming apparatus intended to elude or disrupt speed-measuring

55. ISO Form PP 00 01 09 18, Part D, Exclusion 10.

56. ISO Form PP 00 01 09 18, Part D, § D. The term "custom equipment" includes but is not limited to special carpeting or insulation, furniture or bars, height-extending roof, body, engine, exhaust or suspension enhancers, winches, or anti-roll or anti-sway bars, custom grilles, louvers, side pipes, hood scoops or spoilers, custom wheels, tires or spinners, custom chrome, murals, paintwork, decals or other graphics, or caps, covers, or bedliners. It does not include electronic equipment that reproduces, receives, or transmits audio, visual, or data signals.

57. ISO Form PP 00 01 09 18, Part D, Limit of Liability, § A.

58. ISO Form PP 00 01 09 18, Part D, Limit of Liability, § C.

59. ISO Form PP 00 01 09 18, Part D, Limit of Liability, § B.

60. Linkov & Bartlett, *Why Flooded-Out Cars Are Likely Total Losses* (July 8, 2021), Consumer Reports, *available at* https://www.consumerreports.org/car-insurance/why-flooded-out-cars-are-likely-total-losses/. *See also* Foley v. United Service Auto. Ass'n, 187 Kan. 405, 407, 357 P.2d 824, 826 (Kan. 1960), where the court relates the testimony of automobile dealers about flooded cars.

61. CA 00 01 11 20, § III.B.4.a.

equipment.[62] There is also no coverage for the loss of any electronic equipment, regardless of whether it is permanently installed, that reproduces, receives, or transmits audio, visual, or data signals or any accessories used with that equipment.[63] This exclusion, however, does not apply to equipment designed to be operated solely by use of the power from the vehicle's electrical system that, at the time of loss, is permanently installed in or on the vehicle, is removable from a housing unit that is permanently installed in or on the vehicle, is an integral part of the same unit housing any excluded electronic equipment, or is necessary for the normal operation of the vehicle or the monitoring of its operating system.[64] Finally, the insurer will not pay for loss to a vehicle due to diminution in value.[65] The term "diminution in value" means actual or perceived loss in market or resale value that results from a direct and accidental loss.[66]

Under the business auto policy, the most the insurer will pay for loss to any one covered auto is the lesser of the actual cash value of the damaged property as of the time of the loss or the cost of repairing or replacing the damaged property with other property of like kind and quality.[67] An adjustment for depreciation and physical condition will be made in determining actual cash value when there is a total loss,[68] which as noted above is likely in the event a vehicle is in a flood. If a repair or replacement results in better than like kind or quality, the insurer will not pay for the amount of the betterment.[69] There is a limit of $1,000 for electronic equipment that reproduces, receives, or transmits audio, visual, or data signals in any one loss if at the time of the loss the electronic equipment is permanently installed in or on the covered vehicle in a housing, opening, or other location that is not normally used by the manufacturer for the installation of that equipment, is removable from a permanently installed housing unit, or is an integral part of the equipment.[70]

---

62. CA 00 01 11 20, § III.B.4.b.
63. CA 00 01 11 20, §§ III.B, 4.c & d.
64. CA 00 01 11 20, § III.B.5.
65. CA 00 01 11 20, § III.B.6.
66. CA 00 01 11 20, § V.E.
67. CA 00 01 11 20, § III.C.1.a.
68. CA 00 01 11 20, § III.C.2.
69. CA 00 01 11 20, § III.C.3.
70. CA 00 01 11 20, § III.C.1.b.

12

Recovering from an Insurance Producer

12.1 Introduction

Property owners in the United States know just enough about flooding and flood insurance to be a danger to themselves. Almost all know that the federal government provides flood insurance through the Federal Emergency Management Agency (FEMA). A surprising number of property owners are under the misperception that they only *need* that insurance when it is required by a lender. They likely do not know that the lender is requiring that coverage because their property is in a FEMA high-risk flood zone or that properties outside those zones can still be at considerable risk of flooding. For some reason, residential property owners often do not realize that the limit of coverage in the FEMA policy is only $250,000, an amount far below the value of a great many American homes. Another common misconception is that there is no private flood coverage available. Finally, while sophisticated large organizations are aware that excess coverage is available, many homeowners and small business people do not know that they can ask for coverage that will pay for losses that exceed the coverage of a primary policy whether obtained from FEMA or a private carrier. In other words, they need advice. They very much need an insurance consultant but almost never employ one. Instead, they rely on a broker or agent for advice and then seek to hold the agent or broker liable for failing to provide it. Generally, they are unsuccessful.

After their property has been damaged in a flood, it is not unusual for owners to complain about what they were *not* told by the person from whom the purchased their property insurance. They were not told that their property was in an area at risk for flooding. They were not told that flood insurance was available. They were not told that excess flood insurance was available to cover a loss that exceeds what the Federal Emergency Management Agency's Standard Flood Insurance Policy (SFIP) covers. If they *had* been told, they say they would have purchased insurance for the loss they have suffered. They also often contend that they did not get the coverage for which they asked.

They asked for "the best coverage available" or "the maximum coverage that could be obtained." Instead, they got less coverage than it turned out they needed. Whether they are unhappy about what they were not told or what they asked for but did not receive, they want to sue the person they believe "dropped the ball." That person is known broadly as an insurance "intermediary" or "producer," but more commonly as an insurance agent or broker.

12.2 Agents Distinguished from Brokers[1]

A "producer" in the insurance industry is an agent, a broker, or another licensed representative who sells insurance.[2] Laypeople use the terms "agent" and "broker" interchangeably, but the law does not. An "agent" markets policies of insurance for an insurance carrier or independently.[3] The agent then represents the carrier.[4] Brokers work for the applicant or insured. They are not restricted to selling policies for a particular insurance carrier.[5] They are generally considered an agent of the insured,[6] even though their commissions are paid by the carrier from the premiums received from the policyholder.[7] There are special circumstances in which a broker may be the agent for both the insured and the insurer. If a broker acts under a directive from an applicant to procure coverage from a particular company, the broker can be considered an agent for that company.[8]

---

1. *See generally* Beh & Willis, *Insurance Intermediaries*, 15 Conn. Ins. L.J. 571, 574–81 (2009); Richmond, *Insurance Agent and Broker Liability*, 40 Tort & Ins. L.J. 1 (2004).

2. *Producer*, IRMI, https://www.irmi.com/online/insurance-glossary/terms/p/producer.aspx.

3. *Glossary A*, NAIC, http://naic.org/consumer_glossary.htm#A. *See also Agent*, IRMI, https://www.irmi.com/online/insurance-glossary/terms/a/agent.aspx (agents are individuals or entities that solicit, negotiate, or instigate insurance contracts for insurance companies and can be either independent or employed by the company).

4. American Way Cellular, Inc. v. Travelers Property Casualty Co. of America, 216 Cal. App. 4th 1040, 1052, 157 Cal. Rptr. 3d 385, 395 (2013). *See also* Stars & Bars, LLC v. Travelers Cas. Ins. Co. of Am., 2018 U.S. Dist. LEXIS 228006 (C.D. Cal. Sept. 17, 2018) (agent has ongoing and continuous relationship with insurer).

5. *Broker*, IRMI, https://www.irmi.com/online/insurance-glossary/terms/b/broker.aspx.

6. *See, e.g.*, American Way Cellular, Inc. v. Travelers Property Casualty Co. of America, 216 Cal. App. 4th 1040, 1052, 157 Cal. Rptr. 3d 385, 394–95 (2013) (broker is middleman between policyholder and carrier, which is not liable for broker's acts or omissions). *See also* Jaber v. State Farm Mut. Auto. Ins. Co., 2012 U.S. Dist. LEXIS 102530 (E.D. La. 2012) (negligent actions of broker are not imputable to insurer, so broker may be found independently negligent for client's loss).

7. *Broker*, IRMI, https://www.irmi.com/online/insurance-glossary/terms/b/broker.aspx.

8. Mark Andy, Inc. v. Hartford Fire Ins. Co., 229 F.3d 710, 717 (8th Cir. 2000).

12.3 Liability of Agents and Brokers Generally[9]

[1] Basic Principles

Liability of insurance producers for failure to procure insurance is a topic about which much has been written. It is addressed at length in law review articles,[10] in specialized volumes,[11] and also in the two well-known multi-volume insurance law treatises.[12] Therefore, this chapter provides an overview of the issues and focuses on unique concerns in the procurement of flood insurance.

Coverage procurement actions may be brought as a claim for negligent failure to procure coverage, negligent misrepresentation of the coverage obtained, breach of contract (express or implied), or breach of a fiduciary duty.[13] A negligent procurement claim alleges the defendant failed to procure the coverage the applicant sought.[14] In a negligent misrepresentation claim,

---

9. *See generally* Beh & Willis, *Insurance Intermediaries*, 15 Conn. Ins. L.J. 571, 581–91 (2009).

10. *See* Sumbaly, *An Insurance Broker's Duty: Adopting California's Approach*, 43 Seton Hall Legis. J. 195 (2019); Kanterman, *New Jersey Insurance Producer Liability: Attempting to Define the "Special Relationship" Theory of Liability*, 2016 Rutgers U.L. Rev. Comments 92 (2016); Everett, Martin & Hossellman, *Broker, Advisor, or Both?: When an Expanded Duty Will Be Imposed*, 2015 Orange County Lawyer 22 (2015); Beh & Willis, *Insurance Intermediaries*, 15 Conn. Ins. L.J. 571 (2009); Le Clercq, *Show Me the Money! What Exactly Are the Duties of Insurance Agents and Brokers?*, 54 LA Bar J. 94 (2006); Richmond, *Insurance Agent and Broker Liability*, 40 Tort & Ins. L.J. 1 (2004); Sakall, *Can the Public Really Count on Insurance Agents to Advise Them? A Critique of the "Special Circumstances" Test*, 42 Ariz. L. Rev. 991 (2000); Swift, *How Special Is Special? An Insurance Agent's Duty to Advise*, 21 Hamline L. Rev. 323 (1998); Mandenon, *Insurance Agent Malpractice: The Texas Experience*, 29 Tort & Ins. L.J. 623 (1994); O'Donnell, *An Overview of Insurance Agent/Broker Liability Claims by Policyholders, Insurers, and Third Parties*, 25 The Brief 34 (1992); Pierce, *The Ethical Dilemma Insurance Agents Face Which May Tempt Some to Mislead Their Clients Regarding Coverage, and What to Do to Protect Your Business from the Consequences of Such Conduct*, 19 W. St. U. L. Rev. 507 (1992).

11. *See* Harnett, *Responsibilities of Insurance Agents and Brokers* (Matthew Bender, Rev. Ed. 2021); Weimer, Whitman & Hagglund, *Law of Commercial Insurance Agents and Brokers* (Thomson West 2021).

12. Plitt et al., *Couch on Insurance*, Chs. 44–57 (Clark Boardman Callaghan 2021); 1 Jeffrey E. Thomas, *New Appleman on Insurance Law Library Edition* §§ 2.01–2.09 (LexisNexis 2022). *See also* Bjorkman, Leitner & Simpson, *Law and Practice of Insurance Coverage Litigation* §§ 48:1–48:85 (Thomson West 2021).

13. Actions for fraudulent misrepresentation or concealment can also be brought, but fraud is difficult to prove and policyholders rarely prevail on fraud-based claims. *See generally* 1 Jeffrey E. Thomas, *New Appleman on Insurance Law Library Edition* §§ 2.05[2][d][ii], [iii] (LexisNexis 2022).

14. *See, e.g.*, Landry v. State Farm Fire & Cas. Co., 428 F. Supp. 2d 531 (E.D. La. 2006). *See also* Glazier Group, Inc. v. Nova Cas. Co., 2018 N.Y. Misc. LEXIS 4591 (Oct. 5, 2018), where a principal of the insured met with the broker and provided the broker with a copy of the lease

the plaintiff asserts that scope of the coverage was misrepresented.[15] Negligence claims can be based on a statutory standard of care.[16] In a breach of contract claim, the plaintiff asserts there was a contract between the parties, the producer breached that contract, and the plaintiff was damaged as a result of that breach.[17] Finally, in an action for breach of fiduciary duty, the plaintiff must show that there was a fiduciary relationship between the parties, that the defendant breached its fiduciary duty, and that the plaintiff was damaged by that breach.[18] Plaintiffs often bring all four actions against a producer. However, a breach of fiduciary claim generally cannot be brought against an agent for the insurer because relationship between an insurance agent and clients is an ordinary business relationship, an arm's-length transaction in which an applicant for coverage has no reasonable basis for reposing special confidence or trust in the agent.[19]

The elements of any of these causes of action, and the defenses to them, will vary from state to state. The attorney bringing a procurement-based claim must, therefore, carefully study the law of the pertinent jurisdiction.

[2] The Narrow Duty of Agents and Brokers

In general, the relationship between a producer and client is not a fiduciary one but an ordinary business relationship.[20] Thus, the duty of producers to applicants for insurance is narrow.[21] They usually have no obligation to anticipate the needs of applicants, to advise them about coverage,[22] or to tell them

---

for the property to be insured. The lease specified the insurance that had to be carried on the property, which included flood insurance. The policy the broker procured excluded coverage for flood loss. On the broker's motion to dismiss the insured's negligence suit, the court said the insured had adequately alleged that it informed the broker of the need for flood coverage, that the broker failed to procure it, and that the failure caused damages.

15. *See, e.g.*, Packard v. Farmers Ins. of Columbus, Inc., 672 F. Supp. 2d 817 (S.D. Ohio 2009).

16. *See* 1 Jeffrey E. Thomas, *New Appleman on Insurance Law Library Edition* § 2.05[2][b] (LexisNexis 2022).

17. *See* Richmond, *Insurance Agent and Broker Liability*, 40 Tort & Ins. L.J. 1 (2004) (contract to procure insurance may be oral and to prevail on a breach of contract claim, plaintiff must prove agent or broker agreed to procure coverage effective at a certain time, or of certain breadth or scope, and then failed to do so; plaintiff's promise to pay premiums and accept delivery of policy provide consideration for promise to procure insurance).

18. *See generally* Douglas R. Richmond, *Creating and Navigating Special Relationships between Insurance Brokers and Insureds, New Appleman on Insurance: Current Critical Issues in Insurance Law* (Summer 2021).

19. 1 Jeffrey E. Thomas, *New Appleman on Insurance Law Library Edition* § 2.05[2][c][ii] (LexisNexis 2022).

20. FDT Group, LLC v. Guaraci, 2017 Ohio App. LEXIS 652 (Feb. 23, 2017).

21. *See, e.g.*, Cameron Parish Sch. Bd. v. State Farm Fire & Cas. Co., 2007 U.S. Dist. LEXIS 80423 (W.D. La. Oct. 29, 2007).

22. Mag-Dolphus, Inc. v. Ohio Cas. Ins. Co., 40 F. Supp. 3d 817, 839 (S.D. Tex. 2014) (absent admissible evidence of some specific, affirmative misrepresentation by agency about

about optional coverages,[23] unless they specifically agree to do so.[24] For that reason, requests from an applicant for "full coverage," "the best insurance available," or "the best and most comprehensive coverage" generally impose no obligation on agents or brokers;[25] moreover, courts say that an applicant has the responsibility to specify the coverage and terms he or she desires.[26] For example, in a New Jersey post-Superstorm Sandy case,[27] an insured sued its broker because the flood insurance procured by the broker had a limit of $1 million, which was far less than the loss the insured property suffered in the storm. The broker prevailed. Absent a special relationship, said the court, the broker did not have a common law duty to advise a customer about the need for a higher policy limit. Indeed, noted the court, brokers are not insurance consultants. If the property owner wanted an insurance consultant to advise it of its insurance needs, it could have employed one, said the court.

How explicit does the applicant's request for coverage need to be? In a case before the Louisiana Supreme Court, a producer acknowledged that an applicant for coverage had requested as much coverage on his property as could

---

policy at issue, insured's mistaken belief about scope or availability of coverage is not actionable); Mladineo v. Schmidt, 52 So. 3d 1154, 1163 (Miss. 2010). *But see* Poluk v. J.N. Manson Agency, Inc., 258 Wis. 2d 725, 739, 653 N.W.2d 905, 912 (Wisc. App. 2002), where the court said that when an agent or broker is "presented with information suggesting an exemption clause might be triggered in a policy being renewed, they have a duty to inquire further" and that to hold otherwise would be to absolve the agent of the duty to obtain insurance requested by the insured.

23. *See* Emerson Elec. Co. v. Marsh & McLennan Cos., 362 S.W.3d 7, 13 (Mo. 2012); Houck v. State Farm Fire & Cas. Ins. Co., 366 S.C. 7, 12, 620 S.E.2d 326, 330 (S.C. 2005).

24. *See* Swift, *How Special Is Special? An Insurance Agent's Duty to Advise*, 21 Hamline L. Rev. 323, 327 (1998) (if insured and agent actually agree that agent will give advice to insured, then agent is under duty to advise and counsel insured; generally, these agreements must be accompanied by payment to agent beyond policy premium).

25. *See, e.g.*, L.C.E.L. Collectibles v. American Ins. Co., 228 A.D.2d 196, 643 N.Y.S.2d 102 (1996) (request for "the best and most comprehensive coverage" did not trigger duty to inspect property to determine whether it was near floodplain or swamp or to recommend flood coverage).

26. *See, e.g.*, Isidore Newman Sch. v. J. Everett Eaves, Inc., 42 So. 3d 352, 358 (La. 2010) (it is not agent's responsibility to advise client that it is underinsured; instead, necessary coverages are best determined and calculated by insured, who is charged with primary responsibility to read the policy); City Blueprint & Supply Co. v. Boggio, 3 So. 3d 62, 65–66 (La. App. 2008); Sinex v. Wallis, 611 A.2d 31, 33 (Del. Super. 1991); Kenyon v. Larsen, 205 Neb. 209, 217, 286 N.W.2d 759, 784 (1980).

27. C.S. Osborne & Co. v. Charter Oak Fire Ins. Co., 2017 N.J. Super. Unpub. LEXIS 1051 (May 1, 2017), *cert. den.*, 230 N.J. 563, 170 A.3d 337 (2017). *See also* Mandina, Inc. v. O'Brien, 156 So. 3d 99 (La. App. 2013), where the insured had a flood policy that did not provide business interruption coverage and another policy that did included that coverage but excluded flood losses. After Hurricane Katrina the insured sued its broker for failure to procure business interruption coverage for floods. The court said that an insured who does not inquire about a particular coverage, ask for the coverage, or ask for clarification about that coverage—and who never examines years of policies—has no right to assume that coverage is in place and to then sue the broker because that assumption was incorrect.

be obtained and that the most coverage available was $100,000. Nonetheless, through error, the producer only procured $10,000 in coverage. The producer even sent an invoice for coverage indicating that $100,000 in coverage had been procured. On those facts, the state's highest court agreed that a verdict for the insured in his negligence action against the producer was correct.[28]

[3] Broader Duty of Agents and Brokers

In any profession, including that of insurance agent or broker,[29] the general rule is that anyone who undertakes to render services in the practice of a profession is required to exercise the skill and knowledge normally possessed by members of that profession in good standing in similar communities, unless he or she represents that he or she has greater or less skill or knowledge.[30]

The duties of producers can be broadened by circumstances. When, for instance, a producer prepares an insurance proposal for the applicant to review before purchasing a policy, courts may impose a duty of due care to accurately inform the applicant of the policy provisions unless there is a disclaimer—which there virtually always is—and that disclaimer is a sufficient one.[31]

If an applicant for insurance asks for specific coverage, courts usually hold that the agent or broker is then obliged to use reasonable care to obtain that coverage if the agent or broker *agrees* to procure it,[32] and an agent or broker who does not or cannot obtain the requested coverage has a duty to give the applicant timely notice of that fact.[33] Additionally, "[w]here a special relationship develops between the broker and client, the broker may be liable, even

---

28. Karam v. St. Paul Fire & Marine Ins. Co., 281 So. 2d 728 (La. 1973).

29. *See, e.g.*, Pressley v. Travelers Prop. Cas. Corp., 817 A.2d 1131 (Pa. Super. 2003); Milliken v. Woodward, 64 N.J.L. 444, 448, 45 A. 796, 798 (1900).

30. Restatement (Second) of Torts § 299A (Am. Law Inst. 1977).

31. Eddy v. Sharp, 245 Cal. Rptr. 211, 199 Cal. App. 3d 858 (1988). In *Eddy*, a broker prepared an insurance proposal that described the proffered coverage as all-risk subject to exclusions on a list attached to the proposal. That list did not include losses from water backing up through drains or sewers. After the policy went into effect, the insured property was damaged when the municipal sewer system adjacent to it became clogged during a rainstorm and sewage drained into the basement. The insurer denied coverage because there was an exclusion for water backing up through drains or sewers. The insurance proposal contained a disclaimer that read, "This proposal is prepared for your convenience only and is not intended to be a complete explanation of policy coverage or terms. Actual policy language will govern the scope and limits of protection afforded." The court noted that there was no disclaimer that the proposal was not a complete list of exclusions. It could not say as a matter of law that the disclaimer was sufficient to "override and nullify" the list of identified exclusions and concluded there was a triable issue of material fact as to whether the broker negligently misrepresented the terms of the policy.

32. Star Spa Servs. v. Robert G. Turano Ins. Agency, Inc., 595 F. Supp. 2d 519 (M.D. Pa. 2009); Avery v. Diedrich, 301 Wis. 2d 693, 734 N.W.2d 159 (2007).

33. Bell v. O'Leary, 744 F.2d 1370, 1373 (8th Cir. 1984) (failure to notify client that insurance is not available will render agent liable to client for negligent breach of duty). *See also* Bucksaw Resort, L.L.C. v. Mehrtens, 414 S.W.3d 39, 43 (Mo. App. 2013).

in the absence of a specific request, for failing to advise or direct the client to obtain additional coverage."[34] A duty to advise arises out of that "special relationship" between the parties.[35] Much has been written about the definition of that relationship.[36] The essence of it is "entrustment."[37] An off-cited opinion of the New York Court of Appeals said that a duty of advisement has been recognized by courts in exceptional situations where, for example, "(1) the agent receives compensation for consultation apart from payment of the premiums . . . (2) there was some interaction regarding a question of coverage, with the insured relying on the expertise of the agent[38] . . . or (3) there is a course of dealing over an extended period of time which would have put objectively reasonable insurance agents on notice that their advice was being sought and specially relied on."[39] A Florida federal court asserted that to

34. MAAD Constr., Inc. v. Cavallino Risk Mgt., Inc., 178 A.D.3d 816, 819 115 N.Y.S.3d 385, 388 (2019).

35. Schweitzer v. Am. Family Mut. Ins. Co., 16 N.E.3d 982 (Ind. App. 2014); Garnerville Holding Co. v. Kaye Ins. Assocs., 309 A.D.2d 541, 765 N.Y.S.2d 317 (2003), *app. den.*, 780 N.Y.S.2d 311, 2 N.Y.3d 705, 812 N.E.2d 1261 (2004).

36. *See* Douglas R. Richmond, *Creating and Navigating Special Relationships between Insurance Brokers and Insureds, New Appleman on Insurance: Current Critical Issues in Insurance Law* (Summer 2021); Sumbaly, *An Insurance Broker's Duty: Adopting California's Approach*, 43 Seton Hall Legis. J. 195 (2019); Kanterman, *New Jersey Insurance Producer Liability: Attempting to Define the "Special Relationship" Theory of Liability*, 2016 Rutgers U.L. Rev. Comments 92 (2016); Sakall, *Can the Public Really Count on Insurance Agents to Advise Them? A Critique of the "Special Circumstances" Test*, 42 Ariz. L. Rev. 991 (2000); Swift, *How Special Is Special? An Insurance Agent's Duty to Advise*, 21 Hamline L. Rev. 323 (1998).

37. Kaercher v. Sater, 155 P.3d 437, 441 (Colo. App. 2006) (whether special relationship has been formed turns on whether there is "entrustment," whether agent or broker assumes additional responsibilities beyond those that attach to ordinary, reasonable agent possessing normal competencies and skills). *See also* FDT Group, LLC v. Guaraci, 2017 Ohio App. LEXIS 652 (Feb. 23, 2017) (finding no special relationship where insured was sophisticated businessman running multiple businesses and owning many properties and testified to understanding relationship with broker to be one where broker would make recommendations in his own self-interest; additionally, insured had no personal relationship with and did not communicate directly with broker and had only approximate one-year business relationship with broker prior to proposal at issue); 1049 Asylum L.P. v. Kinney Pike Ins., 2003 Conn. Super. LEXIS 1740 (May 30, 2003) (insured must allege sufficient facts to show that "unique degree of trust and confidence" existed between parties to constitute fiduciary duty).

38. Where the officers of the insured did not discuss the items of coverage at issue with the broker, the court said there was no "identifiable source of a special duty of care" regarding them. Shenorock Shore Club, Inc. v. Rollins Agency, Inc., 270 A.D.2d 330, 705 N.Y.S.2d 56 (2000).

39. Murphy v. Kuhn, 660 N.Y.S.2d 371, 375, 90 N.Y.2d 266, 272–73, 682 N.E.2d 972, 976 (1997) (citations omitted). *See also* Rick Friedman Enters., Ltd. v. Travelers Indem. Co., 2017 N.Y. Misc. LEXIS 144 (Jan. 9, 2017) (where insured conceded broker had no means to determine whether specific property sat within flood zone and thereby to advise prospective client that flood insurance might be required, insured could not claim that it reasonably relied on broker's expertise; insured failed to demonstrate course of dealing between it and broker, giving rise to inference that broker would reasonably understand to be on notice that insured was seeking specific advice or service).

determine whether a broker shared a "special relationship" with a client, one should consider "(1) representations by the broker about its expertise; (2) representations by the broker about the breadth of the coverage obtained; (3) the length and depth of the relationship; (4 the extent of the broker's involvement in the client's decision making about its insurance needs; (5) information volunteered by the broker about the client's insurance needs; and (6) payment of additional compensation for advisory services."[40] How the "special relationship" doctrine is viewed varies from jurisdiction to jurisdiction, so the attorney seeking to apply it must carefully review the law of the pertinent state. A procedural matter that does not appear to be subject to much debate is that the insured bears the burden of proving a special relationship.[41]

[4] Negligent Misrepresentation

Unlike a procurement action, a claim of negligent misrepresentation does not require a request to obtain certain coverage. A negligent misrepresentation action is based on alleged misrepresentation about an aspect of a policy.[42] The general rule is that an insurance agent or broker who undertakes to advise an insured has to use reasonable care to provide accurate information.[43] That undertaking may be expressed or implied.[44] As explicated by the Restatement (Second) of Torts, when in the course of a business, profession, or employment,a person fails to exercise reasonable care or competence in obtaining or communicating information and thus supplies false information for the guidance of another in a business transaction, he or she is subject to liability for pecuniary loss caused by the justifiable reliance of that other party on the information.[45]

[5] Defenses

Damages are an element of most causes of action including breach of contract and negligence. Therefore, if the plaintiff suffers no damages because of the failure of a producer to obtain coverage, there is no liability.[46] For that reason,

---

40. Tiara Condo. Ass'n v. Marsh, USA, Inc., 991 F. Supp. 2d 1271, 1281 (S.D. Fla. 2014).

41. Murphy v. Kuhn, 660 N.Y.S.2d 371, 374–75, 90 N.Y.2d 266, 272–73, 682 N.E.2d 972, 975–76 (1997).

42. 1 Jeffrey E. Thomas, *New Appleman on Insurance Law Library Edition* § 2.05[2][d][i] (LexisNexis 2022).

43. Mladineo v. Schmidt, 52 So. 3d 1154, 1163 (Miss. 2010); Flamme v. Wolf Ins. Agency, 239 Neb. 465, 471, 476 N.W.2d 802, 806 (1991); Trotter v. State Farm, 297 S.C. 465, 471, 377 S.E.2d 343, 347 (1988).

44. Mullins v. Commonwealth Life Ins. Co., 839 S.W.2d 245, 248 (1992).

45. Restatement (Second) of Torts § 552(1) (Am. Law Inst. 1977).

46. *See, e.g.*, Terminal Ventures, Inc. v. Fireman's Fund Ins. Co., 2009 N.J. Super. Unpub. LEXIS 1793 (July 9, 2009) (even if broker erroneously failed to obtain insurance coverage for

if the policyholder sues the insurance company for failure to pay a claim and the agent or broker for failure to procure coverage, success on the former will generally preclude recovery on the latter.[47]

A common defense raised by brokers and agents is that the insured failed to read the policy. The argument is that the agent or broker cannot, therefore, be liable for failure to procure coverage or misrepresenting the coverage because had the insured read the policy, he or she would have discovered the omission or misrepresentation. Courts are split on this "duty to read" contention to the extent that a majority view cannot be stated.[48] Some say that an insured is charged with the knowledge of the terms of policies.[49] Other courts hold that failure to read does not bar a claim against a producer but instead constitutes comparative negligence.[50] Still others say failure of the insured to read a policy does not relieve the agent or broker of liability because the insured has a right to expect the coverage provided will be that which he or she requested.[51] There are many variations on these principles that are discussed elsewhere,[52] but two of note are that the duty to read does not apply

---

business interruption losses due to flood perils, insured suffered no damages as a result of that alleged failure).

47. Mitsui Sumitomo Ins. United States, Inc. v. Gibson Guitar Corp., 2011 U.S. Dist. LEXIS 101260 (S.D.N.Y. Sept. 8, 2011) (stated in *dicta*).

48. 1 Jeffrey E. Thomas, *New Appleman on Insurance Law Library Edition* § 2.05[10] (LexisNexis 2022).

49. *See, e.g.*, Allegis Inv. Servs., LLC v. Arthur J. Gallagher & Co., 371 F. Supp. 3d 983, 1001 (D. Utah 2019) (insured could not fault broker for its own failure to read and understand terms of policies before agreeing to bind itself to proposed coverage); Mladineo v. Schmidt, 52 So. 3d 1154, 1161 (Miss. 2010) (insured is charged, as matter of law, with knowledge of terms of policy on which he or she relies for protection); City Blueprint & Supply Co. v. Boggio, 3 So. 3d 62, 67 (La. App. 2008) (assumption that policy covered flood loss was not justifiable as insured was responsible for reading policy and is presumed to know its terms).

50. *See, e.g.*, American Bldg. Supply Corp. v. Petrocelli Group, Inc., 955 N.Y.S.2d 854, 858, 19 N.Y.3d 730, 736–37, 979 N.E.2d 1181, 1185 (N.Y. 2012) (failure to read policy, at most, may give rise to defense of comparative negligence but should not bar, altogether, action against broker); Zaremba Equip., Inc. v. Harco Nat'l Ins. Co., 280 Mich. App. 16, 33, 761 N.W.2d 151, 162 (2008) (plaintiff's admitted failure to read policy could qualify as comparative negligence, and trial court should have permitted jury to consider whether plaintiff unreasonably failed to read it).

51. *See, e.g.*, Tonkovic v. State Farm Mut. Auto. Ins. Co., 513 Pa. 445, 454, 521 A.2d 920, 925 (1985) (if insurer issues policy differing from what insured requested and paid for, burden is not on insured to read policy to discover those changes, or not read it at his or her peril); Stock v. ADCO Gen. Corp., 96 N.M. 544, 546, 632 P.2d, 1182, 1185 (1981) (insured has right to presume policy is in accordance with application and failure to read it will not relieve insurer or its agent from duty of so writing it); Pfiester v. Missouri State Life Ins. Co., 85 Kan. 97, 104, 116 P. 248, 248 (1911) (insured has right to assume policy is prepared in accordance with the application and fact that insured does not read it until after loss has occurred will not defeat recovery).

52. 1 Jeffrey E. Thomas, *New Appleman on Insurance Law Library Edition* § 2.05[10] (LexisNexis 2022).

where reading the policy would not disclose the misrepresentation at issue[53] or the insured does not receive a copy of the policy before the loss.[54] More importantly, the entire debate over the duty to read is moot when the policy is a FEMA Standard Flood Insurance Policy because the policy is incorporated into the Code of Federal Regulations. The policy is, therefore, law, and policyholders are charged with knowledge of it.[55]

12.4 Liability When the Coverage Sought Is Flood Insurance

When a plaintiff sues a producer for failure to procure flood coverage, the general rules discussed above regarding producer liability apply. For example, a homeowner contacted her broker to acquire a homeowners policy and asked for "the best policy they had." The broker obtained a standard policy that did not include flood coverage. When the plaintiff later suffered a loss that would have been covered by flood insurance, she sued the broker for breach of contract. The court said that it was "too simplistic" for the plaintiff to assert that, in requesting a homeowners policy, a mere direction to obtain "the best policy" amounts to "a direction to procure a policy covering all foreseeable risks which appellees breached by issuance of a standard policy."[56] The flip side of that principle is that when the applicant gives specific instructions regarding coverage, he or she has a right to rely on the producer to obtain it.[57]

One of the leading cases on negligent misrepresentation happens to involve flood insurance. The plaintiffs bought a mobile home. An employee of the defendant insurance agency solicited and sold a policy to the plaintiffs. Subsequently, they move the home to a different trailer court, one proximate to a creek. Concerned about flooding, the plaintiffs visited the agent, who they claim assured them that mobile home insurance was different from regular

53. Mladineo v. Schmidt, 52 So. 3d 1162–63 (Miss. 2010) (where agent allegedly informed insureds that their property was not in floodplain and counseled against flood insurance, duty to read did not bar claim because alleged misrepresentations would not have been disclosed by reading the policy).

54. Industrial Enclosure Corp. v. Northern Ins. Corp., 2000 U.S. Dist. LEXIS 11567 (N.D. Ill. July 25, 2000). *Compare* Mandina, Inc. v. O'Brien, 156 So. 3d 99, 111 (La. App. 2013) (even though insured did not receive policies until after loss, it was charged with knowledge of contents where nothing in those policies would have provided any additional information that could not have been obtained by reviewing prior policies).

55. Cohen v. Allstate Ins. Co., 924 F.3d 776, 781 (5th Cir. 2019).

56. Nowell v. Dawn-Leavitt Agency, 127 Ariz. 48, 617 P.2d 1164 (Ariz. App. 1980). *See also* City Blueprint & Supply Co. v. Boggio, 3 So. 3d 62 (La. App. 2008) (policyholder could not recover for loss arising from failure to obtain coverage because there was no agreement by defendants to procure flood insurance and policyholder's representatives acknowledged that they never specifically requested that agent obtain flood insurance on property).

57. 386 3rd Ave. Partners Ltd. Partnership v. Alliance Brokerage Corp., 2017 N.Y. Misc. LEXIS 2683 (July 11, 2017) (absent any showing that insured is aware of discrepancy between coverage it claims to have requested and that it actually obtained, insured has right to rely on presumed obedience to his or her instructions).

homeowners insurance and had a comprehensive clause—apparently meaning all-risk—that afforded flood protection. In fact, the policy issued to the plaintiffs was not "comprehensive coverage" but instead covered named perils of which flood was not one. Additionally, there was an exclusion for losses resulting from flooding. The mobile home was severely damaged in a flood, and the insurer denied the plaintiffs' claim. They brought an action for negligent misrepresentation against the agency and obtained a verdict awarding them considerable damages. The state supreme court affirmed the judgment and said that on the record the cause of action of negligent misrepresentation was "properly established" in the case.[58]

A post-Katrina case[59] is another example of the application of principles of negligent misrepresentation. The plaintiffs in that case purchased a homeowners policy and claimed the agent for the insurance company expressly represented to them that they would have full and comprehensive coverage for any and all hurricane damage including that caused by storm surge. They also contended they asked the agent whether they needed to purchase additional flood insurance, and one of the agent's employees told them that they did not need additional flood coverage because the home was not in a floodplain and that the policy's hurricane coverage would cover any damage caused by a hurricane. The plaintiffs said they relied on the representations in concluding they did not need flood insurance. After their home was damaged in the hurricane, the company's adjustor found most of the loss to be excluded flood damage. The insurer, therefore, paid a small fraction of the loss. Although it is not clear from the opinion whether the agent was a defendant, the court noted that generally "both a principal and its agent are liable for the torts of the agent committed in the course and scope of the agency." It then reviewed the allegations the plaintiffs made. The court said that while the agent was under no duty to advise the plaintiffs about what coverages were necessary to protect their property, if the plaintiffs made an inquiry of the agent and the agent or her employee made the representations concerning coverage that the plaintiffs alleged, then the insurer could have potential liability for all of the damage to the plaintiffs' property. The court denied the insurer's motion to dismiss.[60]

As previously discussed, an agent or broker is generally only responsible for obtaining the coverage an applicant requests. After suffering an uninsured flood loss, property owners often claim the agent or broker breached that duty. For example, an oceanfront country club obtained a flood policy

---

58. Moore v. Kluthe & Lane Ins. Agency, 89 S.D. 419, 234 N.W.2d 260 (1975).

59. Buente v. Allstate Ins. Co., 422 F. Supp. 2d 690 (S.D. Miss. 2006).

60. *See also* Mladineo v. Schmidt, 52 So. 3d 1154 (Miss. 2010), where the agent allegedly informed the property owners that their property was not in a floodplain and counseled against flood insurance because "hurricane" coverage was sufficient protection against flooding. The Mississippi Supreme Court reversed summary judgment for the agent because the agent offered advice to insureds and had a duty to exercise reasonable care in doing so.

through its broker. Apparently unknown to the club, the policy only covered the clubhouse, not other buildings on the property that were damaged by flood waters during a storm. The club claimed it asked for coverage for all the buildings on its property and their contents. The broker denied it. The court said that a broker's duty is defined by the customer's request for coverage. It found that there was no request and, therefore, no agreement that the broker would procure a policy with flood coverage on the outbuildings.

The potential for flooding is something that often can be observed by an inspection of a property. As discussed above, courts generally hold that agents and brokers have no duty to advise applicants about coverage or to tell them about optional coverages. Thus, they also have been found not to have a duty to inspect a property and advise clients based on that inspection.[61]

When the liability of the producer is clear, it may admit liability, and its errors and omissions (E&O) insurer may cover the loss. For example, homeowners applied for a policy of homeowners insurance with a carrier through its authorized agent and asked the agent to duplicate the water or sewer backup/overflow coverage they had had with their former insurer. The agent neglected to communicate that request to the carrier. The policy issued contained an exclusion for water that backed up through sewer or drains or overflowed from a sump. Heavy rains led to flooding in the basement of the insured home, causing $26,500 in damages, and the carrier denied the claim based on the exclusion. The agent's E&O insurer paid the $26,500.[62]

12.5 Liability When the Coverage Sought Is a FEMA Standard Flood Insurance Policy

When the coverage sought is from a FEMA SFIP, a procurement claim against one of the *private insurance companies* that issue SFIPs on behalf of FEMA may be preempted. Courts look to a FEMA rule that states that representations about the extent and scope coverage that are not consistent with FEMA regulations or the National Flood Insurance Act "are void, and the duly licensed property or casualty agent acts for the insured" not for the insurer.[63] The insurance companies are thus protected from liability for representations

61. Wisniski v. Brown & Brown Ins. Co., 906 A.2d 571 (Pa. Super. 2006), *app. den.*, 591 Pa. 728, 920 A.2d 834 (2007) (broker procured commercial property policy with usual flood exclusion for property located directly across highway from Susquehanna River and with stream running beneath building); L.C.E.L. Collectibles v. American Ins. Co., 228 A.D.2d 196, 643 N.Y.S.2d 102 (1996) (broker had no duty to recommend flood insurance or to inspect location of plaintiff's property to determine whether it was near floodplain or swamp, where plaintiff neither specifically requested that insurance nor communicated area's susceptibility to flood damage).

62. Palkowski v. Acuity, 341 Wis. 2d 491, 815 N.W.2d 407 (Wisc. App.), *rev. den.*, 344 Wis. 2d 304, 822 N.W.2d 882 (Wisc. 2012).

63. 44 C.F.R. § 61.5(e).

made by agents that are inconsistent with the SFIP.[64] On the other hand, many courts have held that state law claims against insurers for *failure to procure* flood insurance is not preempted.[65] FEMA and other courts do not agree.[66] The debate is academic when the defendant is an agent or broker because FEMA has said that procurement disputes involving them or "any allegation of negligence on the part of the agent related to procurement are not subject to preemption."[67] Courts agree.[68] The result is even clearer when an action is based on failure to procure *excess* coverage, as FEMA does not offer that coverage.[69]

However, there is another roadblock for policyholders when the claim is for negligent misrepresentation by the agent or broker. A cause of action for negligent misrepresentation requires reasonable or justified reliance on the representation.[70] There can be no reliance by one who has *actual* knowledge of the matter at issue.[71] Moreover, constructive knowledge may be sufficient to defeat an action.[72] Further, the contents of the SFIP are found in the Code of Federal Regulations making them law. Everyone is charged with knowledge of the law.[73] As the Fifth Circuit Court has said, "[c]laimants dealing with the

---

64. *See, e.g.*, Parker v. Miss. Farm Bureau Cas. Ins. Co., 997 F. Supp. 2d 481 (S.D. Miss. 2014); Uddoh v. Selective Ins. Co., 2012 U.S. Dist. LEXIS 100905 (D.N.J. July 20, 2012); Remund v. State Farm Fire & Cas. Co., 2010 U.S. Dist. LEXIS 49098, at *13 (D. Utah May 18, 2010); Gurevitch v. National Flood Ins. Program, 1983 U.S. Dist. LEXIS 14072 (N.D. Cal. Sept. 2, 1983).

65. Harris v. Nationwide Mut. Fire Ins. Co., 832 F.3d 593 (6th Cir. 2016); Packard v. Farmers Ins. of Columbus, Inc., 672 F. Supp. 2d 817 (S.D. Ohio 2009); Padalino v. Std. Fire Ins. Co., 616 F. Supp. 2d 538, 546 (E.D. Pa. 2008); TAF, L.L.C. v. Hartford Fire Ins. Co., 549 F. Supp. 2d 1282 (D. Colo. 2008); Reeder v. Nationwide Mut. Fire Ins. Co., 419 F. Supp. 2d 750 (D. Md. 2006); Jamal v. Travelers Lloyds of Tex. Ins. Co., 129 F. Supp. 2d 1024 (S.D. Tex. 2001).

66. Davis v. Nationwide Mut. Fire Ins. Co., 783 F. Supp. 2d 825, 833 (E.D. Va. 2011). *See also* Saporito v. Stillwater Prop. & Cas. Ins. Co., 2016 U.S. Dist. LEXIS 173168 (E.D.N.Y. June 2, 2016); Geisler v. Don Hunt & Assocs., 2012 U.S. Dist. LEXIS 37850 (D. Kan. Mar. 20, 2012).

67. *See* https://nfipservices.floodsmart.gov/sites/default/files/w-09038.pdf.

68. Davis v. Nationwide Mut. Fire Ins. Co., 783 F. Supp. 2d 825, 833–34 (E.D. Va. 2011) (no preemption of tort actions against agents or brokers over procurement or alleging procurement-related negligence). *See also* Pittman v. Farmers Fire Ins. Exch., 2015 U.S. Dist. LEXIS 96707 (W.D. Mo. July 24, 2015).

69. Chaudhary v. Arthur J. Gallagher & Co., 2021 U.S. Dist. LEXIS 146707 (S.D. Tex. Aug. 5, 2021) (where claims were about failure to procure or renew *private excess* flood coverage, not interpretation or management of plaintiff's SFIP, there was no preemption).

70. Bull v. Allstate Ins. Co., 649 F. Supp. 2d 529, 540 (W.D. La. 2009); Renaissance Leasing, LLC v. Vermeer Mfg. Co., 322 S.W.3d 112, 132 (Mo. 2010).

71. *See, e.g.*, Goodman v. Fid. Nat'l Ins. Co., 2008 U.S. Dist. LEXIS 68694 (E.D. La. Aug. 14, 2008), where the plaintiff sued his agent and the insurer alleging the agent never discussed or offered him contents coverage and it was undisputed that he knew contents coverage was available, but opted not to purchase it. Summary judgment was, therefore, appropriate.

72. Parker v. Miss. Farm Bureau Cas. Ins. Co., 997 F. Supp. 2d 481 (S.D. Miss. 2014); Sitaram, Inc. v. N.H. Ins. Co., 771 F. Supp. 2d 624, 629 (W.D. La. 2011).

73. Dennis v. Fid. Nat'l Prop. & Cas. Ins. Co., 2010 U.S. Dist. LEXIS 28759 (W.D. La. Mar. 25, 2010) (plaintiff was charged with constructive knowledge of provisions of SFIP including

government are presumed to have full knowledge of the law and cannot rely on the conduct of government officials to the contrary."[74] That should apply with at least equal force to the conduct and representations of non-government officials. On the other hand, constructive knowledge may not preclude reasonable reliance where a policy has not been issued or it was void from inception.[75]

12.6 Liability When the Coverage Sought Is Excess Flood Insurance

After a major flood, many policyholders learn that their loss far exceeds the limits of their SFIP, and as a result suits are initiated that fault agents for either failing to tell applicants about the need for excess coverage or telling them that an SFIP is all the coverage available. Property owners argue that had they been told about the availability of excess coverage, they would have purchased it and received the protection it afforded.[76]

Vague requests from an applicant for "full coverage" or "the best insurance available" generally do not obligate an agent or broker to obtain excess coverage. The agent or broker also has, in general, no duty to advise an applicant of the availability of excess insurance.[77] The need for excess coverage is based on the value of the property to be insured, and courts say that the

---

30-day waiting period and could not rely on assurances of agent regarding effective date of coverage). *But see* Pittman v. Farmers Fire Ins. Exch., 2015 U.S. Dist. LEXIS 96707 (W.D. Mo. July 24, 2015) (because FEMA regulations create legal fiction that agent acts for insured, there may be reasonable reliance on misrepresentations about SFIP by an agent); Royal Inn v. Courtier, 1996 U.S. Dist. LEXIS 11038 (E.D. La. July 31, 1996) (court rejected argument that insured had sufficient notice of contents of SFIP through its publication in Code of Federal Regulations).

74. Cohen v. Allstate Ins. Co., 924 F.3d 776, 780 (5th Cir. 2019).

75. Bell v. O'Leary, 744 F.2d 1370, 1373 (8th Cir. 1984) (even though plaintiffs could have discovered pertinent information in Code of Federal Regulations, broker held himself out to public as one who had superior knowledge of insurance and was charged with knowledge of his business, which included awareness of what facts rendered his clients ineligible for insurance coverage); Padalino v. Std. Fire Ins. Co., 616 F. Supp. 2d 538, 548 (E.D. Pa. 2008).

76. *See, e.g.*, Richmond v. Chubb Group of Ins. Cos., 2006 U.S. Dist. LEXIS 67537 (E.D. La. Sept. 20, 2006), where, after their home was damaged by the flood waters of Hurricane Katrina, homeowners who had maximum SFIP coverage contended their broker never informed them of or offered them excess flood insurance and also claimed that had they known of or been offered excess flood insurance and contents coverage, they would have purchased it to fully cover their home and contents, which were worth millions of dollars.

77. Tufaro v. Fid. Nat'l Prop. & Cas. Ins. Co., 2013 U.S. Dist. LEXIS 178157 (E.D. La. Dec. 18, 2013) (where plaintiff homeowner claimed agent failed to properly advise that excess coverage was available, court held agent had no duty to advise whether client has procured correct amount or type of coverage); Cameron Parish Sch. Bd. State Farm Fire & Cas. Co. v. Derbonne, 560 F. Supp. 2d 485, 488 (W.D. La. 2008) (insurance agents do not have affirmative duty to inform insured about availability of flood coverage in excess of NFIP limits or advise them as to whether they are underinsured).

applicant is in a better position to know if that value exceeds the available primary coverage.[78]

On the other hand, if an applicant asks for specific coverage, courts usually say agents or brokers have a duty of reasonable care to obtain the coverage requested when they agree to procure it.[79] If the agent or broker knows a specific amount of coverage is sought and fails to procure excess coverage that would provide that amount, courts generally find the agent or broker liable.[80] A request for excess coverage can also be implied if an applicant requests flood coverage for the full appraised value of property for which the value exceeds the maximum coverage that can be obtained with an SFIP.[81] When, however, an applicant for coverage does not have primary flood insurance or refuses an offer to procure it, a broker or agent cannot be liable for failing to advise of the availability of excess flood insurance because the applicant lacks the primary coverage to which another policy would be excess and could not have procured it even if advised that it was available.[82] Also, if excess coverage would not have been triggered, it does not matter whether or not the broker or agent discussed excess coverage.[83]

A broker or agent can be liable for failing to advise an applicant for coverage of all the prerequisites to it when that failure causes the applicant to

---

78. Cameron Parish Sch. Bd. v. State Farm Fire & Cas. Co., 2007 U.S. Dist. LEXIS 80423 (W.D. La. Oct. 29, 2007) (plaintiff insured knew that value of its property was in excess of $26 million and was covered for only $8 million in loss by flood, and it was obvious that coverage was not sufficient, yet there was no allegation that plaintiff asked defendant agent to investigate availability of excess coverage and plaintiff was in far better position than agent to know that property was worth more than coverage limits that it selected).

79. Star Spa Servs. v. Robert G. Turano Ins. Agency, Inc., 595 F. Supp. 2d 519 (M.D. Pa. 2009); Avery v. Diedrich, 301 Wis. 2d 693, 734 N.W.2d 159 (2007).

80. *See, e.g.*, Henley v. Love Ins. Group, LLC, 2017 U.S. Dist. LEXIS 26244 (N.D. Tex. Feb. 24, 2017).

81. Botnick v. Vigilant Ins. Co., 2006 U.S. Dist. LEXIS 75441 (E.D. La. Oct. 13, 2006) (broker should have been aware that property owners wanted to obtain excess flood insurance, given their stated request for full coverage up to appraised value of residence, which far exceeded $250,000 available under NFIP; finding "arguably reasonable basis to predict" that under Louisiana law, broker would be found to have breached its duty of reasonable diligence in procuring coverage desired by applicant).

82. Merridth v. Allstate Indem. Co., 2007 U.S. Dist. LEXIS 6853 (E.D. La. Jan. 31, 2007). *Compare* Barash v. Encompass Indem. Co., 2006 U.S. Dist. LEXIS 93074 (E.D. La. Dec. 21, 2006), where the broker argued that the plaintiff homeowners failed to state a cause of action for failure to procure excess flood insurance coverage because they did not request or purchase the maximum limits under the National Flood Insurance Program. The court, however, said that the plaintiffs' claims that they requested flood insurance to cover the value of their property and the broker negligently failed to procure or offer that flood insurance stated a cause of action. The court did note that the homeowners did not explicitly claim that they requested excess flood insurance.

83. Zinsel Co. v. J. Everett Eaves, Inc., 749 So. 2d 798 (La. App. 1999).

be underinsured. That was the result in a Missouri case in which the owner of a corporation told an agent for an insurer that he wanted to purchase flood insurance that would cover 100 percent of the replacement value of the assets of the business. When he went to the agent's office to sign the insurance application, with the imminent threat of a levee breaking, he told her that the listed amount was insufficient but signed it because he thought there was no time to increase the coverage because of the impending flood. Prior to signing the application, he was told of a five-day waiting period and then five days later was told he needed an engineering survey. The court said the testimony showed the applicant was hampered in the ability to obtain flood insurance by the agent's failure to advise him of all the prerequisites during their first meeting and by her inability to obtain a price quote. The court denied the agent's motion for summary judgment because whether she was negligent in failing to provide insurance for 100 percent of the value of the assets was a factual question to be determined by a jury.[84]

There is rarely a written contract between an applicant for insurance coverage and an insurance agent or broker. However, contracts can be oral or implied. For example, the owner of an apartment complex sought $975,000 in flood coverage because that was the amount a lender required to be maintained as a condition of a loan to buy the property. A broker secured a FEMA policy for the maximum coverage of $500,000 but no coverage in excess of that amount even though the applicant paid a premium for excess coverage. The plaintiff/applicant alleged the broker breached an implied contract when it did not secure $975,000 of insurance coverage. The broker argued that there was no evidence of damages in excess of the primary coverage to which an excess policy would have applied. While damages is an element of a breach of contract claim, the court nevertheless granted the plaintiff summary judgment on the breach of contract claim and left the issue of damages for trial.[85]

12.7 Waiver/Checklists

Despite the obstacles, suits against producers for failure to procure flood insurance coverage are increasingly common. In response, many producers have applicants for coverage sign a "coverage" checklist.[86] The attorney representing an insured should try to find out as early as possible in the representation

84. Microdyne Prods. Co. v. State Farm Fire & Cas. Co., 1999 U.S. Dist. LEXIS 23529 (E.D. Mo. Oct. 8, 1999).

85. Henley v. Love Ins. Group, LLC, 2017 U.S. Dist. LEXIS 26244 (N.D. Tex. Feb. 24, 2017).

86. *See, e.g.*, Pine Ridge Realty, Inc. v. Massachusetts Bay Ins. Co., 752 A.2d 595 (Me. 2000) (representative for policyholder signed flood insurance checklist indicating that property was not in an identified flood hazard area and that National Flood Insurance was not being sought).

whether the client has signed one of these checklists and what specifically it says. A coverage checklist lists specific coverages. Applicants for insurance "check off" either the coverage they want or the coverage they reject,[87] and then waive the responsibility of the producer.

One example of a waiver/checklist is called an "Excess Flood Insurance Waiver of Agent's Responsibility." Applicants who sign it agree they have been made aware that the value of their property exceeds the coverage that can be procured through the National Flood Insurance Program—meaning the maximum coverage under an SFIP—and, further, that they are aware that excess flood coverage is obtainable. [88]

It is important to determine exactly what coverages a client rejected when signing a waiver. For example, the document may simply state: "I reject excess building & contents coverage." In that case there are other excess coverages that are not explicitly rejected, for instance, business interruption or extra expense.

12.8 Damages

The general rule is that the liability of a broker or agent is limited to the losses that would have been covered by the policy.[89] That amount may be different from the amount of the loss, as only a part of it might have been covered by the policy.[90] If the loss is greater than the policy limits that an agent or broker allegedly failed to procure, the producer is not liable for the excess.[91] Where an insured settles with insurance companies for less than the damages suffered, the insured may still obtain damages from the broker for negligent procurement.[92]

---

87. Wells, *Excess Flood Insurance—When the Federal Plan Isn't Sufficient* (Aug. 7, 2006), Insurance Journal, http://www.insurancejournal.com/magazines/features/2006/08/07/72126.htm.

88. https://www.wrightflood.net/static/corp/documents/ExcessFloodWaiver.pdf.

89. 1 Jeffrey E. Thomas, *New Appleman on Insurance Law Library Edition* § 2.05[3][d] (LexisNexis 2022). *See, e.g.*, Belmont Commons, L.L.C. v. Axis Surplus Ins. Co., 2008 U.S. Dist. LEXIS 116896 (E.D. La. Oct. 29, 2008) (if insured proves agent or broker breached duty by leading it to believe that excess flood insurance was not available and by not procuring it, damages would be limited to type of coverage included in an excess policy).

90. Henley v. Love Ins. Group, LLC, 2017 U.S. Dist. LEXIS 26244 (N.D. Tex. Feb. 24, 2017) (measure of damages when agent fails to procure insurance is amount that would have been due had agent procured that coverage).

91. 1 Jeffrey E. Thomas, *New Appleman on Insurance Law Library Edition* § 2.05[3][d] (LexisNexis 2022).

92. Bucksaw Resort, L.L.C. v. Mehrtens, 414 S.W.3d 39 (Mo. App. 2013).

12.9 Reformation

[1] Generally

Reformation is an alternative to an action for damages.[93] When an agent errs in procuring coverage, a policyholder may seek reformation of the policy to correct the mistake.[94] The Restatement of Contracts outlines requirements for reformation in two circumstances: mistake or misrepresentation. In the first, when an insurance contract "in whole or in part fails to express the agreement because of a mistake of both parties as to the contents or effect of the writing," the Restatement says a court may reform the contract to express the agreement.[95] Second, if a policyholder's manifestation of assent is induced by misrepresentation about the contents of a policy, a court may reform a policy to express the terms of the agreement providing the policyholder was justified in relying on the misrepresentation.[96]

The point of reformation is to "express the agreement" of the parties, the parties being the policyholder and the insurance company. Reformation is based on there having been an agreement between them on the terms of coverage. For that reason, the policyholder cannot seek reformation when a broker procured the coverage because the broker represents the policyholder. Any mistaken understanding or misrepresentation by the broker cannot be imputed to the insurer, as is the case when the mistake or misrepresentation is that of an agent of the insurer.[97] Additionally, a unilateral mistake may not be the basis of reformation because, again, there is no agreement.[98]

---

93. *See generally Appleman on Insurance Law & Practice Archive* §§ 7607–7610 (1st ed. 2011).

94. Palkowski v. Acuity, 341 Wis. 2d 491, 815 N.W.2d 407 (Wisc. App.), *rev. den.*, 344 Wis. 2d 304, 822 N.W.2d 882 (Wisc. 2012).

95. Restatement (Second) of Contracts § 155 (Am. Law. Inst. 1981). *See also* Johnson, *It's a Mistake!, Correcting Scrivener's Errors in Insurance Contracts*, 44 The Brief 32 (2015).

96. Restatement (Second) of Contracts § 166 (Am. Law. Inst. 1981).

97. Mark Andy, Inc. v. Hartford Fire Ins. Co., 229 F.3d 710, 717 (8th Cir. 2000) (insurance contract could not have been reformed on basis of any objective manifestation of intent by insurance agency because it was agent of policyholder at time contract was formed); Weinisch v. Sawyer, 123 N.J. 333, 340, 587 A.2d 615, 618 (1991) (because broker, unlike agent, is not employed by insurer, broker's breach will not support action for reformation). *See also* Archer Daniels Midland Co. v. Hartford Fire Ins. Co., 243 F.3d 369, 374 (7th Cir. 2001) (policy could not be reformed to cover what broker unilaterally said it would cover); Dugan v. General Acci. Fire & Life Assurance Corp., 421 S.W.2d 717, 720 (Tex. App. 1967) (generally, fact that insured accepts policy without noticing mistake therein would not preclude insured from having that mistake corrected by reformation; however, that rule does not apply where insured has employed experienced agent to represent his interests in matters of insurance protection).

98. Wentwood Woodside I LP v. GMAC Commer. Mortg. Corp., 419 F.3d 310, 316 (5th Cir. 2005) (unilaterally mistaken party alone bears responsibility for consequences of its error).

The burden is on the party seeking reformation to prove that the policy did not conform to the intent of the parties.[99] The cause for reformation must generally be shown by clear and convincing evidence.[100]

There are very few cases discussing reformation of flood insurance policies because most flood insurance is a FEMA Standard Flood Insurance Policy that, as discussed below, severely restricts the use of reformation. Those that have addressed reformation offer limited guidance.[101]

[2] Reformation of a FEMA Standard Flood Insurance Policy

[a] Generally

When the policy is a FEMA SFIP, common law reformation is not available. State law claims for reformation of a flood insurance policy are preempted by federal law.[102] Reformation can only be obtained pursuant to the language of the policy.[103] As one federal court explained:

> reformation of a SFIP contract is governed by different rules than ones that normally apply in an insurance dispute. A SFIP contract is governed by federal regulatory codifications. As such, "strict adherence is required to all terms of the SFIP." There is one limited provision under these regulations for SFIP contract reformation, and it only allows for reformation in certain situations when the policy premium paid is less than what is necessary to receive the requested policy coverage.[104]

The result of that preemption can be harsh. For example, a New Jersey limited liability company was formed to acquire, develop, and manage a

99. Tower Auto., Inc. v. Am. Prot. Ins. Co., 266 F. Supp. 2d 664 (W.D. Mich. 2003); Calvert Fire Ins. Co. v. Hardwicke, 232 Ark. 466, 467, 338 S.W.2d 329, 330 (1960).

100. Paraco Gas Corp. v. Travelers Cas. & Sur. Co. of Am., 51 F. Supp. 3d 379, 391 (S.D.N.Y. 2014); Aetna Life Ins. Co. v. American Zinc, Lead & Smelting Co., 169 Mo. App. 550, 561, 154 S.W. 827, 830 (1913).

101. *See, e.g.*, Mark Andy, Inc. v. Hartford Fire Ins. Co., 229 F.3d 710 (8th Cir. 2000) (insurance contract was not subject to reformation based on any objective manifestation of intent by insurance agent, because that agent was insured's agent when contract was formed); 570 Smith St. Realty Corp. v. Seneca Ins. Co., Inc., 2019 N.Y. Misc. LEXIS 1773 (Apr. 4, 2019) (cause of action for reformation was moot or academic because parties had not mentioned or briefed it); City of Atlanta v. Allianz Global Risks US Ins. Co., 2014 U.S. Dist. LEXIS 201393 (N.D. Ga. Aug. 8, 2014) (where insurer assessed property as being in area not subject to high risk for flooding, and issued policy with sublimit for properties in high hazard flood zone, but property was actually in special flood hazard area that arguably was high hazard flood zone, court found insured's claim for reformation was sufficiently pled to avoid motion to dismiss).

102. Davis v. Nationwide Mut. Fire Ins. Co., 783 F. Supp. 2d 825, 833 (E.D. Va. 2011).

103. Cure v. La. Farm Bureau Cas. Ins. Co., 2007 U.S. Dist. LEXIS 93927 (E.D. La. Dec. 20, 2007) (facts presented for reformation must squarely fit within provisions of policy).

104. Tucard, LLC v. Fid. Nat'l Prop. & Cas. Ins. Co., 567 F. Supp. 2d 215, 221 (D. Mass. 2008).

commercial condominium property comprised of eight free-standing buildings. The LLC controlled the board of the condominium association. It purchased contents and building flood insurance for one of the condominium units, the only one subject to flooding. The insurer issued a FEMA Standard Flood Insurance Policy to the LLC as the named insured. The insured unit suffered flood damage when the Raritan River overflowed its banks. The insurer denied a building coverage claim and returned the premium the LLC paid for the building coverage because the LLC had no insurable interest. The LLC sought reformation to change the named insured, but the court said the SFIP provided no basis for reformation to change the named insured.[105] In another case, a company sought flood coverage for a property it owned, but the application listed the address of the company's corporate office and the SFIP was issued to cover that property. The property the company intended to insure was damaged in a flood, and FEMA refused to allow the policy to be revised to cover that property. The court said that reformation is an equitable remedy available for insurance contracts, but in the context of FEMA policies, it is only available in the limited circumstances provided by the SFIP, and as the reformation request did not fit within the express scope of any SFIP provision, the remedy was unavailable.[106]

[b] The Exception

There is one case in which a court allowed a common law reformation claim to go forward when the policy was an SFIP.[107] The insured in that case owned a service station and a car wash in two separate buildings at the same address. His insurance agency procured an SFIP. On the Declarations Page the property description characterized the building as "one floor with no basement, nonresidential small business, non-elevated building." The application for insurance said the insured building did not have an attached garage and in fact, the service station building had an attached garage, while the car wash building did not. The property was flooded. The adjuster only evaluated the damage to the service station building and assessed its damages at less than the policy deductible. A contractor hired by the insured estimated that the damages to the car wash building at nearly $150,000, far in excess of the deductible. An SFIP can cover only one building, and the insurer decided the policy covered the service station and, thus, paid nothing on the claim. The insured sued the insurer and the insurance agency for, *inter alia*, breach of contract and

105. Branchburg Commerce Park, LLC v. Hartford Ins. Co., 2017 U.S. Dist. LEXIS 17518 (D.N.J. Feb. 8, 2017) (having been provided no legal authority in support of reformation, court was hesitant to reform policy to change parties to contract absent authority explicitly granting it power to award that equitable relief).

106. Tucard, LLC v. Fid. Nat'l Prop. & Cas. Ins. Co., 567 F. Supp. 2d 215, 222 (D. Mass. 2008).

107. Nicol v. Auto-Owners Ins. Co., 2006 U.S. Dist. LEXIS 9502 (D. Minn. Mar. 8, 2006).

reformation of contract. In the reformation claim, the insured contended he relied on the expertise of the agency acting as an agent for the insurer, "for the purpose of writing the policy, and that the policy would cover both the service station and the car wash."

The court discussed the breach and reformation together as the "contract claims." It noted that the SFIP describes the policy as including the Declarations Page and application. It agreed that the SFIP stated that only one building, specifically described in the application, could be insured under the policy, but pointed out that the building description in the application could apply to either building. That ambiguity, said the court, created an issue of material fact. Moreover, an email from the insurance agency to the insurer's adjuster stated that the policy coverage amount of $250,000 represented the amount of insurance on both buildings. That, said the court, manifested "further genuine issues of material fact regarding the resolution of [the] contract claims." Therefore, the court denied the agency's motion for summary judgment on both the breach of contract and reformation claims.

Given the emphatic holdings of other courts that reformation of an SFIP is limited to the circumstances outlined in the policy itself, the case is most certainly an outlier. Nonetheless, it is a reported federal court decision that has never been reversed or indeed cited by any other court.

[c] Reformation Prior to Loss

The SFIP provides that if the premium received by the insurer was not enough to buy the kind and amount of coverage that the insured requested, the insurer will provide only the amount of coverage that can be purchased for the premium payment received.[108] The policy can, however, be reformed to increase the amount of coverage resulting from that reduction to the amount the insured requested.[109] If the insurer discovers that the premium payment was not enough to buy the requested amount of coverage *before the policyholder has a flood loss*, it will send the policyholder and any mortgagee or trustee known to it a bill for the required additional premium for the current policy term.[110] The bill does not have to explain the reason for the additional premium.[111] Moreover, if the carrier fails to send the bill, there is no breach of contract as the insured is charged with constructive knowledge of the policy limit.[112]

---

108. General Property Form Standard Flood Insurance Policy, § VII.G.1.

109. General Property Form Standard Flood Insurance Policy, § VII.G.1.a.

110. General Property Form Standard Flood Insurance Policy, § VII.G.1.a.(1).

111. Connell v. Allstate Ins. Co., 2007 U.S. Dist. LEXIS 87826 (E.D. La. Nov. 28, 2007) (while explanation of additional premium would have been useful, SFIP only requires that insurer send bill stating payment necessary to maintain coverage).

112. Molero v. State Farm Fire & Cas. Co., 2007 U.S. Dist. LEXIS 41976 (E.D. La. June 8, 2007).

If the additional premium is paid within 30 days from the date of the bill, the insurer will reform the policy to increase the amount of coverage to the originally requested amount effective to the beginning of the current policy term.[113] Otherwise, the policyholder will only have the coverage that could be purchased for the premium received.[114]

If, before the policyholder has a flood loss, the insurer determines that the rating information it has is incomplete and prevents it from calculating the additional premium, it will ask the policyholder to send the required information. It must be submitted within 60 days of the insurer's request. Once the insurer determines the amount of additional premium for the current policy term, it will follow the procedure for reforming the policy.[115]

[d] Reformation after Loss

Under the SFIP, if the insurer discovers, *after a flood loss*, that the policyholder's premium payment was not enough to buy the requested amount of coverage, it will send the policyholder and any mortgagee or trustee known to it a bill for the required additional premium for the current and the prior policy terms and, if the bill is paid within 30 days of the date of the bill, it will reform the policy to increase the amount of coverage to the originally requested amount effective to the beginning of the prior policy term.[116]

If, after a flood loss, the insurer discovers that the rating information it has is incomplete and prevents it from calculating the additional premium, it will ask the policyholder to send the required information.[117] That information must be submitted before any claim can be paid. Once the insurer determines the amount of additional premium for the current and prior policy terms, it will follow the procedure for reform of the policy. If it does not receive an additional premium by the date it is due, any flood claim will be settled based on the reduced amount of coverage.[118]

[e] Examples of Situations Requiring Reformation

FEMA provides examples of situations that it says require reformation.[119] These include the following:

---

113. General Property Form Standard Flood Insurance Policy, § VII.G.1.a.(1).

114. Connell v. Allstate Ins. Co., 2007 U.S. Dist. LEXIS 87826 (E.D. La. Nov. 28, 2007).

115. General Property Form Standard Flood Insurance Policy, § VII.G.1.a.(2).

116. General Property Form Standard Flood Insurance Policy, § VII.G.2.b.(1). *See* Englande v. Bradshaw Ins. Agency, 2007 U.S. Dist. LEXIS 62270 (E.D. La. Aug. 22, 2007).

117. General Property Form Standard Flood Insurance Policy, § VII.G.2.b.(2).

118. General Property Form Standard Flood Insurance Policy, § VII.G.2.b.(3).

119. National Flood Insurance Program Flood Insurance Manual, at 2-21 (FEMA Oct. 2021).

- Underpayment of a bill (though not an invalid payment, such as a check returned by the bank for non-sufficient funds) to purchase an initial policy, policy renewal, or endorsement;
- A rating adjustment requiring additional premium after a mid-term event (for example, a renovation or damage from another peril) changes one or more rating characteristics;
- A rating correction requiring additional premium;
- Discovery that an incorrect SFIP form was used (or a different SFIP form is needed now) and the premium paid is insufficient to purchase the originally requested coverage amount under the correct policy form; and
- Endorsement of a policy from a provisional rate to a rating engine rate, if the premium paid is insufficient under the rating engine rate.

These scenarios apply whether before or after a flood.

13

Recovering from a Commercial Landlord or Tenant

13.1 Introduction

When the client who presents with a flood loss is a commercial landlord or tenant of the damaged property, the attorney needs to examine the lease to determine if it addresses the loss. Commercial leases often specify who is responsible for repairs and for insuring the property. Failure of a party to comply with a lease requirement will entitle the other party to bring a breach of contract action.

13.2 Lease Covenants Regarding Repairs

At common law, the tenant took the leased property "as is" and the landlord had no duty to maintain or repair the premises.[1] Thus, if a flood damaged the property, the tenant was not relieved of the duties under the lease. For example, in an Iowa case the lease contained no covenant by the landlord to repair or for abatement of rent in the event of casualty to the premises. The tenant installed bowling lanes on the premises. They were damaged beyond repair when a nearby river overflowed its banks and the premises were flooded. The building itself suffered only minor damage. The court held that the damage caused by the flood to the portion of the building leased to the tenant did not relieve him of the obligation to pay the rent. While the court did not mention repairs, obviously the tenant would have to repair the bowling lanes to continue to use the property for the purpose for which he rented it.[2]

1. 5 *Thompson on Real Property, Third Thomas Edition*, §§ 41.01, 44.07(a) (LexisNexis 2021); *Current Leasing Law and Techniques—Forms*, § 8.02 (LexisNexis Matthew Bender 2021).

2. Osterling v. Sturgeon, 261 Iowa 836, 156 N.W.2d 344 (1968).

The common law, however, is rarely applicable to commercial leases because they address maintenance and repair. In a commercial lease, the parties are free to contract regarding the various responsibilities for repair, maintenance, and improvements.[3] A covenant to repair defines the extent of the duty.[4] Repair covenants may make one of the parties responsible for all repairs[5] or may allocate responsibilities,[6] for example, requiring the tenant to repair the interior and the landlord the roof.[7] Another covenant related to repairs is one that obligates the tenant to surrender the premises at the end of the lease term in the same condition as at the commencement of the term, usually subject to ordinary wear and tear.[8]

It is generally said that an unconditional or unqualified covenant requiring the tenant to maintain and keep the leased premises in good repair or in as good condition as that existing at a time specified in the lease, and to return them at the expiration or termination of the lease in equivalent condition, obligates the tenant to rebuild if the leased building is destroyed by casualty during the lease term.[9] Courts have sometimes specifically mentioned flood damage. For example, the Mississippi Supreme Court has said that "an unconditional express covenant to repair or keep in repair is equivalent to a covenant to rebuild, 'and binds the covenanter to make good any injury which human power can remedy, even if caused by storm, flood, fire, inevitable

---

3. Baird v. Kelley, 250 Ga. App. 393, 395, 551 S.E.2d 811, 812 (2001).

4. Brown v. Hauge, 105 Wash. App. 800, 804, 21 P.3d 716, 719 (Wash. Ct. App. 2001).

5. *See* Dog House Invs., LLC v. Teal Props., 448 S.W.3d 905 (Tenn. App. 2014), where the lease made the landlord responsible for repairs when the property was "damaged by fire or other cause as to be rendered untenantable." The property was damaged in a flood. The landlord collected from his flood insurance, but made no repairs. The tenant made and paid for necessary repairs, and the landlord was aware of the tenant's actions. The tenant sued for, *inter alia*, breach of contract and unjust enrichment. The court said that flooding was an "other cause" that triggered the landlord's repair duties and that the landlord breached the contract by failing to reimburse the tenant for the expenses it incurred.

6. *See, e.g.*, Fernandes v. AGAR Supply Co., 687 F.3d 39, 43 (1st Cir. 2012) (parties to lease are free to limit scope of lessor's contractual repair obligations by specifying which portions of leased property lessor is to maintain and repair).

7. Even where the landlord is obligated to make a specific repair, lease clauses exculpating the landlord from liability and placing the burden on the tenant to procure adequate insurance to cover any loss would apportion the risk of loss. Thus, the tenant of a warehouse claimed the landlord breached a lease covenant to maintain the roof and should be precluded from avoiding liability under an exculpatory clause for damage to property the tenant had stored on the premises. The court, however, found for the landlord. Meyer v. Caribbean Interiors, 435 So. 2d 936 (Fla. 3d DCA 1983).

8. *Current Leasing Law and Techniques—Forms*, § 8.02[1] (LexisNexis Matthew Bender 2021).

9. Anderson v. Ferguson, 17 Wn.2d 262, 271, 135 P.2d 302, 306 (1943). *See also* Hoy v. Holt, 91 Pa. 88, 90 (1879) (where, in lease, there is an express and unconditional agreement to repair and keep in repair, tenant is bound to do so, although premises be destroyed by fire or other accident); Levey v. Dyess, 51 Miss. 501, 509 (1875) (when covenant is to repair, or keep in repair generally, without qualifying words, tenant, according to all authorities, must rebuild).

accident, or the act of a stranger,' and that, while an act of God will excuse the non-performance of a duty created by law, it will not excuse a duty created by contract."[10] Once again, the common law is generally modified by the parties by a lease clause addressing destruction or frustration of purpose, as discussed in the next section.

13.3 Destruction of Leased Premises

The common law rule was that if leased premises were fortuitously destroyed, the tenant remained bound to the lease agreement including the obligation to pay rent because the essence of a lease was the use of the land rather than of any improvements.[11] Courts have, however, departed from the common law by applying the doctrine of "impossibility of performance." An Illinois appellate court explained that the doctrine is applied "if there is an unanticipated circumstance that has made the performance of the promise vitally different from what should reasonably have been within the contemplation of the parties when the contract was entered" and that it "requires that the circumstances creating the impossibility were not and could not have been anticipated by the parties, that the party asserting the doctrine did not contribute to the circumstances, and that the party demonstrate that it has tried all practical alternatives available to permit performance."[12] The burden is on the tenant claiming benefit of the doctrine to prove these elements.[13] The fact that

---

10. Mitchell v. Hancock County, 91 Miss. 414, 418-19, 45 So. 571, 572 (1907). *See also* Metzgar Register Co. v. Thomas Canning Co., 220 Mich. 435, 441, 190 N.W. 245, 247 (1922).

11. Madison, *The Real Properties of Contract Law*, 82 B.U.L. Rev. 405, 423 (2002).

12. Ill.-Am. Water Co. v. City of Peoria, 266 Ill. Dec. 277, 285, 332 Ill. App. 3d 1098, 1106, 774 N.E.2d 383, 391 (2002). *See also* American Aviation v. Aero-Flight Serv., 712 So. 2d 809, 810 (Fla. 4th DCA 1998) (doctrine of impossibility of performance should be employed with great caution if relevant business risk was foreseeable at inception of agreement and could have been subject of an express provision of agreement).

13. *See, e.g.*, Home Design Center-Joint Venture v. County Appliances of Naples, Inc., 563 So. 2d 767 (Fla. 2d DCA 1990), where the tenant signed a five-year commercial lease a condition of which was that the tenant would procure and maintain $100,000 in property damage coverage. The tenant operated an appliance business and did not own its merchandise. Rather the merchandise was owned by a finance company under a "floor plan agreement." Under that agreement, the tenant had to obtain and maintain fire and property insurance on the merchandise. The tenant's initial policy and substitute policy were cancelled. The tenant spent two business days in a search for insurance coverage before it abandoned the task as impossible. The tenant vacated the premises and, in defense of the landlord's breach of the lease action, the tenant claimed impossibility of performance. The court, however, said the tenant failed to prove that it was impossible for it to perform its purpose under the lease when it had difficulty in obtaining property insurance under its floor plan agreement. It could still operate an appliance store without floor plan financing, which would have presented a financial challenge to the tenant, but that economic difficulty, said the court, did not render its purpose "impossible." Further, although the tenant may not have anticipated future problems with its insurer or its floor plan financier, it did not present substantial competent evidence to show these basic business risks were matters that it could not have foreseen at the time it negotiated the terms of the lease.

the tenant purchased flood insurance would show that the tenant anticipated the possibility of a flood.[14] Even though the landlord may have failed to disclose specific prior incidents of flooding, where the tenant was aware of the flood risks associated with the property before executing the lease, it could not argue that a flood was not foreseeable.[15]

The Restatement of Contracts has adopted a version of the doctrine of impossibility of performance. It says that "[i]f the existence of a specific thing is necessary for the performance of a duty, its . . . destruction, or such deterioration as makes performance impracticable is an event the non-occurrence of which was a basic assumption on which the contract was made."[16] Further, "[w]here, after a contract is made, a party's performance is made impracticable without his fault by the occurrence of an event the non-occurrence of which was a basic assumption on which the contract was made, his duty to render that performance is discharged, unless the language or the circumstances indicate the contrary."[17]

Following the foregoing principles, the Pennsylvania Supreme Court has said that:

> It is no longer reasonable to *assume* that in the absence of a lease provision to the contrary the lessee should bear the risk of loss in the event of total destruction of the building. Where the parties do not expressly provide for such a catastrophe, the court should analyze the facts and the lease agreement as any other contract would be analyzed. Following such an analysis, if it is evident to the court that the parties bargained for the existence of a building, and no provision is made as to who bears the risk of loss if the building is destroyed, the court should relieve the parties of their respective obligations when the building no longer exists.[18]

State statutes may also abrogate the common law rule. For example, in New York, where any building that is leased is destroyed or so injured as to be untenantable and unfit for occupancy, the lessee, if the destruction or injury occurred without his or her fault or neglect, may quit and surrender

14. Portnoy v. Omnicare Pharm., Inc., 2004 U.S. Dist. LEXIS 12235 (E.D. Pa. June 25, 2004).

15. Gander Mt. Co. v. Islip U-Slip LLC, 923 F. Supp. 2d 351 (N.D.N.Y. 2013). In the case, after two floods the tenant was unable to secure all-risk property insurance as required by the lease. The court said that because the tenant was aware of the possibility of flooding, it could not have assumed that all-risk insurance would be available.

16. Restatement (Second) of Contracts, § 263.

17. Restatement (Second) of Contracts, § 261.

18. Albert M. Greenfield & Co. v. Kolea, 475 Pa. 351, 357, 380 A.2d 758, 760 (1977). *Accord* Romer v. Topel, 414 N.W.2d 787 (Minn. App. 1987).

possession of the leasehold premises if there is no express agreement to the contrary in writing.[19]

The common law and attempts by legislatures or courts to soften its blow are largely irrelevant in modern commercial tenancies because leases typically address destruction in considerable detail.[20] How those leases allocate the risk of loss from destruction of the property depends on the relative bargaining power of the parties, meaning that leases generally favor landlords. Despite any disparity in bargaining power, courts will not intervene to rewrite a lease that was negotiated by two relatively sophisticated business parties.

One expert commentary recommends that a "destruction" clause specifically address loss of the tenant's ability to use the premises because of conditions that go beyond the building, or arise entirely outside the building, for example a flood, that the clause waive any statutory provision allowing a tenant to terminate the lease in the event of a casualty rendering the premises untenantable,[21] and that if the landlord has the right or obligation to restore, that it measure any deadline for restoration from receipt of insurance proceeds by the landlord, not from the date of the event.[22] However, leases may simply require the landlord to "promptly repair or replace the damage,"[23] or require the same of the tenant,[24] or may allow the tenant to terminate the lease

---

19. N.Y. Real Prop. Law § 227. *See* Tilbern Realty, Inc. v. Lax Drug Co., 59 Misc. 2d 515, 299 N.Y.S.2d 758 (1969) (parties to lease are free, under statute, to agree to some other rule with respect to total destruction; agreement must be in writing and expressly or by necessary implication show parties intended that rent and term should continue notwithstanding destruction).

20. *See generally* Schoenmeyer, *Surrender Dorothy: Restoration Obligations in Office Leases*, Prac. Real Estate. Law (May 2007).

21. Most commercial leases give the landlord the option to restore the premises or terminate the lease after major damage or destruction. 5 *Thompson on Real Property, Third Thomas Edition*, § 44.11(c) (LexisNexis 2021).

22. Compton & Stein, *Landlord's Checklist of Silent Lease Issues (Second Edition)*, 36-2 NYRPLJ 13 (2008).

23. *Current Leasing Law and Techniques—Forms*, § 8.06[1] (LexisNexis Matthew Bender 2021) (if premises are damaged by casualty, landlord must promptly repair or replace damaged portions of premises excluding tenant's personal property or any leasehold improvements, additions, or changes to premises made or installed by or for tenant and within 30 days after landlord has substantially completed its repairs, tenant must repair or replace all of tenant's damaged personal property). However, according to one expert commentary, knowledgeable landlords disclaim any obligation to repair or rebuild in the event of fire or other casualty and instead make restoration at the landlord's option and limited to the proceeds of insurance received by the landlord. 5 *Thompson on Real Property, Third Thomas Edition*, § 44.11(e) (LexisNexis 2021).

24. *See, e.g.*, Gander Mt. Co. v. Islip U-Slip LLC, 923 F. Supp. 2d 351 (N.D.N.Y. 2013) (under repair and restoration provision, if premises were damaged or destroyed in whole or in part by fire or other casualty, tenant was required to promptly repair and restore premises to condition equal to its condition immediately prior to that damage or destruction). *See also* 5 *Thompson on Real Property, Third Thomas Edition*, § 44.11(e) (LexisNexis 2021) (it may be

within a set time after the damage when rebuilding or repairs of the damaged portion cannot be completed within a prescribed time after the date of the damage.[25] These are all provisions that attorneys for either party will want to look for in the lease. The landlord's attorney will want to determine if under the policy language, any lease termination may *not* constitute a covered loss for the landlord.[26] The tenant's counsel will want to discover if the client has business interruption insurance that will cover lost income for the tenant during any period of restoration.[27]

13.4 Landlord's Duty to Warn Tenant of Flood Risk

[1] Generally

Does a landlord have a duty to warn a prospective tenant of the danger of flooding or the need to purchase flood insurance? Under the Restatement a landlord who conceals or fails to disclose to a tenant any condition, whether natural or artificial, that involves unreasonable risk of *physical harm to persons* on the land is subject to liability to the tenant and others on the land with the consent of the tenant or subtenant for physical harm caused by the condition after the tenant has taken possession if the tenant does not know or have reason to know of the condition or the risk involved and the landlord knows or has reason to know of the condition, and realizes or should realize the risk involved, and has reason to expect that the tenant will not discover the condition or realize the risk.[28]

Even though the Restatement applies to "physical harm to persons," it has been discussed in terms of physical harm to property. For example, a flash flood brought substantial flooding to a leased premises resulting in extensive damage to the tenant's stored equipment and materials and temporary suspension of its business. The tenant sued the landlord alleging that the landlord never warned of the possibility of flooding even though the landlord knew of a previous tropical storm and had a mortgage containing a flood insurance contingency. The court, after citing the Restatement, said that any dangerous condition has to be latent. There is no liability for open and obvious hazards. The river that was the source of the flooding was a defect known to the tenant

---

appropriate to allocate duty to repair casualty damages to tenant in case of long-term lease of building to single tenant).

25. *Current Leasing Law and Techniques—Forms*, § 8.06[2] (LexisNexis Matthew Bender 2021).

26. Compton & Stein, *Landlord's Checklist of Silent Lease Issues (Second Edition)*, 36-2 NYRPLJ 13 (2008).

27. See Chapter 6, *supra*.

28. Restatement (Second) of Torts § 358(1).

as it was open and obvious and the landlord, therefore, had no obligation to advise the tenant to retain flood insurance.[29]

[2] Tenant's Duty to Examine Public Record

One potential defense to a landlord when flooding is the danger is that a commercial tenant should, through due diligence, discover the condition or the risk before leasing the premises because flood status is a matter of public record. Flood maps are readily available from local governments or online from the FEMA Flood Map Service Center.[30] A landlord can argue that just as a would-be tenant should check the zoning status of property, he or she should also determine its flood risk. In one case, a trial court held that because a floodplain is a matter of public record, a tenant could have discovered information about it after a reasonable investigation and thus, the landlord owed no duty of disclosure. The appellate court, however, noting that the tenant had leased the premises for five years before the defendant landlord purchased it, found there was no evidence that the tenant relied on the landlord's failure to disclose when it decided to renew its lease. In light of that holding, the appellate court said it did not need to address the "legal consequences, if any, of the floodplain being a matter of public record."[31] A Tennessee federal court subsequently did address those consequences. In that case, the leased property as well as the tenant's equipment and material were damaged by flood waters. After the flood, the tenant learned that the landlord had flood insurance. The tenant sued the landlord for negligence in failing to disclose or warn of the "known dangerous condition" that the property was in a flood zone. The court held that the claim failed because the tenant had not shown the exercise of reasonable care. The prospect of flooding is, said the court, ascertainable from "reasonably accessible public documents," but the tenant did not ask the landlord or neighboring tenants whether the property was prone to flooding and did not claim to have asked anyone, including his own insurance agent, whether the property was in a flood zone.[32]

---

29. Barabas v. Davsco, LLC, 2010 Conn. Super. LEXIS 876 (Apr. 9, 2010). *See also* Gander Mt. Co. v. Islip U-Slip LLC, 923 F. Supp. 2d 351 (N.D.N.Y. 2013) (no duty to warn of prior floods).

30. *FEMA Flood Map Service Center*, FEMA, https://msc.fema.gov/portal/home.

31. Matthews Office Designs, Inc. v. Taub Invs. 647 A.2d 382 (Del. 1994). In the case, a creek behind the leased property overflowed during an unusually heavy rain. The property flooded, destroying inventory and other property stored inside the leased building. Neither the trial nor appellate court mentioned that the creek was open and obvious to the tenant so the landlord should not have had any duty to disclose.

32. Airpro Sys. v. Prologis N.C. Ltd. P'ship, 2012 U.S. Dist. LEXIS 85578 (M.D. Tenn. June 20, 2012). The court also held that the landlord had no duty to disclose, a second basis for dismissing the action.

[3] Duty to Warn of Specific Circumstances

Even though a landlord may have no duty to warn a tenant of a generalized danger of flooding, there may be a duty to warn of specific circumstances that may lead to flooding.[33] For example, a Louisiana federal court found for a tenant whose automobiles were damaged by flood waters while stored on property leased from the defendant landlord. The flood occurred during a hurricane and was caused by a combination of heavy rains and the fact that a gravity drainage system that usually served the property was closed to protect the area from rising waters in an adjacent canal. The landlord was notified promptly by the authorities that the gates were closed, but he neither notified the tenant nor made any effort to remove the stored vehicles from the property. The court said that the possibility that the property might be inundated by rainwater was a defect, a shortcoming not to be expected in normal property. It was not apparent to the tenant and made the property potentially unsuitable for its intended use, the storage of new cars. The landlord knew or should have known of the defect because he had been warned by an engineer for the local government that it was possible that, during some hurricanes, the gravity drainage system might be closed, and the property might then be flooded. The court concluded the property had a defect, the landlord knew of it and also knew that, if it occurred, it would damage the tenant's property, yet neither warned of the peril nor took any steps to avert it and, as the tenant had no obligation to take measures to avoid the risk; the landlord's liability was established and summary judgment was entered in favor of the tenant.[34]

The tenant was unsuccessful in another case. The plaintiff in that case subleased office space in a basement suite for a CT scan facility. Less than two years after the lease was executed, the basement flooded. It was determined that the flood was caused by blockage in an outlet pipe that fed into a drain. Water backed up into an underground detention basin, up through a drain pipe, down a slope, and into the basement-level windows. After that event, the subtenant asked the defendants from whom he sublet if the building had a flooding problem and if they could correct it. They replied that they were working on it and, based on the assurance that the defendants would prevent floods in the future, the plaintiff said he decided to remain in the building. However, only two months later, the basement flooded again after a heavy rainfall, and this time the plaintiff's CT scan machine was rendered inoperable. The plaintiff sued for, *inter alia*, breach of contract and fraud, alleging the

33. *But see* Gander Mt. Co. v. Islip U-Slip LLC, 923 F. Supp. 2d 351 (N.D.N.Y. 2013) (landlord failed to answer questionnaire from tenant that would have revealed several prior floods, but tenant could not argue flooding was unforeseeable because its own investigation prior to executing lease revealed property was in floodplain and was adjacent to tributary of major river).

34. Volkswagen of America, Inc. v. Robertson, 433 F. Supp. 164 (E.D. La. 1977).

defendants failed to correct known deficiencies to the building storm drainage system. The court, however, found that the evidence did not support the contention that the flood was caused by problems with that system. Rather, it showed the county drain became overwhelmed. To the extent the defendants had a duty to use reasonable care to prevent flooding of the basement suite, asserted the court, that duty did not "encompass a guarantee that no flood would ever occur, no matter what the cause." The evidence supported a finding that the defendants made reasonable efforts to prevent future floods after the first incident and were not liable.[35] Arguably, the plaintiff brought the action based on the wrong allegation. Had the plaintiff brought a claim for a misrepresentation as to the likelihood of flooding, no matter the source, the duty of the defendants would have been to warn, not to prevent.

A Louisiana state court stated broadly that potentiality for flooding is a defect against which a landlord warrants but then discussed special circumstances it found to be significant. The case concerned a residential tenancy. The home was inundated during a four-day rain event that caused historic flooding in the area. The landlord acknowledged that at closing, when he purchased the house, he was provided a flood loss history showing three prior National Flood Insurance Program flood claims. The trial court granted summary judgment for the landlord on the grounds of *force majeure* or act of God. The appellate court reversed. It said that there were genuine issues of material fact raised regarding whether the residence was flood prone under ordinary rain conditions so that the tenant's damages were partly or totally caused by a warranty defect in the premises and whether the landlord acted in bad faith in failing to inform the tenant of prior flooding events.[36] The case is distinguishable from others on at least two grounds: (1) it is based on Louisiana residential landlord/tenant law, and (2) the residential tenant arguably should not be held to the due diligence standard of a commercial tenant.

13.5 Agreements to Insure[37]

Commercial leases almost always address insurance, often at some length. They may require either party to insure the property of the landlord.[38] Absent

35. Mid-Michigan Diagnostic Corp. v. Michigan Internal Med., P.C., 2014 Mich. App. LEXIS 386 (Mar. 4, 2014).

36. Milazzo v. Harvey, 245 So. 3d 346 (La. App. 2018).

37. *See generally* Iwamoto, *Insurance and the Commercial Lease*, 22 Prac. Real. Est. Law. 57 (Jan. 2006); Saltz, *Allocation of Insurable Risks in Commercial Leases*, 37 Real Prop. Prob. & Tr. J. 479 (2002); Iwamoto, *Using Insurance in Commercial Leases*, 10 Prac. Real. Law. 81 (1994).

38. McEwan v. Mt. Land Support Corp., 116 P.3d 955 (Utah App. 2005), illustrates how important the specific lease language can be. The lease required the tenant to obtain "casualty" and "liability" insurance for the leased premises. One of the lease insurance provisions

an express agreement, there is no implied obligation on the part of a tenant to insure leased premises.[39] Some leases obligate the *tenant* to obtain property insurance at its expense that names the landlord as an additional insured or loss payee.[40] Sometimes the lease explicitly requires flood insurance.[41] What happens if the tenant fails to obtain that coverage or, unbeknown to the landlord, the coverage is cancelled by the insurer? The landlord has a cause of action for breach of the lease agreement.[42] Failure to obtain insurance may also be grounds for forfeiture of the lease.[43]

The landlord may recover damages for the loss sustained by reason of the breach—in other words, the amount that would have been due under the policy if it had been obtained.[44] The syllabus to a case decided by the United States Supreme Court in 1896 states, "A lessee of a building who contracts in his lease to keep the leased building insured for the benefit of the lessor during the term at an agreed sum, and fails to do so, is liable to the lessor for that

---

requiring the tenant to obtain "casualty insurance" was headed "Property Insurance." The other lease provision was labeled "Liability Insurance." The landlord argued the obligation to obtain casualty insurance was one to obtain property insurance. The court did not agree. The landlord prepared the lease herself by "cutting and pasting" form leases on her computer. It seems likely that the landlord thought that "casualty" insurance was different from liability insurance, but that did not sway the court.

39. Gebhart v. Huffman, 326 N.W.2d 891 (S.D. 1982); Alexander v. Security-First Nat'l Bank, 7 Cal. 2d 718, 62 P.2d 735 (1936); Yoshida v. Security Ins. Co., 145 Ore. 325, 26 P.2d 1082 (1933).

40. *See, e.g.*, Gander Mt. Co. v. Islip U-Slip LLC, 923 F. Supp. 2d 351 (N.D.N.Y. 2013) (on request by landlord, tenant required to provide certificate of insurance naming landlord and any fee mortgagee as additional insureds); Good v. Saia, 967 So. 2d 1161 (La. App. 2007) (lessee required to carry fire, extended coverage, vandalism, malicious mischief, and flood insurance); Rodriguez v. Nachamie, 395 N.Y.S.2d 51, 57 A.D.2d 920 (1977) (lease provided that tenant would maintain fire insurance on building and equipment, with landlord as loss payee). A loss payee is not an insured, is subject to all the defenses an insurer might have against the primary insured, and can only recover if the primary insured pursues a claim. Cargile, *The Basics of Insurance in Leases*, 14 Prob. & Prop. 19 (2000).

41. *See, e.g.*, Good v. Saia, 967 So. 2d 1161 (La. App. 2007); Creque v. Harbor Chevrolet, Oldsmobile, Cadillac, Inc., 1987 U.S. Dist. LEXIS 15999 (D.V.I. Oct. 28, 1987).

42. *See, e.g.*, Good v. Saia, 967 So. 2d 1161 (La. App. 2007); St. Paul Fire & Marine Ins. Co. v. Cumiskey, 665 P.2d 223 (Mont. 1983). *But see* Nichols v. Stone, 2010 U.S. Dist. LEXIS 32162 (D. Md. Mar. 31, 2010) (while landlord should have been named insured, its assets were nonetheless insured and, therefore, no breach of contract occurred).

43. Creque v. Harbor Chevrolet, Oldsmobile, Cadillac, Inc., 1987 U.S. Dist. LEXIS 15999 (D.V.I. Oct. 28, 1987) (failure to obtain flood insurance warranted forfeiture and equity did not prohibit it).

44. Robinson v. Janay, 105 N.J. Super. 585, 591, 253 A.2d 816, 819 (1969). *See also* Louisiana Farm Bureau Mut. Ins. Co. v. Thompson, 719 So. 2d 427 (La. 1998); Cromartie v. Carteret Sav. & Loan, 277 N.J. Super. 88, 649 A.2d 76 (1994); American Trust Co. v. Truck Ins. Exchange, 147 Cal. App. 2d 395, 305 P.2d 73 (1957); Benton v. Alcazar Hotel Co., 352 Mo. 836, 180 S.W.2d 33 (1944); Franck v. Stout, 139 Wis. 223, 120 N.W. 867 (1909). *And see* Kinney v. G. W. Lisk Co., 76 N.Y.2d 215, 557 N.Y.S.2d 283, 556 N.E.2d 1090 (1990) (construction contract).

amount, if the building is destroyed by fire during the term."[45] If, however, the landlord *knows* the tenant failed to procure insurance, in violation of the lease agreement, the damages are limited to the cost of the insurance the tenant was to have obtained.[46]

The landlord may also be able to proceed against the insurer. For example, a Texas appellate court has held that "a breach by a lessee of a contract to insure the leased property for the benefit of his lessor will charge the benefits of any insurance taken out by the lessee on the leased property with a lien in favor of the lessor; and . . . the lessor may proceed directly against the insurer to recover his pro rata share of any funds payable under the policy."[47] Other courts generally agree.[48] However, where a lease agreement did not require that the lessee obtain insurance with loss payable to the lessor, the equitable lien doctrine did not apply and the lessor lacked standing to sue the insurer for coverage.[49]

13.6 Subrogation Claims against Tenants

When the landlord's property is damaged through the negligence of the tenant and the landlord's insurer covers the loss, may the insurer recover from the tenant in subrogation? Different courts have different answers.[50] Some courts

45. Jacksonville, M., P. Ry. & Nav. Co. v. Hooper, 160 U.S. 514, 529, 16 S. Ct. 379, 40 L. Ed. 515 (1896).

46. Rodriguez v. Nachamie, 395 N.Y.S.2d 51, 57 A.D.2d 920 (1977).

47. Farmers Ins. Exchange v. Nelson, 479 S.W.2d 717, 721 (Tex. Civ. App. 1972). In *Nelson*, the tenant agreed to carry property insurance in an amount satisfactory to the landlord with any loss payable to both parties as interest would appear. However, the policy the tenant purchased was issued to him as the named insured and made no reference to the landlord. The insurer was not advised that the landlord owned any interest in the building or its contents and in fact, the written application showed the tenant to be the owner of the property. The landlord did not know that the tenant had failed to comply with the insurance provision of the lease. The building and its contents were destroyed by fire. The tenant closed his business after the fire, did not comply with the terms and conditions of the policy, and made no attempt to recover against the insurer for any loss suffered.

48. *See, e.g.*, Alexander v. Security-First Nat'l Bank, 7 Cal. 2d 718, 62 P.2d 735 (1936) (if there is agreement for insurance between landlord and tenant and party obligated, in violation of that agreement, procures insurance payable to himself alone, other party for whose benefit agreement was made has equitable lien on proceeds of that insurance); Houston Canning Co. v. Virginia Can Co., 211 Ala. 232, 100 So. 104 (1924) (where lessor had contracts with lessee to keep leased machines fully insured for its benefit and, in disregard of contract, lessee insured machines and other property in its own name, and resisted payment of any proceeds to lessor, insurance money was trust fund for benefit of both parties and each was entitled to its proportion of proceeds).

49. Sierra Equip., Inc. v. Lexington Ins. Co., 890 F.3d 555 (5th Cir. 2018).

50. *See* Dattel Family Ltd. P'ship v. Wintz, 250 S.W.3d 883 (Tenn. App. 2007), for a discussion of the three approaches taken by courts and a list of decisions aligned with each. *See generally* Williams, *Insurers' Rights of Subrogation against Tenants: The Begotten Union between Equity and Her Beloved*, 55 Drake L. Rev. 541 (2007); Spake, *The Roof Is on Fire: When,*

hold that unless the landlord and tenant agree to the contrary, the insurer has a right of subrogation.[51] Many courts have no bright line and employ a case-by-case analysis.[52] Finally, other courts rule that, absent an express provision in a lease establishing the liability of a tenant for loss caused by the tenant's negligence, the landlord's insurance is deemed to be held for the mutual benefit of both parties and the insurer, therefore, cannot seek subrogation against the tenant. In other words, the tenant is an "implied coinsured." Some courts limit the implication to residential tenants,[53] while others apply it to commercial tenants as well.[54]

13.7 Allocation of Insurance Proceeds

[1] Generally

The general rule is that, absent a lease covenant requiring a party to obtain insurance, neither one may share in the policy proceeds paid under a policy procured by the other.[55] On the other hand, where, under a lease covenant, one party agrees to obtain coverage, the policy proceeds are usually considered to be for the benefit of both the landlord and the tenant, and they will be entitled to share in the proceeds in proportion to the value of their respective interests.[56] When one party obtains coverage and the policy provides that any proceeds are to be paid to the landlord and tenant "as their respective interests may appear," it will be left to a court to decide what those respective interests were. In one case, the tenants had torn down a building and built a much more costly one.

Absent an Agreement Otherwise, May a Landlord's Insurer Pursue a Subrogation Claim against a Negligent Tenant?, 63 Wash & Lee L. Rev. 1743 (2006).

51. *See, e.g.*, Fire Ins. Exchange v. Geekie, 128 Ill. Dec. 616, 179 Ill. App. 3d 679, 534 N.E.2d 1061, (1989).

52. *See, e.g.*, Bannock Bldg. Co. v. Sahlberg, 126 Idaho 545, 887 P.2d 1052 (1994). *See also* Agra-By-Products v. Agway, 347 N.W.2d 142 (N.D. 1984) (lease clause under which tenant agreed to reimburse landlord for all insurance premiums paid by landlord was clear indication of parties' intent to provide for mutual protection of their insurable interests in leased property; however, tenant was limited in its protection to extent of insurance coverage provided).

53. *See, e.g.*, Seaco Ins. Co. v. Barbosa, 435 Mass. 772, 779, 761 N.E.2d 946, 951 (2002) (declining to extend rule implied coinsured to commercial tenancies and looking to terms of lease and other evidence to ascertain intent of parties).

54. *See, e.g.*, Safeco Ins. Co. v. Capri, 101 Nev. 429, 705 P.2d 659 (1985).

55. 5 *Thompson on Real Property, Third Thomas Edition*, § 40.17 (LexisNexis 2021).

56. Cambron v. Carlisle, 435 So. 2d 1216, 1218 (Ala. 1983) (covenant by lessor to maintain fire insurance was for benefit of both parties to lease); Grand Forks Seed Co. v. Northland Greyhound Lines, Inc., 168 F. Supp. 882, 884 (D.N.D. 1959) (where lease stipulates that one party will keep property insured for benefit of other, each is entitled to proportionate interest in proceeds). *See also* Fred A. Chapin Lumber Co. v. Lumber Bargains, Inc., 189 Cal. App. 2d 613, 617, 11 Cal. Rptr. 634, 636 (1961) (where parties to lease agree that one of them will maintain insurance for their mutual protection and obligated party procures insurance payable to himself alone, other party for whose benefit agreement was made has equitable lien on insurance proceeds).

When that building was destroyed, the trial court held that the landlord was entitled to the value of the original building and the remainder of the proceeds should be paid to the tenants. The Arkansas Supreme Court, however, reversed and concluded the tenants had no insurable interest in the property except the value of their right to occupy it during the remainder of the term and directed that the landlord was to receive the bulk of the proceeds.[57]

Any common law rules, however, are largely immaterial because modern commercial leases often require one party to obtain coverage on the premises and then specify how insurance proceeds will be applied.[58] For example, a sample lease clause in one treatise provides that if the tenant has agreed to assume responsibility for rebuilding in the event of a casualty and obtains insurance, any proceeds payable in a prescribed amount or less are to be paid to the tenant and applied by the tenant to pay for repair and restoration with any balance on completion of the repairs to be the sole property of the tenant while any proceeds payable in excess of a prescribed amount are to be held by the landlord or the first mortgagee and applied to restoration in accordance with the lease procedures.[59] Obviously, the terms of a particular lease will be tailored to meet the needs of the parties, and the attorney representing either a landlord or tenant has to carefully review the language of the particular lease to determine to what his or her client is entitled.

Note that the ability of the landlord to use insurance proceeds to rebuild will depend on the mandates of any mortgage lender. Standard financing documents direct that proceeds have to be paid to the lender and applied by it, at its option, to restoration or reduction of any unpaid principal balance secured by the mortgage.[60]

[2] Tenant as Sole Insured

If the tenant insures the property, and the landlord does not, is the landlord entitled to any of the insurance proceeds?[61] Generally, the answer is no, not

---

57. Hale v. Simmons, 200 Ark. 556, 139 S.W.2d 696 (1940).

58. 5 *Thompson on Real Property, Third Thomas Edition*, § 40.17 (LexisNexis 2021).

59. *Current Leasing Law and Techniques—Forms*, § 9.04[4] (LexisNexis Matthew Bender 2021). *See also* Portnoy v. Omnicare Pharm., Inc., 2004 U.S. Dist. LEXIS 12235 (E.D. Pa. June 25, 2004) (if landlord receives any insurance proceeds from the property insurance maintained by tenant pursuant to the lease, landlord is required to turn them over to tenant to make repairs).

60. 5 *Thompson on Real Property, Third Thomas Edition*, § 44.11(d) (LexisNexis 2021).

61. The tenant, of course, must have an insurable interest in the property that is insured. The general rule is that the insured has to have a substantial economic interest in the safety or preservation of the property from loss or destruction. Many courts have adopted this position, and it is codified in some states. *See, e.g.*, N.Y. Ins. Law § 3401 ("insurable interest" includes any lawful and substantial economic interest in safety or preservation of property from loss, destruction, or pecuniary damage); Nev. Rev. Stat. § 687B.060(2) ("insurable interest" means any actual, lawful, and substantial economic interest in safety or preservation of subject of insurance free from loss, destruction, or pecuniary damage or impairment). An insured having a

unless the landlord is an additional insured or loss payee. Absent an agreement to the contrary, the proceeds of insurance obtained by one party to a lease may not be claimed, in whole or in part, by the other, despite the fact that the policy covers the value of the interests of both.[62]

The California Supreme Court has said that absent a provision in a lease, there is no obligation on a tenant to procure insurance for the benefit of the landlord, and neither party has an interest in the proceeds of insurance obtained by the other on that party's separate insurable interest. However, if there is an agreement for insurance between them, and the party obligated, in violation of that agreement, procures insurance payable to him- or herself alone, the other party for whose benefit the agreement was made has an equitable lien on the proceeds of that insurance. Thus, where a lease requires that all insurance moneys should be used to rebuild and repair the property, the landlord's claim on the insurance proceeds could not be defeated by the subsequent termination of the lease. However, where another lease for a different property provided the tenant at its own cost should keep the building in a "good and safe and secure condition," but did not say that all insurance moneys should be used in repair, the landlord had no claim on insurance procured by the tenant.[63]

In another case, a warehouse owned by a landlord was insured by the tenant. The structure was destroyed in a fire. The landlord filed a proof of claim with the insurance company, which denied it because the landlord was not named as a loss payee or an additional insured in the insurance policy. The court said that if the landlord was an additional insured at the time of the fire, the landlord was entitled to insurance proceeds equal to the cash value of the building, but if it was not, the tenant as named insured was entitled to *all* of the insurance proceeds. The lease required the tenant to obtain coverage at its expense, but nothing in the lease required the tenant to provide insurance protection for the landlord. It placed responsibility for any damage to the building on the tenant's shoulders, said the court, but ensured that the tenant would have insurance to pay for any obligatory repairs. The court concluded that the tenant had submitted sufficient evidence to create a genuine issue of material fact on the question of whether the landlord was an additional insured and, therefore, a jury had to resolve whether the tenant consented to the landlord being named an additional insured on the policy.[64]

---

leasehold interest has been said to be limited in recovery for the loss of the insured property to the value of that interest. National Sec. Fire & Casualty Co. v. Newman, 53 Ala. App. 614, 620, 303 So. 2d 113, 118 (1974). A tenant who has agreed to return the premises to the landlord in good condition or has agreed to keep the premises insured has an insurable interest in the premises leased. Sigola Mfg., Inc. v. Dairyland Ins. Co., 124 A.D.2d 654, 508 N.Y.S.2d 38 (1986).

62. Middleton v. Rush, 764 So. 2d 1276, 1279 (Ala. App. 2000).

63. Alexander v. Security-First Nat'l Bank, 7 Cal. 2d 718, 62 P.2d 735 (1936).

64. Ionian Corp. v. Country Mut. Ins. Co., 836 F. Supp. 2d 1173 (D. Ore 2011).

14

Recovering from a Governmental Entity or Regulated Lender

14.1 Introduction

One observer has noted that courts are increasingly holding governments liable under common law theories for activities that increase flood hazards on adjacent private lands and for "residual" damage from flood control structures.[1] That may be true, but another commentary warns that property owners who seek to recoup damages for flood losses in litigation against governmental entities face long and costly legal battles with uncertain outcomes.[2] This chapter explores the hurdles plaintiffs face, substantive and procedural, when seeking compensation from a government for a flood loss.

14.2 The United States

[1] Generally

There are many activities of the federal government that potentially subject it to liability for flood damage including flood control, roadway and other construction, and even weather forecasting, a subject discussed elsewhere.[3] However, although not mentioned in the Constitution, the United States enjoys immunity from suit. The Supreme Court over a century ago said that it is an "axiom of our jurisprudence" that the government is not liable to suit unless it consents to it, and its liability cannot extend beyond the plain language of

1. Kusler, *Flood Risk in the Courts: Reducing Government Liability while Encouraging Government Responsibility* at 1 (Oct. 24, 2011), *available at* https://biotech.law.lsu.edu/blog/Flood_Risk_in_the_Courts_102411.pdf.

2. Pace, *Unaware, Unprepared, and Unexpectedly Flooded: Improving Louisiana's Capacity to Respond to Flood Hazards*, 6 LSU J. Energy L. & Resources 121, 142 (2017).

3. See Chapter 15, *infra*.

the statute authorizing it.[4] As explained below, the federal government has consented to being sued, but it is an exceedingly narrow consent.

[2] Flood Control Act

[a] Generally[5]

The starting point for determining the potential liability of the federal government for flood damage is the Flood Control Act (FCA).[6] It provides that "No liability of any kind shall attach to or rest upon the United States for any damage from or by floods or flood waters at any place."[7] That language has been described as "at best opaque."[8] The result has been confusion in the courts.

The United States Supreme Court sought to bring some clarity when it interpreted that sentence in *Cent. Green Co. v. United States*.[9] In that case, the petitioner owned 1,000 acres of pistachio orchards in the San Joaquin Valley in California. The Madera Canal flowed through the property. The canal was used for irrigation purposes and was part of a project that had flood control as one of its purposes. The petitioner brought an action against the government alleging that its negligence in the design, construction, and maintenance of the canal had caused subsurface flooding that resulted in damage to the orchards. The Ninth Circuit concluded that because the canal was part of a flood control project, the immunity of the Flood Control Act applied. The Supreme Court granted *certiorari* to address whether the words of the immunity statute encompass all the water that flows through a federal facility designed and operated, at least in part, for flood control purposes, a question to which the Ninth Circuit answered yes. The Supreme Court reversed and said:

> to characterize every drop of water that flows through that immense project as "flood water" simply because flood control is among the purposes served by the project unnecessarily dilutes the language of

4. Price v. United States, 174 U.S. 373, 19 S. Ct. 765, 43 L. Ed. 1011 (1899). *See generally* Schaefer, *Reining in Sovereign Immunity to Compensate Hurricane Katrina Victims*, 40 Ecology L.Q. 411, 412–16 (2013); Duval, *Sovereign Immunity, Anachronistic or Inherent: A Sword or a Shield?* 84 Tul. L. Rev. 1471 (2010).

5. *See generally* Janke, *Government Liability in Tort under a Hundred Year Flood Plan*, 36 S.U. L. Rev. 11, 23-28 (2008); Kusler, *A Comparative Look at Public Liability for Flood Hazard Mitigation* (2008), *available at* https://biotech.law.lsu.edu/blog/Kusler2008.pdf.

6. 33 U.S.C. §§ 701, *et seq. See generally* Schaefer, *Reining in Sovereign Immunity to Compensate Hurricane Katrina Victims*, 40 Ecology L.Q. 411, 421–23 (2013); Hofmann, *An Enduring Anachronism: Arguments for the Repeal of the § 702c Immunity Provision of the Flood Control Act of 1928*, 79 Tex. L. Rev. 791 (2001).

7. 33 U.S.C. § 702c.

8. Duval, *Sovereign Immunity, Anachronistic or Inherent: A Sword or a Shield?* 84 Tul. L. Rev. 1471, 1487 (2010).

9. Cent. Green Co. v. United States, 531 U.S. 425, 121 S. Ct. 1005, 148 L. Ed. 2d 919 (2001).

the statute. The text of the statute does not include the words "flood control project." Rather, it states that immunity attaches to "any damage from or by floods or flood waters . . . ." Accordingly, the text of the statute directs us to determine the scope of the immunity conferred, not by the character of the federal project or the purposes it serves, but by the character of the waters that cause the relevant damage and the purposes behind their release.[10]

The court then concluded that in determining whether the statutory immunity attaches, courts should consider the character of the waters that caused the damage instead of the relation between that damage and a flood control project. In the end, the court may have failed to bring the clarity for which one would hope. As one federal judge said, the nation's highest court has left flood immunity precedent unsettled to say the least.[11]

Subsequent to *Cent. Green*, one of the most important statements about FCA immunity arose in the aftermath of a hurricane. Courts in the Fifth Circuit were swamped by a plethora of lawsuits after Hurricane Katrina. A number of cases were consolidated in what came to be known as the "In re Katrina Canal Breaches Litigation." In a definitive opinion, the Fifth Circuit Court of Appeals explicated *Cent. Green*. First, the court said that within the meaning of the FCA immunity statute, waters that constitute "floods or flood waters" are not all waters that pass through a federal flood-control project, but instead are those of a certain "character." Moreover, under *Cent. Green*, determining whether water that caused damage had that immune "character" has become the heart of the inquiry. After the Supreme Court decision, said the Fifth Circuit panel, waters have the immune character of "flood waters" if the government's link to them is through flood-control activity. In other words, flood-control activity is what gives waters an immune "character." Therefore, concluded the court, immunity under the FCA only applies where damages result from waters released by flood-control activity or negligence in flood-control activity.[12]

10. Cent. Green Co. v. United States, 531 U.S. 425, 434, 121 S. Ct. 1005, 1010–11, 148 L. Ed. 2d 919, 928 (2001).

11. Kroshus v. United States, 2011 U.S. Dist. LEXIS 118797 (D. Nev. Sept. 26, 2011). *See generally* Chizewer & Tarlock, *New Challenges for Urban Areas Facing Flood Risks*, 40 Fordham Urb. L.J. 1739, 1755 (2013) (Supreme Court engrafted significant limitation of § 702c immunity by limiting federal government's liability to damages determined by character of waters that caused harm, as opposed to character of federal flood-control project that was supposed to prevent that harm).

12. Robinson v. United States (*In re* Katrina Canal Breaches Litig.), 696 F.3d 436 (5th Cir. 2012), *cert. den. sub. nom.*, Lattimore v. United States, 570 U.S. 926, 133 S. Ct. 2855, 186 L. Ed. 2d 925 (2013).

[b] Specific Instances of Immunity from Flood Loss

Since *Cent. Green*, courts have found no liability under the FCA in a number of circumstances. The government was immune for releasing water from a dam[13] and for failing to reduce lake levels by a controlled discharge of water through a dam.[14] There was also no liability for damages caused by a beach-replenishment project.[15] When a drain pipe was removed as part of building a flood control levy, there was no liability.[16] It has also been held that FCA immunity extends to activities related to management of a flood control

---

13. Cont'l Ins. Co. v. United States, 2013 U.S. Dist. LEXIS 27292 (M.D. Tenn. Feb. 28, 2013). The plaintiffs in the case contended the dam was not a "flood control project." The court responded that there may be immunity for flood-control activity even where a project is not primarily or substantially related to flood control. In this case, the alleged misconduct, said the court, was flood control activity involving flood waters. The character of the waters was "flood waters," and the alleged actions and inactions were flood control efforts. The government was, therefore, immune under the FCA.

14. Godfrey v. United States, 2012 U.S. Dist. LEXIS 15911 (W.D. Ark. Feb. 9, 2012). In *Godfrey*, the plaintiff claimed property damage after the Army Corps of Engineers abandoned its longtime practice of periodically reducing levels in a lake by controlled discharges of water through a dam. Heavy rains subsequently caused lake levels to become dangerously high, and the Corps released water from the dam, which allegedly resulted in flood damage and destruction to the plaintiff's property. The plaintiff contended there was no immunity because the reason the Corps had previously failed to release water was that it was motivated by the commercial purpose of generating power and that the dam was not a flood control project. The court, however, said that the damage to the plaintiff's property was unquestionably caused by flooding and that release of water that damaged the property was not a release for the commercial purpose of generating electricity. The government was immune from suit for flood damage, and the fact that the water supply of the lake and dam was used at times for multiple purposes did not affect the outcome. *See also* A.O. Smith Corp. v. United States, 2013 U.S. Dist. LEXIS 27299 (M.D. Tenn. Feb. 28, 2013) (even if dam was not characterized as "flood control project," alleged misconduct was flood control activity involving flood waters).

15. Cohen v. United States *ex rel.* U.S. Army Corps of Eng'rs, 2018 U.S. Dist. LEXIS 197588 (D.N.J. Nov. 20, 2018). In *Cohen*, an Army Corps of Engineers beach-replenishment project included elevating the beachfront and modifying stormwater outfalls. On completion of the project, an outfall drained onto a newly constructed beach at the base of a seawall, causing erosion and pooling water near the property of the plaintiff. The plaintiff acknowledged that the seawall damage was caused by "stormwater," and therefore, it was undisputed that the "character of the waters" causing the damage was "flood waters." Further, the flood waters were released on account of "flood-control activity or negligence," and the government was thus immune from liability.

16. *See* PNC Bank N.A. v. United States Army Corps of Eng'rs, 2018 U.S. Dist. LEXIS 52968 (N.D. Ind. Mar. 29, 2018) where after the drain pipe was removed, the plaintiff's property experienced flooding during rainfalls. Plaintiff argued the FCA applied only to flood damage caused by the overflow of water from a nearby river, not to flooding on its property caused by rainfall after the government removed the drain pipe. The court disagreed and said that rightly or wrongly, the FCA statute protects the United States from liability even when its flooding solution in one area causes floods in another.

activity including whether and how to warn of the dangers of that flood control activity.[17]

The Fifth Circuit illustrated the distinction between immune and non-immune events in a case with a large number of plaintiffs.[18] One group of those plaintiffs sued over the Mississippi River Gulf Outlet (MRGO), a shipping channel between New Orleans and the Gulf of Mexico. When Hurricane Katrina struck, the MRGO's size and configuration greatly aggravated the damage caused by the storm. The court said that under the FTC, the government enjoys immunity only from damages caused by flood waters released on account of flood-control activity. Because the design, construction, and maintenance of the MRGO could not be characterized as flood-control activity, the FCA *did not* immunize the government against liability for that flooding.[19] On the other hand, another group of plaintiffs claimed to have been harmed by the breaching of the levees caused by the negligent dredging of canals and negligent design and construction of the levees. Because the canals were designed to prevent flooding by either creating drainage or preventing storm surge with levees, and were fully incorporated in the Lake Pontchartrain and Vicinity Hurricane Protection Plan, their design and dredging were flood-control activities. Thus, the government was immune from liability, as the waters that damaged the plaintiffs' property were allegedly released by negligence in flood-control activity.[20]

[c] National Flood Insurance Act and Section 702c Immunity

Under the National Flood Insurance Act (NFIA),[21] which is administered by the Federal Emergency Management Agency (FEMA), the government does more than provide insurance coverage. It disseminates information about flood insurance,[22] determines whether local land use and control measures

17. Fortner v. TVA, 2005 U.S. Dist. LEXIS 28036 (E.D. Tenn. Nov. 4, 2005).

18. Robinson v. United States (*In re* Katrina Canal Breaches Litig.), 696 F.3d 436 (5th Cir. 2012), *cert. den. sub. nom.*, Lattimore v. United States, 570 U.S. 926, 133 S. Ct. 2855, 186 L. Ed. 2d 925 (2013).

19. No action related to the MRGO, said the court, could be characterized as flood-control activity. The only conceivable flood-control activity was failure of the government to implement timely foreshore protection. That was the very omission complained of by the plaintiffs. Such an omission could not, concluded the court, provide the basis for FTC immunity because otherwise all flood damage caused by government activity would be regarded as a result of, or a lack of, flood-control activity.

20. *See also* Kibler v. United States, 46 F. Supp. 3d 844, 861 (C.D. Ill. 2014) (plaintiff's injuries occurred as direct result of flood waters being kept in lake for flood control purposes, and thus § 702c immunity would apply).

21. 42 U.S.C. §§ 4001, *et seq.*

22. 42 U.S.C. § 4020.

are consistent with the comprehensive criteria for land management and use under the Act,[23] and makes flood elevation determinations and publishes flood hazard maps.[24] Does the immunity of the Flood Control Act apply to these government actions under the NFIA?

In two cases, plaintiffs sued the government, arguing in essence that but for the failure of the government to publicize the availability of flood insurance to them as required by the NFIA, they would have had coverage for their flood losses. A Colorado federal court held that because the NFIA is directed at compensation for, rather than prevention of, flood damages, the FCA immunity statute did not apply.[25] On the other hand, an Alabama federal court found that the "broad and sweeping language" of the FCA immunity statute extended to damages allegedly related to the NFIA. It rejected the reasoning of the Colorado court and characterized that court's review of the NFIA as "cursory."[26]

There have been cases in which plaintiffs have sought to hold the government liable because it produced inaccurate flood hazard maps. For example, in an Alabama case, the plaintiffs alleged the government was negligent in preparing a flood hazard map that erroneously failed to identify a certain area of their community as flood prone. In reliance on that map, they claimed they built and occupied houses in that flood-prone area, and those houses were subsequently severely damaged by flooding. The court said that the alleged negligence involved actions undertaken pursuant to acts of Congress authorizing expenditures of federal funds for flood control. It held that under the FCA, the government was immune from liability.[27]

In addition to initial flood hazard maps, FEMA also issues Letters of Map Revision (LOMR). FCA immunity applies to issuing a LOMR. In a Mississippi case, for instance, the plaintiff business was a store in a floodplain adjacent to another store about half of which was in the floodplain and in a regulatory floodway. A "regulatory floodway" is "channel of a river or other watercourse and the adjacent land areas that must be reserved in order to discharge the base flood."[28] Over a decade after the adjacent store was built in the floodway, it was allowed to remain because FEMA issued a LOMR removing it from the

23. 42 U.S.C. § 4022(a)(1).

24. 42 U.S.C. § 4104.

25. Schell v. National Flood Insurers Ass'n, 520 F. Supp. 150 (D. Colo. 1981).

26. Powers v. United States, 787 F. Supp. 1397 (M.D. Ala. 1992), *aff'd*, 996 F.2d 1121 (11th Cir. 1993).

27. Britt v. United States, 515 F. Supp. 1159 (M.D. Ala. 1981). *See also* Weitzman v. Pima Cty., 2009 U.S. Dist. LEXIS 141003 (D. Ariz. Aug. 6, 2009) (Congress contemplated that FEMA's acts with respect to flood mapping would be covered by immunity provision of FCA).

28. *Floodway*, FEMA, https://www.fema.gov/glossary/floodway.

floodway. The plaintiff argued that the floodway had been drawn correctly in the initial map. The presence of the adjacent store in the floodway, said the plaintiff, caused displacement of water, a rise in the water level, and an alteration of the water flow from standing water to a rushing, forceful water, all of which resulted in extensive flood damages to the plaintiff's store. FEMA argued that issuance of a LOMR is a flood control initiative precluding liability pursuant to the FCA. The court agreed and said that the LOMR at issue was prepared and disseminated pursuant to congressionally mandated flood control initiatives and that it was an "integral part" of those initiatives. Thus, FEMA was immune from suit under the FCA.[29]

In a particularly tragic case, the plaintiffs bought a home in March 2017 without obtaining flood insurance and 40 days later, that home was destroyed by a flood. Before buying the house, the plaintiffs obtained documents from FEMA stating that the home was not in a 100-year floodplain. They failed to obtain flood insurance in part in reliance on that fact. They later learned that in 2010 there had been a floodplain map change that recategorized the house from within the 100-year floodplain to outside it. They alleged that in 2018, FEMA changed the designation back to its pre-2010 status—placing the house within the 100-year floodplain—and backdated documents to suggest the flood status had never changed. They contended that had they known the true status of the property, they never would have bought it and that the 2018 recategorization made it impossible for them to sell the house. They sought to assert claims of, *inter alia*, misrepresentation and negligence against FEMA. The court said the claims were barred by the FCA immunity statute because floodplain mapping was integral to "congressionally mandated flood control initiatives." Although various factors may have contributed to the plaintiffs' loss, said the court, they would not have been damaged but for the flooding of their property, and the alleged negligence of FEMA arose out of its attempt to control the negative effects of flooding.[30]

[3] Waiver of Sovereign Immunity

[a] The Federal Tort Claims Act Generally

If a plaintiff avoids the immunity granted the government under the Flood Control Act, he or she still must contend with the sovereign immunity of the federal government. That immunity is waived under the Federal Tort Claims

29. Kmart Corp. v. Kroger Co., 2012 U.S. Dist. LEXIS 80218 (N.D. Miss. June 11, 2012). The court said, however, that it found FEMA to be immune from suit on other grounds.

30. Christopherson v. Bushner, 2021 U.S. Dist. LEXIS 82593 (W.D. Mo. Apr. 29, 2021).

Act (FTCA).[31] Initially, the Act provides a broad waiver from tort liability, stating that the United States shall be liable in the same manner and to the same extent as a private individual under like circumstances.[32] The government, however, is not liable for pre-judgment interest or punitive damages. The Act contains an expansive exception to the waiver of immunity for

> Any claim based upon an act or omission of an employee of the Government, exercising due care, in the execution of a statute or regulation, whether or not such statute or regulation be valid, or based upon the exercise or performance or the failure to exercise or perform a discretionary function or duty on the part of a federal agency or an employee of the Government, whether or not the discretion involved be abused.[33]

"Employee of the government" includes officers or employees of any federal agency, members of the military or naval forces, members of the National Guard, and persons acting on behalf of a federal agency in an official capacity, temporarily or permanently in the service of the United States, whether with or without compensation.[34]

A discussion of the precise meaning of "discretionary function" is beyond the scope of this treatise. It has been the subject of endless scholarly debate. There are treatises on federal tort claims that address it[35] and many excellent law review articles on the topic.[36] One leading authority explains that there

---

31. 28 U.S.C. §§ 2671, *et seq. See generally* Schaefer, *Reining in Sovereign Immunity to Compensate Hurricane Katrina Victims*, 40 Ecology L.Q. 411, 416–21 (2013).

32. 28 U.S.C. § 2674.

33. 28 U.S.C. § 2680(a). Note that the federal district courts have exclusive jurisdiction of civil actions on claims against the United States for money damages and for injury or loss of property caused by the negligent or wrongful act or omission of any employee of the government while acting within the scope of his or her office or employment, under circumstances in which the United States, if a private person, would be liable to the claimant in accordance with the law of the place where the act or omission occurred. 28 U.S.C. § 1346(b)(1).

34. 28 U.S.C. § 2671.

35. *See* Morris, *Federal Tort Claims* (Clark Boardman Callaghan 2021); Figley, *A Guide to the Federal Torts Claim Act* (2d ed. ABA 2018).

36. *See, e.g.*, Cohen, *Not Fully Discretionary: Incorporating a Factor-Based Standard into the FTCA's Discretionary Function Exception*, 112 Nw. U.L. Rev. 879 (2018); Daley & Duval, *The Discretionary Function: License to Kill? The Federal Tort Claims Act and Hurricane Katrina Implications of the Robinson/MRGO Decisions: Can the King Do No Wrong?* 62 Loy. L. Rev. 299 (2016); Schaefer, *Reining in Sovereign Immunity to Compensate Hurricane Katrina Victims*, 40 Ecology L.Q. 411 (2013); Bruno, *Immunity for "Discretionary" Functions: A Proposal to Amend the Federal Tort Claims Act*, 49 Harv. J. Legis. 411, 419–22 (2012); Nelson, *The King's Wrongs and the Federal District Courts: Understanding the Discretionary Function Exception to the Federal Tort Claims Act*, 51 S. Tex. L. Rev. 259 (2009); Rosenthal, *A Theory of Governmental Damages Liability: Torts, Constitutional Torts, and Takings*, 9 U. Pa. J. Const.

are two elements to the discretionary function exception. First, the government action has to involve an element of judgment or choice, and there can be no judgment or choice if a federal statute, regulation, or policy specifically prescribes a course of action an employee is to follow. Second, the required judgment has to involve social, economic, or political policy. The test is met if the actions taken are susceptible to policy analysis, and it does not matter whether the decision was made at the planning or operational level.[37] An attorney in the United States Department of Justice put it more succinctly. The discretionary function exception does not cover claims alleging violation of an agency's own rules, utter failure to address a clearly hazardous condition, or careless driving.[38] In other words, the exception is decidedly narrow. It is not, however, a license for negligence.[39]

[b] The Federal Tort Claims Act and Flood Damage

[i] Discretionary Function Exception Applied

Courts generally find that decisions about the design and construction of projects are an exercise of an agency's discretionary functions. This includes

---

L. 797 (2007); Niles, *"Nothing but Mischief": The Federal Tort Claims Act and the Scope of Discretionary Immunity*, 54 Admin. L. Rev. 1275 (2002); Weaver & Longoria, *Bureaucracy that Kills: Federal Sovereign Immunity and the Discretionary Function Exception*, 96 Am. Pol. Sci. Rev. 335 (2002).

37. Figley, *Understanding the Federal Tort Claims Act: A Different Metaphor*, 44 Tort & Ins. L.J. 1105 (2009). The author adds that it is the nature of the conduct, rather than the status of the actor, that governs whether the exception applies and that because the exception is applicable whether or not the discretion is abused, a claim is barred, even if it arises from flawed policies or negligent conduct, when the elements are met.

38. *See* Fishback, *The Federal Tort Claims Act Is a Very Limited Waiver of Sovereign Immunity—So Long as Agencies Follow Their Own Rules and Do Not Simply Ignore Problems*, 59 U.S. Attys' Bull. 16, 23–26 (2011).

39. Standler, *Tort Liability in the USA for Negligent Weather Forecasts* at 33 (2003), *available at* www.rbs2.com/forecast.pdf. The author cites to *Indian Towing Co., Inc. v. United States*, 350 U.S. 61, 100 L. Ed. 48, 76 S. Ct. 122 (1955), where the plaintiff alleged its tug boat ran aground because the Coast Guard failed to keep a lighthouse in repair. The court said that once the Coast Guard exercised its discretion to operate a light and engendered reliance on the guidance afforded by it, the agency was obligated to use due care to make certain the light was maintained in good working order. The opinion has been dismissed as no longer persuasive authority on the discretionary function exception. *See, e.g.*, Cranford v. United States, 466 F.3d 955, 959 (11th Cir. 2006).

projects for shoreline protection,[40] dikes,[41] dams,[42] removal of the drain pipe as part of building a flood control levy,[43] and canals and ditches.[44]

Road construction is usually a discretionary function. For example, construction of the surface of a public highway caused the natural flow of surface water, which had previously flowed away from the plaintiffs' property over the surface of the highway, to be diverted to their property. The property owners alleged negligence in raising the level of the surface of the road, in constructing the road base, and in failing to provide culverts, or adequate culverts, underneath the highway. The court said these were acts calling for the exercise of judgment and discretion in the planning of the highway and granted the government's motion to dismiss.[45]

---

40. Vaizburd v. United States, 90 F. Supp. 2d 210 (E.D.N.Y. 2000) (where beach nourishment project involving construction of groin and fillet caused property damage, government was not liable for alleged improper and negligent design and maintenance because its actions were discretionary functions); Devito v. United States, 12 F. Supp. 2d 269 (E.D.N.Y. 1998) (government dredged and constructed jetties and stone groins in shoreline stabilization project, and plaintiffs claimed negligence accelerated erosion and property damage; court found government actions were discretionary functions).

41. McGillic v. United States, 153 F. Supp. 565 (D.N.D. 1957) (plaintiffs alleged construction and maintenance of dike by government impeded or hindered normal passage or runoff of flood waters, causing damage to their land; court found government's actions were discretionary function).

42. Cooley v. United States, 172 F. Supp. 385 (D.S.D. 1959) (plaintiffs alleged construction of dam and reservoir and subsequent impounding of water caused their land to be wrongfully and unlawfully flooded, resulting in loss in their crop yield; court found flooding was result of discretionary act by government); North v. United States, 94 F. Supp. 824 (D. Utah 1950) (where dam constructed by government caused water to back up in reservoir, causing rise in level in underground water that allegedly caused plaintiff's cellar and cesspool to flood, court found that project involved decisions and exercise of discretion and discretionary functions of "the highest order").

43. PNC Bank N.A. v. United States Army Corps of Eng'rs, 2018 U.S. Dist. LEXIS 52968 (N.D. Ind. Mar. 29, 2018). In *PNC Bank* the Army Corps of Engineers designed a flood control levy to include removal of a drain pipe after which the plaintiff's property experienced flooding during rainfalls. The Corps admitted that its engineers designed the project and that the design specifications included removal of the drain pipe. The court said the Corps exercised its delegated discretion, and it was not constrained by any statute or regulation that would prohibit it from deciding to remove the drain pipe and that FTCA exception to the immunity waiver shielded the Corps from all liabilities, be they derived from state or federal laws, so long as it exercised discretion and its decisions involved policy considerations. Clearly, concluded the court, both those conditions applied and the Corps was immune from liability.

44. United States v. Ure, 225 F.2d 709 (9th Cir. 1955) (plaintiffs claimed their land was flooded following breaks in canal constructed by government; court held that decision not to line entire canal with concrete or other impervious material was discretionary function); California v. United States, 146 F. Supp. 341 (S.D. Cal. 1956) (state claimed that construction of canal, pipeline, culverts, ditches, and channels by federal government caused damage to state road; court dismissed case, finding any injury resulted from discretionary acts).

45. Sisley v. United States, 202 F. Supp. 273 (D. Alaska 1962).

How the government chooses to operate or maintain facilities is usually found to be a discretionary function. For example, the discretionary function exception shielded the government from liability for alleged negligent operation of canal locks and control gates by the Army Corps of Engineers.[46] The decision of the United States whether or not to allow greater flows through canals was a discretionary act,[47] as was the decision by the United States Fish and Wildlife Service to open the floodgates of a dam.[48] A decision to forego improvements to an existing project while a study is conducted is the exercise of a discretionary function.[49]

Channeling or changing the course of rivers is usually found to be a discretionary function.[50] A dramatic example occurred when the Army Corps of Engineers dredged and widened a bend in the Tombigbee River in Green County, Alabama. The Corps of Engineers knew that encroachment might result in certain areas, but decided the cost of conducting studies to identify those areas would exceed the cost of any after-the-fact acquisition. The plaintiff alleged that because of the dredging and widening, the river bank was eroded and her home collapsed into the river. She asserted negligent redesign of the course of the river caused her damage, and the government conceded the damage would not have occurred but for the widening of the bend. The court said that the decision to alter the watercourse was a part of an overall decision to improve navigation on the river, and the determination of whether

---

46. Miller v. United States, 583 F.2d 857 (6th Cir. 1978). *See also In re* Ohio River Disaster Litigation, 862 F.2d 1237 (6th Cir. 1988) (discretionary function exception protected government for liability for Army Corps of Engineers' alleged negligent operation of navigational dam).

47. Sauders v. South Carolina Pub. Serv. Auth., 856 F. Supp. 1066 (D.S.C. 1994). *See also* Konecny v. United States, 388 F.2d 59 (8th Cir. 1967).

48. Olson v. United States, 93 F. Supp. 150 (D.N.D. 1950). *See also* Spillway Marina, Inc. v. United States, 445 F.2d 876 (10th Cir. 1971) (intentional drawdown of water level of flood control reservoir was within discretionary function exception); Cont'l Ins. Co. v. United States, 2013 U.S. Dist. LEXIS 27292 (M.D. Tenn. Feb. 28, 2013) (decisions about water levels of reservoir and timing and quantity of releases were committed to discretion of Corps of Engineers and, therefore, claims against government were barred by discretionary function exception to Federal Tort Claims Act).

49. National Union Fire Ins. v. United States, 115 F.3d 1415 (9th Cir. 1997), *cert. den.*, 522 U.S. 1116, 118 S. Ct. 1053, 140 L. Ed. 2d 116 (1998).

50. *See, e.g.*, Coates v. United States, 181 F.2d 816 (8th Cir. 1950) (no liability for flood damages to farms and crops allegedly caused by substantial changes made by government to flow, current, channel, banks, and course of Missouri River by driving pilings, dredging channels, laying rip-raps, and employing mechanical and artificial devices); Chicago and Illinois Midland Ry. Co. v. Marsh, 577 F. Supp. 798 (C.D. Ill. 1984), *aff'd*, 746 F.2d 1482 (7th Cir. 1984) (damming and channelization of Mackinaw River that caused river waters to flow with increased force and velocity and damaging plaintiff's bridges was exercise of discretional function).

or not to conduct a study to determine where specific injury to property might occur was a discretionary function.[51]

Property can be damaged by flooding when owners failed to take precautions against rivers overflowing their banks, against torrential rainfall, or against storm surge from a tropical cyclone. There are federal government agencies that collect and disseminate information about these events. Is the government liable if that information is erroneous or misleading? Property owners in a case decided by the Eight Circuit said the answer should be yes. In that case, the Kansas River entered flood stage, and it was alleged that federal government agencies negligently disseminated misinformation about the course and action of the flood waters. Property owners sued the government, arguing that they were led by that misinformation into a feeling of security that the river would not overflow its banks, dikes, and levees and, therefore, they did not remove portable goods and property from the flood area and thereby prevent damage to that property. The court, however, found that the discretionary function exception applied, and interestingly that another part of the FTCA precluding recovery for claims arising out of misrepresentations[52] also applied, and that together they insulated the government from liability.[53]

A common government function is issuing permits and licenses. Is that a discretionary function? The Eight Circuit addressed that question in a case in which the Army Corps of Engineers issued a permit to a rancher to build two jetties in a river and to reroute the river by excavating a channel through a sandbar on the southern bank. The project was intended to prevent erosion on the ranch property. However, property owners alleged that, under the supervision of the Corps of Engineers, the rancher negligently constructed the jetties, causing severe flooding on their property. The injured property owners argued that the government was liable for their loss for three reasons. First, the Corps, by its own regulations, had a nondiscretionary duty to issue a prohibitory order when its inspector discovered that the rancher was violating his permit. Second, the Corps voluntarily undertook a non-discretionary obligation to enforce the terms of the permit. Third, the Corps violated its

51. Payne v. United States, 730 F.2d 1434 (11th Cir. 1984).

52. 28 U.S.C. § 2680(h). *See also* Christopherson v. Bushner, 2021 U.S. Dist. LEXIS 82593 (W.D. Mo. Apr. 29, 2021) (where property owners alleged that FEMA was negligent in changing base flood elevation before they bought property and then changing it back after flood, crux of allegation was reliance on FEMA's communications, which would fall within misrepresentation exception to FTCA's immunity waiver); Harrah v. Miller, 558 F. Supp. 702 (S.D. W. Va. 1983) (Farmers Home Administration and its employees who approved plaintiff's loan and failed to inform plaintiff that house was located in flood zone and that flood insurance was required were immune from liability for damage caused to house as result of flash flood under misrepresentation exception). *See generally* Fontenot, *Misrepresentation Exception to the Federal Tort Claims Act*, 1988 Army Law. 18 (1988).

53. National Mfg. Co. v. United States, 210 F.2d 263 (8th Cir. 1954).

own regulations by accepting an after-the-fact permit for the completed project when the rancher had failed to perform required remedial work. The court agreed that the Corps had a non-discretionary duty to enforce the permit it issued, and failure to follow its mandatory regulations rendered its conduct actionable under the FTCA. However, the court also held that general promises by the Corps about monitoring and supervision of the rancher's activities did not create non-discretionary duties to enforce the terms of the permit. Finally, the court decided that regulations gave the Corps discretion to determine what remedial work was appropriate and, therefore, the discretionary function exception barred any claim based on the approval of an after-the-fact permit.[54]

When a statute says a federal agency "shall" do a thing, does that mean there is no discretion? A federal court addressed the question in the context of statutes about the duty of FEMA to update its flood hazard maps. While those statutes used the word "shall," it was "conditioned on an exercise of FEMA's discretion." Updating the maps involved an element of judgment or choice and was not controlled by a mandatory statute or regulation.[55]

[ii] Discretionary Function Exception Not Applied

There are cases in which the *design or construction* of a facility has been found not to entail discretion. For example, the government constructed a drainage ditch while building an aircraft maintenance facility. A train derailed in an area abutting the ditch. The railroad company brought suit alleging that negligent design of the drainage system had caused diverted water to undermine the railroad right-of-way and resulted in the derailment. The government argued that its actions were discretionary functions. The Fifth Circuit, however, said that once the government decided to build the ditch, it was no longer exercising a discretionary policy-making function and it had to build the drainage ditch in a non-negligent manner. It held that the trial court correctly found that the government was liable for damages caused by the government's negligent design of the drainage system.[56] In another case, the Army Corps of Engineers built a dike that deflected the current of a river toward a utility line tower. The utility company determined the tower was in danger of being undermined by erosion. It expended funds to stabilize the tower and subsequently brought an action against the government to recover those costs. In the district court, the government successfully argued that the discretionary function exemption insulated it from liability. The Eleventh Circuit reversed.

---

54. Hurst v. United States, 882 F.2d 306 (8th Cir. 1989).

55. Christopherson v. Bushner, 2021 U.S. Dist. LEXIS 82593 (W.D. Mo. Apr. 29, 2021). The court also found that the challenged conduct was grounded in regulatory policy and, thus, the discretionary function exception to the immunity waiver barred claims against FEMA.

56. Seaboard Coast Line Railroad Co. v. United States, 473 F.2d 714 (5th Cir. 1973).

It noted that most cases that find a discretionary function exemption in the *design context* do so because the decision implicated policy considerations. It then held that where the Corps makes a social, economic, or political policy decision about the design of a particular project, there is no liability; however, absent a policy decision, the Corps's design decisions are subject to judicial review under state law tort standards that would normally govern an action for engineering malpractice. In the case before it, the record revealed no policy decision made by the Corps about the effect of the dike. The appellate court did allow that on remand the district court could, in its discretion, allow the government to open the record to show that its actions did in fact involve policy considerations.[57]

The Ninth Circuit drew a distinction between design and construction that illustrates the underlying rationale for the discretionary function exception to the waiver of sovereign immunity. In the case, the plaintiffs sought to recover for property damage arising out of two breaks in a main irrigation canal designed and constructed by the United States Bureau of Reclamation. The government contended that its actions in designing and constructing the canal fell within the discretionary function exception to the waiver of sovereign immunity. The court agreed and held that the discretionary function exception barred a claim based on *design* negligence. However, it also agreed that the contracting officer's discretion in deciding whether to remove unsuitable materials during construction was based not on policy judgments but on technical, scientific, and engineering considerations. The claim based on negligence in construction was, therefore, not barred by the discretionary function exception.[58]

A California federal court has allowed that negligent *operation or maintenance* might not be a discretionary function. The court refused to dismiss an action based on allegations of negligent maintenance of canals. The government argued the claim was based on the performance of, or failure to perform, a discretionary function or duty. The court responded that while the building of the canals at a certain place or in a certain way may have been discretionary, it could not agree that negligent maintenance of them was a discretionary function or duty. The court conceded that discovery could reveal that the claimed damages were the result of discretionary acts, in which case a motion by the government for summary judgment might be in order. However, on a motion to dismiss the court had to accept the allegation of the pleadings as correct, and if the plaintiff's damage did result from the negligent or wrongful act or omission of any employee of the United States in maintaining or repairing the canals, while acting in the scope of his or her office or employment,

57. Alabama Elec. Coop., Inc. v. United States, 769 F.2d 1523 (11th Cir. 1985).
58. Kennewick Irr. Dist. v. United States, 880 F.2d 1018 (9th Cir. 1989).

then the government was liable.[59] The Eighth Circuit reached the same conclusion where the Army Corps of Engineers decided not to maintain the banks of a ditch that was part of a flood control project. A landowner sued the government seeking reimbursement for permanent damage to its land by erosion it alleged was caused by the negligent construction of a flood control ditch that ran through an easement on its land. The court said that even though the corps knew the ditch would cause erosion of adjoining land, it failed to maintain the banks of the ditch in proper fashion. The omission constituted maintenance and operation and involved the most basic form of operational, ministerial conduct. Thus, the decision not to maintain the banks of the ditch was not discretionary and did not come within the protection afforded by the discretionary function exception.[60]

[c] Limited Waiver under the National Flood Insurance Act

Under the NFIA,[61] FEMA makes flood elevation determinations.[62] The NFIA provides that any appellant aggrieved by any final determination on administrative appeal may appeal that determination to the United States district court for the district within which the community is located not more than 60 days after receipt of notice of the determination.[63] This constitutes a limited waiver of sovereign immunity for flood elevation and flood zone classification determinations.[64] Challenges are limited to whether the proposed flood elevations are scientifically or technically incorrect.[65] Exhaustion of the

---

59. Desert Beach Corp. v. United States, 128 F. Supp. 581 (S.D. Cal. 1955). *But see* California v. United States, 146 F. Supp. 341 (S.D. Cal. 1956).

60. E. Ritter & Co. v. Department of Army, Corps of Engineers, 874 F.2d 1236 (8th Cir. 1989).

61. 42 U.S.C. §§ 4001, *et seq.*

62. *See* 42 U.S.C. § 4104(a).

63. 42 U.S.C. § 4104(g). *See* Hofbauer v. Northwestern Nat'l Bank, 700 F.2d 1197, 1201 (8th Cir. 1983) (under 42 U.S.C. § 4104, owners, lessees, and communities objecting to flood-hazard designation can file suit in federal court and seek redesignation); Till v. Unifirst Fed. Sav. & Loan Ass'n, 653 F.2d 152, 160 (5th Cir. 1981) (owners and lessees of property, as well as communities that feel flood hazard designation is incorrect, can appeal from administrative review to federal court for redesignation). The scope of review is as provided by the Administrative Procedures Act (APA). *See* 5 U.S.C.S. §§ 701, *et seq.* This can lead to confusion. *See* Douglas County v. Fed. Emergency Mgmt. Agency, 2011 U.S. Dist. LEXIS 28529 (D. Nev. Mar. 16, 2011) (where procedures required by NFIA conflict with those required by APA, those of NFIA must control because specific controls general, but where procedures required by NFIA and APA can coexist, § 4104(g) is best read as making them cumulative).

64. *See, e.g.*, Barrow v. FEMA, 2015 U.S. Dist. LEXIS 89355 (S.D. Ga. July 9, 2015) (where plaintiff filed suit within 60 days of receipt of FEMA's final determination notice, court had jurisdiction of plaintiff's claims under limited wavier of sovereign immunity of § 4104(g)).

65. 42 U.S.C. § 4104(b). *See, e.g.*, Robinson v. FEMA, 1987 U.S. Dist. LEXIS 3095 (D. Mass. Apr. 7, 1987); City of Biloxi v. Giuffrida, 608 F. Supp. 927, 931 (S.D. Miss. 1985). *See also* Reardon v. Krimm, 541 F. Supp. 187, 189 (D. Kan. 1982) (where plaintiff did not challenge

FEMA administrative appeal process is a prerequisite to falling within the NFIA waiver of sovereign immunity and invoking the court's subject matter jurisdiction.[66] Additionally, the 60-day period within which an appeal to the court must be made is jurisdictional.[67]

Any LOMR affecting flood elevation levels is subject to the judicial review procedures set forth in the NFIA.[68] The decision to accredit or de-accredit a levee or levee system is considered a type of flood elevation determination and could be subject to judicial review pursuant to the NFIA waiver of sovereign immunity once there is a final agency decision.[69] However, claim for failure to provide notice of a flood map change does not fall within the NFIA waiver of immunity.[70]

In an Arizona case, the plaintiff purchased property that was shown on a FEMA floodplain map as being outside of the 100-year floodplain. Because of that, the plaintiff said he did not obtain flood insurance for the property. Years later the property was submerged under several feet of water. The plaintiff alleged that FEMA owed him a duty of care in preparation of the floodplain map, that the agency was aware that he would rely on the accuracy of that map in determining whether to obtain flood insurance, and that as a result of FEMA's negligence he suffered damages. The court said that the sole basis for challenging FEMA's maps was through the NFIA and that the plaintiff had not alleged facts sufficient to bring his claim within the narrow scope of the limited waiver for flood elevation determinations. The court concluded by saying

---

flood elevations on basis of their scientific and technical accuracy at administrative level, there was no appeal at that level and action had to be dismissed for lack of jurisdiction).

66. McCrory v. Adm'r of the Fed. Emergency Mgmt. Agency of the United States Dep't of Homeland Sec., 22 F. Supp. 3d 279 (S.D.N.Y. 2014), *aff'd*, 600 Fed. Appx. 807 (2d Cir. 2015) (NFIA allows federal court challenges to FEMA's flood elevation and flood zone classification determinations; however, only those who have filed administrative appeal with FEMA and are aggrieved by agency's decision on that appeal may further appeal to federal district court). *See also* Normandy Pointe Assocs. v. FEMA, 105 F. Supp. 2d 822, 828 (S.D. Ohio 2000) (by enacting 42 U.S.C. § 4104, Congress provided limited waiver of sovereign immunity in disputes regarding FEMA floodplain determinations, and all such waivers of sovereign immunity must be strictly construed in favor of government; district courts, therefore, may review final agency actions *after* exhaustion of administrative remedies).

67. City of Trenton v. FEMA, 545 F. Supp. 13 (E.D. Mich. 1981). *See also* City of Brunswick v. United States, 1986 U.S. Dist. LEXIS 31291 (S.D. Ga. Jan. 9, 1986).

68. Coalition for a Sustainable Delta v. FEMA, 812 F. Supp. 2d 1089, 1102 (E.D. Cal. 2011). *See also* Great Rivers Habitat Alliance v. FEMA, 615 F.3d 985, 989 (8th Cir. 2010) (revising Flood Insurance Rate Map to move land from one flood zone to another is functionally identical to adjusting base flood elevation and is flood elevation determination); Kmart Corp. v. Kroger Co., 2012 U.S. Dist. LEXIS 80218 (N.D. Miss. June 11, 2012).

69. City of Alexandria v. Fed. Emergency Mgmt. Agency, 781 F. Supp. 2d 340, 349 (W.D. La. 2011).

70. LCP W. Monroe, L.L.C. v. United States, 2018 U.S. Dist. LEXIS 117318 (W.D. La. May 7, 2018).

that "[t]he act of designating flood plains is wholly related to flood control" and that the facts of the case before it "fit squarely within the activities from which Congress intended to immunize the government."[71] The mention of "flood control" would seem to refer to the Flood Control Act immunity.

FEMA hires contractors to assist in flood mapping. Courts have said that under the doctrine of "obstacle preemption," which applies when state law is an obstacle to the accomplishment and execution of the full purposes and objectives of Congress, these contractors are immune from suit. The doctrine applies to statutory and state tort claims alleging violation of a common law duty. For example, FEMA hired a company as an independent contractor to provide engineering services to assist in a remapping effort. A property owner contended that the hydraulic model provided by that company, which was used to determine flood elevations, was flawed and inaccurate. As a result, the property owner alleged, a large part of its property was designated as being in a floodway, which preventing it from being developed. It sued the contractor. The court dismissed the claim under the doctrine of "obstacle preemption." It held that state law causes of action against FEMA independent contractors would undermine the primary purposes of the National Flood Insurance Act and that additionally those causes of action would undermine the "limited appeals process"[72] Congress provided in the Act.[73] The immunity apparently does not extend to companies providing flood certifications.[74]

[4] Takings or Inverse Condemnation

Under the Fifth Amendment to the United States Constitution, private property may not be taken for public use without just compensation. Actions brought under that proscription are generally called "takings claims," but they are also referred to as claims for "inverse condemnation." It should be understood at the outset that the law surrounding takings is extensive, complex, and little known. When a claim is brought, the government attorneys will almost certainly have comprehensive knowledge of takings jurisprudence, including of defenses that are not encountered in ordinary litigation. The private attorney who has a general civil trial practice cannot hope to match that knowledge. He or she should, therefore, either refer the case to an attorney with the requisite knowledge and experience or, in the case of a multi-count complaint,

---

71. Weitzman v. Pima Cty., 2009 U.S. Dist. LEXIS 141003 (D. Ariz. Aug. 6, 2009).

72. *See* 42 U.S.C. § 4104.

73. Columbia Venture, LLC v. Dewberry & Davis, LLC, 604 F.3d 824 (4th Cir. 2010). *See also* Christopherson v. Bushner, 2021 U.S. Dist. LEXIS 82593 (W.D. Mo. Apr. 29, 2021) (applying obstacle preemption to claim against FEMA general contractor who created allegedly erroneous floodplain maps).

74. *See, e.g.*, Harris v. Nationwide Mut. Fire Ins. Co., 2018 U.S. Dist. LEXIS 78214 (M.D. Tenn. May 8, 2018).

seek co-counsel to handle the takings count. That being said, as one expert has pointed out, "Takings law is important for landowners affected by flood control projects because there is no remedy in tort for their damages . . . [and thus] takings claims appear to be the only avenue for relief when government inversely, rather than expressly, condemns property it uses implementing flood control projects."[75]

Takings law is a discrete field of practice. There are treatises solely on the topic.[76] There are many scholarly journal articles discussing it in general[77] and in the context of flooding.[78] Because takings jurisprudence is so specialized and because so much has been written about it, the treatment here will be limited to the examination a few key cases.

It is important to distinguish between torts and takings, a difference explained in a number of articles.[79] The significance of the difference, as one commentary points out, is that an action that is a tort claim, for example, negligence of the government, cannot be brought in the Court of Federal Claims and federal immunity may require dismissal regardless of the venue.[80]

---

75. Greathouse, *Flood Control Takings Litigation from an Owner's Perspective*, at 1 (2013), *available at* https://ppgmrlaw.com/uploads/pages/Julie%20Greathouse%20CLE%20presentation%20-%20Takings%20after%20AGFC.pdf.

76. *See* Martinez, *Government Takings* (Thomson West 2021); Eagle, *Regulatory Takings* (5th ed. LexisNexis 2020).

77. *See* Zellmer, *Takings, Torts, and Background Principles*, 52 Wake Forest L. Rev. 193 (2017); Rosenthal, *A Theory of Governmental Damages Liability: Torts, Constitutional Torts, and Takings*, 9 U. Pa. J. Const. L. 797 (2007). *See also* Treanor, *The Original Understanding of the Takings Clause* (1998), *available at* https://scholarship.law.georgetown.edu/facpub/1048/.

78. *See, e.g.*, Heise, *Floods, Fires, and Inverse Condemnation*, 29 N.Y.U. Envtl. L.J. 1 (2021) (examining application of doctrine of inverse condemnation to flood damage to private property caused by public improvement); Shapiro, *The Flooding of Eagle Lake: But-For Causation and the Doctrine of Relative Benefits in Flood-Based Fifth Amendment Cases*, 34 Tul. Envtl. L.J. 1 (2021); Pippin & Moroz, *But Flooding Is Different: Takings Liability for Flooding in the Era of Climate Change*, 50 ELR 10920 (2020); Wallace, *When (and Why) the Levee Breaks: A Suggested Causation Framework for Takings Claims That Arise from Government-Induced Flooding*, 61 Wm. & Mary L. Rev. 603 (2019); Spellerberg, *St. Bernard Parish Government v. United States: Post-Katrina Flooding Revisited through a Takings Claim*, 32 Tul. Envtl. L.J. 119 (2018); Dana, *Incentivizing Municipalities to Adapt to Climate Change: Takings Liability and FEMA Reform as Possible Solutions*, 43 B.C. Envtl. Aff. L. Rev. 281 (2016); Abrams & Bertelsen, *Downstream Inundations Caused by Federal Flood Control Dam Operations in a Changing Climate: Getting the Proper Mix of Takings, Tort, and Compensation*, 19 U. Denv. Water L. Rev. 1 (2015); Schaefer, *Reining in Sovereign Immunity to Compensate Hurricane Katrina Victims*, 40 Ecology L.Q. 411 (2013).

79. *See, e.g.*, Zellmer, *Takings, Torts, and Background Principles*, 52 Wake Forest L. Rev. 193 (2017); Abrams & Bertelsen, *Downstream Inundations Caused by Federal Flood Control Dam Operations in a Changing Climate: Getting the Proper Mix of Takings, Tort, and Compensation*, 19 U. Denv. Water L. Rev. 1 (2015); Rosenthal, *A Theory of Governmental Damages Liability: Torts, Constitutional Torts, and Takings*, 9 U. Pa. J. Const. L. 797 (2007).

80. Zellmer, *Takings, Torts, and Background Principles*, 52 Wake Forest L. Rev. 193, 194 (2017).

One of the most important recent cases on takings and flooding is a decision by the United States Supreme Court in *Ark. Game & Fish Comm'n v. United States.*[81] In that case, the Arkansas Game and Fish Commission owned forest land that was periodically flooded when the Army Corps of Engineers released water from behind a dam. The repeated flooding damaged or destroyed more than 18 million board feet of the Commission's timber and disrupted the ordinary use and enjoyment of its property, for which it sought compensation from the United States pursuant to the Fifth Amendment. Justice Ginsburg, writing for a unanimous court, said that "recurrent floodings, even if of finite duration, are not categorically exempt from Takings Clause liability."[82] She noted that the Court had first ruled that government-induced flooding can constitute a taking 140 years earlier[83] and had subsequently ruled that seasonally recurring flooding could constitute a taking for which the federal government could be liable.[84] The court did not establish a bright line test but noted that time *could* be a factor and that the Court had previously ruled there was no liability where the damage caused by government action could not have been foreseen.[85] On remand, the Federal Circuit affirmed the decision of the Court of Federal Claims that found a taking had occurred.[86]

When the federal government engages in flood control, it is not required to be perfect. In a 1939 decision by Justice Black the United States Supreme Court said:

> An undertaking by the Government to reduce the menace from flood damages which were inevitable but for the Government's work does not constitute the Government a taker of all lands not fully and wholly protected. When undertaking to safeguard a large area from existing flood hazards, the Government does not owe compensation under the Fifth Amendment to every landowner which it fails to or cannot protect. In the very nature of things the degree of flood protection to be afforded must vary.[87]

---

81. Ark. Game & Fish Comm'n v. United States, 133 S. Ct. 511, 568 U.S. 23, 184 L. Ed. 2d 417, (2012). *See generally* Pippin & Moroz, *But Flooding Is Different: Takings Liability for Flooding in the Era of Climate Change*, 50 ELR 10920 (2020); Abrams & Bertelsen, *Downstream Inundations Caused by Federal Flood Control Dam Operations in a Changing Climate: Getting the Proper Mix of Takings, Tort, and Compensation*, 19 U. Denv. Water L. Rev. 1 (2015).

82. *See generally* Lee, *Draining the Serbonian Bog: Originalism and the Need for Temporary Takings by Floodwaters*, 37 S. Ill. U. L. J. 169 (2012).

83. *See* Pumpelly v. Green Bay Co., 80 U.S. 166, 13 Wall. 166, 20 L. Ed. 557 (1872).

84. *See* United States v. Cress, 243 U.S. 316, 37 S. Ct. 380, 61 L. Ed. 746 (1917).

85. *See* John Horstmann Co. v. United States, 257 U.S. 138, 146, 42 S. Ct. 58, 66 L. Ed. 171 (1921).

86. Ark. Game & Fish Comm'n v. United States, 736 F.3d 1364 (Fed. Cir. 2013).

87. United States v. Sponenbarger, 308 U.S. 256, 265, 60 S. Ct. 225, 228, 84 L. Ed. 230, 237 (1939).

In other words, "when the government undertakes efforts to mitigate against flooding, but fails to provide perfect flood control, it does not then become liable for a compensable taking because its mitigative efforts failed."[88]

Not all takings/flood cases involve flood control projects. For example, the federal government built a Postal Service facility in West Virginia with associated parking lots and driveways. The facility was adjacent to, and uphill from, the largest shopping center and mixed-use commercial development in the state. The shopping center experienced a significant increase in stormwater runoff and was compelled to construct flood control structures to prevent damage to its property. The corporate owner of the shopping center brought an action against the government claiming that the additional water flow caused by the development of the postal facility constituted a taking of a flowage easement entitling it to compensation. The appellate court held that the plaintiff's property did not need to suffer an effectual destruction or a permanent and exclusive occupation by government runoff for a taking claim based on a flowage easement. However, whether there was a compensable taking depended on whether the loss could properly be analyzed under takings law as opposed to tort law, and then on whether the plaintiff had a protectable property interest under state property law that had been violated by government action. The court added that if there were a taking, damages could be assessed based on the cost of constructing "prudent flood control measures."[89]

There is some disagreement over whether a single flood can be the basis of a takings claim or whether the government gets "one free flood." While the latter is thought to be the case,[90] some courts have left the door open for a claim based on a single flood.[91]

---

88. *In re* Downstream Addicks & Barker (Tex.) Flood-Control Reservoirs, 147 Fed. Cl. 566, 582 (2020). In *Downstream Addicks & Barker*, a claim under the Fifth Amendment was brought by Texas property owners to recover for losses they suffered from flooding after Hurricane Harvey. The plaintiffs argued that their property was only inundated after the Army Corps of Engineers opened reservoir gates to prevent additional upstream flooding. The court characterized the plaintiffs' claims as an assertion "that they were entitled to perfect flood control, simply because government set up a flood control system." It held that neither Texas nor federal law creates a protected property interest in perfect flood control in the face of an act of God.

89. Ridge Line, Inc. v. United States, 346 F.3d 1346 (Fed. Cir. 2003). *See generally* Davis, *Strengthening the Floodwalls: Reinterpreting the Federal Circuit's Ridge Line Test to Limit Government Liability in Takings Jurisprudence*, 26 Fed. Cir. B.J. 29 (2016).

90. *See* Big Oak Farms, Inc. v. United States, 105 Fed. Cl. 48 (2012) (where claim is based on single flood that has since receded, plaintiffs have not stated takings claim). *See also* Sher, *A Recipe for Disaster: How Plaintiffs Seeking Compensation for Takings Following Natural Disasters Are Unfairly Burdened*, 93 Tul. L. Rev. 419 (2018) ("one flood free rule" has never been expressly overturned).

91. *See* St. Bernard Par. Gov't v. United States, 121 Fed. Cl. 687, 739 (2016), *rev'd on other grounds*, 887 F.3d 1354 (Fed. Cir. 2018) (temporary taking may arise from one occasion of flooding); Quebedeaux v. United States, 112 Fed. Cl. 317 (2013) (refusing to adopt bright-line rule that would require dismissal of complaint simply because it cites only single recent flooding event).

One potentially emerging inverse condemnation claim is for actions and inaction by governments in the face of climate change. For example, if rising coastal sea levels submerge private property and the government fails to act to prevent that submersion, is there a taking? That is a question beyond the scope of the discussion here, but it is receiving scholarly attention.[92]

There is an important jurisdictional consideration for takings claims because they emanate from the Constitution. Federal district courts have original jurisdiction, concurrent with the United States Court of Federal Claims, of any civil action or claim against the United States *not exceeding $10,000* in amount, founded on the Constitution.[93] The United States Court of Federal Claims has jurisdiction to render judgment on any claim against the United States founded on the Constitution *regardless of the amount at issue*.[94]

14.3 State Governments

[1] Generally

Although state governments enjoy immunity from suit, almost all of them have waived that immunity to some extent. The practitioner, therefore, needs to know the parameters of immunity in the state where suit is to be brought. He or she also has to determine what causes of action can be brought under any waiver of immunity and how the state interprets that cause of action in flood cases.

[2] Sovereign Immunity

The Eleventh Amendment to the United States Constitution says, "The judicial power of the United States shall not be construed to extend to any suit in law or equity, commenced or prosecuted against one of the United States

92. *See* Rosenberg, *Condemn (the) Nation: Holding the United States Accountable through Inverse Condemnation Claims for Its Role in Bringing About—and Then Failing to Mitigate and Adapt to Certain Effects of—Climate Change*, 26 Buff. Envtl. L.J. 85 (2018) (arguing that while federal government should not be insurer of last resort for every natural disaster, it should be liable for just compensation when it has caused, through both its actions in promoting climate change and failing to adapt to particular climate change effects, physical invasion of plaintiff's private properly). *See also* Flynn, *Climate Change, Takings, and Armstrong*, 46 Ecology L.Q. 671 (2019); Lovett, *Moving to Higher Ground: Protecting and Relocating Communities in Response to Climate Change*, 42 Vt. L. Rev. 25 (2017); Serkin, *Passive Takings: The State's Affirmative Duty to Protect Property*, 113 Mich. L. Rev. 345 (2014); Kusler, *Government Liability and Climate Change: Selected Legal Issues Related to Flood Hazards* (2014), *available at* https://biotech.law.lsu.edu/blog/government_liability_and_climate_change_kusler.pdf; Ruppert & Grimm, *Drowning in Place: Local Government Costs and Liabilities for Flooding Due to Sea-Level Rise*, 87 Fla. Bar J. 29 (2013) (discussing whether courts should require local governments to upgrade drainage systems to address rising sea levels).

93. 28 U.S.C. § 1346(a)(2).

94. 28 U.S.C. § 1491(a)(1).

by citizens of another state, or by citizens or subjects of any foreign state." The United States Supreme Court added that the states, absent consent, are immune from suits brought against them by their own citizens or by federal corporations, although those suits are not within the explicit prohibitions of the amendment.[95] Subsequently, the court reiterated that states retain immunity from private suit in their own courts. It said that it had

> sometimes referred to the States' immunity from suit as "Eleventh Amendment immunity." The phrase is convenient shorthand but something of a misnomer, for the sovereign immunity of the States neither derives from nor is limited by the terms of the Eleventh Amendment. Rather, as the Constitution's structure, and its history, and the authoritative interpretations by this Court make clear, the States' immunity from suit is a fundamental aspect of the sovereignty which the States enjoyed before the ratification of the Constitution, and which they retain today (either literally or by virtue of their admission into the Union upon an equal footing with the other States) except as altered by the plan of the Convention or certain constitutional Amendments.[96]

[3] Waiver of Immunity

The majority of states have waived sovereign immunity.[97] The waiver may be found in the state constitution. For example, the Illinois Constitution states that "Except as the General Assembly may provide by law, sovereign immunity in this State is abolished."[98] In other states, for example, Florida[99] and California,[100] the state constitution creates legislative authority for the waiver of sovereign immunity.

The waiver of immunity may be found in a statute. For example, by statute New York "waives its immunity from liability" and consents to have its liability determined in accordance with the same rules of law as applied to actions

95. Principality of Monaco v. Mississippi, 292 U.S. 313, 54 S. Ct. 745, 78 L. Ed. 1282 (1934). *See, e.g.*, Steadfast Ins. Co. v. Agric. Ins. Co., 507 F.3d 1250 (10th Cir. 2007) (where Grand River Dam Authority was sued for damages related to a series of flood incidents, court found it was state agency entitled to Eleventh Amendment immunity).

96. Alden v. Me., 527 U.S. 706, 713, 119 S. Ct. 2240, 2246–47, 144 L. Ed. 2d 636, 652 (1999). *See generally* Berger, *The Collision of the Takings and State Sovereign Immunity Doctrines*, 63 Wash & Lee L. Rev. 493 (2006).

97. *But see* Ala. Const. art. I, § 14 ("the State of Alabama shall never be made a defendant in any court of law or equity"). *See also* Nance v. Matthews, 622 So. 2d 297, 299–300 (Ala. 1993) (state of Alabama and its agencies possess absolute immunity from suit). State officials can, however, be sued in certain cases. *See Ex parte* Ala. DOT, 978 So. 2d 17 (2007).

98. Ill. Const. art. XIII, § 4.

99. Fla. Const. art. X, § 13 ("Provision may be made by general law for bringing suit against the state as to all liabilities now existing or hereafter originating.").

100. Cal. Const. art. III, § 5 ("Suits may be brought against the state in such manner and in such courts as shall be directed by law.").

against individuals or corporations.[101] One then has to refer to case law to determine the extent of the waiver.[102] Texas, on the other hand, has a statute that says that sovereign immunity to suit is waived and abolished to the extent of liability created by the Texas Tort Claims Act,[103] of which it is a part.[104]

The statutes governing waiver of state immunity from suit vary greatly. Before bringing an action against a state government for a flood loss, one has to examine them carefully for specific provisions that may limit the waiver of immunity. These limitations may include

- A discretionary function exception,[105]
- A failure to supervise exception,[106]
- A limitation on liability for failure to discharge a statutory duty,[107]
- A cap on the amount of damages the state must pay if found liable,[108]

---

101. N.Y. Court of Claims Act § 8. *See also* N.Y. Canal Law § 120 (requiring payment to persons sustaining damages from canals or from their use or management, or resulting or arising from neglect or conduct of any officer of state having charge of canals, or resulting or arising from any accident, or other matter or thing connected with canals).

102. For example, the New York Court of Appeals long ago decided that "[w]herever duties of a judicial nature are imposed upon a public officer, the due execution of which depends upon his own judgment, he is exempt from all responsibility by action, for the motives which influence him, and the manner in which such duties are performed." Rochester White Lead Co. v. Rochester, 3 N.Y. 463, 466 (1850). That remains the law in New York today. *See, e.g.*, Mehta v. New York City Dep't of Consumer Affairs, 162 A.D.2d 236, 556 N.Y.S.2d 601 (1990) (withholding of license, even if erroneous, is discretionary exercise of governmental function, and thus immune from liability for money damages).

103. Tex. Civil Practice and Remedies Code Ann. §§ 101.001, *et seq.*

104. Tex. Civ. Prac. & Rem. Code § 101.025(a).

105. *See, e.g.*, Cal. Gov. Code § 820.2 (public employee is not liable for injury resulting from act or omission where that act or omission was result of exercise of discretion vested in that employee, whether or not such discretion be abused); Tex. Civil Practice and Remedies Code Ann. § 101.056 (Texas Tort Claims Act does not apply to claim based on failure of governmental unit to perform act that it is not required by law to perform or decision not to perform act or failure to make decision on performance or non-performance of act if law leaves performance or non-performance to discretion of governmental unit).

106. 745 ILCS 10/3-108(a) (neither local public entity nor public employee who undertakes to supervise activity on or use of any public property is liable for injury unless local public entity or public employee is guilty of willful and wanton conduct in its supervision proximately causing that injury).

107. *See, e.g.*, Cal. Gov. Code § 815.6 (where public entity is under mandatory duty imposed by enactment designed to protect against risk of particular kind of injury, it is liable for injury of that kind proximately caused by its failure to discharge that duty unless it establishes that it exercised reasonable diligence to discharge that duty).

108. *See, e.g.*, Fla. Stat. Ann. § 768.28(5)(a) (neither state nor its agencies or subdivisions shall be liable to pay claim or judgment by any one person that exceeds $200,000 or any claim or judgment, or portions thereof, which, when totaled with all other claims or judgments paid by state or its agencies or subdivisions arising out of same incident or occurrence, exceeds $300,000); Tex. Civ. Prac. & Rem. Code § 101.023(a) (liability of state government is limited to money damages in maximum amount of $250,000 for each person and $500,000 for each single occurrence for bodily injury or death and $100,000 for each single occurrence for injury to or destruction of property).

- A proscription on state liability for punitive damages,[109]
- A limitation on attorney's fees,[110]
- A specific limitations period within which an action has to be brought,[111] and
- A bar on liability for injury caused by misrepresentation by an employee.[112]

In addition to general tort claims statutes, state law may grant immunity to states in particular circumstances. For example, the state of Florida and its Water Management Districts are immunized from liability for damages caused, *inter alia*, by partial or total failure of any stormwater management system, dam, impoundment, reservoir, or appurtenant work.[113]

A number of states have statutes granting immunity from liability for an injury caused by a condition of unimproved public property.[114] The purpose of these statutes is to promote use of public property in its natural condition, without concerns for the financial burden of maintaining it in a safe condition and defending lawsuits.[115] Unimproved land cases almost always concern personal injury, not property damage by flooding. Could the unimproved land immunity protect against liability from damages when governmental negligence related to a natural stream or water body results in flooding? It would appear not. In several cases, trees on government property fell onto adjacent property and courts concluded the natural condition immunity was

109. *See, e.g.*, Cal. Gov. Code § 818 (public entities are not liable for damages awarded under statute governing exemplary or punitive damages or for other damages imposed primarily for sake of example and by way of punishing defendant).

110. *See, e.g.*, Fla. Stat. Ann. § 768.28(8) (no attorney may charge, demand, receive, or collect, for services rendered, fees in excess of 25 percent of any judgment or settlement).

111. The limitation may apply broadly. *See, e.g.*, Fla. Stat. Ann. § 768.28(14) (every claim against state or one of its agencies or subdivisions for damages for negligent or wrongful act or omission forever barred unless civil action is commenced by filing complaint in court of appropriate jurisdiction within four years after claim accrues). A limitation might also be very specific. *See, e.g.*, Ill. Ann. Stat. ch. 745, 15/2 (no civil action shall be commenced against any county engineer or superintendent of highways by any person for any injury to his or her person or property resulting from failure to perform or negligence in performing any official duty and which injury arises out of use of highways, culverts, bridges, or shoulders unless it is commenced within one year after cause of action accrue).

112. *See, e.g.*, Cal. Gov. Code § 818.8 (public entities are not liable for injury caused by misrepresentation by employee of that public entity, whether or not such misrepresentation be negligent or intentional).

113. Fla. Stat. § 373.443.

114. *See, e.g.*, N.J. Stat. § 59:4-8; Cal. Gov. Code § 831.2. The New Jersey and California statutes add "including but not limited to any natural condition of any lake, stream, bay, river or beach." Others make no mention of streams or bodies of water. *See, e.g.*, Kan. Stat. Ann. § 75-6104(p) (governmental entity shall not be liable for damages resulting from natural condition of any unimproved public property of that governmental entity).

115. Rynard, *Insurance and Risk Management for State and Local Governments*, § 16.07[3] (Matthew Bender & Co. 2021).

inapplicable to injuries caused to nonusers of the government property who were on adjacent property.[116]

There may be procedural and jurisdictional requirements under state law that affect the ability of an injured party to bring a claim against the state. For example, before bringing an action, a party may be required to present the claim in writing to the appropriate agency and receive a denial.[117] A state may also grant exclusive jurisdiction to a specific court. For example, under Illinois law its Court of Claims has exclusive jurisdiction to hear and determine all "claims against the State for damages in cases sounding in tort, if a like cause of action would lie against a private person or corporation in a civil suit."[118] Venue may also be an issue when the defendant is a state agency. For example, property owners sued the State of Washington Department of Natural Resources claiming that their property, in a relatively rural area, was damaged by flooding that was caused by the agency's poor forestry practices. The suit was brought in the county where Seattle is located, presumably because the agency had an office there. However, by statute, actions for injury to real property have to be filed in the county where the property is located. The court of appeals held the statute was jurisdictional, and the lower court therefore properly dismissed the action. Fortunately for the plaintiffs, the state's highest court disagreed. It said the statute at issue stated a venue requirement and that when an action for injuries to real property is commenced in an improper county, the result should be a change of venue to the county in which the real property is located.[119] While the plaintiffs ultimately had their day in court, the failure of their counsel to determine the proper venue made their path to trial unnecessarily long and expensive.

[4] Tort Claims for Flood Losses

[a] Generally

This subsection includes cases discussing state government liability for flood losses. The decisions do not present a comprehensive analysis of the law. Rather, they are illustrative. That is necessary because significant variables that determine outcomes differ from state to state. The two most important

---

116. Milligan v. City of Laguna Beach, 34 Cal. 3d 829, 196 Cal. Rptr. 38, 670 P.2d 1121 (1983). *See also* Belton v. Forest Pres. Dist., 347 Ill. Dec. 931, 407 Ill. App. 3d 409, 943 N.E.2d 221 (2011); Bany v. Borough of Haworth, 267 N.J. Super. 591, 632 A.2d 535 (1993).

117. *See, e.g.*, Fla. Stat. Ann. § 768.28(6)(a) (action may not be instituted on claim against state or one of its agencies or subdivisions unless claimant presents it in writing to appropriate agency, and also, except as to any claim against municipality, county, or Florida Space Authority, presents claim in writing to Department of Financial Services, within three years after claim accrues and Department of Financial Services or appropriate agency denies claim in writing).

118. Ill. Ann. Stat. ch. 705, § 505/8(d).

119. Ralph v. Dep't of Nat. Res., 182 Wn. 2d 242, 343 P.3d 342 (2014).

variables are the duty of care imposed and the extent of any immunity from the consequences of a breach of that duty. The cases considered in this subsection will allow the practitioner to issue spot. Beyond that, one has to carefully examine the law of the jurisdiction in which suit is brought.

[b] Pertinent Tort Law Principles

[i] Strict Liability

Under the Restatement of Torts, "[o]ne who carries on an abnormally dangerous activity is subject to liability for harm to the person, land or chattels of another resulting from the activity, although he has exercised the utmost care to prevent the harm."[120] The Reporter's Notes say that typical abnormally dangerous activities would include water collected in quantity in an unsuitable or dangerous place. The Restatement sets forth six factors to be considered in determining whether an activity is abnormally dangerous.[121] A comment to the factors says that while collection of large quantities of water in irrigation ditches or a reservoir in open country is usually not an abnormal danger, if a reservoir is constructed on a bluff overhanging a large city or if water is collected in an enormous standing tank above that city, there is abnormal danger and, therefore, strict liability when, without any negligence, the water escapes and does harm.[122] Under the Restatement, there is strict liability for one carrying on an abnormally dangerous activity even though the resulting injury is caused by an "unexpectable" operation of a force of nature.[123] On the other hand, the Restatement says the rules about strict liability for abnormally dangerous activities do not apply if the activity is carried on in pursuit of a public duty imposed on the actor as a public officer or employee.[124] While the doctrine of strict liability in tort is widely accepted, it is rarely applied to flooding or water damage cases. For example, most courts reject its application to

---

120. Restatement (Second) of Torts, § 519(1). The Restatement also says that "[t]his strict liability is limited to the kind of harm, the possibility of which makes the activity abnormally dangerous." Restatement (Second) of Torts, § 519(2).

121. The factors are a high degree of risk of some harm to the person, land, or chattels of others; likelihood the resulting harm will be great; the inability to eliminate the risk by exercise of reasonable care; the extent to which the activity is not a matter of common usage; the inappropriateness of the activity to the place where it is carried on; and the extent to which its value to the community is outweighed by its dangerous attributes. Restatement (Second) of Torts, § 520. *See also In re* Chicago Flood Litig., 223 Ill. Dec. 532, 176 Ill. 2d 179, 680 N.E.2d 265 (1997), where the court, after considering the factors of § 520, found that pile driving and maintenance of a tunnel that flooded because of pile driving were not abnormally dangerous or ultrahazardous activities.

122. Restatement (Second) of Torts, § 520, comment on clause (d).

123. Restatement (Second) of Torts, § 522(c).

124. Restatement (Second) of Torts, § 521. *Consider* Magnolia 8 Props., LLC v. City of Maple Plain, 893 N.W.2d 658, 668 (Minn. App. 2017) (discretionary-acts exception to municipality liability is absolute and bars all tort claims, including strict-liability claims, when municipality demonstrates that its conduct involved planning-level decisions).

broken water main cases.[125] However, the Iowa Supreme Court has said that if a local government intentionally leaves water mains underground beyond inspection and maintenance until a break occurs, they become "inherently dangerous" and likely to damage neighboring property and the government can be strictly liable.[126]

[ii] Duty Regarding Surface Water

Liability for *surface water* that a defendant causes to enter and damage a plaintiff's property depends on the drainage law doctrine adopted in a particular state. Unfortunately, there are not sharply defined majority and minority rules. As one commentary observes, the law of surface waters is cumbersome and antiquated and "simply confusing to attorneys, clients, and courts."[127] The earliest doctrine to emerge in American courts is called the "common enemy" rule. The Supreme Judicial Court of Maine described the rule in 1877. It said "it is well established that any proprietor of land may control the flow of mere surface water over his own premises, according to his own wants and interests, without obligation to any proprietor either above or below."[128] The common enemy rule produced some disturbing results in response to which courts adopted a number of exceptions and limitations, for example, imposing a duty of due care.[129] Many jurisdictions have rejected the common enemy rule entirely and in its stead adopted the "reasonable use" rule. Under that rule, as explained by the Missouri Supreme Court, "[l]iability arises when the defendant's conduct is either (1) intentional and unreasonable; or (2) negligent, reckless, or in the course of an abnormally dangerous activity."[130] The court cautioned that the rule does not "purport to lay down any specific

125. Quigley v. United States, 865 F. Supp. 2d 685, 695–96 (D. Md. 2012) (predicting Maryland would side with majority of courts that have concluded that maintenance of public water mains is not an abnormally dangerous activity, but acknowledging that there could be certain rare situations in which burst water main would warrant application of strict liability); Summit Hill Associates v. Knoxville Utilities Bd., 667 S.W.2d 91 (Tenn. App. 1983) (refusing to apply doctrine of strict liability to ruptured water mains); John T. Arnold Assoc., Inc. v. Wichita, 5 Kan. App. 2d 301, 318, 615 P.2d 814, 824 (1980) (operation of municipal water system under the facts of case did not constitute abnormally dangerous activity). *See generally* Jones, *Strict Liability for Hazardous Enterprise*, 92 Colum. L. Rev. 1705, 1733 (1992) (with rare exceptions, American courts have refused to apply strict liability to municipal water supply, requiring proof of negligence in case of broken water mains and burst pipes).

126. Lubin v. Iowa City, 257 Iowa 383, 391, 131 N.W.2d 765, 770 (1964).

127. Fraley, *Water, Water, Everywhere: Surface Water Liability*, 5 Mich. J. Envtl. & Admin. L. 73, 76 (2015).

128. Morrison v. Bucksport & Bangor R.R. Co., 67 Me. 353, 355 (1877).

129. See Gerrard, *Environmental Law Practice Guide* § 21.02[1][c] (Matthew Bender 2021) for an overview of the "modified common enemy" rule. *See also* Elliott, *Diffused Surface Water in Wyoming: Ascertaining Property Owners' Rights and Settling Disputes*, 11 Wyo. L. Rev. 409, 414–15 (2011).

130. Heins Implement Co. v. Missouri Highway & Transp. Comm'n, 859 S.W.2d 681, 689 (Mo. 1993).

rights or privileges" but "leaves each case to be determined on its own facts, in accordance with general principles of fairness and common sense." To further confuse matters, regardless of the rule applied in a given jurisdiction, it applies to "diffuse surface water," a phrase that has to be defined in order to apply the rule. One commentary says that:

> Diffuse surface waters are those waters snow and rain normally create. Diffuse waters, which follow no definite course, are those waters which are lost by evaporation, by percolation, or by reaching a substantial body of water or a defined watercourse into which they flow. Additionally, diffuse surface waters are defined as those waters which do not flow in a defined bed, bank, or channel, but seem to wash over the face of the property with no permanent source. Thus, diffuse surface waters may not include waters which are contained within a defined lake, pond, or watercourse.[131]

That description is widely accepted by courts.[132] However, courts may say that water can lose its status as surface water if it is directed into a human-made trench or drainage system. For example, in a South Carolina case, the state Department of Transportation built a new underground stormwater drainage system when it widened and improved a road. However, before the installation was completed, the insured property was damaged when there was a heavy downpour and rainwater exited the incomplete drainage system. The court held that the water was surface water before it was collected in the stormwater system, but once it was deliberately contained, concentrated, and cast onto an adjoining property, it was no longer naturally flowing, diffuse water and lacked the identifiable characteristics of surface water. The court added that the water would not become surface water again after it was discharged from a pipe or collection system.[133]

As can be seen, determining the potential liability of a defendant is dependent on a number of factors. First, what surface water rule applies in the jurisdiction where suit is brought? Second, how do the courts in that state interpret and apply the rule? Third, how do those courts define "diffuse surface water"? Finally, as the Missouri Supreme Court observed, "general principles of fairness and common sense" applied to the particular facts of the case play a role. This discussion cannot explore these factors in depth. Fortunately, there

---

131. Whitmer, *Common Enemy or Unilateral Threat: Why Jurisdictions Need to Become Reasonable in Regards to Diffuse Surface Waters*, 41 Creighton L. Rev. 423, 424 (2008).

132. See § 2.01[4], *supra*.

133. M & M Corp. v. Auto-Owners Ins. Co., 390 S.C. 255, 701 S.E.2d 33 (S.C. 2010) (water spewing in unnatural concentration from stormwater drainage system lacks identifiable characteristics of surface water; naturally falling water that has been intentionally concentrated and cast on insured's property is not surface water for purposes of policy).

are some well-respected treatises on the subject.[134] There are also some state-specific treatises.[135]

[iii] Doctrine of Res Ipsa Loquitur

Res ipsa loquitur is a Latin phrase meaning "the thing speaks for itself."[136] In tort law, it is a doctrine under which a plaintiff can create a rebuttable presumption of negligence by the defendant.[137] The plaintiff has to show that (1) the instrumentality was under the control or management of the defendant; (2) the circumstances, according to common knowledge and experience, created a clear inference that the accident would not have happened if the defendant had not been negligent; and (3) the plaintiff's injury must have resulted from that accident.[138] As one court said, the doctrine means that "the circumstances involved in or connected with an accident are of such an unusual character as to justify, in the absence of any other evidence bearing upon the subject, the inference that the accident was due to the negligence of the one having possession or control of the article or thing which caused the injury."[139] The doctrine creates an *inference of negligence* that the trier of fact, on hearing all the evidence, may or may not choose to accept.[140] When the presumption applies, it falls to the defendant to prove affirmatively that he or she was *not* negligent.[141]

While not often raised in flood-damage cases against state governments, it has been successfully invoked. For example, the Illinois State Department of Agriculture rehabilitated a sewer system on property it owned by separating the sanitary and storm sewers. To accomplish that, diversionary facilities that connected the sanitary sewers and storm sewers and permitted heavy flows in one to be shunted into the other were disconnected. The disconnection of

134. *See* Beck & Kelley, *Waters and Water Rights* (Matthew Bender, 2021); Tarlock & Robison, *Law of Water Rights and Resources* (Clark Boardman Callaghan, 2021).

135. *See, e.g.*, Slater, *California Water Law and Policy* (Matthew Bender, 2021); Brown, Bryan & McElyea, *Montana Water Law* (Rocky Mtn. Mineral Law Found. 2021); Ciliberto & Zilis, *Colorado Water Law Benchbook* (CBA-CLE 2019).

136. *Ballentine's Law Dictionary*, 3rd ed.

137. *Res Ipsa Loquitur*, Legal Information Institute, https://www.law.cornell.edu/wex/res_ipsa_loquitur.

138. *Ballentine's Law Dictionary*, 3rd ed. *See generally* Heckel & Harper, *Effect of the Doctrine of Res Ipsa Loquitur*, 22 Ill. L. Rev. 724 (1928).

139. Hurd v. State, 187 Misc. 662, 666, 64 N.Y.S.2d 896, 899 (1946). *See also* John T. Arnold Assoc., Inc. v. Wichita, 5 Kan. App. 2d 301, 615 P.2d 814 (1980) (court could not say from evidence presented that water main would not have broken except for act of negligence on part of defendant city); Wilkinson v. State, 42 Utah 483, 490, 134 P. 626, 629 (1913) (stating in *dicta* that ditch owner is only liable when break or escape of water occurs if owner was negligent and negligence is not presumed under doctrine of *res ipsa loquitur* from mere fact that break or escape occurred).

140. Maroules v. Jumbo, Inc., 452 F.3d 639, 643 (7th Cir. 2006).

141. Lewis v. Wolk, 312 Ky. 536, 539, 228 S.W.2d 432, 434 (1950).

one of the diversionary facilities caused sanitary sewers to become overloaded during heavy rainfalls and discharge the excess water through a sanitary manhole onto a nearby property that previously had never flooded. The owners of that property sued the state for damages suffered in two floods about a week apart. The court found that application of the doctrine of *res ipsa loquitur* was appropriate because the flooding that caused the damage was from property solely in the possession and control of the state and had not occurred prior to alteration of the particular diversionary facility. It was, said the court, appropriate to infer negligence on the part of the state in the design or construction of the sewer improvements. Further finding that the state failed to rebut the *prima facie* inference of negligence raised by application of the doctrine, the court decided the plaintiffs were entitled to receive an award of damages.[142]

In a New York case, the state would customarily discharge water from a canal by lifting gates, allowing the water to flow into a stream that eventually traversed a farm with an orchard of cherry trees. The owner of the farm contended that in early March the state opened the gates and discharged an excessive amount of water into the stream, which was frozen. The water discharged on the frozen surface of the stream overflowed its banks and poured onto the farm property, destroying 95 trees. A week later it was found that some of the gates were still open and the canal was nearly empty. Prior to the flooding of the farm, the canal had not been drained of water and the farm had flooded only once. The state argued that the property owner has not established that the water that overflowed the farm came from its canal. The court, however, agreed with the farm owner that the case was made by application of the doctrine of *res ipsa loquitur*. The canal and its gates were in the custody, and possession, and under the exclusive control of the state, which had exclusive knowledge of the care exercised in its control and management. Further, said the court, the evidence showed that the overflow of the stream would not ordinarily have happened without the neglect of some duty. Sufficient evidence had, therefore, been produced to justify an inference of negligence and to shift the burden of explanation to the state. Because the evidence offered by the land owner was sufficient, uncontradicted, and unexplained, the court found the state is liable in damages.[143]

142. Bennett v. State, 38 Ill. Ct. Cl. 185 (1986).

143. Hurd v. State, 187 Misc. 662, 64 N.Y.S.2d 896 (1946). The court said that the flooding might have been avoided by the exercise of proper care. It noted that the water in the canal was carelessly allowed to rise to an abnormal height before any of the gates were opened, and that the gates were then opened, not gradually, but all at once, allowing sudden and unnecessarily large volumes of water into the channel of the stream, thus unnecessarily and negligently causing the stream to overflow its banks.

[iv] Public Duty Doctrine

The public duty doctrine is a principle of tort law under which, "[t]o establish a duty in tort against a governmental entity, a plaintiff must show that the duty breached was owed to an individual and was not a general obligation owed to the public."[144] The doctrine applies in negligence and nuisance actions.[145] Some states no longer recognize the doctrine,[146] but most do. In some cases, the rule is codified by statute.[147] Many states also limit the doctrine by the "special relationship" exception.[148] Under that exception, if a plaintiff is able to show that a special relationship existed between him or her and the defendant, application of the public-duty doctrine can be avoided.[149]

[c] Road Construction and Maintenance

Road construction can alter the path of surface water and increase its volume. In a Louisiana case, property owners brought action against the state and its Department of Transportation. The plaintiffs alleged that road construction caused flooding and damage to their property. The appellate court found ample evidence in the record to support the trial court's conclusion that erection of the road by the defendant violated the natural servitude of drainage, and the obstruction caused by a bridge and its embankment was the cause of the flooding of the properties of the plaintiffs.[150] The trial court awarded the plaintiffs nearly $92 million; however, the case serves to illustrate one of the pitfalls in litigation against states: the judgment has not been paid because of limitations on state law judgments.[151]

Failure to properly maintain roads may also result in flooding. For example, in a case before the Hawaii Supreme Court, a drainage culvert that ran under a state highway was often clogged and during a heavy rain, water that

144. Norg v. City of Seattle, 18 Wn. App. 2d 399, 404, 491 P.3d 237, 240 (2021).

145. Bruns, *Resetting the Public-Duty Doctrine: Where Does the Duty Come From?*, 69 Drake L. Rev. 201, 205 (2021).

146. *See, e.g.*, Coleman v. East Joliet Fire Prot. Dist. (*In re* Estate of Coleman), 399 Ill. Dec. 422, 46 N.E.3d 741 (2016) (abandoning public duty rule). *See also* Commercial Carrier Corp. v. Indian River County, 371 So. 2d 1010, 1015 (Fla. 1979) (public duty doctrine does not survive enactment of Tort Claims Act).

147. *See, e.g.*, Carleton v. Town of Framingham, 418 Mass. 623, 627, 640 N.E.2d 452, 455 (1994) (tort claims law amended to adopt what is in effect statutory public duty rule providing governmental immunity after court announced intent to abandon application of its common law public duty rule).

148. *See generally* McMillan, *Government Liability and the Public Duty Doctrine*, 32 Vill. L. Rev. 505, 509–20 (1987).

149. Bruns, *Resetting the Public-Duty Doctrine: Where Does the Duty Come From?*, 69 Drake L. Rev. 201, 206 (2021).

150. Boudreaux v. State, 780 So. 2d 1163 (La. App. 2001).

151. Pace, *Unaware, Unprepared, and Unexpectedly Flooded: Improving Louisiana's Capacity to Respond to Flood Hazards*, 6 LSU J. Energy L. & Resources 121, 140 (2017).

backed up because of the clogged culvert flooded a home. The homeowner sued the state. The court refused to apply the discretionary function exception to the state's waiver of immunity because maintenance of highway culverts is an everyday governmental operation undertaken to protect highways from drainage waters and, therefore not a discretionary function. The court also took the opportunity to adopt the reasonable use rule and hold that a possessor of land may interfere with the natural flow of surface water for the development of his land as long as that interference is not unreasonable under the circumstances of the particular case. In the case before it, the court said the state had knowledge of the specific risk and from the facts, it could not say that the trial court erred in finding that the circumstances required more than a periodic inspection of the particular culvert. The state was, therefore, liable for the damage to the plaintiff's home.[152]

[d] Failure to Make Improvements

Flooding can result from the failure of the state to improve an existing structure. Generally, a government is not required to upgrade a flood control system to provide additional protection.[153] For example, in a Hawaii case, the warehouses of a business were inundated by flood waters when a stream overflowed its banks and allegedly caused substantial damage. The stream flowed beneath a road where a bridge crossed the stream. A number of years after the bridge was constructed, the state contracted for a hydraulic design report that recommended that the bridge be reconstructed and elevated to allow passage of a larger amount of flood waters. That improvement was not made. The plaintiffs contended that when the stream overflowed, the bridge acted as a dam, causing the flood waters to back up, flood over the freeway, and rush down at great velocity through its property. The plaintiff claimed the state was negligent in failing to reconstruct or improve the bridge. The court found that reconstruction or replacement of the bridge would require evaluation of broad policy factors. The decision not to make the improvements was, therefore, discretionary and immune from judicial review.[154]

A California court reached a different conclusion where the failure of a flood control project was due to an unreasonable plan. The state had a levee built with porous, uncompacted mining debris, in a location that encouraged seepage, leading directly to the failure of that levee, which was part of a larger flood control project. The state had never tested the levee, or reviewed the records of its construction, to see if it was as strong as assumed, and the state

---

152. Rodrigues v. State, 52 Haw. 156, 472 P.2d 509 (1970).

153. Paterno v. State of California, 113 Cal. App. 4th 998, 1003, 6 Cal. Rptr. 3d 854, 857 (2003) (public entity cannot be held liable for failing to upgrade flood control system to provide additional protection).

154. Julius Rothschild & Co. v. State, 66 Haw. 76, 80, 655 P.2d 877, 881 (1982).

even ignored specific warnings about the levee's weaknesses. The court found an unreasonable state plan resulted in the failure of the levee. Therefore, the plaintiff's damages were directly caused by the unreasonable plan, and the state was liable to pay for the plaintiff's damages.[155]

[e] Flood Forecast

In a California case, a business owner called the State Department of Water Resources to ask about the anticipated height of a flooding river. The river rose 5 feet higher than the agency said it would. The business owner took precautions based on the information he was given by the agency, and he suffered damage to his property. He sued claiming, *inter alia*, negligence by the agency in the dissemination of inaccurate river height forecasts. The state argued first that a recipient of a weather forecast cannot, as a reasonable person, rely on its accuracy because it is common knowledge that weather forecasts are not statements of fact. Second, the agency contended that its forecasts were for the benefit of the public generally, and the plaintiff could not claim a duty owed him and, thus, could not claim a breach of a duty. The trial court agreed and dismissed the action. The appellate court, however, rejected both arguments and reversed. The court said that the plaintiff was not alleging negligence merely because the forecast turned out to be wrong. Rather, he pleaded specific acts of negligence in the gathering and evaluating of known facts. For example, he alleged the agency had a duty be informed about river heights and that there was a breakdown in the operation of the office and its river depth measuring stations. As to the agency's "public benefit" argument, the court noted that the plaintiff himself called the agency and "identified himself as a businessman with a great deal at stake in a proper estimate in the river height." He suffered damages when he relied on the information he received in that telephone call and was not in the "realm of an amorphous public receiving general information."[156]

[5] Takings or Inverse Condemnation

Under the Fifth Amendment to the United States Constitution, private property cannot be taken for public use without just compensation. That proscription is made applicable to the states by the Fourteenth Amendment. Additionally, virtually every state constitution contains a "takings" clause.[157] An action can be brought under the federal or state constitution, or both.

155. Paterno v. State of California, 113 Cal. App. 4th 998, 6 Cal. Rptr. 3d 854 (2003).

156. Connelly v. State, 3 Cal. App. 3d 744, 84 Cal. Rptr. 257 (1970).

157. *See generally* Saxer, *Paying for Disasters*, 68 U. Kan. L. Rev. 413, 431–41 (2020), for a discussion of state takings jurisprudence and flooding.

The language in some state constitutions is quite similar to the Fifth Amendment, but with differences that should be noted. The exact wording in the federal Constitution is "nor shall private property be taken for public use, without just compensation." The comparable clause in the Pennsylvania Constitution reads "nor shall private property be taken or applied to public use, without authority of law and without just compensation being first made or secured."[158] The language in the Wisconsin Constitution is terse: "The property of no person shall be taken for public use without just compensation therefor."[159] Maryland has four sections in its constitution that address takings. There is one that specifically addresses three counties and the city of Baltimore, another concerning highways, and two more sections that are about acquisition of property in two counties by the Washington Suburban Sanitary Commission.[160]

The majority of state constitutions preclude not only taking property for public use without compensation but also *damaging* or *injuring* property for public use, a prohibition not found in the Fifth Amendment. For example, the California Constitution says that "Private property may be taken or damaged for a public use and only when just compensation, ascertained by a jury unless waived, has first been paid to, or into court for, the owner."[161] Under the Georgia Constitution, "private property shall not be taken or damaged for public purposes without just and adequate compensation being first paid."[162] These "damagings" clauses have received little attention from state courts, but one commentary says that they were intended to address harm "where nothing has been taken or regulated, but landowners are nonetheless unfairly burdened by a project for public benefit."[163]

The takings clauses in state constitutions may contain other provisions of which a practitioner should be aware. The meaning of "just compensation" is defined in some state constitutions. Oklahoma defines it as the value of the property taken and any injury to any part of the property not taken.[164] In Virginia it means no less than the value of the property taken, lost profits, and lost access, as well as damages to the residue caused by the taking.[165] In Michigan, if the property is an individual's principal residence, the amount of compensation may not be less than 125 percent of that property's fair market value, in addition to any other reimbursement allowed by law.[166] In several

158. Pa. Const. art. I, § 10
159. Wis. Const. art. I, § 13
160. Md. Const. art. III, §§ 40–40D.
161. Cal. Const. art. I, § 19(a).
162. Ga. Const. art. 1, § 3, para. 1
163. Brady, *The Damagings Clauses*, 104 Va. L. Rev. 341, 345–46 (2018).
164. Okla. Const. art. II, § 24.
165. Va. Const. art. I, § 11.
166. Mich. Const. art. 10, § 2.

states the takings clauses say that the question of whether the use is "public" is for the courts, not the legislature.[167]

In addition to carefully reviewing the state constitution before bringing a takings claim based on it, counsel also needs to examine the interpretive case law. The need for that review is demonstrated by some illustrative cases. The Virginia Supreme Court held that a *single occurrence* of flooding allegedly caused by straightening and relocation of a stream when the state Department of Transportation constructed a road could support an inverse condemnation claim.[168] A Florida appellate court, on the other hand, said that construction by the state that causes flooding on abutting private property may constitute a taking where the flooding is a *permanent invasion* of land amounting to an appropriation.[169] The courts in some states say that a claim can be brought against a government for its inaction that results in a taking,[170] while others require an affirmative act.[171] This dichotomy is especially important when a taking is alleged to be the result of a government's response, or lack of one, to the effect of climate change, for example, rising sea levels in waterfront communities.[172]

---

167. The exact language typically used is: "Whenever an attempt is made to take private property for a use alleged to be public, the question whether the contemplated use be really public shall be a judicial question, and determined as such without regard to any legislative assertion that the use is public." *See, e.g.*, Ariz. Const. art. 2, § 17; Colo. Const. art. II, § 15. The constitution in Washington state includes that language and adds that "the taking of private property by the state for land reclamation and settlement purposes is hereby declared to be for public use." Wash. Const. art. I, § 16.

168. Livingston v. Va. DOT, 284 Va. 140, 726 S.E.2d 264 (2012).

169. Kendry v. State Road Dep't, 213 So. 2d 23 (Fla. 4th DCA 1968). The court acknowledged that this rule is easier to state than to apply and said the problem of application involves a determination of what constitutes permanent flooding and an appropriation of property as distinguished from damage to property.

170. *See, e.g.*, Litz v. Md. Dep't of the Env't, 446 Md. 254, 267, 131 A.3d 923, 931 (2016) (inverse condemnation claim is pleaded adequately where plaintiff alleges taking caused by failure to act in face of affirmative duty to do so).

171. *See, e.g.*, Hawkins v. City of Greenville, 594 S.E.2d 557, 358 S.C. 280 (Ct. App. 2004) (inverse condemnation claim has to be proved by "affirmative, positive, aggressive" acts by government and allegations of mere failure to act are insufficient). *See generally* Saxer, *Paying for Disasters*, 68 U. Kan. L. Rev. 413, 440–41 (2020); Mulvaney, *Non-Enforcement Takings*, 59 B.C. L. Rev. 145 (2018).

172. *See* Jones et al., *Roads to Nowhere in Four States: State and Local Governments in the Atlantic Southeast Facing Sea-Level Rise*, 44 Colum. J. Envtl. L. 67 (2019) (regarding takings jurisprudence when governments abandon roads because of flooding); Herzog & Hecht, *Combatting Sea Level Rise in Southern California: How Local Governments Can Seize Adaptation Opportunities while Minimizing Legal Risk*, 19 Hastings W.-N.W. J. Env. L. & Pol'y 463, 479–82 (2013) (concerning takings challenges to adaptation strategies implemented to address rising sea levels); Wilkins, *Is Sea Level Rise "Foreseeable"? Does It Matter?*, 26 J. Land Use & Envtl. Law 437 (2011) (discussing state taking jurisprudence and suggesting that governments could be held accountable for failure to control development or to issue strong warnings regarding risky development in hazardous areas).

A property owner in Washington state was denied a permit by the state to re-channel the bed of a creek running through his property. Subsequently, the creek overflowed and damaged his property, and he claimed denial of the permit was the proximate cause of substantial damage to his property. The Washington Supreme Court found his inverse condemnation claim was properly denied because there was no *permanent infringement* preventing the original use of the land nor any total appropriation, the flooding was due to a "force majeure," no action by the state caused the flooding, and there was no project, public improvement, or actual public use.[173] Finally, the California Supreme Court held that when a flood control levee fails to retain waters within its design capacity, plaintiff property owners who suffer damage from the resultant flooding are not entitled to recover absent proof of *unreasonable* conduct.[174]

14.4 Local Governments

[1] Generally

The discussion in this section is not intended to be a comprehensive analysis of the potential liability of local governments for flood losses. That would require a separate multi-volume treatise. Instead, this discussion highlights the two principal variables the practitioner faces in bringing suit: governmental immunity and state court construction of pertinent causes of action. Cases and statutes are cited to identify issues that may arise. In each instance the attorney has to research to determine the law of his or her jurisdiction.

[2] Sovereign Immunity

The Eleventh Amendment sovereign immunity extends to states but not local governments.[175] On the other hand, if the state would have to pay for damages out of its own treasury, immunity would apply.[176] Thus, to determine the extent of a local government's liability, one must look to state law.

For example, in Florida, the state's tort claims statute waives immunity for the state, its agencies, and its subdivisions and defines "state agencies or

173. Rains v. Washington Dep't of Fisheries, 89 Wn. 2d 740, 575 P.2d 1057 (Wash. 1978).

174. Belair v. Riverside County Flood Control Dist., 253 Cal. Rptr. 693, 694, 47 Cal. 3d 550, 554, 764 P.2d 1070, 1071 (1988).

175. *See, e.g.*, Northern Ins. Co. v. Chatham County, 547 U.S. 189, 193, 126 S. Ct. 1689, 1693, 164 L. Ed. 2d 367, 373 (2006) (only states and arms of states possess immunity from suits authorized by federal law and, therefore, Court has repeatedly refused to extend sovereign immunity to counties); Jinks v. Richland County, 538 U.S. 456, 466, 123 S. Ct. 1667, 1673, 155 L. Ed. 2d 631, 642 (2003) ("municipalities, unlike States, do not enjoy a constitutionally protected immunity from suit").

176. Hess v. Port Auth. Trans-Hudson Corp., 115 S. Ct. 394, 404, 513 U.S. 30, 47, 130 L. Ed. 2d 245, 260 (1994).

subdivisions" to include counties and municipalities.[177] Under Texas law, a municipality is liable for damages arising from its governmental functions including, significantly, street construction and design, bridge construction and maintenance and street maintenance, sanitary and storm sewers, waterworks, dams and reservoirs, engineering functions, and water and sewer service.[178] Liability of a municipality is, however, limited to money damages in a maximum amount of $100,000 for each single occurrence for injury to or destruction of property.[179] An Iowa statute excepts from the waiver of immunity claims based on or arising out of an act or omission of a municipality in connection with an emergency response.[180] In New York, the state has waived its immunity from liability,[181] and the New York Court of Appeals held decades ago that because the civil divisions of the state—counties, cities, towns, and villages—have no independent sovereignty, the waiver applies to them.[182] More recently, the court said that even if a plaintiff establishes the elements of a negligence claim, a governmental defendant "engaging in a governmental function can avoid liability if it timely raises the defense and proves that the alleged negligent act or omission involved the exercise of discretionary authority."[183] As these examples demonstrate, determining the extent of local government liability requires a careful examination of state law.

[3] Tort Claims for Flood Losses

[a] Generally

Whether a local government can be held liable in tort varies from state to state partly dependent on the extent of any waiver of immunity, but also on the substantive tort law of a given jurisdiction. For example, when a local government operates a water or sanitary sewer system, the extent of its liability for flooding caused by that system initially depends on whether the function is considered governmental or proprietary, which in turn usually determines immunity from suit. Liability for surface water that a defendant causes to enter and damage a plaintiff's property depends on the drainage law doctrine adopted in a particular state.[184] In each case a practitioner contemplates bringing against a local government, the particular law on immunity and tort liability has to be determined.

---

177. Fla. Stat. § 768.28(2).
178. Tex. Civ. Prac. & Rem. Code §§ 101.0215(a)(3), (4), (9), (11), (19), (30), & (32).
179. Tex. Civ. Prac. & Rem. Code § 101.023(c).
180. Iowa Code § 670.4(1)(k).
181. N.Y. Court of Claims Act § 8.
182. Bernardine v. New York, 294 N.Y. 361, 365, 62 N.E.2d 604, 605 (1945).
183. Valdez v. City of New York, 936 N.Y.S.2d 587, 593, 18 N.Y.3d 69, 76, 960 N.E.2d 356, 362 (2011).
184. See § 14.03[4][b], *supra*.

[b] Negligent Design

State law typically insulates local governments from liability for negligence in the design of projects in either their original construction or any improvements where the design has been approved by a body exercising discretionary authority.[185] Even where there is no explicit statutory statement of immunity, design decisions are often considered to be a discretionary function because the construction of public improvements usually involves policy choices and, therefore, there is immunity.[186] Thus, immunity applies to the decision of whether to construct a public improvement and the discretion exercised with respect to its design.[187] A distinction, however, is generally made between the immunity granted in the designing and planning of a project, for example, a drainage district intended to prevent flooding, and the liability imposed where injury is caused because an improper mode, means, or method was used to carry the plan into execution.[188] In other words, immunity may not extend to negligent failure to construct a public project according to its design.[189] A public project may be adequate to meet its objective when built, but changed circumstance may render it inadequate. Thus, a local government that has notice that a project no longer functions as designed may be liable for failure to remedy the defect.[190] There might, however, be a specific statutory ban on such a claim.[191]

---

185. *See, e.g.*, Cal. Gov. Code § 830.6; N.J. Rev. Stat. § 59:4-6. Some statutes may specifically include construction in the grant of immunity. *See* Iowa Code 670.4(1)(h).

186. Rynard, *Insurance and Risk Management for State and Local Governments*, § 16.06[2][a] (Matthew Bender & Co. 2021).

187. E. B. Metal & Rubber Industries, Inc. v. County of Washington, 479 N.Y.S.2d 794, 796, 102 A.D.2d 599, 601–02 (1984) (town would be entitled to immunity in its lawful exercise of sovereign power in planning and design of dike).

188. Office Park Corp. v. County of Onondaga, 409 N.Y.S.2d 854, 858, 64 A.D.2d 252, 258–59 (1978).

189. *See, e.g.*, Mozzetti v. City of Brisbane, 67 Cal. App. 3d 565, 573, 136 Cal. Rptr. 751, 755 (1977) (public entity may still be liable if damage is unrelated to design, for example, it results from improper construction).

190. F. Koehnen, Ltd. v. Hawaii County, 47 Haw. 329, 388 P.2d 214 (1963) (liability for failure to replace inadequate drains constructed over 35 years earlier when local government learned that drains could not adequately handle surface flow during very heavy rains that could be expected to occur every few years in that locality).

191. *See, e.g.*, Cal. Gov. Code § 830.6 (notwithstanding notice that constructed or improved public property may no longer be in conformity with a plan or design, immunity continues for reasonable period of time sufficient to permit public entity to obtain funds for, and to carry out, remedial work and if public entity is unable to remedy such public property because of practical impossibility or lack of sufficient funds, immunity remains so long as such public entity reasonably attempts to provide adequate warnings of condition not conforming to approved plan or design); Iowa Code 670.4(1)(h) (claim shall not be allowed for failure to upgrade, improve, or alter any aspect of existing public improvement or other public facility to new, changed, or altered design standards).

Both plaintiffs and defendant governments should be aware of requirements imposed by statute. For example, under California law, a government seeking design immunity must prove approval of the design in advance of construction by a legislative body or officer exercising discretionary authority, the reasonableness of that design, and a causal relationship between the plan or design and the flood damage. Failure to prove any of those three elements is fatal to the immunity defense.[192] Pursuant to an Iowa statute, there is immunity from liability for a claim based on negligent design or negligent construction or reconstruction of a public improvement that was constructed or reconstructed in accordance with a "generally recognized" engineering or safety standard, criteria, or design theory in existence at the time of the construction or reconstruction.[193] The Iowa Supreme Court has said that it is the plaintiff's burden to establish that the government did not construct or reconstruct the improvement in accordance with those standards.[194]

[c] Lack of Maintenance or Inspection

Generally, there is no immunity for failure to properly maintain public property.[195] However, the Connecticut Supreme Court has held that absent a legal directive prescribing the specific manner in which a government is required to maintain and repair its storm sewer system, that government is immune from liability because the maintenance of storm drains and drainage systems is a discretionary function.[196]

Maintenance is defined as activity required to preserve the property as it was originally designed and constructed and that has to be performed in a prescribed manner that does not require evaluation of broad policy factors.[197] The mere fact that a public facility fails to perform as expected is not proof of negligent maintenance. For example, the Alabama Supreme Court said that a blockage in a drainage system does not necessarily mean negligent maintenance, as it

---

192. Mozzetti v. City of Brisbane, 67 Cal. App. 3d 565, 574, 136 Cal. Rptr. 751, 756 (1977).

193. Iowa Code 670.4(1)(h).

194. Fischer v. City of Sioux City, 695 N.W.2d 31 (Iowa 2005). In *Fischer*, the basements of several homeowners flooded after an unusually heavy rainstorm resulted in excess surface water. The homeowners sued, alleging the city was negligent in connection with its storm-drainage system. The court agreed that substantial evidence supported the finding of the trial court that detention ponds maintained the storm-drainage system in accordance with a generally recognized engineering standard requiring the system to be able to handle a ten-year storm without flooding. Thus, the city was immune from liability.

195. Rynard, *Insurance and Risk Management for State and Local Governments*, § 16.06[2][c] (Matthew Bender & Co. 2021). *See, e.g.*, Rooney v. City of Phila., 623 F. Supp. 2d 644 (E.D. Pa. 2009) (liability attaches if plaintiff can prove damages resulted from negligence of local government in maintenance of sewer system).

196. Northrup v. Witkowski, 332 Conn. 158, 210 A.3d 29 (2019).

197. Rynard, *Insurance and Risk Management for State and Local Governments*, § 16.06[2][c] (Matthew Bender & Co. 2021).

could occur from the sudden and unforeseeable deposit of some foreign object or material as well as from gradual accumulation of foreseeable debris that prudent maintenance could prevent.[198]

The practitioner contemplating an action for failure to maintain a public project should determine if there are any maintenance standards that may have been violated. For example, under a Minnesota statute, after a drainage system has been constructed, it has to be maintained and repairs necessary to make the system efficient have to be made and open drainage ditches have to be inspected at least every five years when no violation of the law requiring that ditches be planted with perennial vegetation has been found and annually when a violation has been found, until one year after the violation is corrected.[199] A county had a policy under which it would maintain and repair its drainage systems only at the request of an owner of property benefited by that system. A home near one of the county's drainage ditches flooded, and the homeowner sued. The county claimed immunity, asserting it exercised its discretion in adopting its maintenance and repair policy. The court, citing the statute, said the county had no discretion to enact that policy. The county was required by state law to inspect the ditch on a regular basis, and because its policy flouted its statutory duties, its use of the policy did not afford it statutory immunity for exercise of a discretionary function.[200]

Even though a local government may have no maintenance duty, it can assume one. For example, in an Alabama case, a city periodically cleaned out a drainage ditch. It then stopped doing so, after which the ditch became clogged with junk people dumped into it. A home bordering the ditch was flooded. It had never flooded when the city maintained the ditch. The city denied liability for the flood damage. However, the court said that while the city was under no duty originally to keep the ditch free from obstructions, if it subsequently maintained it, the city became liable for damages to adjoining property owners if it negligently failed to keep the ditch reasonably free from obstructions.[201]

A Florida case may have implications for maintenance of public structures that affect flooding. The court held that a county had a duty to reasonably maintain a road as long as it was a public road dedicated to the public use, but not to maintain it in a particular manner or at a particular level of accessibility. The county would, said the court, have to provide a reasonable level of maintenance that affords meaningful access, unless or until it formally abandoned the road.[202] Moreover, the court held that governmental inaction in the face

198. Locke v. City of Mobile, 851 So. 2d 446, 450 (Ala. 2002) (if flooding resulted from some sudden and unforeseeable deposit, issue of negligence would depend on, among other factors, whether or not city had notice of that particular deposit).

199. Minn. Stat. § 103E.705, subd. 1.

200. Blaine v. City of Sartell, 865 N.W.2d 723 (Minn. App. 2015).

201. Prichard v. Lasner, 406 So. 2d 990 (Ala. App. 1981).

202. Jordan v. St. Johns County, 63 So. 3d 835, 839 (Fla. 5th DCA 2011).

of an affirmative duty to act could support a claim for inverse condemnation. One commentary in response to the holding asserts that were courts to determine that local governments have to maintain a "level of service" for drainage rather than maintain existing infrastructure itself, local governments could face legal liability in the form of either an inverse condemnation claim or a tort claim.[203] That could mean that in communities experiencing rising sea levels, local governments would have to improve public facilities to address changing flood threats.[204]

[d] Flood Control and Water Control Structures

Local governments may maintain any number of water or flood control structures including dams, levees, canals, drainage ditches, culverts, and storm drains. The failure of these structures can lead to liability for a local government.[205]

The doctrine of strict liability in tort is occasionally applied to flooding caused by water control structures.[206] For example, in a Minnesota case decided a century ago, a large water main leading from a reservoir broke, allowing a great amount of water to escape and damage the plaintiff's property. The court said that "If a break occurs in the reservoir itself, or in the principal mains, the flood may utterly ruin an individual financially." In that case, said the court, even though negligence is absent, natural justice would seem to demand that the whole community, which benefited by the enterprise, should stand the loss rather than the individual.[207] More recently, an Arizona appellate court said negligence was immaterial where flooding was caused by a canal extension.[208] However, strict liability does not mean there are no possible defenses. In the case of flooding, weather conditions may make a loss an "act of God."[209]

---

203. Ruppert & Grimm, *Drowning in Place: Local Government Costs and Liabilities for Flooding Due to Sea-Level Rise*, 87 Fla. Bar J. 29 (2013).

204. *But see* Paterno v. State of California, 113 Cal. App. 4th 998, 1003, 6 Cal. Rptr. 3d 854, 857 (2003) (public entity cannot be held liable for failing to upgrade flood control system to provide additional protection).

205. *See generally* Thomas, *Liability for Water Control Structure Failure Due to Flooding* (2006), *available at* https://s3-us-west-2.amazonaws.com/asfpm-library/Legal/NAI_Liability_Failure_Facilities_2006.pdf.

206. *But see* Hughes v. King County, 42 Wn. App. 776, 714 P.2d 316 (1986) (refusing application of strict liability).

207. Bridgeman-Russell Co. v. City of Duluth, 158 Minn. 509, 511, 197 N.W. 971, 972 (1924).

208. Green Reservoir Flood Control Dist. v. Willmoth, 15 Ariz. App. 406, 489 P.2d 69 (1971) (canal extension was cause of flooding and resulting damages; while jury found negligence in flood control project was proximate cause of damages, negligence was immaterial because flooded premises were not subject to any easement for flow of water).

209. Smith v. Chippewa County Road Comm'rs, 5 Mich. App. 370, 146 N.W.2d 702 (1966), *aff'd*, 381 Mich. 363, 161 N.W.2d 561 (1968) (where plaintiff claimed defendant, by its

Strict liability is the exception, More commonly, actions for damages caused by failure of a water control facility are brought as negligence claims. Local government liability then depends on whether the government breached a duty owed to the plaintiff and whether the government is immune from suit. Generally, the government has no duty to anticipate an "unusual and catastrophic" flood.[210] There is also generally no duty to upgrade a flood control system to provide additional protection.[211] Local governments also do not generally have a duty to immediately implement specific recommendations of a drainage study. For example, in a Minnesota case, a city commissioned an engineer to review all drainage areas of the city and recommend improvements for the entire drainage system. The lengthy completed report was intended to provide a guide for improvement of the drainage system as needed over an extended period. The report identified a number of potential problem areas, including a holding pond that was identified as important, but not necessarily as a first priority. Several years later the report's recommendations had not been implemented and during an extremely heavy rain storm, that holding pond overflowed and the flood waters damaged a home. The homeowner sued the city for negligence, and the trial and appellate courts sided with the plaintiff. The Minnesota Supreme Court reversed. It said that imposition of liability usurped the city's discretion to decide how or when to act to implement any part of the engineer's report. Notice of inadequacy was not converted into an absolute duty to implement one suggested improvement without properly considering the context of the city's decision or the need to determine which of the many other suggested improvements should be given priority. The court concluded that mere acceptance of the report should not be held to have imposed a duty to act at once to correct every inadequacy identified by it. Receipt of the report alone was an insufficient basis for liability.[212]

The doctrine of *res ipsa loquitur* might apply and permit an inference of negligence from the circumstances of the injury.[213] However, the doctrine

---

actions in repairing road, created artificial reservoir and defendant was absolutely liable for any damages inflicted by escaped water trespassing on plaintiff's land, defense of act of God—hard torrential rains—was valid defense). *See generally* Faure, Jing & Wibisana, *Industrial Accidents, Natural Disasters and "Act of God,"* 43 Ga. J. Int'l & Comp. L. 383 (2015), explaining that while nature may cause a disaster, the scope of the damage can be exacerbated by human mistakes, for example, constructing residences in a floodplain or failing to take preventive measures to minimize harm.

210. Jacoby v. Gillette, 62 Wyo. 487, 174 P.2d 505 (1947). In *Jacoby*, a warm chinook wind accelerated the melting of a large amount of snow. An unprecedented flood of water poured down the city's canal and damaged the plaintiff's property. The court found the city did not breach any duty.

211. Paterno v. State of California, 113 Cal. App. 4th 998, 1003, 6 Cal. Rptr. 3d 854, 857 (2003) (public entity cannot be held liable for failing to upgrade flood control system to provide additional protection).

212. Chabot v. Sauk Rapids, 422 N.W.2d 708 (Minn. 1988).

213. See § 14.03[4][b][iii], *supra*, for a discussion of the doctrine of *res ipsa loquitur*.

generally does not apply unless the government has exclusive control of the instrumentality of the injury.[214]

A state statute may provide that flood control is a governmental function for which there is immunity.[215] However, not every flood control activity may come within that proscription. For example, heavy rains, together with the already saturated ground, contributed to the infiltration of groundwater and stormwater into a city's sewer system, which then backed up and damaged the plaintiff's property. The court found an immunity statute did not apply because normal operation of a sewer system did not constitute "flood control measures," even if one effect of that operation was to reduce the likelihood of flooding.[216]

In an Iowa Supreme Court case, a city had decided not to sandbag or otherwise close a railroad opening in a river levee just prior to a flood and the court said that was an operational decision and not an exercise of a discretionary function. Therefore, the city was not necessarily immune from liability if it were found that it breached a duty to the plaintiff whose property was damaged.[217] However, under Iowa law there was an "emergency response" exception to the general waiver of immunity and the court said it could not say as a matter of law that the city was acting in response to an emergency when it decided not to close the opening in the levee.

Even though an act or omission may be "operational," a government may be immune from liability under state law. In a case before the Texas Supreme Court, the plaintiff brought a claim for flood damage against a city for its failure to maintain culverts clear of debris that might interfere with the flow of water. The court said that while Texas common law classified operation and maintenance of storm sewers as proprietary functions for which a municipality could be sued, under the state's Tort Claims Act as it had been amended, operation of storm sewers had been reclassified as a governmental function for which the city was immune.[218] A state statute can yield the opposite result. For example, in Pennsylvania a statute provides that a local government can be liable for a dangerous condition in a sewer system that it owns provided the claimant establishes that the dangerous condition created a reasonably foreseeable risk of the kind of injury that occurred and that the government had actual notice or could reasonably be charged with it.[219] A storm drainage

---

214. *See, e.g.*, Hughes v. King County, 42 Wn. App. 776, 714 P.2d 316 (1986) (refusing to apply doctrine where no finding suggested county had any control over private drainage system that was located downstream of damaged property and that contained "bottleneck" causing flooding).

215. *See, e.g.*, Ohio Rev. Code 2744.01(C)(2)(r).

216. Inland Prods. v. City of Columbus, 193 Ohio App. 3d 740, 954 N.E.2d 141 (2011).

217. Keystone Elec. Mfg. Co. v. City of Des Moines, 586 N.W.2d 340 (Iowa 1998).

218. City of Tyler v. Likes, 962 S.W.2d 489 (Tex. 1997).

219. 42 Pa. Cons. Stat. § 8542(b)(5).

system in a Pennsylvania community overflowed into the basement of a home. Stormwater had previously flooded the home's basement many times because the sewers were filled with dirt and mud and, although the city had been asked repeatedly to correct the problem, it only responded once by removing large quantities of dirt from the sewer. The court said the statute applied to both sanitary and stormwater sewers and that in the case before it sufficient competent evidence established liability. It pointed to testimony the system had caused street flooding and basement backups in the past and that the city had been notified of the recurring problem and responded only once and had then removed a significant amount of dirt from the system. That was sufficient, said the court, to establish both notice and reasonably foreseeable risk, as required by the statute.[220]

Sometimes a government constructs a water control structure in response to a specifically expected flood. That structure may save some properties from flooding but cause others to suffer damage. Generally, under what is known as the *public necessity doctrine*, the government may take protective measures without liability to those damaged.[221]

A local government might be liable for damage to the plaintiff's water control structure. For instance, a large retail store in New York City had an easement for a storm drainpipe that ran to the main storm sewer. While working on an unrelated project, the city cut the pipe, after which the store began to experience flooding when it would rain heavily. The store brought actions for, *inter alia*, negligence and trespass. The negligence action was dismissed as untimely, but the trespass action went forward. The court said that having established a timely claim of trespass on and interference with its easement, the store "should be allowed to recover for the cost of bringing that trespass to an end and restoring the functionality of the easement."[222]

[e] Water and Sanitary Sewer Systems

[i] Proprietary Functions

It is not uncommon for cities to operate municipal water and sanitary sewer systems. Typically, these systems generate revenues for the government, are in essence a business, and are distinguished from the legislative function of

220. Washington v. Johns, 81 Pa. Commw. 601, 474 A.2d 1199 (1984). *See also* McCarthy v. City of Bethlehem, 962 A.2d 1276 (Pa. Commw. 2008).

221. *See* McKell v. Spanish Fork City, 6 Utah 2d 92, 305 P.2d 1097 (1957) (no liability where, in response to unprecedented runoff and flooding of mountain streams, city raised dyke on existing gravel road, causing greater flooding on plaintiff's property than otherwise would have occurred). *See generally* Craig, *Adapting Water Law to Public Necessity: Reframing Climate Change Adaptation as Emergency Response and Preparedness*, 11 Vt. J. Envtl. L. 709, 738–43 (2010) (explaining public necessity doctrine in detail and citing many cases involving flooding).

222. Bloomingdales, Inc. v. New York City Tr. Auth., 52 A.D.3d 120, 859 N.Y.S.2d 22 (2008).

the government.[223] As the Eighth Circuit has said, "A city has two classes of powers, the one legislative or governmental, by virtue of which it controls its people as their sovereign, the other proprietary or business, by means of which it acts and contracts for the private advantage of the inhabitants of the city and of the city itself."[224] Thus, courts generally hold that sewage treatment[225] and supplying water[226] are proprietary functions.[227] In some statutes a statute may classify water and sewer operations as proprietary.[228] One commentary describes the distinction between "governmental" and "proprietary" functions as one that can be reduced to the difference between immunity and liability and adds that the "concept of liability for torts while engaged in a proprietary function has been adhered to since 1890 in the United States."[229]

Cases in which private property is flooded because of a broken water main or a clogged or broken sewer pipe are quite common. The practitioner planning to litigate the claim of a property owner who has suffered damage because of one of these events needs first to ascertain whether the jurisdiction in which the claim will be brought views the activity as proprietary and whether it thereby grants no immunity to the government.

---

223. *See* Kemp, *The Government's Liability for Tortious Conduct Arising from Proprietary Functions*, 20 DePaul L. Rev. 302, 305 (1970) (government engages in proprietary enterprise when it embarks on enterprise that is commercial in character or that is usually carried on by private individuals or private companies).

224. Omaha Water Co. v. Omaha, 147 F. 1, 5 (8th Cir. 1906), *app. dis.*, 207 U.S. 584, 28 S. Ct. 262, 52 L. Ed. 351 (1907).

225. National Food Stores, Inc. v. North Washington St. Water & Sewer Dist., 163 Colo. 178, 180, 429 P.2d 283, 285 (1967) (services of sewage treatment facilities are proprietary). *But see* City of Douglas v. Cartrett, 109 Ga. App. 683, 685, 137 S.E.2d 358, 360 (1964) (establishment and maintenance of sewerage system by municipality is for protection of public health and is governmental function).

226. City of Chicago v. Ames, 365 Ill. 529, 533, 7 N.E.2d 294, 296 (1937) (when municipality goes into business of furnishing water for sale through contracts made between it and consumer, which contract consumer has option to make or not, municipality does so not in capacity of sovereignty but in private capacity); Taber v. Benton Harbor, 280 Mich. 522, 525, 274 N.W. 324, 325 (1937) (although city may in construction, operation, and maintenance of water works system be acting in governmental capacity, as general proposition weight of authority is that enterprise is exercised in proprietary or private capacity); Eau Claire Dells Improv. Co. v. Eau Claire, 172 Wis. 240, 252, 179 N.W. 2, 7 (1920) (in operating waterworks system city acts in proprietary, not governmental, capacity).

227. *See* Griffith, *Local Government Contracts: Escaping from the Governmental/Proprietary Maze*, 75 Iowa L. Rev. 277, 311 (1990) (courts have traditionally characterized supply of water and sewage treatment as proprietary functions).

228. *See, e.g.*, Ohio Rev. Code §§ 2744.01(G)(2)(c) & (d) ("proprietary function" includes establishment, maintenance, and operation of municipal corporation water supply system and maintenance, destruction, operation, and upkeep of sewer system). Another statute waives immunity. Ohio Rev. Code § 2744.02(B)(2) (political subdivisions are liable for injury, death, or loss to person or property caused by the negligent performance of acts by their employees with respect to proprietary functions).

229. Kemp, *The Government's Liability for Tortious Conduct Arising from Proprietary Functions*, 20 DePaul L. Rev. 302, 303–04 (1970).

[ii] Water Supply Systems

The general rule is that "the operation of a water department for the purpose of supplying water for domestic and commercial purposes is a private or proprietary right, and for negligence in such operation a municipality is liable in like manner as a private individual."[230] However, a local government may be immune under state law when its actions, whether proprietary or governmental, are a discretionary function.[231]

The mere fact that water from a leaking or broken water main damages property does not create *prima facie* liability; liability depends on whether or not the defendant was negligent.[232] Local governments may be liable if they fail to inspect and maintain water mains,[233] when use of heavy equipment causes a water main leak,[234] if government employees mistakenly turn

230. Richmond v. Virginia Bonded Warehouse Corp., 148 Va. 60, 70–71, 138 S.E. 503, 506 (1927). *See also* D & D of Delhi, Inc. v. Village of Delhi, 47 A.D.3d 1117, 849 N.Y.S.2d 716 (2008); Hansen v. City of Pocatello, 145 Idaho 700, 703, 184 P.3d 206, 209 (2008) (city acts in proprietary capacity when it owns, maintains, and operates water system for benefit of its inhabitants); A. Da Prato Co. v. Boston, 334 Mass. 186, 188, 134 N.E.2d 438, 439 (1956) (municipality supplying water at a price is not performing governmental function but is engaging in trade and is liable for its negligence in laying pipes and keeping them in repair).

231. *See, e.g.*, Lamont Bair Enters. v. City of Idaho Falls, 165 Idaho 930, 454 P.3d 572 (2019) (pipe replacement plans were part of city's planning and policy decision, making it discretionary decision exempt from liability).

232. Smith v. City of Morgantown, 289 S.E.2d 223 (W.Va.1982) (lower court erred in instructing jury that city was absolutely liable for water escaping from its water lines without showing of negligence; negligence is standard by which to measure liability for damages caused by leaking water mains); John T. Arnold Assoc., Inc. v. Wichita, 5 Kan. App. 2d 301, 615 P.2d 814 (1980) (majority of courts have either held or tacitly assumed that in cases involving water escaping from water mains, distributor is not an insurer and before recovery may be allowed, negligence must be shown); Jennings Buick, Inc. v. Cincinnati, 56 Ohio St. 2d 459, 384 N.E.2d 303 (1978); Ford v. District of Columbia, 190 A.2d 905, 907 (D.C. App. 1963) (break in water main alone is not sufficient to support inference that break was likely due to negligence); Kind v. Seattle, 50 Wn. 2d 485, 312 P.2d 811 (1957); Allied Realty Co. v. Philadelphia, 95 Pa. Super. 62, 65 (1928). *See generally* Richards, *Water, Water Everywhere: Is a Municipality Liable for Damages Caused by a Leak in Its Water Supply System?*, 26 NYSBA Municipal Lawyer 7 (2012).

233. Lubin v. Iowa City, 257 Iowa 383, 390–91, 131 N.W.2d 765, 770 (1964) (it would be neither just nor reasonable for city to escape liability when it intentionally leaves water main underground beyond inspection and maintenance until break occurs). *See also* Allied Realty Co. v. Philadelphia, 95 Pa. Super. 62 (1928) (negligence may consist of failure to make reasonably careful inspection from time to time or to repair after actual or constructive notice of defective condition). *Compare* Lamont Bair Enters. v. City of Idaho Falls, 165 Idaho 930, 454 P.3d 572 (2019) (while city was required to maintain water pipes in reasonably safe condition, method and plan it adopted to maintain pipes was discretionary decision for which it enjoyed immunity).

234. Magnolia 8 Props., LLC v. City of Maple Plain, 893 N.W.2d 658, 666 (Minn. App. 2017) (city not entitled to statutory immunity based on its decision to use heavy machinery).

a wrong valve,[235] and if government employees fail to turn off water service when a pipe is leaking or to warn the property owner to do so.[236]

Many courts have held that *res ipsa loquitur* is applicable in general to broken water main cases, permitting an inference of negligence from the circumstances of the injury.[237] For example, the Alaska Supreme Court said the jury should have been instructed on the doctrine where the plaintiff introduced evidence that a break in a water main was *probably* caused by frost jacking, which can usually be avoided by the use of safety precautions.[238]

Liability for operating a water supply system is almost always based on negligence, not strict liability. Some courts have explicitly refused to apply the doctrine of strict liability to ruptured water mains.[239] On the other hand, the

---

235. Richmond v. Virginia Bonded Warehouse Corp., 148 Va. 60, 138 S.E. 503 (1927) (company installing sprinkler system needed city to shutoff water, but city employees turned wrong valve and failed to cut water off, which flooded plaintiff's warehouse). *See also* D & D of Delhi, Inc. v. Village of Delhi, 47 A.D.3d 1117, 849 N.Y.S.2d 716, 717 (2008) (city employee mistakenly believed valve would stop flow of water through main line and help isolate water main break, but when he turned that valve, rather than stopping water flow, water was forced to flow from main line through lateral line and into plaintiff's building, causing substantial property damage).

236. Woehrle v. City of Mankato, 647 N.W.2d 549 (Minn. App. 2002). In *Woehrle* the plaintiffs learned the day after a fire that water from burst water pipes had continued to leak onto their possessions overnight and that the firefighters had not shut off the water service or warned the plaintiffs to do so. The court agreed that the firefighters had a duty either to shut off the water or to inform the plaintiffs of the need to do so. However, there was no evidence that the omission caused any water damage that was distinct from that which had already been caused in fighting the fire. *Compare* A. Da Prato Co. v. Boston, 334 Mass. 186, 188–89, 134 N.E.2d 438, 439 (1956) (while it could be found that likelihood of water escaping into building was such that reasonable care by city required immediate shutting off of water and that it was negligent to delay doing so until after access to building was gained some 15 hours later after leak was observed, there was no evidence from which jury could find amount of damage caused to the plaintiff's property by any delay).

237. Pennsylvania Liquor Control Board v. Philadelphia, 17 Pa. Commw. 627, 333 A.2d 497 (1975); Pacific Northwest Bell Tel. Co. v. Port of Seattle, 80 Wash. 2d 59, 491 P.2d 1037 (1971); Koch Bros. Bag Co. v. Kansas City, 315 S.W.2d 743, 746 (Mo.1958); Juchert v. California Water Serv. Co., 16 Cal. 2d 500, 106 P.2d 886 (1940). See § 14.03[4][b][iii], *supra*, for a discussion of the doctrine of *res ipsa loquitur*.

238. State Farm Fire & Casualty Co. v. Anchorage, 788 P.2d 726, 730 (Alaska 1990). *See also* Quigley v. Hibbing, 268 Minn. 541, 543, 129 N.W.2d 765, 768 (1964) (doctrine applied where damage sustained was caused when service line that had been in use for about 40 years broke without warning; service life of line under ordinary circumstances would be about 100 years, and that it failed without the application of some extraordinary force was beyond reasonable expectation absent carelessness).

239. State Farm Fire & Casualty Co. v. Anchorage, 788 P.2d 726, 729 (Alaska 1990) (declining to hold that operation of water delivery system constitutes ultrahazardous activity requiring strict liability); Summit Hill Associates v. Knoxville Utilities Bd., 667 S.W.2d 91 (Tenn. App. 1983). *See* Quigley v. United States, 865 F. Supp. 2d 685, 696 (D. Md. 2012) for a list of jurisdictions in which courts have held strict liability does not apply to maintenance of water mains. *See also* Allied Realty Co. v. Philadelphia, 95 Pa. Super. 62, 65 (1928) (that ruptured water main damages property does not create *prima facie* liability).

Iowa Supreme Court has said that if a local government intentionally leaves water mains underground beyond inspection and maintenance until a break occurs, they become "inherently dangerous" and likely to damage neighboring property and the government can be strictly liable.[240] Pennsylvania acknowledges by statute that a water system can present a dangerous condition and says that liability may be imposed on a local government for a dangerous condition of a water system owned by a government and located within rights-of-way, but the plaintiff has to establish that the dangerous condition created a reasonably foreseeable risk of the kind of injury that was incurred and that the government had actual or constructive notice in time to have taken measures to protect against the dangerous condition.[241]

Liability is more complicated when the source of the water that causes damage is associated with a fire hydrant. That is because fire hydrants are part of a government's fire-suppression efforts, a function courts generally view as governmental rather than proprietary. Nonetheless, some courts say that if a local government owns and operates a water system for the dual purpose of supplying water for revenue and for prevention of fires and keeping the city sanitary and healthful—governmental purposes—the government has a duty to keep pipes and hydrants in repair and free from danger to others.[242] For example, in one case, a hydrant became disconnected from the water pipe to which it was attached and a large amount of water flowed into the plaintiff's basement, destroying merchandise stored there. The city argued that the hydrant was part of its waterworks system operated and maintained in the exercise of a governmental function and, therefore, it was immune from liability. The court responded that if the sole use and function of the hydrant was for fire protection, the city could not be liable for negligence in its construction or maintenance. However, the hydrant was used for a dual purpose: fire protection when needed and continuously for closing the city's water pipe. The city could have closed the pipe by some form of plug or of sealing but chose to so by using the hydrant. If the city, said the court, negligently failed to use a proper and efficient instrumentality to close the flow of water, and if, because of that negligence, water escaped, the city was responsible in damages for that negligence.[243] In another case, a municipal water line broke and caused the basement of a church to flood. The pipe began leaking in early January and finally burst in late February. The line that broke connected a main under the middle of a street with a fire hydrant. The city contended that the

240. Lubin v. Iowa City, 257 Iowa 383, 391, 131 N.W.2d 765, 770 (1964). *See also* Bierman v. City of New York, 60 Misc.2d 497, 302 N.Y.S.2d 696 (1969) (where water poured into plaintiff's basement while work was performed on water main, "substantial justice" demanded rule of strict liability rather than rule of fault).

241. 42 Pa. Cons. Stat. § 8542(b)(5).

242. Koch Bros. Bag Co. v. Kansas City, 315 S.W.2d 743 (Mo.1958).

243. Miller Grocery Co. v. Des Moines, 195 Iowa 1310, 192 N.W. 306 (1923).

hydrant was maintained exclusively for firefighting; that the pipe that broke, while defective, served only to connect with that fire hydrant; and that it was not liable because it was exercising a governmental function. The court, however, said that the hydrant did not cause any injury as the break was not in it but in the pipe leading to it. The negligence of the city was its failure to inspect and repair the pipe after it had ample and repeated notice that the water was leaking into the basement.[244]

[iii] Sanitary Sewer Systems

Generally local governments may be liable for negligent maintenance of sewers as they have a duty to provide an "adequate" sewage system.[245] Cases in which sewers break or back up and damage property are quite common. Property owners frequently lose because they are unable to prove government negligence. Courts often say that a municipality that operates a sewer system is not insurer "and can be held liable only for negligence in the performance of its duty."[246] To succeed in a negligence action the plaintiff must prove the defendant owed a duty and breached that duty. Establishing the standard of care may require expert testimony.[247]

One way that plaintiffs attempt to prove negligence is by asserting that the defendant local government had a duty to inspect or perform maintenance on sewer lines. For example, a city was found liable where an accumulation of grease obstructed a sewer line and a resulting backup damaged the plaintiff's home. It had been at least 15 years since any preventive maintenance had been done on that sewer line. The defendant city said it could not be liable because it did not have actual or constructive notice of the defect in its sewer system. The court said that local governments are liable for damages that result from failure to exercise ordinary or reasonable care to keep sewers in repair and free from obstructions.[248] "The duty of a municipality to keep its sewers in

244. Boyle v. Pittsburgh, 145 Pa. Super. 325, 21 A.2d 243 (1941).

245. Rynard, *Insurance and Risk Management for State and Local Governments*, § 16.08 (Matthew Bender & Co. 2021) (exception to liability applies when activity pertains to decision to provide sewers). *See also* District of Columbia v. Billingsley, 667 A.2d 837, 838 (D.C. App. 1995) (government may be liable for negligence in performance of proprietary function such as maintenance of sewer system).

246. Platter v. Des Moines, 237 Iowa 348, 353, 21 N.W.2d 787, 790 (1946).

247. Biernacki v. Village of Ravena, 245 A.D.2d 656, 664 N.Y.S.2d 682 (1997) (court said that *significantly*, plaintiffs engaged no expert to conduct necessary inspections and analysis and to formulate opinion as to cause of flooding in their basement they alleged was from overflow of sewers); District of Columbia v. Billingsley, 667 A.2d 837, 843 (D.C. App. 1995) (evidence of whether government's maintenance was within standard of care might be best developed through expert testimony).

248. *See also* Pickersgill v. City of New York, 168 Misc. 2d 768, 770, 642 N.Y.S.2d 469, 470 (1996) (city was required to use reasonable care to inspect and repair sewers to prevent damage to its citizens' property and if it fails to do so and sewer becomes obstructed, city can be liable for damages resulting from its acts or omissions).

repair," asserted the court, "involves the exercise of a reasonable degree of watchfulness in ascertaining their condition from time to time and preventing them from becoming dilapidated or obstructed. Where the obstruction or dilapidation is an ordinary result of the use of the sewer which ought to be anticipated and could be guarded against by occasional examination and cleansing, the omission to make such examinations and to keep the sewers clear is a neglect of duty which renders the municipality liable."[249] The court added that the government's duty is not fulfilled by waiting to be notified by citizens that sewers are out of repair. The fact that the government cannot show exactly when it inspected or cleared a sewer line does not change the fact that for it to be liable, it must have actual or constructive notice of a problem and then fail to act.[250]

How often should a government inspect or clear sewers? The Wisconsin Supreme Court said that an annual cleaning of sewer mains that included use of a rotating root-cutting device was satisfactory and refused to hold the defendant city had a duty to make any inspection of the particular sewer main in question in between the dates of its annual cleaning operation.[251]

Because negligence is difficult to prove in sewer backup cases, many plaintiffs invoke the doctrine of *res ipsa loquitur*. The doctrine, when applied by a court, creates a rebuttable presumption of negligence by the defendant. It applies when the plaintiff shows that (1) the instrumentality was under the control or management of the defendant; (2) the circumstances, according to common knowledge and experience, created a clear inference that the accident would not have happened if the defendant had not been negligent; and (3) the plaintiff's injury resulted from that accident.[252] Some courts say that a "backup of [a] sewer into a home is not an event which normally occurs absent some negligence on the part of the municipality charged with operating and maintaining the sewer system" and, therefore, the doctrine is applicable.[253]

249. City of Tucson v. Hughes, 23 Ariz. App. 350. 351–52, 533 P.2d 561, 562–63 (1975) (citing a number of cases from other jurisdictions that agree with holding). *See also* Graham v. Town of Latta, 417 S.C. 164, 789 S.E.2d 71 (S.C. App. 2016) (testimony about sewer system's infiltration problems, unidentified obstruction encountered when camera test was attempted, and town's inability to precisely locate its own sewer line—much less reach it to properly maintain it—supported inference that town failed to exercise due care in operation and maintenance of its system).

250. Ward v. Charlotte, 48 N.C. App. 463, 469, 269 S.E.2d 663, 667 (1980) (no liability where plaintiff offered no evidence to show that dropped pipe or obstruction had been present for sufficient time to place city on constructive notice of defects or to show that inspection would have disclosed their presence; although city could not show when it had made inspections, there was some evidence in the record that city sewer system received periodic cleaning).

251. Freitag v. Montello, 36 Wis. 2d 409, 153 N.W.2d 505 (1967).

252. See § 14.03[4][b][iii], *supra*, for a discussion of the doctrine.

253. *See, e.g.*, Pickersgill v. City of New York, 168 Misc. 2d 768, 771–72, 642 N.Y.S.2d 469, 471 (1996); Hull v. Griggsville, 29 Ill. App. 3d 253, 330 N.E.2d 293 (1975) (malfunctioning of city sewer system damaging plaintiff's property is event that does not ordinarily occur,

However, many courts refuse to apply the doctrine in these cases. One reason is that the first criteria, that the sewer line was under the control of the government, is not shown. Courts hold that when a sewer is clogged with foreign matter *res ipsa loquitur* does not apply because the government does not have exclusive control of that which enter its sewers.[254] The same may be true when unusually heavy rains overwhelmed a sewer system, as a government obviously has no control over the extent of the rain storms,[255] or because a sewer system is "overtaxed" by runoff from adjacent new construction.[256] A court may also refuse to apply the doctrine because the plaintiff's evidence fails to show a clear inference that the accident would not have happened but for the defendant's negligence.[257] On the other hand, when there is a defect or break in a sewer line, the instrumentality of any damage is within the control of the government.[258]

In addition to a negligence action, a plaintiff whose property is flooded after a malfunction in a government sewer system might bring an action in trespass[259] or nuisance.[260]

---

and jury was entitled to draw an inference of negligence). *But see* City of New Smyrna Beach Utilities Comm'n v. McWhorter, 418 So. 2d 261 (Fla. 1982) (by demonstrating that externally introduced objects frequently cause line blockages despite reasonable preventative safeguards, city effectively undercut any argument that sewage backup was of such an extraordinary nature as to preclude any cause other than city's negligence).

254. *See, e.g.*, District of Columbia v. Billingsley, 667 A.2d 837, 841 (D.C. App. 1995) (sewer was not in exclusive control of district as others could throw objects into sewer that might cause blockage); City of New Smyrna Beach Utilities Comm'n v. McWhorter, 418 So. 2d 261 (Fla. 1982) (where accumulation of paper, of unknown origin, caused obstruction that impeded normal flow of sewage, and sewage and water backed up and flooded plaintiff's house, plaintiff failed to allege and prove city had exclusive control over the injury-causing instrumentality as city was clearly not responsible for bundle of papers that caused stoppage and obviously could not control what users flushed down their toilets); Freitag v. Montello, 36 Wis. 2d 409, 153 N.W.2d 505 (1967) (doctrine did not apply where sewer was blocked by temporary obstruction).

255. Davis v. City of Milwaukee, 352 Wis. 2d 574, 842 N.W.2d 537 (2013) (refusing to apply *res ipsa loquitur* even though there had been four sewer backups over two years).

256. Jordan v. Hillsboro, 48 Ore. App. 839, 617 P.2d 970 (1980) (where it was determined that sewer system was overtaxed by muddy water that evidence showed was caused by rainwater runoff from two new housing developments under construction that were upstream from plaintiff's home, it could not be said that instrumentality was within defendant's exclusive control).

257. *See, e.g.*, Ward v. Charlotte, 48 N.C. App. 463, 468, 269 S.E.2d 663, 667 (1980) (that an obstruction occurred or pipe dropped because of broken bell did not exclude *all* inferences other than inference that defendant was negligent).

258. Freitag v. Montello, 36 Wis. 2d 409, 153 N.W.2d 505 (1967) (flooding caused by defect, or break, in sewer main would constitute instrumentality entirely within the control of government).

259. *See, e.g.*, Gleaton v. City of Atlanta, 131 Ga. App. 399, 206 S.E.2d 46 (1974).

260. *See, e.g.*, Fletcher v. City of Independence, 708 S.W.2d 158 (Mo. App. 1986) (affirming award of damages for nuisance where homeowner reported sewer backups that damaged their home to city over course of the 11 years and nothing came of it).

During heavy rainfall, stormwater can infiltrate and overwhelm sewer systems, causing backups that damage property. In those cases, the government has a defense in that the injury was caused by nature or an act of God. However, a New York court said that while it may be argued that rain is an act of God, that alone does not relieve a city of the duty to maintain adequate sewers "foreseeing the likelihood of a heavy rainfall." To invoke the act of God defense, the government has to establish that the weather conditions were so extraordinarily harsh that they could not be anticipated by reasonable design of the sewers and, therefore, where the negligent acts or omissions of the government *contribute* to the injury, the act of God defense should not be applied.[261]

Before bringing an action for flood loss caused by a sewer system, the practitioner should check for any state statutes that specifically address responsibility for sewer systems. For example, a Pennsylvania statute provides that liability may be imposed for a "dangerous condition of the facilities of . . . [a sewer system] . . . owned by the local agency and located within rights-of-way, except that the claimant to recover must establish that the dangerous condition created a reasonably foreseeable risk of the kind of injury which was incurred and that the local agency had actual notice or could reasonably be charged with notice under the circumstances of the dangerous condition at a sufficient time prior to the event to have taken measures to protect against the dangerous condition."[262]

[f] Permitting

Development of property can result in flooding on another property because of either water drainage or water and sewer systems on the newly developed properties. What is the extent of liability of a local government that approves development plans?[263] It is universally held that the initial decision to zone property for a particular use is a legislative decision generally not subject to

261. Pickersgill v. City of New York, 168 Misc. 2d 768, 642 N.Y.S.2d 469 (1996). *See also* Saden v. Kirby, 660 So. 2d 423, 428 (La. 1995) (when act of God combines or concurs with conduct of defendant to produce injury, defendant may be held liable for any damages that would not have occurred but for its own conduct or omission); McCarthy v. District of Columbia, 168 A.2d 910 (D.C. App. 1961) (heavy but foreseeable rainfalls cannot be classified as acts of God).

262. 42 Pa. Cons. Stat. § 8542(b)(5).

263. *See generally* Lachman, *Should Municipalities Be Liable for Development-Related Flooding?*, 41 Nat. Res. J. 945 (2001). *See also* Wilkins, *Is Sea Level Rise "Foreseeable?" Does It Matter?*, 26 J. Land Use & Envtl. Law 437 (2011) (asking if local government has control over planning and zoning decisions and possesses special knowledge about likelihood and severity of risks, but allows development that results in damage or injury from natural hazards that it knew or should have known about, can it be found liable for damages); Kozlowski, *Dams and Levees Are Not Enough: The Case for Recognizing a Cause of Action against Non-Complying NFIP Communities*, 32 Wm. & Mary Envtl. L. & Pol'y Rev. 245 (2007), proposing that property owners be able to sue local governments that fail adopt sound land use ordinances to protect against future flooding as required by the National Flood Insurance Act.

judicial review absent an arbitrary or irrational exercise of authority.[264] With the exception of a handful of states that, under the "change or mistake" rule, treat rezonings as quasi-judicial, the same holds true when a local government changes the zoning category of a property.[265] Approval of subdivisions, on the other hand, is generally characterized as an administrative process.[266]

No matter how characterized, local governments are generally not liable for planning decisions. For example, in a case before the Hawaii Supreme Court,[267] the appellants suffered damages when their house was flooded five times in a little over one year. They believed these floods occurred because of the development of a subdivision and sued the county government that granted final approval of the subdivision. They alleged the county owed them a duty to administer and enforce the applicable laws, rules and regulations, and directives of the county and state and breached that duty by negligently granting final approval of the subdivision. The court held that the primary responsibility of providing an adequate and safe development rested with the developer, not the county whose task it was to review the development plans submitted and assess their compliance with the law. Governments, said the court, are not required to conduct their own engineering studies to ensure the validity and correctness of a developer's plans. If the court were to hold that the county was liable for failure to discover an error in subdivision plans that could only have been discovered by an independent engineering study, it would in effect be impermissibly setting policies that more rightly belong to the legislative body of the county.[268]

The Wyoming Supreme Court reached a different decision in a case in which residents of an approved subdivision were forced to move out of their homes because their water and septic systems were inadequate.[269] They sued the county for negligent approval of the subdivision permit and negligent supervision of the subdividers. Evidence of that negligence, claimed the residents, was that the county failed to comply with a state statute pursuant to which it was to require written certification of a licensed Wyoming engineer that a proposed sewage disposal system was adequate and safe. The court held that the county owed the residents a duty to exercise reasonable care in processing and reviewing the subdivision application and that it could be liable for failing to exercise reasonable care in performing basic tasks—information

264. 2 Yokley, *Zoning Law and Practice*, § 9-3 (LexisNexis Matthew Bender 2017).

265. 2 Yokley, *Zoning Law and Practice*, § 11-3 (LexisNexis Matthew Bender 2017).

266. 3 Yokley, *Zoning Law and Practice*, § 17-5 (LexisNexis Matthew Bender 2018).

267. Cootey v. Sun Inv., 68 Haw. 480, 718 P.2d 1086 (1986).

268. *See also* First Gaston Bank of N.C. v. City of Hickory, 203 N.C. App. 195, 208, 691 S.E.2d 715, 724 (2010) (refusing to hold city liable for damage to privately constructed storm drain when its only involvement in creating additional stormwater volume was in approving private development that, when constructed, resulted in increased runoff).

269. Pickle v. Board of County Comm'rs, 764 P.2d 262 (Wyo. 1988).

gathering, for example—some of which were set forth in statutes. If a relevant statute is violated, said the court, that fact may be evidence of a failure to exercise reasonable care. The county contended that subdivision approval was a "quasi-legislative zoning decision," but the court responded that while the enactment of a zoning ordinance or regulation is a legislative act, the conduct challenged in the case before it did not involve adoption of legislation in any sense. The duty to require an engineer's certification was a purely administrative duty imposed by statute to which quasi-legislative immunity did not apply.

One commentary has suggested that communities that fail to meet National Flood Insurance Program requirements for flood planning should be subject to suit by either the federal government or private citizens for flood losses, but currently no such cause of action is recognized.[270]

[4] Takings or Inverse Condemnation

Under the Fifth Amendment to the United States Constitution, private property cannot be taken for public use without just compensation. That proscription is made applicable to the states by the Fourteenth Amendment. Additionally, virtually every state constitution contains a "takings" clause. An action can be brought under the federal or state constitution, or both. The language in some state constitutions parallels the Fifth Amendment, but with differences that should be noted. The majority of state constitutions preclude not only taking property for public use without compensation but also *damaging* or *injuring* property for public use, a prohibition not found in the Fifth Amendment. Taking claims under state constitutions are discussed elsewhere.[271] Generally, the principles discussed there will apply to a claim brought against a local government.

14.5 Regulated Lender Liability

Under the National Flood Insurance Act, federal agencies that regulate lending are required to adopt rules that prohibit "regulated lending institutions"[272] from making, increasing, extending, or renewing any loan secured by improved real estate or a mobile home in an area with special flood hazards in which flood insurance has been made available under the Act, unless the building

270. Kozlowsk, *Dams and Levees Are Not Enough: The Case for Recognizing a Cause of Action against Non-Complying NFIP Communities*, 32 Wm. & Mary Envtl. L. & Pol'y Rev. 245 (2007).

271. See §14.03[5], *supra*.

272. The term "regulated lending institution" is defined as "any bank, savings and loan association, credit union, farm credit bank, Federal land bank association, production credit association, or similar institution subject to the supervision of a Federal entity for lending regulation." 42 U.S.C. § 4003(a)(10). The coverage has to be in an amount at least equal to the outstanding principal balance of the loan.

or mobile home, and any personal property securing the loan, is covered for the term of the loan by flood insurance.[273] The same restriction applies to "federal agency lenders."[274] The Federal National Mortgage Association (Fannie Mae) and the Federal Home Loan Mortgage Corporation (Freddie Mac) are required by the Act to ensure that for any loan they purchase secured by improved real estate located in an area that, at the time of the origination of the loan or at any time during its term, is in an area with special flood hazards and for which flood insurance under the Act is available, the building, and any personal property securing the loan, is covered by flood insurance for the term of the loan.[275]

One vehicle for a property owner to recover for a flood loss when the lender fails to meet the flood insurance mandate would be to sue the lender. However, as the Fifth Circuit has said, "[e]very single federal court to consider whether a federal private right of action arises under [the statutory mandate] has concluded that the federal treasury, not individual mortgagors . . . is the class the statute intends to protect."[276] Thus, in a post-Katrina case, the plaintiff owned property subject to a mortgage in favor of the defendant lender. The property flooded during the hurricane. The plaintiff alleged that the lender performed a flood survey on the property and advised him that his property was not in a flood zone and, therefore, he did not need flood insurance. The plaintiff actually did acquire flood insurance, but the policy lapsed and the insurer refused to pay. The plaintiff alleged a cause of action against the lender for negligently performing a flood zone determination and failing to advise him that his property was in fact located in a flood zone. While lenders are required under the flood insurance mandate statute to perform a flood zone determination when they make or extend a loan, the court said the lender had no duty to the *borrower* to make a correct flood zone determination.[277] Moreover, any state cause of action is usually preempted by the NFIA,[278] although there are exceptions.[279] What is not preempted is a breach of contract action.

273. 42 U.S.C. § 4012a(b)(1).

274. 42 U.S.C. § 4012a(b)(2). *See also* 42 U.S.C. § 4003(a)(7) (defining "federal agency lender").

275. 42 U.S.C. § 4012a(b)(3).

276. Wentwood Woodside I LP v. GMAC Commer. Mortg. Corp., 419 F.3d 310, 323 (5th Cir. 2005). *See also* Hofbauer v. Northwestern National Bank of Rochester, 700 F.2d 1197, 1200 (8th Cir. 1983) (NFIA does not create implied private cause of action for damages under federal law); R. B. J. Apartments v. Gate City Sav. & Loan Ass'n, 315 N.W.2d 284, 289 (N.D. 1982) (there is no implied private cause of action under 42 U.S.C. § 4012a for lending money secured by real estate that should have been covered by adequate flood insurance).

277. Duong v. Allstate Ins. Co., 499 F. Supp. 2d 700 (E.D. La. 2007).

278. Duong v. Allstate Ins. Co., 499 F. Supp. 2d 700 (E.D. La. 2007).

279. *See* Paul v. Landsafe Flood Determination, Inc., 550 F.3d 511 (5th Cir. 2008), where the appellee company was employed to determine whether the home in Mississippi for which the appellant sought financing was located in a flood zone. The company concluded it was not. The lender, therefore, provided financing without requiring flood insurance. After Hurricane Katrina

Where a mortgagor claimed that her lender escrowed funds for flood insurance and breached the mortgage agreement by failing to make those payments, that she detrimentally relied on that agreement, and that payments for escrow items never decreased, the court found that she alleged a duty to make flood insurance payments that arose from the mortgage agreement, a claim that was not preempted by the NFIA.[280]

struck and caused substantial damage to the home, it was learned that it actually was in a flood hazard area. The appellant sued the appellee for negligence and negligent misrepresentation. The court said that under Mississippi law the question was whether the appellee could have reasonably foreseen that the appellant would rely on the flood determination, not whether she was a member of a limited group for whose benefit the determination was intended. An erroneous flood zone determination, concluded the court, was the kind of professional opinion, developed in the course of a business and supplied for the guidance of others in a transaction, on which justifiable and detrimental reliance by a reasonably foreseeable person might be shown to have occurred. The appellate court, therefore, reversed summary judgment for the appellee company and remanded. *See also* Bagelmann v. First Nat'l Bank, 823 N.W.2d 18, 30 (Iowa 2012) (allegation that loan servicer *knew*, not merely should have known, that property was in flood zone, and that prior representations to the contrary were incorrect could give rise to negligence claim).

280. Blackstone v. Chase Manhattan Mortg. Corp., 802 F. Supp. 2d 732, 737 (E.D. La. 2011) (allegations in complaint did not dispute accuracy of the flood zone determination presented in letter declaring that property was not in a flood zone).

15

Recovering from Weather Forecasters and Those Who Fail to Warn of Weather Dangers

15.1 Introduction

Individuals and businesses rely on weather predictions in a variety of ways. When a forecast turns out to be incorrect, anyone may be annoyed, but some may suffer real harm by trusting in an inaccurate forecast.[1] With increasingly powerful computers and more sophisticated models, forecasts have become demonstrably more accurate.[2] Of course, not all forecasts are the same. "Short-range forecasts about obvious and imminent changes in the weather are distinguishable from longer-range projections about developing changes in the weather. Long-range forecasts involve considerably more guesswork, and no reasonable person would expect them to mirror current conditions to a degree on which he could safely rely."[3] Even with computers and modern models, short-range forecasts can be wrong. As the First Circuit said in one case, "A weather forecast is a classic example of a prediction of indeterminate reliability, and a place peculiarly open to debatable decisions. . . . Weather predictions fail on frequent occasions."[4] Thus, people question "the reliability of the daily

1. "Loper, *"Red Sky in the Morning, Forecasters Take Warning": The Liability of Meteorologists for Negligent Weather Forecasts*, 66 Tex. L. Rev. 683 (1988). *See also* Klein & Pielke, *Bad Weather? Then Sue the Weatherman!: Part I: Legal Liability for Public Sector Forecasts*, Bull. Am. Meteorological Soc. at 1791 (2002), *available at* http://sciencepolicy.colorado.edu/admin/publication_files/2002.21.pdf (inadequate or inaccurate forecasts can lead to financial loss or bodily harm).

2. Klein & Pielke, *Bad Weather? Then Sue the Weatherman!: Part I: Legal Liability for Public Sector Forecasts*, Bull. Am. Meteorological Soc. at 1791 (2002), *available at* http://sciencepolicy.colorado.edu/admin/publication_files/2002.21.pdf.

3. Loper, *"Red Sky in the Morning, Forecasters Take Warning": The Liability of Meteorologists for Negligent Weather Forecasts*, 66 Tex. L. Rev. 683, 711 (1988).

4. Brown v. United States, 790 F.2d 199, 204 (1st Cir. 1986). *See also In re* Hercules Carriers, Inc., 1985 U.S. Dist. LEXIS 16417 (M.D. Fla. Aug. 28, 1985) (weather forecasts are merely predictions and are subject to vagaries of nature and her elements; thus quite often the actual weather experienced is not exactly that predicted).

weather forecasts, not because of any doubt that reasonable methods are used in making such determinations, but because of the vagaries of the weather."[5] There is then a common perception that weather forecasts are not reliable, and "a reasonable person would not rely on a favorable weather forecast as being an absolute assurance that there will be no dangerous storms"[6] The reasonableness of any reliance is important in litigation over inaccurate weather forecasts because the cause of action is often negligent misrepresentation, an element of which is justifiable reliance by the plaintiff on the defendant's representation.[7] Significantly for weather forecast cases, misrepresentation by non-disclosure can also be actionable.[8]

This chapter briefly explores the potential liability of those who forecast weather and those who fail to relay warnings of threatening weather. That liability has relevance to plaintiffs seeking to recover from flood losses because, of course, weather is the frequent cause of flood damage. Unfortunately for plaintiffs, the circumstances in which courts have imposed liability are few.

15.2 Private Weather Forecasters

[1] Generally

Most people, when they hear the word "meteorologist," think of the person on the local evening news who tells them what to expect tomorrow's weather to be like. They understand that forecast is not specific to them, but a regional, generic prediction. Broadcast meteorologists offer a gratuitous service to the public and do not owe a duty to every listener, but they have to use due care when they forecast for *individuals* who have clearly indicated an intent to rely.[9] There are, however, meteorologists who sell their services—including long- and short-range weather forecasts—and they have a "contractual duty to provide their clients with forecasts prepared according to reasonable and professional standards."[10]

When a meteorologist has a tort duty of care, what would that be? One expert describes the duty as issuing "forecasts prepared according to the standards of a reasonably prudent meteorologist, including reporting facts

5. Chanon v. United States, 350 F. Supp. 1039, 1041 (S.D. Tex. 1972), *aff'd*, 80 F.2d 1227 (5th Cir. 1973).

6. Standler, *Tort Liability in the USA for Negligent Weather Forecasts* at 2 (2003), *available at* http://www.rbs2.com/forecast.pdf.

7. Restatement (Second) of Torts, § 552.

8. Restatement (Second) of Torts, § 551.

9. Loper, *"Red Sky in the Morning, Forecasters Take Warning": The Liability of Meteorologists for Negligent Weather Forecasts*, 66 Tex. L. Rev. 683, 698 (1988).

10. Loper, *"Red Sky in the Morning, Forecasters Take Warning": The Liability of Meteorologists for Negligent Weather Forecasts*, 66 Tex. L. Rev. 683, 697 (1988).

about the current state of the weather accurately."[11] The court would focus on whether the defendant used widely accepted forecasting methods that are ordinarily used by recognized forecasters for that purpose.[12] "In a reasonableness inquiry," says one commentator, "the court should concentrate on determining whether the forecaster had enough information to make a reasonable prediction and whether the meteorologist's forecasting process strayed from acceptable standards."[13]

[2] Media Forecasters

The Weather Channel (TWC) is a television network that broadcasts weather forecasts and weather-related news and analysis 24 hours a day. Millions of Americans turn to it each day for weather news and forecasts. A Florida man monitored the channel one morning before going out on a friend's boat. TWC issued no small craft warning that morning, and no bad weather had been forecast. However, adverse weather conditions caused the man to be thrown from the boat and drowned. His personal representative brought a wrongful death action against TWC. The court dismissed the action with prejudice. It said that the plaintiff sought an "unprecedented expansion" of the scope of tort law by imposing on a television broadcaster a general duty to viewers who watch a weather forecast and take action in reliance on it. That duty would chill the First Amendment rights of broadcasters. Moreover, said the court, it is well-settled that mass media broadcasters owe no duty to the general public who may view their broadcasts. Imposition of negligence liability for allegedly incorrect weather forecasts would be, said the court, contrary to public policy.[14] However, one respected commentator and expert in the field of liability for weather forecasting notes that while the court spoke of erroneous or incorrect forecasts, the issue in the case was whether there was a *negligent* forecast, not whether the forecast was incorrect, and negligence requires proof of a minimum standard of care.[15] As for the lack of duty of mass media broadcasters, the commentator pointed out that none of the cases cited by the court for that proposition involved a television network or a source of weather information. Thus, it may be that a practitioner could convince another court that there is a minimum standard of care required of meteorologists just as

---

11. Loper, *"Red Sky in the Morning, Forecasters Take Warning": The Liability of Meteorologists for Negligent Weather Forecasts*, 66 Tex. L. Rev. 683, 684 (1988).

12. Klein & Pielke, *Bad Weather? Then Sue the Weatherman!: Part II: Legal Liability for Private Sector Forecasts*, Bull. Am. Meteorological Soc. at 1804 (2002), *available at* http://sciencepolicy.colorado.edu/admin/publication_files/2002.22.pdf.

13. Loper, *"Red Sky in the Morning, Forecasters Take Warning": The Liability of Meteorologists for Negligent Weather Forecasts*, 66 Tex. L. Rev. 683, 684–85 (1988).

14. Brandt v. Weather Channel, Inc., 42 F. Supp. 2d 1344 (S.D. Fla. 1999).

15. Standler, *Tort Liability in the USA for Negligent Weather Forecasts* at 18 (2003), *available at* http://www.rbs2.com/forecast.pdf.

there is with other professionals. For example, what if a meteorologist in a coastal community fails to report that an approaching squall could produce a storm surge and flooding when indicators of a storm surge well-known in the profession are present? Should that omission not incur liability? The same commentator suggests that if a media outlet regularly broadcasts weather forecasts at fixed times, past broadcasts may be argued to create a justifiable reliance that the outlet will continue to make weather forecasts in the future. The omission of a forecast in the face of threatening weather might then be a basis for liability.[16]

[3] Consulting Forecasters

Some meteorologists work in the private sector but not for media companies. They might, for example, work for insurance companies in risk management and mitigation or as expert witnesses in cases where weather is at issue.[17] They might also work for a company or as an independent contractor and provide weather forecasts. One expert says that these "consulting meteorologists" have a *contractual* duty to provide clients with forecasts prepared consistently with reasonable and professional standards and that if their forecast is inaccurate because of negligence, they have breached a contractual duty to their customer.[18] As for tort liability, another expert says that while no appellate court appears to have addressed that issue, professional malpractice law could apply, requiring the meteorologist to exercise the reasonable degree of care ordinarily exercised by others of the profession under similar circumstances.[19] For example, a meteorologist might be liable for continuing to use known defective meteorological instruments, failing to warn of known hazards, or using untested computer software containing serious errors. The plaintiff, of course, would have to prove that the defendant's negligence was the cause of his or her harm.[20] Another issue that could arise is that if the plaintiff was

16. Standler, *Tort Liability in the USA for Negligent Weather Forecasts* at 10 (2003), *available at* http://www.rbs2.com/forecast.pdf.

17. *Career Opportunities in Meteorology*, NOAA, https://www.weather.gov/media/bro/outreach/pdf/CareerOpportunitiesMeteorology.pdf.

18. Loper, *"Red Sky in the Morning, Forecasters Take Warning": The Liability of Meteorologists for Negligent Weather Forecasts*, 66 Tex. L. Rev. 683, 689 (1988).

19. Klein, *Someone to Blame: Legal Liability for Weather Forecasts* (2003), WeatherWise Magazine, *available at* http://sciencepolicy.colorado.edu/admin/publication_files/2003.31.pdf. *See* Springer v. United States, 641 F. Supp. 913, 934–35 (D.S.C. 1986), *aff'd*, 819 F.2d 1139 (4th Cir. 1987) (National Weather Service owed duty of reasonable care in operating its weather observation and aviation forecast system).

20. Klein & Pielke, *Bad Weather? Then Sue the Weatherman!: Part II: Legal Liability for Private Sector Forecasts*, Bull. Am. Meteorological Soc. at 1804 (2002), *available at* http://sciencepolicy.colorado.edu/admin/publication_files/2002.22.pdf (court would have to decide whether plaintiff relied on forecast and whether it was substantial factor in causing plaintiff's injuries).

not the party for whom the forecast was provided, did the defendant owe the plaintiff any duty, perhaps as a third-party beneficiary? That, of course, is an issue that comes up in attorney malpractice cases where the injured party was not a client of the defendant attorney.

In what appears to be the only reported case of a weather forecasting company being sued because of its weather prediction, the cause of action was conspiracy to defraud the plaintiffs and improperly manipulate the market prices of Frozen Concentrate Orange Juice (FCOJ) contracts in which the plaintiffs had invested. The defendant was a private weather forecasting firm in the business of issuing weather reports to its customers for a fee. One of the plaintiffs called the firm and was told that its low temperature forecast for a particular date for Florida orange groves was around 32 degrees. The plaintiffs contended that figure was out of line with the government data publicly available that forecast a temperature of 44 degrees. The plaintiffs contended the forecast was "'recklessly and fraudulently made without any basis in fact and with the intent to manipulate or aid and abet the manipulation of the FCOJ contract market.'" The court dismissed the claim against the firm because it made "no economic sense." The firm, observed the court, was in the business of providing weather forecasts, mainly to customers in weather-sensitive businesses who would want the most accurate forecasts possible. The firm was in business to make a profit, and it would contrary to its economic and long-term business interests to intentionally issue false and misleading weather forecasts. The plaintiffs, decided the court, failed to sufficiently demonstrate that the firm's conduct caused whatever monetary loss they suffered.[21]

15.3 State and Local Agencies

[1] Negligent Forecast

The leading case on liability of a state for a negligent forecast was brought against the State of California by a businessman who operated marinas on the Sacramento River.[22] After heavy rains, the river rose to unusual heights. The businessman called the State Department of Water Resources to ask about any anticipated change in the level of the river. He was told the river was expected to rise to a maximum height that was five feet below the level at which it actually crested. He took precautions to protect his properties based on the inaccurate forecast and suffered major damage. He sued the state. The court first analyzed whether the plaintiff had stated a cause of action under the general laws of negligence. The state argued that a recipient of a weather

21. Grossman v. Citrus Associates of New York Cotton Exchange, Inc., 706 F. Supp. 221 (S.D.N.Y. 1989).

22. Connelly v. State, 3 Cal. App. 3d 744, 84 Cal. Rptr. 257 (1970).

forecast cannot, as a reasonable person, rely on its accuracy because it is common knowledge that weather forecasts of future conditions are not statements of fact but are subject to the vagaries of nature. The court responded that the plaintiff did not rest his allegation of negligence merely on the fact the prediction turned out to be mistaken, but pleaded specific acts of negligence in the gathering and evaluating of known facts—for example, that an agency employee miscalculated and that those in charge of the office negligently failed to detect that miscalculation. The state also contended that the forecasts of the Department of Water Resources were for the benefit of the public generally, and the plaintiff could not, therefore, claim a breach of duty because no duty was owed him. Again, the court disagreed. The plaintiff pleaded not only that businesses along the river used and relied on flood forecast information but also that he himself telephoned the agency office to determine the maximum height to which the river would rise and identified himself as a businessman with a great deal at stake in the proper estimate of the river height, and that in reliance on the agency's information he secured his marina docks. Therefore, concluded the court, the plaintiff pleaded facts that took him out of the realm of an "amorphous public receiving general information" and placed him in the position of a businessman making a personal inquiry and relying on the information received.

The court next addressed governmental immunity. It held that the determination to issue flood forecasts is a policy-making function, a discretionary activity within the scope of governmental immunity, but gathering, evaluating, and disseminating flood forecast information are administrative or ministerial activities outside the scope of that immunity. Because there was nothing in the pleadings to indicate that the state employees charged with negligence were engaged in policy- or decision-making, the court found the plaintiff's suit could survive a motion to dismiss.

[2] Failure to Warn or Alert

Many government agencies monitor the weather. For example, law enforcement organizations obtain weather warnings to alert officers in the field of approaching weather dangers. Schools use weather reports and warnings to determine if they must close schools for the safety of students. When is a government responsible to transmit warnings of which it is aware to others? The answer is, virtually never. First, mere receipt of weather bulletins or advisories does not amount to assumption of a duty to protect the public from severe weather.[23] Second, state and local governments will generally be immune from liability for discretionary acts.

---

23. Caldwell v. Let the Good Times Roll Festival, 717 So. 2d 1263 (La. App.), *cert. den.*, 729 So. 2d 566 (La. 1998). In *Caldwell* the plaintiffs attended a public festival and were injured by flying debris when a tornadic-force wind arose. One defendant was the city, which received

An especially tragic case in which a government agency was sued for failure to warn was decided by a New York appellate court.[24] Thirty children were killed or injured when an elementary school wall collapsed after it was struck by either high winds or a tornado shortly after noon. Earlier that morning the county government had received a report from the State Police Information Network of a tornado watch issued by the National Weather Service. About 40 minutes before the storm struck, the county emergency manager gave the county public information officer a copy of the report for dissemination to Emergency Broadcast System radio stations. The information officer, however, failed to disseminate the information before the storm struck. The plaintiffs sued the county and contended that because the county had enacted an emergency preparedness plan providing for direct notification of schools in emergencies, it had a duty to inform the school of the tornado watch issued by the National Weather Service and known to the county. The court began by stating there was no disputing the principle that a county is generally immune from liability for acts that involve the exercise of discretion. The plaintiffs argued that the county emergency preparedness plan made notification of the tornado watch a ministerial duty, the breach of which could make the county liable. However, the plan said schools would be notified "as conditions warrant," and the court stated that language, on its face, conclusively demonstrated that the plan fell squarely within the definition of a discretionary act because it required an analysis of a situation and a decision whether notification was warranted.[25] The court further noted that the National Weather

---

a severe weather warning from the National Weather Service that was relayed to the fire and police radio dispatcher who then broadcast it on a fire and police radio band. Off-duty uniformed police officers providing safety and security at the festival heard the broadcast only shortly before the tornadic-force wind was produced. The court found the city was not liable. *See also* Griffin v. Rogers, 232 Kan. 168, 653 P.2d 463 (1982) (plaintiffs contended that sheriff established custom or practice of warning of severe weather conditions, which those affected had right to rely on; however, court found record did not support that contention and that sheriff's office broadcast severe weather information by all-points bulletin, which could be received by sheriff's officers, city police, highway patrol, and state park officers, and others who had their radios tuned to the sheriff's radio frequency, but that sheriff had no means of ascertaining who may have heard broadcast).

24. Litchhult v. Reiss, 583 N.Y.S.2d 671, 183 A.D.2d 1067, *app. dis.*, 81 N.Y.2d 737, 594 N.Y.S.2d 708, 610 N.E.2d 381 (1992).

25. *See also* Griffin v. Rogers, 232 Kan. 168, 653 P.2d 463 (1982) (dissemination of weather information by government agency or officer is generally held to be discretionary function). In some jurisdictions, "emergency preparedness activities" may carry immunity. For example, in Bradley v. Board of County Comm'rs, 20 Kan. App. 2d 602, 890 P.2d 1228 (1995), the National Weather Service issued a tornado warning for a city whose police chief heard the warning and ordered the warning siren sounded. The siren did not function, whereupon the chief ordered police vehicles to drive through city streets sounding their sirens, and one officer went to the vicinity of a mobile home park where the plaintiff lived. She was injured when the tornado hit her home. The court held that the defendants were exempt from liability for their actions or inactions as the claims arose out of emergency preparedness activities.

Service had issued a tornado *watch*—notification that the weather conditions were such that they conceivably could produce a tornado—as opposed to a tornado *warning*, which is given when there is actual evidence of a tornado in the area. The plaintiffs next argued that because the emergency preparedness plan mentioned schools specifically, a special relationship was created resulting in an exception to the governmental immunity rule. However, the court responded that there was "no suggestion in the plan's statement of purpose that special protection of plaintiffs' decedents individually or even schools generally was intended."[26]

As in any negligence action, the plaintiff who brings an action for failure to warn of dangerous weather has to show the government had a duty to warn, breached that duty, and that the breach was the proximate cause of the injuries he or she suffered. For instance, a Florida beachgoer was struck by lightning. She sued the county, alleging its beach lifeguards were negligent in failing to warn her of the risk of lightning. Lightning is a common danger in Florida, so the lifeguards monitored the beach for storm activity and would call a "red light" alert when they learned of an approaching storm. The alert required the lifeguards to get all beachgoers out of the water. The court said that if any duty to warn existed, it arose from the undertaking to provide warnings of lightning to beachgoers, a responsibility the county was obliged to exercise with reasonable care. In this case, the warning was issued about 20 minutes after the county learned that a lightning storm was approaching the beach from the southwest. The lifeguards were monitoring the storm and following their usual procedure to determine when to issue the warning. The court noted that the procedure prioritized persons in the water, and there was no evidence offered that the lifeguards failed to exercise reasonable care in executing the procedure, merely that the procedure failed to protect the plaintiff, who was not in the water. Moreover, all the evidence at trial indicated that the lightning that struck the plaintiff was generated from a western storm, not the one to the southwest. The court concluded that the causal link based on failure to call a red light alert based on the presence of the southern storm was missing.[27]

---

26. The plaintiffs also argued that because the county attempted to notify the *public* through the Emergency Broadcast System, it had to be liable for its negligence in failing to complete the task undertaken. The court, however, decided that it could not be seriously disputed that the decision to notify the public was an immune exercise of discretion, and even if the decision to notify the public through the Emergency Broadcast System could be interpreted as an assumption of a duty where none previously existed, that duty was not one to decedents or the school, but rather to the public.

27. Seelbinder v. County of Volusia, 821 So. 2d 1095 (Fla. 5th DCA 2002).

15.4 Federal Government Agencies

[1] Generally

There are several government agencies that provide information to the public about weather and flooding. The National Weather Service[28] is a part of the National Oceanic and Atmospheric Administration (NOAA) of the United States Department of Commerce. Its mission is to "Provide weather, water and climate data, forecasts, warnings, and impact-based decision support services for the protection of life and property and enhancement of the national economy."[29] Among its forecasts are flood advisories, watches, and warnings; flash flood warnings; tsunami warnings, advisories, watches, and information statements; and severe thunderstorm watches and warnings. The Aviation Weather Center[30] (AWC) of the National Weather Service (NWS) has as its mission delivering "consistent, timely and accurate weather information for the world airspace system." The National Hurricane Center[31] (NHC), another agency of NOAA, issues tropical cyclone watches and warnings. Earthquakes and volcanoes can cause flooding by damaging flood control structures or interfering with the flow of watercourses. The United States Geological Survey[32] (USGS) monitors and assesses a wide range of natural hazards and specifically provides earthquake[33] and volcano[34] notification services.

The warnings and notices these agencies issue are available at their websites, and the public can sign up to receive them directly. Many media outlets do so. One court noted that because government agencies have few facilities for their own broadcasts, the general public does not rely on direct government broadcasts and the government owes no duty to directly broadcast weather information at any time. On the other hand, the government does have a duty to use due care in forwarding forecasts and warnings to the media, although it has no duty to see to it that private sources actually transmit the weather information it provides to them.[35]

---

28. *See National Weather Service*, NOAA, https://www.weather.gov/.
29. *About the National Weather Service*, NOAA, https://www.weather.gov/about/.
30. *Aviation Weather Overview*, NOAA, https://aviationweather.gov/.
31. *National Hurricane Center and Central Pacific Hurricane Center*, NOAA, https://www.nhc.noaa.gov/.
32. U.S. Geological Survey, https://www.usgs.gov/.
33. *See Earthquake Notification Service*, U.S. Geological Survey, https://earthquake.usgs.gov/ens/.
34. *See* https://www.usgs.gov/tools/volcano-notification-service-vns.
35. Chanon v. United States, 350 F. Supp. 1039, 1042 (S.D. Tex. 1972), *aff'd*, 80 F.2d 1227 (5th Cir. 1973).

[2] Weather Forecast Liability

Can the forecasting activities of these agencies lead the federal government to be liable for dissemination of false information or failing to issues warnings? First, the government does have a "duty to use due care in gathering weather information, forecasting and making available for broadcasting, up-to-date weather information," but the fact that a forecast turns out to be erroneous, standing alone, "should not be considered as any evidence of fault on the part of the Weather Service."[36] One observer contends that if individuals contact an NWS office and put the NWS on notice that they are entitled to a duty of due care by indicating that they are staking their safety or the safety of property on the accuracy of the forecast, the agency should be required to act with due care.[37]

Even though the government has some duty in weather forecasting, its actions may be immune from liability. One example of that is the classic weather forecast liability case of *Bergquist v. United States*.[38] In that case a tornado in Illinois resulted in many deaths and enormous property damage. Numerous plaintiffs sued the federal government alleging that the National Weather Service was negligent in forecasting and in issuing warnings about the tornado. The plaintiffs said NWS employees breached a duty to use due care in gathering, forecasting, and making available for broadcasting up-to-date weather information. The court found that all of the negligence allegations clearly fell within the discretionary function exception to liability under the Federal Tort Claims Act (FTCA) because acts and omissions of which the plaintiffs complained were susceptible to any one of the three policy analyses identified by the government: cost/budgetary policy considerations, a general "don't over-warn" policy, and a policy of vesting discretion in forecasters. The exception applies when the government determines how much meteorological information to collect.[39] A number of courts have found that the exception

---

36. Chanon v. United States, 350 F. Supp. 1039, 1041 (S.D. Tex. 1972), *aff'd*, 80 F.2d 1227 (5th Cir. 1973) (finding government was not negligent in manner of assembling pertinent weather facts nor in method of formulating forecasts and warnings as to weather during critical time at issue).

37. Loper, *"Red Sky in the Morning, Forecasters Take Warning": The Liability of Meteorologists for Negligent Weather Forecasts*, 66 Tex. L. Rev. 683, 688–89 (1988).

38. Bergquist v. United States, 849 F. Supp. 1221 (N.D. Ill. 1994).

39. *See* Brown v. United States, 790 F.2d 199 (1st Cir. 1986), where representatives of deceased fishermen sued the government. The deaths happened when fishing boats encountered more severe weather than predicted by the NWS. The action was based on the government's failure to repair or replace a sporadically malfunctioning weather-reporting buoy. The plaintiffs did not allege that forecasters negligently interpreted or compiled data, but that the government failed to collect enough information. The court, however, found that the determination of the number of functioning buoys was a discretionary function. One commentator agrees with the holding and says that "the government should not be liable for any discretionary decisions made in determining the adequacy of the warning provided." Loper, *"Red Sky in the Morning,*

applies to failure of the NWS to provide adequate or timely warnings of looming severe weather, including floods.[40] A Florida court found the government immune when the NWS chose to provide a descriptive forecast, rather than issue a severe thunderstorm warning.[41] The discretionary function exception, however, does not bar negligence actions that focus *not* on the failure of the government to use due care in communicating information but instead on its breach of a different duty.[42]

Even if the discretionary function exception does not apply, the FTCA does not pertain to "[a]ny claim arising out of . . . misrepresentation."[43] The United States Supreme Court has held that as a consequence, the government is relieved of "tort liability for pecuniary injuries which are wholly attributable

---

Forecasters Take Warning": The Liability of Meteorologists for Negligent Weather Forecasts, 66 Tex. L. Rev. 683, 708 (1988).

40. *See, e.g.*, Monzon v. United States, 253 F.3d 567 (11th Cir. 2001) (failure of NWS to warn of rip currents was not actionable as discretionary function), *cert. den.*, 535 U.S. 1035, 122 S. Ct. 1792, 152 L. Ed. 2d 651 (2002); Brown v. United States, 790 F.2d 199, 202 (1st Cir. 1986), *cert. den.*, 479 U.S. 1058, 107 S. Ct. 938, 93 L. Ed. 2d 989 (1987) (government, by issuing weather reports, did not assume duty to invest in that activity whatever resources courts might find necessary to achieve what courts believe to be proper care.); Spencer v. New Orleans Levee Bd., 737 F.2d 435 (5th Cir. 1984) (where Levee Board filed third-party complaint against NWS alleging that it negligently failed to predict weather and tidal conditions accurately and to warn Board, discretionary function exception applied); Williams v. United States, 504 F. Supp. 746, 750 (E.D. Mo. 1980) (weather forecasts, or omission of forecasts, are excepted from the Federal Tort Claims Act); Bartie v. United States, 216 F. Supp. 10 (W.D. La. 1963), *aff'd*, 326 F.2d 754 (5th Cir. 1964), *cert. den.*, 379 U.S. 852, 85 S. Ct. 98, 13 L. Ed. 2d 55 (1964) (plaintiff brought wrongful death action against government alleging federal Weather Bureau was negligent in failing to give adequate, clear, correct, and proper warning of nature, intensity, location, path, velocity, and speed of tidal wave caused by hurricane and court found defendant's action were discretionary and government was immune from liability); Mid-Central Fish Co. v. United States, 112 F. Supp. 792 (W.D. Mo. 1953) (claim alleging government negligently collected, analyzed, and disseminated flood information defeated by discretionary function exception), *aff'd sub. nom.*, National Mfg. Co. v. United States, 210 F.2d 263 (8th Cir. 1954), *cert. den.*, 347 U.S. 967, 74 S. Ct. 778, 98 L. Ed. 1108 (1954).

41. *In re* Hercules Carriers, Inc., 1985 U.S. Dist. LEXIS 16417 (M.D. Fla. Aug. 28, 1985) (weight of evidence illustrated that forecasters on watch acted reasonably and prudently with information available to them at time forecast was made, performing in accordance with Weather Service guidelines and procedures).

42. Block v. Neal, 460 U.S. 289, 297, 75 L. Ed. 2d 67, 74, 103 S. Ct. 1089, 1094 (1983). *See, e.g.*, Kaskaskia River v. United States, 2008 U.S. Dist. LEXIS 81720 (S.D. Ill. Oct. 15, 2008) (where plaintiff sued government claiming it owed duty of care to take certain actions for safety of plaintiff's property in maintenance and control of water levels of lock and dam system and breached duty, in part, when it failed to notify plaintiff of unsafe water levels resulting from its negligent maintenance, complaint clearly alleged negligence, not misrepresentation, claim). *See generally* Loper, *"Red Sky in the Morning, Forecasters Take Warning": The Liability of Meteorologists for Negligent Weather Forecasts*, 66 Tex. L. Rev. 683, 713 (1988) (discretionary immunity should shield government from liability for long-range forecasts that involve significant subjective analysis, but not when forecaster bungles operational chores, for example, reporting facts and following explicit Manual of Operations instructions, or makes short-term forecast that distorts present conditions).

43. 28 U.S.C. § 2680(h).

to reliance on the Government's negligent misstatements."[44] In applying the misrepresentation exception, the question is not whether the government is guilty of an affirmative misstatement or merely an omission.[45] The question is whether the injury resulted from a commercial decision based on a governmental misrepresentation.[46]

The misrepresentation has been applied in the cases of weather forecasts.[47] One notable case is *National Mfg. Co. v. United States*.[48] In that case, the plaintiffs' property was damaged when the Kansas River overflowed its banks. They claimed the government was liable because the Weather Bureau (now the NWS) and other federal agencies negligently assured the plaintiffs immediately prior to the flood that the river would not overflow and negligently omitted and failed to give the plaintiffs notice and warning of the impending overflow in time for them to remove their movable property. The court held that the "activity" of the government employees was misrepresentations—that is, false, improper, or imperfect representations—within the meaning of the exception to the FTCA. The court rejected the argument that the exception applied only to intentional rather that negligent misrepresentations and added that the exception applies to affirmative statements as well as omissions.

---

44. Block v. Neal, 460 U.S. 289, 297, 75 L. Ed. 2d 67, 74, 103 S. Ct. 1089, 1093 (1983). *See also* United States v. Neustadt, 366 U.S. 696, 711, 6 L. Ed. 2d 614, 624, 81 S. Ct. 1294, 1302 (1961) (where plaintiff was furnished statement reporting results of inaccurate Federal Housing Administration inspection and appraisal, claim was one arising out of misrepresentation and hence not actionable against government). *See generally* Fontenot, *Misrepresentation Exception to the Federal Tort Claims Act*, 1988 Army Law. 18 (1988); Shimomura, *Federal Misrepresentation: Protecting the Reliance Interest*, 60 Tul. L. Rev. 596 (1986) (misrepresentation exception poses jurisdictional bar to general averments regarding government's alleged misrepresentations and omissions in its warnings of storm activity and specific allegations about government dissemination of allegedly inaccurate or potentially confusing information, and incomplete reports).

45. Green v. United States, 629 F.2d 581, 584 (9th Cir. 1980).

46. Preston v. United States, 596 F.2d 232, 239 (7th Cir. 1979), *cert. den.*, 444 U.S. 915, 62 L. Ed. 2d 169, 100 S. Ct. 228 (1979). *See also* Schinmann v. United States, 618 F. Supp. 1030 (E.D. Wash. 1985) (decisions of farmers and ranchers to change crops, sell cattle, and invest in wells and additional irrigation equipment were commercial or economic, within scope of misrepresentation exception and absent communication of misinformation to plaintiffs, no damage would have ensued).

47. Bergquist v. United States, 849 F. Supp. 1221 (N.D. Ill. 1994). *See also* Bartie v. United States, 216 F. Supp. 10 (W.D. La. 1963), *aff'd*, 326 F.2d 754 (5th Cir. 1964), *cert. den.*, 379 U.S. 852, 85 S. Ct. 98, 13 L. Ed. 2d 55 (1964) (plaintiff brought wrongful death action against government alleging federal Weather Bureau was negligent in failing to give adequate, clear, correct, and proper warning of nature, intensity, location, path, velocity, and speed of tidal wave caused by hurricane and court found plaintiff sought to hold government liable for claim arising out of misrepresentation, claim not actionable under Tort Claims Act).

48. National Mfg. Co. v. United States, 210 F.2d 263 (8th Cir. 1954). Note that the court said that sovereign immunity applied if there were no comparable private service. That test was proscribed in *Indian Towing Co., Inc. v. United States*, 350 U.S. 61, 100 L. Ed. 48, 76 S. Ct. 122 (1955). *See* Standler, *Tort Liability in the USA for Negligent Weather Forecasts* at 5 (2003), *available at* http://www.rbs2.com/forecast.pdf.

Even though the plaintiff may characterize the action as one for negligent breach of a duty to warn of the existence of a dangerous condition, courts may still construe it as a claim arising out of misrepresentation.[49] If the plaintiff alleges the injury was the result of an independent tort, that tort has to be, of course, the proximate cause of the injury.[50]

[3] Aviation Weather Forecasts

As noted above, the Aviation Weather Center provides weather information for the world airspace system. The Federal Aviation Administration[51] (FAA) of the United States Department of Transportation also manages several weather observation programs. These include the "Aviation Surface Weather Observation Network," which measures weather parameters on the surface and reports conditions; the "Next Generation Weather Radar," which detects, processes, and distributes for display hazardous and routine weather information; the "Terminal Doppler Weather Radar," which provides information and warnings about hazardous wind shear conditions, precipitation, gust fronts, and microbursts; and the "Wind Shear Detection Services," which provides alerts and warnings of hazardous wind shear.[52] The FAA says these weather observation programs increase airspace safety by detecting hazardous conditions and reducing weather-related delays and accidents.

Aviation accidents caused by inclement weather are a unique subset of the cases in which plaintiffs who suffer losses seek to recover from the federal government. That is because plaintiffs occasionally win airline crash cases. One reason may be that, as one expert commentator has observed, government attorneys rarely raise the discretionary function or misrepresentation exceptions to the government's tort liability, and when they are raised, courts apply them inconsistently.[53] He theorizes that the reason for this is that Congress has established a public policy favoring air traffic safety and the Code of Federal Regulations establishes an FAA duty to pilots. An analysis of the case law on liability for air crashes allegedly caused by negligent weather forecasts by federal employees is beyond the scope of this discussion.[54] It is mentioned

---

49. *See, e.g.*, Vaughn v. United States, 259 F. Supp. 286 (N.D. Miss. 1966).

50. Schinmann v. United States, 618 F. Supp. 1030 (E.D. Wash. 1985) (plaintiffs' contention that Bureau of Reclamation's water supply forecast communication was collateral to improper computation of water supply was not well taken, as proximate cause of loss appeared to have been misrepresentation or communication of misinformation, not erroneous calculation of figures).

51. Federal Aviation Administration, https://www.faa.gov/.

52. *Weather Observation*, Federal Aviation Administration, https://www.faa.gov/air_traffic/weather/.

53. Standler, *Tort Liability in the USA for Negligent Weather Forecasts* (2003) at 33, 36, *available at* http://www.rbs2.com/forecast.pdf.

54. There are treatises and law journal articles on the topic. *See* Kreindler et al., *Aviation Accident Law* (Matthew Bender 2021); Harakas, *Litigating the Aviation Case* (American Bar

here because a practitioner may come across a flood case whose facts allow analogizing to the air crash cases. To that end, two illustrative cases are discussed below.

The employees accused of negligence in air crash cases usually work for the FAA, but occasionally National Weather Service employees are also implicated. For example, in one case the plaintiff was a co-pilot injured when his airplane crashed. He alleged that FAA air traffic controllers negligently failed to forward information of significant weather phenomenon to the crew of the aircraft and that employees of the NWS negligently failed to issue a severe thunderstorm warning. The court concluded that none of the government employees was negligent and that in any event, forecasts or omission of them is a discretionary function excepted from the Federal Tort Claims Act.[55] Finally, the court noted that pilots are trained to make their own evaluation of weather conditions and are, therefore, in a much better position than the general public to recognize severe weather and take precautions. In this case the pilots, aware of the weather conditions, chose to land the aircraft and were negligent in doing so.[56]

A different result was reached in a South Carolina case.[57] The plaintiff there alleged that a fatal airplane crash was caused by failure of the government to warn the pilot of a small aircraft of a severe low-level wind shear condition, about which it knew or should have known. The government denied negligence and pled the negligent acts of others and/or the pilot were the sole proximate cause of the accident. The court found that the pilot was not negligent but that both the air traffic controllers and employees of the National Weather Service were negligent. It was negligence for no air traffic controller to relay to the pilot reports of the strong low-level southwest winds and to fail to relay the information to any other FAA or NWS facility. The court also found that the failure of NWS employees to issue an amendment to its forecast was a proximate cause of the crash that resulted from the plane's encounter with low-level wind shear. Had an amendment been issued, said the court, the pilot would have had the information needed to either select a flight path that would have safely traversed the shear zone or abort the flight.

Association 2019); Gesell, *Aviation and the Law* (Coast Aire Publications & Consulting, LLC 2011); Moller & Lasson, *Handling the Turbulence Case*, 64 J. Air L. & Com. 1057 (1999); Alimonti, *Death by Misinformation—Governmental Liability for Faulty FAA Weather Information*, 60 J. Air L. & Com. 961 (1995).

55. *See also* United States Aviation Underwriters, Inc. v. United States, 562 F.3d 1297, 1300 (11th Cir. 2009) (while NWS instruction required issuance of warning once meteorologists determined that sudden severe clear air turbulence (CAT) was occurring or was likely to occur, underlying determination of whether severe CAT was occurring was discretionary).

56. Williams v. United States, 504 F. Supp. 746 (E.D. Mo. 1980).

57. Springer v. United States, 641 F. Supp. 913 (D.S.C. 1986). *See also* Webb v. United States, 840 F. Supp. 1484 (D. Utah 1994) (government liable where FAA employees failed to inform pilot of adverse conditions, including danger of experiencing whiteout).

15.5 Failure of Private Business to Alert Patrons to Weather Dangers

When a business has knowledge of a forecast of threatening weather, does it have an obligation to pass the information along to its customers? The Kansas Supreme Court stated the general rule in the case of patrons of an ice cream store. They claimed that employees "shooed them" out of the store and into the path of a tornado. They were injured while driving home when the tornado threw a truck into their car. They sued the store, alleging its employees were aware that there was a tornado warning in effect when they told the patrons to leave the store. Moreover, the employees learned from a telephone call from persons outside the store that there were reports of a tornado sighting in the area. The plaintiff patrons contended the store had a duty as the possessor of land to warn them of the approaching tornado because it was a foreseeable hazard, and the fact that their injuries actually occurred *off of the premises* was of no consequence because the defendant's negligence consisted of failure to warn and offer shelter while the plaintiffs were still in the store. The court refused to extend premises liability law to hold that a business has a duty to warn and shelter patrons from severe weather they might encounter on their way home from the business premises. The owner of a business, the court said, is not the insurer of the safety of its patrons.[58]

The Wyoming Supreme Court took a different approach in a case in which a family visited a movie theater on an evening in which the community experienced a severe thunderstorm. The storm caused the National Weather Service, civil defense authorities, and local law enforcement officials to issue severe thunderstorm, flash flood, and tornado warnings. The storm worsened, and local emergency management officials demanded that citizens stay indoors and off the streets. The theater employees were aware of the severity of the storm, flooding in the area, and the various warnings. The family was never made aware of the warnings. They left the theater through an exit leading directly into the parking lot and traveled on public streets where their vehicle became struck by flood waters and their daughter drowned. They sued several parties including the theater, seeking to hold it liable for negligently failing to restrain or warn patrons of the foreseeable, dangerous consequences of leaving the theater. The theater filed a motion to dismiss asserting that no duty existed to warn or act for the protection of patrons. The court choose to "depart from the traditional rule that a landowner has no duty to warn an invitee of risks off the landowner's premises." After noting that theater employees were aware that flooding was occurring and warnings issued, the court held the theater

---

58. Cunningham v. Braum's Ice Cream & Dairy Stores, 276 Kan. 883, 80 P.3d 35 (2003). *See also* Grant v. Wakeda Campground, LLC, 631 F. Supp. 2d 120 (D.N.H. 2009) (business generally has no duty to monitor weather for safety of patrons).

owed the family an affirmative duty to exercise reasonable or ordinary care for their safety, including an obligation to advise them of an off-premises danger that might reasonably be foreseeable. The court said it was not suggesting that the theater had a duty to restrain patrons or even to advise them what to do. The duty was only to reveal to its customers what it knew.[59]

A business can be liable when it assumes a duty for the safety of its patrons that it would not otherwise have. Under the Restatement, one who gratuitously or for consideration renders services to another is subject to liability to that other party for physical harm resulting from failure to exercise reasonable care to perform the undertaking.[60] For example, under the terms of a lease, a tenant agreed to make all repairs; however, when pipes in the apartment were broken, the landlord agreed to make the repairs. The water to the building was turned off. Before the repairs were made the landlord, when turning on the water for a new tenant, turned it on for the entire building causing the apartment of the other tenant to flood. The Pennsylvania Supreme Court said that having undertaken to make the necessary repairs to the pipes, the landlord was liable for any damage due to his negligent performance of the work that he voluntarily performed.[61] Thus, in the Kansas case, if the employees had undertaken to warn the store's customers of the tornado, but were negligent in some respect in doing so, the court might have found the business liable.

The Restatement principles were applied in an especially terrible case before the Kansas Supreme Court. Two young golfers were severely injured when they were struck by lightning while on the defendant's golf course. The course had been closed earlier in the day because of a lightning storm. The course had policies in place for inclement weather. The manager on duty was to monitor the local television stations and radar images on the internet, and visually inspect the weather by stepping outside. There was no policy about the frequency with which the managers were to check weather conditions, but one manager acknowledged that they were checked more frequently when storms were in the area. If a manager determined it was necessary to bring golfers in off the course, the procedure was to sound an air horn. The injured golfers began to play shortly after the course was reopened. While they were playing,

59. Mostert v. CBL & Assocs., 741 P.2d 1090 (Wyo. 1987). The court found no liability on the part of the theater's landlord as the theater had exclusive possession of the property and retained complete control of the premises.

60. Restatement (Second) of Torts, § 323.

61. Tarnogurski v. Rzepski, 97 A. 697, 252 Pa. 507 (Pa. 1916). *See also* Mistretta v. Alessi, 45 N.J. Super. 176, 131 A.2d 891 (1957) (defendant who was under no duty to prepare safe place for licensees by sanding walk, and nonetheless sanded alleyway and steps down to cellar door, but not icy front porch was liable for injuries plaintiff suffered because, having undertaken affirmatively to act, defendant was under obligation to act with due care); Walsh v. Hackensack Water Co., 13 N.J. Misc. 815, 181 A. 422 (N.J. 1935) (when defendant undertook removal of water meter, it became its duty to perform that work in reasonably careful manner, even if it was in first instance not obliged to do so).

the manager on duty was monitoring the weather, observed dark clouds and lightning, and sounded the air horn. Unfortunately, lightning struck the young golfers before they could reach the safety of the clubhouse. The court said that the golf course had a policy in place that undeniably was for the protection of its patrons in the event of threatening inclement weather. Therefore, a material factual issue remained on the question of whether the course negligently performed the duty it *assumed* to monitor weather conditions and warn patrons to exit the golf course when the manager on duty deemed it prudent.[62]

All the weather cases discussed in this section concern personal injury and the duty of a business under premises liability concepts. That is quite different from a failure to warn of a danger to the *plaintiff's property*. It seems highly unlikely that a court would impose liability on a business for failure to warn customers of potential damage to their property when there is no business relationship related to protecting the customer's property. Indeed, the Restatement of Torts says that the "fact that the actor realizes or should realize that action on his part is necessary for another's aid or protection does not of itself impose upon him a duty to take such action."[63] Thus, a big box hardware store should have no liability for failing to warn customers that there has been a forecast of flooding and the store has sand bags for sale that could protect the property of those customers. That could hold true even if the store employees mislead customers about the existence or extent of the flooding danger because relying on a store employee for weather information would probably not be considered reasonable. Reliance on a representation, of course, is completely different from selling faulty sand bags that fail to function as intended.

15.6 Establishing Duty, Breach, and Proximate Cause

Assuming a court accepts the proposition that a meteorologist can be liable for professional negligence, the plaintiff still has the burden of showing the duty of care and its breach. There are a number of sources of information available to attorneys for learning about forecasting generally and about professional standards.

The American Meteorological Society has a plethora of publications including a bulletin, journals, meteorological monographs, books, and a glossary of meteorology. The *Bulletin of the American Meteorological Society*

62. Sall v. T'S, Inc., 281 Kan. 1355, 136 P.3d 471 (2006). *Accord* Maussner v. Atlantic City Country Club, Inc., 299 N.J. Super. 535, 691 A.2d 826 (1997). *See generally* Shadiack, *Does a Golf Course Owner and/or Operator Owe a Duty of Care to Their Patrons to Protect Them from Lightning Strikes?*, Maussner v. Atlantic City Country Club, Inc., *691 A.2d 826 (N.J. Super. Ct. Div. 1997)*, 8 Seton Hall J. Sports L. 301 (1998).

63. Restatement (Second) of Torts, § 314. In some cases, there is special relationship between the parties that imposes a duty to take affirmative precautions. Restatement (Second) of Torts, § 314A.

(BAMS) is a monthly magazine.[64] It contains articles on a wide variety of topics including forecasting standards. For example, a recent article discusses the challenges in forecasting excessive rainfall and the flash flooding it often causes.[65] Among the journals the AMS publishes is the *Weather and Forecasting (WAF) Journal*.[66] AMS says the WAF publishes research relevant to operational forecasting including papers on significant weather events, forecasting techniques, forecast verification, model parameterizations, data assimilation, model ensembles, statistical postprocessing techniques, and the transfer of research results to the forecasting community. The scope of the journal, says AMS, includes "research relevant to forecast lead times ranging from short-term 'nowcasts' through seasonal time scales out to approximately two years." The Glossary of Meteorology is an online resource providing definitions for over 12,000 meteorological terms.[67] The AMS bookstore[68] has dozens of offerings including textbooks for undergraduate students[69] that may prove useful in understanding forecast standards. Of particular note is a book written by a forensic meteorologist about his career as an expert witness.[70]

The World Meteorological Organization (WMO) adopts technical regulations that lay down meteorological practices and procedures to be followed by its members. The technical regulations are supplemented by a number of manuals and guides. Manuals contain mandatory practices, while guides contain recommended practices. One guide that may prove useful is the *Guide to Meteorological Instruments and Methods of Observation*.[71]

Expert testimony may be necessary to establish the duty owed and its breach.[72] One expert says that expert testimony "would determine the

---

64. *Bulletin of the American Meteorological Society*, American Meteorological Society, https://www.ametsoc.org/ams/index.cfm/publications/bulletin-of-the-american-meteorological-society-bams/.

65. Schumacher et al., *From Random Forests to Flood Forecasts: A Research to Operations Success Story*, 102 BAMS 1742 (2001), *available at* https://journals.ametsoc.org/view/journals/bams/102/9/BAMS-D-20-0186.1.xml.

66. *Weather and Forecasting*, American Meteorological Society, https://journals.ametsoc.org/view/journals/wefo/wefo-overview.xml.

67. *Glossary of Meteorology*, American Meteorological Society, https://glossary.ametsoc.org/wiki/Welcome.

68. *AMS Bookstore*, American Meteorological Society, https://bookstore.ametsoc.org/.

69. *Bookstore Undergraduate Students*, American Meteorological Society, https://edubooks.ametsoc.org/.

70. Haggard, *Weather in the Courtroom: Memoirs from a Career in Forensic Meteorology* (AMS 2016).

71. *Guide to Meteorological Instruments and Methods of Observation* (World Meteorological Organization, 2008), *available at* https://www.weather.gov/media/epz/mesonet/CWOP-WMO8.pdf.

72. Klein & Pielke, *Bad Weather? Then Sue the Weatherman!: Part II: Legal Liability for Private Sector Forecasts*, Bull. Am. Meteorological Soc. at 1804 (2002), *available at* http://sciencepolicy.colorado.edu/admin/publication_files/2002.22.pdf (expert testimony from other

reasonableness of an actual prognostication."[73] The American Meteorological Society offers two certifications of which attorneys seeking expert witnesses in a weather-related case should be aware. The first is "Certified Broadcast Meteorologist (CBM)" for radio and television meteorologists.[74] The second is "Certified Consulting Meteorologist (CCM)."[75] The AMS says that its Certified Consulting Meteorologist program enable users of meteorological services to select consultants with greater confidence in the quality and reliability of their products and services and that CCMs are considered experts for testimony on weather-related court cases. A list of those holding the CCM certification is available online.[76] There is also an organization called the Association of Certified Meteorologists.[77] It lists the specialties of its members at a web page.[78] Another organization of which to be aware is the National Council of Industrial Meteorologists (NCIM).[79] It is a "professional association of meteorologists, principally engaged in the private practice of industrial and applied meteorological consulting." Its members generally hold the Certified Consulting Meteorologist designation, and their work includes forensic meteorology, operational weather forecasting, air quality and environmental consulting, the collection or dissemination of meteorological data, and weather resources management.

Even if a plaintiff can show a duty and breach, the breach has to be shown to be the proximate cause any injury.[80] However, as one expert says, a "negligent forecast is never the 'nearest' cause of a plaintiff's misfortune because the weather itself is the most immediate cause of harm."[81] He adds that the

---

meteorologists could help determine whether forecasting process strayed from acceptable standards).

73. Loper, *"Red Sky in the Morning, Forecasters Take Warning": The Liability of Meteorologists for Negligent Weather Forecasts*, 66 Tex. L. Rev. 683, 684 (1988).

74. *Certified Broadcast Meteorologist Program (CBM)*, American Meteorological Society, https://www.ametsoc.org/index.cfm/ams/education-careers/careers/ams-professional-certification-programs/certified-broadcast-meteorologist-program-cbm/.

75. *Certified Consulting Meteorologist Program (CCM)*, American Meteorological Society, https://www.ametsoc.org/index.cfm/ams/education-careers/careers/ams-professional-certification-programs/certified-consulting-meteorologist-program-ccm/.

76. *See List of AMS Certified Consulting Meteorologists (CCM)*, American Meteorological Society, https://www.ametsoc.org/index.cfm/ams/education-careers/careers/ams-professional-certification-programs/directories-of-ams-certified-individuals/list-of-ams-certified-consulting-meteorologists-ccm/.

77. *About the Association of Certified Meteorologists*, Association of Certified Meteorologists, http://certifiedmeteorologists.org/about-association-certified-meteorologists.htm.

78. *See Find an Expert*, Association of Certified Meteorologists, http://certifiedmeteorologists.org/find-an-expert-meteorologist.htm.

79. *NCIM Blog*, NCIM, https://ncimorg.wordpress.com/.

80. *See, e.g.*, Schinmann v. United States, 618 F. Supp. 1030 (E.D. Wash. 1985); Seelbinder v. County of Volusia, 821 So. 2d 1095 (Fla. 5th DCA 2002).

81. Loper, *"Red Sky in the Morning, Forecasters Take Warning": The Liability of Meteorologists for Negligent Weather Forecasts*, 66 Tex. L. Rev. 683, 699 (1988).

negligent forecast has to be so substandard that it clearly caused the plaintiff to undertake an action that he or she would not have otherwise, or to forego an action that he or she would have undertaken after receiving a reasonable forecast. Additionally, forecaster liability should require both objective and actual reliance by the plaintiff.[82]

82. Loper, *"Red Sky in the Morning, Forecasters Take Warning": The Liability of Meteorologists for Negligent Weather Forecasts*, 66 Tex. L. Rev. 683, 700 (1988) (actual reliance on negligent forecast is required because some recipients of multiple weather forecasts consistently favor one report over others; if court finds plaintiff would have taken alternative action or no action had the defendant's forecast lacked negligence, then it has to determine whether that alternative action or forbearance would have prevented plaintiff's injuries).